The Good Britain Guide 2001

Edited by Alisdair Aird

Deputy Editor: Fiona Stapley

Associate Editors: Karen Fick, Robert Unsworth

Research Officer: Tom Smith

Walks Consultant: Tim Locke

Additional Research: Elizabeth Adlington

EBURY PRESS
LONDON

Please send reports to:

The Good Britain Guide
FREEPOST TN1569
WADHURST
E Sussex
TN5 7BR

Front cover photograph of Tom and Harry Watson © Helen Hepburn

This edition published in 2000 by
Ebury Press
Random House, 20 Vauxhall Bridge Road
London SW1V 2SA

www.randomhouse.co.uk

3 5 7 9 10 8 6 4 2

ISBN 0 09 187781 4

Typeset from author's disks by Textype Typesetters, Cambridge
Printed and bound in Great Britain by Cox & Wyman Ltd, Reading, Berkshire

Contents

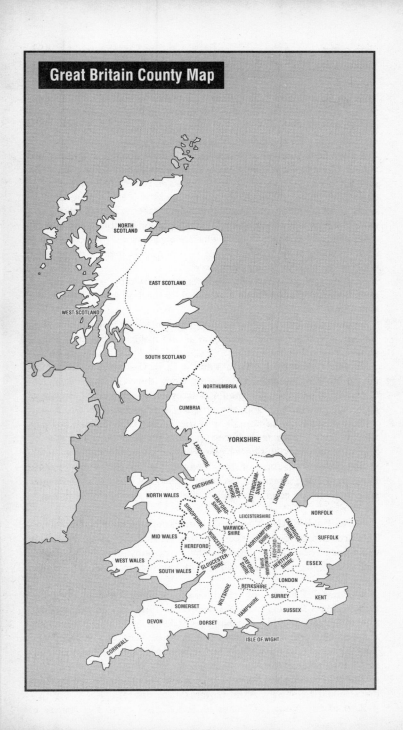

Great Britain County Map

INTRODUCTION

This will be a vintage year for seeing Britain. More than 1,000 projects funded partly by Lottery heritage grants have now come to fruition, and a great many more are now on stream thanks to further Lottery cash earmarked for the Millennium. Forget that sinking flagship the Dome – it's this great fleet of other projects, big and small, which are having a real impact. Many towns and villages have a new, more attractive public face, with restored buildings, parks, greens, piers and so forth. Real money has backed efforts to make many country areas more appealing both to wildlife and to visitors. Hundreds of buildings, galleries and museums have at last been able to afford up-to-date features and facilities – and in many cases add prize new acquisitions which a few years ago they could never have dreamed of being able to buy. And of course there are dozens of entirely new and interesting places to visit.

Lottery money has certainly made its impact on some – but not all – of the following places and organisations, which for their excellence gain our annual awards.

Trip of the Year is Frog Tours of London, for 90 minutes of fun in a yellow amphibious vehicle, taking in all the major central sites before splashing down into the Thames.

Green Attraction of the Year is Earth Centre at Denaby Main (South Yorkshire): despite problems along the way, this Millennium Commission project has turned 400 acres left derelict in the decline of coal-mining into an ambitious and intriguing environmental centre.

Steam Railway of the Year is the Ravenglass & Eskdale Railway, affectionately known as the Ratty, in Cumbria, with lovingly preserved ancient steam trains chugging up one of Lakeland's most beautiful valleys.

Specialist Museum of the Year is the Impossible Microworld Museum in Bath (Somerset): fascinating displays of ingenious microscopic sculpture – makes counting angels on the head of a pin seem child's play in comparison.

Farm Park of the Year is Cogges Farm in Witney (Oxfordshire). This farm-with-a-difference takes you back to Victorian times, with plenty of fun and a good eye for detail – authentic demonstrations by costumed Victorians, even the rather unfamiliar farmyard animals you'd have seen then.

Heritage Centre of the Year is Segedunum in Wallsend (Northumbria), an invigorating new look at Tyneside's surprisingly rich Roman legacy, with an eye-catching new building.

Local Museum of the Year is the Bagshaw Museum in Batley (West Yorkshire): a really rewarding miscellany in this beautiful and beautifully set Victorian Gothic mansion – and it's free.

Thrill of the Year is Oblivion – three minutes of unmitigated terror at that splendid theme park, Alton Towers (Staffordshire).

Zoo of the Year is Colchester Zoo (Essex): masses of animals of course, but also plenty going on for family visitors, including good play areas, a new activity centre, and all sorts of holiday events.

Garden of the Year is the 'Southern Kew', Wakehurst Place at Ardingly (Sussex), with its tremendous variety of immaculately grown plants in lovely grounds; its new Millennium Seed Bank is an extraordinary achievement.

Gallery of the Year is the New Art Gallery Walsall (West Midlands): the collection is great, and the new building housing it is quite stunning, a work of art in itself.

Tour of the Year is Llechwedd Slate Caverns nr Blaenau Ffestiniog (North Wales): plenty of interest on the surface, and riveting rides through the deep caverns.

Heritage Building of the Year is Kentwell Hall in Long Melford (Suffolk): what gains the accolade for this beautiful moated manor house, with rare breeds in its grounds, is its first-class series of re-creations of Elizabethan and 1940s life, informative yet real fun, staged between Apr and Sept.

Living Museum of the Year is the Black Country Living Museum in Dudley (West Midlands): always something eye-opening at this lively reconstructed early 20th-c village.

National Museum of the Year is the Imperial War Museum, London, which has added a grimly enthralling exhibition on the Holocaust to its excellent and exhaustive look at warfare and its effects, from the earliest times to the conflicts of today.

Tourism and Heritage Organisation of the Year is British Waterways, whose bold plans and vigorous commitment to restoration are bringing long-neglected stretches of Britain's canals back to life – and to public enjoyment. An excellent example is its Scottish Millennium Link project, which will reopen 70 miles of canal between Edinburgh and Glasgow, centred on a fantastic boat-lifting Big Wheel being built in Falkirk (East Scotland).

Spectacle of the Year is the London Eye: the capital as you've never seen it before, from one of the Millennium Commission's real successes. What's more, this millennium icon is almost unique among modern structures, in that in itself it doesn't spoil the view - its distinctive shape actually adds to the appeal of many central London views.

Newcomer of the Year will be the National Space Science Centre in Leicester, opening in the spring, and rocketing into the future of museum technology.

Family Attraction of the Year is @Bristol (in our Somerset chapter), an absorbing fusion of the latest interactive technology with science and wildlife – a totally 21st-c place to visit.

To check facts and track down local information, we spend a lot of time each year telephoning Tourist Information Centres (TICs) and other tourist information outfits. We normally make the approach as if we were just any other customer, so as to get an idea of how they vary. And how they do vary! Some are pretty useless. For example, if you try to speak to someone at Bristol you have to wait through to the end of a long recorded message, and then find yourself put on hold for ever (we never succeeded in getting through, even after several attempts). The British Tourist Authority (in charge nationally) sets a fine example, sending out plenty of helpful information; their web site www.visitbritain.com is worth checking. And a dozen others also get our warm applause, for being particularly helpful: Aberdeen & Grampian Tourist Board, Cleethorpes TIC, Guildford TIC, Kent Tourism, Llandrindod Wells Tourist Office, Northumberland Tourism, Perthshire Tourist Board, Scottish Borders Tourist Authority, Shropshire County Council, Suffolk County Council, Wales Tourism (South and West), and York Tourism. Best of all is the TIC in Bath, Somerset. Despite the mass of visitors to the city, this is always friendly and helpful, coping very well with the rush. Bath TIC is our **Tourist Information Centre of the Year**.

GOOD NEWS FOR WALKERS AND RIDERS

Three major initiatives are now helping walkers and riders make the most of the countryside. The most ambitious is the National Cycle Network, which by 2005 will cover the UK with 9,000 miles of cycle routes, quite a few of which are already up and running. Purpose-built paths are linking quiet country lanes, existing cycleways such as disused railway tracks, and traffic-calmed town streets, so that the network is safe even for novice riders. Many parts are suited to walkers who don't want the rough stuff but do want peace and quiet.

English Heritage (in charge of many of historic sites and buildings) has designed several dozen interesting time trails, linking many of their sites. Ring (01793) 414910 for details, or see their web site www.english-heritage.org.uk.

Countryside Stewardship Schemes, under which farmers are paid to manage interesting areas of countryside in an environmentally friendly way, are now making a real impact in many places. One requirement is for public access. These new arrangements have already added some 700 miles of appealing walks and rides to the national footpath network, and the number of schemes is scheduled to expand quite dramatically in this and following years. While controversy surrounds the much better-known 'right to roam' legislation proposals, this little-known but rapidly expanding pattern of growing collaboration between government and farmers on access to interesting countryside seems to us a more fruitful development. Free guides are available from Conservation Management Division, MAFF, Room G15, Nobel House, 17 Smith Sq, London SW1P 3JR.

BARGAIN BRITAIN?

This year, high petrol prices and the weak E have tended to keep European visitors away, and British people have gone abroad instead of spending their holiday money here. Has the holiday industry responded by cutting prices, to lure back its missing customers? Alas, no. The general response has been a series of price increases, on average firmly outstripping other retail prices. We have compared prices charged this year by over 3,600 tourism establishments, with what those same places were charging last year. On average, they have put up their prices by 4½%. That's half as much again as the rise in other retail prices during the same period. The sharpest price hikes were in places to eat in such as restaurants, pubs and tearooms (just over 5%), followed closely by admission fees for places to visit. Places to stay in were slightly less rapacious, but have still increased their prices by more than the retail price index, right across the board from humble B&Bs to posh hotels.

This alarming tide of rising holiday prices has prompted us for the first time to rank all the areas of Great Britain, on the basis of how much you get for your money in each. The first stage was to compare prices of paid attractions, and the cost of holiday accommodation in each main category (hotels, inns, B&Bs and farms), and of light meals out, in pubs, restaurants and tearooms. We then brought into the calculation nearly 3,000 places to visit where no charge is involved (anything from an interesting little village or a lakeside walk to a historic town crammed with fine sights, or one of the great free galleries and museums).

This gave us a preliminary list, based primarily on price. Of course, price alone is sometimes a misleading yardstick. So we then applied our detailed knowledge of what is on offer in each area, to bring sheer quality into the equation, and construct this Value Table:

Britain's Top Holiday Values (masses to see and do, free or attractively priced; excellent value places to stay and eating out) Yorkshire, Wales, Northumbria, Devon

The Undiscovered Bargains (extremely low prices, and plenty to enjoy – if you know where to look) Lincolnshire, Herefordshire

Well Worth While (clearly above average both for places to visit and for attractive prices) Suffolk, Lancashire, Somerset, Worcestershire, Norfolk, Cumbria

Virtually every other area of Britain can also be rewarding to explore. After all, that's what this *Guide* is all about, pointing the way to hidden treasures that you may not know about. What's more, some areas which don't quite make it into these top value ranks score very highly indeed in some particular respects. Staffordshire, for instance, scores top marks for outstandingly good value accommodation. Northamptonshire's hotels stand out as having low prices, and there is excellent value B&B to be had in both Berkshire and Buckinghamshire. Eating out can be very cheap in Cornwall. Scotland has an unrivalled range of free places to visit, and London, where tourism prices have otherwise gone through the roof, has some great free attractions.

One great way of combining pleasure with real value, and at the same time discovering something a bit different, is to stay on a farm. In the last few years a good many of our readers have been enjoying the fun of this. Prices compare very favourably with other B&B establishments (normally under £50 a night for two people). This year we have nearly 100 farms, all firmly recommended, among our other places to stay in.

Which brings us to another price point. Ann Partridge of the Manor Farmhouse nr Yetminster in Dorset earns special praise for using an 0800 telephone number – so potential customers can call her, free. This savings-conscious customer-friendly attitude is almost unique outside of a small handful of much bigger hotel firms. Most places unhelpfully expect their potential customers to pay for the full cost of calling them. If Mrs Partridge in her small establishment can manage this helpful free telephone service for her customers, why is it so rare elsewhere?

We found only two paid-entry visitor attractions, both in the West Country, which operate an 0800 free telephone information service – the Goonhilly Earth Station in Cornwall, and Monkey World in Dorset. The general rule is for an establishment to expect their customers to pay for the full telephone cost of checking anything with them, though the 0870 and 0990 numbers used mainly by some big-name places such as Madame Tussaud's save you a bit if you call off-peak. We did find one rogue, the London Dungeon: their 0891 number is charged at 60p a minute whenever you call, which means that in effect you are paying them through the nose to give you what should be free information about opening times and so forth. We'd suggest a spell in the dungeon as the most appropriate treatment for whichever manager there thought up this piece of chicanery (with the accompanying fine, of course – admission tickets there cost nearly £10). Other even riper candidates for the dungeon are the four Tourist Information Centres which – in our view scandalously – charge telephone callers a premium rate, usually around 50p a minute, to listen through a recorded message before they even have the chance to speak to a real person: Bournemouth, Brighton, Hove and London. Manchester and Liverpool charge this same extortionate rate, but at least put you straight through to an operator.

Using the Guide

The Counties

England has been split alphabetically into county chapters. Scotland and Wales have each been covered in single chapters, and London appears immediately before them at the end of England.

Where to stay

In each section, hotels, inns and other places to stay such as farmhouses are listed alphabetically.

The price we show is the total for two people sharing a double or twin-bedded room with its own bathroom, for one night in high season. It includes full English breakfast (unless only continental is available, in which case we say so), VAT and any automatic service charge that we know about. So the price is the total price for a room for two people. We say if dinner is included in this total price. It is included in some of the more remote places, especially in Cumbria and Scotland, and may also be in some other places where the quality of the food is a main attraction; in these cases, the establishment concerned does not normally offer B&B on its own. In some of the places we list, some or occasionally even all the bedrooms share bathrooms; we say if this is the case.

An asterisk beside the price means that the establishment concerned assured us that that price would hold until the end of summer 2001. Many establishments were unable to give us this assurance; it would be prudent to allow for an increase of around 5% by then.

A few hotels will do a bargain break price at weekends even if you're staying for just one night. If so, that's the price we give, and we show this with a w beside the price. Many more hotels have very good value short break prices, especially out of season, if you stay a minimum of at least two nights; if you plan to stay in one area rather than tour around, it's well worth asking if there's a special price for short breaks when you book. Many hotels also offer short-notice bargains which don't appear on their tariffs if they are underbooked on a particular night, so as to fill their rooms even at a discount. So, especially if you are not booking in advance, ask what price they can quote you for that particular night.

If there's a choice of rooms at different prices, we always give the cheapest, and if we know that maybe the back rooms are the quietest or the front ones have the best views or the ones in the new extension are more spacious then we say so. If you want a room with a sea view or whatever, you should always ask specifically for this, and check whether it costs extra.

If the hotel closes for any day or part of the year, we say so. But especially in outlying areas hotels have been known to close at other times if their business is very slack. And this last year or two we've found some go out of business altogether. So don't head off into an area where there are no nearby alternatives without checking by telephone first. We always mention a restaurant if we know the inn or hotel has one. Note that we always commend food if we have information supporting a positive recommendation. So a bare mention that food is served shouldn't be taken to imply a recommendation of the food.

WHERE TO EAT

The price in ordinary type is for one person having a typical three-course restaurant meal with half a bottle of wine, including any automatic service charge. So double it to get a meal for two. The second price, in **bold** type after the |, is for a more informal single-dish meal, if that's available.

We list any scheduled closing dates. We have found quite a few instances of unscheduled closures in the last year or two, and recommend booking if your plans would be thrown into turmoil by finding a place unexpectedly closed. Moreover, many of the restaurants we list are very popular, and without a booking you may find there's no room for you.

If you want a good meal out in any area, look at the places to stay as well as the restaurants, especially in country areas. When we praise a hotel or inn for its food, that means it's well worth consideration as a place for a good meal out. In some parts of the country, it's in these hotel restaurants that you'll find the best food.

Our brief mentions of places to eat in the text of the **To see and do** sections are based on our own inspections or firm recommendations from readers.

CHILDREN

We asked all hotels, restaurants and other places to stay in and eat at which have full entries in the *Guide* whether they allow children. If the entry doesn't mention children, that means the establishment has told us that it welcomes them, with no restrictions. If there are restrictions (either an age limit, or segregated early evening meals for them), we spell these out. We have found that very occasionally establishments turn out in practice to be more restrictive about children than they claim. And of course managements change, and so do their policies. If you are travelling with children, to avoid misunderstandings it's always worth checking ahead that there will be no problem. Please let us know if you find any difference from what we say. Obviously, too, you should bear in mind the character of the hotel or restaurant, as described, and in relation to your own children. While some children might fit perfectly into the atmosphere of a dignified and old-fashioned country house, others might be fractiously ill at ease there – no fun for you, or for the other guests. This year we've chosen a few places to stay that are really special for families. We've marked these in the text with ☺, our new good for families symbol.

LOCATIONS

Generally, we list places to see (and hotels and restaurants) under the name of the nearest village or town. We use **BOLD CAPITALS** to name the locality, and **bold type** like this to name the establishment. If the village is so small that you probably wouldn't find it on a road map, we've listed it under the name of the nearest sizeable village or town instead.

Places well known in their own right – famous castles, great houses, for example – are shown in **BOLD CAPITALS** instead of the locality name. The maps use the same locality name as the text.

We include places in their true geographical locations – so if a village is actually in Buckinghamshire that's where we list it, even if its postal address is in Oxfordshire.

HERITAGE OPEN DAYS

On Heritage Open Days, many notable buildings will be open to the public which are normally closed. English National Heritage Weekend will be on 7–10 Sept, when some 2,000 properties will be open. As we went to press individual details are undecided, but if 2000 was anything to go by they will range from intriguing follies through all sorts of official and office buildings to even the Chancellor of the Exchequer's office. For regional directories write to Civic Trust, 17 Carlton House Terrace, London SW1Y 5AW, with six 2nd-class stamps or call (020) 7930 0914. The Welsh National Heritage Weekend will be 15–16 Sept, ring (029) 2048 4606 for details. During London Open House Weekend there will be free admission to around 100 buildings; anything from Lloyds of London to Bushy House. For more details write to London Open House, PO Box 6984, London N6 6PY, or call (0207) 267 2070. The Scottish equivalent, Doors Open Days, will run most weekends in September, but precise dates were undecided as we went to press; ring (0141) 221 1466.

PRICES AND OTHER FACTUAL DETAILS

Information about opening times and so forth is for 2001. In some cases establishments were uncertain about these when the *Guide* went to press during the late summer of 2000; if so, we say in the text. (And of course there's always the risk of changed plans and unexpected closures). When we say 'cl Nov–Mar' we mean closed from the beginning of November to the end of March, inclusive; however when we say 'cl Nov–Easter' we mean that the establishment reopens for Easter.

Where establishments were able to guarantee a price for 2001, we have marked this with an asterisk. In many cases establishments could not rule out an unscheduled price increase, and in these cases – i.e., no asterisk against the price – it's probably prudent to allow for a 5% increase in around April 2001. If you find a significantly different price from that shown, please let us know.

🔢 OUR DISCOUNT VOUCHER

In this edition nearly 800 places to visit have a 🔢 symbol immediately after their name. These have said they will honour our discount voucher until the end of 2001 (or of course the end of their season, if they close earlier). To get the discount, you must hand one of the vouchers in at the admissions kiosk; there are six vouchers on the tear-out card in the centre of the book. Usually, the discount is that one child will be admitted free for two adults paying the full price. Please check the text for that entry carefully. If there are any variations from the usual, or any special conditions, we spell them out in a bracket immediately after the 🔢 symbol. Please also note the general conditions on the voucher itself.

NATIONAL TRUST

NT after price details means that the property is owned by the National Trust, and that for members of the Trust admission is free. There is a similar arrangement for properties owned by the National Trust for Scotland (NTS); the two Trusts have a reciprocal arrangement, so that members of one may visit the properties of the other free. Membership is therefore well worth while if you are likely to visit more than a very few properties in the year – quite apart from its benefit to the Trusts' valuable work. NT membership is £30 a year (£51 joint membership); details from National Trust, PO Box 39, Bromley, Kent BR1 1NH, (0208) 315 1111. NTS membership is £27 (£45 family); details from National Trust for Scotland, 28 Charlotte Sq, Edinburgh EH2 4ET, (0131) 243 9300.

FRIENDS OF HISTORIC HOUSES

The Friends of Historic Houses Association has NT-style membership offering free entry to around 280 historic houses and gardens in private ownership throughout Britain – including a high proportion of those we recommend which aren't NT, English Heritage or other national equivalent. Membership is £28 a year (£40 for joint membership), so you only have to go to four or five houses and you've got your money back. Details from Historic Houses Association, Heritage House, PO Box 21, Baldock, Herts SG7 5SH, (01462) 896688.

ENGLISH HERITAGE

A similar membership scheme gives free access to those EH properties (about half) which charge admission. It costs £28 (£46 two adults, £49.50 family). Details from English Heritage Membership Dept, PO Box 570, Swindon SN2 2YR, (01793) 414910/911. Cadw (for Wales) (029) 2050 0200 and Historic Scotland (0131) 668 8600 have similar schemes.

OTHER MONEY SAVERS

In the relevant sections we mention any notable travel bargains and other sightseeing bargains we know of, such as National Museums and Galleries on Merseyside Eight Pass, allowing discounted entry into all Liverpool's finest attractions. It's also worth knowing about the Slow Travel Networks, especially if you're young and on a budget. Very popular with backpackers from overseas, these are coach runs linking all the main tourist cities around Britain – a £129 ticket gets you the whole circuit, though you can get on or off at any stage for as long as you like – there's no time limit, and the drivers are very flexible; (0207) 373 7737.

MAP REFERENCES

Most place names are given four-figure map references, looking like this: NT4892. The NT means it's in the square labelled NT on the map for that area. The first figure, 4, tells you to look along the grid at the top and bottom of the NT square for the figure 4. The third figure, 9, tells you to look down the grid at the side of the square to find the figure 9. Imaginary lines drawn down and across the square from these figures should intersect near the locality itself. The second and fourth figures, the 8 and the 2, are for more precise pin-pointing, and are really for use with larger-scale maps such as road atlases or the Ordnance Survey 1:50,000 maps, which use exactly the same map reference system. On the relevant Ordnance Survey map, instead of finding the 4 marker on the top grid you'd find the 48 one; instead of the 9 on the side grid you'd look for the 92 marker. This makes it very easy to locate even the smallest village.

DISABLED ACCESS

We always ask establishments if they can deal well with disabled people. We mention disabled access if a cautious view of their answers suggests that this is reasonable, though to be on the safe side anyone with a serious mobility problem would be well advised to ask ahead (many establishments tell us that this helps them to make any special arrangements needed). There may well be at least some access even when we or the establishment concerned have not felt it safe to make a blanket recommendation – again, well worth checking ahead. There are of course many places where we can't easily make this sort of assessment – particularly the less formal 'attractions' such as churches, bird reserves, waterside walks, viewpoints. In such cases (which should be obvious from the context) the absence of any statement about disabled access doesn't mean that a visit is out of the question, it simply means we have no information about that aspect. We're always grateful to hear of readers' own experiences. An important incidental point: many places told us that they would give free admission to a wheelchair user and companion.

CHANGES DURING THE YEAR – PLEASE TELL US

Changes are inevitable during the course of the year. Managements change, and so do their policies. We very much hope that you will find everything just as we say. But if you find anything different, please let us know, using the report card in the middle of the book, the forms at the end of the book, or just a letter. This *Guide* depends very heavily indeed on readers reporting back to it. In that sense it's very much a collaborative venture: and the more people that send us reports, the better the book will be. So please do help us by telling us about places you think should be added to the book, or removed from it, or even just confirming that places still deserve their entry. We try to answer all letters (though there may be a delay – and between the end of May and October we put all letters aside until after the end of the hectic editorial rush). People who help us do get a special offer discount price on the next edition. There's a note on the sort of information we need at the back of the book, with report forms; and a tear-out report card in the middle of the book. For letters posted in Britain you don't need a stamp: the address is Good Guide to Britain, FREEPOST TN1569, WADHURST, E Sussex TN5 7BR. Alternatively you can use our web site, www.goodguides.com (see below), to send us reports.

Our web site combines material from *The Good Britain Guide* and its sister publication *The Good Pub Guide*. It additionally includes a list of events that will be taking place throughout 2001. We have included this information on our web site rather than in the *Guide* so that we can keep it more up to date than printed material allows, and we hope to add more events that there would never be room for in a book. We also hope to add further features which will go beyond what is in the printed books – for example, the site includes some recommended day-out tours in the Lake District and Brighton.

SYMBOLS

The multiplicity of symbols which were used in previous editions of the *Guide* could have been more of a confusion than a help. So this year we have used just four in the text:

☺ Good places for families to stay
⊖ London Underground

⇌ Surface rail – former British Rail
▣ Our special offer discount (see details above and tear-out card)

Additionally, the map uses these two symbols:

⊨ places to stay
✗ places to eat

BEDFORDSHIRE

Particularly good for wildlife – some outstanding days out

Most of Bedfordshire's main attractions have plenty to interest people of all ages, with three outstanding animal-based places of particular appeal to families. Woburn Abbey has more than enough for a day visit – from the exciting Safari Park to the quieter glories of the abbey and its collections, and the tranquil deer park. The 2,500 animals in their fine setting at Whipsnade are, of course, a perennial family favourite. Last year's newcomer Bedford Butterfly Park mixes pleasure with education – children especially enjoy the bugs room and summer nature trail.

Other places to head for with children include Woodside Farm at Slip End and Mead Open Farm at Billington, both offering good value family entertainment. The Stockwood Craft Museum and Gardens (comprising the Mossman Collection of Vehicles) have enough to occupy both parents and their children, and picturesque Bromham Mill runs a good programme of events during the school holidays.

Elsewhere, several places have a real variety of appeal. The charming village of Old Warden glories in both the Shuttleworth Collection of vintage aeroplanes, and the unusual Swiss Garden. The Lodge at Sandy is perfect for bird-spotting, or just for a pleasant stroll, and Wrest Park has beautiful gardens.

Leighton Buzzard Museum is one of the better heritage museums (and includes fun train rides). The Cecil Higgins art gallery in Bedford is impressive. There are some charming villages to stroll through.

Dunstable Downs have decent walking and remarkable views, though otherwise the county's scenery is generally not memorable. The relative flatness is a boon to cyclists; a tourist board leaflet details good circular cycle routes. You can get this from local Tourist Information Centres, which stand out in this county for their wide range of helpful information. Other good leaflets cover year-round weekend activities and guided walks through some of the prettier villages and countryside; and the Ivel Valley Countryside Project's Kingfisher Way circular walks and Skylark Ride horse trek.

Where to stay

FLITWICK TL0234 **Flitwick Manor** *Church Rd, Flitwick, Bedford, Bedfordshire MK45 IAE (01525) 712242* **£174**, plus special breaks; 17 thoughtfully decorated rms. 17th-c country house surrounded by interesting gardens, with log fire in entrance hall, comfortable lounge and library, and smart restaurant with fine French wines and imaginative food using home-grown and local produce; tennis, putting, croquet; children over 12 in evening restaurant; limited disabled access

LEIGHTON BUZZARD SP9224 **Swan** *High St, Leighton Buzzard, Bedfordshire LU7 7EA (01525) 372148* **£60**, plus wknd breaks; 38 rms. Handsome Georgian coaching inn with pleasant lounge, relaxed bars, and attractive conservatory restaurant with English cooking; limited disabled access

SANDY TL1651 **Highfield Farm** *Tempsford Rd, Sandy, Bedfordshire SG19 2AQ (01767) 682332* **£50**; 6 rms (2 in former stables), 4 with own bthrm. Neatly kept whitewashed house set well away from A1 and surrounded by attractive arable farmland with plenty of room for children to run around; friendly helpful owner, open fire in comfortable sitting room, and communal breakfasts in pleasant dining room ☺

WOBURN SP9433 **Bell** *21 Bedford St, Woburn, Milton Keynes, Buckinghamshire MK17 9QB (01525) 290280* **£70**, plus wknd breaks; 23 attractively decorated rms, some with antiques. Lovely, friendly old inn, carefully restored, with beamed evening restaurant, long narrow bar/dining area, good changing food, and well kept ales; also, residents' own lounge and bar

To see and do

Bedfordshireshire Family Attraction of the Year

SLIP END TL0818 **Woodside Farm & Wildlife Park** 🖼 This good value, friendly farm has expanded quite a bit since the days when it was just an egg production centre, but not so much that it's lost its warmth or got too big for its muddy boots. Children can still collect eggs from the hen house, but there are now around 250 different breeds of animals and birds for them to meet, and sometimes touch. If you miss one of their handling sessions, you can still usually pick out rabbits or guinea pigs from the warrens, and, from spring to autumn, you might be able to feed a baby goat or handle a new-born chick; when we last called you could touch their young raccoons, but they're likely to be too big by the time this edition hits the shops. They have a monkey house with particularly friendly lemurs and marmosets – some have been hand-reared, so aren't at all perturbed by people. It's nicest on a dry day (they do tractor and pony rides for a very small extra charge), but much of the farm is under cover, and on wetter days animals normally found outside are usually moved to indoor barns. A new indoor play area should be finished by the end of the year; they already have a good one outside. You can buy feed for the animals from their very well stocked farm shop. Like most farms, it's best for small children; some will want to stay for a good chunk of the day, others may have had enough in two or three hours. If they're itching for a pet, you might want to steer them quickly past the shop selling all sorts of potential furry friends, but if they've already got one, you're bound to find something useful to look after it. Clowns, magicians or other special events on bank holidays or the summer school break. Restaurant, indoor and outdoor picnic areas, shops (quite a stock of farmyard toys), good disabled access; open daily (from 8am in summer), cl 25–26 Dec, 1 Jan; (01582) 841044; *£3, *£2 children.

AMPTHILL PARK TL0239
Former hunting grounds of Henry VIII, surprisingly heathy but landscaped by Capability Brown, with lovely trees and a water-lily lake.

BEDFORD TL0549
Really a straightforward modern town despite its long history, but there are decent riverside gardens and a few nice buildings. The Corn Exchange (St Paul's Sq) has a bronze bust of Glenn Miller,

who made many of his morale-boosting broadcasts from here. Lincolns (Goldington Green) is an interesting old place for lunch.
Bedford Museum (Castle Cl) Traditional museum next to the Cecil Higgins; cl Sun am, all Mon, and 25 Dec; (01234) 354954; £2.
Cecil Higgins Art Gallery & Museum (Castle Cl) Bedford's outstanding attraction, very rewarding,

boasting the kind of paintings most other museums can only dream about, inc great works by Turner, Constable, Rembrandt, Matisse, Picasso, and Dali. The Victorian mansion's beautifully furnished rooms make it look as if the family that lived here have just popped out – it's clear lots of thought has gone into the displays, and nothing seems unnatural or out of place. An award-winning extension has collections of local lace and European glass and ceramics; changing exhibitions. Snacks, shop, disabled access; cl Sun am, all day Mon (exc pm bank hols), 25–26 Dec, 1 Jan, Good Fri; (01234) 211222; *£2.

John Bunyan Museum (Bunyan Meeting Free Church, Mill St) Housed in a building in the grounds of the church where John Bunyan was minister, visitors can walk through a series of tableaux of his life (there's also a trail around Bunyan-related sites in the town). Snacks, shop, disabled access; cl Sun, Mon, Good Fri, Nov–Feb; (01234) 213722; free.

BILLINGTON SP9422
Mead Open Farm (Stanbridge Rd) Plenty of fun for children here including trailer rides, indoor and outdoor play areas and a variety of hands-on activities; falconry displays twice a month exc Jan. Meals, snacks, shop, disabled access; cl Weds–Fri Nov–Jan, 24–27, 31 Dec, 1 Jan; (01525) 852954; £3.75.

BROMHAM TL0050
Bromham Mill 🖾 (Bridge End) Picturesque working 17th-c watermill on River Ouse, with Sunday milling demonstrations (weather permitting), and a gallery with local art and crafts. Lots of events throughout the year, esp in school hols – phone for more information. Snacks, shop, disabled access to ground floor only; open Sun and bank hols, pm Weds–Sat (Sun only Nov–Feb); (01234) 824330; £1.25 (£2.50 Sun and bank hols). The Swan is a popular food pub.

COLMWORTH (BUSHMEAD) TL1160
Bushmead Priory Ruins of late 12th-c Augustinian priory, well preserved, with medieval wall paintings and timber-framed roof. Open wknds and bank hols, July and Aug; (01234) 376614;

£1.85; EH.

DUNSTABLE TL0221
Priory Church of St Peter (Church Street) This remarkable priory church incorporates part of a 12th-c abbey (where Henry VIII's first marriage was dissolved); shop, disabled access; cl bank hols; free. The Old Sugarloaf (High St) is useful for lunch.

DUNSTABLE DOWNS TL0019
Very popular with kite-fliers and gliders at wknds or in summer; there's a countryside centre (cl Mon exc summer school hols, and winter wkdys), two car parks, and lots of space to run around. The downs give great views from a spectacular escarpment path, amid ancient grasslands. The downs can be linked to a circuit incorporating Whipsnade village and the nearby Tree Cathedral – the best walk in Beds. **Five Knolls** is an important Bronze Age burial mound, excavated by Agatha Christie's husband Sir Mortimer Wheeler and Gerald Dunning. The Horse & Jockey (A5183) is a good family food pub.

ELSTOW TL0447
The county's finest village, with a very handsome core of fine old timbered houses by the green. Bunyan was baptised in the attractive church, which has an unusual detached tower and a 'Pilgrims Progress' window. The Three Tuns at Biddenham is the closest good place for lunch.

Moot Hall Outstanding brick-and-timber medieval market house with a collection of John Bunyan's works (he was born nearby), and a reconstruction of his writing room. Shop; cl am, all day Mon (exc bank hols), Fri and Sat, and Oct–Mar; £1.

FELMERSHAM SP9957
A lovely church by a medieval tithe barn, a fine old thatched pub and some attractive old houses, with the River Ouse below. Nearby Pavenham is also pretty, with a stroll down to the river.

HARROLD SP9556
Pretty riverside village with 13th-c church and pack-bridge, and an early 19th-c lock-up on the village green. The Magpie is useful for lunch, and in Odell the Bell is good.

Harrold and Odell Country Park (Carlton Road) Highly recommended

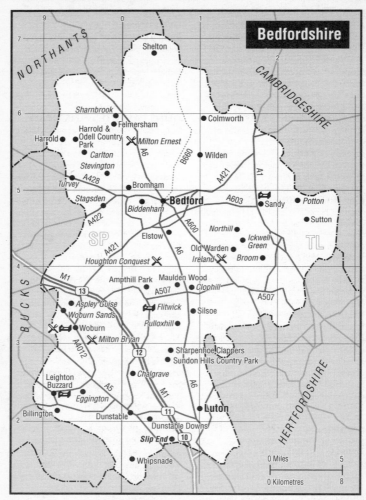

Bedfordshire

NORTHANTS

CAMBRIDGESHIRE

BUCKS

SP

TL

HERTFORDSHIRE

Shelton

Sharnbrook
Felmersham
Colmworth
Harrold & Odell Country Park
Harrold
Milton Ernest
Carlton
Wilden
Stevington
Turvey
Bromham
Stagsden
Bedford
Sandy
Potton
Biddenham
Sutton
Elstow
Northill
Ickwell Green
Old Warden
Houghton Conquest
Ireland
Broom
Ampthill Park
Maulden Wood
Clophill
Aspley Guise
Flitwick
Woburn Sands
Silsoe
Woburn
Pulloxhill
Milton Bryan
Sharpenhoe Clappers
Sundon Hills Country Park
Leighton Buzzard
Chalgrave
Eggington
Luton
Billington
Dunstable
Dunstable Downs
Slip End
Whipsnade

A6, B660, A421, A1, A428, A422, A603, A600, A507, M1, A5, A4012, A5120

0 Miles 5
0 Kilometres 8

for bird-watching; with a lake and nature reserve, it's especially good for waterfowl, particularly in winter. Bedfordshire CC publish a circular route incorporating three waymarked walks up to 13 miles long. Snacks, disabled access; visitor centre; cl Christmas week; (01234) 720016; free.

LEIGHTON BUZZARD SP9224
Leighton Buzzard Railway (Pages Park Station, Billington Rd) Good collection of over 50 locomotives from around the world, with a fleet of 11 steam trains to trundle you through gently varied countryside.

The Stonehenge Works terminus has industrial heritage displays. Meals, snacks, shop, disabled access; open Sun and bank hols Easter–Sept, plus Weds Jun–Aug, Tues, Thurs and Sat in Aug, and wknds in Dec; (01525) 373888 for timetable; £5 (discount not valid over Christmas season). The Globe in Linslade is a nicely set canalside food pub, with pleasant nearby walks.

LUTON TL0820
Stockwood Craft Museum & Gardens (Stockwood Country Park, Farley Hill) Ideal for a restrained and uncomplicated day out. Besides a

museum and several lovely period garden settings (inc a 17th-c knot garden and a Victorian cottage garden), there's a refreshingly witty sculpture garden, and an adjacent children's play area. Also here, the **Mossman Collection** of restored old vehicles has plenty of vintage cars. Snacks, shop, disabled access; cl Mon (exc bank hols), wkdys Nov–Mar, 25–26 Dec, 1 Jan; (01582) 738714; free.

MAULDEN WOOD TL0638
Ancient woodland with a picnic site, marked walks and muntjac deer.

OLD WARDEN TL1343
An attractive village in its own right, built deliberately quaintly in the 19th c, and especially worth visiting for the Shuttleworth Collection. The village church has a number of European wood carvings, inc some from the private chapel of Henry VIII's wife Anne of Cleves. The Hare & Hounds is a useful food pub.

Shuttleworth Collection Nearly 40 working historic aeroplanes covering the early history of aviation, from 1909 Bleriot to 1942 Spitfire in purpose-built hangars on a classic grass aerodrome. Several exhibits are the only surviving examples of their type, and it's worth trying to go on one on the days when some of them are flown (usually the first Sun of the month and Sat evenings, May–Oct; best to phone). Meals, snacks, shop, disabled access; cl Christmas week; (01767) 627288; £6, higher charges on flying days.

Swiss Garden 🔊 Early 19th-c romantic wilderness garden, with pretty vistas and colourful trees and shrubs – a nice place for a stroll. Meals, snacks, shop, disabled access; open Sun and bank hols Jan–Oct, plus pm daily Mar–Sept; (01767) 627666; £3. Now approached from Old Warden Park via Shuttleworth Mansion.

SANDY TL1847
The Lodge (RSPB Nature Reserve) The elegant 19th-c Tudor-style house is the headquarters of the RSPB, and isn't open to the public, but is surrounded by formal gardens, a wildlife garden, and a nature reserve covering 106 acres of heath, lake and woodland, with plenty of birds, animals and trails spread all over. Perfect for

watching rare species undisturbed, but even if bird-spotting's not your thing, this is a relaxing place to wander through, especially charming in spring when the woods are carpeted with bluebells. Snacks, shop, some disabled access; cl 25–26 Dec; (01767) 680551; £2.50 (free for RSPB members). The Locomotive nearby is useful for lunch, and in the town the Kings Arms is good.

SHARPENHOE CLAPPERS TL0629
Steep-sided downland with chalkland flora and butterflies, crowned with a fine beechwood and Iron Age hill fort; the area is owned by the National Trust and is laced with paths.

SHELTON TL0368
Pretty little cottages, hall and rectory grouped around the delightful church, with 13th-c work inside, wall paintings, and a 14th-c font on seven legs.

SILSOE TL0935
Wrest Park House & Gardens (off A6) Inspired by French chateaux, the 19th-c house has several ornately plastered rooms open to visitors, but it's the enormous formal gardens that are the main attraction. They go on for over 90 acres and give a good example of the changes in gardening styles between 1700 and 1850. Perhaps best of all is the Great Garden, designed by the Duke of Kent between 1706 and 1740 and later modified by Capability Brown, with lovely views down the water to the baroque pavilion. Snacks, shop, limited disabled access (some electric buggies available); open wknds and bank hols Apr–Oct; (01525) 860152; £3.40; EH. The George Hotel is a friendly place for family lunches.

SLIP END TL0818
Woodside Farm & Wildlife Park
See separate family panel on p.2.

SUNDON HILLS COUNTRY PARK TL0528
Sheep-cropped downland with good views and walks (some quite steep).

SUTTON TL2247
Notable for its steeply humpbacked packhorse bridge, looking more like a part of Devon or Derbys; ironically, cars have to use a more ancient crossing, the shallow ford beside it. A decent pub nearby is named after John o' Gaunt, the village's former owner.

WHIPSNADE TL0018
Tree Cathedral Tucked just off the
village road is this most unusual war
memorial, trees planted in the plan of a
cathedral in the 1930s, with continuing
more recent plantings.
Whipsnade Wild Animal Park
Plenty of space for the animals at this
splendid 600-acre zoo; the elephant
paddock is reckoned to be Europe's
biggest. Altogether 2,500 creatures
roam the beautiful downs-edge
parkland, from tigers, giraffes and
rhinos to monkeys, wallabies, peafowl
and Chinese water deer. You'll need a
full day to see everything, and it's too
big to get round completely on foot –
you can drive round the perimeter road
and walk from various stopping points,
or there's a free open-topped tour bus,
but the best way of getting around is on
their railway, which takes you past
herds of Asian animals. Younger visitors
enjoy the elephant walk, penguin feed
and sea lion demonstrations, and
there's a hands-on children's farm, as
well as indoor discovery centre with
dwarf crocodiles, snakes and spiders.
Play areas include a bear-themed maze.
Meals, snacks, shop, disabled access; cl
25 Dec; (0990) 200123; £9.90. The Bell
at Studham is the best nearby place for
lunch; the Old Hunters Lodge is very
handy.
WILDEN TL0954
Bedford Butterfly Park (off B660
just N of town) Well organised place
with quite an emphasis on children inc a
very good adventure playground and
separate play area for younger children.
The hot house is full of exotic plants and
flowers, as well as colourful butterflies
and caterpillars, ponds with carp and
water-lilies, and a cascading waterfall.
Children enjoy the bugs room with
tarantulas, scorpions and other creepy-
crawlies all safely kept behind glass; hay
meadow nature trail (most colourful in
July), children's quiz sheets from the gift
shop. A British butterfly garden should
be open by the time this book comes
out. Meals, snacks, disabled access; cl 24
Dec–18 Feb (last admission 4.30pm);
(01234) 772770; £4.
WOBURN SP9433
Some lovely 18th-c houses and good
antiques shops.

Woburn Abbey & Deer Park 🏛
One of England's grandest stately
homes – everything from the lovely
English and French 18th-c furniture to
the splendid range of silver seems to
have the edge over most assemblages
elsewhere, and the art collection, taking
in sumptuous paintings by Rembrandt,
Van Dyck and Gainsborough, is
outstanding (where else can you see 21
Canalettos in just one room?). The
3,000 acres of surrounding parkland
were landscaped by Humphrey Repton,
and today are home to several varieties
of deer. Swans, ducks and other
waterfowl on the lake and aviary with
free-flying budgies; pottery and huge
antiques centre. Meals, snacks, shop,
disabled access by arrangement; cl
Nov–Dec and wkdys Oct and Jan–Mar;
(01525) 290666; £7.50. The drive
into the park, through Froxfield, is
most attractive, with a wealth of
rhododendrons in June.
Woburn Safari Park Always exciting,
the highlight here is the drive-through
safari – you can almost imagine you are
driving through African plains, with
lions and tigers (if you're lucky) just on
the other side of the windscreen – pick
your day carefully however: readers
who've visited on bank hols have found
themselves in slow-moving traffic jams,
so it's probably best to avoid coming
then if you can. The 300 acres of abbey
parkland also feature giraffes, rhinos,
bears, sea lion, penguin and elephant
shows, animal encounters, a train ride,
new toboggan run and a boating lake.
Birds swoop down and feed from your
hand in a walk-through aviary, and a
woodland walk takes you among fallow
and sika deer. Meals, snacks, shop,
disabled access; cl wkdys Nov–Feb;
(01525) 290407; £12 (£8.50 children,
free for under-3s in cars).
Other attractive villages include
Aspley Guise SP9335, spacious
Biddenham TL0249 (nice 12th-c
church), Broom TL1743, Clophill
TL0837, Eggington SP9525, Northill
TL1546, Sharnbrook SP9959
(interesting specialist shops), Pulloxhill
TL0634, Turvey SP9452 (the interesting
church has Saxon origins) and Woburn
Sands (good wooded walks nearby)
SP9235; all have pubs we can

recommend for lunch. Carlton SP9555 is also pleasant. Ickwell Green TL1545 nr Northill is well worth a look, too, with its colourful thatched houses around a broad green; Stagsden SP9849 is attractive, with a good few thatched houses, and strolls in the woods nearby.

Stevington SP9853 has a handsomely restored windmill, and a holy well opposite the handsome church. **Other churches** worth investigating include Chalgrave TL0027 and Potton TL2449 (it's the gravestones that are worth the visit).

Where to eat

HOUGHTON CONQUEST TL0441 **Knife & Cleaver** *The Grove (01234) 740387* Civilised 17th-c dining pub with welcoming comfortable bar, blazing winter fire, attentive, friendly service, smartly stylish bar food (lovely fresh fish and shellfish), 26 good wines by the glass, well kept real ales, good choice of whiskies, no smoking conservatory restaurant, and neat garden; good bdrms; cl Sun pm, 27–30 Dec; disabled access. £32|**£6.25**

IRELAND TL1341 **Black Horse** *(01462) 811398* Busy and attractive beamed pub in lovely setting, with a good choice of plentiful piping hot food in sizeable lounge or family dining area, helpful, friendly staff, and lots of tables in lovely front garden with play area; cl Sun pm; disabled access. £20.25|**£5.95**

KEYSOE TL0763 **Chequers** *Pertenhall Rd (01234) 708678* Friendly and unpretentious village local with two comfortably modernised beamed bars, consistently good food, well kept beer, and terrace and garden with children's play equipment; cl Tues, and maybe some time in Sept; disabled access. £17|**£6**

MILTON BRYAN SP9730 **Red Lion** *Toddington Rd (01525) 210044* (South End) Relaxed, comfortable pub with spotless beamed bar area, fresh flowers, good popular food inc quite a few fresh fish dishes and very good value OAP wkdy lunches, no smoking dining areas, real ales, and plenty of seats on terrace and lawn, with pretty hanging baskets; disabled access. £19.50|**£7**

MILTON ERNEST TL0156 **Strawberry Tree** *3 Radwell Rd (01234) 823633* 18th-c thatched cottage with low beams and open fires, very good interesting lunchtime and evening food using the best ingredients from a sensibly short menu in the no smoking dining room, and very popular afternoon teas, too; cl Mon, Tues, 2 wks winter, 2 wks summer. £40/3-course lunch £17

WOBURN SP9533 **Paris House Woburn Park** *(01525) 290692* Lovely black and white timbered house in Woburn's deer park with a neat garden for pre-meal drinks, and serving enjoyable modern French food with exotic touches and a mainly French wine list; cl Sun pm, Mon, all Feb; disabled access. £53 dinner, £25 lunch

Special thanks to Mr and Mrs Michael Back

We welcome reports from readers

This *Guide* depends on readers' reports. Do help us if you can – in return, we offer a discount on the next edition to people who've helped us with reports for it. Tell us what you think about places already in it, and anything extra you think we should say about them. And send us your ideas for inclusion in the next edition: places to visit, eat at or stay in, attractive drives or walks, maybe even unusual interesting shops you know of. Use the card in the middle, the report forms at the end, or just write – no stamp needed: *The Good Britain Guide*, FREEPOST TN1569, Wadhurst, E Sussex TN5 7BR.

BERKSHIRE

The home of the monarchy and the world of Lego draw most people to Windsor and its surroundings, but some unique family attractions elsewhere have great appeal – and the west of the county has possibilities for quiet breaks

Windsor Castle is a favourite destination, and the town has plenty to fill a day or more's busy sightseeing. Legoland is a very popular day out for children – outstanding when it first opened, it's improved significantly each year since. For a complete change of pace nearby, Dorney Court is a fine ancient building with the traditional charm of a proper family home. Windsor Great Park, the Savill Garden and the Valley Gardens have memorable vistas, and can be returned to again and again without exhausting their possibilities.

Children also really enjoy the Look Out discovery park in Bracknell, a good combination of hands-on science with nature and outdoor adventure. Prettily set Bucklebury Farm Park is more suited to smaller children, who'll be encouraged to handle the animals. Horse-lovers will enjoy the shire horses and racing pedigrees at Littlewick Green and Lambourn respectively. There's much more than just fishing at Trilakes Country Park and Fishery. Wellington Country Park has plenty for families.

The innovative Wyld Court Rainforest at Hampstead Norreys is quite an eye-opener, and Beale Park at Lower Basildon is most rewarding for anyone with an interest in wildlife. Basildon Park, also here, provides a pleasant afternoon's excursion. All of these are towards the west of the county. This part has quite a good range of walking possibilities, from gentle strolls to long hikes – with some comfortable and attractive places to stay in, and plenty of good food. Its rolling downland and civilised small villages linked by pleasant minor roads make for attractive drives – the Lambourn Valley and Lambourn Downs, the B4009 and B4494, and the back road from Pangbourne to Aldworth are among the best.

The rural life museum on the edge of Reading is one of the best in Britain. Those who fancy a flutter at the races can choose between Ascot, Newbury and Windsor.

The finest stretch of the Thames is between Marlow and Henley, with easy towpath sauntering and plenty of boating activity. In holiday time the river does get very busy, but is idyllic on a fine early summer or autumn afternoon. Away from the Thames, there are also boat trips in Hungerford, Newbury and Kintbury.

Please let us know what you think of places in the Guide. *Use the report forms at the back of the book or simply write us a letter.*

Where to stay

BRAY SU9179 **Monkey Island** *Old Mill Lane, Bray, Maidenhead, Berkshire SL6 2EE (01628) 623400* **£160**, plus wknd breaks; 26 comfortable rms. Set on an island in the River Thames and reached only by footbridge or boat, this peaceful 18th-c former fishing lodge built by the 3rd Duke of Marlborough is made up of two smart white buildings surrounded by beautifully kept gardens with peacocks, ducks and geese; some fine original features inc an original painted ceiling in the lounge showing monkeys in 18th-c sporting gear, helpful friendly staff, and enjoyable food in restaurant overlooking the water; disabled access

EAST ILSLEY SU4981 **Crown & Horns** *Compton Rd, East Ilsley, Newbury, Berkshire RG20 7LH (01635) 281205* **£58**; 8 rms, some in converted stable block; 6 more to be added. Bustling and friendly old pub in horse-training country with interesting beamed rooms, well liked bar food, 160 whiskies from all over the world, and pretty paved stable yard

HAMSTEAD MARSHALL SU4165 **White Hart** *Hamstead Marshall, Newbury, Berkshire RG20 0HW (01488) 658201* **£85***; 6 beamed, comfortable rms in converted barn. Civilised country inn in quiet village with a log fire open on both sides of the L-shaped bar, a partly no smoking restaurant, good Italian food (the daily specials are the thing to go for), decent Italian wines, friendly service, and very pleasant walled garden; cl 25–26 Dec, 1 Jan

HUNGERFORD SU3369 **Bear Hotel** *41 Charnham St, Hungerford, Berkshire RG17 0EL (01488) 682512* **£93**w, plus special breaks; 41 comfortable, attractive rms with antiques and beams in older ones. Civilised hotel with fresh flowers, open fires, a fantastic huge clock, plentiful bar food, well kept real ales, and a relaxing restaurant; disabled access

HUNGERFORD SU3268 **Marshgate Cottage** *Marsh Lane, Hungerford, Berkshire RG17 0QN (01488) 682307* **£55***; 10 individually decorated rms. Family-run little hotel backing on to Kennet & Avon Canal with residents' lounge and bar, super breakfasts, a friendly atmosphere, and seats overlooking water and marsh, and in sheltered courtyard; plenty to see nearby; disabled access

LAMBOURN SU3278 **Lodge Down** *Ermin St, Lambourn Woodlands, Hungerford, Berkshire RG17 7BJ (01672) 540304* **£50**; 3 rms. Country house in lovely grounds with views over the gallops of Lambourn Downs, open fire in spacious elegant sitting room, friendly owners, and good breakfasts around communal table; visits to stables on request; tennis court and swimming pool

MAIDENHEAD SU8880 **Fredricks Hotel & Restaurant** *Shoppenhangers Rd, Maidenhead, Berkshire SL6 2PZ (01628) 581000* **£210**, plus wknd breaks; 37 luxurious rms, many with garden views. Smart red-brick hotel next to the greens of Maidenhead Golf Club, with champagne on arrival in reception with its stylishly modern chandeliers and marble waterfall, plush cocktail bar, fine professional cooking in luxurious restaurant, and good formal service from long-standing staff; lush conservatory overlooking gardens, and refurbished terrace where you can take meals in warm weather; cl 24 Dec–3 Jan; disabled access

STREATLEY SU5980 **Swan Diplomat** *High St, Streatley, Reading, Berkshire RG8 9HR (01491) 878800* **£105**w, plus special breaks; 46 attractive rms, many overlooking the water. Well run, friendly riverside hotel with comfortable, relaxed lounges, consistently good food in attractive restaurant, popular leisure club, restored Magdalen College Barge, and flower-filled garden; disabled access

WINDSOR SU9277 **Oakley Court** *Windsor Rd, Water Oakley, Windsor, Berkshire SL4 5UR (01753) 609988* **£160**w, plus special breaks; 115 spacious, individually furnished rms. Splendid Victorian country-house hotel in 35 acres of grounds by the Thames with 9-hole golf course, croquet lawn, tennis, fishing, boating, and health club; log fires in the elegant lounges, a panelled library, and particularly good food in smart restaurant; used in 200 films, notably the 'St Trinians' series and Hammer 'Dracula' films; disabled access

YATTENDON SU5574 **Royal Oak** *The Square, Yattendon, Newbury, Berkshire RG18 0UG (01635) 201325* **£115**, plus special breaks; 5 pretty rms. Elegant and comfortable old inn in peaceful village with fresh flowers and log fire in prettily decorated panelled bar, a relaxed atmosphere, interesting modern food, real ales, a good wine list, and a pleasant walled garden

To see and do

Berkshire Family Attraction of the Year

BRACKNELL SU8666 **Look Out** (3 miles from centre, Nine Mile Ride; off B3430) Let's be honest, nothing in Berkshire beats Legoland for the majority of under-12s, but this busy centre should satisfy both lively minds and legs. It's the starting point for 2,600 acres of woodland, great for running around and exploring, but the main feature is now very much the hands-on science centre, all under cover, so just as good on a rainy day. Visitors can enjoy climbing through a giant mole hole, try the Puzzle Carousel, or have a go at launching a miniature hydrogen rocket or hot-air balloon. Children between 5 and 12 can easily spend at least an hour playing on the displays, more if they have an interest in science, or if you come at a weekend or during school holidays when they have a very full timetable of extra shows and particularly well organised activities. Mainly conifer plantations, the forest is full of nature trails and wildlife; one walk leads to an Iron Age hill fort. As the centre's name suggests, there is a rather dramatic 22-metre look-out tower, with good views of the surrounding area – hardly England's most beautiful, but surprisingly wooded and green. If you can't face climbing the 88 steps, cheat and see the scenery from a monitor at the bottom. You can hire mountain bikes (from £2.50 for two hours) and the many tracks, some based on Roman roads, allow long, if not particularly varied walks and rides. Snacks, shop, disabled access; cl Christmas week; (01344) 354400; £3.85, £2.55 children over 4. A saver ticket – for two adults and two children or one adult and three children – is good value at £10.20. It's half price after 4 o'clock (but shuts at 5). If you've got the energy, a particularly fun day out is to combine this with the very jolly Coral Reef swimming complex just across the road.

ARBORFIELD SU7566
Henry Street Garden Centre
Specialist rose and bedding plant grower, with a well stocked garden centre. From Jun–Sept you can wander through the fragrant rose fields. Meals, snacks, shop, disabled access; cl 25–26 Dec, and Easter; (0118) 976 1223; free. The George & Dragon over at Swallowfield is good for lunch.

ASCOT SU9268
Royal Ascot Probably the most famous racecourse in the world, though most visitors spend as much time watching the people as the horses. The four-day Royal Meeting in mid-June is still one of the highlights of the English season; to try for admission to the Royal Enclosure, British citizens should apply to Ascot Races (Royal Enclosure and Members' Stand), St James's Palace, London SW1, foreign citizens to their embassy. For the other stands contact the Racecourse; tickets must be booked in advance and are available from 1 Jan. Plenty of other top-class races throughout the year, when ticket prices range from £6 to £45 depending on the enclosure (the Silver Ring is the cheapest). Meals, snacks, shop, disabled access; (01344) 876876 for dates. The Thatched Tavern at Cheapside is the best nearby place for lunch.

BISHAM SU8484
Bisham church Well worth a look; sitting on a seat in the churchyard by the Thames on a fine evening is rather special.

BOULTER'S LOCK SU9082
An excellent starting-point for leisurely strolls by the River Thames (head upstream).

BRACKNELL SU8767

Coral Reef Across the road from the Look Out centre, this is a wacky swimming pool complex, great for younger members of the family; the Wild Water Rapids are the best bit. Meals, snacks, shop, disabled access; wkdys outside school holidays slides only operate from 3.30pm; cl 2 weeks before Christmas; (01344) 862484; £5.40.

Look Out *See separate family panel on p.10.*

BUCKLEBURY SU5570

Bucklebury Farm Park Perhaps the best time to visit this friendly place, attractively set in the Pang Valley, is in June when the red deer calves are born. A free tractor-drawn trailer takes you right up to the herd (some are tame enough to feed), which now numbers around 100 animals. Children can bottle-feed lambs and calves in the spring, handle rabbits and guinea pigs in the pets' corner or watch a sow suckle her litter; also chickens, geese, goats and donkeys. They own five acres of woodland and a two-mile way-marked walk crosses an ancient common; two adventure playgrounds. You can pick your own strawberries between mid-Jun and mid-July. Snacks, shop, disabled access; cl Nov–mid-Mar; (0118) 9714002; £3.50 (£2.50 children).

BURGHFIELD SU6668

Old Rectory Plantsman's garden inc oriental rarities and cottage-garden plants. Plant centre selling plants from other gardens in the area. Snacks, disabled access to most of garden; open last Weds of month Feb–Oct; (0118) 983 3200; £2. The Hatch Gate here is a friendly pub for lunch.

COOKHAM SU8985

The village, leading down to the Thames, is attractive, and has several decent pubs of which the very smart if expensive Bel & the Dragon, and Uncle Toms Cabin at Cookham Dean, are the current pick. There are plenty of opportunities in this area for **walks** combining the Thames with its hinterland, including great views from the chalk escarpment of Winter Hill. Cock Marsh (NT), by the Thames, is a fine lowland marsh, with breeding wading birds and wetland flora. Paths in this area are very well kept, and it is

hard to lose the way seriously, although woodland walking sometimes means you have to keep your eyes skinned for arrow markers painted on trees.

Stanley Spencer Gallery (King's Hall) Cookham really made its mark on Spencer and his art: it was his birthplace and he spent most of his working life here. This rewarding little gallery has a good range of his unique work, with highlights including *The Last Supper* and the curious *Christ Preaching at Cookham Regatta*. Shop, disabled access; cl wkdys Nov–Easter; (01628) 520890; £1.

DORNEY SU9279

Dorney Court Engaging partly 15th-c timber-framed manor house with pleasant gardens and some very fine furniture, as well as the Elizabethan Palmer Needlework tapestry. The same family have lived here for over 450 years. In the 16th c they grew the first pineapple raised in England, and still have pick-your-own fruit and vegetables every day in season (usually daily Jun–Sept – discounts on Mon, Tues or Weds). Also plant centre, with plants from Blooms of Bressingham, and teas. Meals, snacks; open pm bank hols and preceding Suns in May, and daily pm in Aug exc Sat; (01628) 604638; *£5. The Pickwick at Eton Wick is handy for lunch.

EASTHAMPSTEAD SU8667

Easthampstead church The church here is notable for the fine pre-Raphaelite stained glass by William Morris, Edward Burne-Jones and others.

ETON SU9677

So close to Windsor it's pretty much part of it, this has a restrained and decorous High St with a mix of interesting old shops and houses. Its glory is **Eton College**, the famous public school, whose stately Tudor and later buildings in graceful precincts are marvellously calm during the school's holidays. The chapel is an outstanding late Gothic building in the Perpendicular style, and a museum tells the story of the school from its foundation in 1440 up to the present, with fascinating videos on life for pupils here today (inc Prince Harry). Bizarre information is turned up by the various historical documents – in the 17th c, for

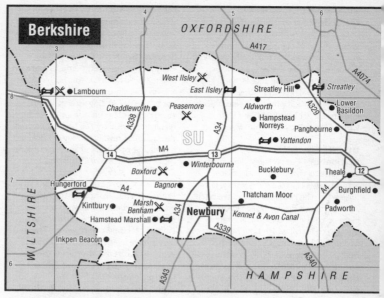

example, smoking was compulsory for all scholars as a protection against bubonic plague. The Brewhouse Gallery has some good watercolour drawings and changing exhibitions, and next door there's an exhaustive collection of Egyptian antiquities. Shop, some disabled access; cl am in term-time, and all Oct–Mar; (01753) 671177; from £2.70 (guided tours from £4). The college runs residential courses in summer on topics as diverse as rowing and choral singing. The Pickwick at Eton Wick has good value food.

FINCHAMPSTEAD RIDGES SU7863

A steepish chunk of heather and pinewood, not big but with a good natural character, good views and sheltered picnic spots; the fine avenue of wellingtonias just above it is well worth seeing too. To the N, Simons Wood NT woodland, with a walk to Heath Pool and Devil's Highway Roman road, now a track. The Golden Pot in Eversley has good food.

HAMPSTEAD NORREYS SU5376

Wyld Court Rainforest (B4009 slightly out of village) Very highly praised by readers, an unusual and quite fascinating tropical rainforest reconstructed under glass, with thousands of weird-looking plants currently in danger of extinction. They're spread over two different areas, Lowland Tropical and Amazonica, each with its own climate and atmosphere. Particularly strange are the giant 8-ft lily pads (best from Jun to Oct), which start life the size of a pea, and the orchid collection is exceptional. Quite a few of these plants can't be seen anywhere else in Europe. Also rare monkeys, varied fish, tarantulas, a chameleon and even a dwarf crocodile. As it's so warm, this is particularly handy on a cold day. Snacks, good shop (with plants for sale), mostly disabled access (though hard work in gravel car park); cl 25–26 Dec; (01635) 200221; *£4.50. The White Hart has good value food.

HAMSTEAD MARSHALL SU4667

Period Plants Small nursery laid out in the style of a 16th-c garden producing plants grown in British gardens until 1700. Dated beds show garden-sized samples of each plant (all for sale); rough farmland may prove difficult for wheelchairs. By appointment only; phone (0467) 411611 to arrange a visit; free.

HUNGERFORD SU3368

Attractive small town with some interesting antiques shops (there's a

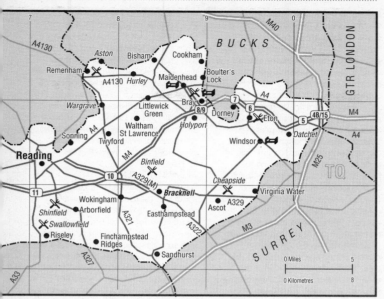

large arcade on the High Street (01488)
683701), some general, others
specialising in items as diverse as
fireplaces, kitchen furnishings and
billiard tables; antiques fairs in the town
hall. The Kennet & Avon Canal Trust
run **canal trips** from the Wharf at
2.30pm wknds Easter–Oct (also Weds
pm Jun–Sept, £4; maybe also 4.30pm
trips July and Aug). The Tally Ho
towards the motorway is a friendly
place for lunch.

INKPEN BEACON SU3562
The high escarpment between here and
Walbury Hill gives some dramatic
ridgeway walking; best reached from
the minor road S of Inkpen (where the
Swan is handy for lunch). The gibbet on
top of the hill is a macabre relic from
highwayman days. Immediately S lie
some lovely rolling downlands laced
with gentle and mostly well marked
tracks, field paths and woodland paths
overlapping into Hants and Wilts.

KINTBURY SU3866
Horse-drawn barge trips 🎫 1½-hr
trips along the restored Kennet & Avon
Canal, Easter–Sept; (01635) 44154;
£4.75.

LAMBOURN SU3278
Quiet streamside racehorse-training
village below the downs. The parish

church of St Michael and All Angels is
worth a look (originally Norman, with
Perpendicular additions), and the Hare
& Hounds (on the B4000 S), with strong
racing connections, is good for lunch.
Lambourn Trainers Association
🎫 (Windsor House) Guided tours
around this successful racehorse
training centre; you meet individual
horses and see them put through their
paces. Wear suitable shoes, and you
must make an appointment. Snacks,
shop, disabled access; open 10–12am,
daily exc Sun and bank hols; (01488)
71347; *£5 plus VAT.

Seven Barrows Up on the downs
off the Lambourn–Kingston Lisle rd
(OS Sheet 174 SU329827), this
Bronze Age cemetery has at least
32 barrows – a spectacle even for the
uninitiated.

LITTLEWICK GREEN SU8580
Courage Shire Horse Centre 🎫
(A4, 2 miles W of Maidenhead) You can
go right up to the horses at this friendly
place, and watch them being groomed
and plaited up; also small animals and
birds, working forge on some days,
children's playground, daily dray rides
at 12pm and 3pm. Meals, snacks, shop,
disabled access; cl Nov–Feb; (01628)
824848; *£3.50.

LOWER BASILDON SU6178
Basildon Park (off A329) Elegant Bath stone Palladian mansion used as a hospital during World War I, with delicate plasterwork on the ceilings and walls, unusual Octagon room, and intriguing collection of rare sea shells in the Shell Room. Outside are old-fashioned roses, a pretty terrace, and pleasant grounds beyond. The classical frontage is particularly impressive. Summer teas, light lunches, shop, disabled access to garden and grounds only; open pm Weds–Sun and bank hols, Apr–Oct; (0118) 9843040; £4.20, £1.80 grounds only; NT.
Beale Park 🅳 (Church Farm) Good, reliable and informative wildlife gardens, with a varied range of birds and mammals – many rare. Just about all their animals were born here in conditions as near as possible to the wild. The surroundings well deserve their listing as an Area of Outstanding Beauty, and there's a lot going on – attractions include a narrow-gauge railway, a model boat collection with exhibits displayed both in and out of the water, paddling pools and a children's playground. Readers get a great deal of pleasure from coming here. Meals, snacks, shop, disabled access; cl Dec–Feb; (0118) 984 5172; *£4.50. In summer there are short river cruises and you can get a boat to here from Caversham Bridge in Reading (two hrs each way, (0118) 948 1008, £5.50 return).

MAIDENHEAD SU9081
Boating on the Thames Though busy in summer, this is a lovely stretch of the river, flowing through lively towns and villages, past grand houses in imposing grounds to idyllic reaches by steep quiet woodland – with islets where you can picnic. A particularly pretty trip is from Wargrave to Henley to Medmenham Abbey to Hambleden, Hurley and Marlow Reach. A good shorter stretch is Cliveden Reach (the two miles between Cookham and Boulter's Lock). As well as motor launches, you can hire very attractive (not to mention silent and quite environmentally friendly) electric launches, though for the purists – and the energetic – only a rowing boat will do. Bray Boats in Ray Mead Rd, Maidenhead, (01628) 637880, have small boats/motor launches ranging from £20 an hour to around £150 a day; they also run half-hour or two-hour trips as far as Cookham. Kris Cruisers in Datchet have rowing boats from £6 an hour and electric launches from £15 – they do good discounts during the week; (01753) 543930. A recorded information service (updated weekly) has details of events and estimated conditions on the river; (0118) 9535520.

NEWBURY SU4667
Busy shopping town famed for its notorious bypass, which generally seems to have reduced congestion in the centre. Some nice old parts, with interesting older buildings among the high street shops. **St Nicolas** is a fine early 16th-c Perpendicular church with a magnificent pulpit. West Mills is the best evocation of the town's 18th-c prosperity, and leads to the attractively rejuvenated canal. **Boat trips** occasionally run from the old wharf, beyond the market square on the other side of the high street; (01635) 44154. The town has an excellent **racecourse**, with midweek and wknd races all year; (01635) 40015 for dates; prices from £5 to £18. **Donnington Castle** (just N off B4494) is actually the tall, ruined medieval gatehouse of a much larger fortress destroyed in the Civil War. The Old Waggon & Horses (Market Pl) has a friendly family dining area above the river, and the Lock Stock & Barrel (also waterside) an afternoon coffee shop as well as bar meals.
West Berkshire Museum (The Wharf) Handsome museum, good on the Civil War battles fought here, and on the development of ballooning. Shop, disabled access to ground floor only; open Mon–Sat, exc Weds in school hols, plus pm some Suns and bank hols April–Sept; free.

PADWORTH SU6067
Kennet & Avon Canal Visitor Centre (Aldermaston Wharf) Set in a nice little house beside the canal, exhibitions on the history and usage of the waterway, and useful information on things to do along its various stretches (of which some would say the

Berkshire bits are the prettiest). Good trails and walks. Snacks (in picnic garden), shop, limited disabled access; cl wkdys Nov–mid-Mar, and all Jan; (0118) 971 2868; free. Nearby quietly placed Padworth church feels very ancient and peaceful, and the Round Oak has decent food. See also Hungerford, Kintbury and Newbury entries for boat trips. And besides other places we mention, there's good access from Aldermaston Wharf SU6067, Marsh Benham SU4267, Thatcham SU5167 and Woolhampton SU5767, all of which have decent pubs. The railway makes a useful method of return, after a walk along the canal from Hungerford to Kintbury, for example.

PANGBOURNE SU6376
Pangbourne Meadow Traditional meadow by the Thames, scythed after flowering and seeding to preserve its wide range of wild flowers. The attractive riverside Swan has food all day, and the village has some decent shops; it was the home of Kenneth Grahame, who perhaps found inspiration around here for *The Wind in the Willows*.

READING SU7173
Berkshire's county town, largely 19th-c red brick, and not really a tourist town, but with museums worth visiting. The abbey ruins in Forbury Gardens are worth a look if passing. In West St, Vicars & Sons is an old-fashioned game butcher's established in the 19th c, an interesting shop with good food. For the extravagant, a **balloon trip** gives a very different view of Berkshire; lift off from town-centre parks daily (weather permitting) in summer, dawn and dusk; (0208) 840 0108; £130. Sweeney & Todd in Castle St has excellent value home-made pies, and the canalside Fishermans Cottage (Kennet Side – walk through from Orts Rd off Kings Rd) is also very popular for lunch.
Blake's Lock Museum (Gasworks Rd) Very well organised, concentrating on Reading's waterways, trade and industries, with reconstructed bakery (the town was well known for biscuit-making), barber's shop and printer's workshop, and a Victorian turbine house. Shop, snacks, disabled access; open pm wknds and bank hols, plus all day Tues–Fri in school hols; (0118) 939 0918; free.
Museum of English Rural Life (Univ of Reading, Whiteknights Park; 2m SE on A327, so you don't have to go into the busy centre) You won't find a better exploration of life in the English countryside over the last couple of centuries than this, taking in farm tools, rural crafts, and domestic room settings. Shop, disabled access; cl 1–2pm, all day Sun and Mon, and 25 Dec–1 Jan; (0118) 931 8663; *£1.
Museum of Reading (Blagrave St) Housed in a showy neo-Gothic building, with hands-on displays and good reconstructions, and a unique Victorian copy of the Bayeux Tapestry. Recently extended and refurbished to include displays from biscuit tins to Roman pottery. Meals, snacks, shop, disabled access; cl Mon exc bank hols (open till 7pm, Thurs); (0118) 939 9800; free.

REMENHAM SU7682
A good start for gentle strolls along the Thames towpath, showing to full effect the river's nostalgic qualities of boating and Edwardian England. There are spectacular period riverside mansions towards Maidenhead. This reach is the course of the Henley regatta; you can instead start a walk from Henley itself (coming back over the bridge).

RISELEY SU7164
Wellington Country Park (off B3349 Reading–Basingstoke) Plenty for families in this big country park; the 350 acres of meadows, woodland and lakes include marked nature trails, a miniature railway, deer park, collection of small domestic animals, and an adventure playground. You can fish and hire rowing and pedal boats on the lake. Meals, snacks, shop, some disabled access, cl Nov–Feb; (0118) 932 6444; £4. The George & Dragon at Swallowfield does good lunches.

SANDHURST SU8262
Trilakes Country Park and Fishery (Yateley Rd) Not just for fishermen, these attractive lakes and surrounding park and woodland have lots of animals and birds, some of which you can feed. Shetland pony rides for children on summer Suns, and in spring you can bottle-feed the lambs. Also model railway. Meals, snacks, shop, limited

disabled access; cl wkdys Nov–Mar; (01252) 873191; £2.25, £7.50 fishing. The Bird in Hand at Little Sandhurst is useful for lunch.

SONNING SU7575
A charming village, with a pleasant walk through the churchyard and past the lovely church to the River Thames, and to Sonning Lock.

STREATLEY HILL SU5580
The NT car park below here gives access to NT downland for fine views over the Thames Valley. The long-distance downs-top Ridgeway Path, one of the oldest tracks in England, follows surfaced farm roads in places hereabouts, but takes in some quiet countryside.

THATCHAM MOOR SU5066
Nature Discovery Centre
Surprisingly, the largest area of inland freshwater reed beds in England; lots of birds (some rare), moths, and marshland and aquatic plants. Car park S of A4. The Nature Discovery Centre explains more about the environment and has a good programme of special events. Snacks, shop, disabled access; cl Mon and 25–26 Dec; free.

THEALE SU6271
Englefield House (A340) The striking house itself is open only to groups, but the surrounding woodland is attractive, with interesting trees, water and formal gardens, and deer park. Some disabled access; open Mon all year, plus Tues–Thurs Apr–Sept; (0118) 930 2221; £2. The Old Boot over at Stanford Dingley has very good food.

TWYFORD SU7975
Thames Valley Vineyard (Stanlake Park, B3018) English wines made by a pioneering blend of tradition and technology. Snacks, shop; cl Sun am, 25 Dec–2 Jan; (0118) 934 0176; free. The Bull near the Thames at Sonning is pleasant for lunch.

VIRGINIA WATER SU9768
Very beautiful, particularly in autumn; the Long Walk gives glorious perspectives of Windsor Castle. Best access via Valley Gardens or Savill Garden car parks.

WALTHAM ST LAWRENCE SU8377
Shottesbrooke church A magnificent 14th-c building, unusually set in a park just E of Waltham St Lawrence – itself an attractive quiet village with an ancient centre.

WINDSOR SU9676
Well worth an expedition (though a tremendous magnet for visitors), the town is dominated by its famous castle, the largest inhabited one in the world. The little streets to the S have many pretty timber-framed or Georgian-fronted houses and shops. The High St, by contrast, is wide and busy. You can walk by the Thames (for example, from Home Park, beyond the station); or across to Eton. The good evening racecourse is best approached by boat – shuttle services run from Barry Avenue Promenade; (01753) 865234 for race dates. The Trooper in St Leonards Rd and Two Brewers in Park St are useful for a bite to eat, but for a better meal we'd recommend going out to the Rose & Crown in Woodside – handy for the various Windsor Park attractions. The Union and Oxford Blue are good pubs in the quieter nearby Thames-side village of Old Windsor.
Frogmore House (Home Park) This lesser known former Royal residence is definitely worth catching on one of its few open days – usually a few days in May (when they have snacks) and Aug bank hol; shop; (01753) 869898); £5. It was a favourite with Queen Victoria, who is buried in a mausoleum in the grounds (open annually on Weds nearest to 24 May), alongside her beloved Albert.
Legoland (B3022, 2m SW of the town centre; shuttle-bus from the station at Windsor and Eton Riverside, which connects with London Waterloo) Ever expanding and truly imaginative, Legoland tops even Windsor Castle in number of visitors; it's one of the most visited attractions in Britain. Divided into several differently themed areas (all built with those amazingly versatile coloured bricks), highlights include the driving school at Lego Traffic (where the best drivers earn their own licence), the Rat Trap – a first-class labyrinth of wooden walkways, climbing nets and slides – and an excellent steep water chute. Children over nine can create robotic models in the more sophisticated Mindstorms Centre,

which gets very busy (particularly mid-afternoon), so entrance is by timed ticket – try and sort out your slot as soon as you arrive. The colourful Duplo Gardens appeal to younger children, while My Town has some jolly fairground rides and a circus. Best of all though is Miniland, where 20 million Lego bricks charmingly re-create European capitals in miniature, with moving people, vehicles and animals, and wonderful attention to detail. You'll need a full day to stand even a chance of seeing everything (it stays open later in the summer holidays); a two-day ticket (£7 extra) helps to avoid rushing. Book in advance and you'll miss the long wait at the entrance. Meals, snacks, shops, good disabled access; open daily from mid-Mar to early Jan; (08705) 040404; £18 (£15 children). Be warned – they close the doors when they feel there are enough visitors.

Savill Garden (Wick Lane, Englefield Green – where the Sun is a good lunch break) On the eastern edge of Windsor Great Park, 35 peaceful acres taking in woodland, formal rose garden, rock plants, herbaceous borders and so forth, and punctuated with a number of rare trees, shrubs and perennials. The range of colours can be quite dazzling. Perhaps best in spring but quite stunning at any time of year. Meals, snacks, good shop, plant sales, disabled access; cl 25–26 Dec; (01753) 847518; £5 Apr–May, £4 Jun–Oct, £3 Nov–Mar.

Valley Gardens Lovely for a relaxing stroll, with over 400 acres of woodland – 50 of which are devoted to rhododendrons, making this the largest planting of the species in the world. Also an outstanding collection of trees and shrubs, a heather garden, waterfowl lakes, and attractive landscaping. It's free for pedestrians (the mile-long walk from Savill Garden is pleasant), though cars can enter by a gate on Wick Rd, Englefield Green, for a fee of £5, £3.50 outside summer – change needed for the automatic barrier).

Windsor Castle A mass of towers, ramparts and pinnacles, this splendid palace is the official residence of the monarch, though it's changed considerably since William the Conqueror built his original wooden fort here. Henry II constructed the first stone buildings, inc the familiar Round Tower, but for many the highlight is the magnificent **St George's Chapel**, a splendid example of Perpendicular architecture, with intricate carvings on the choir stalls, fine ironwork, an amazing fan-vaulted ceiling, and the arms and pennants of every knight entered into the Order of the Knights of the Garter. This is closed Sun and occasional other dates, often at short notice – best to check on the number below. The **State Apartments**, used for ceremonial and official occasions, are decorated with carvings by Grinling Gibbons and ceilings by Verrio, and full of superb paintings from the Royal collection (inc notable Rembrandts and Van Dycks), porcelain, armour, and exceptionally fine furniture. This area (which may be closed when the Queen is in residence) was badly damaged by the disastrous fire in 1992, but you'd hardly know it now, with St George's Hall restored beyond its former glory. Entrance to **Queen Mary's Dolls' House**, an exquisite creation by Edwin Lutyens, built for Queen Mary in the 1920s, with perfectly scaled furniture and decoration, is now also included in the general admission price. Shop, disabled access (exc Dolls' House); occasionally closed for official events, so best to phone (01753) 869898; £10.50. The guards generally change daily Mon–Sat (alternate days only in winter), at 11 o'clock – again, phone for exact dates.

Windsor Great Park Miles of well kept parkland, so sensitively landscaped that it takes the occasional surprising find (statues, even a totem pole) to remind you that it's not natural. It's the only real prospect in this eastern part of the county for walks that'll make you feel genuinely exercised.

WOKINGHAM SU7865

California Country Park (B3016 S of Wokingham, turning R at Wick Hill opp B3430) These woods and open spaces are very useful for young children to let off steam in.

Holme Grange Craft Village (Heathlands Rd) Expanding craft centre with paintings, sculpture, rugs, and even a circus shop; Widget the pot-bellied pig is a favourite with children. Snacks, shops, disabled access; cl 25 Dec–1 Jan; (0118) 977 6753; free. Heathlands Rd has a couple of farm shops and pick-your-own plots; the Crooked Billet on Gardeners Green, Honey Hill, just SE of Wokingham, is a friendly place for lunch.

Other attractive villages, all with decent pubs and pleasant local walks, include Aldworth SU5579, Aston SU7884, Bagnor SU4569 (with a well regarded theatre in a lovely old watermill), Bray SU9079, Chaddleworth SU4177, Datchet SU9876, Holyport SU8977, Hurley SU8283, Wargrave SU7878, Winterbourne SU4572 and Yattendon SU5574.

Where to eat

BINFIELD SU8471 **Stag & Hounds** *Forest Rd (01344) 483553* Little low-beamed rooms (one no smoking) with log fires, interesting furnishings and pictures, some fine sporting prints, a good bustling atmosphere, real ales, great wines, daily papers, and lots of interesting daily specials – plenty of fish and vegetarian dishes, too. £21|**£8.95**

BOXFORD SU4271 **Bell** *Lambourn Rd (01488) 608721* Civilised and neatly kept mock-Tudor village inn with long snug bar, a nice mix of racing pictures, smaller old advertisements, and interesting bric-a-brac, a rather smart restaurant, thoughtful modern cooking, well kept real ales, and decent wines; bdrms; cl 26 Dec. £25|**£4.95**

BRAY SU9079 **Fat Duck** *1 High St (01628) 580333* Really innovative food cooked with immense care and based on traditional French cooking (some perfectly cooked more straightforward dishes as well) in this black and white former pub, with a relaxed if slightly sophisticated feel, knowledgeable helpful staff, and a well chosen wine list; cl Mon, 2 wks Christmas; disabled access. £55/3 course lunch £23.50

BRAY SU9079 **Fish** *Old Mill Lane (01628) 781111* Converted pub with two stylish but relaxed rooms and a no smoking conservatory, candles and fresh flowers, particularly good fish dishes, lovely puddings, real ales, and a good wine list; cl Sun pm, Mon, Christmas; children over 12 in evening; disabled access. £27|**£10.50**

CHEAPSIDE SU9469 **Thatched Tavern** *Cheapside Rd (01344) 20874* Smartly civilised dining pub (not actually thatched!) with low old beams, polished flagstones, and a big inglenook, pretty gingham cloths on the tables in the long dining room, a large choice of good food inc local game and fresh fish, well kept real ales, and polite friendly service. £28|**£11**

ETON SU9677 **Gilbey's Bar and Restaurant** *82 High St (01753) 854921* Bustling, revamped wine bar with an airy and relaxed bar overlooking the High St, a restaurant and conservatory with bookable tables and friendly, helpful staff, an elegant private dining room, imaginative, modern food, and a super wine list; cl one wk Christmas. £28.35|**£7.50**

LAMBOURN SU3275 **Hare & Hounds** *Ermin St (01488) 71386* Stylish dining pub in the heart of horse country, with colourful and idiosyncratically decorated rooms leading off narrow bar, imaginative food, well kept real ales, good wines, and friendly service. £24|**£10.50**

MARSH BENHAM SU4267 **Red House** *(01635) 582017* Attractively set old thatched pub with comfortable bar, no smoking dining room, and front orangery restaurant, good carefully cooked food, well kept ales, decent wine list, lots of malt whiskies, and quite a few brandies and ports; seats on terrace and long lawns that slope down to water meadows and River Kennet; cl Sun pm, Mon; children over 8; disabled access. £27.50|**£6.50**

PEASEMORE SU4577 **Fox & Hounds** *(01635) 248252* Tucked-away downland pub with hunting prints and fox masks in the two bars, a log-effect gas fire open to both rooms, a relaxed atmosphere, enjoyable bar food, real ales, singer/guitarist Fri evenings, and seats outside with far-reaching views; cl Mon. £19.50|**£6.95**

REMENHAM SU7682 **Little Angel** *Remenham Lane (01491) 574165* Cosy little restaurant with good seafood, splendid range of wines by glass, and helpful service; also bar food and well kept real ales in old low-beamed and panelled bar; floodlit terrace; cl winter Sun pm; children must be well behaved. £25|**£8**

SWALLOWFIELD SU7364 **George & Dragon** *Church Rd (0118) 988 4432*
Attractive, cottagey dining pub, cosily old-fashioned, with a smart décor of stripped
beams, rugs on flagstones, red walls, good solid wooden furnishings, and a big log
fire; good seasonal food inc imaginative daily specials; a no smoking dining
conservatory; well kept real ales, decent wines, and friendly, prompt service.
£25|**£9**

WEST ILSLEY SU4782 **Harrow** *(01635) 281260* Popular white-tiled village inn
overlooking duck pond and green, with very good home-made bar food (super
vegetables), no smoking dining area, real ales, a relaxed and welcoming atmosphere,
and big garden; no food winter Sun/Mon pms; children over 10; disabled access.
£25|**£9.50**

Special thanks to M G Hart

We welcome reports from readers

This *Guide* depends on readers' reports. Do help us if you can – in return, we
offer a discount on the next edition to people who've helped us with reports for
it. Tell us what you think about places already in it, and anything extra you think
we should say about them. And send us your ideas for inclusion in the next
edition: places to visit, eat at or stay in, attractive drives or walks, maybe even
unusual interesting shops you know of. Use the card in the middle, the report
forms at the end, or just write – no stamp needed: *The Good Britain Guide*,
FREEPOST TN1569, Wadhurst, E Sussex TN5 7BR.

BUCKINGHAMSHIRE

Plenty of enjoyable family outings and some unusual museums, as well as lovely Chilterns scenery and grand houses and gardens

A new entry last year, Gulliver's Land in Milton Keynes is this year's family attraction, with lots to entertain young children. The Roald Dahl Gallery in Aylesbury is outstanding, providing information through fun and inventive displays. Odds Farm Park at Wooburn Common, St Tiggywinkles wildlife centre in Haddenham and the Bucks Goat Centre at Stoke Mandeville are all good animal attractions. Many older children join adults in enjoying the open-air Chilterns museum in Chalfont St Giles, the railway centre at Quainton and the extraordinary Hell Fire Caves at West Wycombe — happily combined with a walk in the nearby beechwoods. Conversely, people who take children to see the Bekonscot model village in Beaconsfield tend to end up fascinated themselves.

Pitstone has a variety of diversions: the country's oldest windmill, museum activity days on the second Sunday of the month, and boat trips along or walks by the canal.

Claydon House at Middle Claydon was brought to the public's attention by the BBC TV adaptation of *Vanity Fair*. Waddesdon Manor and Ascott at Wing are both rich testaments to the Rothschild alliance of wealth with taste; Chenies Manor has a quieter charm. The landscape gardens of Stowe and Cliveden are memorable fine-weather outings. Bletchley Park has intriguing memories of World War II secrets, presented in a friendly and untouristy way. A smaller place, the Old Gaol Museum in Buckingham, has been carefully upgraded, and the new Milton Keynes Gallery promises bold changing exhibitions of contemporary art.

The Chiltern Hills give the south of the county a special charm: quiet valleys, lovely tucked-away villages with pretty brick and flint houses, endless walking possibilities. This scenery is at its best in spring and autumn through to November, when the beechwoods are at their most beautiful. Some of the best stretches of the Thames are in this area — the finest reaches of all are best seen from a boat. Coombe Hill, the highest point, is an excellent spot for kite-flying.

Where to stay

AYLESBURY SP7812 **Hartwell House** *Oxford Rd, Aylesbury, Buckinghamshire HP17 8NL (01296) 747444* **£232**, plus special breaks; 46 rms, some huge and well equipped, others with four-posters and fine panelling, inc ten secluded suites in restored 18th-c stables with private garden and statues. Elegant Grade I listed building with Jacobean and Georgian façades, wonderful decorative plasterwork and panelling, fine paintings and antiques, a marvellous Gothic central staircase, splendid morning room, and library, exceptional service, and excellent food; 90 acres of parkland with ruined church, lake and statues, and spa with indoor swimming pool, saunas, gym and beauty rooms, and informal restaurant; croquet, fishing; children over 8; dogs accepted; good disabled access

HAMBLEDEN SU7886 **Stag & Huntsman** *Hambleden, Henley-on-Thames, Oxfordshire RG9 6RP (01491) 571227* **£68**; 3 attractive rms. Peaceful brick and flint pub opposite church in very pretty village surrounded by Chilterns beechwoods; compact half-panelled lounge, large fireplace, attractively simple public bar and cosy snug, good food, well kept real ales, and spacious pretty garden (summer barbecues); cl 25 Dec

MARLOW SU8586 **Compleat Angler** *Bisham Rd, Marlow, Buckinghamshire SL7 1RG (01628) 484444* **£205**, plus special breaks; 65 pretty, individually furnished rms overlooking garden or river. Famous Thames-side hotel with comfortable panelled lounge, balconied bar, spacious beamed restaurant with marvellous view, imaginative food, and friendly, prompt service; tennis, croquet, coarse fishing, and boating; disabled access

MURSLEY SP8128 **Richmond Lodge** *Mursley, Milton Keynes, Buckinghamshire MK17 0LE (01296) 720275* **£50***; 3 attractive rms, some with own bthrm. Carefully run Edwardian house in big neat garden with tennis and croquet, open fire in sitting room, lovely breakfasts (super dinner if ordered in advance), and friendly owners; no smoking; cl Christmas/New Year; children over 6

TAPLOW SU9185 **Cliveden** *Taplow, Maidenhead, Berkshire SL6 0JF (01628) 668561* **£364** (plus £5.50 per person paid to the National Trust), plus special breaks; 39 luxurious, individual rms with maid unpacking service and a butler's tray. Superb Grade I listed stately home with gracious, comfortable public rooms, fine paintings, tapestries and armour, and a surprisingly unstuffy atmosphere; lovely views over the magnificent NT Thames-side parkland and formal gardens (open to the public); daily-changing imaginative food in the two no smoking restaurants with lighter meals in the conservatory, friendly breakfasts around a huge table, and impeccable bright staff; pavilion with swimming pool, gym and so forth, tennis, squash, croquet, riding, coarse fishing, and boats for river trips; good disabled access ☺

WINSLOW SP7627 **Bell** *Market Sq, Winslow, Buckingham, Buckinghamshire MK18 3AB (01296) 714091* **£54**; 43 rms. Elegant black and white timbered inn with beams and open fires, plush hotel bar, all-day coffee lounge, enjoyable bar food, and good lunchtime carvery in restaurant; disabled access

WOOBURN COMMON SU9087 **Chequers** *Kiln Lane, Wooburn Green, High Wycombe, Buckinghamshire HP10 0JQ (01628) 529575* **£102.50**, plus special breaks; 17 stripped pine rms in mock-Tudor wing. Popular inn with unchanging traditional atmosphere in cosy low-beamed bar, standing timbers and alcoves, log fires and comfortable sofas, well kept real ales, good daily-changing food in busy dining room, nice breakfasts, and spacious garden

---

Please let us know what you think of places in the *Guide*. Use the report forms at the back of the book or simply write us a letter.

To see and do

Buckinghamshire Family Attraction of the Year

MILTON KEYNES SP8839 **Gulliver's Land** (Newlands, M1 junction 14) Designed very much with children in mind, this friendly, family-run place is hardly Alton Towers, but most under-12s will happily spend a very enjoyable day here (the rides are a little tame for anyone older). Like its sister parks at Matlock Bath and Warrington, it's loosely based on Jonathan Swift's tale of the shipwrecked surgeon taken prisoner by the pint-sized population of Lilliput. Some bits focus on the story, but they certainly haven't restricted themselves to that: the spinning cups ride is called the Mad Hatters Tea Party, and live performances include a Wild West show. Most of the 30 or so rides and attractions are scaled-down versions of what you'd expect (swinging pirate ships, gentle rollercoasters, log flumes, dodgems, and crazy golf), but some have been created with real thought and some flair: you can travel on musical instruments, flying boots, or a nicely conceived balloon-styled ferris wheel. The central castle and surrounding streets are very well put together, and this year they added a fun new water ride that whisks you through waterfalls and whirlpools. Very young children are well catered for, with face painting, rides like the Flying Fish, and a good play area for the under-5s. Most rides are under cover, but they say some can close in particularly bad weather. They do big events and special activities around Hallowe'en, Bonfire Night and Christmas; it may be worth booking for some of these. Restaurants, cafés, shops, disabled access; open wknds Easter–Jun and daily Jun–mid-Sept – maybe best to ring outside peak summer times; (01908) 609001; £8.50 adults and children, includes unlimited goes on everything all day. Free for children under 90cm (they may not be able to go on some rides).

AMERSHAM SU9597
Older part, especially the High St, retains a number of well preserved buildings from several periods inc the charming Tudor-fronted Kings Arms (good value food), and the Crown, fronted by a Georgian façade, but containing some 16th-c wall paintings and original beams inside.

AYLESBURY SP8113
Buckinghamshire County Museum & Roald Dahl Children's Gallery (St Mary's Sq, Church St) Roald Dahl lived in Buckinghamshire for most of his life, and this museum celebrates the connection with a gallery of hands-on displays that use Dahl's novels and characters to teach children about insects, light and any number of other topics; visitors can crawl through the tunnel of Fantastic Mr Fox, discover Willy Wonka's inventions, and even go inside the Giant Peach to find out what things look like under the microscope. Also a good collection of regional art and a walled garden. Snacks, shop, good disabled access; cl Sun am and

25–26 Dec (Dahl gallery cl until 3pm wkdys in term-time); (01296) 331441; £3.50 (£1.50 without Dahl gallery). The Bottle & Glass out on the A418 at Gibraltar is the closest good dining pub.

BEACONSFIELD SU9391
Bekonscot Model Village 🖼 (Warwick Rd) Popular with readers, this miniature portrayal of rural Britain in the 1930s includes scaled-down churches, castles, zoo and even a racecourse, as well as a gauge-1 model railway. Snacks, shop, disabled access; cl Nov–mid-Feb; (01494) 672919; £4.50. The Greyhound is good for lunch.

BLETCHLEY SP8633
Bletchley Park 🖼 (turn off B4034 at Eight Bells pub, then turn right into Wilton Ave) Victorian mansion featured in the Robert Harris novel *Enigma*, where 12,000 men and women worked cracking German codes during World War II. It now has a series of genuine and untouristy wartime exhibitions and displays, warmly praised by contributors. Some of the code-breaking bits are a little technical, but

there's plenty more to see, inc a toy collection, landscaped grounds, wartime fire engines and a working tank. Snacks, shop, disabled access; open alternate wknds; (01908) 640404; £5. The Crooked Billet (Westbrook End, Newton Longville) has decent food.

BOARSTALL SP6214
Boarstall Duck Decoy Displays and working demonstrations of one of only three remaining 17th-c working duck decoys. Also woodland walks and nature trail. Open wknds and bank hols plus 5–8pm Weds, Apr–Aug; (01844) 237488; £2.10; NT. Brill is the nearest useful place for lunch.

BOOKER SU8390
Blue Max Collection (Wycombe Air Park) We hope you'll still be able to admire the 15 or so aircraft here next summer – the air park was closed for filming as we went to press, which is hardly surprising as the planes, inc a 1917 Sopwith Camel and 1940 Battle of Britain Spitfire, are all veterans of films or TV, from *Indiana Jones* to *Poirot*. There are some displays of film props and memorabilia. Snacks, shop, disabled access; usually open Mon–Fri and Sun, April–Nov, but phone to check; (01494) 529432; £2.75. The George & Dragon in West Wycombe is fairly handy for lunch.

BRADENHAM SU8396
This pretty village is surrounded by ancient woodland, with pleasant strolling possibilities.

BRILL SP6514
The **windmill** (open summer Suns pm) is in a magnificent position right on the edge of the Chilterns, with distant views across Oxford; there's been a mill on this site for over 700 years. In the distinctive and quietly attractive village the Pheasant (with a view of the windmill) is handy for lunch. There's a decent walk up nearby Muswell Hill, or along the ridge and down to Boarstall.

BUCKINGHAM SP6933
Quite a lot of attractive early 18th-c brick buildings, and much of the nostalgic charm of a once important town that has been eclipsed by rivals (in this case Aylesbury and Milton Keynes). The thatched Wheatsheaf out at Maids Moreton does good steaks.

Old Gaol Museum ⊞ (Market Hill) New improvements to this small local history museum include a glazed exercise courtyard and a lift for disabled people. Housed in an extraordinary early Gothic-Revival gaol, the museum has a good audio-visual show in an intact original cell. Shop, disabled access; open Mon–Sat April–Dec, best to ring for Sun opening; (01280) 823020; *£1.50.

BURNHAM BEECHES SU9485
A supreme example of a Chilterns beechwood, splendid in spring and autumn colours, and with maybe a glimpse of deer; maps are posted throughout the forest, but it is quite easy to lose one's bearings. The main starting-point is at East Burnham Common car park, opposite the W end of Beeches Rd at Farnham Common. There are several decent pubs dotted around the forest.

CHALFONT ST GILES TQ0193
Chiltern Open-Air Museum ⊞ (Newland Park, Gorelands Lane) A good few traditional Chilterns buildings that would otherwise have been demolished have found their way here in the last 20 years or so, painstakingly dismantled and rebuilt again piece by piece. Dotted about the 45 acres are structures as diverse as an Iron Age house, a Victorian farmyard, an Edwardian public convenience and a 1940s prefab, with useful displays on their original use; also a pretty woodland walk, and a children's playground. Usually hands-on activities every day, and special events on some bank hols (may have extra charges). Snacks, shop, some disabled access; open Apr–Oct; (01494) 872163; £5.50 (£3 children 5–16). Nearby, the smart Ivy House (London Rd) has good food.

Milton's Cottage (Deanway) The writer brought his family to this timber-framed 16th-c cottage to escape the Plague in 1665, and while here completed *Paradise Lost* and began *Paradise Regained*. Displays of first editions, other rare books and memorabilia, and a charming cottage garden full of plants and flowers mentioned by Milton in his poetry. Shop, disabled access to ground floor; cl 1–2pm, all day Mon (exc bank hols), and

Nov–Feb; (01494) 872313; *£2. The nearby White Hart (Three Households) has decent food.

CHENIES TQ0198
Chenies Manor House Rewarding 15th-c house with Tudor rooms, doll collection, tapestries, priest's hole, and 13th-c crypt; the gardens include a physic garden, herbs and a maze. Home-made teas, shop (good for dried flowers and herbs), disabled access to gardens only; open pm Weds, Thurs and bank hol Mons Apr–Oct; (01494) 762888; £4.80 house and garden, £2.50 garden only. The neighbouring church has the rich family monuments of the Bedfords (viewed through a glass panel), 15th-c brasses, and a Norman font. The Red Lion is good for lunch.

CHESS VALLEY TQ0298
Shared between Bucks and Herts, this is miniature and unspoilt, and handily reached from Chalfont & Latimer station on the Metropolitan Underground line; Chenies and Latimer in Bucks, and Sarratt just over the Herts border, are the villages to head for.

CHETWODE SP6430
Chetwode church A handsome church, notable for its fine Early English windows.

CHILTERNS SU7295
The well wooded Chiltern Hills offer plenty of easy-going walks, with a good scattering of rural pubs and pretty villages, though sometimes you have to choose your path carefully to avoid the numerous suburban developments. Even so, it's easy to escape into idyllic landscapes which some rate above all others for wknd walks. The escarpment where the hills drop sharply down to the plain gives some very distant views, for instance from above Bledlow (useful pub). The signposted Ridgeway takes in the most dramatic features.

CHURCH WOOD SU9786
On the edge of the immaculate village of Hedgerley, this is a nature reserve managed by the RSPB, with over 80 species of birds in 34 acres.

COOMBE HILL SP8506
The highest point in the Chilterns, with its Boer War Memorial (an excellent place for views – and for kite-flying). Wendover Woods with some well marked nature trails are adjacent. The

town of Wendover (the Red Lion Hotel here is walker-friendly) gives nearby access, or you can follow paths from Ellesborough and sneak views of Chequers (the Prime Minister's country retreat (emphatically private); an alternative path in is from Dunsmore.

FAWLEY SU7684
Fawley Court Not the typical English stately home it appears to be; though it does boast some fine Wyatt interiors and an elaborate ceiling by Grinling Gibbons, it's owned by a Polish religious group, and has a unique museum dedicated to their homeland, particularly strong on Polish military history. The grounds (landscaped by Capability Brown) run down to the river, and you can stay here, B&B or half and full board. Shop, limited disabled access; open pm Weds, Thurs and Sun May–Oct (maybe not Whitsun week – phone to check); (01491) 574917; *£4. The Walnut Tree has good food.

FINGEST SU7791
Fingest church This brick and flint church is famous for its huge Norman tower with a twin saddleback roof. The Chequers opposite is nice for lunch, and, below the landmark windmill to the N, this is a particularly delectable valley – try the road round through Turville.

FORTY GREEN SU9291
Royal Standard of England The pub stands out as a quite remarkable old building, full of interesting furniture – crowded at wknds, it's well worth a quiet prowl during the week.

HADDENHAM SP7408
St Tiggywinkles Visitor Centre 🐾 (Aston Rd) A video system in the new visitor centre at this wildlife hospital lets you watch the animals being treated without disturbing them. Outdoors there are gardens with enclosures for the animals that they can't release back into the wild, inc hedgehogs, ducks, badgers and foxes. Snacks, shop, disabled access; cl wknds Christmas–Easter; (01844) 292292; £1.50.

HAMBLEDEN SU7886
Thames walk The footbridge over the weir below the charming Chilterns village of Hambleden is attractive, and is the best starting point on the

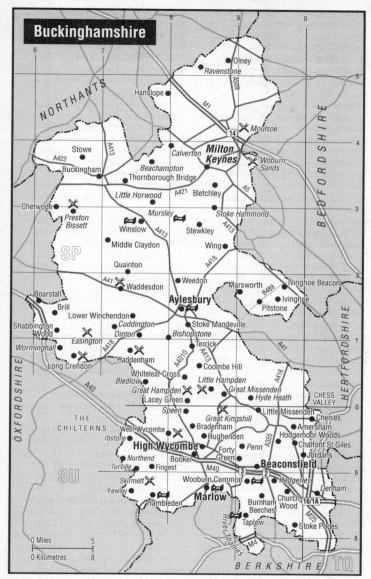

Buckinghamshire

Olney
Ravenstone
Hanslope
Moulsoe
Stowe
Calverton
Milton Keynes
Buckingham
Beachampton
Woburn Sands
Thornborough Bridge
Chetwode
Little Horwood
Bletchley
Preston Bissett
Mursley
Stoke Hammond
Winslow
Stewkley
Middle Claydon
Wing
Quainton
Weedon
Marsworth
Ivinghoe Beacon
Boarstall
Waddesdon
Aylesbury
Ivinghoe
Brill
Pitstone
Lower Winchendon
Shabbington Wood
Cuddington
Stoke Mandeville
Easington
Dinton
Bishopstone
Worminghall
Terrick
Haddenham
Coombe Hill
Long Crendon
Whiteleaf Cross
Little Hampden
Bledlow
Great Hampden
Great Missenden
Lacey Green
Hyde Heath
Speen
Little Missenden
Chenies
Great Kingshill
Bradenham
Amersham
West Wycombe
Hughenden
Hodgemoor Woods
Ibstone
High Wycombe
Penn
Chalfont St Giles
Northend
Booker
Forty Green
Jordans
Turville
Fingest
Beaconsfield
Skirmett
Wooburn Common
Hedgerley
Denham
Fawley
Marlow
Church Wood
Hambleden
Burnham Beeches
Stoke Poges
Taplow
River Thames

NORTHANTS
BEDFORDSHIRE
HERTFORDSHIRE
OXFORDSHIRE
THE CHILTERNS
CHESS VALLEY
BERKSHIRE
SP
SU
TQ

0 Miles   5
0 Kilometres   8

Buckinghamshire bank for riverside walks.

HANSLOPE SP8046
Hanslope church Attractive in its own right, but the most striking feature is its unusually tall spire.

HIGH WYCOMBE SU8593
Wycombe Museum (Castle Hill House, Priory Ave) 18th-c house telling the history of the town's furniture industry which started with chair-making, using beechwood from the Chilterns. There's an unusual collection of various styles of chair produced nearby, as well as pretty landscaped gardens; local history displays with

hands-on exhibits. Shop; disabled access to ground floor; cl Sun am and all day bank hols; (01494) 421895; free.

HODGEMOOR WOODS SU9693 (W of Chalfont St Giles) This ancient woodland has three colour-coded nature trails, giving enjoyable walks of varying lengths.

HUGHENDEN SU8695

Hughenden Manor The home of Benjamin Disraeli until his death in 1881, this imposing old house still has many of the ex-Prime Minister's books and other possessions, as well as related memorabilia, portraits of friends, and formal gardens; he's buried in the grounds. One room should be restored to resemble an original gentleman's smoking room, by the time this book comes out. Snacks, shop, some disabled access; open pm Weds–Sun and bank hol Mons Apr–Oct, wknds only in Mar, cl Good Fri; (01494) 755565; £4.30, garden only £1.50, NT. The Red Lion at Great Kingshill does good fish lunches.

IVINGHOE SP9416

Attractive old village giving its name to the beacon hill high above, with splendid views (esp to the north) and an Iron Age earthwork on top. The Rose & Crown does fresh bar lunches. This enclave is a fragment of Buckinghamshire almost encircled by Hertfordshire.

Ford End Watermill (Station Rd) 18th-c, the only remaining working watermill in the county. An unusual feature is the sheep wash, a special pool into which sheep were dropped and cleaned to make shearing easier. Shop; open pm Easter Mon, then first Sun and bank hols May–Sept, with milling (water level permitting) 3–5pm on bank hols and second Sun in May; £1.20.

IVINGHOE BEACON SP9616

This is a protruding finger of the Chilterns, and the finish of the long-distance Ridgeway Path which begins in Wiltshire. The slopes, too steep for ploughing, comprise woodland, scrub and unspoilt downland; from the beacon itself you look down over eight counties. The Old Swan at Cheddington is the nearest good pub.

JORDANS SU9791

Interesting as a quiet tree-filled village built mainly this century in honour of

the first 17th-c Quaker meeting place here – a simple, evocative building. The nearby Mayflower Barn is built with timbers from the famous ship.

LACEY GREEN SP8100

Lacey Green Smockmill (off A4010) The oldest surviving smock mill in the country, and indeed the third-oldest windmill of any type, built in 1650. It's been well restored. Shop; open Sun pm and bank hols May–Sept; (01844) 343560; 70p. The Pink & Lily does good food – and has kept its little tap room much as Rupert Brooke enjoyed it. Other well restored windmills can be seen at nearby Pitstone and Loosley Row. The mill at Ibstone is unusual for having 12 sides.

LITTLE MISSENDEN SU9298

The church of this pretty village has some wall paintings from the 12th c and some pre-Norman traces, and the village itself has charming old timbered and tiled houses. The attractive old Crown does good sandwiches.

LONG CRENDON SP6909

The cottages in the High St are very pretty, some little changed since the village was a rich wool centre in the 15th c. The Angel is a good dining pub.

Courthouse A particularly lovely timber-framed building, early 15th-c; probably built as a wool store. Open wknds, bank hols and Weds pm, Apr–Sept; £1; NT. There are snacks in the nearby church house.

LOWER WINCHENDON SP7312

This secluded old place has carefully restored houses and a charming, simple church – the walk over the hill to Upper Winchendon gives interesting views.

MARLOW SU8586

Thames Boating Marlow Reach is lively and attractive, and a good centre for trips in either direction. Salters (01865) 243421 operate 40-min cruises May–Sept, £3.75. The Compleat Angler right on the river is a fine place for lunch; on a humbler plane the Two Brewers back over the bridge and the Hare & Hounds out towards Henley are good bets.

MARSWORTH SP9114

Canalside walk Marsworth gives good towpath access to an imposing flight of locks; there's a useful family pub at Startops End.

MIDDLE CLAYDON SP7125
Claydon House 🏛 The wonderfully
over-the-top rococo décor is the prime
attraction of this mainly 18th-c house
(featured in BBC's *Vanity Fair*) – quite a
surprise given the classical simplicity of
the exterior. Highlights are the carvings
by Luke Lightfoot and the fantastic
walls, ceilings and overmantles, though
there are also portraits by Lely and Van
Dyck, and mementoes of Florence
Nightingale, a frequent guest. The
original owner's tastes were
considerably richer than his pockets;
but though his ambitious plans for the
house eventually bankrupted him, his
family still live here. Snacks, disabled
access to ground floor; open pm
Sat–Weds Apr–Oct; (01296) 730349;
£4.20; NT. The Seven Stars between
Twyford and Calvert is a pleasant place
for lunch.

MILTON KEYNES SP8742
Britain's largest New Town is perhaps
also the most successful example of the
idea, with roads well laid out to keep
traffic moving easily and well away from
pedestrians, and a lot of greenery.
Locals are proud of the remarkable
number of public sculptures dotted
around, from the endearing Wounded
Elephant to the famous concrete cows
in a field on the N side of the H3 road
(Monks Way, or A422) near the A5
junction. There's a very swish shopping
centre at Midsummer Boulevard,
named for its alignment with the
summer solstice; a new theatre
development with a gallery, information
centre and restaurants is a recent
addition here. Tucked around the city
are various villagey corners, and the
Swan (Broughton Rd in the Old Village)
and canalside Black Horse at Great
Linford are both pleasant retreats for
lunch.
City Discovery Centre (Bradwell
Abbey) Tells you all you could need to
know about the New Town
development (lots of slides, maps and
old photographs), in a 16th-c
farmhouse in the 17-acre grounds of a
former abbey. Also 14th-c barn and
chapel, medieval fishponds, herb
gardens, and nature trail. Meals, snacks,
shop, disabled access; open Mon–Fri
and some Sun pms, but advisable to

phone in advance to avoid large school
groups; (01908) 227229; free.
Gullivers Land See *separate family
panel on p. 22.*
Milton Keynes Gallery New
contemporary art gallery with changing
exhibitions, in a sleek modern building;
shop, disabled access; cl Mon and bank
hols, maybe other times too – call
(01908) 676900; free.
Milton Keynes Museum (McConnell
Drive, H2 Millers Way) Includes
Victorian and Edwardian room settings,
a school-room, a steam tram, print
shop and a transport hall. A Victorian
Christmas week (pm) starts on the first
Sat in Dec. Snacks, shop, disabled
access; open pm Weds–Sun,
Easter–Oct; (01908) 316222; £3.50.
MILTON KEYNES (WILLEN)
SP8839
Willen Lakeside Park (Brickhill St)
Two lakes – one with water sports,
hotel and restaurant, and the other for
bird-watching; also a Japanese peace
pagoda built by Buddhist monks, turf
maze, and nature trail.

OLNEY SP8951
Pleasant stone-built extended village
with Thurs market and a nice riverside
stroll to the Robin Hood at Clifton
Reynes; the Bull, HQ for the town's
famous Shrove Tuesday pancake race, is
an alternative for lunch, as are the Swan
and Two Brewers.
Cowper and Newton Museum 🏛
(Market Pl) Enthusiastically run, in the
former home of hymn-writer William
Cowper. Several of his personal
possessions, manuscripts and poems
are on display, along with some
belonging to his friend John Newton,
curate of Olney and composer of
'Amazing Grace'. There's a notable
lace-making exhibition, and a restored
period summerhouse in the little
garden. Shop, limited disabled access to
building; cl 1–2pm, all day Sun (exc pms
Jun–Aug) and Mon, and Christmas–Feb;
(01234) 711516; £2.

PITSTONE SP9415
As well as a decent little **agricultural
museum** (open some summer Suns
and bank hols, (01296) 662151) and an
interesting old church, this small village
has the oldest **windmill** in the country,
built in 1627. Open Sun pm and bank

hols Jun–Aug; £1, NT. You can hire canal boats for a day from the Wharf (over the B489), and there are pleasant canal walks from there to the Red Lion or White Lion at Marsworth.

QUAINTON SP7419

Bucks Railway Centre 🏠 (Quainton Rd Station) One of the largest collections of engines and rolling stock we know of, with examples from all over the world attractively displayed in a restored country station; also vintage steam-train rides, workshops, miniature railway, and small museum. Regular half-day steam driving courses (not cheap at £145, but people come away converted for life). Snacks, picnic area, shop; open Sun and bank hols Apr–Oct, plus Weds July–Aug and some wknds in Dec; (01296) 655720; £3.50 (£5 bank hols). Waddesdon is the closest good place for lunch.

Quainton Hill This prominent viewpoint is one of the main features on the 30-mile North Bucks Way, a long-distance footpath from Chequers Knap above Great Kimble to Wolverton in Milton Keynes; the Way also runs past Waddesdon.

Quainton Tower Mill 🏠 Particularly tall 19th-c mill on the edge of the village green; you can watch the continuing restoration work. Shop; open Sun am; (01296) 655348; *£1.

SHABBINGTON WOOD SP6210 (nr Oakley) Designated a Site of Special Scientific Interest because of its rich butterfly habitats; a special butterfly trail helps you to spot some of the 40-odd species here.

STEWKLEY SP8525

The church in this unusually long village has good examples of late Norman work; the village also has two decent pubs, and hour-long **balloon trips** for two far over the countryside – (01525) 240451, £130 per person.

STOKE MANDEVILLE SP8309

Bucks Goat Centre 🏠 (Layby Farm, just off A4010) Goats galore as well as a pig, poultry, sheep, donkeys and pets; you can feed the animals (they sell bags of cut-up vegetables in the shop). Many animals are under cover, so good for a rainy day. Pony rides most wknds. Also farm shop (with cheese and fudge made from goat's milk), and various others

inc a specialist motor-bike shop. Meals, snacks, disabled access; cl Mon (exc bank hols); (01296) 612983; £2.50. The Chequers over at Weston Turville does good lunches.

Oak Farm Rare Breeds Park 🏠 (off A41, E edge of Aylesbury) Friendly little working farm, with animals to feed, walks and nature trails. Snacks, shop, disabled access; open Weds–Sun (plus bank hol Mons) mid-Feb–Oct; (01296) 415709; £2.50. The Chequers in Weston Turville has enjoyable food.

STOKE POGES SU9782

Stoke Poges church The graveyard inspired Thomas Gray's elegy (he's buried here); the church itself has 17th-c stained heraldic glass in the 16th-c chapel.

STOWE SP6737

Stowe Landscape Gardens Stunning gardens stretching over 350 acres, first laid out between 1713 and 1725. Capability Brown was head gardener for ten years, and the monuments and temples that adorn the grounds are by the likes of James Gibb, Sir John Vanbrugh and William Kent. Several suitably grand events throughout the year, but at any time this is a spectacular place to visit, the scale of its artistry quite staggering. Meals, snacks, shop, disabled access (inc electric-powered cars at no extra charge). Meals, snacks, shop, disabled access; open Weds–Sun Apr–Oct, 2–23 Dec, plus Tues July–early Sept; (01280) 822850; £4.60; NT. The house itself (a public school since 1923) is open pm daily (exc some wknds) during the Easter and summer hols (phone to check extra opening times (01280) 818000). You may feel it's outclassed by its surroundings, though it is very elegant from the outside; £2. The Bull & Butcher at Akeley has a good value buffet lunch (not Sun, when the Wheatsheaf at Maids Moreton would be a good substitute).

TAPLOW SU9185

Cliveden 🏠 Nearly 400 acres of lovely formal gardens, woodland and parkland overlooking the Thames. The magnificent house used to belong to the Astors and is now a luxury hotel (and extremely enjoyable as such), although non-resident visitors can see three of the rooms with their family portraits and elegant furnishings and décor. Meals and snacks (not Mon or Tues), shop, very good disabled access; gardens open daily mid-Mar–Dec, house open only Thurs and Sun Apr–Oct from 3–6pm; (01628) 605069; £5, house £1 extra; NT. The village too is attractive.

TERRICK SP8408
Chiltern Brewey Small traditional brewery with guided tours at noon every Sat. Shop, disabled access; cl Sun, 25–26 Dec, 1 Jan; tour £3.50.

THORNBOROUGH BRIDGE SP7433
(A421) A 4½-mile walk starting and ending here, and well described in a leaflet from Bucks County Council, takes in a mill, the site of a medieval village, and the Buckingham Arm Canal. Leaflets (25p) from information centres, or from the County Hall, tel (01280) 823020.

WADDESDON SP7316
Waddesdon Manor One of the spectacular mansions built for Baron Ferdinand de Rothschild at the end of the 19th c. Plenty of rooms to see, each as lavish as the last, and filled with a dazzling array of furnishings, porcelain, portraits, and other objects; there's an unrivalled display of Sèvres china. Parts of the Bachelors' Wing are now fully restored and other improvement work continues. Quite splendid late Victorian formal gardens surround the house, and there's a cast-iron rococo aviary (still in use). The fabled wine cellars have huge vintage bottles, and a collection of labels designed or painted by some of the century's greatest artists. A very satisfying place to visit, but it does get busy; they operate a timed ticket system for the house (can be bought in advance, but £3 booking charge), so if you arrive too late it's possible you won't get in at all. Good meals and snacks, shop, disabled access; house open Weds–Sun and bank hol Mons Apr–Oct (grounds Mar–24 Dec); (01296) 651282; £7, Bachelors' Wing £1, grounds only £3; NT. No under-5s in house. The Five Arrows does very good lunches (and has some good Rothschild wines in all price ranges).

WEEDON SP8018
This is a lovely little village, well worth walking around for the variety of its 17th- and 18th-c houses.

WEST WYCOMBE SU8394
The whole village was bought by the NT in 1929 when it was threatened with road-widening. It's still beleaguered by traffic, and you risk getting run over as you step back to admire the architecture along the village street – all the sites we mention are just off street. The busy George & Dragon in W Wycombe is good for lunch. A visit to the caves and village here can be easily combined with a walk into the beechwoods just N; the pretty village of Bradenham makes a good objective for longer circular walks.

Hell Fire Caves Great fun, these spooky old caves were extended in the 1750s by Sir Francis Dashwood to provide work for the unemployed. Legend has it that the Hell Fire Club he founded met in the tunnels for their drinking, whoring and sorcery. Once through the atmospheric Gothic entrance the tunnels extend for about a third of a mile underground, and are filled with colourful models and tableaux. Underground café, shop; cl wkdys Nov–Feb; *£3.50.

St Lawrence church On the site of an Iron Age fort, adapted by Dashwood, and crowned with a golden ball so big (it can seat six people) that it too served as a meeting-place for the Hell Fire Club. The view from the top of the tower is impressive, and the church's interior has a number of unusual features.

West Wycombe Park 300 acres of beautifully laid-out parkland surround this splendid 18th-c Palladian house, parts of which are currently being restored. The magnificent rooms have a good collection of tapestries, furniture and paintings, and the Italianate painted ceilings are particularly notable. Some disabled access; house and grounds open pm Sun–Thurs Jun–Aug, grounds also open pm Sun, Weds and bank hols Apr–May; (01494) 513569; £4.60, grounds only £2.60; NT.

WHITELEAF CROSS SP8204
A large ancient hill cross dug out of the chalk on the Chilterns escarpment, above which is a neolithic barrow. The Red Lion below is good for lunch, and

the houses of the surrounding hamlet are quite pretty.

WING SP8922

Ascott Another Rothschild mansion, its black and white timbers and jutting gables quite a contrast to the luxuriant opulence of nearby Waddesdon. Once again it's crammed full of treasures, but it feels more like a home and less like a museum; indeed it's still lived in. Ming and K'ang Hsi porcelain, paintings by Hogarth, Rubens and Gainsborough, Dutch art by Hobbema, Cuyp and others, and French and Chippendale furniture. The 260-acre grounds have extensive gardens with rare trees and shrubs, and some intriguing astrological topiary. As we were going to press, they were reviewing their opening times, so best to phone (01296) 688242; £5.60 (£4 garden only), NT.

All Saints church has a fine monument to Sir Robert Dormer (died 1552), a 10th-c apse, crypt and nave, and 12th-c font. The Queens Head has good value home cooking.

WINSLOW SP7627

Keach's Meeting House Fine example of a 17th-c dissenters' chapel; you'll need to get the key from Wilkinson's the estate agent on Market Sq, or from Mr Williams, (01296) 715746. The Bell is useful for lunch.

Winslow Hall Striking house almost certainly designed by Wren, and unusually surviving without any major structural changes. A modest but friendly place, with a collection of Chinese art. Open pm bank hol wknds Easter–Aug, or by appointment; (01296) 712323; £5.

WOOBURN COMMON SU9387

Odds Farm Park Cheery rare breeds centre developed with children in mind. They can go right up to the rare breeds, and join in bottle-feeding the lambs, hand-milking the goats, or collecting the chickens' eggs. Younger children can pet rabbits and guinea-pigs in the pets' corner, while older ones can learn a lot about farm life – displays are instructive as well as fun; also quite a bit of thought has gone into the indoor and outdoor play areas. Special events range from sheepdog demonstrations to parachuting teddy bears. Snacks, shop, disabled access; cl 25–26 Dec, and Mon–Weds mid-Nov–Feb; (01628) 520188; £3.95 (£2.95 children over 2). The Chequers is a good place for lunch.

Other attractive villages, all with decent pubs, include Beachampton SP7737 (stream along main street), Bishopstone SP8010 (pleasant country walks), Bledlow SP7702 (great views; Norman church with early wall-paintings), Calverton SP7939, Cuddington SP7311, Denham TQ0386, Dinton SP7611, Great Missenden SP8901, Hedgerley SU9686, Hyde Heath SU9399, Ibstone SU7593, Little Hampden SP8503, Little Horwood SP7930, Northend SU7392, Penn SU9193 (interesting church), Preston Bissett SP6529, Ravenstone SP8450, Speen SU8399, Stoke Hammond SP8829, Turville SU7690 (perhaps the most lovely valley of all here) and Worminghall SP6308.

Where to eat

EASINGTON SP6810 **Mole & Chicken** *Easington* *(01844) 208387* Bustling country dining pub with very attractively furnished beamed bar, winter log fires, candles on tables and a relaxed atmosphere, particularly good interesting food served by neatly dressed young staff, and a fine range of drinks; cl 25 Dec; partial disabled access. £25|£7

GREAT HAMPDEN SP8401 **Hampden Arms** *(01494) 488255* Comfortable two-room country pub by cricket green with civilised atmosphere, interesting reasonably priced food, real ales, quietly obliging service, and a tree-sheltered garden; good for nearby walks; partial disabled access. £20|£4.95

GREAT KINGSHILL SU8798 **Red Lion** *Missenden Rd* *(01494) 711262* Little brick and flint cottage with simple furnishings, very fresh fish from Billingsgate served by friendly Spanish landlord and his staff, and good house wines; cl Sun pm, Mon. £25

HADDENHAM SP7408 **Green Dragon** *8 Churchway (01844) 291403* Civilised dining pub with particularly imaginative food in its two attractively decorated, high-ceilinged rooms, a French brasserie-type atmosphere, well chosen wines, real ales, a winter log fire, and seats outside on the big sheltered terrace; cl Sun pm; children over 6; disabled access. £28|**£8.50**

LITTLE HAMPDEN SP8503 **Rising Sun** *(01494) 488393* Secluded upmarket dining pub surrounded by fine walks, with consistently excellent interesting food, a short but decent wine list, real ales, and an attractive terrace; bdrms; cl Sun pm, Mon (open bank hol am); disabled access. £22.50|**£5.95**

LONG CRENDON SP6909 **Angel** *Bicester Rd (01844) 208268* Carefully restored and civilised partly 17th-c dining pub, really now a restaurant, with big sofas in comfortable lounge, very good interesting food in bar and no smoking conservatory dining room, real ales, a big wine list, and friendly staff; bdrms; cl Sun pm. £28

MOULSOE SP9141 **Carrington Arms** *Cranfield Rd (01908) 218050* Well refurbished old brick house with comfortable traditional furnishings, delicious meat and fish displayed in refrigerated glass case with friendly staff who guide you through what is on offer (it is then sold in pounds and ounces and cooked on a sophisticated indoor barbecue), separate bar menu as well, an oyster bar, well kept real ales, and a good range of wines inc champagne by the glass; bdrms; disabled access. £23|**£7.50**

PRESTON BISSETT SP6529 **White Hart** *Pound Lane (01280) 847969* Friendly 18th-c thatched and timbered house with three cosy little rooms, traditional atmosphere and furnishings, tasty often interesting bar food inc lunchtime snacks, real ales and a dozen malt whiskies, and chatty helpful staff; best to book evenings; cl Tues am, and no food Mon or Tues pms. £22|**£7.95**

SKIRMETT SU7790 **Frog** *(01491) 638996* Brightly modernised country inn with the atmosphere of a smart rural local, a mix of comfortable furnishings and open fire in neat beamed bar area, good popular interesting food, efficient service, no smoking restaurant, real ales and a fair range of wines, and lovely garden; bdrms; cl Sun pm from Oct–May; disabled access. £25.70|**£7.50**

WADDESDON SP7416 **Five Arrows** *High Street (01296) 651727* Rather grand small hotel – part of the Rothschild estate – with an informally pubby bar made up of several open-plan rooms, a relaxed but civilised atmosphere, Rothschild family portraits and old estate-worker photographs on the walls, sturdy furnishings on parquet flooring, newspapers and magazines, delicious imaginative food, a no smoking country-house-style restaurant, a formidable wine list, well kept real ales, efficient service, and sheltered back garden; good bdrms; cl 25 Dec pm, 26 Dec. £25.80|**£5.95**

WEST WYCOMBE SU8394 **George & Dragon** *High St (01494) 464414* Striking partly Tudor inn with a cheerful bustling atmosphere in rambling main bar, big log fire, popular food inc very good home-made pies, and big peaceful garden; bdrms (not Christmas, New Year or Easter). £19|**£6**

WOBURN SANDS SP9235 **Spooners** *61 High St (01908) 584385* Smart, pretty restaurant with good value French and English cooking, and a welcoming atmosphere; good value snacks downstairs; cl Sun, Mon, 24 Dec–early Jan; disabled access. £25 dinner, £18 lunch|**£7.95**

Special thanks to Norman Fox

CAMBRIDGESHIRE

A good mix of attractions for all ages and most tastes, plus the city of Cambridge – great for a short visit, with plenty of interest as well as its free-of-charge world-class museums

Cambridge is arguably Britain's most attractive ancient university city, graceful and charming, with plenty of interest to fill a short stay – and it's an easy day out from London. The city is at its best during the university terms, when the college students put life and context into the medieval lanes, buildings and gardens. In summer, when it is host instead to foreign language students, its popularity with coach tours means that particular places can suddenly overflow with visitors, so perhaps the best time of all is spring or autumn. Spring is a particular delight in the University Botanic Garden. In winter, like the rest of the county, it can be very chill. Punting with a picnic is a great summer pastime.

Elsewhere, families are well catered for by a broad range of places. Ever-improving and with a constant flux of new inmates, Hamerton Wildlife Centre earns itself this county's Family Attraction of the Year award. Friendly Linton Zoo is best for children in the summer holidays, and the new Waterworld & Bug City at Willers Mill Wildlife should appeal to those with a soft spot for creepy-crawlies.

Stately Wimpole Hall and its friendly farm wrap together plenty of variety for a good day out. Medieval Denny Abbey at Chittering and its associated farm museum has village reconstructions and summer events. Stepping back even further in time, a museum and reconstructed farm puts into context the ongoing discoveries at Flag Fen Bronze Age Excavation site.

The Duxford Air Museum goes from strength to strength: flying history on a massive scale, right up to the present. The Nene Valley Railway is another good family outing.

Some good wildlife reserves include Wicken Fen, parts of Grafham Water, and Wood Walton Fen, new to the book this year, and developed around the remains of old brick pits. Older people like quiet Ely with its graceful cathedral and most unusual stained-glass museum, Anglesey Abbey at Lode, Elton Hall and the haunting American War Cemetery at Coton. There are some lovely villages to stroll through, often with fine churches. Evensong at King's College Chapel or Ely Cathedral is very special.

The countryside is a touch monotonous – especially the north's flat silt fens and vast level fields. But there are those who love the misty bleakness in autumn, say, and this area has a lot to offer bird-watchers. To the west, the land's drier and more rolling, with stone-built villages more reminiscent of Leicestershire.

Where to stay

CAMBRIDGE TL4459 **Arundel House** *Chesterton Rd, Cambridge CB4 3AN* (01223) 367701 **£93**; 105 comfortable rms, 3 without bthrm, some overlooking the river. Carefully preserved terrace of fine early Victorian houses overlooking the River Cam and parkland; comfortable, attractive bar with two fires, elegant restaurant, large and airy plant-filled conservatory, good imaginative food, and seats in the pleasant garden

CAMBRIDGE TL4359 **Cambridge Lodge** *139 Huntingdon Rd, Cambridge CB3 0DQ* (01223) 352833 **£77.50**; 15 rms, 12 with own bthrm. Mock-Tudor house on the outskirts, with open fire in relaxed and comfortable lounge, friendly service, and good freshly prepared food in the popular restaurant

DUXFORD TL4845 **Duxford Lodge** *Ickleton Rd, Duxford, Cambridge CB2 4RU* (01223) 836444 **£89**w; 15 good-sized rms. Carefully run Victorian hotel in an acre of neatly kept gardens, with a restful little lounge, spacious bar, relaxed atmosphere, and enjoyable modern cooking in the airy no smoking restaurant

ELY TL5480 **Lamb** *2 Lynn Rd, Ely, Cambridgeshire CB7 4EJ* (01353) 663574 **£90**; 32 comfortable rms. Pleasant, neatly kept old coaching inn nr the cathedral, with two smart bars, enjoyable food in an attractive restaurant, very friendly staff, and good car parking

HUNTINGDON TL2471 **Old Bridge** *1 High St, Huntingdon, Cambridgeshire PE18 6TQ* (01480) 452681 **£95***, plus wknd breaks; 24 excellent rms with CD stereos and power showers. Creeper-covered Georgian hotel with pretty lounge, log fire in panelled bar, imaginative British cooking and extensive wine list in the partly no smoking restaurant and more informal lunchtime room (nice murals), and quick courteous service; riverside gardens; disabled access

LITTLE GRANSDEN TL2853 **Gransden Lodge Farm** *Longstowe Rd, Little Gransden, Sandy, Bedfordshire SG19 3EB* (01767) 677365 **£40**; 4 attractive rms, most with own bthrm. Set on a working farm of 860 acres, this no smoking friendly house has a big lounge with open fire, well appointed dining room, and gardens; no evening meals (plenty of pubs and restaurants locally)

NEEDINGWORTH TL3571 **Pike & Eel** *Overcote Lane, Needingworth, St Ives, Huntingdon, Cambridgeshire PE17 3TW* (01480) 463336 **£70**; 11 rms. 17th-c inn in very peaceful riverside spot with spacious lawns and grounds by marina, roomy plush bar, big open fire and easy chairs in smaller room, glass-walled restaurant, carvery, real ale, good breakfasts, and friendly staff; disabled access

SIX MILE BOTTOM TL5857 **Swynford Paddocks** *Six Mile Bottom, Newmarket, Cambridgeshire CB8 0UE* (01638) 570234 **£135**, plus wknd breaks; 15 individually furnished rms with good bthrms. Gabled country house in neat grounds overlooking stud paddocks; carefully furnished rooms with fresh flowers and log fires, a relaxed atmosphere, good food, and friendly service; tennis, putting, and croquet

STILTON TL1689 **Bell** *7 High St, Stilton, Peterborough, Cambridgeshire PE7 3RA* (01733) 241066 **£89.50***; 19 rms. Elegant, carefully restored coaching inn with attractive rambling bars, big log fire, generous helpings of good food using the famous cheese (which was first sold from here), and seats in the sheltered cobbled and flagstoned courtyard; cl 25 Dec

WANSFORD TL0799 **Haycock** *London Rd, Wansford, Peterborough, Cambridgeshire PE8 6JA* (01780) 782223 **£80**, plus special breaks; 50 attractively decorated rms. Old-fashioned golden stone inn with relaxed, comfortable, carefully furnished lounges and pubby bar; pretty lunchtime café, smart restaurant with good food, excellent wines and efficient friendly service; garden with boules, fishing and cricket; disabled access. The little village it dominates is attractive, with a fine bridge over the Nene, and a good antiques shop

---

Please let us know what you think of places in the *Guide*. Use the report forms at the back of the book or simply write us a letter.

To see and do

Cambridgeshire Family Attraction of the Year

HAMERTON TL1481 **Hamerton Wildlife Centre** Much expanded since it opened in 1990, but still a nicely manageable size, this dedicated centre has a splendidly varied collection of rare and endangered species from all over the world; some are now extinct in the wild, and others can't be seen anywhere else in the UK. Set over 15 acres of pretty countryside, it's a real favourite with some readers; we know of one couple who come here almost every month. They've established quite a reputation for successful breeding, and exchange programmes with other zoos mean regular visitors will generally see something new; they do a season ticket to save on repeat visits. Some of the enclosures have windows at child height so that younger visitors have an easy view of the animals, and another is full of tame animals that children can stroke. There are over a hundred different species, from playful marmosets, lemurs and gibbons, through cheetahs, wolves and boa constrictors, to smaller animals such as tortoises and porcupines; they also have plenty of birds. They've recently started having talks from the keepers at feeding times at wknds and school holidays – the schedule varies, so it's worth calling ahead to see what's going on. Wellies may be useful in winter, though there are good paved paths throughout. Decent play area. Not much is under cover (there is a covered picnic area, or you can eat on the lawns), but if it rains they generally give you free tickets to come back another day. Sensibly priced tearoom (closed in winter), small shop, disabled access (when dry); cl 25 Dec; (01832) 293362; £4.95, £3.95 children 3–12. Their website, www.hamertonzoopark.com, usually has money-saving offers, such as a voucher for free entry for a child accompanied by two paying adults.

BARNACK TF0704
Barnack has interesting dotted-about clusters of stone-built houses, a windmill, a part-Saxon church, and a fine pub (the Millstone).

BARRINGTON TL3949
Superb village green surrounded by pretty timbered houses, an interesting church and a good pub; the nearby village of Foxton is especially interesting if you know the book *The Common Stream* by Rowland Parker (an intricate account of the village through the ages).

BOURN TL3158
The working **windmill** here is thought to be the oldest trestle post mill in the country. Usually open pm last Sun of month, Mar–Oct; (01223) 243830; £1. The Duke of Wellington has good food.
Wysing Arts Lively arts centre set in 11 acres of farmland, with contemporary art exhibitions and a continuous programme of events. Also workshops in sculpture and ceramics studios (£1.50–£100). Good disabled access; (01954) 718881; free.

BURWELL TL5866
Burwell church This handsome and airy building has a fine oak roof. The village also has a restored windmill.
CAMBRIDGE TL4458
Quieter and prettier than Oxford (which the colleges here were founded to escape), the centre is dominated by ancient and graceful university buildings: you get a real sense of centuries of study. It still has the character of a small, old-fashioned market town, almost untouched by the modern world; Cambridge's hi-tech light industry is kept firmly on the outskirts. Between the colleges and university buildings are numerous less imposing but attractive old buildings, often grouped together quite picturesquely. The architecture has a striking diversity (continuous development of the colleges means that most have much-loved or maligned modern blocks), though isn't always shown off at its best, thanks to layers of muck and grime that rather spoil some of the libraries and faculty buildings.

Happily, one of the most delightful parts of town, **The Backs**, where the river snakes through the colleges, never looks less than charming, with its delightful lawns, trees, college gardens, punts gliding past the weeping willows and sometimes even grazing cattle opposite King's. Don't try to drive around town; there really is no parking, and apart from the pedestrianised centre there's a frustrating tangle of congested one-way streets. Head for one of the big out-of-town car parks and use the excellent park and ride system. If you don't plan to take a car at all, it's worth noting that the railway station is far from central, although there is a frequent bus service into the historic centre. Chauffeured trishaws can offer a pleasant alternative way to get around. For a first-time visit, the Tour Bus (about an hour) is a good introduction. Walking tours set off from the Tourist Information Centre (Wheeler St) four times a day in summer (£7 inc entrance to King's Chapel, last tour £6 inc entrance to St John's – best to book in advance). Cyclists will enjoy the towpaths here; nettle-free, and safe if you have children with you. Quite a few shops are that bit different and worth popping into. In term-time, there are countless events; any college notice-board will show what's on. West Road concert hall has outstanding acoustics, while a concert in one of the smaller college chapels can be a charmingly intimate experience.

Cambridge & County Folk Museum ▣ (2–3 Castle St) Useful exploration of local life in a handsome 16th-c former inn nr the river – a touch-screen database includes contemporary residents' diaries and 'virtual' city tours. Shop; cl winter Mon; (01223) 355159; *£2.

Cambridge churches Of the many churches here, it's worth noting **St Bene's**, one of the city's oldest, the popular **Holy Sepulchre** or Round Church (which has brass-rubbing), and **Great St Mary's** with its fine roof and good city views from the tower.

Cambridge colleges The colleges look private, but you can usually wander into the courtyards (not at exam time, and expect to be charged by

many during the summer). Be warned though, college porters will get terribly agitated if you even look at the grass let alone accidentally step on it. Several of the dining halls and chapels are worth seeking out. The largest, finest and richest college is Trinity, where the imposing Great Court is usually open to the public, and the Wren Library (open wkdys 12–2pm) in Neville's Court is definitely worth a visit. King's is probably the best known, with its magnificent chapel, and is pleasant to walk through. Gonville & Caius (pronounced 'keys') is small and slightly snooty, but very pretty. Queen's has a half-timbered courtyard and an eye-catchingly gaudy painted hall, as well as the famous Mathematical Bridge (reputedly built without any bolts or fastenings, until curiosity got the better of some engineers who dismantled it and found they couldn't put it back together in the same way). Peterhouse is the oldest, founded in 1284; the buildings carry their years very gracefully, although these days its deer park is devoid of deer. Opposite, Pembroke's chapel is one of Wren's first buildings. St John's has the very photographed Bridge of Sighs. Jesus, a bit off the main beat, is huge and grandly impressive, and Emmanuel has notable gardens. Clare and Trinity Hall are smaller yet charming colleges, next to each other by The Backs.

Fitzwilliam Museum (Trumpington St) This is a wonderful place, a grand and impressive building, crammed with more dazzling treasures than you could hope to examine in one visit. Downstairs are Greek, Egyptian, and Roman antiquities, European ceramics, English glass, carvings, and armour, while upstairs you'll find furniture, sculpture and paintings by Titian, Canaletto and French Impressionists; both galleries are open all day. Decent café, shop, disabled access; cl Mon (exc bank hols), 24 Dec–1 Jan, Good Fri; (01223) 332900; free.

Kettle's Yard (Castle St) Lively arts centre with temporary exhibitions in the gallery and permanent displays in the avant-garde yet surprisingly welcoming house, taking in 20th-c paintings and sculptures (interesting St

Ives connections), lovely 18th-c furniture and oriental carpets, and collections of shells and stones. Lots of activities and workshops, several designed especially for the blind or hard of hearing. Devotees say the sunlight on winter afternoons illuminates the exhibits to extraordinary effect. Shop, some disabled access; cl am, all Mon (exc bank hols); (01233) 352124; free.

King's College Chapel The annual Festival of Nine Lessons and Carols has made the interior and something of the atmosphere familiar to most visitors, but you're still not fully prepared for the grandeur and scale of the fan-vaulted ceiling, or the miraculously preserved 16th-c stained glass. The overall effect is marred slightly by the unique dark oak screen added by Henry VIII, but the chapel's other famous feature – Rubens's *Adoration of the Magi* – is quite breathtaking. Try to attend choral evensong at 5.30pm Mon–Sat in term-time, or one of the Sun services (3.30pm and 6pm). Shop, disabled access; cl most of Sun during term-time, Easter Sun and 24 Dec–3 Jan – phone to check other times; (01223) 331155; *£3.50.

Other Cambridge museums Most of the town's other museums have a rather academic bent, but are no less rewarding for that: the **Sedgwick Museum** (Downing St) is the university geology museum, with an outstanding collection of fossils, and rocks from Darwin's journey in HMS *Beagle*. The curator not so long ago proved that iguanadons were put together differently from how scientists had previously thought; the bones of his museum's 20-ft specimen have not been rearranged for historical reasons although theoretically, he claims, it is currently in agony. Shop, limited disabled access; cl 1–2pm, Sat pm, all Sun, Christmas–New Year, Easter; free. Down the same street is the **Museum of Archaeology & Anthropology**, home to a 50-ft totem pole (open pm Tues–Sat, cl Christmas, Easter; free) and a **Museum of Zoology**, where a 70-ft whale skeleton hangs above the entrance inside (cl wknds and 1–2pm outside term-time; free). The **Museum of Classical Archaeology** on

Sidgwick Ave has one of the few surviving collections of casts of Greek and Roman sculpture (cl wknds; free), while the various scientific instruments and apparatus at the **Whipple Museum of Science** (Free School Lane) quickly make you thankful we need no longer rely on sundials and abacuses (open pm wkdys though best to check outside term; (01223) 334500; free).The **Scott Polar Research Institute** (Lensfield Rd) houses fascinating exhibits from the fateful polar expedition inc diaries, letters, clothing and an Eskimo carving. Shop, disabled access; open pm Mon–Sat (exc bank hols); free. The exhibition centre at the towering and austere **University Library** (West Rd) has occasional displays of rare and ancient manuscripts; cl Sat pm and all Sun; free.

Punting 🖾 The only way to travel, though if your skills in this department were picked up in Oxford you'll find they do things a little back to front here. You can punt right along The Backs, and even down to Grantchester, a pleasant little village still much as described in Rupert Brooke's poem of the same name, with the civilised Orchard Tea Gardens (lovely in summer – and does other drinks too, inc champagne) and three pubs. Hire punts from Scudamores on Mill Lane (01223) 359750 or other stations along the water; prices are generally around £10 an hour (£35 if you require a chauffeur). Bumps races (several rowing eights start off in a line and have to catch up with the one in front) take place on the river in Feb, Jun and July.

Shopping There are lots of **secondhand bookshops** worth a look. Heffers children's bookshop is particularly good, and the general bookshops are as fine as you'd expect in this university town. On the first Sat of the month there's a **craft fair** on St John's Green, and **Primavera Contemporary Craftwork** (10 King's Parade) has changing exhibitions of contemporary British painting and craftwork. The decent **Cambridge Darkroom** (photography) is relocating, so phone to check new address; (01223) 566725.

Snacks in Cambridge Many

attractive snack places include Clowns (King St, off Sidney St), Roof Garden (top floor of Arts Theatre – side entrance in St Edward's Passage opposite King's), Boards (down a floor), the tiny Little Tea Room (All Saints Green), Copper Kettle (King's Parade), King's Pantry (King's Parade), Hobbs Pavilion (fantastic pancakes), Parker's Piece and Browns (Trumpington St). Decent **riverside pubs** include the Anchor (Silver St Bridge), Boathouse (Chesterton Rd), Fort St George (Midsummer Common) and the Mill (Mill Lane). The best pubs away from the river are the smoke-free Cambridge Blue (Gwydir St) and atmospheric Eagle (Bene't St).

Towpath walks From Magdalene Bridge right in Cambridge itself there's a pleasant walk by the towpath out into the meadows – tranquil, with only punts as far as the lock. Beyond that, you could walk as far as Ely, with oarsmen setting an altogether more vigorous tone – though the Ancient Shepherds or the Plough at Fen Ditton might be a gentler target. Another pleasant stroll out from Cambridge – in the opposite direction – is the walk along the Cam to Grantchester.

University Botanic Garden (Cory Lodge, Bateman St) Founded in 1762 and moved to its present site in 1831, now covering 40 acres, with some marvellous mature trees, a geographic rock garden, scented garden, water and winter gardens, and many rare plants inc several National Collections. Rarely crowded, and very pleasant to stroll through. Snacks (wknds only in winter), summer shop, disabled access; cl 25–26 Dec; (01223) 336265; *£2.

CASTOR TL1298
Ancient village with a pleasantly relaxed mood. It has a fine church, several handsome thatched stone-built houses, and two pleasant pubs – both thatched too.

CHITTERING TL4868
Denny Abbey & Farmland Museum (off A10) 12th-c Benedictine abbey with some impressive Norman remains and a 14th-c nuns' refectory. The museum focuses on farming and the county's rural history, with reconstructions of a village shop, pub,

kitchen and dairy. Workshops and events Easter–Sept; wknd snacks, shop, disabled access; open pm Apr–Oct; (01223) 860489; £3.40. The Travellers Rest has decent food.

COTON TL4059
Cambridge American War Cemetery Established in 1944 on land donated by Cambridge University, this beautiful haunting tribute to the American servicemen and women who lost their lives in World War II covers 30 acres, framed by woodland to the W and S. The Portland stone memorial chapel has some intriguing features inc a map of air assaults over the Atlantic and stained-glass windows depicting the seals of the States arranged from left to right in the order that they entered the Union. Disabled access; (01954) 210350; free. The John Barleycorn in the village is a useful lunch stop.

CROYDON TL3149
Croydon church Quietly charming, a proper country church with a timeless feel. The Queen Adelaide is a popular dining pub.

DEEPING ST JAMES TF1410
Exotic Pet Refuge Quite impressive pet sanctuary, solidly improving as it gathers funds; adequate and well built enclosures inc a bat house, easily the equal of many zoos; other animals range from jungle cats and lemurs to snakes and monitor lizards. Open on only a few wknds throughout the year, when they provide refreshments, best to phone (01778) 345923; £2.

DEVIL'S DITCH TL5765
This miles-long ancient embankment lets you fuel a walk with speculations on whether it was built to fight off the Romans, or some centuries later to protect the riches of East Anglia from Midlands warlords. A good start or finish might be the Kings pub in Reach, at its N end: expert German cooking. It's not much of a topographical feature, and is crossed by one or two very busy roads.

DUXFORD TL4546
Duxford Airfield Very handy from Cambridge, this branch of the Imperial War Museum is home to Europe's best collection of military and civil aircraft, with over 140 flying machines from

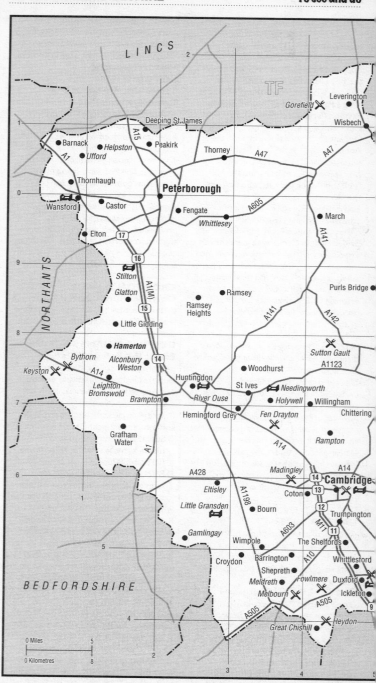

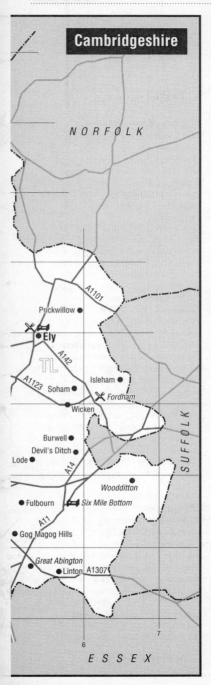

Cambridgeshire

NORFOLK

A1101
Prickwillow •
Ely
A142
TL
A1123   Soham •   Isleham •
Fordham
Wicken •
SUFFOLK
Burwell •
Devil's Ditch •
Lode •   A14
Woodditton •
• Fulbourn   Six Mile Bottom
A11
• Gog Magog Hills
Great Abington
• Linton   A1307

6   7

ESSEX

flimsy-looking biplanes to state-of-the-art Gulf War jets. Children particularly enjoy the fun hands-on section, where they can go into the cockpits of some exhibits; preserved hangars, control towers and operations rooms create something of the atmosphere Duxford must have had when it was a working World War II air base. A realistic hi-tech flight simulator re-creates a Battle of Britain dogfight, and there's also the prototype Concorde, a summer narrow-gauge railway, pleasure flights, and an adventure playground; airshows in summer – phone for details. Meals and snacks (or plenty of space for picnics), shop, disabled access; cl 24–26 Dec; (01223) 835000; £7.40 (children are free). The Green Man close by at Thriplow makes for an interesting pub lunch.

ELTON TL0892
Elton Hall From the back a splendid 'gothick' fantasy, this is a fascinating lived-in house dating back to Tudor times, with lovely furnishings, porcelain and paintings, inc works by 15th-c Old Masters and Gainsborough and Constable. The library has a Prayer Book that belonged to Henry VIII (his writing is inside), and the gardens are especially pleasant in summer when the roses are in bloom. New shop, adjacent garden centre and tearoom, disabled access to garden only; open pm 27–28 May, Weds pm Jun–Aug, plus Thurs and Sun pm July–Aug, and pm 27 Aug (usually antiques fairs on bank hols); (01832) 280468; £5, £2.50 garden. The Black Horse nearby has good interesting food, and the attractive stone-built village has a lovely Saxon church.

ELY TL5480
Busy little market town with good shops and some lovely old buildings; it well repays a leisurely stroll. The Prince Albert, handy for the cathedral, has a nice garden. The Cutter, out at Annesdale off the A10, is an attractively placed riverside family pub.

Ely Cathedral One of England's most striking, its distinctive towers dominating the skyline for miles; especially good views coming in on the Soham road. Complete by the late 12th c, it was restored in a surprisingly sympathetic manner mainly in the mid-19th c. The façade, covered in blind arcading, is fantastic, but most remarkable perhaps is the Octagonal Tower, over 400 tons suspended in space without any visible means of support; it looks especially impressive from inside. The Lady Chapel has the widest medieval vault in the country, and the walls are carved with hundreds of tiny statues which were all somewhat brutally beheaded in the Reformation. The splendid Norman nave seems even longer than it really is because it's so narrow. Also not to be missed are a couple of elaborately sculpted medieval doors – and see if you can spot the railwayman's epitaph, with its unique imagery. Readers have particularly enjoyed the evensong here, every day (exc Weds) at 5.30pm. Meals, snacks, shop, disabled access; (01353) 667735; £4.

Ely Museum (Old Gaol, Market St) Displays include one on Hereward the Wake, who led the Anglo-Saxon resistance to the Norman Conquest from here. Shop; disabled access; cl 2 wks over Christmas; (01353) 666655; £2.

Oliver Cromwell's House 🖼 (St Mary's St) Next to the unexpectedly grand church of St Mary's, this fine old house was the home of Oliver Cromwell and his family from 1636 until shortly before he became Lord Protector. Period furnished rooms, useful videos (one on the draining of the Fens), and information centre in the downstairs front room. Shop; cl 25–26 Dec, 1 Jan; (01353) 662062; *£3.

Stained Glass Museum 🖼 Housed in the cathedral's south triforium, this preserves fine medieval and more modern stained glass rescued from redundant buildings and churches. Good displays on how the windows are made, and a bonus is the unusual view down over the cathedral. Shop; cl Sun am, 25 Dec and Good Fri; (01353) 660347; *£3.50.

FENGATE TL2199

Flag Fen Bronze Age Excavation 🖼 (Fengate, 2m E of Peterborough) Fascinating and well organised prehistoric site, with an excellent Bronze Age museum displaying finds

from the ongoing excavations. In summer you should be able to watch archaeologists painstakingly uncovering more secrets, and a reconstructed Bronze Age farm (inc primitive breeds of sheep and pigs) puts the discoveries in context. Snacks, shop, mostly disabled access; cl 25 Dec–2 Jan; (01733) 313414; £3.50, EH.

FULBOURN TL5155
This is an attractive largely thatched village, with a windmill on the Cambridge road, a good farm shop with pick-your-own fruit, and a pretty church; a path takes you eastwards to the wooded line of the Fleam Dyke, a miles-long Dark Ages defence earthwork.

GOG MAGOG HILLS TL4953
Not exactly a towering range, these are worth a passing visit; among tall trees you can trace the main rampart and ditch of **Wandlebury Iron Age fort**, and there are good views of the city's distant towers and spires.

GRAFHAM WATER TL1667
Well liked by readers, this offers fishing and sailing, cycle hire, a nature reserve with bird-watching hides and trails (you'll see a lot more birds in winter); exhibition centre. There's an attractive waterside path along the northern shore. Snacks, good disabled access; £2 car parking charge; (01480) 812154; free. The Wheatsheaf at West Perry is a popular refreshment stop, and if you're travelling on the B661 from here to Staunton, look out for the roadside stall at the Dillington crossroads – excellent pickled onions and the like, reasonably priced.

HAMERTON TL1481
Hamerton Wildlife Centre See *separate family panel on p. 34.*

HEMINGFORD GREY TL2970
Charming village with a peaceful view of the church over the willow-bordered river (the odd church tower is the result of its spire being lopped off by an 18th-c storm); one stone house among the thatched brick ones is Norman and said to be England's oldest. Nearby Hemingford Abbots is also pretty, and the Axe & Compass here is useful for lunch.

HUNTINGDON TL2371
After considerable recent growth the

old centre now feels a bit sidetracked, but has one or two fine buildings such as the George, a particularly handsome Georgian coaching inn. The Old Bridge is a good civilised place for lunch. **Cromwell Museum** (Grammar School Walk) Two of Huntingdon's MPs can claim to have run the country for a while, and this commemorates the first. The restored Norman building is where the future Lord Protector went to school (as did Pepys), and many of his possessions are on display. Shop; cl 1–2pm, all Mon, am winter Sun and wkdys, 24–26, 31 Dec and 1 Jan; (01480) 425830; free.
Hinchingbrooke Country Park (a couple of miles W) Good for a walk, a run-about or picnic. Guided walks or events most wknds, and there are water sports on the lake. Wknd snacks, disabled access; (01480) 451568; free.
Hinchingbrooke House Now a school, this is where some reckon Cromwell and Charles I met as children. Snacks, disabled access; usually open pm summer Suns from first May bank hol–Aug bank hol; (01480) 375700; £2. The Olde Mill opposite is a delightfully set family dining pub.
ICKLETON TL4944
This attractive village has a fine church, with Roman columns as bases for its arches, and interestingly carved pews. The churchyard is lovely, and around the church and small green are several beautiful old houses – often a good deal older than their Georgian refacing suggests.
ISLEHAM TL6474
Isleham church Attractive from the outside, but its best feature is its wonderful roof.
LEVERINGTON TF4411
Leverington church The tower and its spire are noteworthy, as is the very unusual two-storey 14th-c porch.
LINTON TL5648
Chilford Hall Vineyard (towards Balsham) A friendly 18-acre winery with interesting old buildings and tours on the hour. Snacks, shop, disabled access; cl Christmas–Feb; (01223) 892641; £4.50 (inc tastings and a little souvenir glass). The Pear Tree in Hildersham does decent family food.

Linton Zoological Gardens (B1052, just off A604) Well liked by readers, this friendly family-run zoo has a firm emphasis on conservation and breeding. Current residents include giant tortoises, snow leopards, a couple of Grevy's zebras, tigers, and marabou storks, all housed in enclosures as close to their natural habitats as possible. Family quiz trails in school holidays, play area for smaller children, picnic areas around the prettily landscaped grounds (some under cover), and children's pony rides on summer wknds. Snacks, shop, disabled access; cl 25 Dec; (01223) 891308; £5.
LITTLE GIDDING TL1281
Little Gidding church Archetypal small-village country church, well worth a look inside; if it's closed, ask at the farmhouse.
LODE TL5362
Anglesey Abbey All that remains of the original priory is a medieval undercroft, but the handsome 17th-c house has an engaging collection of clocks and eclectic range of furniture and paintings; it's definitely worth pausing at Constable's view of the Thames and the landscapes by Claude. The bookshelves in the library are made from Rennie's Waterloo Bridge. The lovely gardens were laid out in Georgian style from 1926 by the first Lord Fairhaven, and a restored watermill in the grounds still produces flour. Varied events and activities, inc highly regarded open-air theatre and opera. Meals, snacks, shop, some disabled access; house open pm Weds–Sun and bank hols late Mar to mid-Oct, grounds open from 10.30am (also open Mon and Tues most of July to mid-Sept; the new winter walk through part of the grounds is open Oct–Mar). Restaurant, shop and plant centre; (01223) 811200; £6.10 (£7.10 Sun and bank hols), £3.75 grounds only; NT. The Red Lion at attractive Swaffham Prior does decent fresh food.
MARCH TL4195
Pleasant country town, market day Weds; a good base for exploring the Fens. St Wendreda's church with its wonderful angel roof was described by Betjeman as being 'worth cycling 40 miles in a headwind to see'. The Acre

(Acre Rd) has good home cooking.

PEAKIRK TF1606

Waterfowl World Over 100 different species of waterfowl inc rare and unusual breeds, all in a lovely setting. Most were reared in captivity and can be fed by hand – always fun; they sell corn in the gatehouse but the birds seem to prefer bread, so take some along. A good outing even if you're not exactly a twitcher, fascinating if you are. Snacks, shop, disabled access; last entry 2pm Nov–Mar, cl 24–25 Dec; (01733) 252271; £3.50. The Ruddy Duck is popular for lunch.

PETERBOROUGH TL1998

Has preserved much of its long history and fine old buildings, though it expanded hugely in the mid-1970s and is now a thriving industrial town (with a good pedestrianised shopping centre). Sculptures have been commissioned for the new network of cycleways, footpaths and bridleways that links tourist attractions and nature reserves with residential areas. Charters (by Town Bridge) is an enjoyable floating pub/restaurant in a converted barge. The best place for lunch is some miles outside the town – the Haycock, along the A47 at Wansford.

City Museum & Art Gallery (Priestgate) Among other interesting exhibits are some unusual models made from fishbones by Napoleonic prisoners of war. Shop, disabled access; open Tues–Sat; (01733) 343329; free.

Ferry Meadows Country Park (off A605 W of Peterborough) Useful for children to let off steam; 500 acres with children's play areas, two big lakes with water sports, fishing and boat trips, bird reserves, pony rides, miniature railway and two golf courses and pitch and putt nearby. Visitor centre; summer snacks, shop, disabled access; (01733) 234443; free. Parking charge wknds and bank hols Apr–Oct, £2.30.

Longthorpe Tower (Thorpe Rd, W of centre) 13th/14th-c fortified house with rare wall paintings (open pm wknds and bank hols Apr–Oct; £1.60); EH.

Peterborough Cathedral One of the most dramatic in the country, its extraordinary west front a medieval

masterpiece, with a trio of huge arches. Despite the damage inflicted by Cromwell (he is said to have looked on approvingly as prayer books were torn up and the organ smashed), the richly Romanesque interior has preserved its original fabric to a remarkable degree; especially worth a look are the elaborately vaulted retro-choir and the fine early 13th-c painted wooden nave ceiling – though you'll probably need good light and glasses to see this at its best. Meals, snacks, shop, some disabled access; cl 26 Dec, 1 Jan; *£3 donation suggested.

Railworld 🔁 (Oundle Rd) Friendly railway museum; snacks, shop, disabled access; cl wknds Nov–Feb, and 25 Dec–1 Jan; (01733) 344240; *£2.50.

St Margaret's Church (Fletton) On the southern edge of Peterborough, this has some exceptionally fine little Anglo-Saxon sculptures.

PRICKWILLOW TL5982

Drainage Engine Museum 🔁 The story of water, pumping and fen drainage in the area since the last Ice Age, especially interesting when the engines are running, phone for dates. Snacks, shop, disabled access; open daily May–Sept, and wknds and bank hols Oct–Nov and Mar–Apr; (01353) 688360; £2 (£3 when engines running).

PURLS BRIDGE TL4787

Highly recommended for diehard bird-watchers; there's an RSPB reserve off the B1093 with several hides (one with disabled access) and big mugs of coffee.

RAMSEY TL2984

Abbey Gatehouse The ruins of an ornate Gothic gatehouse with buttresses and friezes, along with the 13th-c Lady Chapel (all that's left of the abbey itself). Cl Nov–Mar; free. Some of the stone from the abbey is thought to have made up the nearby local history **museum** (open pm Thurs and Sun Apr–Sept; (01487) 815715; £1). The Cross Keys at Upwood (where there's a windmill) has good value food.

RAMSEY HEIGHTS TL2384

Wood Walton Fen (off B1040 W of Ramsey) Quiet and peaceful nature reserve, developed around the overgrown remains of old brick pits and kilns; nature trails lead through several meadows and along a dyke, and you may spy some of the many small woodland birds from a hide overlooking a marshy area; boardwalks over ponds for a closer look; parking in meadow nearest the lane.

RIVER OUSE TL2772
The stretch between St Ives and Hemingford Grey is a popular wknd stamping-ground, with **Houghton Mill** as a charming set piece – a lovely building in pretty setting; the Three Horseshoes nearby has decent food.

SHELFORDS, THE TL4552
The interlinked villages of Great and Little Shelford will reward a slow stroll for those with an eye for architectural detail, and even a quick drive through will show up several delightful timbered houses.

SHEPRETH TL3847
Docwra Manor Gardens Tranquil gardens, at their best Apr–Jun but always with a variety of unusual plants grown and for sale. The highlight is perhaps the lovely intimate walled garden. Disabled access (although gravel paths may be hard work); open Weds and Fri, plus pm first Sun of month Apr–Oct; (01763) 261557; *£2. The Plough is popular for lunch.

Willers Mill Wildlife Park 🖼
Genuine little wildlife rescue centre with all sorts of unwanted or injured animals and birds from pine martens to parrots. There's a monkey house, and fish farm where the koi will feed from your hand; pony rides summer wknds. Some of the enclosures have been restored since last year, and a new Waterworld & Bug City has scorpions, praying mantis and leaf-cutter ants at work. The entrance isn't that well signed, so keep an eye out. Snacks (in shop and elevated tree-top café), disabled access; cl 25 Dec; (01763) 262226; £4.50.

SOHAM TL5872
As well as a rather grand church, this has two surviving mills – you can buy flour ground here.

ST IVES TL3171
Pleasant little town, with a graceful church, small local museum, and walks by the curving river. There's an unusual tiny chapel on the old bridge, rising straight out of the water; key from museum. In the town, the Royal Oak

does generous food, and the riverside Pike & Eel out at Needingworth is attractively placed for lunch.

THORNEY TF2804
Rises from the flatlands like an island – which it was, when this was all half-submerged marsh. Much older than most villages in the area, it has a Norman-modified Saxon church on its green, and some interesting yellow-brick workers' houses put up by the Duke of Bedford. The friendly **Heritage Museum** has good displays, and organises tours of the village and abbey. Shop, limited disabled access; open pm wknds Easter–Sept, or by appointment; (01733) 270908; museum free, tours £1.50. The Rose & Crown does freshly made food.

THORNHAUGH TF0700
Sacrewell Farm and Country Centre 🖼 (off A47) Based around an old working watermill, with demonstrations and displays of rural crafts, tools and machinery and discovery centre, as well as gardens, children's maze and nature trails, lots of animals, and pick-your-own fruit in season. Pleasantly simple and undeveloped, this is a friendly place, well liked by visitors, and very organised for children. Snacks, shop, disabled access; cl 24 Dec–4 Jan; (01780) 782254; £3. Wansford is very handy for lunch.

TRUMPINGTON TL4454
Trumpington church Attractive in its own right, but perhaps most famous for having the second oldest memorial brass in England.

WANSFORD TL0997
Nene Valley Railway 15-mile round trip on steam trains through delightful countryside to Peterborough. Also a fine collection of steam locomotives and rolling stock, and a small museum. The railway is a favourite with film-makers. Meals and snacks on steam days, shop, disabled access; cl Mon exc bank hols, best to phone for train times, (01780) 784444; £2 site admission (refundable against train fare), £8 for the train. It's easy to extend this into an all-day trip by breaking your journey at one of the country parks alongside stations en route, or by taking a stroll around Peterborough. At the

Wansford end (pretty village), the Haycock is particularly good for lunch.

WHITTLESFORD TL4748

Whittlesford church The interior is a rich testament to the former agricultural wealth of this area. The Tickell Arms, a little way off, is a most unusual pub.

WICKEN TL5670

Wicken Fen (Lode Lane) After an absence of over 60 years, otters have been spotted again at this, the last of the undrained fens. Surrounded in plastic to prevent it from drying out, it is an outstanding area for bird-watching (there are hides). The marshy and open fen landscape is one of the oldest nature reserves in the country, originally safeguarded in 1899 as an example of what the fens were like before they were turned over to intensive agriculture. Beautiful at all times of year, it's home to a remarkable range of plants, insects, birds and other wildlife; some good trails (one for wheelchairs), along with the last fenland windpump (moved here from elsewhere), and tiny fen cottage (open Sun and Bank hols Apr–Oct). Reserve open every day, visitor centre with snacks, shop and disabled access cl Mon exc bank hols, and 25 Dec; (01353) 720274; £3.70; NT. The Maids Head overlooking the village green is a handy dining pub.

WILLINGHAM TL4070

Willingham church Lots to notice here: outside are the fine tower and spire, and inside it has many early wall paintings, and some fine early screens.

WIMPOLE TL3350

Wimpole Hall and Home Farm (off A603) The varied attractions at this huge estate can easily fill most of a day. Children like the working stock farm best, its thatched and timbered buildings designed by Sir John Soane when it was at the forefront of agricultural innovation. A restored barn houses machinery and tools from those days, and there are plenty of farm animals (with younger ones to pet and feed) inc various rare breeds; separate play areas for older and younger children. Popular heavy horse wagon rides run the short distance to the mainly 18th-c house, one of the most striking mansions in the whole of East Anglia. Behind its imposing and harmonious Georgian façade is a lovely trompe l'oeil chapel ceiling, and rooms by James Gibbs and Sir John Soane. Perfect for a relaxing stroll, the gardens are good for spring daffodils and summer roses; vegetables now grow in the restored walled garden. Best of all perhaps are the 360 acres of parkland, home to the National Walnut Collection, and designed by several different notable landscapers inc Capability Brown and Repton; the remains of a medieval village are under the pasture. Good programme of concerts and events in the hall or grounds. Meals, snacks, shops, some disabled access (not to house). Hall open pm Tues–Thurs and wknds mid-Mar to late Oct, plus bank hol and Fri pm in Aug. Farm open same times plus mornings, wknds in winter, and Fri in July and Aug; (01223) 207257; £8.50 hall, farm and garden (£5.90 hall, £4.70 farm, £2.70 gardens); NT. The surrounding park is open all year, with walkers welcomed free of charge to the extensive paths and tracks through its farmland and woodland, past a folly and up to a surprisingly elevated ridge path.

WISBECH TF4609

The North Brink along the River Nene has handsome Georgian houses (among them the Red Lion has decent food, and serves beer from the nearby brewery – see below – in fine condition).

Elgoods Brewery Museum & Gardens (North Brink) Watch traditional brewing methods in practice at this 200-year-old Georgian brewery on the banks of the River Nene. Behind, four acres of gardens include a hot-house, lake and lawns leading to a maze. Snacks, shop, disabled access to gardens only; open pm Weds–Sun and bank hols May–Oct, brewery tours pm Weds–Fri Jun–Sept; (01945) 583160; £5 inc tasting, £2 gardens only.

Peckover House (North Brink) Lovely early 18th-c house with rococo decoration, restored Victorian library, contemporary art exhibitions, and a two-acre Victorian garden with a pond, ornamental ironwork arches, rose gardens, kitchen garden and greenhouses – where orange trees are still fruiting after 250 years. Afternoon

teas when house open, shop; open Apr–Oct, Weds pm, wknds and bank hols, plus garden only pm Mon, Tues and Thurs; (01945) 583463; £3.80 (£2.50 on garden only days); NT.
Wisbech & Fenland Museum (Museum Sq) Honest and thorough local history museum, with several early manuscripts, and an exhibition on the slave trade. Improvements over the next year will include a new display on the fens, and greater disabled access. Shop; cl Sun, Mon; (01945) 583817; free.
WOODHURST TL3375
Raptor Foundation 🏛 Sanctuary and breeding centre for over 300 birds of prey inc owls, buzzards and falcons; flying displays three times a day. Snacks, shop, disabled access; cl 25–26 Dec, I Jan; (01487) 741140; £2.50.
Other attractive villages include Alconbury Weston TL1776, Brampton TL2170, Eltisley TL2659, Helpston TF1205, (John Clare's Village), Glatton TL1585, Leighton Bromswold TL1175, Gamlingay TL2452, Great Abington TL5348, Great Chishill TL4239 (well restored windmill), Holywell TL3370, Meldreth TL3746, Rampton TL4268, Ufford TF0904 (lovely area at bluebell time), Whittlesey TL2797 and Woodditton TL6659.

Where to eat

BYTHORN TL0575 **White Hart** *(01832)* 710226 Civilised dining pub with a friendly welcome, several linked smallish rooms, magazines and cookery books to read, open fire, imaginative food, real ales, and a sensible wine list; cl Sun pm, Mon, New Year. £27|**£7.50**
CAMBRIDGE TL4557 **Browns** *23 Trumpington Street (01223)* 461655 Cheerful and informal sizeable restaurant with cushioned wicker chairs and sofas, well spaced tables, candles, ceiling fans, big potted plants, a good range of enjoyable food, efficient, helpful service, and tables on small front roadside terrace; branches in Bath, Brighton, Edinburgh, London, and Oxford. £20 ☺
CAMBRIDGE TL4559 **Twenty Two** *22 Chesterton Rd (01223)* 351880 Simple and pretty candlelit evening restaurant in Edwardian house with imaginative modern cooking from a set menu, a fine wine list, and friendly service; cl Sun, Mon, I wk Christmas; children over 10. £28.30
DUXFORD TL4746 **John Barleycorn** *3 Moorfield Rd (01223)* 832699 Pretty, early 17th-c thatched country pub, attractively furnished, with a quietly chatty bar, good food and courteous service; fine hanging baskets and flower-filled back garden; no children. £26|**£8**
ELY TL5380 **Old Fire Engine House** *25 St Marys St (01353)* 662582 Former fire station next to the cathedral, with good hearty English cooking inc nice puddings, an interesting wine list, simple furnishings and a relaxed atmosphere; large walled garden, also an art gallery; cl Sun pm, bank hols, 24 Dec–7 Jan. £27.50
FEN DRAYTON TL3368 **Three Tuns** *High St (01954)* 230242 Pretty thatched inn with two inglenook fireplaces and heavy Tudor beams and timbers in its unpretentious and cosy bar; well kept real ales, generous helpings of good, reasonably priced bar food, and a neat back garden with children's play equipment; children until 8pm. £17.45|**£6.45**
FORDHAM TL6270 **White Pheasant** *Market St (01638)* 720414 Well converted, fresh-feeling dining pub with simple decorations, flowers in bottles on tables, farmhouse chairs on bare boards, and a cheerful log fire; creative food, generously served on big white plates, super daily specials, well kept real ales, and good house wines. £18.50|**£6.10**
FOWLMERE TL4245 **Chequers** *High St (01763)* 208369 Civilised old coaching inn with smartly dressed waiters, ambitious food in galleried restaurant, good puddings, and excellent wines; two comfortably furnished rooms with an open log fire, some interesting photographs of local World War I and II airfields, and a no smoking conservatory overlooking the neat garden; cl 25 Dec; disabled access. £22.45|**£7.80**

GOREFIELD TF4111 **Woodmans Cottage** *Main St (01945) 870669* Busy village pub with a wide choice of enjoyable food inc lots of good puddings in spacious modernised bar, a comfortable eating area, and separate restaurant; cl 25 Dec; well behaved children only; disabled access. £22|**£7.25**

HEYDON TL4243 **King William IV** *Chrishall Rd (01763) 838773* Bustling village pub with nooks and crannies in rambling rooms, neatly kept agricultural implements on standing props, wall timbers and dark oak beams, and a log fire; notably interesting vegetarian dishes (plus some meaty dishes, too), well kept real ales, and friendly efficient staff. £23.50|**£8**

KEYSTON TL0475 **Pheasant Village** *Loop Rd (01832) 710241* Pretty thatched former smithy, full of character, with a nice civilised atmosphere, a relaxed bar with informal service, a slightly more formal, no smoking room with linen napkins, delicious imaginative food, a particularly good wine list, and real ales; cl pm 25 Dec; partial disabled access. £27.15

MADINGLEY TL3960 **Three Horseshoes** *High St (01954) 210221* Thatched dining pub, smart and well run, with a relaxed and civilised atmosphere, open fire in the charming bar, and an attractive conservatory; very good imaginative food, well kept real ales, a thoughtful wine list (many by the glass inc champagne), and efficient, attentive service; pretty summer garden; disabled access. £25|**£7.95**

MELBOURN TL3844 **Pink Geranium** *25 Station Rd (01763) 260215* Very pretty 15th-c thatched cottage, pink inside and out, with consistently good sophisticated cooking; a cosy and relaxed atmosphere, a carefully chosen wine list with helpful notes, cottagey garden, and chauffeur service; good value set lunches, and cookery courses, too; disabled access. £45 dinner, £19 lunch

MELBOURN TL3844 **Sheene Mill** *39 Station Rd (01763) 261393* Lovely late 17th-c watermill on the River Mel (owned by celebrity chef Steven Saunders) and just 200 yards from its sister restaurant, the Pink Geranium; relaxed and informal bar and conservatory, airy restaurant decorated in yellow and terracotta, with pretty blue dining chairs around yellow-clothed tables, and lovely gardens with seats on the terrace; delicious modern cooking inc vegetarian and fish dishes, and light lunches or snacks; bdrms; partial disabled access. £33

SUTTON GAULT TL4279 **Anchor** *Bury Lane (01353) 778537* Very friendly, popular dining pub with gas lamps and candles in four heavily beamed rooms (two are no smoking), log fires and stripped pine furniture; delicious imaginative modern cooking (good value two-course wkdy lunches), well kept real ales, very good wine list (10 by the glass), helpful service, and riverbank tables; bdrms; cl 27 Dec; no children under 7 after 8pm; disabled access. £28|**£6.50**

Special thanks to Michael and Jenny Back, Richard Lewis, Gaynor Hulme, B and K Hypher, Helen Dixon, Mary and Peter Lister

CHESHIRE

A county of great charm; wonderfully varied countryside, pretty villages, and a real diversity of attractions – from the Romans to the Space Age

Chester Zoo and Blue Planet (Ellesmere Port), Europe's largest aquarium, are outstanding animal attractions run by helpful staff, and with enough to look at to occupy a whole day's family outing; the impressive Stapeley Water Gardens are home to piranhas and sharks, too.

The Jodrell Bank Centre & Arboretum is similarly absorbing, combining star-gazing with sufficient scope for an afternoon outdoors – our family attraction of the year.

The lively Quarry Bank Mill & Country Park at Styal has a new working steam engine, and other heritage centres here include the Salt Museum in Nantwich and the lively Paradise Mill and Silk Museum in Macclesfield. Catalyst in Widnes has plenty to intrigue a young enquiring mind.

Tatton Park in Knutsford, with its lovely grounds and working historic farm, is good for a traditional family day out, as is Arley Hall & Gardens and Stockley Farm, where tractors drive you between attractions. Lyme Park near Disley makes for another good excursion, and other rewarding places include Tabley House (and the remarkable clock and fairground organ collection nearby), Little Moreton Hall near Congleton, Gawsworth Hall (ideal places to enjoy outdoor summer theatre), Norton Priory in Runcorn, the Ness botanic gardens, and the spectacular garden centre at Bridgemere. On a quieter scale, newcomer Foxhill Arboretum is pleasant for a short stroll among some rare trees.

Chester itself is a must. Very pedestrian-friendly, it has beautifully restored and preserved medieval buildings, lots of interest, and a lively feel. The Dewa experience re-creates the city's Roman heyday, while the Grosvenor Museum deserves congratulation for its much improved disabled access.

With many charming thatched and timbered villages, Cheshire's countryside varies from the picturesque castle-topped wooded hills of the west, through the lush parkland, leafy lanes and meres (shallow lakes) of the central plain to the rugged eastern Peak District – small steep stone-walled pastures, shaggy sheep, deep twisty valleys, austere moorland. An intricate network of canals takes in some of the most interesting countryside, with well kept towpaths.

Industry is largely confined to the Mersey, with chemical works at Northwich and engineering around Crewe.

Please let us know what you think of places in the *Guide*. Use the report forms at the back of the book or simply write us a letter.

BEESTON SJ5559 **Wild Boar Hotel** *Whitchurch Rd, Beeston, Tarporley, Cheshire CW6 9NW (01829) 260309* **£90**, plus special breaks; 37 rms with appealing touches such as fresh fruit and sherry. Attractive half-timbered 17th-c former hunting lodge, carefully extended over the years, beneath the 12th-c castle, with relaxed and comfortable bars and lounges, enjoyable food in the beamed restaurant, and good helpful service; disabled access

BICKLEY MOSS SJ5450 **Cholmondeley Arms** *Cholmondeley, Malpas, Cheshire SY14 8HN (01829) 720300* **£65***, plus special breaks; 2 rms with bath, 4 with showers. Airy converted Victorian schoolhouse close to castle and gardens, with lots of atmosphere, very friendly staff, interesting furnishings, open fire, excellent imaginative bar food, and very good choice of wines (famously, Cholmondeley is pronounced Chumley); disabled access

CHESTER SJ4065 **Castle House** *23 Castle St, Chester CH1 2DS (01244) 350354* **£48***; 5 comfortable rms, 3 with own bthrm. Small, carefully preserved 16th-c guest house in the middle of the city, with helpful friendly owners, and fine breakfasts

COTEBROOK SJ5765 **Alvanley Arms** *Cotebrook, Tarporley, Cheshire CW6 9DS (01829) 760200* **£60***; 7 newly refurbished rms. Handsome creeper-covered Georgian inn with pleasant beamed bars (one area is no smoking), big open fire, a chintzy little hall, generous helpings of good food, and a garden with pond and trout

FULLERS MOOR SJ4854 **Frogg Manor** *Nantwich Rd, Broxton, Chester CH3 9JH (01829) 782629* **£110**, plus special breaks; 6 lavishly decorated rms with thoughtful extras. Enjoyably eccentric Georgian manor house full of ornamental frogs and antique furniture, open fires and ornate dried-flower arrangements, a restful upstairs sitting room, cosy little bar, a large library of 30s/40s records, and good English cooking in elegant dining room which leads to conservatory overlooking the gardens; dogs by arrangement

HIGHER BURWARDSLEY SJ5257 **Pheasant Higher Burwardsley,** *Burwardsley, Chester, Cheshire CH3 9PF (01829) 770434* **£70**, plus special breaks; 10 rms in comfortably converted sandstone-built barn. Pretty half-timbered 17th-c inn on top of Peckforton Hills with marvellous views, a huge fireplace in the attractive old-fashioned bar, no smoking conservatory, good food, and friendly staff; lots of walks nearby; disabled access

HIGHER WYCH SJ4943 **Mill House** *Higher Wych, Malpas, Cheshire SY14 7JR (01948) 780362* **£40**; 2 rms, 1 with own bthrm. Very welcoming and friendly B&B in former farmhouse on the Welsh/English border, with relaxed atmosphere and good breakfasts – evening meals by arrangement; self-catering cottage; cl Dec

HOOLE SJ4167 **Hoole Hall** *Warrington Rd, Hoole, Chester, Cheshire CH2 3PD (01244) 350011* **£75**w, plus special breaks; 97 well equipped rms, some no smoking. Extended and attractively refurbished 18th-c hall with 5 acres of gardens, good food in two restaurants, and friendly service; good disabled access

KNUTSFORD SJ7479 **Longview** *51–55 Manchester Rd, Knutsford, Cheshire WA16 0LX (01565) 632119* **£85***; 26 rms. Friendly Victorian hotel with attractive period and reproduction furnishings, open fires in original fireplaces, pleasant cellar bar, ornate restaurant, and good well presented food; cl 24 Dec–10 Jan

MACCLESFIELD SJ9271 **Sutton Hall Hotel** *Bullocks Lane, Sutton, Macclesfield, Cheshire SK11 0HE (01260) 253211* **£90**; 10 marvellous rms. Welcoming and secluded historic baronial hall, full of character, stylish rooms with tall black beams, stone fireplaces, suits of armour and so forth, friendly service, and good food; can arrange clay shooting/golf/fishing

MACCLESFIELD FOREST SJ9471 **Hardingland Farm** *Macclesfield Forest, Macclesfield, Cheshire SK11 0ND (01625) 425759* **£48***; 3 rms. Neatly kept Georgian stone farmhouse set in the Peak National Park with wonderful views, an elegantly furnished lounge and Regency-style dining room, helpful owners, and delicious food using their own lamb and beef; cl Nov–Mar; no children

MOBBERLEY SJ7779 **Laburnum Cottage** *Knutsford Rd, Mobberley, Knutsford,*

Cheshire WA16 7PU (01565) 872464 **£50**; 4 pretty rms. Neatly kept and friendly no smoking country guest house in an acre of landscaped gardens; relaxed atmosphere in comfortable lounge with log fire and books, sunny conservatory, and very good food; disabled access (with prior notice)

MOLLINGTON SJ3869 **Crabwall Manor** *Parkgate Rd, Mollington, Chester CH1 6NE (01244) 851666* **£150**, plus special breaks; 48 very comfortable, individually decorated rms. Partly castellated largely 17th-c hotel in landscaped grounds with restful, attractive day rooms, open fires, very good modern British cooking in elegant restaurant, and friendly professional service; disabled access

POTT SHRIGLEY SJ9478 **Shrigley Hall** *Shrigley Park, Pott Shrigley, Macclesfield, Cheshire SK10 5SB (01625) 575757* **£150***, plus special breaks; 150 smart, well equipped rms, some with country views. Set in over 260 acres of parkland, this impressive country house has a splendid entrance hall with several elegant rooms leading off, enjoyable food in the orangery and restaurant, and good service from friendly staff; championship golf course, fishing, tennis, and leisure centre in former church building; plenty to do nearby; disabled access

PRESTBURY SJ9077 **White House** *The Village, Prestbury, Macclesfield, Cheshire SK10 4HP (01625) 829376* **£100***, plus wknd breaks; 11 individual, stylish and well equipped rms with antiques, in separate manor just a short walk from the restaurant. Exceptionally friendly and pretty restaurant, with spacious bar, low-ceilinged dining room, imaginative modern British cooking, and a thoughtful wine list; breakfast in small conservatory lounge or in room; cl 25 Dec; children over 10

ROWTON SJ4464 **Rowton Hall** *Whitchurch Rd, Rowton, Chester CH3 6AD (01244) 335262* **£135***, plus wknd breaks; 38 attractive rms; 18th-c country house in 8 acres of award-winning gardens with tennis courts and croquet lawn; conservatory lounge, comfortable bar, log fires, a relaxed atmosphere, and smart restaurant; leisure club with swimming pool, gym, sauna and solarium; disabled access

SANDBACH SJ7560 **Old Hall** *High St, Sandbach, Cheshire CW11 1AL (01270) 761221* **£75**; 14 comfortable rms. Fine Jacobean timbered hotel with lots of original panelling and fireplaces, relaxing lounge, pianist, friendly welcome, and popular restaurant; disabled access

SANDIWAY SJ5968 **Nunsmere Hall** *Tarporley Rd, Oakmere, Northwich, Cheshire CW8 2ES (01606) 889100* **£190**; 36 individually decorated rms. Luxurious lakeside hotel on wooded peninsula with elegantly furnished lounge and library, oak-panelled cocktail bar, very good modern cooking, and a warm welcome from courteous staff; children over 12 in evening restaurant; disabled access

TARPORLEY SJ5562 **Swan** *50 High St, Tarporley, Cheshire CW6 0AG (01829) 733838* **£75***; 17 rms. Well managed Georgian inn with a good mix of individual tables and chairs in attractive bar, well kept real ales, decent wines, and quite a few malt whiskies, good food from extensive menu, nice breakfasts, and friendly staff; limited disabled access

TILSTON SJ4650 **Tilston Lodge** *Tilston, Malpas, Cheshire SY14 7DR (01829) 250223* **£64***; 3 thoughtfully equipped rms. Warmly friendly and beautifully restored Victorian house in 16 acres with a collection of rare breed farm animals, comfortable and attractive public rooms, open fire in dining room, and good breakfasts

WESTON SJ7352 **White Lion** *31 Main Rd, Weston, Crewe, Cheshire CW2 5NA (01270) 500303* **£68**, plus wknd breaks; 16 comfortable rms. Pretty 17th-c timbered inn with low beams (several no smoking areas), a friendly relaxed atmosphere, well kept real ales, and popular food; own bowling green; no accommodation 25 Dec; disabled access

WETTENHALL SJ6261 **Boot & Slipper** *Wettenhall, Winsford, Cheshire CW7 4DN (01270) 528238* **£48**; 4 attractive rms with showers. Cosily refurbished 16th-c coaching inn on small country lane, with low beams and open fire in quiet bars, a relaxed friendly atmosphere, and good breakfasts

WHEELOCK SJ7558 **Grove House** *Mill Lane, Wheelock, Sandbach, Cheshire*

CW11 4RD (01270) 762582 **£80**; 8 rms, some refurbished this year. Family-run Georgian restaurant-with-rooms, with relaxed homely atmosphere, quietly furnished lounge and restaurant, personal friendly service, and very good modern cooking in popular restaurant; plenty to do nearby; cl 27–30 Dec

WORLESTON SJ6555 **Rookery Hall** *Main Rd, Worleston, Nantwich, Cheshire CW5 6DQ (01270) 610016* **£105***, plus special breaks; 45 individually decorated rms. Fine early 19th-c hotel in 38 acres of lovely parkland, with elegant lounges, log fires, intimate panelled restaurant with enjoyable food, and friendly service; disabled access

To see and do

Cheshire Family Attraction of the Year

JODRELL BANK SJ7970 **Jodrell Bank Centre & Arboretum** (off A535, near M6 junction 18) Instantly recognisable, the huge radio telescope here is still the second largest in the world – as big as the dome of St Paul's. Over its 43 years of operation it has been responsible for some vital astronomical discoveries. It's unusual for a working research establishment like this to welcome so many visitors; its popularity is down to the fact that there's quite a range of things for visitors to do, from the exemplary planetarium to the rather incongruous (but very welcome) 35-acre arboretum. It's older children who'll get the most out of a visit (younger children have a play area, though it isn't huge), and if they're at all interested in what really makes the world go round they'll find it fascinating. A science centre has eight galleries exploring the mysteries of the universe, with models and interactive displays illustrating the earth's cycles of day, night and seasons, and secrets of the moon, solar system and space exploration. One gallery is entirely hands-on. Intriguing shows in the planetarium reveal a perfect night sky and close-up views of the sun and the moon. Except on very busy days you can see the show again as often as you like throughout your visit (or pay a small extra charge if a different show is playing). When they're busy you may be allocated a specific time to enter the planetarium, and if you're visiting in term-time it's worth checking the shows aren't restricted to school parties. The 2,000 species of tree in the arboretum are quite a contrast to the indoor exhibits; you can spend quite a while following the various trails – the best for families has the solar system laid out to scale, so you can hunt around for the next planet. There's a busy programme of events and special activities; you can count on extra goings-on during the summer holidays. Meals and snacks (the café has fine views of the telescope), picnic area, shop, good disabled access (outside too); (01477) 571339; cl Mon Nov–Mar, and 18–22, 25–26 Dec, 1, 8–12 Jan (opening hours are much shorter in winter); £4.60, £2.30 children (children under 5 are free, but won't be admitted to the planetarium).

ARLEY SJ6780

Arley Hall & Gardens and Stockley Farm The dramatic-looking house is Victorian Jacobean, but the same family have lived on the estate for over 500 years, so there are older furnishings and mementoes. Outside, the charming grounds include walled, scented, and herb gardens, shrub rose collection, a more informal woodland area, and craft workshops; also an interesting private chapel. Meals, snacks, shop and nursery, disabled access; open Easter to Sept, Tues–Sun, house open Tues pm and Sun only; (01565) 777353; £4.40 grounds and gardens, hall £2.50 extra. From the car park, tractor and trailer rides take you to nearby Stockley Farm, a friendly working dairy farm that's ideal for children; falconry displays at wknds in school hols. Open pm Weds, Sat, Sun and bank hols Easter–Sept, plus daily exc Mon in Aug; (01565) 777323; £4.

ASTBURY SJ8461

A delightful village, and its church is well worth a look – graceful detached spire, spectacular roofing, rich carving.

AUDLEM WHARF SJ6543
For walkers, a good access point for the **Shropshire Union Canal** which threads through this area, giving interesting stretches for strolls; just outside the village is an impressive flight of over a dozen locks.

BARTHOMLEY SJ7752
This charming village has lots of thatch, black and white timbering, quiet up-and-down lanes, a fine church, and delightfully unspoilt pub.

BEESTON SJ5459
Beeston Castle Well worth the steep climb, there are wonderful views from this ruined 13th-c fortress, perched atop dramatically rising crags, and said to be where Richard II left buried treasure. Good exhibition covers site's 4,000-year history. Snacks, shop; cl 24–26 Dec, 1 Jan; (01829) 260464; £2.80, EH. The pub of the same name, handy for the canal, does good value generous food.

BOLLINGTON SJ9377
Bollington is well worth a stroll: handsome stone milltown buildings, unchanged 19th-c shops and houses, and overhead a great stone aqueduct and its later rival the railway viaduct. The Church House is a useful pub. In summer you can **hire bikes** along a traffic-free ten-mile stretch of the Middlewood Way bordering the Peak District (£5.25 for three hours – £9.50 full day), (01625) 572681. Just outside, the Cheshire Hunt in Spurley Lane at Pott Shrigley is a good place for lunch, and near it you can pick up the long-distance Gritstone Trail for walks among high stone-walled pastures. The Poachers (Ingersley Rd) or Redway (Kerridge) are good start points for the viewpoint Kerridge Hill (crowned by a curious folly known as White Nancy) just E of the town.

BRIDGEMERE SJ7243
Bridgemere Garden World (A51) A garden-lover's paradise – 25 acres of gardens (inc the WI cottage garden), plants, glasshouses, and garden furniture, with more plants in more varieties than anywhere else in Britain (indoor and outdoor), and professional help on hand for any sort of query. Art and crafts shop and water garden features new this year. Best to visit in the morning before the coach parties arrive. Good meals and snacks, excellent shop, disabled access; cl 25–26 Dec; (01270) 520381; free.

BUNBURY SJ5758
Bunbury has pretty cottages around its 14th-c church, and a well restored 19th-c watermill.

BURWARDSLEY SJ5257
Cheshire Candle Workshops
Popular demonstrations of candle-making and other crafts, and a big craft shop. Meals, snacks, disabled access; cl 25 Dec and maybe winter Mons; (01829) 770401; free. The Pheasant is good for lunch, with great views.

CAPESTHORNE SJ8473
Capesthorne Hall 🏛 18th-c family home of the Bromley-Davenports, who have lived on the site since Domesday; fine paintings include Lowry's unusual interpretation of the house's striking exterior, and there's a good collection of Roman and Greek busts and vases. Also lovely Georgian chapel and 60 acres of gardens and woodland. Snacks, disabled access; open pm Weds, Sun and bank hols Apr–Oct; (01625) 861221; £6, £3.50 garden and chapel only. The Blacksmiths Arms at Henbury (A537 towards Macclesfield) is a decent family dining pub, if you don't want the longer trip to the Dog over at Peover Heath. Discount only valid until Oct.

CHESTER SJ4066
One of Britain's most rewarding cities, Chester was the site of an important fort in Roman times, and later plentiful river traffic kept it rich. The old centre is ringed by a medieval **town wall** that's more complete than any other in Britain. You can walk the whole way round, enjoying marvellous views; there are summer exhibitions in some of the towers along the way. Partly because of the limit set by the wall, the centre of town is easy to get around on foot, not too big, and with the main streets pretty much free of cars (there may be a few buses), although in summer the sheer number of tourists and shoppers can still make them appear congested. Guided walks leave the Tourist Information Centre on Town Hall Sq at

10.30, 11.45 and 2.30 each day; £3. If you're driving in, you'll be shunted round to one of the big car parks, and you may have to queue a while to get a space. Chester's racecourse, the Roodee, is the oldest in the world; it still has fashionable races in May and a summer Sun meet that's become a lively event for families. The quaint Albion (Park St) has good food, and Watergates (Watergate St), in a fine medieval crypt, is useful for lunch. The ancient Blue Bell (Northgate St) has been licensed to sell alcohol since 1494.

Chester Castle Though now largely moated by car parks and occupied by civil servants, this has some impressive buildings, both medieval and grand-manner late 18th-c. There's a small military museum here; cl 21 Dec–2 Jan; £1.

Chester Cathedral Not unlike an ordinary church at first glance, this is far more impressive inside, with some marvellous medieval carving in and above the choir stalls, and some fine vaulting. Many of the former abbey buildings survived the Reformation, so the precincts still include peaceful arcaded flagstoned cloisters, a medieval chapter house, and older Norman parts inc a refectory – brought back into use as an excellent café (which even has a resident pianist Tues, Fri and Sat lunchtimes). All the carved bosses have been gilded recently, and a model of the cathedral has a Braille text. Shop, disabled access; cl for Sun am services; (01244) 324756; £2 suggested donation. There are quiet cobbled Georgian lanes around Abbey Sq, behind the cathedral a little way down Northgate.

Chester viewpoints The tree-shaded Groves look out to the medieval bridge over the River Dee – very photogenic and a pleasant place for a stroll or picnic. Several companies offer boat trips on the river from here, (01244) 325394). The bridge at the N end of Northgate gives a close view of the so-called Bridge of Sighs over the canal far below.

Chester Zoo 🖼 (A41, 2m N of Chester) Very well liked by readers, this is the biggest and undoubtedly one of the best zoos in Britain, constantly developing and improving. Its several thousand animals are housed in spacious, near-natural enclosures spread over 80 acres of glorious gardens, with 11 miles of pathways. Over 200 of the species here are classed as rare or endangered, and they put a great deal of effort into breeding, so there's usually quite a range of baby animals (a new baby elephant had just been born as we went to press). Highlights include the splendidly laid out Chimpanzee Island, the Komodo dragons and Amazon parrots in the new Islands in Danger tropical habitat, and the remarkable free-flying bat cave, with around 200 inhabitants. A new jaguar enclosure will be open by the time this book comes out. There's a full programme of feeding sessions throughout the day; times can change, so best to check the day's events on the main information boards. Smaller children can pet the animals at the well organised farm. In summer a waterbus can ferry you between the attractions, or there's an overhead train that zips around the grounds (both £1.70 extra). Meals, snacks, shops, good disabled access, tactile maps and Braille guides; cl 25 Dec; (01244) 380280; £10*.

Dewa Roman Experience (Pierpoint Lane, off Bridge St) Re-creation of Chester's Roman heyday, with the sights, sounds and smells of streets, fortresses, and even bathhouses. It starts off as though you're on board a Roman galley, and at the end is an exhibition of Roman, Saxon and medieval relics found on the site. Shop, disabled access; cl 25–26 Dec, 1 Jan; (01244) 343407; £3.95.

Grosvenor Museum (Grosvenor St) By the time this book is published, this newly refurbished museum will have significantly improved its disabled access. The ground floor will be fully accessible, and touch-screen computers will allow visitors in wheelchairs to get a virtual view of the exhibits upstairs. A surprising highlight is a gallery of huge Roman tombstones. A new conservatory shop leads from here to a Georgian house with restored Georgian and Victorian rooms, an art gallery, and displays of locally made silver and furniture. A series of exhibitions inc one on life in Chester from 1900 to 2000 will accompany the relaunch. Cl Sun am and a few days over Christmas; (01244) 402008; free.

Roman Chester Recent research has led to speculation that Emperor Hadrian ordered Chester to be built as a 'beautiful new city' – a reflection of Rome's glory. This certainly helps to explain the city's grandiose walls, constructed with unusually large sandstone blocks in a manner designed to impress, with imposing ornamental gateways. Other remains include some broken Roman columns in a neat and peaceful garden running along the town wall by the gate at the bottom of Pepper St. Nearby is the excavated part of a very large Roman amphitheatre – probably big enough to seat nearly 10,000 people. Other relics can pop up in unexpected places: Spud-U-Like and Miss Selfridge show off well preserved sections of hypocaust.

The Rows Giving Chester's heart a magnificently Tudor look, these are sets of timbered two-storey shops – with open upper arcaded galleries – radiating from the central Cross. Parts are thought to be at least 700 years old. Besides being attractive to look at and charming to walk through, they form the heart of the city's shopping centre (and include a useful pub, the Boot, on Eastgate Row N). Watergate is one of the finest stretches, with some of Chester's most glorious timber-framed buildings, though more fine buildings jetty out over the pavement in Lower Bridge St (for instance, the late 17th-c Falcon, once a house used by the Duke of Westminster's ancestors but now a good pub), and in St Werbergh St off Eastgate (built in the 1890s, despite their Elizabethan look).

Toy & Doll Museum 🖾 (Lower Bridge St Row, Chester) One of the best such collections we've come across, not least because of the hard-to-beat assemblage of Matchbox cars and toys (the company's HQ are here). Lots of Dinky toys and Hornby trains, as well as dolls, teddies, and some vintage amusement machines. Shop (good for doll's house furniture); cl Sun Jan–Mar, and 25 Dec; (01244) 346297; *£2.

CHOLMONDELEY SJ5351

Cholmondeley Castle Gardens Very pretty to stroll through, with acres of colourful ornamental gardens around elegant castle buildings (not open). Also fine woodland and lakeside walks, llamas and entertaining pygmy goats among the rare breeds, and an ancient private chapel. Snacks, shop and plant centre, limited disabled access; open pm Sun, Weds, Thurs and some bank hols Apr–Sept, best to check; (01829) 720383; £3. The Cholmondeley Arms is excellent for lunch.

CHRISTLETON SJ4465
Though now almost part of Chester, this is still very much a distinct village, with a classic green, pond, almshouses, and medieval packhorse bridges.

CLOUD SJ9063
There are good hilly walks here, and the craggy summit, with steep drops to the Cheshire Plain, gives grand views; the Coach & Horses at Timbersbrook is a useful nearby pub.

CONGLETON SJ8358
Little Moreton Hall (Scholar Green; A34 S) One of Britain's best-preserved half-timbered buildings, its splendid black and white exterior pretty much unchanged since it was built in 1580, and covered with such a profusion of lines the effect is almost dizzying. The inside, though largely unfurnished, has some interesting features too, especially the wainscoted Long Gallery, Great Hall and chapel. There's a re-creation of a typical 17th-c knot garden – and make sure you don't miss the built-in dog kennel. Regular open-air theatre and concerts. Meals, snacks, shop, disabled access to ground floor only; open pm Weds–Sun and bank hols Apr–Oct, then wknds up to Christmas; (01260) 272018; £4.40; NT. The Brownlow Arms nearby or Rising Sun in Scholar Green itself are popular for lunch. **Heritage Narrow Boats** at Kent Green have electric narrow boats to hire by the day; maybe cl Nov–Easter; (01782) 785700; £80 wkdys for up to 12 people (£95 wknds) – very satisfying, gliding along in silence.

CREWE SJ7055
A 19th-c railway town, smartened up a lot in the last decade or two, with bargains esp china in the market, a pedestrianised centre, colourful

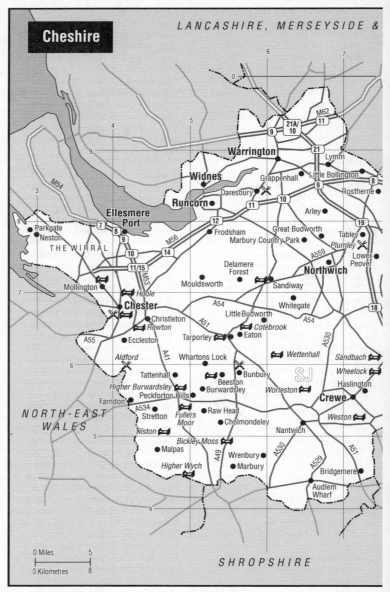

Queens Park and useful foyer restaurant in the Victorian theatre. The Crewe Arms is good value for a comfortable lunch.

Railway Age (Vernon Way) Rapidly developing exhibition with one of the widest ranges of preserved electric and diesel locomotives in the country, along with models, miniature and standard-gauge railways and other displays. Shop (not always open), some disabled access; cl Nov–mid-Feb; (01270) 212130; £2.50 wkdys, £3.50 wknds (when there's more going on).

MANCHESTER

DARESBURY SJ5882
Daresbury church The 'Alice in Wonderland' stained-glass window commemorates Lewis Carroll, who was born here. There are pleasant canalside strolls, and the Ring o' Bells is useful for lunch.

DELAMERE FOREST SJ5571
Several square miles of mainly coniferous plantation, with some older oak and other woodland, inc plenty of open stretches and picnic places, and some small stretches of reedy water. A section of the 30-mile **Sandstone Trail** long-distance path takes in much of the best bits, with good access from several places inc Delamere and Hatchmere, with decent prettily placed pubs in both villages.

DISLEY SJ9682
Lyme Park Wonderful country estate outside the pleasant hillside village of Disley. The Hall at its centre is a magnificent blend of Elizabethan, Georgian and Regency architecture and styles. Tours are unguided, so you can take your time looking at the intricate carvings, and lovely tapestries, paintings and furniture. There's a particularly grand staircase, and a fine collection of English clocks. Around the house (its exterior used as Pemberley in the BBC's *Pride and Prejudice*) are 17 acres of Victorian gardens with orangery, sunken Dutch garden and wilderness garden, and a sprawling ancient park with a newly restored hunting tower, herds of red deer and nature trails inc a new one suitable for wheelchairs. Pleasant walk down to the canal. Snacks, shop, disabled access (with notice); house and gardens open Apr–Oct, garden cl am Weds and Thurs, house cl all am plus all Weds and Thurs, gardens also open some winter wknds – ring for dates; the park is open all year; (01663) 762023; £3.50 per car to go in the park, then £4.50 house and garden, £2 garden only; NT. The White Horse is a useful food stop (with OAP lunch days). The long-distance **Gritstone Trail** starts from the Park and runs along the western flanks of the Peak District. It's well marked and offers a few days' walking of the highest quality.

EATON SJ5763
Eaton is a classic Cheshire village, with unassuming but charming picture-postcard combinations of thatch, stone and timbering.

ECCLESTON SJ4162
This romantically eclectic estate village was built in the last century for the Duke of Westminster, with a richly

expansive sandstone church that's a culmination of Victorian ecclesiastical architecture.

ELLESMERE PORT SJ4076

Boat Museum 🏛 (Dockyard Rd) Nicely set in a historic dock complex, a huge floating collection of canal boats, as well as steam engines, a blacksmith's forge, workers' cottages, stables, big indoor exhibitions, and boat trips. Snacks, shop, disabled access; cl winter Thurs and Fri, 24–26 Dec; (0151) 355 5017; £5.50. Parts of the surrounding docks have been redeveloped with craft workshops and the like. The Woodland (Chester Rd) is a useful pub/restaurant (with its own bowling green). On the S edge of town (nr M56 junction 10) Cheshire Oaks claims to be Europe's biggest factory outlet shopping village, with familiar brands and bargains.

Blue Planet Aquarium (off A5117, N J10, M53) The most obviously dramatic feature at this splendid aquarium is the 71-metre (233-ft) walk-through tunnel, surrounded by sharks, stingray, and 3½ million gallons of water; a moving walkway lets you trundle along gawping without having to look where you're going. Knowledgeable staff (many are marine biologists) are on hand at each exhibit to answer questions and give talks at various times of the day. A big draw is the Aquatheatre, rather like a cinema with the screen replaced by a window into one of their biggest tanks; divers regularly go down to feed the creatures, and have microphones to chat with the audience as they do it. The main sections represent water environments and their occupants from trout streams to mangroves, with touchpools in some areas, where children can handle starfish and the like. As well as fish they have plenty of reptiles and insects. Most displays are at a height younger children can appreciate, and there's free face-painting. Meals, snacks, shop, good disabled access; cl 25 Dec; (0151) 357 8800; £6.95 (£4.95 children over 3). Various good value family tickets.

FARNDON SJ4154

Charming rustic two-mile riverside walk from car park by arched Dee bridge; good food at the Nags Head.

FRODSHAM SJ5075

Foxhill Arboretum (off B5393, S of Frodsham). Begun in 1962, this includes a mix of rare conifer and broadleaf trees, from dawn redwood and Spanish firs to native elms. Be warned, some of the steeper paths can be very slippery; (01928) 739189; *£2. In town the Helter Skelter (Church St) has good food.

GAWSWORTH SJ8969

Gawsworth Hall Exceptionally pretty timbered manor house dating back to Norman times, the former home of Mary Fitton, possibly the Dark Lady of Shakespeare's Sonnets; plenty of fine furniture, stained glass, pictures and sculptures. In summer the open-air theatre has a well chosen range of concerts and plays; good gardens and park too. Snacks, shop, disabled access to gardens; cl am, some Sats in May and Sept, and all Oct–late Apr; (01260) 223456; £4.20. The village has fine houses in parkland, ponds, an interesting church, and an unusual unspoilt farm pub, while the Sutton Hall Hotel over at Sutton Lane Ends is quite handy for lunch.

GRAPPENHALL SJ6386

This attractive village is worth a visit for the ancient grinning cat on its church tower; there are peaceful canalside strolls here.

GREAT BUDWORTH SJ6677

Set in attractive rich countryside, this is a quaint purpose-built estate village; the church is imposing (as is the pub), and there are many pretty cottages.

HASLINGTON SJ7358

Lakemore Country Park (Lane End Farm) Readers enjoy this country park with rare breeds inc miniature donkeys and endangered birds of prey. Nature trails link five man-made lakes; pets' corner, outdoor and indoor playgrounds – extra charge for children's rides. Open daily Apr–Oct, and maybe wknds in Christmas hols; (01270) 253556; £3. The friendly Fox nearby has decent food.

JODRELL BANK SJ7970

Jodrell Bank Centre & Arboretum *See separate family panel on p.50.*

KERRIDGE HILL SJ9477

Above Bollington, and with fine views, this is topped by the curious folly known as White Nancy. Good walks here, and to the E – where the quaint Highwayman pub (B5470 N of Rainow) also has good views, and is handy for the long-distance Gritstone Trail path.

KETTLESHULME SJ9879
Dunge Valley Gardens ⌸ (off B5470) Colourful gardens in Peak District countryside, esp good for rhododendrons (May, Jun), roses and unusual perennials. Teas, plant sales; cl Sept–Mar (exc plant sales) and Mon exc bank hols; (01663) 733787; £2.50 wknds and bank hols, £2 wkdys (free plant if £10 spent on plants). The Crag at nearby Wildboarclough does decent food, and fits in well with a walk to the Three Shires Head and the summit of Shutlingsoe.

KNUTSFORD SJ7578
Despite obvious present-day prosperity and some rather heavy traffic, this has a pleasantly old-world feel, with lots of striking Georgian and other period buildings. It quickly conjures up schoolday memories of reading Mrs Gaskell's *Cranford*, its alias.
Tatton Park On Knutsford's northern edge, a busy estate with a handsome neo-classical Georgian mansion at its centre. Magnificent collection of furnishings, porcelain and paintings (inc two Canalettos) in the opulent State rooms, and restored kitchens and servants' quarters; the Tudor Old Hall hints at the long history of the estate. The lovely grounds boast an Edwardian rose garden, Italian and Japanese gardens, orangery and fern house, leading to a big country park with mature trees, lakes, signposted walks and deer and waterfowl; you can fish, hire bikes, or take a carriage ride. There's also a Home Farm that works as it did 60 years ago, with vintage machinery and rare breeds of animals; children's playground. You could easily spend most of an undemanding day here (good family activities in summer school hols), or take a carload for a picnic in the park. Meals, snacks, shop, some disabled access; park and gardens open all year (exc winter Mons), rest cl Mon (exc bank hols), all Nov–Mar (exc farm open Sun), mansion and Tudor Hall also cl am (mansion open some wknds in Dec with seasonal

decorations); (01625) 534435; entry to park £3.50 per car (free for cyclists and pedestrians), then £3 for the mansion or gardens, and £2.50 for the farm or Tudor Hall. A ticket allowing entry for any two attractions is £4.50; NT (though as the site is managed by the county council members still have to pay for all exc the mansion and garden).

LITTLE BOLLINGTON SJ7286
This peaceful hamlet gives strolls by the Bridgewater Canal and in Dunham Massey deer park.

LITTLE BUDWORTH SJ5867
Cheshire Herbs Award-winning specialist herb nursery growing and selling over 200 different varieties from agrimony to yellow melilot. Shop, disabled access; cl 24 Dec–2 Jan; (01829) 760578; free. The Shrewsbury Arms has good value food.
Little Budworth Common This country park is a strong (and oddly refreshing) contrast to most of this area's richly manicured countryside: poor wild heath with young bogs and scrawny birchwoods.

LOWER PEOVER SJ7474
Many people's favourite Cheshire village: cobbled lanes, glorious 14th-c black and white timbered church, quiet watermeadows and a fine pub.

LOWER WITHINGTON SJ8169
Welltrough Dried Flowers (signed off A34) Well praised by readers, a helpful and friendly dried and silk flowers specialist based on a working arable farm, with waterfowl and calves for children. Snacks, shop, disabled access; cl 25–27 Dec, 1–3 Jan; (01477) 571616; free. Further along the A34 at Marton is a simple 14th-c shingle-roofed black and white timbered **church** in unpromising surroundings; readers recommend the adjacent **craft centre**, where a farm shop sells home-made ice-cream.

LYMM SJ6887
There are pretty cottages in The Dingle, and you can take **boat trips** on the Bridgewater Canal, for example from the new Admiral Benbow pub at Agden Wharf. The walk up to the lake at Lymm Dam is a pleasant stroll, and the Spread Eagle (Eagle Brow) has good value food.

MACCLESFIELD SJ9173
Away from the modern shopping streets are plenty of fine old buildings associated with the early industrial revolution and the silk industry; the weavers' cottages on Paradise St with their wide garret windows are of special note. Behind St Michael's church is a more ancient core with quaint little cobbled alleys, the famous 108 steps, and fine views across the town to the Pennines. The tea shop at Arighi Bianchi (Silk Rd) is highly recommended. The Sutton Hall Hotel just S is best for lunch, and other moorland pubs are in fairly easy reach.
Hare Hill (off B5087 NW of Macclesfield) Acres of lovely parkland with walled garden, pergola, fine spring flowers, and an abundance of rhododendrons and azaleas in May. Some disabled access; cl Nov–Mar, plus Mon (exc bank hols), Tues and Fri Apr–Oct; £2.50; NT. A footpath leads to Alderley Edge.
Paradise Mill 🏛 (Park Lane) Good fun; enthusiastic guides (many of whom are former silk workers) demonstrate the silk production process on the mill's restored handlooms, and room settings give a good idea of 1930s working conditions. Shop, good disabled access; cl am, all day Mon (exc bank hols), 24 Dec–2 Jan, Good Fri; (01625) 618228; £2.80. A joint ticket with the Silk Museum £4.90.
Silk Museum 🏛 (Roe St) The best place to learn about the industry, with some fine examples of the end product. Snacks, shop, some disabled access; cl Sun am, Good Fri, 25–26 Dec, 1 Jan; (01625) 613210, £2.80.
West Park Museum (Prestbury Rd) Small museum with a decent range of decorative arts and some interesting Egyptian antiquities. Adjacent West Park is pleasant and has one of the largest bowling greens in the country. Shop; cl am, all day Mon (exc bank hols), 24–26 Dec, 1 Jan, Good Fri; free.
MACCLESFIELD CANAL SJ8965
With good more or less level towpath walks, this tracks through fine high countryside from the Cheshire county boundary nr Disley to pass Bollington, Macclesfield and Congleton, with plenty of access points. One of the most

interesting places is S of the A54 just W of its junction with the A523, where a staggering flight of ten locks leads down to a sturdily elegant iron aqueduct.
MALPAS SJ4847
The most striking thing in this attractive place is the extraordinarily uplifting ceiling in its 14th-c hilltop church. There's also a fragmentary castle ruin nearby, as well as pretty cottages and almshouses, and some grander buildings.
MARBURY SJ5645
Some delightful landscapes open up in this village, with its attractive church, lake, wood and canal surroundings.
MARBURY COUNTRY PARK SJ6576
With some quiet short walks, this gives on to the extensive **Budworth Mere**, with sailing, and herons, ducks, grebes and coots pottering around the rushes; good pubs nearby at Comberbach (pronounced Comberbatch) and Great Budworth.
MIDDLEWOOD WAY SJ9482
A sort of linear country park near Macclesfield, this runs along a former railway; attractively bordered with wild flowers and trees, with cycle tracks (bicycle hire at Lyme Park or Bollington) and horse rides (can also be hired by the hour, around £10); several decent pubs in Bollington, one at Whiteley Green. The pleasant stretches around the Poynton inclines are underrated, and the Boars Head here is a good value refreshment stop.
MOBBERLEY SJ7979
Hillside Bird Oasis (Damson Lane) Excellent private collection of wildfowl with rare species such as white-headed stifftail and the Abyssinian black duck, as well as aviaries of softbills, flamingos and other exotic birds. Children should enjoy the penguin pool, and they have a pair of white wallabies. Under-cover picnic area, snacks, shop; open Apr–Oct exc Thurs, and Weds and Sun only Nov–Mar; (01565) 873282; £4.50. The church has a magnificently carved Tudor rood screen. The Bird in Hand and Church Inn are useful for lunch.
MOLLINGTON SJ3869
Cheshire Cheese Experience (The Grange) Demonstrations of Cheshire cheese-making; which stages of the

process you see depends on the time of day you visit, but a museum will fill you in on the rest. Snacks, shop, disabled access; cl 24 Dec–1 Feb; (01244) 851982; free, tours inc samples £1.

MOULDSWORTH SJ5070
Mouldsworth Motor Museum 🅰
(Smithy Lane) Splendid changing collection of cars, everything from vintage MGs to gleaming Ferraris. It's a notably friendly place, and you really don't have to be a car fiend to enjoy it – the 1930s art deco building and its grounds are very attractive in themselves, and there's plenty to amuse children, with quizzes, play areas and space to run around. There's also a collection of unusual teapots, many from the 1920s and 30s. Shop; disabled access; open Sun pm and bank hols Feb–Nov, plus Weds pm July and Aug; (01928) 731781; £2.50. The White Lion at Alvanley is a popular nearby dining pub.

MOW COP SJ8557
Right on the Staffs border is a shaggy steep hill with a castellated folly on top, and a rock pinnacle left by former quarrying; rich views over Cheshire (the village just behind, which is in Staffs, is a reminder of the contrast with Cheshire's richness). Worth a look if passing.

NANTWICH SJ6552
A pedestrian-only centre protects the splendid 14th-c church, with its exceptional carved choir-stalls; look out for the devil forcing open a nun's mouth, and the wife threatening her husband with a ladle. Much of the town, destroyed by a firestorm in 1583, was rebuilt then in intricate black and white timbering, and with countless window-boxes in flower in spring and summer is a fine sight esp around the centre. Quite a few decent antiques shops, and the central Crown has good value lunchtime food. As most of south Cheshire's roads seem to intersect at the town, traffic can be a problem.
Firs Pottery (Aston; A530 towards Whitchurch) Friendly place organising one-day pottery workshops (half-days for children). Booking essential; (01270) 780345; £26 for a day course, inc lunch and tea and coffee (£10 children, during school hols). A good

shop sells all sorts of useful pots; disabled access to ground floor only. The nearby Bhurtpore has enjoyable food and a good range of real ales. Readers enjoy the vast array of different flavours of ice-cream available at
Snugbury's Ice-Cream Farm (Hurleston, A51 N); cl 25–26 Dec, 1 Jan.
Hack Green Secret Nuclear Bunker 🅰 (Baddington) Built in the 1950s, this concrete labyrinth is where civil servants and military commanders would have hidden in the event of a nuclear war. An ordinary utility building on the surface, inside it is crammed with gadgets and interactive displays conjuring up a picture of what life would be like during a nuclear fall-out – you can even view the original TV broadcasts that would have been transmitted on all channels before a strike; children's trail. Snacks, shop, disabled access; cl wkdys Nov, Jan–late Mar, plus all Dec; (01270) 629219; *£4.90.

Stapeley Water Gardens (A51 about a mile SE) The world's largest and best-regarded water-garden centre, with display pools, fountains (the dancing ones are popular with younger visitors), waterfalls, gardens, coldwater and tropical fish, and a huge heated glasshouse full of over 350 sorts of water-lily (at their best Jun–Sept), piranhas, sharks, palms and parrots. Plenty of other gifts (lots for fishermen) as well as plants, and frequent special events. Meals, snacks, shop, disabled access; cl 25 Dec; (01270) 623868; gardens free, palm house £3.65.

NESTON SJ3075
Ness Gardens Liverpool University's extensive collection of specimen trees and shrubs, herbaceous plants, renowned heather, rock, rose and water gardens; visitor centre, good children's adventure playground, and picnic area. Meals, snacks, shop and plant sales (not over Christmas), wheelchair route; cl 25 Dec; (0151) 353 0123; £4.50. The Red Lion is the nicest place in nearby Parkgate for a light lunch.

NETHER ALDERLEY SJ8476
Nether Alderley Mill Lovely 15th-c watermill with carefully preserved atmosphere, and restored working

water wheels. The Victorian machinery still grinds flour (water supplies permitting). Shop; open pm Weds, Sun and bank hols Apr–Oct, plus pm bank hol Mons, Tues, Thurs, Fri and Sat Jun–Sept; (01625) 523012; £2; NT. Nearby Alderley Edge SJ8677 (not to be confused with the straggling suburban settlement named after it) rises high out of the plain, with good walks through the woodland and fine views of the higher hills to the E. The local caving-club members are working towards opening some of the former copper mines which honeycomb the area.

NORTHWICH SJ6674

Salt Museum ▣ (London Rd) Cheshire is the only British county to produce salt on a large scale, and much of it comes from this town. This interesting museum has the industry pretty well covered; microscopes let you see the intricacy of each crystal. Snacks, shop, disabled access to ground floor only; cl am wknds, all day Mon (exc bank hols and in Aug), 24–26 Dec; (01606) 41331; £2.10. You can follow the Salt Heritage Trail around some of the other buildings. From the Quay there are cruises down the river. The Smoker at Plumley (A556 E) is a reliable dining pub.

PARKGATE SJ2879

This interesting village is the country's only inland seaside resort, the Dee estuary having retreated since its palmy days at the end of the 18th and early 19th c. Before that, it was a more important port than Liverpool, and there's an eerie charm in sitting in the Boathouse or Red Lion on the 'Promenad', looking out over the marshes to the distant waters and the Welsh hills on the far side. A similar sense of stranded time can be had at the Harp by the ruined marshside quay near Little Neston; you can walk between the two (and on to Ness Gardens at Ness) along the Dee Estuary 'coastal' path.

PECKFORTON HILLS SJ5256

These are tracked by a particularly fine section of the 30-mile **Sandstone Trail**, with splendid views of real and real-looking romantic castles, and good pubs usefully placed at Bulkeley and Higher Burwardsley. The Trail offers very varied scenery, following the romantically wooded sandstone ridges, crags and outcrops stretching from Overton in the N (the church here is pretty, and the Ring o' Bells is a most attractive pub, with Mersey views) to the Shropshire border S of Malpas (the ancient Bell o' the Hill pub nr Tushingham down there is another good stop).

POYNTON SJ9183

Brookside Garden Centre (Macclesfield Rd) A splendid miniature railway chuffs its way through an authentically detailed circuit in a pretty garden setting to a replica West Country station, packed with railway memorabilia. There's also a pottery. Parking is not always easy. Meals, snacks, shop, disabled access (not train); railway runs wknds all year (exc in Christmas hols) plus Weds Apr–Sept and daily mid-July–Aug; (01625) 872919; train £1, garden centre free. A mile away at Higher Poynton, Coppice Fruit Farm has **pick-your-own**.

PRESTBURY SJ9077

Very prosperous-feeling now, with leafy surroundings, good shops, and for refreshment the smart Legh Arms and homelier Admiral Rodney. There are pleasant riverside walks to the S, along the Bollin.

RAW HEAD SJ5154

From the A534 nr Harthill a section of the 30-mile Sandstone Trail ascends Raw Head, the most spectacular natural feature of the central Cheshire ridge, with sandstone cliffs weathered into bizarre shapes, and a cave to explore.

ROSTHERNE SJ7483

As well as charming brick cottages along its quaint cobbled pavement, this picture-postcard village gives a lovely view over one of the county's broadest meres from the graveyard of its attractive timbered church.

RUNCORN SJ5481

Apart from Norton Priory, this New Town has some enjoyable surprises – such as the Sunday-afternoon **miniature train rides** in the Park on Stockham Lane (Halton), popular with children. There are views from the nearby ruins of Halton Castle up on its grassy hill.

Norton Priory Museum and

Gardens (Tudor Rd, Manor Park) Lovely 12th-c priory that developed into a Georgian stately home, with exhibitions on medieval monastic life, and sculpture inc a 12-ft sandstone statue of St Christopher, said to be carved by a member of the priory 600 years ago. Outside is an enchanting 18th-c walled garden, and beautiful woodland gardens. Snacks, shop, disabled access; cl am, 24–26 Dec, 1 Jan, walled gdn cl Nov–Feb; (01928) 569895; £3.30.

SANDIWAY SJ6070
Blakemere Craft Centre (Chester Rd) Much better than average craft centre based around a restored Edwardian stable block, with interesting range of goods in the 25 shops, aquatic and falconry centre, garden centre and indoor play area. Wknd craft fairs, meals, snacks, disabled access; cl Mon (exc bank hols); (01606) 883261; free.

STRETTON SJ4453
Stretton Watermill Working watermill in lovely countryside, which still produces corn, powered by two ancient wheels. Shop, snacks, some disabled access; cl am, all Mon and Oct–Mar (open wknds and bank hols only Apr and Sept); (01606) 41331; £1.80. The Cock 'o Barton up on the A534 is quite useful for lunch (and a good base for walks – as is the Farndon Arms in the attractive Dee-side village of Farndon).

STYAL SJ8383
Quarry Bank Mill & Country Park 🖼 One of the best and most extensive places in the country to get to grips with the Industrial Revolution – you can easily spend the best part of a day here. The 18th-c cotton mill that's the centrepiece still produces cloth (you can buy it in the shop), and as well as demonstrations of spinning and weaving has lively exhibitions looking at factory conditions for the millworkers and their bosses. A hands-on exhibition explains how the 1840 beam engine (joined this year by a slightly later model) in the original engine house was restored, while the 50-ton working water wheel remains an impressive sight. The surrounding village has carefully preserved workers' cottages, chapels and shop, and they grow rare types of fruit and vegetables in the garden. At the Apprentice House enthusiastic guides in period dress explain the lifestyle and 12-hour working days faced by young pauper children (you can even try out their beds); there are timed tickets in operation here, so it makes sense to see this bit at the start of your visit. Good woodland and riverside walks in the park, lots of events throughout the year. Meals, snacks, shop, disabled access; cl winter Mons, apprentice house cl am wkdys and Mon during school terms; (01625) 527468; all-in ticket £6, mill only £4.80, apprentice house only £3.80; NT. The Ship is pleasant for lunch.

SWETTENHAM SJ8067
One of Cheshire's tucked-away comfortable villages – rich paddocks with wrought-iron fences, daffodils in spring in a dell by an old mill, a good dining pub (the Swettenham Arms) behind the partly 13th-c church.

TABLEY SJ7177
Cuckoo Clock Collection 🖼 (Old School House, Nether Tabley) A unique collection of these and other mechanical timepieces from all over the world. They currently have over 500 rare and beautiful clocks, most of them working, but the number constantly increases as the owners nip off to Europe to track down more. Four working historic fairground organs are among the other mechanisms on show. By appointment (phone to order snacks). Shop, disabled access; (01565) 633039; £5.

Tabley House 🖼 (off A5033) Probably the finest Palladian House in the North-West, with a splendid collection of paintings. Sir John Fleming Leicester (whose family lived here for over 700 years) was the first great collector of British art, and though plans to turn his home into a National Gallery came to nothing, most of the works he assembled are still here, inc pictures by Turner (the one of a pineapple shows why he is remembered for his landscapes), Reynolds, Henry Thompson and James Ward. Snacks, shop, very good disabled access (though they prefer notice); open Apr–Oct, Thurs–Sun pm and bank hols; (01565) 750151; £4. The Smoker at

Plumley is good for lunch. Discount entitles one child free for every full paying adult.

TARPORLEY SJ5562
Largely bypassed and quietly attractive, with very individual shops inc antiques shops; the Rising Sun is a fine pub, the Swan a well restored old coaching inn.

TATTENHALL SJ5059
Cheshire Farm Ice Cream
(Drumlan Hall Farm) Watch the cows being milked then sample the delicious end product; snacks, shop, disabled access; cl two wks mid-Jan; (01829) 770995; free. The Egerton Arms down the A41 at Broxton is a good lunch stop.

TEGGS NOSE COUNTRY PARK
SJ9472
Cheshire's hilly eastern edge forms part of the Peak District, and offers some grand views westwards towards North Wales. This country park has a useful summer information centre, and good walks with far views, punctuated by relics of the former quarrying here. By the turn off the A537, the Setter Dog is a good pub. From the park, a well marked track heads off S into the Macclesfield Forest, with steep deep green pine plantations around neatly walled small reservoirs; on the far side of this the isolated Leathers Smithy E of Langley is a warmly welcoming moorside refuge with superb views, and the Stanley Arms tucked away at Bottom of the Oven is also good. This track is actually part of the long-distance Gritstone Trail.

WARRINGTON SJ5990
Gulliver's World (Old Hall) Theme park very similar to its sister parks in Milton Keynes and Matlock Bath (see **Buckinghamshire** and **Derbyshire** chapters), with rides and entertainment aimed at the under-12s. Meals, snacks, shop, disabled access; open wknds Apr–Oct, daily Jun–mid-Sept and during school hols, phone to check; (01925) 444888; £6.50.

Warrington Museum & Gallery
(Bold St) The refurbished geology and botany galleries contain hands-on displays and a 'breathing' model dinosaur. Other weird and wonderful exhibits include a model mermaid, cannibal's flesh hook, an Egyptian mummy, a toy-packed nursery, and a number of beetles and other creepy-crawlies. Snacks, shop, disabled access; cl Sun and bank hols; free. The Ferry at Fiddlers Ferry down by the Mersey off the A562 at Penketh is prettily placed for lunch. A new arts centre will have opened on recently revamped Palmyra Sq, just off Bold St, by the time this book comes out.

WHARTONS LOCK SJ5360
With a handy family dining pub nearby, this is a good place for walks along the **Shropshire Union Canal**; this is a charming section, winding through the richly wooded farming country below Beeston Castle.

WHITEGATE SJ6168
An interesting village, with thatched houses around the village green, fragmentary remains of what was once the biggest Cistercian monastery in the whole of England opposite its church, and a lakeside walk along a nearby derelict railway.

WIDNES SJ5183
Catalyst (Mersey Rd) Award-winning centre exploring the chemical industry and how it affects our lives. Put like that it doesn't sound too gripping, but children who enjoy museums where you poke, press and push things will really get a lot out of it. It's all presented in a splendidly enjoyable and entertaining way, with interactive games and displays such as Apples and Maggots, where you battle against maggots, gales and floods to grow a successful crop of apples, or the Game of Health, which involves travelling from the past to the present without falling victim to any deadly diseases. A glass lift whisks you up to a roof-top Observatory with splendid views. There's an adjacent waterside park, with wildlife and brightly coloured fishing boats. Meals, snacks, shop, disabled access; cl Mon exc bank and school hols, 25–26 Dec, 1 Jan; (0151) 420 1121; £4.65.

WRENBURY SJ5947
Canal walks The pretty **Llangollen Branch** is a relaxing canal for gentle waterside walks, with access at Wrenbury, for example; the good Dusty Miller dining pub here has an interesting lifting bridge by it.

Where to eat

ALDFORD SJ4158 **Grosvenor Arms** *Chester Rd (01244) 620228* Sizeable but friendly Victorian pub, attractively decorated, with huge panelled library and several quieter rooms, airy conservatory, good interesting food from a daily-changing menu, well kept real ales, lots of New World wines (and malt whiskies), and large elegant sun-trap terrace and neat lawn; best to get there early; children allowed until 6pm; disabled access. £24|**£6.50**

BOLLINGTON SJ9377 **Mauro's** *88 Palmerston St (01625) 573898* Friendly Italian restaurant with lots of good pasta, excellent fresh fish and lovely puddings; cl Sun, Mon, 25–26 Dec; disabled access. £30|**£5**

BUNBURY SJ5758 **Dysart Arms** *Bowes Gate Rd (01829) 260183* By the village church, this neat former farmhouse has a civilised, old-fashioned atmosphere, log fires, lots of antique furniture, cosy alcoves, a no smoking library area, well kept ales and house wines, interesting food, friendly service, and tables in lovely elevated big garden; children over 10 in evenings; disabled access. £19.45|**£7.50**

CHESTER SJ4066 **Francs** *14 Cuppin St (01244) 317952* Cheerful timbered brasserie on two floors of old converted warehouse with very good French country food; partial disabled access. £17|**£6.95**

CHESTER SJ4166 **Old Harkers Arms** *1 Russell St (01244) 344525* Attractive conversion of an early Victorian canal warehouse with lofty ceiling, tall windows and well spaced tables and chairs, lots to look at, a comfortably busy atmosphere, friendly efficient staff, a changing choice of nicely presented, sometimes unusual food (inc interesting sandwiches), well kept real ales, and New World wines; disabled access. £17.70|**£5.95**

DARESBURY SJ5782 **Ring o' Bells** *(01925) 740256* Roomy pub with plenty of places to sit inc no smoking dining rooms and a down-to-earth part for walkers; reasonably priced and interesting daily specials, well kept real ales, 12 wines by the glass, a dozen malts, efficient, friendly service, and roaring fire; tables in long, partly terraced garden; this is an attractive village where Lewis Carroll's father was vicar. £19.70|**£6.95**

HASSALL GREEN SJ7758 **Canal Centre & Tearoom** *Canal Centre (01270) 762266* 200-year-old house with tearoom offering breakfasts, snacks, lunches, cream teas, and evening restaurant – and you can sit on the lawn and watch the narrow-boats going through the locks; gift shop and towpath walks; bdrms; disabled access. £15|**£5.95**

KNUTSFORD SJ7578 **Belle Epoque Brasserie** *60 King St (01565) 633060* Popular restaurant with rooms decorated in art nouveau style with lavish drapes, marbled pillared alcoves, and smartly set tables, enthusiastic friendly staff and lovely modern cooking; cl Sun, bank hols; children over 12. £25|**£5.50**

PEOVER HEATH SJ7973 **Dog** *Wellbank Rd (01625) 861421* On a quiet lane, this bustling pub has two big no smoking areas, a cosy, comfortable tap room with darts and pool, open fires, well kept real ales, a good choice of whiskies, a comprehensive wine list, and well liked, often interesting food using local produce; bdrms; cl pm 25 Dec; disabled access. £24|**£5.50**

PLUMLEY SJ7176 **Smoker** *Chester Rd (01565) 722338* Popular thatched 16th-c pub with open fires and comfortable sofas in three well decorated connecting rooms, good swiftly served food, a wide choice of whiskies, well kept real ales, and friendly service; big garden; disabled access. £19.50/evening and Sun lunch 2-course menu £9.95|**£6.95**

SWETTENHAM SJ8067 **Swettenham Arms** *(01477) 571284* Tucked-away country dining pub with three spacious beamed bar areas, winter log fires, nice furnishings, real ales, a no smoking restaurant, and huge range of very popular food; cl pm 25–26 Dec; partial disabled access. £24|**£5.50**

WHITELEY GREEN SJ9178 **Windmill** *Holehouse Lane (01625) 574222* Close to canal and other walks and with plenty of seats in the attractive four-acre garden, this large slate-roofed white house has a 16th-c heart with wooden-floored open-plan extensions, country kitchen-style furnishings, a welcoming atmosphere, very good well prepared interesting food, well kept ales, and friendly service. £22|£7.50

Special thanks to E G Parish

We welcome reports from readers

This *Guide* depends on readers' reports. Do help us if you can – in return, we offer a discount on the next edition to people who've helped us with reports for it. Tell us what you think about places already in it, and anything extra you think we should say about them. And send us your ideas for inclusion in the next edition: places to visit, eat at or stay in, attractive drives or walks, maybe even unusual interesting shops you know of. Use the card in the middle, the report forms at the end, or just write – no stamp needed: *The Good Britain Guide*, FREEPOST TN1569, Wadhurst, E Sussex TN5 7BR.

CORNWALL

Ideal holiday country, from sandy family resorts through picturesque creeks, coves and quaint fishing villages to wild majestic cliffs and bleak moors; masses of family attractions, some spectacular gardens, a fine choice of places to stay in

Great places for enjoyable family outings include Dobwalls adventure park, Flambards theme park near Helston (entertaining for all ages), and Dairyland near Newquay. Paradise Park (HQ of the World Parrot Trust) makes for an entertaining day out, too. Animal-lovers will be pleased to see excellent conservation work at Newquay Zoo, the monkey sanctuary near Looe, Tamar Otter Park, and the seal sanctuary at Gweek. The expanding animal centre at Trecangate is refreshingly uncommercial.

Cornwall is noted for its great gardens, and the monumental Eden Project at Pentewan will provide a showcase for 21st-century horticulture when it opens later this year. Older, more established gardens here are best in late spring but gorgeous at almost any time, and quite unlike those elsewhere in England — altogether more exotic, almost subtropical. Among many splendid examples, the Lost Gardens of Heligan (Mevagissey), Lanhydrock (the house too is special), Trelissick and Trebah (Mawnan Smith) are outstanding. Having opened to the public only a few years ago despite its long history, the graceful Trevarno estate is a welcome addition to the *Guide* this year.

The fairy-tale castle on St Michael's Mount off Marazion is a most enjoyable outing, and other unusual places to note include the Minack open-air theatre at Porthcurno, the bizarre collection of stuffed animals at Bolventor, the space-age Goonhilly Earth Station, the distinctly Cornish Poldark Mine & Heritage Centre, and the National Lighthouse Centre.

Cotehele, near Calstock, is Cornwall's most lovely house, and Trerice, Pencarrow at Bodmin and Antony House at Torpoint, are all well worth visiting.

There are many delightful seaside villages and towns, keeping their charm even in summer, as the strolling crowds never quite override their friendly local character. Readers like the gently picturesque south coast best — very sheltered, with wonderful places to stay in. East of the Lizard Point are plenty of interesting little coves, winding estuaries and creeks rich in bird life, and boat and fishing trips from virtually every harbour. There are some dramatic cliffy stretches too, interspersed with fine sandy beaches, especially west of the Lizard.

The north coast scores for uncomplicated family beach holidays, around the attractive town of St Ives (with its two first-class art galleries), and between Padstow (appealing combination of fishing port and resort) and lively Newquay (Cornwall's biggest resort and increasingly a surfing centre). This stretch is an almost continuous line of resort developments, with plenty of family attractions nearby.

West of St Ives are rugged stretches of windswept empty clifftop moorland, with a hinterland exceptionally rich in well preserved visible archaeology – Bronze Age burial chambers and standing stones, Iron Age hill forts and village sites, ancient stone crosses. Small rather withdrawn-looking granite villages and farmsteads among wind-beaten pastures give this western part a rather clannish feel, almost like the more nationalistic parts of Wales; but though visitors are clearly seen as outsiders, the locals are far from unfriendly. Another stretch of wild grandeur is up towards Devon, north of commercialised Tintagel – towering precipices, dramatic surfing beaches and much unspoilt seaboard, with no development, little car access, just wildlife, wind, waves and the occasional walker. Port Isaac and Boscastle are the pick of this part's few settlements.

Away from the sheltered south-east, the inland parts are largely treeless, with rolling pasture and moorland. Windswept Bodmin Moor is the county's most untouched inland area. In the more exposed spots the towering alloy propellers of the new windfarms are becoming a striking landscape feature.

In high summer Cornwall's better for long stay-put holidays than for short breaks or touring: with lots of traffic on the narrow roads (and some serious parking problems), getting there, back and around can overshadow a short summer visit. On a longer holiday, it's surprisingly easy to escape the crowds that go with the big family attractions, honey-pot fishing villages and famous beaches. With 500 miles of coastal walks here, much of the land owned and beautifully preserved by the National Trust, you can always quickly escape into solitude. Incidentally, few roads actually follow the coast – good for walkers, if disappointing for drivers (or cyclists). The relatively warm sea makes Cornwall popular bathing country in summer: we pick out reliably clean beaches in the text.

Out of high season, Cornwall comes into its own for those prepared to spend the time getting there: lots to do, a very relaxed pace of life, and attractive prices. Generally well sheltered, most of the coastal places can be pleasantly mild when other parts of the West Country are cold. Late May and early June is an ideal time for a short break here, with the scenery at its best, and relatively few other visitors. In spring and early summer, the tall roadside hedged banks which block the view from many byroads compensate by being virtual walls of wild flowers. September and October is seal pup time. From London, you should allow about five hours' driving out of season to get well into the county; it's about three hours from Bristol – across just a couple of counties. The A30 is now a good fast long-distance route (much better than the A390).

If you'd rather avoid the roads altogether, a Cornish Rail Rover ticket is good value for eight days (which don't have to be consecutive) of unlimited train journeys throughout the county for around £40 (less in winter); you can also get a ticket for three days.

The Isles of Scilly are ideal for a really quiet and relaxing holiday, with Penzance the quickest jumping-off point.

Where to stay

BODINNICK SX1352 **Old Ferry** *Bodinnick, Fowey, Cornwall PL23 ILX* (01726) 870237 **£60**; 12 comfortable and spacious rms, most with own bthrm and river views. 400-year-old inn in lovely situation overlooking Fowey estuary; back flagstoned bar partly cut into the rock, real ales, comfortable residents' lounge with French windows opening on to a terrace, and decent food in both bar and little evening restaurant; quiet out of season

BOTALLACK SW3632 **Botallack Manor Farm** *Botallack, St Just In Penwith, Penzance, Cornwall TR19 7QG* (01736) 788525 **£50***; 3 rms. Blissfully quiet and friendly 17th-c local granite farmhouse on working farm, with a medley of furnishings in reading room, good breakfasts with home-baked bread, and safe walled garden; no pets; marvellous cliff walks, ruined mines and small coves

BURYAS BRIDGE SW4427 **Rose Farm** *Chyenhal, Buryas Bridge, Penzance, Cornwall TR19 6AN* (01736) 731808 **£44***, plus winter breaks; 3 delightfully furnished rms. Relaxed, informal and friendly 200-year-old farmhouse tucked away down remote country lane with excellent breakfasts around big table; can see lots of animals (working farm), and children love it; cl 24–25 Dec; disabled access ☺

CARNE BEACH SW9040 **Nare Hotel** *Carne Beach, Veryan, Truro, Cornwall TR2 5PF* (01872) 501279 **£236**, plus special breaks; 36 lovely rms to suit all tastes – some stylish ones overlook garden and out to sea. Attractively decorated and furnished hotel in magnificent clifftop position with secluded gardens, outdoor and indoor swimming pools, tennis, sailboarding, and fishing; antiques, fresh flowers and log fires in the airy, spacious day rooms, very good food inc wonderful breakfasts, and run by staff who really care; ideal for quiet family hols, with safe sandy beach below; cl Jan; disabled access ☺

CONSTANTINE BAY SW8674 **Treglos Hotel** *Constantine Bay, Padstow, Cornwall PL28 8JH* (01841) 520727 **£126**, plus special breaks; 44 light rms, some with balcony. Quiet and relaxed hotel close to good sandy beach, and in the same family for 30 years; comfortable traditional furnishings, log fires, good food, friendly helpful staff, sheltered garden plus playground and adventure equipment, indoor swimming pool, table tennis, table football, and pool table, and children's playroom with electronic games; lovely nearby walks; self-catering apartments; cl mid-Nov–mid-Mar; children over 7 in restaurant; disabled access ☺

CRACKINGTON HAVEN SX1496 **Manor Farm** *Crackington Haven, Bude, Cornwall EX23 0JW* (01840) 230304 **£60***; 3 pretty rms. Lovely Domesday-listed, no smoking manor surrounded by 25 acres of farmland and carefully landscaped gardens; antiques in four lounges, a log fire, a house-party atmosphere, big breakfasts, and a delicious 4-course dinner at 7pm; cl 25 Dec; no children

FALMOUTH SW7932 **Penmere Manor** *Mongleath Rd, Falmouth, Cornwall TR11 4PN* (01326) 211411 **£95**, plus special breaks; 37 spacious rms. Run by the same owners for 29 years, this quietly set Georgian manor has 5 acres of subtropical gardens and woodland, heated outdoor swimming pool, giant chess, croquet, and leisure centre with indoor swimming pool, gym, sauna, and woodland fitness trail; particularly helpful friendly staff, an evening pianist, and enjoyable food in restaurant and informal bar; cl 24–27 Dec

FOWEY SX1151 **Carnethic House** *Lambs Barn, Fowey, Cornwall PL23 IHQ* (01726) 833336 **£70***, plus special breaks; 8 rms. Warmly friendly Regency house in lovely gardens with heated swimming pool, badminton and putting; relaxed and informal atmosphere, very helpful owners, attractive lounge, and good home-made food (local fish is popular); cl Dec–Jan; limited disabled access

FOWEY SX1251 **Fowey Hall** *Fowey, Cornwall PL23 1ET* (01726) 833866 **£165**; 25 rms inc 9 suites and 5 pairs of interconnecting rms. Fine Gothic-style mansion in five acres of grounds overlooking the harbour and run along the same lines as their other hotels – Woolley Grange, Bradford-on-Avon, Moonfleet Manor at Fleet, and Old Bell, Malmesbury; marble fireplaces, baroque plasterwork, panelling, antiques, big potted plants, two restaurants offering good, enjoyable food, marvellous facilities for children inc supervised nursery, and covered swimming pool, croquet, and badminton ☺

FOWEY SX1251 **Marina Hotel** *17 Esplanade, Fowey, Cornwall PL23 1HY* (01726) 833315 **£84**, plus special breaks; 12 rms, several with lovely views (some with balcony). Homely, friendly hotel in fine position overlooking Fowey River and open sea (private access from secluded walled garden), comfortable lounge, attractive dining room overlooking the water, good food, and helpful service; cl mid-Dec–mid-Feb; children over 12

GERRANS BAY SW8938 **Pendower Beach House** *Ruan High Lanes, Truro, Cornwall TR2 5LW* (01872) 501241 **£141** inc dinner, plus special breaks; 15 rms. Family-run hotel dating back to 16th c in eight acres by lovely sandy beach, with superb sea and coastal views, and plenty of seats on sunny terrace; a friendly atmosphere in attractive and comfortable rooms, good food in cosy restaurant (super fresh local fish and shellfish), and tennis court; cl Nov–Feb; disabled access

GILLAN SW7825 **Tregildry** *Gillan, Manaccan, Helston, Cornwall TR12 6HG* (01326) 231378 **£140*** inc dinner, plus special breaks; 10 attractive rms with fine views over Falmouth Bay. Elegantly furnished hotel in four acres of grounds with private access to the cove below; spacious comfortable lounges, fresh flowers, books and magazines, a restful atmosphere, good food in attractive restaurant, enjoyable breakfasts, and courteous service; cl Nov–Feb; children over 8

GUNWALLOE SW6522 **Halzephron** *Gunwalloe, Helston, Cornwall TR12 7QB* (01326) 240406 **£64**; 2 cosy rms. 500-year-old former smugglers' inn run by knowledgeable and friendly Cornish landlady, with imaginative food in bar areas and bistro-style restaurant, open fire, and fine views of Mounts Bay; lots of walks, nearby beaches, golf, and boating; cl 25 Dec; no children for accommodation (allowed in pub)

LAMORNA COVE SW4424 **Lamorna Cove** *Lamorna Cove, Penzance, Cornwall TR19 6XH* (01736) 731411 **£69**; 12 well furnished rms, most with cove views. Beautifully placed hotel overlooking gardens to the sea, with comfortable homely rooms, a light, airy restaurant using fresh local food (esp seafood), warmly welcoming owners, and outdoor heated swimming pool; marvellous walks; cl Nov–end Feb, but open at Christmas and New Year; no children

LISKEARD SX2460 **Well House** *St Keyne, Liskeard, Cornwall PL14 4RN* (01579) 342001 **£135**, plus special breaks; 9 individually designed rms with fine views. Light and airy Victorian country house with warmly friendly owners, courteous staff, comfortable drawing room, cosy little bar, and particularly good food and fine wines in dining room overlooking terrace and lawns; three acres of gardens with hard tennis court, swimming pool and croquet lawn; children over 8 in evening restaurant

LITTLE PETHERICK SW9172 **Old Mill Country House** *Little Petherick, Wadebridge, Cornwall PL27 7QT* (01841) 540388 **£60***, plus special breaks; 5 rms. 16th-c corn mill in lovely riverside gardens with waterwheel and other original features, enjoyable breakfasts in beamed dining room, lounges, and attentive service; plenty of places nearby for evening meals; cl Nov–Mar; no children

LOOE SX2251 **Talland Bay Hotel** *Porthallow, Looe, Cornwall PL13 2JB* (01503) 272667 **£112**, plus special breaks; 23 charming rms with sea or country views. Down a little lane between Looe and Polperro, this restful partly 16th-c country house has lovely subtropical gardens just above the sea; comfortable drawing room with log fire, smaller lounge with library, fresh flowers, courteous service, good food in pretty oak-panelled dining room, and pleasant afternoon teas; heated outdoor swimming pool, putting, croquet; cl Jan/Feb; children over 5 in evening restaurant (high tea for younger ones); dogs by prior arrangement

MAWNAN SMITH SW7828 **Meudon Hotel** *Mawnan Smith, Falmouth, Cornwall TR11 5HT* (01326) 250541 **£170**, plus special breaks; 29 well equipped comfortable rms in separate wing. Run by the same caring family for over 30 years, this is an old stone mansion with a newer wing set in beautiful subtropical gardens laid out by Capability Brown; fine views from the dining room, comfortable lounge with log fire and fresh flowers, good English cooking, and old-fashioned standards of service; cl Jan; dogs by arrangement (not in public rooms); limited disabled access

MAXWORTHY SX2492 **Wheatley Farm** *Maxworthy, Launceston, Cornwall PL15 8LY (01566) 781232 £36**, plus special breaks; 5 attractive rms with showers. In the same family for five generations, this working sheep and dairy farm has comfortable, pretty furnishings, log fires, good 4-course evening meals using local produce in spacious dining room, and hearty breakfasts; games room with table tennis and toys, animals to visit, pony rides, and safe play area for children; cl Nov–end Jan; self-catering cottages, too

MITHIAN SW7450 **Rose-in-Vale Country House Hotel** *Mithian, St Agnes, Cornwall TR5 0QD (01872) 552202* **£89**, plus special breaks; 18 pretty rms. Secluded and quietly set Georgian house in four acres of neatly kept gardens, with comfortable spacious day rooms, a friendly atmosphere, helpful, long-standing local staff, and good food in enlarged dining room; ducks on ponds, a trout stream, outdoor swimming pool, badminton, and croquet, plus a sauna and solarium; children over 7 in evening in public rooms and restaurant (high tea for smaller ones); well behaved dogs welcome; cl Jan–Feb; disabled access

MULLION SW6818 **Meaver Farm** *Mullion, Helston, Cornwall TR12 7DN (01326) 240128 £45*; 3 individual rms with super bthrms, and one with little private garden. 17th-c stone farmhouse (no longer a working farm), with good Aga-cooked breakfasts in beamed kitchen, log fire, plants and antiques in sitting room, and friendly helpful owners; dogs welcome and have their own fenced acre field

MULLION SW6718 **Polurrian Hotel** *Mullion, Helston, Cornwall TR12 7EN (01326) 240421* **£190** inc dinner, plus special breaks; 39 rms, some with memorable sea view. White clifftop hotel in lovely gardens with path down to sheltered private cove below, a restful atmosphere in the comfortable lounges and bright cocktail bar, fresh flowers, good food using fresh local ingredients (pianist and sea views in the dining room), enjoyable breakfasts, leisure club with heated swimming pool, and heated outdoor pool, badminton, tennis, mini-golf, squash and croquet; particularly good for families; disabled access ☺

PADSTOW SW9175 **Treverbyn House** *Station Rd, Padstow, Cornwall PL28 8DA (01841) 532855 £50*; 5 refurbished rms with lovely views over the Camel estuary. Carefully restored Edwardian house opposite the famous Seafood Restaurant, with friendly owners, open fires in comfortable public rooms, and good breakfasts; cl Christmas

PELYNT SX2055 **Jubilee** *Pelynt, Looe, Cornwall PL13 2JZ (01503) 220312* **£65**, plus special breaks; 12 rms. Neat 16th-c inn with Queen Victoria mementoes, oak tables and a mix of nice seats under the beams in the relaxed lounge bar, log fire, gleaming brass and fresh flowers, and good waitress-served bar food; well equipped play area

PENZANCE SW4730 **Abbey Hotel** *Abbey St, Penzance, Cornwall TR18 4AR (01736) 366906* **£100**, plus winter breaks; 7 charming rms. Stylish little 17th-c house close to harbour with marvellous views, a relaxed atmosphere in comfortable drawing room full of flowers, fine paintings and antiques, a good set menu in small restaurant, and pretty garden; cl 20–27 Dec; children over 7

PENZANCE SW4729 **Summer House** *Cornwall Terrace, Penzance, Cornwall TR18 4HL (01736) 363744* **£55**, plus special breaks; 5 charming rooms with fresh flowers and antiques. In a mews 50 metres from the sea, this Regency restaurant-with-rooms (flooded with light by a curving glass tower) has a relaxed, informal atmosphere, lots of cheerful yellows and blues, wooden floors, comfortable sofas and local paintings, and wonderful Mediterranean-style food (the owner/chef worked in some top London restaurants); pretty walled garden; cl Jan; children over 12

PILLATON SX3663 **Weary Friar** *Pillaton, Saltash, Cornwall PL12 6QS (01579) 350238 £55*, plus special breaks; 12 rms. Pretty 12th-c inn by church in pleasantly remote village; lots of character in its four knocked-together rooms (one no smoking), attractive furnishings, well kept real ales, and good food in both bar and restaurant; children over 10

POLPERRO SX2051 **Landaviddy Manor** *Landaviddy Lane, Polperro, Looe, Cornwall PL13 2RT (01503)* 272210 **£50***, plus special breaks; 7 pretty rms. Attractive and carefully furnished no smoking 18th-c manor house with fine views over the two acres of peaceful gardens and over the bay beyond; comfortably furnished lounges, open fire, a relaxed atmosphere, and Aga-cooked breakfasts in beamed dining room; cl Oct–mid-Mar; no children and no pets

POLPERRO SX2051 **Old Mill House** *Mill Hill, Polperro, Looe, Cornwall PL13 2RP (01503)* 272362 **£55**, plus special breaks; 8 attractive rms. Pretty white cottagey pub with a nice civilised feel, solid stripped pine furniture on polished boards, log fire in big fireplace, fishing boat pictures, well kept real ales, good enjoyable food inc fresh fish (no food winter lunchtimes), cosy little bistro, and friendly service; fishing trips/boating outings arranged

PORT ISAAC SX0080 **Port Gaverne Hotel** *Port Gaverne, Port Isaac, Cornwall PL29 3SQ (01208)* 880244 **£110**, plus special breaks; 16 comfortable rms. Lovely place to stay and an excellent base for area (dramatic coves, good clifftop walks, and lots of birds); big log fires in well kept bars, relaxed lounges, decent bar food, good restaurant food, and fine wines; also, restored 18th-c self-catering cottages; children over 7 in restaurant; dogs allowed

PORT ISAAC SW9980 **Valencia House** *Rose Hill, Port Isaac, Cornwall PL29 3RL (01208)* 880677 **£50**; 3 rms with thoughtful extras. Carefully renovated Victorian house up on a hill overlooking the harbour, with warmly welcoming, helpful hosts and good hearty breakfasts in homely dining room; lots of walks; cl Dec–Feb

QUINTRELL DOWNS SW8360 **Manuels Farm** *Quintrell Downs, Newquay, Cornwall TR8 4NY (01637)* 873577 **£40**; 3 rms. Comfortable and relaxed 17th-c farmhouse with log fires, candlelit dinners, and pretty garden; good for children – bottle-feed calves, collect eggs and so forth (free babysitting); cl Christmas/New Year; limited disabled access

ROCK SW9375 **St Enodoc Hotel** *Rock, Wadebridge, Cornwall PL27 6LA (01208)* 863394 **£145**, plus special breaks; 19 individually designed rms with lovely views. Quietly set hotel overlooking the Camel estuary and next to two 18-hole golf courses; stylish Mediterranean décor with plenty of paintings and fresh flowers, delicious modern cooking in bar and split-level restaurant, a relaxed informal atmosphere, a gym, sauna and billiards room, and heated swimming pool in big garden; good for families; lovely nearby beaches and walks; cl Dec–Feb ☺

RUAN HIGH LANES SW9039 **Crugsillick Manor** *Ruan High Lanes, Truro, Cornwall TR2 5LJ (01872)* 501214 **£80**, plus special breaks; 3 rms. One of the loveliest houses in Cornwall, this Queen Anne manor is extended from a pre-Elizabethan farmhouse and surrounded by a big quiet garden with wooded valley views; log fire in drawing room with Napoleonic ceiling, candlelit dinners in 17th-c dining room using home-grown produce where possible, fine breakfasts, and charming owners; self-catering cottages in grounds – excellent disabled access, and children welcome (but must be over 12 in main house); cl Christmas/New Year

SALTASH SX3957 **Erth Barton** *Elmgate, Saltash, Cornwall PL12 4QY (01752)* 842127 **£70**; 3 rms. Lovely old manor house with its own chapel, peaceful rooms with lots of books, pictures and big fireplaces, good enjoyable food, bird-watching in the surrounding estuaries, and riding (you can bring your own horse); children over 12

SENNEN SW3425 **Lands End Hotel** *Sennen, Penzance, Cornwall TR19 7AA (01736)* 871844 **£100**, plus special breaks; 33 elegant airy rms, many with splendid sea views. Comfortable hotel right on the cliff top with fine sea views, good food in attractive conservatory-style restaurant, elegant seating areas, informal bar with lots of malt whiskies, and helpful staff

ST AUSTELL SX0552 **Boscundle Manor** *Tregrehan, St Austell, Cornwall PL25 3RL (01726)* 813557 **£130**, plus special breaks; 10 rms with CD players. Mainly 18th-c rambling manor run by the same caring owners for over 20 years – with country house atmosphere in its low-beamed and carefully furnished rooms, enjoyable food under a new chef, a good wine list, and breakfasts in pretty conservatory; 14 acres of grounds inc two acres of terraced gardens, croquet, badminton, outdoor heated swimming pool, indoor swimming pool, golf practice area with two greens and two all-weather teeing positions, and barn with gym, snooker, table tennis, and darts; woodland walks, too; cl Nov–Mar

ST BLAZEY SX0655 **Nanscawen House** Prideaux, St Blazey, Par, Cornwall PL24 2SR (01726) 814488 **£78***; 3 spacious, pretty rms overlooking the garden. Attractive creeper-covered no smoking Georgian house in five acres of quiet grounds with helpful owners, big drawing room with small bar, and plenty of places nearby to eat at in the evening; heated outdoor swimming pool and outdoor whirlpool bath; cl 25–26 Dec; children over 12

ST IVES SW5239 **Blue Hayes** Trelyon Avenue, St Ives, Cornwall TR26 2AD (01736) 797129 **£84**, plus special breaks; 9 rms, most with own bthrm. Long-standing and friendly guest house in wonderful clifftop position overlooking the sea, quiet flower-filled garden leading to beach, comfortable rooms, and enjoyable breakfasts (lots of nearby restaurants for evening meals); cl Nov–end Feb; children over 5

ST IVES SW5437 **Countryman** Old Coach Rd, Trink, St Ives, Cornwall TR26 3JQ (01736) 797571 **£60***, plus special winter breaks; 6 rms. Small friendly no smoking hotel in two acres of gardens with log fire in comfortable lounge, bright flower-filled conservatory, and cosy little restaurant; walks, golf and Tate Gallery nearby; children over 9

ST IVES SW5040 **Garrack** Burthallan Lane, St Ives, Cornwall TR26 3AA (01736) 796199 **£116***, plus winter breaks; 18 rms, some in more modern wing. Friendly hotel in two acres of gardens with wonderful sea views, cosy lounges with antiques, books and open fires, a family room, good food inc fresh shellfish, helpful staff, and indoor leisure centre; disabled access

ST IVES SW5140 **Kandahar** 11 The Warren, St Ives, Cornwall TR26 2EA (01736) 796183 **£54**; 5 rms with sea views. No smoking B&B in splendid water's-edge position overlooking the harbour and up the coast to Newquay, with comfortable old-fashioned lounge and good breakfasts in small dining room overlooking the sea; cl Nov–March; children over 6; no pets

ST KEYNE SX2460 **Old Rectory** St Keyne, Liskeard, Cornwall PL14 4RL (01579) 342617 **£75**, plus special breaks; 6 comfortable rms. Friendly little hotel in four-acre grounds, with open fire in comfortably furnished lounge, cosy bar, good homely atmosphere, and enjoyable food; cl Christmas/New Year; no children; pets by prior arrangement; disabled access

ST MARTIN SX2755 **Bucklawren Farm** St Martin, Looe, Cornwall PL13 1NZ (01503) 240738 **£46***, plus special breaks; 6 rms. Spacious farmhouse on 500-acre beef and arable working farm with coastal and sea views, croquet and putting in the big garden, large homely lounge, south-facing sun lounge, and enjoyable food in restaurant; cl Nov–end Feb; children over 5; disabled access

ST MAWES SW8433 **Rising Sun** The Square, St Mawes, Truro, Cornwall TR2 5DJ (01326) 270233 **£100**; 8 rms. Small attractive hotel in popular picturesque waterside village, with harbour views, large comfortable newly refurbished lounge bar area, airy conservatory, charming terrace; partial disabled access

ST MAWES SW8432 **Tresanton** Lower Castle Rd, St Mawes, Truro, Cornwall TR2 5DR (01326) 270055 **£220**; 26 rms all with individual furnishings and sea views. Hidden away behind a discreet entrance, with elegant terraces (heating for cool weather), little bottom bar, steps up to the main building and its stylish lounge with deeply comfortable sofas and armchairs, big bowls of flowers, log fire, daily papers and sophisticated but relaxed atmosphere; excellent food, a fine (if rather pricey) wine list, and friendly informal service; several boats for hire inc the beautiful 48-foot yacht, Pinuccia; plenty of cliff walks (and smart wellington boots of all sizes to borrow)

TREGONY SW9244 **Tregony House** Tregony, Truro, Cornwall TR2 5RN (01872) 530671 **£46***, plus winter breaks; 5 individually furnished rms, some with own bthrm. Partly 17th-c no smoking house with very friendly and helpful owners, big breakfasts and good evening meals in low-beamed dining room, cosy sitting room with open fire, and pretty cottagey garden; cl Nov–Feb; children over 12

TRENALE SX0787 **Trebrea Lodge** *Trenale, Tintagel, Cornwall PL34 0HR* (01840) 770410 **£86***, plus special breaks; 7 pretty rms with views across fields to the sea. Handsome manor house in wooded hillside grounds, with log fire and honesty bar in comfortable smoking room, elegant first-floor drawing room, and good set dinner in oak-panelled dining room; lots of walks; cl Jan; children over 12; dogs welcome by prior arrangement

TREVAUNANCE COVE SW7251 **Driftwood Spars** *Trevaunance Cove, St Agnes, Cornwall TR5 0RT* (01872) 552428 **£66**; 17 attractive, comfortable bdrms, some with sea view, 8 in separate building. Friendly family-owned hotel just up the road from the beach and dramatic cove, with woodburning stove in comfortable lounge, main bar with large open fire, upstairs gallery, helpful staff, and enjoyable food; live music wknds

To see and do

Cornwall Family Attraction of the Year

DOBWALLS SX2165 **Dobwalls Family Adventure Park** (off A38) A reliable bet for 6- to 11-year-olds who like running around, this nicely undemanding place stands out for its unusual pricing policy that, provided you make the most of it, can be very good value indeed. Designed to appeal to families staying in the area for a few days, tickets are valid for a week after you buy them, so you can keep popping back for a couple of hours each day rather than feel obliged to do everything at once. It started life as a miniature railway, and the two miles of scaled-down American-style railroad are still very much the hub of activity; ten different steam and diesel trains chuff up and down the track, and there's an accompanying video. Active visitors may prefer to head straight for Adventureland, an extensive adventure play area full of ropes, aerial walkways and so on; in a pleasant woodland setting, it's got sections for children at both ends of the age range. The skydome, a complex climbing frame of latticed ropework, is particularly unusual. There's another good play area under cover. Three costumed bears provide unsophisticated entertainment for younger visitors, and, for an extra £2, there's a children's driving school, where over-5s can drive a tiny London bus and take a driving test (don't worry, most children have no trouble getting their licence). Next door is a gallery specialising in art with birds and animals, and there are occasional sheepdog trials – more frequent ones in a neighbouring field. Children who don't like miniature trains and big play areas won't get much out of a visit here; those who do will happily come back for more. Meals, snacks, shop, some disabled access; open Easter–Oct, but may be closed occasional dates Sept–Oct; (01579) 320325; a week-long ticket for two people (ie an adult and one child) is £11.25, three people £16.75, and four people £22. Under-2s are free. After 2.30pm on Fri, Sat and Sun, you can get tickets valid for just that afternoon for £2.50.

ALTARNUN SX2281
Altarnun church The church has an enchanting set of 16th-c carved bench ends, much humanity and humour. The unpretentious Rising Sun just N does decent simple food. Nearby **Wesley's Cottage**, just off A30 at Trewint, the world's smallest Methodist place of worship, has a primitive time-warp room used by Wesley in 1744.

BEDRUTHAN STEPS SW8469
(off B3276 Newquay–Padstow) Really special, with their dramatic rocky pinnacles, cliffs and lovely sandy coves. A splendid place for walks.
BODMIN SX0766
Bodmin & Wenford Railway (General Station, St Nicholas St) Restored steam locomotives take you back to the glory days of the Great Western Railway

when hordes of holiday-makers travelled this route to the sun. As well as enjoying the view, you can stop off for pleasant woodland walks. Regular trains connect with Bodmin Parkway station. Snacks, shop, disabled access; cl Jan–late Mar, and Nov, with a limited service in May, Oct and Dec – best to phone for train times; (01208) 73666; from £5.

Bodmin Gaol (Berrycombe Rd) The former county prison, built in 1778, with spooky underground dungeons; the Crown Jewels were stored here in World War I. Meals and snacks (pub on site), shop; (01208) 76292; £3. There's a sacred well in the churchyard of St Petroc's church. The Borough Arms (A389 NW) is good value for lunch.

Pencarrow (Washaway, 3m N of Bodmin off A389) Notable 18th-c house with fine paintings and furniture, rococo ceiling in the music room, and, perhaps the highlight, 50 acres of lovely formal and woodland gardens with over 600 different rhododendrons and an acclaimed conifer collection. Also marked trails, children's play area, peacocks, chickens and other birds, craft centre and ancient British encampment. Snacks, shop, limited disabled access; house open all day (exc Fri, Sat) early Mar–mid-Oct; gardens open daily; (01208) 841369; £5, garden only £2.50.

BODMIN MOOR SX1875
This windswept expanse is not as richly endowed as Dartmoor for walking, and much is boggy and rough. It does have its own bleak character, with strange tors, prehistoric traces, wind-bent trees, granite walls, lonely lakes, and, despite official denials, continuing tales of black panthers. The main A30 actually gives more striking views of the moor than the small side roads, which tend to burrow along wooded coombes or between rather high dykes or walls. Riding is popular on the moor, and quite a few stables on or around it cater for all levels of riding ability.

The Cheesewring A striking megalithic tomb, the massive stones now left high and dry by a fall in the soil level over thousands of years, its several improbably overhanging granite slabs making an appealing camera subject with Bodmin Moor stretching

into the distance. There is a clear track to the nearby Hurlers stone circles.

BOLVENTOR SX1673
Colliford Lake Park Complex 🖾 (off A30 just S of Bolventor) Barn owls and red squirrels are among the animals being reintroduced at this family-oriented place; also rare breeds of birds, cattle, poultry, and sheep, indoor and outdoor pets, adventure play areas, under-cover assault course, museum, and lakeside walks. Meals, snacks, shop, some disabled access; cl Oct–Easter (exc wknds); (01208) 821469; *£4.95. About a mile away, Dozmary Pool is one of two Cornish lakes that claim to be where a legendary arm rose from the depths and reclaimed Excalibur (the other is Loe Pool near Porthleven), and it's an easy starting point for Bodmin Moor.

Potters Museum of Curiosity 🖾 Set in the little complex that's sprung up around Jamaica Inn, the pub immortalised by Daphne du Maurier, this is a bizarre Victorian collection of stuffed animals and other assorted oddities. Rather than simply displaying them in cases, Mr Potter constructed elaborate tableaux around the bodies brought to him by local farmers, with the animals positioned as if they were tiny humans. Guinea-pigs play cricket, rabbits sit in a classroom, and squirrels carouse in a pub in this weird little world – while the Kittens' Wedding has to be seen to be believed. Meals, snacks, shop, disabled access; cl Jan–Feb half-term; (01566) 86838; *£2.50. The pub itself is still atmospheric despite the developments. The A30, incidentally, has better views of the moor than any of the byroads.

BOSCASTLE SX0991
Pretty harbour with 16th-c pier squeezed into a rocky creek, cottages converted from warehouses, gift shops, a witchcraft museum; the Cobweb and (a stiff climb) Napoleon are useful for lunch. The cliffs nearby afford some fascinating views. Not far from here at Trevalga, Tredole Farm will arrange coastal or country **horse and pony trekking** (inc a ride to a pub); non-riders welcome; (01840) 250495; from £12.50. Nearby **St Juliot church** was restored by Thomas Hardy in his career

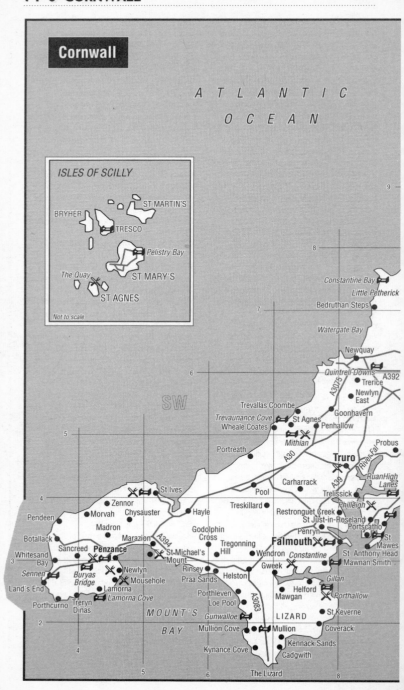

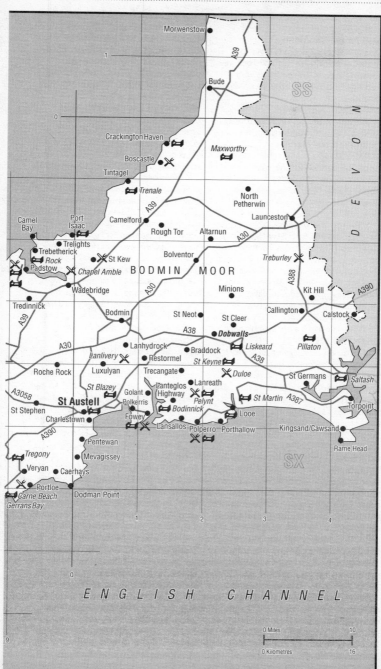

Morwenstow

Bude

SS

D E V O N

Crackington Haven

Boscastle

Tintagel

Trenale

Maxworthy

North
Petherwin

Launceston

Camel
Bay

Port
Isaac

Camelford

Rough Tor

Altarnun

Trelights

Trebetherick

St Kew

Rock

Padstow

Chapel Amble

Bolventor

B O D M I N   M O O R

Treburley

Kit Hill

Wadebridge

Minions

Tredinnick

Bodmin

St Neot

St Cleer

Callington

Calstock

Roche Rock

A30

Lanhydrock

Lanlivery

Restormel

Dobwalls

Braddock

St Keyne

Liskeard

Pillaton

Luxulyan

Trecangate

Duloe

St Blazey

Lanteglos
Highway

Lanreath

St Germans

Saltash

St Austell

St Stephen

Golant

Polkerris

Bodinnick

Pelynt

St Martin A387

Torpoint

Charlestown

Fowey

Lansallos

Looe

Polperro

Porthallow

Kingsand/Cawsand

Pentewan

Rame Head

Tregony

Mevagissey

SX

Veryan

Caerhays

Portloe

Carne Beach

Dodman Point

Gerrans Bay

E N G L I S H   C H A N N E L

0 Miles   10

0 Kilometres   16

as an architect; he described the area later in *A Pair of Blue Eyes*.

BOTALLACK SW3632
On a wild day this rugged corner of West Cornwall, with its ruined engine house right down by the sea, is very dramatic, and there are fine steep walks all around.

BRADDOCK SX1662
Braddock church Hardly striking as a building, but well worth visiting for its handsome wood carvings.

BUDE SS2106
A popular area for surfing, with great beaches beyond the dunes; Sandy Mouth slightly N has clean water for bathing, and there's a nature trail close to surfers' favourite Duckpool. Otherwise it's an unremarkable resort, though the **Bude and Stratton Museum** (The Wharf) is a decent rainy-day retreat (shop, disabled access; open daily Easter–Sept, and Thurs and Sun Oct; 50p). The Falcon Hotel does good value quick food. The carved bench ends up at **Poughill church** (pronounced poffle) are entertaining; the Preston Gate is a decent pub here.

CADGWITH SW7214
This picturesque village on its pretty cove has photogenic fish stores, thatched cottages, and a decent pub. A rewarding short stroll on the coast path leads S to Chynhalls Point past the aptly named Devil's Frying Pan, where the waves foam into a spectacular collapsed cavern.

CAERHAYS SW9741
Caerhays Castle Gardens Relatively undiscovered, these magnificent spring gardens are beautifully set around the back of a striking castle, with lovely coastal views. Renowned especially for their rhododendrons, magnolias and camellias, they're easily combined with a visit to the better-known Lost Gardens of Heligan. Tearoom, shop, some disabled access; open wkdys from mid-Mar to late May; (01872) 501310; £3.50. Depending on where you're coming from, the Crown over at St Ewe and Kings Arms at Tregony up on the main road are handy for lunch.

CALLINGTON SX3769
Dupath Holy Well (off A388 S) The best-preserved of Cornwall's many holy wells, its unappetising water said to

cure whooping cough. The town is not in itself remarkable.

CALSTOCK SX4268
Cotehele (1m W by footpath, 6m by road) Tucked away in a network of twisting roads high above the Tamar, this rambling granite house has hardly changed since being built in the late 15th c; there's no electricity, so the dark rooms – with fine furniture, armour and tapestries – have an authentically medieval atmosphere. Outside are lovely terraced gardens, a medieval dovecote, restored watermill, and miles of peaceful woodland walks. Down at Cotehele Quay a National Maritime Museum outpost shows the quay's history, and the last of the Tamar ketch-rigged barges has been restored here. One of the most rewarding places to visit in Cornwall, but now so over-visited that to protect it the National Trust have had to limit entrance to 600 people a day. Best to come midweek out of high season, or at least early in the morning; at other times you'll have to wait, and may not get in at all. Meals, snacks (tearoom in pleasant riverside setting with good cream teas), shop, some disabled access; house cl Fri and Nov–Mar, mill as house (but cl am and open Fri July–Aug), garden open daily all year; (01579) 351346; *£6, *£3.20 garden and mill only; NT. Pleasant walks along the Tamar from the village. The Carpenters Arms at Lower Metherell and unusual Who'd Have Thought It at St Dominick are good for lunch.

CAMEL BAY SW9280
On the E side, sand dunes suddenly give way to a rocky headland, Rumps Point, which can be walked round in an hour or so; or at low tide there's a pleasant sandy walk between Rock and Polzeath (which has one of Cornwall's best beaches, popular with surfers).

CAMELFORD SX1083
Locals will tell you this is the site of Camelot, and send you a mile N to the otherwise unremarkable Slaughter Bridge, where Arthur supposedly fell at his last battle. The Masons Arms has good value food.
British Cycling Museum 🅰 (The Old Station – B3266 N) Comprehensive (and still growing) collection of over 400 bicycles, tricycles

and even a five-wheeled Hen and Chickens bike, ranging from an original 1819 hobby-horse through boneshakers and penny-farthings to the hi-tech bikes of today. The couple who run it met through cycling, and really know their stuff. Outside is a sculpture made up of old bicycles. Shop, disabled access; usually cl Fri and Sat, and 25 Dec; (01840) 212811; £2.50.

North Cornwall Museum & Gallery 🖼 (The Clease) Good exploration of regional life over the past century, with displays of cider-making and farming, and collections of pottery and even early vacuum cleaners. Shop; cl Sun and Oct–Mar; (01840) 212954; *£1.50.

CARHARRACK SW7341

Carharrack church Has an exhibition on Cornish Methodism and John Wesley, who preached at the chapel that used to stand here. Disabled access; open by appointment; (01209) 820381; free. Wesley preached more regularly at nearby **Gwennap Pit**, which still has services (2.30 Suns in July and Aug), and a visitor centre. Shop, snacks, disabled access; centre usually cl Sat pm and all Oct–Apr, though best to check; (01209) 821390. The peaceful grass amphitheatre itself is open all the time; free. The Fox & Hounds at Lanner is useful for lunch.

CHARLESTOWN SX0351

A picturesque working china clay port, with sailing ships as well as modern cargo boats; it's much used as a film/TV setting, featuring in *Poldark* and ITV's *Moll Flanders*. Two square-rigged sailing ships, stars of many films inc *1492: Conquest of Paradise* maybe in the harbour. The **Shipwreck & Heritage Centre** (Quay Rd) has an exhibition about the *Titanic* and is good for local history (cl Nov–Feb; (01726) 69897; *£4.45). The waterside Harbour Inn is useful for lunch.

CHYSAUSTER SW4735

Chysauster Ancient Village (off B3311 N of Gulval) On a windy hillside overlooking the coast, these stunted remains of nine courtyard houses give some impression of village life 2,000 years ago. The site is also notable for its large untreated meadow, popular with wild birds, and, depending on the

season, bright with bluebells, heather or unusual orchids. Snacks, shop; cl Nov–Mar; (07831) 757934; £1.60; EH.

COVERACK SW7818

An attractive coastal village, with a decent pub. A rewarding walk takes you down to Black Head and maybe beyond, or to Lowland Point, for dramatic views of The Manacles – striking offshore rocks.

CRACKINGTON HAVEN SX1496

With a superbly sited dining pub, the Coombe Barton, to set you up (or reward you afterwards), this has a good walk to High Cliff, Cornwall's highest.

DOBWALLS SX2165

Dobwalls Family Adventure Park *See separate family panel on p. 72.*

DODMAN POINT SX0039

Reached from Gorran Haven, or one of the closer car parks – for instance, at Hemmick Beach – this allows a round walk mainly along clifftops.

FALMOUTH SW8132

The county's biggest town has a huge natural harbour full of sailing boats of every description, big sea-going ships, little passenger ferries (to St Mawes and Truro – great fun) and boat trips (2-hour trip £5.50; (01326) 374241); it's also a busy but pleasant shopping centre with some nice old-fashioned streets, ships' chandlers and a good bustling atmosphere, though surprisingly few sea views. Broad avenues of spiky-leaved dracaena trees away from the centre give it quite a foreign feel. The Quayside and Chain Locker by the inner harbour do useful food, and the Warehouse is an enjoyable waterside restaurant. The A39 here from Truro can be tiresomely slow.

Pendennis Castle (1m SE of Falmouth) Superb views from this well preserved fort, one of Henry VIII's chain of coastal defences. Snacks, shop, some disabled access; cl 25–26 Dec, 1 Jan; £3.80; EH.

FOWEY SX1251

(pronounced 'Foy') Steep, lively and bustling, in an exceptional riverside position, with pretty views from up the hill on either side, some interesting shops in its maze of quaint alleys and tiny lanes, and a choice of good value food pubs – King of Prussia, Ship and Galleon. The harbour has yachts to ocean-going ships, also car ferry to Bodinnick, and foot ferry to Polruan, the similarly steep little harbourside hamlet opposite – less interesting, but with lovely views of Fowey (both have decent pubs). **St Catherine's Castle** is a ruined stronghold built by Henry VIII, restored mid-19th c; free. The NT owns most of the coastline in these parts, so count on clean beaches; just around from the harbour, the secluded cove at Lantic Bay (reached by a steep coastal path) is particularly nice. A popular circular route takes walkers across on the Bodinnick car ferry, then takes the path through the steep creekside woods round to Polruan, and comes back on the other foot ferry.

GODOLPHIN CROSS SW6031
Godolphin House As we went to press, building work was just about to start at this 15th-c house of the Earls of Godolphin, well known for its colonnaded front; you'll be able to watch the ongoing restoration, and the gardens, dating back to Tudor times, will be open as usual. Snacks; should be open pm Tues, Thurs, Sun and bank hols May–Sept, but best to check first; (01736) 762409; £4. The Queens Arms down at Breage does decent food.

GOLANT SX1254
This waterside village has its attractions – particularly the church, unusual for its complete 15th-c fittings.

GOONHAVERN SW7853
World in Miniature The world's landmarks at a fraction of the normal cost – and size; and some much larger dinosaurs. Beautiful gardens with thousands of plants, and children's fairground rides. Meals, snacks, shop, disabled access; cl Nov–Mar; (01872) 572828; £5.

GWEEK SW7027
National Seal Sanctuary 🖾 The biggest seal sanctuary in Europe, the National Seal Sanctuary provides a home for dozens of injured or orphaned seals that they hope to be able to release back into the wild, all with their own names and character traits. Underwater observatories, feeding-time fun, woodland walks, play area, as well as donkeys, ponies and goats, an audio-visual display and a nature trail. Snacks, shop, disabled

access; cl 25 Dec; (01326) 221361; £5.99. The Gweek Inn, with home-made food, is handy, and the Trengilly Wartha at Nancenoy is excellent for lunch, with a nice walk down to Scotts Quay on the creek.

HAYLE SW5536
Paradise Park Headquarters of the World Parrot Trust, with some of the beautiful residents showcased to spectacular effect in the huge Parrot Jungle, a splendid mix of waterfalls, swamps and streams. You can try feeding lorikeets in the Australian aviary (nectar for sale in the shop), and there are lots of other exotic birds and numerous animals too, some of which you can feed at the Fun Farm. Daily free-flying bird show (usually at 12.30), summer bird of prey displays (not Sat exc July–Aug), entertaining penguin and otter feeding shows, children's quiz trails, big play area, and a narrow-gauge railway gently rattling through the park. Adults may prefer the Victorian walled garden (lovely clematis arches in May) or the pub that brews its own real ale. Recently, the park initiated a scheme to reintroduce the rare Cornish chough to its native countryside, after an absence of 26 years. Meals, snacks, shop (and plant sales), mostly disabled access; (01736) 757407; £5.95 (£3.95 children over 4), usually with return.

HELFORD SW7526
There's an undemanding coast path E to **Dennis Head** and beyond. This NE part of the Lizard is appreciably leafier, with some intricate coves.

HELSTON SW6626
Flambards Village Theme Park (off A394, S edge of village) Beautifully kept leisure park, a clear cut above the average theme park. One of the best parts is the very good reconstructed Victorian village; once just three period rooms, it now has over 50 authentically furnished and stocked houses, shops and settings, complete with cobbled streets, carriages and other period pieces. Also a state-of-the-art time travel exhibition from the Big Bang to the present day, a life-size 'Britain in the Blitz' street, a collection of aircraft, adventure playground and play areas, award-winning gardens, displays on topics from wedding fashions to antique

prams, and rides, inc a few new ones, to suit all ages. A place which lets adults get at least as much out of it as children, and you could quite easily spend a day here. Meals, snacks, shop, disabled access; cl Nov–Easter, and Mon and Fri at the start and end of season; (01326) 564093; £7.95 (less off-season or from mid-afternoon).

Goonhilly Earth Station Very un-Cornish, this space-age complex is one of the planet's foremost telecom centres, and the vast dishes rising out of the heath are an awesome sight. In the control room you can see information and images sent out and received from all over the world, while the visitor centre lets you operate one of the tracking dishes yourself. Also bus tour round the site (which is a nature reserve), audio-visual show, and free internet surfing. A well presented, interesting and genuinely exciting place, though probably not ideal for younger children. Meals, snacks, shop, disabled access; cl Nov–Mar; (0800) 679593; £4. The B3293 past here and the byroad to Kuggar are unusual for Cornish roads, in giving some quite distant views. The White Hart at St Keverne is the best place around for lunch.

Helston Folk Museum World-famous for its annual Furry Dance in early May, it has a popular Saturday market and a little folk museum in the Old Butter Market; shop, disabled access; cl Sun; £2. The simple Blue Anchor pub has a 15th-c working brewhouse which you can usually look around at lunchtime; the best food nearby is at the Halzephron at Gunwalloe, off the A3083 S – a good road with views, and usually signs of action from the Culdrose helicopter base.

Trevarno Estate & Gardens After 700 years of private ownership, these enchanting gardens finally opened to the public in 1998. Parts are still being restored, but there are some lovely walks around a tranquil lake with Victorian boathouse, through a yew tunnel, and in a wood carpeted with bluebells in spring. A small museum houses a collection of gardening tools, and various workshops inc wax-making in the bee centre. The attractive conservatory has a fountain, and serves good value snacks and cream teas. Shop, some disabled access; cl 25 Dec; (01326) 574274; £3.50.

KENNACK SANDS SW7316 (just E of Kuggar) One of the cleanest beaches in Britain, with beautifully clear water; it can get crowded.

KINGSAND/CAWSAND SX4350 Appealing seaside village with higgledy-piggledy charm, near great cliff walks; the Halfway House and Rising Sun both have good local fish.

KIT HILL SX3771 (off the A390 N of Callington) With a huge chimney stack and mine shafts, this gives breezy walks, and impressive views across to Dartmoor.

KYNANCE COVE SW6813 A particularly fine beach below the spectacular cliffs – a long walk down from the car park, but well worth it for the strange rock formations, caves and sandy coves. There are lovely views from the cliff walk S.

LAMORNA SW4424 The cove is pretty, with good walks along the coast path. There's a good view of the Merry Maidens stone circle from the B3315. The Lamorna Wink is useful for lunch.

Lamorna Pottery As well as the pottery there's a garden with acclaimed cream teas. Meals, snacks, shop, disabled access; cl 25–26 Dec; (01736) 810330; free.

LAND'S END SW3425 The most westerly point of England, with wild and blustery walks along dramatic clifftops, and on a clear day views out as far even as the Isles of Scilly. You may not be able to stand and contemplate it on your own – the 200-acre site has been extensively developed for families over the years, and it's become almost like a theme park, with 'multi-sensory experiences', gift shops, craft centres, farm animals and burger bars. It's not as bad as it sounds – the exhibitions and hi-tech displays are a useful enough introduction to the folklore of the area, and there's plenty to amuse children. An RSPB observation hide has information on the coastline's wildlife. Meals, snacks, neat shopping arcade, good disabled access; cl 24–25 Dec; (01736) 871501; £8 for all attractions, less off-season. A public right of way goes through here to Land's End itself, so you're not obliged to buy a ticket if you just want to walk to the end of England. The same goes for the fine cliff walks in both directions – the one to Sennen is lovely, and the cove there is worth looking around. Some of the wildest and most formidable cliffs in Britain are between here and Treen.

LANHYDROCK SX0863

Lanhydrock House A staggering 50 rooms to visit in this splendid old house, well liked by readers; the highlight is the Long Gallery, with its magnificently illustrated Old Testament scenes – it's one of the few original 16th-c parts left, as a disastrous fire in the 19th c resulted in major changes and refurbishments. Do leave time to explore the pretty formal **gardens** (glorious around May) and grounds with Victorian coach house stables; it's a lovely walk down to the river and back through the woods. Good meals and snacks, shop and plant sales, disabled access; house cl Mon (exc bank hols) and Nov–Mar; (01208) 73320; £6.60, £3.60 grounds only; NT. The Crown down at Lanlivery is most enjoyable for lunch, in a Jane Austen village setting.

LANREATH SX1856

Pretty village with some remarkable woodwork in its exceptional medieval church. The Punch Bowl has a fascinating old bar.

Folk Museum Most fun for its summer demonstrations and workshops – corn dolly making (Mon), Cornish pasty crimping (Weds) and egg decorating (Fri); all activities 2–4pm. Snacks, shop, disabled access; cl Nov–Easter; (01503) 220321; £2.50.

LANSALL SX1751

Lansallos church The attraction here is inside the church – the ancient carved bench ends, each individual but all sharing a style.

LANTEGLOS HIGHWAY SX1453

Lanteglos Highway church A curiosity, Perpendicular but not – subsidence has left the arches at drunken angles.

LAUNCESTON SX3285

The most attractive inland town in Cornwall, with winding old hillside streets and an untouristy feel; it was once Cornwall's capital. The White Hart does popular food.

Launceston Castle Set on a Norman motte, the ruined 12th- and 13th-c hilltop castle is substantial and commanding – it was captured four times during the Civil War. Snacks, shop, some disabled access; cl Nov–Mar exc Fri–Sun, 24–26 Dec and 1 Jan; (01566) 773277; £1.80; EH.

Launceston Steam Railway 19th-c locomotives running on a 2-ft gauge line along the trackbed of the old North Cornwall Railway, through 2½ miles of scenic valley – open carriages on sunny days; also transport museum. A network of footpaths leads off from Newmills Station. Snacks, bookshop, disabled access; open Easter, then Sun and Tues until spring bank hol, after which daily (exc Sat) to end of Sept, Sun and Tues only in Oct, and some trains Dec wknds; (01566) 775665 for times; £5.20.

Lawrence House (Castle St) Set in a Georgian house with useful displays on the town's past; cl wknds and mid-Oct–Mar; free.

Trethorne Leisure Farm 🔁 (Kennards House, off A30 3m W of Launceston) 140-acre farm good for children, who can milk Daisy the cow, play with the rabbits, take a pony ride or bottle-feed the lambs. Also roller-blading, ten pin bowling, good 18-hole golf course, and big indoor and outdoor play areas. Meals, snacks, shop, disabled access; cl Sun (exc golf); (01566) 86324; £4.50, golf £22 round.

LIZARD SW7012

This peninsula S of Helston is famous as the most southerly part of mainland Britain, and though the inland parts can be rather flat and dull and not really worth extended walks, the coastline is altogether more attractive. The National Trust have improved the area around Lizard Point, the southern tip, in recent years, and it's a good start for bracing cliff walks in either direction, with good views. Readers very much enjoy exploring the Lizard's dramatic western and eastern edges. The W side has mighty cliffs, with roads down to beautiful Mullion Cove and Kynance Cove. The E side is more sheltered and lusher, with wooded creeks. **Lizard**

village itself is pretty uninspiring (there's a very civilised pub, and they sell interesting local serpentine rock carvings), but is well placed for longer walks encompassing Church Cove to the E and Kynance Cove to the W. On top and inland the Lizard is disappointing, a big flat peninsula; although the Goonhilly satellite station is a remarkable landmark.

LOE POOL SW6424
Cornwall's largest lake, a haven for waterfowl, is blocked from the sea by an NT shingle bank called Loe Bar (only breeding place of the rare sandhill rust moth – and favourite place of worship of a German evangelical sect); a path leads round the lake. There's a coast walk from here to Gunwalloe fishing cove.

LOOE SX2553
Seaside resort packed with tourist shops, teashops and pubs, but with a nice easy-going atmosphere even in high season. The old fishing village with its picturesque harbour and narrow little back streets is now immersed in tourism, and is the main shark-fishing place (on 'shark-fishing' trips you watch others doing the catching). From the quay there are summer **boat trips**, the easiest out to nearby St George's Island. The Olde Salutation has plenty of atmosphere and good simple food; the Smugglers is a decent friendly restaurant, and the quayside Trawlers has very good unusual seafood.
Monkey Sanctuary (signed off B3253 at No Man's Land, just E of Looe) One of the most fascinating places to visit in the entire county; established in 1964, its wooded grounds are home to the world's first colony of Amazonian woolly monkeys to breed successfully outside their natural habitat. All of the animals were born here, and talks by staff give an intriguing insight into the dynamics and politics of the monkey community. Meals, snacks, shop, disabled access; cl Fri, Sat, and Oct–wk before Easter; (01503) 262532; *£4.

LUXULYAN SX0558
The village has an attractive church, and from the village you can walk along the lush wooded valley to the S, strewn with huge granite boulders and crossed by an impressive viaduct; if you feel adventurous you can climb up the valley to the top of the viaduct.

MADRON SW4431
Trengwainton Garden (B3312) The name in Cornish means 'Farm of the Spring' and it does always seem to be spring at this lovely place, the climate favouring plants not usually found outside in England. Magnolias, azaleas, rhododendrons, unusual southern hemisphere trees and shrubs inc a delightful tree-fern grotto, walled gardens, good views to Mounts Bay and the Lizard. Cream teas, shop, interesting plant sales, some disabled access; open Sun–Thurs (and Good Fri) Mar–Oct; (01736) 362297; £3.50; NT. The King William IV has enjoyable food. The road to Morvah passes a very photogenic prehistoric burial chamber at Lanyon Quoit; a bit further along by a phone box a signed path on the right takes you to a great Bronze Age stone hoop at Men-An-Tol, and the lane opposite leads to Chun Castle, an Iron Age fort with great views.

MARAZION SW5130
St Michael's Mount There's something particularly awe-inspiring about this medieval castle, rising majestically from the sea. On gloomy or stormy days the picturesque silhouette seems even more dramatic. The little island is reached by ferry (it doesn't go in bad weather), or at low tide on foot along a causeway; the walk up to the castle, still the home of the family which acquired it in 1660, is quite steep. Fine Chippendale furniture, plaster reliefs, armour and paintings, audio-visual show. Summer meals, snacks, shop; open wkdys and some wknds Apr–Oct, and Mon, Weds and Fri only Nov–Mar, phone to check; (01736) 710507; £4.40; NT (members may have to pay some wknds). The Cutty Sark has decent food.

MAWGAN SW7223
Trelowarren This manor house is worth a look for its elaborate Strawberry Hill gothick chapel (usually only open Weds pm and bank hols), and the surrounding estate (open all the time) has plenty going on in summer inc woodland walks, craft shops and pottery, campsite, Thurs evening concerts, and good meals and snacks in

the Yard Bistro; (01326) 221224; £1.50.

MAWNAN SMITH SW7728

This sheltered coastal village is pretty, and the Red Lion is good for lunch. From nearby Mawnan a fine if blowy stretch of the coast path takes you around Rosemullion Head and on N to Maenporth, where there's a sheltered sandy cove with decent modern pub/restaurant.

Glendurgan Garden Lovely sub-tropical garden in valley above Helford River, started by Alfred Fox in 1820; fine shrubs from all over the world, mature trees, walled garden and restored laurel maze. Shop, snacks; cl Sun, Mon (exc bank hols), Good Fri, all Nov–Feb; (01326) 250906; £3.50; NT.

Trebah Garden ⊞ This steeply wooded ravine garden is widely reckoned to be one of the finest in the world. At times it really feels as if you've strayed into a benign, exclusive jungle. Huge subtropical tree ferns and palms, giant gunnera, lots of blue and white hydrangeas, 100-year-old rhododendrons, some fine rare trees. Several activities for children, and at the bottom end a private beach on the Helford River – good for a picnic or secluded swim. Snacks, shop (plants for sale), disabled access; (01326) 250448; £3.50.

MEVAGISSEY SX0144

This bustling place is a picturesque fishing village much expanded into quite a commercialised resort, but fun, with hillside cottages, narrow streets, gift shops, a busy working harbour. The Ship, Fountain and Harbour Lights are all worthwhile pubs, and the harbourside Mr Bistro does mainly fresh fish.

Folk Museum This decent local museum in an 18th-c boat-builder's shed on East Quay has a comprehensive wartime exhibition; shop, disabled access to ground floor; cl Nov–Easter; *60p.

Lost Gardens of Heligan (off B2373, just NW of Mevagissey) Forgotten and neglected between 1914 and 1991, these highly acclaimed gardens have now been fully restored. Some very fine mature trees, Victorian walled gardens, lots of rhododendrons, lakes, and big collection of tree ferns, bamboos and palms. It's a friendly place, and they're more than happy to talk about their work. Meals, snacks, shop/nursery, disabled access; cl 24–25 Dec; (01726) 845100; £5.50. The Crown at St Ewe is useful for lunch.

World of Model Railways ⊞ (Meadow St) Over 50 model trains trundling through a realistic little world that takes in Cornish china-clay pits, ski resorts, fairgrounds, towns and country. Shop, some disabled access; cl Mon–Sat Nov–early Mar; (01726) 842457; £2.95.

MINIONS SX2571

Prehistoric monuments Above Minions, the highest village in Cornwall, the **Hurlers** are three Bronze-Age stone circles – the central one still has 14 stones standing. Close by is the **Rillaton Barrow** where the lovely Rillaton gold cup (now in the British Museum) was found, along with other interesting relics. There is a clear track to the nearby **Cheesewring**; not far off, the track between Sharptor and Kilmar Tor affords fine views.

MORVAH SW4035

The moors nearly reach the sea around here, and in a few miles walkers can take in the cliff path, the moors close to the ruin of Ding Dong Mine, the prehistoric stone hoop of Men an Tol and the Iron Age hillfort of Chun Castle (close by Chun Quoit, a Bronze Age burial chamber).

MORWENSTOW SS2015

The church, in an idyllic setting, has Norman arches and 16th-c bench ends, with shipwrecked sailors' headstones in the graveyard. A driftwood shack built for contemplation by a Victorian parson over the impressive cliffs is preserved by the NT. The Bush is an interesting old pub, and the rectory tearoom is delightful.

MOUSEHOLE SW4626

Attractive working fishing village with steep little roads – too many summer visitors, but lovely out of season, with spectacular Christmas lights in the little harbour; the harbourside Ship (with good value bedrooms) is fun for lunch, though the Old Coastguard has more interesting food and a lovely garden.

MULLION SW6719

This attractive village has an enjoyable

family pub (the Old Inn) and a possibly unique feature in its church – a dog flap. You can hire bicycles at Atlantic Forge (*£5 half-day, *£7 day); (01326) 240294 – open all year, but check first out of season. This is a good way to explore the Lizard.

MULLION COVE SW6617

This dramatic fusion of rock, sand and sea is most rewardingly reached by a there-and-back walk along the cliff from Porth Mellin; for the energetic, the extension S to Kynance Cove is outstanding.

NEWLYN SW4629

Cornwall's busiest working fishing port – it's great fun watching the boats come in – and home to the last working **Salt Pilchard Works** 🖼, a tour of which passes a surprisingly entertaining hour or so; shop; cl wknds and Nov–Mar; (01736) 332112; £2.95. There's an unusual art deco swimming pool, and an excellent and occasionally rather avant-garde **Art Gallery** (New Rd) in a lovely coastal setting with fine views (cl Sun, 25–26 Dec and 1 Jan; (01736) 363715; donations). At Christmas the fishermen decorate the harbour and its boats with spectacular lights. The Dolphin and Fishermans Arms are useful for lunch.

NEWLYN EAST SW8655

Lappa Valley Steam Railway and Leisure Park 🖼 15-inch gauge steam train trips through pretty countryside to an old lead mine. It's surrounded by parkland with lakes, woodland walk, a maze, and play areas; a section of the old branch line leads to a nine-hole golf course. Meals, snacks, shop, some disabled access; cl Nov–Easter, and some days in Oct – best to check train times; (01872) 510317; £5.90, covers fare and all attractions exc golf. The backstreet Pheasant has good home cooking.

NEWQUAY SW8261

Now famed as England's surfing capital, a thorough-going seaside resort with excellent safe golden beaches below fine cliffs; Crantock Beach is the best and least crowded, with great views from the Bowgie family pub up on West Pentire headland. There's no shortage of souvenir shops, an alcohol-free zone declared on the streets, theme parks on the edge, and older houses around the

harbour; there's decent food all day at the Fort Hotel (Fore St). Thanks in part to the surfers, the town has quite a cheery young feel these days. Fistral Beach is reckoned by some to be the best surfing beach in Europe; a couple of surfing schools here can get beginners started.

Dairyland 🖼 (A3508 4m SE) Much expanded since it first opened 20 years ago, this bustling dairy farm is a huge favourite with families. Its showpiece remains the daily milking sessions, when cows step aboard a bizarre merry-go-round milking machine and are milked to the strains of classical music. Also well labelled nature trails, farm park, rural bygones, brass rubbing centre and plenty of activities for children. Meals, snacks, shop, disabled access; cl Nov–late Mar (exc around Christmas); (01872) 510246; £4.95.

Holywell Bay Fun Park (off A3075 SW of town) Active children should enjoy the go-karts, bumper boats, rides, indoor play area, golf; cl Nov–Apr; (01637) 830095; separate charges for various attractions.

Newquay Zoo (Trenance Leisure Park, off A3075 Edgcumbe Ave) The emphasis is very much on conservation here, with carefully designed enclosures for monkeys, penguins, lions and tortoises, as well as gardens, and summer activities. Feeding displays are well timetabled so there's something to see throughout the day. Also children's farm, play areas, and a maze. Meals, snacks, shop, disabled access; cl 25 Dec; (01637) 873342; £5.50. **Water World**, a lively fun pool, is just up the road – joint tickets available; (01637) 853829.

Sea Life Centre (Towan Promenade) Another in the reliable chain – a see-through tunnel creates the illusion of walking along the sea bed, and bubble windows bring you face to face with fish, sea-horses and sharks. There should be more displays once it reopens in Apr following refurbishment; meals, snacks, shop, some disabled access; cl 25 Dec; (01637) 872822; £4.50.

NORTH PETHERWIN SX2889

Tamar Otter Park 🖼 Friendly place breeding otters then releasing them back into the wild; it's fun to watch the attractive Asian short-clawed otters playing. Three species of deer roam free, and there are waterfowl lakes, wallabies, and nature trails. The otters are fed at noon and 3pm. Snacks, shop, some disabled access; cl Nov–Mar; (01566) 785646; *£5.

PADSTOW SW9175

Quaint streets, old buildings clustered around the working fishing harbour, and attractive slate houses; Rick Stein's restaurants are currently drawing the crowds (you'll need to book well in advance). The Golden Lion, London Inn and Old Custom House are useful for lunch. The Camel estuary is popular for sailing: gentle dreamy scenery with lots of little boats. Plenty of good clean beaches near here; Constantine Bay is the best, and popular with surfers. The B3276 has the best roadside coastal views in this part of Cornwall.

Prideaux Place 🏠 Still a lived-in family home, this fine old house has changed little since it was built in the late 16th c. Highlights include the elegant ceilings, atmospheric library and the intricate biblical tableaux in the Great Chamber. Notable concerts and special events in the grounds. Cream teas, shop, disabled access to ground floor only; cl Fri and Sat, a week after Easter, and Oct–Easter (subject to change, best to phone); (01841) 532411; £4.50, gardens only £2.

Shipwreck Museum (South Quay) Not far from the town's little harbour, a collection of relics and tales of the plentiful shipwrecks along this coast. Snacks, shop, disabled access; open Mar–Oct; (01726) 69897; £4.45.

PENDEEN SW3733

Levant Mine (B3306, 1m W) Unusual mine beneath the sea, powered by the oldest steam engine in Cornwall, all explained by knowledgeable and enthusiastic staff. Shop, disabled access with notice; open every Fri (steaming Mar–Sept only), plus Easter and May bank hol Sun and Mon, Weds, Thurs and Sun in Jun, and daily exc Sat July–Sept; (01736) 786156; £3; NT. The nearby **Pendeen Watch lighthouse** is worth a look, and the Radjel is useful for something to eat.

PENHALLOW SW7650

Callestock Cider Farm Traditional working cider farm producing scrumpy, country wines and jam, with seasonal demonstrations, and friendly horses, rabbits, goats, pigs and donkeys. Also cider museum with ancient presses, and hives of the bees needed for pollination; guided tours. Summer snacks, shop (with samples of everything they make), disabled access; cl Sat Oct–Easter, Sun Oct–Whitsun, and 3 wks over Christmas; (01872) 573356; free, £2 for museum and tractor ride. The Miners Arms at Mithian is useful for lunch.

PENRYN SW7834

Appealing waterside village, quite sizeable, with pretty houses dropping down to the estuary.

PENTEWAN SX0149

Eden Project (Watering Lane Nursery, Pentewan) Interest in this £74m attraction was so great that the managers opened the doors nearly a year before their official opening date. The ongoing project involves the transformation of a 60-metre deep china clay pit into a dramatic 34-acre garden. Giant conservatories known as biomes, big enough to accommodate full-size mahogany trees and made up of hexagonal steel panels covered in triple-glazed foil, will eventually contain thousands of plants from all over the planet inc the humid tropics and warm temperate regions. Outside, a lake will form the centrepiece of a 12-acre garden, planted with species from temperate climates. The whole place has been developed with the environment and education in mind – even run-off rainwater from the roof will be used for humidification in the hothouses – and experts will be on hand in the classrooms and hands-on exhibition centre. Following further development over winter, the centre hopes to reopen fully in spring/early summer, so best to phone for opening times. Good snacks, plant sales, disabled access; (01726) 222900; £3.

PENZANCE SW4730

The area's main shopping centre, a pleasantly relaxed town by the sea. The prettiest part is Chapel St, where there's a decent **Maritime Museum** (cl Sun; (01736) 368890; *£2), the extravagantly designed early 19th-c Egyptian House deserves a passing look,

and the Turks Head is a good pub.
Harris's restaurant on New St has good
local fish. In summer you can take **boat
trips** around the coastline or across to
the Isles of Scilly, and there are regular
helicopter flights to the islands.
National Lighthouse Centre 🏛
(Old Buoy Store, Wharf Rd) Easy to
spot thanks to the big buoys outside,
this has an excellent collection of
lighthouse equipment, and a good
audio-visual display on what it was like
to live in one; a typical room is
reconstructed, with original curved
furniture. Many of the staff are ex-
lighthouse personnel so a good source
of information and anecdote – and
there is a lighthouse opposite. Shop,
disabled access; cl Sat and all Nov–Apr;
(01736) 360077; £2.50.
Penlee House Gallery & Museum
🏛 (Morrab Rd) Formerly the Penzance
& District Museum, this was extended
last year and has paintings that are
certainly worth a look – mainly by the
Newlyn School. Meals, snacks, shop,
disabled access; cl Sun; *£2 (free Sat).
POLKERRIS SX0952
Little seaside hamlet – scarcely more
than the waterside inn – with terrific
view, almost even better in winter,
across St Austell bay from well restored
ancient quay.
POLPERRO SX2150
Almost unbelievably pretty, tiny streets
around a very quaint sheltered fishing
harbour, little cottages perched on
rocks – once a busy smuggling place,
now some enjoyable craft shops tucked
away, one or two tourist attractions,
oddities like the shell-encrusted Shell
House, and unspoilt harbourside
fishermen's locals (the Blue Peter and
Three Pilchards); the Crumplehorn Mill
does decent food, and the Old Mill
House is good. The beaches around
here are some of England's cleanest. It
gets very busy in summer, with little
electric buses (or horse and cart)
shuttling in from the out-of-village car
park. A sensible alternative to sweating
out summer traffic jams in the village
itself is to park instead in Talland Bay,
for an easy one-mile walk along the
coast to enter this harbour feeling
you've earned it.
Land of Legend & Model Village

(The Old Forge, Mill Hill) A useful
enough distraction for children, with
two model railways (another is planned
for next year), and a scaled-down
version of Polperro. Shop, some
disabled access; cl Sat and all
Nov–Easter; (01503) 272378; *£2.50.
POOL SW6741
Cornish Engines (A3047)
Developing site based around two big
beam engines, originally used for
pumping water from tin and copper
mines. Shop, visitor centre (open all
year), some disabled access; open
Apr–Oct, phone for winter opening;
(01209) 315027; £3.50; NT. The
Cornish Choughs (at Treswithian, just
off the far end of the Camborne bypass)
has interesting food inc good fresh fish.
PORT ISAAC SX0080
Delightful steep fishing village, a
favourite with many: tiny streets, and
houses hanging high over the pretty
harbour – the Golden Lion's terrace
overlooks it. Park at the top and walk
down (at low tide you can park on the
beach). There are some particularly fine
stretches of cliffs for walking around
here, and just up the coast Port
Gaverne is a beautiful NT cove.
PORTHALLOW SX2251
This is snugly set above a little fishing
harbour, with a beautifully set pub, the
Five Pilchards; the beach is notoriously
polluted, and swimming in the sea is not
recommended. A friendly little
vineyard here has self-guided tours,
free samples of their wines and cider,
and a particularly tasty birch country
wine; cl 1–2pm, all day Sun, and
Nov–Easter; (01326) 280050; 50p.
PORTHCURNO SW3822
Porthcurno's lovely silver sands –
among Cornwall's best beaches – are
the property of the National Trust, in
common with so much of the coastline
round here. If you walk their length, be
careful not to get cut off by high tide.
The Logan Rock at Treen is good for
lunch and ideal for cliff walkers.
Minack Theatre & Exhibition Centre
There are few better backdrops for
plays than the one at this famous little
open-air theatre – dramatic cliffs and
blue sea stretching into the distance
make this a magical setting. Varied
summer season, and an exhibition on

the life of Rowena Cade, the remarkable woman who built the theatre, cut into these steep cliffs, with her own hands. Tickets go on sale in May, but aren't for particular seats – if you've booked you'll still need to get there early to bag the best. Evening shows are more atmospheric. Shows are cancelled only in extreme conditions, so take a waterproof. Snacks, shop, disabled access to café and exhibition; performances May–Sept, exhibition cl during matinees, and 25–26 Dec; (01736) 810181; shows £6.50, exhibition £2.50.

Museum of Submarine Telegraphy 🖼 Don't let the name put you off – this museum housed in the secret wartime communications centre in underground tunnels is a good deal more interesting than you'd think. Meals, snacks, shop, disabled access, cl Sat (exc July–Aug) and Nov–Mar (exc Mon); (01209) 612142; £3.50.

PORTHLEVEN SW6225
Pretty working fishing village; the Ship built into the cliffs is a good pub, and the long stretch of rocky beach S is a good walk if the surf's not beating in too fiercely.

PORTLOE SW9339
Tiny unspoilt village wedged into a precipitous cove, with splendid cliff walks in rugged scenery, and stiffish climbs on to Nare Head; good teashop/small restaurant.

PORTREATH SW6545
A good base for long bracing clifftop walks, with a decent pub; along this whole section of coast, between St Ives Bay and Trevose Head (nr Padstow), the coast path is rich in rugged views, and very rewarding to those with sturdy legs.

PORTSCATHO SW8735
Very sheltered fishing village with a picturesque little harbour, and some fine nearby beaches – excellent for families. Virtually the whole of Gerrans Bay around here is good easy walking, with some lovely clifftop stretches; there's a good sandy stretch at Pendower Beach.

PRAA SANDS SW5828
A popular summer family beach.

PROBUS SW9247
Trewithen (off A390 between Probus and Grampound, where the Dolphin has good value food) Justly famous landscaped gardens, with many rare trees and shrubs. The early 18th-c house is a little unfairly overshadowed by what's outside, and is an interesting obviously lived-in family home. Snacks, rare plants for sale, disabled access; gardens open Mar–Sept (cl Sun exc Apr and May), walled garden open Mon and Tues in Jun, house open only Mon and Tues pms Apr–July (plus Aug bank hol); (01726) 883647; gardens £3.50, house another £3.50, joint ticket £6.

RAME HEAD SX4248
Jutting far out at the E end of Whitsand Bay, this is capped by a primitive hermitage chapel – a worthwhile walk from the pretty village of Kingsand.

RESTORMEL SX1060
Restormel Castle Very well preserved Norman castle with notable round keep and fine views over Fowey Valley. Lots of flowers in spring. Snacks, shop, mostly disabled access; cl Nov–Mar; (01208) 872687; *£1.60; EH. The Royal Oak in Lostwithiel is good for lunch.

RESTRONGUET CREEK SW8137
Though the waterside village is mainly of no great age, its pub the Pandora has a lovely location – you can park in Mylor Bridge for a leisurely two-mile waterside walk there and back, or drive all the way.

RINSEY SW5927
The coast path passes two magnificently sited ruined tin and copper mine buildings, Wheal Prosper and Wheal Trewavas, both now maintained by the NT.

ROCHE ROCK SW9959
This small but picturesque crag is worth the short walk from the B3274, with a 14th-c ruined ivy-covered chapel built into it, and a ladder up (decent pub nearby, past the station).

ROUGH TOR SX1284
(pronounced 'Roe Tor') The summit, reached from a signed car park off the A39 nr Camelford, gives views of Brown Willy, the highest point in Cornwall.

SANCREED SW4129
Carn Euny Ancient Village Dating from the 1st c, substantial traces of a little village of stone courtyard houses, and a 20-metre underground passage

leading to a circular chamber (some very minor roads to get here).

ST AGNES SW7150

A former mining town, now with a holiday role; some attractive steeply terraced cottages, fine cliff scenery nearby, and great views from the St Agnes Beacon hilltop, just W of town. The Railway Inn has some interesting collections.

Presingoll Barns (Penwinnick Rd) Craft centre with demonstrations of glass painting, candle and fudge-making, good picnic areas. Snacks, shop, limited disabled access; cl 25–26 Dec; (01872) 553007; free (a small charge for candle-dipping).

ST ANTHONY HEAD SW8431

On the E side of the Fal estuary, by the **Zone Head lighthouse**, this has superb views, and easy walks along low, level cliffs; parking at the head itself, or near Porth Farm on the way down.

ST AUSTELL SX0352

The centre of the china-clay industry and a busy modern shopping town. **Holy Trinity church** has a fine tower and interesting font, and you can tour the **St Austell Brewery** on Trevarthian Rd (booking recommended – (01726) 66022; £5, inc samples of beer). **Pine Lodge Gardens** (Holmbush) cover 30 acres, with rhododendrons and magnolias, arboretum, Japanese garden, and several ponds and water features; snacks, plant sales, disabled access; open Weds–Sun and bank hols Apr–Sept; (01726) 73500; £3.50. The area N is a strange bleak moonscape of whitish spoil heaps with metallic blue lakes dotted among them; the B3279 St Stephen–Nanpean gives some of the best views over this.

Wheal Martyn Museum 🏛 (B3274 N of St Austell – you don't have to go into the town) Interestingly restored 19th-c clayworks showing the 250-year history of china-clay production. Working waterwheels and other equipment, steam locomotives, nature trails with a spectacular viewpoint over a huge clay pit, and children's adventure trail. Meals, snacks, shop; cl Nov–Mar and Sat (exc bank hol wknds); (01726) 850362; £4.50 (a good value family ticket gets 2 adults and up to 4 children

in for £12.50).

ST CLEER SX2568

Trevethy Quoit This is a very photogenic megalithic tomb, its massive stones now left high and dry by a fall in the soil level over thousands of years. The Crows Nest down near Darite is handy for lunch.

ST GERMANS SX3657

St Germans church Wonderful Norman doorway and particularly fine east window; worth a look if you're passing this waterside village. There's a good view towards Port Eliot, a stately home designed by John Soane (not open).

ST IVES SW5039

A pretty place, despite the summer crowds, with its attractive working harbour and narrow streets and alleys (the cobbled Fore St is the prettiest). It has good wide beaches, and plenty of bird life along the Lelant Saltings (RSPB reserve). Besides the Pig 'n' Fish, the waterside Sloop (interesting pictures for sale) does reliable food. The best beach for surfers is Porthmeor slightly N, while in the other direction the B3306 to Land's End has great coast and moorland views. Out of season, when the caravan and camp sites are empty, the magnificent sands around St Ives Bay are well worth walking, with good cliff walks to the west.

Barbara Hepworth Museum & Sculpture Garden (Porthmeor Beach) This tranquil escape from the holiday hordes, devoted to the artist's work and life, has sculptures in the house, studio and subtropical garden, as well as photographs and letters. Shop; cl Mon (exc July–Aug, and bank hols), and 24–26 Dec; (01736) 796226; *£3.75. Other works by Hepworth are dotted about the town.

Tate Gallery St Ives (Porthmeor Beach) St Ives's famous popularity with artists is best explored at this gallery, which can take a lot of the credit for the town's recent tourism boom. Works by the familiar St Ives School names are regularly joined by new displays of 20th-c art with a Cornish connection. It's an impressive building, outside and in, fully exploiting its spectacular cliffside setting – views are best from the café. Meals, snacks, shop, disabled access; cl

Mon (exc bank hols and July–Aug), maybe first 2 wks in Nov, and 24–26 Dec, phone to check; (01736) 796226; *£3.95.

ST JUST-IN-ROSELAND SW8435

An unspoilt spot, with its church in an idyllic creekside setting; the steep graveyard is like a lost subtropical garden – well worth a visit on a quiet sunny day, or in spring with the baby rooks blethering and the smell of wild garlic. The words on the inscribed stones by the path seem quite fitting.

ST KEVERNE SW7921

Set around a little square, this is a pleasant village with a lovely little **working farm** just S at Tregellast Barton, undeveloped and tranquil, with pleasant walks through woods and meadows, afternoon milking (4.30), and a good farm shop with samples of their unusually flavoured ice-cream; phone for opening times; (01326) 280479; free. There's a good walk to Lowland Point, for dramatic views of The Manacles – striking offshore rocks.

ST KEW SX0276

Delightful quiet leafy village with old-fashioned feel, and agreeably low-key **Donkey and Pony Sanctuary**. Shop and visitor centre cl Nov–Easter; (01208) 841710; £3.95. The St Kew Inn is a nice place for a meal.

ST MAWES SW8433

Very pretty harbourside and estuary views, a long waterfront to stroll along, clean bathing waters, a foot-passenger ferry to Falmouth and other boat trips (full of yachtsmen and others in summer, lots of guesthouses). The 16th-c **castle** is remarkably well preserved (cl 1–2pm and Weds–Thurs Nov–Mar; £2.50; EH). The Victory does good value lunches. Readers recommend taking the ferry across to St Anthony-in-Roseland for some remote and unspoilt views and walks. The King Harry chain-drawn car ferry on the B3269 N of St Mawes is a favourite family crossing, and on the way the Roseland at Philleigh is one of Cornwall's nicest pubs.

ST NEOT SX1867

The village church is well known for its early stained glass, and also has an unusual stone vault in the south porch. Nearby ancient remains include the five impressive **Brown Gelly Barrows** and some hut circles. **Carnglaze Slate Caverns** are big long-abandoned mining chambers, with a lake at the far end of one; guided tours (cl Sat; (01579) 320251; £3). The London Inn is good for lunch.

ST STEPHEN SW9353

Automobilia (A3058 about 4m W of St Austell) Over 50 cars, motorcycles and other vehicles from 1904 to the 1960s, inc a vintage Bentley and Aston Martin, with a permanent auto-jumble that vintage-car owners may find useful. Snacks, shop, disabled access; cl Sats in Apr, May and Oct, and all Nov–Mar; (01726) 823092; £3.50.

TINTAGEL SX0588

King Arthur's Great Halls (Fore St) Arthurian legends are taken as fact here, and treated very earnestly – far from being a light-hearted romp. There's no denying the impressive craftsmanship, especially in the 72 stained glass scenes. Decent shop, disabled access; cl 25 Dec; (01840) 770526; £2.75.

Old Post Office Small saggy-roofed 14th-c manor used in 19th c as a post office; shop; cl Nov–Mar; (01840) 770024; £2.20; NT.

Tintagel Castle Forgetting the myths and legends, these dramatic 12th- and 13th-c ruins have a spectacular setting and unrivalled views. A good start is from Rocky Valley, a craggy valley leading from the B3263 to the sea. Try to come out of season, when the crowds are fewer and the mist and crashing waves add a touch of mystery. There's quite a lot of climbing involved, and the often steep steps among the crags can be slippery in wet weather. As for King Arthur, latest theories suggest he was a Shropshire lad, but a small exhibition makes the most of the Cornish case. Shop; cl 24–26 Dec and 1 Jan; (01840) 770328; *£2.90; EH. In summer, a Land Rover can ferry you to the site from the village (a tourist trap since the 19th c) at regular intervals throughout the day. The Cornishman is useful for lunch, and the parish church worth a look.

TORPOINT SX4156

Antony House (2m NW) A pleasant ferry ride from Devonport in Plymouth (it's a lot harder to get to by road), this is the finest Classical house in Cornwall, little changed since the early 18th c, with interesting contents and paintings in its panelled rooms; also riverside gardens redesigned by Humphrey Repton, and a dovecote. Snacks, shop, some disabled access to ground floor only; open pm Tues–Thurs and bank hols Apr–Oct, plus Sun Jun–Aug; (01752) 812191; £4, woodland garden £3; NT.

Mount Edgcumbe ⬚ (B3247 E of Kingsand) A short walk up from the Cremyll pedestrian ferry from Plymouth, this mansion was reconstructed after World War II bombing, with period furniture and (the main attraction) acres of lovely gardens and parkland, divided into English, French and Italian sections. Great views to Plymouth. Meals, snacks, shop, disabled access; house cl Mon (exc bank hols), Tues, and Oct–Mar (but park and gardens open then, free); (01752) 822236; £4.50. The charmingly furnished Edgcumbe Arms by the ferry has good value food.

TREBETHERICK SW9277
St Enodoc's church Tucked well away from the roads under a seaside hill off the Rock road, looking out to Padstow Bay. A nice stroll from the village, it's the burial place of John Betjeman. Daymer Bay near here is a very clean and attractive beach, and as it's so shallow, ideal for families wanting a paddle. The Carpenters Arms is useful for lunch, and down on the water at Rock the Mariners Hotel has lovely views over to Padstow.

TRECANGATE SX1759
Porfell Animal Land ⬚ Delightfully unspoilt and friendly, this expanding centre has deer, wallabies, racoons, lemurs, meerkats and a capybara called Bart, as well as rabbits, guinea-pigs, goats, ducks and chickens in 15 acres of sloping fields and woodland. Readers very much enjoy the peaceful and remote feel. Snacks, shop, disabled access; cl Nov–Mar; (01503) 220211; *£3.75. The Ship over at Lerryn is fairly handy for lunch and often has good watercolours for sale; the stepping stones over the river there are a hit with children, and good circular walks

are signposted from the car park.
TREDINNICK SW9270
Shire Horse Adventure Park Far more to this busy complex than just the magnificent horses: there's a children's farm, an exhibition of rural antiquities, nature trails, watermill and working craftsmen, and very big indoor and outdoor adventure playgrounds inc animated animal shows. The horses are displayed in an indoor arena, and you can see them being groomed in their stables – along with shetland ponies. Lots for all ages, but ideal for children. Meals, snacks, shop, disabled access; cl Nov–Easter and Sat in Oct; (01841) 540276; £6. The Ring o' Bells at St Issey is handy for lunch.

TREGONNING HILL SW6029
Takes only a few minutes to climb but has an impressive view; here in 1746 William Cookworthy made the first discovery of china clay in England, and went on to make porcelain.

TRELIGHTS SW9879
Long Cross Victorian Gardens Slightly inland at Trelights (but with good views down to the sea) the prettily restored gardens by the Long Cross Hotel, intricately hedged against the sea winds, have interesting granite and water features, a maze, and playground and pets' corner for children. Meals, snacks, plant sales (not Nov–Easter), disabled access; (01208) 880243; £1.50 (donations only in winter).

TRELISSICK SW8339
Trelissick Garden (B3289) Woodland park with beautifully kept gardens of camellias, magnolias and hydrangeas, also subtropical garden and other unusual plants; good views of the King Harry Passage and over to Pendennis Castle. There's a pretty orchard, and good walks in the surrounding woodland. Meals, snacks, shop, disabled access; cl Sun am, and all Jan–late Feb; (01872) 862090; £4.30; NT. The NT have four holiday cottages on the estate. The Punch Bowl & Ladle at Penelewey on the King Harry Ferry road is popular for lunch.

TRERICE SW8458
Trerice House ⬚ Pretty Elizabethan house with unusual Dutch-style gables, and elaborate plasterwork ceilings in the magnificent Hall and Great

Chamber. Fine furnishings from the 17th and 18th c, notable paintings, early embroideries, Oriental and English porcelain, and in the grounds an unusual collection of lawnmowers; lovely colourful gardens with Cornish fruit trees. Snacks (in a barn with activities for toddlers), shop, very good disabled access; cl Sat and Tues (exc summer school hols), and all Nov–Mar; (01637) 875404; £4.20; NT. The Two Clomes at Quintrell Downs is quite handy for lunch.

TRERYN DINAS SW4022
The most stunning of Cornwall's headlands, capped by the precariously balanced Logan Rock; it's a fairly easy walk from the Logan Rock pub (good food) in Treen.

TRESKILLARD SW6739
Shire Horse Farm & Carriage Museum 🔲 Refreshingly uncommercialised; most displays are indoors, and there are working blacksmith's and wheelwright's shops. Snacks, shop, disabled access; cl Sat and all Nov–Easter; (01209) 713606; *£3.50.

TREVALLAS COOMBE SW7351
Blue Hills Tin Streams Tours of this family-run outfit include demonstrations of vanning, panning and jigging. Snacks, shop, disabled access; cl Sun (bookings only Nov–Mar), and 25–26 Dec; (01872) 553341; £3.

TRURO SW8244
A busy but civilised town with good shops; Lemon St is a particularly fine Georgian street, and Boscawen St is cobbled. The **cathedral** is one of the newer Anglican ones, designed in 1880 in Early English style and finished in 1910; the twin spires of the west front are handsome, and pop up dramatically from behind shops and houses; meals, snacks, shop. **The Royal Cornwall Museum** (River St) tells tales of local characters such as Black John of Tetcott, an 18th-c dwarf whose party piece was apparently tying mice together by their tails, swallowing them whole, and then pulling them up again; also natural history and textile galleries. Meals, snacks, shop, disabled access; cl Sun, bank hols; (01872) 272205; *£3. Just outside the centre, **Bosvigo** (Bosvigo Lane) is a charming

plantsman's garden, with most colour Jun–Sept; small nursery; open Thurs–Sat Mar–Sept; (01872) 275774; *£3. The Old Ale House and Wig & Pen are good for lunch.

VERYAN SW9139
Lovely village famous for its five devil-proof thatched round houses; also a water garden sheltered by holm oaks. The New Inn has good value food. Nearby, 16th-c **Melinsey Mill** is a nicely restored watermill in a lovely setting, with good afternoon teas and basket-weaving demonstrations (not Sat); open Easter–Sept; (01841) 540604; £3. The prettiest approach is to walk along the streamside 'Secret Valley' from Pendower Beach (off A3078 S) rather than go from the village itself.

WADEBRIDGE SW9673
The disused railway track between Wadebridge and Padstow is a level six miles along the edge of the Camel Estuary, with banks of wild flowers, birds, and lovely views between cuttings – you can walk or cycle (bike hire at either end), or picnic on the small beaches at low tide. Those with less energy could park at Wadebridge, walk to Padstow, have lunch and get the bus back (2.12pm from the old station). You might then walk on through scenic countryside beyond Bodmin (worth stopping at Helland pottery, just by the path at Helland Bridge).

WENDRON SW6831
Poldark Mine & Heritage Centre
A fun feature of this old tin mine is its underground post box, the deepest in Britain. More serious attractions include a tour of the mine, an 18th-c village, a film on the history of Cornish mining, old cottages, collection of working beam engines, and plenty of children's amusements. Varied enough to interest most members of the family. Meals, snacks, craft shops, limited disabled access; cl Nov–Mar; (01326) 563166; guided tour £5.25.

WHEALE COATES SW6949
One of the most photogenic **mine ruins** on the Cornish coast; for walkers, the diversion up St Agnes Beacon is well worth it for the commanding views.

WHITESAND BAY SW3526
Long expanses of wonderfully clean sands below the cliffs here give good

walks, stretching away N of Sennen Cove (very popular with surfers; the Old Success here has a great view).

ZENNOR SW4538
The church here is best seen in its granite landscape from the hills above. The Tinners Arms is useful for lunch. Around here you can walk for miles without seeing another soul; Gurnards Head juts dramatically into the Atlantic,

and the hotel there is a good base for cliff walks (with unusual bar snacks).

Wayside Folk Museum 🏛 Readers enjoy this decent little local history museum which has chatty descriptions and information scattered through the exhibits; children's quiz trails. Teas, shop (specialising in Cornish books and crafts); cl Nov–Mar and Sat (exc school and bank hols); (01736) 796945; *£2.20.

Where to eat

BOSCASTLE SX0991 **Carpenters Kitchen** *The Harbour (01840) 250595* In a picturesque village and actually built on the site of an old carpenter's workshop, this is a super (no smoking) place for morning coffee, light lunches and cream teas with everything made on the premises; polished tables, matching china, neatly uniformed staff, hard-working friendly owners, delicious local crab in sandwiches, a daily changing winter soup, and plenty of cakes, gateaux, scones, Cornish splits, and so forth; cl end Oct–beginning of Apr but open wknds Mar and Nov and open 27 Dec–1 Jan; disabled access. £10

CHAPEL AMBLE SW9975 **Maltsters Arms** *(01208) 812473* Popular family-run pub with attractively knocked-together rooms (one is no smoking), flagstones, beams and a big stone fireplace, good interesting food inc lots of fish, afternoon summer cream teas, 20 wines by the glass, well kept real ales, a no smoking main restaurant, and helpful friendly staff; cl 25 Dec pm; children in family room or over 8 in restaurant; disabled access. £25|**£5.95**

CONSTANTINE SW7328 **Trengilly Wartha** *(01326) 340332* Extremely well run, tucked-away inn with a woodburner in the relaxed and civilised bar, a bright no smoking family conservatory, very good imaginative food, a fine range of changing real ales, a thoughtful wine list with 20 by the glass (they also operate a retail business), 40 malt whiskies, and a pretty, landscaped garden; nice bdrms; no food 25 Dec. £29.50|**£7.80**

DULOE SX2358 **Olde Plough House** *(01503) 262050* Very neatly kept pub with lovely slate floor in both communicating bar rooms, three woodburners, a mix of pews and chairs, good interesting food inc fishy specials and steaks cooked on hot stones, real ales, sensibly priced wines, and attentive service; cl pms 25–26 Dec; disabled access. £20.75|**£4.95**

FALMOUTH SW8135 **HMS Ganges** *Mylor Yacht Harbour (01326) 374320* Not actually a ship though obviously named after one, this friendly little restaurant looks across the River Fal and specialises in fresh fish and seafood – they also serve breakfast for the many yachtsmen who sail into the harbour; good choice of wines from around the world at reasonable prices, and helpful service; cl Sun pm, all Feb; disabled access. £24|**£5.95**

FOWEY SX1251 **Food for Thought** *4 Town Quay (01726) 832221* Carefully run quayside evening restaurant with generous helpings of attractively presented food inc fine fish and some simple as well as other elaborate dishes, and lovely puddings; cl Sun, cl Jan/Feb; children must be well behaved. £25

LANLIVERY SX0759 **Crown** *(01208) 872707* Pretty 12th-c inn with friendly licensees, a rambling series of rooms with open fires and a chatty atmosphere, good food using home-grown and local produce, well kept real ales, and a nice garden; disabled access. £20|**£5.50**

MITHIAN SW7450 **Miners Arms** *(01872) 552375* Secluded Tudor pub with lots of character, fine old furnishings and warm winter fires, popular food, a no smoking dining room, real ales, and friendly service. £18|**£6**

MOUSEHOLE SW4626 **Cornish Range** 6 *Chapel St (01736) 731488* Very friendly and neatly kept restaurant with a relaxed atmosphere and carefully cooked food inc plenty of good local fish dishes and enjoyable puddings; cl Mon/Weds during Nov, Jan, Feb; disabled access. £25

NEWLYN SW4628 **Smugglers** *12–14 Fore St (01736) 331501* In a fine setting on the edge of the fishing-boat harbour, this simply furnished little restaurant has candles on pine tables, a friendly atmosphere, and an interesting menu inc delicious fresh fish and super puddings; cl some winter evenings; partial disabled access. £21

PADSTOW SW9175 **Seafood Restaurant** *Riverside (01841) 532700* Wonderfully fresh seafood straight from the boats in busy (and famous – hence having to book so far in advance) airy quayside restaurant, good puddings, nice cheeses, a long, interesting and fairly priced wine list, and friendly service; conservatory for aperitifs; bdrms; cl Christmas, May Day; children over 3. £50/3-course lunch £30

PADSTOW SW9175 **St Petroc's** *4 New St (01841) 532700* Attractive little hotel (under the same ownership as the Seafood Restaurant) with a cheerfully and informally decorated dining room, good quickly served food from a short bistro-type menu (plenty of fish), a sensible wine list, and friendly atmosphere; bdrms; cl Mon, 1 wk Christmas. £30|**£6.50**

PENZANCE SW4730 **Harris's** *46 New St (01736) 364408* Long-standing and boldly decorated cosy restaurant in a narrow cobbled street, with good enjoyable food using local produce (popular fish and shellfish), well liked puddings, and a decent wine list; cl Mon, 3 wks in winter. £28

PHILLEIGH SW8739 **Roseland** *(01872) 580254* Friendly little 17th-c pub just up the hill from the King Harry ferry, with old photographs, insects in glass cases, several small atmospheric rooms, a good winter fire, well kept real ales, and good, popular home-made food; disabled access. £17.50|**£5.95**

POLPERRO SX2051 **Kitchen** *The Coombes (01503) 272780* Cottagey, informal no smoking evening restaurant with really enjoyable interesting food inc vegetarian and daily-changing fresh fish dishes (lovely fresh lobster and crab), and good value wines; may cl Sun, cl Nov–Easter; children over 12. £25

POLPERRO SX2051 **Plantation Café** *The Coombes (01503) 272223* Popular beamed tea shop with good cream teas, a wide choice of interesting teas inc herbal and fruit, lunchtime sandwiches, and evening meals; cl Sat, cl Nov–Mar; disabled access. £12.95|**£3.95**

PORTHALLOW SW7923 **Taranaki Tea Rooms** *Porthallow (01326) 280671* Lovely flower-filled tropical gardens (complete with stick insects that managed to find their way on to tree ferns from New Zealand), with seats under covered pergola or in conservatory; home-baked scones and cakes, cream teas and light lunches (super crab sandwiches) all prepared by friendly owner; no licence but can bring drinks from nearby pub; cl end Sept–Easter; partial disabled access. 2 courses £8|**£3.50**

PORTLOE SW9339 **Tregain** *(01872) 501252* Small, friendly, no smoking restaurant serving interesting well cooked food using local produce inc daily specials (fresh fish in the evening and lovely home-made crab soup at lunchtime), light lunches and super cream teas, a decent wine list, and local cider; 2 bdrms; cl Sun pm exc bank hol wknds, Nov–Mar. £27|**£7**

ST IVES SW5140 **Porthminster Beach Café** *(01736) 795352* Bustling, popular café open all day for morning coffee with home-baked pastries, cream teas, light lunches and more substantial evening meals offering good Mediterranean-style cooking (nice daily specials) using local produce, and a wide choice of coffees and teas; kind to children; cl Nov–Easter. £22|**£6**

ST KEW SX0276 **St Kew Inn** *(01208) 841259* Rather grand-looking stone pub with a friendly welcome, nice old-fashioned furnishings in neatly kept bar, good popular food, and peaceful garden; lovely church next door. £19|**£7**

ST MICHAEL'S MOUNT SW5130 **Sail Loft** *The Harbour (01736) 710748* Converted boat house with enjoyable home-made cakes, Cornish cream teas, more substantial meals, and friendly service; no smoking; cl Oct–Apr; disabled access. £13.50|**£3.50**

TREBURLEY SX3477 **Springer Spaniel** *(01579) 370424* Lovely relaxed atmosphere in main-road pub with totally home-made interesting food inc delicious puddings (some home-grown produce), very friendly service, simply furnished bars, well kept real ales, 7 good wines by the glass, and attractive no smoking restaurant; cl 4 days over Christmas. £25|**£5.75**

TRURO SW8244 **Old Ale House** *7 Quay St/Princes St (01872) 271122* Appealing, bustling and friendly back-to-basics pub, popular with a good cross-section of people, with interesting bric-a-brac and engaging old furnishings, up to 24 real ales, and enterprising, freshly prepared and very cheap food from a spotless kitchen. £14|**£5**

Isles of Scilly

The islands, about 30 miles W of Land's End, are charmingly unspoilt and a great place for utter relaxation. They have beautiful scenery, an almost subtropical climate, and a variety of shorelines giving excellent coastal walks. In a lazy day you can comfortably walk round the largest, St Mary's, which is just six square miles. Tresco and St Agnes are the other main populated ones, though that means small undeveloped communities rather than any towns or big settlements. There are over 100 islands in all, some just strange-shaped rocks jutting out of the sea, their only visitors seals, dolphins and puffins.

You can get there from Penzance by ferry (£34 day return) or more spectacularly by helicopter, a 20-minute ride with really beautiful views of the Cornish coast and of the islands (return fares start at £64). The islands also have their own little airline Skybus which leaves from Land's End, Newquay or Exeter several times a day. The trip from Land's End is quickest and cheapest (from £59 return; no flights Sun). They also do combined air and rail tickets – (0845) 710 5555 for details.

Where to stay

PELISTRY BAY SV9311 **Carnwethers Country House** *Carnwethers, Pelistry Bay, St Mary's, Isles of Scilly TR21 0NX (01720) 422415* **£104*** inc dinner – good value weekly terms, too; 9 rms. Well run no smoking country guesthouse nr very fine beach, with an acre of lovely gardens, heated swimming pool, and croquet, lounge with helpful books about the islands, well stocked bar, good freshly cooked set 4-course dinner using local produce served at 6.30pm, sound wine list, and games room with pool table and table tennis; sauna; lots of coastal walks; cl Nov–Mar; children over 12

TRESCO SV8915 **Island Hotel** *Tresco, Isles of Scilly TR24 0PU (01720) 422883* **£220** inc dinner; 48 rms, many with balconies and terrace overlooking gardens or sea. Tiny private island, renowned for its wonderful subtropical Abbey Gardens and reached by helicopter or boat – hotel tractor-drawn bus (no cars allowed though bike hire available) takes you to spacious, very friendly modern hotel with colonial-style bar, library, fine food and wine, panoramic views, swimming pool, and private beach; no dogs; cl Nov–Mar

---

Please let us know what you think of places in the *Guide*. Use the report forms at the back of the book or simply write us a letter.

To see and do

As each of the islands is so small, few apart from Tresco have many specific attractions — visitors come mainly to 'get away from it all', and there can be a refreshing feeling of complete isolation. By far the best activity is walking — there are plenty of white sandy beaches (the sea is cold but clean), or unusual plants and birds to track down. Hiring bikes is another good way of exploring and enjoying the scenery. Thanks to the climate — the name means Sun Isles — flowers come out early, and spring and autumn sunsets can be particularly beautiful. A good plan is to island-hop — there are regular ferries between the larger islands, though it can prove expensive. Every Fri evening and some Weds in summer you can watch the racing of the traditional six-oar gigs that used to dash out to shipwrecks.

BRYHER SV8715

A tiny quiet place, even by Scilly standards. The S bay has lots of wild flowers, and Watch Hill has wonderful views. The Hell Bay Hotel is good value.

ST AGNES SV8708

The most south-westerly community in the British Isles, joined to a smaller island called Gugh by a sandbar, awash at high tide. The sheltered cove here is especially popular. The 17th-c **lighthouse** is the second oldest in Britain. The views from here out to the rocks and islets are very atmospheric especially when you remember more ships have been wrecked here than anywhere comparable in the world.

ST MARTIN'S SV9315

A narrow rocky ridge with flowers stretching down to the main attraction — the extensive beaches, very popular for picnics. There's a diving school, and the St Martin's Hotel has lovely sunset views.

ST MARY'S SV9010

The hub of Scilly Isles life, though its centre, Hugh Town, is little more than a village by mainland standards. Most ferries and planes arrive here, and you can get pleasure cruises from the Old Quay out to the bird and seal colonies on the outer islets and islands; there are fishing trips from here too. There's a museum, and 9-hole putting green with fine views. The **Longstone**

Papers Past Exhibition has a huge collection of archive newspapers; snacks, shop; cl Sun and all early Sept–late May; 99p. The Bishop & Wolf is a pleasant pub, and the Atlantic Holt has a good pub part. Up in the N at Bant's Carn there's a burial chamber and ancient village. Back down S, walk out to Penninis Head for good views of the Wolf and Bishop's Rock lighthouses. Just along the coast is Star Castle.

TRESCO SV8915

The highlight here is the amazing **subtropical garden** around the grounds of the abbey, begun in 1834, which, despite storms, contains a magnificent collection of exotic plants, bananas even. Also in these grounds is **Valhalla**, a collection of carved figureheads from wrecked ships, many dating back to the 17th c. Helicopters from Penzance land just outside the garden gate, so it's possible (though not cheap) to come here just for a day. The southern parts of the island are mainly sandy, but in the north it's more wild and rugged, with the remains of the castles of both Charles I and Oliver Cromwell, and a cave known as the Piper's Hole. Cycling and walking are real pleasures — not least because there aren't any cars. The New Inn, embellished with a mystery cargo of pine planking which washed ashore a while back, has good food inc seafood.

Where to eat

ST AGNES SV8807 **Turks Head** The Quay (01720) 422434 Idyllically placed pub (a pleasant place to stay) with outstanding views over sweeping bay, enjoyable food in simple pine-panelled bar inc legendary huge locally made pasties, afternoon teas, evening barbecues, real ales, and decent wines; you can walk down to the slipway and sit right on the shore — or enjoy the wonderful views from seats on the lawn; cl Nov–Mar. £15|£5.50

CUMBRIA

Some of Britain's finest scenery; outstanding access to open country – ideal for outdoor activities, with lots of interesting places to visit too, and excellent places to stay in

The splendid countryside is what draws most tourists here. Each lake has its own character, and the landscape around them varies greatly too. Windermere, the longest and busiest, has always been a general favourite; it's picturesquely dotted with villas built by Victorian magnates, and has masses of accommodation on its eastern side. Ullswater approaches the grandeur of Scottish lochs, and has some excellent (if not cheap) places to stay right by the lake shore. Buttermere and Crummock Water also have scenery on the grand scale, perhaps without quite matching Ullswater's scenic perfection. Derwent Water wavers charmingly between highland and lowland in flavour, and its islands and manageable proportions make it a favourite for idle boating as well as for bankside strolls. Coniston Water, quite well wooded, also appeals to both boaters and walkers, with some fine views – in some ways it's a junior version of Windermere, smaller and quieter. Wastwater, England's deepest lake, is austere, surrounded by towering screes. Bassenthwaite is altogether gentler, lowland in feel. Some much smaller lakes, notably Grasmere, Rydal Water and Elterwater, are idyllic.

The most beautiful scenery is concentrated thickly around the central area, especially around the towns of Ambleside and Windermere. Both places are quite intensively developed for visitors and very busy indeed in summer; Keswick too has lots going on for all ages. These parts really come into their own at quieter times of year – you need a degree of peace and quiet to enjoy the beauty of the delicious central area between Windermere and Grasmere. Cockermouth to the NW has plenty of attractions to fill a rainy day.

The best coastal scenery is around Morecambe Bay. The west coast is untouristy, with miles of unfrequented beaches (as well as some run-down looking places – and the big nuclear power plant at Seascale, which has an excellent visitor centre).

Cumbria is very good territory for children who get a kick out of doing outdoor things. Grizedale Forest Park is great for letting off steam, with sculpture trails, orienteering and great potential for cycling. Worth noting, too, are the several historic buildings which provide considerable scope for family fun such as Holker Hall & Gardens, Mirehouse near Bassenthwaite, Dalemain at Dacre and Appleby Castle. Most impressive this year, with its owl centre, beautiful gardens and fun new maze, is Muncaster Castle & Owl Centre – Cumbria's Family Attraction of the Year.

Families who need more in the way of amusements laid on will not be disappointed. Among plenty of farm and wildlife centres, the South Lakes

Wild Animal Park at Dalton-in-Furness, Amazonia (with its exotic creatures) in Windermere, and the aquarium at Newby Bridge stand out. The Lowther Leisure Park at Hackthorpe will amuse most younger kids, the Lakeland Sheep & Wool Centre is surprisingly entertaining, and children enjoy the reconstructions at Carlisle's Tullie House.

We'd recommend a look at the villages of Hawkshead, Troutbeck and Cartmel, and Hutton-in-the-Forest and Townend at Troutbeck are satisfying places to wander around.

The literary trail is heavily trodden in summer, and though very well managed is specially rewarding at quieter times. The main Wordsworth focus is on Grasmere, Rydal and Cockermouth. Beatrix Potter is well served at her home at Near Sawrey, and in Ambleside and Hawkshead, and for young children in Windermere. Admirers of Ruskin may head for the museum at Coniston, but his house Brantwood, across the water, has a more general appeal.

The county has many good craft centres – the Brougham Hall craft centre is perhaps the best, and readers enjoy browsing at the Kirkstone Galleries in Skelwith Bridge, new to the *Guide* this year. Wetheriggs Pottery has plenty for children to get stuck into.

The area's local history is well represented; the new Rheged centre at Penrith presents the region's past on a giant scale, and the attractive Abbot Hall in Kendal is good for showing the influence of the Lakes on famous artists – Kendal has a good value inclusive-price ticket for its museums. Boat enthusiasts will appreciate the Dock Museum at Barrow-in-Furness, car fans won't want to miss the celebrity vehicles at Keswick, and the Laurel & Hardy Museum at Ulverston has been lovingly put together.

The Florence Mine Heritage Centre gives a fascinating glimpse of an industrial world, and at Ravenglass is England's oldest, and one of its finest, steam railways. Whitehaven's friendly heritage centre, the Beacon, is fascinating for anyone with a weather obsession – all too easy to acquire in Lakeland.

The National Trust controls over a quarter of the land in the Lake District National Park. So preservation of and access to the countryside here is first-class (and it's an area where membership of the Trust really pays off in terms of free admission). You could stay here for weeks every year of your life and never walk the same path twice – so our walks suggestions are really just initial pointers. Also, many of the recommended places to stay here have been chosen for the grand walks right from their doorsteps. There's an excellent choice of places to stay, many of which serve really good food. We have gone out of our way to recommend places that are strong on peace and quiet; there's a splendid range of styles and prices.

For a quiet break with plenty of walking on your doorstep, the Langdales, particularly Great Langdale, and Borrowdale are outstanding. The west is even quieter, separated from the central Lake District by high ridges with tortuous roads over the few passes. British rock-climbing was born over here, with England's highest mountain, Scafell Pike, surrounded by other awesome peaks – serious walking country.

Another area where you can reckon on peace and quiet even in summer is the part east of the M6. This is one of England's least-known areas, and though overshadowed by the Lake District proper has a lot of charm, and some excellent value places to stay in. Quiet river valleys shelter below more awesome open country and high moors, and there are some attractive and untouristy places to visit. Much of the high country is too bleak and boggy for most walkers, but moorland roads give drivers good views (eg A683 Kirkby Lonsdale–Kirkby Stephen, B6260 Tebay–Appleby, B6413 Lazonby–Brampton, A689 Brampton–Alston). The railway crossing the moors between Carlisle and Settle is perhaps the best way of all of seeing this unusual part of England.

Lakeland generally is at its best out of season. May (sheets of wild flowers on the hills) and June are ideal: more sun, no crowds. The views are often clearest (and the ground firm and dry for walkers) in October and November, though afternoons are short then. In the summer holidays and at other peak times crowds make the best places less enjoyable, and indeed put a real strain on the environment. If you're determined to go at that time of year, you've more chance of finding peace in the west, or over by the Pennines east of the M6. For all but the hardiest expert outdoorsmen, winter up here is too bleak for pleasure – unless you plan to stay indoors. Whenever you come bring something waterproof – the Lake District has more annual rainfall than any other part of the country.

Public transport in the Lakes is good and useful for round-trip long walks. Local information leaflets offer plenty of choice of well guided walks; information too from National Park visitor services (015394) 46601, and from the National Trust (015394) 35599. Bicycles can be hired by the day in the main towns (considering the scenic grandeur, you can cycle for a surprisingly long way, at least in the central area, without having to struggle up steep hills). Many places offer riding: around £10 an hour for adults, £8 for children.

Where to stay

ALSTON NY7646 **Lovelady Shield Country House** *Nenthead Rd, Alston, Cumbria CA9 3LF (01434) 381203* **£170** inc dinner, plus special breaks; 12 rms. In a lovely setting with River Nent running along bottom of garden (tennis and croquet), this country house has a tranquil atmosphere, courteous staff, log fires in comfortable rooms (no smoking in sitting room or restaurant), and very good food inc fine breakfasts; children over 7 in evening restaurant; dogs by prior arrangement
AMBLESIDE NY3703 **Rothay Manor** *Rothay Bridge, Ambleside, Cumbria LA22 0EH (015394) 33605* **£120**, plus special breaks; 18 attractive rms, many overlooking garden. Family-run Regency-style country house in neatly kept mature grounds, with open fires and fresh flowers in quietly civilised and comfortable day rooms, very good English food in no smoking dining room, a thoughtful wine list, super big breakfasts, and helpful friendly service; windsurfing/waterskiing etc close by, free use of nearby leisure club; cl 3 Jan–9 Feb; good disabled access
AMBLESIDE NY3804 **Rowanfield Country House** *Kirkstone Rd, Ambleside,*

Cumbria LA22 9ET (015394) 33686 **£62***, plus special breaks. 8 rms. Charming carefully restored Lakeland house looking across Lake Windermere to distant hills, with a woodburner in the comfortable and attractively furnished sitting room, enjoyable interesting food at 7pm in the flagstoned and candlelit dining room (bring your own wine), super breakfasts, and friendly owners; cl mid-Nov–mid-Mar, but open Christmas and New Year; children over 8

AMBLESIDE NY3703 **Wateredge Hotel** *Borrans Rd, Ambleside, Cumbria LA22 0EP (015394)* 32332 **£110**, plus special breaks; 23 good, comfortable rms. Beautifully placed, warmly welcoming hotel with neat gardens running down to Lake Windermere (embarkation point for cruising the lake), light airy lounges, good meals in cosy beamed no smoking dining room, and excellent service; free fishing permits; cl mid-Dec–early Jan; children over 7; dogs by prior arrangement

APPLEBY NY6920 **Appleby Manor** *Roman Rd, Appleby, Cumbria CA16 6JB (01768)* 351571 **£114***, plus special breaks; 30 well equipped rms in original house (the nicest), coach house annexe or modern wing. Very friendly family-run hotel with fine views over Appleby Castle and Eden Valley, log fires in two of the three comfortable lounges, relaxed bar with wide range of whiskies, excellent service, good interesting food in panelled restaurant, and leisure centre; enjoyed by families; cl 24–26 Dec; disabled access ☺

BARBON SD6282 **Barbon Inn** *Barbon, Carnforth, Cumbria LA6 2LJ (015242)* 76233 **£60**; 10 simple but comfortable rms, some with own bthrm. Small friendly village inn in quiet spot below fells, with relaxing bar, traditional lounge, good meals in candlelit dining room, and helpful service

BASSENTHWAITE LAKE NY2032 **Armathwaite Hall Hotel** *Bassenthwaite Lake, Keswick, Cumbria CA12 4RE (017687)* 76551 **£124***; 43 rms. Turreted 17th-c mansion in 400 acres of deerpark and woodland; handsome public rooms with lovely fireplaces, fine panelling, antiques, paintings and fresh flowers, good French and English cooking, a super wine list, and helpful staff; snooker room, croquet, pitch-and-putt, tennis court, indoor swimming pool, gym and beauty salon; also fishing and riding, archery and clay pigeon shooting, and jogging and mountain-bike tracks ☺

BASSENTHWAITE LAKE NY1930 **Pheasant** *Bassenthwaite Lake, Cockermouth, Cumbria CA13 9YE (017687)* 76234 **£120**, plus special breaks; 18 rms. Civilised hotel with delightfully old-fashioned pubby bar, restful lounges with open fire, antiques, fresh flowers and comfortable armchairs, and interesting gardens merging into surrounding fellside woodlands; cl 24 Dec pm, 25 Dec; disabled access

BRAMPTON NY5760 **Farlam Hall** *Hallbankgate, Brampton, Cumbria CA8 2NG (016977)* 46234 **£230** inc dinner, plus special breaks; 12 comfortable rms. Charmingly Victorian (though parts are much older) and very civilised country house with log fires in spacious lounges, excellent attentive service, good 4-course dinner, marvellous breakfasts, and peaceful spacious grounds with croquet lawn and small pretty lake; cl 25–30 Dec; children over 5; dogs by prior arrangement; partial disabled access

BUTTERMERE NY1716 **Bridge** *Buttermere, Cockermouth, Cumbria CA13 9UZ (017687)* 70252 **£100** inc dinner, plus special breaks; 21 rms. Comfortable hotel surrounded by some of the best steep countryside in the county, with beamed bar (the flagstoned part is popular with walkers), log fire and deep armchairs in sitting room, good food in bar and no smoking restaurant, real ales, decent malt whiskies, and a friendly atmosphere; self-catering also

CARLISLE NY4055 **Number Thirty One Howard Place** *31 Howard Pl, Carlisle, Cumbria CA1 1HR (01228)* 597080 **£75***; 3 well equipped individually decorated rms. Carefully restored no smoking Victorian townhouse with a relaxed informal atmosphere, open fire and plenty of books in the cosy lounge, delicious interesting food using the best local produce, breakfast with home-baked bread, home-made preserves and home-made Cumbrian sausages, and helpful courteous owners; cl Jan–Feb; no children; partial disabled access

CARTMEL SD3977 **Uplands** *Haggs Lane, Cartmel, Grange-over-Sands, Cumbria*

LA11 6HD (015395) 36248 **£152** inc dinner, plus special breaks; 5 pretty rms. Comfortable Edwardian house in two acres of garden with views over to the Morecambe Bay estuary, attractively decorated rooms, and helpful service; the main draw is undoubtedly the richly imaginative food in the no smoking dining room; cl Jan–Feb; children over 8; well behaved dogs welcome

CASTERTON SD6279 **Pheasant** *Casterton, Carnforth, Lancashire LA6 2RX (015242) 71230* **£72**, plus special breaks; 11 comfortable rms, most with countryside views. Small civilised inn with pleasant atmosphere, good food in no smoking panelled dining room, cheerful staff, and small but sound wine list; dogs allowed; disabled access

CATLOWDY NY4676 **Bessiestown Farm** *Penton, Carlisle, Cumbria CA6 5QP (01228) 577219* **£50**; 5 rms. Friendly no smoking farmhouse close to the Scottish borders, with two comfortable lounges, conservatory, good home-made food and big breakfasts in attractive dining room, indoor heated swimming pool, and games room; self-catering also; children must be well behaved

CROOK SD4395 **Wild Boar** *Crook, Windermere, Cumbria LA23 3NF (015394) 45225* **£132***; 36 rms. Comfortable, well run extended hotel with period furnishings and log fires in its ancient core, attentive service, and good food in no smoking dining room; free access to nearby leisure club and discounts on watersports

CROSBY ON EDEN NY4459 **Crosby Lodge** *High Crosby, Crosby on Eden, Carlisle, Cumbria CA6 4QZ (01228) 573618* **£115***, plus wknd breaks; 11 spacious rms (2 in stable conversion). Imposing and carefully converted country house in attractive mature grounds, with comfortable and appealing individual furnishings, a good choice of tasty food in bar and no smoking restaurant, friendly long-established owners, and nice surrounding countryside; cl 24 Dec–20 Jan; limited disabled access

DENT SD7686 **Sportsmans** *Cowgill, Dent, Sedbergh, Cumbria LA10 5RG (01539) 625282* **£45**, plus winter breaks; 6 rms with shared bthrm. Unassuming comfortable pub notable for its wonderful position in Dentdale by the River Dee with the Settle–Carlisle railway close by, and walks in all directions; open log fires and good value home-made food; well behaved dogs allowed

DERWENT WATER NY2618 **Hilton Keswick Lodore** *Borrowdale, Keswick, Cumbria CA12 5UX (017687) 77285* **£136***, plus special breaks; 71 well equipped rms. Long-standing but well updated big holiday hotel with lots of facilities in 40 acres of lakeside gardens and woodlands, open fires in comfortable day rooms, elegant restaurant, leisure club, tennis and squash, outdoor swimming pool, and games room; particularly well organised for families with NNEB nannies and so forth; self-catering house too ☺

DOCKRAY NY3921 **Royal** *Dockray, Penrith, Cumbria CA11 0JY (017684) 82356* **£62**, plus special breaks; 10 rms. Friendly family-run hotel with open fires in big modernised open-plan bar, good value hearty meals, and well kept beers; in fine spot between hills and lake with walks from the doorstep; children must be well behaved

ELTERWATER NY3204 **Britannia Inn** *Elterwater, Ambleside, Cumbria LA22 9HP (015394) 37210* **£72***, plus special breaks; 13 rms, most with shower, some in quiet annexe opposite. Simple charmingly traditional pub in fine surroundings opposite village green, with a happy friendly atmosphere (it does get very busy at peak times), hearty home cooking inc superb breakfast, comfortable no smoking lounge and bustling bar, real ales, and Sun evening quiz; fine walks all around; cl 25–26 Dec pm; well behaved dogs allowed

ESKDALE GREEN SD1199 **Bower House** *Eskdale Green, Holmrook, Cumbria CA19 1TD (019467) 23244* **£74**, plus special breaks; 24 comfortable rms, some in annexe. Relaxed and pleasantly isolated old stone inn with nicely tended sheltered garden, a lounge bar with log fire and a comfortable separate one with sofas and easy chairs, several bar rooms, popular good value food inc wonderful puddings, no smoking restaurant, and friendly staff; disabled access

FAR SAWREY SD3895 **Sawrey** *Far Sawrey, Ambleside, Cumbria LA22 0LQ* (015394) 43425 **£59**; 18 rms. Friendly hotel well placed at the foot of Claife Heights, with simple pubby and smarter bars, friendly staff, good straightforward food, and seats on pleasant lawn with good views of Lake Windermere; cl Christmas; kind to children; dogs allowed; partial disabled access

GARRIGILL NY7441 **George & Dragon** *Garrigill, Alston, Cumbria CA9 3DS* (01434) 381293 **£40**; 4 small rms, shared bthrm but clean and comfortable. Friendly 17th-c pub on dead-end road in beautiful countryside, with informal flagstone bar, stone-and-panelled dining room, log fire in smashing fireplace, and good service; children over 10

GRANGE-OVER-SANDS SD4077 **Graythwaite Manor** *Fernhill Rd, Grange-over-Sands, Cumbria LA11 7JE* (015395) 32001 **£90***, plus special breaks; 21 individually furnished rms, many with fine views. Set in flower-filled landscaped gardens with views over Morecambe Bay, this comfortable hotel (run by the same family since 1937) has a particularly relaxed friendly atmosphere, elegantly furnished lounges with flowers and antiques, open fires, and good carefully prepared food in the attractive no smoking dining room; cl 7–26 Jan; no dogs; disabled access

GRASMERE NY3408 **Michael's Nook Hotel** *Grasmere, Ambleside, Cumbria LA22 9RP* (015394) 35496 **£130** inc dinner, plus winter breaks; 12 lovely rms and 2 suites. Beautifully furnished hotel with fine antiques, paintings and rugs (the owner is a former antiques dealer), lovely flowers, comfortable sofas by open fires in cosy bar or elegant drawing room, excellent food, landscaped garden with specimen rhododendrons, and good walks; also, great danes and exotic cats; free use of indoor pool and health facilities at nearby Wordsworth Hotel (under the same ownership, and listed below); children over 7

GRASMERE NY3308 **Swan** *Keswick Rd, Grasmere, Ambleside, Cumbria LA22 9RF* (015394) 35551 **£108**; 38 rms, most with fine views. Smart and friendly 17th-c hotel in beautiful fell-foot surroundings, with beams and inglenooks, elegant no smoking dining room, enjoyable food, and attractive garden; lovely walks; partial disabled access

GRASMERE NY3307 **Wordsworth Hotel** *Grasmere, Ambleside, Cumbria LA22 9SW* (015394) 35592 **£138***, plus special breaks; 37 comfortable, pretty rms. Well run hotel, right in village next to the churchyard where Wordsworth is buried; stylish lounges and airy restaurant overlooking landscaped gardens, a relaxed conservatory and popular pubby bar, friendly service, enjoyable food, and heated indoor pool, mini-gym, and sauna; good disabled access

GRIZEDALE SD3394 **Grizedale Lodge** *Hawkshead Hill, Grizedale, Ambleside, Cumbria LA22 0QL* (015394) 36532 **£70***, plus special breaks; 9 no smoking rms. Friendly, comfortable B&B hotel in the middle of the magnificent Grizedale Forest with lots of walks from the front door, a winter log fire in lounge bar, and hearty breakfasts in attractive breakfast room; children over 5; disabled access

HAWKSHEAD NY3501 **Drunken Duck** *Barngates, Hawkshead, Ambleside, Cumbria LA22 0NG* (015394) 36347 **£90**, plus special breaks; 11 comfortable rms. Attractive 17th-c Lakeland inn alone in 60 hillside acres, with several cosy, beamed, mainly no smoking rooms, open fires, views of Lake Windermere in distance, home-brewed ales, over 50 malt whiskies, and good interesting lunchtime food (more elaborate in the evening); fishing in private tarn; cl 25 Dec pm; limited disabled access

HAWKSHEAD SD3498 **Highfield House** *Hawkshead Hill, Ambleside, Cumbria LA22 0PN* (015394) 36344 **£89***, plus winter breaks; 11 pretty rms. Welcoming Victorian country house in spacious woodland garden with fine views (good walks from the door), open fire in comfortable lounge, cosy bar, and enjoyable food inc packed lunches and children's high tea; cl Jan

IREBY NY2335 **Overwater Hall** *Ireby, Carlisle, Cumbria CA5 1HH* (017687) 76566 **£85**, plus special breaks; 12 rms. Relaxed and friendly, partly castellated, family-run hotel in 18 acres of gardens and woodland, with log fire in elegant comfortable drawing room, good imaginative food in cosy dining room, and lots of walks; children over 5 in restaurant (high tea 5 pm); well behaved dogs welcome; cl first 2 weeks Jan; partial disabled access

KENDAL NY5401 **Low Jock Scar** *Selside, Kendal, Cumbria LA8 9LE (01539) 823259* £58*; 5 rms, most with own bthrm. Relaxed and friendly little country guesthouse in six acres of garden and woodland, with residents' lounge, and good home cooking (picnic lunches on request); no smoking; cl Nov–Feb; children over 12

KESWICK NY2623 **Shu-le-Crow Cottage** *7 Penrith Rd, Keswick, Cumbria CA12 4HF (017687) 75253* £40*; 3 attractive rms. Pink-washed no smoking 18th-c cottage with plenty of original features, cheerful owners who can advise on local walks, and super breakfasts (vegetarian options); plenty of places to eat nearby

KESWICK NY2421 **Swinside Lodge** *Newlands, Keswick, Cumbria CA12 5UE (017687) 72948* £89, plus special breaks; 7 comfortable rms. Victorian hotel in own grounds surrounded by wonderful unspoilt scenery at the foot of Cat Bells, and a few minutes from shores of Derwent Water; hearty breakfasts and super home-made evening meals in candelit dining room, helpful friendly service, and two relaxing sitting rooms; cl end Nov–beginning of Feb; children over 12

KIRKCAMBECK NY5269 **Cracrop Farm** *Kirkcambeck, Brampton, Cumbria CA8 2BW (016977) 48245* £50; 3 rms overlooking garden and open fields. Friendly Victorian farmhouse on 425 acres with stock animals and very good marked farm trails (they are keen on conservation), comfortable and homely rooms, good traditional breakfasts (other food arranged in advance) and games room and sauna; no smoking; cl Christmas; children over 12

LANERCOST NY5563 **Abbey Bridge** *Lanercost, Brampton, Cumbria CA8 2HG (016977) 2224* £60; 7 simple rms, most with own bthrm. Beautifully placed small country inn in quiet spot nr ancient priory, with enjoyable food in informal converted forge which also houses cheerful bar, and pleasant staff; cl 25 Dec; disabled access

LANGDALE NY2806 **Old Dungeon Ghyll** *Great Langdale, Ambleside, Cumbria LA22 9JY (015394) 37272* £72, plus special breaks; 17 rms, some with shared bthrm. Friendly, simple and cosy walkers' and climbers' inn dramatically surrounded by fells, wonderful views and terrific walks; cosy residents' lounge and popular food – best to book for dinner if not a resident; cl 3 days over Christmas

LINDALE SD4180 **Greenacres Country Guest House** *Lindale, Grange-over-Sands, Cumbria LA11 6LP (015395) 34578* £50*, plus special breaks; 5 appealing rms. Charming 19th-c cottage with friendly atmosphere, pretty sitting room, conservatory, log fire, good home-made food and big breakfasts in cosy dining room, and packed lunch on request; kind to families and will set aside the whole house for family parties; cl Christmas and New Year ☺

LITTLE LANGDALE NY3103 **Three Shires** *Little Langdale, Ambleside, Cumbria LA22 9NZ (015394) 37215* £66, plus special breaks; 10 rms. Family-run stone-built country inn with beautiful views, comfortably old-fashioned residents' part, separate walkers' bar with real ales, decent food, and pretty gardens; no accommodation Jan (bar is open)

LORTON NY1522 **New House Farm** *Lorton, Cockermouth, Cumbria CA13 9UU (01900) 85404* £80, plus special breaks; 5 rms with wonderful hillside views. Friendly no smoking 17th-c house (not a working farm) in 15 acres, with beams and rafters, flagstones, open fires, and three residents' lounges, very good food inc game and fish caught by owner, home-made scones and preserves, a thoughtful wine list – and lots of walks; children over 8.

MUNGRISDALE NY3630 **Mill Hotel** *Mungrisdale, Penrith, Cumbria CA11 0XR (017687) 79659* £75; 9 rms, most with own bthrm. Very friendly small streamside hotel beautifully placed in lovely valley hamlet hidden away below Blencathra, with open fire in cosy and comfortable sitting room, good imaginative 5-course evening meals, and a small carefully chosen wine list; cl Nov–beginning of Mar; dogs welcome by arrangement; disabled access

POOLEY BRIDGE NY4521 **Sharrow Bay** *Pooley Bridge, Penrith, Cumbria CA10 2LZ* (017684) 86301 **£300** inc dinner; 28 lovely rms with antiques, books, and games. Country-house hotel in quiet idyllic spot by Ullswater with lovely views of the lake and mountains, and showing the years of loving care the owners put into its distinctive style, furnishings and décor; unobtrusively attentive service and excellent English cooking in the two contrasting dining rooms; cl Dec–beginning of Mar; no children

RAVENSTONEDALE NY7401 **Fat Lamb** *Cross Bank, Ravenstonedale, Kirkby Stephen, Cumbria CA17 4LL* (015396) 23242 **£70**, plus special breaks; 12 comfortable rms. Welcoming moorland inn in beautiful open countryside, with log fire and good local photographs in cheerfully modernised two-room bar, enjoyable food, and 17 acres of land, seven of which is nature reserve; very good disabled access

RYDAL WATER NY3406 **White Moss House** *White Moss, Ambleside, Cumbria LA22 9SE* (015394) 35295 **£130** inc dinner, plus special breaks; 8 thoughtfully furnished and comfortable little rms in main house plus separate cottage let as one unit with 2 rms. Bought by Wordsworth for his son, this attractive stripped-stone country house – set in charming mature grounds overlooking the lake – is a marvellously relaxing place to stay, with owners who have been there for over 20 years, a comfortable lounge, excellent fixed price 5-course meals in pretty no smoking dining room, a fine wine list, and exemplary service; free fishing and free use of local leisure club; cl Dec–early Feb; no toddlers

SEATOLLER NY2413 **Seatoller House** *Borrowdale, Keswick, Cumbria CA12 5XN* (017687) 77218 **£57**; 9 spotless, comfortable rms. Friendly house-party atmosphere in 17th-c house that has been a guesthouse for over 100 years, with self-service drinks and board games in comfortable lounges (no TV), and good no-choice fixed-time hearty dinner (not Tues) served at two big oak tables; packed lunches; two acres of grounds and many walks from doorstep as house is at the foot of Honister Pass; cl end Nov–Mar

TALKIN NY5557 **Hullerbank** *Talkin, Brampton, Cumbria CA8 1LB* (016977) 46668 **£46***; 3 rms. Comfortable and very friendly no smoking Georgian farmhouse in unspoilt countryside, with a relaxed atmosphere in homely lounge, and good food using home-grown and local produce inc home-produced lamb (packed lunch on request); cl Christmas–Feb; children over 12; no pets

THIRLMERE NY3117 **Dale Head Hall** *Thirlmere, Keswick, Cumbria CA12 4TN* (017687) 72478 **£90**, plus special breaks; 16 pretty rms, most with lake views, and 7 in new wing. Peaceful partly 16th-c country house in lovely lakeside grounds, with comfortable lounges, log fire, friendly owners, and home-cooked food using produce grown in own walled garden; children over 10 for evening meals; cl Jan

TIRRIL NY5026 **Queens Head** *Tirril, Penrith, Cumbria CA10 2JF* (01768) 863219 **£50**, plus special breaks; 7 lovely rms, most with own bthrm. Bustling inn with flagstones and exposed floorboards in the bar, spacious back restaurant (mostly no smoking), low beams, black panelling, inglenook fireplace and old-fashioned settles in older part, good interesting food inc snacks and OAP specials, and well kept real ales (inc their own brews); babies welcome but older children must be over 13

WASDALE HEAD NY1607 **Wasdale Head Hotel** *Wasdale Head, Seascale, Cumbria CA20 1EX* (019467) 26229 **£90***; 9 simple but warmly comfortable pine-clad rms, with 3 more luxurious ones in farmhouse annexe. Old flagstoned and gabled walkers' and climbers' inn in magnificent setting surrounded by steep fells, with civilised day rooms (inc a new garden room), popular home cooking, good wine list, huge breakfasts, and cheerfully busy public bar; steam room; self-catering cottages; partial disabled access

WATER YEAT SD2889 **Water Yeat** *Water Yeat, Ulverston, Cumbria LA12 8DJ* (01229) 885306 **£57***; 5 pretty rooms. Friendly new owners have redecorated much of this attractively converted and neatly kept 17th-c farmhouse by Coniston Water, in three acres of garden and woodland; there's an especially relaxing atmosphere, log fire in lounge, enjoyable breakfasts, and particularly good food in heavily beamed dining room; cl Dec–mid-Feb; children over 4; self-catering cottage

WATERMILLOCK NY4421 **Leeming House** *Watermillock, Ullswater, Penrith, Cumbria CA11 0JJ (017684) 86622* **£138**, plus special breaks; 40 cosseting rms, many with beautiful views. Well run extended hotel in 20 acres of quiet lakeside grounds, with log fires in comfortable lounges, cosy panelled bar, fine food in lovely no smoking dining room, and good courteous service; boating and fishing; high teas for young children; good provision for disabled

WATERMILLOCK NY4321 **Old Church Hotel** *Watermillock, Penrith, Cumbria CA11 0JN (017684) 86204* **£204** plus special breaks; 10 rms, some with lovely Ullswater view. Attractive 18th-c Lakeland house peacefully placed in waterside gardens, with log fires and individual furnishings in civilised day rooms, kind service, and excellent English dinners at 8pm in no smoking dining room; rowing/windsurfing boats; cl Dec–Feb

WATERMILLOCK NY4523 **Rampsbeck Country House** *Watermillock, Penrith, Cumbria CA11 0LP (017684) 86442* **£120**; 20 rms. Run by friendly helpful people, this 18th-c hotel is set in 18 acres by Lake Ullswater, and has an open fire in the cosy sitting room, French windows into the garden from the plush, comfortable lounge, and carefully prepared food in the attractive dining room; croquet; lots to do nearby; cl Jan–mid-Feb; children over 8 in evening restaurant

WINDERMERE SD4097 **Fir Trees** *Lake Rd, Windermere, Cumbria LA23 2EQ (015394) 42272* **£56***; 7 attractive spotless rms inc 2 big family ones. Well run and comfortable no smoking Victorian house with an informal relaxed atmosphere, antiques, fine prints and fresh flowers, warmly helpful service (detailed suggestions of what to do), and good hearty breakfasts and vegetarian meals by prior arrangement, high chairs

WINDERMERE SD4295 **Gilpin Lodge** *Crook Rd, Windermere, Cumbria LA23 3NE (015394) 88818* **£110**, plus special breaks; 14 marvellous rms with lots of space, sitting areas, super bthrms, and fine views. Impeccably run country house hotel with lovely gardens and grounds that take in ponds, woodlands and moor; big peaceful sitting rooms with antiques, fresh flowers, magazines, and open fires (no formal bar or reception desk), delicious food in three charming restaurant rooms, exceptional breakfasts and afternoon teas, and genuinely friendly, professional but unpretentious staff; free use of nearby Parklands Country & Leisure Club; children over 7; partial disabled access

WINDERMERE NY3902 **Holbeck Ghyll Country House** *Holbeck Lane, Windermere, Cumbria LA23 1LU (015394) 32375* **£170** inc dinner, plus special breaks; 20 individual rms with fresh flowers and sherry, many with fine views – 6 in new building (could be self-catering). Charming and warmly friendly country house in mature landscaped gardens and seven acres of woodland overlooking Lake Windermere, with tennis court, putting green, and croquet – their labradors like to walk with you; immaculate comfortable lounges (refurbished this year) with antiques and panelling, log fires, and very good food (vegetarian too) and wine in oak-panelled restaurant; health spa; children over 8 in evening restaurant; disabled access

WINDERMERE NY3801 **Langdale Chase Hotel** *Windermere, Cumbria LA23 1LW (015394) 32201* **£160**; 28 rms, many with marvellous lake view. Welcoming family-run hotel in lovely position on the edge of Lake Windermere with water-skiing and bathing from the hotel jetty; tennis, croquet, putting and rowing, afternoon tea on the terraces, gracious oak-panelled rooms with antiques, paintings, fresh flowers, open fires, very good food (huge breakfasts, too), and friendly service; disabled access

WINDERMERE SD4098 **Miller Howe** *Rayrigg Rd, Windermere, Cumbria LA23 1EY (015394) 42536* **£250** inc dinner, plus special breaks; 12 comfortable well equipped rms, many with fine views. Splendid, immaculately kept (and recently refurbished) Edwardian country house set high over the lake with unbeatable views from day rooms, conservatory and sloping garden, excellent evening meals, a remarkably wide-ranging New World wine list with helpful tasting notes, and super breakfasts; children over 8; cl Jan

WINTON NY7810 **Bay Horse** *Winton, Kirkby Stephen, Cumbria CA17 4HS (017683) 71451* **£35**; 2 clean, good value rms. Well kept unpretentious moorland pub in lovely setting, with welcoming low-ceilinged rooms, friendly owners, and good generous home cooking; well behaved children over 5

WITHERSLACK SD4384 **Old Vicarage** *Witherslack, Grange-over-sands, Cumbria LA11 6RS (015395) 52381* **£98**, plus special breaks; 13 individually decorated rms – some in the modern Orchard House are more spacious and have their own woodland terraces. Late Georgian vicarage in five acres of peaceful gardens and woodland, with two comfortable lounges, a log fire, good interesting food in cosy restaurant inc home-made bread, cakes and preserves, and hearty breakfasts; tennis and lots of surrounding walks; dogs welcome by arrangement

To see and do

Cumbria Family Attraction of the Year

RAVENGLASS SD1096 **Muncaster Castle & Owl Centre** (A595, 1m E) With its castle, owl centre, beautiful gardens and fun new maze, this grand old place has something to appeal to most members of the family, and its varied summer activities should easily fill an unhurried afternoon. The same family have lived in the elegant house since 1208, and will continue to do so as long as a magical glass drinking bowl remains intact. Extended over the centuries (esp the 19th) from its original tower, it still feels very lived in, and the rich furnishings and décor include some fine Elizabethan furniture and embroidery. The Walkman tour is particularly entertaining, narrated by the owner and enlivened by nuggets of family history and explanations of how they came across their various treasures (a painting by Gainsborough was the result of a bet). Young children will probably get the most out of the maze that opened in the old bear pit not too long before we went to press: the idea is they're a vole trying to cross a meadow, which they do by answering various environment-themed questions along the way, scratching the answers off a card. The owl centre also delights younger visitors: Muncaster is the HQ of the World Owl Trust, and they have over 180 birds from 50 different species. An interpretation centre has closed circuit TV of nesting owls, along with talks and flying displays at 2.30pm every afternoon Apr–Oct, weather permitting. Lots of rescued birds of prey in the lovely 77-acre grounds, which are rich in species rhododendrons; there are also some unusual trees, and a good adventure play area, with aerial runways and so on. Lots of walks and trails: best is the Terrace Walk, with hard-to-beat views of the Esk and surrounding mountains. Another takes in a number of plants more typically found in the Himalayas; they've been planted in an area where the soil and weather are roughly equivalent to an altitude of 11,000 ft in the Far East. Various special events, inc occasional open air theatre. Meals, snacks, shops, good plant centre, mostly disabled access; house open pm daily (exc Sat) from mid-Mar to early Nov, garden and owl centre open all year; (01229) 717614; £6 for everything (£4 children 5–15). The family ticket is good value at £17, and you can buy tickets just for the garden and owl centre.

Please let us know what you think of places in the *Guide*. Use the report forms at the back of the book or simply write us a letter.

ABBEY TOWN NY1751
Holme Cultram (B5302
Wigtown–Silloth) Remains of
formidably rich Cistercian abbey –
extraordinarily grand for this quiet
village. The New Inn at Blencogo has
good food – must book, on (016973)
61091.

ALSTON NY7146
This interesting little well weathered
Pennine market town is the highest of
its kind in England, with a surprising
number of pubs up and down its very
steep cobbled main street (the Angel is
best), and a couple of craft shops. *Oliver
Twist* was recently filmed here, and a
leaflet marks out the main sites that
were used (available from the gallery
below).
Gossipgate Gallery (The Butts) Local
art and crafts, with changing
exhibitions, a good big shop, and a new
garden with a tea terrace, and cultivated
flowers planted alongside their wild
ancestors; disabled access (though no
facilities); cl Jan–mid-Feb, most wkdys
mid-Feb–Easter and am wkdys
Nov-Dec, best to phone; (01434)
381806; free.
Hartside Nursery (A686 W of
Alston) Beautifully placed alpine
nursery with small streamside garden
and rare plants for sale; it's quite a draw
for birds and wildlife. Shop, some
disabled access with notice; cl Nov–Feb
(exc by appointment); (01434) 381372;
free.
South Tynedale Railway The chief
attraction around here, with diesel and
occasionally steam vintage narrow-
gauge train trips along a lovely winding
valley. They now also run a service up
to Kirkhaugh in Northumberland. Teas,
shop, disabled access by arrangement;
open wknds and bank hols Apr–Oct,
daily July–Aug (exc most Mons and
Fridays in July), and some wknds in Dec
– best to ring for timetable; (01434)
381696; fares from £3.50.

AMBLESIDE NY3704
A busy holiday-oriented shopping
centre inc excellent outdoor
equipment shops strung along its
central one-way system, with the
quaintest information centre in the
Lakes – the little NT shop in the tiny
stone Bridge House over Stock Ghyll by
the main car park. In the side lanes
above here are one or two attractive
older buildings. Traditional **glass
blowing** at Adrian Sankey, Rydal Rd;
good demonstrations and shop, but no
pressure to buy; (015394) 33039.
Hayes Garden World (Lake Rd) is a
big garden centre in landscaped
gardens; café, disabled access. The
Queens Hotel is good value for lunch.
Armitt Ambleside Museum 🖼
Decent local history museum with the
largest collection of Beatrix Potter's
watercolours, plus works by local
artists, photographers, several original
manuscripts by local writers, and
numerous archaeological remains.
Shop, disabled access; cl 25 Dec;
(015394) 31212; £2.50.
Brockhole (A591 S of Ambleside, or
launch from town pier) National Park
information centre in country house
with well landscaped gardens and
attractive lakeshore grounds; also
audio-visual show, exhibitions, and
adventure play area. Special talks and
events throughout the year. Meals,
snacks, shop, disabled access; visitor
centre cl Nov–Apr, gardens and
grounds open all year; (015394) 46601;
free, but charge for parking (£4 all day).
Stagshaw Garden (Waterhead, just
S) Hillside woodland garden with lovely
lake views, mature camellias,
rhododendrons, magnolias and
heathers; best in spring. Open daily
Apr–Jun then by appointment July–Oct;
(015394) 35599; £1.50; NT. Parking is
very limited. There's little left of the
Roman fort in nearby Borrans Park.

APPLEBY NY6820
An attractive riverside village; the main
street, rising from the harmonious
12th-c church to the castle, is still a
grand sight despite the cars, with a good
few handsome buildings inc a lovely
courtyard of almshouses. Pleasant
strolls by the River Eden. The Royal
Oak is most enjoyable for lunch.
**Appleby Castle Conservation
Centre** One of the best-preserved
Norman keeps in the country (the rest
of the buildings are later additions);
terrific views from the ramparts. The
Clifford family lived here for nearly 700
years, though they moved later to the
grander house next door, the Great

Hall of which has antiques, paintings and Chinese porcelain on display. The main feature of the attractive grounds is the big collection of birds, waterfowl and farm animals, in a lovely setting above the river; also brass rubbing, exhibitions and falconry displays. Meals, snacks, shop, limited disabled access; cl Oct–Easter (exc wknds); (017683) 51402; £4.50.

ARNSIDE SD4578

A good start for the 20-minute train trip along the N shore of Morecambe Bay to Ulverston: long viaducts, stupendous views. The Ship at nearby Sandside also has glorious views.

ARNSIDE KNOTT SD4577

Near Arnside, this looks across Morecambe Bay to the southern Lakeland fells – very rewarding views for walkers.

ASKHAM NY5123

An attractive village in fine scenery, with not one but two village greens – each with a good pub.

BARBON SD6282

An unpretentious village given appeal by its fine setting, just below the fells; the road from here to Dent via Gawthrop leads through lonely Barbondale, dominated by the Barbon Fell. The Barbon Inn is good.

BARROW-IN-FURNESS SD1969

The town shows the effects of the virtual collapse of shipbuilding in this country, on which it depended. The railway from here to Whitehaven hugs the coast and has good views, missed by the road, though in the other direction the A5087 to Ulverston has fine views across Morecambe Bay. The Anchor out at Lindal has decent food.

Dock Museum (North Rd) Futuristic-looking museum exploring how Barrow developed from a tiny hamlet to the biggest iron and steel centre in the world, before becoming renowned for shipbuilding; displays range from simple fishing boats to Trident submarines; also interactive displays and an adventure playground. Recent Lottery-funded additions include the rare Vickers ship model and photography collection. New café, shop, good disabled access; cl Mon (exc bank hols), plus Tues Nov–Easter; (01229) 894444; free.

Furness Abbey (slightly NE, towards Dalton) Impressive warm sandstone Norman remains of the one-time second richest monastery in England, with lovely arched cloisters, peaceful lawns, and views of pretty valley. Small museum, shop, disabled access; cl winter Mon and Tues, 24–26 Dec; (01229) 823420; £2.60; EH.

Sandscale Haws (SD1875) These dunes are protected as a **nature reserve**.

BASSENTHWAITE NY2332

Attractive close-set little village – the 12th-c parish church is three miles S; the Sun is an enjoyable pub. Escorted woodland **horse-riding** can be arranged from £14 an hour; (017687) 76949 for details. You can also hire rowing boats on Bassenthwaite Water. Readers tell us they know of few nicer sites for a caravan than the one at Englethwaite Hall near here.

Mirehouse (off A591 S) The family that still live in this modest 17th-c house once had excellent literary connections, so the fine rooms have mementoes of Wordsworth, Carlyle and Tennyson among others. Piano recitals in the music room, and on Weds in Jun, July and Sept they usually have displays of lace-making. Interesting garden (bee/butterfly plants) with changing poetry exhibitions in the verandah, as well as peaceful lakeshore grounds, lakeside church, and woods with well thought-out adventure play areas. Lots to do, with a surprising number of activities for children – they may even let them ring the gong in the house. Good home cooking in ex-mill tearoom, shop, disabled access; open Apr–Oct, house Sun and Weds pm, plus Fri pm in August, garden daily; phone for winter opening; (017687) 72287; £4, garden only £1.70.

BASSENTHWAITE LAKE NY2032

Trotters & Friends Animal Farm (Coalbeck Farm) Excellent for families; there are milking demonstrations, children can join in feeding, and there are plenty of other opportunities to get close to the animals. The 23-acre deer park is good for a picnic, and there are birds of prey and a reptile house. Indoor areas make it a good bet on drizzly days. Meals, snacks, shop, disabled access; cl wkdys Nov–Feb; (017687) 76239; £3.75.

BEETHAM SD4979

Heron Cornmill and Papermaking Well organised working watermill, dates back to 1096, though the current building is 18th-c; baking exhibition. Displays about the papermaking industry are in a converted barn next door. Shop; cl Mon (exc bank hols), and Oct–Mar; (015395) 65027; *£1.50. Beetham itself is attractive, with an interesting church, and the Wheatsheaf is good for lunch. From the village, a woodland walk leads to the Fairy Steps with rewarding views over the bay.

BINSEY NY2235

A pathless lump of a hill, but it rewards walkers with splendid views of the Lakes and Solway Firth (and into southern Scotland) by virtue of its geographical isolation.

BOOT NY1801

The steam railway from Ravenglass ends here, at Dalegarth Station, and Dalegarth Falls here are lovely. The Burnmoor Inn, very well placed for walkers, has extremely good value food; the Bower House and King George IV further down Eskdale at Eskdale Green are also good.

Eskdale Watermill Guided tours of attractively set 16th-c working two-wheeled mill, with a picnic area nr woodland waterfalls. Snacks, shop; cl Mon (exc bank hols), all Oct–Mar; (019467) 23335; £1.25.

BORROWDALE NY2517

Many people's favourite Lakeland base for walks, with good paths along or just above the River Derwent, especially from Grange (useful teashop). For lazier souls, the drive along the B5289 gives glorious views. Other prized walks giving or leading to fine views include mossy Johnny Wood (from Rosthwaite or Seatoller, where there's an NT centre exc in winter), and the two famous waterfalls, both best after rain, Taylorgill Force and Lodore Falls (behind Lodore Hotel).

BRAMPTON NY5563

Lanercost Priory (signed from town) Impressive and extensive remains of Norman priory, built with stone recycled from Hadrian's Wall. Shop, some disabled access; cl Nov–Easter;

£2; EH. The nave, picturesquely framed by an arch, was restored in the 18th c as a red sandstone church, and has stained glass by William Morris and Burne-Jones. The Abbey Bridge Inn by the priory has good food.

BROUGH NY7914

Brough Castle Classic ruined Norman fortress, in a romantic setting on moors above the village, with great views; free. The Golden Fleece is useful for lunch.

BROUGHAM NY5329

Brougham Castle (off A6 S of Penrith) A sturdy Norman ruin on steep lawns above riverside sheep pastures; climb to the top of the keep for the best view. Traces of Roman remains too, with a small exhibition of tombstones. Snacks, shop, disabled access; cl Nov–Mar; (01768) 862488; £2; EH.

Brougham Hall Craft Centre 13 different craft workshops inc metal workers, furniture restoration and home-made chocolates, in the attractive stone courtyard of a 15th-c Hall. Plenty to see around the house and grounds inc Cromwellian chapel and a collection of dolls and dolls' houses. Meals and snacks (in summer), shop, disabled access; cl 25 Dec; (01768) 862488; *£2 suggested donation.

BROUGHTON-IN-FURNESS SD2187

Small town with a local feel, and a busy little market square. A handy base for exploring the Duddon and other quieter Lakeland valleys. The Blacksmiths Arms has good food.

BUTTERMERE NY1815

A splendid varied flat walk circles the lake, with glorious views, plenty of safe opportunities for children aged 6 or more to let off steam, and even a tunnel; weather has to be really savage to spoil it. Parking at Gatescarth. The Bridge Hotel in the little village is good for lunch, and you can hire rowing boats.

Hay Stacks To the south of Buttermere and high above it, this is a challenging walk, but a rewarding one for the changing views, continuing on to Fleetwith Pike.

The ceiling of the Lakes The green slatey fells N of Buttermere offer keen

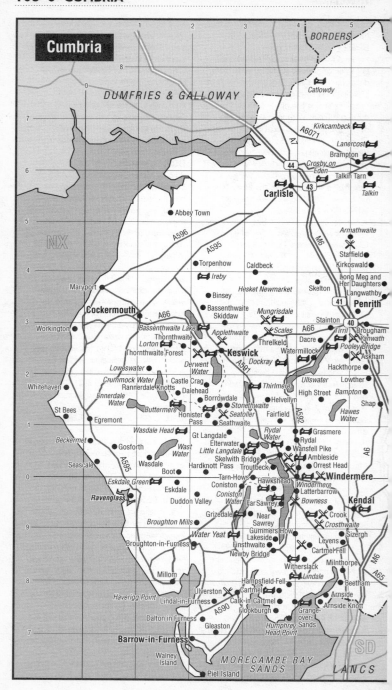

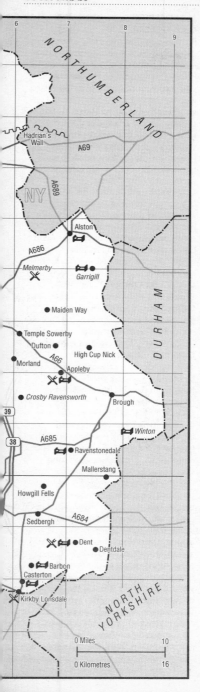

walkers superlative routes along high ridges: Whiteless Pike, Causey Pike, Crag Hill and Grasmoor are among the most exciting points.

CALDBECK NY3239
John Peel's grave can be found in the churchyard here, and the Oddfellows Arms has good generous food. There's a pretty drive to attractive Mungrisdale; alternatively, a pleasant stroll to a peaceful spot with a waterfall called the Howk.

CARK-IN-CARTMEL SD3577
Holker Hall & Gardens Opulently built and furnished mainly Victorian mansion with appealingly unstuffy feel despite the beauty. The glorious 25-acre formal and woodland gardens are among the best in the country, with spectacular water features, rose garden, rhododendron and azalea arboretum and rare plants and shrubs. Also deer park, entertaining motor museum, adventure playground, and a collection of old tools and gardening implements – enough to take up most of the day. Meals, snacks, shop, disabled access; cl Sat, and Nov–Mar; (015395) 58328; £3.50 gardens, grounds and exhibitions; Hall, motor museum. The nearby Engine is useful for lunch.

CARLISLE NY3956
A sizeable town, but not an obvious holiday destination, but plenty to interest the visitor, with several quietly attractive old buildings (and a very helpful visitor centre in one of them, the Old Town Hall). Work has begun on a new crossing over the River Eden as part of the National Cycleway, and on a riverside walkway along the West Wall.
St Cuthbert's church is remarkable for its mobile pulpit. The Crown & Mitre (English St) has a good value lunchtime buffet, and there's good home cooking in the Black Lion out at Durdar, where the attractively placed racecourse has meetings every month exc July; (01228) 522973 for dates.
Carlisle Castle This extensive medieval fortress, rather gaunt and forbidding, is surprisingly well kept considering its violent history. Interesting period furnished rooms, a portcullised gatehouse, lots of staircases and passages, and centuries of prisoners' carved graffiti in the

dungeons; good views from the ramparts. Snacks, shop, limited disabled access; cl 24–26 Dec; (01228) 591922; £3; EH.

Carlisle Cathedral This unpretentious abbey church, founded in 1122 and severely damaged in the Civil War, has fine stained glass; try to go on a bright morning when the sunlight comes streaming colourfully through the east window. Also medieval carvings inc the Brougham Triptych, painted panels and stonework, and crypt treasury. Meals, snacks, good shop (some tasty local foods), disabled access (exc to restaurant); free but donations encouraged.

Guildhall Museum (Green Market) A handsomely restored medieval timbered hall; worth a look inside if passing – some displays including interesting Guild silver. Cl Mon (exc bank hols) and all Nov–Easter; free.

Settle–Carlisle railway Running up Ribbledale and into the Cumbrian Pennines, stopping at Dent Station, Garsdale Head, Kirkby Stephen, Appleby, Langwathby and other Eden Valley villages, this is a memorable 70 miles of grand scenery, best from Appleby to Settle; (0345) 484950 for times and fares.

Solway Aviation Museum 🖃 (Aviation House, Carlisle Airport; on A869 between Carlisle and Brampton) Exhibits include several aircraft, Whittle's prototype jet engines and various displays on local airports used as airbases during the war. From the airport bar, you can watch planes taking off and coming in to land; snacks, shop, disabled access (not to aircraft); open Sun Apr–Oct; (01228) 573823; £2.50.

Tullie House (Castle St) Great fun: dramatic displays of Border history, using state-of-the-art techniques of sight, sound and smell. Children especially find lots to do, from exploring mine tunnels to trying out a Roman crossbow. The ground floor has a more conventional art gallery/museum, and a new gallery housing various millennial exhibits is due to open under Castle Way. Meals, snacks, shop, good disabled access; cl Sun am, 25–26 Dec, 1 Jan; (01228) 534781; £3.75 (get there between 10

and 11am Mon–Sat, and it's half-price).

CARTMEL SD3778
Picturesque little alleys lead off the delightfully harmonious central square – esp the one out through the former Priory gatehouse. The **Priory church**, which towers massively over the village, is an interesting mix of architectural grandeur from 12th to 16th c, inc fine carving. Lots of arts and crafts in the village, and Cartmel Village Store sells wickedly good sticky toffee pudding and Penrith fudge. The Cavendish Arms is good for lunch. The village can get particularly busy in summer.

CARTMEL FELL SD4189
In a wonderful tucked-away country location, **St Anthony's church** here has interesting early pews and a fine triple-decker pulpit. The Masons Arms is deservedly very popular indeed for lunch. The road here from Winster is very pretty.

CASTERTON SD6279
Brontë fans will want to see **Casterton School**; attractive pre-Raphaelite stained glass and paintings in the church result from enthusiastic Brotherhood holidays here. The Pheasant is good.

CASTLE CRAG NY2416
This impregnable-looking pinnacle can be reached by a path winding up the back, from Grange. It's a challenging hike, but gives terrific lake views.

COCKERMOUTH NY1130
Quietly attractive riverside town, increasingly worth a holiday visit, with a good wide range of places to visit. The comfortable Trout does good food.

Castlegate House (Castlegate) Friendly lived-in Georgian house opposite the castle, home to changing exhibitions of modern art, with Adam ceiling, warming winter fires, and sculpture in walled garden. Sales of paintings, disabled access; cl Thurs, Sun, and all Jan–Feb; (01900) 822149; free.

Jennings Brewery 🖃 Tours of traditional Castle Brewery, where the water for brewing is still drawn from the well that supplied the castle at the time of the Norman Conquest. Shop; tours 11am and 2pm Mar–Oct (plus 12.30pm mid-July–Aug) – booking advisable; (01900) 821011; £3. No children under 12.

Lakeland Sheep & Wool Centre

⊞ (off the A5086 slightly S)
Entertaining live show starring 19
different species of sheep and maybe a
few geese; they demonstrate shearing
and sheepdog trials, and an adjacent
exhibition is a worthwhile introduction
to the area. Show times 10.30am, noon,
2pm, and 3.30pm; no shows Mon or
Tues mid-Feb–Easter, and none at all
from mid-Nov–mid-Feb; meals, snacks,
shop, disabled access; cl 25 Dec, and
4–14 Jan; (01900) 822673; show *£3,
exhibitions free.

Printing House (next to
Wordsworth House) This working
print museum has a good range of
historic presses and equipment; you can
try out various printing methods. Shop,
disabled access; cl Sun, and all
Christmas–Easter; (01900) 824984;
*£2.75. The Norham opposite is a good
teashop.

Toy & Model Museum ⊞ (Market
Pl) Good expanding collection of mainly
British toys from the 20th c; shop,
limited disabled access; cl Dec and Jan
exc by appointment; (01900) 827606;
£2.60 (discount valid until Nov).

Wordsworth House (Main St) The
poet's happy childhood home, a
handsome restored 18th-c town house
with fine furniture, pictures by friends
and contemporaries, good original
panelling, and walled garden above
river. Well worth a visit in its own right
as well as for its Wordsworth
associations, and interesting to see how
different it is from the places he lived in
later on. Snacks, shop, some disabled
access (not to house); cl wknds (exc
Sats from Jun–Aug or before bank hols),
and Nov–Mar; (01900) 824805; £3; NT.

CONISTON SD2997
Unpretentious village at the foot of its
mountain, the Old Man. From Spoon
Hall there's **pony trekking** on the fells
above; cl Nov–Easter; (015394) 41391;
from £12 an hour.

Brantwood ⊞ Ruskin's rambling
Victorian house, with lots of his
furniture, books and paintings. It's
appealingly unstuffy, but the real
attraction is the surroundings and
setting, especially the very extensive
informal hillside woodland gardens
(best in late May/Jun). Good hour's walk
on nature trail, and mouth-watering

views of lake and fells. Meals, snacks,
good shop, disabled access (grounds
steep in places); cl winter Mon and Tues
and 25–26 Dec; (015394) 41396; £4.

Coniston Water walks There's a
lovely path on the W side, S of
Coniston; you can combine this walk
with one on a higher-level route along
the Walna Scar 'road' (an ancient hard
track closed to through traffic) beneath
the **Old Man of Coniston**, the
outstanding viewpoint of the vicinity.
Climb the Old Man from Coniston, go
up past the remains of copper mines,
and return down the Walna Scar Road.

Ruskin Museum ⊞ Eclectic mix of
displays, from local architecture and
lace-making to a video of Donald
Campbell's water speed record
attempts, and a virtual tour of local
copper mines on CD-rom. Naturally,
much is given over to the eponymous
Victorian philosopher, inc a look at his
watercolours, essays, and even his
funeral pall. Shop, disabled access; cl
mid-Nov–Mar (tel for winter opening);
(015394) 41164; £3. The nearby Black
Bull is good for lunch.

CONISTON WATER SD3197
An opulent Victorian **steam yacht**
sails daily end Mar–Oct, from Coniston
Pier, Brantwood and Park-a-Moor;
(015394) 41288 for times – best to ring
between 9 and 10.30am or you're likely
to get the answerphone; £4.70 for a 45-
minute trip. Or hire rowing or other
boats from the **boating centre** run by
the National Parks, 15 minutes' walk
from the village; usually cl Nov–Mar but
worth ringing; (015394) 41366; rowing
boats from £5 an hour (£1 each extra
person), motorboats from £10.

CRUMMOCK WATER NY1518
The scenery is less rewarding than
around Buttermere, but it's not to be
sniffed at. A good start for a walk is the
car park by **Lanthwaite Wood**, off
the B5289 towards Loweswater at the
N end; there's a pretty view from the
hill above the wood. You can hire
rowing boats on this lake, and if you're
keen to swim in one of the lakes this is
probably the best.

DACRE NY4626
Dalemain House Largely Elizabethan
despite the Georgian façade, and with a
number of even older features, so an

appealing variety of periods and style. Some rooms are grand, others are charming, with splendid furnishings and paintings and a good deal for children to enjoy. Particularly interesting Chinese Room with hand-painted wallpaper. There's an adventure playground, and deer in the carefully landscaped park with lake and mountain views. Atmospheric restaurant, shop, plant centre, disabled access to ground floor only; cl Fri and Sat, and mid-Oct to Mar; (017684) 86450; £5, £3 grounds. The village church has pre-Norman sculpture, and quaint medieval stone bears in the graveyard. The Horse & Farrier has decent food (and unusually an integral Post Office).

DALEHEAD NY2215
From Howtown there's a good walk up Martindale (where the church has attractive primitive stonework), then up over the fells to Bedafell Knott and down into Patterdale; hard work, but gorgeous views, Herdwick sheep, buzzards, ring ouzels.

DALTON-IN-FURNESS SD2273
The village has a rather austere square castle; the Black Dog (Broughton Rd) has decent food.

South Lakes Wild Animal Park 🖼
(Crossgates) Very committed and rapidly expanding wildlife centre, well placed for fine views of the entire Furness peninsula. A particular highlight is watching their Sumatran and Amur tigers clamber up a 20-ft vertical pole to hunt their meat (daily at 2.30). Also fun is the chance to hand-feed their big collection of kangaroos, the only place you can do this outside Australia. Gathered together according to the continents they hail from, residents include rhinos, zebra, giraffe, cheetah and wolves, with lots of smaller creatures such as meerkats, pandas, coatis and porcupines. A four-acre section has wallabies and emus waiting to be fed; play area, and a miniature railway (Apr–Sept). Snacks, shop, disabled access; cl 25 Dec; (01229) 466086; *£6.50 (*£3.50 children 3–15). Admission is half-price Nov–Feb.

DENT SD7087
Inside the modern outskirts is a delightful cobbled village (thought by some readers to be the prettiest in Lakeland), a rewarding end to an attractive drive – though now on the tourist trail, so busy in summer. During its heyday the town had a thriving knitting industry – Robert Southey even referred to the incessant knitters of Dent. The welcoming Sun brews its own beer, and the church is well worth a look; the views from the churchyard are spectacular. E of the village, towards Denthead, Colin Gardner (Stone House, Cowgill; cl wknds) makes traditional furniture. Dentdale has easy to middling walks, in the shadow of Whernside.

DENTDALE SD7586
Just on the Cumbrian side of the Yorkshire border, this offers walks along a lonely green track above the S side of the dale.

DERWENT WATER NY2523
With all its inlets and little islets, a pleasant place for pottering about in boats. It has gorgeous lakeside scenery, romantic little islets, ancient woodland, a variety of mountain backdrops. You can hire **rowing boats** and launches in Keswick (not Nov–Easter); from around £3 per hour. Regular launches run all year from Keswick to half a dozen points around the lake. Walks along the lake's west shore, best reached from car parks off the back road between Grange and Swinside, can be combined with the more demanding walk up Cat Bells for the best views of the lake.

Watendlath This lovely 'lost village' is little more than a tarn, a farm and a very modest café. There is a narrow road up from the B5289 by Derwent Water, but the village makes a very rewarding destination for a walk over the hills – for instance from Rosthwaite, where the Scafell is a fine walkers' local.

DUDDON VALLEY SD2296
This is a favourite starting point for rather more demanding walks, either by the river or up into the heights, with the Newfield Inn at Seathwaite a good base.

DUFTON NY6926
The High Pennines Over to the E of the Lakes, these have few walking routes and are extremely bleak: this is the reserve of the dedicated peat-bog enthusiast. An easy way to get an idea of the remoteness of these hills is to walk

along paths encircling **Dufton Pike** from Dufton (the Stag has good food).

EGREMONT NY0110
Dominated by its very ruined Norman castle; as so often, the gatehouse is the best preserved part. **Lowes Court Gallery** Georgian house with local arts and crafts for sale, disabled access; cl Sun, Weds pm and wkdys pm Jan–Feb; (01946) 820693; free.

Florence Mine Heritage Centre 🅰 (A595 just SE) Based around the last working iron ore mine in Europe. Tours of the pit (wknds and bank hols at noon – tel for wkdy times), and visitor centre with reconstructions of pit life at the start of the last century. Snacks, shop, disabled access to visitor centre; open wknds Apr–Oct, plus some wkdys in Apr, early May, and summer hols (best to phone), by appointment only Nov–Mar; (01946) 820683; *£6.50 pit tour, £1 visitor centre.

ELTERWATER NY3204
Idyllically placed village, with lake views. The Britannia is very popular for lunch. The B5343 past here gives awesome mountain views; you can keep on a poorer steeper road, passing pretty Blea Tarn, and coming back down through the gentler Little Langdale.

ENNERDALE WATER NY1016
Gentle walks by the lake (no boating) and through forestry, with high peaks above; the Fox & Hounds at Ennerdale Bridge is a good pub.

ESKDALE NY1700
Excellent for walks, esp around Boot. Here, a prime objective is the **Stanley Ghyll Force** waterfall, approached by a series of bridges and visible from a dizzying view-platform high above. From Trough House Bridge car park nr the waterfall you can walk along one side of the river to Doctor Bridge, then return the other side, for an easy route – with delectable views throughout. Other walks take you up towards the open fells (the landlord of the Burnmoor Inn is helpful with route suggestions). You can use the Ravenglass & Eskdale railway as part of a round trip.

FAIRFIELD NY3511
Rewarding for determined fell-walkers, climbed by a horseshoe layout of ridges from Rydal.

FAR SAWREY SD3895
Between the ferry here and the Wray Castle estate to the N can be found the cream of Windermere's waterside strolls, along the lake's W shore. The estate is a large NT tract with general public access. The forested slope rising from this shore has several well signposted routes, with Far Sawrey and Near Sawrey villages, and Latterbarrow, worthwhile objectives for circular walks.

FINTHSWAITE SD3788
Stott Park Bobbin Mill (just N) Set in coppiced woodland, this former water-and-steam mill made wooden cotton reels from 1835 right up to 1971; enthusiastic guides give excellent demonstrations of 19th-c industrial techniques. The mill is still powered by steam Tues–Thurs: the lathes look lethal. Snacks, shop, disabled access; cl Nov–Mar; (015395) 31087; £3; EH. The Swan at Newby Bridge is attractively set for lunch.

FLOOKBURGH SD3675
This peaceful village has excellent potted local shrimps, and a decent craft shop.

GLEASTON SD2671
Watermill 🅰 Well restored working watermill in peaceful surroundings, with a working corn mill, and a pleasant streamside walk. Good meals and snacks, shop, some disabled access; cl Mon (exc bank hols), plus Tues–Fri in winter; (01229) 869244; £1.50. The ruins of a partly built medieval castle are nearby.

GOSFORTH NY0603
The churchyard has a 10th-c carved cross, one of Britain's finest; there are more ancient carved hogback tombstones in the church. The working **pottery** may let you try making a pot (only in school hols); good shop. Cl Mon Oct–May plus Tues and Weds Jan–Feb, 25–26 Dec; (01946) 725296.

GRANGE-OVER-SANDS SD4077
This sedately old-fashioned resort is the start for summer guided walks over **Morecambe Bay Sands**, oddly other-worldly; glistening tidal flats, quick-stepping patrols of wading birds, distant hills, grisly tales of people and horses sucked under – a guide really is essential; phone Cedric Robinson, the

official guide appointed by the Queen, on (015395) 32165 for times.

GRASMERE NY3407

The pretty village swarms with visitors in summer, most of them here to see **Dove Cottage** – still much as Wordsworth had it in his most creative years (he completed 'The Prelude' here), with sister Dorothy's journals and his extensive cottage garden. Informative guided tours cope well with the bustle, but in early morning (opens 9.30) out of season you may get some space to yourself. The place always was crowded; barely big enough for two, with the poets' children and friends it often had a dozen or more people living here. The adjoining **Wordsworth Museum**, included in the price, has changing exhibitions and possessions of the poet and his family and friends, as well as a reconstructed Lakeland kitchen. Meals, snacks, shop, limited disabled access; cl Jan to first wk in Feb, 24–26 Dec; (015394) 35544; £5. Wordsworth is buried in the graveyard of the robust old church, which has quite an unusual interior. Sarah Nelson's gingerbread shop by the church is wonderfully old-fashioned. The Travellers Rest (A591) is our current pick for lunch. The lake itself, with Rydal Water and Elter Water, is the very heart of picturesque Lakeland. All three are famous for their lovely settings, and there are pleasant walks all around; you can even link all three together in a long afternoon's walk filled with glorious views. The walk up the good track to Easedale Tarn from Grasmere quickly gets you away from the crowds, into a fine valley; the lake itself is romantically set below rocks.

GREAT LANGDALE NY2806

Dominated by the awesome Langdale Pikes, this is the area's main centre for more serious fell-walking in grand scenery. One very popular shorter walk here is up the good track to Stickle Tarn, from the car park by the Stickle Barn (useful for refreshments), and Bow Fell and Crinkle Crags are two longer fell walks. Wainwrights, in the not specially graceful settlement of Chapel Stile off the B5343, another useful refreshment place, is particularly popular with many of our contributors

as a base for walks along here.

GRIZEDALE SD3394

Grizedale Forest Park Visitor Centre Woodland trails from short strolls to half-day walks, punctuated by 80 or so often hard-to-spot timber and rock sculptures. These trails are good when rain cuts off more open views; the sculptures are set in various spots throughout the forest (map from visitor centre). Lots of other activities too: craft centre, good information centre, orienteering, bike hire (it's an ideal area for cycling), and adventure play area. In all, six or seven square miles of mainly coniferous hillside timber to get lost in. Meals, snacks, shop, some disabled access; cl 25–26 Dec and 1 Jan; (01229) 860373; parking charge, £2 for 4 hrs. The Eagles Head at Satterthwaite (some winter closures) is good value for lunch, and the back roads through this area are quiet and pleasant.

GUMMERS HOW SD3988

An easy 20-minute climb from the road, for a fine lake view.

HACKTHORPE NY5224

Lowther Leisure Park 🎫 (signed off A6 S of Penrith) Plenty to keep children up to around 11 amused for most of the day (the pace is too sedate for teenagers). Some features have a refreshingly old-fashioned appeal: there's a circus with trapeze and clown acts, and the rides are more along the lines of a traditional funfair than gravity-busting roller-coasters. The attractive parkland has a developing wildlife area, as well as boating, miniature train rides, challenging play areas, and an archery range. Meals, snacks, shop, disabled access; open daily in Easter hols, wknds in May, then daily from spring bank hol till early Sept; £7.45. The Punch Bowl at Askham does interesting food.

HADRIAN'S WALL NY5664

Surviving traces of this far less known western section of the Roman wall can be reached on well signed paths from the lanes between the A69 and B6318 N of Brampton. For the Birdoswald Roman fort at Gilsland, see **Northumbria** chapter (the **goat farm** at Holme View nearby sells prize-winning traditional cheeses).

HAMPSFIELD FELL SD3979

A pleasant walk up through the woods

from Grange-over-Sands, giving terrific views over the bay from its limestone pavements and summit 'hospice' inscribed with 19th-c words of wisdom.

HARDKNOTT PASS NY2101
Hardknott Roman Fort Quite well preserved and interestingly restored, but most notable for its staggering lonely position high in the mountains; magnificent views to sea and even the Isle of Man. The drive up here is not for the faint-hearted – it's very steep and twisting, through this pass and Wrynose Pass, but the scenery makes it worthwhile; the Woolpack Inn at Bleabeck just W is good value.

HAWKSHEAD SD3598
Don't miss this virtually unchanged Elizabethan Lakeland village, with sturdy outside walls, and sheltered flower-filled inner courtyards. Though very popular with summer visitors, even at its busiest it has a pleasantly foreign 'different' feel, and the fact that cars are kept out helps a lot. The church has some eye-catching early 18th-c murals. The best nearby pub for lunch is the Drunken Duck up at Barngates. **Trout fishing** and **boat hire** on nearby Esthwaite Water, the largest stocked lake in the region.

Beatrix Potter Gallery (Main St) A generous annually changing selection of the original illustrations of Benjamin Bunny and other favourites, as well as rather different more acutely (almost acidly) observed drawings. A timed ticket system keeps it uncrowded – during holiday periods you may have to wait to get in. Shop; cl Fri, Sat, and Nov–Mar; (015394) 36355; £3; NT.

Old Grammar School Museum Now a museum, this is worth poking your nose into, if only to see where Wordsworth carved his name on a desk (he attended 1779–83); limited disabled access; cl 12.30–1.30, Sun am, and Nov–Easter; £2.50.

HELVELLYN NY3415
This famous Lakeland landmark is most easily (and crowdedly) tackled from Thirlmere, but much more exciting when reached from Glenridding and **Striding Edge**, where the path follows a narrow rocky edge (mild scrambling needed – best ascended rather than descended) above a great post-glacial

corrie; it's a day's severe walking, for perhaps the grandest and certainly the most popular of all Lakeland panoramas, with dramatic ridges leading off for miles.

HIGH CUP NICK NY7426
A great scoop in the ridge of the Pennines, this is one of the most dramatic features in the whole of the range, well worth the long but easily followed walk from Dufton.

HIGH STREET NY4515
One of Lakeland's great fell walks, this is a Roman ridge road, reached best from Hawes Water reservoir (the hotel here is a good stop).

HONISTER PASS NY2213
From the top of the pass stout-hearted and well equipped walkers can tackle Brandreth, and perhaps head on via Windy Gap for the least taxing ascent of **Great Gable**. Even if you decide not to go the whole way, the views in clear weather are spectacular.

HOWGILL FELLS SD6897
Bold 2,000-footers, empty and tough going even for hardened walkers; the easiest walks into them are up Winder from Sedbergh, and from the A683 N of Sedbergh to majestic **Cautley Spout** waterfall.

HUMPHREY HEAD POINT SD3874
This ¾-mile-long headland protruding into the sea gives walkers stunning views of Morecambe Bay.

KENDAL SD5192
A real town as opposed to a tourist centre, busy, with hectic traffic, but lots of small closes leading off the main street, some of them attractively restored to give a feel of what the place was like in the 18th-c heyday of the wool-weaving industry. The mint cake that takes its name comes in a surprising number of varieties. The Gateway (Crook Rd) is a good pub/restaurant.

Brewery Arts Centre (Highgate) Good changing events and exhibitions, café, bar, and landscaped garden; (01539) 725133 for what's on. K Shoes have a **factory shopping centre** at Netherfield (cl 25 Dec). Lakeland Canoes (Hollins Lane, Burneside) hire them by the day, and will take them to and fro for you. **Webbs Garden Centre** (Burneside Rd) is big, with lots of plants; decent café, disabled access.

Abbot Hall Art Gallery & Museum
(Kirkland) Beautifully restored
Georgian house with period furniture,
silver, china and glass and most
importantly an art collection that
reflects Kendal's importance in the 18th
c as the centre of an artists' school, and
includes works by Ruskin, Turner,
Constable, and esp George Romney.
Meals, snacks, good craft shop, disabled
access; cl 22 Dec–8 Feb; (01539)
722464; £3 (or £1 if you have visited
one of Kendal's other two museums).

Kendal Castle Ruin on a small hill on E
edge of town, the birthplace of Henry
VIII's wife Katherine Parr. There's little
more now than parts of the outer wall
with some towers – but children enjoy
it, and there are fine views. A humble
building associated with it is the **Castle
Dairy** (Wildman St), an unspoiled
Tudor house with some period
furniture, inc the oldest bed the V&A
have ever recorded. It's a restaurant
but they are happy to let people look
around.

Kendal Museum (Station Rd) Less
immediately appealing than the town's
other museums, this traditional place
takes a comprehensive look at local and
natural history and archaeology, with
lots of realistically mounted stuffed
animals, and a gallery devoted to the
work of Alfred Wainwright, the
walkers' guru. Shop, disabled access to
ground floor only; (01539) 721374; cl
Sun and 24 Dec–mid-Feb; *£3 (or £1 if
you have visited one of Kendal's other
two museums).

Museum of Lakeland Life (behind
Abbot Hall, Kirkland) Lovingly re-
created period rooms, shops and
workshops, and an almost palpable feel
of the past. Subjects as diverse as
shoemaking, Arthur Ransome and
Postman Pat. Snacks, shop, some
disabled access; cl 25 Dec to mid-Feb;
(01539) 722464; £3 (or £1 if you have
visited one of Kendal's other two
museums).

Quaker Tapestry Exhibition 🔄
(Friends Meeting House, Stramongate)
Bayeux-style tapestry history of the
Quaker movement. There are also
embroidery demonstrations. Shop,
disabled access; cl Sun and all Jan–Mar;

(01539) 722975; £3.

KESWICK NY2623
The tourist centre of the northern
Lakes, handy for Derwent Water, with
lots of Victorian villas (many of them
now guesthouses and small hotels)
outside quite a traditional centre, with
small cobbled closes running off the
main streets. It's full of breeches, boots
and backpacks in high season, with good
outdoor equipment shops, and is a
routine stop on coach tours. The Dog &
Gun and older-fashioned George Hotel
are very popular for lunch, with the
Pheasant out towards Crosthwaite also
good. The **Wild Strawberry** is a
quaint tearoom with an upstairs gallery;
cl Sun and Weds evenings. **Lakeside
Tea Gardens** (Lake Rd) have home
baking, lots for children, pleasant
modern furniture and crockery inside
and in garden with trees and
chaffinches; cl about 6pm. George
Fisher (Borrowdale Rd) is a good big
outdoors shop. The new Theatre by the
Lake seats 400 people; cl some Suns;
box office (017687) 74411. The back
road around Swinside is pretty, and in
clear weather is worth following up the
gauntly formidable Keskadale Pass.

Cars of the Stars Motor Museum
🔄 (Standish St) Unusual collection of
cars from film and TV dating back to
Laurel & Hardy's Model T Ford, taking
in Chitty Chitty Bang Bang, the
Batmobile and cars used by James Bond,
the Flintstones and Postman Pat along
the way. Shop, disabled access; open
Easter–New Year (wknds only in Dec)
plus Feb half-term; (017687) 73757; £3.

Castlerigg stone circle (just E) This
neolithic monument is well preserved,
and gives photogenic perspectives of
the mountains (the best times for
pictures are morning and evening); take
a map to identify the peaks it aligns with.
There's a brief explanation of the
stones' history. NT.

Dodd Wood (off A591 N) Marked
walks through the woods, or on open
hillside, with Bassenthwaite views.

Friar's Crag An easy walk S, this gives
exquisite views of Derwent Water,
with more prospects unfolding as you
walk up to Castlehead Wood (there's
more direct access to this from a car
park on the B5289 S).

Keswick Museum & Art Gallery 🔲
(Fitzpark, Station Rd) Thoroughly
traditional; the Poets Corner stands
out. Shop, disabled access; cl
Nov–Easter; (017687) 73263; £1
(discount valid until Nov).

Pencil Museum (Southey Works)
Alongside the Derwent pencil factory,
this surprisingly interesting museum has
some unexpected exhibits inc, at 7 ft,
the world's tallest pencil. Shop, disabled
access; cl 25–26 Dec, and 1 Jan;
(017687) 73626; £2.50.

Teapottery (Central Car Park Rd)
The only shape you won't see among
the often ludicrous examples here is the
traditional one we all have in our
kitchens; shop, disabled access to
ground floor only; cl 25–26 Dec, 1 Jan;
(017687) 73983; free.

Walla Crag S of town and a steep walk
up above Great Wood (often teeming
with red squirrels), this gives fairly high
views over Derwent Water; a
moorland path heads to the photogenic
Ashness Bridge, from where a
rewarding return walk is one down to
the shore and back again.

KIRKBY LONSDALE SD6178
Small and usually quiet town of
considerable character, interesting old
yards and ginnels and good country
shops; it's more lively on Thurs
country-market day. Behind the fine
church of St Mary is a pretty stretch of
the River Lune, good for walking or just
lazing about – even swimming if it's hot.
Along here 87 steps lead up to Ruskin's
View, a beautiful panorama over the
Lune Valley, appealing countryside little
visited by tourists. The Snooty Fox has
good food. The lovely old Devils' Bridge
that spans the River Lune just below the
town dates from the 12th c.

KIRKOSWALD NY5541
This attractive village has the ruins of a
13th-c castle, views towards the
Pennines, and a useful pub.

LAKE WINDERMERE SD4096
The most popular boating lake, so the
easiest place to hire **rowing boats** and
other vessels. However, the
Government's decision to implement a
10mph speed limit from 2005 will
significantly reduce the scale of water
sports on the lake. Lots of launches, of
all sorts of shapes and sizes, run cruises

of varying lengths from Bowness Bay,
Ambleside, Waterhead and (not
Nov–Mar) Newby Bridge. The pick of
the sightseeing boat trips is the 45-min
tour on the silent steam launch *Osprey*,
though it's available only to visitors to
the Steamboat Museum (see separate
entry). The pier at the S end of the lake
is the terminus for the Haverthwaite
steam railway. Rowing boats can be
hired from the Bowness Bay Boating
Co; from £2.50 an hour. They also have
motorboats, and a number of launches
– at least one of which is equipped to
take disabled people; (015394) 43360
to check. Lake Holidays Afloat do
motorboats too; (015394) 43415; from
£14.20 per hour. A pleasant place to
hire rowing boats (not Nov–Easter) is
Fell Foot Park nr Newby Bridge, an
18-acre park with plenty of room for
lakeside picnics; café and shop (cl
Nov–Easter), some disabled access;
(015395) 31273; parking charges (from
£1.50), rowing boats £5 per hour for
two people; NT. They can provide
details of boating and fishing on other
NT waters. Maples (Marina Village,
Bowness) do day, wknd or longer
cruises and courses on large sailing
yachts; (07889) 773292; from £135 a
day. Windsurfing or waterskiing can be
arranged at Low Wood Water Sports
Centre, Windermere; windsurfing,
canoeing or dinghy sailing Mar–Oct at
Windermere Sailing Centre, Rayrigg
Rd, Windermere. The chain ferry
linking the ferry road below Bowness
with the Hawkshead road below Far
Sawrey is a utilitarian way of taking to
the water; but though it runs every 20
mins and saves miles of driving, queues
mean that it saves time only out of
season.

LAKESIDE SD3791
Graythwaite Hall Gardens (2m N)
Well kept late Victorian garden, strong
on rhododendrons and late-spring
shrubs. Open Apr–Jun only; (015395)
31248; *£2.

Lakeside & Haverthwaite Railway
A short steam trip running up to
Haverthwaite. There's a small
collection of steam and diesel
locomotives. Meals, snacks, shop,
disabled access; trains daily Apr–Oct;
(015395) 31594 for times; £3.70 return.

The White Hart at Bouth does good food.

LANGWATHBY NY5734

Eden Ostrich World 🖽
(Langwathby Hall Farm) Pigs, shire horses, ducks, geese and of course ostriches at this friendly farm. Meals, snacks, shop, disabled access; cl Nov–Feb; (01768) 881771; £3.75.

LATTERBARROW SD3699

A dwarf in comparison to the great Lakeland fells, but elevated enough above a relatively low-lying area to give views over Windermere and Langdale.

LEVENS SD4985

Levens Hall (A6) Impressive Elizabethan mansion based around older core, with fine carved oak chimney-pieces, ceiling plasterwork, Spanish leather panelling, period furnishings and interesting paintings. The magnificent topiary gardens in their original layout of 1692 are perhaps the highlight, the fantastic shapes really standing out against the ancient grey stone of the house. Also model and other steam engines (pm only; in steam, some bank hols and some summer Suns), play area, grand beech trees, and deer park. Snacks, plant sales, shop, disabled access to grounds only; open Sun–Thurs, Apr–mid-Oct (plus gardens open wkdys till end Oct); (015395) 60321; £5.50, £4 grounds only. The Hare & Hounds is good for lunch.

LINDAL-IN-FURNESS SD2576

Colony Country Store View the candlemakers at work then browse among the vast array of candles and other gifts in the shop; disabled access; cl Sun am, 25 Dec and 1 Jan; (01229) 461102. Chandlers Café next door has good value home-made food.

LONG MEG AND HER DAUGHTERS NY5737

There's access off the lane N of Little Salkeld to this quaintly named **stone circle**.

LOWTHER NY5323

Lakeland Bird of Prey Centre 🖽
Set in the huge Victorian walled garden at Lowther Castle, hawks, eagles, owls, buzzards and falcons, with flying displays at 11.30am, 2 and 4pm. Also craft gallery. Teas, shop, disabled access; cl Nov–Feb; (01931) 712746; £5.

MAIDEN WAY NY6433

The back road from Langwathby on the A686 through Skirwith to Kirkland leads to this **Roman road**, still sound for walkers, which plunges northwards into the bleak high Pennines, giving a great feeling of solitude. There are other walks from the clusters of sheep farms along the foot of the Pennines between here and Appleby.

MALLERSTANG NY7800

This area, which the B6259 S of Kirkby Stephen runs through, is reckoned by some readers to be one of the best places to stay for a short break.

MARYPORT NY0336

There's a straightforward **maritime museum** on Senhouse St (cl Sun exc summer pms, and Fri and Sat lunchtimes; donations) and an **aquarium** on South Quay (snacks, shop, disabled access; cl 25–26 Dec; £4.25). Elizabeth Dock is home to two fully restored **steamships**, bought from the council for £1 by local volunteers; best to check opening times on (01900) 815954; £2 recommended donation. The B5300 N has good views across to Scotland.

Senhouse Museum 🖽 (The Battery, Sea Brows) Impressive collection of Roman military altar stones and inscriptions, dug from the former fort next door from the 1570s onwards, making it one of the oldest collections of antiquities in the country; also other artefacts inc a Celtic serpent stone. Snacks, shop, disabled access; open Fri–Sun all year, plus Tues and Thurs Apr–Jun, bank hols, and daily July–Oct; (01900) 816168; *£2.

MILLOM SD1779

Not much of a town, but there's an interesting **church**, and ruined **castle** around what's now a farm (A5093 N: ask at the house for permission to look round the ruins). The decent **folk museum** on St George's Rd should have moved to another site in town by the time you read this; tel (01229) 772555 for new details. S of the town a broad lagoon built to protect former mineworks is now a bird reserve (also home to natterjack toads), the loneliness exaggerated out of season when the nearby unsmart but enjoyable little resort of Haverigg SD1678 (great beaches, good sailing and fishing) has closed down; the Harbour Inn has good cheap food, good walks in the wildflower dunes.

Haverigg Point (nr Millom) This huge stretch of impressive dunes is a high point on this section of coast, but virtually the whole length from Ravenglass down to Hodbarrow Point is good for breezy seaside walks – lots of long beaches, deserted except in high season.

MILNTHORPE SD5078

Lakeland Wildlife Oasis 🖼 (Hale; A6 S of Milnthorpe) Millions of years of evolution flash before your eyes at this lively jungle house, a fascinating cross between zoo and museum. Interactive displays alongside the brightly coloured and unusual fish, birds, insects and animals, and woodland where children can crawl along tunnels overlooking the meerkat enclosure. Activities include fossil rubbing and an animal rubber-stamping trail. Snacks, shop, disabled access; cl 25–26 Dec; (015395) 63027; £5.50. The B5282 to Arnside has quiet estuary and mountain views.

MORLAND NY6022

Highgate Farm 🖼 Cheerful farm with plenty of fun activities from cuddling bunnies and egg collecting to pony rides, pig feeding and sheep racing; children's quad bikes, and indoor play barn with go-karts and a sandpit. Snacks, shop, disabled access; cl Nov–Easter; (01931) 714347; £5.95.

NEAR SAWREY SD3795

Hill Top Small, remote 17th-c farmhouse, kept exactly as it was when owned by Beatrix Potter, who wrote many of her stories here. The NT is worried about the effect of too many visitors, so limit the daily number to 800. It's so small they don't allow many people in at once, so if you do decide to visit be prepared to queue. Shop, disabled access to ground floor by prior arrangement; cl Thurs, Fri, and all Nov–Mar; (015394) 36269; £4; NT. The old-fashioned NT-owned Tower Bank Arms (with nicely furnished bedrooms) is pictured in *The Tale of Jemima Puddle-Duck*.

NEWBY BRIDGE SD3787

Aquarium of the Lakes By the steamer stop is this imaginatively laid out aquarium-style centre which vividly demonstrates the story of a local river. You can walk in see-through tunnels along a re-created lake bed, with the area's animal (inc otters), insect, bird and plant life all around, and there's a water lab with microscopes for close-up examinations of tadpoles, plankton and larvae. Snacks, shop, disabled access; cl 25 Dec; (015395) 30153; £5.25.

ORREST HEAD SD4199

A short steep walk (half-hour each way) from Windermere (opposite station), this gives spectacular views over the lake and the Pennines, lovely at sunset.

PENRITH NY5130

A real locals' rather than tourists' town, and the biggest in Lakeland. It's very much a northern country town, with solid stone streets, farmers from far and wide descending on its Skirsgill agricultural market (Sat), and genuinely traditional Lakeland shops selling real fudge and toffee, rich cakes (Birketts), local cheeses (Grahams), prize Cumberland sausages (Cranstons), local antiquarian books, and cheap and sturdy country clothes. John Norris (21 Victoria Rd) is the outstanding fishing/outdoor wear shop, with something for everyone at good prices. A **museum** on Middlegate is a useful introduction to the area, and the George does decent lunches.

Oasis Holiday Village Six miles out of Penrith in Whinfell Forest is the Rank Organisation's Center Parcs style holiday village. It's been very well thought out as far as visitors are concerned, and for small groups the lodges are pretty good value; (01768) 893000.

Penrith Castle Built in the 14th c as a defence against Scottish raids, and the home of Richard III when he was Duke of Gloucester. The ruins are surrounded by a park; free.

Rheged Discovery Centre (Redhills) Named after the Celtic kingdom which once stretched from Strathclyde to Cheshire, this vast new development – Britain's largest grass-covered building – is set right into a hillside, and pays homage to all things Cumbrian. The history of the county is brought to life on a cinema screen the size of six double-decker buses, and a separate video display takes a look at contemporary life through the eyes of six local people. Also changing exhibitions of local art (some of it for sale), an in-house potter, workshops, and specialist shops and restaurants promoting local produce. A hands-on exhibition devoted to the history of mountaineering should open later this year. The huge glass atrium gives views across to the High Pennines. Meals, snacks, shop, disabled access; (01768) 868000; cinema £4.95.

St Wilfred's church (B6262 E of Eamont Bridge) A striking exception to the usual Lakeland rule of simplicity in churches, filled with magnificent furnishings inc Continental treasures; candlelit.

Wetheriggs Pottery 🖼 (Clifton Dykes, signed off A6 S) Interesting and very smart working pottery – one of the oldest in the country – with 19th-c steam engine and equipment; children can try their hands at the wheel, and there's a play area, birds of prey and rare breeds of pig. Restaurant, shop, disabled access; cl Tues, plus Weds Nov–Easter, 25–26 Dec, and 1 Jan; (01768) 892733; free (exc Aug, £2.50).

PIEL ISLAND SD2363
Small island shared by a basic inn and a grand 14th-c ruined fortress commanding Barrow Harbour and Morecambe Bay. It's reached by ferry (by arrangement only in winter) from Roa Island nr Barrow.

RANNERDALE KNOTTS NY1618
Best reached by a walk via Low Bank from Buttermere village, this vantage point gives good views of Crummock Water and the hills surrounding it. The green slatey fells N offer walkers superlative routes along high ridges: Whiteless Pike, Causey Pike, Crag Hill and Grasmoor are among the most exciting points.

RAVENGLASS SD0896
Pretty sailing harbour by the well sheltered Esk estuary; in summer a local fishing boat sells freshly caught fish on the shore. The so-called **Walls Castle** just outside the village is actually a Roman bath house; its walls stand taller than any other building of its age so far north.

Muncaster Castle & Owl Centre

See separate family panel on p. 104.
Muncaster Mill (A595 NE) A well restored working watermill with Victorian machinery, and flour for sale. Cl Nov–Easter (exc some wknds); (01229) 717232; *£2. They also do good value B&B.

Ravenglass & Eskdale Railway
England's oldest narrow-gauge steam trains, lovingly preserved, with open carriages chugging up seven miles of unspoilt valley to Dalegarth; admirers say it's the most beautiful train journey in England. Cafés each end, and a small museum at Ravenglass. Shop, disabled access (with notice); cl most of Nov–Mar, but best to phone for train times and dates; (01229) 717171; £6.80 return. Good three-hour summer walk back from Boot (walks booklets from stations).

RAVENSTONEDALE NY7203
The village is notable more for its pleasant riverside scenery than for its buildings – apart from the unspoilt church which escaped Victorian refitting; longitudinal pews, three-decker pulpit, steeply pitched gallery (steep stairs up), and fine east window memorial to Fothergill family (one was last female Protestant martyr to be burned at the stake). Choose a bright day for best light. The Black Swan and Kings Head both have decent food.

RYDAL NY3606
Rydal Mount 🖼 (A591)
Wordsworth's sister Dorothy described Rydal as 'a paradise' when the family moved here from Grasmere in 1813; they stayed for the rest of their lives. The house itself is rather modest, with family portraits and period furniture, and it's what's outside that really stands out – the good-sized garden is still much as the poet laid it out, consciously picturesque, with original ideas that people are still rediscovering today. The setting is lovely, overlooking mountains and lakes, and they often have readings of the poetry it inspired. Shop, limited disabled access; cl Tues Nov–Feb, and the last three weeks of Jan; (015394) 33002; £3.75. Decent campsites nearby. The Glen Rothay Hotel does respectable lunches.

SEASCALE NY0204

Sellafield Visitor Centre (off A595) Not everyone approves of the pro-nuclear PR, but children certainly enjoy the hands-on Disney-style approach to the industry at this nuclear power visitor centre with imaginative exhibitions and displays. Meals, snacks, shop, disabled access; cl 25 Dec; (019467) 27027; free. Seascale itself has a pleasant beach, and a singularly scenic golf course, where every hole offers views of the sea or the mountains; the third tee ironically puts Sellafield into the same frame as a ring of prehistoric stones.

SEATHWAITE NY2109
Packhorse track Determined fell-walkers enjoy the unspoilt packhorse track from Seathwaite over **Styhead Pass** down into Wasdale. The summit of the pass is a start point for a fiercely dramatic route up Scafell Pike.

SEDBERGH SD6390
Hardy small town at the foot of the Howgill Fells, with a helpful Yorkshire Dales National Park Centre on Main St (cl Dec–Easter). A while ago it replaced its picturesque cobbles with an ordinary surface – much to the chagrin of the National Parks and English Heritage, who only a few years previously paid for new cobbles. The Dalesman is good for lunch.
Holme Farm 🔳 (Middleton, just SW of Sedbergh) 2pm tours of traditional hill farm, with plenty of young animals and nature trail. They do occasional evening tours with badger watch. Disabled access; cl Oct–Feb exc by arrangement; (015396) 20654; *£2. You may be able to camp here.

SHAP NY5514
Shap Abbey (left towards Keld off A6 going N out of village) The best feature is the unspoilt and undeveloped riverside seclusion; the abbey itself is very ruined, but you can trace the 13th-c layout in some detail. Nearby **Keld Chapel** is a lonely untouched shepherds' church in a riverside hamlet, and the gated Swindale road signed off the Bampton road nr Rosgill is pretty. The Greyhound is good value for lunch.

SIZERGH SD4888
Low Sizergh Barn Plenty of fresh farm foods (cheese, meat, ice-cream, sausage and bread), and other local produce inc Morecambe Bay shrimps. Also craft shop and pick-your-own strawberries (late Jun–July). A nature trail around the farm will be ready later this year. The tearoom overlooks the milking parlour and makes a handy place for lunch. Meals, snacks, shop; cl 25–26 Dec and 1 Jan; (015395) 60426; free.
Sizergh Castle Lovely lakeside house, over the centuries harmoniously extended from its original sturdy 14th-c tower by the family who have lived here for generations. Fine Tudor and Elizabethan carving, panelling and furniture, Jacobite relics, and terraced gardens surrounding a grand flight of steps down to water. Lots to interest a gardener, inc an enormous rock garden, Japanese maples, water garden, wild flowers, and daffodils in the crab-apple orchard; the autumn colours are lovely. Snacks, shop, disabled access to garden and ground floor of house; open pm Sun–Thurs Easter–Oct; (015395) 60070; £4.60, £2.30 garden only; NT.

SKELTON NY4635
Hutton-in-the-Forest (B5305) Some say this formidable mansion was the castle of the Green Knight of Arthurian legend. Grandly extended in the 17th c from its 14th-c peel tower core, then castellated more recently, it has a magnificent panelled gallery. A terraced garden runs down to the lake; there's an 18th-c walled formal garden, and a more romantic Victorian garden with grand trees, dovecot and woodland nature walk. Snacks, shop; garden open daily (exc Sat), house open pm Thurs, Fri and Sun Apr–Sept, plus Easter wknd and all bank hols; (01768) 484449; £4, £2.50 garden only.

SKELWITH BRIDGE NY3403
Kirkstone Galleries Stylish displays reflecting current fashions in home furnishing, from kitchen paraphernalia to mirrors and lamps. The extensive shop sells a range of good quality gifts (not cheap) inc ornaments made from the attractive green Kirkstone, quarried only in Cumbria. Coffee shop, some disabled access; (015394) 34002; free. The Skelwith Bridge Hotel does good value bar lunches.

SKIDDAW NY2629
One of Cumbria's great peaks, but more accessible than many – quite an

easy haul up from Applethwaite, for far views.

ST BEES NX9511

Cliffs and birds The Cumbrian coast has one particular lure for walkers and bird watchers: the cliff path between Whitehaven and St Bees – each town has a railway station. From the beach car park NW of St Bees an easy walk takes you up the nature-reserve sandstone headland, famous for its bird life, and with magnificent sea and hill views.

STAFFIELD NY5342

Nunnery Walks These are private paths through old woodland, taking you through a lovely **Eden Valley** river gorge with waterfalls and quiet pools; teas; £1.75. There are other good free walks in this delightfully wooded sheltered valley, for instance from Armathwaite and Wetheral. The Eden Valley has the reputation of staying dry when it's pouring over in Lakeland.

STAINTON NY4827

Alpaca Centre The first centre for this fleecy Andean animal in Britain; you can view them in their paddocks, from the tearoom, or get up close on a field walk (£1). Shop, disabled access; cl 25–26 Dec, 1 Jan; talks by prior arrangement; (01768) 891440; free. The Kings Arms is good for lunch.

TALKIN TARN NY5457

Lovely lake with partly wooded shores, peaceful mountain views, plenty of space for strolling; nature trail, orienteering and rowing boats; disabled access, teas. The village is pretty; the Blacksmiths Arms is popular for food.

TARN HOWS SD3299

An easy hour's walk from Hawkshead, this is a gorgeously photogenic small lake; particularly beautiful on a still clear autumn day.

TEMPLE SOWERBY NY6128

Acorn Bank Garden Richly planted terraced and walled garden with 250 varieties of medicinal and culinary herbs, clematis, unusual old fruit trees, and herbaceous borders; the steep wild garden drops down to the stream. The wheel of the restored mill down here turns at wknds. This is a lovely spot at daffodil time. Shop, tearoom, disabled access; cl Nov–Mar; (017683) 61893; £2.30; NT. The B6412 to Lazenby and

then the back road through the Eden valley to Armathwaite and on up to Wetheral gives delicious quiet views.

THORNTHWAITE NY2225

Thornthwaite Galleries Fine art, pottery and other crafts, as well as teas, summer try-your-hand-at-it demonstrations, and a play area. Snacks, shop, disabled access (but no facilities); cl Tues, Mon–Thurs in Nov, and all Dec–Feb; (017687) 78248; free. The Coledale Inn at Braithwaite is good for lunch (and walkers).

THORNTHWAITE FOREST NY2124

The first-ever Forestry Commission plantation: walks through it, and up to the fells above (with lake and mountain views), are best started with a visit to the Whinlatter Visitor Centre (B5292 above Braithwaite). This has good explanatory forestry displays, shop, forest maps, teas.

THRELKELD NY3123

Scenic road The B5322 Threlkeld–Thirlmere is pretty, with a very photogenic view of Clough Head from the Brigham/Keswick side road turning off just past Yew Tree Farm.

TORPENHOW NY2039

Torpenhow church A formidably Norman building, striking in itself but worth looking at closely, for the even older Roman masonry.

TROUTBECK NY4100

Holehird Garden (off A592 S of Troutbeck) The Lakeland Horticultural Society's hillside garden – five acres of well grown plants in wide variety, inc National Collections of hydrangeas and some other families; lovely views. Open all year (exc 25 Dec, 1 Jan), but manned in summer only; (015394) 46008; donations (they rely on these to maintain the gardens). Rookin House Farm has accompanied **horse-riding**, beginners welcome; (017684) 83561; £11.50 an hour. The quaint Queens Head is an excellent place.

Townend The perfectly preserved home of a comfortably off, very traditional farming family who lived here for 300 years till the 1940s, the house showing little change over all that time. Solid simple unshowy comfort, and a sensible, down-to-earth and entirely self-sufficient layout. This is one of several such beautifully placed 'statesmen's' farms making up this lovely village strung along the steep valley below high fells. Braille guide; cl am, all day Mon (exc bank hols) and Sat, and Nov–Mar; (015394) 32628; £3; NT.

ULLSWATER NY4421
Here elegant Victorian steamers converted to diesel run between Pooley Bridge, Howtown and Glenridding; disabled access, cl Dec–Mar. Motor boats can be hired from Ullswater Marina at Watermillock, (017684) 86415, and the sailing school at Glenridding has a range of canoes and sailing dinghies for hire – some experience of sailing necessary to hire a sailboat though they do give introductory lessons – (017684) 82541; cl winter. Rowing and other boats can be hired from Tindals in Glenridding; (017684) 82393; around £5.50 per hour, motorboats around £14.

Aira Force waterfall This is the best-known walk on Ullswater's W side – a pleasant if rather populated stroll of a mile or so from the car park on the A592 just NE of the A5091 junction, through NT lakeshore woods to the waterfalls themselves, and the Gothick folly of Lyulph's Tower, with Wordsworth's daffodils a bonus in spring; above here, Gowbarrow Park has the best lake views on this side. Aira Force is a 20-metre (65-ft) waterfall, at its best after rain or on a misty morning; restaurant and shop, £1.50 (£3 all day) parking charge. The Royal Hotel at Dockray is handy.

Ullswater walks The E shore is outstanding; there are many different views, with a rewarding combination of waterside stretches and higher ground – from which to see more sweeping vistas. On the best and most popular stretch, Howtown–Patterdale– Glenridding, you will meet quite a few other people in summer (when it can be combined with the steamer for a round trip; best to take the steamer on the way out in case the service is cancelled). The charmingly old-fashioned Howtown Hotel is a good break in a stunning setting, and Hallin Fell nearby gives an aerial view of the lake.

ULVERSTON SD2878
This town holds the bizarre double claim of being the birthplace of both pole-vaulting and the Quaker movement. The Pork Pie Shop at the N end of Market Pl is very good indeed, while the Dolls' House Man (Furness Galleries, Theatre St) makes dolls' houses, farms, wooden animals and so on, and usually has examples on display. The **Heritage Centre** on Lower Brook St has local history displays (cl Sun, and most Weds Oct–Easter; £2). The Farmers Arms (Market Pl) has good food, and the Bay Horse out at Canal Foot is very good for lunch.

Conishead Priory (Priory Rd) There's a Buddhist Temple in the grounds here; guided tours of the priory around £2; open pm most wknds and bank hols Easter–Oct.

Lakes Glass Centre (Oubas Hill) Watch the craftsmen blowing, cutting and engraving. The factory shop is good value, with cheap seconds. Meals, snacks, shop, disabled access; cl 25–26 Dec; (01229) 584400; £2.

Laurel & Hardy Museum (Upper Brook St) The owner of this unique exhibition (a former mayor) really knows his subject, and it's his obvious enthusiasm that makes this one of Lakeland's best-loved attractions. Fittingly in Stan Laurel's home town, with delightfully informally presented mementoes and all-day films. Shop, disabled access; cl Jan; (01229) 582292; £3.

Swarthmoor Hall Elizabethan manor known as the birthplace of Quakerism, after George Fox was sheltered here in 1652. The interior has been lovingly restored with period furnishings, and they've rebuilt an old barn within the grounds. Guided tours available pm Thurs, Fri and Sun Apr–Sept; (01229) 583204; £2.50.

WALNEY ISLAND SD1869
Over the bridge from Barrow, this has some long roads of low houses but is mostly a windswept sweep of duney grass, very offshore-feeling; nature reserves at both ends, with excellent bird-watching and interesting plants. The George has decent food.

WANSFELL PIKE NY3904
Gained by a path from Ambleside, this is

toylike in size compared with the bigger fells, but the view is as good as from many more imposing peaks.

WASDALE NY1808

The start for many magnificent fell walks, inc the ascents of Great Gable and Scafell Pike; one less taxing walk is straight up the head of the valley to the summit of Black Sail Pass and back. Apart from around the interesting churchyard, it's not so good for gentle strolls, and parking at Wasdale Head can be a problem in summer or at holiday times. Besides the Wasdale Head Hotel, the Strands lower down is a useful stop for food.

WATERMILLOCK NY4422

The church is worth stopping at for its evocative photographs of all its 1930s parishioners. **Sailing dinghies** can be hired by competent sailors from Ullswater Marina here.

WHITEHAVEN NX9718

Planned as an 18th-c industrial town and major port, the restoration of this interesting place continues after its decline. The harbour is attractive at high tide (a bit dirty at low tide). Michael Moon's **bookshop** (Lowther St) has a vast and rewarding secondhand stock, the best in the Lakes; cl Sun, bank hols, and Weds Jan–Easter. There are some other interesting shops in side streets, and the Richmond (Hensingham) is useful for lunch. Just S at Sandwith, the Lowther Arms is recommended by readers for good homely food and accommodation, handy for the coast-to-coast walk.

The Beacon ⊞ (West Strand) Whitehaven's history is well covered here, but what really makes this friendly heritage centre worth a look is the Met Office Weather Gallery on the top floor, full of hi-tech monitoring and recording equipment, and excellent hands-on displays explaining how weather forecasts are put together. The building itself is striking, with good views over the town and harbour from the top floor. Shop, snacks, disabled access; cl Mon (exc bank hols) and 25 Dec; (01946) 592302; £4.20.

WINDERMERE SD3996

An extensive largely Victorian development of guest houses and small hotels spreads up between the older village of Bowness and the hillside station. It has a touristy feel right through the year, especially around the main street down to the steamer piers. In Bowness itself there is an inner core of narrower much older streets and buildings – one of the most ancient is the engaging Hole in t' Wall pub. **Horse riding** can be arranged from Wynlass Beck Stables (bottom of Patterdale Rd). The Tourist Information Centre on Victoria St has a useful range of locally produced crafts if you haven't time to look properly, and the Birdcage (College Rd) is a good **antiques shop** – mostly small things, especially lamps.

Amazonia (Glebe Rd) Fascinating changing collection of reptiles – all shapes and sizes inc snakes, crocodiles and brightly coloured lizards. All housed among koi and turtle ponds, waterfalls and free-nesting tropical birds. Meals, snacks, shop, disabled access; cl 25 Dec, 1 Jan; (015394) 48002; £3.75.

Steamboat Museum ⊞ (Rayrigg Rd) Nearly three dozen gleamingly restored graceful antique steamboats, inc the 1850 SL *Dolly*, the oldest mechanically powered steamboat in the world, and the record-breaker *Miss Windermere IV*. Also a few boats that comfortably predate steam, and events like vintage boat rallies and model boat regattas. Snacks, shop, disabled access; cl Nov to mid-Mar; (015394) 45565; £3.25. For an extra £5, there are stately 50-minute tours of the lake on the silent steam launch *Osprey* or *Swallow*, weather permitting.

World of Beatrix Potter (Old Laundry, Crag Brow, Bowness) Much enjoyed by young children, delightfully detailed re-creations of characters and scenes from *Peter Rabbit* and other tales. Some bits have smells, so you can get more of the atmosphere of Mrs Tiggywinkle's laundry or nasty old Mr McGregor's Potting Shed. Meals and snacks (in the Tailor of Gloucester's tea room), shop, disabled access; cl 25 Dec, and last 3 wks Jan; £3.50.

WITHERSLACK SD4384

Halecat Garden (A590) Good example of modern landscaping with fine views from the mainly herbaceous garden; plants for sale (esp hydrangeas).

Some disabled access with notice; cl Sat am ; (015395) 52229; free.

WORKINGTON NY0028

Helena Thompson Museum (Park End Rd) Some antique and Georgian costumes, as well as pottery, silver, furniture and local history, in period surroundings. Disabled access to ground floor only; cl Sun; (01900) 326255; free. Cobbled Portland Sq is pretty, and the Alamin Indian restaurant (Jane St) is good.

Workington Hall [🏛] (Curwen Pk, NE edge of town) Former mansion, now ruinous hulk around Norman tower, in public park – an odd conjunction. A famous letter by Mary Queen of Scots to her cousin Elizabeth I was written here. Small shop, limited disabled access; cl am, and Nov–Easter; (01900) 326408; £1.

Other attractive villages in fine scenery, all with good pubs, include Armathwaite NY5146, Bampton NY5118, Beckermet NY0207, Broughton Mills SD2290, Crosby Ravensworth NY6215 (Maulds Meaburn is also pretty), Garrigill NY7441, Hesket Newmarket NY3438, Langwathby NY5734 and Stonethwaite NY2613. The comfortable Kirkstile Inn at Loweswater NY1222 deserves a mention for its glorious setting.

Where to eat

AMBLESIDE NY3704 **Sheila's Cottage** *The Slack (015394) 33079* 250-year-old cottage and converted barn run by the same owners for over 30 years, with very good and enjoyable food served all day inc popular afternoon teas; cl 2 wks mid-Jan. £21|£5.95

APPLEBY NY6820 **Royal Oak** *Bongate (017683) 51463* Friendly, popular, partly 14th-c coaching inn, with open fire in oak-panelled public bar, beamed lounge, panelled and glass snug, enjoyable food, well kept real ales, and a decent wine list; comfortable bdrms. £20|£6.95

APPLETHWAITE NY2725 **Underscar Manor** *(01768) 775000* Italianate Victorian house in wonderful position with panoramic views, a comfortable sitting room, two pretty restaurants with ornate drapes and lovely fresh flowers, very good beautifully presented classical cooking, and a mainly French wine list; smart dress; no smoking; children over 12. £25 lunch, £34 dinner

ARMATHWAITE NY5046 **Dukes Head** *(016974) 72226* In an attractive village, this is a comfortable and friendly inn with a civilised lounge bar, a warm coal fire, good home cooking, well kept real ales, and decent wines; bdrms; disabled access. £18|£6.50

ASKHAM NY5123 **Punch Bowl** *(01931) 712443* Attractively set by a village green, this bustling pub has an interestingly furnished rambling bar, open log fire, friendly atmosphere, generous helpings of good bar food, and well kept beers; cl pm 25 Dec; disabled access. £17|£7

BOWNESS SD4096 **Porthole** *3 Ash St (015394) 42793* Long-established bustling bistro with consistently good meals (mainly Italian), genuinely personal service, simple furnishings, and decent wine – a reliably enjoyable evening out; cl Sat am, Tues, Christmas–beginning of Feb; limited disabled access. £30|£6

CARTMEL FELL SD4189 **Masons Arms** *(015395) 68486* Old-fashioned building in unrivalled setting with wonderful views, a wide range of beers inc summer own-brew and interesting continental real ales, and very popular food, much vegetarian; self-catering accommodation; cl 25 Dec. £23|£8

CROOK SD4695 **Sun** *(01539) 821351* Friendly and relaxed pub away from the Windermere bustle, with two opened-up rooms (one no smoking) and a wide range of imaginative food inc proper puddings; cheerful efficient staff, well kept ales, and good value interesting wines. £21|£8.50

CROSTHWAITE SD4692 **Punch Bowl** *(015395) 68237* Prettily set Lakeland inn with an interesting series of nicely furnished rooms, and concentrating very much on excellent food; a good pubby atmosphere, well kept real ales, and friendly service; bedrooms; cl Sun pm Oct–Mar, cl Mon, last 3 wks Nov; disabled access. £25|£7.50

DENT SD7087 **Stone Close** *Main St (015396) 25231* Cottagey 17th-c tea shop with pine furniture on the flagstones, cast-iron ranges, beams, and local crafts, home-made meals served from mid-morning until early evening inc delicious cakes and pastries, and a relaxed friendly atmosphere; bdrms, plus self-catering cottage next door; cl mid-Jan—early Feb. £16|**£4.75**

KESWICK NY2623 **George** *3 St John's St (017687) 72076* Fine old inn with attractive traditional black-panelled side room with interesting Wordsworth connection, and a good log fire; open-plan main bar with old-fashioned settles and modern banquettes under Elizabethan beams, and daily newspapers to read; enjoyable, often interesting bar food, well kept real ales, and a no smoking restaurant. £19.45|**£7.95**

KESWICK NY2623 **Maysons** *33 Lake Rd (017687) 74104* Busy restaurant with an interesting range of highly enjoyable food inc good vegetarian dishes, nice salads, and yummy cakes; cl evenings Nov—May (exc Easter). £15|**£4.50**

KIRKBY LONSDALE SD6178 **Snooty Fox** *33 Main St (015242) 71308* Rambling inn with plenty of interest in the various relaxed pubby rooms, good interesting food, a no smoking dining annexe, well kept beers, and pretty garden; cl pm 25 Dec; children must be well behaved; disabled access. £20.75|**£6.65**

MELMERBY NY6137 **Shepherds** *(01768) 881217* Friendly place in unspoilt sandstone village, with popular home-made food inc a marvellous range of cheeses, delicious puddings, and lots of daily specials using only local produce; quick friendly table service; cl 25 Dec; fair disabled access. £18|**£6.50**

MELMERBY NY6137 **Village Bakery** *(01768) 881515* Converted stone barn selling wonderful organic bread and cakes for cream teas, super breakfasts (until 11am) and good home-made restaurant food using produce grown organically behind the bakery; craft gallery upstairs; cl 25—26 Dec, 1 Jan; disabled access. £15|**£5**

MUNGRISDALE NY3630 **Mill Inn** *(017687) 79632* Friendly inn in high, secluded valley, with warm fire in simply furnished main bar, separate restaurant, enjoyable food. Well-kept real ales and good choice of wines by the glass, and friendly service. £18|**£7**

SCALES NY3426 **White Horse** *(017687) 79241* Cosy and isolated farmhouse inn in dramatic setting under Blencathra, perfect haven after walks; best to book as generously served food, using fresh local produce, is very popular; cl Mon, and Nov—Apr. £18|**£6**

SEATOLLER NY2413 **Yew Tree** *(017687) 77634* Set at the foot of a lovely valley, this restaurant was originally two 17th-c miners' cottages, and has fine oak beams, a slate floor, an open range and brick bread oven, lots of interesting old photographs and memorabilia, a super atmosphere, and good interesting food using local produce; cl Mon, Jan; disabled access. £23|**£4.95**

TROUTBECK NY4103 **Queens Head** *(015394) 32174* Popular gabled 17th-c coaching inn with several rambling bar rooms, some fine antique carving, a log fire and woodburner, efficient staff, particularly good first-class bar food, and well kept real ales; bdrms; cl 25 Dec. £24|**£5.95**

ULVERSTON SD3177 **Bay Horse Hotel and Restaurant** *Canal Foot (out past Glaxo) (01229) 583972* Civilised, nicely placed inn overlooking Morecambe Bay, with beautifully presented innovative food, well kept real ales and good wine list; bdrms; children in bar lounge only; cl Mon am; partial disabled access. £30|**£9.50**

WINDERMERE SD4198 **Oregano** *4 High St (015394) 44954* Intimate well liked little evening restaurant with good Mediterranean-influenced English cooking, candlelit tables on wooden floors, a relaxed bistro-type atmosphere, and helpful service; good value set menus; cl Sun. £20

YANWATH NY5127 **Gate** *(01768) 862386* Unpretentious village local with really good inventive food, well kept real ales, obliging service, log fire in simple chatty bar, and no smoking dining room; cl 25 Dec. £20|**£6.50**

Special thanks to Arthur and Margaret Dickinson, Audrey Lee, B and K Hypher

DERBYSHIRE

Spectacular scenery, from valleys and dales to deep caverns, with plenty of rewarding walks and bike rides. Great days out too, with several grand houses, interesting industrial heritage and some unusual museums; very good places to stay in

While most people are drawn to the marvellous countryside here, a handful of quirky museums offer enjoyable indoor alternatives for rainy days. Among them, the National Stone Centre provides a lively look at fossils, with activities such as gem-panning or fossil-rubbing; Derby's Pickfords House Museum combines a decent look at life in the Georgian era, with displays of costumes and toys to interest children. There are more toys and dolls at the National Trust Museum of Childhood, Sudbury Hall, where smaller children can try their luck as a chimney sweep. The National Tramway Museum, with its enthusiastic mix of facts and fun – not to mention rides on the lovely old vehicles – makes for a good value family day out.

One of Britain's richest pre-industrial areas, this has some splendid stately homes. Magnificent Chatsworth (excellent family entertainment), Hardwick Hall (some impressive restoration with heritage funding), Calke Abbey, charming Haddon Hall, Kedleston Hall, Bolsover Castle and – less lofty but no less enjoyable – Eyam Hall, are all well worth a visit, and each quite distinctive. Ruined Wingfield Manor at South Wingfield puts an ironic twist on past glories.

Underground Derbyshire is also quite special, laced with remarkable subterranean caverns. The Heights of Abraham in Matlock Bath is a great family draw. Poole's Cavern in Buxton is the most striking of all, Treak Cliff Cavern the best of several good ones around Castleton.

The county's industrial heritage is well represented at Derby's Industrial Museum, Middleton Top Engine House, the lively Peak District Mining Museum, and at proto-industrial Cromford, home to the oldest surviving railway workshops in the world.

Other family highlights include the Chestnut conservation park in Chapel-en-le-Frith, the enjoyable Peak Rail at Darley Dale, and the theme parks at Ilkeston and Matlock Bath.

The best of the scenery is in the central area, more or less south of the A625, known as the White Peak. This limestone country, picturesquely cut by the intricate channels of the dales, has an abundance of generally gentle walking – and is very rewarding for drivers too. High, flat pastures have small fields of rich grassland enclosed by silvery stone walls, clusters of often very photogenic pale stone farm buildings, and small old-fashioned villages. In summer the loveliest dales do have almost a crocodile of walkers snaking along them, though even then you can find quiet areas. Further north, up in the High Peak, the scenery becomes bleaker and more forbidding – daunting for all but the most committed walker, though exhilarating for drivers – the A6024, A628 (rather slow), A57, A5002, A624 and A625 all have outstanding views.

Peak Cycle Hire offer good value bike hire at various centres throughout the county, as well as a decent leaflet detailing six traffic-free cycle routes; phone (07000) 732529 for more information.

Where to stay

ASHBOURNE SK1746 **Callow Hall** *Mappleton Rd, Ashbourne, Derbyshire DE6 2AA (01335) 300900* **£130,** plus special breaks; 16 lovely well furnished rms, excellent bthrms. Quietly smart and friendly Victorian mansion up a long drive through grounds with fine trees and surrounded by marvellous countryside; comfortable drawing room with open fire, fresh flowers and plants, and period furniture, very good traditional food using home-grown produce, excellent breakfasts, and kind hosts; good private fishing; cl Christmas; disabled access

ASHFORD IN THE WATER SK1969 **Riverside Country House Hotel** *Fennel St, Ashford in the Water, Bakewell, Derbyshire DE4 1QF (01629) 814275* **£125,** plus special breaks; 15 individually decorated pretty rms. Creeper-covered Georgian house in delightful village with attractive riverside gardens, a relaxed house party atmosphere, antiques and log fires in cosy sitting rooms, good modern English cooking, and good service; children over 8; disabled access

BAKEWELL SK2272 **Hassop Hall** *Hassop, Bakewell, Derbyshire DE45 1NS (01629) 640488* **£94.90,** plus winter breaks; 13 gracious rms. Mentioned in the Domesday Book, in lovely parkland surrounded by fine scenery, this handsome hotel has antiques and oil paintings, an elegant drawing room, oak-panelled bar, good food and friendly service; tennis; no accommodation 3 nights over Christmas; partial disabled access

BASLOW SK2572 **Cavendish Hotel** *Baslow, Bakewell, Derbyshire DE45 1SP (01246) 582311* **£146.20,** plus winter wknd breaks; 24 spotless, comfortable and individually furnished rms (varying in size). Charming hotel with magnificent views over Chatsworth estate, most attractive well furnished day rooms (some furnishings come from Chatsworth), an eclectic collection of the owner's pictures, open fires and fresh flowers, fine food in two restaurants, very courteous staff

BASLOW SK2572 **Fischer's Baslow Hall** *Calver Rd, Baslow, Bakewell, Derbyshire DE45 1RR (01246) 583259* **£100,** plus special breaks; 6 comfortable, pretty rms. Handsome Edwardian manor house with individually chosen furnishings and pictures, open fires, fresh flowers and plants, beautifully presented fine food using the best ingredients (some home-grown and lots of game and fish) in airy dining room or in lunchtime Café Max (both no smoking), and courteous attentive service; cl 25–26 Dec; children over 12 in evening restaurant

BIGGIN-BY-HARTINGTON SK1559 **Biggin Hall** *Biggin-by-Hartington, Buxton, Derbyshire SK17 0DH (01298) 84451* **£59,** plus special breaks; 19 spacious rms with antiques, some in converted 18th-c stone building and in bothy. Cheerfully run 17th-c house in quiet grounds with a very relaxed atmosphere, two comfortable sitting rooms, log fires, freshly cooked straightforward food with an emphasis on free-range wholefoods served at 7pm in the attractive dining room, and packed lunches if wanted; children over 12; limited disabled access

BIRCH VALE SK0287 **Waltzing Weasel** *New Mills Rd, Birch Vale, High Peak, Derbyshire SK22 1BT (01663) 743402* **£69.99;** 8 lovely rms. Attractive traditional inn with open fire, some handsome furnishings, daily newspapers and plants in quiet civilised bar, very good food using the best seasonal produce in charming back restaurant (fine views), excellent puddings and cheeses, obliging service; children over 7; disabled access

CASTLETON SK1582 **Bargate Cottage** *Market Pl, Castleton, Hope Valley, Derbyshire S33 8WQ (01433) 620201* **£43*;** 3 well equipped rms. Lovely, beautifully restored old cottage with beams, an inglenook fireplace, delicious breakfasts, super packed lunches, and pretty terraced garden; no smoking; cl 24–25 Dec; children over 12

DOVE DALE SK1550 **Peveril of the Peak** *Thorpe, Ashbourne, Derbyshire DE6 2AW (01335) 350333* **£104**, plus special breaks; 46 rms. Relaxing hotel in pretty village with comfortable sofas and log fire in lounge, modern bar and attractive restaurant overlooking the garden, and good English cooking; tennis; wonderful walking nearby; disabled access

DOVERIDGE SK1237 **Beeches Farmhouse** *Doveridge, Ashbourne, Derbyshire DE6 5LR (01889) 590288* **£62**; 10 rms with home-made biscuits, fruit and flowers. 18th-c farmhouse with an open fire in the rustic beamed bar, several cosy beamed eating areas with original brickwork, good English food, and hearty breakfasts; cl Christmas; partial disabled access

GLOSSOP SK0593 **Wind in the Willows** *Derbyshire Level, Sheffield Rd, Glossop, Derbyshire SK13 7PT (01457) 868001* **£119**; 12 individual rms with thoughtful extras. Set in five acres of grounds on the edge of the Pennines, this early Victorian house has a restful atmosphere in its tranquil traditionally furnished sitting rooms, log fires and antiques, enjoyable set dinners (the restaurant is not open to the general public), particularly good breakfasts, and charming, helpful service; adjoining golf course; cl Christmas and New Year; children over 10

GRINDLEFORD SK2478 **Maynard Arms** *Main Rd, Nether Padley, Grindleford, Hope Valley, Derbyshire S32 2HE (01433) 630321* **£79***, plus special breaks; 10 rms. Comfortable hotel with log fire and good Peak District views from the first-floor lounge, smart welcoming bar, good choice of food, particularly attentive service; good walks nearby

HATHERSAGE SK2281 **George** *Main Rd, Hathersage, Hope Valley, Derbyshire S32 1BB (01433) 650436* **£99.50**, plus special breaks; 19 pretty rms (the back ones are quietest). Substantial and comfortably modernised old inn with attractive airy lounge, beamed friendly bar, popular food, and a neat flagstoned back terrace by rose garden; good walks all around

HOPE SK1783 **Underleigh House** *Edale Rd, Hope, Castleton, Derbyshire S33 6RF (01433) 621372* **£66***, plus special breaks; 6 thoughtfully decorated rms. In unspoilt countryside, this spotlessly kept converted barn has fine views from the comfortable sitting room, hearty breakfasts with good home-made preserves enjoyed around communal table in flagstoned dining room, friendly cheerful owners, attractive gardens; terrific walks on the doorstep and packed lunches can be arranged; children over 12

KIRK IRETON SK2650 **Barley Mow** *Kirk Ireton, Ashbourne, Derbyshire DE6 3JP (01335) 370306* **£45**; 5 rms. Tall, Jacobean, walkers' inn with lots of woodwork in straightforward series of interconnecting bar rooms, a solid fuel stove in beamed residents' sitting room, and well kept real ales; close to Carsington Reservoir; cl Christmas wk

MATLOCK SK3059 **Riber Hall** *Matlock, Derbyshire DE4 5JU (01629) 582795* **£139**, plus special breaks; 14 lovely beamed rms with antiques, chocolates, and baskets of fruit. Elizabethan manor house in pretty grounds surrounded by peaceful countryside, with antiques-filled heavily beamed rooms, fresh flowers, two elegant dining rooms with reliable food and fine wines, and tennis and clay pigeon shooting; children over 10

MONSAL HEAD SK1871 **Monsal Head Hotel** *Monsal Head, Buxton, Derbyshire DE45 1NL (01629) 640250* **£55**, plus special breaks; 8 very good rms, most with own bthrm. Comfortable and enjoyable small hotel in marvellous setting high above the River Wye, with horsey theme in bar (converted from old stables), freshly prepared decent food, and good service; cl 25 Dec; dogs welcome

ROWLAND SK2172 **Holly Cottage** *Rowland, Bakewell, Derbyshire DE45 1NR (01629) 640624* **£46***, plus special breaks; 2 pretty rms, shared bthrm. 200-year-old, no smoking cottage on a quiet lane, surrounded by peaceful rolling countryside; open fire in large lounge, woodburner in panelled hall, attractive dining room and homely relaxed atmosphere, excellent breakfasts with home-made rolls, bread and preserves; lovely gardens, and friendly black labrador; lots of walks; cl Nov–Feb

ROWSLEY SK2565 **Peacock** *Rowsley, Matlock, Derbyshire DE4 2EB (01629) 733518* **£110**, plus special breaks; 17 comfortable rms. 17th-c country house hotel by River Derwent (private fishing in season), with well kept gardens, friendly staff, interesting old-fashioned inner bar, spacious comfortable lounge, and very popular restaurant

SHIRLEY SK2241 **Shirley Hall Farm** *Shirley, Ashbourne, Derbyshire DE6 3AS (01335) 360346* **£46**; 3 rms. Timbered and part-moated farmhouse on family-run dairy and arable farm, with homely sitting room, and good breakfasts with home-made bread, jam and marmalade, and local organic sausages; private coarse fishing and lots of walks; nearby pub for evening meals; cl Christmas; self-catering cottages

SHOTTLE SK3050 **Dannah Farm** *Bowmans Lane, Shottle, Belper, Derbyshire DE56 2DR (01773) 550273* **£76***, plus special breaks; 8 rms with old pine and antiques, and some with private sitting rooms, four-posters, and whirlpool baths. Carefully restored and friendly Georgian farmhouse with two comfortable sitting rooms, and popular imaginative cooking in attractive no smoking dining room; calves, hens, a nanny goat, hairy kune-kune pigs and farm dogs and cats; cl 25 Dec; disabled access

To see and do

Derbyshire Family Attraction of the Year

CRICH SK3455 **National Tramway Museum** 🖼 A favourite with several readers, this enthusiastically run place is much more than just a collection of nostalgic vehicles, and they put a good deal of effort into making sure children enjoy their visit. The staff are keen to get everyone interested and involved, and there's a good balance between facts and fun. When you come in you're given a genuine old penny (or half-penny for children), which you use to pay for unlimited rides on the lovingly restored vintage trams that run up and down a one-mile period street and beyond, through lovely parts of the Derwent Valley (familiar to viewers of *Peak Practice*). Trams run every few minutes, and you rarely have to wait very long. A comprehensive exhibition has more trams, from all over the British Isles and further afield, as well as related memorabilia, from ticket offices to uniforms and posters. And there are plenty of play areas: a big one outside, with bridges, ropes and balancing poles, and a tram-themed one inside – not terribly elaborate, but good fun for younger children especially (there's a dedicated section for under-5s). Nice walks through the surrounding woodland. They do regular special events, and it's particularly atmospheric in the run-up to Christmas. Dogs on leads are welcome. Meals, snacks, picnic areas, disabled access (one tram has been adapted for wheelchairs, and they have a guide book in Braille; open daily Apr–Oct, just Sun and Mon in winter; (01773) 852565; £6.70 (£3.30 children 4–15). The family ticket, covering two adults and three children, at £18.20 offers a much better than usual saving.

ALKMONTON SK1839
Bentley Fields Open Farm Unspoilt traditional livestock farm stretching over 245 acres; they milk their cows at 1 and 4pm. In spring you may see calving or lambing – or chicks pecking their way out of their eggs. Teas, shop, some disabled access; open daily Easter wk and May half-term, bank hol Suns and Mons, but best to check (01335)

330240; £2. The Holly Bush over at Church Broughton is quite handy for lunch.

ASHBOURNE SK1846
A good few interesting Georgian buildings in the streets off the hillside market place, esp leading to its elegantly proportioned church, which has a famous white marble statue of a sleeping child. The Gingerbread Shop

sells the town's long-standing speciality. Smiths Tavern, the Green Man and White Lion are good for lunch. The B5056 towards Bakewell and B5053 to Wirksworth have characteristic views. You can hire bicycles by the half-day or day from Ashbourne Cycle Hire, Mapleton Lane; (01335) 343156.

Derwent Crystal Centre (Shaw Croft) Quality glassworks and engravers, with demonstrations (9am–2.30pm Mon–Thurs) and factory shop. Disabled access; cl Suns, 25–26 Dec, 1 Jan; (01335) 345219; free.

Tissington Trail This path for walkers and cyclists follows a disused railway track from Ashbourne up to Parsley Hay on the A515, where it joins the similar High Peak Trail from Buxton to near Cromford. You can hire cycles in Ashbourne, or from Parsley Hay Cycle Hire, Parsley Hay. This has a particularly interesting finale from Middleton Top engine house (cycle hire here, too) to High Peak Junction, dipping down a great incline past old engine houses to reach the Cromford Canal.

ASHFORD IN THE WATER
SK1969

One of the area's more appealing villages, with decent food in the Bulls Head.

BAKEWELL SK2168

Away from the traffic this is a civilised small town, especially around the church. You can still get those famous tarts here, though there has been some dispute over the original recipe – two shops have claimed rights to the authentic Bakewell Pudding, and the case even went to court. The Castle Inn and Aitch's are useful for lunch.

Haddon Hall One of the most perfectly preserved medieval manor houses in England, still with its 12th-c painted chapel, 14th-c kitchen, and banqueting hall with minstrels' gallery. Some rooms can seem rather bare (there aren't many furnishings or pictures), but a bright spot is Rex Whistler's painting of the house in the silver-panelled long gallery. It's a particularly pretty location in summer when the long terraced rose gardens are in full bloom. Several films and TV adaptations have had scenes shot here in recent years. Meals, snacks, shop; cl Fri–Sun in Oct, and all Nov–Mar; (01629) 812855; £5.75. The Lathkil Hotel up in Over Haddon is good for lunch, and nearby roads have attractive views.

Magpie Mine (3m W) Surface remains of a mine last worked in 1958 and stabilised in the 1970s give a good idea of a 19th-c lead mine; free.

Old House Museum (Cunningham Pl) Folk collection in the 16th-c house convered by pioneer industrialist Richard Arkwright, still with its original wattle-and-daub interior walls and open-timbered chamber. Shop, limited disabled access; open pm daily Good Fri–Oct, plus am July–Aug; (01629) 813642; £2.50.

BERESFORD DALE SK1259

Not so popular as the downstream parts of Dove Dale (of which this is an upstream continuation), this wooded section rewards walkers with a real sense of peace, even though it's easily reached from the B5054 between Hulme End and Hartington.

BIRCHOVER SK2362

The starting point for an extraordinary walk over **Stanton Moor**, where among quarry workings and prehistoric burial mounds are the Nine Ladies stone circle, a folly tower and a huge boulder known as the Cork Stone, equipped with metal steps for the courageous and adorned with at least four centuries' worth of graffiti (the earliest we found was 1613); there are good views into Darley Dale from the edge of the escarpment. Behind the Druid Inn in Birchover are **Rowtor Rocks**, a gritstone outcrop into which one Rev Eyre cut steps, benches and a stone armchair for contemplation.

BOLSOVER SK4770

Bolsover Castle 🏰 The original ruined castle dates back to the 12th c, but was rebuilt in 1613 as a spectacular mock castle – about 200 years ahead of this fashion. Battlements and turrets outside, and inside allegorical frescoes, fine panelling and ornate fireplaces; visitor centre and newly restored fountain garden. Snacks, shop, some disabled access; cl Mon and Tues Nov–Mar, and 24–26 Dec; (01246) 823349; £4.20, inc Walkman tour. Just on the other side of the M1 at Sutton

Scarsdale (and in fact looking down on the motorway), the ruins of a once-grand 17th-c hall are quite evocative.

BRADBOURNE SK2152
Appealing dales village, with an ancient Saxon cross outside its Norman church.

BUXTON SK0572
Much changed, but it still has some handsome buildings dating from its days as a flourishing spa, with Georgian terraces (the Crescent is a noble Georgian streetscape) and a restored Edwardian opera house. St Ann's Well is the only direct reminder of its water-based heyday – you can take the water for free here (it's naturally warm). Many of the grander buildings come back to life during the town's excellent annual festival. The Columbine (Hall Bank) is good for lunch. An enjoyable self-guided walk takes you around the town's attractions inc the Pavilion Gardens, currently being restored; available from the Tourist Information Centre (The Crescent); 30p.

Buxton Museum & Art Gallery (Terrace Rd) A useful introduction to the area; shop, disabled access; cl Mon (exc bank hols) and winter Sun, 25–26 Dec and 1 Jan; £1.

Grin Low Woods (just S) Well landscaped, with mature woodland and the Victorian folly of Solomon's Temple (good views from the top), though it's not always open.

Poole's Cavern (Buxton Country Park, Green Lane) The best show cave in the Peak District and the longest in Britain, a spectacular natural limestone cavern in 100 acres of woodland, with well lit stalactites and stalagmites, and exhibitions on caves, woodland and Romans. As in other caverns, wrap up well. Snacks, shop, some disabled access with notice; cl Nov–Feb; (01298) 26978; £4.75.

CALKE SK3622
Calke Abbey One of the most rewarding NT properties in Britain, an unusual baroque mansion still in pretty much the same state as when the last baronet died here in 1924. You might expect the splendidly decorated rooms with their fascinating displays (inc an extensive natural history collection), but it's quite a surprise to find the more

dilapidated corridors and areas where family possessions were just bundled together in heaps. This gives you a better appreciation of how the abbey was a much-loved family home – and of how things forgotten in the attic can quickly become social history. Also extensive parkland and walled gardens. Meals, snacks, shop, disabled access; cl Thurs, Fri, and Nov–Mar, house cl am; (01332) 863822; £5.10, garden only £2.40 – there's a £2.50 vehicle charge on entering the park, refundable on entry to the house (which has a timed ticket system); NT. The nearby Saracens Head (Heath End Lane) has great value snacks.

CARSINGTON WATER SK2552
Britain's newest reservoir is beginning to tone into the landscape; good visitor centre, watersports, walks, cycling, etc. Meals, snacks, shop, disabled access; cl 25 Dec; (01629) 540696; car park charge, £1.50 all day. The Red Lion at Hognaston has good food.

CASTLETON SK1482
Very much geared to visitors, and filled with walkers and cavers in summer; plenty of cafés, and shops selling expensive worked pieces of the Blue John fluorspar that's found only in the nearby mine workings. The village's attractive dark stone buildings (one of the most impressive now a youth hostel) are dominated by the ruins of **Peveril Castle**, built high above in the 11th c – magnificent views. Shop, snacks; cl Mon and Tues from Nov–Mar, 24–26 Dec and 1 Jan; (01433) 620613; £2.20; EH. The Rose Cottage, Castle, Olde Nags Head (a remarkable Blue John table is housed in the craft shop opposite) and Peak all do decent food, and in the pretty nearby village of Hope the Cheshire Cheese is good. The B6061 to Sparrowpit (where the Wanted Inn has good value home cooking) has fine views. The most varied walks in the High Peak are found around Castleton and Hope. The great walk here takes in Castleton, the Lose Hill/Mam Tor ridge, the caves, and Winnats Pass; Mam Tor is so shaly and prone to landslips that it's dubbed the Shivering Mountain – the abandoned section of the A625 is a testament to the victory of the mountain over man.

Cave Dale is an optional side trip from the back of Castleton. Quarrying has had an unfortunate effect on the local landscape in the area, and limits walks further afield, though there are some pleasant walks to be had in the gentler high pastures of the limestone country to the south.

Blue John Cavern & Mine ⌂ (Buxton Rd) Containing eight of the 14 known veins of Blue John, this has been the main source of the precious stone for nearly 300 years. It's an impressive example of a water-worn cave, over a third of a mile long, with chambers 45 metres (150 ft) high. Snacks, craft shop; cl 25 Dec, 1 Jan; (01433) 620638; £6.

Peak Cavern Right in the village, this is the biggest natural cavern in the country and really does seem huge – the entrance hall is so large it used to house an entire village. From there it's a half-mile walk along lighted subterranean passageways to the Great Cave, 45 by 27 metres (150 ft wide, 90 ft long). By the time you reach the Devil's Staircase you'll be nearly 140 metres (450 ft) underground. Rope-making demonstrations; shop; cl wkdys Nov–Easter (exc school hols); (01433) 620285; £4.75.

Speedwell Cavern ⌂ (Winnats Pass – ex A625 W of Castleton) Very atmospheric former lead mine, with 105 steps down to a half-mile underground boat trip along floodlit passages, finishing up in a cathedral of a cavern with an impressive 'bottomless pit'. Good fun, though you may have to queue. Shop, snacks; (01433) 620512; cl 25 Dec; £5.25.

Treak Cliff Cavern (off ex A625 W) Informative tours of the first Blue John mine, worked since 1750, with rich veins of the mineral and quite staggering stalactites and stalagmites. Well placed lights create spooky shapes and atmospheric shadows. The entrance is narrow, and it's quite steep, but readers prefer this to many of the other caverns nearby. They're developing a visitor centre and workshop. Snacks, shop; cl 24–26 Dec and 1 Jan, but worth checking for times; (01433) 620571; £5.

CHAPEL-EN-LE-FRITH SK0580
Chestnut Centre ⌂ (A625)

Warmly recommended conservation park, concerned especially with breeding otters and barn owls, but other animals and birds of prey too. Good observation platforms. Snacks, shop, disabled access; cl wkdys Jan and Feb; (01298) 814099; *£4.95. The Cross Keys has decent food (all day Sun).

CHATSWORTH SK2670
Chatsworth (off B6012) Splendidly grand home of the Duke and Duchess of Devonshire prettily set on the banks of the River Derwent. Sumptuously furnished, the 17 rooms on display show off a superb collection of fine arts, including memorable paintings by Rembrandt and Van Dyck, and all sorts of intriguing decorative details. The lovely gardens cover over 100 acres and are full of surprises, with a maze, and brass bands playing on summer Sunday afternoons. The surrounding park was landscaped by Capability Brown. Also a farmyard (milking 3.30pm) and elaborate adventure playground. Meals, snacks, shops, garden centre, disabled access to garden only; cl Nov–mid-Mar; (01246) 582204; £6.75 house and garden, £3.85 garden only, and £3.50 for just the farmyard and adventure playground. Also in the grounds, at Stud Farm, 1½ m from the house towards Pilsley, is one of England's best farm shops, and the estate village of Edensor opposite the main gate is a marvellous mix of styles, with fine views from the lane leading up out of it. Around Chatsworth are two more most attractive small estate villages, Baslow and Beeley (which has a good food pub). The B1602 (busy in summer) has pleasant views.

CHESTERFIELD SK3871
Not a tourist town, but its largely 14th-c **church** has a really striking leaning spire, and is a rich building inside; the **town museum** (Corporation St) has the full angle on it; cl Weds and Sun; free. The **Victorian market hall** has flourishing indoor and outdoor markets every day exc Sun (flea market Thurs, street entertainment summer Sats). Nearby **Grassmoor Country Park** is a pleasant place to stroll; fishing lake. The Derby Tup (Sheffield Rd) is an enjoyable ale house with simple food.

CRESWELL CRAGS SK5374
Beside Crags Pond, these form the basis of a short but attractive there-and-back walk through woodland.

CRICH SK3455
National Tramway Museum See separate family panel on p. 130.

CROMFORD SK2956
A good example of an 18th-c cotton-milling village, little developed after its original building, and rewarding to stroll through. Carefully preserved North St is the first true industrial street in the world (built in 1777). The restored **canal** is a quiet and attractive early Industrial Revolution setting with a restored steam-powered pumping house and a fine aqueduct over the river; there are pleasant walks along here. Branching off at Roystone Grange is an archaeological trail. The Boat, an 18th-c traditional local, has well priced food. The A5012 to Grangemill gives evocative views.

Cromford Mill 🖼 (Mill Lane) Richard Arkwright established the world's first successful water-powered cotton mill here in 1771 – the true beginning of the factory age. Wholefood restaurant, shops, limited disabled access; cl 25 Dec; (01629) 825776; site free, tours *£2.

High Peak Junction Workshops Oldest surviving railway workshops in the world. The visitor centre includes exhibitions and a film; snacks, shop, disabled access; cl wkdys Oct–Easter; (01629) 822831; *50p.

DALE ABBEY SK4338
Abbey ruins, Hermits Cave and remarkable All Saints church, part of which was formerly the village inn; the Carpenters Arms has good value food, and the village is attractive.

DARK PEAK SK2575
The eastern edges include the abrupt ramparts of Curbar Edge and Froggatt Edge, popular with rock-climbers and easily accessible from the road. Birchen Edge and Wellington's Monument are obvious objectives for walkers from the Robin Hood at Curbar.

DARLEY DALE SK2762
Carriage Museum 🖼 (Red House Stables) Collection of vehicles and equipment, some of which you can ride in. Also horse and pony rides – booking essential. Teas, disabled access; cl 25 Dec; (01629) 733583; £2.75.

Peak Rail 🖼 Private railway, very popular with readers. Trains run between here and Matlock, then on to Rowsley. The eventual aim is to run as far as Buxton. Wknd restaurant car, shop, disabled access; usually open wknds all year (not Sat in depths of winter), plus most of summer hols, but best to check times; (01629) 580381; *£6. The Grouse (A6 N) is handy for a snack.

DERBY SK3536
A big busy city, but not too daunting for a visitor to penetrate, and with several things worth visiting; it's got far more open spaces than you'd expect, and a pedestrianised centre.

Derby Cathedral The 16th-c tower is the second highest in the country; the rest of the building was replaced in the 18th c. Bess of Hardwick is buried in the vaults, and there's a delightful early Georgian screen. New restaurant opening this year, shop, disabled access; £2 suggested donation. The quaint nearby Olde Dolphin (Queen St) has bargain food all day.

Derby Museum & Art Gallery (The Strand) Stands out for its collections of porcelain and the paintings of local artist Joseph Wright. Shop, disabled access; cl Sun am and over Christmas; free.

Heritage Centre (St Peter's churchyard) Once a Tudor grammar school, ghost walks through the city's tunnels and other themed tours leave here (and from the Old Gaol, Friargate) 7pm in summer; booking essential, (01332) 299321; £13 inc meal. Centre cl Sun and bank hols; free.

Industrial Museum (Full St) Warmly praised by some readers, this restored early 18th-c silk mill and adjacent flour mill has probably the world's finest collection of Rolls-Royce aero engines, and a Power Gallery with lots of hands-on displays. Shop, disabled access; cl am Sun and bank hols, and some time over Christmas – phone to check; (01332) 255308; free. The nearby Old Silk Mill is an interesting pub, open all day.

Pickfords House Museum (Friargate) Gives a very good idea of 18th-c domestic life, with period furnished rooms and Georgian garden; also costume display and a collection of toy theatres. Shop, some disabled access; cl Sun and bank hol am, and over Christmas – phone to check; (01332) 255363; free.

Q Gallery (Queen St) City-centre gallery showing contemporary visual art, photography and new media; shop, disabled access; cl Sun–Tues, plus Weds–Fri am and between exhibitions – best to phone; (01332) 385601; free.

Royal Crown Derby Visitor Centre 🏛 (Osmaston Rd) Cheerfully informative twice-daily tours of a bone-china factory, celebrating 250 years of porcelain production. A museum traces the industry's development from its origins. Meals, snacks, shop (lots of bargain seconds), disabled access (exc museum); open daily, no tours wknds, bank holidays or factory shut-down weeks; (01332) 712800; £5.50 (£2.75 without tour) – no under-10s on tours.

DOVE DALE SK1452

Shared between Derbyshire and Staffordshire, with the River Dove as the boundary, this is the most popular of all the dales. Partly wooded, it has a beautifully varied mixture of water, trees and pastures, and is lined with crags and curiously shaped outcrops of rock. To see fewer people, head further upstream. Handy nearby refreshment places are the Okeover Arms at Mapleton (with a domed church, and a nice riverside walk to Thorpe), the Coach & Horses at Fenny Bentley and (to be found on the Staffordshire side) the Izaak Walton Hotel nr Ilam (cosier inside than it looks from out).

EDALE SK1285

Famous as the start of the 256-mile Pennine Way to the Scottish border, with a good information centre and decent food in the Old Nags Head. It tends to be packed with expectant long-distant walkers on Sunday mornings. For a taste of the Dark Peak proper, this can be the start for half-day walks that quite quickly take you up through the stone-walled pastures of the valley on to the edge of the dark plateau above. The track signed as the alternative Pennine Way route up Jacob's Ladder is easier to find, and has more to see, than the official Pennine

Way plod across a huge blanket bog.

ELVASTON SK4032

Elvaston Castle Country Park (B5010) 200 acres of lovely 19th-c landscaped parkland, with formal and Old English gardens, wooded walks, and wildfowl on the ornamental lake. Also museum with traditional craft workshops, and nature trails. Meals, snacks, shop, disabled access; open all year, but museum open only Weds–Sat pms plus Sun and bank hols May–Oct; (01332) 571342; museum £1.20, car park 70p wkdys, £1.30 wknds. Shardlow is convenient for lunch.

EYAM SK2276

Attractive secluded village with a dark past: in the Great Plague sick villagers confined themselves here for fear of infecting people outside – plaques record who died where, and stones on the village edge mark where money was disinfected. The Miners Arms is very good for lunch. Just up the B6521 at Upper Padley, **Padley Chapel** is an interesting 15th-c revival, effectively restored in 1933.

Eyam Hall 🏛 Sturdy-looking 17th-c manor house, still very much a family home, with furniture, portraits and tapestries, fine Jacobean staircase and impressive stone-flagged hall. Small craft centre in the stables. Meals, snacks, shop, some disabled access; house open Weds, Thurs, Sun and bank hols July–Aug, craft centre open daily exc Mon; (01433) 631976; *£4.25 – timed ticket system.

GOYT VALLEY SK0177

The well wooded valley with its three miles of reservoirs is a man-made landscape, but nonetheless charming for walks or picnics; reached off the A54 W of Buxton.

HARDSTOFT SK4264

Herb Garden (B6039, nr M1 junction 29) Big main garden with lots of herbs and old English roses, smaller gardens specialising in rare medicinal herbs, pot-pourri or lavender. Meals, snacks, shop, disabled access; cl Tues (exc after bank hol wknds) and mid-Sept–mid-Mar; (01246) 854268; *£1.

HARDWICK HALL SK4663

Hardwick Hall The marriages of the redoubtable Bess of Hardwick couldn't necessarily be described as happy but

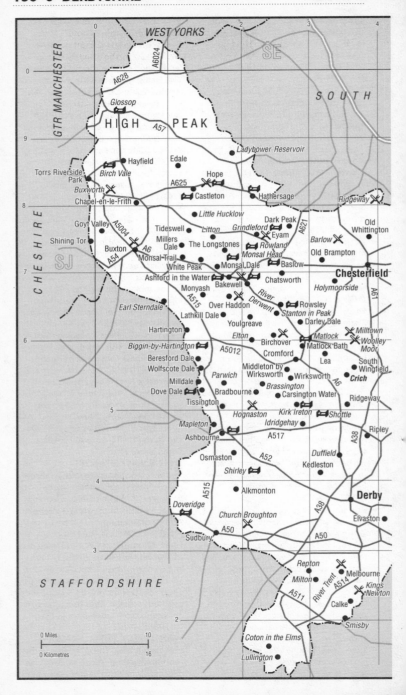

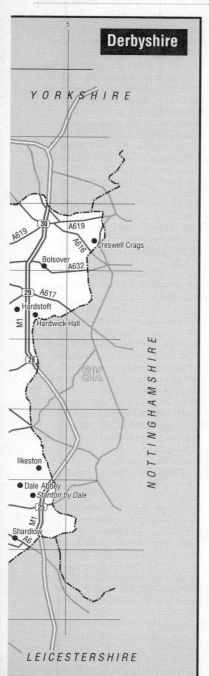

she certainly did very well out of them, the fourth leaving her enough money to build this triumphant Elizabethan prodigy house. The beautifully symmetrical towers are crowned with the monogram ES, and there's an amazing expanse of glass (her sight was dimming). Also fine tapestries and needlework, large park, and gardens laid out in walled courtyard. Heritage funding is helping to restore the huge and ancient Gideon tapestries which run the length of the 50-metre (167-ft) Long Gallery, a silk canopy, and the garden walls; a gazebo houses an exhibition on garden history; guided walks to stonemason's yard (Weds and Thurs at 1, 2 and 3.30 pm). Meals, snacks, shop, disabled access; open pm Apr–Oct, house cl all day Mon (exc bank hols), Tues and Fri; (01246) 850430; £2 vehicle charge to enter the grounds; £6 house and garden, £3.20 garden only, operating on a timed ticket; NT. Not far from this 'new' house is the shell of Hardwick Old Hall, Bess's birthplace; (01246) 850431; £2.60 (NT members free). A joint ticket is available for both houses (£8). Also on the estate is a restored watermill (another £1.80, NT). The park is attractive for walks, and at the end of it the Hardwick Inn, also NT-owned, is useful for lunch.

HARTINGTON SK1260

This attractive village has a good cheese shop selling local Stilton, and a pottery on Mill Lane.

HATHERSAGE SK2281

Charlotte Brontë wrote *Jane Eyre* here. The church is the legendary site of Little John's grave. It's a good village for walkers and climbers, with good walks inc the attractive moorland, pastures and woodland making up Longshaw, nr the Fox House Inn up on the Sheffield road; or, closer and gentler, down along the River Derwent towards Grindleford. Besides the George, the Plough (A622) is useful for lunch. The B6001 S is a pleasant drive.

HAYFIELD SK0387

This moorland village and its attractive nearby smaller sister Little Hayfield have good walks around them, both up towards Kinder Scout and to the Lantern Pike viewpoint in the opposite direction. There's also a popular walk or cycle ride – the **Sett Valley Trail** – along a hillside former railway to New Mills, looking down on the mill buildings by the River Sett. There's a handy bike shop in Hayfield itself, and an information centre for the Trail. The welcoming Lantern Pike Inn in Little Hayfield has decent food.

HIGH PEAK SK1092
These dark moors are one of England's great wildernesses. But they have few easy circular routes, are largely very bleak indeed, and often consist of private grouse moor with no right of public access yet. The car park at the top of Snake Pass (A57 Glossop–Hathersage) is near the centre of the biggest of the National Trust's moorland holdings here, giving free access to the miles of Hope Woodlands (there aren't actually many trees).

ILKESTON SK4444
American Adventure Theme Park (Pit Lane) Excellent theme park with around 100 rides and attractions; all supposedly have an American theme, though this can be rather tenuous – ever so English Sooty stars in a Wild West show. Highlights include dropping 13 metres (42 ft) at 62 mph on the Nightmare Niagara triple log flume, and the Missile, a stomach-churning roller-coaster that twists and turns at unfeasible angles, before going the whole route again backwards. Live shows include a Wild West saloon and a Mexican fiesta, and there's a huge indoor play area for younger children; some extra charges for go-karts, crazy golf and so on. Meals, snacks, shops, good disabled access; cl Nov–wk before Easter; (01773) 531521; £13.50 (children under 1 metre, free).
Shipley Country Park Medieval estate developed and landscaped in the 18th c, with 600 acres of woodland, lakes and fields. A pleasant place to wander, with railway lines transformed into leafy walkways; you may be able to hire bikes from here by the time this book comes out. Snacks, shop, disabled access; visitor centre cl 25 Dec; (01773) 719961; free.

KEDLESTON SK3140
Kedleston Hall 🏛 This 18th-c

Palladian mansion is thought by many to be the finest example of Robert Adam's work – it's certainly the least altered. Interesting objets d'art, original furnishings, good collection of paintings, and a museum of items collected by Lord Curzon when he was Viceroy of India. Adam designed a charming boathouse and bridge in the park outside, which also has extensive formal gardens with marvellous rhododendrons, and long woodland walks. Meals, snacks, shop, disabled access (best to phone in advance); open Apr–Oct, house pm Sat–Weds, grounds daily plus wknds Nov–Dec; (01332) 842191; £5, £2.20 grounds only; NT. The Joiners Arms in Quarndon now does good value weekday lunches.

LADYBOWER RESERVOIR SK1788
Pretty enough to drive past; also the lane up to the car park by the Derwent Reservoir (with a summer minibus service beyond to Howden Reservoir) gives plenty of easy waterside-forest walking on the relatively sheltered stone-walled slopes of the upper parts of Derwent Dale, with access to the higher moors for better views – for example, up on to Win Hill, or on a kind day on to the formidable Derwent Moors to the E. The Ladybower pub down on the main road is useful.

LATHKILL DALE SK1865
Charming combination of woods, steep pastures and more well weathered signs of old mines; its short tributary Bradford Dale is also very attractive for walks.

LEA SK3258
Lea Gardens Beautiful woodland gardens with rhododendrons inc rare species and cultivars, azaleas and rock plants. Home-baked snacks, shop and garden centre, limited disabled access; open 19 Mar–29 Jun, other times by appointment only; (01629) 534380; £3.

LONGSTONES, THE SK1871
Little Longstone and nearby Great Longstone are charming steep stone-built villages, and the back road from Baslow through here to Tideswell is a pretty drive.

MATLOCK BATH SK2958
Pleasantly busy place, with lots to do. A

spectacular wooded cliff looks across the lower roadside town to pastures by the Derwent; up the side of the gorge, quiet lanes climb steeply past 18th and 19th-c villas. The Temple Hotel (Temple Walk) has great views and decent food.

Gulliver's Kingdom & Royal Cave
(1m S, off A6) Family theme park with chair lift and hectic rides, cave tour, and cowboy and ghost towns; it's aimed at the under-12s, so don't expect white knuckles. Meals, snacks, shops, limited disabled access; open wknds and school hols Easter–Sept; (01629) 580540; £6.

Heights of Abraham Country Park
Derbyshire is full of stunning show caverns, but few are as good for families, and none can boast as thrilling an introduction as the one here: cable cars whisk you up from the Derwent Valley to a 60-acre country park, with dramatic views over the ancient limestone gorge (not to mention a railway and the busy A6). At the end of the 5-minute trip a multi-media show explains how the rock was formed 325 million years ago, then guides escort you into the two show caverns. Outside are nature trails, the Prospect Tower to climb, dinosaur displays, and a few play areas (inc a maze), as well as great views and nicely laid out woodland walks; usually clown shows or similar entertainments. Good meals and snacks, shop, limited disabled access – best to phone beforehand; open most wknds from mid-Feb–Easter (best to check first as dates can depend on the weather), then daily mid-Mar to Oct; (01629) 582365; £6.50.

Matlock Bath Aquarium & Hologram A useful family attraction if you're staying in the area; cl winter wkdys; (01629) 583624; £1.80.

Peak District Mining Museum 🏛
(Temple Rd) Lively exploration of mining, with a unique early 19th-c water-pressure pumping engine, and interactive display on the pitfalls of working in a mine. Also tours of the old Temple Mine workings, and the chance to pan for minerals – in the past they've even found a tiny amount of gold. Snacks, shop, disabled access; cl 25 Dec; (01629) 583834; *£2.50, joint ticket inc mine tours *£4.

MELBOURNE SK3825
This pleasant small town has a good relaxed feel and villagey lanes; the White Swan and Railway Hotel are good for lunch. The **church of St Michael and St Mary** is impressive, more like a cathedral than an ordinary parish church.

Melbourne Hall Behind its 18th-c façade, this grandly extended house dates back in part to the 13th c, and has twice been the home of British prime ministers; fine pictures and furnishings. Glorious formal gardens with fountains, pools, and famous yew tunnel; interesting craft centre (open all year). Meals, snacks, shop, limited disabled access; Hall open pm daily in Aug (exc first three Mons), plus gardens open Weds, Sat, Sun and bank hol Mon pms Apr–Sept; (01332) 862502; *£3 (with gardens, *£5).

MIDDLETON-BY-WIRKSWORTH SK2755
Middleton Top Engine House
Home to a beam engine built in 1829 to haul waggons up a steep incline on the Cromford & High Peak Railway. Snacks, shop, disabled access; engine in motion first wknd of month and bank hol wknds; cl wkdys Oct–Easter; (01629) 823204; *£1 (50p when engine is static). The Knockerdown Inn out on the B5035 is pleasant for lunch.

MILLDALE SK1354
This section of Dove Dale has barer pastures and steeper hillsides than the lower sections – but fewer other walkers to keep you company. Handy refreshment places on the Staffordshire side of the river are the Watts Russell Arms at Hopedale and George at Alstonefield.

MILLERS DALE SK1573
The B6049 N off the A6 SE of Buxton gives access to Millers Dale, just past the little village of that name (the Anglers Rest is a decent pub); upstream of Monsal Dale, this is rather less visited but also a lovely spot for walks – as is its continuation Chee Dale.

MONSAL DALE SK1771
This winding valley is the outstanding place for walks in this central part of the White Peak area, its pastoral quality emphasised by the disused limestone cotton mills along the way. It's

especially lovely in May and June with wild flowers enriching the pastures along the broader stretches. Don't expect to have it to yourself. There's good access from the A6 a couple of miles towards Buxton from Ashford in the Water; and from Monsal Head (friendly hotel), where a disused railway viaduct adds interest. This viaduct forms part of the Monsal Trail.

MONSAL TRAIL SK1172
This outshines the other former railway-track walks in the Peak District, though like them is in parts more exposed to the winds than walks down in the dales. It runs from Wye Dale E of Buxton to Coombs Road viaduct S of Bakewell. W of Millers Dale Station, the trail leaves the old railway and takes a stepping-stone route along the river beneath the towering cliffs of Chee Tor before rejoining the railway track.

MONYASH SK1566
Quiet village with good value home cooking at the Bulls Head, and (2m S) the mysterious **Arbor Low stone circle**.

OLD BRAMPTON SK3371
The village itself is attractive, and has one special curiosity: count the minutes between one and two o'clock on its church clock.

OLD WHITTINGTON SK3874
Revolution House (High St) Innocuous-looking thatched cottage, 300 years ago the birthplace of what came to be known as the Glorious Revolution. Good audio-visual display, period rooms and furniture. Shop, disabled access to ground floor only; open Good Fri–Oct and last 2 wks in Dec (exc 25–26); (01246) 453554; free. The White Horse is useful for lunch.

OSMASTON SK2043
This village of pretty thatched cottages has a pleasant path through a lakeside park. The Shoulder of Mutton has good value food.

OVER HADDON SK2066
Lathkill Dale Craft Centre (Manor Farm) Set in a pretty village, this has plenty of craft shops and demonstrations; café, disabled access; cl 25 Dec; (01629) 813589; free.

RIPLEY SK3947
Denby Pottery Visitor Centre (B6179 S) Guided factory tours (10.30am and 1pm – Mon–Thurs;

booking essential) show the intricate skills of potters and craftsmen. Big factory shop, and children's play area. Meals, snacks, shops and garden centre, disabled access; cl 25–26 Dec; (01773) 740799; full tours £3.75, otherwise free.

Midland Railway Centre 🔄 (Butterley Station) Regular steam-train passenger service through country park, and developing railway museum. Meals, snacks, shop, disabled access; cl 25 Dec; best to ring for train timetable, (01773) 570140; £7.95 (£8.95 bank hols and special events). It's good for families – not only are there a few farm animals on the adjacent farm (you can visit here free without having to go on the railway), but two children are admitted free with every adult ticket during special events. The Excavator on the A610 out at Buckland Hollow is a good value family dining pub.

RIVER DERWENT SK2666
You can walk along pleasant stretches where Izaak Walton fished, either upstream from Rowsley, or from the B6012 N of there at the Calton Lees car park – there's open access to Chatsworth Park on this W side of the river, which is particularly lovely.

RIVER TRENT SK3427
This impresses with its silent power – perhaps Britain's most formidable river. Ingleby is one good access point – for example, from the big garden of the John Thompson pub, which brews its own beer.

ROWSLEY SK2565
Caudwell's Mill & Craft Centre Working 19th-c flour mill, powered by water turbines, with crafts such as glass-blowing and wood-turning. Meals, snacks, shop; cl wkdys Jan; (01629) 734374; mill *£3, craft centre free. Rowsley also has an interesting **stone circle** called the Nine Ladies. The Grouse & Claret does decent food (all day wknds).

Peak Village Developing designer shopping village in the heart of the Peak District with a *Wind in the Willows* attraction and related merchandise; also craft and other shops; there are plans for an indoor play area. Meals, snacks, disabled access; (01629) 735326; free.

SHARDLOW SK4430
Shardlow – canal basin Attractive, with some handsome former wharf buildings – one now an antiques warehouse, another, the Malt Shovel, a good pub.

SHINING TOR SK1454
A breezy but undemanding moorland walk from the summit of a minor road.

SOUTH WINGFIELD SK3754
Wingfield Manor (B5035) Substantial ruin with virtually complete banqueting hall, tower and undercroft. The 16th-c Babington Plot is thought to have been hatched here, leading to the final downfall of Mary, Queen of Scots. Used as a filming location for Zeffirelli's *Jane Eyre*. Snacks, shop, some disabled access; cl Mon and Tues, 24–26 Dec and 1 Jan; (01773) 832060; £3, inc audio tour. The White Hart at Moorwood Moor has reasonably priced food.

SUDBURY SK1532
Sudbury Hall Individual but attractive Stuart mansion with elaborate carving, frescoes, murals and plasterwork in splendidly elegant rooms; the interiors featured in the BBC's *Pride and Prejudice* as the home of Mr Darcy. It's worth a visit just for the excellent **National Trust Museum of Childhood**, which has a chimney climb for sweep-sized children, and a fine collection of toys and dolls. You can play with some exhibits, and at wknds the schoolroom is staffed by an Edwardian teacher. Meals, snacks, shop, disabled access (bear in mind, new car park is 400 yds from Hall); open pm Weds–Sun (and bank hol Mons) Apr–Oct, plus museum open a few wknd pms in Dec; (01283) 585305; £5.90 for everything, or £3.70 house and grounds or museum only; NT. The Boars Head Hotel is useful for lunch.

TIDESWELL SK1575
The spacious 14th-c **church** is known as the Cathedral of the Peak; the village is attractive, with an excellent butcher, and this is good walking country. The B6049 across Millers Dale has nice views.

TISSINGTON SK1752
The Peak District's most beautiful village, its broad main street wonderfully harmonious, with wide grass verges, handsome stone houses inc a Jacobean hall (open Tues–Thurs

pm late Jun to late Aug; (01335) 352200; £5, gardens only £2) and interesting church. The grey stone gardener's cottage is familiar from many calendars; garden centre, decent homely café.

TORRS RIVERSIDE PARK SJ9984
This deep gorge below New Mills is a good place to potter among the ivy-covered remains of former mills and other industrial relics; the canal basin has been restored over at Buxworth – the Navigation here is a very enjoyable pub. The **Goyt Way** is a track heading N towards and beyond Marple, partly following the Peak Forest Canal – a pretty walk.

WHITE PEAK SK1572
This area, picturesquely cut by the intricate channels of the dales, has high, flat pastures with small fields of rich grassland enclosed by silvery stone walls, clusters of often very photogenic farm buildings, and small old-fashioned villages. It gives an abundance of generally gentle walking.

WIRKSWORTH SK2755
National Stone Centre (Porter Lane, Middleton) Surprisingly enjoyable centre, featuring 330-million-year-old tropical lagoons and limestone fossil reefs, as well as an exhibition, guided fossil trails, and, for an extra charge, activities like gem-panning or fossil-rubbing. Snacks, shop, some disabled access; cl 25–26 Dec; (01629) 824833; £1.80.

Wirksworth Heritage Centre (Crown Yard, Market Pl) Attractive old silk and velvet mill, with displays on quarrying and local customs such as well-dressing and clypping the church, and a few children's activities. Meals, snacks, shop; cl Mon (exc bank hols and mid-July–mid-Sept), Tues (exc Apr–mid-Sept), and all Dec–mid-Feb; (01629) 825225; *£2. The town boasts a lot of restored old buildings; the Blacks Head (Market Pl) is a useful local pub.

WOLFSCOTE DALE SK1357
One of the quieter sections of Dove Dale, its dramatic rocky gorge and still trout pools are best reached on foot from Hartington, where the Devonshire Arms and Minton House are both reliable hotels.

YOULGREAVE SK2164
A charming dales village, with an

interesting church.

Other attractive villages include Brassington SK2354, Coton in the Elms SK2415, Duffield SK3443, Earl Sterndale SK0967, Elton SK2261, Holymoorside SK3469, Idridgehay SK2849, Kirk Ireton SK2650, Little Hucklow SK1678, Litton SK1675, Lullington SK2513, Mapleton SK1648 (domed church, nice riverside walk to Thorpe), Milton SK3126, Parwich SK1854, Repton SK3026, Ridgeway SK3551, Smisby SK3419, Stanton by Dale SK4638 and Stanton in Peak SK2464.

Decent country pubs perfectly placed for walkers include the Peacock at Barlow SK3474, Robin Hood at Baslow SK2572 (handy for the ridge of Baslow Edge), Kings Head at Bonsall SK2858 (very child-friendly, by the Limestone Way), Bowling Green at Bradwell SK1781 in Smalldale, Barrel on the ridge at Bretton SK2077, Church at Chelmorton SK1170, Beehive at Combs SK0478 (lovely valley), Bridge at Ford SK4080, Grouse nr Froggatt Edge SK2577, Queen Anne at Great Hucklow SK1878, Royal Oak at Millthorpe SK3276, Miners Arms at Milltown SK3561, Bulls Head at Monyash SK1566, Grouse at Nether Padley SK2577, New Napoleon by Ogston Reservoir SK3761, Little Mill nr Rowarth SK0189 (particularly for Lantern Pike), Queens Arms at Taddington SK1472 and Bulls Head at Wardlow SK1874 (for well wooded Cressbrook Dale).

Where to eat

BAKEWELL SK2168 **Byways** *Water Lane* *(01629) 812807* Olde-worlde tea room with several separate areas, roaring log fire, well presented good value food from snacks to meals, and warmly friendly staff. £11|**£3**

BAKEWELL SK2168 **Renaissance** *Bath St (01629) 812687* Overlooking a little walled garden where fresh herbs are grown, this beamed restaurant serves imaginative French dishes inc gourmet specials and a fresh fish of the day, and delicious puddings; friendly service; cl Sun pm, Mon, first 2 wks Jan, first 2 wks Aug; disabled access. £25

BARLOW SK3474 **Trout** *33 Valley Rd (01742) 890893* More inviting than you'd guess from outside, this dining pub has plenty of brocaded banquettes and neat tables, beamery and old-world prints, a proper pubby part and second dining room, good genuinely home-made food inc delicious puddings, no smoking restaurant, well kept real ales, and quick competent service. £17.50|**£5.85**

BIRCHOVER SK2362 **Druid** *(01629) 650302* Civilised and pleasantly remote creeper-covered dining pub with huge choice of very popular interesting food (best to book), well kept real ales, and friendly service; bustling little bar with big coal fire, no smoking Garden Room, and spacious and airy two-storey dining extension; children must leave by 8pm; cl 25 Dec. £22|**£8.90**

BUXTON SK0673 **Coffee Bean Café** *50 Spring Gardens (01298) 27345* Small bustling café, long and narrow, with old tea and coffee advertisements, 15 types of coffee, all-day breakfasts, savouries and light lunches, and delicious cakes; cl evenings; disabled access. |**£4**

BUXTON SK0573 **Old Sun** *33 High St (01298) 23452* Old coaching inn with several small cosy rooms leading off central bar, open fires, low beams, comfortable leather armchairs and chesterfields, fresh flowers and carefully chosen bric-a-brac, a good choice of real ales, a dozen wines by the glass, adventurous food inc excellent puddings, and friendly staff; children until 8pm; disabled access. £18.20|**£7.15**

BUXWORTH SK0282 **Navigation** *(01663) 732072* Very welcoming extended pub by restored canal basin, with low-ceilinged rooms, plenty to look at, good fires, well kept real ales, good value generous food, and cheerful staff; tables on sunken flagstone terrace; disabled access. £16.25|**£5.95**

CHURCH BROUGHTON SK2033 **Holly Bush** *Main St (01283) 585345* Neat brick village pub, nicely refurbished, with well kept real ale and good value, home-

made, simple but tasty food in both bar and separate dining room; disabled access.
£10|£3.50

EYAM SK2276 **Eyam Tea Rooms** *The Square (01433) 631274* Family-run tea
shop with sandwiches, salads and good cream teas, and lots of speciality teas; cl
winter Weds, cl Nov–mid-Feb; partial disabled access. |£3.50

EYAM SK2276 **Miners Arms** *Water Lane (01433) 630853* Carefully refurbished
pub with a restful atmosphere in its three little plush beamed rooms, good
interesting lunchtime food served by attentive staff, well kept ales, and decent
nearby walks; bdrms; cl Mon am, no food Sun or Mon pm, cl 1st 2 wks Jan; disabled
access. £17.25|£6.95

HOGNASTON SK2350 **Red Lion** *Main St (01335) 370396* Carefully renovated
open-plan oak-beamed dining pub with a friendly welcome and relaxed
atmosphere, attractive mix of candlelit tables on ancient flagstones, three open
fires, a collection of teddy bears, well presented imaginative food (book at wknds),
well kept real ales, and attentive staff; attractive bdrms; cl Mon am; children over 10;
disabled access. £22.80|£5.95

HOPE SK1783 **Cheshire Cheese** *Edale Rd (01433) 620381* 16th-c village pub
with three cosy beamed rooms, each with its own coal fire, well kept real ales, a
decent choice of house wines, good food (esp evenings), obliging service, and two
small no smoking dining rooms. £19.45|£4.95

KINGS NEWTON SK3826 **Hardinge Arms** *(01332) 813808* Civilised and
attractive old inn with beams, open fires and comfortable rambling rooms, popular
lunchtime carvery and other enjoyable bar food, and well kept real ales from a fine
panelled and carved bar counter; bdrms; disabled access. £18|£6.95

MELBOURNE SK3825 **Bay Tree** *4 Potter St (01332) 863358* Small family-run
cottagey restaurant with beams and simple furnishings, carefully presented popular
food (Sun lunch is booked up weeks ahead), and thoughtful relaxed service; cl Sun
pm, Mon. £33

MILLTOWN SK3661 **Miners Arms** *(01246) 590218* Impeccably kept and
comfortable stone-built dining pub with L-shaped layout, a back bar, and no
smoking dining room; particularly good home-made food, well priced, with
especially good interesting vegetables (a choice of half-a-dozen), and three sorts of
potato, well kept real ales, decent value wines, and friendly efficient service.
£16.30|£6.50

OVER HADDON SK2066 **Lathkil** *(01629) 812501* Comfortable inn with
stunning views and plenty of surrounding walks; open fires, beams and comfortable
furnishings, partly no smoking dining area which doubles as an evening restaurant,
enjoyable food and well kept real ales, and helpful service; children lunchtime only.
£23|£7.25

RIDGEWAY SK4081 **Old Vicarage** *Ridgeway Moor (0114) 247 5814* Big
Victorian house in lovely gardens with a marvellously relaxing welcoming
atmosphere, cosy sitting room for pre-dinner drinks and beautifully presented,
quite exceptional cooking using home-grown produce in candlelit dining room or
light and airy less formal conservatory; cl Sat am, Sun pm, Mon (though they will
open then for private parties of over 10 people); disabled access. £51/3-course Sun
lunch £32

WOOLLEY MOOR SK3661 **White Horse** *Badger Lane (01246) 590319*
Popular old pub run by very friendly people – and much liked by locals; very good
food using best local produce, lots of daily specials, decent wines and beers, new
conservatory, lovely view from garden (pleasant Ashover Valley walks), good play
area; disabled access. £15.50|£4.95

Special thanks to Mrs J Davidson, R A Smith, John Lucas, S T Reynolds

DEVON

Devon has so much to see and do, and such a wonderful variety of scenery, that we have divided it into three areas. East Devon is classic family holiday country, with Exeter a charming small city for a short break. South Devon, with Dartmoor, has the widest appeal of all, with a mass of interesting places to visit, and glorious vistas of coast and moor. North Devon, with Exmoor, is mainly less touristy than the other areas, but is also very rewarding.

In all three areas, there are some splendid family days out. Crealy Country at Clyst St Mary is an East Devon favourite. In South Devon, the National Marine Aquarium and the Plymouth Dome (both in Plymouth), the Woodland Leisure Park (Blackawton), and Morwellham Quay are all engrossing in their very different ways, and children aren't left out even in more grown-up places such as Powderham Castle and Buckland Abbey. In North Devon, the vibrant Torrington 1646 heritage centre stands out, and adults may be surprised to find out that they're enjoying the Big Sheep near Bideford or the Gnome Reserve near Bradworthy as much as the children.

Of course, Devon isn't all family fun; with some fine gardens, remarkable historic buildings, and unusual and enthusiastic museums, and a lot of excellent food, it's very rewarding for adults. And there are some outstanding places to stay in, at all price levels.

Some of the best views here are from trains; besides vintage steam trains puffing through gorgeous river valleys, the standard railway Devon Rover is a good deal, with unlimited train journeys in the area at a reduced rate for either a week or any three days out of seven; phone Great Western trains on (08457) 000125.

Exeter & East Devon

Good for seaside holidays, with plenty to keep families busy; we include Exeter here – a most charming small city with a very distinctive atmosphere

Farway Countryside Park, with its decent mix of animals and play areas, joins Crealy Adventure Park (several new attractions here this year inc a runaway train ride), the World of Country Life in Exmouth and the Pecorama Pleasure Gardens at Beer, as safe bets for family days out.

Escot Aquatic Gardens (animals and birds too) near Ottery St Mary has wide appeal, and the Great Exmouth Model Railway is worth an outing if only to see the amazingly detailed craftsmanship.

The gardens at Killerton, Bicton Park and Bicton College of Agriculture are all most attractive, and Exmouth's A la Ronde is a rewarding example of architectural whimsy; the Court of Sovereigns at beautiful Cadhay is unusual too.

The coast has four main beach resorts, each quite different from the others. Exmouth is the liveliest and biggest, and doubles as a working port. Seaton, quieter, is a more typical family resort, with much less of a beach. Budleigh Salterton, the quietest, is rather retiring and genteel. Sidmouth is slightly busier, with a good deal of character as well as plenty for families – the broadest all-round appeal. Branscombe is the prettiest coastal village. Inland, coastal downs give a gently varied landscape of charming wooded valleys with views and high pastures between, and several attractive villages. N of the A30/A35 is more self-contained farmland, mainly well hedged traditional stock and dairy farms. Cullompton farmers' market has a refreshing appeal in this supermarket age.

Exeter is civilised and gently attractive, with a decidedly relaxed and easy-going West Country feel. It has a lot to see, with good free guided walks, and an intriguing tour through underground passages. Its museums are interesting and particularly well organised: the Royal Albert Memorial Museum, with several fine recently added galleries, is now one of the best in the country. Film buffs will enjoy the Bill Douglas Centre. Served by fast trains and the M5, the city can be reached quickly from far away – and good roads bring the other parts of Devon within comfortable reach for a day out.

Where to stay

EXETER SX9292 **Edwardian Hotel** *30–32 Heavitree Rd, Exeter, Devon EX1 2LQ* *(01392)* *276102* **£48**, plus special breaks; 12 individually furnished rms, four with four-posters. Popular guest house close to cathedral and city centre, with pretty lounge, enjoyable breakfasts in attractive dining rooms, and warmly friendly and knowledgeable resident owners; plenty of places nearby for evening meals; cl 25–26 Dec; disabled access

EXETER SX9192 **St Olave's Court** *Mary Arches St, Exeter, Devon EX4 3AZ* *(01392)* *217736* **£75**w, plus special breaks; 15 well equipped rms. Handsome Georgian style house just 400 yds from the cathedral in its own walled garden, with a warm welcome from helpful friendly staff, comfortable rooms, enjoyable evening meals in candlelit restaurant, and good breakfasts

EXETER SX9292 **White Hart** *66 South St, Exeter, Devon EX1 IEE (01392)* *279897* **£64**w, plus special breaks; 57 modern but slightly dated rms. Rather splendid 14th-c inn with lots of different eating areas (wine-bar-type as well as a proper restaurant), marvellous atmospheric bar, open fires, beams, antiques, good range of wines, friendly service, attractive courtyard with proper barbecues, and enjoyable breakfasts; no accommodation 24–26 Dec

GITTISHAM SY1497 **Combe House** *Gittisham, Honiton, Devon EX14 0AD* *(01404)* *540400* **£108**, plus winter breaks; 15 individually decorated, pretty rms with lovely views. Peaceful and newly refurbished Elizabethan country hotel in gardens with 700-year-old Lebanese cedars and walks around the 3,000-acre estate; elegant day rooms with antiques, pictures and fresh flowers, a happy relaxed atmosphere, very good food using some home-grown produce, and fine wines (the cellar is popular for wine tastings); can use the house for special occasions and meetings

LYMPSTONE SX9884 **River House** *Lympstone, Devon EX8 5EY (01395) 265147* **£86**, plus special breaks; 3 pretty rms. Warmly welcoming restaurant-with-rooms with marvellous river views from big picture windows, good imaginative food (wonderful fresh fish and interesting vegetable dishes) in first-floor restaurant using some home-grown produce, thoughtfully chosen wines, and kind service; practical cookery courses, too; cl 25–28 Dec, 1 Jan, bank hol Mons; restaurant cl Sun/Mon pm (though open if residents want to eat and open for private parties of 6 or more); children over 6; limited disabled access

MEMBURY ST2703 **Lea Hill** *Membury, Axminster, Devon EX13 7AQ (01404) 881881 £92*, plus special breaks; 11 rms, inc 2 suites, in carefully converted barns, mostly with private garden areas or terraces. Set in eight acres in lovely countryside, this thatched 14th-c longhouse has comfortable beamed rooms, a convivial bar, relaxed and friendly owners, particularly good evening meals, and nice breakfasts; well behaved dogs by special arrangement; cl Jan/Feb; children over 12

SIDFORD SY1489 **Blue Ball** *Sidford, Sidmouth, Devon EX10 9QL (01395) 514062 £60*; 5 rms with nice touches like free papers, fruit and fresh flowers, shared bthrm – they hope to add private bthrms and add another 2 rms. Welcoming thatched 14th-c inn run by the same family since 1912, with lovely winter log fire in low partly panelled lounge bar, heavy beams, lots of bric-a-brac, no smoking snug, very friendly service, and decent food inc hearty breakfasts; dogs by arrangement

STOCKLAND ST2404 **Kings Arms** *Stockland, Honiton, Devon EX14 9BS (01404) 881361 £50*; 3 rms. Cream-faced thatched pub with elegant rooms, open fires, first-class food in bar and evening restaurant food (esp fish), and interesting wine list; skittle alley, live music Sun pm; cl 25 Dec; well behaved children only

WHIMPLE SY0497 **Woodhayes** *Whimple, Exeter, Devon EX5 2TD (01404) 822237 £75*; 6 lovely spacious rms. Big Georgian country house in neat grounds, with comfortable quietly decorated lounges, small library, open fires, flagstoned bar and pretty dining room, fine food, afternoon teas, and excellent breakfasts; tennis, croquet; cl 2 wks over Christmas/New Year; children over 12

To see and do

BEER SY2289
Rather cottagey resort village, still with fishing boats pulled up on the shingle beach (summer boat hire, too), and a stream channelled down the main street. The village was famous from Roman times for its cavernous whitestone quarries, which can be visited, and the B3174 inland passes lots of Bronze Age burial mounds. The Dolphin here is good value.
Pecorama Pleasure Gardens Fun for railway lovers, with models and train collections in the house, and outside a miniature steam and diesel passenger line with stunning views of the bay. Also crazy golf, aviary, children's maze and assault course, a multi-themed garden, live entertainment and maybe children's pony rides. Meals, snacks, shop, mostly disabled access; cl Sat pm, Sun (exc Jun–Aug), and outdoor features cl Oct–Easter (exc Oct half-term); (01297) 21542; £4.25 (less for just outside features).
BRANSCOMBE SY1988
The church has a magnificently carved

oak gallery, and a Norman tower with distinctive stair-turret. The village is notably pretty – a series of largely unspoilt thatched hamlets strung along a lovely seaside valley. Branscombe, lying just inland, is linked to the coast path by other paths, and has the good Masons Arms in the main part of the village, as well as the NT Old Bakery tea room opp the unique NT thatched smithy.
BROADCLYST SX9897
Pretty thatch-and-cob village, with a marvellous old church, photogenic outside, interesting in. The Red Lion has good food – and the post office has a unique computer information kiosk.
CLYST ST MARY SY0090
Crealy Adventure Park 🖼
(Sidmouth Rd) There's plenty to amuse children of all ages at this bustling family complex. The Magical Kingdom, a delightfully constructed area aimed mostly at under-7s, has play areas and a soaring gondola swing, while among the attractions to occupy older children are bumper boats, go-karts and a farm where you can milk the cows (and

always meet baby animals). Many of the attractions are indoors, inc some of the animals, and a very good varied adventure playground, with plenty of slides (one has a practically vertical drop) and things to swing on. Several new attractions include a family roller-coaster, toddlers' garden play area, multi-colour meadow and splash zone. Other features include pony rides and lakeside walks, and they have a particularly wide range of special events and activities (usually on summer Suns). Meals, snacks, shop, disabled access; (01395) 233200; cl 25–26 Dec, 1 Jan; £5.50; several family tickets available. Our discount voucher entitles you to a free go-kart race before noon. If you don't want to eat in the park, the Half Moon has decent food.

CULLOMPTON ST0207
The church is notable for its remarkable painted screen; the busy little town has an attractive feel, and a famers' market (the first of its kind in the West Country) is held in Station Rd on the 2nd Sat of every month (exc Jan and Feb).

CULMSTOCK ST1013
The village has a handsome church, a prettily placed old pub, and a pleasant riverside walk to Uffculme.

DALWOOD ST2400
Burrow Farm Gardens 🖼 (half a mile or so off A35, turn off at Taunton Cross signs) Part of this 6-acre site has been created from an ancient Roman clay pit, and there are spacious lawns, borders and unusual shrubs and trees as well as a woodland garden, pergola walk with old-fashioned roses, and super views. There is a new rill garden, and a wildlife lake will be opening this year. Cream teas, snacks, nursery, disabled access; cl Oct–Mar; (01404) 831285; *£3. The pretty Tuckers Arms is good for lunch.

DOWLANDS CLIFFS SY2889
The steeply tumbled brambly wooded wilderness of this undercliff 3m E of Axmouth has numerous small birds.

EAST BUDLEIGH SY0684
Attractive and quietly placed cob and thatch village; the pleasant church has fascinating Jacobean carved pew ends – some grotesque, some hilarious, some frankly rude. The Sir Walter Raleigh has

good food.
Bicton College of Agriculture The gardens here are of great if rather specialised appeal; long monkey-puzzle avenue through parkland, rich collection of magnolias, camellias and flowering cherries, national pittosporum and agapanthus collections, and 17-acre arboretum with woodland garden. Snacks, plant centre; usually cl winter wknds, 25 Dec and Good Fri; (01395) 568353; £2.
Bicton Park 🖼 63 acres of lovely gardens, shrubs, lakes and woodland. A futuristic-looking glass Palm House turns out to be early 19th c, and has a fine collection of tropical trees and plants; also fuchsia, geranium and orchid houses, bird garden, pinetum, magnificent Italian gardens, miniature train rides and nature trails. Meals, snacks, shop and plant centre, disabled access; cl 25 Dec; (01395) 568465; *£4.95. The Salterton Arms is handy, in nearby Budleigh Salterton – a peaceful seaside resort; the bottom end of its beach is a haven for nudists.

EXETER SX9292
Though large parts of the centre were devastated by World War II bombing, some choice streets and buildings survive, with picturesque partly Tudor narrow lanes leading from the mainly pedestrianised High St into the serene tree-shaded cathedral close. The atmosphere is distinctive – relaxed and liberal yet responsible, buoyed up by the thriving university. In the centre, modern shops are integrated into the old layout very discreetly indeed. With many smaller churches, decent book and other shops, pubs and so forth nearby, this is a very pleasant part for browsing around. Particularly attractive streets include Southernhay at the end of the close, and Stepcote Hill, a picturesque detour from Fore St. The Quay, beyond the streams of fast traffic on the ring road (there are quiet underpasses), has become lively and entertaining, with handsomely restored buildings, resurgent cafés and pubs (the Prospect and Port Royal are worth knowing), and a growing number of craft shops and the like; the Old Quay House has a visitor centre with audio-visual show. Apart from the White

Hart, civilised pubs and wine bars with decent food include the sumptuous Imperial (New North Rd), Chaucers (High St, under C&A), Ship (14th-c, Martins Lane), Well House (The Close – cathedral view and Roman well) and Papermakers (Exe St). There are boat trips down the ship canal to Exminster; or you can walk down, passing the Double Locks (a favourite pub) and ending at the Turf Hotel looking out over the estuary. Daily free guided tours leave the Royal Clarence Hotel (Cathedral Close) throughout the day (tel (01392) 265203 for details, or pick up a programme from the Tourist Information Centre, Paris St). The quickest way into the city from either the M5 or the A38 is to keep on round to the westbound A30 and go into the city from the Alphington roundabout.

Bill Douglas Centre (Old Library, Exeter University, Prince of Wales Rd) Display of almost 1,000 cinema-related objects amassed by the late film-maker Bill Douglas; items inc film star dolls, 19th-c optical toys and oriental shadow puppets. Disabled access; cl all wknds (inc bank hols), Easter and Christmas weeks; (01392) 264321; free (guided tours £2).

Exeter Cathedral England's finest example of Decorated Gothic architecture, with its magnificent nave soaring to the vaulted roof, and intricately carved choir stalls; the 13th-c misericords are thought to be the oldest set in the country. It also boasts the longest unbroken Gothic vaulting in Europe, superbly atmospheric. Lots of colourfully embroidered cushions, chronologically illustrating English and local history. The façade has three tiers of sculpted figures, inc the Apostles. Meals, snacks, shop, disabled access; guided tours 11am and 2.30pm wkdys, just 11 Sat; £2.50 suggested donation.

Guildhall This medieval municipal building with its ornately colonnaded Elizabethan façade is one of the oldest still in use; it has displays of civic regalia and so on. Disabled access to ground floor only; cl 1–2pm, Sat pm (and all day Sats in winter), all day Sun and bank hols, during civic functions and over Christmas; free.

Royal Albert Memorial Museum

(Queen St) Wonderful Gothic exterior, and inside notable displays of regional silver, African carvings, archaeology, paintings, natural history and ethnology: three recently added galleries include touch-screen computer displays and intriguing exhibits such as materials collected during Captain Cook's voyages. Snacks, shop, disabled access; cl Sun, Good Fri, 25–26 Dec and 1 Jan; (01392) 265858; free.

St Nicholas's Priory (Mint Lane) 11th-c Benedictine monastery with unusual Norman undercroft, Tudor room and 15th-c kitchen. Shop, disabled access to ground floor only; open 3–4.30pm Mon, Weds and Sat Easter–Oct, occasionally cl for private functions; (01392) 665858; *50p (children free).

Underground Passages 🖾 (entrance via Boots Arcade in High St) An unusual medieval attraction is this atmospheric network, built in the 14th c to bring water into the city; there's an introductory exhibition and video, then a guided tour of the passages themselves, still much as they were centuries ago. The guides can be very entertaining, and clearly enjoy their work. Flat shoes are recommended. Shop; cl am wkdys (exc July–Sept and school hols), all day Mon (exc school hols) and Sun; (01392) 265887; £2.50 (£3.50 in summer).

EXMOUTH SY0080 Good family seaside holiday town, worth a visit for its lively harbour and marina, its long sandy beach and its stately church. Summer cruise trips go from the harbour up to Topsham, and there are sea fishing trips from the clock tower (they supply rod and bait); (01395) 222144 for both. The Seafood Restaurant (Tower St) has nothing but the freshest fish and shellfish; the Grove (attractive seafront garden) and seafront Deer Leap are useful too.

A la Ronde (A376 2m N) Extraordinary 16-sided house, built around 1795 and decorated in part with feathers, seashells, seaweed and sand. A charmingly whimsical place, the outside looking not entirely unlike a giant biscuit barrel. The curator has come up with a novel way to fund the restoration of the roof – by asking visitors to sponsor the 20,000 ceramic tiles at £1 a go. Meals, snacks, shop, disabled access to ground floor only; cl Fri, Sat, and all Nov–Easter; (01395) 265514; £3.30; NT.

Great Exmouth Model Railway (Sea Front) Home to the world's biggest 00 gauge model railway, nearly 1½ miles of track indoors with outside trains running round a pond of koi carp. It took 14 years to build and is constantly updated; some of the detail is amazing, right down to the birds in the trees. Shop, some disabled access; cl Nov–Feb; (01395) 278383; £2.25.

High Land of Orcombe Reached by the shore road E out of Exmouth and protected against campsite encroachment by its National Trust ownership, this gives walkers a short stroll with sea views.

World of Country Life (Sandy Bay) 40 acres of decent family-based activities, with friendly animals, adventure playground and undercover play areas, safari rides through deer and llama paddocks, reconstructed Victorian street, classic motorcycle collection, crafts, steam engines, and falconry centre (no displays Sat). Meals, snacks, shop, disabled access; cl Nov–Easter; (01395) 274533; £5.50.

FARWAY SY1896

Farway Countryside Park (off A3052 W of Colyford) Prettily set over 100 acres, this bustling place is home to a real jumble of animals. Children can feed calves and lambs twice a day, and other baby animals to pet include goslings, turkeys and guinea pigs. Elsewhere you'll find more unusual creatures from water buffalo to pot-bellied pigs, as well as indoor and outdoor play areas, donkey and pony rides and a 9-hole pitch and putt course. Meals, snacks, shop, disabled access; open daily Apr–Oct, plus wknds and school hols in winter; (01404) 871367; £3.95, small extra charge for golf and rides.

HEMBURY HILL FORT ST1103
A walk up from the A373 NW of Honiton, for good views.

HONITON ST1600
Some handsome Georgian buildings along this country town's long high street, and some interesting shops. The Red Cow (High St) is good value for lunch. Fine views from the A375 S.

Allhallows Museum 🏛 (High St) This refurbished 13th-c building has useful displays of Honiton lace, and lace-making demonstrations in Jun, July and Aug. Shop, disabled access to ground floor only (they hope to add a lift this year); cl Sat pm, all Sun, and Nov–Easter; (01404) 44966; *£2.

KILLERTON SS9700
Best of all in spring, 15 acres of beautiful hillside gardens, shrub borders and planted beds, with an impressive avenue of beech trees. The 18th-c house has an annually changing costume exhibition in period furnished rooms, but it's the gardens that really give the place its special appeal. Meals, snacks, shop and plant centre, good disabled access (with buggies round the grounds); house cl Tues, and all Nov–mid-Mar; (01392) 881345; £5.10, £3.50 garden only; NT. The Three Tuns in Silverton has enjoyable food, esp vegetarian, and readers recommend the antiques centre at nearby Hele (towards Bradninch).

OTTERTON SY0785
Otterton Mill Centre 🏛 Working watermill still grinding flour for the bread, cakes and pies sold on the premises. Also craft workshops, display of local lace, and interesting evening events. Enjoyable meals and snacks, shop, garden centre, some disabled access; cl 24–27 Dec; (01395) 568521; £1.50 (free entry to wheelchair users). The village itself is pretty.

OTTERY ST MARY SY1095
Restrained small town – or extended village – with some attractive old buildings around its interesting twin-towered church. The circular tumbling weir by an 18th-c mill signed off Mill St is unusual, and photogenic. The London Inn is useful, and the Otter Nurseries (award-winning lavatories) have good plants.

Cadhay (just NW) Beautiful Tudor and Georgian manor house, with fine timbered 15th-c roof in its Great Hall, and unusual Court of Sovereigns – a pretty courtyard with statues of various monarchs. Disabled access to garden and downstairs; open pm Tues–Thurs July and Aug, plus Sun and Mon spring and Aug bank hol; (01404) 812432; £4.

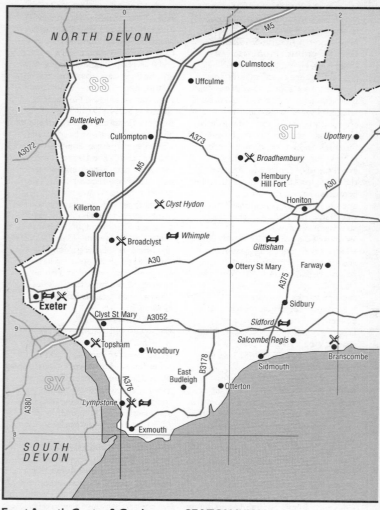

Escot Aquatic Centre & Gardens
(Parklands Farm, Escot) Tropical and coldwater fish from koi carp to piranhas, as well as rabbits and other pets, otters (fed at 11 and 3), Victorian walled rose garden, wild boar enclosures, walks, views and parkland. Also wetlands and waterfowl park, birds of prey, play area and pet centre with all you'll need for any kind of pet, inc the animals themselves. Meals, snacks, shop, disabled access; cl Mon Jan–Mar and 25–26 Dec; (01404) 822188; £3.50.

SEATON SY2391
Lyme Bay Cider (Manor Farm; A3052 just N) Vintage equipment and free tastings of cider, country wines and traditional liqueurs; cl winter wknds and some summer Suns; (01297) 22887; free. Open-top trams run from Seaton to Colyton, where the Kingfisher is a good pub; back in town, the Fisherman's (Marine Crescent) has decent cheap food all day.

SIDBURY SY1391
A pretty village, with a charming church, and a very good pub nearby at Sidford.

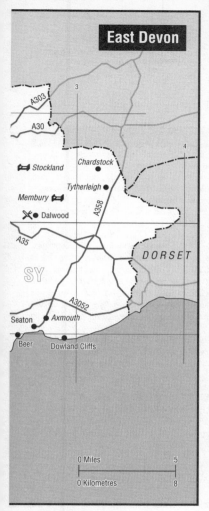

East Devon

Stockland

Chardstock

Tytherleigh

Membury

Dalwood

A303
A30
A358
A35
A3052

DORSET

SY

Seaton · Axmouth
Beer · Dowland Cliffs

0 Miles 5
0 Kilometres 8

SIDMOUTH SY1287

Attractive old streets, very 18th-c, running back from the seafront, and grander Regency buildings facing the sea. It was a fashionable upper-class resort in the early 19th c, and many of the town's buildings show undoubted architectural verve – there's very little seaside tat. The pebbly beach has fishing boats pulled up on it, and the town is protected by warm red sandstone cliffs; it stretches back along the river valley, though away from the sea the buildings are less interesting. The partly 14th-c

Old Ship is the best pub here, and Sue's Pantry (High St) has tasty cakes and pastries. The dedicated **Donkey Sanctuary** is a useful free attraction for families, with an unbelievable number of donkeys; meals, snacks, shop, disabled access. The **Heritage Centre** (in a fine Regency house on Church St, cl am Mon and Sun and all Nov–Easter; £1) organises summer walking tours round the town, Tues and Thurs at 10.15 am. **Cliff walks** The long stretch of red sandstone cliff between Sidmouth and Branscombe can be reached from either place (or, steeply but very prettily, from Salcombe Regis).

SILVERTON SS9502

An attractive village, with a particularly handsome church. The friendly old Three Tuns has good value food.

TOPSHAM SX9688

Old-world seaside village, well worth a quiet potter, its buildings showing its past importance as a port – as do its large number of good pubs and inns. The Passage House is currently the best for food, and readers like the fresh fish at the Galley restaurant. There's a small maritime museum.

UFFCULME ST0612

A large pleasant village above the Culm River, with a magnificent carved screen in the attractive church. The B3397 to Culmstock and then the turn to Hemyock is a pretty drive; beyond at Clayhidon the Half Moon has good food, by a footpath to the Blackdown Hills visitor centre.

Coldharbour Mill Working Museum Every stage in the production of wool, in a well restored 18th-c mill building. Also restoration of a steam engine, and the New World Tapestry, one of the largest tapestries in the world – for a donation you can add your own stitch. Meals, snacks, shop, limited disabled access; cl winter wknds, and at least a week at Christmas; (01884) 840960; £5.50.

WOODBURY SY0387

Lonely heathland, fine views (off B3180 E). Miles of heath with some pinewoods, a place to get away from people even in high summer (red flags warn if there's firing on one section which is a shooting range). From the highest points, nr the road, there are far views along the coast and to Dartmoor. The wooded hill fort right by the road is worth a look, and it's a bit eerie tracing the ramparts through the beech trees. The village of Woodbury itself is attractive, with a decent pub.

Other attractive villages, all with decent pubs, include seaside Axmouth SY2591, Broadhembury ST1004, Butterleigh SS9708, Chardstock ST3004, Lympstone SX9984, Salcombe Regis SY1488, Tytherleigh ST3103 and Upottery ST2007.

Where to eat

BRANSCOMBE SY1988 **Masons Arms** (01297) 680300 Popular, well run inn with no smoking bar, two-sided wood-burning stove, stripped original pine woodwork, low beams in main bar with massive central hearth (spit-roasts Tues and Sun lunch, Fri evenings), no smoking restaurant, particularly enjoyable imaginative food, well kept real ales inc summer beer festival, 14 wines by the glass, and outside tables under little thatched roofs; good bdrms, some with four-posters; self-catering cottages; disabled access. £27.50|£11

BROADCLYST SX9897 **Red Lion** (01392) 461271 Ochre-washed pub in quiet village setting with popular, straightforward food, very good wines, well kept ales, heavy-beamed long bar, and skittle alley; picnic-sets on front cobbles and seats in small enclosed garden across lane. £15|£6.50

BROADHEMBURY ST1004 **Drewe Arms** (01404) 841267 Charming 15th-c pub in attractive village with carved beams and handsome stone-mullioned windows in the bar, several other interesting rooms, excellent fresh fish dishes, lovely puddings, well kept beers, fine wines, and charming garden; cl Sun pm, 25 Dec; disabled access. £24|£8

CLYST HYDON ST0300 **Five Bells** (01884) 277288 Charming spotless thatched pub, with long bar divided by standing timbers, lots of plates on shelves, sparkling brass and copper, fresh flowers and candles in bottles, very good popular food, warmly friendly service, and lovely cottagey gardens; cl pms 25–26 Dec; children over 10 in pretty evening restaurant. £30|£7.50

DALWOOD ST2400 **Tuckers Arms** (01404) 881342 Delightful thatched medieval longhouse with fine flagstoned bar, lots of beams, log fire in inglenook, woodburner, a good mix of dining chairs, window seats and wall settles, huge collection of miniature bottles, well prepared enterprising bar food and lots of colourful hanging baskets; bdrms; no children; disabled access. £27.50|£6.95

EXETER SX9390 **Double Locks** Canal Banks (01392) 56947 Friendly and very relaxed lock-side country pub, popular with students, with good simple bar food (all day), summer barbecues, and up to 10 real ales on handpump; disabled access. £18|£4.95

EXETER SX9292 **St Martin's Café Bar** Cathedral Yard (01392) 310130 Attached to the Royal Clarence Hotel and overlooking cathedral precinct, attractive, light and airy with lots of pine, helpful young service, relaxed atmosphere, and enjoyable food usefully served all day (from breakfast until last orders 11pm). £21|£5.50

LYMPSTONE SX9884 **Globe** (01395) 263166 Attractive extended dining pub with simple furnishings, a thriving local feel in bar, good interesting food inc imaginative daily specials (plenty of fish), well kept real ales, and cheap spirits. £22|£9

TOPSHAM SX9688 **Georgian Tea Room** 35 High St (01392) 873465 18th-c house with pretty embroidered tablecloths and fresh flowers, and good food all day – breakfasts, morning coffee, snacks, lunchtime meals inc a popular roast on Tues, Thurs and Sun, cream teas with home-made cakes and cookies, and a wide range of teas and coffees with home-made lemonade. |£4.50

South Devon & Dartmoor

Lovely coastline from desolate beaches to the bustle of the Torbay riviera, magnificent Dartmoor, charming villages, plenty of family attractions, and beautiful places to stay in

Families are very well catered for here, with the rides and animals at Woodland Leisure Park or industrial re-creations at Morwellham Quay easily filling an enjoyable day out. Combining several activities in one day is also fun – such as catching a steam train to the enjoyable Butterfly Park & Dartmoor Otter Sanctuary at Buckfastleigh or swapping steam trains for river boats between Dartmouth and Totnes. Some excellent wildlife attractions include Plymouth's outstanding National Marine Aquarium, the attractive Paignton Zoo, Pennywell animal centre, and the mixture of animals at Dunstone's shire horse centre. The Plymouth Dome is one of the snappier heritage centres around, and military-minded children will enjoy roaming around the ramparts and adventure playground of Crownhill Fort (with wonderful views of the city). Gorse Blossom Railway Adventure Park has gentler distractions for younger children.

Rewarding places for adults include Overbecks near Salcombe with its lush seaside gardens and bizarre inventions; the remarkable Benedictine craft shop at Buckfast Abbey; magnificent Saltram near Plympton; the exotic gardens at Plantworld near Newton Abbot; romantic Coleton Fishacre garden at Kingswear; Castle Drogo at Drewsteignton, Buckland Abbey and the Garden House at Buckland Monachorum.

Kents Cavern show caves near Torquay have spooky summer evening tours, and daytime walks along Lydford Gorge take in some dramatic scenery.

For those after more tranquillity, the lawns in front of Berry Pomeroy Castle are ideal for picnics, and there's no better place for quiet contemplation than under the Meavy oak – planted near the end of the first millennium.

Free samples of the end product are the welcome rewards for touring Brimblescombe cider farm (where they still follow 16th-c methods) or Sharpham Barton Vineyard – both newcomers to the *Guide* this year.

Dartmoor is a powerful brooding wilderness, with complete walking freedom in most parts (you're not confined to footpaths), and all sorts of points of interest – especially its strange-shaped tors and its prehistoric remains. Around its edges are intimate and picturesque valleys and villages, delightful to explore. There's a similar intimate appeal in the small coves, stretches of cliff, sheltered boating creeks and estuaries cut deeply into the hills of the S and W coast. Here, relaxed and welcoming small towns such as Dartmouth and Totnes offer plenty to see and do. Some of England's best and cleanest beaches are to be found here, too, such as

Slapton Sands.

Torbay and its English Riviera offer a complete contrast: spacious promenades, low cliffs, bright gardens and palm trees.

Away from Dartmoor, the inland landscape is made up largely of well hedged hilly pastures, steeply wooded valleys and occasional vivid red-earth fields.

Where to stay

ASHBURTON SX7270 **Holne Chase** *Ashburton, Newton Abbot, Devon TQ13 7NS* *(01364) 631471* **£125***, plus winter breaks; 17 comfortable and individually furnished rms, many with views over the Dart Valley, and some split-level suites in converted stables. Marvellously peaceful ex-hunting lodge of Buckfast Abbey in 70 acres with sweeping lawns and plenty of woodland walks, a mile of Dart fishing, shooting and riding on Dartmoor; cheerful welcoming owners, comfortable public rooms with log fires, very good modern English cooking using home-grown vegetables, and enjoyable breakfasts and afternoon teas (home-made breads, marmalades and so forth); children over 10 in evening restaurant; disabled access

AVETON GIFFORD SX6947 **Court Barton Farmhouse** *Aveton Gifford, Kingsbridge, Devon TQ7 4LE (01548) 550312* **£52***; 7 rms. Pretty creeper-clad 16th-c farmhouse on small mixed farm, with cosy homely lounge, log fires, a warm welcome, farmhouse breakfasts, and flower-filled garden; cl 25 Dec

BANTHAM SX6743 **Widcombe House** *Bantham, Kingsbridge, Devon TQ7 3AA (01548) 561084* **£60***; 3 well equipped neat rms. In lovely countryside with fine views down to the sea, this modern no smoking house is spotlessly kept and very relaxing, with a log fire in chilly weather, very good breakfasts and delicious evening meals in the dining room using home-grown produce (bring your own wine); cl Nov–Jan; no children

BLACKAWTON SX8050 **Normandy Arms** *Blackawton, Totnes, Devon TQ9 7BN (01803) 712316* **£52**, plus special breaks; 5 pretty rms. Quaint, friendly pub in quiet village, with cosy main bar, log fire, some interesting displays of World War II battle gear, generous food in bar and restaurant, real ales, and seats in garden

BOVEY TRACEY SX8078 **Edgemoor Hotel** *Haytor Rd, Bovey Tracey, Newton Abbot, Devon TQ13 9LE (01626) 832466* **£100***, plus special breaks; 16 charming rms. Ivy-covered country house in neatly kept gardens on the edge of Dartmoor, with comfortable lounge and bar, log fires, good food in elegant restaurant, and high tea for children under 8; cl 1 wk after Christmas; limited disabled access

BURGH ISLAND SX6443 **Burgh Island Hotel** *Burgh Island, Bigbury-on-Sea, Devon TQ7 4AU (01548) 810514* **£208** inc dinner; 14 art deco seaview suites, most with balconies. Extravagantly decorated and restored 1929 hotel on cut-off small island – access by hotel Land Rover (or foot) at low tide, and on sea-going summer tractor-on-stilts at high tide; domed palm court, sun lounge, classic cocktail bar, art deco furniture, kind helpful hosts, good food, and super breakfasts. Tennis, mini gym, snooker, water sports, natural pool and private beach, walks, and sea fishing. Island has 14th-c pub – and summer day crowds. No dogs; cl Jan and wkdys Feb; no children under 8 for ballroom dining; disabled access

CHAGFORD SX7189 **Easton Court** *Sandy Park, Chagford, Newton Abbot, Devon TQ13 8JN (01647) 433469* **£96**, plus special breaks; 8 rms. Creeper-clad thatched 15th-c house with beams, inglenook fireplace, granite walls, and big library (literary connections inc Evelyn Waugh writing *Brideshead Revisited* here), cosy bar, charming sitting room, good breakfasts, delicious evening meals in candlelit restaurant; cl Jan; children over 12; disabled access

CHAGFORD SX7087 **Gidleigh Park** *Chagford, Newton Abbot, Devon TQ13 8HH (01647) 432367* **£370** inc dinner, plus winter breaks; 15 opulent and individual rms with fruit and flowers. Exceptional luxurious Dartmoor-edge mock Tudor hotel with deeply comfortable panelled drawing room, wonderful flowers, conservatory overlooking the fine grounds (40 acres, with walks straight up on to the moor), log fires, particularly fine cooking and a fine wine list, and caring staff

DARTMOUTH SX8751 **Ford House** *44 Victoria Rd, Dartmouth, Devon TQ6 9DX (01803) 834047* **£75***, plus special breaks; 4 individually decorated rms. Nr the harbour, this Regency town house has a log fire in the comfortable drawing room, antiques, good interesting food using fresh local produce eaten around a big table, delicious breakfasts, helpful service, and sheltered garden; you can take over the whole house for a wknd party; cl Nov–Mar

DARTMOUTH SX8751 **Royal Castle** *11 The Quay, Dartmouth, Devon TQ6 9PS (01803) 833033* **£107.90**, plus special breaks; 25 individually furnished rms. Well restored mainly Georgian hotel (part 16th-c) overlooking the inner harbour – great views from most rooms; lively and interesting public bar with open fires and beams, quiet library/lounge with antiques, drawing room overlooking the quayside, winter spit-roasts in lounge bar, elegant upstairs seafood restaurant, decent bar food, and friendly staff

DODDISCOMBSLEIGH SX8586 **Nobody Inn** *Doddiscombsleigh, Exeter, Devon EX6 7PS (01647) 252394* **£70**; 7 rms, some in a Georgian manor house 150 yds down the road, and most with own bthrm. Friendly 16th-c pub with beams, heavy wooden furniture, and inglenook fireplace in the attractively furnished two-roomed lounge bar, an outstanding cellar running to 800 wines and 250 malts, and popular food in bar and restaurant inc huge range of Devon cheeses; good views from garden, and the church is worth visiting for fine stained glass; cl 25–26 Dec; no children

EAST PORTLEMOUTH SX7537 **Gara Rock** *East Portlemouth, Salcombe, Devon TQ8 8PH (01548) 842342* **£64**; 17 rms, some can convert to family suites, and 20 self-catering apartments. Originally a coast-guard station and look-out with its own beach at the foot of the cliffs; marvellous for families with daily clubs and rooms for every age, baby-listening and sitting, acres of grassy garden with heated outdoor swimming pool and paddling pool, tennis, an adventure playground with wooden boat, various pets, lots of entertainments, children's menus, early suppers, and so forth; enjoyable food all day inc barbecues, helpful friendly staff, and an informal and relaxed atmosphere; lots to do nearby (though so much in the hotel, you might not leave the grounds); cl Dec–Jan; disabled access ☺

GALMPTON SX6940 **Burton Farm** *Galmpton, Kingsbridge, Devon TQ7 3EY (01548) 561210* **£50**; 10 rms. Welcoming working farm in lovely countryside with dairy herd and pedigree sheep (guests welcome to look around and help), and traditional farmhouse cooking using home-produced ingredients; they are kind to children with their own tea time and play area; no smoking; cl Christmas; disabled access ☺

GOVETON SX7546 **Buckland-Tout-Saints** *Goveton, Kingsbridge, Devon TQ7 2DS (01548) 853055* **£170**, plus special winter breaks; 10 luxuriously period rms. Handsome Queen Anne mansion in five well kept acres of gardens with croquet/putting, and relaxing rooms with antiques, fine panelling and plasterwork, chintzy furniture and roaring log fire, imaginative food using good local produce in lovely no smoking restaurant, notable wines, and excellent personal service; dogs by arrangement; cl 3 wks Jan/early Feb; children over 6 in restaurant

HAYTOR SX7777 **Bel Alp House** *Haytor, Newton Abbot, Devon TQ13 9XX (01364) 661217* **£120***, plus special breaks; 8 spacious rms. Handsome Edwardian country house with elegant drawing room, comfortable sitting room, log fires, friendly atmosphere, and fine careful cooking in pretty restaurant; wonderful views and peaceful garden; disabled access

HAYTOR VALE SX7777 **Rock** *Haytor Vale, Newton Abbot, Devon TQ13 9XP (01364) 661305* **£76.50**, plus special breaks; 9 rms. Civilised old inn on the edge of Dartmoor National Park, with good food (inc fresh fish), a nice mix of visitors and locals in the two rooms of the panelled bar, open fires, no smoking restaurant, courteous service, and big garden; walking, fishing, riding and golf nearby; cl 25–26 Dec

HAZLEWOOD SX7251 **Crannacombe Farm** *Hazlewood, Loddiswell, Kingsbridge, Devon TQ7 4DX (01548) 550256* **£46***; 2 rms. Quietly set and comfortable Georgian farmhouse on working stock farm in a lovely unspoilt valley with half a mile of river frontage; own prize-winning organic cider and apple juice, and hearty food; no smoking; babysitting; cl Christmas

HOLNE SX7170 **Wellpritton Farm** *Holne, Ashburton, Devon TQ13 7RX (01364) 631273* **£40**; 4 pretty rms, 3 with own bthrm. Small friendly Dartmoor farm with horses, goats and chickens and lovely views from terrace and garden; comfortable sitting room, good food (packed lunches if you want), and small swimming pool; children under 5 by arrangement

HOPE COVE SX6739 **Hope Cove Hotel** *Hope Cove, Kingsbridge, Devon TQ7 3HH (01548) 561233* **£57**, plus special breaks; 7 rms with fine sea views. Neatly kept and welcoming little hotel in tranquil spot with sandy beaches and plenty of walks; lovely views from lounge or dining room, helpful owners and staff, and enjoyable food; cl Oct–Easter; children from 6

KINGSTON SX6347 **Dolphin** *Kingston, Kingsbridge, Devon TQ7 4QE (01548) 810314* **£55**; 3 rms. Peaceful 16th-c inn with several knocked-through beamed rooms, a warmly welcoming atmosphere, a small no smoking area, very good home-made food, and real ales; tracks down to the sea

LEWDOWN SX4586 **Lewtrenchard Manor** *Lewdown, Okehampton, Devon EX20 4PN (01566) 783256* **£160**, plus special breaks; 9 well equipped rms with fresh flowers and period furniture. Lovely Elizabethan manor house in garden with fine dovecot and surrounded by peaceful estate with shooting, fishing and croquet; dark panelling, ornate ceilings, antiques, fresh flowers, and log fires, a friendly welcome, relaxed atmosphere, and candlelit restaurant with very good food; children under 8 by arrangement; partial disabled access

LIFTON SX3885 **Arundell Arms** *Fore St, Lifton, Devon PL16 0AA (01566) 784666* **£113**, plus special breaks; 28 well equipped rms, 5 in annexe over the road. Carefully renovated old coaching inn with 20 miles of its own waters – salmon and trout fishing and a long-established fly-fishing school; comfortable sitting room, log fires, super food in both bar and elegantly refurbished restaurant, carefully chosen wines, and kind service from local staff; new eating area in attractive terraced garden; dogs welcome away from restaurant and river bank; cl 4 days over Christmas; dogs welcome

MALBOROUGH SX7039 **Soar Mill Cove Hotel** *Malborough, Salcombe, Devon TQ7 3DS (01548) 561566* **£144** inc dinner, plus special breaks; 21 comfortable rms, some opening on to garden. Neatly kept single-storey building in idyllic spot by peaceful and very beautiful cove on NT coast (excellent walks), with lovely views, extensive private grounds, tennis/putting, and warm indoor pool; outstanding service, log fires, very good food (marvellous fish), and they are particularly kind to children of all ages: microwave, fridge, and so forth for little ones, own high tea or smaller helpings of most meals, fully equipped laundry, a play room, table tennis and snooker, swings, and donkey and pony; cl Jan; small, mature, well behaved dogs by arrangement; disabled access ☺

MORETONHAMPSTEAD SX7386 **Great Sloncombe Farm** *Moreton-hampstead, Newton Abbot, Devon TQ13 8QF (01647) 440595* **£46***; 3 rms – the big double is the favourite. Lovely 13th-c farmhouse on a working dairy and stock farm, with friendly owners, carefully polished old-fashioned furniture, decent food, log fires, a relaxed atmosphere, and good nearby walking and bird-watching; no smoking; children over 8; dogs by arrangement

MORETONHAMPSTEAD SX7586 **White Hart** *Moretonhampstead, Newton Abbot, Devon TQ13 8NF (01647) 440406* **£60**, plus special breaks; 18 rms. Comfortable former Georgian posting house with interesting furnishings in civilised lounge bar and hall, lively back bar, good bar food, and no smoking restaurant; well placed for Dartmoor

NORTH BOVEY SX7483 **Gate House** *North Bovey, Newton Abbot, Devon TQ13 8RB (01647) 440479* **£56**; 3 charming rms. 15th-c thatched cottage in picturesque village, with huge granite fireplace in attractive beamed sitting room, breakfasts and candlelit evening meals served in beamed dining room, tea with home-made cakes, friendly owners, and outdoor swimming pool in peaceful garden; plenty to do nearby; no children

PRESTON SX8773 **Sampsons Farm** *Preston, Newton Abbot, Devon TQ12 3PP (01626) 54913* **£50**, plus special breaks; 10 rms, most with own bthrms. Thatched 14th-c longhouse with beams, panelling and big open fires in cosy sitting rooms, a very relaxed welcoming atmosphere, most enjoyable food in popular restaurant, and lots of nearby walks; children over 3; disabled access; self-catering too

SALCOMBE SX7338 **Tides Reach** *Cliff Rd, South Sands, Salcombe, Devon TQ8 8LJ (01548) 843466* **£146**, plus special breaks; 35 rms, many with estuary views. Unusually individual resort hotel run by long-serving owners in pretty wooded cove by the sea, with airy luxury day rooms, big sea aquarium in cocktail bar, good restaurant food using fresh local produce, friendly efficient service, and squash, snooker, leisure complex, health area, and big heated pool; windsurfing etc, beach over lane, and lots of coast walks; cl Dec/Jan; children over 8

SANDY PARK SX7189 **Mill End** *Sandy Park, Chagford, Newton Abbot, Devon TQ13 8JN (01647) 432282* **£110***, plus special breaks; 17 refurbished, neat rms, most with views. Quietly set former flour mill with waterwheel in neatly kept grounds below Dartmoor; comfortable lounges, carefully prepared interesting food and fine breakfasts, and good service; well behaved dogs welcome away from public rooms; cl Jan; partial disabled access

SOUTH ZEAL SX6593 **Oxenham Arms** *South Zeal, Okehampton, Devon EX20 2JT (01837) 840244* **£70***, plus special breaks; 8 rms. Grandly atmospheric old inn dating back to 12th c and first licensed in 1477 (a neolithic standing stone still forms part of the wall in the TV room); elegant beamed and panelled bar with chatty relaxed atmosphere and open fire, decent food and wines, and charming ex-monastery small garden; well behaved dogs welcome

STAVERTON SX7964 **Sea Trout** *Staverton, Totnes, Devon TQ9 6PA (01803) 762274* **£74**; 10 cottagey rms. Comfortable pub in quiet hamlet nr River Dart with two relaxed beamed bars, log fires, popular food in bar and airy dining conservatory, and terraced garden with fountains and waterfalls; cl Christmas

STOKE GABRIEL SX8457 **Gabriel Court** *Stoke Gabriel, Totnes, Devon TQ9 6SF (01803) 782206* **£80**, plus special breaks; 19 rms, some in former hay lofts. In a walled Elizabethan garden, this attractive family-run manor has quiet relaxing lounges (winter log fire), enjoyable traditional English food, and courteous helpful staff; outdoor heated swimming pool and grass tennis court; dogs welcome

TEIGNMOUTH SX9372 **Thomas Luny House** *Teign St, Teignmouth, Devon TQ14 8EG (01626) 772976* **£75***, plus special breaks; 4 pretty rms with flowers and books. Lovely little no smoking Georgian house nr fish quay; open fires in spacious, comfortable drawing room and elegant dining room, a relaxed friendly atmosphere, enjoyable food around big dining table, and sunny walled garden; children over 12

THURLESTONE SX6742 **Thurlestone Hotel** *Thurlestone, Kingsbridge, Devon TQ7 3NN (01548) 560382* **£92**; 65 comfortable rms with sea or country views. Owned by the same family since 1896, this well run hotel is in lovely grounds with marvellous views over the coast, and tennis and squash courts, badminton court, swimming pool, par-three golf course, and super play area for children; stylish and spacious public rooms, relaxing cocktail bar, imaginative food in attractive no smoking restaurant, and courteous helpful staff; lots for families with an indoor paddling pool, their own club, playpens for both swimming pools, well equipped laundry room, and baby-listening that extends to the 16th-c pub next door; marvellous nearby beaches and walks, and fishing, riding, and sailing on request. ☺

TWO BRIDGES SX6274 **Prince Hall** *Two Bridges, Yelverton, Devon PL20 6SA (01822) 890403* **£100**; 9 attractive, spacious rms. Surrounded by Dartmoor National Park, this tranquil 18th-c country house is run by caring friendly owners and their helpful staff; lovely views from convivial bar, comfortable sitting room, and cosy dining room, open fires, very good evening meals, enjoyable breakfasts, and lots of fine walks; cl mid-Dec to mid-Feb; children over 10

To see and do

ASHBURTON SX7370
Probably the best of the small towns around Dartmoor, with distinct character. The **River Dart Country Park** (Holne Park) is pleasant for walking or fishing, with adventure playgrounds for children. Snacks, shop; cl Oct–Mar; (01364) 652511; £4.75.

BANTHAM SANDS SX6643
A gentle walk from Bantham through dunes (good picnic spots) to the broad stretch of rivermouth sand facing Burgh Island. You can go on above the rocks S, for views of Bolt Tail and the coves between.

BERRY HEAD SX9356
Tremendous coast, sea and shipping views from ex-quarry country park; squat lighthouse, formidable Napoleonic War battlements with cannon (and guardhouse café), nature trail takes in kittiwakes and guillemots on cliffs, uncommon plants.

BERRY POMEROY SX8361
Berry Pomeroy Castle (off A385 just E of Totnes; keep on past village) Reputedly Devon's most haunted castle, hidden away on a crag over a quiet wooded valley. Appropriately spooky Norman gatehouse and walls around the ruins of an imposing and unexpected Tudor mansion, with an interesting 15th-c fresco inside. The lawns in front are ideal for a picnic. Meals, snacks, shop, disabled access; cl Nov–Mar; (01803) 866618; £2.20; EH. The red sandstone 15th-c village church is worth a look on the way; odd monument in Seymour Chapel. The road through here from Ashburton via Littlehempston and on to Stoke Gabriel is a nice drive.

BICKINGTON SX7972
Gorse Blossom Railway Adventure Park Rides on 7¼-inch gauge steam railway through acres of woodland; also nature trails, play areas, and indoor model railway. Meals, snacks, shop, some disabled access; cl Nov–Easter, phone (01626) 821361 to check times; £5. The Toby Jug is useful for lunch.

BLACKAWTON SX8052
Woodland Leisure Park (off A3122) One of the best family days out in Devon. A highlight is the Twister, an exhilarating spiralling and plunging water-coaster – be prepared to get wet. There are several other rides and lots of well thought out play areas (inc several for younger children), as well as a honey farm with millions of bees behind glass, daily falconry displays, and a small zoo with wallabies, llamas and foreign birds. There are boats on the lake and plenty of quieter areas for woodland walks. Meals, snacks, shop, disabled access; open wknds and school hols and daily mid-Mar–early Nov; (01803) 712598; £5.95.

BOVEY TRACEY SX8178
An unassuming small Dartmoor-edge town; the Devon Guild of Craftsmen have a good varied **craft centre** at Riverside Mill (cl most winter bank hols; free. **House of Marbles and Teign Valley Glass** (Pottery Rd) Demonstrations of glass-blowing at factory specialising in marbles, with a fantastic array of these and some interesting marble runs in its recently refurbished museum inc, they claim, the largest marble run in the world. Meals, snacks, shop, disabled access; no glass-blowing Sat and winter Sun; (01626) 835358; free. The **Lowerdown Pottery** (off B3344) does fine decorated pottery; it's open by appointment only, (01626) 833408; free. The Cromwell Arms does generous food.

BRIXHAM SX9256
Busy fishing port, perhaps the prettiest of the Riviera resorts, with some attractive narrow streets on the hill above. Lots of activity (and summer seaside shops and cafés) in the harbour, inc (for no apparent reason) a full-size reconstruction of Drake's *Golden Hind*, and summer boats around Torbay. The local history **museum**

(Bolton Cross) has something of a maritime emphasis (shop; cl Sun and pm Sat, cl Nov–Jan, reduced opening Feb–Mar). The quaint Quayside Inn is handy for lunch, and Shoalstone beach nr here has some of the cleanest bathing water in the UK.

Scabbacombe Head A blowy but rewarding day's walk from Brixham to Kingswear, 12 miles of stunning wild scenery (and some steep climbs), passing the oasis of Coleton Fishacre gardens.

BUCKFASTLEIGH SX7467
Buckfast Abbey Originally established in 1018 but after the Dissolution of the Monasteries left abandoned until 1882, when it was refounded by four remarkable monks, who then did most of the rebuilding work themselves over a period of 32 years. It's now one of the most visited religious sites in Britain, with an interesting exhibition, and several services each day. An excellent shop sells not just their own famous honey, but goods produced at other Benedictine monasteries around Europe, inc Bavarian beer, French cakes, and Irish linen; many people feel this alone is worth a special journey. Good meals and snacks, disabled access; cl Good Fri and 25 Dec; guided tours (01364) 645500; free.

Butterfly Park & Dartmoor Otter Sanctuary (Dart Bridge Rd) You can watch otters swimming and playing from an underwater viewing tunnel, or see them on land in the six big landscaped enclosures; summer feeding times (readers enjoy this part most) 11.30am, 2 and 4.30pm. Also under-cover tropical garden with free-flying butterflies and moths. Meals, snacks, shop, disabled access; cl Nov–Feb; (01364) 642916; £4.95. Combined with a trip on the South Devon Railway (the trains stop here), this makes for a very pleasant day out.

Pennywell ⊞ (Lower Dean, off A38 just S) Friendly and unfussy, with over 750 animals in 80 acres, as well as lovely scenery, wildlife viewing hides, and barn owl demonstrations. Different events every half hour, from milking and feeding to ferret racing and worm charming, so always something for children to get involved in; also play areas, an assault course, pony and donkey rides and an area where children can try out crafts like basket weaving. New go-kart ride and theatre. Meals, snacks, shop, disabled access; open wknds in Nov and Feb (tel for Christmas opening), Feb half-term, then daily from late Mar–Oct; (01364) 642023; £5.95.

South Devon Railway GWR steam train trips through lovely unspoilt scenery along the wooded River Dart (some of which is hard to see any other way). It stops just outside Totnes as well as at Staverton, and they do tickets combining it with a Dartmouth–Totnes river trip; also a small museum, play area and a chance to see the ongoing restoration of rolling stock. Shop, disabled access; trains run roughly every 1¼ hrs summer (eight trains a day Tues, Weds and Thurs throughout Aug), less often other times; best to check dates; (01364) 642338 for timetable (or pick one up from local Tourist Information Centres); £6.50. The Dartbridge opp is a popular family dining pub.

BUCKLAND MONACHORUM SX4866
Buckland Abbey The home of Francis Drake until his death in 1596, and of his family until 1946. They still have the famous drum said to sound whenever England is in danger, as well as craft workshops, a brass rubbing centre, herb knot garden, thyme garden (an Elizabethan garden should open in the spring), good walks, and entertaining summer activities for children. In summer, weather permitting, you can play bowls on the lawn for a small extra charge. Meals, snacks, shop, disabled access to ground floor only; cl Thurs, and Nov–Mar exc pm wknds; (01822) 853607; £4.50, £2.30 grounds only; NT.

Garden House Profusion of unusual plants beautifully laid out in warm garden sheltered by picturesque partly ruined walls of former abbey buildings; also a spring garden, quarry garden, rhododendron walk and wildflower meadow. Interesting plant sales, meals, teas Apr–Sept; cl Nov–Feb; (01822) 854769; £4. The Drake Manor is good for lunch.

BURGH ISLAND SX6544
Connected at low tide by a causeway to
Bigbury-on-Sea (undistinguished for
much save its clean sandy beaches);
spectacular cliffs on the seaward side, a
true island and quite remote-seeming
when the tide's in. At high tide an odd
giant tractor-on-stilts wades back and
forth with passengers. The Pilchard is a
quaint seaview pub, and you can
windsurf or fish nearby.

CHAGFORD SX7087
A large village, quite busy, and an
attractive jumping-off point for the
moor; even the bank is thatched, and
the two old-fashioned general stores
are fun. The Ring o' Bells is good for
lunch, the Bullers Arms is useful too,
and for non-meat-eaters, the small
vegetarian Courtyard Café is well
recommended. If you eat at the luxury
country-house hotel **Gidleigh Park**,
you can stroll around their lovely
grounds, with colourful woodland
walks and immaculate formal gardens.

CHUDLEIGH SX8678
Despite the 1807 fire which destroyed
lots of the buildings, this is a pleasant old
wool town with pretty cottages in
narrow, winding lanes.
Rock Garden and Cave 🏛 Three
acres of wild gardens in an ancient
quarry, populated by a good range of
birds and wildlife. The cave has some
interesting calcite formations, and they
are still digging in search of legendary
larger caverns. From the pretty
neighbouring waterfall it's a short walk
up Chudleigh Rock for dramatic vistas
of the surrounding countryside and
moors. Snacks, nursery, craft shop,
limited disabled access; cl Christmas
week, and some bits may be cl in winter;
(01626) 852134; £2. You can arrange
abseiling or caving on (01626) 852717.
Ugbrooke Park (off A380 just SE) An
interesting early example of the work of
Robert Adam, in lovely Capability
Brown parkland. Delightfully informal
guided tours (2pm and 3.45pm). Teas,
disabled access; open pm Sun, Tues,
Weds, Thurs and bank hols mid-July to
early Sept; (01626) 852179; £4.80.

DARTINGTON SX7862
Dartington Cider Press Centre
(Shinners Bridge) Cluster of 16th- and
17th-c buildings with craft shops, farm
foods, herbs and such, and restaurants,
inc a good vegetarian one. The
surroundings add a lot to the attraction,
with nearby medieval great hall on
photogenic lawned courtyard,
sculpture gardens, and streamside
nature trail. Disabled access; cl Suns
Jan–Easter; (01803) 864171; free. The
Cott, good for lunch, is close by.

DARTMOOR SX5880
Classic moorland, where distant vistas
of changing greens and browns fade into
the austere grey-blues of far shoulders
and edges. The moor is punctuated with
all sorts of interesting focal points and
features: numerous easily traceable
prehistoric remains; strange wind-
sculpted, eroded granite tors which
crown many of the slopes; the little
streams that thread over boulders;
tamed water-courses where leats or
miniature canals (dating back to the
16th-c one cut by Drake to supply
Plymouth) curl carefully around the
contours; sheltered valleys cut into the
moors, where white houses crouch
among sycamores and oaks; occasional
higher clusters of much more stunted
oaks mark abandoned tin-mine
workings with ruined wheelhouses, and
shaggy ponies hope for a hand-out.
Good roads over the moor are the
B3212 and B3357, and the back road
towards Ashburton off the B3344 just
NW of Manaton. The villages around it
are well worth exploring: typically
thatched white-plastered stone
cottages clustered around an ancient
stone church beside its church-house
inn. The towns ringing the moor have
useful facilities. A big chunk of NW
Dartmoor is used by the Ministry of
Defence for firing practice; it's marked
out by red and white posts, and you can
go in when there are no red lights or
red flags. Dartmoor is outstanding for
walking, but mist can come down very
suddenly, so on the open moor you
must carry a compass. A lot of the
moor is a long way from the road,
hence rather inaccessible. There are
more paths for walkers than the right-
of-way network suggests, but don't
assume a right of way marked on the
OS map will be visible on the ground
(the black dashed lines on these maps
are generally more reliable). Old

mineral railways and cart tracks make for some good walkers' routes. There are plenty of things to head for, to give a moorland walk a sense of purpose – most obviously, one of the many tors of naked rock rising out of the moor (beware: the rounded rocks can be a good deal more slippery than they look).

Ancient sites SX5866 The upper valley of the River Plym has numerous visible hut circles, stone rows and cairns.

Bowerman's Nose SX7480 This quaint tor, looking snootily out over a patchwork of pastures, makes a pleasant objective for a Dartmoor walk.

Brentor church SX4780 (above back road Lydford–Tavistock, just S of North Brentor) 12th-c, one of England's smallest churches, notable for its lonely hilltop position with remarkable coast and Dartmoor views.

Burrator Reservoir SX5568 This gives a 5-mile walk in beautiful woodland and moorland surroundings. Sheepstor church on the way has interesting memorials to the Brookes family, former rajahs of Sarawak.

Clapper bridge SX6578 By the road at Postbridge, this ancient stone packhorse bridge is an attractive – and in summer very popular – focus for Dartmoor strolls, often complete with hopeful ponies.

Devonport leat SX5975 This watercourse, still largely complete, was first engineered 200 years ago to give Devonport a water supply. A path along the gently graded channel takes in some remote scenery in Dartmoor's western moors, and makes getting lost quite difficult; it's easily reached off the B3212 NE of Yelverton.

Dr Blackall's Drive SX7073 This specially created carriage drive from Bel Tor Corner to New Bridge gives splendid views of the Dart Valley, and is among Dartmoor's finest paths for walkers.

Great Mis Tor SX5676 In the lonely terrain N of Dartmoor Prison, this gives walkers panoramic views over much of the moor – though access may be barred by army firing practice (red flags give warning).

Grimspound SX7080 By a stream,

this is one of the most impressive of Dartmoor's ancient sites, with a fine old lichened granite cross nearby to mark the way for later medieval travellers; great views from the round walk to Widecombe.

Haytor Rocks SX7577 This fortress-like collection of rocks makes a striking and popular objective for walks; nearby is an abandoned quarry served by an unusual 19th-c tramway with grooved-granite rails.

Honeybag Tor SX7278 Marvellous views over Widecombe – and though the OS map doesn't show this, there's a path over to Hound Tor to the E, along the spine of the ridge.

Hound Tor SX7478 Majestically monumental and a good destination for a walk, with an interesting excavated abandoned medieval village nearby.

Hunter's Tor SX7682 The ridge path to this landmark gives panoramic views of Lustleigh Cleave and the Bovey Valley.

Shovel Down SX6585 These open moorland expanses harbour some of Dartmoor's richest concentrations of antiquities. You'll need a map just to find the car park at Scorhill, SW of Gidleigh and W of Chagford; from there, a path brings you out on to the moor within sight of Scorhill stone circle. Close by are stone slab bridges over clear brooks; among the litter of rocks by one river is the Teign Tolmen, a natural boulder through which the water has gouged a perfectly circular hole. You can walk over to nearby Kes Tor, close to which is the Long Stone and a fine stone row of about 2500–1500 BC.

Vixen Tor SX5474 Towering up from the bracken, this looks unclimbable, but is quite easily reached from behind. This area of the Walkham Valley is relatively lush and green, and walkers can explore the old railway tracks which once served local quarries.

Yarner Wood SX7778 (nr Bovey Tracey) This National Nature Reserve has a good nature trail despite an arson attack several years ago.

Yes Tor SX5890 Up in the lonelier northern part of the moor, this landmark gives great views over Dartmoor. This area of Okehampton

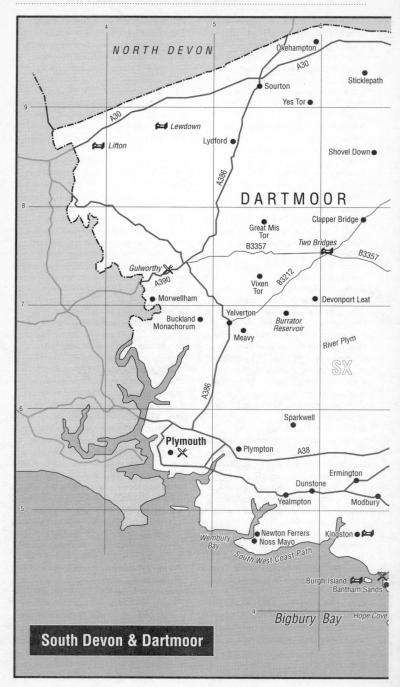

South Devon & Dartmoor

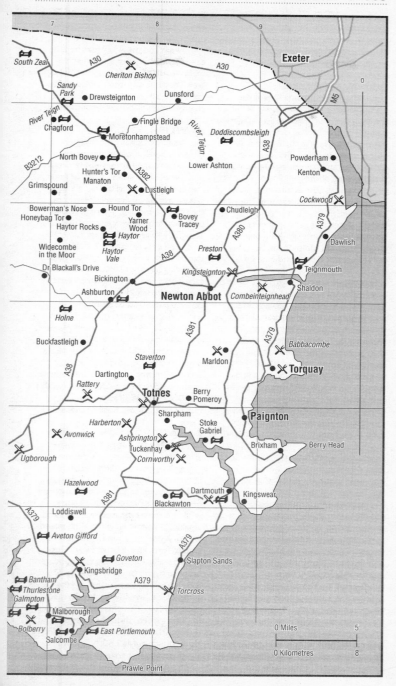

7 8 9

South Zeal

A30 Cheriton Bishop A30 Exeter

Sandy Park

Drewsteignton Dunsford

M5

0

River Teign

Chagford Fingle Bridge

River Teign Doddiscombsleigh

Moretonhampstead

North Bovey Lower Ashton Powderham

B3212 Kenton

Hunter's Tor A382

Grimspound Manaton Lustleigh Cockwood

Bowerman's Nose Hound Tor Chudleigh

Honeybag Tor Yarner Bovey A379

Haytor Rocks Wood Tracey A380

Haytor Dawlish

Widecombe Haytor Preston

in the Moor Vale A38 Teignmouth

Dr Blackall's Drive Kingsteignton Shaldon

Bickington Newton Abbot Combeinteignhead

Ashburton

Holne A381 A379 Babbacombe

Buckfastleigh Torquay

A38 Staverton Marldon

Dartington

Rattery Totnes Berry Paignton

Pomeroy

Harberton Sharpham

Avonwick Stoke Brixham Berry Head

Ashprington Gabriel

Ugborough Tuckenhay

Cornworthy

Hazelwood

A381 Dartmouth Kingswear

Loddiswell Blackawton

A379

Aveton Gifford

A379

Goveton Slapton Sands

Bantham Kingsbridge

Thurlestone A379

Galmpton Torcross

Malborough

Bolberry East Portlemouth

Salcombe

0 Miles 5

0 Kilometres 8

Prawle Point

Common is the highest terrain in southern England, though as throughout this northern area access is often barred by army firing practice – look out for red flags on approach roads.

DARTMOUTH SX8751
Charming waterside small town with many exceptional buildings, esp around the inner harbour. Though so popular, it's kept its own strong character, and stays very much alive through the winter. Cobbled Bayards Cove, with old fort and steep wooded hills behind, is particularly photogenic, as is pedestrianised Foss St. Markets Tues, Fri: Old Market is picturesque. The Royal Naval College is a striking building. Interesting shops, plenty of waterside seats, lots of action on the river. Parking in summer can be trying: best to use good park-and-ride on B3207 Halwell Rd.

Dartmouth Castle (slightly SE of town, off B3205) Classic late 15th-c battlemented fortress, virtually intact, with cannon and later gun batteries (a video display shows it firing), and great views out into the Channel. Snacks, shop; cl winter lunchtimes, and all day Mon and Tues Nov–Mar; (01803) 833588; £2.90; EH. In summer a little ferry leaves the South Embankment for here every 15 minutes or so. Otherwise it's an enjoyable and fairly gentle 20-min walk from Dartmouth itself, though the immediate hinterland is unremarkable.

Dartmouth Museum 🖾 (Duke St) Well restored 17th-c timbered house, with mainly nautical displays; shop; cl Sun, 25–26 Dec, and 1 Jan; £1.50.

Newcomen Engine House 🖾 (Royal Ave Gdns) Huge steam-powered atmospheric beam-engine pump, thought to be the world's oldest, worked 1720–1913. Shop, disabled access; cl Sun Nov–Mar, 25 Dec and 1 Jan; (01803) 834224; *50p.

River trips to Totnes 🖾 Pass some of Devon's prettiest scenery, much of which can't be seen on foot or by car; you can combine this with steam trains or a connecting bus back – which saves hearing the commentary a second time. You can also go on circular tours of the surrounding area. There are some

boats in winter – (01803) 832109 to check; £6.90 return to Totnes. Also quaint car and pedestrian ferries to Kingswear and the A379 (can be 2-hr car wait at peak summer times).

St Saviour's Lots of charming detail, well worth a close look, inc altar, pulpit, painted rood screen, brasses on chancel floor, elaborate 14th-c hinges on the south door.

DAWLISH SX9576
Old-fashioned small resort with modern developments and camps outside; red sandstone cliffs, waterside parks with black swans, small summer museum, prom, pier; the mainline railway cut through the cliffs right by the water is striking. There have been pollution problems at nearby beaches.

Dawlish Warren Sandy grassy spit (with golf course) largely blocking in Exe estuary, with glistening tidal flats full of wading birds, and dunes with some rare plants. In summer get well out to the point, to avoid the crowds and caravan parks at the station end; in winter it's splendidly wild and blowy, with thousands of ducks, brent geese and waders (even avocets) congregating at high tide to wait till the mudflats show again. Shop, disabled access to visitor centre; visitor centre cl winter wkdys; free, guided nature walks £2; (01626) 863980 for times. The Mount Pleasant out here has decent food.

DREWSTEIGNTON SX7290
Castle Drogo Above the charming village of Drewsteignton is this impressive granite castle, designed by Lutyens and built early last century as a bizarre and brilliantly inventive mixture of medieval style and 20th-c luxury, with cunningly disguised radiators and amazing details even in the kitchen and lavatory. Lovely grounds with yew hedges form an outer barbican. Good guided walks through the surrounding woodland, and super views – it's 275 metres (900 ft) up overlooking the gorge of the River Teign. Meals, snacks, shop; cl Nov–Mar, plus castle cl Fri (though garden, shop and tearoom still open); (01647) 433306; £5.40, garden and grounds only £2.60; NT. A well signposted minor road W of the village takes you to **Spinster's Rock**, a well

preserved neolithic burial chamber and the most easily accessible prehistoric feature in the area.

DUNSFORD SX8389

Brimblescombe Farm Cider (Farrants Farm, off B3212 W of Exeter) Watch cider being made the traditional way at this working farm, parts of which pre-date Saxon times; cl Nov–Apr; (01647) 252783; free (inc sample).

DUNSTONE SX5951

National Shire Horse Centre Shire horses and foals, wagon rides, reptile house, falconry displays (in season only – best to ring), adventure playground, pets' corner and special wknd events. Meals, snacks, shop, disabled access; tel (01752) 880268 for winter opening; £3.95; reduced rates and displays in winter. The Dartmoor Union in Holbeton is quite handy for lunch, and the road from there to Noss Mayo has good views.

ERMINGTON SX6353

Ermington church Notable for the crooked 14th-c stone spire above its tower – Victorian rebuilding kept the tilt. The B3210 from Totnes is pretty, the First & Last an attractive pub.

FINGLE BRIDGE SX7489

From the Anglers Rest a lovely 'Fisherman's Path' winds along a wooded stretch of the River Teign; you can return at high level on the 'Hunter's Path', passing nr Castle Drogo and gaining tremendous views.

KENTON SX9583

Kenton church A delightful church, its harmonious medieval sandstone masonry photographing well against blue sky; fine carving inside.

KINGSBRIDGE SX7344

Small town of character, pretty cobbled lanes diving off steep Fore St, arcaded shops, pillared market house (various markets Mon–Thurs), interesting monuments in church, boats on tidal estuary (and ferry to Salcombe); the waterfront Crabshell is very popular for seafood. At the head of the nearby creek, pretty South Pool has a fairly interesting church, with a delightfully ghoulish story attached, and a good pub.

Cookworthy Museum of Rural Life (Fore St) Collection of rural artefacts from Victorian kitchen implements to modern farming equipment, housed in a 17th-c grammar school. Shop, some disabled access; cl Sun, and all Nov–Mar; (01548) 853235; *£1.80.

KINGSTON SX6347

There are several walks from the village down to an unspoilt beach.

KINGSWEAR SX9051

Coleton Fishacre (3m E, off Lower Ferry Rd at Tollhouse) D'Oyly Carte's romantic and lush subtropical garden, with 20 colourful acres dropping down to a pretty cove; formal terraces, walled garden with stream-fed ponds, unusual trees and shrubs, grassy woodland paths. Meals, snacks, shop, limited disabled access; open Weds–Sun Apr–Nov, plus bank hols, and Sun pms in Mar; (01803) 752466; £3.70 (house £1 extra); NT. More ambitious marked paths beyond the gardens take you along the cliffs, showing how wild this part was before the garden was planted. The Royal Dart in the pretty waterside village of Kingswear has good seafood upstairs, and the Dart Valley Railway runs between the village and Paignton.

LODDISWELL SX7248

If you cross the river by the lane towards Woodsleigh, there's a quiet walk upstream by riverside pastures and woods towards Topsham Bridge.

LOWER ASHTON SX8382

Canonteign Falls 🖼 Pleasant country park covering 80 acres of ancient woodland, with a spectacularly high waterfall; also lakes, wildfowl, and children's commando course. Meals, snacks, shop; cl mid-Nov–Mar (exc most Suns and Feb half-term); (01647) 252434; £4.25. The Manor pub in the village is useful for lunch (no children inside).

LUSTLEIGH SX7881

One of the most attractive villages in the whole of England, with charming riverside walks in utterly unspoilt woodland around it, or up to Hunter's Tor on Dartmoor. Primrose Cottage is hotly tipped for cream teas, and the Cleave Inn is good.

LYDFORD SX5084

Lydford Gorge 🖼 Spectacular gorge formed by the River Lyd cutting into the rock, causing boulders to scoop out potholes in the bed of the stream. Walks along the ravine take you to dramatic sights such as the White Lady Waterfall and the Devil's Cauldron whirlpool (summer crowds around this bit). Children like it but need to be watched carefully, and paths can be narrow and slippery. Meals, snacks (in ingeniously designed tearoom), shop, special walk for the disabled; most parts cl Nov–Mar; (01822) 820441; £3.50; NT. The forbidding ruined castle has a daunting 12th-c stone keep, its upper floor once used as a court, and the lower as a prison; free. The Dartmoor Inn has good food.

MALBOROUGH SX7039
Yarde Medieval Farmhouse (just outside, towards Salcombe) Although it is somewhat delapidated – a programme of restoration proceeds as finances allow – readers enjoy visiting this attractive old farmhouse complete with brewhouse and stables; also shetland ponies, goats, hens, ducks and a pets' corner. Tea and cakes, some disabled access; open Sun pm, Easter–Sept; (01548) 842367; £2. In the lovely village the Old Inn is popular for food.

MANATON SX7580
A pretty village, with the private riverside woodland around **Becky Falls Woodland Estate** (B3344 to Bovey Tracey) useful enough for undemanding family walks if you don't plan to take advantage of the countryside proper. Meals, snacks, shop, some disabled access; cl Nov–late Mar (exc wknds, weather permitting); (01647) 221259; £4.80 (less in winter). The prettily placed Kestor has decent food.

MARLDON SX8962
Compton Castle (1m N, off A3022; or off A381 at Ipplepen turnoff) Formidably fortified and rather picturesque 14th-, 15th- and 16th-c manor around courtyard with portcullised entrance, particularly interesting for its completeness. The exterior was used as Willoughby's house in the film of *Sense and Sensibility*. Shop, very limited disabled access; open Mon, Weds and Thurs Apr–Oct, cl 12.15–2pm; (01803) 875740; £2.80; NT. The Church House Inn is handy for lunch.

MEAVY SX5367
This clear wooded river has some pleasant spots for strolling. Meavy itself (pronounced 'Mewy' locally) is an attractive village with one of the oldest oak trees in Britain, and the parish still owns the (good) pub (whose locals dance around the tree on New Year's Eve). Another useful pub for people walking in this valley is the Skylark at Clearbrook.

MODBURY SX6551
Attractive buildings esp in steep Church St, with quite photogenic church at top and pretty Exeter Inn at bottom. Brownston St is quite interesting too, esp ornate water conduit at top.

MORWELLHAM SX4470
Morwellham Quay Thriving and meticulously researched open-air museum in lovely countryside, with costumed guides convincingly re-creating the boom years when Morwellham was the greatest copper port in the Empire. The restored cottages come complete with pigs in the backyard, and you can watch the work of a blacksmith, cooper, coachmen and quay workers. Also rides into the mines, horse-drawn carriages, and lovely walks. Very popular in school hols – a visit can easily last all day. Meals, snacks, shop, disabled access limited but reduced price admission; cl Christmas wk; (01822) 832766; £8.50 (reduced price and operations in winter). The Ship (part of the centre) is good, with period waitresses and drinks.

NEWTON ABBOT SX8670
A working town rather than a holiday centre, but several interesting places here or nearby.
Bradley Manor (off A381 S) Peaceful 15th-c house nr stream through extensive wood-fringed grounds, quiet walks. Open Weds pm Apr–Sept, plus some Thurs at start and end of season – best to phone; (01626) 354513; £2.60; NT.
Orchid Paradise (Forches Cross, A382 N) Colourful place, with lots of rare and endangered species in elaborate indoor reconstructions of their natural habitats. Snacks, nursery and shop, some disabled access (but no facilities); cl winter bank hols; (01626) 352233; *£1.50.
Plant World 🖼 (St Marychurch Rd;

signed from Penn Inn roundabout)
Unusual four-acre garden built and
planted as a giant map of the world, with
the countries containing their correct
native plants, trees and flowers – many
of them quite rare in this country, but
flourishing in the mild Devon climate.
Also plant centre (with seeds of some
of the rarest plants), old-fashioned
English garden and fine views from
picnic area. Snacks; cl Oct–Mar;
(01803) 872939; *£1.50. The Linny in
nearby Coffinswell is a charming old
thatched pub.

Tuckers Maltings (Teign Rd) One of
the few remaining working malthouses
in the country, and the only one open to
the public – every year they produce
enough malt for 15 million pints of beer.
Tours show all aspects of malting (you
can touch the grain and taste the malt);
they also have their own brewery.
There's a hands-on section for children.
Snacks, shop with over 145 speciality
bottled beers; last guided tour starts
3pm (3.45 July–Sept and bank hols), cl
Nov–Easter; (01626) 334734; £4.35
(inc sample of beer).

NEWTON FERRERS/NOSS
MAYO SX5548

Picturesque twin villages on very
sheltered rocky wooded creek of
Yealm estuary; besides modern
development, there are some attractive
whitewashed cottages. Lots of yachting
in summer. The Old Ship, Dolphin and
Swan are all pleasant places for lunch.

NORTH BOVEY SX7184

A delightful peaceful spot, not usually
invaded by tourists: oak-shaded green
with mounting block, stone cross,
pump, ancient cottages and attractive
pub. **Miniature Pony Centre**
(Wormhill Farm) Lots of friendly and
engaging tiny ponies, happy to give
children steady rides. Also bigger
horses, pigs, donkeys, and pigmy goats,
bird garden, and good adventure
playground. The setting is lovely. Meals,
snacks, shop, good disabled access; cl
Nov–Easter; (01647) 432400; £4.95.

NOSS MAYO SX5449

Yealm estuary There are attractive
walks by this wooded estuary from
Noss Mayo, then beyond to Gara Point
and exposed cliff; largely NT. This can
be reached in sections via the Noss

Mayo–Holbeton coastal ridge road.

OKEHAMPTON SX5895

This Dartmoor-edge working town has
a couple of things worth stopping for.
Museum of Dartmoor Life (West
St) Well converted old watermill with
interactive displays on local life, Tourist
Information Centre and working craft
studios next door. Tearoom, shop,
some disabled access; cl Sun (exc
June–Sept) and end Oct–Easter;
(01837) 52295; £1.90.

Okehampton Castle The tower on a
steep grassy mound above the river is
remarkable for the way it stays standing
– a balancing act of ruined masonry
zigzagging up into the sky. It's the
biggest medieval castle in Devon, with
sections dating from 11th to 14th c;
good woodland walks. Snacks, shop; cl
all Nov–Mar; (01837) 52844; £2.30.

PAIGNTON SX8861

Largely a typical resort, with long
promenade between good sandy beach
and green; the little harbour is pretty,
with working fishing boats as well as
yachts. The original inland core has an
attractive red sandstone church with
some interesting buildings nearby, esp
Kirkham House, a handsome
sandstone Tudor merchant's house
with lofty hall. The formal and
subtropical lakeside gardens at
Oldway are colourful; on summer
wkdy mornings there are guided tours
of the Versailles-style colonnaded
mansion at their centre (tel (01803)
201201 and ask for Oldway House
details). Attractive Elberry Cove
between Paignton and Brixham is
altogether quieter. Decent places for
lunch include the Embassy (Colin Rd)
and Ship (Manor Rd, Preston).

**Paignton & Dartmouth Steam
Railway** (Queens Park Station, Torbay
Rd) One of the nicest such steam train
trips we know of – GWR steam trains
run from here right by the sea along Tor
Bay (halts at Goodrington Beach, which
has closer parking, and Churston), then
along the Dart estuary to Kingswear. The
front Pullman coach is less crowded, and
there's a model railway at the Paignton
end. You can combine this with a boat
Dartmouth– Totnes, and bus
Totnes–Paignton. Snacks, shop, disabled
access; open Apr–Oct (daily Jun–Sept)

and selected dates out of season, (01803) 555872 for timetable; £6.40 return.

Paignton Zoo (St Michael's) Well run and shown, with over 1,300 animals and birds (many of them breeding) in 75 acres of beautifully planted surroundings; it's perhaps the country's most visually appealing zoo, and lays a decent emphasis on conservation. Also lakeside miniature railway, and splendid hands-on animal education centre for children. Lots of events and feeding displays throughout the day. Meals, snacks, shop, good disabled access; cl 25 Dec; (01803) 557479; £7.50.

PLYMOUTH SX4753

Apart from the area round the Barbican most of the old parts of the city were destroyed in the war, and in parts it is like lots of other busy modern towns. There are some interesting escapes from the bustle, and in places the Hoe has something of the feel of smaller seaside promenades, with great views out over the Sound; decent food from the Yard Arm (looking out in suitably nautical style) and the Waterfront bar/restaurant. A statue of Drake is a reminder that he's supposed to have played his famous game of bowls here; there's still a bowling green close by. A tour bus can take you to the main attractions, though it's perhaps more fun on one of the **boat trips** run by Tamar Cruises from Mayflower Steps, off Madeira Rd, Barbican; (01752) 822105. There are also boats from here to **Mountbatten Peninsula**, a former Ministry of Defence area now open to the public; you can walk along the breakwater, which goes right out into the sound with views back towards the city. The ferries over to Torpoint in Cornwall put Antony House and Mt Edgcumbe in very easy reach. The Bank (behind Theatre Royal) does good value food all day, and the Tourist Information Centre is one of the most efficient we've come across.

Barbican Carefully restored since the war, a series of narrow twisty streets of old buildings W of working Sutton Harbour; photogenic – and evocative even in wet weather. New St is its oldest core. The Dolphin pub has original Beryl Cook paintings.

Barbican Glassworks The old

fishmarket has been redeveloped as a visitor centre. You can watch glass-blowing demonstrations by Dartington Crystal, and there are exhibitions on the local area. Large shop, disabled access; cl 25 Dec, 1 Jan and Easter Sun; free.

Black Friars Distillery (60 Southside St) Photogenic home of Plymouth Dry Gin, now the only English gin still made in its original distillery, founded in 1793. The building itself dates back much further, and has had periods as a monastery and a prison; tours include demonstrations of production, a film of the town's history and, of course, a sample of the gin itself. Shop; cl Sun Sept–May, and all Jan–Easter; (01752) 665292; *£2.75.

City Museum & Art Gallery (Drake Circus) Well shown collections of mostly West Country interest. Snacks, shop, good disabled access; cl Sun, Mon (exc bank hols); free.

Crownhill Fort 🏛 (Crownhill Fort Rd) Just N of town, the biggest and least altered of Plymouth's Victorian forts, though from the road it looks little more than a wooded hill. Used by the army right up to 1986, it's been well restored by the Landmark Trust, with barrack rooms, underground tunnels, secret passageways, and lookout towers to explore; children can run around quite freely, and there's an adventure playground. You can stay here in a Victorian officer's flat (all year), and have the run of the place after dark. Snacks, shop, limited disabled access (lots of steep steps); cl Nov–Mar; (01752) 793754; £3.50.

Elizabethan House (32 New St) Splendid timber-framed Tudor sea-captain's house with period furniture. Shop; cl Mon and Tues; (01752) 304774; £1. There's an Elizabethan garden just down the road at number 39.

Merchant's House (St Andrew St) Well restored 16th-c jettied house, telling the city's day-to-day history in displays themed on tinker, tailor, soldier, sailor; also early Victorian apothecary's shop and schoolroom. Shop; cl 1–2pm, Sun, Mon (exc bank hols), and Oct–Mar; (01752) 304774; £1.

National Marine Aquarium 🔲 (Barbican) The hundreds of fish at this excellent aquarium are shown in elaborate reconstructions of their natural habitats, starting with a moorland stream and bog, and progressing over the three floors through an estuary, seashore, and coral reef. Plenty of sound and other effects make the environments as authentic as possible – there's even a moorland mist rolling down the tor side. Most impressive of all is the huge two-storey deep reef tank, designed to represent the deeper offshore waters around the British Isles, and containing over half a million litres of water. Divers descend into the depths to feed the fish by hand at various times. Also discovery pools for children, and Europe's largest collection of seahorses. The Shark Theatre has spooky lighting to create an appropriate air of menace. They usually feed the sharks Mon, Weds and Fri – check in advance to make sure. Café with nice views over Plymouth Sound, shop, disabled access; cl 25 Dec; (01752) 220084; £6.50 (£4 children 4–15; good value family ticket, £19). Tickets usually allow same day re-entry.

Plymouth Dome 🔲 (The Hoe) State-of-the-art evocation of Plymouth's past and present using feel-part-of-it technology – you can stroll along lively Elizabethan streets, dodge press gangs, meet Drake and the Pilgrim Fathers, and come bang up to date with satellite and radar monitoring of current harbour action and weather. Good fun as well as interesting, and well worth two hours (you may have trouble parking nearby for longer than that). Particularly good for families – children don't mind learning about a place's heritage when it's presented like this. Snacks, shop, good disabled access; cl 25 Dec and Mon Nov–Easter ; (01752) 603300; £4.10 (inc admission to Smeaton's Tower).

Prysten House 🔲 (Finewell St) The city's oldest house, an austere late 15th-c granite building with galleried courtyard. Unpretentious but quite atmospheric restored rooms feature a model of 17th-c Plymouth, and several yards of an ambitious tapestry showing American colonisation. Cl Sun, and Nov–Mar; (01752) 661414; *70p.

Royal Citadel (The Hoe) Unrivalled views of the city and sea from the ramparts of this magnificent 17th-c battlemented fortress. The gateway is striking, and the barracked parade-ground is still in use. Disabled access (though no facilities); admission by guided tour only, at 2.30pm May–Sept (this may change – best to check), starting from the main gate – get tickets at least 15 mins earlier from the Dome or the Tourist Information Centre; (01752) 304849; £3.

Smeaton's Tower 🔲 (The Hoe) Colourfully striped 18th-c former Eddystone Rocks lighthouse, moved here 110 years ago, with a good view from the top if you like steps. Cl Nov–Mar, and maybe in bad weather; (01752) 600608; 75p.

St Andrew's (St Andrew St) Bombed but lovingly restored, with stained glass by John Piper illustrating the city's history.

PLYMPTON SX5255
Saltram (2m W, off A38/A379 at Marsh Mills roundabout) Magnificent mostly 18th-c mansion still with pretty much all the original contents, esp notable for its unaltered Robert Adam rooms. George II furnishings, decoration and paintings (strong on Reynolds, who as a regular guest advised on which other pictures to buy), interesting period kitchen, stately garden with orangery, and parkland by wooded Plym estuary. The house has attracted lots of extra visitors since starring as Norland Park in *Sense and Sensibility*. Meals, snacks, shop, local-art/crafts gallery, disabled access; cl Fri, Sat, and all Nov–Mar (house cl am), best to check; (01752) 333500; £6, garden only £3; NT. The old town around St Maurice Church is worth a look if you're here: attractive partly arcaded streets, very ruined motte and bailey castle, decent food at the George.

POWDERHAM SX9684
Powderham Castle 🔲 The ancestral home of the Earls of Devon, badly damaged in the Civil War but elaborately restored in the 18th and 19th c. The richly decorated state rooms were used in the film *The*

Remains of the Day. Spectacular rose garden, home to Timothy the 157-year-old tortoise, spring woodland garden, a secret garden designed for children, with ducks, rabbits, guinea pigs and chinchillas, and broad deer park with views over Exe estuary. Good guided tours, lots of special events, and a new farm shop. Meals, snacks, some disabled access; cl Sat, and Nov–Mar; (01626) 890243; £5.85. The ancient waterside Anchor has good seafood.

PRAWLE POINT SX7735
Impressive scenery: wind-blasted gorse, grass and thrift above low but fierce cliffs, lending itself to a round walk, with a useful network of green lanes leading inland to the village of East Prawle (good food at the Freebooters Arms).

SALCOMBE SX7438
Steep narrow-streets fishing village, full of enjoyable holiday bustle in summer, with lots of souvenirs, bric-a-brac, boating shops, teashops and pubs overlooking sea, nearby beaches and coves, boat trips and boat hire. The Ferry, Victoria and Fortescue are all popular for food.

Bolt Head/Bolt Tail Six miles of one of the best coast-path sections, with remote exposed clifftops, glorious coves, far views, well preserved Iron Age earth ramparts on Bolt Tail; all NT. Best access is via Overbecks, Soar Mill Cove or Hope Cove.

Overbecks (South Sands; signed from Salcombe and Malborough) Named after the eccentric research chemist who lived here until 1937; among his possessions and inventions you can still see the Rejuvenator which he claimed 'practically renewed' his youth. For most the chief attraction is the luscious subtropical gardens, with terraced plantings among woodland, many rarities and plenty of palms and citrus fruits; outstanding late May–Jun for the magnolias, but worth a trip any time of year. Glorious views out to sea, also colourful statue garden, picnic belvedere and collections of dolls and lead soldiers. Snacks, shop; cl Sat (exc Aug), Fri in Oct, and all Nov–Mar (garden open all year); (01548) 842893; *£4.10, *£2.90 garden only; NT. Mill Bay nr here has one of the area's safest bathing beaches.

SHALDON SX9372
Interesting and colourful mix of seaside houses spanning 200 years of architectural fancy; some lovely corners esp down by water away from the centre, also much older cottages in Crown Sq. The Clifford Arms has good local fish. High grassy sandstone Ness overlooks the sea and Teignmouth, with a tunnel cut by the 19th-c landowner to a sheltered beach; the beautifully set Ness House up here is useful for food. The A379 to Maidencombe has sea views.

Wildlife Trust 🅰 (Ness Drive) Nicely low-key breeding collection of rare and endangered foreign birds, and small mammals inc monkeys. Shop; cl 25 Dec; (01626) 872234; *£3.

SHARPHAM SX8158
Sharpham Barton Vineyard Two self-guided trails (one alongside a river) take you through the award-winning vineyard at this attractive 500-acre estate that also comprises a Jersey dairy farm (not open to the public). Shop; cl Sun and Dec–Feb; (01803) 732203; £2.50 (inc wine tasting).

SLAPTON SANDS SX8343
One of the finest beaches in the country, six miles of almost straight shingle N of the lighthouse at Start Point, backed by hills in the S and by road, shingle bank, lake (Slapton Ley nature reserve, marked nature trail) and marsh, then low cliffs, in the N. Good for out-of-season desolation, sheltered from W winds, with a storm-ruined village at Hallsands, and salvaged tank memorial to a US Normandy landings practice disaster at Torcross.

SOURTON SX5390
Highwayman An extraordinary pub, one bar recalling a galleon, the other a sort of fairy-tale fantasy, and the garden demonstrating yet more exuberant imagination – all meticulously done by the owners, not some brewery theme pub.

SOUTH-WEST COAST PATH SX5446
The finest part of Devon's S coast for walkers is between Plymouth and Brixham – much of it quite unspoilt. In summer ferries cross the rivers (exc the River Erme S of Ermington, which you have to cross at low tide).

SPARKWELL SX5858
**Dartmoor Wildlife Park &
Westcountry Falconry Centre** 🖻
Various animals inc big cats (feeding
time 3.30pm) in 30 acres of
countryside. Also falconry centre with
displays at 12pm and 4pm (Easter–Oct
exc Fri), adventure playground and
picnic area. Meals, snacks, shop,
disabled access; (01752) 837209; £6.95.
STICKLEPATH SX6494
Finch Foundry 🖻 No longer
producing the sickles, shovels and tools
for which it was known in the 19th c,
but the waterwheels and machinery are
all still working. Snacks, shop, limited
disabled access; cl Tues, and Nov–Mar;
(01837) 840046; £2.70; NT. The
thatched Devonshire Inn in the village is
good value.
STOKE GABRIEL SX8457
Steep village above a sheltered side-
pool of the Dart estuary, with 14th-c
church (with ancient yew) and Church
House (pleasant for lunch) perched
prettily on a high cobbled terrace.
TEIGNMOUTH SX9473
Popular resort for family holidays, with
good beaches, windsurfing and so on,
some handsome 19th-c streets and
active docks, and on French St a decent
local history **museum** (cl Sun am, and
third week in Oct–Apr; £1).
TORQUAY SX9163
The busiest of the area's resorts, good
for evening strolling, with palm trees
and rocks, promenades, colourful
gardens, decorous guesthouses and
huge hotels, broad Victorian streets
and upmarket shops. The sheltered
beaches around here are cleaner than
many along this coast. Summer bustle
centres around the attractive harbour,
with lots of shops, boat trips, and an
aquarium. In summer a **cliff railway**
takes care of a dizzy swoop from
Oddicombe Beach to the high wooded
clifftop (75p one way, £1.25 return).
The quaint Hole in the Wall (Park Lane)
and smart new London (Strand) do
good value food.
Bygones (Fore St, St Marychurch)
Enthusiastically reconstructed life-sized
Victorian street, with well stocked
period shops and rooms, model
railway, and re-created World War I
trench, replete with sound effects and

cooking smells. Open till 9pm(6pm Fri
and Sat) July–Aug. Café, shop; cl 25 Dec;
(01803) 326108; £3.75
Cockington Winding lanes of olde-
worlde thatched cottages and bric-a-
brac/craft shops in sheltered village
with millpond etc, well preserved by
Torbay Council; adjoining 500-acre
park. The Drum pub (a useful stop) was
designed to match by Lutyens in 1934.
Terribly pretty, and very touristy in
season, with open horse-drawn carriages.
Kents Cavern Showcaves 🖻
(Ilsham Rd, Wellswood) The oldest
directly dated archaeological site in
Britain; continuing excavations often
make scientists reconsider their
theories about prehistoric life. Good
guided tours really bring out the
mystery of the caves, and colourful
stalagmites and stalactites add to the
eerie atmosphere. In summer they do
spooky evening tours (booking essential).
Very well presented, and definitely
worth an hour or so if you're in the
area. Special visits at Christmas. Summer
meals, snacks, shop, disabled access
(with prior notice); cl 25 Dec; (01803)
215136; £4.75 (£5.50 evening tours).
Model Village (Hampton Ave,
Babbacombe) Hundreds of one-twelfth
scale buildings in four acres of
miniaturised landscape, beautifully
done. Try coming at dusk between
Easter and Oct, when the scenes are
prettily floodlit. Snacks, shop, good
disabled access; cl 25 Dec; (01803)
328669; £4.80 – a little pricey, but it's
probably the best of its type (you may
also have to pay for parking). The beach
here has safe bathing water, and the
Cary Arms (Beach Rd) is good.
Torquay Museum (529 Babbacombe
Rd) Re-opening in April following
refurbishment inc improvements to
disabled access, this will have new
galleries, plus finds from ancient local
caves, local history, Victoriana and a
cannon that turns out to be a clock,
designed to fire its charge at midday.
Shop; cl Sun am, winter wknds and
Christmas week; (01803) 293975; £2.
Torre Abbey 🖻 (Kings Drive) Some
of the earlier parts of the abbey remain,
inc the medieval barn, gatehouse,
undercrofts and ruined Norman tower,
but they've been eclipsed by the later

house with its 18th- and 19th-c period rooms. The main feature now is Devon's largest art gallery, along with a showy garden and palm house and an Agatha Christie room, full of possessions of the locally born author. Snacks, shop; cl Nov–Mar; (01803) 293593; *£3.

TOTNES SX8060
Busy in summer, but still keeping most of its charm then, particularly early in the morning. The picturesque Elizabethan area known as **The Narrows** is very atmospheric, esp along the High St down to the arch at the top of Fore St, with quaint pillared arcades. On Tues mornings May–Sept some traders wear Elizabethan costume, and the main streets are closed to traffic then, delighting visitors but infuriating some local traders. There's a working harbour (see Dartmouth for excellent river trips), and you can walk some way downstream on either side of the River Dart. Behind the church of St Mary's (which has a super rood screen), several rooms in the 11th-c guildhall may be open; it was originally part of a Benedictine priory. Perhaps unexpectedly, Totnes has quite a New Age flavour; there's even a flotation tank to wash away city stresses. The Kingsbridge Inn (Leechwell St), Royal Seven Stars Hotel (Fore St) and Albert (Bridgetown) have decent food. The South Devon Railway, which stops here, is described under Buckfastleigh.
Bowden House (Ashprington Rd, S of town) Tours by costumed guides of handsomely restored grand Tudor and baroque rooms (plenty of weaponry, and well documented tales of ghosts), and separate **photography museum** with still and moving pictures (inc cartoons) in attractive grounds. Meals, snacks, shop, disabled access to museum only; open pm Mon–Fri and possibly bank hol Suns from May–Oct; (01803) 863664; £4.95.
Devonshire Collection of Costume ▣ (43 High St) Period costumes and accessories from the 18th c to the present, from ordinary work clothes to high fashion, with changing annual exhibitions. Shop; cl wknds, and Nov–mid-May; £1.75.
Totnes Castle Part Norman, part

14th-c, these classic circular remains were lucky enough to avoid any battles, so the keep is pretty much intact. There's a tree-shaded inner lawn, and lovely views of the town and down to the river. Shop, snacks, very limited disabled access; cl Mon and Tues and lunchtimes Nov–Mar; (01803) 864406; £1.60.
Totnes Museum ▣ (70 Fore St) Stately Elizabethan merchant's house with galleried courtyard, herb garden, and display on the inventions of Totnes boy Charles Babbage, creator of one of the earliest computers. Shop, some disabled access with prior arrangement; cl wknds, and Nov–Mar; (01803) 863821; £1.50.
TUCKENHAY SX8156
This gives a pretty one-mile stroll E along wooded Bow Creek, from the Maltsters Arms – good food here.
WEMBURY BAY SX5148
A walk here gives good views, starting from Wembury past the church at the start of NT clifftops; woods and pastures on opposite shore, Plymouth shipping in the distance.
WIDECOMBE IN THE MOOR SX7176
One of the most visited villages on Dartmoor, immortalised by the trip of Uncle Tom Cobbleigh and all to Widecombe Fair. The granite-carved village sign shows them all crowded on to their old grey mare. The **church**, known as the Cathedral of the Moors, has a distinctive disproportionately high tower. The adjoining 16th-c church house, now the church hall, is worth a look. Next door, the **Sexton's Cottage** is a NT and Dartmoor National Park information centre and gift shop; cl 24–26 Dec and first week in Mar. The Post Office Stores has good ice-cream and local honey. The reconstructed Olde Inne in the village is very popular with tourists, but for more of a Tom Cobbleigh flavour try the Rugglestone Inn just S. The **Shilstone Rocks Riding Centre** organises horse-riding over Dartmoor, beginners welcome. Disabled access; (01364) 621281; from £14 an hour.
YEALMPTON SX5751
They now open the stunning illuminated **Kitley caves** here only to

small groups or individuals with a special interest in the subject; tel (01752) 880885 to book free guided tour. Above ground are 50 acres of pretty woodland and riverside walks with many varieties of plants, shrubs and trees. The Rose & Crown does decent food. Nearby is a good farm shop, and seasonal pick your own fruit and veg (inc courgettes,

spinach and pumpkins).
YELVERTON SX5167
Paperweight Centre (Buckland Terrace) Odd collection of hundreds of glass paperweights, all sizes and designs, inc collector's pieces. Shop, disabled access; open wknds and daily Apr–Oct and Dec; (01822) 854250; free. The Rock (A386) is a good family pub.

Where to eat

ASHPRINGTON SX8157 **Durant Arms** (01803) 732240 Friendly dining pub, opposite the church, with two attractive bar rooms, open fires, good bar food, well kept beers, and friendly service; cl pm 25 Dec; disabled access. £21|**£7.50**

AVONWICK SX7158 **Avon Inn** (01364) 73475 Popular dining pub with comfortable fairly modern furnishings, a wide range of good food inc lots of interesting pasta dishes, plenty of fish, and lovely puddings, good Italian wines, well kept real ales, and pleasant riverside garden; cl Sun, 1 wk Jan; children in restaurant only; disabled access. £23|**£5.45**

BABBACOMBE SX9265 **Tea Rose Tea Rooms** 49 Babbacombe Downs Rd (01803) 324477 Charming small tearoom with inside and outside tables set in a garden opposite the sea, with waitresses in period dress, and generous cream teas and snacks; disabled access.

BANTHAM SX6743 **Sloop** (01548) 560489 Nr sandy beach (good for surfing), this 16th-c nautical village inn has good bar food inc lots of fish, hearty breakfasts, and decent beers and wines; bdrms and self-catering cottages. £21.50|**£5.65**

BOLBERRY SX6939 **Port Light** (01548) 561384 Popular even on dismal winter wkdys, this clifftop former RAF radar station (easy walk from Hope Cove) is warmly friendly with good home-made food in attractive bar and restaurant, super sea views, woodburner, and good outdoor children's play area; bdrms; cl 1–10 Dec, and all Jan; disabled access. £21|**£6.95**

CHERITON BISHOP SX7695 **Old Thatch** (01647) 24204 Welcoming 16th-c inn with good bar food from big menu, interesting puddings, winter themed food evenings, beamed bar and big open stone fireplace, real ales from small independent breweries, and friendly service; bdrms; cl 25 Dec. £21.50|**£4.95**

COCKWOOD SX9780 **Anchor** (01626) 890203 Friendly and very popular pub by the harbour with small low-ceilinged rambling rooms and lots of good fresh fish dishes – 30 ways of serving mussels, 12 of serving scallops, 10 of oysters, and so forth, no smoking restaurant, well kept real ales, 10 wines by the glass, and 50 malt whiskies; disabled access. £25|**£5.95**

COMBEINTEIGNHEAD SX9271 **Coombe Cellars** (01626) 872423 Big bustling family pub with lots for children inc an indoor play area, their own menu, fun days with entertainment, outside play galleon and fenced-in playground; lovely estuary setting with tables on jetties and big terraces, a roomy and comfortable bar with plenty of nautical bric-a-brac, well kept real ales, lots of wines by the glass, enjoyable food, and friendly, efficient staff.|**£7** ☺

CORNWORTHY SX8255 **Hunters Lodge** (01803) 732204 Welcoming and popular country local with a low-ceilinged bar, cottagey restaurant with 17th-c fireplace, tasty lunchtime food and imaginative evening meals, well kept real ales, decent wines, and plenty of seats outside; partial disabled access. £20|**£4.95**

DARTMOUTH SX8751 **Café Alf Resco** Lower Rd (no telephone) On three levels (the one on street level is partly open-air), this is a bustling café offering hearty breakfasts, morning coffee and lunchtime snacks; bdrms; cl Mon, Tues, last wk Jan and first 2 wks Feb; disabled access. £12|**£4.50**

DARTMOUTH SX8751 **Carved Angel** 2 South Embankment (01803) 832465 Black and white timbered restaurant, airy and attractive, overlooking the quay, with wonderful meals using carefully chosen absolutely fresh produce – superb fish, delicious puddings and lovely cheeses – fine wines in every price range, and a smart yet friendly atmosphere; no smoking. See also the cheerful (and much cheaper) new **Carved Angel Café** at 7 Foss St, under the same owners, which offers imaginative, very good simpler food in the form of morning coffee, light lunches, afternoon tea, and wknd evening meals. Main restaurant cl Sun pm, Mon, 3 days Christmas; children lunchtime only; partial disabled access. £50

DARTMOUTH SX8751 **Cherub** *10 Higher St* (01804) 832571 Dartmouth's oldest building (already 300 years old when Sir Francis Drake used it), this has a bustling bar, liked by locals, an upstairs dining room, decent food, and well kept ales; children in upstairs restaurant only. £19.50|**£5.50**

GULWORTHY SX4473 **Horn of Plenty** (01822) 832528 On the edge of Dartmoor in quiet flower-filled gardens, this relaxed, refurbished Georgian no smoking restaurant-with-rooms has excellent carefully cooked food using top quality local produce inc lovely puddings and cheeses (wonderful breakfasts, too), a good wine list, and vine-covered terrace for aperitifs; comfortable bdrms; cl Mon am, 25–26 Dec; disabled access. £27 lunch, £37 dinner

HARBERTON SX7758 **Church House** (01803) 863707 Ancient village pub with magnificent medieval panelling, attractive old furnishings, generous helpings of interesting daily specials, well kept beers, and decent wines; bdrms; children in family room; cl pm 25–26 Dec, 1 Jan. £19.65|**£7.95**

KINGSBRIDGE SX7443 **Crabshell** *The Quay, Embankment Rd* (01548) 852345 Famous old dining pub, very popular for its lovely waterside position and fresh fish and shellfish – they also do picnics and take-aways; friendly staff, well kept real ales, decent wines, warm winter fire, and live music Thurs; disabled access. £20|**£6**

KINGSTEIGNTON SX8773 **Old Rydon** *Rydon Rd* (01626) 54626 Cosy old pub with wide choice of constantly changing imaginative bar food, winter log fire, well kept real ales, helpful service, and pretty dining conservatory. £28.80|**£7.45**

LUSTLEIGH SX7881 **Primrose Cottage** (01647) 277365 Thatched 15th-c cottage by the old village church with seats in riverside garden, clotted cream teas, lovely home-made cakes and pastries, and tasty all-day light meals; cl Tues, cl Nov–Feb. £14|**£6.95**

MARLDON SX8663 **Church House** (01803) 558279 Under new licensees, this well run bustling pub has several different attractive bar areas and restaurant, candles on tables, bare boards, hops and dried flowers, imaginative daily-changing food, well kept real ales, 10 wines by the glass, and seats outside; bdrms; children over 10 in evening. £20|**£6.50**

PLYMOUTH SX4754 **Chez Nous** *13 Frankfort Gate* (01752) 266793 Informal and friendly Michelin-starred French bistro with long-standing owners, careful cooking of fresh local produce, esp fresh fish and fine puddings, some distinguished wines, and friendly atmosphere; cl Sun, Mon, Sat am, 3 wks Feb, 3 wks Sept; children over 10; partial disabled access. £45

RATTERY SX7461 **Church House** (01364) 642220 One of Britain's oldest pubs, with open fires, friendly staff, good bar food, decent wines and beers, fine malt whiskies, and nice dog and cats; peaceful setting; disabled access. £17|**£4.95**

TORCROSS SX8241 **Start Bay** (01548) 580553 Notable and very popular fresh seafood generously served in busy thatched pub overlooking 3-mile pebble beach; farm cider; family room; cl pm 25 Dec; partial disabled access. £15|**£5**

TORQUAY SX9064 **Mulberry Room** *1 Scarborough Rd* (01803) 213639 Popular no smoking restaurant-with-rooms, with good interesting food using local produce, and very enjoyable home-made cakes and scones for afternoon tea; bdrms; cl Mon, Tues (except to residents); disabled access. £21|**£4.50**

TOTNES SX8060 **Greys Dining Room** *96 High St* (01803) 866369 No smoking Georgian house with pretty china on a handsome dresser and partly panelled walls, lots of teas plus herb and fruit ones, sandwiches, salads and omelettes as well as lots of cakes and set teas; cl Weds; no pushchairs and children must be well behaved; partial disabled access. £12|**£6**

TUCKENHAY SX8156 **Maltsters Arms** *(01803) 732350* Very well run creekside pub with enthusiastic friendly owners, particularly good interesting food – though they are keen to keep it as a pub where people also feel comfortable dropping in for a drink – well kept real ales, 12 wines by the glass, and relaxed, airy bars; seats by the water; super bdrms; open all day Sat/Sun and all day during summer hols. £25|£5

UGBOROUGH SX6755 **Anchor** *Letterburn St (01752) 892283* Friendly pub, oak beams and log fire, a wide choice of very good food inc unusual things such as ostrich, alligator, emu and bison, lots of fresh fish, courteous service, and well kept real ales; disabled access. £25|£7

North Devon & Exmoor

Great for escaping the crowds, with good walks, some unusual family attractions, and outstanding coastal scenery; easy to find peace and quiet even in summer

Although much of the area is untouched by tourism, there are plenty of things to occupy families here, inc what must be some of the most whimsical attractions in the country: children can try on pixie fashions at the Gnome Reserve in Bradworthy, take a driving test at Once Upon A Time (more elfin fun at its sister park, Watermouth Castle, too), and watch sheep racing and duck trials at The Big Sheep, Tiverton. More closely grounded in fact, but no less interesting or fun for that, is the county's Family Attraction of the Year, Torrington 1646 – an enthusiastically run heritage centre with excellent costumed guides.

Wildlife fans will enjoy Exmoor Falconry & Animal Farm (Allerford) and Exmoor Zoological Park (South Stowford), as well as the birds and butterflies at Ashford Butterfly House & Gardens, and the mix of rare animals and models of their extinct forebears at Combe Martin Wildlife & Dinosaur Park.

Arlington Court is an interesting day out for any age, and Bickleigh has the joint attractions of its castle and mill with a new summer maze. There are fine woodland gardens at Downes and RHS Rosemoor, both near Torrington, and also at spooky-looking Knightshayes Court. Tapeley Park has a few attractions to occupy children while their parents stroll around the pretty grounds.

Clovelly, and Combe Martin with its odd Pack of Cards pub, are legendarily pretty (and do draw the summer crowds), and Lynton (good walks) and Hartland Quay are other places to head for.

Long stretches of coastline here – there's a magnificent coastal path – remain empty even in summer. Even Ilfracombe, the main resort, is not too touristy; it's pleasant and distinctive, with plenty for families, and stays active all year. The lower-key beach resorts such as Woolacombe and Westward Ho! virtually shut down when the season's over, their marvellous beaches then ideal for lonely walks; elsewhere there are fine bracing cliff walks. Lundy Island is a relaxing windswept wilderness.

Exmoor itself is full of interest for walkers (and drivers), and quieter in summer than Dartmoor; the Exmoor Natural History Society organise decent leisurely strolls. Though part lies in Somerset, we've covered the whole of the moor area in this chapter (some places such as Dunster within the boundary of the National Park but outside the moor itself are described in the Somerset chapter). Some of the best parts of the Tarka Trail, a growing destination for walkers and cyclists, are on and around the moor. Other inland parts are largely secluded farmland. The twisty wooded Taw Valley is pretty; the A377 gives drivers some good views here, though not quite so outstanding as the Exeter–Barnstaple rail journey, one of England's finest.

Where to stay

ASHWATER SX3697 **Blagdon Manor** *Ashwater, Beaworthy, Devon EX21 5DF* *(01409) 211224* **£110***; 7 pretty rms. Standing in rolling countryside, this carefully restored and tranquil 17th-c manor has eight acres of grounds (croquet and 4-hole practice golf course), beams and flagstones, log fires, fresh flowers, lovely food in a dinner-party atmosphere, and kind staff; cl Christmas; dogs by arrangement; no children

BISHOP'S TAWTON SS5928 **Halmpstone Manor** *Bishop's Tawton, Barnstaple, Devon EX32 0EA (01271) 830321* **£100***; 5 pretty rms. Quietly relaxing small country hotel with log fire in comfortable sitting room, enjoyable food in panelled dining room, good breakfasts, caring service, an attractive garden, and nice views; plenty to do nearby; cl Christmas/New Year; no children

BUCKLAND BREWER SS4220 **Coach & Horses** *Buckland Brewer, Bideford, Devon EX39 5LU (01237) 451395* **£50***; 2 rms above bar (so could be noisy for children until 11.30pm). Welcoming well preserved 13th-c thatched village pub with cosy beamed bar, log fires in inglenook fireplaces, enjoyable food, dining room, and pleasant garden; children over 8; no dogs; partial disabled access

CADBURY SS9005 **Beers Farm** *Cadbury, Exeter, Devon EX5 5PY (01884) 855426* **£38**; 2 rms. Set in several acres with lovely views across to the Raddon Hills, this non-working farm is quiet and comfortable (and no smoking) with friendly, helpful owners and good breakfasts; packed lunches on request; garden plants for sale; lots to do nearby

CHITTLEHAMHOLT SS6520 **Highbullen** *Chittlehamholt, Umberleigh, Devon EX37 9HD (01769) 540561* **£130***, plus special breaks; 40 comfortable and elegant, often spacious rms in main building and various attractively converted outbuildings. Victorian Gothick mansion set in huge wooded parkland and gardens with lots of wildlife, fishing (several beats), 9-hole golf course, indoor tennis court' and swimming pool, table tennis, and squash court; consistently good food in intimate restaurant overlooking the valley, busy little bar, library, and relaxed informal service (no reception, you ring a bell and wait); children over 8; no dogs

CLAWTON SX3499 **Court Barn Hotel** *Clawton, Holsworthy, Devon EX22 6PS (01409) 271219* **£68**, plus special breaks; 8 individually furnished rms. Charming country house in five pretty acres with croquet, 9-hole putting green, small chip-and-putt course, and tennis and badminton courts; comfortable lounges, log fires, library/TV room, good service, imaginative food and award-winning wines (and teas), and a quiet relaxed atmosphere; dogs allowed away from public rooms; cl 2–12 Jan

DULVERTON SS8631 **Ashwick House** *Ashwick, Dulverton, Devon TA22 9QD (01398) 323969* **£96***, plus special breaks; 6 peaceful rms with thoughtful extras. Quietly set Edwardian house in six lovely acres overlooking the Barle Valley (they've created a woodland trail), with personal service from caring owner, comfortable old-fashioned furnishings, fresh flowers, log fires and candlelight, enjoyable food, hearty breakfasts (which can be taken on the south-facing terrace), and a really relaxing atmosphere; children over 8

HATHERLEIGH SS5404 **Tally Ho** *Market St, Hatherleigh, Okehampton, Devon EX20 3JN* (01837) 810306 **£50**, plus wknd breaks; 3 rms. Friendly and interesting old inn with genuinely old-fashioned fittings in opened-up beamed rooms, good food and own-brew beers

HAWKRIDGE SS8632 **Tarr Steps Hotel** *Dulverton, Somerset TA22 9PY* (01643) 851293 **£130** inc dinner, plus special breaks; 11 rms, most with own bthrm. Former Georgian rectory in 11 acres of gardens, surrounded by 500 acres of land with rough shooting and trout-filled river, riding, and clay-pigeon shooting; carefully refurbished comfortable drawing room with log fires and flowers, oak-panelled bar, good food in attractive dining room (popular locally) using own organic vegetables, a relaxed happy atmosphere, and friendly staff; self-catering cottage also; cl end Jan/early Feb; disabled access; well behaved dogs allowed

HEDDON'S MOUTH SS6548 **Heddon's Gate Hotel** *Martinhoe, Parracombe, Barnstaple, Devon EX31 4PZ* (01598) 763313 **£88***, plus special breaks; 14 comfortable rms named for their original use and many with views. Victorian country house hotel in interesting large gardens on the edge of Exmoor, with marvellously relaxed and friendly atmosphere, comfortable sitting room with lovely views, good library/Victorian morning room, attractive dining room, very good home cooking inc 6-course dinners and proper afternoon tea, and friendly helpful service; cl Nov–Easter; children welcome if able to eat at 8pm (no special meals for them); dogs by prior arrangement; disabled access in annexe cottage

HORNS CROSS SS3823 **Lower Waytown** *Horns Cross, Bideford, Devon EX39 5DN* (01237) 451787 **£52***; 3 rms. Beautifully converted barn and roundhouse in five acres with ornamental waterfowl on stream-fed ponds, round sitting room with beams and inglenook fireplaces, and lovely breakfasts in big dining room; no smoking; self-catering cottages; cl Christmas/New Year; children over 12; partial disabled access

LYNMOUTH SS7249 **Rising Sun** *Mars Hill, Lynmouth, Devon EX35 6EG* (01598) 753223 **£90**; 16 comfortable and cosy rms. Thatched 14th-c inn with lovely views over the little harbour and out to sea, oak-panelled dining room, beamed and panelled bar with uneven oak floors, good food and wines, charming terraced garden, and lots of nearby walks; children over 8

LYNTON SS7149 **Highcliffe House** *Sinai Hill, Lynton, Devon EX35 6AR* (01598) 752235 **£50***, plus special breaks; 6 well equipped attractive rms. Carefully refurbished no smoking Victorian house with wonderful views over Lynton, the sea, and wooded countryside; two comfortable sitting rooms, good food in candlelit dining conservatory, and kind staff; cl first 2 wks Jan; no children and no pets

MORCHARD BISHOP SS7508 **Wigham** *Morchard Bishop, Crediton, Devon EX17 6RJ* (01363) 877350 **£150** inc dinner, plus special breaks; 5 rms. Picturesque thatched longhouse on 30-acre farm, with house-party atmosphere, two sitting rooms, big log fires, and snooker room; dining room with honesty bar, and good set dinner and breakfasts using home-grown organic fruit and veg, home-made butter, breads and jams, and own free-range eggs; no smoking and no pets (they have their own); outdoor heated swimming pool; cl sometime over Jan/Feb; children by arrangement

NORTHAM SS4528 **Yeoldon House** *Durrant Lane, Northam, Bideford, Devon EX39 2RL* (01237) 474400 **£90**, plus special breaks; 10 cosy rms. At the end of a long private drive, this quietly set hotel by the River Torridge has a warmly friendly and relaxed atmosphere, a comfortable lounge where you can enjoy a free sherry before dinner, good food using local produce in the attractive dining room, and helpful service; lots to do nearby; cl Christmas

OAKFORD SS9122 **Newhouse Farm** *Oakford, Tiverton, Devon EX16 9JE* (01398) 351347 **£45***, plus special breaks; 2 rms. 17th-c longhouse on edge of Exmoor, part of farm with small flock of friendly sheep; cottage sitting room, inglenook fireplace, beams, and country dining room serving home-made food inc good bread, pâtés and puddings; cl Christmas; no children or pets; disabled access

PORLOCK SS8846 **Oaks** *Doverhay, Porlock, Minehead, Somerset TA24 8ES* (01643) 862265 **£100***, plus special breaks; 9 airy and pretty rms. Particularly welcoming and spotless Edwardian country house looking down from Exmoor to Porlock Bay, with surrounding lawns and oak trees, a relaxed atmosphere and log fire in attractive lounge, and good unpretentious cooking in attractive no smoking restaurant; cl Nov–Mar; children over 8

PORLOCK SS8846 **Seapoint** *Redway, Porlock, Minehead, Somerset TA24 8QE* (01643) 862289 **£50**, plus winter breaks; 3 rms. Surrounded by the Exmoor hills and with views of Porlock Bay, this Edwardian guesthouse has a comfortable sitting room with winter log fire, a friendly and relaxing atmosphere, enjoyable home-made food in candlelit dining room, and fine breakfasts; cl Dec/Jan

PORLOCK SS8746 **West Porlock House** *Porlock, Minehead, Somerset TA24 8NX* (01643) 862880 **£55**; 5 rms. Nicely proportioned no smoking former manor house in four acres, with spacious carefully furnished rooms, and kind personal service; cl Nov–Feb; children over 6; no pets

SELWORTHY SS9346 **Hindon Farm** *Selworthy, Minehead, Somerset TA24 8SH* (01643) 705244 **£44***; 3 rms, 1 with own bthrm. Relaxed and friendly organic Exmoor farm of 500 acres with sheep, pigs, and cattle, lawn with volleyball and small unheated swimming pool, donkeys and ducks, lots of lovely surrounding walks inc award-winning conservation trail, riding (can bring your own horse), and mountain biking; attractive sitting room and dining room, games barn with table tennis, and snooker, log fires, and fine breakfasts using their own eggs, bacon and honey; dogs welcome; self-catering wing also; cl Christmas; children under 11 by arrangement in B&B

SHEEPWASH SS4806 **Half Moon** *Sheepwash, Beaworthy, Devon EX21 5NE* (01409) 231376 **£78***, plus special breaks; 15 rms. Civilised heart-of-Devon hideaway in colourful village square with 10 miles of private salmon, sea trout and brown trout fishing on the Torridge, a neatly kept friendly bar, solid old furnishings and big log fire, good wines, lovely evening restaurant, lunchtime bar snacks; dogs welcome; 24–26 Dec; limited disabled access

WEST BUCKLAND SS6630 **Huxtable Farm** *West Buckland, Barnstaple, Devon EX32 0SR* (01598) 760254 **£50***, plus special breaks; 6 rms. 16th-c farmhouse surrounded by carefully converted listed stone buildings, open fields, fine views, sheep, chickens, and rabbits; candlelit dinner with wholesome home-made food using home-grown produce, home-made wine and bread, a relaxing sitting room, and beams, open fireplaces with bread ovens, and uneven floors; sauna, fitness room, tennis court, games room, and outside children's play area with swings, sandpit and Wendy house; good for families; cl Dec/Jan (but open New Year) ☺

WEST PORLOCK SS8746 **Bales Mead** *West Porlock, Minehead, Somerset TA24 8NX* (01643) 862565 **£66***; 3 comfortable rms with sherry, fresh flowers, and thoughtful little extras. This quiet and relaxing no smoking Edwardian house has lovely Exmoor views towards the sea, a particularly pretty garden, charmingly decorated sitting room with log fire and baby grand piano, super breakfasts (no evening meals), and friendly, helpful owners; cl Christmas/New Year; no children

WOOLACOMBE SS4543 **Woolacombe Bay Hotel** *Woolacombe, Devon EX34 7BN* (01271) 870388 **£170**, plus special breaks; 65 rms. Carefully extended Victorian hotel in six acres of grounds by a splendid 3-mile beach; quiet, comfortable lounges, a relaxed bistro and high-ceilinged more formal restaurant, two bars, and splendid facilities for children: indoor and outdoor pool (with flume), a children's club plus teenage activities, discos and bands, board games and books, and riding and fishing can be arranged; tennis, 9-hole approach golf, croquet and swing ball, billiard room and pool tables, squash, and gym, solarium and steam room, and lovely unspoilt surrounding countryside ☺

Please let us know what you think of places in the *Guide*. Use the report forms at the back of the book or simply write us a letter.

To see and do

Devon Family Attraction of the Year

TORRINGTON SS4919 **Torrington 1646** (South St car park) Still relatively new, this lively heritage centre entertainingly brings to life one of the lesser-known battles of the English Civil War, fought here in February 1646. It's run by a charity keen to encourage visitors to Torrington, and their enthusiasm and genuine interest in the subject quickly proves infectious. What makes it special is the way the four or five actors, all in period clothes, work so hard to get children involved, and though they rarely step out of character, they'll interact and chat with visitors at every opportunity (don't be surprised if they quiz you on your clothes or other modern oddities). The scene-setting first part is a fairly traditional exhibition of Civil War history, where you can try on a helmet or find out from touch-screens whether you'd have been a Cavalier or Roundhead. A video shows a recent large-scale reconstruction of the battle by the Sealed Knot. But it's in the back room that the fun really begins. Groups of 12 are ushered in and told to imagine they're back in the 17th c; the guide disappears and is replaced by a 17th-c local keen to usher you away from the battle to safety. He'll take you through various reconstructions and situations, until you get to the church, used (unwisely as it turns out) to store gunpowder. . . Outside, army stragglers will try and sell you their armour and weapons; they'll show you how to charge into battle, let you examine their swords, and maybe introduce you to period games. Finally you're shown around a reconstructed 17th-c garden. With so many hands-on activities, this really is a place children enjoy, and it's good to come across a new attraction that focuses so well on the basics of entertainment and value for money. It's amazing how many places with more money spent on them or with more elaborate facilities don't get that right. Teas, snacks, picnic area, shop, disabled access; cl Sun and Mon outside school hols, and all mid-Dec to mid-Jan; (01805) 626146; *£3.50, children *£2 (under-5s are free, but they probably won't enjoy it so much as older ones). The family ticket, £10 for two adults and three children, is good value.

ALLERFORD SS9047
Pretty stone-built village with lovely packhorse bridge, and enthusiastic **West Somerset Museum of Rural Life** (cl Sun (exc school hols), Sat, and Nov–Easter, £1) with occasional summer craft demonstrations.
Exmoor Falconry & Animal Farm
🏠 Friendly place with rare breeds, pony rides, baby animals for children to feed, and birds of prey. Twice daily flying displays and summer evening hawk walks up on Exmoor, when you may be able to fly the birds yourself (£35 for 2 hrs inc light supper). B&B in the 15th-c farmhouse. Snacks, shop, disabled access; cl Nov–Feb; (01643) 862816; £4.95.
APPLEDORE SS4630
A pretty centre of narrow cottagey streets off the quayside road which looks out over the Taw estuary, and

ship- and boat-building in the yard just upstream. There's a pedestrian ferry over to Instow. The Royal George has lovely views and decent food, and the Beaver is also good for lunch.
North Devon Maritime Museum (Odun House, Odun Rd) Good museum exploring a different topic in each room. Shop, disabled access to ground floor only; cl 11–12.30pm, and Nov–Easter; (01237) 422064; £1.
ARLINGTON SS6140
Arlington Court (A39) From its Victorian heyday up to 1949 Rosalie Chichester filled this early 19th-c house with model ships, stuffed birds, holiday souvenirs – in fact anything she could get her hands on; her assemblages have been watered down since, but there's still quite a fascinating medley. Covering 3,500 acres, the grounds have attractive landscaped gardens and a number of

Shetland ponies and sheep, along with Victorian garden and conservatory, woodland and lakeside nature trails, and an unusual collection of carriages and horse-drawn vehicles (rides available). Meals, snacks, shop, disabled access to ground floor only; cl Sat (exc bank hol wknds), and Nov–Mar; (01271) 850296; £5.30, garden only £3.30; NT. The Pyne Arms at East Down is useful for lunch.

ASHFORD SS5235

Butterfly House & Gardens Well looked after collection of tropical butterflies, with plenty of plants and birds, and two acres of landscaped gardens outside. Meals, snacks, shop, disabled access; cl Oct–Easter; (01271) 342880; £2.50, gardens free. The Ring of Bells at Pilton is useful for lunch.

BARNSTAPLE SS5533

The main regional shopping centre, with a good deal of unforced charm in the older parts. Interesting buildings include an imposing 18th-c colonnaded arcade on the Great Quay, a lofty Victorian market hall (market days Tues and Fri), almshouses behind the church, more off the square by the long old stone bridge, and some interesting shops. It's still a working port, though in a very small way now. The best nearby pub is the Chichester Arms up in Bishops Tawton. On Pilston Causeway there's a good sheepskin shop; you can tour the adjacent factory. In summer you can hire bikes at the main railway station – a good ride is the one along the disused rail track up to Torrington. The surviving mainline Exeter–Barnstaple line (known as the **Tarka Line**), mostly tracking along closer to the River Taw than the road does, is one of the finest of all train rides for scenery.

Art Hotel (off B3230, from Barnstaple towards Ilfracombe) There's an appealing blend of old and new at this friendly late Victorian hotel surrounded by woodland. Inside, the house is decorated with antiques and contemporary art, while new works are continually added to the evolving sculpture garden; they also run a programme of lectures, music recitals and poetry readings. Meals, snacks, shop; garden and gallery cl Mon and Tues; (01271) 850262; £3.50. The hotel has a tennis court and heated outdoor swimming pool; B&B £25 (wknd £30).

Barnstaple Heritage Centre 🏛 (Queen Anne's Walk) You pass through an ornate Georgian colonnade to reach this centre which relates the 1,000-year history of the town with the help of computer and hands-on displays; occasional historical re-enactments. Shop, disabled access; cl Sun and winter Mons; (01271) 373003; *£2.50.

Brannam's Pot Factory (Roundswell Industrial Estate) Guided tours of big pottery (their terracotta pots are indispensable to many gardeners) with a chance to throw your own pot. Meals, snacks, shop, disabled access; no tours wknds, but shop open Sat and summer Sun; (01271) 343035; £3.50.

Disused railway paths Down at sea level sections of the former track from Barnstaple and Bideford can be walked or cycled (local bicycle hire around £6.50 a day, more for mountain bikes). The best section is the one from Barnstaple through Instow and Bideford up to the Puffing Billy at the former Torrington Station. In autumn and winter particularly this gives close views of the wading birds massed on the tidal sands of the estuary, and year-round the section up to Torrington is very attractive.

Marwood Hill Gardens (Marwood; off A361 towards Braunton) 18 well kept and colourful acres inc rare trees and shrubs, small lakes, extensive bog garden, clematis, camellias, alpines and eucalyptus, and national collections of astilbes (best in July) and tulbaghia. Cream teas on Sun and bank hols Apr–early Oct, plant centre, some disabled access; (01271) 342528; *£3. The New Ring o' Bells at Prixford is very handy for lunch.

Museum of North Devon (The Square) Some interactive displays, and an exhibition on the local environment. Shop, disabled access; cl Sun, Mon, Christmas wk and bank hols; (01271) 346747; *£1 (free Sat am).

BICKLEIGH SS9306

Bickleigh Castle Charming moated and fortified manor house, still very much a family home; the 11th-c chapel is said to be Devon's oldest complete building. Also medieval hall, armoury and guard room, Tudor bedroom, 17th-c farmhouse, and exhibitions on maritime history and the Civil War. All done with great enthusiasm, and with a fair bit to amuse children. Good cream teas, plant sales in the Victorian walled garden, shop, limited disabled access; open pm Weds, Sun and bank hols Easter–May then pm daily (exc Sat) till early Oct; (01884) 855363; £4. The Fisherman's Cot is a beautifully placed riverside dining pub.

Bickleigh Mill and Maize Maze (Bickleigh Mill Farm) Bustling family-run place with a working water wheel, resident potter (not Sat), animals inc pigs and donkeys, and an 11-acre maize labyrinth (which can grow over head-height). Meals, snacks, shops, some disabled access; open daily (maze July–Sept only); (01884) 855419; free (exc maze, £3).

BIDEFORD SS4526
Quiet hillside town now bypassed, with notable medieval bridge and some pleasant old streets, partly pedestrianised, behind the Quay. The day-trip boat for Lundy (a good long day) sails from here year round, though not every day, and only rarely in March. One of the oldest streets is Bridgeland St, and up towards the top of Bridge St there are quite a few antiques or antiqueish shops. The Joiners Arms (Market Sq) has decent food, and readers recommend the Vagabond Cavalier (Cooper St) for good value Italian meals.

The Big Sheep 🖼 (A39, 2m W) Exuberant sheep centre, best known for its splendidly entertaining sheep steeplechasing (usually around 3.20pm), when sheep with knitted jockeys on their back race 200 yards from their field towards the prize of extra food. Even better are the duck trials half an hour later, miniature sheepdog trials with the sheep replaced by ducks; there are more traditional sheepdog demonstrations too. Other events and displays take in everything from shearing and bottle-feeding to milking, with plenty of opportunities to get close to the animals (lambs are born

throughout the year, so always some to cuddle). Decent adventure play area, and a couple of puppet shows. Lots under cover, and it's good value – tickets are valid for unlimited return visits for a week for £1. Home-made meals and snacks (good teas), shop, disabled access; cl wkdys during winter except school holidays (01237) 477916; £4.95. The Thatched House family dining pub at Abbotsham is handy for lunch.

BOLHAM SS9615
Knightshayes Court 🖼 Lovely woodland garden with acres of unusual even unique plants, esp lovely in spring but a glory at any time of year. Alpine and more formal gardens, ancient yew topiary, attractive walks, and good Exe Valley views. The spooky-looking house itself is extravagantly ornate Victorian Gothick, with elaborate painted ceilings and décor and a restored minstrels' gallery. The original plans were even more over-the-top, but when the horrified owner saw them he sent the architect packing. Meals, snacks, shop and plant centre, disabled access; cl Nov–mid-Mar, plus house cl Fri (exc Good Fri); (01884) 254665; £5.30, garden only £3.70; NT. The Rose & Crown over at Calverleigh is a pleasant place for lunch.

BRADWORTHY SS3213
A pleasant jumping-off point for walks, with some quiet local strolls on the common, or over by the Tamar Lake a couple of miles SW.

Gnome Reserve 🖼 (West Putford, 2¼m E) One of the most delightfully silly places in the area, woodland and wildflower meadows populated by hand-painted and individually modelled pixies. They lend you gnome hats and fishing rods so that resident gnomes will think you're one of them. The setting is pretty (flowers and plants are labelled), and small children love it. Shop, snacks, limited disabled access; cl Nov–mid-Mar (exc shop); (01409) 241435; £1.95. Coming from the N you could stop for something to eat at the thatched Farmers Arms at Woolfardisworthy.

BRATTON FLEMING SS6638
Exmoor Steam Railway (Cape of Good Hope Farm) Enthusiastically run family-owned narrow-gauge railway

with half-sized steam trains winding through a mile of countryside, and a small display of traction engines. Meals, snacks, shop, disabled access; cl Mon, Fri in low season, all Sats, and Nov–mid-Mar (exc Dec specials); (01598) 710711; £3.75. The White Hart is useful for lunch.

BRAUNTON BURROWS SS4532
This vast nature reserve expanse of great swelling dunes is easily reached from the B3231 W of Braunton (red flags warn if there's shooting on the range here). The Mariners Arms in South St in Braunton itself is a useful pleasantly untouristy pub, and the Coffee Shoppe (Copperfields) has good local seafood.

BROWNSHAMS, THE SS2825
These isolated farmhouses, now NT property, give walkers good quiet access to the woods, cliffs and clifftop farmland W of Clovelly.

BULL POINT SS4646
There's a lighthouse here, and dramatic cliff walks between here and Morte Point; the Ship Aground public house by the interesting church in Mortehoe is a useful break, or a starting point.

CALVERLEIGH SS9214
An attractive village with a fine church and decent pub.

CHITTLEHAMPTON SS6127
Cobbaton Combat Collection 🏛
(off A377) Growing private collection of British and Canadian World War II vehicles, quite tightly packed under cover but looking ready for action; also mock-ups of wartime scenes, wartime memorabilia, and play area with Sherman tank. Summer snacks, shop, some disabled access; open daily Easter–Oct, usually open wkdys in winter but best to check; (01769) 540740; £4. The Exeter Inn at Chittlehamholt has good food.

CHULMLEIGH SS6814
Lovely unspoilt village with a decent pub, the Old Court House. It's a good base for touring the coast and Taw Valley.

CLOVELLY SS3124
One of Devon's most famous views, down the very steep old cobbled street, free from traffic and with flower-covered cottages either side, to the tiny harbour below. It's a delightful village,

best appreciated out of season. At any time of year you'll have to park up at the top, outside the village, then pay £3.50 to pass through a turnstile, and walk down. The Red Lion down by the quay is pleasant; if you can't face the climb back up a Land Rover can drive you back from behind here (summer only, £1.60). You may be able to get boats to Lundy in summer. Up towards the A39 is a big Iron Age hill fort, Clovelly Dykes, and along the coast the beachside hamlet of Bucks Mills is well worth a visit. The woods, cliffs and clifftops farmland W of Clovelly is attractive walking country. The moorland road down from Stibb Cross on the A388 via Woolfardisworthy is good, and the woodland Hobby Drive toll road is the area's best coast drive.

Clovelly Court 🏛 These parkland gardens have tranquil sea views, and a fine walled garden and restored Victorian greenhouse. Open Apr–Sept; (01237) 431200; *£1.

Milky Way (Downland Farm) One of the biggest covered attractions in the region, losing a bit of its original character as it grows, but still friendly, and very good for families. They guarantee all children will be able to feed a lamb or kid, and there's also cow-milking, a working pottery, golf driving nets, laser clay pigeon shooting, birds of prey (twice-daily displays), sheep dog training centre (no demonstrations Sun) and a little railway. Good indoor and outdoor play areas and a Clone Zone interactive ride game. Meals, snacks, shop, disabled access; cl wkdys Nov–Mar; (01237) 431255; £6.

COMBE MARTIN SS5846
A string of former smallholdings and cottages scattered down a lovely sheltered valley, with an odd pub, the Pack of Cards, built to celebrate a cards win – four floors, 13 doors, 52 windows. There's a little fishing harbour in the shingly cove between the cliffs, and the Dolphin and Fo'c'sle are useful for lunch.

Combe Martin Motorcycle Collection 🏛 (Cross St) British bikes displayed against old petrol pumps, signs, garage equipment and other motoring nostalgia. Shop, mostly disabled access; cl Nov–mid-May;

(01271) 882346; £2.90.

Combe Martin Wildlife & Dinosaur Park 🅐 (A399) Good range of animals and birds in over 30 acres of woodland inc a pair of rare snow leopards, and meerkats in a huge desert enclosure. Also meticulously researched life-size dinosaurs, some of which move and roar – like the towering Tyrannosaurus rex, and a new dinosaur museum. A themed train ride (they assure us that you don't actually get wet) runs through the gardens, which have rare and tropical plants, and there's a petting zoo for children. Meals, snacks, shop; cl Nov–Easter; (01271) 882486; £6.95.

CROYDE SS4439
A magnet for surfers, this clean-sand village has a good family pub, the Thatch. Baggy Point W of here has a path good enough for wheelchairs.

EGGESFORD SS6811
This quiet Taw Valley village has a 14th-c church, and a garden centre prettily set in the walled garden of a ruined house; refreshments on a terrace with lovely views. A good base for inland walks (and a stop on the Barnstaple–Exeter rail line): in Flashdown Wood, up wooded Hayne Valley to Wembworthy (the Odd Wheel is a decent family pub), or through Heywood Wood, where the mound of the former castle gives good views (and there are picnic sets).

EXMOOR SS7739
Excellent walking, less busy than Dartmoor in summer. In some places it's been more tamed than Dartmoor – drained and resown with richer-growing grasses for better pasture. But it's still a wild place, with hawthorns and low oak trees bent and gnarled by the winds, and (unlike Dartmoor) wild deer. Where it drops away sharply to the sea, fast streams and rivers cut deeply into beautiful wooded valleys. Note that some of Exmoor's moorland paths have a disconcerting habit of fizzling out without warning. It's rewarding territory for drivers, with plenty of good views; the B roads are generally less congested.

Badgworthy Water SS7944 This Exmoor stream is the focus of a walkers' path from Malmsmead which takes you into the very heart of Lorna

Doone country – it gets wilder and more remote with every step southwards (the surrounding moors provide a handful of return routes).

Dulverton SS9128 The main town for Exmoor is a civilised place, with a handsome old stone market house, and a fine bridge over the river which has cut this steeply wooded valley. The Lion Hotel is useful for lunch, and the area's main information centre is at the S end of Fore St, (01398) 323841.

Dunkery Hill SS8941 Exmoor's great ridge walk, with Dunkery Beacon as its high point surveying a huge chunk of SW England and S Wales (as tramping boots have worn three feet off the top of the Beacon, walkers are now asked to take a bag of stones and earth up to deposit there). It is easily walked from the nearby road; a splendid place to leave the car is Webbers Post (which is also good for local pottering). It can also be incorporated into longer walks from Horner Woods or Luccombe.

River Exe The peace of inland Exmoor is perhaps best appreciated from along paths by the rivers. A notable stretch of the Exe is between Exford and Winsford.

Exford SS8538 Prettily set in a sheltered valley by a small streamside green; the church up the hill a bit is well worth a look. The White Horse and Crown are useful for lunch.

Malmsmead Natural History Centre SS7947 The Exmoor Natural History Society run leisurely two-hour strolls through the striking scenery around their Natural History Centre every Weds and Thurs mid-May–mid Sept at 2pm. Very enthusiastically done, and esp worth knowing about as they're free (inc a cup of tea afterwards for a small donation); Mrs Waite has full details on (01643) 703470. Shop, disabled access. The best way of finding the Centre is from the County Gate National Park centre on the A39. Jan Ridd brought his bride Lorna around here in *Lorna Doone*. The Exmoor Sandpiper at Countisbury up towards Lynton has decent food.

Parracombe SS6644 A lovely little village worth visiting in its own right, but particularly interesting is **St Petroc's church**, one of the few

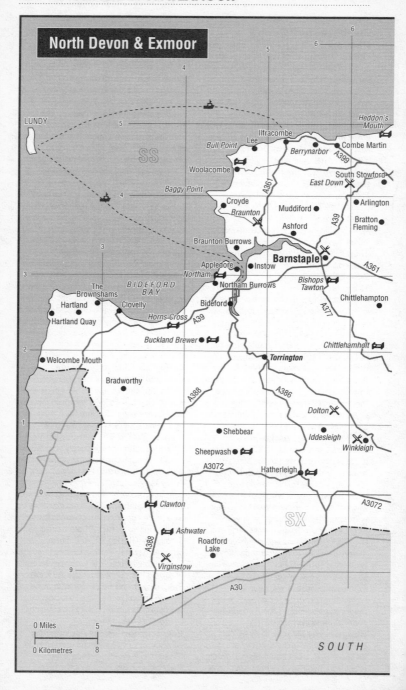

North Devon & Exmoor

LUNDY

SS

Heddon's Mouth

Ilfracombe
Lee
Bull Point
Berrynarbor
Combe Martin
A399
Woolacombe
South Stowford
East Down
Baggy Point
Arlington
Croyde
Braunton
Muddiford
Bratton Fleming
Ashford
A39

Braunton Burrows

Barnstaple
A361
Appledore
Instow
Northam
Bishops Tawton
BIDEFORD BAY
Northam Burrows
Chittlehampton
The Brownshams
Hartland
Clovelly
Bideford
A377
Hartland Quay
Horns-Cross
A39
Chittlehamholt
Buckland Brewer
Torrington
Welcombe Mouth
A388
A386
Bradworthy
Dolton

Shebbear
Iddesleigh
Winkleigh
Sheepwash
A3072
Hatherleigh
A3072

SX
Clawton
A388
Ashwater
Roadford Lake
Virginstow

A30

0 Miles 5

0 Kilometres 8

SOUTH

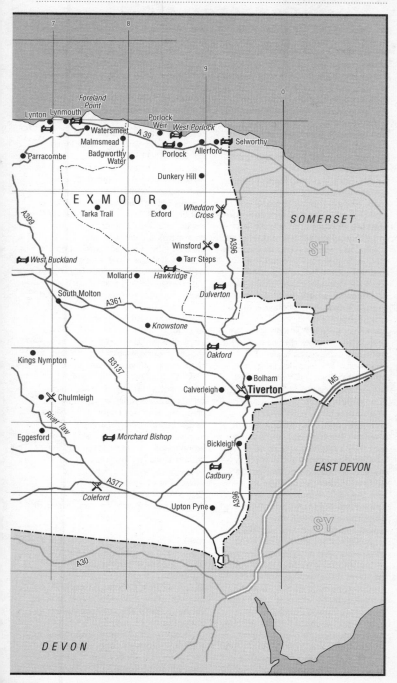

churches to have a completely unspoilt medieval fabric with Georgian interior; locked Nov-Easter, but key available from custodian then. The Fox & Goose is useful for lunch.

Selworthy SS9146 Gloriously unspoilt village, rated by a number of our contributors as the most attractive they've ever seen, with groups of white thatched cottages around a prettily planted hillside green looking out over Exmoor, and trees behind. The church is a gem, with a fine waggon ceiling with roof bosses.

Tarka Trail This long-distance figure-of-eight signed path runs nearly 200 miles linking Exmoor, Dartmoor and the N Devon coast, following the route of Henry Williamson's *Tarka the Otter* – and is most enjoyable with a copy of the book. One beautiful section is the route around Pinkworthy Pond and The Chains, reached from the car park a couple of miles along the B3358 E of Challacombe (where the Black Venus is good). It's even more popular with cyclists than walkers.

Tarr Steps SS8632 The River Barle's most famous feature, the finest of all the stone-and-slab clapper bridges for packhorses. The path along the river, which runs between Simonsbath and Dulverton, is uneven and surprisingly slow-going in places.

Watersmeet SS7448 Paths run eastward out of Lynton along the Lyn River to Watersmeet (1½m E), where the Farley Waters tumble down to meet the East Lyn in a series of rocky cascades among steeply picturesque oak woods (there's a discreet NT refreshment pavilion here).

Watersmeet House, a 19th-c fishing lodge, is itself not particularly remarkable (though has interesting local wildlife displays), but the estate that surrounds it really is attractive – a perfectly relaxing wooded valley, with the house at the meeting point of the rivers. Just right for an afternoon's pottering (and forming one of the best parts of the Tarka Trail long-distance walk), though some of the walks can be steep. Meals, snacks, shop, disabled access with notice; cl Nov–Mar; (01598) 753348; free; NT. Another scenic path leads high above the same

valley along its S side, and riverside paths head on further upstream, to the prettily set Rockford Inn (a good base for walks – food finishes at 2pm). Just N of Watersmeet, the Foreland Cliffs are the highest in the country – a good walk with dramatic views.

Winsford SS9034 A quiet and attractive village below high hills, with the River Exe lacing through its countless bridges. The carefully restored Royal Oak is good for lunch.

HARTLAND SS2424

Hartland Abbey 🏛 Fine old house on the site of an Augustinian abbey, with elegant rooms (the drawing room is modelled on the House of Lords), paintings by Gainsborough and Joshua Reynolds, several interesting historic documents, exhibition of old photography, woodland walks and peacock-filled parkland. Along with the walled gardens there's a newly restored Victorian fernery. Snacks, shop; open Easter Sun and Mon pm, and Weds, Thurs, Sun and bank hols May–Sept, plus Tues July and Aug (garden cl Sats and daily am); (01237) 441264; £4.50, grounds only £3. The village has craft shops inc working pottery and Windsor chair-maker (children's sizes too).

HARTLAND QUAY SS2324

Grand isolated spot at foot of toll road, on jagged coast which looks a dramatic cross between illustrations for geology textbooks and ones for a shipwreckers' manual. Down by the sea is a wonderfully maritime old inn, and the **museum** covers four centuries of shipwrecks – even big ships still go down here – and smuggling; cl Oct–Whit (exc Easter); *£1. For walkers, the cliffs around here are much more dramatic than those at nearby Hartland Point (which also has a toll gate). Just S at Spekes Mill Mouth the sea-eroded valley leaves the river spewing down the cliff in a seaside waterfall.

Docton Mill 🏛 (Milford) Extensive and interesting sheltered streamside garden, largely naturalised, beside an ancient restored watermill. It's particularly attractive in spring. Meals, snacks (good cream teas), plant sales; cl Nov–Feb; (01237) 441369; *£3.30. They have a couple of bedrooms you can stay in.

HATHERLEIGH SS5404

An attractive hillside village – even the church slopes – with fine inns (the Tally Ho, brewing its own beer, and George) and a good pottery (20 Market St).

ILFRACOMBE SS5147

Picturesque resort around busy harbour sheltered by high cliffs, with terraces of late Victorian boarding houses and small hotels looking out over it from their perches among the trees of the steep bay. There are period resort buildings and gardens, and even tunnels cut through the rock to a former Victorian bathing place. The 14th-c chapel above the harbour mouth has doubled as a lighthouse for over 450 years; the lifeboat station can be visited (donation requested). Holy Trinity church (Church St) is worth a look for its richly carved 15th-c waggon-roof, one of the most striking in the area. The ancient George & Dragon has decent food. In summer the paddle steamer *Waverley* or the traditional cruise ship *Balmoral* run cruises from the pier to Lundy, Minehead, and other places – even as far as Swansea. Bicclescombe Park (A361 just S) has a restored 18th-c cornmill; the Coach House nearby also has decent food. The best cliff walks are to the W of the town, towards Lee Bay.

Hele Mill 🖼 (A399 just E) Well restored early 16th-c mill still producing wholemeal flour. Pottery demonstrations and the chance to throw your own pot. Snacks, shop, disabled access to pottery and tearoom only; cl Oct–Easter, and Sat exc July–Aug; (01271) 863185; *£2.50.

Ilfracombe Museum 🖼 (Runnymede Gardens) Cheerful and enthusiastic town museum, if unsurprising (cl winter wknds; £1).

Old Railway This disused railway trail above Ilfracombe is popular with walkers and cyclists, with a tunnel, interesting plants, and attractive scenery inc the lakes of Slade Reservoirs. For a one-way walk it's best to do it in reverse, for better views – and it's downhill all the way; Red Bus 31 or Filers 303 up from the town to Lee Bridge or Lee Cross (or to the Fortescue Hotel for a preliminary bracer).

Watermouth Castle 🖼 'Devon's Happy Castle', this is a fine 19th-c structure overlooking the bay, transformed into a world of gnomes, goblins, trolls and fairy tales, with slides, carousels and a musical water show. Very much for families, with young children the ones who'll enjoy it most. Meals, snacks, shop, disabled access; cl Sat, plus Fri at the start and end of the season, and all Nov–Apr; (01271) 867474; £6.

INSTOW SS4728

At the mouth of the Torridge estuary, this has an expanse of tidal sands, with dozens of moored boats beached on them at low tide. The Boathouse has good food and views.

Tapeley Park 🖼 The very pretty Italianate garden with rococo features and walled kitchen garden is the main draw, though there's also a pets' corner, play area, and woodland walk. Lovely views down to the sea. Teas and snacks in period dairy, plant sales, disabled access; cl Sat, and Nov–Easter; (01271) 342558; *£3.50.

KING'S NYMPTON SS6819

An attractive village with a fine church and decent pub.

LEE SS4846

This pretty village in a sheltered woody valley has an attractive ancient pub, the Grampus. There are good cliff walks between Lee Bay and Ilfracombe.

LUNDY DAY TRIPS SS1344

(boat from Bideford or, in summer, Ilfracombe) Well worth considering if you're in Devon for more than just a few days. The island's best known for the migrant birds that come here in spring and autumn, but the remoteness and loneliness is also a powerful draw – the permanent population is around a dozen. Lovely walks along its seven miles of formidably high cliffs, windswept rough pastures, small church, evocative castle ruins, two lighthouses (one the highest in Britain), wandering goats, small soay sheep and ponies, and the chance of seeing seals (especially in autumn), the introduced small sika deer, and, in Apr and May, the island's trademark puffins. Accommodation can be arranged through the Landmark Trust (01628) 825925. The Marisco Tavern is a good place to eat. The return boat trip (about 2 hrs each way) is £25; (01237) 423365 for sailing times.

LYNMOUTH SS7249

Exmoor Boat Cruises Informative boat trips, inc talks about sea birds and coastal geography, leave from the harbour from 11am daily weather and tide permitting, Apr–Oct; (01598) 753207; from £4.

LYNTON SS7249

Merging into its harbourside extension, Lynmouth, down at the bottom of the cliff railway track, this beautifully placed steep village tucks into the wooded seaside gorge where the East and West Lyn tumble down to the sea. The most delightful walks in N Devon are around here. Lynton clearly shows its origins as a Victorian resort in one of the many areas then known as Little Switzerland, with hillside villas now quiet boarding houses, photogenic corners and some older cottages. Pretty cottages down by the little tidal harbour, as well as craft shops and so forth (there's a friendly hands-on pottery); lots of trippers during the day in summer. The Olde Cottage Inne (B3234 – lovely walk up The Lynway from Sinai Hill) is useful for lunch, and the Rising Sun down by the harbour has a good restaurant. The Valley of Rocks is an easy walk from the village, and Watersmeet is also within reach.

Glen Lyn Gorge Carefully restored after the tragic flood of 1952, with pretty walks and an exhibition on water power. Some disabled access. Exhibition cl Nov–Mar (reduced admission £2), gorge cl 3rd Weds in Jan, and possibly in bad weather; (01598) 753207; £3. They have decent holiday flats and cottages in a peaceful setting.

Heddon's Mouth Cleave This secretive wooded combe runs up through the rugged seaside moorland hills by the sea W of Lynton. This and others like it are prime territory for walkers. There's a good walk down from the beautifully placed Hunters Inn W of Martinhoe, and another fine one in this area is the terraced walkway known as the Ladies' Mile which runs along a charming valley near Trentishoe.

Lyn & Exmoor Museum 🏛 (Market St, Lynton) In the old part of the upper village, this engagingly simple museum of local history is in an 18th-c cottage with a scale model of the former Lynton–Barnstaple narrow-gauge railway (you can still walk much of its track bed). Shop; cl 12.30-2pm, Sun pm, Sat, and Nov-Easter; (01598) 752205; £1.

Valley of Rocks A great valley bowl with steep crags and pinnacles of rock dividing it from the sea (and a dreadful unscreened car park smack in the middle). It's reached by an easy coast path from Lynton, or by paths over Hollerday Hill (wooded, but opens out dramatically on top).

MOLLAND SS8028

An attractive village with a fine church and decent pub.

MUDDIFORD SS5540

Blakewell Trout Farm Good for experts and beginners, with a little pool where you're practically guaranteed a bite. Meals, snacks, shop, disabled access; cl 25 Dec; (01271) 344533; free.

NORTHAM BURROWS SS4430

Dunes, sand slacks and meres behind a pebble ridge, with the Atlantic rollers swinging in along the rock-strewn Saunton Sands beyond – deserted out of season and stimulating then for lonely walks; in summer a popular family beach.

PORLOCK SS8846

A lot of traffic, but some attractive cottages with distinctive lighthouse-like chimneys and thatched roofs.

PORLOCK WEIR SS8647

This harbour tucked below wooded cliffs is much quieter than nearby Porlock, though it does get a lot of summer visitors; decent food at the thatched Ship. There are long walks along the coast: heading W along the shore at the foot of the wooded cliffs, even the most avid pebble-hunter would find all he wanted. Another good walk is through the woods up to the tiny and quite isolated **Culbone church**.

ROADFORD LAKE SX4290

Trout fishing Serious trout fishing in this carefully landscaped reservoir; cl Nov–Mar; £12.50 day permit.

SHEBBEAR SS4409

An interesting and attractive tucked-away village, with the odd Devil's Stone by the green (and a decent pub named after it), and a working pottery.

SHEEPWASH SS4806
Quiet village with cob-and-thatch houses around the green; the Half Moon is good for lunch. A mile N is Duckpool Cottage traditional wood-fired pottery.

SOUTH MOLTON SS7126
An attractive central square and imposing church – and its farming roots show in the Thurs cattle market. The 18th-c Guildhall has a local history **museum** (cl Fri, Sun, and Dec–Feb, limited hours Sat, Wed; free), and monthly art-and-craft shows. The Corn Dolly (East St), is nicely decorated with its namesakes and is ideal for afternoon tea, while the Castle at George Nympton has generous home cooking. **Hancock's Devon Cider** (Clapworthy Mill, 3m SW) Exhibition and film showing how they produce their good scrumpy. It's a nice spot for a picnic. Snacks, shop, good disabled access; cl 1–2pm, all day Sun, and Oct–Easter; (01769) 572678; £2.30.
Quince Honey Farm £ (North Rd) The biggest wild-bee farm in the world, with observation hives looking right into the centre of the colonies. Meals, snacks, shop (lots of honey and their own beeswax skin and hair care products); cl Nov–Easter (though shop stays open); (01769) 572401; £3.

SOUTH STOWFORD SS6540
Exmoor Zoological Park £ (off B3226 N of Bratton Fleming) Good-sized collection of rare and endangered creatures, many of which breed successfully throughout the year. Children can feed the smaller animals or play on the assault course, and there are good views from the well landscaped grounds. Snacks, shop, disabled access; cl 25–26 Dec, and maybe Dec–Jan for refurbishment – best to check; (01598) 763352; £4.55. The Old Station House at Blackmoor Gate is a pleasant dining pub.

TIVERTON SS9512
Formerly prosperous wool town, well worth wandering round; **St Peter's church** is magnificently decorated with rich carving, and other grand buildings include the Jacobean council offices.

The four showrooms of the **Tiverton Craft Centre** showcase the work of over 170 local craftsmen (cl Sun). In summer there are 2½-hr **horse-drawn boat trips** along the attractively restored canal from the wharf; booking advisable, (01884) 253345; £6.65. They also hire out rowing boats and motor-boats.
Tiverton Castle The handsome castle was built in 1106 as a Royal fortress dominating the River Exe, and still has its Norman tower and gatehouse, as well as an interesting clock collection and one of the best assemblages of Civil War armour and arms. You can stay in apartments in the oldest parts of the building. Shop, limited disabled access; open pm (from 2.30) Sun, Thurs and bank hol Mons Easter–Sept, plus pm Mon–Weds July and Aug; (01884) 253200; *£3.50.
Tiverton Museum (St Andrew St) A 19th-c school houses this local history museum, with two waterwheels, an excellent railway gallery and a display about the work of the wheelwright (shop, disabled access; cl Sun, and Christmas–Jan; £2). Following refurbishment, they hope to reopen around Easter.

TORRINGTON SS4919
Quiet dairy-farming town on a ridge above the River Torridge, with some attractive buildings inc 14th-c Taddiport Chapel (for a former leper colony), the imposing Palmer House, and a rather grand church built to replace the original blown up in the Civil War. There are good views from the neatly mown hill above the river, and other nearby strolls on the preserved commons surrounding the town. The Black Horse is useful for lunch.
Dartington Crystal £ (Linden Cl) On wkdys you can tour the factory (last tour 3.15pm); there's a useful visitor centre, and shop with well priced goblets and decanters. They get very busy on wet days in summer – best to phone and check tour availability. No tours wknds, bank hols or 2 weeks at Christmas, shop cl 25–26 Dec, Easter Sun; meals, snacks, disabled access (prior arrangement); (01805) 626242; £3.50.

Downes (A386 Torrington–Bideford, nr Monkleigh) Fine big woodland garden with interesting flowering trees and shrubs and lovely landscaped lawns. Wknd teas, plant sales; open early Apr–mid-Jun, by appointment till Sept; (01805) 622244; *£2.

RHS Garden Rosemoor (off B3220 just S) A wonderful place, constantly being developed and updated by the Royal Horticultural Society; marvellous rare trees, shrubs, and other plants in charmingly landscaped sheltered woodland setting, rose, stream and bog gardens, foliage and plantsman's garden, and trails for children. Meals, snacks, picnic area, smart shop, disabled access; cl 25 Dec; (01805) 624067; £4.

Torrington 1646 See separate family panel on p. 179.

UPTON PYNE SX9197 Appealingly unspoilt village, the basis of Barton in Sense and Sensibility.

WELCOMBE MOUTH SS2118 Rather a rough drive down, but an attractive spot, and the cliffs around have possibilities for wild coast walks.

WOOLACOMBE SS4843 The beach here is particularly nice, and its Atlantic breakers now draw quite a few surfers. The Rock at Georgeham and Mill at Ossaborough are pleasant for lunch, and the back road to Mortehoe is scenic.

Once Upon a Time (Old Station, B3343 inland) Run by the same people as Watermouth Castle at Ilfracombe, this is a super place for children up to about 11, with lots of rides and other activities; there's a driving school that even offers tests. Meals, snacks, shop, disabled access; cl Sat, plus Fri at start and end of season, and all Oct–Mar; (01271) 867474; £2.75 (£5.20 children).

Other attractive villages with decent pubs include Berrynarbor SS5646, Buckland Brewer SS4220, Iddesleigh SS5708, Knowstone SS8223 and Winkleigh SS6308.

Where to eat

BARNSTAPLE SS5533 **Foodco@** 18 Bear St (01271) 322221 Interesting light and airy modern art restaurant with sculptures, ceramics, and paintings on walls and plinths, simple stylish furniture, fresh flowers, traditional food with a contemporary international twist, and a decent wine list; well behaved children by arrangement; disabled access. £25 dinner, £15 lunch

BARNSTAPLE SS5631 **Lynwood House** Bishops Tawton Rd (01271) 343695 The same family have run this no smoking restaurant-with-rooms for 31 years, and the elegant Victorian dining room specialises in popular fresh local seafood (though meaty and vegetarian dishes are covered, and there's also a lighter menu); bdrms; cl Sun, 26 Dec, 1 Jan. £30

BRAUNTON SS4836 **Squires Fish Restaurant** Exeter Rd (01271) 815533 First-class fish and chip take-away and restaurant with really excellent fish, good wines, friendly service and attractive airy surroundings; cl Sun (but open school summer hols then), 25–26 Dec, 1 Jan; disabled access. |£4

CHULMLEIGH SS6814 **Old Bakehouse** South Molton St (01769) 580137/580074 Thatched 16th-c merchant's house with lots of beams, a flower-filled courtyard, and dining room serving morning coffee, light lunches and afternoon teas (plus breakfast and dinner for residents); bdrms. cl Sun pm, Mon, all Feb; children over 5; disabled access. £23.50|£6

COLEFORD SS7701 **New Inn** (01363) 84242 Comfortable thatched 14th-c inn with good interesting food, an extensive wine list, well kept real ales, four nicely furnished areas, winter log fire, and attractive garden with stream; bdrms; cl 25–26 Dec; disabled access. £27.50|£6.95

DOLTON SS5712 **Union** Fore St (01805) 804633 Relaxed and friendly old pub with good interesting genuinely home-made food using first-class produce, well kept real ales, and decent wines; comfortable little lounge, characterful lower bar with chatty drinking area and tables for eating, and charming owners; bdrms; cl Weds 1 Oct–Easter, cl Weds am Easter–1 Oct; first 2 wks Feb. £21

EAST DOWN SS6041 **Pyne Arms** *(01271) 850207* Popular pub with lots of nooks and crannies in low-beamed bar, small no smoking galleried loft, games area, good food, and well kept real ales; cl 25 Dec; no children; disabled access. £15.40|**£5.95**

TIVERTON SS9512 **Four and Twenty Blackbirds** *43 Gold St (01884) 257055* Friendly teashop with beams, a mix of old tables and chairs, lots of interesting things to look at, delicious food (everything is home-made), and upstairs antiques shop; cl Sun. |**£4.20**

VIRGINSTOW SX3892 **Percy's at Coombeshead** *(01409) 211236* Carefully renovated restaurant-with-rooms in 16th-c longhouse set in 40 acres (which provide some of the organic produce used in the no smoking evening restaurant); good imaginative modern cooking (super bread and puddings) and a well chosen wine list; comfortable, spacious bdrms; children over 10; disabled access. £33.50|**£14.50**

WHEDDON CROSS SS9238 **Rest & Be Thankful** *(01643) 841222* Helpful staff and varied bar food in comfortably modern two-room bar with two good log fires, big jug collection, aquarium, and restaurant; good bdrms; cl 25 Dec, am 26 Dec; disabled access. £18|**£5.50**

WINKLEIGH SS6308 **Pophams** *Castle St (01837) 83767* Tiny bustling place for morning coffee and lunch — bring your own wine — with particularly good, interesting food, and relaxed happy atmosphere; cl Sat–Tues, and Feb; no children. £27

WINSFORD SS9035 **Royal Oak** *(01643) 851455* Beautiful thatched inn in quiet spot with attractively furnished cosy bars, a smartly civilised atmosphere, log fire, enjoyable home-made bar and restaurant food, well kept real ales, and friendly staff; lots of surrounding walks; bdrms; disabled access. £25|**£7.50**

Special thanks to Michael and Jenny Back, S G and O M Barber, Jody and Bruce Davie

DORSET

Great for families, with attractions as varied as the coastline, from bustling Bournemouth through character family resorts to striking unspoilt fossil-strewn beaches; some untouched countryside makes for rewarding walks

One of the county's greatest appeals is the diversity of its attractions, with plenty to keep children and their parents happy. Abbotsbury is a good place to head for, with its gardens, swannery and more, and Kingston Lacy House, Kingston Maurward Park and Stapehill Abbey all stand out as fun places to visit for the whole family.

Dorset has a good range of animal attractions, from the enjoyable Monkey World at Wool (enthusiastically run, with good play areas for children) to the cheery Dorset Heavy Horse Centre at Edmondsham, decent aquariums in Bournemouth, Poole and Weymouth, and the unique butterfly-filled Elizabethan Hall at Worldlife & Lullingstone Silk Farm. Children can really muck in at Putlake Adventure Farm, the county's Family Attraction of the Year.

There's a wonderfully eclectic mix of museums here, too. Military matters are given zesty treatment at the Royal Signals Museum in Blandford Forum and at Bovington Camp's Tank Museum, while Dorchester boasts an eminent Dinosaur Museum, intriguing Tutankhamun Exhibition, and a cheery Teddy Bear House. Wimborne Minster's Priest's House Museum has yet more well researched period rooms, and the Museum of Electricity at Christchurch jump-starts a potentially lustreless subject.

Smaller children will enjoy the Alice in Wonderland Family Park in Hurn; there are occasional flying displays at the airport's aviation museum opposite. Splashdown in Poole is great for cooling off children.

The green-fingered should head for Poole's Compton Acres, popular Knoll Gardens (very environmentally minded), the fabulous water-lilies at Bennetts Water Gardens and Mapperton Gardens near Beaminster.

Ideal places for picnics include the idyllic ruins of Sherborne Old Castle and the peaceful waterside White Mill at Sturminster Marshall, new to the *Guide* this year.

Dorset has some great scenery. Striking coastal features include Lulworth Cove, the rugged Isle of Purbeck, Portland Bill, and the tremendous sweep of Chesil Beach and its great lagoon near East Fleet. A coastal path, often with magnificent views, runs the length of the county. Inland, the countryside has a subtle understated appeal, with secluded valleys, narrow lanes threading through peaceful farmland and tucked-away villages (Milton Abbas best of all – a good day out). The central area's chalk uplands cut by intricate valleys give some splendid high viewpoints – not to mention the prehistoric giant cut into the hillside north of Cerne Abbas. In May the bluebell woods at Bere and Delcombe make lovely walks. The west's intimate farming country feels very untouched by passing time, with ancient monuments such as the impressive earth ramparts of Eggardon Hill. The heathland W of Poole Harbour, partly planted with conifers, has a quite different character – largely flat tank-training ground W of Weymouth, a more interesting roaming ground for nature-lovers towards Studland Bay with its fine beach. Brownsea Island off Poole is particularly good for nature. A nationwide lottery-funded project to conserve dwindling heathlands includes the landscape that Hardy knew as Egdon Heath.

Bournemouth has miles of good beaches, with plenty to see and do, and a civilised and spacious spread of comfortably sedate resort areas and leafy suburbs; on summer evenings especially, the town centre clubs and bars spill over with a younger crowd. Tethered balloon flights give a good aerial perspective of the town. Other smaller places – nearby Poole and Christchurch, and particularly Weymouth and Wimborne Minster – have a lot to offer families who want something a bit different.

Dorchester is an interesting county town with a wealth of attractions and some traces of its Roman occupation. There's plenty for Thomas Hardy fans here and elsewhere; his books (and films of them) are vividly conjured up by particular Dorset villages and tracts of countryside. Sherborne, Shaftesbury and Blandford Forum are smaller towns well worth visiting.

An Explorer ticket is a good buy here if you're going to be doing much travelling on buses.

Where to stay

ABBOTSBURY SY5785 **Ilchester Arms** *9 Market St, Abbotsbury, Weymouth, Dorset DT3 4JR (01305) 871243* **£56.90**; 10 comfortable rms. Handsome old stone inn nr abbey, with log fire and hundreds of swan pictures in rambling beamed bar, breakfasts in attractive no smoking conservatory, restaurant, and pleasant staff; plenty of walks; no accommodation Christmas; disabled access

BOURNEMOUTH SZ1091 **Langtry Manor** *26 Derby Rd, Eastcliff, Bournemouth, Dorset BH1 3QB (01202) 553887* **£129.50***, plus special breaks; 28 pretty rms, some in the manor, some in the lodge. Built by Edward VII for Lily Langtry with lots of memorabilia, relaxed public rooms, helpful friendly staff, and good food inc Edwardian dinner every Sat evening; disabled access

BRIDPORT SY4691 **Britmead House** *West Bay Rd, Bridport, Dorset DT6 4EG (01308) 422941* **£60**, plus special breaks; 7 rms. Extended Victorian hotel with lots to do nearby, comfortable lounge overlooking garden, attractive dining room, good food, and kind helpful service; dogs by prior arrangement

CORFE CASTLE SZ0080 **Knitson Old Farmhouse** *Corfe Castle, Wareham, Dorset BH20 5JB (01929) 422836* **£40***; 3 rms, shared bthrm. Big ancient cottage on working farm with sheep and Jersey cows, large garden with hens and horses; comfortable sitting room with flagstones and woodburner, and good evening food, by arrangement, using home-reared pork and lamb served in the spacious kitchen; no smoking and free babysitting; cl Christmas

CRANBORNE SU0513 **Fleur-de-Lys** *5 Wimborne St, Cranborne, Wimborne, Dorset BH21 5PP (01725) 517282* **£55**, plus special breaks; 8 rms. Nicely placed old creeper-clad pub with oak-panelled lounge bar, simply furnished beamed public bar, lots of historical documents and mementoes of past customers such as Thomas

Hardy, and decent food

DORCHESTER SY6990 **Casterbridge** *49 High East St, Dorchester, Dorset DT1 1HU (01305) 264043* **£70***, plus wknd breaks; 14 rms. Small Georgian hotel in town centre with modern annexe across little courtyard; elegant drawing room, cosy library, attractive dining room and conservatory, and good breakfasts; no evening meals (lots of nearby restaurants); cl 25–26 Dec; disabled access

DORCHESTER SY6990 **Kings Arms** *High East St, Dorchester, Dorset DT1 1HF (01305) 265353* **£59.40**, plus special breaks; 31 rms – the Lawrence of Arabia and the Tutenkhamun suites are extraordinary. Smart, thriving coaching inn made famous by Hardy; different menus in restaurant, coffee shop and bar, old-fashioned public bar with real ales, live music twice a week; disabled access

DORCHESTER SY6889 **Maiden Castle Farm** *Dorchester, Dorset DT2 9PR (01305) 262356* **£50**; 4 rms. Victorian farmhouse on big working farm set beneath the prehistoric earthworks from which it takes its name; views of the castle and countryside, and comfortable traditionally furnished sitting room which overlooks the garden

EAST KNIGHTON SY8185 **Countryman** *East Knighton, Dorchester, Dorset DT2 8LL (01305) 852666* **£55**; 6 rms. Attractively converted and much liked pair of old cottages, with open fires and plenty of character in the main bar which opens into several smaller areas, no smoking family room, half a dozen real ales, imaginative, generously served food inc nice breakfasts, and courteous staff; cl 25 Dec

EVERSHOT ST5704 **Summer Lodge** *Evershot, Dorchester, Dorset DT2 0JR (01935) 83424* **£203**, plus special breaks; 17 big, individually decorated rms. Beautifully kept, peacefully set former dower house with lovely flowers in the comfortable and elegantly furnished day rooms, excellent food using the best local produce in most attractive restaurant overlooking pretty garden, delicious breakfasts and afternoon tea, and personal caring service; outdoor swimming pool, tennis and croquet; dogs by prior arrangement and away from public rooms; children over 7 in evening restaurant; partial disabled access

FLEET SY6280 **Moonfleet Manor** *Fleet Rd, Fleet, Weymouth, Dorset DT3 4ED (01305) 786948* **£150** inc dinner; 40 rms. Overlooking the Fleet (no beach access), with coastal walks and lovely surrounding countryside, this handsome stuccoed Georgian manor has a very relaxed atmosphere, friendly helpful staff, Edwardian furnishings, and log fires and plants in large public rooms; enjoyable food in restaurant and Verandah Bar, residents' nightclub in Georgian cellars, and swimming pool, sauna, sunbed, tennis, squash and badminton; particularly good for families with plenty of inside and outside activities for them; disabled access ☺

GILLINGHAM ST7827 **Stock Hill Country House Hotel** *Wyke, Gillingham, Dorset SP8 5NR (01747) 823626* **£242** inc dinner, plus special breaks; 8 lovely, very comfortable rms. Marvellously relaxing carefully run Victorian manor house in 11 acres of wooded grounds, with antiques and paintings in opulent day rooms, particularly welcoming service, and excellent food in the no smoking restaurant using home-grown herbs and vegetables, local meat and fish; all-weather tennis court, croquet; children over 7

HALSTOCK ST5308 **Halstock Mill** *Halstock, Yeovil, Somerset BA22 9SJ (01935) 891278* **£56***; 4 rms. Attractive 17th-c house quietly set in 10 acres with lots of surrounding walks; log fire in cosy beamed lounge, pleasant little dining room, and good food using home-grown fruit and vegetables, local fish and cheese; stabling; cl Christmas; children over 5

LOWER BOCKHAMPTON SY7290 **Yalbury Cottage** *Lower Bockhampton, Dorchester, Dorset DT2 8PZ (01305) 262382* **£78**, plus special breaks; 8 rms overlooking garden or fields. Very attractive family-run 16th-c thatched house with a relaxed friendly atmosphere, and low beams and inglenook fireplaces in comfortable lounge and dining room; carefully cooked often imaginative food, good wines

LYME REGIS SY3392 **Charnwood Guest House** *21 Woodmead Rd, Lyme Regis, Dorset DT7 3AD (01297) 445281* **£49***, plus special breaks; 8 rms with showers. No smoking Edwardian house with covered verandah, recently modernised rooms, friendly owners who will help with walks and other local info, and decent breakfasts; children over 5; cl part of Nov and Jan

MELBURY ABBAS ST8720 **Melbury Mill** *Melbury Abbas, Shaftesbury, Dorset SP7 0DB (01747)* 852163 **£50***; 3 rms, 1 in the main house and 2 in beautifully converted mill building. Quietly set and welcoming 18th-c stone farmhouse with an open fire and flagstones in the dining room, a comfortable sitting room with windows looking on to the garden and mill pond (lots of waterfowl), and traditional English breakfast; cl Christmas; children over 8; partial disabled access

POOLE SZ0090 **Mansion House** *Thames St, Poole, Dorset BH15 1JN (01202)* 685666 **£98**, plus special breaks; 32 cosy rms with lots of little extras. Close to waterfront, this civilised old merchant's town house has a lovely sweeping staircase, antiques in the pretty residents' lounge, convivial cocktail bar, good food in the attractive restaurant, and courteous, old-fashioned service; children over 5 in restaurant but can dine in bistro

SHAFTESBURY ST8522 **Old Rectory** *St James, Shaftesbury, Dorset SP7 8HG (01747)* 853658 **£66***; 3 rms. Elegant 18th-c house with a friendly informal atmosphere, comfortable sitting room with log fire, very good food and an interesting wine list, a sunny conservatory, and quiet walled garden; cl Christmas; dogs welcome

STUDLAND SZ0383 **Knoll House** *Studland, Swanage, Dorset BH19 3AH (01929)* 450450 **£114.80** inc dinner; 80 comfortable rms. Spacious, very well run hotel owned by the same family for over 40 years, and set in 100 acres with marvellous views of Studland Bay and direct access to the fine three-mile beach; relaxed and friendly atmosphere, particularly helpful staff, super food in dining room with windows overlooking the gardens, cocktail bar, TV lounge, and excellent facilities for families: attractive children's dining room (with proper food and baby food, microwave, own fridge, etc), well equipped play room, table tennis, pool and table football, heated outdoor pool, tennis courts, small private golf course, marvellous adventure playground, and nearby sea-fishing, riding, walking, sailing and windsurfing; health spa; cl end Oct–Easter; children over 5 in dining room; dogs very welcome (wonderful surrounding walks); disabled access ☺

STURMINSTER NEWTON ST7711 **Plumber Manor** *Hazelbury Bryan Rd, Plumber, Sturminster Newton, Dorset DT10 2AF (01258)* 472507 **£145**, plus special breaks; 16 very comfortable rms. Handsome 17th-c house in quiet countryside with tennis and trout stream; warm fires, resident Labradors, good uncomplicated food, a relaxed atmosphere, and friendly helpful service; dogs allowed away from public rooms; cl Feb; children welcome by prior arrangement; disabled access

SYDLING ST NICHOLAS SY6399 **Lamperts Cottage** *Sydling St Nicholas, Dorchester, Dorset DT2 9NU (01300)* 341659 **£42**; 3 little rms under the eaves, shared bthrm. Charming, mainly no smoking, 16th-c thatched cottage in unspoilt village, with friendly welcome from helpful owner, good breakfasts in beamed dining room with huge inglenook fireplace and bread oven, and pretty garden; children over 8

UPLYME SY3194 **Amherst Lodge Farm** *Uplyme, Lyme Regis, Dorset DT7 3XH (01297)* 442773 **£65***, plus special breaks. 4 rms. Comfortable long house surrounded by 140 acres of gardens, woodlands, fields and seven lakes; rod room and trout fishing available; relaxed friendly country-house atmosphere, oak-panelled lounge with fire, books and magazines, and occasional evening meals; self-catering also; no children

WAREHAM SY9380 **Bradle Farmhouse** *Bradle, Wareham, Dorset BH20 5NU (01929)* 480712 **£44**, plus special breaks; 3 spacious rms. Fine Victorian stone-built house on 550 acres of working farmland with long views, good breakfasts in homely dining room with its woodburner, unlimited tea with home-made cake, and welcoming owners; good nearby pub for meals; cl 25–26 Dec; children over 8

WAREHAM SY9287 **Priory Hotel** *Church Green, Wareham, Dorset BH20 4ND (01929)* 551666 **£160**, plus special breaks; 19 very comfortable rms – the best being in the converted boathouse with its own landscaped gardens. Beautifully converted medieval buildings in four acres of carefully kept riverside gardens; two elegant lounges with antiques, delicious English cooking served in the converted abbot's cellar (exceptional English cheese board), and genuinely welcoming service; children over 8

WEST BEXINGTON SY5386 **Manor** *Beach Rd, West Bexington, Dorchester, Dorset DT2 9DF (01308) 897616* **£100**, plus special breaks; 13 cottagey rms. Handsome and civilised old stone hotel mentioned in Domesday Book in a pleasant setting not far from beach; relaxed informal atmosphere, comfortable lounge, popular pubby cellar bar, log fires, good bar food, excellent restaurant, and friendly service

WIMBORNE MINSTER SZ0199 **Beechleas** *17 Poole Rd, Wimborne, Dorset BH21 1QA (01202) 841684* **£89**, plus special breaks; 9 attractive, comfortable rms. Carefully restored Georgian house with open fires in cosy sitting room and charming dining room, airy conservatory overlooking walled garden, enjoyable Aga-cooked food using organic produce, nice breakfasts, and friendly helpful owners; lots to do and see nearby; cl Christmas–New Year; disabled access

YETMINSTER ST5910 **Manor Farmhouse** *High St, Yetminster, Sherborne, Dorset DT9 6LF (0800) 0566761* – free in UK **£70***; 4 rms. Fine, carefully modernised, no smoking 17th-c building, with beams and oak panelling, inglenook fireplaces, helpful owners, and good fresh traditional cooking; no children or dogs; partial disabled access

To see and do

Dorset Family Attraction of the Year

LANGTON MATRAVERS SZ0078 **Putlake Adventure Farm** 🖭
Children are encouraged to get really involved with the lively activities at this friendly unspoilt farm, which makes it a good deal more enjoyable than some of the better-developed rural attractions we've come across. Every day they can join in hand-milking the cows, collecting eggs from the chickens, or bottle-feeding the lambs and goats; several activities take place more than once, but if there's something you'd particularly like to do it's worth checking the times in advance. They do pony rides twice a day (unusually, there's no extra charge for this), and there are plenty of delightful small animals to fuss over. A more novel feature is the daily ferret racing at 1.30, when two ferrets compete to see which will be the faster through their tube; it's hard to know which one to support, but young children enjoy trying to pick the winner. The tractor rides are fun, with a commentary about the surrounding scenery; these are 60p extra, but the views over the Isle of Purbeck make it really worthwhile. They keep all the animals you might expect, and there are plenty of things to play on, from miniature or full-sized tractors to scramble over, to an adventure playground and indoor play area. They were about to add a bouncy castle as we went to press, and there may be face-painting some days. Though it's best in fine weather, when it's wet just about everything but the tractor rides carries on: the pony rides and most of the animals simply move into barns. Meals, snacks, indoor and outdoor picnic areas, shop (look out for the colourful sand art), disabled access; open daily Apr–Oct, plus maybe wknds in Nov, Dec and Mar; (01929) 422917; £3.95 (£2.95 children). A family ticket for two adults and two children is £12.80.

Please let us know what you think of places in the *Guide*. Use the report forms at the back of the book or simply write us a letter.

ABBOTSBURY SY5982
Delightful Dorset village with several
worthwhile places to visit – most
famous are the unique ancient
swannery and subtropical gardens (see
separate entries). The 14th-c hilltop
chapel (not always open), with a bare
earth floor, belonged to the abbey, of
which there are a few medieval
fragments around the church. A huge
medieval thatched **tithe barn** now
houses a friendly children's farm. Shop,
disabled access; (01305) 871817; £4.
After visiting one of Abbotsbury's
attractions you get discounts on the
others. The village also has an **oyster
farm** (cl am winter), and the Ilchester
Arms is good for lunch. Abbotsbury is
the start for strolls around Chapel Hill
and on to the massive shingle bank of
Chesil Beach (exhausting to walk any
distance along – see also East Fleet entry
below). Paths leading N from the village
get lovely views from the chalk downs.
The B3157 W also has fine views.
Abbotsbury Subtropical Gardens
⊞ Twenty acres of beautiful woodland
with very mild coastal climate letting
rare and record-breaking plants and
trees flourish. The central walled
garden in spring is a mass of azaleas,
camellias and rhododendrons. Also
woodland trail, aviary and play area.
Meals, snacks, shop and plant centre,
some disabled access; cl 25–26 Dec;
(01305) 871387; £4.50 summer, less in
winter.
Abbotsbury Swannery ⊞
(Newbarn Rd) Home to the only
sizeable colony of swans in the world
that can be seen during nesting time.
The swan families quite happily come
right up to visitors, and during the
cygnet season (late May–Jun) you might
see some of the hundreds of eggs
hatching right next to you. All year
there are mass feedings of the herd at
noon and 4pm; they sometimes choose
a visitor to help, and it can be rather
dramatic – certainly a far cry from the
average trip to feed the swans. An ugly
duckling trail keeps younger children
amused, and there are interesting reed
bed walks; also the country's oldest
duck decoy, and an audio-visual show.
No dogs. Restaurant (reached by a little
bridge), shop, good disabled access; cl

Nov–mid-Mar; (01305) 871684; £5. A
joint ticket with the sub-tropical garden
is £8.20.
ARNE SY9788
This relatively undiscovered little village
has a good **toy museum**, Arne House
⊞ ; cl Oct–Mar, plus ams and all Mon
and Sat Apr–Jun and Sept; £2.75.
There's also a quiet beach and a nature
trail.
ASHLEY HEATH SU1006
Moors Valley Country Park Good
for families, nearly 400 hectares of
forest, with river and lakeside walks,
fishing, nature trails (inc a playful one
for children), plenty of wildlife, narrow-
gauge steam railway, unusual treetop
walkway, and 18-hole golf course.
Meals, snacks, shop, disabled access; cl
25 Dec; (01425) 470721; *£4 car
parking charge (£2 after 4pm), free
winter wkdys (£2 wknds then). The Old
Barn Farm at Three Legged Cross is
handy for families, with good value
food.
ATHELHAMPTON SY7794
Athelhampton House ⊞ (A35)
Readers enjoy coming to this
magnificent 15th-c house, built on the
legendary site of King Athelstan's
palace. The great hall has a fantastic
roof. You'd never know now there was
a disastrous fire here in 1993 – most of
the beautiful furnishings and contents
(even much of the panelling) were
saved, and are back in their original
positions. An added bonus is the acres
of wonderful formal and landscaped
gardens with rare plants, topiary and
fountain pools. Meals, snacks, shop,
disabled access; open daily (exc Sat)
Mar–Oct, Sun only Nov–Feb; (01305)
848363; £5.40 house and gardens,
£3.80 garden only. The young Thomas
Hardy helped design the church across
the road, host to Greek Orthodox
services since the local vicar's
conversion last year. The Martyrs at
Tolpuddle has good home cooking and
a nice garden.
BEAMINSTER ST4602
Horn Park (A3066 N) Unusual plants
in series of gardens with bluebell
woods, ponds, wild flowers and good
views. Plant sales, some disabled access;
open Sun-Thurs pm Apr–Oct; (01308)
862212; *£3.50 (free for wheelchairs).

Mapperton Gardens 🏛 (off B3163 E) Several delightful acres of hillside gardens in grounds of 16th-c manor house; specimen trees and shrubs, fountains, grottoes, fishponds, orangery, good walks and views. Occasional musical events in summer. Snacks, shop, some disabled access; cl am, and all Nov–Feb; (01308) 862645; *£3.50.

Parnham 🏛 (A3066 Beaminster–Bridport) Surrounded by 14 acres of lovely gardens, a fine Tudor mansion famous as the home of John Makepeace the furniture-maker. His workshop is open, with completed pieces shown around the house, along with exhibitions by other craftsmen. The mix of modern furniture with period rooms is refreshingly different. Also formal gardens and play area. Meals, snacks, shop, mostly disabled access; open Apr–Oct, Sun, Tues–Thurs, and bank hols; (01308) 862204; *£5.50. The nearby woods of Hooke Park are pleasant for a stroll. In Beaminster, Pickwicks and the Greyhound are good bets for food.

BERE REGIS SY8494
Bere Regis church This boasts the finest timbered roof in Dorset, with extraordinary carved figures; 20p in a slot lights these up to remarkable effect. It also contains the Turberville tomb and window mentioned in *Tess of the D'Urbervilles*. The Drax Arms is good value for lunch.

BERE WOOD SY8794
At the W end of Bloxworth, this is a fine bluebell wood, at its best in May; the track can be followed right through to Bere Regis.

BLANDFORD FORUM ST8806
Georgian market town, rebuilt in 1731 after the older buildings were destroyed by fire – very interesting to walk round. The Dolphin and Nelsons have decent food.

Mrs Penny's Cavalcade of Costume (The Plocks) 250 years of fashion housed in Georgian Lime Tree House. Snacks, shop, disabled access to ground floor only; cl Tues, Weds and 5 wks from mid-Dec; (01258) 453006; £3.

Royal Signals Museum 🏛 (Blandford Camp) A lively look at the history of army communications, with an exhibition on SAS codes and code-breaking, plus several interactive displays and fun trails for children. Snacks, shop, disabled access; cl wknds exc Mar–Oct; (01258) 482248; £4.

BOURNEMOUTH SZ0890
Still has something of the 'very salubrious air' that Queen Victoria recommended to Disraeli. Neatly kept streamside gardens in the centre, a pier that's one of the few to look as fresh as when it was built, long promenades below the low cliff, and miles of well organised sandy beach (no dogs in summer, and children's activities then). The best beaches, with water safe for swimming and good wrist-band schemes to prevent children from getting lost, are at Durley Chine and Southbourne. All this, along with the mild climate and a good local orchestra, has made the town expansively popular both as a civilised place to retire to and as a centre for regular development, with recent additions such as a seafront IMAX cinema (Pier Approach), palm trees, Edwardian furniture, and a camera obscura at Bournemouth Sq; and one of England's cheekiest statues, depicting the town's founder on one side and, perched on a lavatory facing the other direction, its first sanitation inspector (outside the International Centre, Exeter Rd). It's a big, busy town surrounded by suburbs, with tall modern buildings and monumental traffic schemes. But down by the sea you're well insulated from all of that. Tethered balloon flights in Lower Gardens are a nice way to take it all in (£9.95, £7 before 9am; (01202) 399939). The western residential suburbs of Westbourne and particularly Branksome Park are quiet, with pinetree valleys winding down to the sea; it's virtually impossible to tell here when Bournemouth becomes Poole. Butlers Crab & Ale House (Old Christchurch Rd) is useful, the Moon in the Square (Exeter Rd) is good value, and the Durley (Durley Chine) is a very well run beachside pub.

Hengistbury Head By far the best place close to Bournemouth for a stroll: not a long walk, but the feeling of space and views over Christchurch harbour and beyond are outstanding. It has traces of an Iron Age hill fort, and a good beach below.

Oceanarium (Pier Approach, West Beach) An impressive range of fish from all around the world, with an emphasis on the environment and conservation. Snacks, shop, disabled access; cl 25 Dec; (01202) 311993; £5.75.

Russell-Cotes Art Gallery & Museum Newly refurbished Victorian mansion with a good collection of 17th- to 20th-c paintings, ceramics and furnishings. A new extension has exhibitions on Japanese art, and a story-telling gallery aimed at children. Café, shop, disabled access; cl Mon, 25 Dec, and Good Fri; (01202) 451800; free.

Shelley Rooms (Boscombe Manor, Beechwood Ave) Small museum devoted to the life and work of the poet, esp the later part of his life. Disabled access; cl am, all Mon, and 25 Dec; (01202) 303571; free. Shelley's heart is buried beneath the impressive tombstone of Mary Shelley in St Peter's churchyard.

BOVINGTON CAMP SY8290

Clouds Hill A mile or so up the road from Bovington Camp is the cottage Lawrence of Arabia lived in as a private in the Tank Corps, and his sleeping bag, furniture and other memorabilia can be seen in the three ascetic little rooms on display. Open Weds–Fri pm, Sun and bank hols mid-Apr–Oct; (01929) 405616; £2.30; NT.

Tank Museum Over 260 armoured fighting vehicles from 23 countries, some of which you can go inside, as well as a tank simulator (the screen can be a bit fuzzy), costumes, medals, weapons and videos. Many of the tanks are now put through their paces, complete with simulated gunfire (Thurs July–Sept, plus Fri in Aug); there are armoured vehicle rides on summer wkdys. There's an exhibition on Lawrence of Arabia, and an assault course for children. Meals, snacks, shop, disabled access; cl Christmas wk; (01929) 405096; £6.90. The very child-friendly Countryman at East Knighton has good food.

BRADFORD PEVERELL SY6593

New Barn Field Centre 🈯 Authentic re-creation of an Iron Age homestead, complete with animals and so on; also working potter, wildflower reserve and nature trails. Summer meals and snacks, shop, some disabled access; cl Oct–Easter; (01305) 268865; *£3.50.

BRIDPORT SY4692

Still the country's main rope producer, and its old harbour is now the busy fishing port of nearby West Bay, a restrained small resort (where the West Bay Hotel has good local seafood). The recently revamped Harbour Life Exhibition (Salt House) tells the story of the area with the aid of pictures, photographs and videos. Shop, disabled access; cl Nov–Mar; (01308) 420997; £1.25.

Bridport Museum (South St) Usually has displays of rope and net-making and loom weaving; free activity sheets for children. The upstairs art gallery is currently being refurbished. Shop, disabled access to ground floor only; cl Sun, and Nov–mid-May; (01308) 422116; £2.

BROADWINDSOR ST4302

Craft & Design Centre Good centre in former farm buildings; woodworkers, hatters, painters and so forth. Meals, snacks, shop, disabled access; cl 23 Dec–1 Feb; (01308) 868362; free. The White Lion has generous home cooking. The B3164 W to Birdsmoorgate and then the B3165 through Marshwood (good country pub) is an unspoilt scenic drive through a little-known valley.

BULBARROW HILL ST7705

Memorable viewpoint on the narrow lanes just S of Woolland, esp on a summer evening with the sun going down over Somerset. Around here, a scenic drive runs from Piddletrenthide through Plush (the Brace of Pheasants is a very good lunchtime stop) and Mappowder to Hazelbury Bryan, then through Ansty and Melcombe Bingham, to turn right at Cheselbourne for Piddletrenthide again.

CERNE ABBAS ST6701

Attractive village with a fine church, fragments of the old abbey, several good pubs (the Royal Oak is the best), and its famously indelicate prehistoric giant cut into the chalk above, best seen from the main road N. There's a working **pottery** (cl Mon, best to phone Nov–Mar; (01300) 341865) on the way up to the giant; above it, the old Dorchester–Middlemarsh ridge road has some bracing views.

CHARMOUTH SY3693

The beach here is famous for fossil-hunting. A small museum exhibits locally found relics; good shop, hammers for hire. The George has good value food.

CHETTLE ST9513

Chettle House Fine baroque country house, with beautifully laid out gardens and a vineyard; various craft wknds and special events. Snacks, disabled access to garden only; open Sun Easter–Sept; (01258) 830209; £2.50.

CHICKERELL SY6580

Bennetts Water Gardens 🏛 (Putton Lane) Eight acres of landscaped lakes renowned for their summer water-lilies – over 100 varieties, plus a replica of Monet's famous bridge at Givenchy; also a museum covering the gardens, local history and the Chickerell brickworks. Home-made teas, shop, disabled access; cl Mon, Sun in Sept, and all Oct–Mar; (01305) 785150; *£4.80.

CHRISTCHURCH SZ1592

At the 'Hampshire' end of the Bournemouth complex, with attractive Georgian brick buildings in its old centre, a restored watermill, and a quay looking out over the yachting harbour, busy in summer. Beyond the harbour mouth, long beaches stretch way into Hampshire from the vast Mudeford car park (the Haven House by the sea here is well worth knowing for its unrivalled position, and there's an excellent fishmonger nearby). Pleasant walking out of season.

Christchurch Castle & Norman House All that remains is a ruined keep, and the ruins of the Norman house probably used by the castle constable. It's quite well preserved, with one of the earliest chimneys in the country, and an ancient midden by a millstream; free.

Christchurch Priory Magnificent medieval monastic church, at over 90 metres (300 ft) the longest parish church in the country; very striking inside, with remarkable carving. The 'Miraculous Beam' apparently fitted in the roof only with divine assistance, so

prompting the renaming of the borough to Christchurch (it used to be called Twynham). Free recitals most Thurs lunchtimes; shop, mostly disabled access; £1 suggested donation. The church has a small museum open in the summer, and good views from the tower (50p) – though with 176 spiral steps you have to earn them.

Knights of Christchurch Sadly the organisers of this lively two-hour mock-jousting spectacle weren't able to tell us where they would be based this summer, but it's well worth checking nearer the time (usually July–Sept); (01202) 483777.

Museum of Electricity 🏛 (opposite Castle's Ironmongers, Bargates) Housed in an Edwardian power station, this has a range of electrical exhibits from antique washing machines to power generators. A transport gallery houses vehicles as diverse as the fully restored No 85 tram (which ran in Bournemouth from 1914–35), a 1970s electric car, and Sir Clive Sinclair's much ridiculed Sinclair C5; interactive displays, and occasional demonstrations of early electrical experiments. Shop, some disabled access; cl wknds, and Oct–Easter; (01202) 480467; £1.50.

Red House Museum & Gardens 🏛 (Quay Rd) Georgian house with local history and archaeology, Victorian bric-a-brac, costumes, and a walled herb garden. Snacks, shop, disabled access to ground floor only; cl Sun am, Mon (exc bank hols), Christmas wk; (01202) 482860; £1.50.

CORFE CASTLE SY9681

The castle is the most spectacular ruin in the area, and gives superb views from its dramatic hilltop position. The site is remarkably atmospheric considering how little of the castle is left, with remnants of portcullises and menacing murder holes. Meals, snacks, shop; cl 25–26 Dec and two days at end of Jan; (01929) 481294; £4; NT. The Swanage Railway runs to here; a joint ticket is available; (01929) 425800. A Tudor building on West St has a decent local history **museum**, with dinosaur footprints; cl wkdys Nov–Apr; free. Parking can be a problem in the attractive ancient small town in summer. The Halfway at Norden Heath (A351 towards Wareham) has good food. The road W through Church Knowle is pretty.

Corfe Castle Model Village Set in attractive gardens, with a faithful reconstruction of how the Norman castle looked like before the Parliamentarians destroyed it in 1646. Meals, snacks, shop, disabled access; cl Nov–Easter; (01929) 481234; £2.25.

CRANBORNE SU0513

A peaceful place, with the Fleur-de-Lys a good pub well known to Hardy and the subject of an entertaining poem by Rupert Brooke (framed inside).

Cranborne Manor Gardens

Delightful 17th-c gardens originally laid out by Tradescant; Jacobean mount garden, herb garden, lovely river garden and avenues of beech and lime. Particularly attractive in spring. Snacks, shop and garden centre, disabled access (limited in gardens); gardens open Weds Mar–Sept, garden centre open daily all year; (01725) 517248; £3. The B3078 has good country views, as does the minor rd crossing it to Three Legged Cross and the Gussages.

CRANBORNE CHASE ST9116

Shared between Dorset and Wiltshire, this offers good walking with some fine views, especially around Ashmore.

DELCOMBE WOOD ST7805

A lovely bluebell wood, sheets of colour in May; but the only public track just skirts the W edge of the wood.

DORCHESTER SY6990

Thriving country town, with busy shopping streets and Weds market, and several worthwhile antiques and print shops. Though most of the more attractive Georgian buildings are just out of the bustle, there are a few distinguished buildings on the main streets, inc the timbered building of **Judge Jeffreys' Lodgings** in High West St; he stayed here during his notorious Bloody Assizes. The trial of the Tolpuddle Martyrs also took place on High West St, in the **Shire Hall**; the room is preserved as a memorial, and is open wkdys in summer hols; for an extra £1.50 you can look round some of the cells (open wkdy pms, not Mon). There are one or two traces of the Romans' occupation, inc the

fragmentary remains of a town house behind the County Hall (you can usually walk around the site on wkdys; a booklet from the County Hall fills you in on its history), and of an amphitheatre on Weymouth Ave. The Napper's Mite restaurant (South St), a former almshouse, has good value food.

Dinosaur Museum (Icen Way) The best of Dorset's dinosaur-related exhibitions, a well displayed and entertaining collection very much designed with younger visitors in mind. There are full-size skeletons and reconstructions, lots of opportunities to handle bones, fossils and the like (not many exhibits have barriers), and fun activities such as Dinosaurs and You, where you put in your height and weight and the computer works out how you compare with a couple of dinosaurs. Look out for the intriguing Dinosaurid – a Canadian expert's idea of what dinosaurs would have evolved into if they hadn't become extinct. Shop, disabled access to ground floor only; cl 24–26 Dec; (01305) 269880; £4.25 (£2.95 children).

Dorset County Museum 🖾 (High West St) Hardy's study from Max Gate has been reconstructed at this comprehensive museum. The writer's gallery looks at the lives of Hardy and other Dorset novelists such as Sylvia Townsend Warner, with touch-screen computer displays. Shop, disabled access to ground floor only; cl Sun Nov–Apr, plus 25–26 Dec and 1 Jan; (01305) 262735; £3.30. Along in High East St the Kings Arms Hotel, full of Hardy associations, is a good place for lunch.

Hardy's Cottage (Higher Bockhampton, just off A35 3m E) The writer's 1840 birthplace is just outside town; the thatched house hasn't changed much since. Cl Fri and Sat and all Nov–Mar; (01305) 262366; £2.60; NT. The surrounding heath is now largely forested. You can walk into the plantations, and just SE of the cottage are stretches of open heathland much as he knew it on Black Heath and Duddle Heath, parts of the 'untamed and untameable' Egdon Heath of his novels. A path from the river at Lower Bockhampton leads to the village, and a

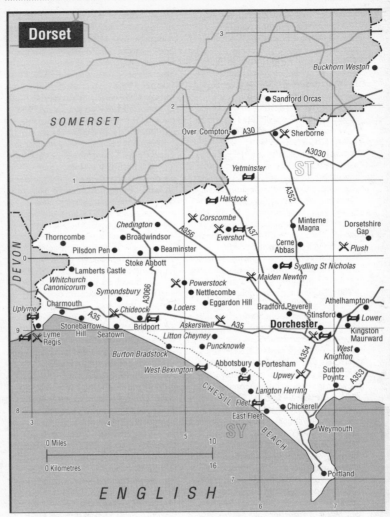

Dorset

SOMERSET

Buckhorn Weston ●

● Sandford Orcas

Over Compton ● A30 ✗ Sherborne

A3030

Yetminster 🏛

A352

🏛 Halstock

✗ Corscombe

Chedington ● Minterne Magna

● Broadwindsor *Evershot* 🏛 A37

Thorncombe ● Cerne Abbas

Pilsdon Pen ● ● Beaminster Dorsetshire Gap

Stoke Abbott ✗ Plush

Lamberts Castle

Whitchurch Canonicorum ● Sydling St Nicholas 🏛

Symondsbury ✗ *Powerstock* ✗ Maiden Newton

Charmouth ● Nettlecombe

Uplyme ✗ Chideock ● *Loders* ● Eggardon Hill Bradford Peverell Athelhampton

A35 Stinsford 🏛 Lower

Stonebarrow ● *Askerswell* A35 **Dorchester** ✗ Kingston

Lyme Hill Seatown Bridport Maurward

Regis *Litton Cheyney* ● A354 West

● Puncknowle Knighton

Burton Bradstock Sutton

Abbotsbury ● Portesham Upwey ✗ Poyntz

West Bexington 🏛 *Langton Herring* A353

CHESIL 🏛 Fleet ● Chickerell

East Fleet ●

BEACH Weymouth

SY

● Portland

ENGLISH

0 Miles 10

0 Kilometres 16

DEVON

ST

---

nature trail leads through Thorncombe Wood to Hardy's cottage.

Keep Military Museum (Bridport Rd) More interesting than most military museums, in a handsome Victorian barracks gatehouse; splendid views from the battlements. Snacks, shop, disabled access; cl Sun (exc July–Aug), plus two wks at Christmas; (01305) 264066; £3.

Maiden Castle (off A354 S) One of the best examples of an Iron Age fort, a massive series of grassy ridges covering 47 acres. It's so vast that the tour of its grassy ramparts almost qualifies as a fully fledged walk.

Max Gate (Alington Ave, A351 1m E) Among the places still associated with Thomas Hardy (who lived in Dorchester for most of his life, using the town as the centre of events in *The Mayor of Casterbridge*), this is the house he designed and lived in from 1885 to his death in 1928, and where he wrote *Tess* and *Jude the Obscure*. You can see only the dining and drawing rooms (the

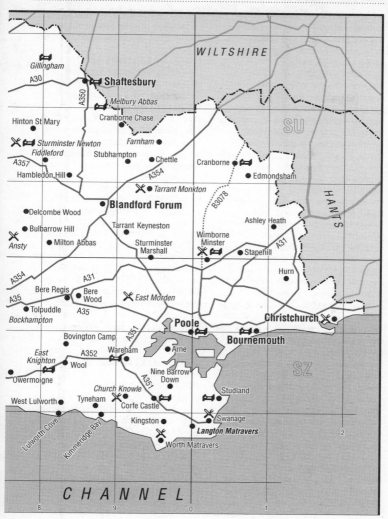

study has been moved to the County Museum), but the gardens are fascinating, not least because they inspired so much of Hardy's poetry. Shop, disabled access; open Sun pm, Mon and Weds Apr–Sept; (01305) 262538; £2.10; NT. The Trumpet Major food pub is very handy.

Teddy Bear House (Antelope House) Tucked away in an old coaching house behind a good teddy shop, a family of human-sized bears dwell in blissful oblivion to the outside world.

You can snuggle up next to a dozing Grandpa on the sofa, go upstairs to see Mother and her ever-increasing brood of baby bears, or head downstairs to the cellar, where the Dorset Teddy Bear Museum collection includes every kind of teddy imaginable; enthusiastically run, this is a must for all teddy-lovers. Shop; cl 25–26 Dec, ring for winter hours; (01305) 263200; £2.95.

Tutankhamun Exhibition (High West St) Readers are impressed by the exhibits here, which re-create the discovery of ancient treasures using a mix of sights, sounds and smells. Shop, some disabled access; cl 24–26 Dec; (01305) 269880; £4.25.

DORSETSHIRE GAP ST7403
The downland W of Binghams Melcombe is attractive for walkers; the dry ground of the Gap comes as a pleasant surprise on those days when it seems as if all Dorset is turning to chalky mud. Despite the ultra-English charm of much of inland Dorset – chalk downs, sleepy thatched villages, clumps of beechwoods and fine views – the area is surprisingly little walked, so field routes are often not obvious, careful map-reading is necessary, and even then the longer paths can sometimes be difficult to follow.

EAST FLEET SY6380
Interesting, particularly for the tiny ruined church which was wrecked by a legendary 1824 storm. Nearby Chesil Beach, its pebbles and boulders immaculately graded by millennia of storms, is emphatically not for swimmers – the undertow will suck you straight down – but with its long lagoon behind is very interesting for beach-combers and nature-lovers. Swans nest on the great lagoon, which was used for trying out the World War II dam-busting bouncing bomb; now a peaceful spot, with lots of other birds too. The vicinity's pleasant walks are especially interesting if you've read J M Faulkner's *Moonfleet*. The Elm Tree at Langton Herring is handy for lunch.

EDMONDSHAM SU0611
Dorset Heavy Horse Centre (well signed from Verwood) Cheery place with five different breeds of huge heavy horse, and miniature Shetland ponies at the other extreme as well as llamas, miniature donkeys and pygmy goats. Snacks, shop, disabled access; cl Nov–Feb; (01202) 824040; £4.95, maybe less out of season. Dogs welcome. The Albion is handy for lunch.

EGGARDON HILL SY5494
On the summit of Eggardon Hill, this has wonderful views and – still after thousands of years – impressive earthen ramparts.

HAMBLEDON HILL ST8412
In a commanding position just above

Child Okeford, this has a winning view, and still gives a strong sense of how formidable it must have been thousands of years ago.

HINTON ST MARY ST7816
One of Dorset's many attractive villages, this has a superb manor house and a striking medieval tithe barn.

HURN SZ1197
Alice in Wonderland Family Park ⌨ (opposite Bournemouth Airport) Lots of thought and effort have been put into this park, especially suited to younger children. Attractions include a huge maze with 5,200 bushes shaped into Alice characters, several fairground rides, adventure play areas, croquet lawns, herb gardens, rare breeds, and pantomime-style interpretations of the famous stories (12 and 3pm). Meals, snacks, shop, some disabled access; open Easter–Oct (cl wkdys from mid-Sept, exc half-term); (01202) 483444; £5.25 (children, £4.75). The Avon Causeway Hotel does decent food. The **Bournemouth Aviation Museum** at the airport has a collection of aircraft inc vintage planes and helicopters, and occasional flying demonstrations. Snacks, shop, disabled access; (01202) 580858; cl Christmas and New Year; *£4.

KIMMERIDGE BAY SY9179
A lovely spot with intriguing rock strata, kept quieter than it might be by the toll. The New Inn up at Church Knowle is good for lunch.

KINGSTON SY9579
From here there's an easy level path to **Hounstout Cliff**; fortify yourself beforehand at the Scott Arms, a good family pub with superb views of Corfe Castle. Turn left at the end and you are into Dorset fossil country, presided over by the primitive hermitage chapel on St Aldhelm's Head; the path here is of the switchback sort, and the chalk mud can make it tough going in wet seasons. A gentler circular walk down to Chapman's Pool and on to Kingston gives outstanding coastal views in both directions.

KINGSTON MAURWARD SY7191
Kingston Maurward Park Popular with some readers, this feels like the heart of the countryside despite its proximity to Dorchester, with peaceful

woodland and lakeside walks, visitor centre, farm park (children can feed the animals), and plenty of garden variety inc Elizabethan and Edwardian gardens, penstemon and salvia national collections. Meals, snacks, shop, some disabled access; cl Christmas; (01305) 215000; *£3.75.

LAMBERTS CASTLE SY3799
This unspoiled **hill fort** is charming for strolls, especially in late summer when the heather is out; it's quite hard to spot the turning from the road.

LANGTON MATRAVERS SZ0078
Putlake Adventure Farm See separate family panel on p. 196.

LULWORTH COVE SY8279
This beauty spot, a magnet for summer visitors and really best appreciated out of season, has a classic mini-walk W along the cliffs to Durdle Door, a natural arch eroded by the sea; the unusually shaped rocks are surrounded by particularly good beaches. Inland is prairie-like monotony, and it is best to return the same way. Exhibitions on smuggling and country wines in the **Lulworth Cove Heritage Centre** (cl 24–25 Dec; nearby parking £2 for two hours). E of Lulworth Cove is army training land, which means high-security fences and dire warning notices, but you are allowed in most wknds and daily in Aug and during Easter (keep to the paths; firing times are published in local papers). Information boards by road junctions off the A351 and A352 nr Wareham give opening times; or ring (01929) 462721 ext 4824 and ask for the Guardroom. The coast walk between Lulworth Cove and Kimmeridge Bay is very strenuous but excellent, heading past the surreal 'fossil forest' (formed of petrified algae that once clung to tree-trunks) to Mupe Bay. Another path ascends Bindon Hill, looking down over the semi-circular cove.

LYME REGIS SY3492
Enchanting old seaside town, well liked by readers, with rather an elegant, steep main street and interesting side streets; the esplanade is pretty, and there's a lively little fishing and yacht harbour. The sea has been cleaned up by a sewage treatment plant, tempting some quite varied animals to make the occasional visit. A coast path snakes W through an intriguing nature-reserve undercliff, still subject to landfalls; this is a celebrated area for fossils and flora (several shops sell fossils, with show collections too). There are pleasant walks in the valley. The Pilot Boat on the front is the best place for lunch; the enjoyable old Royal Standard has a lighted terrace leading to the beach. The town gets very busy in summer, but it is worth braving the crowds. The Jane Austen cliffside gardens have peaceful sea views.

Dinosaurland (Coombe St) An excellent collection of fossils, and they can tell you about any you may have at home. They do two-hour fossil walks along the beach. Shop; cl 25–26 Dec; (01297) 443541; £3.20, guided beach walks £4.50 (booking recommended).
Lyme Regis Marine Aquarium (The Cobb) As we went to press, the future of this decent aquarium right on the historic harbour wall was uncertain; best to call the Tourist Information Centre on (01297) 442138.

MILTON ABBAS ST8001
Lovely thatched village built in the 18th c to replace an earlier one which had spoilt the view from the big house; the 17th-c almshouses were moved here at the same time. Pleasant stroll past the lake through the Capability Brown park to the fine 15th-c **abbey church** of a former Benedictine monastery (it now serves the public school in the nearby house). There's an attractive signed walk over the lane to a former chapel in the wood. Another pleasant walk through the abbey estate leads into Green Hill Down Nature Reserve, and a longer walk continues NW to **Bulbarrow Hill**, which looks far into Somerset and Wiltshire.
Downland views The road through the Winterbornes to Okeford Fitzpaine has good downland views.

MINTERNE MAGNA ST6604
Minterne Gardens (Minterne House, A352) Beautiful landscaped gardens, with lakes, cascades, streams, rare trees and impressive spring shows of azaleas, rhododendrons and bulbs; the autumn colours can be quite spectacular. Open Mar–mid-Nov; (01300) 341370; *£3. The road W up Gore Hill and

Batcombe Hill to Holywell has memorable views.

NETTLECOMBE SY5295

A sleepy village in charming walking country, little touched by agricultural improvement – delectable downland and valley landscapes, with a reasonably good path network – and has a good pub.

NINE BARROW DOWN SY9982

The main Purbeck ridge, this has far-ranging two-way views – good from a car, and also a pleasing goal for walks from Corfe Castle.

OVER COMPTON ST5916

Worldlife & Lullingstone Silk Farm 💷 Superb collection of butterflies, flying free in reconstructions of their natural habitat inside Elizabethan Compton Hall. The silk farm demonstrates production of English silk used for coronations and Royal weddings. Snacks, shop, some disabled access; cl Oct–Mar; (01935) 474608; £4.50.

OWERMOIGNE SY7685

Mill House Cider Museum & Dorset Clock Collection 💷 Cider museum with fully restored 18th- and 19th-c equipment, and video demonstrating the process. Also a collection of locally made 18th- and 19th-c clocks. Shop with local ciders, some disabled access; cl 25 Dec–2 Jan; (01305) 852220; £1.50 cider museum, £2 clocks, £2.90 both. The beautifully placed Sailors Return at East Chaldon is good value for lunch.

PILSDON PEN ST4101

Not a place for long walks, but ideal for those who want a rewarding view in a very short stroll – Dorset's highest point, capped by a hill fort, and looking over Lyme Bay and N towards the Mendips. It is reached within minutes from the layby.

POOLE SZ0190

Merging indistinguishably into Bournemouth on the edges, its centre is wholly distinct, with a more lively feel, especially around The Quay. The broad natural harbour is still busy with the comings and goings of boats and small ships (several decent pubs to watch them from – the nautical Portsmouth Hoy is best for lunch); launch ferries around the harbour, and out to Brownsea Island. There are interesting old buildings along here; the streets

behind, some pedestrianised, are well worth strolling through. The Old Harry (High St) has good local fish, the Guildhall Tavern (Market St) has good value family food, and the Custom House (The Quay) has a marvellous quayside location. The town is also well served for cyclists, with plenty of signed routes.

Aquarium Complex (Hennings Wharf, The Quay) Busy indoor centre well liked by readers, with an enormous 00 gauge model railway as well as the aquarium; also smuggling and space exhibitions, and insectarium. Good for families on rainy days. Meals, snacks, shop; cl 24–25 Dec; (01202) 686712; £4.95, £3.95 aquarium only.

Brownsea Island Unspoilt 500-acre island in the middle of the huge natural harbour, famous as the site of the first scout camp in 1907. Lots of birds (inc peacocks), animals and butterflies in heath and woodland (you may spot red squirrels), large heronry, nature reserve, and fine views back towards the coast from its beaches. It's a really splendid place to explore. Guided walks 2.45pm daily in July and Aug, and from mid-July to mid-Aug maybe open-air Shakespeare or opera. Snacks, shop, disabled access; cl early Oct–Mar; (01202) 707744; *£3.50; NT. Ferries to the island run every half-hour from Poole Harbour (£4 return, takes half an hour) or Sandbanks (£3 return, takes only six minutes); don't forget to check the time of the last one back.

Chain ferry This runs from Sandbanks, by the harbour mouth, to the Studland side – a spectacular entrance to Dorset proper; it's quickest to go as a foot passenger or by bus (they have priority; 90p each way). The beach at Sandbanks is regularly lauded as one of the best in Britain.

Compton Acres Gardens 💷 (Canford Cliffs) Perhaps Poole's outstanding attraction, with lovely statuary among fine plants landscaped in an eclectic variety of styles – the Japanese garden is the foremost in Europe. Good views of the hills and Poole harbour. Sat is the least busy day to visit. Snacks, shop and plant sales, disabled access; cl Nov–Feb; (01202) 700778; £4.95. The Nightjar has decent food.

Poole Pottery 🖼 (The Quay)
Distinctive china has been produced
here since 1873. Good factory tours
(exc wknds and Fri pm), and a museum
and film; you can have a go at throwing
and decorating your own pot. Other
craft demonstrations too. Restaurant
with harbour views (open evenings),
shop, disabled access; cl 12.30–1.30pm,
25 Dec, and some winter wknds, phone
to check; (01202) 666200; £2.50.

Splashdown (Tower Park, 2m NE on
A3049) Good for children, a water park
with 11 rides and slides (indoor and
out), inc a near-vertical drop in total
darkness. Snacks; cl wkdy ams outside
school hols (in peak periods they may
have limits on how long you can stay),
also 25, 31 Dec, 1 Jan, and for 3 or 4 wks
at the start of Jan – best to ring; (01202)
716123; £5.90.

Waterfront Museum (High St) Four
floors of well laid out local history;
disabled access; (01202) 262600; cl Sun
am, and 25–26 Dec (reduced hours in
winter); £2). For £2 extra in July and
Aug, you can go next door to
Scaplen's Court, a well restored
medieval merchant's home with
exhibitions upstairs.

PORTESHAM SY6086
The high heathland above here is good
walking territory, with a view covering
the entire sweep of the West Dorset
coast.

Hardy Monument As hideous as it is
prominent, this commemorates
Nelson's admiral, not the Dorset
author; it has tremendous views. A
track along Bronkham Hill SE from the
car park feels truly ancient, with
prehistoric burial mounds flanking it. If
you don't feel like leaving the car, the
Black Down rd passing the monument
towards Martinstown also gives fine
views.

PORTLAND SY6973
This odd, much-quarried promontory
with its narrow neck and long naval
connections gives tremendous views
from its peak. Nearer at hand, the
remarkable sea defences of Portland
Harbour laid out below are a fine sight –
and you may glimpse Britain's first
prison ship for generations moored off
here. The Pulpit and the Lobster Pot,
both handy for a stroll to the

lighthouse (visitor centre, only open
Sun in winter; (01305) 861233) and
cliffs, are useful for lunch.

Portland Castle You may be able to
try on armour at this fortress, built
under Henry VIII to defend the south
coast. Audio tour, snacks, shop, limited
disabled access; cl Nov–Mar; (01305)
820539; £2.80; EH.

Portland Museum (Wakeham St) A
cottage used by Hardy in *The Well-
Beloved* is now a local history museum
which was founded by Dr Marie Stopes,
the birth control pioneer. Shop, some
disabled access; cl 1–1.30pm, Weds and
Thurs (exc Aug), and all Nov–Mar;
(01305) 821804; £1.80.

SANDFORD ORCAS ST6221
Manor House Interesting lived-in
Tudor manor house, largely unaltered
since the 16th c, with fine furnishings
and family portraits, and pleasant
gardens, at their best May and Jun.
Open Easter Mon, then Sun pm and all
day Mon May–Sept; (01963) 220206;
*£2.50. The Mitre has decent food.

SEATOWN SY4291
This seaside hamlet has some charming
stone cottages and a perfectly placed
seaside pub. There's a steep walk up to
the **Golden Cap**, the highest point on
the county's coast, and another good
walk along to the New Inn at Eype. Just
inland, the village of Chideock is pretty
– or would be, if it weren't sadly ripped
in half by the busy A35.

SHAFTESBURY ST8623
Hilltop town with good views from
Castle Hill and Park Walk; there are
several craft shops and workshops. The
most famous street is Gold Hill –
thatched cottages stepped down a
steep cobbled street, familiar from
those Hovis TV advertisements. At the
bottom, St James (where the Two
Brewers is the town's best family food
pub) is attractive.

**Shaftesbury Abbey Museum &
Garden** You can still see the ancient
gravestones at this abbey set up by
Alfred the Great; excavated remains
from the site (inc stonework for
children to touch) can be seen at an
adjacent museum, along with an Anglo-
Saxon herb garden; audio tour. Shop,
disabled access; cl Nov–Apr; (01747)
852910; £1.50.

Shaftesbury Town Museum At the top of Gold Hill the local history museum includes an 18th-c fire engine and a collection of old farm implements. Limited disabled access to ground floor only; cl Oct–Easter; (01747) 852157; £1.20.

SHERBORNE ST6316
An attractive town to wander through, given a feeling of unchanging solidity by the handsome stone medieval abbey buildings that mix in with later ones of the public school here, and by many other fine old buildings in and near the main street. The **abbey** itself is a glorious golden stone building with a beautifully vaulted nave; at the Dissolution the townspeople raised the money to buy it, and it's been the parish church ever since. Locals remain very much involved in its fortunes: a while ago they won their campaign to rid the church of a 19th-c stained-glass window by Pugin, in which Old Testament prophets were said to resemble Mr Blobby. The unspoilt Digby Tap (handy for the abbey but no food Sun) and Skippers (Horsecastles) are useful for lunch. Several craft shops include a working saddlery in the main street.

Sherborne Castle 🎟 (just E of town) Striking old house built by Sir Walter Raleigh in 1594, standing out particularly for its wonderful period furnishings, though there are also interesting paintings and porcelain. Outside are gardens designed by Capability Brown, and beautiful parkland with an enormous lake. Meals, snacks, shop; open pms Apr–Oct, grounds cl Weds, house same, plus Mon and Fri; (01935) 813182; £5 house and gardens, £2.50 grounds only.

Sherborne Museum (Abbeygate House, Church Ave) An eclectic collection includes a reconstruction of the old castle in its heyday, as well as a Victorian dolls' house and Roman remains. Shop, disabled access to ground floor only; cl Sun am, Mon (exc bank hols), and Nov–Easter; (01935) 812252; *£1.

Sherborne Old Castle (Castleton) Facing Sherborne Castle across the lake is the original 12th-c castle, now a beautifully evocative ruin. Good for a picnic, and especially appealing in Apr

when the dry ditch is full of wild primroses. Snacks, shop, disabled access (but no facilities); cl 1–2pm, winter Mon and Tues, 24–26 Dec, and 1 Jan; (01935) 812730; £1.60.

STAPEHILL SU0500
Stapehill Abbey 🎟 Just right for a relaxed, unhurried afternoon, a 19th-c Cistercian abbey (the nuns moved out in 1989, although the chapel has been preserved) now houses craft workshops and exhibitions on monastic life; acres of park and landscaped grounds inc a new Japanese garden, with waterfalls and woodland walk, and play area and farm animals for children. Meals, snacks, shop, limited disabled access; cl Mon and Tues Oct–Mar, Christmas hols and all Jan; (01202) 873060; *£7 (less in winter). The Barley Mow at Colehill is a good food pub.

STINSFORD SY7191
On the Thomas Hardy trail: he featured the village as Mellstock, and at the church his heart is buried beside the body of his first wife.

STOKE ABBOTT ST4500
With thatched houses, a good deal of charm, and a pleasant pub, this offers walkers attractive undisturbed surrounding countryside, with a reasonably good path network.

STONEBARROW HILL SY3893
Reached by a steep narrow road just E of Charmouth, this has good easy walking, fine sea and inland views, a disabled WC, and NT shop in season.

STUBHAMPTON ST9214
In good weather the bridleway from here along Ashmore Bottom to Ashmore is well worth exploring; but it can be muddy in a wet spring.

STUDLAND SZ0482
The most remarkably varied short walk in Dorset. In a couple of hours you can take in Ballard Down (huge views over Poole Harbour), Old Harry Rocks (tooth-like chalk pinnacles detached from the cliff) and the Agglestone (a rock standing solitary on Dorset's largest surviving heath). The **beach** is lovely, with two areas set aside for dog owners and a parking charge in summer (expensive exc for NT members, less after 2pm); behind is a nature reserve, with a nearby NT visitor centre with snacks and shop, and decent food at the

Manor House Hotel (where Churchill and Eisenhower watched D-Day rehearsals). Next to the ferry, the simple Shell Bay is good for seafood.

STURMINSTER MARSHALL ST9500

White Mill Rebuilt in 1776 and restored over 200 years later, this waterside cornmill still retains its original wooden machinery (too fragile to operate); delightfully set on the banks of the River Stour, it's a very pleasant spot for a picnic. Disabled access; open wknd and bank hol pms Easter–Sept; (01258) 858051; *£2.

SUTTON POYNTZ SY7083

This attractive thatched village, with a decent pub, has a good path to the nearby village of Osmington (also thatched, pretty and with a decent pub). The path gives views of the **White Horse** – an equestrian portrait of George III etched into the hillside. You can walk back along the Dorset coastal path, which here leads along the top of the downs rather than along the coast itself.

SWANAGE SZ0278

Fairly quiet 19th-c resort, which, for reasons hotly disputed by locals, seems to be losing much of the sand from the northern end of its beaches. The seaview Mowlem Theatre restaurant (Shire Rd) is good.

Durlston Country Park On the edge of Swanage, this has spectacular clifftop scenery and unspoilt countryside, with good views from the headland, the **Great Globe** (a 40-ton global representation in Portland stone), and good spots to watch seabirds, butterflies or deer (let them know if you see dolphins, seals or whales). Snacks, shop, some disabled access; information centre cl wkdys Nov–Mar; (01929) 424443; free, though there's a parking charge of £2.50 in summer (£1 in winter).

Swanage Railway ⊞ Steam trains now run along six miles of track to Corfe Castle (a joint ticket is available): a nice way of approaching the ruins – or you could walk there and ride back. The Swanage station has an exhibition of old railway memorabilia, and, more unusually, a travel agency where the commission goes to the railway's

upkeep. Parking is easier at the Norden end of the line. Snacks, shop, disabled access; cl 25 Dec, and winter wkdys exc school hols, best to ring for timetable; (01929) 425800 for train times; £6.

TARRANT KEYNESTON ST9104

Keyneston Mill Fruit Farm Interesting vineyard and farm shop, with 21 different kinds of pick-your-own. Meals, snacks, disabled access; usually open summer wknds (and maybe other times throughout the year, best to check); (01258) 452596; free. The True Lovers Knot has decent food and a big garden.

THORNCOMBE ST3504

Forde Abbey The extensive gardens here really are special, with glorious trees and shrubs, a fine collection of Asiatic primulas, many interesting plants, and sweeping lawns, as well as a new visitor centre and Ionic-style temple. The striking abbey buildings still retain some of the features of the original 12th-c Cistercian monastery, but it was modernised in 1520 by Abbot Chard, and it's his great hall and tower that remain. Cromwell's Attorney-General later turned the abbey into a house, and the interior has changed little since, with magnificently furnished rooms, unusual plaster ceilings and a set of Raphael tapestries. Meals and snacks (in 12th-c undercroft), shop, disabled access to gardens only; house open pm Tues–Thurs, Sun and bank hols Apr–Oct, garden and nursery all year; (01460) 220231; £5.20, £4 garden only. Thorncombe Wood is awash with bluebells in spring.

TOLPUDDLE SY7894

Famous for the agricultural workers who were transported to Australia after they united to improve their working conditions and terms of employment. The Martyrs' Tree under which they supposedly met still remains, and more of their story is explained in interactive displays in a little museum between the six cottages built by the TUC as a memorial. Disabled access; cl Mon, and Christmas; (01305) 848237; free. With the bypass completed, the village is now much quieter. The Martyrs pub is useful for lunch.

TYNEHAM SY8880

Tyneham Abandoned Village On the army's Purbeck firing ranges (open holidays and most wknds), this is quite poignant; there's an explanatory exhibition in the former church.

WAREHAM SY9287

This largely modern town has a few striking old buildings, inc the church of St Martin, with a finely carved memorial to Lawrence of Arabia. The church of Lady St Mary not far from the quay has the coffin of Edward the Martyr, murdered at nearby Corfe Castle in 978. Two very traditional old inns, the Black Bear and Kings Arms; another, the Quay, is in a fine position. The attractive road over the West Creech Hills may sometimes be closed for army firing practice.

Blue Pool 🖽 (Furzebrook, 3m S) Curiously, the water in this peaceful beauty spot (formerly a claypit) changes colour with the weather; it's bluest on an overcast day. There are some rare plants and animals among the surrounding 25 acres of heathland, plus a museum and a small play area. Snacks, shop, plant sales, some disabled access; facilities and museum cl Oct–Easter, site cl Dec–Feb; (01929) 551408; £3. Discount valid until Oct.

WEST LULWORTH SY8280

A lovely spot, though hardly undiscovered (parking can be a nightmare), just above a very beautiful cove with extraordinary nearby rock formations; the thatched Castle Inn is useful for lunch. The Lulworth Equestrian Centre can arrange horse-riding; (01929) 400396; around £12 an hour.

Lulworth Castle Fully restored 17th-c castle with splendid views over the wooded park from its SE tower; the formal gardens are a nice spot for a picnic. The Catholic chapel was the first to be built in England after the Reformation, and an Anglican church was built in part by Thomas Hardy, about whom there's an exhibition inside; also children's summer farm and play area. Meals, teas, shop, limited disabled access; cl Sun and 25–26 Dec; (01929) 400352; £4.50.

WEYMOUTH SY6878

Elegant 18th- and 19th-c terraces along its curving esplanade, and some older buildings in the narrower partly pedestrianised streets behind. The harbour is lively, with big ferries leaving from the outer quay, and the town's inner ring road running one-way around the inner harbour. The Old Rooms has good value food and interesting harbour views. On the far side of the harbour the narrow streets of the old town are worth exploring; there's a **Tudor house** on Trinity St. The resort has a good beach, and lots of lively family attractions.

Brewers Quay In the heart of the Old Harbour, this is a skilful conversion of harbourside Victorian brewery into shopping and leisure complex, with plenty of good year-round activities. **Timewalk** 🖽 imaginatively re-creates scenes from the town's history, and a new interactive gallery takes an interesting look at its brewing heritage (£4.25). There's also a craft market, ten-pin bowling, microbrewery, and lively hands-on science centre. Several places to eat, and good specialist shops, disabled access (exc to Timewalk); cl 25–27 Dec, and last two wks in Jan; (01305) 777622; free admission to centre.

Deep Sea Adventure 🖽 (Custom House Quay) Fascinating look at underwater exploration, shipwrecks, and the search for buried treasure, with lots of interactive displays. There's an exemplary exhibition on the *Titanic*, and a first-class indoor play area (£2.75 extra). Meals, snacks, shop, disabled access; cl 25–26 Dec and 1 Jan; (01305) 760690; £3.50.

Model World 🖽 (Lodmoor Country Park, Preston Rd) Set in landscaped gardens, this miniature world includes a model airport, funfair, space centre, zoo and 0 gauge railway (runs daily, weather permitting); also plenty of models to operate yourself, and an aviary. Snacks, shop, disabled access; cl Nov–Apr; (01305) 781797; £2.75.

Nothe Fort (Barrack Rd) Interesting armed Victorian fort on three levels, spread over a staggering 70 rooms. Children can clamber over some of the vehicles and guns, and there are fine views of the harbour and coast. Snacks, shop, some disabled access; open daily mid-May to mid-Sept, Easter hols and Oct half-term, plus Sun pm and bank hols rest of year; (01305) 787243; *£3. Good views too from the garden of the Nothe Tavern (with tasty fresh fish), and from the pleasant nearby Nothe Gardens.

Sea Life Park (Lodmoor Country Park) One of the most elaborate in the excellent Sea Life Centres chain. As well as the stunning marine displays and touch pools, features include a Shark Academy, with fun interactive games and quizzes leading to a scholarship, a new seal sanctuary, and a splendid outdoor play area. Meals, snacks, shop, disabled access; cl 25 Dec (reduced hours in winter); (01305) 788255; £6.50.

WIMBORNE MINSTER SZ0199 Georgian houses (and decent antiques shops and auctions) in the narrow central streets around the **Minster** – a fine, well preserved, largely Norman church with contrasting red and grey masonry, twin towers, and a brightly coloured jack striking the clock bell every quarter. Inside, an interesting Norman crypt, a distinctive astronomical clock and the original chained library. Further along King St is an entertaining model town (cl Oct–Easter; £3). Dormers (Hanham Rd) and the Cross Keys (Victoria Rd, W) are best for lunch. Just W of town at Pamphill is a good big farm shop, and just E there are pleasant country walks around the Fox & Hounds at Little Canford.

Iron Age hill fort The once formidable hill fort of **Badbury Rings**, just off B3082 NW of Wimborne, is associated by some with King Arthur. It's a good strolling ground with an impressive range of wild flowers – and if you feel more energetic, a Roman road lets you strike out for miles N.

Kingston Lacy House 🏛 (B3082 NW) Impressive 17th-c mansion later remodelled by Charles Barry, with grand Italian marble staircase and superb Venetian ceilings; outstanding paintings such as the *Judgement of Solomon* by Sebastiano del Piombo, and others by Titian, Rubens and Van Dyck. The enormous grounds have landscaped gardens, a herd of Red Devon cattle in the park, and summer concerts and plays. Lovely snowdrops in Feb and early Mar. There's easily enough here to fill up a good day out. Meals, snacks, shop, disabled access to park and gardens; open Apr–Oct, house cl am and Thurs, Fri; (01202) 883402; £6, £2.50 grounds only; NT.

Knoll Gardens 🏛 (Stapehill Rd) Rare and exotic plants in various colourfully themed well developed gardens, with over 6,000 different named species, many of which can be bought in the expanding nursery. They maintain a good working relationship with the Dorset Wildlife Trust. Good value meals and snacks, shop and garden centre, disabled access; cl Dec–Jan, wkdys in Feb, and Mon and Tues in Mar and Oct; (01202) 873931; £3.75. Adjacent Trehane Nurseries have a great range of camellias.

Priest's House Museum (High St) Historic town house with carefully researched period rooms inc a new gallery on local villages; regular cooking displays in the Victorian kitchen, and charming walled garden. Summer teas, shop, disabled access to ground floor and garden; cl Sun (exc pm Jun–Sept and bank hol wknds), and Nov–Mar (exc special 2-wk exhibition after Christmas – best to phone); (01202) 882533; £2.20.

Walford Mill (Stone Lane) Former 18th-c flour mill with exhibitions and local crafts. Meals, snacks, shop, disabled access; cl 25–26 Dec, 1 Jan, and Mons Jan–Mar; (01202) 841400; free.

WOOL SY8589

Monkey World (off A35 towards Bere Regis) As enjoyable as it is worthwhile, this enthusiastic rescue centre for apes and chimps delights visitors of all ages. The centre looks after all kinds of primates that are gradually reintroduced to natural surroundings. As well as the biggest group of chimpanzees you'll see outside Africa, residents usually include ring-tailed and ruffed lemurs, Barbary macaques, capuchins and vervets, orang-utans and gibbons, all roaming and climbing freely in decent-sized open enclosures. Keepers give useful talks, and you can see baby chimps playing in their nursery. There's quite a range of

play areas inc a 15-stage obstacle course, plus a pets' corner, mini motor-bikes, and jet boats – it's a very satisfying fine weather half-day out for families. There may be a clown some afternoons in summer. Snacks (and picnic area), shop, disabled access (a few steep paths); cl 25 Dec; (0800) 456600; £5.50 (£4 children). The village itself was used by Thomas Hardy as the ancient seat of the D'Urbevilles.
WORTH MATRAVERS SY9677
In this prettily set coastal hamlet the unpretentious Square & Compass has lovely views, and is a good base for coast walks. Near here, the rock pool at Dancing Ledge is said to have been cut

by a local schoolmaster.
Other attractive villages with decent pubs include Buckhorn Weston ST7524, Burton Bradstock SY4889, Chedington ST4805, Church Knowle SY9481, Evershot ST5704, Farnham ST9515, Fiddleford ST8013, Langton Herring SY6182, Litton Cheyney SY5590, Loders SY4994, Powerstock SY5196, Puncknowle SY5388 (pronounced Punnel), Sydling St Nicholas SY6399, Symondsbury SY4493, Tarrant Monkton ST9408, West Knighton SY7387 and Whitchurch Canonicorum SY3995 (fine church).

Where to eat

ANSTY ST7603 **Fox** *(01258) 880328* Country inn in lovely peaceful spot with a good mix of walkers, cyclists and locals who enjoy its warm, relaxed atmosphere; high-ceilinged main bar with interesting photographs and pictures, Toby jugs and decorative plates, well kept real ales, eight wines by the glass, and very good interesting bar food; a nice place to stay. £20.15|**£7.95**

ASKERSWELL SY5293 **Spyway** *(01308) 485250* Former smugglers' look-out with exceptional value, very popular bar food, lots of salads, and cheesecake; good views, big garden, walks nearby; no children inside; cl Mon exc bank hols. £15.50|**£5**

CHIDEOCK SY4292 **Betchworth House** *(01297) 489478* Welcoming, no smoking, 17th-c house with attractive tearoom and pretty cottagey garden, offering morning coffee and home-made clotted cream teas; bdrms; cl Mon–Thurs Nov–Feb.|**£3.20**

CHRISTCHURCH SZ1592 **Splinters** *12 Church St (01202) 483454* Fine old building near priory with three attractively decorated rooms, international modern cooking, lovely puddings, a fine British cheese choice, good value wines, and friendly helpful owners; also run Pommery's (next door) with delicatessen and lively upstairs café-bar; cl Sun, Mon, 26 Dec. £40

CHURCH KNOWLE SY9481 **New Inn** *(01929) 480357* Very attractive, partly thatched old pub with two nicely furnished main bar areas, lots of bric-a-brac, log fires, and relaxing dining lounge; very good fresh fish (and other food), well kept ales, decent wines, and skittle alley; camping in field behind (need to book). £19|**£7.50**

CORSCOMBE ST5205 **Fox** *(01935) 891330* Popular thatched pub with new dining room opened in old kitchen (Aga, Welsh dresser, etc), with lovely polished copper pots and pans, scrubbed pine tables, candles in champagne bottles, open fires in one room and woodburner in another, imaginative popular food, well kept real ales, local cider, and a super wine list; nice surrounding walks; well behaved children welcome; bdrms. £25|**£5**

DORCHESTER SY6990 **Potter In** *19 Durngate St (01305) 260312* All-day food inc English breakfast, enjoyable lunchtime meals and snacks, and afternoon teas; walled garden for summer, open fire and fresh flowers, and a friendly welcome; disabled access.|**£3.40**

EAST MORDEN SY9194 **Cock & Bottle** *(01929) 459238* Popular dining pub with several beamed communicating areas, a nice mix of old furnishings, good log fire, enjoyable food inc interesting daily specials with plenty of fish and seasonal game, well kept beers and good wines; disabled access. £25.50|**£6.95**

EVERSHOT ST5704 **Acorn** *28 Fore St (01935) 83228* Well run old coaching inn with a comfortable L-shaped bar, two fine old fireplaces and copies of the inn's deeds going back to the 17th c; imaginative daily specials, well kept ales, home-made damson vodka and sloe gin, and a thoughtful wine list; nice village and good nearby walks. £25|**£8.25**

LYME REGIS SY3492 **Pilot Boat** *1 Bridge St* (01297) 443157 Welcoming place across from beaches, with a bustling atmosphere, light comfortable dining bar decorated with fishing and nautical memorabilia, good food, no smoking restaurant, and decent wines and liqueurs; cl 25 Dec; disabled access. £15.25|**£6.50**

MAIDEN NEWTON SY6097 **Petit Canard** *Dorchester Rd* (01300) 320536 Welcoming little restaurant (they prefer you not to smoke) with simple furnishings, good very interesting food inc fine puddings, and a well chosen wine list; cl am, Sun and Mon pm, first 2 wks Jan; children over 12. £30.50

PLUSH ST7102 **Brace of Pheasants** *(01300) 348357* Long, low, 16th-c thatched cottage with a civilised but relaxed atmosphere, good solid furnishings, fresh flowers and a good log fire in the airy beamed bar; interesting food, well kept real ales; swings and an aviary in the garden; children in the family room. £22.50|**£7.95**

POWERSTOCK SY5196 **Three Horseshoes** *(01308) 485328* Popular stone and thatch pub with comfortable L-shaped bar, warm fires, lovely sea views, well kept ales, 20 wines by the glass, and (depending what the local fishermen bring in) a very good choice of well prepared interesting fish dishes. £21.50|**£9**

SHERBORNE ST6316 **Pheasants** *24 Greenhill* (01935) 815252 Georgian restaurant-with-rooms in attractive town, with friendly staff, enjoyable modern English cooking, good breakfasts; cl Mon, 2 wks beginning Jan; well behaved children welcome; disabled access. £30|£16 3 courses

STURMINSTER NEWTON ST7814 **Red Rose** *Market Cross* (01258) 472460 Long-standing family-run lunchtime restaurant with proper English cooking using their own lamb and local produce, and with a very relaxed and happy atmosphere; popular locally; cl evenings, Sun; disabled access. £8.40

SWANAGE SZ0278 **Galley** *9 High St* (01929) 427299 Enjoyable little evening restaurant not far from the seafront with emphasis on fresh local fish and game, good reasonably priced wines, and helpful service; cl Nov–Mar; no children. £25.75

TARRANT MONKTON ST9408 **Langton Arms** *(01258) 830225* Charmingly set, welcoming, 17th-c thatched pub with beams and an inglenook fireplace, no smoking bistro restaurant in an attractively reworked barn, no smoking family room with play area in skittle alley, well kept interesting real ales, popular enjoyable bar food, and garden with another play area; good nearby walks; bdrms. £18.15|**£6.50**

UPWEY SY6785 **Old Ship** *(01305) 812522* Pretty and friendly whitewashed cottagey pub with several interconnected beamed rooms, fresh flowers and an open fire, very good bar food, well kept beer, a fine range of wines, attentive service, and seats in the garden; cl 24 Dec. £16|**£6.50**

UPWEY SY6684 **Wishing Well** *Church St* (01305) 814470 Nice little restaurant, popular locally, with good interesting lunchtime food and afternoon teas, and friendly service; bring your own wine; cl Mon–Tues Mar–Easter, cl mid-Dec–beginning Mar; disabled access. £12|**£5.95**

WIMBORNE MINSTER SZ0199 **Cloisters** *40 East St* (01202) 880593 Friendly restaurant with pleasant décor and enjoyable food inc breakfast with home-made marmalade, lunchtime snacks and meals, and afternoon tea; cl 25–30 Dec; disabled access. £20|**£4.25**

WORTH MATRAVERS SY9776 **Worth Café & Craft Centre** *(01929) 439360* Welcoming converted barn with enthusiastic staff, good home-made lunches (lots for vegetarians) and cakes, and good locally made crafts; walkers welcome; cl winter Tues, 2 wks end Jan; disabled access. £25|**£5.95**

Special thanks to R J Cox, B and K Hypher, Paul Kennedy, A Keys and Phyl and Jack Street

ESSEX

Pleasantly unassuming, with some nice surprises, from quirky museums to ancient forests

Colchester, Britain's oldest recorded town, is the best bet for family attractions here, with an excellent ever-expanding zoo (inventive play areas and free children's activities) and the enjoyable Castle Museum. Among several other interesting places to visit in the town, current refurbishments at Hollytrees Museum promise to boost its family appeal. Happy half-days can be readily spent at Lee Valley Park Farms, Colne Valley Railway, Mangapps Farm Railway, Layer Marney Tower, the wildlife park at Widdington, and Barleylands Farm Museum & Visitor Centre; reconstructed Mountfitchet Castle & 1066 Village is a good fair-weather outing.

Magnificent Audley End is also good for families, though the pleasant old town of Saffron Walden nearby has a more adult appeal.

Southend-on-Sea, the main seaside resort, has plenty to do and a buoyant appeal in summer – the Central Museum has a fun new discovery centre, and medieval moated Southchurch Hall Museum is an unexpected find; Brightlingsea has the best beach.

Gardeners can choose between the charming Gardens of Easton Lodge (new to the *Guide* this year), those at Elmstead Market (Beth Chatto), Lamarsh (plenty to keep children occupied here), and Rettendon, with the more frivolous heading for the gnome forest at Dedham, another newcomer. The Gibberd Garden in Harlow joins the similarly titled art collection as one of Harlow's several surprises for visitors. The eventual fusion of the town's museum and Marks Hall cycle collection should prove rewarding too.

Essex has many beautiful villages, especially Finchingfield, Thaxted and Great Bardfield (all of which have windmills). Coggeshall has some fine medieval buildings, and attractive Burnham-on-Crouch is lively in summer. Many of the churches are well worth a look. North Essex has a real East Anglian flavour. Driving through, you pass lots of attractive houses right by the road, often with fine old timbering and distinctive colour-washed plasterwork – the intricate patterning is known as pargeting. Constable's Stour Valley still enchants, though the unspoilt character which makes its landscapes so attractive is under growing threat from the sheer number of visitors. In stark contrast, the two nuclear war command bunkers at Kelvedon Hatch and Mistley have a chilling fascination.

The Blackwater/Crouch coast has a surprisingly remote feel, given the closeness of densely urban South Essex. Further north, there are good coastal walks at Walton on the Naze.

Where to stay

BROXTED TL5827 **Whitehall** *Church End, Broxted, Dunmow, Essex CM6 2BZ* (01279) 850603 **£145**, plus special breaks; 26 pretty rms. Fine Elizabethan manor house in lovely walled gardens, with restful spacious lounge, a smaller cosier one with log fire, pleasant bar, good food in big, heavily-timbered restaurant, and friendly service; cl 25–31 Dec; disabled access

BURNHAM-ON-CROUCH TQ9595 **White Harte** *The Quay, Burnham-on-Crouch, Essex CM0 8AS* (01621) 782106 **£58**; 19 rms, 11 with own bthrm. Old-fashioned 17th-c yachting inn on quay overlooking the River Crouch with its own jetty; high ceilings, oak tables, polished parquet flooring, sea pictures, panelling, residents' lounge, and restaurant

COGGESHALL TL8422 **White Hart** *Market End, Coggeshall, Colchester, Essex CO6 1NH* (01376) 561654 **£75**, plus wknd breaks; 18 attractive rms. 15th-c hotel with beamed lounge bar and residents' bar, log fires, friendly staff, and good food in bar and restaurant

DEDHAM TM0433 **Maison Talbooth** *Stratford Rd, Dedham, Colchester, Essex CO7 6HN* (01206) 322367 **£155**, plus special breaks; 10 luxuriously furnished rms. Tranquil Victorian country house in fine Constable country, with deeply comfortable seating and fresh flowers in elegant lounge, very good imaginative food in lovely timber-framed restaurant overlooking river and gardens, and marvellous breakfasts; partial disabled access

MALDON TL8407 **Blue Boar** *Silver St, Maldon, Essex CM9 4QE* (01621) 852681 **£80**, plus wknd breaks; 28 comfortable rms. Fine 14th-c coaching inn with cosy little beamed and oak-panelled rooms, roaring log fires, good food (nice breakfasts), and friendly staff; limited disabled access

RICKLING GREEN TL5029 **Cricketers Arms** *Rickling Green, Saffron Walden, Essex CB11 3YG* (01799) 543210 **£70**; 10 rms, some in modern block behind. Cheerful family-run pub by village green with cricketing mementoes, beamed bar with open fires, home-made food in bar and attractive restaurant; handy for Stansted Airport; partial disabled access

THAXTED TL6131 **Swan** *Bull Ring, Thaxted, Dunmow, Essex CM6 2PL* (01371) 830321 **£75**; 20 comfortably modernised rms. Four-gabled late 15th-c inn with views towards the church and almshouses; pleasantly pubby big bar area with warm atmosphere, well kept real ales, and good food

WEST MERSEA TM0012 **Blackwater Hotel** *20 Church Rd, West Mersea, Colchester, Essex CO5 8QH* (01206) 383358 **£60**, plus special breaks; 9 pretty rms. Creeper-covered hotel with neat little sitting room, fresh flowers, attractive beamed restaurant with mainly French food (emphasis on fresh fish), the relaxed and informal Mussel Pan Bistro (which specialises in mussels), big breakfasts, and friendly service

We welcome reports from readers

This *Guide* depends on readers' reports. Do help us if you can – in return, we offer a discount on the next edition to people who've helped us with reports for it. Tell us what you think about places already in it, and anything extra you think we should say about them. And send us your ideas for inclusion in the next edition: places to visit, eat at or stay in, attractive drives or walks, maybe even unusual interesting shops you know of. Use the card in the middle, the report forms at the end, or just write – no stamp needed: *The Good Britain Guide*, FREEPOST TN1569, Wadhurst, E Sussex TN5 7BR.

To see and do

Essex Family Attraction of the Year

COLCHESTER TL9522 **Colchester Zoo** ▣ (Maldon Rd, Stanway, 2m E of Colchester by B1002) You can't possibly see everything at this exemplary zoo in one visit; the timetable of events and feeding sessions is enormous, and though several things are repeated throughout the day (the elephants in particular have a number of mealtimes you can catch), others do clash, so best to decide as soon as you arrive which things you'd most like to watch. One of the country's most satisfying animal collections, it also stands out in the value for money stakes: even extra activities such as face-painting and brass-rubbing are included in the price. Over 200 rare and endangered species live in enclosures as close to their natural environment as possible — several splendidly improved in recent years, with the cheetahs, penguins, chimps and tigers among those finding themselves in smart new homes. It's not the sort of place to rest on its laurels and much more work is under way: they're hoping to add warthogs and flamingos over the next few months, and they've planted 25,000 new trees around the gardens and grounds. Several good play areas (our favourite is the Kalahari Capers under-cover complex), and a new activity centre with changing animal-related or Native American crafts. One enclosure has shire horses, pigs, rabbits and other tame animals for children to get close to. During the summer holidays they might add Punch and Judy and magic shows, and there are themed activities around Hallowe'en and Christmas. The zoo is particularly good on cats and primates, so note they don't do the big cat feed on Fridays. Meals, snacks, shops, indoor and outdoor picnic areas, mostly disabled access (though there are some steep bits; they do a leaflet marking the easier routes); cl 25 Dec; (01206) 330253; £8.50 (£5.50 children 3–13). You can save up to £1.75 off the normal adult price by booking more than 48 hours in advance on their website, www.colchester-zoo.co.uk; the tickets stay valid for two years.

ABRIDGE TQ4897
Crowther Nurseries (Ongar Rd) Working garden with decorative shrub beds, flower borders, a vegetable plot, greenhouses and over 400 varieties of clematis; also pets' corner inc sheep, goats, a donkey, and a Lego corner to keep children occupied. Meals, snacks, plant sales, disabled access; cl 2 wks over Christmas; (01708) 688581; free.
BATTLESBRIDGE TQ7894
Attractive village, with popular antiques and crafts centre, walks to head of Crouch estuary, and a good pub.
BILLERICAY TQ6991
Barleylands Farm Museum & Visitor Centre ▣ (A129 SE) Expanding series of attractions, from farm animals and rural life displays to working glassworks, craft studios and miniature railway (summer Sun only). Meals, snacks, shop, disabled access; cl Nov–Feb; (01268) 282090; £3.25. Discount voucher not valid for special

events. The nearby Duke of York (South Green) has decent food.
BLACKWATER ESTUARY TL9610
Vast skies, with boats and bird life punctuating the flat sea and landscapes; the pick of local walks include paths along the dykes from Tollesbury, and the one we describe from Bradwell-on-Sea. The Chequers at Goldhanger is another good starting point. Like other parts of this low-lying much indented coast, the immediate hinterland is generally too dull to make circular walks worthwhile — usually best to come back the way you went.
BOCKING TL7623
Windmills As well as the one here in Churchstreet, good examples can be found in Aythorpe Roding TL5815, and Mountnessing TQ6397.
BRADWELL-ON-SEA TL9907
Worth the long drive for the sense of being right out on the edge of things —

the timeless emptiness if anything exaggerated by distant views of vast industrial installations (there are free tours of the nuclear power station; cl Nov–Feb; (01621) 873395). The walk E down the old Roman rd across the marshes takes you to a little restored **Saxon chapel** of St Peter right on the sea wall, the scene of an annual pilgrimage in July. The Green Man is a good traditional pub.

BRAINTREE TL7622

Working Silk Museum 🖼 (South St) Silk production demonstrated from start to finish, in a well restored old mill building; the hand looms they use are over 150 years old. Shop, disabled access; cl 12.30–1.30pm, wknds, bank hols, and Christmas–New Year; (01376) 553393; £3.30. The Green Dragon just S at Youngs End has good food.

BURNHAM-ON-CROUCH TQ9595

Attractively old-fashioned yachting station, lively in summer (packed around the Aug bank hol for its regatta), but nice in winter too with rigging clacking forlornly against the masts of those yachts left to ride at anchor. There are pleasant walks along the banks of the River Crouch. The White Harte on the quay is good for lunch, and there is a decent little craft centre (where they filmed some episodes of *Lovejoy*) at Blake End, a little W on the A120.

Mangapps Farm Railway Museum (B1021 towards Southminster) Friendly and growing collection of vintage rolling stock and railway memorabilia. They have a station formed from railway buildings from sites all over East Anglia and steam rides along 1¾ miles of track. Mostly under cover, snacks, shop, limited disabled access; open pm wknds, daily in Aug and Easter school hols – best to ring for winter opening; (01621) 784898; £4 (£1 extra when the steam trains are running – usually Sun). Further along, The Limes is a decent **farm shop**, with nature trails and pick-your-own.

CASTLE HEDINGHAM TL7736

The town, which has some attractive buildings, is named for the Norman **castle** which dominates it, the

magnificent four-storey keep towering above the surrounding trees. Exceptionally well preserved, it still has its roof, banqueting hall and minstrels' gallery. Teas, shop; cl Oct–Easter; (01787) 460261; *£4. The **church** has grand Norman masonry and interestingly carved choir seats. There's a good working pottery in St James St, and the Bell is good for lunch. The B1058 towards Sudbury, then left through Gestingthorpe and the Belchamps is a pleasant excursion.

Colne Valley Railway & Museum (A1017 N) Lovingly restored Victorian railway buildings with collection of vintage engines and carriages; short steam-train trips Sun pm mid-Mar to mid-Oct, and Weds and Thurs pm in hols; diesel rides Tues, Fri and Sat pm in hols – best to ring for timetable. Admission price now includes entry to rare breeds farm park. Meals on Pullman coaches, snacks, shop, limited disabled access; cl 23 Dec–Feb; (01787) 461174; £6, £3 when trains not running.

CHAPPEL TL8927

The prettily sited Swan has good food, in sight of the Chappel Viaduct (reputedly the biggest brick structure in Europe), and there's a decent **railway museum** 🖼 – maybe rides on a short demonstration line – best to ring for timetable. Wknd snacks, shop, disabled access; cl 25–26 Dec; (01206) 242524; £6 (£3 non-steam days).

CHELMSFORD TL7007

A big busy city with little for visitors, but its 15th-c **cathedral**, consecrated as such only in 1914, has particularly harmonious Perpendicular architecture.

CLACTON TM1714

Roomy family seaside resort, with long stretches of gently shelving sandy beach and all the usual amusements. The pier has an aquarium, reptile house and various rides (cl winter); and watching the fishing at its end has a curiously mesmerising charm. The Robin Hood (London Rd) is the best family dining pub in the area.

COGGESHALL TL8422

Attractive small town with a good few antiques shops, and a working **pottery**. The Woolpack out by the church is a magnificent timbered building.

Grange Barn (Grange Hill; B1024 S edge) 12th-c, the oldest surviving timber-framed barn in Europe, originally part of a Cistercian monastery. Disabled access; hours as Paycocke's; (01376) 562226; £1.60, or joint ticket with Paycocke's £3; NT.

Marks Hall (B1024 N) Gradually being restored, this estate is recommended by readers for an attractive and undemanding stroll. There's a massive 13th-c oak and a developing arboretum, and work is under way on re-creating a 17th-c walled garden. Meals, snacks, shop, disabled access; cl Mon, and wkdys Nov–Apr; (01376) 563796; £3 per car.

Paycocke's (West St) A fine timber-framed medieval merchant's home with unusual panelling and carvings, and pretty garden behind. Open pm Tues, Thurs, Sun and bank hols Apr–mid-Oct; (01376) 561305; £2 (joint ticket with Grange Barn £3); NT. The Fleece next door has decent food.

COLCHESTER TL9925

Britain's oldest recorded town, the capital of Roman Britain. You can trace the Roman wall (the Hole in the Wall, Balkerne Gdns, is a decent pub built into the one surviving fragmentary gatehouse). The High St has handsome buildings, some extravagantly timbered, and plenty more historical buildings inc **St Botolph's**, the oldest Augustinian priory in the country; readers have enjoyed the contemporary art gallery at No 74. Town tours leave the Tourist Information Centre (Queen St) at 11am (Easter–Sept; £2.50). The Rose & Crown (East St) is popular for lunch, and the Crown (Lexden Rd) has good food and a pretty garden.

Bourne Mill (just off B1025 S) Delightfully quaint restored watermill by pretty millpond, worth a look from the outside even when it's not open. Open pm Sun and Mon bank hol wknds, plus pm Sun and Tues Jun–Aug; (01206) 572422; £2; NT.

Colchester Castle Museum 🏛 (Castle Park, off High St) Ideal for families, they let you try on Roman togas and helmets, or touch 2,000-year-old pottery excavated nearby; also splendid collection of Roman relics from jewellery to military tombstones.

The castle itself has the biggest Norman keep in Europe, and stands on the site of a colossal Roman temple (you can still see the vaults). They've made a valiant attempt to bring grisly moments in its history to life: you can hear a dramatisation of one of the forced confessions of the suspect witches incarcerated here. For £1.25 extra a guided castle tour takes you up on the roof as well to the vaults and chapel. Good shop, mostly disabled access (to castle museum but not to vaults or castle roof); cl Sun am; (01206) 282931; £3.80.

Colchester Zoo See *separate family panel on p. 216.*

Hollytrees Museum (High St) When it reopens in July following lottery-funded improvements, this Georgian town house will include new displays on its history and famous local figures, as well as its existing collection of toys, costumes and curios from the last two centuries. Shop, improved disabled access; cl 12–1pm, all Mon and Sun; (01206) 282940; free.

Natural History Museum (All Saints church, High St) Lots of hands-on displays, with an emphasis on man's impact on the environment. Shop, disabled access; (01206) 282941; free.

Rollerworld (Eastgates) Children like this place, the only international-standard roller-skating rink in Britain; evenings only during the week (also pms in school hols), cl Mon; (01206) 868868; from £3.80; also Quasar and ten-pin bowling.

Tymperleys Clock Museum (Trinity St) A particularly unusual selection in a lovely 15th-c house; there's something very special about coming here and hearing all the ticking; also reconstructed Tudor herb garden. Shop, disabled access; cl over Christmas; (01206) 282931; free.

COPFORD TL9222

Copford church Worth a visit, particularly for its well restored 12th-c wall paintings.

CRESSING TL7918

Cressing Temple (Witham Rd) Medieval barns with exhibitions on medieval husbandry, surrounded by a 16th-c style garden. Snacks, shop, disabled access; cl Sat and all

Nov–Easter; (01376) 584903; £3.
DEDHAM TM0533
Several fine old buildings, especially the
15th-c flint **church**, its pinnacled tower
familiar from so many Constable
paintings. There's also the school
Constable went to, and good walks
through the protected riverside
meadows to his father's mill at Flatford
(across the river lock, so in Suffolk, and
described in that chapter). The partly
medieval Sun has decent food, and the
handsome Marlborough Head, a wool
merchant's house dating from 1475,
deserves a look. Worries about the
hordes of visitors the Constable
connection attracts have led local
tourist boards to cut down on the
publicity they give the village in their
literature.
Dedham Art & Craft Centre 🖼
(High St) A number of crafts, growing
collection of dolls' houses, stained-glass
workshop and candle-making;
wholefood café; cl 25 Dec, and Mon
Jan–Mar; (01206) 322666; 50p.
Gnome Magic (Ipswich Rd) This
attractive garden extends into woods
where 500 gnomes live; picnic site;
open Apr–Sept; (01206) 231390; £3.
Sir Alfred Munnings Art Museum
(Castle House, Castle Hill) The house
itself is a mix of Tudor and Georgian,
and inside the artist's own furniture
gives a real sense of how it would have
looked when he and his wife lived here.
His paintings are hung throughout the
house, and you can also view his studios
and stroll through the pleasant gardens.
Shop, disabled access to ground floor
only; open pms Sun, Weds and bank hol
Mon Easter–mid-Oct, plus Thurs and
Sat pm in Aug; (01206) 322127; £3.
ELMSTEAD MARKET TM0623
Beth Chatto Gardens A riot of
colour in summer, it's hard to believe
that these attractive gardens were once
four acres of wasteland. Lots of
gardening ideas, and unusual varieties of
plants for sale. Snacks during summer;
cl Sun, bank hols and winter Sats, 2 wks
over Christmas; (01206) 822007; *£3.
Over at Great Bromley the Old Black
Boy has good value food.
EPPING FOREST TQ4197
A magnificent survival, an expansive
tract of ancient hornbeam coppice,

mainly tucked between the M25 and
outer London. There are miles of leafy
walks (and rides – you can hire horses
locally), with some rough grazing and
occasional distant views. There are so
many woodland paths that getting lost is
part of the experience; the long-
distance Forest Way is, however, well
marked. On the W side there's a
pleasant diversion to High Beach, from
where a few field paths lead SW.
FEERING TL8620
Feeringbury Manor 🖼 (Coggeshall
Rd) Fine big riverside garden with
ponds, streams, a little waterwheel, bog
gardens and a range of plants. Disabled
access; open Thurs and Fri May–July;
(01376) 561946; *£2. The Sun towards
Kelvedon has interesting food.
FINCHINGFIELD TL6734
The county's prettiest village, with
charming houses spread generously
around a sloping green that dips to a
stream and pond; just off stands a
pristine-looking small windmill. The Fox
(one of the most attractive buildings) is
useful for lunch. There's a pleasant
easily followed path along the
Finchingfield Brook to nearby Great
Bardfield.
FRINTON-ON-SEA TM2419
A pleasant family seaside resort, with
long stretches of gently shelving sandy
beach; it's a quieter place than its
neighbour Clacton. Beyond, the blowy
open space of The Naze is pleasant for
strolling, especially out of season when
you're likely to have its 150 acres
virtually to yourself.
GREAT BARDFIELD TL6730
Known as the Montmartre of Essex
because of the group of artists who
once lived here, this has several
attractive pargeted houses, a village
green, a church with a rare 14th-c
carved stone screen, and a windmill.
The tiny Cottage Museum (Dunmow
Rd) has a collection of rural bygones;
open wknd pms and bank hols
Apr–Sept.
GREAT LEIGHS TL7217
Great Maize 🖼 (Rochester Farm, 2m
S of Braintree) Every year they try to
outgrow the previous year's crop
labyrinth here; also children's swings
and slides. Open daily mid-July to early
Sept; (01245) 361411; £4.

GREAT SALING TL7025
Saling Hall Gardens 12 acres of tranquil gardens created over the last 50 years. There is a fine walled garden and water features, but the aboretum is the main draw here. Disabled access; open Weds pm May–July; (01371) 850243; £2.50. The White Hart has decent food.

GREAT WALTHAM TL6913
Pleasant village, with an attractive and interesting church.

GREENSTED TL5302
St Andrew's church Tests have established that it was probably built around the time of the Norman Conquest – the oldest wooden church in the world; shop, disabled access. The nearby Green Man at Toot Hill has decent food (and fine wine).

HARLOW TL4611
A New Town, and not perhaps top of most itineraries, but has a couple of surprisingly good museums.
Gibberd Collection Housed on the first floor of the town hall, this surprisingly fine collection of British modern art includes works by Graham Sutherland, Elizabeth Blackadder and John Nash, to name but a few. Some disabled access; open wkdys; (01279) 446763; free.
Gibberd Garden (Marsh Lane, Gilden Way) The master planner of Harlow New Town designed these gardens in the late 1950s and continued to develop them until his death in 1984. Planned as a series of individual 'rooms', the glades, groves, pools and alleys provide settings for sculpture, architectural salvage, a gazebo and even a moated castle. Snacks, disabled access – there are plans for a shop; open wknd pms Easter–Sept but best to check; (01279) 446611; £3.
Harlow Museum (Third Ave) This has an important Roman collection, and a butterfly garden. Shop; cl Sun, Mon and Sat lunchtime; (01279) 454959; free. There are plans to combine the exhibits here with the collection of bicycles at Mark Hall (Muskham Rd).
Mark Hall (Muskham Rd) Reopening, they hope, near the end of the year as the new Harlow Museum, with a greater emphasis on local history (see details above). Meanwhile the Tudor herb garden and three walled gardens remain

open Mon–Fri; disabled access; free.
HARWICH TM2430
The Redoubt here is a circular fort built in 1808 in case of invasion by Napoleon, with three small museums. Shop; cl Sept–Apr; (01255) 503429. Harwich's two lighthouses both have small museums, one a **maritime museum** (times as above; 50p), the other a collection of vintage radios and TVs (times as above; £1). Also a little lifeboat museum (times as above, 50p), and ferry rides. From the A120 W there's an unusual sight for this part of Essex – a tall narrow **windmill** (actually an interloper, as it was brought from Suffolk).

HATFIELD FOREST TL5320
(just S of Stansted Airport) An unexpected survivor, ancient mainly hornbeam woodland, not on quite the same scale as Epping Forest but still extensive enough, with a nature trail and boating lake.

HULLBRIDGE TQ8193
Jakapeni Rare Breeds Farm Small rare breeds park, specialising in pigs and sheep; you can fish on the lake (around £3 a day). Snacks, shop, disabled access; open Sun and bank hols Easter–Oct, but best to check times and prices; (01702) 232394; £1.75. The Bull nearby at Hockley has decent food, and is handy for walks in Hockley Woods.

INGATESTONE TQ6598
Ingatestone Hall 🔢 Interesting old house, nothing too remarkable but enthusiastic tours by the family that live here, and lovely grounds. Teas, shop; open pm wknds, bank hols and Weds–Fri in school hols Easter–beginning Sept; (01277) 353010; £3.50. The Cricketers Arms out at Mill Green is a handy food pub.

KELVEDON HATCH TQ5599
Secret Nuclear Bunker 🔢 (off A128) Who'd have thought that a three-storey Cold War underground complex lay beneath this innocuous 1950s bungalow? Knowledgeable tours take you through all parts of this clinically self-sufficient little world, and are done with real relish, but you can't help feeling relieved when you're back in the surrounding woodland. Wknd meals, snacks, shop; cl wkdys Oct–Mar; (01277) 364883; *£5. The Black Horse

in Pilgrims Hatch is a good handy dining pub.

LAMARSH TL8836
Paradise Centre 🖼 (Twinstead Rd) Fascinating for gardeners, with a very wide variety of unusual plants beautifully laid out and for sale, particularly woodland ones; also miniature goats, bantams and play area. Open wknds and bank hols Easter–Oct, or by appointment; (01787) 269449; *£1.50 (free to customers). The Lion is good for lunch, and the Bures–Henny Street rd is a pretty drive.

LAYER DE LA HAYE TL9517
Abberton Reservoir Wildlife Centre (B1026, Layer de la Haye) Popular wetland stop for wildfowl; observation room and hides, nature trails, and events for families in summer. Snacks, shop, disabled access; cl Mon and 25–26 Dec; (01206) 738172; £1 suggested donation (more for special events). The Donkey & Buskins (B1026) is handy for a meal.

LAYER MARNEY TL9217
Layer Marney Tower 🖼 The mansion here was never completed, but its eight-storey Tudor gatehouse is very impressive – one of the most striking examples of 16th-c architecture in Britain. Around it are formal gardens, a rare breeds farm, medieval barn, farm shop and deer park. Tearoom, shop, disabled access to grounds; cl am, all day Sat, and mid-Oct–Mar; (01206) 330784; £3.50.

LITTLE BADDOW TL7707
Blakes Wood Ancient woodland of hornbeam and chestnut coppice, with lovely bluebells in spring. The Generals Arms is useful for lunch.

LITTLE DUNMOW TL6521
Little Dunmow church Unusually stately for such a relatively small village – it's the surviving part of a priory founded in 1106. The Flitch of Bacon is a good pub.

LITTLE EASTON TL5924
Gardens of Easton Lodge Queen Elizabeth I once owned the 14th-c deer park in which these charming gardens are set. Handed down through generations of the Maynard family who lived in the apparently doomed Easton Lodge (both the original and its Victorian predecessor were destroyed

by fires), they were redeveloped by the current owners in the mid-1990s, and are a nice reflection of changing tastes in gardening. Harold Peto possibly left the biggest impression in the early 1900s, with his sunken Italian garden, unique courtyard and adults' tree-house (now a ruin). They're currently developing a flower bed inc every plant mentioned in Shakespeare's works. Snacks (maybe cream teas with morris men in summer), shop, disabled access (can be tricky in wet weather); open Fri–Sun pms Feb–Oct; (01371) 876979; *£3.80.

Little Easton Manor Pleasant summer gardens (a shame they're not open on the same day as Easton Lodge's); snacks, shop, disabled access; open Thurs pm Jun–Sept; (01371) 872857; *£2. Little Easton church just beside the manor is also worth a visit. Great Easton nearby is attractive, good for strolling through.

LITTLE MAPLESTEAD TL8234
Little Maplestead church Very different from most in the area – an unusual round building modelled on the Holy Sepulchre in Jerusalem.

MALDON TL8506
The **Maeldune Centre** (junction Market Hill/High St) houses an ambitious tapestry commemorating the 1,000th anniversary of the crucial Battle of Maldon; shop, (01621) 851628; £1.50. The **Millennium Gardens** are named for the same event, and re-create what a garden might have looked like at the time of the battle. Also a **church** with an unusual triangular tower, some decent bits, a couple of small museums, and a riverside stroll past the golf course to the pretty weir by Beeleigh Abbey.

Hythe Quay Full of life, and the best chance to see one of the classic Thames barges with its ox-blood sails in action.

MERSEA ISLAND TM0012
Linked to the mainland by a little causeway, which can get covered by the tide; much of its coast is a National Nature Reserve for its shore life, and there's a bracing coastal walk from East Mersea along the sea dyke overlooking the Colne estuary. It does feel very much an island, and away from the extended village of West Mersea,

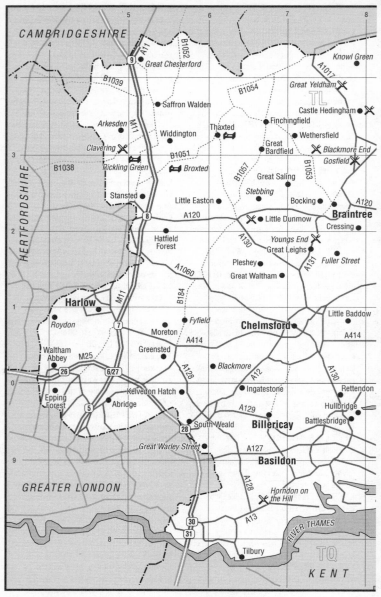

popular for retirement homes, there are few people about out of season (in summer the caravan parks bring in lots of families). The Willow Lodge has good food; the Blackwater and Fox are good value too.

MISTLEY TM1031

Environmental & Animal Centre

(New Rd) Very friendly animal rescue centre: Ping and Pong the Vietnamese pot-bellied pigs may come to greet you as you go in. Snacks (not

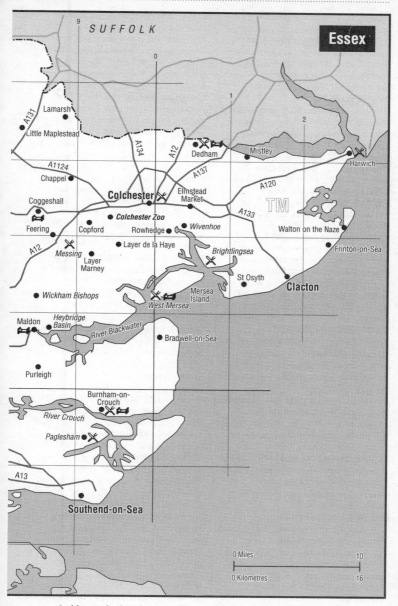

summer Mons, wknds only in winter), shop, disabled access; (01206) 396483; £2.50. The village has the remains of a Robert Adam church (known locally as the Mistley Towers). If you come by train, don't miss the splendid station

buffet at Manningtree.
Essex Secret Bunker (B1352) Much of its original equipment has been returned by the government and other groups, so the operations centre at this nuclear war command centre looks

especially authentic. Odd seeing something so contemporary consigned to history, especially when similar establishments are still in operation. Snacks, shop, disabled access; cl end Dec–beginning Jan and wkdys Nov–Mar; (01206) 392271; *£4.95.

MORETON TL5306
This is an attractive village, and helpfully the pubs here usually have a leaflet detailing an interesting walk through and around it.

PLESHEY TL6614
This attractive village has a ruined castle, charming churchyard, country walks – and a good pub.

PURLEIGH TL8302
New Hall Vineyards Covering 85 acres, this 30-year-old vineyard is reputedly the largest in East Anglia; free tastings, guided group tours (by arrangement). They host an annual English wine festival (craft fair, live music, art exhibitions) on the wknd before Aug bank hol. Shop, disabled access; cl wknd pms; (01621) 828343; free.

RETTENDON TQ7899
RHS Garden (Hyde Hall) Eight acres of year-round hillside colour, with woodland garden, big rose garden, ornamental ponds, shrubs, trees, and national collections of malus and viburnum. Meals and snacks in thatched barn, plant sales, limited disabled access; cl Nov–Mar; (01245) 400256; £3. The Barge at Battlesbridge is quite handy for lunch.

RIVER CROUCH WALKS TQ8596
The Ferry Boat Inn down near the River Crouch at the end of the lane through North Fambridge is a good base for lonely waterside walks.

ROWHEDGE TM0221
The village itself is well worth a visit; and nearby is a nature reserve among former gravel workings at Fingringhoe, where the Whalebone (beside the county's oldest oak) has good food. There's a pedestrian ferry to Wivenhoe.

SAFFRON WALDEN TL5438
The finest small town in the region, with prime examples of warmly colour-washed pargeting throughout. Walking around looking at buildings, you'll find it difficult to avoid being tempted into one of the many antiques shops (or David Prue, the fine cabinet-maker in Radwinter Rd; cl Suns and some Sats). The grand airy **church** has a magnificent spire, the very ruined **castle** up on a grassy mound is worth prowling around, and children will enjoy the maze on the Common. The Crown just N at Little Walden is nice for lunch. The town has a goodish network of tracks for walks around it, extending into the parkland of nearby Audley End House. Longer rambles can take in Newport, where the houses have characteristic pargeted plaster walls, and Wendens Ambo. The B184 to Chipping Ongar is a pleasant country drive; about 4m along, Grace's Farm Shop at Wimbish is good, with **pick-your-own** in summer. Another enjoyable drive is the B1053 to Braintree.

Audley End House (B1383, 1m W) Spectacular Jacobean mansion and former Royal palace remodelled by Robert Adam, serenely surrounded by splendid gardens landscaped by Capability Brown – from the town you can walk straight into the park. Nothing inside can compete with the quite breathtaking façade, but it's not for want of trying – there are around 30 rooms to see, crammed with fine furnishings inc a magnificent dolls' house, and art. Suitably grand concerts and other events in the grounds. Meals, snacks, shop, disabled access to gardens and ground floor; cl Mon (exc bank hols), Tues, and end Oct–Mar; (01799) 522842; £6.50, £4.50 grounds only.

Bridge End Gardens (Bridge St) Pleasant early Victorian gardens spread over 3½ acres, with rose garden, formal Dutch garden, kitchen garden and an atmospheric wilderness leading to a little grotto. You'll need to get a key from the Tourist Information Centre (Market Pl) to explore the yew tree maze. Limited disabled access; cl 25 Dec; free.

Saffron Walden Museum (Museum St) Notable natural history section in the town museum as well as social history and toys and dolls; shop, good disabled access; cl Sun am and bank hols, 24–25 Dec; (01799) 510333; £1.

SOUTH WEALD TQ5992
Attractive village; the Tower Arms is a

decent food pub. **Old Macdonald's farm park** (Weald Rd) Very extensive range of animals, with 30 breeds of sheep alone. Demonstrations, nature trails and craft displays, and plenty of opportunities to stroke the animals. Meals, snacks, shop, disabled access; cl 25 Dec and 1 Jan; (01277) 375177; £2.75. Nearby is a country park with deer enclosure, lakes, woods, and visitor centre.

SOUTHEND-ON-SEA TQ8885
Traditional seaside resort long favoured by East Londoners, with many of the attractions you'd expect to find. Most famous is the pier, the longest in the world, excellent for fishing, with a museum and happily a restored train service – it's a long walk there and back. Like many such resorts, Southend in winter has a special appeal for people who wouldn't like it in summer – seafront shops by the endless promenade looking closed for ever, the sea itself a doleful muddy grey. Readers enjoy the Westcliff part of town, with its decent art gallery (cl 1–2pm; Sun and Mon, free). Summer **boat trips** include occasional runs on a vintage paddle-steamer; (01634) 827648 for dates. There are year-round ferries to Felixstowe.

Cabaret Mechanical Theatre
Tucked away in the heart of the former market buildings, an appealing collection of unique hand-made working automata, operated by the touch of a button or by inserting a coin. Great fun – though several exhibits are quite bizarre, notably the incredible Last Judgement by Paul Spooner. Shop, some disabled access; cl 25–26 Dec; (020) 7379 7961; £1.50.

Central Museum & Planetarium
(Victoria Ave) The only planetarium in the South-East outside London, with a local history museum and a new hands-on discovery centre. Shop; cl Sun, Mon, inc bank hols (planetarium also cl Tues); (01702) 215131; planetarium £2.25, museum and discovery centre free.

Leigh-on-Sea Though attached to Southend, this has a quite distinct character, altogether more intimate, with wood-clad buildings and shrimp boats in the working harbour; Ivy

Osborne's cockle stall here is justly famous, and the Crooked Billet overlooking the water has real old-fashioned character.

Prittlewell Priory Museum (Priory Park, slightly N of centre) 12th-c Cluniac priory in nice grounds, with eclectic collections of local and religious history; shop; cl 1–2pm, all day Sun and Mon; free.

Southend Aquarium (Eastern Esplanade) New owners had just taken over this fun look at underwater life, formerly the Sea Life Centre, as we went to press; highlights include a walk-through tunnel along a reconstructed sea-bed, and shark exhibition. They hope to have finished refurbishments by Mar, for reopening then. Snacks, shop, disabled access; cl 25 Dec; (01702) 462400; £5.25.

Southchurch Hall Museum (Park Lane) An unexpected find, a medieval moated manor house in an attractive park, with period room settings and fun talks on Tudor life; occasional lute demonstrations. Shop, limited disabled access; cl 1–2pm, all day Sun and Mon (and Tues after bank hols), 25 Dec, 1 Jan and Easter; (01702) 467671; free (small charge for talks).

ST OSYTH TM1215
This pretty village is distinguished by the remarkable crenellated flint gateway leading to **St Osyth Priory**. Unfortunately, the lovely buildings and grounds behind are no longer open to the public. The White Hart towards Point Clear has decent food, and not too far away, the beach at Brightlingsea is probably the county's best.

STANSTED TL5125
House on the Hill Museum Adventure Home to what we think is the biggest privately owned toy collection in the world, with over 30,000 toys, games and playthings from Victorian times to the 1970s. Quite a few toy museums attract parents more than children (which might explain why so many have closed over the last couple of years), but this one avoids that by making its very well thought out displays entertaining to look at; lots of them are animated, and it's great fun watching the soldiers, trains and Meccano in action. There are a few

coin-operated slot machines and puppet shows, a new collection of celebrity memorabilia, and a good collectors' shop. All indoors, so good in any weather. Cl 24–26 Dec; (01279) 813237; £3.50 (£2.50 children).

Mountfitchet Castle & 1066 Village Intriguing, an authentically reconstructed Norman castle and village, complete with thatched houses, and deer, sheep, goats and chickens wandering around between them. The castle includes a small chunk of the original, and there are dummies displaying gruesome examples of torture and punishment. Cheerful and enthusiastic rather than particularly sophisticated, it's a good introduction to life a thousand years ago, though you will need to visit on a dry day. Snacks (and space for picnics), shop, some disabled access; cl mid-Nov–mid-Mar; (01279) 813237; £4.50 (£3.50 children). It's under the same management as the toy museum five mins' walk up the hill.

Stansted Mountfitchet windmill The well preserved 18th-c windmill still has much of its original equipment (though isn't working). Shop; open pm first Sun of month Apr–Oct, plus pm every Sun in Aug, and pm bank hol Sun and Mons; *50p. The Cricketers Arms at nearby Rickling Green is good for lunch.

THAXTED TL6131
This engaging small town has a graceful, airy **church** (where Holst was organist) with a tremendous spire, several handsome buildings inc nearby almshouses, a fine **guildhall** (small local museum), and a restored **windmill**. The **Raven Armoury** (B184 towards Dunmow) does hand-forged steel and weaponry. The 15th-c Swan has decent food.

TILBURY TQ6475
Tilbury Fort Well preserved 17th-c fort with unusual double moat; good views of the Thames estuary. The most violent episode in its history was a 1776 cricket match that left three dead. Snacks, shop, some disabled access; cl Mon and Tues Oct–Mar, 24–26 Dec and 1 Jan; (01375) 858489; £2.60. For an extra £1 you can fire a 1943 anti-aircraft gun – irresistible for several children of our acquaintance. There is a

pleasant 3-mile walk along the Thames to **Coalhouse Fort** (off the A1013, Orsett–Stanford-le-Hope; open last Sun of month and bank hols, cl Nov–Feb; £2.50).

WALTHAM ABBEY TL3800
Despite the surrounding housing developments, the centre has some handsome buildings – especially the **Abbey church** with its famous peal of 13 bells (and a museum in the crypt; shop, disabled access to ground floor only; open Tues–Fri Apr–Oct and Mon, Tues, Fri and Sat Oct–Mar). Associated ruins include part of a Norman cloister, and the bridge dates back to the abbey's time.

Epping Forest District Museum (Sun St) Lively holiday activities for children and archeological displays, in two timber-framed old houses. Shop, limited disabled access; cl Weds–Thurs, (Weds, Thurs and Sun Oct–Mar); (01992) 716882; free.

Lee Valley Park Farms 🖼 (B194, 2m N) Takes in Hayes Hill children's farm with plenty of traditional animals, a pet centre and play area, and Holyfield Hall working farm and dairy, with 150 cows milked every afternoon around 3pm and seasonal events like sheep-shearing and harvesting. Meals, snacks, shop, disabled access; (01992) 892781; £3.

WALTON ON THE NAZE TM2623
There's a pleasant walk N from this quiet seaside town, along the coast, round the tip of The Naze – with views of shipping entering and leaving Harwich and Felixstowe – to a **nature reserve** harbouring migrant birds; there is a nature trail here.

WETHERSFIELD TL7131
Boydells Dairy Farm 🖼 Working dairy farm where you may be able to join in milking the goats and cows – or even the sheep. Also working beehive, various other animals, and ice lollies made from their own sheep yoghurt. Snacks, shop, disabled access; open Fri–Sun pm Easter–Sept, plus May half-term and summer hols pm; (01371) 850481; £3.

WIDDINGTON TL5431
Mole Hall Wildlife Park 🖼 Family-run place with a wide variety of animals

around moated manor house. Otters a speciality, but also free-roaming wildfowl, deer paddock and butterfly house. There may be a bouncy castle some days in summer. Summer snacks, shop, some disabled access; park only cl 25 Dec, but butterfly house cl Nov–mid-Mar; (01799) 540400; £4.50 (£3.20 children) – less in winter. **Other attractive villages**, all with decent pubs, include Arkesden TL4834, Blackmore TL6001, Fuller Street TL7416, Fyfield TL5606, Great Chesterford TL5143, Great Warley Street TQ5890, Knowl Green TL7841, Paglesham TQ9293, Roydon TL4109, Stebbing TL6624, Wickham Bishops TL8412, and waterside Heybridge Basin TL8707 and Wivenhoe TM0321.

Where to eat

BLACKMORE END TL7330 **Bull** *(01371) 851037* Comfortable tucked-away dining pub with pretty, cottagey restaurant area, good snacks, excellent meals, and a thoughtful choice of wines; cl Mon exc bank hols; children in restaurant only. £23.70|**£5.95**

BRIGHTLINGSEA TM0816 **Coffee Pot** *Victoria Pl (01206) 305738* Spotless place with very good breakfast, lunch and tea – everything freshly made daily; helpful friendly staff; cl pm, Sun; disabled access. |**£3.55**

BURNHAM-ON-CROUCH TQ9595 **Contented Sole** *80 High St (01621) 782139* Long-standing, family-run evening restaurant (though they do Sun lunch), very popular for consistently good imaginative food with emphasis on fine seafood; popular wine tastings all year; cl Sun pm, 2 wks July; disabled access. £30

CASTLE HEDINGHAM TL7835 **Bell** *St James's St (01787) 460350* Run by the same family for over 30 years, this interesting old coaching inn has a log fire in the beamed lounge bar, a traditionally furnished public bar, no smoking area, enjoyable traditional bar food, and lovely big walled garden behind; disabled access. £17|**£5**

CLAVERING TL4832 **Cricketers** *(01799) 550442* Run by the parents of TV chef Jamie Oliver, this smart comfortably modernised 16th-c dining pub has an L-shaped beamed bar with standing timbers on new brickwork, gleaming copper, dried flowers in big fireplaces, and a wide choice of interesting and elaborate food inc super puddings; pretty bdrms; cl 25–26 Dec; disabled access. £30|**£7**

COLCHESTER TL9925 **Clowns** *61–62 High St (01206) 578631* Huge helpings of good straightforward food in clean spacious restaurant; nice children's menu, too; cl 25–26 Dec; disabled access. £20|**£4.95**

COLCHESTER TL9925 **Warehouse Brasserie** *12 Chapel St N (01206) 765656* Bustling bistro with friendly, relaxed atmosphere, pine settles and chairs, an upper gallery area, prints on warm red walls, real ales, enjoyable, interesting food, and decent wines; cl Sun, last Mon of month, 20 Aug–3 Sept, 24 Dec–7 Jan (but open Sat pm); disabled access. £25/£2 courses £8.95

DEDHAM TM0533 **Millstream** *Riverside Cottage (01206) 322066* Little no smoking riverside restaurant with a homely relaxed atmosphere and a good choice of popular food; also, morning coffee and cream teas; cl winter Mon and Tues; children over 8 in evening. £23|**£6**

GOSFIELD TL7829 **Green Man** *The Street (01787) 472746* Smart dining pub with a relaxed chatty atmosphere, two little bars and no smoking dining room, enjoyable food inc marvellous lunchtime cold buffet and delicious puddings, well kept real ales and decent wines, many by the glass; no food Sun pm; partial disabled access. £20|**£7**

GREAT YELDHAM TL7637 **White Hart** *Poole St (01787) 237250* Striking black and white timbered building with beams, oak panelling, and stone or wooden floors, ambitious food cooked by the new landlord which can be eaten in bar or restaurant, a remarkable range of wines inc lots by the glass, real ales; best to book; seats in the attractive garden. £19.50|**£6.95**

HARWICH TM2532 **Pier at Harwich** *The Quay (01255) 241212* Attractive restaurant overlooking the Stour and Orwell estuaries, with particularly good fresh fish dishes (and lobsters from their salt-water tanks); more informal, brightly decorated Ha'penny Pier downstairs, and first-floor dining room with more ambitious dishes; thoughtful choice of wines; cl 24–26 Dec pm. £30|**£7.50**

HORNDON ON THE HILL TQ6783 **Bell** *(01375) 673154* Flower-decked medieval inn with welcoming licensees, open-plan beamed bar with polished oak floorboards and flagstones, carefully prepared imaginative food that changes twice daily, five real ales, good choice of wines; restaurant cl 25–26 Dec pm. £26|**£5.95**

LITTLE DUNMOW TL6521 **Flitch of Bacon** *(01371) 820323* Friendly pub with small, attractively furnished, timbered bar, decent reasonably priced food, several wines by the glass, and real ales; comfortable bdrms; children away from bar area; disabled access. £15.70|**£5.50**

MESSING TL8918 **Crispin's** *The Street (01621) 815868* Friendly Elizabethan restaurant with open fire in beamed lounge, candles on the walls and tables, good food inc fish and vegetarian choices, monthly themed evenings, a growing wine list, helpful service, and quiet back garden; bdrms; cl Sun pm and Mon. £25

PAGLESHAM TQ9492 **Plough & Sail** *East End (01702) 258242* Beautifully kept white weatherboarded 17th-c dining pub with pine tables and seats under its rather low beams, lots of brasses and pictures, big log fires, and pretty flower arrangements; consistently good imaginative food, well kept real ales, decent house wines, friendly attentive staff, and tables in an attractive neatly kept garden with an aviary. £19.20|**£5.95**

WEST MERSEA TM0012 **Willow Lodge** *108 Coast Rd (01206) 383568* Large busy restaurant with wide range of very good food inc lots of fresh fish; cl Sun pm, Mon; well behaved children welcome; disabled access. £23|**£6**

YOUNG'S END TL7319 **Green Dragon** *London Rd (01245) 361030* Well run dining pub with attractive understated barn theme in no smoking restaurant area, extensive range of very good interesting bar food, well kept real ales, and plenty of seats in back garden. £20|**£5.75**

Special thanks to Dr J Howard-Griffin

GLOUCESTERSHIRE

Perfect Cotswold countryside, some of the prettiest villages in Britain, and a good mix of places to visit, from farm parks to elegant gardens

Ideal for a relaxing short break, Gloucestershire is particularly strong on quietly rewarding places for adults – including lovely places to stay and eat in. But if you know where to look, there are good family days out, too.

While most children's attractions here revolve around animals, this year's pick of the bunch is the recently refurbished National Waterways Museum in Gloucester's docks, offering lots of opportunities for hands-on fun with a good balance of enthusiastically presented history thrown in too. The Museum of Advertising & Packaging, also part of the lively waterfront development, might provide a comforting dose of nostalgia to parents (and indeed grandparents).

The county caters well for bird-lovers, with the excellent Wildfowl & Wetlands Trust at Slimbridge adding several new attractions this year including a children's discovery centre, and Newent's National Birds of Prey Centre housing one of Britain's leading collections in the country.

Elsewhere there's a chance to feed farmyard animals at Butts Farm in South Cerney, and Oldown County Park at Tockington (good play areas) and Kineton's Cotswold Farm Park both offer excellent value entertainment. Folly Farm at Bourton-on-the-Water is an unusual spot for a family picnic.

When people think of Gloucestershire, they usually think 'Cotswolds', with their broad landscapes and charming stone-built villages. The one snag is that the Cotswolds tend to be expensive – particularly in the north. In the summer they do attract a great many visitors, though even then you can find delightful villages that have escaped the crowds – especially in the south.

The county's other speciality is its fine range of handsome stone-built Cotswold towns of real individuality. Chipping Campden, Cirencester, Northleach, Painswick and Stow-on-the-Wold all bulge with sightseeing possibilities – and antiques shops; Tewkesbury too is attractive.

Cheltenham still has a considerable degree of Regency elegance – Holst's Birthplace Museum and the Pittville Pump Room are just two examples. It's a useful base for exploring the area; the tourism office does a good leaflet detailing how to get to most Cotswold attractions by public transport.

Favourite houses to visit include Snowshill Manor and its extraordinary bric-a-brac, beautiful Stanway House, Sudeley Castle near Winchcombe (new exhibitions), the Roman villa at Yanworth, and the never-finished Gothic mansion at Nympsfield. The county also boasts some unforgettable gardens and parks, with Kiftsgate Court near Mickleton, the magnificent arboretums at Westonbirt and Batsford near Moreton-in-Marsh, and, in late May especially, the gardens of Lydney Park, particularly outstanding. The Nature in Art collection at Twigworth is very unusual.

There are two or three intriguing natural phenomena to be seen here as well. The uninitiated will marvel at the Severn Bore, Symonds Yat Rock is a spectacular landmark (and a favourite spot of peregrine falcons), and the labyrinthine caves at Clearwell are good for an adventure.

The Cotswolds are great for cyclists. Extended walks over the Cotswold plateau are not always rewarding, with unchanging views of arable fields often the rule; however, there are plenty of really enjoyable walks through choice scenery, with the long-distance Cotswold Way between Chipping Campden and Bath tracing through much of the best. Most TICs should also keep copies of the new Severn Way guide, detailing a walk from Mid-Wales to Bristol (£6.95).

Away from the Cotswolds, some less well known parts are delightful (and generally cheaper): the tortuously steep hills and valleys around Stroud, the quiet water-meadows of the upper Thames, the unspoilt orchard and farming countryside around the Severn Valley (so few river crossings that the little villages down by the W bank, with few people passing through, have a very secluded and unchanging feel). The Forest of Dean's hilly woodland is punctuated with all sorts of interesting features, and is flanked by a spectacular stretch of the Wye Valley.

Where to stay

ASHLEWORTH SO8125 **Ashleworth Court** *Ashleworth, Gloucester, Gloucestershire GL19 4JA (01452) 700241* **£44***; 3 rms, shared bthrms. Set by a small elegant church and NT tithe barn, this striking ancient house is part of a working farm and has a homely kitchen with an Aga, a comfortable sitting room, enjoyable breakfasts served in what was originally part of the Great Hall, and chickens in the back garden; two good pubs in the village; cl Christmas

BERKELEY ST6899 **Old Schoolhouse Hotel** *Canonbury St, Berkeley, Gloucestershire GL13 9BG (01453) 811711* **£65***; 8 rms. Carefully converted former schoolhouse and chapel with fine views and surrounded by the grounds of Berkeley Castle; friendly relaxed atmosphere, log fire in comfortable lounge, imaginative food in popular restaurant, and seats on the terrace; disabled access

BIBURY SP1106 **Bibury Court** *Bibury, Cirencester, Gloucestershire GL7 5NT (01285) 740337* **£123.90**, plus special breaks; 19 individual rms. Lovely peaceful mansion dating from Tudor times and set in beautiful gardens, with an informal friendly atmosphere, panelled rooms, antiques, huge log fires, conservatory, a fine choice of breakfasts, and good interesting food; cl Christmas and New Year

BIBURY SP1106 **Swan** *Bibury, Cirencester, Gloucestershire GL7 5NW (01285) 740695* **£175***, plus special breaks; 18 very pretty individually decorated rms. Handsome creeper-covered hotel on the River Coln, with private fishing and attractive formal gardens; lovely flowers and log fires in carefully furnished comfortable lounges, a cosy no smoking parlour, good food in opulent dining room, nice breakfasts, and attentive staff; disabled access

BLEDINGTON SP2422 **Kings Head** *The Green, Bledington, Chipping Norton, Oxfordshire OX7 6XQ (01608) 658365* **£65***; 12 rms (2 over the kitchen can be noisy). Very nicely placed 15th-c Cotswold inn by duck-filled stream; spotless bar full of ancient beams and appropriate furnishings, log fire in inglenook, a nice sitting room with comfortable sofas and magazines, excellent imaginative food (inc enjoyable breakfasts), several real ales, an extensive wine list with 11 by the glass, lots of malt whiskies, a partly no smoking restaurant, and friendly service; cl 24–25

Dec; limited disabled access

BUCKLAND SP0835 **Buckland Manor** *Buckland, Broadway, Worcestershire WR12 7LY (01386) 852626* **£215***, plus special breaks; 13 sumptuous rms. Really lovely 13th-c building in 10 acres of beautifully kept gardens, comfortable lounges with magnificent oak panelling, flowers and antiques, and elegant restaurant with fine food using home-grown produce; outdoor swimming pool, riding, tennis, croquet, putting; children over 12

CHARINGWORTH SP1939 **Charingworth Manor** *Charingworth, Chipping Campden, Gloucestershire GL55 6NS (01386) 593555* **£150**, plus special breaks; 26 lovely rms with thoughtful extras. Early 14th-c manor with Jacobean additions set in fine grounds, with mullioned windows, antiques, and log fires and heavy oak beams in relaxing sitting room; good modern cooking in charming restaurant, excellent breakfasts, friendly staff, and leisure spa with indoor swimming pool, gym, and all-weather tennis court

CHELTENHAM SO9523 **Hotel on the Park** *Evesham Rd, Cheltenham, Gloucestershire GL52 2AH (01242) 518898* **£123**, plus special breaks; 12 lovely rms. Warmly welcoming and handsome Regency house with elegantly furnished drawing room and dining room, pretty flowers and antiques, and imaginative food in stylish restaurant – good breakfasts, too; children over 8

CHELTENHAM SO9421 **Lypiatt House** *Lypiatt Rd, Cheltenham, Gloucestershire GL50 2QW (01242) 224994* **£65**, plus wknd breaks; 10 attractive rms. Carefully restored Victorian house in its own grounds, with an open fire, books and plants in light, comfortable drawing room, little conservatory bar, and friendly personal service

CHELTENHAM SO9421 **Wyastone Hotel** *Parabola Rd, Montpellier, Cheltenham, Gloucestershire GL50 3BG (01242) 245549* **£75**, plus special breaks; 13 pretty rms. Quietly set Victorian house with a panelled bar and cosy pink-coloured lounge, plenty of period features, friendly owners, enjoyable breakfasts, and traditional French evening meals; charming little terraced garden; no meals over Christmas period

CHIPPING CAMPDEN SP1539 **Badgers Hall** *High St, Chipping Campden, Gloucestershire GL55 6HB (01386) 840839* **£55**; 3 beamed rms. Opposite the historic market hall, this fine old stone house has friendly helpful owners, a relaxed atmosphere, particularly good breakfasts plus a thriving tea shop with home-made lunches and afternoon teas, and a display of local artists' work for sale; no smoking; plenty of pubs and restaurants nearby for evening meals; cl Christmas and New Year; children over 10

CHIPPING CAMPDEN SP1539 **Eight Bells** *Church St, Chipping Campden, Gloucestershire GL55 6JG (01386) 840371* **£60**; 6 rms. Neatly restored heavy-beamed 14th-c pub by church; three log fires, interesting food with fresh local produce, friendly staff, decent wines and beers, a new terrace, and pleasant courtyard; cl 25 Dec; disabled access

CLAPTON SP1617 **Clapton Manor** *Clapton, Cheltenham, Gloucestershire GL54 2LG (01451) 810202* **£70**; 2 charming rms. Fine 16th-c Cotswold stone house in lovely interestingly planted gardens with marvellous views across the Windrush Valley; large inglenook fireplaces, heavy beams, mullioned windows, antiques, and a relaxed, informal family atmosphere; log fire and TV in residents' sitting room, and good breakfasts with home-made jams and their own eggs served in the dining room or on the terrace; no smoking; several restaurants and pubs nearby for dinner; cl Christmas

CLEARWELL SO5708 **Tudor Farmhouse** *Clearwell, Coleford, Gloucestershire GL16 8JS (01594) 833046* **£65**, plus special breaks; 21 cottagey rms. Carefully restored Tudor farmhouse and stone cottages with landscaped gardens and surrounding fields; lots of beams, sloping floors and oak doors, delicious food in candlelit restaurant, and friendly staff; cl 23 Dec–30 Jan; disabled access

CLEARWELL SO5708 **Wyndham Arms** *The Cross, Clearwell, Coleford, Gloucestershire GL16 8JT (01594) 833666* **£80***, plus special winter and wknd breaks; 18 well equipped rms and luxury penthouse suite. Smart and neatly kept old country inn with comfortable beamed bar, open fire, particularly good food (much home-grown), helpful service, and friendly dogs – you stay free on Sun if you eat in the restaurant; good disabled access

CORSE LAWN SO8330 **Corse Lawn House** *Corse Lawn, Gloucester GL19 4LZ (01452) 780771* **£120**, plus special breaks; 19 pretty, individually furnished rms. Magnificent Queen Anne building with comfortable and attractive day rooms, a distinguished restaurant with imaginative food and excellent wines (there's a less pricey bistro-style operation too), warmly friendly staff, a relaxed atmosphere, and an indoor and outdoor swimming pool, tennis court, croquet, and horses in 12 acres of surrounding gardens and fields; dogs welcome; cl 24–26 Dec; disabled access

GREAT RISSINGTON SP1917 **Lamb** *Great Rissington, Cheltenham, Gloucestershire GL54 2LP (01451) 820388* **£65**, plus special breaks; 14 pretty rms – several are suites with own lounge. Civilised 17th-c inn with a bustling and friendly atmosphere and nice mix of customers in the cosy two-roomed bar, some interesting things to look at, residents' lounge with log fire, enjoyable bar food and a more extensive choice in no smoking restaurant, seats in the sheltered hillside garden, and good nearby walks; cl 25–26 Dec; dogs by prior arrangement

GREET SP0230 **Manor Farm** *Market Lane, Greet, Cheltenham, Gloucestershire GL54 5BJ (01242) 602423* **£50***; 3 rms. Carefully restored 16th-c manor house on mixed farm, with nice breakfasts, fine views, a big garden with croquet, and caravan site; also, self-catering cottages; cl Christmas

HAZLETON SP0818 **Windrush House** *Hazleton, Cheltenham, Gloucestershire GL54 4EB (01451) 860364* **£49***; 4 rms, 2 with own bthrm. Warmly friendly and neatly kept no smoking guest house, with exceptionally good imaginative food, lovely breakfasts, log fire, and traditional furnishings; cl mid-Dec to mid-Feb; no children, no dogs

KINETON SP0926 **Halfway House** *Kineton, Guiting Power, Cheltenham, Gloucestershire GL54 5UG (01451) 850344* **£50**; 4 rms. Friendly little stone pub with a good mix of customers, a warm fire, farm tools and pictures in the unpretentious bar, tasty food (served all day at wknds), and well kept real ales; large garden

LEONARD STANLEY SO8003 **Grey Cottage** *Leonard Stanley, Stonehouse, Gloucestershire GL10 3LU (01453) 822515* **£60***, plus special breaks; 3 rms overlooking garden or countryside with chocolates, fruit and biscuits. Carefully restored 170-year-old cottage with a pretty garden, really kind and thoughtful owners who cosset you, interesting furnishings and fresh flowers, comfortable sitting room, marvellous breakfasts, and enjoyable evening meals by prior arrangement

LITTLE BARRINGTON SP1913 **Inn For All Seasons** *Little Barrington, Burford, Oxfordshire OX18 4TN (01451) 844324* **£85**; 10 rms. Handsome old inn with low beams, stripped stone and flagstones, a big log fire, old prints, particularly good fresh fish and other food, well kept real ales and wines, lots of malt whiskies, and a pleasant garden surrounded by lots of walks; children over 10

LITTLE RISSINGTON SP1919 **Touchstone** *Little Rissington, Cheltenham, Gloucestershire GL54 2ND (01451) 822481* **£36***; 3 rms with thoughtful extras. Attractive traditional Cotswold stone house with very friendly owners, good breakfasts in dining room with doors on to terrace, and lots of nearby walks; no children; cl Jan–Feb

LOWER SLAUGHTER SP1522 **Lower Slaughter Manor** *Lower Slaughter, Cheltenham, Gloucestershire GL54 2HP (01451) 820456* **£175**; 16 luxurious rms with thoughtful extras. Grand 17th-c manor house with four acres of neatly kept grounds, a 15th-c dovecot, all-weather tennis court, croquet, and indoor pool; lovely flower arrangements, log fires, fine plaster ceilings, antiques and paintings, excellent modern cooking and award-winning wines in the elegant restaurant, and attentive welcoming staff; children over 8; disabled access

LOWER SWELL SP1725 **Old Farmhouse Hotel** *Lower Swell, Cheltenham,*

Gloucestershire GL54 1LF (01451) 830232 **£70***, plus special breaks; 12 rms, some in main building but most in various barns, stables and outbuildings, and most with own bthrm. Peaceful and unpretentious 16th-c manor farm with log fire in cosy beamed lounge bar, good interesting food (for groups of 10 or more if booked in advance), a thoughtful wine list, friendly staff, and walled rose garden; they are very kind to children and also have a special leaflet for families showing things to do and see in the area; cl 24 Dec–7 Jan ☺

MORETON-IN-MARSH SP2032 **White Hart Royal** *High St, Moreton-in-Marsh, Gloucestershire GL56 0BA (01608)* 650731 **£68**; 19 good rms. Busy and comfortable, partly 15th-c inn with interesting Civil War history, oak beams and stripped stone, big inglenook fire in lounge area just off main bar, friendly helpful staff, well kept real ales, and decent food in bar and pleasant restaurant; attractive courtyard; disabled access

NAILSWORTH ST8599 **Egypt Mill** *Stroud Rd, Nailsworth, Stroud, Gloucestershire GL6 0AE (01453)* 833449 **£75***, plus special breaks; 17 comfortable airy rms. Carefully converted 16th-c watermill with original millstones and lifting equipment in the spacious lounge, a split-level restaurant, ground floor bar where two waterwheels can be seen, enjoyable food, friendly service, and seats in the waterside gardens

NORTH CERNEY SP0107 **Bathurst Arms** *North Cerney, Cirencester, Gloucestershire GL7 7BZ (01285)* 831281 **£50**; 5 pleasant rms. Civilised and handsome old inn with lots of atmosphere, notably friendly staff, a nice mix of polished old furniture and a fireplace at each end of the beamed and panelled bar, small no smoking dining room, imaginative food, 11 well chosen wines by the glass (inc two champagnes), well kept real ales, and an attractive garden running down to the River Churn; lots of surrounding walks

NORTHLEACH SP1114 **Market House** *The Square, Northleach, Cheltenham, Gloucestershire GL54 3EJ (01451)* 860557 **£48**, plus special breaks; 4 rms, mostly shared bthrm. Pretty 400-year-old stone house with beams and an inglenook fireplace, and good breakfasts; plenty of nearby restaurants; cl Dec–Jan; children over 12

PAINSWICK SO8609 **Painswick Hotel** *Kemps Lane, Painswick, Stroud, Gloucestershire GL6 6YB (01452)* 812160 **£135**, plus special breaks; 19 well equipped comfortable rms. 18th-c Palladian mansion – once a grand rectory – with fine views, antiques and paintings in the elegant rooms, open fires, good food using the best local produce, a thoughtful wine list, and a relaxed, friendly atmosphere; garden with croquet lawn; they are kind to families ☺

PARKEND SO6108 **Edale House** *Folly Rd, Parkend, Lydney, Gloucestershire GL15 4JF (01594)* 562835 **£49**, plus special breaks; 5 rms. Georgian house opposite cricket green and backing on to Nagshead Nature Reserve; comfortable, homely sitting room, little bar, very good food in attractive dining room (overlooking the garden), and a relaxed atmosphere; cl New Year; children over 12

PUCKRUP SO8836 **Hilton Puckrup Hall** *Twyning, Tewkesbury, Gloucestershire GL20 6EL (01684)* 296200 **£130**, plus special breaks; 112 comfortably spacious rms. Handsome Regency mansion in over 140 acres of parkland with its own par 71, 18-hole golf course, and leisure club inc indoor swimming pool, crèche, gym and so forth; elegant lounge with fine plasterwork, a relaxed bar overlooking croquet lawn, and good food in four different dining areas; disabled access

SHURDINGTON SO9217 **Greenway** *Shurdington, Cheltenham, Gloucestershire GL51 5UG (01242)* 862352 **£119**, plus special breaks; 19 well equipped, spacious and pretty rms. Very well run, lovely 16th-c manor house with antiques, fresh flowers and comfortable seats in the attractive drawing room, a cosy cocktail bar, particularly good modern British cooking, an excellent wine list, and attentive service; neatly kept gardens; children over 7; limited disabled access

ST BRIAVELS SO5504 **George** *St Briavels, Lydney, Gloucestershire GL15 6TA (01594)* 530228 **£45**; 4 rms. Pleasant old pub in particularly interesting village overlooking 12th-c castle, with three rambling rooms, big stone fireplace, a Celtic coffin lid dating from 1070 (found in a fireplace here and now mounted next to the bar counter), cosy dining room, real ales, and good food; outdoor chessboard

STOW-ON-THE-WOLD SP1925 **Grapevine** *Sheep St, Stow-on-the-Wold, Cheltenham, Gloucestershire GL54 1AU (01451) 830344* **£110**, plus special breaks; 22 well furnished no smoking rms. Warm, friendly and very well run hotel with antiques, comfortable chairs and a relaxed atmosphere in the lounge, a beamed bar, and good food in the attractive, sunny restaurant with its 70-year-old trailing vine; disabled access

STOW-ON-THE-WOLD SP1925 **Old Stocks** *The Square, Stow-on-the-Wold, Cheltenham, Gloucestershire GL54 1AF (01451) 830666* **£80**, plus special breaks; 18 rms. Well run 16th/17th-c Cotswold stone hotel with cosy welcoming small bar, beams and open fire, good food, friendly staff, and sheltered garden; cl 18–29 Dec; disabled access.

TETBURY ST8494 **Calcot Manor** *Calcot, Tetbury, Gloucestershire GL8 8YJ (0666) 890391* **£130**, plus special breaks; 27 attractive rms inc 9 super family ones and suites in old Granary Barn. Charming former farmhouse with country house décor and log fires in comfortable lounges, extremely helpful friendly staff, imaginative food in conservatory restaurant and Gumstool brasserie, enjoyable breakfasts, and smallish outdoor swimming pool in enclosed courtyard; they are particularly kind to families, with a qualified nanny in the playroom (stuffed with toys and games), computers and Playstation, tasty high teas, two tennis courts, an outdoor play area with bikes and lots of equipment, and plenty to do nearby; disabled access ☺

THORNBURY ST6390 **Thornbury Castle** *Castle St, Thornbury, Bristol BS35 1HH (01454) 281182* **£175**; 20 opulent rms, some with big Tudor fireplaces or fine oriel windows. Impressive and luxuriously renovated early 16th-c castle with antiques, tapestries, huge fireplaces and mullioned windows in the baronial public rooms, two restaurants (one in the base of a tower), fine cooking, extensive wine list (inc wine from their own vineyard), thoughtful friendly service, and vast grounds; cl 4 days Jan; partial disabled access

UPPER SLAUGHTER SP1523 **Lords of the Manor** *Upper Slaughter, Cheltenham, Glos GL54 2JD (01451) 820243* **£145**, plus special breaks; 27 rms carefully furnished with antiques, Victorian sketches and paintings. Warmly friendly hotel with mid-17th-c heart (though it's been carefully extended many times), lovely views over eight acres of grounds from very comfortable library and drawing room, log fires, and fresh flowers; fine modern English cooking in attractive candlelit restaurant overlooking the original rectory gardens, good breakfasts, and kind service; cl New Year; children over 7 in restaurant

WILLERSEY SP1039 **Old Rectory** *Church St, Willersey, Broadway, Worcestershire WR12 7PN (01386) 853729* **£89**, plus special breaks; 6 attractive, well equipped rms. Quietly set and friendly 17th-c house opposite church (nice walks from the churchyard), with a log fire in dining/sitting room and pretty flower-filled walled gardens with an ancient mulberry tree; good breakfasts, but no evening meals – though several places nearby; self-catering also; cl 22–28 Dec; children over 8; disabled access

WINCHCOMBE SP0327 **Sudeley Hill Farm** *Sudeley Rd, Winchcombe, Cheltenham, Gloucestershire GL54 5JB (01242) 602344* **£48***; 3 no smoking rms. Friendly 15th-c farmhouse on working mixed farm of 800 acres, with log fires, a guest sitting room, and dining room overlooking the large garden; cl Christmas; no dogs

WINCHCOMBE SP0228 **Wesley House** *High St, Winchcombe, Cheltenham, Gloucestershire GL54 5LJ (01242) 602366* **£70**, plus special breaks; 6 pleasantly furnished rms with individual antiques and showers. Pretty, half-timbered 15th-c town house with quiet, friendly atmosphere, log fire in comfortable front lounge, attractively presented, very good food (inc lovely puddings) in beamed restaurant, enjoyable breakfasts, and friendly informal service; old-fashioned garden furniture on small back terrace with pretty view; cl 10–30 Jan

WINSTONE SO9609 **Winstone Glebe** *Winstone, Cirencester, Gloucestershire*

GL7 7JU (01285) 821451 **£60**; 3 rms. Small Georgian rectory in quiet countryside with five acres of gardens and paddocks, tennis, and lots of surrounding walks; friendly hosts, traditional furnishings, and delicious food (by arrangement); dogs welcome; cl Christmas

To see and do

Gloucestershire Family Attraction of the Year

GLOUCESTER SO8218 **National Waterways Museum** ⬚ (Llanthony Warehouse, Gloucester Docks) Housed in the largest and the last of Gloucester's big waterside warehouses, this comprehensive collection of canal memorabilia is a good deal more appealing to children than you might expect. Focusing on the history of Britain's network of inland waterways, it has quite an emphasis on hands-on exhibits: one new gallery is completely interactive, with lots of touch-screen activities ranging from building your own canal, to a more infuriating share certificate game where you're allocated a company and then follow its fortunes. Elsewhere, a highlight is the miniature lock chamber, where you can try steering a narrow boat safely through the locks. You can get a good idea of the heavy demands of canal work by hoisting sacks on a pulley system, and clamber aboard some of the exhibits. A particularly interesting gallery looks at the way boats have been decorated from ancient times; you can create your own design. They've had an extensive refurbishment in recent months, with several improvements to the galleries and facilities. Most displays are under cover, though there are some historic boats outside, and in summer (for an extra charge) you can take 45-min boat trips along the canal. Videos tell the story of how the rise and fall of canals affected people's lives; some are narrated by people who've worked on the waterways themselves. There are no play areas as such, but in school holidays they often have extra activities for younger children such as brass-rubbing, and canal-related jigsaws and colouring. There's usually a fully working traditional forge. Snacks, shop, disabled access (not to floating exhibits); cl 25 Dec; (01452) 318054; £4.75 (£3.75 children over 5). They do family tickets that include the boat trip as well: £22 for two adults and three children. You can easily extend a visit to the Docks by calling at the other museums and attractions nearby; see main Gloucester listings below for full details.

ASHLEWORTH SO8125
A **tithe barn** of some note, a good dining pub, the Queens Arms; and a splendidly traditional pub, the Boat, right on the River Severn – in the same family for centuries.

BARNSLEY SP0805
Barnsley House Garden (B4425) Lovely little herb, vegetable and knot gardens, fruit trees and decorative plants, laburnum and lime walks and 18th-c summerhouses; esp attractive spring blossom and autumn colours. Plant sales, some disabled access; cl Tues, Sun, and Christmas–Jan; (01285) 740561; £3.75. The Village Pub is good.

BELAS KNAP SP0125
There's a pleasant walk up to Belas Knap and its steep grassy slopes – and

great views – from the Craven Arms in Brockhampton (a good pub, with a nice garden in a lovely setting); this could be tied in with a walk past some very surprising ruins of a Roman villa tucked away in the woods.

BERKELEY ST6899
Berkeley Castle ⬚ (off A38) Excellently preserved castle, very much a family home, but still keeping a flavour of its days as a Norman fortress. Impressive paintings, furnishings and silver, fine old keep and Great Hall, terraced gardens, park, extensive butterfly farm – and the dungeon where Edward II was murdered in 1327. Snacks, shop, limited disabled access; open Sun pm and all day bank hol Mons Apr–Oct, all day Tues–Sat Jun–Sept,

plus all day Mon July–Aug; (01453) 810332; £5.40, £2 butterfly farm. The Pickwick at Lower Wick is a popular dining pub.

Cattle Country Adventure Park 🎟 (off B4066 E) Various cattle inc American bison, yaks, and you can feed the wild boar; also farm trail and indoor and outdoor adventure playgrounds. Snacks (they hope to add a new restaurant), shop, disabled access. Usually open daily but best to check during term time; (01453) 810220; *£5 (less out of season).

Jenner Museum 🎟 (High St) Largely unchanged Georgian home of Edward Jenner, who discovered the vaccine against smallpox here. He gave free vaccinations from the thatched hut in the attractive grounds. Shop, some disabled access; cl am, all day Mon exc bank hols, Oct exc Sun, and all Nov–Mar; (01453) 810631; £2.80.

BIBURY SP1106
One of the most popular villages in the area (William Morris thought it the most beautiful in England), with lovely golden streamside houses. Nowadays, summer crowds can rather blunt its appeal. The **River Coln** lets you approach Bibury more quietly and prettily, along the path from the toll-house just S of Coln St Aldwyns. This route takes you in by the mill and bridge over the Coln itself. Besides Bibury Court, the Catherine Wheel is the best place here for lunch.

Arlington Mill Museum The 18th-c machinery of this well restored watermill is demonstrated every day, with guided tours by arrangement; at the back, a developing herb garden overlooks the river. Meals, snacks, shop, disabled access to tearoom; cl 25 Dec; (01285) 740368; £2.

Bibury Trout Farm 🎟 Long-established working farm breeding rainbow trout in 20 ponds. You can feed the fish, or try to catch your own. Snacks, good shop, limited disabled access; cl 25–26 Dec; (01285) 740215; *£2.

River Coln villages By the same trout-stream as over-visited Bibury, a pleasant drive links other villages that are just as engaging, but bypassed by most visitors, particularly Coln St

Aldwyns (the New Inn is excellent) and Quenington (a decent village pub). On the far side of Bibury the back road tracking along the river passes through a string of pleasant little villages such as Coln Rogers, Coln St Dennis and Yanworth, eventually reaching the pretty village of Withington (delightful pub right on the stream).

BIRDSWOOD SO7418
Old Ley Court 🎟 (Chapel Lane) Working farm producing double and single Gloucester cheese – you can watch them make it on Tues and Thurs, 9.30–11am and 12.30–4pm. Some disabled access (but no facilities); (01452) 750225; £1.50. The Apple Tree at nearby Minsterworth is a pleasant dining pub, and the lane past it leads to a good quiet spot for watching the Severn Bore.

BOURTON-ON-THE-HILL SP1732
Bourton House Unusual plants inc tender ones in attractive garden around fine old house (not open). Teas in 16th-c tithe barn, shop; open Thurs and Fri late May–3rd wk in Oct; *£3.50. The Horse & Groom does decent food.

Sezincote House and Garden (off A424 about 1m S) Exotic onion-domed forerunner of Brighton Pavilion, stunning from the outside, less interesting inside. Also classic early 19th-c water garden, and a more recent Indian-style garden to match the building. Garden open pm Thurs, Fri and bank hols (cl Dec), house Thurs and Fri pm May–July and Sept; *£5, £3.50 garden only. Children are not allowed in the house.

BOURTON-ON-THE-WATER SP1620
One of the best-known Cotswold villages, but disfigured by sprawly crowds in summer unless you get there very early in the morning – when it's enchanting. There is a wealth of attractions aimed at visitors. The Old Manse has decent food and garden tables overlooking the Windrush; the riverside Kingsbridge Arms is useful, too. The best walk out of the village is the exit by the church, heading out W past the school and over the old railway line, then following the lanes and tracks S of Upper Slaughter to rejoin the River

Windrush and back to Bourton.

Birdland 🖼 (Rissington Rd) Rare and exotic birds on banks of meandering River Windrush, inc a large colony of penguins and over 50 aviaries. Meals, snacks, shop, disabled access; cl 25 Dec; (01451) 820480; £4.25.

Cotswold Motor Museum and Toy Collection 🖼 (Sherbourne St) Housed in an old watermill, the collection here includes cars and motorcycles from vintage years to the 1950s, along with advertising signs, automobilia, and toy collection. It's also the home of Brum the children's TV character. Shop, disabled access; the new owners hope to finish expanding the museum by March – best to phone for opening hours; (01451) 821255; £2.25.

Dragonfly Maze (Rissington Rd) Follow clues on engraved flagstones to find your way through a yew tree maze to an ornate central pavilion filled with charming animated sculptures. Shop, disabled access; open daily in summer, best to check in winter; (01451) 822251; £2.

Folly Farm Waterfowl (A436 3m W) Lakes and pools with 160 species of waterfowl, as well as friendly ducks, geese and poultry, and hand-reared animals. Good for children, and a nice spot for a picnic (or to camp). Their lavender fields are in full bloom July. Shop, disabled access; cl 25 Dec; (01451) 820285; £3.50.

Model Village (High St) Charming replica of the village, modelled from Cotswold stone in the 1930s to a scale of one-ninth, complete with working waterwheel and music in the church. Good home-made food (and lovely river view) in adjacent welcoming Old New Inn, snacks, shop, limited disabled access; cl 25 Dec; (01451) 820467; £2.

Perfumery Exhibition 🖼 (Victoria St) Includes the origins of perfume, a cinema with smells and perfume quiz and garden. Shop, disabled access; cl 25–26 Dec; (01451) 820698; *£2.

CHELTENHAM SO9523
Beautiful spa town useful for exploring Cotswolds, shopping, or admiring the elegant Regency architecture of its tree-lined avenues. These days Cheltenham is best known for its races,

and the racecourse at Prestbury Park (N on A435) has an exhibition on Gold Cup winners; (01242) 513014; cl wknds; free. Lots of antique shops, esp around the Montpellier area. Tailors (Cambray Pl), the Montpellier Wine Bar (Montpellier St), Moon Under Water (Bath Rd) and Belgian Monk (Clarence St) have decent food, and the well run café in the beautiful Imperial Gardens is suitable for families.

Art Gallery & Museum (Clarence St) Excellent Arts and Crafts collection inspired by William Morris, fine paintings inc 17th-c Dutch works, and rare porcelain and ceramics. Special exhibitions throughout the year. Meals, snacks, shop, disabled access; cl Sun and bank hols; (01242) 837431; free.

Holst Birthplace Museum 🖼 (Clarence Rd) Nr the Pump Room, this interesting Regency house is where the composer was born in 1874; you can see the piano on which he composed *The Planets*. Worthwhile even if you're not mad about Holst, as the rooms are all carefully furnished in period style. Shop, some disabled access; cl Sun, Mon and bank hols; (01242) 524846; *£2.25.

Pittville Pump Room (Pittville Park) A short walk from the centre, this is generally regarded as the town's finest building, 19th-c Greek Revival with a colonnaded façade and balconied hall. It's easy to imagine the place's Regency heyday, especially strolling round the super park and gardens, or during concerts in the July music festival; on summer Suns they may have teas accompanied by live music. You can still sample the spa water – rather salty. Shop, disabled access to ground floor only; cl Tues; (01242) 523852.

CHIPPING CAMPDEN SP1539
Extremely attractive town, with interesting old buildings inc an ancient covered open-sided market hall, a grand Perpendicular church typical of the area's rich 'wool churches', enjoyable shops, and fine old inns. Many of our contributors would put it among the country's most delightful small towns, though until they get the cars out of the centre not all would agree. The Eight Bells, Volunteer, Noel Arms and Lygon Arms are all good for lunch. The **Cotswold Way**, a 100-mile path

from here all the way to Bath, carefully picks out some of the choicest Cotswold scenery – a worthwhile aid for those planning a shorter stroll.

CIRENCESTER SP0202

A busy country town, particularly on its Mon and Fri market days, with a succession of fine Cotswold stone streets off the long market place. It has many attractive buildings, and interesting antiques and other shops inc traditional country saddlers' etc. Though one of the most handsome of all the Cotswold towns, it isn't too touristy. The **church** of St John the Baptist (Market Pl) is wonderfully grand, and has a striking late Gothic tower. **Brewery Court** has 16 independent craft businesses and shops in former brewery (cl Sun and some bank hols), along with theatre, gallery and café. Also worth a look are the 12th-c remains of **St John's Hospital**, the **Norman arch**, and the various well preserved wool merchants' houses. Cecily Hill, one of the town's most attractive streets, gives on to the pleasant strolling-ground of Cirencester Park. Decent places for lunch include the Slug & Lettuce, Corinium Court, Tatyans (Chinese) and (very local but good value) Golden Cross.

Corinium Museum (Park St) Cirencester was one of the most important cities in Roman Britain, and this spacious museum has one of the finest collections of antiquities from the period (all clearly displayed and labelled). Reconstructed period dining room and kitchen (complete with menus), with Saxon and medieval galleries too. They hope to have meals and snacks, shop, excellent disabled access; cl Christmas week, 19 and 26 Mar and 5 Nov; (01285) 655611; £2.50.

CLEARWELL SO5708

Clearwell Caves ▨ (off B4228) Tours of nine huge caverns, a source of ore from the Iron Age right up to the present day; deeper trips for the more adventurous. It's quite a labyrinth, with many miles of passageways, so stout shoes recommended. Lively themed displays down here at Christmas. Meals, snacks, shop; open Mar–24 Dec, and wknds Jan–Feb; (01594) 832535;

*£3.50. The Wyndham Arms is good for lunch, and though the village is not in itself particularly pretty it's a very good centre for the lovely surrounding countryside.

CLEEVE COMMON SO9924

The steep grassy slopes of the W escarpment of the Cotswolds make for some of the area's best walking. This, the highest point of the Cotswolds, has breezy, unkempt grassland on its open expanses and can either be reached from the nearby village of Cleeve Hill on the A46, or integrated into a circular walk past Belas Knap long barrow and through the Sudeley Castle estate into Winchcombe.

COTSWOLDS SP0912

It's the countryside above all which delights here – especially the rolling hills themselves, with their traditional dry stone-walled fields, occasional beechwoods, meandering streams, beautiful villages of warm golden-tinted stone picturesquely roofed in heavy stone slabs. Many villages have handsome medieval churches, and their cottages and houses don't hide away behind gardens and high walls, but tend to be right by the road. Often, there's a strip of daffodil-planted grass between pavement and road (the area is particularly attractive in spring), and sometimes a little stream. *The Romantic Road*, a guide to the prettiest villages in the area, is available from Cheltenham Tourism (01242) 522878, or from Tourist Information Centres in the area. For cyclists, the Cotswolds are great – quiet village-to-village lanes with ever-changing views. Campus Holidays not only hire bikes but can arrange your route and accommodation too; (01242) 250642.

DEERHURST SO8729

Ancient remains here include **Odda's Chapel**, a restored 11th-c chapel discovered as part of a farmhouse, and the **Priory Church of St Mary**, a mainly Saxon church with a lovely atmosphere and some intriguing original carvings and features. The Farmers Arms at Apperley is a decent dining pub (brewing its own beers).

DEVIL'S CHIMNEY SO9418

On the Cotswold Way, a viewpoint rock pinnacle amid old quarries on

Leckhampton Hill, perched above Cheltenham.

DYRHAM ST7475

Dyrham Park In an ancient park grazed by fallow deer, this fine William and Mary house has hardly changed since the late 17th c. The interiors have Dutch-style furnishings, Delft ware, Dutch bird paintings and a remarkable trompe l'oeil by Hoogstraten. Victorian domestic rooms including a bakehouse, larders, kitchen and dairy are also now open. Meals, snacks, shop, disabled access to ground floor; house cl am, all day Weds and Thurs, and all Nov–Mar, park open all year; (0117) 937 2501; £7.50, garden and deer park only £2.60; deer park only £1.80; NT. The Bull at Hinton Dyrham and Crown at Tolldown (A46) are handy for lunch.

EASTLEACH SP2005

Delightful Cotswold village; a lovely ancient clapper bridge links the two Norman churches, very photogenic when the daffodils are out.

FAIRFORD SP1501

Pleasant riverside meadows, and a wonderful 15th-c Perpendicular **church**, well known for its remarkable medieval stained glass (inc a fascinating depiction of Hell), and comical misericords. The Bull has decent food.

FOREST OF DEAN SO6212

The Forest of Dean has a unique landscape: hilly woodland that shows many traces of the way it has provided a livelihood for the people living around it. Its woodland colours are at their best in late May and autumn. Still largely ancient oak woodland despite encroaching pine plantations, the forest rolls over many miles of hilly countryside, giving plenty of space – even in summer you can often have much of the woods to yourself. There are ponds, streams with stepping stones, cattle and maybe fallow deer, sudden distant views, the humps and gouges that mark ancient iron workings, the tracks of abandoned railways and tramways, and still one or two of the freeminers, who've been digging coal by hand from surface seams for hundreds of years. The forest scenery has most impact on those prepared to delve into its past a bit – a good start is the **heritage centre** at

Upper Soudley; the forest is well equipped with car parks, picnic sites and forest trails. The **Sculpture Trail** takes a four-mile route passing nearly 20 specially commissioned sculptures hidden deep in the forest (from picnic site nr the comfortable Speech House Hotel). The **Kidnalls Forest Trail** is a good way of tracking down some early industrial sites. The **Foundry Wood Trail** passes Soudley fish ponds and gains some fine views. The **Wench Ford Forest Walk** leads past a series of quite interesting rock outcrops. Signed paths ensure easy route-finding up to the open summit of May Hill, where on a clear day you can see the Cotswolds, Malverns, Welsh Marches and Severn Estuary. Around the edges of the forest the scenery changes to a patchwork of steep pastures – also very attractive. It's well worth getting a forest map, either from the Dean Heritage Centre or direct from the Forestry Commission in Coleford (01594) 833057; these outline walks (inc the sculpture trail), and mark the best spots for views or picnics. The information centres can also provide details of canoeing, caving, cycling or fishing in the forest. The B4432 to Symonds Yat does give some good views, the B4228 down past St Briavels is a pleasant country road, and the little lanes around the edges of the forest are rewarding drives – but need a large-scale map.

Conifer arboretum SO6212 This makes an interesting change from the forest's predominantly broad-leaved trees; nr Speech House.

Dean Heritage Centre 🏛 SO6513 (Camp Mill, Upper Soudley) Useful introduction to the Forest of Dean, set around an old watermill in pretty wooded valley. Plenty going on, inc a working beam engine, a collection of clocks, craft displays, adventure playground, and occasional traditional charcoal burning. Meals, snacks, shop, disabled access; cl 24–26 Dec and 1 Jan; (01594) 822170; *£3.50.

Hopewell Colliery 🏛 SO5911 (B4226 E of Broadwell) 45-min underground tours of the 'free' mine guided by ex-miners, and display of mining tools and equipment. You'll

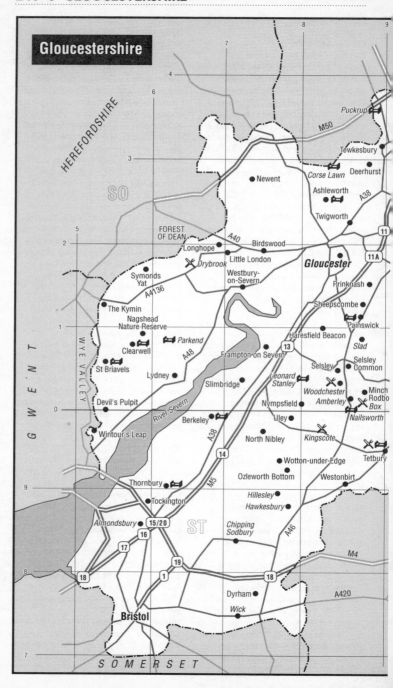

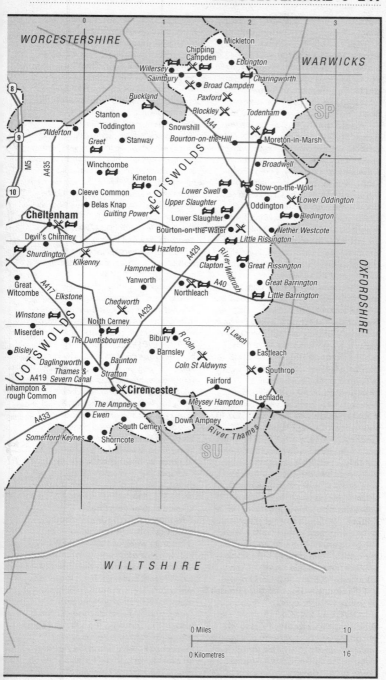

need sturdy shoes and warm clothing. Snacks, shop; cl Nov–Easter; (01594) 810706; £3.

Puzzle Wood SO5808 (just off B4228 S of Coleford) Wooded paths arranged as a stroll-along puzzle, landscaped in the 19th c nr remains of Roman iron mines. Snacks, shop; cl Mon (exc bank hols), and Nov–Easter; (01594) 833187; £3. Across the road is the **Treasure Train**; steam trains run along a ¾-mile stretch of narrow-gauge track, with children solving clues that lead to treasure along the way. There are four stops, with footpaths through the woods nearby. Snacks, disabled access; open some wknds and bank hols Easter–Oct, and some days in summer hols, best to check; (01594) 834991; £3.10 for unlimited train journeys, plus £1.75 for the treasure trail. The Dog & Muffler at Joyford is a pretty place for lunch; good walks nearby.

Roman road SO6508 You can track the remarkably durable paving of this just off the B4431 at Blackpool Bridge.

Symonds Yat Rock SO5615 Perhaps the Forest of Dean's most spectacular feature, where the River Wye rolls around a monumental wooded cliff barrier, a favourite spot with peregrine falcons; tremendous views in all directions from the top, and at the bottom a ferry runs between two inns.

FRAMPTON ON SEVERN SO7407 **Frampton Court** Elegant lived-in Georgian house, with original furniture, porcelain and paintings, and fascinating gardens. The 18th-c orangery has been converted into self-catering holiday flats. Snacks (by prior arrangement), disabled access to gardens; personal tours all year by appointment, (01452) 740267; *£4.50. The village green is said to be the longest in the country, with the orangery on one side, and the civilised Bell (good range of food) on another. Just outside the village the Gloucester & Sharpness Canal passes grand colonnaded lock keepers' houses by pretty swing bridges.

GLOUCESTER SO8318
A busy modern city despite its long history – you have to search out the old buildings among today's big shops (for instance the splendid timber-framed house tucked down a passageway off 26

Westgate St). The Tourist Office at St Michael's Tower (itself a fine ancient building at the central Cross) is particularly good at sending you off well equipped for the hunt. The Waterfront (Llanthony Rd, S end of docks), and – all handy for the cathedral – Fountain, New Inn and Tailors House (Westgate St) are useful for a quick lunch.

City Museum & Art Gallery (Brunswick Rd) Local history (inc the oldest known backgammon set), and paintings by Gainsborough and Turner. Shop, disabled access; cl Sun (exc July–Sept); (01452) 524131; £2. Guided tours of the ancient **City East Gate** leave here on Sats May–Sept – best to ring for times; free.

Docks The revitalised waterfront deserves much of the credit for the city's tourism renaissance; guided walks, summer boat trips along the canal or up the river as far as Tewkesbury (contact National Waterways Museum below). Attractions here include the unusually interesting **Soldiers of Gloucester Museum** (cl Mon exc Jun–Sept and bank hols; (01452) 522682; £4), and a big **antiques centre**, with 110 varied antiques shops in Dickensian arcades (limited disabled access; cl Sun am; free wkdys, 50p wknds and bank hols).

Folk Museum (Westgate St) Social history in a group of Tudor and Jacobean timber-framed houses; Victorian classroom, reconstructed ironmonger's shop and a toy gallery. In summer there may be Gloucestershire Old Spot pigs in the yard. Shop, limited disabled access; cl Sun exc July–Sept; (01452) 526467; £2 (children and Gloucester residents free).

Gloucester Cathedral Expecting a flood of small visitors after its temporary transformation into Harry Potter's Hogwarts school for wizards, this towers majestically over the city's more recent buildings. It has lovely fan-vaulted cloisters, the second largest medieval stained-glass window in the country, and a fine collection of church plate in the Treasury. In 1330 the Abbot astutely purchased the remains of murdered Edward II, and the resulting stream of pilgrims paid for elaborate rebuilding, an early example of

Perpendicular style. Meals, snacks, shop, some disabled access; (01452) 528095; £2.50 recommended donation. Not far from here are what's left of 9th-c **St Oswald's Priory**, the city's oldest structure, and other ecclesiastical remains inc **Greyfriars** and **Blackfriars**, the latter pretty much unchanged since the 13th c, with a rare scissor-braced roof.

Gloucester Prison Museum (Barrack Sq) This museum in the old Gate Lodge – the only one of its type attached to a fully operational prison – was closed as we went to press, but hopes to reopen later this year; best to phone to check; (01452) 529551.

House of the Tailor of Gloucester (College Court) Inspiration for Beatrix Potter's story; exhibition and shop. Disabled access to ground floor only; cl Sun, bank hols and 25 Dec; £1.

Jet Age Museum 🖭 (Airport, Cheltenham Rd E) The working surroundings make this collection seem more ready for action than some; children can climb into some of the cockpits. Snacks, shop, disabled access; open daily Easter–Oct, plus Weds and wknds in winter; (01452) 715100; *£3.

Museum of Advertising & Packaging (Albert Warehouse, Docks) Great for nostalgia-lovers, an enormous and quite fascinating assembly of packets, tins, bottles, posters, street signs and more from Victorian days onwards. Also continuous showing of vintage TV commercials. Snacks, shop, disabled access; cl winter Mons, 25–26 Dec; (01452) 302309; £3.50.

National Waterways Museum See *separate family panel on p.235.*

Over farm shop (1m W) A good one, with local produce and pick-your-own in summer (plus, depending on the harvest, a PYO pumpkin festival in Oct half-term); disabled access; cl 25–26 Dec.

Robinswood Hill Country Park (2m S) A little outcrop of the Cotswolds, with 250 acres of walks and trails, a wildlife information centre (fun talks and events), and wonderful views of the city from the summit. Snacks, shop, disabled access; (01452) 303206; free. Not far away is a dry ski slope.

GREAT WITCOMBE SO9316
Crickley Hill Country Park (just N of village) Has a few ancient sites, as well as nature trails, lovely clearly marked woodland walks, and fine views. Some disabled access; visitor centre cl winter; (01452) 863170; free.
Roman villa The outlines of a substantial Roman villa can still be traced here, around a courtyard, with several mosaics and evidence of an underfloor heating system. The Royal George Hotel at Birdlip has decent food, and the Golden Heart at Brimpsfield is good.

GUIDED HORSE-RIDING SO8412 Ongers Farm at Brookthorpe organise this, (01452) 813344, from £10 an hour.
HARESFIELD BEACON SO8108 (3m NW of Stroud), 450 acres of NT woodland and grassland on the Cotswold escarpment, with spectacular views; free, and just a short ascent from the road.

KINETON SP0926
Cotswold Farm Park (off B4077) Full of delightfully odd-looking species of sheep, cattle, pigs, goats, horses and poultry, it's very much a working farm rather than a more developed leisure attraction, but is particularly well organised as far as children are concerned, and excellent value too. Rabbits and piglets to cuddle or feed, tractor and trailer rides, good safe rustic-themed play areas and even a designated children's shop, with items from 5p to around £2. Try to visit close to the start of the season (up to the end of Apr), when the lambs are being born. You can easily spend most or all of a day here; nature trails and woodland walks are ideal for a break from the animals, and there are 19 acres where you can have a picnic, kick a ball around, or relax on the grass. Lots under cover, so still good when the weather isn't perfect (best to wear wellies then). Meals, snacks, shop, disabled access; open mid-Mar–Oct; (01451) 850307; £4.50 (children £2.30). A family ticket is £12.
LECHLADE SU2199
Graceful village with one or two decent antiques shops, good traditional toy shop, pleasant walks, and access to the quiet reed-fringed Thames for footpath walks – especially along to Kelmscot in

Oxfordshire. The New Inn, with a Thames-side garden, is good value.

LITTLE LONDON SO6918
Angora Goat and Mohair Centre
(Blakemore Farm) This unusual goat farm will reopen at Easter after refurbishment – phone to check times and prices. Snacks, shop selling clothes made from goat and other fleeces, and disabled access; (01452) 830630. The Red Hart at Blaisdon is attractive for lunch.

LONGHOPE SO6818
Harts Barn Flower and Craft Centre Smart craft workshops, inc dried flowers, jewellery and ceramics, set in an attractive Norman hunting lodge with landscaped grounds and lake. Courtyard tearoom, picnic area, disabled access; cl Mon exc bank hols; (01452) 830954; free.

LOWER SLAUGHTER SP1622
With its sister village Upper Slaughter, this is perhaps the prettiest village in Britain – a perfect harmony of stone, water, grass and trees. It's not as overwhelmed by summer visitors as its nearby rival Bourton-on-the-Water, though it certainly gets its fair share. The riverside stroll from Lower to Upper Slaughter is a leisurely mile or so; to make a longer walk for a circuit of a couple of hours, you can follow the signposted Warden's Way.

LYDNEY SO6304
Dean Forest Railway ⌗ (New Mills, slightly N of Lydney) Lots of locomotives, wagons and equipment at the station, and steam trips through the forest (mainly just wknds, best to ring for dates). They are currently building a new track to Parkend. Snacks, shop, disabled access; static displays open Apr–Dec; (01594) 843423; £4.20. The Woodman at Parkend has decent food and good nearby walks.

Lydney Park Extensive sheltered spring garden rich with flowering shrubs, rhododendrons, azaleas and magnolias; also lakes and deer park. Tucked away among the trees are the remains of a Roman temple, and a museum with finds from the site, inc the astonishingly intricate Lydney dog. Snacks, shop, plant sales; open Sun, Weds and bank hols late Mar–early Jun; (01594) 842844; £3 (£2 Wed).

MICKLETON SP1743
Hidcote Manor Garden (off B4081) Series of small gardens separated by walls and hedges of different species, with rare shrubs, trees and roses. Very popular even midweek, despite the price. Meals, snacks, good shop, some disabled access; best to phone for opening times; (01684) 855370; £5.60; NT. The Kings Arms is good value for lunch.

Kiftsgate Court Garden ⌗ (off B4081) Renowned for its old-fashioned roses (best Jun and July), inc reputedly the largest rose in England, this has many other rare plants, shrubs and trees, good views across the Vale of Evesham, and that special feel that comes from generations of care by a gifted gardening family. Snacks, rare plant sales; open pm Weds, Thurs, Sun and bank hols, Apr–Sept, plus Sat pm Jun and July; (01386) 438777; *£4.

MINCHINHAMPTON & RODBOROUGH COMMON ST8699
900 acres of open land with fine views and a wide range of wildlife; NT, free. The Halfway Inn at Box on the N edge has good food, and the steep lanes all around are interesting drives.

MISERDEN SO9308
Misarden Park Views over the wooded Golden Valley from handsome gardens of 17th-c manor house (not open), with Lutyens topiary, mature shrubs and trees, and colourful walled garden. Snacks, nursery, some disabled access; open Tues–Thurs Apr–Sept; (01285) 821303; *£3. The quiet village is charming, with good food in the Carpenters Arms.

MORETON-IN-MARSH SP2032
Attractively bustling old place, once an important linen weaving centre and coaching town, now with popular Tues market. For food, besides the good Marsh Goose, the Inn on the Marsh is useful – and the Farriers Arms out at Todenham is worth the trip.

Batsford Arboretum (Batsford Park, just NW) Well grown private collection of over 1,000 rare and beautiful species of tree spread over 50 acres; hundreds of maples, 90 different magnolias, flowering cherries. Best in May and autumn, but relaxing any time.

Meals, snacks, garden centre, disabled access; open Mar–mid-Nov and wknds in Feb; (01386) 701441; *£3.50. The park is home to plenty of deer.

Cotswold Falconry Centre 🔲 (Batsford Park, just NW) Flying demonstrations throughout the day, with a chance to handle some of the birds. Close-circuit TVs give a bird's-eye view of life in the nest. Snacks, shop, disabled access (but no facilities); open Mar–Nov; (01386) 701043; £3.50.

Wellington Aviation Museum (Broadway Rd) World War II aircraft pictures, sculpture and related material. Shop, disabled access; cl 12.30–2pm, all day Mon, 25 Dec, and Jan–Feb; (01608) 650323; £1.50.

NAGSHEAD NATURE RESERVE SO5909

A good place to see deer and other wildlife.

NEWENT SO7225

Small country town with some timbered buildings which have a bit of a Worcestershire or Herefordshire look.

National Birds of Prey Centre (Great Boulsdon, just S) Exceptional collection of birds of prey, with flying displays and breeding aviaries. Meals, snacks, shop, some disabled access; cl Dec, Jan (exc for special events); (01531) 820286; £5.50. The Yew Tree at Cliffords Mesne a bit further on this road has decent food, and is handy for May Hill.

Shambles Museum of Victorian Life Enthusiastic re-creation of Victorian cobbled square, with shops and furnished tradesman's house. Summer snacks, shop, limited disabled access; cl Mon (exc bank hols), Jan–mid-Mar; (01531) 822144; £3.50. The George opposite is handy for lunch.

St Annes Vineyard (Oxenhall, off B4221) Grow and sell 100 varieties of vine, and make wines; cl some winter wkdys, best to check on (01989) 720313; free.

Three Choirs Vineyard (off B4215 towards Dymock) Now one of the six largest vineyards in the country; meals, snacks, shop, disabled access; cl 25–26, 31 Dec and 1–5 Jan; tastings free, tour and exhibitions *£3. The Vineyard Restaurant also has accommodation.

NORTH CERNEY SP0207

Cerney House 🔲 Expansive old garden behind 13th-c church, with old roses, trees, shrubs, walled and herb gardens, a few animals (they make tasty goat's cheese), and a water garden. The surrounding woods are lovely at bluebell time. Teas, shop, some disabled access; open Tues, Weds and Fri Easter–Sept; (01285) 831300; £3. The village is attractive, and the Bathurst Arms is good for lunch.

NORTH NIBLEY ST7496

Hunts Court Informal gardens with over 400 varieties of old roses, plus unusual shrubs and other plants; fine views. Plant sales, disabled access; open Tues–Sat (though cl Aug) – best to check; (01453) 547440; £1.50. The walk up to the Tyndale Monument gives even better views, and the Black Horse is handy for lunch.

NORTHLEACH SP1114

Fine example of an unspoilt small wool town, with a particularly interesting **church**, renowned for its collection of brasses. A while ago they installed an automatic winder to the church clock, allowing retirement for the man who'd faithfully wound it for the last 65 years. The Red Lion is useful for lunch.

Cotswold Heritage Centre (Fosseway) Decent collection of rural bygones; snacks, shop, mostly disabled access; cl Sun am except bank hol, and all Nov–Mar; *£2.50.

World of Mechanical Music (Oak House, High St) Quite captivating collection of clocks, musical boxes and automata in old wool merchant's house, displayed and played in period settings. It's quite spooky watching the instruments work themselves. Shop, good disabled and blind access; cl 25–26 Dec; (01451) 860181; £5.

NYMPSFIELD SO8000

Woodchester Mansion (B4066) Construction of this splendid unfinished Gothic mansion was inexplicably abandoned virtually overnight in 1870. It's being repaired but not finished, and you can usually see traditional building techniques like stonemasonry. Five species of bat add to the atmosphere. Readers report excellent guided tours. No children inside, for safety reasons. Snacks, shop, disabled access to ground floor only; open first wknd of month

Easter–Oct, plus bank hol wknds, and Sun July–Sept (they also hope to open in May – best to check); (01453) 860661; £4. You can explore the surrounding valley, recently purchased by the NT. The walk up Coaley Peak gives tremendous views over the Severn Valley.

ODDINGTON SP2325

Charming Cotswold village; the 11th-c **church** has an interesting mural, and there are pleasant walks, esp from the Fox at Lower Oddington – very good food there, too.

OZLEWORTH BOTTOM ST7992

This valley, not far from Wotton-under-Edge, has a nostalgically forgotten quality about it, providing an interesting walk between Lasborough Manor and Ozleworth Park, with its unusual Norman church endowed with a hexagonal tower.

PAINSWICK SO8609

Readers really enjoy this delightful little town, sometimes referred to as 'Queen of the Cotswolds'. There's been a settlement here since Celtic times, and **Painswick Beacon** has the remains of the earliest structures; it's a short ascent from the road, with great views towards the Malvern hills. Plenty of old buildings to look at, such as the 15th-c **Post Office**, and several antique shops and craft workshops. The **church of St Mary** has fine interesting tombs and a fascinating churchyard where 99 immaculately clipped yews form gateways and canopies. The Falcon opposite is popular for lunch.

Rococo Garden (The Stables, Painswick House) Careful restoration of sizeable 18th-c garden to match a 1748 painting showing its fanciful mix of precisely trimmed hedging, paths and shrubs with unrestrained trees; also a maze and slightly zany garden buildings. Pleasant vistas, children's walks – a cheery-feeling place. Snacks, shop, plant sales, some disabled access; cl Mon–Tues Oct–Apr, and Dec; (01452) 813204; £3.30.

PRINKNASH SO8713

Prinknash Abbey Visitors Centre (off A46) Unusual 20th-c Benedictine monastery and earlier house, now home to the world-famous pottery; you can watch production

from the viewing gallery. Snacks, shop, disabled access; cl 25–26 Dec, Good Fri; (01452) 812239; £2 for pottery tours. The abbey buildings aren't to everyone's taste but the grounds are attractive, with good views over the Severn Vale. The Black Horse in the very steep village of Cranham has enjoyable food.

Prinknash Bird Park (Prinknash Abbey) Exotic pheasants, peacocks and other birds, as well as deer, goats and waterfowl; most animals feed from your hand (the fallow deer are particularly friendly). Snacks, shop; cl 25–26 Dec, Good Fri; (01452) 812727; £3.60.

SELSLEY SO8203

Strung-out Cotswold village in the steep country just S of Stroud; William Morris, Maddox-Brown, Burne-Jones and Rossetti all worked on the **church windows**.

SELSLEY COMMON SO8303

Selsley Herb Farm This friendly herb garden closes to the public in Mar, but the owner's son plans to open a new nursery at nearby Bisley around that time; phone Rob Wimperis for details (0773) 3000 309. The family also has a herb shop just up the A46 in Nailsworth (which has plenty of trails around its old mills). The grassland common itself is quite high, with good views and pleasant walks; the Bell is a handy refreshment stop.

SEVERN BORE SO6904

Tidal wave surging upstream at high tide, which can sometimes reach up to six feet in height around the spring and autumn equinox. The Environment Agency produce a calendar listing the best times and places to catch the phenomenon, with a rating of how spectacular it's likely to be; (01684) 850951. A good quiet spot to get down to the river is from Purton.

SEVERN ESTUARY ST6196

This makes for some lonely walks along the sea wall, with power station cooling towers and the vast Severn bridges emphasising the emptiness of the tidal flats. The White Hart in Littleton-upon-Severn, Anchor in Oldbury-on-Severn and right by the embankment the Windbound at Shepperdine are useful starting points. Further upstream

Arlingham is locked within a big bend of the Severn, about a mile from the river, with the river path looking across to the Forest of Dean; the Ship at Upper Framilode nearby is a good family dining pub.

SHEEPSCOMBE SO8910
Delightful Cotswold village, clinging to picturesque hillsides; the cricket ground's so steep that fielders can scarcely see the bowler.

SHORNCOTE SU0296
Cotswold Water Park 2,000 acres of lakes with facilities for angling, windsurfing, sailing and other watersports, country parks and walks, bird-watching and nature reserves. Snacks at some lakes, shop, disabled access; some activities cl winter; (01285) 861459; £5 (£3 wkdys) car parking, less in winter. The Eliot Arms in the prettily preserved 16th-c village has good food.

SLIMBRIDGE SO7204
Wildfowl & Wetlands Trust 🖾 (off A38) The first of the Wildfowl and Wetlands Trust's nine centres, and still the best, this enormous place is a lot more than just a bird and nature reserve. Thoughtfully upgraded in recent years, it shows off probably the world's most comprehensive collection of geese, swans and ducks, as well as six species of flamingo (you won't see so many anywhere else in Europe), rare and wild birds, and a tropical house that re-creates the sights, sounds and smells of a rain forest. In the Pond Zone children are encouraged to learn about wetland environments by taking part in pond-dipping and seeing what they fish out of the water magnified on to TV screens. Also lots of touch screen computers, video displays and games, and extra events and talks in the school hols. Recent additions include an impressive discovery centre for children, a tower with a telescope, and an art gallery. It's unusual in being somewhere that you might get more out of visiting in the winter, when up to 8,000 wild birds fly in; several of the excellent hides and viewing facilities are heated then. Some birds can be fed by hand, and you may be lucky enough to hear the amazing belch of the macoa duck. It's one of the most visitor-

friendly bird reserves in the country, with plenty of activities specifically aimed at primary school children, and a play area. They'll hire out binoculars if you've left your own at home. Meals and snacks, shop, disabled access; cl 25 Dec; (01453) 890333; £5.75 (£3.50 children over 4, free to WWT members). A family ticket for two adults and two children is £15. The Tudor Arms by the swing bridge across the canal is useful for food, and the village Post Office has details of pleasant little walks.

SNOWSHILL SP0933
Snowshill Manor It looks like an ordinary Cotswold manor house, but inside is one of those extraordinary collections of ephemera great eccentrics somehow amass. Each room is carefully themed, full of maybe toys, musical instruments, bikes hanging from the ceiling – and even suits of Japanese samurai armour, spookily arranged to look like a group of warriors meeting in the gloom. There's a charming cottage garden, and you can stay in one of three cottages. Meals, snacks, shop and secondhand books by the entrance, disabled access to garden only; open Weds–Sun and bank hols Apr–end Oct (plus Mons July–Aug); (01386) 852410; £6; NT. This is one of the Trust's busier properties, and there's a timed ticket system; try to come midweek or out of season. The nearby Snowshill Arms is popular for lunch (busiest 12–1.15 pm), and the drive along the River Windrush to Ford, Kineton and Naunton is delightful.

SOUTH CERNEY SU0698
Butts Farm 🖾 (1m NE, on A419) Notably friendly, with a good range of animals for children to feed, and daily pony or cart rides and goat-milking. New dairy and wartime farming exhibitions, along with spinning demonstrations, and a straw tunnel to play in. Snacks, shop, disabled access; cl Mon and Tues outside school hols, phone for winter opening; (01285) 862205; £3.50. The Eliot Arms in the prettily preserved 16th-c village has decent food.

SOUTHROP SP2003
Charming Cotswold village that really comes into its own when the daffodils

appear, with a delightful riverside church.

ST BRIAVELS SO5504

Attractive and unusual small village focused on the ruins of its 13th-c castle (the inhabited part is a youth hostel), with a steeply grassy former moat and views from the ramparts of the curtain wall. The George is good for lunch, and there are various circular walks around the parish, devised by Mr McGubbin in the **craft shop**.

STANTON SP0734

One of the prettiest Cotswold villages, very small – and rarely overrun with visitors. The best views over it are from the Mount pub, up the steep no through road beyond the village centre. This is the start of a trio of timeless villages on the **Cotswold Way**, a well marked track that conveniently picks out some of the best scenery for walkers. The next two are Stanway and Buckland; field paths and farm track let you detour to Snowshill, and from there it's a pleasant 3-mile walk to Broadway just over the Worcs border.

STANWAY SP0632

Stanway Water Garden ⊞ One of the most beautiful 16th-c manor houses in the country, a cluster of gabled buildings popping up unexpectedly from the countryside, with charming and clearly lived-in rooms. The early 18th-c grounds have fine trees, a recently restored canal and cascade, and interesting buildings inc a folly pyramid on a steeply wooded hill. Open pm Tues and Thurs Aug–Sept; (01386) 584469; £3.

STOW-ON-THE-WOLD SP1925

Handsome market town with fine stone buildings around its square and in the narrow lanes around, and a good few antiques shops, book shops and so forth. It's something of an antidote to the more sweetly pretty Cotswold villages, on quite a high plateau and altogether more austere in style – not for nothing was it known as 'Stow-on-the-Wold, where the wind blows cold', and the ancient stocks on the village green add a touch of quaint severity. The Queens Head and Talbot are both good for lunch.

TETBURY ST8993

A splendid raised **market house**, some interesting little lanes, quite a few

antiques shops and craft workshops, and decent food in the Crown.

Chavenage ⊞ (2m NW) Friendly unspoilt 16th-c manor house with entertaining tours by the owner. It's a popular location for TV programmes, providing a backdrop for characters from *Poirot* to *Casualty*. Shop, disabled access to ground floor only; open pm Easter Sun and Mon then pm Thurs, Sun and bank hols May–Sept; (01666) 502329; *£4. Out this way the Gumstool (A46/A4135) has very good food.

TEWKESBURY SO8832

Severnside town, site of the last battle in the Wars of the Roses in 1471, still full of attractive half-timbered medieval buildings in a maze of little alleyways. Two of these old places now house museums. Most impressive is the **abbey**, its massively confident Norman tower one of the finest in existence. Also splendid vaulting, some 14th-c stained glass, and regular concerts. The historic Bell Hotel and (simpler) ancient Black Bear are good for lunch.

THAMES & SEVERN CANAL SO9303

The rich, steeply sheltered valleys around Stroud make up a complicated landscape, seen to best advantage for example between Chalford and Sapperton. British Waterways recently unveiled plans to restore the atmospherically overgrown derelict canal here – its towpath forming an attractive wooded walkway. The Crown at Frampton Mansell, Butchers Arms at Oakridge Lynch or Daneway at Sapperton are useful jumping-off points.

THORNBURY ST6094

Oldbury Power Station Tours of nuclear power station, with hands-on displays, multi-media show, and nature trail. Snacks, shop, disabled access (not on tour); cl Nov–Feb (though will usually do tours on wkdys if you phone); (01454) 419899; free. The Anchor at Oldbury-on-Severn has good food.

TOCKINGTON ST6187

Oldown ⊞ (B4461) Lively country park with good adventure play areas for older children – lots of rope bridges, tube slides and climbing nets. Play area for younger children too, who'll probably get the most out of the animals and demonstrations at the farm. Several picnic areas, pleasant walks, summer **pick-your-own**, and excellent farm shop – organic meat, local cheeses, home-made honey and so on. Meals, snacks, shop, disabled access; cl Mon (exc bank and summer hols), and all Nov–Feb (exc shop and restaurant); (01454) 413605; £4.25. The quiet village itself is attractive, with good value food in the Swan.

TODDINGTON SP0432

Gloucestershire–Warwickshire Railway Steam and diesel train trips through around six miles of quiet countryside, departing from restored GWR stations either here or in Winchcombe. Snacks, shop, good disabled access (though parts of the car park are uneven); phone for timetable (01242) 621405; around £7. The Pheasant has good value food.

TWIGWORTH SO8223

Nature in Art ▣ (Wallsworth Hall, A38) In an imposing Georgian mansion, a growing collection of well displayed paintings, sculpture, and mosaics inspired by nature; more interesting than you'd expect – besides David Shepherd, artists represented include Picasso, Henry Moore and Graham Sutherland. Readers very much enjoy coming here. Good meals and snacks, shop, disabled access; cl Mon (exc bank hols), 24–26 Dec; (01452) 731422; £3.40.

ULEY ST7898

Attractive former weaving village with some 18th-c or older stone houses; the Old Crown is good value (ditto its bedrooms), and a good base for walkers.

Uley Tumulus (off B4066 N) Quite daunting 55-metre (180-ft) long burial mound known as Hetty Pegler's Tump, with stone central passage and three burial chambers; key from nearby house.

Owlpen Manor (B4066, just E) Charming Tudor manor house, with lovely formal gardens and peaceful woodland. Restaurant; cl Mon (except bank hol), ams and mid-Oct–Mar; (01453) 860261; £4.50. Good views from this road.

WESTBURY-ON-SEVERN

SO7114

Westbury Court Formal Dutch garden with canals, yew topiary, etc, restored to its 1700s layout using pre-1700 cultivars inc old fruit varieties. Disabled access; cl Mon (exc bank hols), Tues and all Nov–Mar; (01452) 760461; £2.90; NT. The Red Lion has good generous food, by the **church** with its unusual detached tower. The village is a good spot for catching the Severn Bore.

WESTONBIRT ST8588

Westonbirt Arboretum ▣ Over 18,000 numbered trees and shrubs fill the 17 miles of pathways at this magnificent collection, begun in 1829. Outstanding in spring and autumn, but worth a stop any time, with lots of wildlife hidden away among the trees. Meals, snacks, shop, disabled access; open all year, though visitor centre cl Christmas–New Year; (01666) 880220; £4. The Hare & Hounds is handy for food.

WINCHCOMBE SP0228

Very peaceful and photogenic – once the capital of Mercia, now worth a stop for a look at the **church** with its grotesque and sometimes rather rude gargoyles, or just to soak up the tranquil atmosphere. The Plaisterers Arms (High St) has good food, and there are interesting craft and other shops here. Splendid views of the area from Belas Knap.

Folk & Police Museum In the Old Town Hall, this has a sometimes surprising collection of British and international police uniforms as well as local history displays; shop; cl Sun, and Nov–Mar; 80p.

Hailes Abbey (Hailes, B4632) Graceful ruins of 13th-c Cistercian abbey, once a centre for pilgrims who flocked to see a phial containing what they believed to be Christ's blood. Walkman tour, shop, some disabled access; cl wkdys Nov–Mar; (01242) 602398; £2.60; NT. Hayles Fruit Farm down the road is good for snacks, and has **pick-your-own**.

Railway Museum & Garden ▣ (Gloucester St) Victorian garden full of lovingly rescued railway memorabilia inc booking office, working signals and signal box. Snacks, shop, disabled access; usually open wknd pms

Easter–Oct and daily in Aug, plus Weds–Fri in between, and 2nd Sun of month in winter; (01242) 620641; *£2.25.

Sudeley Castle & Gardens 🔳 (off B4632) Once home to Catherine Parr, the luckiest of Henry VIII's wives, the remains of the original medieval castle were skilfully blended into a 19th-c reconstruction. Rich furnishings, porcelain and tapestries, and notable paintings by Turner, Van Dyck and Rubens. The ten gardens are splendid, and include a knot garden constructed using flowers shown on a 16th-c tapestry on view in the library; there's an exhibition on World War I, and displays in a former workshop look at the life of Emma Dent, the woman responsible for the most attractive of the Victorian improvements. Meals, snacks, shop and specialist plant centre, disabled access to garden; house open Apr–28 Oct (gardens from Mar); (01242) 602308; *£6.20, *£4.70 grounds and exhibition only, audio tours £2. There's a working pottery nearby (cl winter Suns).

WOTTON-UNDER-EDGE ST7693

More small town than village, and full of charm, with a fine Schreider organ in its church, a little **heritage centre**, and some handsome old buildings; the B4058 is a good drive.

WYE VALLEY SO5309

The lower Wye Valley on the W side of the Forest of Dean cuts through a gorge giving some very picturesque views. As there are few crossing points, and the scenery away from the gorge is relatively unspectacular, walks along it are generally of the there-and-back sort. On the Gloucestershire side the valley is tracked by the Offa's Dyke Path; the Wye Valley Walk takes in the western bank. S of Monmouth, the A466 tracks through the valley below the paths.

Devil's Pulpit ST5499 A great viewpoint on the Offa's Dyke Path, where trees frame a perfect vista of Tintern Abbey far below on the opposite bank of the Wye.

The Kymin SO5212 Can be climbed from May Hill just across the river border opposite Monmouth; at the summit is the Naval Temple, a quaint

rustic conceit put up in 1800 to commemorate admirals of the Napoleonic Wars.

Wintour's Leap ST5496 A highlight of the Offa's Dyke Path: a sheer cliff over the Wye N of Chepstow with dizzy views downwards.

YANWORTH SP0713

An attractive village, especially at daffodil time.

Chedworth Roman Villa The best example of a 2nd-c Roman house in Britain, excavated in 1864 and nicely set in secluded woodland. Well preserved rooms, bath houses and 4th-c mosaics, with smaller remains in museum. Shop, some disabled access; cl Mon (exc bank hols), and end Nov–Feb; (01242) 890256; £3.60; NT. The Mill at Withington and Seven Tuns in Upper Chedworth are quite handy for lunch – and the walk from each is very picturesque and unspoilt, with Chedworth Woods providing further scope for short walks.

Other attractive villages, all with decent pubs, include Alderton SP0033, Almondsbury ST6084, Amberley SO8401, Bisley SO9005, Bledington SP2422, Broad Campden SP1637, Broadwell SP2027, the Duntisbournes SO9709, Ebrington SP1840, Ewen SU0097, Great Barrington SP2013 (good cheap bedrooms at the Fox, lovely walks), Great Rissington SP1917, Lower Swell SP1725, Meysey Hampton SU1199, Nether Westcote SP2120, Slad SO8707 (the setting for Laurie Lee's *Cider With Rosie*), Somerford Keynes SU0195, South Woodchester (particularly for the views) SO8302, Todenham SP2436, Wick ST7072 (pleasant walks) and Willersey SP1039. Though there's no pub to recommend there, Saintbury SP1139 is a winner when the daffodils are out. The B4060 N of Chipping Sodbury ST7282 and the side roads through Hawkesbury ST7786 and Hillesley ST7689 take you through attractive Cotswoldy scenery. Many villages have most attractive **churches**, few of them as yet locked. Cirencester is a good base for planning circuits of these. One such group E of the town consists of Ampney Crucis SP0602, Ampney St Peter SP0801, Ampney St Mary SP0802, Down

Ampney SP1097 (Vaughan Williams was the vicar's son) and Hampnett SP1015. Another group, NW of Cirencester, has Elkstone SO9612, Duntisbourne Abbots SO9707,

Duntisbourne Rouse SO9806, Daglingworth SO9905 (with its finely preserved Saxon carving of Christ on the cross), Stratton SP0103, Baunton SP0204 and North Cerney SP0208.

Where to eat

BLOCKLEY SP1634 **Crown** *High St* (01386) 700245 Smart and civilised Elizabethan stone inn, long bar counter stretching from the front door, through two inter-connecting snug areas and into a big atmospheric room with comfortable sofas and newspapers to read; good, often interesting bar food inc fresh fish dishes, quite a few wines, and real ales; children allowed if well behaved; pretty bdrms. £35|**£6.95**

BOURTON-ON-THE-WATER SP1620 **Vernes** *Riverside* (01451) 822005 Pretty 17th-c cottage with enjoyable light breakfast, lunch and early evening meals, all-day savouries, and cream teas; cl winter Mon, 2 wks Jan; disabled access. £16.50|**£6**

BOX SO8600 **Halfway Inn** (01453) 832631 Recently refurbished, extended tall house on edge of the common; attractive open-plan bar with simple but sturdy chairs and tables, woodburner, fresh flowers and décor; enjoyable imaginative food, well kept real ales, well chosen wines, and friendly helpful service; newly landscaped garden. £19.45|**£7.25**

BROAD CAMPDEN SP1537 **Bakers Arms** (01386) 840515 Atmospheric ex-granary in tranquil village with good value bar food (inc children's menu), a fine range of real ales, cosy beamed bar, log fires, friendly cats, pleasant service, and nice garden; cl 25 Dec, pm 26 Dec.|**£5.50**

CHEDWORTH SP0609 **Hare & Hounds** *Fosse Cross* (01285) 720288 (A429) Rambling dining pub with enthusiastic hard-working licensees, main area with low beams and soft lighting, well spread good-sized tables on stripped boards, and two big log fires in stone fireplaces; a further area has similar furnishings, and yet another log fire with two sofas; well kept real ales, 10 wines by the glass from a thoughtful list, and particularly good imaginative food; cl 25 Dec. £22|**£9**

CHELTENHAM SO9421 **Champignon Sauvage** 24–26 Suffolk Rd (01242) 573449 Classic French cooking in quietly and simply decorated restaurant with helpful service and good thoughtful wine list; cl Sun, Mon, 2 wks Christmas, 3 wks June; partial disabled access. £43.45 dinner, £24.45 lunch

CHIPPING CAMPDEN SP1539 **Brasserie** *Cotswold House Hotel, The Square* (01386) 840330 Fine 17th-c hotel with stylish and attractive brasserie offering good interesting meals and light snacks, plus morning coffee and afternoon tea – more formal restaurant, too; pretty bdrms; partial disabled access. £24|**£6**

CIRENCESTER SP0202 **Swan Yard Café** 6 Swan Yard, W Market Pl (01285) 641300 Popular with shoppers, this small simple family-run café has friendly service, and very good value totally home-made food (inc vegetarian choices); disabled access. £13.50|**£5**

COLN ST ALDWYNS SP1405 **New Inn** (01285) 750651 Civilised ivy-covered inn with beautifully presented restaurant-standard food served in a relaxed pubby atmosphere; attractively decorated rooms, a central log fire, well kept real ales and good wines, a no smoking restaurant, and split-level garden; nice surrounding countryside and walks; comfortable bdrms; children over 10 in restaurant. £32|**£8.50**

DRYBROOK SO6417 **Cider Press** (01594) 544472 Enjoyable little country restaurant specialising in delicious interestingly cooked fresh fish, often using home-grown herbs; free-range meat dishes, too, lovely puddings, excellent cheeses, reasonably priced wines, and friendly owners; cl Tues, cl early Jan; disabled access. £25

GUITING POWER SP0924 **Hollow Bottom** (01451) 850392 Snug old cottage with a friendly homely atmosphere, a comfortable beamed bar full of horse-racing memorabilia, a winter log fire, flagstoned public bar, well kept ales, enjoyable food in bar and separate restaurant, and pleasant helpful service; good nearby walks. £20|£4.95

KILKENNY SP0018 **Kilkeney Inn** *(01242) 820341* Comfortable dining pub, airy and spacious, with extended and modernised bar (drinking area at one end), an open fire, imaginative food under new owners, well kept ales, an interesting wine list, and no smoking dining conservatory; children must be well behaved; disabled access. £21.45|£7

KINGSCOTE ST8196 **Hunters Hall** *(01453) 860393* Civilised old creeper-covered inn with some fine furniture and big log fires in high-beamed connecting rooms, good bar and restaurant food, enjoyable breakfasts, and quite a few wines by the glass; big garden with play area; bdrms. £21|£6

LOWER ODDINGTON SP2326 **Fox** *(01451) 870555* Carefully restored elegant inn with wine-related antiques in one room and fresh flowers, flagstones, hops, an inglenook fireplace, and daily newspapers in other spotless, simply furnished rooms, imaginative and enjoyable food served by uniformed staff, well kept beers, and an excellent wine list. £22.15|£7.95

MORETON-IN-MARSH SP2032 **Marsh Goose** *High St (01608) 652111* Cotswold stone house with local artists' work in the several eating areas, good inventive cooking inc lovely puddings, a thoughtful wine list, and quick young staff; weekly cookery lessons; cl Sun pm, Mon, Tues pm; disabled access. £40 dinner, £25 lunch

NORTHLEACH SP1114 **Red Lion** *Market Pl (01451) 860251* Good value well presented generous food in comfortable and friendly pub, with a straightforward bar, open fire, well kept ales, and friendly service; cl pm 25 Dec; disabled access. £17.50|£5.50

PAXFORD SP1837 **Churchill** *(01386) 594000* Busy yet friendly dining pub with a simply furnished flagstoned bar – low ceilings, assorted old tables and chairs, and a snug warmed by a good log fire in its big fireplace; also, a restaurant extension; well kept real ales, eight good wines by the glass, and constantly changing interesting food; in the best pub tradition, they don't take bookings, but your name goes on a chalked waiting list if all the tables are full; seats outside; bdrms; £22.75|£8.50

SOUTHROP SP2003 **Swan** *(01367) 850205* Civilised creeper-covered old stone-tiled pub in pretty village, with good interesting food, a respectable wine list, little no smoking restaurant, friendly service, and log fires; cl Sun pm. £23|£5.50

TETBURY ST8494 **Gumstool** *Calcot (01666) 890391* Bustling pubby bistro (actually part of rambling Calcot Manor) with stripped pine, flagstones and neatly modern furnishings, a relaxed but civilised atmosphere, delicious interesting food, well kept real ales, a thoughtful choice of wines by the glass, and good service; comfortable bdrms; disabled access. £25|£8

WOODCHESTER SO8402 **Ram** *Station Rd (01453) 873329* Bustling cheerful pub with spectacular valley views from terrace, attractive beamed bar, very enjoyable bar food inc interesting daily specials, prompt friendly service, and lots of real ales; they are hoping to build an extension which will include disabled facilities. £16.40|£5.95

Special thanks to Norman Fox, Mark Holman, Sandra and John Dawkins

HAMPSHIRE

Portsmouth's maritime bustle, plenty of enjoyable historic places to visit, and attractive countryside, especially the New Forest

Perhaps surprisingly, much of the family fun to be had here centres around the county's remarkable military heritage, and its association with the navy in particular – with Portsmouth as its focus. The huge-scale rejuvenation of the harbour is nearing completion, with several new attractions opening as a result. As well as its wonderful collection of old and modern ships, the excellent HM Naval Base has new galleries in its Royal Naval Museum, and an interactive look at the modern navy (inc an IMAX cinema), opening around April. Elsewhere around the harbour, the new Millennium Promenade links other sites of interest such as Explosion!, a lively hands-on museum largely devoted to naval weaponry, opening at Priddy's Hard, Gosport, in the spring.

The pick of the county's other military museums include Fareham's Fort Nelson (a good value destination), the Museum of Army Flying at Middle Wallop, Aldershot's Airborne Forces Museum, the Royal Navy Submarine Museum at Gosport (you can tour the beached HMS *Alliance*), and the lively Royal Marines Museum at Southsea (with a junior commando assault course and lots of special events). Forget dusty old cases of medals and indecipherable battle maps: these places are enthusiastic and up-to-date, with plenty to grab the attention. Hampshire County Council publish 'Defence of the Realm', a brochure detailing discounted entry to over 40 military-linked attractions; available from individual sites, most Tourist Information Centres, or call their hotline (023) 8061 1010.

Southsea, Portsmouth's resort part, caters well for families with a beachfront amusement park and one of England's best Sea Life Centres; sadly the future of Cumberland House Natural History Museum hangs in the balance as we go to press.

Although not yet open, Milestones Living History Museum in Basingstoke so impressed us with its energetic ideas to re-create bygone scenes as well as amuse children, that we've chosen it as Hampshire's Family Attraction of the Year.

Other ideas for family entertainment include Marwell Zoo at Colden Common, the lovely Watercress Railway Line from Alresford (they do decent Thomas the Tank Engine specials), the cheerful Hollycombe Steam Collection near Liphook, the working Iron Age farm at Chalton, and the imaginative Hawk Conservancy at Weyhill. Paultons Park at Ower is a treat for younger children.

The Queen Elizabeth Country Park and Finkley Down Farm Park are good for outdoor activities, and Bursledon holds enough appeal to fill a pleasant summer afternoon.

The New Forest countryside, mainly rolling heathland, is great for free-form wandering among ponies and deer, and ideal for children to romp around in. Its coast has sheltered yachting harbours, the pleasant waterside town of Lymington with warm Georgian buildings (the rest of Hampshire's coastline is largely built up), and the interesting Bucklers Hard. Excellent places to visit in and around it include Beaulieu with its great range of subsidiary attractions, the farm and nature centres at Ashurst, the owl sanctuary at Ringwood (lots of flying displays; new to the *Guide* this year), the grounds of waterside Exbury (irresistible in late spring), the newer gardens of Spinners at Boldre (exciting for plantsmen), and Breamore House.

Winchester is a lovely city, with a charming old quarter around its cathedral, and plenty of opportunities for strolls nearby; a possibility for a quiet city break. Though Southampton is big and busy, it has some surprisingly fine medieval heritage.

Elsewhere, there are some magnificent houses and gardens. Broadlands near Romsey, Hinton Ampner, the Vyne at Sherborne St John, Stratfield Saye and the tranquil ruins of Basing House are all very rewarding. Mottisfont Abbey has wonderful old-fashioned roses, Houghton Lodge just upriver towards Stockbridge is a peaceful spot, and the gardens and arboretum at Ampfield are very fine. The Sandham Memorial Chapel at Burghclere is thought by some to be the greatest masterpiece of 20th-c British art.

Inland, a broad belt of gentle countryside stretches from Andover, Stockbridge and Romsey along the Test Valley in the W, through Winchester and Alresford, to Alton and Petersfield in the E. This is a quietly charming mix of rolling blowy chalk downland, a patchwork of hedged fields and clumps of steep beechwood, the rich valleys of the clear chalk streams, and attractive small villages often of brick and flint, with plenty of peaceful walking opportunities.

The Millennium Pilgrim's Trail passes through areas of historic and natural interest between Winchester and Portsmouth (a cross-Channel continuation is available for the more adventurous); available from Winchester Tourist Information Centre, or phone (01962) 870500 to order a copy; £2.99.

Where to stay

BEAULIEU SU3902 **Montagu Arms** *Palace Lane, Beaulieu, Brockenhurst, Hampshire SO42 7ZL (01590) 612324* **£125**, plus special breaks; 24 individually decorated pretty rms. Attractive creeper-clad hotel with lovely terraced garden, comfortable sitting room, conservatory lounge, very good food in beamed restaurant and more informal brasserie, and attentive staff; their health club is in the nearby village of Brockenhurst

CHERITON SU5828 **Flower Pots** *Cheriton, Alresford, Hampshire SO24 0QQ (01962) 771318* **£50**; 5 rms. Unspoilt and quietly comfortable village local run by very friendly family, with two pleasant little bars, log fire, decent bar food, super own-brew beers, and old-fashioned seats on the pretty lawns; no accommodation 24–26 Dec, 31 Dec, 1 Jan; children over 12

DROXFORD SU6018 **White Horse** *South Hill, Droxford, Southampton, Hampshire SO32 3PB (01489) 877490* **£55**; 3 rms, 1 with own bthrm. Rambling 16th-c inn with a relaxed atmosphere, small cosy lounge bars, log fires, a sizeable public bar, good reasonably priced bar food, no smoking restaurant areas, well kept real ales, and seats in a flower-filled courtyard; no accommodation 25 Dec–1 Jan; no dogs

HURSTBOURNE TARRANT SU3954 **Esseborne Manor** *Hurstbourne Tarrant, Andover, Hampshire SP11 0ER* (01264) 736444 **£112***, plus special breaks; 14 individually decorated rms. Small stylish Victorian manor with a calm relaxed atmosphere, comfortable lounge and snug little bar, good modern cooking, log fires in elegant dining room, and friendly staff; neat gardens with tennis, croquet and golf; disabled access

LYMINGTON SZ3094 **Efford Cottage** *Milford Rd, Everton, Lymington, Hampshire SO41 0JD* (01590) 642315 **£48***, plus winter breaks; 3 comfortable rms. Spacious Georgian family home nr forest, and in an acre of garden, with marvellous breakfasts inc freshly baked bread and home-made jams, enjoyable evening meals (only as part of winter special breaks), and good parking; no children; well behaved dogs welcome by arrangement

LYMINGTON SZ3295 **Stanwell House** *High St, Lymington, Hampshire SO41 9AA* (01590) 677123 **£105**; 28 pretty rms. Handsome townhouse with comfortable attractively furnished lounge, cosy little bar, good imaginative food, and pretty walled back garden; 50-ft yacht for charter

LYNDHURST SU3107 **Poussin at Parkhill** *Beaulieu Rd, Lyndhurst, Hampshire SO43 7FZ* (023) 8028 2944 **£115**, plus special breaks; 20 carefully furnished rms, some overlooking the lawns. Under new owners, this 13th-c hunting lodge was rebuilt by the Duke of Clarence in the 18th c, in parkland with fine views; comfortable lounges, antiques, flowers, and a civilised atmosphere; good food in attractive dining room, and friendly professional staff; mainly no smoking; disabled access

MIDDLE WALLOP SU2837 **Fifehead Manor** *Middle Wallop, Stockbridge, Hampshire SO20 8EG* (01264) 781565 **£130**, plus special breaks; 17 spacious rms. Friendly and comfortable old brick manor house in several acres of lovely gardens; a restful atmosphere, pleasant small lounge and bar, fine food in candlelit restaurant, enjoyable breakfasts, and friendly staff; croquet; disabled access

NEW MILTON SZ2294 **Chewton Glen** *Christchurch Rd, New Milton, Hampshire BH25 6QS* (01425) 275341 **£365** inc dinner; 55 really beautiful rms. Luxurious hotel in lovely grounds with fine antiques in sumptuous day rooms, excellent modern French cooking, and very good service; gardens include nine-hole golf course, swimming pool, tennis (two indoor courts as well) and croquet; also health club with indoor swimming pool, gym, saunas, treatment rooms; children over 6; disabled access

NEW MILTON SZ2497 **Yew Tree Farm** *Bashley Common Rd, New Milton, Hampshire BH25 5SH* (01425) 611041 **£75***; 2 lovely spacious rms. Marvellously warm and comfortable, well run traditional thatched smallholding on forest edge; small cosy hall, friendly welcome, extensive breakfasts (taken in bedroom on tables laid with fine china and crisp napery), and enjoyable home-made dinners (if required) using top-quality produce; riding nearby; no smoking, children or dogs

OWER SU3318 **Ranvilles Farm House** *Pauncefoot Hill, Romsey, Hampshire SO51 6AA* (023) 8081 1483 **£50***; 3 attractively decorated rms with extra-large beds. Dating from the 13th c when Richard de Ranville came from Normandy and settled with his family, this Grade II* listed house is in five quiet acres of gardens and paddock, with open fire and antiques in appealing sitting room, warmly friendly owners; no evening meals; cl Christmas and New Year; disabled access.

PORTSMOUTH SZ6299 **Fortitude Cottage** *51 Broad St, Portsmouth, Hampshire PO1 2JD* (023) 9282 3748 **£50**; 3 neat and attractive rms. Comfortable B&B in cottage named after an old ship, with pretty beamed breakfast room overlooking fishing boats; no evening meals but places nearby; cl 25–26 Dec; children over 9

PORTSMOUTH SZ6399 **Sally Port** *High St, Portsmouth, Hampshire PO1 2LU* (023) 9282 1860 **£65**, plus special breaks; 10 rms, most with own bthrm. Beautifully kept 16th-c inn in quiet spot, with good food and very friendly efficient service; said to have been a favourite of Nelson; disabled access

ROCKBOURNE SU1118 **Shearings** *Rockbourne, Fordingbridge, Hampshire SP6 3NA (01725) 518256* **£60**; 3 rms plus garden annexe. Beside a winter stream, this warmly welcoming and pretty 16th-c thatched cottage has inglenook fireplaces, ancient beams (some nearly 1,000 years old), and comfortable sitting room; good pub just up the road; cl mid-Dec to end Jan; children over 12; no dogs

ROTHERWICK SU7155 **Tylney Hall** *Rotherwick, Basingstoke, Hampshire RG27 9AZ (01256) 764881* **£152**, plus special breaks; 110 comfortable well equipped rms. Grand Victorian mansion in 66 acres of lovely gardens and parkland; gracious rooms with oak panelling, oil paintings, log fires in big ornate fireplaces, fresh flowers, and fine ceilings, interesting modern cooking in candlelit restaurant, and good attentive service; tennis, golf, indoor and outdoor swimming pools, gym and sauna; disabled access

SPARSHOLT SU4431 **Lainston House** *Sparsholt, Winchester, Hampshire SO21 2LT (01962) 863588* **£156**, plus wknd breaks; 41 spacious, individually decorated rms. Close to Winchester, this elegant William and Mary hotel stands in 63 acres of fine parkland, with tennis court, croquet, fishing, archery, and clay pigeon shooting; fresh flowers and paintings in relaxing, elegant lounge, panelled bar and restaurant, a fine wine list, and good British cooking; new gym; disabled access

SWAY SZ2798 **Nurses Cottage** *Station Rd, Sway, Lymington, Hampshire SO41 6BA (01590) 683402* **£95**, plus special breaks; 3 rms with thoughtful extras. Small, immaculately kept and no smoking restaurant-with-rooms with emphasis on personal service by the resident chef/owner; hearty but healthy breakfasts in Garden Room restaurant (which is also open to non-residents for afternoon tea, Sun lunch, and dinner), an impressive wine list, and imaginative food using herbs and vegetables from the neat garden; cl 2 wks Mar, 3 wks Nov; children over 10; disabled access

THRUXTON SU2945 **May Cottage** *Thruxton, Andover, Hampshire SP11 8LZ (01264) 771241* **£50***; 3 rms. Creeper-clad early Georgian house in quiet village, with friendly owners, residents' sitting room, good breakfasts, afternoon tea with home-made cake in pretty garden, and dinner by arrangement; no smoking; cl Christmas; children over 6

WICKHAM SU5711 **Old House** *The Square, Wickham, Fareham, Hampshire PO17 5JG (01329) 833049* **£85**, plus special breaks; 9 rms. Lovely ivy-clad early Georgian house fronting the village square, with beamed and panelled rooms, antiques, fresh flowers and open fires, reliably good French cooking in the restaurant (once the timber-framed outhouse and stables), and pretty back garden; cl 10 days over Christmas

WINCHESTER SU4729 **Hotel du Vin & Bistro** *14 Southgate St, Winchester, Hampshire SO23 9EF (01962) 841414* **£112**; 23 rms, real quality, and each sponsored by a well known wine company with relevant paintings, labels and old photographs. An engaging early 18th-c town house with enthusiastic owners and hard-working staff, deeply comfortable sitting room, two relaxed and pretty eating areas with good bistro-style cooking and an exceptional wine list, and a lovely walled garden for summer dining; disabled access

WINCHESTER SU4828 **Wykeham Arms** *75 Kingsgate St, Winchester, Hampshire SO23 9PE (01962) 853834* **£79.50**; 13 well equipped attractive rms. Very well run, smart old town inn, close to cathedral, with interestingly furnished bustling bars, two small dining rooms serving delicious, daily-changing food (very good breakfasts, too), fine wines (lots by the glass), and prompt friendly service; several no smoking areas; cl 25 Dec; no children

Please let us know what you think of places in the *Guide*. Use the report forms at the back of the book or simply write us a letter.

To see and do

Hampshire Family Attraction of the Year

BASINGSTOKE SU6252 **Milestones Living History Museum** (Leisure Park, off B3400, Churchill Way W) We don't often stick our neck out and recommend somewhere that hasn't opened yet, but this £10-million social history museum — set to open just after this edition is published — sounds so intriguing we couldn't resist making an exception. A network of streets and authentically assembled buildings has been constructed to re-create the sights, sounds and smells of local life since Victorian times, with three factories, a railway station, brewery (an attached pub will serve ales from Hampshire brewer Gales), fire station, and 17 shops, their windows crammed with hats, silverware and toys. To make it seem just that bit more realistic, period lampposts have been moved here from Winchester, and they've dotted around freeze-dried mice and stuffed pigeons. Staff in period clothes will explain things, so it will be almost like a fully populated little town — except for the fact it never rains: the whole thing is indoors, in a splendid, very modern-looking glass building. The idea is to showcase dozens of previously undisplayed collections and items, and they've gone to some trouble filling in any gaps. Something that particularly stands out is the way they're designing some parts very much with children in mind: an interactive post office for under-5s, where children will be able to sort and stamp letters for posting throughout the museum, a big toy area where six activity trucks will compare today's toys and games with those from the past, and a hands-on history section for 7- to 11-year-olds, with a fun old-fashioned photographer's studio. There will be some emphasis on local industries, with vehicles and collections relating to Thornycroft, Willis and Stevens, steam engines from Taskers of Andover, and early examples of clothing from Burberrys, whose first shop opened in Basingstoke in 1856. They say a typical visit will last about three hours. As we went to press it was due to open on 25 November 2000, but the opening has already been put back once, so best to check first. Meals, snacks, shop, disabled access; cl 24–26, 31 Dec, and 1 Jan; (01256) 477766; *£5.95 (£2.95 children). The surrounding leisure park has ice-skating, cinemas and ten-pin bowling.

ALDERSHOT SU8651
Airborne Forces Museum 🏛
(Browning Barracks) Up to now the best of Aldershot's profusion of military museums (most of which have been of rather specialist appeal), looking at the parachute forces. Lots to take in, with very traditional displays. Snacks, shop, some disabled access; cl Christmas and 1 Jan; (01252) 349619; £2.50.
Military Museum (Queens Ave) Following a generous lottery-funded refurbishment, this will reopen in early summer, perked up with new galleries inc one looking at early flying experiments, to accompany the existing displays on the development of the local military camps and their impact on civilian and military life. Shop, disabled access; (01252) 314598; *£2. The Swan out at Ash Vale is a decent dining pub.

ALRESFORD SU5832
Watercress Line One of the nicest steam railways in the country, with 10-mile trips between Alresford and Alton through wonderful countryside and its watercress beds. They try to create a pre-war feel, with stations decked out accordingly. Their Thomas the Tank Engine weeks around Easter and in Aug are extraordinarily popular; several railways organise something similar, but the Thomas here is unusual in being built to the design and proportions in the books, and there may also be other characters such as James the Red Engine, Diesel and the Fat Controller. Properly called the Mid-Hants Railway, it runs special main-line monthly trips to places as far away as Brighton and Bristol. Meals, snacks, shop, disabled access; phone for timetable, (01962)

733810, no trains Nov–Jan (exc Dec Santa specials); £8. Alresford itself is a charming little town, from the Roman ponds teeming with wildfowl in Old Alresford to the so-called New Alresford founded around 1200; good antiquarian bookshop here. The Globe overlooking the ponds does decent lunches, and the Café Cressdon is good. The Itchen road W through Ovington and Easton is pretty, the B3046 N shows high Hampshire farmland well, and the old road E past Ropley and Monkwood to Steep gives a fine downland impression.

ALTON SU7139

Allen Gallery (Church St) Superb collection of pottery, and a little herb garden. Snacks, shop, disabled access to ground floor only; cl Mon and 2 wks over Christmas; (01420) 82802; free. The town is the other terminus of the Watercress steam line (see Alresford entry). Bass Brewery (Turk St) offers wkdy tours (inc snacks) 11.30 am–3pm and 7.30–10pm (not Fri pm); (01420) 520158; £9. A church bears scars from one of the last battles of the Civil War. The French Horn (The Butts) is a friendly food pub.

AMPFIELD SU3824

Sir Harold Hillier Gardens (Jermyns Lane, off A31) Impressive collection of trees and shrubs, the biggest of its kind in Britain, covering 180 beautifully landscaped acres. Full of colour and surprises all year, but particularly delightful in spring; good walks and events (esp first Sun of month). Summer meals, snacks, nursery, disabled access; cl Christmas bank hols; (01794) 368787; *£4.25 (*£3.25 Nov–Mar). The White Horse nearby is a comfortable lunch break.

ANDOVER SU2744

Fast Helicopters The most exciting (and expensive) way to take in the local sights, with a chance to test your piloting potential; (01264) 772508; half-hour flight £125.

Finkley Down Farm Park (just NE) Well laid out working farm with wide range of animals and poultry inc rare breeds; they encourage you to touch the tamer animals, and there are varied activities every half-hour. Also countryside museum, adventure

playground and picnic site. Readers rate this very highly, and it has lots for children (inc space for them to run around). Meals, snacks, shop, disabled access; cl Nov–Feb; (01264) 352195; £4. There are well stocked trout fishing lakes around Andover, inc Rooksbury Mill. Poplar Farm (A343 at Abbotts Ann) is a useful food stop.

Museum of the Iron Age 🖼 Nr the church at the top of the impressive High St of this very extended country town, the museum looks particularly at finds from nearby Danebury Ring, giving a vivid impression of life for the pre-Roman Celts. Snacks, shop, limited disabled access; cl Sun (exc summer pm), Mon (exc summer bank hol pm), and Christmas; (01264) 366283; free (they may introduce an admission price in Apr). There's an adjacent more general **museum** (open same hours, free).

Test Valley Tapestry (Weyhill Rd – B3402) The local authority's conference room houses this remarkable textile, each of its panels embroidered by a different village to show a scene relating to that community. Disabled access; open by appointment only; (01264) 368839; free.

ASHMANSWORTH SU3758

Hampshire's high country There are fine views from many of the lanes around Ashmansworth and Linkenholt – best explored by car, though there are good walks too. The Plough does simple home cooking.

ASHURST SU3310

Longdown Dairy Farm (Deerleap Lane) This friendly place has plenty of animals to feed; their herd of Jersey cows is milked from 2.30pm every day. There's a small play area. Snacks, shop, disabled access; cl Nov–Easter; (01703) 293326; £4.30. The Happy Cheese (A35) has good value food.

New Forest Otter and Owl Park 🖼 (Longdown, off A35) Large collection of otters, owls and other indigenous wildlife; woodland nature trails. Meals, snacks, shop, disabled access; cl wkdys Jan–Feb; (023) 8029 2408; *£5.50. The Pilgrim is an attractive thatched dining pub.

AVINGTON SU5332

Avington Park 🏚 Georgian mansion with Tudor origins, set in lovely parkland. Teas in the orangery, disabled access; open pm Sun and bank hols May–Sept; (01962) 779260; *£3.50. The Bush at Ovington is a nicely placed nearby pub.

BASING SU6652

Basing House Ruins Peaceful ruins of what was once the country's largest house, destroyed during a two-year siege during the Civil War. Also remnants of a Norman castle, a 16th-c barn, dovecotes, an exhibition explaining the eventful history of the site and a re-created 17th-c garden. Nice walks from here along the River Loddon. Snacks, shop, disabled access with notice; open pm only, Weds–Sun and bank hols Apr–Sept; (01256) 467294; £1.50. The Gamekeepers at nearby Mapledurwell is handy for lunch.

BASINGSTOKE SU6250

Milestones Living History Museum *See separate family panel on p.257.*

Viables Craft Centre Fourteen craft workshops housed in the grounds of an 18th-c timber granary; ceramics studio, craft gallery, miniature railway, and various courses and events all year. Meals, snacks, shop, disabled access; usually open Tues–Sat pm Easter–Dec, but best to check; (01256) 473634; free.

BEAULIEU SU3802

Beaulieu Abbey 🏚 A justifiably popular family day out, its centrepiece still the National Motor Museum, a collection that from humble beginnings has grown to become one of the most comprehensive in the world. Other features have a motoring theme too: a hands-on gallery explains how cars work, and Wheels is probably the highlight for children – you sit in a pod-like vehicle and trundle through 100 years of motoring. For an extra £2 a simulator ride gives you a more robust driving experience. A monorail whizzes round the grounds, and in summer you can ride on a replica 1912 London bus. Also go-kart style mini-bikes, radio-controlled cars, and some hi-tech arcade-style driving games. Meanwhile the Palace House is a fine old mansion based around the gatehouse of the huge Cistercian Abbey that stood here until the Reformation (still with what are thought to be the original monastic fan-vaulted ceilings). The surrounding lakeside parkland and gardens are rewarding to explore, with ruins of other abbey buildings, and an exhibition on the monks who lived here. Meals, snacks, shops, disabled access; cl 25 Dec; (01590) 612123; £9.25. In the village facing the Palace House gates, the Wine Press is popular for lunch, and a marked trail leads from it down to Bucklers Hard.

BEAULIEU ROAD STATION SU3506

New Forest walks A good starting point, for its surrounding remote-feeling heaths.

BEDLAM BOTTOM SU6246

Pleasant partly wooded valley walks, particularly pretty in spring; just W of Ellisfield SU6345 (where the Fox has good food), with more downland walks above.

BEECH SU6838

Alton Abbey (signed off A339) The home of a community of Benedictine monks, in peaceful woodland so a relaxing place for a stroll. The grounds have mature specimen trees and shrubs, especially rhododendrons and azaleas. The traditional Sun at Bentworth does good food.

BINSTED SU7740

Binsted church Where Field Marshal Montgomery is buried; after the war he lived a mile away at Islington Mill – a pretty spot. The Cedars has decent food.

BISHOP'S WALTHAM SU5517

Bishop's Waltham Palace Impressive ruins of Bishop of Winchester's majestic 12th-c palace, with the remains of state apartments round a cloister court, and William of Wykeham's great hall and tower. Snacks, shop, disabled access to ground floor; cl Nov–Mar; (01489) 892460; £2; EH. The Barleycorn (Basingwell St) has decent food, and the downs N of here between Owslebury, Beauworth and Warnford give scenic drives.

BOKERLEY DITCH SU0419

This acted as a bulwark from raiders into Dorset in the 4th c; still impressive to walk along, it marks the county boundary and can be reached by walking up from Martin. Towards Pentridge Hill is a nature reserve.

BOLDRE SZ3298

Spinners 🏛 (School Lane) Wonderful gardens created since the 1960s. The nursery is famed for its rare trees (especially maples and magnolias), shrubs and plants. Some disabled access; gardens open Tues–Sat mid-Apr–mid-Sept, or by appointment, nursery open all year exc Sun and Mon Sept–Apr; (01590) 673347; *£2. The Red Lion (no children) is good for lunch.

BREAMORE SU1519

Breamore House Late Elizabethan manor house, with fine furnishings, tapestries and paintings (mainly 17th- and 18th-c Dutch school), and better than average countryside museum with displays of Roman artefacts found within the estate, and a rare 16th-c Bavarian turret clock, currently being restored. Children aren't left out – there's a maze and adventure playground. Snacks, shop, disabled access; open pm only Easter wknd, Tues, Weds, Sun and bank hols Apr–Sept, plus Thurs and Sat May–Sept, and daily in Aug; (01725) 512468; *£5. The village has many thatched houses, and is within a pleasant walk of Breamore House – and the mysterious Mizmaze, cut in the turf. The home cooking at the Horse & Groom at Woodgreen is good, with more lovely wood and riverside walks.

BROCKENHURST SU2902

New Forest walks The village is well placed for walks; you can also hire bicycles here – the forest is a good place for cycling.

BUCKLERS HARD SZ4099

Bucklers Hard Maritime Museum Very pretty little waterside village, with long red-roofed cottage rows flanking a wide, grassed waterside street. It was once an important centre for shipbuilding, and the Maritime Museum tells the story of the industry, right up to the voyages of Sir Francis Chichester. You have to pay to come into the village, though admission includes entry to the museum and the various other exhibitions and reconstructions dotted around, inc the

carefully restored 18th-c homes of a shipwright and labourer, and a typical inn scene complete with costumed figures, smells and conversation. Meals, snacks, shop; cl 25 Dec; (01590) 616203; £4.50. There are summer boat trips, and the Master Builders House is useful for lunch. A pleasant 2½-mile riverside walk takes you to Beaulieu, run by the same people.

BURGHCLERE SU4761

Sandham Memorial Chapel Stanley Spencer's moving masterpiece, built in memory of H W Sandham, killed in World War I. The final resurrection scene is especially dramatic, best on a bright day as the room is quite dark. Open Weds–Sun and bank hols Apr–Oct, wknds only Nov and Mar, best to phone for winter opening; (01635) 278394; *£2.50; NT. The Carpenters Arms opposite is pleasant for lunch, with superb views.

BURITON SU7320

Quiet village below the South Downs north-facing scarp slope nr Petersfield; enjoyable walks in all directions, and handy for the Queen Elizabeth Country Park and Butser Hill. The Five Bells is a good food stop.

BURLEY STREET SU1904

New Forest walks A good starting point for forest walks; the White Buck, and Burley Inn in busier nearby Burley, are both comfortable food pubs.

BURSLEDON SU4911

Manor Farm Country Park (Pylands Lane) Woodland and riverside walks based around traditional working farm, with lots of animals, crafts and activities inc a forge and a wheelwright. Meals, snacks, shop, mostly disabled access; park open all year, farm cl Nov–Easter exc Sun and Feb half-term; (01489) 787055; £3.90. There may be **boat trips** on some summer Sats from here along the Hamble. Bursledon also has a **windmill**; open Sun and summer Sats; £1.50. The Jolly Sailor is a beautifully placed food pub.

CALSHOT CASTLE SU4802

Down past the oil refineries and power stations, this Tudor fort stands on the end of the spit of land out over the tidal mudflats at the end of Southampton Water; splendid views of the shipping and the Isle of Wight. The Jolly Sailor at

Ashlett Creek nr Fawley is a pleasant waterside food pub.

CHALTON SU7117

Butser Ancient Farm 🔁 (Bascombe Copse) Reconstructed Iron Age farm, with period crops, animals and crafts, demonstrations, and ongoing excavations. You can try your hand at grinding corn on a stone, and there's a Celtic maze (planted with period herbs). Shop, disabled access; cl Nov–Mar; (023) 9259 8838; £3.50. The ancient Red Lion, Hampshire's oldest pub, is good for lunch.

CHAWTON SU7037

Jane Austen's House Enjoyable unpretentious 17th-c house where the author lived and worked between 1809 and 1817, still with some of her letters and possessions. Rooms are furnished in period style, and the pleasant garden is good for picnics. Good bookshop, disabled access to ground floor and garden; cl wkdys Jan and Feb, 25–26 Dec; (01420) 83262; £3. The Greyfriar opposite has reasonably priced food, and there are good walks here. Just up the road, Chawton House, the former home of Jane Austen's brother Edward, is now the Centre for the Study of Early English Women's Writing.

CHEESEFOOT HEAD SU5327 (locally pronounced 'Chesford') Good for walks; a natural amphitheatre where Eisenhower and Montgomery addressed the troops before the Normandy invasion.

CHILBOLTON SU3940

An attractive village where the common is being carefully preserved. The Abbots Mitre (open all day Sun) is a good pub.

COLDEN COMMON SU5121

Marwell Zoological Park (Colden Common, off B2177 towards Bishops Waltham) Too many supposedly conservation-minded animal attractions still shove their animals into overcrowded cages or enclosures, so it's particularly nice to find one like this where – at least in places – the tables are turned; visit the lemurs for instance and they'll be enjoying plenty of space and freedom while you watch from covered walkways. Other well conceived viewing areas include a glass wall at the end of the tiger enclosure

and underwater windows into the Penguin World. Residents range from kangaroos to hippos and include some animals which no longer exist in the wild. Children can handle the animals – from snakes to stick insects – during the summer holidays. The acres of parkland are attractively laid out, with particularly pleasant picnic areas; there's a good adventure playground, and road and rail trains whisk you between the different enclosures. *Fierce Creatures*, the less successful follow-up to *A Fish Called Wanda*, was filmed here. Meals, snacks, shop, good disabled access; cl 25 Dec; (01962) 777407; £8.80 (£6.30 children aged 3–14). On the downs above, the Ship at Owslebury is good for a family lunch – quieter than the big nearby Fishers Pond.

DAMERHAM SU1016

Damerham churchyard Well worth a February visit, to see the carpet of snowdrops. The Compasses has good food.

DANEBURY RING SU3237

Iron Age hill fort rich in (excavated) remains. The Peat Spade at Longstock to the E has good food.

EAST MEON SU6822

This appealing village has a splendid Norman church; the George is a good pub.

Snowdrop woods Many of the woodlands in this part of Hampshire fill with snowdrops in February.

EASTON SU5031

This attractive village is well placed for pleasant Itchen Valley walks; we can recommend both the Cricketers and the Chestnut Horse.

EXBURY SU4200

Exbury Gardens Wonderful 200-acre landscaped woodland gardens on E bank of the River Beaulieu, with splendid rock garden, heather garden and river walk, and above all the Rothschild collection of rhododendrons, azaleas, magnolias and camellias – one of the world's finest, at its best May and early Jun. Meals, snacks, shop, disabled access; cl early Nov–Feb; (023) 8089 1203; price varies with the season, from £3.50 in summer, to £5 in spring. The Jolly Sailor at Ashlett Creek nr Fawley is quite handy.

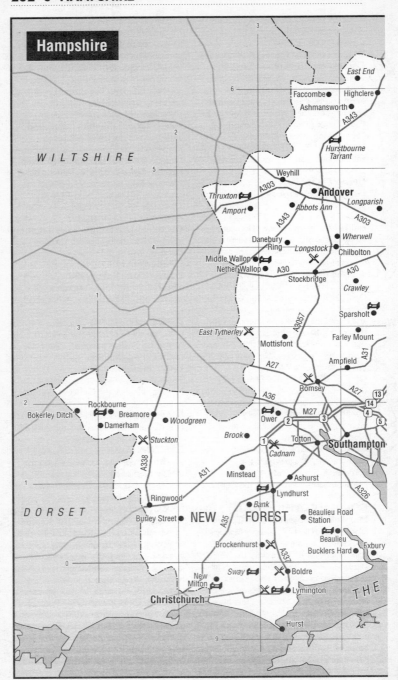

Hampshire

WILTSHIRE

DORSET

East End
Faccombe ● ● Highclere
Ashmansworth ●
A343
Hurstbourne Tarrant
Weyhill ●
A303
Thruxton ● **Andover**
Amport ● Abbots Ann ● *Longparish*
A343 A303
Wherwell
Danebury Ring *Longstock* Chilbolton
Middle Wallop A30
Nether Wallop ● Stockbridge A30
Crawley
Sparsholt ●
East Tytherley ✕ A3057 Farley Mount
Mottisfont ● Ampfield ●
A27 A31
Romsey
A36 ✕ A27 [13]
[14]
Rockbourne [4]
Bokerley Ditch Breamore ● Ower M27 [5]
Damerham ● *Woodgreen* [2] [3] **Southampton**
Stuckton *Brook* ● Totton
A338 Cadnam
A31 Minstead ● Ashurst
Ringwood Lyndhurst A326
NEW *Bank* Beaulieu Road
Burley Street ● **FOREST** Station ●
A35 Beaulieu
Brockenhurst ● ✕ Bucklers Hard ● Exbury
A337
New *Sway* ✕ Boldre
Milton ✕ Lymington T H E
Christchurch
Hurst ✕

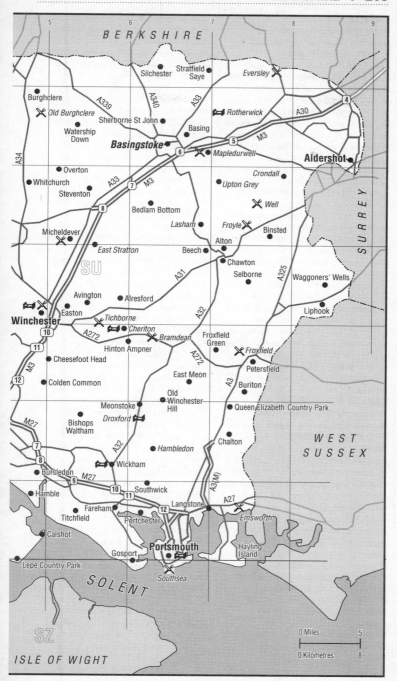

FACCOMBE SU3957

Bright with daffodils in spring, this attractive village has a decent pub, and great views from Pilot Hill.

FAREHAM SU6007

Fort Nelson (Downend Rd) You don't have to be interested in weaponry to enjoy a trip to this restored 19th-c fort, built in response to fears of an attack from France, and now part of the Royal Armouries Museum. It has been known as the noisiest museum in the world, thanks mainly to the roar of the two huge cannon fired twice a day, usually at 12 and 3pm, and the lingering smell of gunpowder adds to the atmosphere. Children aren't discouraged from clambering over the building and even some of the exhibits, and with plenty of underground tunnels to investigate, it's not unlike an enormous adventure playground. Occasional battle re-enactment days (best to ring for dates), and regular guided tours. Good views of Portsmouth Harbour from the ramparts. Meals, snacks, shop, disabled access; cl Mon–Weds Nov–Mar; (01329) 233734; £4.25 (though this may be reduced to £1 in Sept), children free. The Osborne View (Hill Head) has superb views, and is handy for the beach and walks in Titchfield Haven nature reserve.

FARLEY MOUNT SU4229

An attractive area of downland and woodland, with good views and walks.

FROXFIELD GREEN SU7124

Bluebells In May much of the woodland around Froxfield Green is carpeted with bluebells, as are woods elsewhere in the area – for example at East Tisted and Ropley.

GOSPORT SZ6099

Several millennium grant-funded attractions are coming to fruition here. Explosion! – a museum looking at the history of armaments – opens at Priddy's Hard in spring (see below); there's a giant new 15-metre sundial by the harbour, and the Millennium Promenade (see also Portsmouth) takes in some of the town's naval heritage.

Explosion! (Priddy's Hard, Priory Rd) Set within 18th-c former naval stores at the N end of the Millennium Promenade, this lively new museum is part of the project to rejuvenate Portsmouth Harbour. Using interactive and hands-on displays, it aims to trace the history of naval firepower, with exhibits from 18th-c muskets to the Exocet missile. It's not entirely restricted to things which go bang, however; the effects of war and the social history of the local area also get a look. Children should enjoy the more energetic displays – inc the chance to see what it was like to fire a big gun at sea. As the site develops, they hope to add more galleries, as well as shops and restaurants in the outlying buildings. The views from here across to Portsmouth Harbour are most rewarding. Snacks, shop, disabled access; open daily from spring 2001, best to phone Michael Nutt for details; (023) 9250 2490; *£5.

Fort Brockhurst A good overview exhibition of how the various forts protected Portsmouth. Shop, some disabled access though gravel tricky for wheelchairs; open wknds Apr–Nov; £2. The Dolphin (Fort Rd) has popular food.

Gosport Museum (Walpole Rd) Recently refurbished with an imaginative geology department; snacks, shop, disabled access; cl Sun and Mon; (023) 9258 8035; free.

Royal Navy Submarine Museum (Haslar Jetty Rd) The highlight here is the tour of beached World War II submarine HMS *Alliance*, still in full working order, and fascinating inside to boys of any age. More conventional features include an audio-visual show giving the flavour of diving into the depths. Snacks, shop, some disabled access; cl 24 Dec–1 Jan; (023) 9252 9217; £3.75. You can get a Waterbus across to Portsmouth (Apr–Oct), and the sea at Stokes Bay is probably Hampshire's cleanest for swimming in. The Clarence (A32) is a good newish pub brewing its own beer.

HAMBLE SU4806

This pleasant village in *Howard's Way* country has interesting views of the yachts, and you can walk a long way up river or towards The Solent; the simple Olde Whyte Harte has decent food. There's a friendly little ferry to Warsash taking about 10 people at a time, where the riverside Rising Sun has good food, and there's a wildfowl nature reserve just N. Nearby Netley has a coastal **country park** and the extensive ruins of a 13th-c abbey.

HAYLING ISLAND SU7201
Readers enjoy this holiday resort popular for water-sports.

HIGHCLERE SU4360
Highclere Castle 🔳 (best approached from A34 rather than Highclere itself) Magnificent pastiche of a medieval castle, impressively grand inside and out. Elaborate saloon and main staircase, a desk that belonged to Napoleon, and a Van Dyck of Charles I. Exhibitions of Egyptian relics (the 5th Earl discovered Tutankhamun's tomb with Howard Carter), and horse racing (the current Earl is the Queen's racing manager). The lovely gardens and grounds include a Victorian tropical conservatory and walled garden. Meals, snacks, shop and plant centre, disabled access; open daily July–early Sept, plus most bank hols wknds; (01635) 253210; £6.50, £3 gardens only. The Yew Tree (A343 S of village) is a good value dining pub.

HINTON AMPNER SU5927
Hinton Ampner Attractive Georgian house, but it's the impressive grounds that impress most, with tranquil 20th-c shrub gardens. Teas, disabled access; gardens may be open last two Suns in Mar (good for daffodils), then pm only Tues, Weds, wknds and bank hols Apr–Sept, house open pm only Tues and Weds, plus Sat and Sun in Aug; (01962) 771305; £4.50 house and garden, £3.50 garden only; NT. The neighbouring Hinton Arms has good food.

HURST CASTLE SZ3189
This was one of the most sophisticated fortresses around when built by Henry VIII, on a little spit commanding the Solent, and best reached on foot or by summer ferry from Keyhaven (there's a pleasant walk from the 17th-c Gun pub – good value food). Fortified again in the 19th c, it still has two huge 38-ton guns. Summer snacks, shop, disabled access to ground floor; cl wkdys Nov–Mar, 24–26 Dec, 1 Jan; (01590) 642344; £2.50.

LANGSTONE SU7104
Thatched cottages, an old tidal mill, and a couple of decent pubs looking out over the thousands of acres of silted harbour – winter sunsets are memorable. Swans float up at high tide, with oystercatchers and droves of darting dunlins on the low-tide mud flats. Interesting walks along the old sea wall.

LEPE COUNTRY PARK SZ4598
A pleasant spot for mild saunters along the coast.

LIPHOOK SU8330
Bohunt Manor Lovely woodland gardens owned by Worldwide Fund for Nature, with water garden, roses and herbaceous borders, lakeside walk, and unusual trees and shrubs. Disabled access; (01428) 722208; suggested donation £1.50.

Hollycombe Steam Collection 🔳 (Midhurst Rd) Huge collection of steam-driven equipment, from paddle-steamers to an entire Edwardian fairground, inc the big wheel. Occasional open evenings when the fairground is delightfully lit. Traction engine rides, and woodland steam train trips. Snacks, shop; open pm Sun and bank hols Easter–late Oct, and usually daily last wk July–Aug; (01428) 724900; £6.50. The nearest place for a good lunch is the Red Lion over at Fernhurst.

LYMINGTON SZ3295
Handsome and relaxed waterside town, very popular in summer with yachting people; it has quite a number of attractive Georgian buildings and some good shops. The Angel (High St) and Fisherman's Rest (All Saints Rd) have decent food. You can get ferries to the Isle of Wight from here, and the B3054 to Dibden Purlieu is a pretty road.

LYNDHURST SU2908
The tourist centre of the New Forest, as well as the main shopping town for people living here, so lots of tea shops, cafés etc. The car park has a good information centre for the area. The Royal Oak in the pretty hamlet of Bank just outside has a good choice of food.

New Forest Museum (High St) From outside it looks like a modern supermarket but inside there are very good themed displays and audio-visual exploration of the forest's history and wildlife, and a 25-ft embroidery. Decent children's features too. Shop, disabled

access; cl 25 Dec; (023) 8028 3914;
£2.75.

MEONSTOKE SU6119
An attractive village, with a decent pub.
The road from here down through
Soberton runs by the River Meon, and
is quiet enough to suit walkers; the old
Meon Valley railway line nearby is now
open as a walkway.

MICHELDEVER SU5138
Village of lovely thatched cottages and
colourful gardens. There are fine walks
in open countryside to the S, and up the
River Dever valley to the E. The Half
Moon & Spread Eagle has good food.

MIDDLE WALLOP SU3038
Museum of Army Flying 🖼 One of
the country's best military museums,
with kites, balloons, vintage aircraft,
World War II gliders, helicopters, and
an interactive science centre. Meals,
snacks, shop, disabled access; cl
Christmas week; (01980) 674421;
£4.50.

MINSTEAD SU2711
Furzey Gardens 🖼 Eight peaceful
acres, with developing young
arboretum, sensory garden and lake,
around charming 16th-c thatched
cottage and local craft gallery. Snacks,
plant sales, very limited disabled access;
cl 25–26 Dec; (01703) 812464; £3
(£1.50 winter). The village is quiet and
pretty, with a fine old church at the top
of the hill; the Trusty Servant by the
green has good food.

MOTTISFONT SU3227
Mottisfont Abbey 12th-c priory
salvaged from the Reformation as a
delightful family house, in wonderful
peaceful surroundings. The gardens are
a delight, housing a national collection
of old roses (largely scented). You can
usually see a few of the rooms, inc one
richly decorated by Rex Whistler.
Meals, snacks, shop, good disabled
access; open Sat–Weds pm mid-Mar to
Oct, and daily during the rose season
(usually mid–end of June); (01794)
340757; *£5 rose season; NT. The Bear
& Ragged Staff up on the A3057 does
good value food all day, and the road
along the Test through Houghton and
on to the attractive village of Wherwell
is pretty.

NETHER WALLOP SU2936
An attractive sleepy village with an
interesting Saxon church; surprisingly
Leopold Stokowski died here, not in
Hollywood. The Five Bells is a
pleasantly modest place for lunch.

NEW FOREST SU2605
The New Forest countryside has great
charm. Only parts of it are in fact
wooded; the rest is unspoilt rolling
heathland. Walkers can head off in
virtually any direction without worrying
about trespassing. Once away from the
roads, it does give a great feeling of
untrammelled space. Children like it:
there are free-running ponies and deer,
and plenty of scope for generally
running riot without coming to grief.
This unchanging blend of woodland and
heath covers nearly 150 square miles,
designated a Royal hunting preserve by
William the Conqueror not long after
the Battle of Hastings. The two best
drives are the slow back road from
Brockenhurst N through Bolderwood
and then round past Linwood to
Rockford, and the road from
Brockenhurst to Burley; main roads can
get very busy around the more popular
areas, especially on summer wknds. Still
with quite a medieval feel, the ancient
woodlands are very atmospheric to
stroll through, especially when you
come across an unexpected sunlit leafy
glade. It's most fun just to potter
around, but you'll also get a lot out of a
guided tour with people who've lived or
worked in the forest all their lives; (023)
8028 3141 for details. Many of them
have ancient forest rights and privileges,
such as letting their pigs forage for
acorns. The path network in the New
Forest is remarkably comprehensive,
and in most places there's no obligation
to stick to rights of way (of which there
are very few). The lack of major
objectives can be a problem for purists:
there are no obviously defined hills, and
long walks in the eastern woodlands,
many of which are coniferous, can
become monotonous. Further W, the
scenery is more intricate and a touch
more varied. It is often a good idea to
use routes which have plenty of
landmarks to guide the way; the heath
and forest can be fiendishly disorienting.
Besides the ponies, you may see fallow
deer, especially at the Bolderwood
Deer Sanctuary (and in the woods, very

occasionally, the smaller, shyer roe deer; even in some places red deer). The best walks alternate mixed forest with heathland; isolated ponds and country pubs provide focal points. In summer you can usually go on guided badger watch evenings; (01425) 403412. The Museum and Visitor Centre at Lyndhurst is a good place to start, and has details of watersports, riding and campsites. Handy pubs include the Royal Oak at Bank, Red Lion at Boldre (nr Roydon Woods nature reserve), Royal Oak at Fritham, Foresters Arms at Frogham, High Corner Inn or Red Shoot nr Linwood, Royal Oak at North Gorley, Alice Lisle at Rockford, Sir Walter Tyrell at Upper Canterton, and perhaps Turf Cutters Arms at East Boldre and Filly at Setley.

NEW MILTON SZ2394
Sammy Miller Museum 🖼 (Bashley Manor) Well regarded changing collection of fully restored motor cycles, many the only surviving examples of their type in the world. Snacks, shop, disabled access; cl 25–26 Dec; (01425) 620777; £3.50. There's an adjacent craft shop and beauty salon.

OLD WINCHESTER HILL SU6420
This hill fort gives wide views of Hampshire, The Solent and Isle of Wight, with nature trails through natural downland that's never been ploughed and resown; fairly busy on fine wknds, wonderfully remote on a blustery spring or autumn weekday. The George & Falcon at Warnford is popular for food.

OVERTON SU5149
There's a charming **drive** along the B3400 to Hurstbourne Priors and B3048 to Wherwell; Overton though quite large is an attractive stop along the way, with a decent pub.

OWER SU3116
Paultons Park Agreeable family theme park with 140 acres of rides, gardens, animals, birds and wildfowl, as well as model dinosaurs set in marshland, a 10-acre lake with working waterwheel, hedge maze, animated scenes from The Wind in the Willows, and unique Romany Experience with the sights, sounds and smells of traditional gypsy life. A new roller-coaster joins rides such as the Raging

River log flume, tea-cups, go-karts (the only thing with an extra charge), bumper boats and several good play areas, many ideal for toddlers. Meals, snacks, shop, disabled access; cl wkdys Nov and Dec (exc Christmas specials), and all Jan–mid-Mar; (023) 8081 4455; £9.50 adults (£8.50 children under 14; children under 1 metre tall are free – though can't go on everything).

PETERSFIELD SU7423
Bear Museum (Dragon St) Teddies, dolls and toys in a nursery setting. Children (or anyone else for that matter) can cuddle the exhibits; shop; cl Sun, Mon and bank hols; (01730) 265108; free. There's an interesting **church** on Market Sq, and the 16th-c Good Intent has a wide choice of food.

PORTCHESTER SU6204
Portchester Castle The imposing high walls and towers stretching right down to the waterfront were originally part of a 3rd-c Roman fort – they're the best example of their type in Europe. Other remains include a 12th-c church and 14th-c great tower, and what's left of a palace built by Richard II. Snacks, shop, disabled access; cl 24–26 Dec, and 1 Jan; (023) 9237 8291; £2.70. The nearby Cormorant has good value food.

PORTSMOUTH SZ6299
Most of the city's £85m harbour redevelopment should be completed by the time you read this, with several interesting new places to visit, and opening up parts of the city which have been closed to the public for centuries. Its great claim on the imagination is its place at the heart of English naval history, and it is this heritage that forms the focus of the city's rejuvenation. The new six-mile **Millennium Promenade** forms part of a trail linking the two parts that are interesting to visitors: the Old Town and the Historic Dockyard, on either side of the ferry berths and well away from the traffic. Overlooking the narrow harbour neck, Georgian buildings on an old-fashioned cobbled hard give a good feel of the old days, and the little inner Camber Harbour still has fishing boats. The naval base has been revitalised in recent years, and there are new shopping and leisure facilities at

Gunwharf Quays – a huge waterfront leisure complex inc a cinema, bowling alley and permanent craft market. By summer 2002, you'll be able to soak up the lively maritime bustle from the top of the striking 165-metre **Spinnaker Tower**. A lot of development is also under way across the harbour in Gosport (see separate entry), and a new Waterbus service will link the two towns from the start of the year (an existing service already runs Apr–Oct). There may be an all-in-one ticket (inc ferry fare) covering all the new attractions. By the harbour, the Still & West is a beautifully placed food pub, and the Dolphin's a nice old place in the old High St behind. The **cathedral**, dating from the 13th c to the present, is a delightful departure from the traditional layout. Portsmouth is an island city, with just two roads and the motorway bridging it and its residential/resort part Southsea to the mainland – traffic can be very slow indeed on the main approaches.

City Museum (Museum Rd) Very good displays on the city's history, in an astonishing former barracks that looks rather like a French chateau. Also decorative art and crafts. Snacks, shop, disabled access; cl 25–26 Dec; (023) 9282 7261; free.

Cumberland House Natural History Museum (Eastern Parade, Southsea) The future of this interesting place will be decided in Mar, so it's not certain whether the splendid butterfly enclosure will be open to visitors this summer; shop, very limited disabled access; best to phone before visiting; (023) 9282 7261; £1.50 (more in butterfly season).

D-Day Museum (Clarence Esplanade, Southsea) The most notable of the museums devoted to Portsmouth's fighting history; it vividly recalls and explains the Normandy landings from the point of view of both sides. Very realistic in places – you almost panic when the sirens sound. There's a remarkable 84-metre (272-ft) D-Day embroidery inspired by the Bayeux Tapestry. Snacks, shop, disabled access; cl Mon am Nov–Mar, 24–26 Dec; (01705) 827261; £4.75, free winter Mon pms.

Dickens' Birthplace Museum (Old Commercial Rd, in the main town) Restored to the modest middle-class style it had when the author was born here in 1812. Still various Dickens-related objects such as the couch on which he died. Shop; cl Nov–Mar (exc seasonal readings three wks before Christmas, and 7 Feb, his birthday); (01705) 827261; £2.

Guildhall (Guildhall Sq) Contains what's said to be the world's biggest glass mural; snacks, disabled access; free tours, usually 10 and 11.30am Mon, Weds and Fri Apr–Oct; (023) 9283 4092.

HM Naval Base The main stop for most visitors, with lots to see. It houses **HMS** *Victory*, the *Mary Rose*, **HMS** *Warrior*, and the **Royal Naval Museum**. The flagship is of course **HMS** *Victory*, still in commission, and manned by regular serving officers. Guided tours bring those Trafalgar days very close, and include the spot where Nelson died. The raising of the *Mary Rose* from the Solent silt where it had sat for 437 years provided a wealth of material and information about the Tudor period. The discoveries are well shown in an airy hall, while the great oak hull itself is in a separate shed, sprayed almost constantly to prevent the timbers from drying out (there are plans to build a new hall as part of the harbour redevelopment). HMS *Warrior* when launched 140 years ago was the most fearsome battleship in the world; she's been immaculately restored, and is manned by tars in period uniform. Again, tours are very vivid. Housed in handsome 18th-c dockside buildings, the **Royal Naval Museum** has lively displays on the development and history of the navy up to and beyond the Falklands War (or as it's called here the South Atlantic Campaign), with new galleries looking at Nelson, the sailing navy, and HMS *Victory* (and its role in the Battle of Trafalgar). Lots of Nelson memorabilia, and a very jolly gallery looking at popular images of the sailor. Action Stations, a new look at the modern navy through an IMAX film and interactive displays, should open around Apr. Each ship costs £6 to visit individually (though the HMS *Victory* ticket also includes entry to the museum, which on its own costs £3.50), but if you want to see more than one it's well worth getting the all-in ticket at £15.50, which covers all three ships and the museum. The site – which itself costs nothing to enter, after a security check – has a restaurant and shop, and there's disabled access to all the ships; cl 25 Dec; (023) 9287 0999.

Royal Garrison church (French St) Roofless now, this once-grand place was where Charles II was married in 1662; open wkdys Apr–Sept; free.

Royal Marines Museum 🖭 (Royal Marines Eastney, Southsea) This vigorous place couldn't be more different from the usual military exhibitions – lively re-creations of major amphibious actions, a junior commando assault course, and a jungle room with a real snake and scorpions. Also lots of changing exhibitions – one on the photography of the Falklands War runs until the end of Sept – and special events. Snacks, shop, disabled access; cl three days over Christmas; (023) 9281 9385; *£4.

Sea Life Centre (Clarence Esplanade, Southsea) Excellent for families, this is one of the most hi-tech of these centres, with all sorts of multi-sensory experiences and displays, and an exciting shark encounter. Children complete a scratchcard trail as they go round, and there's an indoor soft play area. Snacks, shop, disabled access; cl 25 Dec; (023) 9273 4461; £5.50 (they'll stamp your hand and let you come back later in the day). **Boat trips** round the harbour from nearby.

Southsea Castle The fortifications in defence of Portsmouth Harbour, here, around Gosport, and up on Portsdown, give a remarkably complete picture of the development of defensive strategy from Tudor times to the fears of French invasion in the 1860s, though they have more appeal to people interested in warfare than to those who like the romantic idea of a regular 'castle'. Southsea Castle and Museum is the best place to start, built in 1545 as part of Henry VIII's coastal defences. Good displays on Portsmouth's military history, and some splendid fish-bone model ships made by Napoleonic

prisoners-of-war; special events (esp summer). Snacks, shop; cl wkdys Nov–Mar, 24–26 Dec; (023) 9282 7261; £2. On the seaward side of Southsea are sturdy Tudor and later towers, bastions and batteries, alongside the resort's gardens and entertainments, giving interesting sea views. Good guided walks around the Tudor fortifications and the best parts of the Old Town leave the Square Fort at 2pm on Sun (mid-Apr–late Sept).

Spitbank Fort Wind up an exploration of Portsmouth's naval past with the boat trip from the Naval Base to this granite, iron and brick fortress a mile out to sea. Its two floors are linked by a maze of passages, and there's a 130-metre (420-ft) deep well which still draws fresh water. The inner courtyard is now a sheltered terrace for summer refreshments from the café. Cl Mon (exc bank hols), Tues, and Oct–Apr; (023) 9252 9952; £6.50 inc boat trip (they do packages inc lunch and dinner, too). Ferries leave from Gosport ferry terminal and the pontoon beside HMS *Warrior*, phone for times. For quite a price, you can stay overnight out on the fort if you really do want to get away from it all (great views from comfortable rooms).

QUEEN ELIZABETH COUNTRY PARK SU7117
Lots going on all year, with woodland walks and rides (stables at the park), open downland, an adventure play trail, and events such as Easter egg rolling. You can arrange horse riding (023) 9259 9699. Disabled access; park open all year, visitor centre, shop and café cl wkdys Nov–Mar; (023) 9259 5040; £1.50 parking charge Sun and bank hols, £1 rest of wk. The good Five Bells at Buriton is nearby.

RINGWOOD SU1604
New Forest Owl Sanctuary A real mix of owls and hawks, not always easy to see as some enclosures are deliberately overgrown to resemble natural habitats. It can get a little congested when busy; four flying displays a day, and occasional lectures. Snacks, shop, disabled access; cl Nov–early Feb; (01425) 476487; £4.50. The Elm Tree (Hightown) has good value food.

ROCKBOURNE SU1117
Rockbourne Roman Villa (off
B3078) Remains of largest known
Roman villa in the area, found by chance
50 years ago by a farmer digging out a
ferret. Interesting mosaics in the
museum. Shop, disabled access; cl wkdy
am exc July–Aug, and all Oct–Mar;
(01725) 518541; £1.75. In the charming
thatched village, the Rose & Thistle is
useful for lunch.

ROMSEY SU3520
Broadlands (just S) Elegant Palladian
mansion on banks of the River Test,
surrounded by beautiful landscaped
grounds. Fine furnishings and paintings,
and good exhibition on former resident
Earl Mountbatten. You can fish on an
adjacent stretch of the River Test.
Snacks, shop, mostly disabled access;
open pm mid-Jun–early Sept; (01794)
505010; £5.95. The nearby Dukes Head
(A3057) is an attractive dining pub.
Mountbatten is buried in the interesting
13th-c **abbey**, bought by the
townspeople for their parish church at
the Dissolution. There are some
notable Saxon crosses and a 16th-c
panel painting.

SELBORNE SU7433
Gilbert White's House (The
Wakes) Impressive 18th-c home of
naturalist Gilbert White, furnished in
period style. The restoration of the
extensive gardens to their original form
is almost complete, and separate
galleries commemorate the explorers
Captain Oates and Frank Oates.
Impressive teas and 18th-c style snacks,
good shop, plant sales, disabled access
to ground floor and garden; cl 25–31
Dec; (01420) 511275; £4. The Queens
Hotel is handy for lunch. There are
good pockets of scenery nearby – the
countryside White recorded in such
detail. The zigzag path he created with
his brother in 1753 still climbs Selborne
Hanger (the hangers hereabouts are
beechwoods which cling to the abrupt
escarpments). Noar Hill close by has
been designated a nature reserve for its
chalkland flora, and from Selborne
churchyard, a path leads into The Lythe,
a wooded hillside that was another
favourite haunt of White's.

SHERBORNE ST JOHN SU6356
The Vyne Tudor mansion with
splendid 17th- and 18th-c
embellishments: see if you can spot the
stonemason's error which grafted a
parrot's beak on to an eagle. The
gardens include a 19th-c walled garden
and a summer house garden; there are
pleasant woodland walks. Meals, snacks,
shop, disabled access; cl am, Mon and
Fri (exc bank hols), and all Nov–Mar,
(grounds open wknds Feb–Mar);
(01256) 881337; £5, grounds only
£2.50; NT.

SILCHESTER SU6262
Calleva Museum The site of Roman
town Calleva Atrebatum has been
excavated nearby; 1½ miles of city wall
to walk along (tricky in places), as well
as a 9,000-seat amphitheatre, 12th-c
church on the site of the Roman
temples, and **museum** with small
collection of finds from the site
(disabled access; cl 25 Dec; free). The
Calleva Arms (with a family dining
conservatory) does cheap lunches, and
sells good guides to the site; the Red
Lion at Mortimer West End is a good
dining pub.

SOUTHAMPTON SU4111
Known early last century (through its
shipping importance) as the Gateway to
the World, this huge bustling city rather
unexpectedly has one of the three best-
preserved medieval town walls in the
country. The best stretch is along the
western side of the old core, around
from the magnificent partly Norman
Bargate (which has a small local
museum); there are usually guided
walks along here at 10.30 Sun and bank
hol Mon (daily in summer hols), or you
can walk it yourself at any time. Lots of
other old buildings dotted around the
less appetising modern townscape,
though if you're short of time it's best
to concentrate your efforts on the area
around St Michael's Sq, Bugle St and
perhaps the old High St. Parking around
the centre is metered. The quayside
nearest here has been cleaned up, with
modern café-bars overlooking yachting
berths.

City Art Gallery (Civic Centre,
Commercial Rd) Extensive and
distinguished collection of British and
European paintings and sculptures from
the last 600 years, with particular
emphasis on the 20th c. Snacks, shop,

disabled access; cl Mon, 25–26 Dec and Good Fri; (023) 8083 2277; free.

God's House Tower (Winkle St) An early 15th-c prototype gun battery, now housing an archaeology museum with displays on the city's Saxon forebear, Hamwic; shop, cl 12–1pm, Sun am, all Mon, and Christmas–New Year; free. The nearby bowling green is said to be the oldest in the world.

Hall of Aviation (Albert Rd S) Various aircraft of local interest – inc prototype helicopters and the Spitfire. Shop, some disabled access; cl Sun am, all day Mon (exc bank and school hols), 25 Dec; (023) 8063 5830; £3.

Maritime Museum (Bugle St) A fine 14th-c warehouse with an impressive timber ceiling, and useful displays on the history of the port. Especially good on the great liners. Shop, disabled access to ground floor only; cl 1–2pm, Sun am, Mon, and some days over Christmas and New Year; (023) 8022 3941; free. The pretty 15th-c **Tudor house** on the same road has been restored (disabled access to ground floor and garden; cl 12–1pm, otherwise as above; free). The ancient nearby Duke of Wellington has decent food.

Medieval Merchant's House (French St) Fine timbered building ¼ mile from city centre, splendidly refurbished with period furnishings which vividly re-create what life must have been like for a wealthy merchant's family; free audio tour. Shop; cl Nov–Mar; (023) 8022 1503; £2.10; EH.

SOUTHWICK SU6208
This attractive village, with a decent pub, is well placed for good walks on Portsdown Hill – fine views.

SPARSHOLT SU4331
Attractive village very close to Farley Mount, with good woodland and downland walks, and good food at the Plough.

STEVENTON SU5447
Steventon church 12th-c, with a memorial to Jane Austen, who was born in the village.

STOCKBRIDGE SU3433
Houghton Lodge Gardens 🖼 (just SW) Pretty and very peaceful gardens running down to River Test, with fine trees and lawns, a peacock statue made from recycled car metal, and a topiary dragon that breathes 'steam'. An intriguing hydroponicum demonstrates how to grow plants without soil, and there are plans to restore the 18th-c shrubbery. Snacks, plant sales, disabled access; open all day wknds and bank hols Mar–Sept, plus wkdy pms (exc Weds); (01264) 810177; £5 (children free). The Boot in Houghton has decent food; walks by this lovely stretch of the Test, or up on the downs. In the pleasant nearby town of Stockbridge, the Grosvenor, Vine and White Hart are all useful for lunch. Discount allows two adults admission for the price of one.

STRATFIELD SAYE SU6962
Stratfield Saye House 🖼 (off A33) A grateful nation granted the Duke of Wellington the money to buy this 17th-c house after Waterloo. Perhaps surprisingly, the Duke had a taste for French furniture, lots of which is still here as is his splendid funeral carriage, and his hearing aid – needed after prolonged exposure to cannon. His beloved horse Copenhagen is buried in the grounds. Snacks, shop, disabled access; usually open Weds–Sun Jun–Aug, though subject to change, so best to ring; (01256) 882882; £5.50. The elegant Wellington Arms has good food. There are pleasant walks on Heckfield Heath E of the estate, and Wellington Country Park in Berks is nearby.

TITCHFIELD SU5305
Titchfield Abbey Ruined 13th-c abbey, almost overshadowed by the grand Tudor gatehouse built after the Dissolution. Some of Shakespeare's plays were reputedly first performed here. Disabled access; cl 25 Dec; free; EH. The riverside Fisherman's Rest opposite does food all day, and there's a fine walk by the old canal to the coast at Meon Shore nr Hill Head.

TOTTON SU3612
Eling Tide Mill (Eling Toll Bridge) There's been a mill on this causeway for over 900 years, and the present one still uses tidal energy to produce flour. Heritage centre, snacks, shop, disabled access to ground floor only; cl Mon (exc bank hols), Tues, and 25–26 Dec – ring for milling times, which of course depend on the tide; (023) 8086 9575;

£1.65. In unpromising surroundings, the Anchor on Eling Quay is a good cheap place for something to eat.

WAGGONERS' WELLS SU8534
A series of hammer ponds, a legacy of the medieval Wealden iron industry, set in charming heathy woodlands in a valley, and perfect for a picnic. Paths skirt these NT-owned ponds, which are a haven for wildlife.

WATERSHIP DOWN SU4957
(just S of Kingsclere) The home of the rabbits in the novel by Richard Adams – their final adventure was down at Freefolk, where the eponymous pub often has live rabbits. Pleasant wooded walks through this area.

WEYHILL SU3046
Hawk Conservancy One of the best birds of prey centres we've come across; you can handle some of the birds, and there are three daily flying displays (the best at 2pm). Wildflower meadow, ferret-racing in school hols, and toddlers' play area. Snacks, shop, disabled access; cl Nov–mid-Feb; (01264) 772252; £5.75. The Weyhill Fair is handy for lunch, and the lanes N take you into a particularly unspoilt corner of Hants.

WHITCHURCH SU4648
Whitchurch Silk Mill (Winchester St) Interesting working silk mill, producing fabric for theatrical costumes, interior designers and historic houses using Victorian machinery and traditional processes. There's a self-guided audio tour, and visitors have a chance to work on a loom. Prettily set on an island in the River Test, where you can watch the trout or feed ducks. Helpful staff, good value snacks, shop; cl Mon exc bank hols, 24 Dec–2 Jan; (01256) 892065; £3. The Red House (London St) is the best pub here, and you can get a good cup of coffee at the White Hart Hotel (The Square).

WICKHAM SU5711
An attractive village despite the traffic, notable for its huge village square; at nearby Droxford there's a good farm shop with pick-your-own.

WINCHESTER SU4829
The compact and fascinating medieval centre still has two city gates intact; it was capital of England in Saxon times.

Guided walks around the sights from the Tourist Information Centre at 11am and 2.30pm Mon–Sat, 11.30am Sun May–Sept (2.30pm Mon–Fri, 11am Sat in Apr and Oct), and 11am Sat in winter; £2.50. There's a multi-storey car park at the top of the High St, or a Park & Ride nr the junction with the M3. The most attractive part of the city is the glorious and peaceful cathedral close, surrounded by a very harmonious and distinguished collection of buildings; the handsome old Eclipse Inn nr the NE edge is a useful refreshment break. The Brooks Shopping Centre has a few jolly dioramas and displays on the city's history (cl Sun; free), with the chance for children to make their own Roman mosaic. There are pleasant walks up rounded St Catherine's Hill, which has a small medieval turf maze and traces of a hill fort.

City Mill (Bridge St) Restored 18th-c working watermill, with timbered and raftered ceilings and a pretty little island garden. Shop; cl Mon (exc bank hols) and Tues, wkdys in Mar, and all Nov–Feb; (01962) 870057; £1; NT.

City Museum (The Square) This recently refurbished well organised museum is good for local history and archaeology, with a telling Roman mosaic. Shop, good disabled access; cl Sun am, Mon Nov–Mar, and 25–26 Dec; (01962) 863064; free.

Great Hall of Winchester Castle All that now remains is its huge 13th-c great hall, where Raleigh was tried and condemned to death; hanging on one wall is a round table they call King Arthur's (actually much the same date as the castle, and painted with its Arthurian scenes later). The roof, stone parapets and stained glass have recently been restored, and there's a small but interesting re-created medieval garden S of the hall. Shop, disabled access; cl 25–26 Dec; (01962) 846476; free.

Guildhall Gallery (Broadway) 19th-c building with changing exhibitions of fine art, crafts and photography. Snacks, shop, disabled access; cl Sun am, all Mon Nov–Mar, 25–26 Dec, and 1 Jan; (01962) 848269; free.

Gurkha Museum 📷 Anyone interested in military history will enjoy the three Light Infantry museums in Winchester, but of these only the Gurkha Museum (Romsey Rd) could be said to have a wider appeal. Shop, disabled access; cl Sun am, Christmas week; (01962) 842832; *£1.50.

Hospital of St Cross 🏛 A short stroll from the city centre, along the water-meadows by the River Itchen. Very attractively set around two quadrangles, the quaint 15th-c almshouses still provide bread and ale to travellers who ask at the massive gate (you have to ask for 'wayfarer's dole'). 19th-c scandals here inspired Trollope's *The Warden*. Summer snacks, shop, disabled access; cl Sun, 25 Dec; £2. The Bell out here is useful for lunch.

Westgate Museum (High St) Local history above a formidable medieval city gate – the panorama of the city and surrounding countryside is rewarding. Shop; cl Sun am, Mon in Oct and Feb, and all Nov–Jan; (01962) 869864; 30p.

Winchester Cathedral Awesome and full of interest – one of Europe's finest, with the longest of all Gothic naves, and quite a mixture of architectural styles. Among many rare books and manuscripts in its library is a wonderful 12th-c illuminated Bible, while the sculpture gallery contains some outstanding late Gothic work. William of Wykeham paid for much of the rebuilding, so his tomb is appropriately the finest; also memorials and monuments to Jane Austen, King Canute and St Swithin. The cathedral hosts changing exhibitions of modern art throughout the summer months, and a new sculpture by Antony 'Angel of the North' Gormley beautifully exploits reflections in the winter flood waters of the crypt. Good guided tours,

and first-rate visitor centre in 16th-c coach house, with very good meals and snacks (not cheap) and distinguished shop, disabled access; *£3 suggested donation. Close by are the appreciable remains of Wolvesey Castle, the original Bishop's Palace begun in the 12th c, and beside it (not open, but a handsome sight), the present Bishop's Palace of 1684. The best way out of the Close is through the medieval King's Gate, which includes the upper-floor church of St Swithin. This takes you into Kingsgate St, calm and old-fashioned, with an excellent dining pub, the Wykeham Arms. Down on the left a lovely riverside path takes you along to the City Mill and a mighty statue of King Alfred.

Winchester College All along Kingsgate St are buildings connected with this, the oldest school in the country. Most of the original school buildings remain intact, especially around the grand 14th-c chapel and its calm, tilting cloisters with a delightful two-storey chantry in their centre, and a glimpse of the Warden's garden through one gate. Good shop in former Tuck Shop, some disabled access; guided tours Apr–Sept, cl 1–2 pm, Sun am (winter tours by appointment only); (01962) 621217; £2.50.

Other attractive villages with decent pubs include Abbots Ann SU3243, Amport SU2944, Bank SU2807, Brook SU2714, Cheriton SU5828, Crawley SU4234, Crondall SU7948, East End SU4161 (the one nr Highclere), East Stratton SU5439, Hambledon SU6414, Lasham SU6742, Longparish SU4344, Mapledurwell SU6851, Upton Grey SU6948, Wherwell SU3840 and Woodgreen SU1717.

Where to eat

BOLDRE SZ3198 **Red Lion** *Boldre Lane* (01590) 673177 Very busy, friendly pub with four black-beamed rooms, interesting bric-a-brac and bygones, impressive bar food, prompt service, a fine choice of wines by the glass, and well kept beer; worth getting there early; cl 25 Dec; no children; disabled access. £24|**£6.50**

BRAMDEAN SU6127 **Fox** *(01962) 771363* Welcoming 17th-c dining pub with famous fox masks in modernised and neatly cared for open-plan bar, highly enjoyable imaginative food (quite a few fresh fish dishes), an extensive wine list, well kept real ales, and obliging service; no children; cl winter Mon, 25 Dec. £22.45|**£8.95**

BROCKENHURST SU2902 **Simply Poussin** *The Courtyard, Brookley Rd (01590)* 623063 Popular little restaurant with carefully cooked interesting food using the best local produce, good cheeses and puddings, friendly service, and chicken-themed decorations; cl Sun, Mon; disabled access. £30/2 courses £10.50

BROCKENHURST SU3002 **Thatched Cottage** *16 Brookley Rd (01590)* 623090 Charming 400-year-old thatched cottage with cosy beamed lounge, good dried and fresh flower arrangements, pretty no smoking restaurant, and enjoyable well presented imaginative food served by friendly staff; super cream teas in neat garden, morning coffee too; individually decorated bdrms; cl Sun pm, Mon, Jan; children over 12 lunchtime only. £55/3 set courses £15

CADNAM SU2913 **White Hart** *Old Romsey Rd (023) 8081 2277* Comfortable, popular dining pub with country prints and New Forest pictures in spacious multi-level lounge; good food served by efficient friendly staff, well kept real ales, quite a few wines by the glass, and a skittle alley; seats in garden with fish pond, and horses in next-door paddock. £22.40|**£8.95**

EAST TYTHERLEY SU2927 **Star** *East Tytherley Rd (01794) 340225* 16th-c dining pub with new licensees who have introduced a stylish new menu of imaginative food – you can eat the same menu in the bar or restaurant; well kept real ales, a thoughtful wine list with 10 by the glass, pretty no smoking restaurant, and a mix of comfortable furnishings, log fires, horse brasses and saddlery; skittle alley; seats on smartly furnished terrace, play area; comfortable cottage-style bdrms overlook the village cricket pitch. £20.35|**£7.90**

EMSWORTH SU7405 **36 On The Quay** *47 South St (01243) 375592* Charming cheerfully decorated quayside restaurant with exceptional modern cooking, friendly helpful service and a sound wine list; cl Sat am and Mon, all Sun, 1st 2 wks Jan, 1st wk Oct; disabled access. £40.50 dinner, £27 lunch/2-course lunch £16.50

EVERSLEY SU7861 **Golden Pot** *(0118) 973 2104* Little brick pub with a comfortable easy-going atmosphere in the different spreading areas, bowls of lilies, candles in bottles, fireside sofa; pretty no smoking restaurant, and good interesting food inc special Mon evening rösti menu (landlady is Swiss) with lots of different toppings; well kept real ales and 12 wines (some from Switzerland) by the glass; picnic-sets out in front. £19.45|**£6.95**

EVERSLEY SU7662 **New Mill Restaurant & Grill Room** *New Mill Rd (0118) 973 2277* 16th-c watermill by the Blackwater River with working waterwheel and grinding equipment; big windows overlooking the river and its wildlife, open fires and candlelit tables, a good range of interesting carefully cooked food, and a thoughtful wine list with many by the glass; the beamed Grill Room is more informal and cheaper; cl Sat am, 26–29 Dec; partial disabled access. £38|**£9.75**

FROXFIELD SU7227 **Trooper** *(01730) 827293* (NW of Steep) Interesting pub transformed by very jolly landlord, big windows looking across rolling countryside, airy feel, little Persian knick-knacks, lit candles all around, fresh flowers, log fire; attractive raftered restaurant, good food, well kept real ales, decent house wines; lots of picnic-sets on lawn and partly covered sunken terrace; the horse rail in the car park ('horses only before 8pm') does get used; no children inside. £21.95|**£7.50**

FROYLE SU7542 **Hen & Chicken** *Upper Froyle (01420) 22115* Old coaching inn with interconnecting rooms, hops on beams, candles on tables, daily papers, neat staff serving imaginative food, a partly no smoking restaurant, well kept real ales, and big garden with children's play equipment. £22|**£7.50**

LONGSTOCK SU3537 **Peat Spade** *(01264) 810612* Lively, popular dining pub with airy attractive bar, toby jugs around the fire, an elegant little dining room, no smoking area, imaginative enjoyable food, well kept real ales, and decent wines; bdrms; cl Sun pm, Mon, 25–26 Dec; disabled access. £26|**£6.75**

LYMINGTON SZ2996 **Gordleton Mill** *Silver St, Hordle (01590) 682219* 300-year-old converted watermill under new ownership; lovely romantic gardens, attractive bars and restaurant, a relaxed bustling atmosphere, good modern English cooking, a carefully chosen wine list, and friendly staff; you can sit on the terrace and enjoy a meal by the water; comfortable bdrms. £20

MAPLEDURWELL SU6851 **Gamekeepers** *Tunworth Rd (01256)* 322038 Neatly kept pub run by helpful welcoming licensees, with dark beams and timbers throughout, and a relaxed friendly atmosphere; country pictures, horse tack and fox masks, partly stripped brick walls, some flagstones, two-way log-effect gas fire and a large no smoking dining room with carp at the bottom of a glass-topped well; good popular food, well kept real ales, and a Lhasa Apso dog called Barney; picnic-sets on terrace and back grassy area. £21.15|**£7.95**

MICHELDEVER SU5138 **Half Moon & Spread Eagle** *Winchester Rd (01962) 774339* Attractive country pub with simply decorated beamed bar, woodburners each end, solid furniture, generous helpings of interesting food inc lots of good daily specials, well kept real ales, and decent wines; seats on terrace and by cricket green; disabled access. £21

OLD BURGHCLERE SU4658 **Dew Pond** *(01635)* 278408 Beautiful 16th-c country house with log fires, friendly atmosphere, and imaginative attractively presented evening meals using fresh local produce on a frequently changing small menu – good game, fish and lovely puddings; no smoking; cl Sun, Mon, Christmas and New Year, 2 wks Aug; no under-5s; disabled access. £31

ROMSEY SU3521 **Old Manor House** *21 Palmerston St (01794)* 517353 Long-established Italian restaurant with comfortable lounge and tiny restaurant, consistently enjoyable food (inc home-made salami) using the best local ingredients, classic puddings, and some interesting Italian wines; cl Sun pm, Mon, 1 wk Christmas. £35

SOUTHSEA SZ6499 **A Fistful of Tacos** *31–35 Albert Rd (023)* 9229 3474 Evening restaurant with good Californian/Mexican food; cl 25–26 Dec, 1 Jan; partial disabled access. £17

SOUTHSEA SZ6598 **Tenth Hole** *Eastern Parade (023)* 9283 0009 Bustling café by the pitch-and-putt with snacks, light lunches and generous teas served by friendly staff; cl Jan; children over 12; disabled access.|**£5.50**

STUCKTON SU1613 **Three Lions** *(01425)* 652489 Warmly welcoming restaurant with informal atmosphere, a neat airy bar, fresh flowers, very imaginative food inc local fungi and lovely puddings, a fine wine list, superb breakfasts, and charming owners; good atmosphere and friendly efficient service; cl 2 wks Jan, 2 wks Feb; disabled access; comfortable bdrms. £35

TICHBORNE SU5730 **Tichborne Arms** *(01962)* 733760 Neat and attractive thatched country pub with latticed windows, a log fire in the stone fireplace, and interesting pictures in the comfortable square-panelled bar, and a bigger more lively dining room; good bar food, well kept real ales, and wines by the glass or carafe; picnic-sets in big well kept garden, and plenty of surrounding walks; no children; disabled access. £22.50|**£5.50**

WELL SU7646 **Chequers** *(01256)* 862605 Neatly kept and rather smart country pub with relaxed atmosphere, snug rooms, beams, lots of 18th-c country-life prints, and a wide range of enjoyable bar food; partial disabled access. £15|**£5.95**

WINCHESTER SU4829 **Cathedral Refectory** *Visitor Centre (01962)* 853224 Excellent totally home-made food in bright airy modern conservatory, lovely breads and soups, afternoon cream teas, good children's menu, a friendly informal atmosphere, and nice staff; cl 25–26 Dec, 1 Jan, Good Fri; disabled access. £15.75|**£3.95**

Special thanks to M G Hart, B and K Hypher, Michael and Jenny Back, Phyl and Jack Street

HEREFORDSHIRE

The essence of traditional England, with classic unspoilt scenery, peaceful countryside, beautiful black and white villages – great for restorative short breaks

While adults will undoubtedly benefit most from the county's quietly relaxing charms, some places here deserve special recognition for their efforts to include children. This year, Berrington Hall, an elegant 18th-c house with an attractive woodland garden but also children's orienteering course, adventure playground and several fun trails, ranks as our top family attraction here. Splendid Eastnor Castle, a close second, offers similar fun, including a children's maze.

Herefordshire also does well for enjoyable working farms, where the emphasis is on mucking in and finding out; Pig Pen at Linley Green and Shortwood Dairy Farm at Pencombe are good examples. Younger children will love the miniature cow and other rare breeds at Kington's Small Breeds Farm Park and Owl Centre, too.

The maze and fairytale adventure playground at Symonds Yat should keep little ones amused for a good half-day.

Some of the treasures for adults to enjoy are best taken in through quiet scenic drives or inspiring walks with long gentle views. As you head W the countryside becomes almost bewitchingly untouched – not at all showy, but the sort of peaceful world that elsewhere tends to survive only in people's memories. Not many tourists or second-homers have penetrated here, even at the height of summer, yet there's an abundance of art galleries and bookshops (Hay-on-Wye, that town-sized bookshop, is an attractive drive just over the Welsh border) in the civilised and appealing small towns.

The county is now making a great name for its good locally produced food and drink, and the English Tourism Council is hoping to draw more visitors by promoting a cider trail through the county. Of the many cider-related attractions, Weston's Cider Farm at Much Marcle will suit the enthusiast most (liberal tastings), and those who enjoy craft demonstrations will find fulfilment at the Hop Pocket Craft Centre, Bishops Frome, and Leominster's Herefordshire Cheesemaking, among other places.

The county boasts a number of fine gardens, from attainably small ones such as Kingstone Cottages near Ross-on-Wye or relatively young ones such as the one at Kimbolton, to products of several generations such as Hergest Croft near Kington or the arboretum at Queenswood Country Park.

Lower Brockhampton House, Croft Castle and Goodrich Castle make pleasant outings.

Hereford is engaging and relaxing, with plenty of varied attractions – the cathedral has a splendid display of its great treasures. Ledbury is attractive, with several appealing places to visit. Kington, Leominster and Ross-on-Wye are also agreeable to wander around.

In winter big log fires and generous central heating are the rule – people here really seem to appreciate their warmth. By contrast, summers are relatively hot here.

Where to stay

BRIMFIELD SO5267 **Roebuck** *Brimfield, Ludlow, Shropshire SY8 4NE (01584)* 711230 **£70***; 3 rms. Smart country dining pub with an impressive inglenook fireplace in the quiet, old-fashioned locals' snug, two other civilised bars with small open fires, a cosy no smoking dining room, super, stylish food, well kept real ales, carefully chosen wines, and caring staff; dogs welcome by arrangement

BROMSBERROW HEATH SO7333 **Grove House** *Bromsberrow Heath, Ledbury, Herefordshire HR8 1PE (01531)* 650584 **£75***; 3 spacious rms, 2 with four-posters. Wisteria-clad 15th-c manor house with dark panelling, open fires, beams, fresh flowers and polished antiques, and good evening meals at huge dining table using home-grown produce; 13 acres of fields and garden, hard tennis court, and neighbour's outdoor swimming pool; cl Christmas and New Year

CAREY SO5631 **Cottage of Content** *Carey, Hereford HR2 6NG (01432)* 840242 **£48**; 3 rms. Very pretty medieval country cottage in peaceful setting, with a good mix of tables and chairs on the flagstones or bare boards of the timbered bars, imaginative popular food served by friendly staff, well kept real ales, a good wine list, and seats on flower-filled front and back terraces; cl 25 Dec

FOWNHOPE SO5734 **Green Man** *Fownhope, Hereford HR1 4PE (01432)* 860243 **£64***, plus special breaks; 20 rms. Attractive Tudor inn with impressive oak-beamed lounge (the residents' lounges are no smoking), log fire, and generously served popular bar food; adjoining leisure club with large swimming pool, squash court, solarium, and so forth; partial disabled access

GRAFTON SO4936 **Grafton Villa Farm** *Grafton, Hereford HR2 8ED (01432)* 268689 **£43***; 3 rms. Early 18th-c farmhouse with an acre of lawns and garden, panoramic views, and lots of animals; an open fire in lounge, enjoyable hearty breakfasts in large dining room using their own free-range eggs, and friendly owners; nearby inn for evening meals; cl Christmas; self-catering; disabled access

KINGTON SO3156 **Penrhos Court** *Lyonshall, Kington, Herefordshire HR5 3LH (01544)* 230720 **£80**, plus special breaks; 19 elegant rms. Beautifully restored 13th-c Hall in six acres, with fine beams and flagstones, a magnificent hall for dining, and very good carefully cooked food using seasonal organic home-grown herbs and vegetables; they run regular food and health courses; cl Jan; disabled access

KINNERSLEY SO3349 **Upper Newton Farmhouse** *Kinnersley, Hereford HR3 6QB (01544)* 327727 **£50***, plus special breaks; 3 prettily decorated rms with hand-crafted items. Attractive 17th-c farmhouse in the middle of a working farm, with a particularly welcoming helpful landlady (an award-winner this year), log fires, beams, sloping floors, good food (inc vegetarian) using fresh farm vegetables, colourful garden, and lots of walks; no smoking or pets; self-catering cottage

LEDBURY SO7137 **Feathers** *25 High St, Ledbury, Herefordshire HR8 1DS (01531)* 635266 **£95**, plus special breaks; 19 carefully decorated rms making the most of the old beams and timbers. Very striking, mainly 16th c, black and white hotel with a relaxed atmosphere, log fires, comfortable lounge hall with country antiques, beams and timbers, particularly enjoyable food and friendly service in hop-decked Fuggles bar, a good wine list, and a fine mix of locals and visitors; health and leisure spa with indoor swimming pool

LEYSTERS SO5762 **Old Vicarage** *Leysters, Leominster, Herefordshire HR6 0HS (01568)* 750574 **£68***; 2 rms. Comfortable and friendly 17th-c farmhouse with Victorian additions, set in 18 acres with a two-acre garden, all-weather tennis court, and surrounded by the unspoilt N Herefordshire hills; antiques, enjoyable dinner on request, often using home-grown produce, and eaten around a big dining table; cl Christmas and New Year; children over 12; dogs by prior arrangement

ROSS-ON-WYE SO6024 **Brookfield House** *Over Ross St, Ross-on-Wye, Herefordshire HR9 7AT (01989) 562188* **£46.50**, plus special breaks; 8 rms, some with own bthrm. Part Queen Anne and part Georgian house with sunny terrace and little garden, and a view over the town; very welcoming owners, a log fire in lounge, and super breakfasts in big airy breakfast room; children over 8; pets allowed

RUCKHALL COMMON SO4438 **Ancient Camp** *Eaton Bishop, Hereford HR2 9QX (01981) 250449* **£70**; 5 rms, two with pretty river views. Smart country inn in a pleasantly remote spot with good views of the River Wye and beyond from the rose-fringed terrace; a beamed and flagstoned bar and two other attractive rooms, a log fire, imaginative food from a seasonal menu, well kept real ales, and fine wines; cl 2 wks Jan; children over 12

ULLINGSWICK SO5849 **Steppes Hotel** *Ullingswick, Hereford HR1 3JG (01432) 820424* **£80***, plus special breaks; 6 spacious, pretty rms in barn and restored stone stable. Attractive 14th-c country house hotel with heavy beams, flagstones, and inglenook fireplaces in cellar bar, lounge and dining room, very good food, fine breakfasts, and hospitable helpful owners; cl Dec–Jan; children over 12

WEOBLEY SO4051 **Salutation** *Market Pitch, Weobley, Hereford HR4 8SJ (01544) 318443* **£69***; 4 pretty rms. Friendly 500-year-old inn with good bar and elaborate restaurant food, a quiet lounge with standing timbers and log fires, and small public bar; they now grow their own vegetables and herbs

WOOLHOPE SO6135 **Butchers Arms** *Woolhope, Hereford HR1 4RF (01432) 860281* **£39**; 2 neat, attractive rms with fruit and chocolates (shared bthrm). Family-run 14th-c timbered building with low oak beams and log fires in bars, friendly staff, lots of flowers, and decent food (good breakfasts); lovely surrounding walks

To see and do

Herefordshire Family Attraction of the Year

ASHTON SO5164 **Berrington Hall** [£] (A49) You wouldn't think a National Trust property would hold much appeal for children, but this elegant 18th-c house has a few activities that make it a reliable bet for families – especially in an area not terribly geared up for younger visitors. There are a good few quiz sheets and trails to follow going round the house (50p extra), some designed for under-7s, others for older children, as well as an I Spy sheet (10p) for the beautifully laid out grounds. They recently introduced a children's orienteering course for age 6 and up. The house itself has lots of interest – much more than you'd imagine from the rather severe neo-classical exterior; the finely painted ceilings and Regency furnishings are memorably elegant, and there's a splendid staircase. Many of the rooms are furnished in such a way that you could almost think they were still in use: there's a fully equipped Victorian nursery, a tiled dairy, and a well stocked nursery. For children over 5 there's a good adventure playground, and there are plenty of walks and pathways; one of the prettiest, a pleasant circular route through the park, is open only from July. Capability Brown laid out the grounds (the house was built by his son-in-law); the most famous feature is the 14-acre lake with picturesque views, but there's also an attractive woodland garden, and rows of yew trees. The walled garden has some venerable apple trees. Meals, snacks, shop, some disabled access; open pm Sat–Weds from Apr–Oct – though the shop and restaurant are also open wknds up to Christmas; (01568) 615721; £4.20 (£2.10 children). The family ticket (£10) has a decent saving, and you can get tickets for just the garden.

ABBEY DORE SO3830
Primarily the impressive surviving part
of a once-huge 12th/13th-c Cistercian
abbey church, with Early English
features and an awesome stone altar.
Abbey Dore Court Garden
Attractive riverside lawns and gardens,
with good views across to the ruins.
Snacks (in 17th-c stables), disabled
access; cl Weds and Mons, and
Oct–Mar; (01981) 240419; £2.50. The
Neville Arms is a pleasant nearby stop.
ALMELEY SO3351
Early 18th-c half-timbered Quaker
Meeting House, contemplative feel; key
in porch.
ASHTON SO5164
Berrington Hall See separate family
panel on p.278.
BISHOP'S FROME SO6647
Hop Pocket Craft Centre
Traditional hop farm, its hundred acres
a hive of activity in the harvest season,
with pretty gardens and a new plant
centre. The craft centre has recently
been extended to include wine,
jewellery and card shops – you can also
buy hop bines, and their hop pillows for
poor sleepers are particularly popular.
Restaurant, tearoom, disabled access; cl
Sun am, Mons exc bank hols, plus
Mon–Tues Jan–Feb; (01531) 640323;
free.
BODENHAM SO5151
Queenswood Country Park 170
acres of woodland and arboretum with
over 500 tree varieties; also wildlife
displays and good views. Meals, snacks,
shop and info centre, disabled access; cl
25–26 Dec; (01568) 798320; free. The
Three Crowns between Ullingswick
and unspoilt Little Cowarne has very
good food.
BROCKHAMPTON SO5931
Extraordinary turn-of-the-century Arts
and Crafts church designed by Lethaby;
note that this is in the little village
between Hereford and Ross-on-Wye.
CAREY SO5630
Delightful tucked-away village, with a
charming pub.
CREDENHILL SO4443
Escargot Anglais (A480) Part of the
National Snail Farming Centre, with
snail trails showing various species
(even hairy ones) and exhibitions. Shop;
usually open summer wknds, Mon,

Thurs and Fri by appointment only;
(01432) 760218; £2.80. The Bell at
Tillington does more orthodox food.
CROFT SO4565
Croft Castle The walls and turrets
date from the 14th and 15th c, but the
inside is mostly 18th-c, with an
interesting staircase and plastered
ceilings. Attractive parklands with
avenue of 350-year-old chestnuts. Tea
room, shop, disabled access; openpm
Weds–Sun and bank hols May–Sept,
plus wknds Apr and Oct; (01568)
780246; *£3.90; NT. The picturesque
Bell at Yarpole is handy for lunch. The
brackeny expanse of Leinthall
Common, scattered with cottages, is a
quiet corner of Herefordshire where
you can walk around the castle's estate,
and scale the modest heights of Croft
Ambrey, an Iron Age hill fort with a
view into Shropshire.
EARDISLAND SO4158
A gorgeous riverside black and white
village; the once spectacularly wonky
weather-vane on one ivy-clad dovecote
has now been straightened out. The
friendly Cross Inn has decent food.
EARDISLEY SO3149
Eardisley church 12th-c font with
wonderfully vivid carvings of sinner
being wrested from clutches of evil.
GOLDEN VALLEY SO3141
The B4348/B4347 Golden Valley road is
a pretty drive, with particularly
satisfying walks in the surrounding hills;
the tucked-away village of Dorstone
has an impressive prehistoric burial
mound nearby (and Herefordshire's
oldest pub). The remoter roads parallel
to this, to the W, are also well worth
the drive, through Clodock (delightful
church) and Michaelchurch Escley
(another good pub down by the river),
or passing Craswall, with its memorably
good Bulls Head pub.
GOODRICH SO5719
Goodrich Castle Readers are very
fond of this proper-looking 12th-c
castle, built using the same red
sandstone rock it stands on so that it
seems almost to grow out of the
ground. Still plenty to see, with towers,
passageways, dungeon and marvellous
views of the surrounding countryside.
Snacks (summer only) shop; cl 24–26
Dec and 1 Jan; (01600) 890538; £3.20.

These formidable ruins are a feasible objective for stout-hearted walkers from Symonds Yat – or could be a start point for Wye Valley gorge walks. The partly Norman Mill Race at Walford has good value food.

HEREFORD SO5039
Grew as a regional market centre, and still has its busy livestock and general market every Weds. For the rest of the week it feels very quiet-paced and old-fashioned, its streets (some pedestrianised now) lined with handsome Georgian and other buildings (Church St is almost wholly medieval). Guided walks leave the Tourist Information Centre every day from May–mid-Sept at 10.30am (2.30pm Sun). Wye-side walks give a pleasing view of the city, its spires and towers. Saxtys, the Green Dragon Hotel and Lichfield Vaults are all useful places for lunch.

Bulmer's Cider Mill (Plough Lane) This enormous modern plant has tours and tastings; snacks (Easter–Christmas), shop; cl wknds, bank hols and Christmas–New Year; tours (10.30 am, 2.15 pm, 7.30 pm) by appointment; (01432) 352000; £3.95 ticket includes the Cider Museum (see below).

Churchill House Museum (Venns Lane, northern outskirts) Regency house in fine grounds, with good local history, room settings, and 18th- and 19th-c furniture, costumes and paintings. Shop, some disabled access; cl ams, Mon–Tues and Sat, plus Oct–Mar; (01432) 267409; free.

Cider Museum 🔟 (Ryelands St) Cider-making through the ages, with huge 17th-c French press, original champagne-cider cellars, and a working cider-brandy distillery – the first licensed for over 250 years. Shop, disabled access to ground floor only; cl winter Mon, 25–26 Dec and 1 Jan (reduced opening times Nov–Mar); (01432) 354207; £2.50.

City Museum and Art Gallery (Broad St) Natural history and archaeology, interesting bee-keeping display, and changing art exhibitions. Shop, disabled access; cl Mon (and winter Suns) 25–26 Dec, 1 Jan and Good Friday; (01432) 260692; free.

Hereford Cathedral Nicely placed on the bank of the Wye, this largely Norman building has a lovely 13th- and 15th-c chapel, as well as the country's biggest chained library (the second biggest is at All Saints church, at the opposite end of the main street), and the famous Mappa Mundi, the largest surviving 13th-c world map. There's a splendid interpretative exhibition, with some computer displays; the map itself is shown in a specially dimmed room to preserve it. Meals, snacks, shop, disabled access; cl Good Fri, 25 Dec; (01432) 374200; cathedral free, exhibition £4. Guided tours at 11am and 2pm Mon–Sat, (£2.50), Easter to end Sept.

Old House (High Town) Glorious Jacobean house with period furnishings and paintings. Shop, limited disabled access; cl Sun (exc Apr–Sept), Mon (exc bank hols), 25–26 Dec, 1 Jan and Good Fri; (01432) 260694; free.

Waterworks Museum (Broomy Hill) Restored Victorian pumping station, with giant steam pumping engines, and smaller handpumps; you can try working some. Snacks, shop, disabled access; open in steam pm last Sun of month Apr–Sept, 2nd Sun Jun–Sept, plus bank hols Easter–Aug (not in steam open Tues Apr–Oct); (01432) 361147; *£2.50.

HOARWITHY SO5429
Glenda Spooner Farm This friendly and caring place, former home of the jockeys Michael and Peter Scudamore, is now a centre for the International League for the Protection of Horses, offering care and rehabilitation for equine victims of maltreatment. Snacks, shop, some disabled access; open Sat and Weds 11am–4pm or any time by appointment; (01953) 498682; free.

Hoarwithy church Remarkably Italianate, full of mosaics etc. The village, nr the River Wye, is attractive.

HOW CAPLE SO6130
How Caple Court 🔟 Eleven acres of peaceful formal and woodland Edwardian gardens overlooking the river, with old roses and unusual herbaceous plants for sale. Snacks; open daily Easter–end Sept; (01989) 740626; *£2.50. Also interesting medieval church and fabrics shop. The Green Man at Fownhope is popular for food.

KILPECK SO4430
Kilpeck church This small Norman church in a delightful little hamlet has amazing sandstone carving inside and out, beautifully preserved (except for the more uncomfortably pagan bits which prudish Victorians tried to remove).

KIMBOLTON SO5161
Stockton Bury Gardens (A4112 S) Attractive and developing garden complex covering four acres, good for a gentle wander. Snacks, plant sales, disabled access; cl am, all Mon (exc bank hols) and Tues, plus Nov–Mar; (01568) 613432; *£3.

KINGTON SO2956
Attractive border town by the River Arrow, well placed for walks (for example up the Hergest Ridge). Antiques and bric-a-brac are noticeably cheaper here than – say – in Gloucestershire; one shop specialises in cigarette cards, by the thousand. The Queens Head has good value food. NE of town at Bradnor Hill, the Kington Golf Club (in 240 acres of NT-owned land) is the highest in the country, and has good views.

Hergest Croft Gardens (just W, off A44) The splendid result of inspired work by several generations of keen gardeners; some of the centenarian rhododendrons in the woods are of almost incredible size. Famous kitchen garden with colourful flowerbeds, and the national collections of birches and maples. Snacks, shop, some disabled access; cl am, and all Nov–Apr; (01544) 230160; £3.50.

Hergest Ridge Reached via a cul-de-sac from Kington, this is NW Herefordshire's answer to the Malvern Hills – and like them (allegedly) triggered Elgar, in this case to write his *Introduction and Allegro for Strings*, as well as Mike Oldfield with his album *Hergest Ridge*; the less-known composer Moeran also walked here frequently, and his *Sinfonietta* was inspired by the area. It's another of those ridges for walkers who can't decide whether they prefer the gentle lowland textures of England or the more rugged offerings of Wales. The walk gets better with every step, as the wide ridge tapers into horseback width at the far end, above

Gladestry in Powys.
Small Breeds Farm Park and Owl Centre (off A4111 S) Friendly little farm with rare and unusual miniature horses, goats, poultry, pheasants and waterfowl, as well as a family of playful chipmunks and a pair of Kune Kune pigs. A particular favourite is Dorrie, the miniature Dexter cow, who even on tiptoe is just 81cm (32 in) high; she has a strapping daughter, Delores. All the animals can be displayed under cover if it's raining, and there's a heated barn for picnics. The views and setting are a bonus, and the extensive collections of owls and waterfowl are set in an attractively landscaped garden. Snacks, shop, disabled access; open daily Feb half-term, then wknds until Easter, and daily Easter–Oct; (01544) 231109; *£3.50.

LEDBURY SO7137
The spaciously leisured High St has some fine buildings: the old Market House, the Feathers Hotel and Ledbury Park House are famous for their well balanced 15th- and 16th-c timbering, and there are plenty of similar structures. From the Market House an exceptional alley of ancient jettied buildings leads to the partly Norman church of St Michael and All Angels, with an unusual spire tower detached from the main building, and its carillon ringing out a well known hymn every third hour. The Old Grammar School along here has been restored as a heritage centre (cl Nov–Easter). The council offices must be the only ones in the country decorated with medieval wall-paintings; you can see these any wkdy (exc Thurs) between 11am and 2pm; free. There are craft workshops, antique shops, national Playmobile specialist and a decent book shop, and the Feathers has good food. The road N towards Mathon through Wellington Heath (where the Farmers Arms is a good dining pub) has some good views.
Eastnor Castle (just E) Splendid neo-Gothic castle, especially dramatic in autumn, when the Virginia creeper that all but envelops the stirring battlements turns a fierce red. Designed by Pugin, the richly decorated rooms are breathtaking, with fine collections of armour, tapestries, furniture and

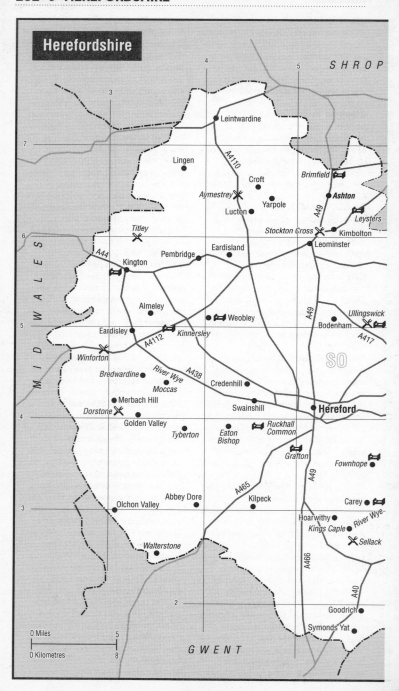

Herefordshire

SHROP

Leintwardine

Lingen

Croft

Brimfield

Aymestrey

Yarpole

Ashton

Lucton

Leysters

Stockton Cross

Kimbolton

Titley

Eardisland

Leominster

Kington

Pembridge

Almeley

Weobley

Ullingswick

Eardisley

Kinnersley

Bodenham

Winforton

Bredwardine

River Wye

Moccas

Credenhill

SO

● Merbach Hill

Swainshill

Hereford

Dorstone

Golden Valley

Tyberton

Eaton Bishop

Ruckhall Common

Grafton

Fownhope

Abbey Dore

Kilpeck

Carey ●

Olchon Valley

Hoarwithy ●

Kings Caple ●

River Wye

Walterstone

Sellack

GWENT

Goodrich ●

Symonds Yat ●

0 Miles   5

0 Kilometres   8

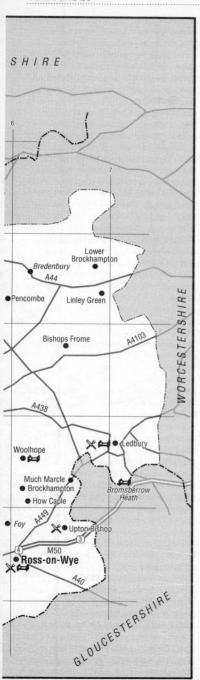

paintings. The attractive grounds have an arboretum, 300-acre deer park, woodland walks, adventure playground, children's maze and garden centre. Meals, snacks, shop; open Sun and bank hol Mons Easter–end of Sept, and every day exc Sat in July and Aug; (01531) 633160; £4.75. Eastnor village's thatched Post Office is lovely.

LEINTWARDINE SO4074
This appealing riverside village is notable partly for its church – much bigger than usual for this county.

LEOMINSTER SO4958
An attractive centre, the medieval streets almost lined with black and white timbered houses. The red priory church still has many of its original Norman features, and the handsome old Talbot has decent food.

Herefordshire Cheesemaking 🖼 (A44, 2m W) You can watch cheese being made by hand using traditional methods. Snacks (inc ploughman's with their own cheese), shop, disabled access; shop and café cl winter Sun and Mon (cheesemaking only Mon, Weds and Fri 10am–2.30pm); (01568) 720307; *£1.75.

LINGEN SO3667
Attractive village prettily set among hills, with Kim Davis's renowned alpine nursery and garden.

LINLEY GREEN SO6953
Pig Pen 🖼 (Hareley Farm) Enthusiastically run fun working pig farm, with lots of piglets to handle (lambs too in early spring), tours of pens and yards, play area, and for a small extra charge, quiz trails around the attractive surrounding woodlands; wear wellies in wet weather. Plenty of space for picnics; snacks, shop, some disabled access; open pm Apr–Sept; (01886) 884362; *£2.75.

LOWER BROCKHAMPTON SO7055
Brockhampton Idyllic moated and timber-framed 14th-c manor house in attractive secluded countryside. Particularly interesting 15th-c gatehouse, and the ruins of a 12th-c chapel. Tearooms, shop, some disabled access; cl am, Mon exc bank hols, Tues, and Nov–Mar; (01885) 488099; £2.50; NT. The Trust also own the surrounding 1,720-acre Brockhampton

Estate, with splendid views from its park and woodlands, marked trails and a sculpture trail. The Talbot at Knightwick is a nice place for lunch.

LUCTON SO4263

Mortimer's Cross Mill Charming watermill on banks of River Ludd, still in working order, with exhibition on the decisive Wars of the Roses battle fought here in 1461. Open Thurs pm Apr–Sept; (01568) 708820; £2. The Riverside at Aymestrey has good food.

MERBACH HILL SO3143

Reached by driving up from Bredwardine, and then walking from the top of the lane, this gives a view right over the Black Mountains, Herefordshire and Radnorshire. A short stroll along the lane SE brings you to Arthur's Stone, a prehistoric burial chamber.

MUCH MARCLE SO6433

Hellens Unspoilt manor house dating from the 13th c; you can see the portrait of Catherine of Braganza that convinced Charles II to marry her. Teas; open pm Sat, Sun, Weds and bank hols Easter–Sept; (01531) 660668; £3.50 (£1 for gardens only).

Weston's Cider Farm 🈯 Still alongside the family house, this has an engaging combination of modern equipment and old-fashioned atmosphere. Enthusiastic guided tours, liberal tastings, interesting ciders and perries. Meals, snacks, good shop with wide range of ciders, tours by appointment; cl Sun and pm Sat and Christmas wk; (01531) 660233; *£3. The nearby Slip has good dishes of the day and outstanding gardens; the memorial monuments in the village church are unrivalled in the area.

OLCHON VALLEY SO3029

Perhaps the remotest place in Herefordshire, a magnificent dead-end valley beneath the E flank of the Black Mountains. From the well signed picnic site nr Longtown a path heads up the Black Hill, an exciting knife-edge ridge, its end-on aspect strikingly triangular – this bit is known as the Cat's Back; after the trig point you can make a circuit by dropping down from the very head of the Olchon Valley, or carrying on over peaty terrain to join the Offa's Dyke Path.

PEMBRIDGE SO3958

One of Herefordshire's most striking black and white villages, full of fine timbered buildings inc a medieval market hall, the ancient New Inn, and a lovely church with an unusual detached belfry where you can watch the clock mechanism.

Dunkerton's Cider Farm (Luntley) Uses ancient traditional local cider-apple and pear cultivars, for distinctive ciders and perries; welcoming atmosphere, free tastings, and good restaurant; shop, disabled access; cider mill cl Sun; restaurant cl Jan–Feb.

PENCOMBE SO5951

Shortwood Dairy Farm Working farm ideal for children, with hands-on afternoon activities like milking Daisy or feeding the pigs and calves, usually sheep-shearing May bank hol. Good play area. Snacks, shop; cl Oct–Easter (though open Oct half-term for cider-making and in the Christmas hols for special events); (01885) 400205; £3.50. The Three Crowns at Ullingswick has very good food.

ROSS-ON-WYE SO5924

Picturesquely perched on a sandstone cliff by the river, with twice-weekly markets at the striking 17th-c market hall. The lower riverside part has attractive waterside walks; the Hope & Anchor here has decent food and Oat Cuisine on Broad St has substantial vegetarian food. There are pleasant woodland walks in Penyard Park, SE of the town.

Kingstone Cottages (Bury Hill, Kingstone; off A40 E) Charming, exuberant cottage garden, not to be missed at midsummer for its profusion of old-fashioned pinks and border carnations. Also fine views, and tucked-away little grotto – looking out it seems as though you're waist-high in water. Unusual plants for sale; open wkdys early May–early July, or by appointment; (01989) 565267; £1.

SWAINSHILL SO4341

Weir Gardens Delightful riverside gardens at their best in spring, with displays of bulbs set in woodland walks, and fine views from clifftop walks. Paths can be steep in places. Open Weds–Sun (and bank hols) mid-Feb–Oct; £2; NT. The Ancient Camp at Ruckhall is handy.

SYMONDS YAT SO5517
Shared with Gloucestershire on the other side of the river, this is a spectacular bend of the River Wye through a steep wooded rock gorge, where peregrine falcons nest (the RSPB have a demonstration area); splendid Wye views, nature trails. Two inns on either side of the river are linked by a hand-pulled ferry, and there's ample (walkers would say over-generous) parking. It's a big tourist draw. There's potential for more ambitious walks into the gorge, where an old railway line follows the river; to the SW an entertainingly rickety wire-mesh suspension bridge at the Biblins gives access to the W bank, in addition to the chain ferry at Symonds Yat village.
Jubilee Park 🖼 Centres on a hedge maze created for the Queen's Silver Jubilee; a lively maze museum tells the history of similar labyrinthine creations. Meals, snacks, shop, disabled access; open daily Good Fri–end Sep, wknds only in Mar and Oct, best to check for winter opening times; (01600) 890360; £3.50.
Splendour of the Orient On the same site as Jubilee Park, this has oriental water gardens, and an indoor tropical garden area with a fairytale-themed adventure playground; £2.50 (summer treasure hunts; £1.50 extra). Snacks, shop (specialising in cane furniture), disabled access; cl 25–26 and 31 Dec and 1 Jan; (01600) 890668; free

entry to gardens.
UPTON BISHOP SO6327
Wobage Farm Craft Workshops
Several potters, a furniture-maker, wood-carver and jeweller; open Thurs–Sun; (01989) 780233; free. The Moody Cow is a good individual lunch stop.
WEOBLEY SO4051
In the very top rank of the county's black and white villages, with its long sloping green, and idyllic stroll out past the bowling green to the church; the Olde Salutation is good for lunch.
WOOLHOPE SO6135
The elevated country around here has a good variety of scenery for walkers; the views from Ridge Hill E and the more densely wooded hills nr Mordiford are among the highlights.
YARPOLE SO4765
The church of this attractive streamside village has an uncommon free-standing medieval bell tower.
Other attractive villages, all with decent pubs, include Bredenbury SO6056 (despite the main road) and Walterstone SO3425 (peaceful walks). Quiet country drives can link several attractive **churches**, such as Bredwardine SO3344, Moccas SO3543, Tyberton SO3839 and Eaton Bishop SO4439; or perhaps Fownhope SO5834, Kings Caple SO5528 and even Foy SO5928 with Brockhampton and Hoarwithy.

Where to eat

AYMESTREY SO4265 **Riverside Inn** *(01568) 708440* Black and white timbered riverside inn with rambling beamed bar, some fine furniture, log fires and a relaxed atmosphere; popular, ambitious food, well kept own-brewed beers, decent wines, and obliging service; seats by the water and in steep garden; comfortable bdrms and fly-fishing for residents; does get very busy at peak times. £25|**£7.95**
DORSTONE SO3141 **Pandy** *(01981) 550273* Ancient half-timbered pub (Herefordshire's oldest), with a good mix of customers in the heavily beamed and neatly kept main room, a no smoking area, and side extension; also, Oscar the parrot; enjoyable bar food inc some South African dishes (the licensees come from there), well kept real ales, and lots of malt whiskies; picnic-sets and a play area in the neat side garden, and pretty surrounding countryside. £19.50|**£7.25**
LEDBURY SO7137 **Market Place Restaurant** *1 The Homend (01531) 634250* Pleasant bustling restaurant open all day for morning coffee, lunch and afternoon tea with home-made cakes, flans and puddings; cl pm, 25–26 Dec, 1 Jan. £9.50|**£3.20**
ROSS-ON-WYE SO5924 **Faisan d'Or Brasserie** *52 Edde Cross St (01989) 565751* Attractive little restaurant with an art nouveau feel, an expanded menu

offering good interesting food (inc nice cheeses), and relaxed atmosphere; cl Sun, Mon, 25 Dec–end Jan; well behaved children welcome. £25.50

SELLACK SO5526 **Lough Pool** *(01989)* 730236 Attractive black and white timbered cottage in lovely countryside, with a log fire at each end of the beamed central room, flagstones and bunches of dried flowers, other individually decorated rooms leading off, interesting food, well kept real ales, several malt whiskies, local farm ciders, and a well chosen wine list; cl pm 25 Dec; well behaved children in snug or restaurant only; disabled access. £19.15|**£6.35**

STOCKTON CROSS SO5161 **Stockton Cross Inn** *(01568)* 612509 Neatly kept, black and white timbered pub with an old-fashioned atmosphere in its heavy-beamed long bar, a huge log fire and woodburner, solid furnishings, a wide choice of enjoyable food, well kept beer, and good welcoming service; seats in garden; cl Mon pm (exc bank hols); children over 6. £20|**£5.95**

TITLEY SO3359 **Stagg** *(01544)* 230221 Attractive old pub under new licensees, and quickly building up a great local reputation for particularly good food; main emphasis on the two dining rooms, one quite big, the other intimate; well kept real ales, up to 10 wines by the glass from a carefully chosen list, a fine collection of malt whiskies, and good light snacks, a formidable cheese range, tasty bar snacks, and imaginative restaurant dishes (which you can eat in the bar); helpful service; tables out in the garden, and lovely surrounding countryside; bdrms; cl Mon. £18.75|**£6.50**

ULLINGSWICK SO5948 **Three Crowns** *(01432)* 820279 As well as a place for local farmers to enjoy their well kept ales, this bustling pub is very popular for its good imaginative food from an extensive seasonally changing menu (the choice is smaller at lunchtime); charming, cosy traditional rooms with hops on low beams, open fires, some no smoking areas, and carefully chosen wines; tables outside; cl Tues; children must be well behaved. £25|**£6**

UPTON BISHOP SO6326 **Moody Cow** *(01989)* 780470 In a quiet village, this friendly pub has several snug separate areas, a pleasant medley of stripped country furniture, a big log fire, no smoking rustic candlelit restaurant and second small dining room, a good choice of enjoyable food, and well kept beers; cl Sun pm, Mon; children must be well behaved; partial disabled access. £25|**£5.95**

WINFORTON SO2947 **Sun** *(01544)* 327677 Very friendly and neatly kept little pub with beamed rooms, individual assortment of furniture, two woodburning stoves, particularly good interesting food, real ales, and a sheltered garden; good bdrms; cl Tues; children over 10. £20.50|**£7**

HERTFORDSHIRE

Peaceful patches away from the bustle, grand houses, some eccentric attractions, and open spaces good for letting off steam

Places here with real family appeal include sumptuous Knebworth House with its excellent adventure playground, Hatfield House (extensive parkland and the National Collection of Model Soldiers), and the unusually lively Van Hage garden centre at Great Amwell (its children's farm and occasional miniature railway fill a pleasant summer afternoon). Aldenham Country Park and the uncluttered expanses of the Ashridge Estate (very good for wildlife) are great for letting off steam, and the grounds of ruined Berkhamsted Castle make a nice spot for a picnic on a sunny day.

Standalone Farm at Letchworth places a good emphasis on finding out about animals and farming; it's especially good for younger animal lovers, but has playful elements which will appeal to all small children. The friendly little zoo at Broxbourne has plenty to please children, too.

St Albans is rewarding to visit; the recently extended Verulamium Museum is a lively introduction to the town's Roman heritage, and there are fine views from the top of the striking Clock Tower.

The rose gardens just outside St Albans are delightful in summer, and Much Hadham's surrounding gentle landscape provides an attractive backdrop for the sculpture at the Henry Moore Foundation.

Elsewhere, pleasant surprises include the outstanding zoological museum at Tring, the shell-encrusted 'gothick' caverns under Ware, the unusual Forge Museum & Cottage Garden at Much Hadham, and the Roman bath hiding under the A1(M) near Welwyn. Cheslyn Gardens are an oasis of calm among the modern developments of Watford.

Though much of the county is built up, there are some very pretty villages dotted about, and clearly waymarked footpaths allow good escapes into protected countryside.

Where to stay

CHIPPERFIELD TL0401 **Two Brewers** *Chipperfield, Kings Langley, Hertfordshire WD4 9BS (01923) 265266* **£79.40**w; 20 comfortable rms. Comfortable and very neatly kept country hotel with relaxing views of pretty village green, dark beams, bow windows, antique settles, sofas and easy chairs, log fires, and good bar and restaurant food; pleasant nearby walks; disabled access

ST ALBANS TL1407 **White Hart** *Holywell Hill, St Albans, Hertfordshire AL1 1EZ (01727) 853624* **£67.90**w; 11 rms, most with own bthrm. Civilised former coaching inn with two bar areas, antique panelling, handsome fireplaces and furnishings, residents' lounge reached by barley-twist staircase, courteous friendly service, and good restaurant

To see and do

Hertfordshire Family Attraction of the Year

LETCHWORTH TL2033 **Standalone Farm** (Wilbury Rd) A little more earnest than some working farms we've been to, but none the worse for that, this simple, unfussy place, run by the Letchworth Garden City Heritage Foundation, is one of the county's best attractions aimed at children. Quite small, it's got something of an educational bent, so appeals most to younger children with a genuine interest in animals, who'll get an unaffected look at life and activities down on the farm. Spring is definitely the best time to come, when you'll find new-born calves, chicks and other animals, and can watch the lambs being bottle-fed (usually at 12 and 4pm). Plenty of animals to enjoy the rest of the year too, from shire horse and Shetland ponies to rabbits, chipmunks and guinea-pigs. Pigs, free-range chickens and rare breeds of poultry wander around the farmyard, and there are paddocks of sheep and goats. Two friendly Jersey cows take part in milking demonstrations every day at 2.30pm. An exhibition farm has a working beehive, model dinosaurs and various creepy-crawlies, and there's an outdoor play area next to a decent spot for picnics. There are picnic areas indoors too, and most animals and displays are under cover on a wet day. Children can also climb on Fergie, a red static play tractor, and there are 170 acres of farmland to explore, with walks and an arboretum. Snacks, shop, disabled access; open daily Mar–Sept, and Oct half-term; (01462) 686775; £2.95 (£1.90 children over 3).

ALDBURY SP9612
A perfect village green, stocks etc, attractive houses, teas, two good pubs; good walks nearby.

ALDENHAM COUNTRY PARK TQ1695
Plenty of space for children to run around in, with adventure play area, nature trails and a herd of longhorn cattle.

ARDELEY TL3027
Attractive thatched village with good food at the Jolly Waggoner, and a pleasant quiet drive along the lane down through Wood End, Haultwick and Dane End. This rolling countryside is very rural, with quite an East Anglian flavour; some of Hertfordshire's best walking territory.

Cromer Windmill 🔳 (just NW)
Partly 13th-c, lovingly restored, the last remaining post-mill in the county, its sails turning again after standing idle for nearly 80 years. Snacks, disabled access ground floor only; open pm Sun, bank hols and alternate Sats mid-May to mid-Sept; (01438) 861662; £1.50.

ASHWELL TL2639
Attractive village with some fine houses and an unusually tall church tower; the Bushel & Strike just beside it and the Three Tuns are both useful for lunch.

AYOT ST LAWRENCE TL1916
Delightful little backwater, with a very picturesque 12th-c ivy-covered ruined church nr its old-fashioned inn; the

existing church is an incongruously grand neo-Grecian affair. The village is conveniently close to link to a walk along the River Lea, which has been dammed at Brocket Hall to form a lake (in view from the public right of way). Shorter walks can start from Ayot Green, where an abandoned railway line is open to walkers and forms a useful link.

Shaw's Corner Much as it was when GBS lived here, 1906–1950; Shaw devotees will enjoy seeing his exercise machine, pen, spectacles, and even the soft homburg he wore for 60 years. The tiny writing shed at the bottom of the garden was designed to revolve and so maximise sunlight. Shop, ring to arrange disabled access; open pm Weds–Sun and bank hols (exc Good Fri), Apr–Oct; (01438) 820307; £3.50; NT.

BENINGTON TL2923
Benington Lordship Seven acres of Edwardian terraced gardens with many unusual plants, fine herbaceous borders, roses and rock garden, and a particularly lovely splash of snowdrops in spring. The grounds include a very picturesque early 19th-c 'Norman' ruined gatehouse, actually put together from stones of the genuinely Norman ruined moated keep. Snacks, limited disabled access; open Weds pm Jun–Sept and Sun May–Aug, plus pm bank hols, 3rd Sun in Oct for plant sales, and some dates in early spring for snowdrops – ring for details; (01438) 869668; *£3. The village is one of the county's prettiest and most interesting, its church lovely when the snowdrops are out in late Feb. The handsome old Bell has generous food. The countryside around offers some of Hertfordshire's better walking, with quite an East Anglian flavour.

BERKHAMSTED SP9908
Berkhamsted Castle (next to railway station) The remains of this Norman castle boast a proud history – William the Conqueror acceded to the English throne here in 1066, and it lays claim to some of the finest earthworks from that time, inc the only double moat in Europe, quite striking when flooded. When the sun is shining, it's a pleasant spot for a picnic. An enthusiastic keeper gives group guided tours for a price; (01442) 871737; free; EH.

BRAUGHING TL3924
(pronounced 'Braffing') Attractive village with pretty 14th-c riverside church; decent pub.

BROXBOURNE TL3306
Paradise Wildlife Park 📷 (White Stubbs Lane) Friendly little zoo and leisure park with lions, monkeys, camels and zebras, events from meeting the python to feeding the lions and falconry displays; adventure playground, crazy golf, woodland walk and paddling pool. Meals, snacks, shop, disabled access; cl 25 Dec; (01992) 468001; £7.50. The Coach & Horses at Newgate Street does enjoyable food, and there are good woodland walks around here.

ESSENDON TL2708
The mildly hilly partly wooded country around here is popular with wknd walkers, with pleasantly varied village-to-village paths.

GREAT AMWELL TL3612
Pretty conjunction of church, pre-Norman Emma's Well and pool with islets.

Van Hage Garden Co (A1170) An unusually lively place, good for an afternoon out, with children's farm, and plenty to look at in addition to their excellent range of plants. Miniature railway some summer wknds. Meals, snacks, shops, disabled access; cl Easter Sun, 25–26 Dec and 1 Jan; (01920) 870811; free.

GREAT HORMEAD TL4029
An attractive village, plenty of thatch and timbering.

GREAT WOOD TL2704
(off B157 N of Northaw, where the Two Brewers is a useful stop) Pretty walks in ancient woodland.

HATFIELD TL2308
Hatfield House A great Jacobean house built in 1611 on the site of a childhood home of Elizabeth I; the splendid State Rooms include portraits of that queen, and even her silk stockings, perhaps among the earliest worn in this country. Also the National Collection of Model Soldiers, with over 3,000 exhibits. The scented garden and knot garden contain plants that were typical between the 15th and 17th c.

Alongside is an extensive park. Meals, snacks, shop, disabled access; open Apr–Sept, park and gardens every day, house cl am and all day Mon exc bank hols and Fri (except to booked parties). No guided tours pm Sat, Sun or bank hols; (01707) 262823; *£6.40, park and garden only £1.50. The nearby church has a window by Burne-Jones, and the attractive village of Old Hatfield has a fine old pub (the Eight Bells). Beyond is the extensive modern built-up area that has now taken the Hatfield name.

HERTFORD TL3212

Some quiet older parts include the old main Fore St, which has handsomely pargeted buildings. There are several antiques shops in St Andrew St (one in a fine 15th-c house). So-called **Hertford Castle** is in fact the 15th-c gatehouse for Edward IV's original moated castle, carefully restored and now occupied by the council; usually open pm first Sun in month May–Sept, for guided tours (and throughout the year for private tours and special events). (01992) 584322; free. The extensive riverside grounds (with the massive flint walls of Henry II's castle) are always open. McMullens Brewery is a striking Victorian building on the river. The Old Barge by the Lee Navigation Canal has a wide choice of vegetarian food among other dishes. Nearby Hertingfordbury is an attractive village, between river and beechwoods.

Hertford Museum (Bull Plain) Cheery local history museum, in an elegant 17th-c building; it has a graceful Jacobean knot garden. Shop, disabled access to ground floor and garden; cl Sun, Mon, 23–26 Dec, 1 Jan and Good Fri; (01992) 582686; free.

KING'S WALDEN TL1623

This quiet village and the rolling farmland around it is pleasant walking territory.

KNEBWORTH TL2221

Knebworth House (Old Knebworth) The splendid house at the centre of this 250-acre park was originally a straightforward Tudor mansion, but was spectacularly embellished by Victorian author Sir Edward Bulwer Lytton; he wanted it to be a castle fit for the romantic characters in his novels. Still a lived-in home (the same family has been here for over 500 years), the grand rooms include a

splendid Jacobean great hall, an exhibition on the great days of the Raj, and mementoes of former guests like Dickens and Churchill. The well restored gardens were designed by Lutyens, and include a herb garden laid out to plans by Gertrude Jekyll; there's also a deer park, a Victorian maze, and a miniature railway (extra). There's an exceptionally good adventure playground – in addition to the usual wooden climbing equipment and so forth there are quite a few exciting slides, inc the monorail suspension slide, and the twisting Corkscrew, plus a special enclosure for younger children. Lots of special events throughout the year. Meals, snacks, shop, limited disabled access; open wknds Easter–Sept, daily from Jun–early Sept and during school hols but best to check; (01438) 812661; £7 for everything (£6.50 children 5–16) – £5.50 grounds only. Along the outer edge of the park is the pretty little hamlet of Old Knebworth; the Lytton Arms here is a very good pub.

LETCHWORTH TL2232

First Garden City Heritage Museum 🖾 The country's first garden city, begun in 1903. The First Garden City Heritage Museum (Norton Way S), set in the architects' charming Arts and Crafts thatched cottages, shows the thinking behind this uniquely 20th-c idea. Shop, mostly disabled access; cl Sun, 25–26 Dec; (01462) 482710; *£1. The nearby Three Magnets (Leys Ave) is a good newish pub.

Standalone Farm See separate family panel on p.288.

LONDON COLNEY TL1604

Aylett Nurseries (A414 N) Enthusiastically run garden centre specialising in geraniums, fuchsias and esp their award-winning dahlias. Meals, snacks, disabled access; cl 25–27 Dec and Easter Sun; (01727) 822255.

De Havilland Aircraft Centre 🖾 (adjacent to Salisbury Hall, off B556) The Mosquito bombers were developed here in secret from 1939, and the site now houses a collection of 20 different De Havilland aircraft, as well as engines and other memorabilia; there's also a new education centre with the story of De Havilland and an engine exhibit. Snacks in verandah-style area in main hangar, shop, disabled access; open Mar–Oct, pm Tues, Thurs and Sat, all day Sun and bank hols; (01727) 826400; *£4. There are pretty riverside gardens down by the bridge.

MILL GREEN TL2309
Mill Green Museum & Mill Well restored working watermill with craft demonstrations most Suns Apr–Sept and Sats July and Aug, from paper-quilling to love-spoon carving. Shop, disabled access to ground floor only; cl am wknds, all day Mon, milling Sun pm, Tues and Weds; (01707) 271362; free.

MUCH HADHAM TL4219
Forge Museum & Cottage Garden (High St) Based around a working blacksmith, the story of such craftsmen through the ages, with an unusual bee shelter in the Victorian-style garden. Snacks, shop, some disabled access; open Fri–Sun and bank hols in summer, in winter by appointment; (01279) 843301; £1.

The Henry Moore Foundation 🖼 Dane Tree House, Perry Green) The excellent sculpture garden here is much enjoyed by readers. Several works are displayed in the studios where they were made, while the larger ones are shown off against a backdrop of woodland, pasture and hedgerows. Shop, disabled access; open daily for 90-min guided tour, must book; (01279) 843333; *£3. The Hoops opposite has good food. Much Hadham is attractive, with fine Tudor and Georgian houses, and a good specialist nursery (Hopleys).

NORTHCHURCH SP9609
Largely swallowed up in Berkhamsted, but notable for the ancient church where Peter the Wild Boy is buried; the George & Dragon is handy for lunch.

PIRTON TL1431
Attractive village; the village green is actually the remains of a Norman motte and bailey.

RAVENSBURGH CASTLE TL1029
Up in the woods above Hexton, this is an easily traced Iron Age hill fort – a pleasant stroll.

RINGSHALL SP9912
Ashridge Estate Right on the county border and nr Whipsnade Zoo in Bedfordshire, 4,000 acres of unspoilt woodlands and open spaces. Plenty of deer and other wildlife (inc dormice, though you won't see them in daylight), and a monument to the Duke of Bridgewater. Teas summer wknds, shop and information centre, disabled access; monument and facilities cl am, Fri, and Nov–Mar; (01442) 851227; monument £1; NT. The Greyhound and Valiant Trooper at Aldbury just below are good for lunch.

ROYSTON TL3540
Royston Cave (Melbourn St) Tucked beneath the pavement, this cave is thought to have been cut into the 60-metre layer of chalk which underlies the town by the Knights Templar in the 13th c; fascinating figures of saints and kings are carved into the walls. Open pms wknds and bank hols Easter–Sept (otherwise by appointment); (01763) 242223; *£1.

SARRATT TQ0498
Long and attractive village green; the church is partly Saxon, and the Cock nearby is good. There are pleasant unspoilt walks from here into the Chess Valley in Buckinghamshire.

SCALES WOOD TL4133
(nr Anstey) A useful strolling ground.

ST ALBANS TL1407
Though modern shops dominate your first impressions, corners of real antiquity are tucked away between and behind them. This was one of the most important Roman towns in northern Europe, and has some fine well excavated remains in peaceful surroundings. A stroll in search of other notable buildings (the tourist information office in the Town Hall, Market Pl, has helpful guide maps) is rewarded by the surprisingly large number of decent pubs here. Down between abbey gate and park, the Fighting Cocks is based on an ancient building which had some connection with the abbey, and its interesting layout includes the clearly discernible shape of a cockpit. In the quietly attractive largely Georgian St Michael's St, the Rose & Crown is very civilised, and the Six Bells is on the site of a

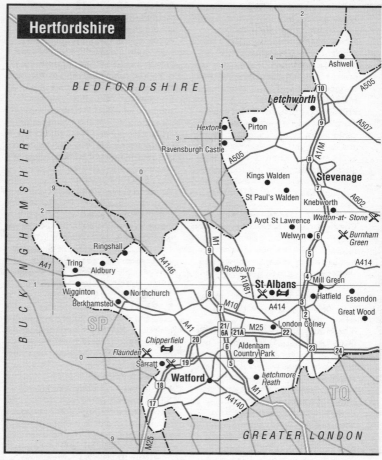

Roman bath house, though not visibly so. The Cock (Hatfield Rd) is worth looking out for because of its bizarre history; its floors were found to rest on thick foundations of human bones. Worth a look if you're nearby are the **museum** (Hatfield Rd), covering the town's post-Roman history (shop, disabled access to ground floor; cl am Sun, 25 Dec; free), and **Grebe House** in the park nr Verulamium, a regional wildlife trust HQ with a woodland garden (cl wknds and bank hols; free). The B651 N towards Hitchin is quite a scenic country drive.

Clock Tower This striking free-standing stone building has a bell, striking on the hour, even older than the tower itself. Exhibitions on the way up and fine views from the top; open wknds and bank hols Easter–Oct; small donation suggested. Nearby, French Row is a narrow alley of striking timbered buildings jettied out over the street, right by a modern shopping centre. The Fleur de Lys pub here is a remarkable medieval building.

Gardens of the Rose 🏛 (B4630 S) The showgrounds of the Royal National Rose Society, with over 1,600 cultivars, many in mass plantings. Plenty of interesting cultivation trials going on, new roses from all over the world, lots of clematis, and an iris garden. Snacks,

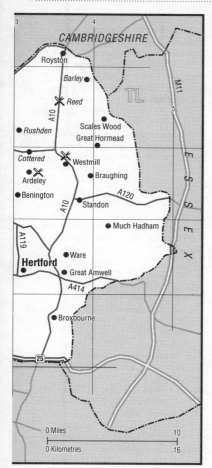

museum. Good meals and snacks, shop, disabled access; cl over Christmas; (01727) 853502; £1.10.

Organ Museum (Camp Rd, 2m from centre) Tuneful collection of automatically operated organs and other musical instruments, inc Wurlitzer and Rutt theatre organs. Recitals every Sun 2–4.30pm, and concerts once a month. Shop, disabled access (but no facilities); open Sun pm only; (01727) 869693; £3.50.

St Albans Cathedral Up on a mound, this has good views; its 11th-c reddish exterior uses flint recycled from the Roman remains. Once the country's premier abbey, it suffered a little after the Reformation, and its fortunes didn't revive until Victorian times. It was touched up a lot then, but the majestic interior does have some earlier features, inc 13th- and 14th-c paintings in the long nave, and some Saxon transept pillars. Meals, snacks, shop, disabled access; cl pm 25 Dec, cathedral free, around £1.50 for audio-visual show. The great 14th-c abbey gatehouse beyond leads down to a neat park, its lake and willow-edged stream packed with ducks.

Verulamium Museum This was the name of the Roman city; its remains are down in the SW corner of town, past the cathedral and attractive park (coming from outside, most easily reached by the A4147 off the Hemel Hempstead exit from M1 junction 7). The place to start is the excellent Verulamium Museum (St Michael's) which has been recently extended, with its lively interpretation of everyday Roman life, as well as jewellery, wall paintings and domestic items found nearby. Shop, disabled access; cl am Sun, 25–26 Dec; (01727) 751810; £3.05. Follow signs from here into the adjacent playing-fields: an unassuming brick building looking like a garage or changing rooms houses the carefully restored mosaic floor and hypocaust underfloor heating system of an excavated Roman villa; free. Further on is a well preserved section of the Roman town wall.

Verulamium Roman Theatre Most impressive; not large by the

shop, disabled access; cl end Sept–end May; (01727) 850461; £4. The Holly Bush at nearby Potters Crouch has decent food (not Sun).

Gorhambury Two miles out (the other side of Verulamium's park) but peaceful enough to make you think it's the heart of the country, an 18th-c house with extensive assemblage of 17th-c family portraits, and some 16th-c enamelled glass. Shop; open pm Thurs May–Sept; (01727) 855000; £6.

Kingsbury Watermill (St Michael's St) 16th-c watermill half a mile from the city on the banks of the River Ver, still with one working waterwheel and a standards of some others in England (room for 1,600), but taking into account its good state of preservation it's unique. Shop, limited disabled access; cl 25–26 Dec, 1 Jan; (01727) 835035; £1.50.

ST PAUL'S WALDEN TL1922
Birthplace of the Queen Mother, a quiet village which with the rolling rather East Anglian feeling surrounding countryside offers some of Hertfordshire's most pleasant walking.

STANDON TL3822
Has some good timbered buildings in its curving High St.

TRING SP9211
Walter Rothschild Zoological Museum (Akeman St, off High St) Part of the national Natural History Museum, this is made up primarily of the remarkably eclectic collections of the second Lord Rothschild, started when he was a little boy; thousands of preserved mammals, insects, birds, fish and reptiles. Snacks, shop, limited disabled access; cl Sun am, and 23–26 Dec; (01442) 824181; £3.50, children free (under-5s might find the displays slightly startling). Entry is free after 4.30pm wknds and bank hols, though as it shuts at 5 you'd have to dash round a bit to see everything then. The Cow Roast (A4521 towards Berkhamsted) has good food (and popular family barbecues). Tring has a choice of canal towpath walks from nr the Grand Junction Arms pub (B488 at Bulbourne), where the Grand Union Canal branches into a part-abandoned offshoot, the Wendover Arm, and the still-operational Aylesbury Arm. (There's also canal access from the Boat down Ravens Lane in Berkhamsted, and the Fisheries at Boxmoor.) For more ambitious walkers, the Royal Hotel on Station Rd stands by the Ridgeway long-distance path, which heads off W right across southern England.

WALKING IN HERTFORDSHIRE TL3206
Large areas of this county are taken up by the northwards spread of London with continuous swathes of development, and also by the first early 20th-c New Towns, the garden cities of Letchworth and Welwyn, and their more modern successors Hatfield,

Hemel Hempstead and Stevenage. But between and beyond these are good green windows of carefully preserved farmland and some more wooded countryside. These yield pockets of good walking terrain, though there is little that is really outstanding. A good point is that even in the prairie-like arable farmland that characterises large chunks of the county, the field paths are often in remarkably good condition and very adequately waymarked. Pubs handy for walks include the Clarendon Arms at Chandlers Cross TQ0698, Two Brewers on Chipperfield Common TL0401, Stag at Chorleywood TQ0295, Fish & Eels at Dobbs Weir TL3808 nr Hoddesdon, Three Blackbirds at Flamstead TL0714, Bricklayers Arms and Green Dragon at Flaunden TL0100, Alford Arms at Frithsden TL0110, Huntsman at Goose Green TL3509 (for Hertford Heath), Cross Keys at Gustard Wood nr Wheathampstead TL1716, Five Horseshoes at Little Berkhamsted TL2908, Bridgewater Arms at Little Gaddesden SP9913, Cabinet at Reed TL3636, Harvest Moon at Thorley TL4718 and White Lion at Walkern TL2826.

WARE TL3513
Scott's Grotto (Scotts Rd) Built in the 1760s by the poet John Scott, this is one of the finest bits of romantic gothickry in the world, extending 20 metres (67 ft) into the hillside under a modern housing development, with underground passages and chambers decorated with flints, shells, stones and minerals. Wear flat shoes and bring a torch. Open pm Sat and bank hols Apr–end Sept, or by appointment; (01920) 464131; suggested donation £1. Several private gardens running down to the quiet River Lea have antique gazebos over the water, neatly restored with crisp white paintwork. The A10 N of here is quite a pleasant road, with decent food at the Sow & Pigs.

WATFORD TQ1097
Cheslyn Gardens An unexpected pleasure in this largely modern urban area, with 3½ acres of woodland and formal gardens, and an aviary; cl 25 Dec; free. From Cassiobury Park you can

watch the canal boats on the Grand Union Canal. The local museum (High St) has a display on the Watford Home Guard, the basis for the TV series *Dad's Army*. Shop, disabled access; cl Sat 1–2pm, all day Sun, bank hols; free.

WELWYN TL2315
Welwyn Roman Baths (just off A1(M) junction 6 – towards Welwyn on A1000, and counting M-way slip roundabout as 1st roundabout go nearly all way round 2nd roundabout – car park through two five-barred gates) Excavated before the construction of the A1 and since then rather ingeniously preserved within the motorway embankment, this Roman bath house is all that remains of a 3rd-c villa. Very good condition, with explanatory displays. Shop, disabled access; open pm wknds and bank hols Jan–Nov, and pms daily during school hols (exc Dec); (01707) 271362; *£1.

WESTMILL TL3627
A happy combination of neat green-tiled cottages and fine old church; the Sword in Hand, well restored after fire damage, has decent food, and there are pleasant walks nearby.

WIGGINTON SP9310
The landlord of the Greyhound here is very helpful with suggestions for walks; the 18th-c summerhouse in the woods is an odd find.

Other attractive villages, all with decent pubs, include partly thatched Barley TL3938, Cottered TL3129, Hexton TL1230, Letchmore Heath TQ1597, Redbourn TL1012 (despite motorway noise Church End with its workhouse and Norman church is pretty) and Rushden TL3031.

Where to eat

ARDELEY TL3027 **Jolly Waggoner** *(01438) 861350* Cream-washed dining inn in pretty, tucked-away village, with lots of woodwork, beams and an open fire, a restaurant newly extended into the cottage next door, a relaxed and civilised atmosphere, well presented food using local produce, a good range of wines, well kept Greene King ales, and attractive garden; cl Mon; children over 7. £23|£6.75

BURNHAM GREEN TL2616 **White Horse** *White Horse Lane (01438) 798416* Busy, popular dining pub with attractive original black-beamed part by bar counter, big two-floored extension (no smoking downstairs), log fire, well prepared reasonably priced food and more elaborate restaurant menu, real ales, and a gentle country view at the back, where there are seats by outdoor heaters. £16.95|£5.50

FLAUNDEN TL0101 **Bricklayers Arms** *Hogpits Bottom (01442) 833322* Cottagey pub with roaring log fires, snug low-beamed rooms with stubs of knocked-through oak-timbered walls, and a couple of life-size bronze dogs, five real ales, decent bar food and more elaborate restaurant menu (which can be eaten anywhere in the pub), and friendly efficient service; it does get busy at wknds; old-fashioned garden. £16.25|£6

REED TL3636 **Cabinet** *High St (01763) 848366* Tiled and weatherboarded village house, now a civilised dining pub, with a small cosy main bar and newly refurbished snug, no smoking restaurant with stripped floors, winter log fire and simple mix of wooden tables and chairs, enjoyable changing bar food, real ales, and decent wines; they now have an exhibition of local sculptors' work. £16.95|£5.25

SARRATT TQ0398 **Cock** *Church Lane (01923) 282908* Cosy white 17th-c country pub, with a carpeted snug, oak-panelled lounge, and inglenook fireplaces; restaurant in a nicely restored thatched barn, generous helpings of well liked food (esp the daily specials), and real ales; benches in front, and seats on a pretty back lawn with country views; disabled access. £30|£5.75

ST ALBANS TL1307 **Waffle House** *Kingsbury Watermill, St Michael's St (01727) 853502* Little restaurant attached to mill (see *To See and Do* section), serving delicious sweet and savoury waffles, and a good choice of drinks inc fresh milk shakes and pure fruit juices; riverside terrace; disabled access. £10|£5

WATTON-AT-STONE TL2919 **George & Dragon** *82 High St (01920) 830285* Civilised pub first licensed in 1603, with a smart but relaxed atmosphere, antiques, open fires, and daily papers, friendly efficient service, first-class imaginative food in bar (good value daily specials) and no smoking restaurant, and good house wines; cl Sun pm; children must be well behaved. £22|**£7.25**

WESTMILL TL3627 **Sword in Hand** *(01763) 271356* In a very attractive village, this 14th-c colour-washed pub is full of character, with exposed beams, log fires, and traditional-style furniture – the partly no smoking dining room has nice views over the garden and church; well presented, very good food, well kept real ales, decent wines, and plenty of seats on the terrace and in garden, with a play area for children. £20|**£7.50**

Please let us know what you think of places in the *Guide*. Use the report forms at the back of the book or simply write us a letter.

ISLE OF WIGHT

A holiday island with a great deal for families, from traditional theme parks to innovative wildlife centres, good beaches, better than average weather, and appealingly varied countryside – some dramatic coastal scenery

Amazon World at Newchurch wins the title of the island's Family Attraction of the Year – lively and interesting, and good for a rainy day. Elsewhere, enjoyable Yafford Watermill provides a novel setting for a farm park, Sandown Zoo is about to open a new dinosaur attraction, the attractively set Rare Breeds & Waterfowl Park at St Lawrence has lots to look at, and Brickfields Horse Centre hosts fun events from piglet racing to cowboy and Indian horse shows. Ruined Appuldurcombe House provides an atmospheric setting for the developing owl and falconry centre.

Blackgang Chine and its Downend counterpart, Robin Hill County Park, are good family retreats, and a decent mix of attractions make Fort Victoria Country Park a worthwhile destination. Up for sale as we went to press, Haseley Manor at Arreton (an enjoyable day out for young and old) may not stay open to the public this year.

Many of the more child-oriented places close for six months over winter.

Osborne House at East Cowes was Queen Victoria's favourite residence, and is popular with many older people today. Lovely Nunwell House at Brading gave Charles I his last comfortable night's sleep, and the Dimbola Lodge arts centre (Freshwater Bay) has interesting Victorian associations.

Some excellent more specialised places worth seeking out include the dinosaur museum near Brighstone, the Lilliput Doll and Toy Museum at Brading (some exhibits date back to 2000 BC), and the combined appeals of the botanical gardens (new visitor centre) and the Museum of Smuggling History at Ventnor.

In high summer the main resorts and places to visit get very busy, yet even then, away from the main tourist haunts, much of the island is surprisingly unspoilt and little visited. The most attractive scenery is in the west, the largest concentration of things to do in the east.

At other times the island feels fresh, uncrowded and leisurely. The coastal walks are the finest in south-east England – worth coming just for these. Inland are long curving chalk ridges (tracks often follow the crests) and forestry plantations with many signposted woodland trails. The crossing takes about 30 mins – half that for the Portsmouth–Ryde catamaran, even less for the Southsea Hovercraft.

The Lymington–Yarmouth trip is the most rewarding (you'll need to book in summer). Foot fares start at around £9, cars from £34 – though the very cheapest fares are usually at pretty anti-social times: (0990)

827744 for bookings from Portsmouth to Fishbourne or Ryde, and Lymington to Yarmouth; (01703) 334010 for Southampton–Cowes; (01705) 811000 for Hovercraft Southsea–Ryde. Once you're there, prices are rather on the low side compared with the mainland, and for longer stays some hotels do good value package deals that include the ferry fare.

The island bus service is excellent, especially between May and September; a week's bus pass is good value, as is a daily Rover road/rail ticket; £6.25 (family ticket, £16.95).

Where to stay

BONCHURCH SZ5777 **Lake Hotel** *Bonchurch, Ventnor, Isle of Wight PO38 1RF* (01983) 852613 **£60***, plus special breaks; 20 rms. Early 19th-c country house in two acres of pretty gardens and 400 metres from the beach; lots of flowers and plants in three light and airy lounges (one is an attractive conservatory), a well stocked bar, and enjoyable food in neat restaurant; cl Nov–Feb; children over 3; dogs by prior arrangement

BONCHURCH SZ5778 **Winterbourne** *Bonchurch Village Rd, Ventnor, Isle of Wight PO38 1RQ* (01983) 852535 **£133** inc dinner; 15 rms, most with own bthrm, many with sea views, and some in the coach house. Charming creeper-covered house with four acres of pretty grounds inc waterfalls, a stream, and small heated swimming pool; restful day rooms, good food in attractive restaurant, and friendly staff and resident owners; Charles Dickens wrote *David Copperfield* here; cl Nov–Mar (though open wknds in Nov/Dec, and open Christmas and New Year); dogs welcome

CHALE SZ4877 **Clarendon** *Chale, Ventnor, Isle of Wight PO38 2HA* (01983) 730431 **£80***, plus winter breaks; 21 rms inc 3 suites. Warmly friendly hotel (and very well run Wight Mouse family pub, attached) with engaging helpful owners, lots of charm and character, comfortable sun lounge and cocktail bar, good food, wines and real ales, and an extraordinary collection of 365 whiskies; excellent for families; disabled access ☺

SEAVIEW SZ6291 **Seaview Hotel** *High St, Seaview, Isle of Wight PO34 5EX* (01983) 612711 **£95***, plus special breaks; 16 attractively decorated rms, some with sea views and private drawing rooms. Small, friendly and spotlessly kept hotel with fine ship photographs in the chatty and relaxed front dining bar, an interesting old-fashioned back bar, good imaginative bar food, and a highly regarded evening restaurant; cl 4 days over Christmas; proper high tea for children (must be over 5 in evening restaurant); well behaved dogs allowed away from public rooms; partial disabled access

SHANKLIN SZ5779 **Luccombe Chine House** *Luccombe, Shanklin, Isle of Wight PO37 6RH* (01983) 862037 **£80**, plus special breaks; 6 rms, all with four-posters and sea or garden views. Very friendly small hotel at the end of a long drive and surrounded by large wooded grounds – you can watch foxes and badgers at night taking food left for them on the lawn; homely lounge with help-yourself drinks tray, beams and inglenook fireplaces, and very good food in cosy dining room; enjoyable walks; cl Dec–Jan; no children or dogs

SHORWELL SZ4582 **Westcourt Farm** *Shorwell, Newport, Isle of Wight PO30 3LA* (01983) 740233 **£38***; 3 rms. Fine Elizabethan manor connected to a farm of 250 acres, with comfortable lounge/dining room, and a restful atmosphere; no smoking; lots of surrounding walks; cl Nov–Mar; children over 12 – though may take younger ones out of season

ST LAWRENCE SZ5476 **Lisle Combe** *Bank End Farm, Undercliffe Drive, Ventnor, Isle of Wight PO38 1UW* (01983) 852582 **£39***; 3 rms, shared bthrm. Elizabethan-style farmhouse in five-acre coastal garden with lovely sea views, friendly courteous staff, and lovely paintings and furniture – it was once the home of poet Alfred Noyes and is still owned by the family; they keep their own rare breeds and waterfowl park, and are close to coves and beaches; must book months ahead (so popular with return customers); self-catering cottage; cl Christmas and New Year; no dogs ☺

VENTNOR SZ5577 **Royal Hotel** *Belgrave Rd, Ventnor, Isle of Wight PO38 1JJ* (01983) 852186 **£110**; 55 well equipped rms. Friendly Victorian hotel with fine sea views, neat gardens with heated outdoor pool, spacious and comfortable day rooms, cosy candlelit bar with open fire, good food in attractive restaurant, and helpful service; cl 2 wks Jan; disabled access

YARMOUTH SZ3589 **Bugle** *The Square, Yarmouth, Isle of Wight PO41 0NS* (01983) 760272 **£68**; 8 rms, most with own bthrm (best to have one not above the lively bar). Bustling inn with bar decorated like a galleon stern, other panelled rooms, a friendly atmosphere, good bar and restaurant food (restaurant closed Sun, Mon), children's room, and sizeable garden

YARMOUTH SZ3589 **George Hotel** *Quay St, Yarmouth, Isle of Wight PO41 0PE* (01983) 760331 **£145**; 17 comfortable rms. 17th-c house by the harbour, with gardens leading to little private beach; a fine flagstoned hall, fresh flowers and open fires, a convivial bar and attractive residents' sitting room with marvellously relaxing atmosphere, imaginative and enjoyable food in informal brasserie and smart restaurant, hearty breakfasts, and prompt courteous service; motor yacht for hire; children over 8; disabled access

To see and do

Isle of Wight Family Attraction of the Year

NEWCHURCH SZ5685 **Amazon World** (Watery Lane, A3056) An effective mix of entertainment and environmental awareness, this is an expanding collection of the kind of animals, birds and insects you'd find in an Amazon rain forest, housed in lively animal and jungle settings. Free-flying birds swoop overhead, and you can imagine snakes slithering through the grass and trees (they do have snakes – but they're kept safely out of the way). Among the 200 species are everything from marmosets and crocodiles, through toucans and flamingos, to tarantulas and terrapins. There are some bigger animals outdoors, but as most of the exhibition is under cover, it's enjoyable in any weather. Divided into several areas, it starts with the story of the rain forests, then goes on to look at how man lives and works in them, the damage that's been done to rain forests in recent years, and a look at the campaigns to reverse that. Outside is a petting area, where children can touch and feed rabbits, goats and the like, as well as twice-daily falconry displays (weather permitting) at 12.30 and 3.30pm. They have meet-the-animal sessions every day at 2pm, where a keeper shows off two animals at a time. There's a good adventure playground (improved and extended this year), with a separate area for under-5s. Meals, snacks, picnic areas, shop, disabled access; cl 25–26 Dec, 1 Jan, and maybe a week in Jan too; (01983) 867122; £4.95 (£3.60 children 3–14).

ALUM BAY SZ3085
The beach here is famous for its multi-coloured sands from the different rock strata in the cliff that runs down to it; 20 shades of pinks, greys and ochres, showing up most vividly after rain. The High Down Hotel towards Totland has decent food.
Needles Old Battery From Needles Pleasure Park it's a ¾-mile walk to this 19th-c Palmerstonian fortress (you can't go by car); the parade-ground shows off two 12-ton gun barrels salvaged from the sea, and there is an exhibition about World War I. A longish underground tunnel leads to an look-out spot that gives stunning views of the Needles themselves, a group of

wave-battered chalk pinnacles, and their lighthouse. Snacks; cl Fri and Sat (exc Easter wknd and July–Aug), all Nov–Mar, and in bad weather; (01983) 754772; £2.50; NT.

Needles Park Clifftop pleasure park which stands out for its spectacular chairlift down to the beach, with wonderful views along the way. They sell little glass tubes with the sands carefully layered inside. Meals, snacks, shop, disabled access; cl early Nov–Easter; (01983) 752401; park entry free (though car parking is £3), then individual charges for attractions (return trip on the chairlift is £2.75). Glass-blowing demonstrations at adjacent Alum Bay Glass (cl 3 wks over Christmas; 80p), and tours of the Sweet Manufactory (also 80p); both have good factory shops.

ARRETON SZ5386

A pleasant place with a delightful 13th-c **church** (which has a brass-rubbing centre). The lovely Elizabethan mellow stone manor house here is no longer open to the public, but nearby, the Country Craft Village has craft workshops, pub, and restaurant with home baking. The White Lion is good for lunch, and the cross-island Wootton Bridge–Niton back road through here has quietly attractive views.

Haseley Manor ⊞ This, the largest and oldest manor house open on the island, was up for sale as we went to press, so we can't be certain of its opening times (or whether indeed it will be open) next year. Dating back in parts to the early 14th c, it's been enthusiastically restored, and the 20 or so rooms are carefully decorated in period style. A reconstructed 18th-c farm has lots of crafts displays and archaeological exhibits housed in two barns, animals, herb gardens, pottery and adventure playground. Snacks, shop, disabled access; best to phone for times and prices; (01983) 865420; £4.95.

BEMBRIDGE SZ6488

Even in summer this is quiet for a coastal place, though with plenty going on in its yachting harbour, and a lifeboat station nearby. Though most of Wight's E coast is heavily developed, with the coastal path sometimes following roads and skirting large residential areas, Bembridge has the best opportunities for walks. Out on the Foreland the magnificent rock pools would keep any beachcomber happy for hours. The clifftop Crab & Lobster (Forelands), an easy walk up from the beach, has fabulous views. There's also a good walk S to Culver Cliff, for more views – the isolated clifftop Culver Haven pub nr the Yarborough Monument there commands a great panorama.

Shipwreck Centre Maritime Museum (Sherbourne St) Six galleries of salvage and shipwreck items, and tales of pirates and mermen. Shop, disabled access ground floor only; cl Nov–Mar; (01983) 872223; £2.50.

Windmill The only surviving windmill on the island, built in 1700 and used until 1913. Shop; cl Sat (exc Easter Sat and July–Aug) and Nov–Mar; £1.50; NT.

BINSTEAD SZ5792

Brickfields Horse Country ⊞ Two daily parades of horses in the indoor arena (noon and 3.30), livened up by the appearance of a medieval knight, and a cowboy and Indian, who chase each other around firing pistols and flinging tomahawks. Also tours of stables, wagon rides, rabbits and guinea pigs, and a collection of Shetland ponies. They also have a nifty line in pigs, with races three times a day. Show-jumping displays from 7pm on summer Weds evenings (car boot sales Mon evenings), and on three evenings in mid-Dec they put on a lively Christmas show, which might include a pantomime and Shetland pony Grand National. Meals, snacks, shop, disabled access; cl 25–26 Dec; (01983) 566801; £4.50. The old White Hart at Havenstreet is handy for lunch.

BLACKGANG SZ4876

Blackgang Chine Fantasy Park Run by the same team as the Robin Hill Country Park (see Downend entry), this 40-acre family leisure park has an excellent policy on return visits: each ticket allows free entry for a second visit within four days. The liveliest attraction is an enjoyable high-speed water chute, and there are plenty more gentle rides to suit younger children, inc a new badger-themed fairground. The most interesting parts are the maritime museum at the restored quayside, and the complete replica of a Victorian sawmill, inc working steam and oil engines. The plentiful models of dinosaurs, goblins, and nursery rhyme scenes dotted around the gardens have been done with a fair bit of flair and panache, and the gardens are well illuminated on summer evenings. Also fossils and gemstones, a hedge maze, and several play areas, inc one for toddlers. Meals, snacks, shop, disabled access (some steep hills); open late Mar–Oct; (01983) 730330; £5.95 (children 3–13 £4.95). The Wight Mouse at Chale is an excellent family pub, and the A3055 in both directions gives fine sea and coast views.

BONCHURCH SZ5778

Much quieter than nearby Ventnor, with leafy lanes hugging the slopes and passing an unexpected tree-shaded pond; steep steps connect the different levels, and there's a quiet cove down below the cliff. The small 13th-c church has a lovely peaceful graveyard, and above the cliff St Boniface Down has tremendous views. The Bonchurch Inn is rather unusual, with its Italian landlord and food. For several miles along this section of coast, the cliffs have been and to some extent still are subject to massive landslides.

BRADING SZ6086

Busy and attractive, with interesting monuments in its Norman church, and a pretty graveyard. The Bugle food pub is very well organised for families. The remains of a **Roman villa** have good mosaics (cl Nov–Mar; £2.75). The road out over Bembridge Down to Culver Cliff gives fine views, especially from the Culver Haven pub at the end.

Isle of Wight Waxworks Set in the partly 11th-c Ancient Rectory Mansion, this is largely what you'd expect from a wax museum, with an adjacent collection of stuffed animals and birds. In the summer there are candle-carving demonstrations. Shop, mostly disabled access; open daily, but best to ring for opening Dec–Jan; (01983) 407286; £4.75.

Lilliput Doll and Toy Museum Excellent private collection, with over 2,000 exhibits dating from as far back as

2000 BC, and examples of almost every seriously collectable doll in Britain. Shop, disabled access; cl 25 Dec; (01983) 407231; £1.95.

Morton Manor 🏠 (off A3055 S) Friendly partly 13th-c manor house, in lovely landscaped gardens with ornamental ponds and Elizabethan turf maze. The little vineyard has an exhibition of winemaking relics. Tearooms, shop, some disabled access; cl Sat, and Nov–Mar; (01983) 406168; £4.

Nunwell House and Gardens 🏠 (West Rd, off A3055 NW) Lovely lived-in 16th-c house with five acres of charming gardens, and interesting furniture and family memorabilia. Charles I spent his last night of freedom here. Light snacks with notice, shop; open Mon–Weds pm July–1st wk Sept, plus 2nd May bank hol Mon; (01983) 407240; *£4 (inc guide book), *£2.50 garden only.

BRIGHSTONE SZ4282

Dinosaur Farm (A3055 SE) One of the most important dinosaur skeletons to be found in the UK was discovered here in 1992. There's an enthusiastic museum dedicated to the find, and you can watch the experts at work, preparing the bones for scientific research and display. Snacks, shop, disabled access; open Thurs and Sun Easter–Sept and Oct half-term, plus Tues and Fri July–Aug; (01983) 740401; £2.

Inland walks Inland, the island is characterised by long curving chalk ridges (tracks often follow the crests) and forestry plantations (with many signposted woodland trails). The hills N of Brighstone represent some of the pick of the scenery. The Countryman on Limerstone Rd is a good refreshment break, with fine views down to the sea.

CALBOURNE SZ4186

Attractive village with photogenic streamside thatched cottages, 13th-c **church**, and the enjoyable working **Chessell Pottery** 🏠; snacks, shop, disabled access; cl two wks at Christmas; 50p. It's worth getting here early to avoid the coach tours. Fine views from the Blacksmiths Arms, a good family pub on the Carisbrooke road.

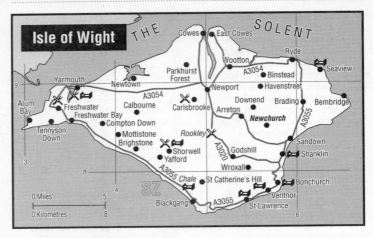

Watermill and Rural Museum 🏛
(B3401) A six-metre (20-ft)
waterwheel still powers this 17th-c mill,
and the grounds have tame peacocks.
Home-baked snacks, shop with stoneground flour, etc, some disabled access;
cl Jan to mid-Feb; (01983) 531227; *£3.
CARISBROOKE SZ4888
Carisbrooke Castle Ruins of the only
medieval castle on the island, between
1647 and 1648 home to the imprisoned
Charles I (his daughter died here in
1650). Some later buildings behind the
imposing gatehouse and walls, and
entertaining demonstrations of how
donkeys drew water from one of the
medieval wells. Snacks, shop, summer
café, disabled access to ground floor; cl
24–26 Dec; (01983) 522107; £4.50; EH.
The Eight Bells above the waterfowl
lake has decent food and good Solent
views.
COMPTON DOWN SZ3785
Another good place for walks on this S
coast, a hogsback grassy hill E of
Freshwater Bay; circular walks can take
in the coast path along Compton Bay –
one of the island's best beaches, not
touristy, with impressive cliff views (NT
car park).
COWES SZ4995
Stylish and lively, very much centred on
its yachting connections, with
interesting buildings and shops inc
fascinating ships' chandlers in the long
narrow High St, and the battery of over
20 brass cannon used to start the yacht

races down by the harbour. The Union
(Watchhouse Lane) has good value
food. Seafaring collections at the small
Maritime Museum in the public
library on Beckford Rd (disabled access;
cl Thurs and Sun, Christmas and 1 Jan;
free), and at the pretty **Sir Max
Aitken Museum** 🏛 (open Tues–Sat
May–Sept; *£1 – one child free for
every two full-paying adults).
DOWNEND SZ5387
Robin Hill Country Park A very
useful retreat for families, particularly
those with younger children who want
to run around. Like its stablemate
Blackgang Chine, it has a few rather
dated-looking representations of trolls
and the like, but scores more highly for
rides such as the pirate ship, the 400-
metre toboggan run (best for older
children, £1 extra) and the motion-
platform cinema. Boasting good play
areas, with underground tunnels and
assault course equipment, the park also
has a pitch and putt course, look-out
tower, wooden maze, and plenty of
space for football and basketball. Paths
and trails wind through the woodland.
Meals, snacks, shop, disabled access but
rather hilly in parts; cl Nov–Mar;
(01983) 527352; £4.95 (a good value
return ticket for £1, allows a second
visit within four days). The nearby Hare
& Hounds is a good family dining pub,
open all day.
EAST COWES SZ5194
Osborne House (1m SE) Queen

Victoria's favourite residence, where she died in 1901; the state and private apartments haven't changed much since. Designed to resemble an Italian villa, by Prince Albert with professional help from Thomas Cubitt, it's a striking place. Albert and his wife were also responsible for the original layout of the fine gardens, which seem filled with every conceivable English plant. A horse-drawn carriage conveys you in style to the Swiss cottage, where the Royal children learnt cooking and gardening. The house featured in the film *Mrs Brown*. Snacks, shop, disabled access to ground floor only; open daily Apr–Oct, phone for winter opening; (01983) 200022; £6.90; EH. Down on the River Medina, the beautifully placed Folly Inn has an appropriately nautical atmosphere.

Whippingham church Said to have been another of Prince Albert's designs, and is a good deal more eccentric than Osborne House: a bizarre mix of different styles.

FRESHWATER SZ3386

A very extended rather sprawling village, with a charming quiet core. The picturesque 20th-c thatched church includes quite a few Tennyson family memorials, and beyond it a causeway crosses the head of the Yar estuary. The Red Lion has good food, and the Vine has a pleasant terrace for warm days. There are fine walks nearby, and Hill Farm has riding.

FRESHWATER BAY SZ3485

Dimbola Lodge (Terrace Lane) When the photography pioneer Julia Cameron lived here in the 1860s/70s regular guests (and sitters) included Edward Lear, Lewis Carroll, Ellen Terry and her next-door neighbour Alfred Lord Tennyson. Vacant for years (and very nearly demolished), the restored house now proudly displays her famous portraits, with changing exhibitions by contemporary artists; summer music recitals. Restaurant (good vegetarian meals), shop, disabled access; cl Mon (exc bank hols), and five days over Christmas and New Year; (01983) 756814; *£3.

GODSHILL SZ5281

Best appreciated in winter, when the coach parties that descend on the

teahouses and quaint little streets have gone home. Plenty of famously pretty thatched cottages, and a good 15th-c church, with interesting 15th-c wall painting. The Cask & Taverners has good food. Godshill is an inland starting point for a good walk via the Worsley Trail on to Stenbury Down (radio masts, but redeemed by wide views), then back via the atmospherically ruinous Appuldurcombe House and passing through a huge estate gateway.

Model Village 🔳 (High St) Painstakingly re-creates old Shanklin, its Chine Valley, and Godshill in miniature (there's even a model model village). Shop, disabled access; cl Nov–Feb; (01983) 840270; £2.60.

Natural History Centre 🔳 (High St) Decent collection of fossils and minerals, and some tropical fish and sea shells; shop, disabled access; cl Jan and first 2 wks Feb; *£1.50.

Nostalgia Toy Museum (High St) Lots of post-war toys and die-cast model cars; cl Nov–Easter; £1.25.

Old Smithy Tourist Centre (Shanklin Rd) Based around a former blacksmith's forge, this has an aviary of exotic birds, and a garden in the shape of the island itself. Snacks, shop (with local crafts), disabled access; cl 25–26 Dec, gardens cl Oct–Mar; (01983) 840362; free.

HAVENSTREET SZ5589

Isle of Wight Steam Railway Well restored railway with very pleasant 10-mile trip from Wootton to Smallbrook Junction nr Ryde (where you can change directly on to the main line). Vintage engines and rolling stock, and related memorabilia displayed in the old gasworks at Havenstreet Station. Meals, snacks, shop, disabled access if accompanied; open Apr–Oct (daily Jun–Sept), and over Christmas/New Year, phone for timetable, (01983) 884343; £6.80. The Island Line day ticket (£8) includes the steam railway with travel on all regular trains on the island. The White Hart does good generous food.

MOTTISTONE SZ4083

Charming old village with a well in the centre of the green; even the bus shelter is stone-built. The Bluebell Wood opposite the church is lovely in spring.

Mottistone Manor 🖼 The fine gardens are open pm only Sun, Tues and bank hols Apr–Oct; on fine days there are teas; (01983) 741302; £2.10; NT. The medieval and Elizabethan manor house itself is open Aug bank hol only.

NEWCHURCH SZ5685
Amazon World See separate family panel on p.299.

NEWPORT SZ5089
The island's capital, with a good deal of character, some fine old Georgian houses, and warm red brick 18th-c buildings down by the quay. It's the main place on the island for antiques shops. The **parish church of St Thomas** is worth a look – it has an interestingly carved Jacobean pulpit and a 19th-c memorial to Charles I's daughter. The 17th-c Wheatsheaf nearby is good for lunch. The Quay Arts Centre (Sea St) has craft fairs some Sats. The back road to Brading has pleasant views.

Classic Boat Museum 🖼 (The Quay) Collection of vintage motor and sailing boats inc the oldest lifeboat in the country, and a 1910 wooden launch used for Thames cruises; you can watch some of the boats being restored. Meals, snacks, new shop and chandlers, disabled access; cl Nov–Apr exc Tues and Sat ams; (01983) 533493; £2.50.

Roman Villa 🖼 (Cypress Rd) Well preserved baths and reconstructed rooms on the site of 3rd-c Roman villa, with an informative museum; also Roman garden. Shop, disabled access; cl Sun (exc July–Aug) and all Nov–Mar; (01983) 529720; £2.

NEWTOWN SZ4290
For a while this was the island's capital, but it began a slow decline after a disastrous fire in 1377, and eventually faded out altogether – what used to be rich merchants' streets are now just grassy tracks. The **Old Town Hall**, rebuilt in 1699 but now left stranded and unusually isolated from any houses, is all that's left to mark the once thriving town; open pm Mon, Weds and Sun Apr–Oct, plus pm Tues and Thurs in July and Aug, Good Fri and Easter Sat; £1.40; NT. Rewarding walks for bird-watchers at the nearby nature reserve. The New Inn at Shalfleet, open all day in

summer, has good seafood.

Newtown Nature Reserve On the N coast, this has walks around the tranquil Norfolk-like creeks of the Newtown/Clamerkin estuaries, but there are few circular routes; from the village a boardwalk leads out into the heart of the reserve within a few minutes.

PARKHURST FOREST SZ4891
Just W of the prison, this is a couple of miles across, with plenty of signposted paths and a good chance of seeing red squirrels.

RYDE SZ5992
Now the biggest town here, with a long triple pier, good sandy beaches, and a full set of holiday-resort amusements – just right for a straightforward family holiday. English Heritage is set to restore some of the buildings in the Old High St as part of its nationwide 'humble heritage' scheme. Free tours and tastings at the **Rosemary Vineyard** on Smallbrook Lane; (01983) 811084.

National Wireless Museum (Puckpool Hill, off Seaview toll road) This tells the story of broadcasting from 1922 onwards, inc demonstrations of how the first radio sets sounded. Snacks, shop, disabled access; usually open wknds Apr–Sept, but best to check; (01983) 567665; free.

SANDOWN SZ6084
All the usual things for a family beach holiday – pier, boat trips, canoeing lake, discos – and a fine beach. You can usually tour the partly underground winery of **Adgestone Vineyard** on Upper Rd, but you'll need to book on (01983) 402503; free.

Museum of Isle of Wight Geology (High St) Small but interesting collection of local fossils and rocks, with recently excavated dinosaur fossils. Shop, some disabled access; cl Sun, 25–26 Dec and 1 Jan; (01983) 404344; free.

Sandown Zoo Rare and endangered animals such as tigers, panthers and leopards, as well as a notable collection of poisonous snakes and primates. A new dinosaur attraction with static and animatronic models opens later this year, when the prices will go up, so best to phone to check these (and winter opening times) before visiting; (01983)

403883. Summer meals, snacks, shop, disabled access.

SEAVIEW SZ6291

A timelessly quiet retreat, with sedate streets of unassuming villas; the Seaview Hotel does very good lunches.

Flamingo Park One of the biggest draws to this developing place, set in spacious landscaped grounds, is the chance to feed some of the hundreds of birds by hand. Children are bound to enjoy watching the penguin chicks splash around in their new nursery pool. Snacks, shop, disabled access; cl Nov–Easter; (01983) 612153; £4.75.

SHANKLIN SZ5881

Shanklin Chine 🔄 Quite glorious natural gorge with magnificent 14-metre (45-ft) waterfall. A heritage centre gives details of rare flora, nature trails and life in Victorian Shanklin. Meals, snacks, shop, some disabled access; cl Nov–Mar; (01983) 866432; *£2.50. Down on the beach, the thatched Fisherman's Cottage is charmingly placed for lunch (cl Nov–Mar), and up at the top the Chine Inn is a good value family pub (no food Sun evening, Tues or Sat).

SHORWELL SZ4583

One of the few really pretty villages on the island to have escaped a flood of tourist interest, with charming streamside thatched cottages and a fine church; the attractive Crown is very good for lunch.

ST CATHERINE'S HILL SZ4978

Capped by the ruins of a 14th-c oratory, a short walk up from the coast path further E; you can walk on along a ridge to the prominent Hoy's Monument at the far end of St Catherine's Down. The coast path meanwhile skirts the undercliff of St Catherine's Point, the isle's S tip, which has a modern working lighthouse; there are several other paths through the undercliff here.

ST LAWRENCE SZ5276

Isle of Wight Glass (Old Park Rd) Offers demonstrations (not wknds), lovely displays, and shop. Disabled access (but no facilities); cl winter wknds and for 3 weeks at Christmas; (01983) 853526; *60p.

Rare Breeds & Waterfowl Park (Undercliff Drive) Good rare breeds

centre in a really lovely setting, covering 30 secluded coastal acres, with fine views out to sea. The range of animals takes in miniature horses, deer, pigs, otter, llamas, meerkats, owls, and delightful pygmy goats. There are a hundred or so species of waterfowl and poultry, an under-cover temperate waterfall house with free-flying birds, a play area, and plenty of animals to pet. Snacks (with lots of space for picnics), shop, some disabled access; open wk before Easter–Oct; (01983) 852582; £3.70 (£2.20 children over 5). They do B&B in the attractive old house, and there's a bus stop just outside.

TENNYSON DOWN SZ3285

On Wight's W tip, the best place of all for walkers here: a friendly grassy ridge and cliff walk rolled into one, with views over most of the island and across to the mainland. You pass the monument to Alfred Lord Tennyson (who lived nearby and loved this place), and the walk culminates in spectacular fashion above The Needles. You can walk the entire ridge from Freshwater Bay (summer bus service from Alum Bay to bring you back), or make a round walk from Alum Bay car park, past the Needles Old Battery and along to the monument, then up on to Headon Warren before going down to Alum Bay. The High Down Hotel (B3322) is another jump-off point.

VENTNOR SZ5476

Relatively untouristy little town up on the cliff, the fairly restrained and decorous seafront down below linked to it by a tortuously steep loop of road; between them perched on ledges among the trees is quite a number of Victorian villas – many of them still private houses rather than guesthouses. Its great pride is the **Botanic Garden**, where an exceptional collection of subtropical plants make the most of the mild climate (new visitor centre; free). The Garden Tavern here has decent food and sea views. The **Heritage Museum** on Spring Hill is good for local history (limited disabled access; cl 12.30–2pm, Weds and Sat pm, all Sun, and Nov–mid-May; 75p). The Spyglass is an interesting pub with superb sea views, and the seafront Mill Bay is good too.

Bonchurch Down Above Ventnor, this has unsightly radar installations but gives walkers fine views.

Museum of Smuggling History In the Botanic Garden (or more correctly under it), this demonstrates the tricks smugglers past and present have used to sneak in wool, brandy, tobacco or drugs. Meals, snacks, shop; cl Oct–Mar; (01983) 853677; *£2.40.

Undercliff Formed from the irregular masses of earth which have come to rest below, with often rocky chasms between each other and the cliff itself. Sometimes planted and sometimes with profuse natural vegetation, the resulting scenery is unlike anything else on the island, with quite a subtropical aspect. Some of the attractions along here we've listed under St Lawrence.

WOOTTON SZ5290
A terminus for the steam railway (see Havenstreet entry). It has an attractive partly Norman church. The Sloop down overlooking the creek is a reliable food pub.

Butterfly World & Fountain World (Staplers Rd) Tropical butterfly house, next to a five-acre garden centre with water gardens and fountains. The new Small World attraction has fairylit fairytale scenes and jumping jet fountains. Snacks, shop, disabled access (but no facilities);cl Nov–Easter; £4.

WROXALL SZ5484
Appuldurcombe House (off B3327 W) Intriguing shell of Palladian house, nestling among grounds beautifully landscaped by Capability Brown. You can still catch something of the atmosphere of the days when this was one of the grandest houses on the island. The stables have been converted into holiday cottages, and the old laundry and brewhouse into an owl and falconry centre (daily flying displays at 11am, 2pm and also 3.30pm in summer) – Henry VIII is said to have stayed here with his falconers. Snacks, shop, some disabled access, though gravel paths may prove difficult for wheelchairs; cl

mid-Dec to mid-Feb; (01983) 852484; *£4 for house, grounds and falconry centre (less in winter), *£2 house, grounds only.

YAFFORD SZ4481
Yafford Water Mill Farm Park A farm park with a fun twist: a seal lives in a special enclosure beside the millpond of the working 18th-c watermill, various species of waterfowl fill the pools of the stream, and rare breeds of sheep and cattle graze along its banks. Also nature trails, wagons and traction engines (sometimes in steam), an adventure playground across the lane, and a recently constructed 2ft 6in gauge railway. Meals and snacks, shop, disabled access; cl 25 Dec; (01983) 740610; £3.70.

YARMOUTH SZ3589
A lively place, its old harbour busy with yachts in summer. The **castle** was built as part of Henry VIII's coastal defences; it's in an excellent state, and you can see the Master Gunner's surprisingly homely parlour and kitchen. Outside, the open gun platform has good views of the harbour. Shop, snacks, disabled access to ground floor; cl Nov–Mar; (01983) 760678; £2.10; EH. The Wheatsheaf serves popular food all day.

Fort Victoria Country Park Surrounding a 19th-c fortress, this has good views down over The Solent, as well as 50 acres of woodland and a mile or so of pebbly beach. In the grounds are a maritime heritage centre (£1.50), planetarium (£1.80), and excellent aquarium (£1.90). Snacks, shop, disabled access (exc planetarium); not all parts open winter – best to check first; (01983) 760860; park free. The adjacent Fort Victoria model railway is reckoned to be the biggest model railway in the country, and the only one completely controlled by computer. Good shop, disabled access; open Easter–Oct; (01983) 761553; £3.30.

Yar estuary The unspoilt reed-fringed estuary is skirted by a footpath along the former railway line S from Yarmouth.

Please let us know what you think of places in the *Guide*. Use the report forms at the back of the book or simply write us a letter.

Where to eat

CARISBROOKE SZ4888 **Blacksmiths Arms** *Calbourne Rd (01983) 529263*
Very neatly kept pub with fine views over The Solent from the simply built and furnished dining extension, and from tables in the smallish back garden; several bars, four real ales, varied and imaginative food cooked by the welcoming Bavarian landlord (Bavarian-sized helpings, too) inc enjoyable platters and various German dishes, and polite helpful service. £16.75|**£5.95**

FRESHWATER SZ3487 **Red Lion** *Church Pl (01983) 754925* Civilised white painted house with a comfortably furnished open-plan bar, lots of local pictures and photographs, open fires, and extremely popular very imaginative food – best to book ahead; well kept real ales, a fine choice of 16 wines by the glass, and tables on a grassy back area (behind which is the kitchen's herb garden); walks nearby, especially around the River Yar. £19.10|**£6.95**

ROOKLEY SZ5083 **Chequers** *Niton Rd (01983) 840314* Former customs and excise house that's marvellous for families, with a large no smoking family room, a large play area outside with toboggan run and bouncy castle, and mother and baby room; cottagey ornaments and log fire in comfortable carpeted lounge bar, lively locals' bar, well kept real ales, and generous helpings of interesting bar food. £19.20|**£6.95**

SHORWELL SZ4583 **Crown** *(01983) 740293* Friendly and very popular old pub in an attractive rural setting, with a traditional atmosphere in four bustling rooms, individual furnishings, winter log fires, lots of houseplants, and several no smoking areas; enjoyable food (nicely presented daily specials), well kept real ales, and efficient service; picnic-sets and white garden chairs in the peaceful tree-sheltered garden, and decent children's play area. £16.50|**£5.95**

YARMOUTH SZ3589 **Jireh House** *The Square (01983) 760513* 17th-c guest house with friendly owners, a relaxed atmosphere, and a range of home-made meals, snacks and afternoon tea inc daily specials and fresh fish; bdrms; cl Nov–Easter; disabled access (restaurant only). £10.50/special afternoon tea £5.95

YARMOUTH SZ3589 **Wheatsheaf** *Bridge Rd (01983) 760456* Handy for the ferry, this bustling inn has a splendidly relaxing atmosphere in its three spacious bar rooms and light and airy no smoking conservatory; reliably good generous helpings of bar food from an extensive menu, well kept real ales, and cheerful staff; you can eat in the garden. £18.15|**£6.95**

We welcome reports from readers

This *Guide* depends on readers' reports. Do help us if you can – in return, we offer a discount on the next edition to people who've helped us with reports for it. Tell us what you think about places already in it, and anything extra you think we should say about them. And send us your ideas for inclusion in the next edition: places to visit, eat at or stay in, attractive drives or walks, maybe even unusual interesting shops you know of. Use the card in the middle, the report forms at the end, or just write – no stamp needed: *The Good Britain Guide*, FREEPOST TN1569, Wadhurst, E Sussex TN5 7BR.

KENT

An excellent mix of family attractions, wonderful castles and gardens, seaside resorts with traditional appeal, some charming countryside

Kent's rewarding family destinations range from the atmospheric castle and enjoyable White Cliffs Experience at Dover, to the maritime merriment of Chatham's Historic Dockyard (improving all the time with the aid of lottery grants), and the mixture of attractions at Hop Farm Country Park, Beltring (with its new display of military vehicles and an interactive time exhibition) and Maidstone's Museum of Kent Life.

John Aspinall has left behind an admirable legacy of conservation at his excellent wildlife parks at Bekesbourne and Lympne, a spirit which is also preserved at the remarkable Wingham Bird Park and at Herne Bay's Wildwood, new to the *Guide* this year. Leading the county's other animal-oriented places is the friendly South of England Rare Breeds Centre at Woodchurch, with its happy blend of intriguing animals, decent play areas and good range of special events. Farming World at Boughton has a new hawking centre, and for a completely different wildlife experience, try a seal-spotting trip at Herne Bay; (01227) 366712.

The county is peppered with grand houses, and has more than its fair share of well preserved castles; those at Leeds and Hever are particularly outstanding, and Tonbridge's unexpected Norman example has been recently restored. The country homes here are especially stately, too, inc magnificent Knole, grand Penshurst Place (with lots for families), lovely Ightham Mote and Squerryes Court. Churchill's Chartwell and Darwin's Down House (both attractive in their own right), give interesting insights into the lives of their former owners.

Grand Groombridge (lots for families here, if it reopens – see text), romantic Sissinghurst and peaceful Doddington Place number among the fine gardens here. For a diverse range of trees and plants head for Bedgebury Pinetum, and the student-designed gardens at Hadlow. The comprehensive Brogdale fruit tree collection near Faversham and the unusual organic gardens at Yalding are quite eye-opening.

Canterbury has many fine buildings besides the cathedral itself, inc two interesting heritage centres, and well shown Roman remains. Rochester makes the most of its Dickens connections, and has a dramatic castle and cathedral. A good round-trip bus service links some excellent attractions outside Tunbridge Wells, an attractive town in itself.

There are unique collections at Birchington's Powell-Cotton Museum & Quex House, Goudhurst's Finchcocks (working keyboard instruments) and Rolvenden's motor museum (3-wheeled Morgans), a new entry this year.

The NE seaside resorts date from pre-railway Victorian days, and have kept a certain dignified charm that gives them an unusual appeal. Broadstairs is a fine example. On the S coast, Folkestone's Museum & Art

Gallery takes a lively new look at the town's history, with more local knowledge (not to mention good views) at the Martello Tower Visitor Centre, another newcomer.

Inland, the Weald (roughly W of the M20) has peaceful and intimate landscapes of little hills and valleys, small pasture fields and oak woods, timeless windmills and villages with attractive tile-hung and weatherboarded houses, early medieval stone-built churches, and a good smattering of antiques shops, teashops and so forth – pleasant territory for pottering about by car. The North Downs between the M20 and M2, also N of the M25/M26, are more open; the best parts are above Wye. The flatlands of Romney Marsh have a certain bypassed-by-time appeal.

Where to stay

BIDDENDEN TQ8435 **Bishopsdale Oast** *Biddenden, Ashford, Kent TN27 8DR* (01580) 292321 **£50**; 4 large, homely rms with king-size beds and country views. Large double-kiln oast house in four acres of wild and cultivated gardens, beams and original features, good breakfasts and imaginative dinner (excellent cheeseboard and home-grown vegetables) eaten on terrace or in dining room, and friendly owners; cl Christmas; children over 10; disabled access

BOUGHTON LEES TR0147 **Eastwell Manor** *Eastwell Park, Boughton Lees, Ashford, Kent TN25 4HR* (01233) 219955 **£180**, plus special breaks; 23 prettily decorated, spacious rms in the hotel and 19 courtyard cottages with their own garden and garden furniture (can also be booked on self-catering basis). Fine Jacobean-style manor (actually built in the 1920s) in 62 acres of grounds with 20-metre pool, croquet lawn, tennis court, and boules; grand oak-panelled rooms, open fires, comfortable leather seating, antiques and fresh flowers, courteous helpful service, and extremely good food; new health and fitness centre, and lots of walks; disabled access

CANTERBURY TR1557 **Cathedral Gate** *36 Burgate, Canterbury, Kent CT1 2HA* (01227) 464381 **£93***, plus special breaks; 27 rms, 12 with own bthrm and some overlooking cathedral. 15th-c hotel that predates the adjoining sculpted cathedral gateway; bow windows, massive oak beams, sloping floors, antiques and fresh flowers, and a restful atmosphere

CANTERBURY TR1457 **Thanington Hotel** *140 Wincheap, Canterbury, Kent CT1 3RY* (01227) 453227 **£72***, plus winter breaks; 15 rms, 5 large ones in the original house, 10 purpose-built ones linked to main building by Georgian-style conservatory. Thoughtfully run and warmly welcoming hotel with elegant little rooms, enjoyable breakfasts, a games room, sun-trap walled garden, and indoor swimming pool; cl 25–26 Dec

CHARING TQ9247 **Barnfield** *Barnfield Rd, Charing, Ashford, Kent TN27 0BN* (01233) 712421 **£44**; 5 beamed rms, shared big bthrm. Delightful early 15th-c farmhouse with fine beams, big open fires, comfortable sitting rooms, lots of books, antiques and homely knick-knacks, good breakfasts, friendly owners, and big garden; cl Christmas

CHIDDINGSTONE HOATH TQ4842 **Hoath House** *Penshurst Rd, Chiddingstone Hoath, Edenbridge, Kent TN8 7DB* (01342) 850362 **£50**; 3 rms, 1 with own bthrm. Wonderful medieval house – added to over the years – with huge beams and plastered walls in the sitting room, family portraits, open fire in the library, heaps of interest and atmosphere, homely suppers, welcoming owners, and a big garden with fine views; they are kind to children; cl Christmas ☺

CRANBROOK TQ7637 **Kennel Holt Hotel** *Goudhurst Rd, Cranbrook, Kent TN17 2PT* (01580) 712032 **£145**, plus winter breaks; 10 beamed rms with good antique furniture. Set in neatly kept five-acre gardens, this partly Tudor and partly

Edwardian hotel is run by charming helpful owners; there's a marvellously relaxing atmosphere, a beamed lounge with big sofas in front of the open fire, an honesty bar, fresh flowers, a panelled library with lots of Edwardian and antique books, and a huge collection of music; excellent modern English cooking using fresh local ingredients, and a carefully chosen wine list; children over 10 in restaurant in evening; restaurant cl Mon

DOVER TR3241 **Churchill** *Waterloo Crescent, Dover, Kent CT17 9BP (01304) 203633* **£97**, plus special breaks; 66 comfortable rms, several with balconies. Overlooking the harbour, this Regency terrace hotel has a congenial bar, sun lounge and terrace, friendly staff, and enjoyable food (lots of fresh fish) in bright little restaurant overlooking the Channel; new health club; disabled access

EAST PECKHAM TQ6651 **Roydon Hall** *East Peckham, Tonbridge, Kent TN12 5NH (01622) 812121* **£42**; 14 rms, some with own bthrm. Fine Tudor manor offering vegetarian B&B (vegetarian lunch and light supper by arrangement); 10 acres of woodlands and garden, original oak panelling in the public rooms, and regular meditation courses; no smoking

FRITTENDEN TQ8041 **Maplehurst Mill** *Mill Lane, Frittenden, Cranbrook, Kent TN17 2DT (01580) 852203* **£76**; 3 rms with views over the water and surrounding countryside. Carefully restored 18th-c watermill attached to a 15th-c mill house with original machinery, millstones and waterwheel; big comfortable drawing room, delicious imaginative food using home-grown organic produce in beamed and candlelit dining room, and 11 acres of gardens and grounds with heated outdoor swimming pool; no smoking; no dogs; cl Christmas and New Year; children over 12; disabled access

GOUDHURST TQ7237 **Star & Eagle** *High St, Goudhurst, Cranbrook, Kent TN17 1AL (01580) 211512* **£55***; 10 character rms, 9 with own bthrm. Striking medieval inn with comfortable Jacobean-style furnishings in heavy-beamed day rooms, pretty views, polite staff, good food, and well kept ales

GROOMBRIDGE TQ5337 **Crown** *The Green, Groombridge, Tunbridge Wells, Kent TN3 9QH (01892) 864742* **£40***; 4 rms, shared bthrm. Carefully preserved Elizabethan inn on village green, with snug timbered bar rooms, a log fire in big brick inglenook, traditional furnishings, good popular food, well kept beers, reasonably priced house wines, and quick service; children over 4

LITTLESTONE TR0825 **Romney Bay House** *Coast Rd, Littlestone, New Romney, Kent TN28 8QY (01797) 364747* **£75**, plus winter breaks; 10 rms. 1920s house on a private road facing the sea with log fire in comfortable drawing room, first-floor 'look-out' with telescope, games and a library, charming friendly owners, and a relaxed atmosphere; enjoyable set evening meal, a thoughtful little wine list, afternoon teas, and garden with tennis court and croquet; golf close by; cl 1 wk Christmas; no children

MARDEN TQ7341 **Tanner House** *Goudhurst Rd, Marden, Tonbridge, Kent TN12 9ND (01622) 831214* **£40***; 3 rms (showers). Quietly set Tudor farmhouse on 150-acre, family-run mixed farm, with residents' lounge, inglenook dining room, large garden, and walks and picnic areas around farm; they breed shire horses; cl Christmas; children over 12; no pets

PLAXTOL TQ6054 **Jordans** *Sheet Hill, Plaxtol, Sevenoaks, Kent TN15 0PU (01732) 810379* **£66**; 3 rms, 2 with own bthrm. 15th-c no smoking house with leaded windows, beams, and an inglenook fireplace, good breakfasts, and pretty garden; the helpful owner is a qualified tourist guide, and can tell you about the many historic houses and lovely gardens nearby; cl mid-Dec to mid-Jan; children over 12

PLUCKLEY TQ9243 **Dering Arms** *The Grove, Pluckley, Ashford, Kent TN27 0RR (01233) 840371* **£40***; 3 rms, shared bthrm. Attractive Dutch-gabled old inn with friendly and relaxed bars, and super food with emphasis on excellent fresh fish; monthly vintage-car rally; cl 26–29 Dec

PLUCKLEY TQ9145 **Elvey Farm** *Pluckley, Ashford, Kent TN27 0SU (01233) 840442* **£59.50**; 9 rms, some in the oast house roundel, some in original barn and stable block. 15th-c farmhouse in secluded spot on 75-acre working family farm, with timbered rooms, inglenook fireplace, and French windows from lounge on to sun terrace; ample play areas for children; well behaved pets welcome; disabled access

SANDGATE TR1935 **Sandgate Hotel** *Wellington Terrace, The Esplanade, Sandgate, Folkestone, Kent CT20 3DY (01303) 220444* **£58**; 14 restful, elegant rms. Smart, impeccably kept Victorian hotel overlooking the beach, with huge picture windows, open fires, fresh flowers, and antique mirrors, exceptional French cooking in pretty restaurant, enjoyable breakfasts, and friendly mainly French staff; cl Jan, 2nd wk Oct

SISSINGHURST TQ8037 **Sissinghurst Castle Farm** *Biddenden Rd, Sissinghurst, Cranbrook, Kent TN17 2AB (01580) 712885* **£54**; 5 rms, some with own bthrm. Gabled Victorian farmhouse in the grounds of Sissinghurst Castle Garden, with an attractively furnished sitting room, and a pretty garden; winter house parties available; cl Christmas; children over 8

SMARDEN TQ8842 **Chequers** *The Street, Smarden, Ashford, Kent TN27 8QA (01233) 770217* **£60**; 6 rms, 3 with own bthrm. Comfortable olde-worlde pub in lovely village, with plenty of character and space in various rooms, beams, a log fire, and a chatty atmosphere (no noisy machines or music), a varied choice of good reasonably priced food, and big breakfasts; cl 25 Dec

ST MARGARET'S AT CLIFFE TR3444 **Wallett's Court** *Dover Rd, Westcliffe, Dover, Kent CT15 6EW (01304) 852424* **£80**, plus special breaks; 16 rms, some in converted stable block with gentle views. Fine old manor house with 13th-c cellars, beams, antiques, comfortable seating and open fires, helpful service, charming owners, and marvellous food; swimming pool and leisure facilities; very close to ferries

TENTERDEN TQ8733 **Brattle House** *Cranbrook Rd, Tenterden, Kent TN30 6UL (01580) 763565* **£74***; 3 rms. Partly 17th-c tile-hung house – where Nelson's illegitimate daughter, Horatia, was entertained by Thomas Brattle – standing in 11 acres of garden, meadow and woodland; charming owners, low-beamed sitting room, enjoyable breakfasts in conservatory, and delicious imaginative dinners in candlelit dining room; no smoking; cl Nov–Mar; no children

TUNBRIDGE WELLS TQ5839 **Hotel Du Vin and Bistro** *Crescent Rd, Tunbridge Wells, Kent TN1 2LY (01892) 526455* **£100**; 32 very attractive individually decorated rms with CD players, satellite TV and power showers. Handsome sandstone building, extended in the 19th c, with a relaxed atmosphere in the two rooms of the bar, comfortable sofas and chairs in the lounge rooms, good modern cooking in the airy, high-ceilinged and informally French-feeling restaurant, and particularly good wines; disabled access

TUNBRIDGE WELLS TQ5739 **Spa Hotel** *Langton Rd, Tunbridge Wells, Kent TN4 8XJ (01892) 520331* **£119.50**, plus wknd breaks; 71 comfortable rms. Run by the same family for three generations, this Georgian hotel stands in 14 acres of landscaped gardens; comfortable and quietly decorated, partly no smoking lounge, a popular and attractive bar, good food in Regency-style restaurant, a nice old-fashioned atmosphere, and friendly long-serving staff; leisure centre with indoor heated swimming pool, gym, and so forth; floodlit hard tennis court; disabled access

WEST MALLING TQ6857 **Scott House** *High St, West Malling, Kent ME19 6QH (01732) 841380* **£69***; 3 pretty little rms. No smoking Georgian town house (from which the family also run an antique business) with big comfortable lounge, good breakfasts in dining room, a friendly atmosphere, and helpful owners; cl Christmas; children over 10

Please let us know what you think of places in the *Guide*. Use the report forms at the back of the book or simply write us a letter.

To see and do

Kent Family Attraction of the Year

WOODCHURCH TQ9534 **South of England Rare Breeds Centre** 🔲
(B2067) Particularly well organised and a great favourite with readers, this 90-acre working farm has one of the largest collections of rare farm animals in Europe. Despite its popularity, it feels notably friendly and not at all over-developed; it's excellent value, too. They encourage children to have contact with the animals, so depending on when you visit, younger visitors may be able to cuddle baby pigs, meet the goats or get close to the residents in the children's barn. It's hard to believe some of the odder-looking breeds were once more common: spotty pigs and cows with handlebar horns delight children used to the more familiar sights of the farmyard. And it's amazing seeing the different varieties of one species: rabbits here range from the Netherlands Dwarf (weighing in at around 2 lb) to the British Giant (a more hefty 30 lb). The Tamworth Two, the plucky pigs who fled from the abattoir in 1998, have found a home here. Under-5s are well catered for, with paddling pool and sandpit, and there's a good playground for older children nr a picnic area. Lots of walks and trails, the nicest perhaps in the woodland, liberally coated with bluebells in the spring; some fine views of the Kentish countryside. Also trailer and tractor rides. They do a very wide range of special events, from Easter Bunny hunts and carol singing to larger-scale displays in the summer. Disabled access is particularly good (they do a lot of work with people with physical or learning disabilities). Note they don't allow dogs. Meals, snacks, shop, plant centre; cl 24–26 Dec and every Mon Oct–Mar; (01233) 861493; £3.50 (£1.90 children 3–15).

ASH TR2858
A handsome partly 12th-c church can be found on the Street.

AYLESFORD TQ7258
Friars These carefully restored 13th/14th-c buildings are once again the home of a group of Carmelite monks. Fine cloisters and chapels, sculptures and ceramics by modern artists, working pottery, and beautiful grounds. Snacks, shop, disabled access; cl Good Fri; (01622) 717272; free. The Little Gem pub is very quaint and ancient. **Kits Coty House** (towards A229) A massive Stone Age tomb chamber which 'mightily impressed' Pepys when he saw it; free.

BARHAM TR1947
Elham Valley Vineyards (Barham) Run by the Vale of Elham Trust which aims to provide work for adults with learning disabilities, this friendly little vineyard set in a pretty sheltered valley offers guided tours and tastings for around £2.50. Also friendly farmyard animals and chipmunks, and a new pottery (demonstrations wkdys only); snacks, wine sales, good craft shop;

excellent disabled access; cl am wknds Oct–Mar, and 2 wks over Christmas; (01227) 831266. The Duke of Cumberland has decent food, and the B2065 through this valley is a pretty drive.

BEDGEBURY TQ7233
Bedgebury Pinetum 🔲 Lakeside landscaped valley full of magnificent conifers, with walks up through forest plots designed to try out the commercial possibilities of all sorts of little-known species. Meals, snacks, shop; visitor centre cl 25 Dec and 1 Jan; (01580) 211044; *£3.

BEKESBOURNE TR1956
Howletts Zoo 🔲 (signed off A2) The first of the excellent wildlife parks founded by the late John Aspinall. Well spread over lovely grounds, it's well known (along with its bigger sister park at Lympne – see below) for its genuinely dedicated approach to looking after the rare or endangered animals and, more controversially, the bonds developed between the keepers and the animals. Highlights include the world's largest colony of breeding gorillas (over 60

have been been born here, and two have been successfully released into the wild), and a unique herd of breeding elephants. Other animals include deer, antelope, leopards, gibbons, and snakes. Meals, snacks, shop, disabled access; cl 25 Dec; (01227) 721286; £9.80.

BELTRING TQ6746

Hop Farm Country Park (off A228) A popular and very well organised family outing, based around the largest surviving group of Victorian oast houses and galleried barns. Clearly laid out exhibitions on hop-farming, rural bygones and somewhat incongruously the water industry, easy nature trails, a mini metal detector treasure hunt, animals (they have more than you'll find in quite a few farm parks), shire horses, pottery, and special events most summer wknds. New attractions include a display of military vehicles and an interactive walk through time. Meals, snacks, shop, some disabled access (not into oast houses); cl 25–26 Dec; (01622) 872068; £5.80. Brookers next door has decent food in a smart conversion of another oast house – used for drying hops (though usually now converted into homes); these with their tall white cowls turning with the wind are a trademark of the Weald of Kent and E Sussex.

BEWL WATER TQ6733

Boat trips and trout fishing, picnic areas, and cycle hire (and a great adventure play area); summer events; can be very busy on bank hols. Interactive displays and videos about the reservoir, and their extensive dry garden is interesting, overlooked by a glazed walkway beside. Meals, snacks, shop, disabled access; £4.50 parking charge summer wknds and bank hols, less other times. The reservoir, dissected by the Kent/Sussex boundary, is skirted by a 14-mile path around its banks.

BIDDENDEN TQ8538

Attractive village with several interesting old houses on the S side of the High St, and a handsome 13th-c **church** with a bold tower. The picturesque old Three Chimneys just W has good food.

Biddenden Vineyards and Cider Works (Benenden rd) Thriving wine-

and cider-producing vineyard – reputedly Kent's oldest. All-year tastings, harvesting in late Sept and bottling in Mar. Snacks, shop, disabled access (but no facilities); cl Sun Jan–Feb and 24 Dec–1 Jan; (01580) 291726; free, guided tours from £2.85 (groups only, book in advance).

BIRCHINGTON TR3068

Powell-Cotton Museum & Quex House 🏛 (off A28) Fascinating museum attached to fine Regency house with furnished period rooms. Nine galleries display the collections of Victorian explorer and naturalist Maj Powell-Cotton, with hundreds of well mounted animals, ethnic artefacts and oriental art. The walled gardens have been restored, and the grounds have an odd early 19th-c bell tower with bizarre wrought-iron spire (open odd Suns in summer). Summer snacks, shop, disabled access; open Tues–Thurs, Sun and bank hols Apr–Oct (house open pm only), plus gardens and museum open 1st 3 Suns in Mar, Nov and Dec; (01843) 842168; £3.50, £2.50 in winter. The Mortons Fork Hotel inland at Minster does worthwhile lunches, and the Minnis Bay beach is good.

BLEAN TR1161

Druidstone Wildlife Park 🏛 (A290) Farmyard and small exotic animals, and birds, with woodland trails, and a couple of adventure playgrounds (one for under 5s). Snacks, shop, disabled access; cl end Nov–Mar; (01227) 765168; £3.50. Nearby Blean Woods are protected as a nature reserve, with well signed walks in the RSPB area.

BOROUGH GREEN TQ6356

Great Comp Garden 🏛 (St Mary's Platt, 2 miles E) Interesting collection of trees, shrubs, herbaceous plants and heathers with fine lawns and paths. Snacks, plant shop, disabled access; cl Nov–Mar; (01732) 886154; *£3.50. The Plough at Ivy Hatch a few miles S is a good restaurant.

BOUGH BEECH TQ4846

Bough Beech Nature Reserve At the N end of the reservoir, with wildlife exhibitions in a 19th-c oast house. Open Weds, wknds and bank hols Apr–Oct; (01732) 750624; limited disabled access; free. The Wheatsheaf has good food, and there are pleasant walks around here.

BOUGHTON TR0459

Farming World 🏠 (Nash Court) Friendly farm with traditional and rare breeds and heavy horses, tractor and wagon rides, nature trails, adventure playground, walled garden, and pick-your-own fruit and veg (Jun–Oct). Also a new hawking centre with daily flying displays and bird handling (summer only). Meals, snacks, farm shop, disabled access; cl Nov–Feb; (01227) 751144; *£4. The White Horse at Boughton Street has decent food all day.

BRASTED TQ4852

Emmetts Garden (Toys Hill, 3m S) Charming hillside shrub garden with magnificent views – it's one of the highest gardens in Kent. Full of bluebells in spring and a riot of colour in autumn. Meals, snacks, shop, some disabled access; open wknds, Weds and bank hols Apr–Sept (Weds–Sun Apr–May); (01732) 868381; *£3.40; NT. The quaint Fox & Hounds out here has good cheap snacks, and there are good walks around here; back in the attractive village are quite a few antiques shops.

BRENCHLEY TQ6840

Marle Place 🏠 Pretty garden around a fine 17th-c house (not open), with interesting plants, a walled scented garden, artists' studios and a new art gallery, mosaic terrace, woodland walk, and ponds. Teas, some disabled access; cl Oct–Mar; (01892) 722304; £3.50. The village has some attractive old houses and a venerable inn.

BRIDGE TR1953

Higham Park 🏠 It is claimed that this restored Palladian manor was the first house in the world to have a wireless radio. The friendly owners are more than willing to pore through albums celebrating the house's colourful history with their visitors. Although the gardens are being restored, the grounds are pleasant to stroll around: a highlight is the yew-lined Italian water garden with water-lilies, secret garden, and extensive terraced rose garden. Meals, snacks, shop, some disabled access; cl Fri and Sat, and all Oct–Mar; (01227) 830830; £3 garden, £2 for tour of the house. In the attractive village, the White Horse is a good value dining

pub, and the Plough & Harrow (open all day Sat) is useful.

BROADSTAIRS TR3967

The NE Kent coast has some pleasant seaside resorts dating from pre-railway Victorian days, when well-to-do Londoners came by boat. When the early coastbound railways took people further afield, these forerunners – most notably Broadstairs – settled into a tranquillity that at least to a degree they've kept till today. Broadstairs is still appealingly unspoilt, attractively meandering up among the trees on the low hill behind, with pleasant gardens, old-fashioned bathing-huts on its central beach, and a good relaxed atmosphere. There are fishing boats and yachts in the lively little harbour (where the Tartar Frigate has good views from its upstairs restaurant), seven sandy bays (Joss Bay, slightly E from the centre, is excellent for families), refreshing clifftop walks (even to Ramsgate if you're feeling energetic), and lots of Dickens connections ('Our watering place', he called the town). Bandstand concerts at 2.30pm on summer Suns.

Bleak House Dickens Museum 🏠 (Fort Rd) Dickens's favourite seaside residence, where he wrote *David Copperfield*, and which he used as the title for another novel. Lots of his belongings and related memorabilia, plus displays on local wrecks and smuggling. Shop, some disabled access; cl mid-Dec–mid-Feb exc wknds in Jan; (01843) 862224; £3.

Dickens House Museum (Victoria Parade) Former home of Miss Mary Strong, the basis for Betsey Trotwood in *David Copperfield* – the parlour is furnished as in the book. Also more of Dickens's letters and possessions. Shop; open pm beginning Apr–mid-Oct; (01843) 862853; £1.50.

BROOKLAND TQ9626

Fairfield church Standing quite alone in the Walland Marsh NW of Brookland, this is a tent-roofed brick and timber building, remarkable for its utterly lonely surroundings – and attractive inside.

Philippine Village Craft Centre (A259 SW) Unique centre selling crafts from the Philippines, with occasional special events. Snacks, limited disabled access; open wknds Easter–1st May bank hol, then daily till end Sept, other times by arrangement; (01797) 344616; free. The Walland Marsh here is an extension of Romney Marsh; the sign off the A259 to the Woolpack leads you to a particularly good pub with the right sort of atmosphere for the area.

CANTERBURY TR1457
One of Britain's most satisfying places to visit – but as around 100,000 visitors arrive each day in summer, you'll find it much more pleasant out of season. Redevelopment after World War II air-raid damage has been rather unsympathetic, but there's still a wealth of historic buildings tucked away in surviving narrow medieval streets. Much of the centre is pedestrianised, with good car parks on the fringes of the old centre (and a reliable Park and Ride). Interesting guided walks leave from the very helpful Visitor Information Centre, 34 St Margaret's St (11.30 and 2pm, 2pm only in winter); if you're making your own way, don't miss Palace St, Burgate with the Buttermarket Sq, and St Peter's St, all of which have fine buildings, and you can follow quite a lot of the ancient city wall on a walk passing the remains of the Norman castle (some info panels, not always open). The city's Roman and ecclesiastical heritage is well known, but there are other remains here too, notably a prehistoric tumulus in Dane John Garden. The Canterbury Tales (just off St Peter's St) is the best pub here for lunch.

Canterbury Cathedral Dramatically floodlit at night, this spectacularly lives up to expectations – for the most overwhelming first impression, it's best approached from Queningate. The earliest parts are Norman, with much added in the 15th c. Rewarding features are everywhere – an airily impressive nave, fascinating stained glass, the Bell Harry Tower, lovely cloisters, and the shrine of Thomas à Becket, murdered here in the 12th c. In the crypt are some wonderfully grotesque carvings, full of strange animals and fantastic fighting monsters. The recently added education centre has audio-visual theatres, seminar rooms, an auditorium

and exhibition gallery. Snacks, shop, disabled access; may be closed for services at certain times, limited opening Sun; *£3 – note this isn't a donation, you'll be charged this just to enter the precincts. There are additional charges for guided tours, audio tours, photo permits and lavatories. It also charges on Sun – the first British cathedral to do so. Entry to the services is free and the choir's singing is then a bonus. In the precincts are fine buildings connected to the cathedral, inc the ruins of the former monastery in Green Court, and the impressive Norman Staircase. Not far outside is the medieval Kings School (The Borough).

Canterbury Heritage Museum (Stour St) Housed in the medieval Poor Priests Hospital (look out for the magnificent oak roof), a splendid interpretation of the city's history, told with deft use of lavishly up-to-date display technology inc holograms, leaving many vivid visual impressions – one of the most rewarding places in SE England. There's a gallery devoted to Rupert Bear. Shop, disabled access to ground floor only; cl Sun Nov–May, Good Fri and Christmas wk; (01227) 452747; £2.40. Hidden away through an arch beside the building is the charming Greyfriars, above the River Stour.

Canterbury Tales (St Margaret's St) Well put together, Chaucer's characters brought enthusiastically to life with smells, sound effects and lively celebrity voices. Meals, snacks, very good unusual shop, disabled access (prior notice preferred); cl 25 Dec; (01227) 454888; £5.50. They also organise evening ghost tours (phone for details), and have children's events during most school hols. The **Chaucer Centre** on St Peter's St also has an interesting shop, and an antiques fair on Sat; cl Sun, Mon and Christmas wk; free.

Roman Museum (Longmarket) Splendid underground museum, by the remains of a Roman town house; lively reconstructions of a market and aromatic kitchen, as well as lots of hands-on and hi-tech displays. The house's mosaic floor is very well displayed. Shop, disabled access; cl Sun

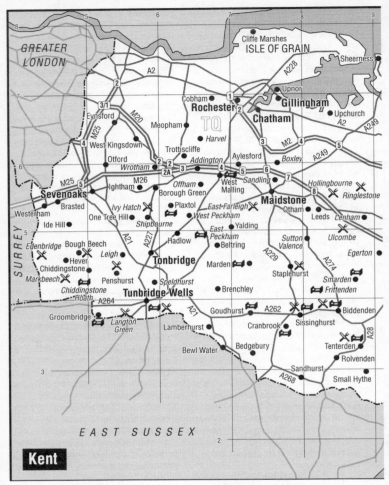

Kent

(exc Jun–Oct), Good Fri and Christmas wk; (01227) 785575; £2.40.

Royal Museum & Art Gallery (High St) Fine porcelain, glass, clocks and watches, Roman and Anglo-Saxon jewellery, and Victorian animal paintings by T S Cooper. Shop; cl Sun, Good Fri and Christmas wk; (01227) 452747; free.

St Augustine's Abbey (Longport) Founded at the end of the 6th c, but most of the remaining ruins date from the Benedictine rebuilding in the 11th c. A free audio tour takes you around the ruins and adjacent museum. Snacks, shop, disabled access; cl 24–26 Dec, 1 Jan; (01227) 767345; £2.50; EH.

St Martin's church (North Holmes Rd) The country's oldest church in continual use; the Venerable Bede says it was built by the Romans, and there are certainly Roman bricks in the walls. The Roman road S to the coast (B2068) is a good drive.

West Gate Museum (where St Peter's St meets St Dunstan's St) The city's last remaining fortified gatehouse, built in the late 14th c, with interesting cells, and excellent views from the battlements. Children can do brass rubbing or try on replica armour. Shop; cl 12.30–1.30pm, all day Sun, Good Fri,

Christmas wk; (01227) 452747; £1.
CHALLOCK TR0152
Beech Court Gardens Peaceful
gardens surrounding a medieval
farmhouse; and lots of spring and
autumn colour; the firs and pines reflect
the designer's admiration for Inverewe
in Scotland. They hold the national
record for the biggest prunus. Teas in
oast house, picnic areas, plant sales and
craft shop, disabled access; cl am Fri and
wknds, and Nov–Easter; (01233)
740735; £2.50. The 17th-c Chequers by
the pretty village green has good value
food.
CHATHAM TQ7568

Fort Amherst (Dock Rd) Perhaps the
finest surviving 18th-c fort in the
country, with massive ditches, gun
emplacements, a warren of tunnels and
a firing gun battery. 18 acres of
parkland, and live re-enactments the
first three Suns of each month. Meals,
snacks, shop; cl 25–26 Dec, 1 Jan;
(01634) 847747; £4. The Command
House below by the water does limited
but decent food.
Historic Dockyard Excellent 80-acre
working museum set in the most
complete Georgian dockyard in the
world. Lots to see and do: the Wooden
Walls exhibition uses sights, sounds and

smells to show how 18th-c warships such as HMS *Victory* were built here, and there's an exhibition on the RNLI, with 15 lifeboats. An exhibition centre in the Flagship Brewery (Building 64) explores the role of beer in the navy (disabled access; open most wkdys; free). Also restorations, rope-making demonstrations, craft workshops, and lively events. A recent £17m lottery grant will go towards a new gallery charting Chatham's historic relationship with the navy, the building of a dockyard steam railway (both hoping to open around Easter), and the complete restoration of HMS *Cavalier* and the Victorian sloop *Gannet*. A visit here can easily fill most of the day. Meals, snacks, shop, disabled access; open daily Apr–Oct, plus wknds and Weds in Nov, Feb and Mar; (01634) 823800; £8.50. You can get a ticket that includes **boat trips** on the paddle steamer *Kingswear Castle*, and may be able to tour the submarine *Ocelot* moored in Chatham Maritime.

CHIDDINGSTONE TQ5045
A favourite Kentish village, an unspoilt cluster of Tudor houses and buildings owned by the NT, in lovely countryside. The church and the mysterious stone which one story claims gives the village its name are worth a look. The Kentish Horse over at Markbeech has good food.

Chiddingstone Castle ⌨ 17th-c house rebuilt in castle style at the start of the 19th c; renowned paintings and antiquities from England, Egypt and the Orient, inc fine collections of Japanese swords and Buddhist art. Attractively restored landscaped grounds, and you can fish in the lake (£8 a day). Tearoom, shop, disabled access to ground floor only; open pm Weds–Fri and Sun Easter–Sept, Sun and public hols only in Easter and spring; (01892) 870347; *£4.

CHILHAM TR0653
The lovely village square is the prettiest in Kent, and several antiques shops reflect its popularity with visitors – in summer, get there early to catch it at its most photogenic. The Woolpack just down the hill is useful for lunch.

Badgers Hill Farm (New Cut Rd – towards Selling) Cheerily unspoilt spot, with cider-making, local crafts, a barrel

merchant, free-roaming pigs (you may find them in the shop) and other animals, play area, and pick-your-own apples (ten types, Aug–Oct). Snacks, farm shop, disabled access; cl 24 Dec–early Mar; (01227) 730573; free. Further towards Selling, the Rose & Crown at Perry Wood is a nice pub, with woodland walks nearby.

CHISLET MARSHES TR2366
Thousands of geese and ducks; duck food by the bag from the nice little Gate Inn at Boyden Gate.

CLIFFE MARSHES TQ7279
N of Rochester, these are bounded by a long sea wall-cum-footpath which feels (and is) extraordinarily remote and not a little surreal – perhaps the best Thames Estuary walk in N Kent.

COBHAM TQ6570
Another attractive village, with a good mix of unspoilt buildings from various centuries – an excellent place to walk round (as Dickens liked to do). The partly 13th-c church is worth examining, with its magnificent brasses and tombs, as is the 14th-c **New College**, like a miniature Oxford college but far less known to visitors (disabled access; free). The Leather Bottle has decent food, interesting Dickens memorabilia and a good garden.

Cobham Hall The Earls of Darnley once lived in this impressive place, now a girls' school. The décor is quite splendid in parts (some notable marble fireplaces), and the lovely grounds are being restored. Snacks, shop; open pms on selected Weds and Suns in Mar, Apr, July and Aug; (01474) 824319; £3.50.

Owletts At the S end of Cobham, this modest 17th-c yeoman's house has an interesting staircase – and in the garden the grandest bird-bath we've ever seen. Open pm Weds and Thurs Apr–Oct; (01892) 890651; £2; NT.

CRANBROOK TQ7736
Cranbrook Union Mill This very good working **windmill**, picturesquely set almost in the centre, still grinds corn. The newly restored workshop has visual displays, while upstairs you can discover the history of the mill and its owners; shop; open pm Sat and bank hols Apr–Sept, plus Sun pm mid-July–end Aug; (01580) 712256;

donations. The attractive miniature town, with largely unspoilt lanes of tile-hung buildings, also has a friendly local history museum, and for picnics Perfect Partners (Stone St) is the best delicatessen for many miles. The walk to Sissinghurst and back is a pleasant way of joining two very interesting places.

DEAL TR3752
Once the busiest harbour in SE England, and Caesar's landing point in 55BC; now a pleasantly understated seaside resort, full of pretty little streets and alleys – but beware of vigilant traffic wardens. The seaview Kings Head (Beach St) has good value food (and bedrooms).

Deal Castle The biggest in Henry VIII's chain of coastal defences, uniquely shaped like a Tudor rose with every wall rounded to deflect shot. Snacks, good audio tour, shop, disabled access ground floor only; cl Mon and Tues Nov–Mar, 24–26 Dec; (01304) 372762; £3, EH.

Time-Ball Tower (Victoria Parade) Museum of time, telegraphy and maritime communication, with time-ball dropping on the hour. Shop; open July–Aug (not Mon); (01304) 360897; £1.25.

Walmer Castle (just S) Another of Henry VIII's coastal defence fortresses, later the official residence of the Lord Warden of the Cinque Ports (one was the Duke of Wellington, who left behind his famous boot). It became more stately home than fortress, with rooms furnished in 18th-c style, and pretty gardens laid out mainly by a niece of William Pitt (a more recent one is dedicated to the Queen Mother). Snacks, shop, some disabled access; cl Mon and Tues Nov–Dec and Mar, wkdys Jan and Feb, Christmas wk and whenever Lord Warden is in residence; (01304) 364288; £4.50; EH.

DODDINGTON TQ9357
Doddington Place Gardens Grand garden with formal plantings, some massive topiary, Edwardian rock garden, rhododendrons in woodland, broad views, and delightfully peaceful atmosphere. Plant sales, café, disabled access; open Weds, bank hols, and pm Sun May–Jun; (01795) 886101; *£3.50.

The George at Newnham is nice for lunch, with good walks nearby.

DOVER TR3241
The busiest ferry port in Europe, with a new £17.5m cruise liner terminal, Dover is not in itself an attractive town but has several extremely interesting places to visit, reflecting the fascinating history it owes to its strategic importance. Blakes (Castle St) is useful for lunch, and there is fast and helpful service at Valentino's on Townland St.

Crabble Corn Mill (Lower Rd) Beautifully restored working 19th-c watermill. Fairs held year round. Snacks (made with their own flour), shop, limited disabled access; open daily Easter–end Sept, wkdys Nov–mid-Dec and Feb–Mar; (01304) 823292; tours £2.

Dover Castle Not to be missed, a magnificent and excellently preserved Norman fortress with its original keep, 74-metre (242-ft) well and massive walls and towers. There's a lot to see inc the atmospheric complex of underground tunnels that played a vital role in World War II, and an exhibition which dramatically re-creates an early 13th-c siege. Also included are the Pharos Tower, a Roman lighthouse using a 4th-floor flaring brazier as a guide-light, and a restored Saxon church. A walk round the battlements gives interesting views of the comings and goings down in the harbour (something which captivates small children); you can get an audioguide to listen to as you stroll. Meals, snacks, shop, disabled access; cl 24–26 Dec; (01304) 211067; £6.90 (£3.50 children), family ticket (two adults and up to three children) £17.30; EH.

Grand Shaft An unusual spiral stone staircase which links top and bottom of Dover's famous cliffs; open Tues–Sun pms July–Aug; £1.25.

Old Town Gaol 🏛 (High St) Hi-tech effects re-create courtroom scenes and life in a Victorian prison; they'll even lock you (albeit briefly) in a tiny cell; tours leave every half-hour. Shop, disabled access; cl Mon, and Sun am; (01304) 242766; £3.50.

Roman Painted House 🏛 (New St) Well preserved remains of Roman hotel with unique wall paintings and panels, and elaborate underfloor heating system. Brass rubbing, shop, disabled access; cl Mon (except bank hols and July–Aug), and Oct–Mar; (01304) 203279; *£2.

White Cliffs Experience (Market Sq) Refreshingly lively museum where children can press, poke and push things, and inadvertently learn about Dover's history while they're doing it. Splendid Roman Encounter and World War II section, as well as 20-min animatronic show bringing the town's history to life. In summer there may be outdoor activities like archery. Snacks (and picnic site), shop, disabled access (they prefer notice); cl Nov–Feb; (01304) 214566; £5.95. Included in the same ticket is a more conventional museum and a gallery based around the Dover Bronze Age boat (discovered during roadworks in 1992).

White Cliffs of Dover These provide an exhilarating walk (and interesting views of the harbour – you can even see France on a clear day) from Dover Castle to St Margaret's at Cliffe, passing the Roman lighthouse above Dover, and a curious scaled-down windmill at St Margaret's. There's a bus back to Dover (no point making a circuit, as the inland scenery here is not worth while), or you can press on to Kingsdown (the Rising Sun is a handy stop) or to Deal.

DUNGENESS TR0817
Fascinatingly odd, a real curiosity and quite foreign-feeling, its acres of shingle colonised by fishing shacks and railway carriages converted into homes (Derek Jarman used to live here). It's a terminus for the little steam railway described under New Romney. And there are more pebbles than you could ever imagine.

Dungeness Nature Reserve RSPB, on the shingle headland, interesting for its unusual plants and in late spring for the nesting terns. Snacks, shop, disabled access; cl 25–26 Dec; (01797) 320588; £3, RSPB members free.

Dungeness Visitor Centre and Power Stations Tours of either the A or the B nuclear power station, with interactive displays, videos, and nature trail. Snacks, shop, disabled access (but must be booked well in advance); open Mar–Oct (Nov–Feb by appointment

only); no children under 5, as everyone has to wear a hard hat; (01797) 321815; free.

Old Lighthouse Fine views from the top of its 167 steps; shop; open most summer days depending on weather – best to check; (01794) 321300; £2. The friendly Britannia nearby has fresh local fish.

ETCHINGHILL TR1638
Saxon Shore Way This long-distance path gives some good views and interesting walks. A section starting at Etchinghill crosses under an old railway line, heads up an unspoilt dry valley, and leads along the top of the slope for sightings of Dungeness and the French coast (Cap Gris Nez in Picardy).

EYNSFORD TQ5365
Eagle Heights ⊞ Readers enjoy this informative birds of prey centre, good in any weather as many displays are indoors (outdoor ones at 12 and 3.30pm). You can handle snakes and reptiles (1.45pm) and meet the owls (2.15pm). Snacks, shop, disabled access; cl wkdys Nov–Feb; (01332) 866466; £5.

Eynsford Castle Norman knight's fortress with impressive 9-metre (30-ft) walls, and remains of the hall and ditch; free. There are organised trails from the nearby countryside centre along the River Darent and into woods above the golf course. The Malt Shovel has good seafood.

Lullingstone Castle ⊞ Historic family mansion with fine state rooms, great hall, staircase and library, and beautiful grounds. The 15th-c gate tower was one of the first buildings to be made entirely of brick. Shop, disabled access; open pm wknds and bank hols May–Aug; (01322) 862114; *£4.

Lullingstone Roman Villa (just SE off A225) Remains of rather well-to-do 1st- and 2nd-c family's villa, with exceptionally well preserved floor mosaics and an extensive bath complex. Also an early Christian chapel – the only one so far found in a private house. Snacks, shop, limited disabled access; cl 24–26 Dec and 1 Jan; (01322) 863467; £2.50.

FAVERSHAM TR0161
Delightfully photogenic small town ideal for a stroll: plenty of colour-washed

timbered old buildings such as the Elizabethan grammar school and the Guildhall (one of the few raised market halls still to shelter stallholders in the pillared market court beneath it – Tues/Fri/Sat). The Albion (Front Brents) has good food, and just N of the town, a track off the road to Oare leads to a remote waterside pub, the Shipwrights Arms: charming setting on summer evenings.

Belmont (Throwley, 4m SW) A pleasant 18th-c mansion in well placed parkland, with a walled garden, and collection of unusual clocks – one looks like a church steeple. Teas, shop, disabled access; open pm wknds and bank hols Easter–Sept; (01795) 890202; £5.25, £2.75 garden only.

Brogdale Orchard (Brogdale Rd, S of A2) This mammoth fruit farm, inc the National Fruit Collection, is beautiful but baffling to stroll through (guided walks available), its 30 acres of orchards produce hundreds of distinct varieties of every hardy fruit imaginable; there are 2,500 variants of apple alone. The shop sells trees, bushes and flowering plants, as well as crops from pears, plums and cherries to cobnuts, quinces and medlars. Meals, snacks, disabled access; orchards cl Nov–Easter, though shop and tearoom open then; (01795) 535286; £2.50.

Chart Gunpowder Mills
(Westbrook Walk) Well restored old gunpowder mills, reputedly the last left in the country. Small shop; open pm wknds and bank hols Apr–Sept, by appointment at other times (01795) 534915; donations.

Fleur de Lis Heritage Centre 🔳
(Preston St) Enthusiastically run recently extended centre with colourful displays, reconstructions and a working vintage-telephone exchange. Shop (good for books on Kent), disabled access to ground floor only (though there are plans to improve facilities later this year); cl some bank hols, and 25–26 Dec, limited hours on Sun; (01795) 534542; £1.50 for museum. Walking tours of Faversham leave here at 10.30am every Sat Apr–Sept (£1).

FOLKESTONE TR2335
🔳 Despite much development of this major cross-Channel port, there is an intact pre-19th-c area called the Bayle around the interesting old **church** – very pretty and Kentish, with the British Lion a nice old pub. The part around the harbour, previously a picturesque warren, was badly bombed in World War II, but the fish stalls there contribute authentic local colour, the Old High St has a Cornish-type quaintness, and Carpenters (The Stade) has good fresh fish. The remains known as **Caesar's Camp** in fact long predate the Roman invasion. Particularly pleasant is a walk along The Leas, a clifftop expanse of lawns and flower gardens with good views. A water-balanced cliff-lift operates between here and the seafront. You can watch sweet- and rock-making in the afternoons (exc Weds and Sun) at **Rowlands Confectionery** on the Old High St; free. The **Rotunda Amusement Park** has traditional fairground rides, crazy golf and roller-coasters, with lots under cover.

Battle of Britain Memorial Just W on the B2011, this is worth a look. The huge stone figure looking out in contemplation across the Channel gives this place an extraordinary air of calm solemnity. New conservatory and Memorial Wall engraved with Churchill's unforgettable tribute to the airmen. Snacks, shop, disabled access; cl Nov–Mar; (01303) 276697; free (parking £1, free to coaches).

Folkestone Museum & Art Gallery
(Grace Hill) New museum bringing the town's local and natural history to life through audio-visual displays and hands-on activities. A contemporary art gallery shows works by local and international artists; shop, disabled access; cl Sun and bank hols; (01303) 850123; free.

Martello Tower Visitor Centre
(East Cliff) One of 74 towers built to defend the south coast from Napoleon's advances in the early 1800s, and later used as a command post during World War II, this now houses a time trail for Folkestone and various local history and archaeological displays; rewarding views from the top. Open daily May–Sept; (01303) 242113; *£1.

Warren This intriguingly jungly tumbledown undercliff is reached from the East Cliff at Folkestone by a walk out past the Martello Tower; once there you can cross a railway footbridge and reach the shore, or go up a flight of steps and on to the clifftop, to return along the cliffs past the Battle of Britain Memorial. The cliff path also makes for a good bracing walk from Folkestone all the way to Dover for the train or bus back.

GILLINGHAM TQ7669
Royal Engineers Museum (Brompton Barracks, Prince Arthur Rd) More appealing than you might think, with sound effects, and art and oddities brought back from various countries, inc a Harrier jump jet and displays relating to mine clearance. Snacks, shop, disabled access; cl Fri, 25–26 Dec, 1 Jan; (01634) 406397; £3.50. The town has a partly Norman church. Off the A2 between here and Boughton Street village, any of the little lanes take you deep into orchard country, with foody pubs at Dargate, Selling and Eastling; blossom-time Apr and early May, many farm shops with local apples Sept onwards.

GOODNESTONE TR2653
Goodnestone Park Old-fashioned roses in traditional walled garden recalling Jane Austen's stays in the fine 18th-c house (not open). Also woodland garden with good trees. Teas, nursery, disabled access; cl Tues, Sat, and Nov–Mar; (01304) 840107; £3. The Fitzwalter Arms has good value food.

GOUDHURST TQ7237
Charming Wealden village, with quite a few antiques shops and so forth, and spectacular views from the graveyard of the 14th-c hilltop church (but during the day too much traffic for comfort). The Spread Eagle up by the church, one of the village's most handsome old buildings, is useful for lunch.
Finchcocks 🖾 (off A262 W of Goudhurst) The early Georgian house and its lovely gardens are attractive, but the main draw is the big collection of working keyboard instruments from the 17th c onwards. Some of these are played whenever the house is open, the well organised recitals really adding to

the atmosphere. Meals (by arrangement), snacks, shop, some disabled access; open Weds and Thurs pm Aug, as well as Sun pm and some bank hols Easter–Sept (otherwise by appointment) – phone to check; (01580) 211702; *£6.50. Under new management, The Green Cross Inn up by the main road is very good for fish.

GREAT STOUR MARSHES TR2462
Interesting for their thousands of geese and ducks; access from the good Grove Ferry pub just off the A28 near Upstreet.

GROOMBRIDGE TQ5337
Groombridge Place Gardens (B2110) As we went to press this estate was on the market, so there is a chance that these beautiful walled gardens may not reopen (the details we give assume that they will). They are among the country's most spectacular, around 17th-c moated mansion, the parkland and forest inspiring generations of artists and writers. Drunken topiary garden, oriental garden, rose garden, sculpture garden (the flowerpot men are in a different league to Bill and Ben), paths patrolled by peacocks, and a moat guarded by black swans. The developing fantasy wilderness is best for children, complete with magic pools, teepees, gipsy caravans and wind chimes. Families are in general better provided for than at most gardens, with play areas, birds of prey (daily displays 11.30am, 1 and 3.30pm), lots of animals (with many roaming free), and canal boat rides. Snacks, gift shop; cl Nov–Mar; (01892) 863999; £7.50. Nr the entrance, the prettily placed Crown does good food.

HADLOW TQ6249
Broadview Gardens A good mix of traditional and imaginatively themed gardens put together by students at Hadlow College; the atmospheric Heaven and Hell Garden is one of our favourites. National collections of hellebores and Japanese anemones, and a well stocked plant centre. Meals, snacks, shop, disabled access; cl Nov–Mar; (01732) 850551; £2; free car parking. Hadlow's church has the interesting Hop Pickers Memorial, dedicated to the 30 hop pickers who

one wet day in 1853 drowned on their way back from the fields; the enormously tall folly of Hadlow Tower is worth a look, and the Artichoke has decent food.

HAWKINGE TR2039
Kent Battle of Britain Museum
Plenty of aeroplanes, and extensive collection of relics and memorabilia of British and German aircraft involved in the fighting, inc relics of more than 600 crashed aircraft. Snacks, shop, disabled access but no facilities; cl Mons, and Nov–Easter; (01303) 893140; £3. The Valiant Sailor at Capel le Ferne (A20) saves you going into Folkestone for lunch.

HERNE BAY TR1868
Not terribly exciting, but a decorous and spaciously laid-out 19th-c resort. Mike Turner runs **boat trips** around the bay and out to see seals from May–Oct; best to book for the seal trip, (01227) 366712. There's a decent art gallery on William St; shop, disabled access; cl Sun exc pm July–Aug; free. The Old Ship (Central Parade) and Rose (Mortimer St) both have decent food. The working **windmill** is also worth a visit; shop; open pm Sun and bank hols Easter–Sept, plus Thurs July–Aug; £1.
Wildwood (Herne Common) Decent woodland wildlife park, strong on conservation, with the only breeding pack of European wolves in Britain; other animals to spot include deer, badgers, polecats, rabbits and hedgehogs. Costumed artists demonstrate ancient crafts in the developing re-created Saxon village, and there's an enjoyably varied programme of events throughout the year; also picnic and play areas. Snacks, shop, disabled access; cl Oct–Mar; (01227) 712111; £4.50.

HERNHILL TR0659
Mount Ephraim Gardens 🏡 Eight acres of pleasant gardens, with Japanese-style rock garden, topiary garden, water garden, woodland walk and small vineyard; good views. Teas, gift shop; cl am, Tues, Fri, and Oct–Easter; (01227) 751496; *£3. There's a craft centre on Sun. By the church and small green of this charming village, the ancient Red Lion has decent food.

HEVER TQ4745
Hever Castle & Gardens In 30 acres of beautiful gardens, double-moated 13th-c castle little changed externally since Anne Boleyn lived here as a child. Inside it's a different story, as the rooms were magnificently restored by the Astor family in the early 1900s. Antiques, furnishings and art mostly from the 16th c, plus a room dedicated to Henry VIII's wives. Another building is home to an exceptional collection of astonishingly detailed miniature houses, furnished and decorated in authentic period styles. The grounds are a draw in their own right, with lakes, Italianate garden with antique sculptures, walled rose garden and maze; also summer splashing water maze and adventure playground. Meals, snacks, shop, good disabled access to gardens; cl Dec–Feb, castle cl am; (01732) 865224; £7.80, £6.10 gardens only. The Henry VIII is popular for lunch.

HYTHE TR1634
This hillside town, served by the classic Romney Hythe & Dymchurch light railway, is well worth a look, with attractive old houses in its narrow High St and the pretty lanes around the church. Its beach stretches to Sandgate, also pleasant to stroll through; the Clarendon, up a steep cobbled lane on the way, has enjoyable food.
St Leonard's church The crypt houses an amazing collection of 2,000 skulls and 8,000 thigh bones, dating from before 1500 and all neatly arranged on shelves or carefully stacked in a large heap (cl lunchtime, Sun am, and Oct–Apr; *50p).
West Hythe walk From West Hythe the towpath of the Royal Military Canal takes you up into Hythe itself, where a path from the junction of Station Rd (B2065) and Mill Lane enters parkland and continues up to Saltwood Castle (not open to public), which still has its impressive medieval curtain wall.

IDE HILL TQ4851
With its pubs and picture-book green, this is on the scarp slope of the lower greensand escarpment, and on the Greensand Way: a good walking area.

IGHTHAM TQ5853
Ightham Mote (off A227, 2m S)

Lovely medieval manor house, still with its surrounding moat, a unique survival that looks esp beautiful on a sunny day. Fascinating great hall, Tudor chapel and 14th-c crypt, while the drawing room has a striking Jacobean fireplace, frieze and windows. Pretty courtyard, garden and woodland walks. Snacks, shop, some disabled access; cl Tues, Sat, and all Nov–Mar; (01732) 810378; £5; NT. The George & Dragon in the village is a good dining pub.

ISLE OF SHEPPEY TR0469
Walkers may enjoy the E end, with a path along the sea dyke S from Leysdown-on-Sea to Shell Ness, at the mouth of the Swale.

LAMBERHURST TQ6436
Bayham Abbey 🖼 (2m W, just over Sussex border) Impressive ruins of 13th-c Premonstratensian abbey and gatehouse in pretty wooded valley. Occasional outdoor theatre and special events. Snacks, shop, disabled access; cl 25 Dec and wkdys Nov–Mar; (01892) 890381; £2.10. The Elephants Head at Hook Green is a useful nearby pub.
Lamberhurst Vineyard (Ridge Farm) One of the biggest vineyards in SE England, no tours but you can wander round; Meals, snacks, shop, disabled access; cl Christmas wk; (01892) 890286; free. Also, a useful if short public path skirts the vineyards. The attractive village now has got government go-ahead for a bypass.
Owl House Gardens (off A21 NE) 16 acres of sweeping lawns, flowers, shrubs and fruit trees around timber-framed 16th-c wool smugglers' house; sunken water gardens and woodlands. Teas, shop, disabled access; cl 25 Dec, 1 Jan; (01892) 890230; £4.
Scotney Castle Garden (A21 just S) Beautiful 19th-c gardens surrounding the ruins of a small 14th-c moated castle, with impressive rhododendrons, azaleas and roses – a really romantic place. Shop, some disabled access (they recommend a strong pusher); open Weds–Fri and pm wknds and bank hols Apr–Oct (exc Good Fri), castle open same hours May–mid-Sept; (01892) 891081; £4.20; NT. A public footpath strides through the estate's woods and pastures, which can form a basis for circular walks from Kilndown to

Lamberhurst and back. The Brown Trout, on the B2169 nearly opposite the main entrance, has good fish.

LEEDS TQ8353
Leeds Castle Long renowned as one of the loveliest castles in the country, perfectly placed on two little islands in the middle of a lake in 500 acres of landscaped parkland. It dates from the 9th c, and was converted into a royal residence by Henry VIII. Lots of paintings, furniture and tapestries, and a unique dog-collar museum in the gatehouse. The enormous grounds have gardens (inc a new Mediterranean one), a maze and grotto, duck enclosure and aviary (well liked by readers), golf course; as this suggests, it's a busy place, not quite as idyllic as it appears from a distance, but very satisfying for a day out. Special events from wine festivals to open-air concerts. Meals, snacks, shop, good disabled access; cl 25 Dec, and the day prior to evening ticketed events (three days a year, usually inc the last wknd in Jun and the first in July but best to check first); (01622) 765400; £9.50, £7.50 park and gardens only. The Pepper Box nr Ulcombe is the best nearby place for lunch.

LYMPNE TR0935
Port Lympne Wild Animal Park 🖼 Set in wonderful ornamental parkland around a well restored house, Port Lympne and its sister park Howletts are well known for their genuinely dedicated approach to looking after the rare or endangered animals in their care; animals are kept in enclosures as close to their natural habitat as possible, with an aim to return them to the wild if they can. More controversially, they try and develop a real bond between the keeper and animal (there have been casualties). There's a lot to see, paths can be steep and there are 300 acres altogether so the free Safari Shuttle trailers between enclosures is a welcome improvement. As we went to press, work had begun on creating a new family gorilla enclosure in order to continue the breeding programme (shared with Howletts) of the 65 lowland gorillas, the most successful of its kind in the world. The park is also

home to the country's largest breeding herd of black rhino. Other animals include tigers, elephants, lions and tapirs, and they hold occasional special talks and events. The house has a number of unusual features, inc the Hexagonal Library used to sign the Treaty of Paris after World War I, but most remarkable must be the incredible Tent Room by Rex Whistler; there's also a room entirely covered by a mural showing south-east Asian animals and birds – they are due to open another similarly decorated room this year. Meals, snacks, shop; cl 25 Dec; (01303) 264646; £9.80.

Royal Military Canal Built along the N fringe of Romney Marsh as a defence against Napoleon, this forms a section of the Saxon Shore Way long-distance path. You can combine it with a path along the escarpment at Lympne Castle; the Botolphs Bridge Inn just S has decent home cooking.

MAIDSTONE TQ7555
Busy modern town, but worth penetrating for its good museums. The Muggleton (King St) is an exemplary pub converted from a very grand Victorian building in conjunction with English Heritage, and the White Lion just out at East Farleigh has good food. You may be able to go on a **boat trip** along to Allington.

Archbishop's Palace (Mill St) Striking edifice used by the Archbishops of Canterbury as a stopping-place on their way from London but now mostly converted offices. If there are no functions occurring, you can visit the Great Hall; cl 25–26 Dec; (01622) 663006; free.

Maidstone Museum & Art Gallery (St Faiths St) Handsome Elizabethan manor house with period original room settings. Shop, some disabled access; cl Sun am, 25–26 Dec; (01622) 754497; free.

Museum of Kent Life ⊞ (Sandling) The story of the Kent countryside, entertainingly told over 27 acres, taking in farming tools, crafts, gardens, animals, and an oast house. A fair bit for children and lots of special events. Snacks, shop, disabled access; cl end Oct–Feb; (01622) 763936; £4.50. Nearby, the well restored 17th-c

Tyland Barn on Bluebell Hill is the HQ of Kent Wildlife Trust, with information on the area's nature reserves; cl Jan; (01622) 662012; free. The Kings Arms in the pretty neighbouring village of Boxley does decent lunches, with pleasant walks nearby.

Tyrwhitt Drake Museum of Carriages Notable collection of horse-drawn vehicles housed in the Palace stables. Shop, disabled access to ground floor only; cl am winter, 25–26 Dec; (01622) 754497; £1.50. The site also includes the old parish **church** of All Saints.

MARDEN TQ7444
This attractive village has a 12th/14th-c ragstone church with a unique white weatherboarded tower, and other buildings going back to the 14th c.

Marden Meadow (Staplehurst Rd) A lovely unimproved hay meadow, alive with wild flowers and butterflies in late spring and early summer. The Wild Duck just S (Pagehurst Lane) has good food.

MARGATE TR3571
⊞ Often rather brash seaside resort, past its best, though huge grants from the European Union are having a noticeable effect, and there's plenty for families, inc excellent sandy beaches. The Old Town Hall (Market Pl) has a local history **museum** (cl winter wknds; £1.50), and nearby is a well preserved **Tudor House**, open only on special occasions, but worth a look from outside. The Spread Eagle (Victoria Rd) has popular food. To the E of town on College Rd there's a working **windmill** (open pm Easter Sun, pm Sun May–Sept and Thurs evening July and Aug, 80p).

Dreamland Theme Park Once through the inauspicious entrance, this is a very satisfactory and well laid out fairground with rides from dodgems to roller-coasters and a log flume; meals, snacks, shop; cl Nov–Mar; (01843) 227011; £9.99.

Margate Caves These huge caverns are atmospheric – with wall-paintings and spooky shapes and shadows; shop; open Easter–Oct; (01843) 220139; £1.80.

Shell Grotto (Grotto Hill) An unexpected puzzle is this 185 sq metres

(2,000 sq ft) of winding underground passages and exquisitely decorated tunnels leading to a mysterious ancient shell temple, thought to be the only one in the world. No-one really knows its origins or what it was for. Shop; cl Nov–Easter; (01843) 220008; £1.80.

MEOPHAM TQ6365

Meopham windmill Unusual both for its six sides and for the fact that its base is a meeting place for the parish council. Shop; open pm Sun and bank hols May–Sept; 70p. The Cricketers prettily set on the green is a useful chain food pub.

MINSTER IN THANET TR3164

Minster Abbey Site of one of the earliest nunneries in the country, with ruins and cloisters of the 7th-c building. The current house is still run by Benedictine nuns. Shop, some disabled access; open 11am–noon, then 2.30–4pm, am only Oct–Apr, cl Sun and Sat pm; (01843) 821254; free. The Mortons Fork hotel does interesting bar food.

NEW ROMNEY TR0724

Romney Hythe & Dymchurch Railway 🏛 The world's smallest-scale public railway, with 13½ miles of 15in-gauge track between Hythe and Dungeness. The station has a toy and model museum with two magnificent model railways. Engines are often changed en route, and the carriages are comfortable. Well run and friendly, it's quite a favourite with readers. Meals, snacks, shop, disabled access (they prefer notice); trains daily Apr–Sept, wknds Oct and Mar – ring for timetable; (01797) 362353; £9 full fare (but wide range of lower ones).

ONE TREE HILL TQ5653

Reached from an NT car park S of Godden Green, this gives walkers a grand view over the Weald. From here the Greensand Way (look for GW markers) follows the very edge of the lower greensand escarpment which dips gently down to Ightham Mote, two miles E; Ivy Hatch and Stone Street have handily placed pubs to make this into a circuit.

OTFORD TQ5159

This charming village has a ruined archbishop's palace, and pleasant walks along an easy track to the attractive nearby village of **Shoreham**, which has a lovely church. There are decent pubs in both villages. The downlands to the E give scope for longer walks across Magpie Bottom and past Romney Street.

OTHAM TQ7953

Stoneacre Lovely half-timbered 15th-c manor house, restored in 1920s, with charming cottage garden. Open pm Weds and Sat Apr–end Oct; (01622) 862871; £2.50; NT.

PENSHURST TQ5244

A pretty village, with antiques shops, teas and so forth, and, above all, **Penshurst Place**, a great medieval manor house, unchanged since the Sidney family first came here centuries ago. Interesting combination of architectural styles, huge chestnut-beamed baronial hall, extensive collections of portraits and furnishings, toy museum, and marvellous formal gardens with woodland trail and adventure playground. Meals, snacks, shop, disabled access to grounds (inc a garden for the blind); house cl am, wkdys in Mar, all Nov–Feb; (01892) 870307; *£6, grounds only £4.50. The Leicester Arms in the village is good for lunch, and above it up on Smarts Hill the Spotted Dog has lovely views down over Penshurst Place. The Bottle House and the Rock out in this direction are also both well worth tracking down if you're walking in this attractive area, which has some of the Weald's most luscious lowlands, predominantly pasture, the cottages characteristically tile-hung, and the paths just elevated enough to gain charming views. As with much of the rest of the area, route-finding for walks is fiddly and patient map-reading is in order. One of the best circular routes, passing several good pubs, is Penshurst–Chiddingstone Hoath–Chiddingstone.

Penshurst Vineyards 🏛 (Grove Rd) Self-guided tours, tastings and various animals inc wallabies and unusual breeds of sheep. Cl 25 Dec–2 Jan, and wknds Jan and Feb; (01892) 870255; *£1.50 to see the animals (children free). Discount entitles one adult free for every full paying adult.

PLAXTOL TQ6154

Old Soar Manor An ancient oak door

at this 13th-c knight's dwelling has graffiti spanning the ages, and there's also a very well preserved chapel and barrel-vaulted undercroft; cl Fri, Oct–Mar; free; NT. This general area is attractive orchard country, not too hedged, with good value apples from the farm shops, from Sept onwards; many here also have fresh cobnuts in Sept. The old Kentish Rifleman (Silver Hill, Dunks Green) has enjoyable food and a good garden.

PLUCKLEY TQ9245
This attractive village has had quite a flood of visitors since *The Darling Buds of May* was filmed here; well marked walks, good pubs for refreshment.

RAMSGATE TR3864
Quietly civilised seaside resort, with some elegantly colonnaded Georgian buildings and other fine houses up on the cliffs (Pugin, the architect of the Houses of Parliament, designed the church – where he's buried – and the house next door), and a historic harbour (bustling now with its yacht marina). Churchills (Paragon) has harbour views and good value food.

Maritime Museum (Pier Yard) Good collection of historic ships and boats in a handsome early 19th-c clock-house in the harbour; shop, limited disabled access; cl wknds Oct–Mar; (01843) 587765; £1.50.

Motor Museum 🖭 (West Cliff Hall, The Paragon) Vintage cars, motorbikes and bicycles in cheerful period settings (shop, disabled access; cl Nov–Mar exc Sun; £2.50).

RECULVER TR2269
Reculver Towers & Roman Fort Built in the 3rd c, this was well preserved until the 18th c, when cliff erosion collapsed some of it into the sea; some parts remain, though it's the proud pair of tall Saxon towers of the former church on the mound above the beach that stay in the memory. Surrounding these remains is a **country park**, with a visitor centre (cl all Mon exc bank hols, plus Tues Sept–Mar and Mon–Sat Oct–Mar); Snacks, shop, disabled access; (01227) 740676; free.

RICHBOROUGH TR3260
Richborough Castle Another evocative ruined Roman castle – lots of walls and foundations, and a small museum. Snacks, shop, disabled access. Cl Mon and Tues Nov and Mar and all wkdys Dec–Feb; (01304) 612013; £2.50 (inc Walkman tour).

ROCHESTER TQ7468
A busy town, but well worth walking round, with several attractive buildings besides those we mention; one of the quaintest is Kent's oldest pub, the Coopers Arms (St Margaret's St; cheap lunches) and many of those on the High St are featured in Dickens's novels.

Charles Dickens Centre 🖭 (High St) Late Tudor house used in both *Pickwick Papers* and *Edwin Drood*, with scenes and characters from the author's books brought vividly to life using impressive hi-tech effects. Shop; cl 3 days at Christmas; (01634) 844176; £3.60.

Gad's Hill School (Higham, A226 NW) Dickens fans should also try to visit this, the only house the writer ever owned. He wrote many of his novels here, and his first sight of the house, many years before he lived there, is described in *A Christmas Carol*. Meals, snacks, shop; open pm first Sun of month Easter–Oct, plus bank hol Suns, during Broadstairs' summer and Christmas Dickens festivals, and other times – out of school hours – by arrangement; (01474) 822366; £2.50.

Guildhall Museum (High St) Impressive decorated plaster ceilings, and some hands-on exhibits for children. Shop, disabled access to ground floor only; cl 24–26 Dec; free.

Rochester Castle 🖭 One of the best examples of 11th-c military architecture – dramatic too; the great square keep looks a little like the Tower of London, only more forbidding. Shop; cl Christmas wk; £3.60.

Rochester Cathedral Spectacularly Norman, with original richly carved door, vaulted crypt, St Gundolph`s tower, tombs and effigies and huge 15th-c window. A new fresco should be completed this year – the first to be painted in an English cathedral for 800 years. The choir sings Evensong at 5.30pm wkdys, 3.15pm wknds. Snacks, shop, good disabled access; (01634) 401301; £2 suggested donation.

ROLVENDEN TQ8331

Good walking territory, with consistently appealing Wealden scenery, a windmill and oast houses gracing the landscape.

C M Booth Collection of Vehicles (High St) Some unusual features inc a unique collection of 3-wheeled Morgans and a 1930s caravan; also toy and model cars and other automobilia. Shop; cl Sun, 25–26 Dec; (01580) 241234; *£1.50.

SANDHURST TQ7828

Sandhurst Vineyard (Hoads Farm, Crouch Lane) Tours of vineyard and hop gardens (£2); hop-picking in Sept. Tastings and shop; cl am, and Jan–Easter exc by arrangement; (01580) 850296; free. They do B&B in a 16th-c farmhouse. The village has a fine 14th-c **church** with good views from the graveyard.

Tile Barn Nursery (Standen Street, Iden Green) The only nursery in the world to specialise in wild cyclamen, with four greenhouses filled with over two dozen miniature species, most of them hardy, in flower Sept–Apr. Usually cl Sun–Tues, best to ring first to check; (01580) 240221. The 17th-c Woodcock signed nearby has decent food.

Wealden walk E of the village (which has a fine 14th-c church with good views from the graveyard) an attractive round walk runs from Burnt House Farm on the A268, via Cledge Wood and Marsh Quarter Farm to the Kent Ditch and the River Rother, to take you round to Bodiam Castle in Sussex, and back via Northlands Farm and Silverden.

SANDWICH TR3358

Pleasant quiet town with a surprising number of medieval remains, inc some sections of the old town wall and three handsome medieval churches, one part-Norman. In its day it was one of England's main commercial ports; the sea's now left it far behind. The best timbered buildings are in Strand St, with some by the attractive former quay on the River Stour (the old Bargate is very photogenic). The Red Cow (Moat Sole) is a decent pub, and the St Crispin in the pretty village of Worth just S, not far from the sands, is pleasant for lunch.

White Mill ⊞ (A257 just outside) A cheerful place with a little folk museum; shop, disabled access; open all year am Fri and Sun, plus daily pm Easter–mid-Sept; (01304) 612076; *£2.

SEVENOAKS TQ5453

This commuters' town has little to see apart from the handsome old buildings of Sevenoaks School. However, the area around it has more walk potential than a glance at the OS map might suggest. The terrain is complicated, the Wealden villages unspoilt to a remarkable degree, and the path network dense and very well kept. Orchards, hop gardens, tile-clad timber-framed cottages and oast houses set the Kentish theme. Newcomers may be surprised to find such attractive and deeply rural countryside so close to London.

Knole (just E) Originally a simple medieval manor house, this was transformed into a palace by a 15th-c archbishop, Henry VIII, and several generations of the Sackville family. It's now a magnificent set piece, the largest – some would say the grandest – still lived-in private house in the country. It's a calendar house, with 365 rooms, 52 staircases and 7 courtyards. Wrap up well: some of the beautifully furnished rooms can get a little chilly. Outside are 26 acres of attractive grounds and a 1,000-acre deer park. Meals, snacks, shop, some disabled access; open pm Weds–Sun and bank hol Mon Apr–Oct; the garden is open only on the first Weds of each month May–Sept; (01732) 450608; £5, £2.50 car park; NT. The park is criss-crossed with public paths and tracks encompassing the deer park, as well as the great house itself; free. The Bucks Head at nearby Godden Green has decent food.

Riverhill House Gardens ⊞ (A225 S) Hillside gardens with rose and shrub terraces, woodland walks among fine trees, rhododendrons, bluebells in spring, and fine views. Teas, plant sales; open pm Weds, Sun and bank hol Sat and Mon Apr–Jun; (01732) 458802; *£3.

Sevenoaks Wildfowl Reserve ⊞ (Bradbourne Vale Rd) 135 acres of lakes, ponds, woodland and reedbeds, several viewing hides and a satisfying nature trail. Snacks, shop, disabled access; open Weds, wknds and bank hols; (01732) 456407; *£4.

SISSINGHURST TQ8037

Sissinghurst Garden Created by Vita Sackville-West and her husband Sir Harold Nicolson, these several charming gardens are themed according to season or colour and cared for by obviously loving hands, all offset by the lovely tall-towered Elizabethan gatehouse (not open). Get there early – a timed ticket sytem is in operation, and they may close once capacity has been reached. Meals, snacks, shop, disabled access; cl am wkdys, all day Mon, and Oct–Mar; (01580) 712850; £6.50; NT. The Three Chimneys on the way to Biddenden is good for lunch.

SMALL HYTHE TQ8930

Smallhythe Place (B2082) Handsome half-timbered house, now a museum of the life of former resident, the actress Dame Ellen Terry. Charming rose garden. Shop; open pm Sat–Weds Apr–Oct; (01580) 762334; *£3.20; NT.

Tenterden Vineyard Park 🏬 (Small Hythe) Acres of vines, attractive lakes ideal for picnics, winery, herb garden, agricultural museum and children's adventure trail; group guided tours £3 (discount voucher applies). Meals, snacks, shop, some disabled access; cl 25 Dec–2 Jan; (01580) 763033; free.

Wittersham windmill (B2082 S) The tallest post mill in Kent with good views over Romney Marsh and the Isle of Oxney; shop; open pm Sun and bank hols May–Sept, other times by appointment; around £1. The nearby Crown at Stone has decent food.

ST MARGARET'S BAY TR3844

Pines Garden 🏬 (Beach Rd) Six acres of trees, shrubs, flowers, an ornamental lake and waterfall and a Romany caravan, with small local history museum. Summer snacks, shop, disabled access; museum cl am, Mon and Tues and all Sept–end of May, garden cl 25 Dec; (01304) 852764; £1.50. The spectacularly sited Coastguard is useful for refreshments.

South Foreland Lighthouse Clifftop exhibition on Marconi, who used the lighthouse in his early radio experiments, plus a visitor centre and

excellent views from the top. Cl Tues, Weds, and all Nov–Feb; *£1.80; NT.

STAPLEHURST TQ7842

Iden Croft Herbs (Frittenden Rd) Peaceful walled herb gardens, thyme rockery, and gardens designed for the blind or disabled. Snacks, plant sales; cl winter Suns; (01580) 891432; £2 gardens. The Lord Raglan (Chart Hill Rd) has good food.

STELLING MINNIS TR1446

Stelling Minnis windmill Working mill with small museum; open Sun pm and bank hols Easter–Sept; around 50p.

SWINGFIELD TR2142

Butterfly Centre (MacFarlane's Garden Centre) Family-run garden centre and butterfly house; snacks, plant sales, shop; open Apr–early Oct (exc Easter Sun); (01303) 844244; £2.

TENTERDEN TQ8833

Busy but attractive small town with lots of charming old buildings, especially 17th- and 18th-c character cottages on the N side of the very broad High St. A few antiques shops, and the striking 15th-c Woolpack has good food.

Kent & East Sussex Railway (A28 W) Thanks to a generous millennium grant and a great deal of work by volunteers, steam trains now run from here as far as Bodiam Castle in Sussex; lovely Wealden views. Meals, snacks, shop, disabled access; phone (01580) 765155 for timetable; £7.50. Over the crossing, a Nissen hut houses a small museum looking at the history of the railway (usually open with the railway, best to phone; £1.50, discounted entry with railway ticket). There's a small local history **museum** further up the road (usually open pm wknds Easter–end Apr and Oct, daily May–Sept; £1).

TONBRIDGE TQ5946

Tonbridge Castle 🏬 (just off High St) Two floors have recently been added and a staircase in the East Tower rebuilt at this splendid Norman castle with interactive displays, audio tours and re-created medieval scenes. Shop; cl Christmas–New Year; (01732) 770929; £3.60 (free to motte and bailey castle site) The commuter town is perked up a bit by the distinguished buildings of Tonbridge School, and with an outdoor area the swimming pool is a cut above the average municipal baths. In summer you can hire rowing boats on the river.

TROTTISCLIFFE TQ6561 (pronounced 'Trosley') There's a good walk E to the **Coldrum Stones**, a 4,000-year-old burial chamber, with an extension on to the North Downs (Trosley Country Park), densely wooded except on the steep slope itself. A problem for walkers elsewhere around here is that as you head E the farmland soon gets arable, with tedious slogs over ploughed fields.

TUNBRIDGE WELLS TQ5838 Very much a busy commuters' shopping centre nowadays, but parts still show its former character as a genteel spa town. The allegedly health-restoring water still trickles through the Pantiles, the former centre of the town, full of elegant buildings and interesting shops. You can try the water at the Chalybeate Spring here, 40p a glass; cl end Oct–Mar. The **church** of King Charles the Martyr is an interesting chapel built in the late 17th c for the gentry visiting the Pantiles; it has a remarkable plaster ceiling. Above the Pantiles the hillside Common is pleasant for strolls, with plenty of trees and rocks.

A Day at The Wells 🖾 (The Pantiles) The town's Georgian heyday elaborately re-created using very up-to-date display technology. Meals, snacks, shop, disabled access (prior notice preferred); cl 25 Dec; (01892) 546545; £4.95.

High Rocks 🖾 (off A264 just W) On the edge of town, this former Stone Age camp has impressive sandstone formations in scenic woodland; take care when wet. Cl 26 Dec and 1 Jan; (01892) 515532; *£2.

Spa Valley Railway 🖾 (Old West Station, by Sainsburys off A26 just S of centre) Developing railway running steam train trips as far as Groombridge. Snacks, shop, disabled access; best to ring (01892) 537715 for timetable; £3.50 return.

Tunbridge Wells Museum & Gallery (Civic Centre, Mount Pleasant Rd) Examples of Tunbridge ware, the area's speciality small-scale woodware, as well as local and natural history. Shop, disabled access; cl Sun and bank

hols; (01892) 526121; free.

UPCHURCH TQ8467 **Upchurch church** 13th-c, with a unique 'candle snuffer' tower. An attractive village, with a decent pub.

UPNOR TQ7570 **Upnor Castle** Well preserved Elizabethan castle notorious for failing to protect the Medway from the Dutch in 1667; attractive turrets, gatehouse and windows. Snacks, shop; open Apr–Oct; (01634) 718742; £3.60. Up towards the Thames marshes, the Black Bull at Cliffe has authentic Malaysian food.

WEST KINGSDOWN TQ5763 **Saxon church** Largely Saxon, given great appeal by its unique tranquil setting, secluded in the middle of a wood. The yew tree by the W door looks very old indeed.

WEST MALLING TQ6857 Attractive village, most of which is a conservation area thanks to its many old timbered houses and wells; lots of nice alleyways to explore. Particularly worth a look are the **abbey**, one of the country's oldest ecclesiastical buildings, and **St Leonard's Tower**, a fine Norman tower from an 11th-c castle. The Five Pointed Star has a good choice of food.

WESTERHAM TQ4454 This pleasant country town is perhaps best known to visitors for Chartwell nearby; there are pleasant walks in the surrounding countryside.

Chartwell (off B2026 S) The home of Winston Churchill until his death. Still much as he left them, the rooms are full of his possessions and reminders of his career, and the gardens are very attractive, with the famous black swans on the lakes. Though this is one of the NT's most popular houses (entry is by timed ticket), you need at least a passing interest in the statesman really to enjoy it. Meals, snacks, shop, disabled access; house and garden cl Nov–Mar, all Mon and Tues (exc bank hols and Tues July–Aug); (01732) 866368; £5.50 house and garden, gardens and studio only £2.75; NT. This is good walking country.

Down House 🖾 (Luxted Rd, towards Downe) Attractive restored house, former home of Charles Darwin who lived here with his family for 40 years, during which he wrote most of his major works inc *On the Origin of Species*. Filled with his personal belongings, notes and journals, the ground floor is much as it was when the Darwins were in residence, while upstairs there is an exhibition on Darwin's life and work; the gardens have also been restored. Snacks, shop, disabled access; cl Mon, Tues (except bank hols), and 24 Dec–early Feb; best to pre-book on (01689) 859119; £5.50; EH. The Queens Head up the road in Downe is good.

Quebec House Gabled boyhood home of General Wolfe with exhibitions on his life and the battle that made his name. Disabled access to ground floor; open pm Tues and Sun Apr–Oct; (01892) 890651; £2.50; NT.

Squerryes Court ⓔ Overshadowed by its more famous neighbour Chartwell but for some people more satisfying, this fine 17th-c manor house overlooks attractive grounds and has excellent collections of paintings, china and furniture. The garden was first laid out in 1689 and is being painstakingly restored; some of the magnificent lime trees are as old as the house. Teas, shop, best to phone for disabled access; open Weds pm, wknds and bank hols Apr–Sept; (01959) 562345; £4.20, grounds only £2.50.

WHITSTABLE TR1066
The focus here is still very much the busy working harbour. **Oyster Fishery Exhibition** (East Quay) Looks at the traditional Kentish industry of oyster fishing, with live shellfish, and hands-on seashore exhibit for children. Snacks, shop, disabled access (though no facilities); open daily Easter–Oct and wknds Nov–Easter; (01227) 272003; £1.50. They sell fresh oysters (which you can order by mail), and a recipe book with ideas for cooking them.

Whitstable Museum & Art Gallery (Oxford St) This explores the town's maritime history and traditions. Shop, disabled access; cl 1–2 pm, Sun (except Sun pm July–Aug), Good Fri, Christmas wk; free. Pearsons fish restaurant is good value.

WILLESBOROUGH TR0342
Willesborough windmill ⓔ
Working mill, open pm wknds and bank

hols Apr–Sept; snacks; shop; £1.

WINGHAM TR2558
Wingham Bird Park Endangered birds from all over the world, with the emphasis very much on breeding and conservation; they have a large walk-through aviary. Also raccoons, wallabies and other animals, and a good adventure playground. Snacks, shop, disabled access; cl 25–26 Dec; (01227) 720836; £4.50. The village is attractive, with decent food in two medieval inns, the Dog and Red Lion.

WOODCHURCH TQ9534
South of England Rare Breeds Centre See *separate family panel on p.312*.

Woodchurch windmill Well restored, still grinding corn for occasional demonstrations, and its sails turning. Shop, disabled access to ground floor only; open Sun pm and bank hols Easter–Sept, other times by appointment; (01233) 860043; *£1.

WYE DOWNS TR0746
Some of Kent's nicest walks are on the North Downs – not that high, but steep enough along the escarpment to give some great views. The Wye Downs, designated a nature reserve for their chalkland flora that includes a variety of orchids, look across the orchards below to both the Thames Estuary and the Channel. The road above Wye through Hastingleigh, Bodsham Green, Sole Street (where the Compasses is a pleasant stop-off) and along the Crundale Downs is a nice drive.

YALDING TQ6949
Yalding Gardens (B2162 just S) Interesting series of gardens maintained by the Henry Doubleday Research Association, the organic farming and gardening organisation (see also Ryton Gardens in Warwickshire); each looks at how people have cultivated land in a given period, from medieval physick gardens to modern organic vegetable plots. Snacks, shop, disabled access; open wknds Apr and Oct, Weds–Sun May–Sept, and Easter and bank hols; (01622) 814650; £3. In the attractive village, the Walnut Tree has good value food inc wkdy OAP bargains.

Other attractive villages, all with decent pubs, include Addington TQ6559, Alkham TR2542,

Bishopsbourne TR1852, Bodsham TR1045, Boughton Lees TR0247, Boxley TQ7758, Chillenden TR2653, Egerton TQ9047, Elham TR1743, Harvel TQ6563, Ickham TR2257, Leigh TQ5446, Lenham TQ8952, Martin TR3346, Offham TQ6557, Sandling (despite the M20) TQ7558, Shipbourne TQ5952, Smarden TQ8842, Speldhurst TQ5541, Stalisfield Green TQ9553, Sutton Valence TQ8149, West Peckham TQ6452, Wickhambreaux TR2158 and Worth TR3356.

Pubs useful for walkers include the Woolpack at Benover TQ7048, Pepper Box at Fairbourne Heath above Ulcombe TQ8550, Woodman on Goathurst Common TQ4952, Bucks Head at Godden Green TQ5555, Ringlestone Inn TQ8755 N of Harrietsham, Rock at Hoath Corner TQ4943, Cock at Ide Hill TQ4851, Cock at Henley Street nr Luddesdown TQ6667, Kentish Horse at Markbeech TQ4742, Horns and Bull at Otford TQ5359, Fox & Hounds at Toys Hill TQ4751, Harrow at Warren Street TQ9253 and Rising Sun at Woodlands TQ5560.

Where to eat

BIDDENDEN TQ8238 **Three Chimneys** *Hareplain Rd (01580) 291472* Ochre-coloured country pub with rambling, low oak-beamed small rooms, interesting furniture inc old settles on flagstones and coir matting, some harness and sporting prints on exposed brick walls, and good winter log fires; well kept real ales, good wines, friendly helpful service, and highly enjoyable imaginative food; smart garden terrace area with seats by outdoor heaters; classic car meetings; Sissinghurst Gardens nearby. £23.45|**£8.95**

BOUGH BEECH TQ4846 **Wheatsheaf** *Hever Rd (01732) 700254* Lovely old pub – thought to have started life as a hunting lodge belonging to Henry V – with oak timbers in unusually high ceilings, several bars and some interesting decorations, a massive stone fireplace, and piles of smart magazines to read; nice nibbles, chestnuts to roast in winter, summer Pimms and mulled wine in winter, and popular, interesting bar food (served all day); real ales, decent wines, and lovely gardens; children in Long Bar only; disabled access. £21|**£5.95**

CANTERBURY TR1556 **Bonne Cuisine** *Canterbury Hotel, 71 New Dover Rd (01227) 450551* Run by the same family for over 20 years, this neat little hotel is warmly friendly and comfortable and serves beautifully presented very good French food in the cheerfully yellow dining room; attractive bdrms; children over 6. £30

CANTERBURY TR1457 **Sully's** *County Hotel, High St (01227) 766266* Part of the County Hotel, this slightly old-fashioned looking restaurant has imaginative, seasonally changing cooking inc two- and three-course set menus (plenty of choice), and a generous lunchtime roast; disabled access. £35|**£12.50**

DARGATE TR0861 **Dove** *Plum Pudding Lane (01227) 751360* Charming, bustling pub with daily changing imaginative food and well kept real ales in rambling rooms, a winter log fire, plenty of seats on the bare boards, and a sheltered pretty garden. £25|**£6**

EAST FARLEIGH TQ7453 **White Lion** *Dean St (01622) 727395* Charming little white cottage with country pictures, a growing collection of jugs hanging from beams, an inglenook fireplace, and plenty of tables set for dining; imaginative food (simpler at lunchtime), real ales, several wines by the glass, and very pretty flowering tubs and baskets; cl Sat am, Sun, Mon. £22|**£5.25**

EDENBRIDGE TQ4446 **Honours Mill** *87 High St (01732) 866757* Charmingly converted watermill with lots of beams in downstairs bar and upstairs restaurant, good interesting food (the wkdy set menus are popular and good value), and a mainly French wine list; cl Sat am, Sun pm, Mon, 2 wks Christmas. £25 dinner, £20.50 lunch

FAVERSHAM TR0161 **Albion** *Front Brents (01795) 591411* Creekside pub with a pleasant chatty atmosphere in airy open-plan bar, big windows with waterside views, well kept beer, a carefully chosen wine list, and very imaginative, highly popular food prepared by French chef; lots of outside seats for summer evenings; cl

Sun and Mon pm in winter; disabled access. £25.95|**£5.50**

FINGLESHAM TR3353 **Crown** *The Street (01304) 612555* Pleasant and attractively refurbished 16th-c country pub with a wide choice of reasonably priced bar food, popular old-world restaurant with inglenook fireplace and flagstones, and good friendly service; cl 25 Dec pm. £17.50|**£5.75**

FOLKESTONE TR2235 **Paul's** *2a Bouverie Rd (01303) 259697* Popular, enjoyable restaurant run by the same owners for well over 20 years, with very imaginative food inc good fish, game and vegetarian options, and a decent wine list; cl 2 wks Christmas; disabled access. £22.90|**£4.95**

HOLLINGBOURNE TQ8455 **Dirty Habit** *Upper St (01622) 880880* Early 15th-c inn with quite a bit of character in the various rooms, a panelled and candlelit dining room with an interesting mix of seats, enjoyable bar food, well kept real ales, a relaxed atmosphere, and friendly staff; cl 25 Dec pm; disabled access. £18.20|**£5**

IVY HATCH TQ5854 **Plough** *High Cross Rd (01732) 810268* Relaxed and friendly tile-hung house with good, imaginative and constantly changing French food (using French produce), carefully chosen wines and well kept beers, and efficient service; front dining bar with dark panelled walls, an old brick fireplace, and dining chairs and settles, separate little room to left of door, and popular conservatory restaurant; nearby walks; best to book; disabled access; cl Sun pm. £27.50|**£6**

LANGTON GREEN TQ5439 **Hare** *Langton Rd (01892) 862419* Popular, civilised dining pub with light, airy knocked-through rooms, a chatty atmosphere, imaginative generously served food from a menu that changes twice daily, attentive waitress service, and decent wines and beers; outside terrace; children in restaurant (not in bar); cl pm 25 Dec, 1 Jan pm; partial disabled access. £22.15|**£7.95**

MARKBEECH TQ4742 **Kentish Horse** *Cow Lane (01342) 850493* Partly white weatherboarded country pub with particularly good interesting food from a modern menu, well kept ales, a simply furnished bar, woodburner in restaurant, with French windows to terrace and garden; safe play area. £20.95|**£6.95**

NEWNHAM TQ9557 **George** *44 The Street (01795) 890237* Distinctive 16th-c pub with a spreading series of attractive and interesting rooms, open fires, friendly staff, imaginative food using fresh local produce, well kept beers, and good wines; cl 25 Dec. £23|**£6.95**

PAINTER'S FORSTAL TQ9958 **Read's** *(01795) 535344* Excellent restaurant with a comfortable bar and airy dining room, and lovely views from the back terrace; exceptionally good innovative English cooking using the best local ingredients, wonderful puddings, a marvellous wine list, and neat young staff; cl Sun, Mon; disabled access. £30 wkdys, £45 Sat pm

PENSHURST TQ5142 **Bottle House** *Coldharbour Lane, Smarts Hill (01892) 870306* Relaxed and friendly 15th-c pub with huge beams, stone pillars, and big windows in the unpretentious bars, quite a collection of china pot lids and old paintings and photographs, excellent popular food, efficient service, and well kept local ales; cl 25 Dec. £24.50|**£7.50**

PENSHURST TQ5242 **Spotted Dog** *Smarts Hill (01892) 870253* Quaint tiled house with fantastic views over Penshurst Place from terrace, particularly good food from a constantly changing menu, very good wines and real ales, a popular restaurant, and fine inglenook, and a bustling atmosphere in the neatly kept beamed and timbered bar; cl Mon pm, 25–26 Dec. £23|**£7.95**

RINGLESTONE TQ8755 **Ringlestone Inn** *Ringlestone Rd (01622) 859900* Well run and very popular country pub with lots of character and some interesting decorations, enjoyable food (especially the hot and cold lunchtime buffet), lots of real ales and country wines, beautifully landscaped gardens, and comfortable bdrms; cl 25 Dec. £30|**£5.75**

SELLING TR0455 **Rose & Crown** *Perry Wood (01227) 752214* Quietly civilised, tucked-away woodland pub with stunning tubs, pots and window-boxes, and a pretty, cottagey garden; lots of beams, hops and interesting corn-dolly work, a huge fireplace, comfortably cushioned seats, a relaxed atmosphere and friendly helpful service, good generously served food, well kept real ales, and decent wines; nearby walks; cl 25 Dec pm; children in restaurant/family room; limited disabled access. £19.70|£5.90

SISSINGHURST TQ7937 **Rankins** *The Street (01580) 713964* Interesting enjoyable food from a fixed evening and Sun lunch menu in pretty white clapboarded cottage inc lovely puddings and vegetarian choices; no smoking until food service has finished; cl Mon, Tues, bank hols; partial disabled access. £32

STAPLEHURST TQ7844 **Lord Raglan** *Chart Hill Rd (01622) 843747* Unpretentious yet quite civilised country inn with hops along low beams, comfortably worn dark wood furniture on nice parquet flooring, a coal fire, a pleasantly relaxed atmosphere, and charming licensees; very generous attractively presented food (the imaginative daily specials are the thing to choose), well kept real ales, and a good wine list; small French windows lead to an enticing little sheltered terrace; wooden picnic-sets in side orchard. £22.20|£8.95

STONE IN OXNEY TQ9327 **Crown** *(01233) 758789* Friendly, tucked-away pub which manages to strike a good balance between drinking and dining, with dark wooden pews and a big inglenook fireplace in the bar, a longish lounge with two big bay windows looking over country views, a relaxed atmosphere, and tasty imaginative food; cl Sun pm, Mon. £22|£6.95

TENTERDEN TQ8833 **Kent & East Sussex Railway** *Tenterden Town Station (01580) 765155* Steam-hauled and ornately decorated Pullman dining car with good English food served by authentically dressed stewards – most Sat evenings, some Weds evenings, Sun roast lunches and afternoon teas, and Christmas dinners; great fun; open Apr–Sept daily and weekends Oct–Mar; disabled access. £28/£12 lunch inc train fare

TUNBRIDGE WELLS TQ5739 **Mount Edgcumbe Hotel** *The Common (01892) 526823* Bustling tucked away hotel on top of one of several large rocky outcrops; small cosy bar with lots of exposed brick and grotto-like rock, enjoyable very popular brasserie food in big-windowed restaurant looking over the Common, cheerful staff, well kept real ales and a good wine list. Book at wknds. £19.40

TUNBRIDGE WELLS TQ5839 **Sankeys** *39 Mount Ephraim (01892) 511422* Excellent fresh fish and seafood cooked in all sorts of ways in several cosy and relaxed rooms, very good wines, real ales, and friendly service; cheaper lively downstairs cellar wine bar too (get there early for a seat), and seats in the walled garden; cl Sun, Christmas. £25|£8.50

TUNBRIDGE WELLS TQ5839 **Thackeray's House** *85 London Rd (01892) 511921* Civilised detached house with two beamed upstairs rooms, pretty paintings, a mix of tables with crisp white cloths, very relaxed comfortable atmosphere, friendly but carefully professional service, interesting and enjoyable food, and very good house wines; downstairs, the small wine bar does simpler (and cheaper) food; cl Sun pm, Mon, Christmas. £35

ULCOMBE TQ8550 **Pepper Box** *Windmill Hill (01622) 842558* Cosy old country inn with timbers and low beams hung with hops in friendly homely bar, copper kettles and pans on window sills, two armchairs and a sofa by the splendid inglenook fireplace, several cats, and a snug little no smoking dining room; good food (esp the daily specials), well kept real ales, and courteous service; nice country views from terrace and garden with small pond, swing and tables among trees, shrubs and flower beds; no children. £22.30|£8

WHITSTABLE TR1066 **Pearsons** *Sea Wall (01227) 272005* Cheerful little upstairs restaurant with sea views and super fresh fish and seafood; the bar downstairs (no view) offers more usual pub food and has nautical décor, well kept real ales, and decent wines. cl 25 Dec. £22|£7.25

Special thanks to Dave Irving

LANCASHIRE

Cosmopolitan cities, famous seaside resorts, marvellous countryside, and a wealth of places to visit

Successful urban regeneration, a combination of grand Victorian and bold modern architecture, and some world-class museums make Manchester and Liverpool ideal for day visits. Perhaps most satisfying of all is the fact that they never seem to rest on their laurels: Liverpool's top attractions boast a most commendable bargain in the Merseyside Eight Pass, while this year sees the completion of Manchester's Millennium Quarter. The epic and inspiring Museum of Science and Industry continues to add new galleries (seemingly by the year). Both cities have good public transport too.

A big bonus in Lancashire is sheer value for money. Prices here have always been attractive. This year, we have been struck by the way that Lancashire prices (particularly in hotels, inns and farms to stay in, and pub meals) have increased less than elsewhere.

The variety of family attractions highlights the county's manifold charms (and explains its appeal to all ages), from the giggles and screams of Blackpool's Pleasure Beach (Britain's most popular theme park, the county's Family Attraction of the Year), to the quieter allure of Croxteth Hall & Country Park just outside Liverpool, splendid Hoghton Tower, and Leighton Hall with its birds of prey, nature trails, and beautifully kept gardens. Wigan Pier has engrossing re-creations of 1900s life, the Birkenhead warships have plenty to amuse children, and Knowsley Safari Park has added yet more animals and some amusement park attractions since last year; the National Wildflower Centre nearby engenders a pioneering spirit of 21st-c conservation. Welcome newcomers, Hat Works in Stockport and the World of Glass at St Helens, both exploit their town's industrial heritage to surprisingly fun effect.

There's glorious countryside even just outside the big cities, where the moors have plenty of scope for exhilarating drives and walks, and bewitched Pendle Hill still holds the imagination. Other areas of fine countryside include the great whaleback of Longridge Fell, the wooded Beacon Fell country park, the magnificent Pennine moorland of the Forest of Bowland (as yet very little known to visitors, though right-to-roam legislation may change that), and the equally peaceful Silverdale/Arndale area up beyond the attractive town of Lancaster.

The area's vast stretches of sand have of course spawned household-name traditional seaside resorts. Brassy Blackpool has lots of discos, fun pubs and so forth as well as its vivid array of entertainments – more a place for young adults to have summer fun than for family beach holidays. Out of season, Lancashire's long stretches of beach and dune are empty, with a lonely charm for walkers; year-round, there's an element of fascination about the treacherous tidal sands of Morecambe Bay.

Where to stay

ASHWORTH VALLEY SD8512 **Leaches Farm** *Ashworth Rd, Rochdale, Lancashire OL11 5UN* (01706) 41117 **£40***; 3 rms, shared bthrm. Creeper-clad 17th-c hill farm with really wonderful views, massive stone walls, beams and log fires; cl 22 Dec–2 Jan; children over 7 and dogs by arrangement

BILSBORROW SD5039 **Guy's Thatched Hamlet** *St Michael's Rd, Bilsborrow, Preston, Lancashire PR3 0RS* (01995) 640010 **£42.99***, plus wknd breaks; 53 smartly modern rms. Bustling complex of thatched buildings by the canal, comprising a restaurant and pizzeria, a tavern, and Guy's Lodgings; craft shops and outside entertainment, a play area, all weather cricket pitch, and crown green bowling; a good base for exploring the area; open all day; cl 25 Dec; disabled access

BLACKPOOL SD3037 **Imperial Hotel** *North Promenade, Blackpool, Lancashire FY1 2HB* (01253) 623971 **£100**, plus special breaks; 181 well equipped pretty rms, many with sea views. Fine Victorian hotel overlooking the sea, with spacious and comfortable day rooms, lots of period features, enjoyable food and fine wines, and a full health and fitness club with indoor swimming pool, gym, sauna and so forth; during the summer and Christmas and Easter, a children's club is open; lots to do nearby; cl during Conservative Conference parties; disabled access ☺

BROMLEY CROSS SD7213 **Last Drop Village Hotel** *Hospital Rd, Bromley Cross, Bolton, Lancashire BL7 9PZ* (01204) 591131 **£78**; 128 rms. Big well equipped hotel complex cleverly integrated into olde-worlde pastiche village complete with stone-and-cobbles street of gift and tea shops, bakery, etc, even a spacious creeper-covered pub with lots of beamery and timbering, popular one-price hot and cold buffet, and heavy tables out on attractive flagstoned terrace; disabled access

CAPERNWRAY SD5371 **New Capernwray Farmhouse** *Capernwray, Carnforth, Lancashire LA6 1AD* (01524) 734284 **£64**; 3 comfortable rms. Pretty 300-year-old ex-farmhouse with helpful friendly owners, cosy lounge, stone walls and beams, and candlelit dinner in what was the dairy; cl Nov–Feb; children over 9

CHIPPING SD6343 **Gibbon Bridge Hotel** *Green Lane, Chipping, Preston, Lancashire PR3 2TQ* (01995) 61456 **£100**, plus special breaks; 29 spacious individual rms, inc 22 split-level suites, with views of the Bowland Hills. Country hotel on the edge of the Forest of Bowland, with beautiful landscaped gardens (plus a popular bandstand which can be used for private dining or for music events), and old-fashioned values of quality and personal service; attractively presented food using home-grown produce in airy restaurant and adjoining conservatory, a quiet relaxing atmosphere, and fine wines; health and gym area; a good base for walking and short driving trips; licensed for marriages, they have a thriving weddings trade; good disabled access

COLNE SD8741 **Higher Wanless Farm** *Red Lane, Colne, Lancashire BB8 7JP* (01282) 865301 **£44**; 2 rms, one with own bthrm. Warmly welcoming farmhouse with beams, log fires and lovely surrounding farmland used mainly for breeding of shire horses, as well as sheep; cl Christmas and New Year; children over 5

COWAN BRIDGE SD6475 **Hipping Hall** *Cowan Bridge, Kirkby Lonsdale, Carnforth, Lancashire LA6 2JJ* (01524) 271187 **£92**, plus special breaks; 7 pretty rms, 4 in main hotel, 3 cottage suites across courtyard. Relaxed country-house atmosphere and delicious food in handsome small hotel with help-yourself drinks in conservatory, an open fire, a lovely beamed Great Hall with minstrel's gallery where guests dine together (plus a new dining room with individual tables), and four acres of walled gardens; fine walks from front door; may close in winter if quiet; children over 12; disabled access

DARWEN SD7222 **Old Rosins** *Long Hey Lane, Pickup Bank, Darwen, Lancashire BB3 3QD* (01254) 771264 **£52.50**, plus wknd breaks; 15 well equipped rms. Friendly old pub tucked below moors, ideal as base for exploring the area; good views from cosy open-plan bar, interesting food in neatly refurbished bar and restaurant, and seats on the terrace also with fine views; partial disabled access

HURST GREEN SD6938 **Shireburn Arms** *Whalley Rd, Hurst Green, Clitheroe,*

Lancashire BB7 9QJ (01254) 826518 **£65**, plus special breaks; 18 rms. Lovely 17th-c country hotel with a refined but friendly atmosphere, an airy and neatly modernised bar, comfortable lounge, open fires, well presented enjoyable food in restaurant, good service, and fine view of the Ribble Valley from the conservatory; disabled access

LANGHO SD7034 **Northcote Manor** *Northcote Rd, Langho, Blackburn, Lancashire BB6 8BE (01254) 240555* **£110**, plus special breaks; 14 attractive rms with antiques and board games, reached up a fine staircase. In pretty countryside, this neatly kept redbrick Victorian house is more of a restaurant-with-rooms, with beams and oak panelling, big log fires, and two comfortable lounges, wonderful breakfasts, and delicious food in the civilised dining room; cl 25 Dec and 1 Jan; partial disabled access

MANCHESTER SJ8498 **Malmaison** *Piccadilly, Manchester M1 3AQ (0161) 278 1000* **£131.50**; 112 chic rms with CD player, in-house movies, smart bthrms, and really good beds. Stylishly modern hotel with comfortable contemporary furniture, exotic flower arrangements, bright paintings, very efficient service, French brasserie, generous breakfasts, and free gym; other hotels in the same small chain in Edinburgh, Glasgow and Newcastle; good disabled access

MANCHESTER SJ8398 **Victoria & Albert Hotel** *Water St, Manchester M60 9EA (0161) 832 1188* **£115**w, plus special breaks; 156 rms, individually styled and named after TV programmes. Carefully converted Victorian warehouse opposite Granada TV studios (free entry if staying here, when they reopen for visits); original iron pillars, oak beams and exposed brickwork, particularly good service, comfortable bar overlooking river, and good imaginative food in restaurant and all-day brasserie; disabled access

WADDINGTON SD7243 **Backfold Cottage** *The Square, Waddington, Clitheroe, Lancashire BB7 3JA (01200) 422367* **£46***; 3 rms. Tiny 17th-c cottage in cobbled street, beautifully furnished with antiques; very good service, all-day snacks, and candlelit evening meals (bring your own wines); nearby walks; children at owner's discretion

WADDINGTON SD7144 **Peter Barn** *Cross Lane, Waddington, Clitheroe, Lancashire BB7 3JH (01200) 428585* **£48***, plus special breaks; 3 lovely rms. Converted old stone tithe barn with beamed sitting room, antiques, lovely home cooking, warmly welcoming owners and a gentle atmosphere; surrounded by a delightful garden in fine walking country; cl Christmas; children over 12

WHITEWELL SD6547 **Inn at Whitewell** *Whitewell, Clitheroe, Lancashire BB7 3AT (01200) 448222* **£94***; 17 rms, some with open peat fires. Civilised stone inn in the Forest of Bowland on the bank of the River Hodder, with seven miles of trout, salmon and sea trout fishing, and grounds with views down the valley; interesting period furnishings, plenty of room, highly praised food (as well as coffee and cream teas all day), fine wines (they house a wine merchant), courteous service, and an art gallery; friendly dogs welcome; partial disabled access

YEALAND CONYERS SD5074 **Bower** *Yealand Rd, Yealand Conyers, Carnforth, Lancashire LA5 9SF (01524) 734585* **£55***; 2 attractive rms. Charming no smoking Georgian house in big garden with views of Ingleborough and the surrounding hills; friendly owners (keen bridge players), open fire and piano in comfortable sitting room, and enjoyable food served around a large table in the dining room; children over 12; dogs by prior arrangement

---

Please let us know what you think of places in the *Guide*. Use the report forms at the back of the book or simply write us a letter.

To see and do

Lancashire Family Attraction of the Year

BLACKPOOL SD3038 **Blackpool Pleasure Beach** Who can resist Blackpool Pleasure Beach? Certainly not the millions of visitors that consistently make it Britain's most visited attraction. It fulfils whatever preconceived idea you may have of the place: if you expect it to be noisy, crowded and expensive, you won't be proved wrong, but if you hope to experience some of the most thrilling fairground rides in the world then there's no real alternative, certainly not in this country. More high thrills than highbrow, it's a fascinating experience, unbearable on busy days (when queues for the more popular features can last much longer than the rides themselves), yet strangely appealing even if scary rides aren't really your bag. Founded in 1896, the park never rests on its laurels, every year adding something new and seemingly more unpleasant: latest addition is the £15 million dark ride, Valhalla, loosely themed around someone's idea of the Viking afterlife. You enter through a Scandinavian church (hand-carved by Russian craftsmen), then it's a hi-tech water ride full of drops and effects that include real fire. At six minutes, it's currently the longest dark ride in the world. You get very wet; eyebrows were raised initially about a 60p charge for poncho hire, especially when the ride uses up two of the most valuable A-ride tickets. There's still nothing to top the Big One, a monster roller-coaster that climbs to 72 metres (235 ft) at speeds of up to 85mph. Altogether 145 rides and attractions are squeezed into the park's 42 acres, inc several other roller-coasters that can whizz you through 360 degrees, backwards, or in the dark, their own Millennium Dome (a simulator here allow you to design your own fairground ride), bungee trampolines, ice-skating, and traditional rides such as ghost trains, River Caves, a Hall of Mirrors and dodgems. Most of the more exciting rides have height restrictions, and younger smaller children won't be able to go on; instead they have a whole section of the park, Beaver Creek, devoted to rides that are more suitable – inc a fine miniature wooden roller-coaster, the Zipper Dipper. Clearly it's not for everyone: if you hate fairgrounds (and Blackpool) you'll loathe it, but if you like them, you'll love it. How long you stay depends on how much you can take: you may have had enough in an hour, you may want to stay all day. Meals and snacks (not just the expected fish and chips and takeaways), shops, disabled access (it's worth getting their detailed brochure in advance); open daily Easter–early Nov, plus wknds in Mar; (0870) 444 5566. Entry to the park is free (so no charge if you're just being supportive), then there are several ways of paying for rides – either individually, starting at £1.25 for the more gentle C rides, and £2.25 for the more dramatic A rides, or by buying sheets of tickets (around £22), or a wristband offering unlimited rides on everything for £25, not cheap but the best option if you've plenty of time. A child's wristband offering unlimited rides at Beaver Creek and the park's C rides is £10.95.

ACCRINGTON SD7627
Haworth Art Gallery (Haworth Park, Manchester Rd) Notable for its collection of Tiffany glass, the biggest in Europe (an Accrington man used to manage the Tiffany studios), this was closed for major improvements as we went to press, but should be fully open again, by the time you read this. Nice setting, with nature trail through grounds. Snacks, shop; check opening times on (01254) 233782; free.

ALTRINCHAM SJ7587
Dunham Massey Hall (off B5160 W) Early Georgian manor house extensively remodelled in the early 20th c, with impressive silverware, paintings and furnishings, and restored kitchen, pantry and laundry. The largely unaltered grounds have plenty of deer, formal avenues of trees, and a working Elizabethan saw mill (usually Weds and

Sun only). Concerts and events even in winter when the house is closed. Meals, snacks, shop, disabled access to ground floor of hall; open Sat–Weds Apr–Oct, house cl am; (0161) 941 1025; £5 house and garden, £3.20 garden only; NT. The Vine at Dunham Woodhouses has popular home cooking.

ASTLEY GREEN SJ7099

Astley Green Colliery Museum (Higher Green, just off A580) The only visible reminder of Lancashire's mining heritage, with its 100-ft steel headgear still intact, plus the largest steam winding engine in Europe (currently being restored), a narrow gauge railway, working stationary steam engines, and displays on coal mining inc an exhibition of photography from 1908–1970. Shop; museum open Sun, Tues and Thurs pm, engines in steam first Sun of month Mar–Oct only; (01942) 828121; free (exc for special events).

BARNOLDSWICK SD9046

Bancroft Mill Engine Museum ⊞ The last working steam mill in the area – not that long ago Barnoldswick had 13. Snacks, shop, disabled access; open 11–3 most Sats for static viewing, (01282) 865626 for dates of steam days; £2. The Fanny Grey (B651 towards Colne) has decent food.

BARROWFORD SD8639

Pendle Heritage Centre Growing local history centre, with 18th-c walled gardens, small farm, country trails, 14th-c barn with pot-bellied pig, and a museum with an exhibition on the Pendle witches – the house itself looks appropriately witchy. Snacks, shop, limited disabled access; cl 25 Dec; (01282) 661701; £2.20, gardens only £1.20. This is picturesque, evocative countryside; the **church** at nearby unspoilt Newchurch has the witches' grave, and there's good food at the Forest Inn at Fence and Bay Horse at Roughlee – a stone's throw from Alice Nutter's home. A few miles upstream from here, just below Blacko, the Water Meetings is an ideal place for a picnic and a paddle.

BIRKENHEAD SJ3288

Waterfront views over to Liverpool, of course, but a surprise in **Birkenhead Priory** (Priory St), a ruined 12th-c

Benedictine priory with notable visitor centre. Shop, mostly disabled access; open wknd pms all year, plus pm daily (exc Mon) in school hols; (0151) 666 4010; free. Good views from the tower of the neighbouring church. The rejuvenated Hamilton Quarter is home to various craft and art galleries. Laid out in 1853 and now being restored, Birkenhead Park is the world's first public park. The Shrewsbury Arms out in Claughton Firs is the best place for lunch.

Historic Warships ⊞ (Birkenhead Docks) HMS *Plymouth* and the Submarine *Onyx* both took part in the Falklands War. You can peep up the periscope on the *Onyx*, and there's plenty for children to fiddle with. A few ladders to negotiate, but don't be put off – readers find this a very satisfying afternoon out. Snacks, new shop with interactive displays, disabled access to visitor centre only; cl 24–26 Dec, 1 Jan; (0151) 650 1573; £5 for both ships. The German U-boat displayed alongside spent the last 50 years on the seabed.

Shore Road Pumping Station (Woodside, nr ferry terminal) This unusual **steam pumping station** has an adjacent small transport museum with a working tram. Open pm wknds, and daily (exc Mon) in school hols but best to check; (0151) 650 1182; £1.

Williamson Art Gallery & Museum (Slatey Rd) English watercolours and art by the Liverpool school, sculpture and ceramics, model ships, and a collection of cars and motorcycles in period garage setting. Shop, disabled access; cl am, all day Mon, Good Fri, 25 Dec and 1 Jan; (0151) 652 4177; free. On summer Suns in Aug there are generally free concerts either here or at the priory.

BLACKBURN SD6828

Put firmly on the map by the Industrial Revolution, this has bustling shops and market, some fine buildings, and lots of beautiful unspoilt countryside around. The parish **church** (actually now a cathedral) is very handsome – grand yet elegant, and will soon be home to a window commemorating Diana, Princess of Wales.

Blackburn Museum & Art Gallery (Museum St) Quite a mixture – English watercolours, Japanese woodblock prints, Greek and Russian orthodox icons, and a fantastic collection of beetles, some pretty scary. Shop, disabled access; cl Sun, Mon, 25–26 Dec, 1 Jan, Good Fri; (01254) 667130; free.

Witton Country Park (off A674 W) 480 acres of attractive countryside to explore. Snacks, shop; (01254) 55423; visitor centre cl am Mon–Sat, plus all Mon–Weds Oct–Mar, 25–26 Dec, and 1 Jan; free.

BLACKPOOL SD3036
Britain's most loved and loathed seaside resort, in summer offering more bed spaces than the whole of Portugal. The atmosphere then is unashamedly boisterous (it's pretty dreary in winter), and though it's now more geared to young adults, most children love it, with plenty for them to do from donkey rides along the beaches (best not to swim here) to days at the **Sandcastle** leisure complex. The tram to Fleetwood is a must for tram freaks. The civilised Bispham Hotel (Red Bank Rd) has good value bedrooms.

Blackpool Pleasure Beach See separate family panel on p.338.

Blackpool Tower The outstanding landmark has several lively attractions geared towards families, inc a circus, laser shows, aquarium (rare giant sea turtles), science gallery, dinosaur dark ride, a lift to the top, replica Crown Jewels and the Walk of Faith – a 5-cm thick glass floor 385 ft above the ground. Perhaps most fun at night (they're open till 11pm in summer). Meals, snacks, shop, limited disabled access; cl winter wkdys; (01253) 622242; £10, more during the Illuminations. These famous autumn light displays are the best of their kind – if you don't mind travelling at a snail's pace along the Golden Five Hundred Yards (or Mile as they call it here).

Blackpool Zoo (East Park Drive) Over 400 animals in 32 acres of landscaped gardens inc a walk-through lemur wood, and free-flying bird hall. The big cats are usually fed at 3.30pm (not Fri), the sealions at 11am and 2.30pm, and there are parrot displays at 11.45am and 2.15pm. Meals, snacks, shop, disabled access; cl 25 Dec;

(01253) 830830; £6.

Grundy Art Gallery (Queen St) This decent gallery away from the crowds is proof that there's more to Blackpool than ice-creams and eyesores; shop, disabled access but no facilities; cl Sun and bank hols; free.

Sea Life Centre (Golden Mile Centre) Broadly similar to others in the chain, but with a bonus: one of the biggest displays of tropical sharks in Europe, with a walk-through tunnel underneath so you feel you're in there with them. Meals, snacks, shop, disabled access; cl 25 Dec; (01253) 622445; £6.99 (they stamp your hand so you can come back later that day if you keep your receipt).

BOLTON SD7109
Quite a few places to visit here, and you can tour **Warburtons Bakery** (Hereford St) by arrangement, Tues–Thurs only; (01204) 523551; free. The Kings Head (Junction Rd, Deane), with a bowling green behind, is useful for lunch, as is the restaurant of the Queens Moat House – an interesting church conversion.

Bolton Museum and Art Gallery (Le Mans Crescent) Quite good, with Egyptian mummies, lots of watercolours and 20th-c sculpture. Shop, disabled access; cl Sun and bank hols; free.

Hall i'th' Wood (Crompton Way) 15th-c, where Samuel Crompton developed his Spinning Mule in 1779; it was refurbished by the first Lord Leverhulme in 1902. Shop, disabled access to ground floor; cl Sun am, all day Mon (exc bank hols), all Oct–Mar; (01204) 332370; £3 (£5 joint ticket with Smithills Hall Museum, below).

Smithills Hall Museum (Smithills, Dean Rd) Interesting (though much restored) old manor house with 14th-c Great Hall and splendid panelled drawing room. Shop, disabled access to ground floor only; cl Sun am, all day Mon (exc bank hols), all Oct–Easter; (01204) 332377; £3.

BOLTON BY BOWLAND SD7849
Attractive streamside Forest of Bowland village, with a fine **church**, and quaint cottages leading off its two village greens. The Coach & Horses has good fresh food.

BRAMHALL SJ8886

Bramall Hall One of the finest houses in the area (particularly from the outside), a splendid timber-framed 14th-c hall with rare 16th-c wall paintings and furniture, and extensive parkland; there was a fair bit of prettifying restoration in the 19th c. Meals, snacks, shop, disabled access to ground floor; cl am Mon–Sat Good Fri–Sept, plus Mon Oct–Dec, then every day exc pm wknds; (0161) 485 3708; £3.50, park free. The Davenport Arms at Woodford does decent lunches.

BROMLEY CROSS SD7213

Last Drop Village (N of Bolton) Pastiche of an 18th-c village, very rustic and quaint, with cottages, shops, decent pub and craft centre. The B6391 and old Roman road through Edgworth N of here are fine moorland roads, as are the A675 N of Bolton itself (good detours off at Belmont), and A666 to Darwen.

BURNLEY SD8530

The **canal wharf** (Manchester Rd), which has a small museum, allows short towpath walks along the Leeds & Liverpool Canal, giving a vivid impression of the towering old weaving mills; the raised canal embankment across the valley is a remarkable sight.

Rockwater Bird Conservation Centre 🖾 (Foxstones Lane, Cliviger – above Mereclough SE) Expanding collection taking in waterfowl, pheasant, foreign birds and owls as well as rabbits, chipmunks, goats and sheep. Children can feed some animals. Snacks, limited disabled access; cl Mon (exc bank hols), wkdys Mar and Oct, all Nov–Feb; (01282) 415016; £2.50. Nearby **Cliviger Gorge** has pleasant walks, with stream, woodland and farmland; moors above. The Kettledrum at Mereclough has good home cooking, and the moorland roads around it are attractive – especially the old packhorse road from Mereclough up Stansfield Moor; good views from the back road angling off SE from the A52 to the junction of the A671 and B6238.

Towneley Hall (A646 S) A striking 14th-c building housing a decent museum (summer snacks, shop, disabled access; cl Sat, Sun am,

Christmas and New Year; free).

BURY SD8010

East Lancs Railway (Bolton St Stn) Well regarded by enthusiasts, a scenic 17-mile steam journey along the pretty Irwell Valley; you can get on or off along the way. Meals, snacks, shop, disabled access; open wknds, bank hols, and Fri in July and Aug; (0161) 764 7790 for timetable; £6 full return. The Lord Raglan up at Nangreaves (off A56/A666 N) has great moorland views and hearty food.

CARNFORTH SD4970

The dilapidated station at this otherwise unremarkable little town starred in *Brief Encounter* in 1945; a £1m project to restore it to its cinematic heyday (complete with visitor centre, café and shop) should be finished later this year. A mile or so N are the ruins of a 14th-c manor house, **Warton Old Rectory**.

Warton Crag (just N) Fine views over Morecambe Bay and the coast, and enjoyable walking.

CATFORTH SD4735

Lancaster Canal Between Preston and Carnforth, this is ideal for boating – 40 miles without a single lock; often through quiet countryside, with herons and even occasional kingfishers – best in spring or early summer, with ducklings and cygnets bobbing about, and lambs in the fields alongside. This is also a good departure point for pleasant towpath walks, largely through quiet countryside. The Running Pump has good home cooking.

CHARNOCK RICHARD SD5415

Camelot Adventure Theme Park 130-acre park themed around the mythical world of Camelot and Arthurian legend – the rides and shows have on the whole been carefully thought out to fit in with this; a dizzying swing-boat ride is in the shape of Excalibur, and in Pendragon's Plunge, you sit in an inflatable boat and drop 9 metres (30 ft) through a series of twists and turns at speeds of up to 25mph – there are three different routes. Also a driving school for younger children, a new maze, jousting displays in a full-sized arena, a very good farm, and dozens of other attractions. Meals, snacks, shop, disabled access; open daily

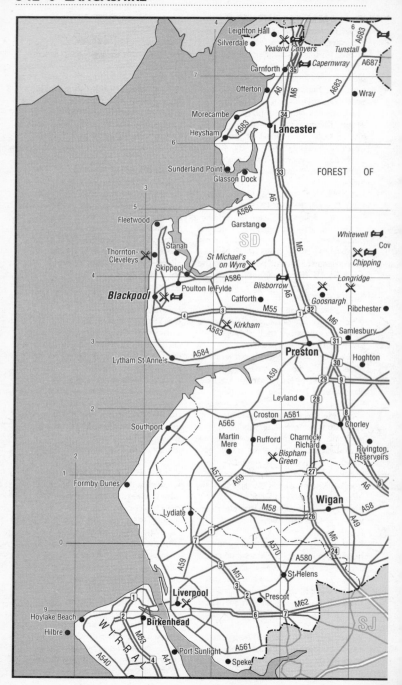

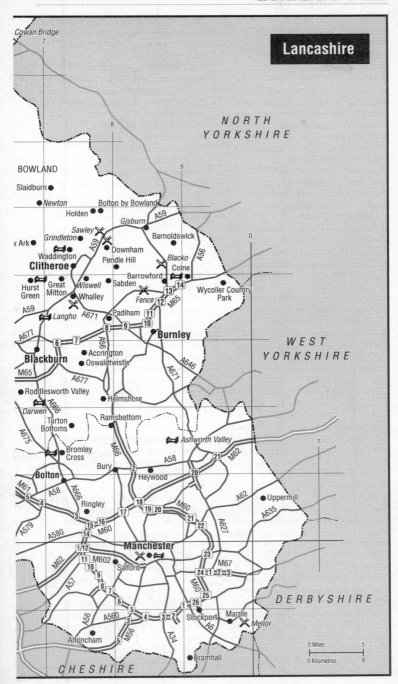

Lancashire

Cowan Bridge

7

NORTH
YORKSHIRE

8

BOWLAND

Slaidburn ●

9

● *Newton*   Bolton by Bowland

Holden ●●

Gisburn   A59

v Ark ●   *Grindleton* ●   *Sawley*   Barnoldswick ●

Waddington ●   A59   ● *Downham*   *Blacko*   0

Clitheroe   Pendle Hill ●   Colne

Hurst   Great   *Wiswell*   Barrowford   Wycoller Country

Green   Mitton   Sabden   13 14   Park

A59   *Whalley*   *Fence* 12   M65

Langho   A671   Padiham 11

8   9   10

A677   6   7   A56   **Burnley**

● Accrington

Blackburn   ● Oswaldtwistle

M65   A677

A646

● Roddlesworth Valley

A671

WEST
YORKSHIRE

Darwen   ● Helmshore

Turton

Bottoms   ● Ramsbottom

A675   A666

Bromley   *Ashworth Valley*

Cross   M66   21   M62

Bolton   Bury   2   A58   20

M61   A58   Heywood

5   A666   18   A62   ● Uppermill

4   Ringley   17   19 20   M60   A635

3   15 16   21   A627

A579   14   M60   22

A580   1/12   Manchester   23   M67

M62   11   M602   24 1 2 3

10   Salford   M60

A57   9   25

8   7   26

A56   6   Stockport   DERBYSHIRE

A560   5   4   3 2   Marple

3   1   A6   Mellor

● Altrincham   M56   A34   ●

5   ● Bramhall

CHESHIRE

0 Miles   5

0 Kilometres   8

Easter–Aug, plus wknds and half-term Sept–Oct – best to check; (01257) 452100; £8.99.

CHORLEY SD5718

Astley Hall (Astley Park) Unusual-looking timber-framed 16th-c house with particularly elaborate carvings and plasterwork, interesting pottery and paintings, and extensive gardens and woodland. It was used in the TV adaptation of *Moll Flanders*. Shop, disabled access to ground floor only; cl am, Mon (exc bank hols), and wkdys Nov–Mar; (01257) 515555; £2.90, free for Chorley residents. The Malt 'n' Hops behind the station in the town itself is useful for a bite to eat.

CLITHEROE SD7441

Bustling old market town: every Weds evening hundreds of poultry and small livestock enthusiasts come to the auctions, some from as far away as Scotland. The High St is dominated by the **castle** perched on its limestone rock. One of the oldest buildings in Lancashire, it has one of the smallest Norman keeps in the country. The **Castle Museum** has an extensive geology exhibition, and good views of the Ribble Valley. Shop, limited disabled access; cl Thurs and Fri Oct–Mar, and all Jan; (01200) 424635; £1.50. Cowmans on Castle St has an incredibly wide range of traditional and speciality sausages, and Byrne's on King St stocks a remarkable range of wines. The Swan & Royal (Castle St) is handy for lunch, and readers enjoy the sculpture trail in Bungerley Park. There's a lovely drive through Bashall Eaves, the Trough of Bowland and Quernmore.

COLNE SD8839

Go-Karts (Holker Mill, Burnley Rd) Exciting and fun, and the only indoor track in the area. Meals, snacks, shop; cl Sun am; (01282) 865675; rides from £12 for 20 mins.

COW ARK SD6845

Browsholme Hall 🖼 Unpretentious-looking Tudor house on the edge of the Forest of Bowland, with surprisingly rich range of contents. Good guided tours by members of the family. Shop, disabled access to ground floor; open Sun and Mon pm spring bank hol, plus pm first two wks in July and second two wks in Aug, best to check; (01254)

826719; £3.50. The Inn at Whitewell in one direction and Red Pump at Bashall Eaves in the other offer a choice of good places to eat.

CROSTON SD4918

A good village to visit, with a very old church surrounded by cobbled paths. The Black Horse has hearty home cooking.

DOWNHAM SD7844

Below Pendle Hill, carefully preserved by the Assheton estate and outstandingly pretty, on the side of a steep pasture valley with a stream winding along the bottom; the Assheton Arms is good.

FLEETWOOD SD3448

Developed as a rather elegant 19th-c resort, with landscaping by Decimus Burton, plenty of smart buildings, lively harbour, excellent market, two elegant if not entirely practical lighthouses (one's in the middle of the street), decent summer museum (cl am exc Tues, Fri, Sat July–Aug, all day Weds exc July–Sept, and all Nov–Good Fri; £1.20), Freeport factory shopping centre (indoor and outdoor play areas), and trams from Blackpool right through the town. The architecturally interesting North Euston Hotel by the terminus is a safe bet for food. The Marine Hall exhibition centre on the front has a decent bar (the Wyre – no food) with excellent views of the harbour and Morecambe Bay.

Farmer Parr's Animal World (Wyrefield Farm, Rossall Lane) Children can feed the lambs at this 20-acre farm with over 200 animals inc llamas, wild boar, emu and owls; pony and tractor rides, children's play area, and a small rural heritage centre. Snacks, shop, disabled access; cl 25–26 Dec; (01253) 874389; *£3.25.

FOREST OF BOWLAND SD6650

Magnificent Pennine moorland, less visited than most areas of comparable scenery, as much of the moorland, privately owned, is closed to walkers. Only a few paths cross the impressive massif that forms some of the county's most significant scenery; Ramblers Association has often organised mass trespasses as demonstrations against denial of access, and hopes for big changes here from right-to-roam legislation. Development in some of the villages (also in private hands) is controlled too strictly for any significant expansion of holiday accommodation – let alone a proliferation of camp sites and so forth. These restrictions make the area particularly appealing for people who want peace and quiet, and it's not impossible to find good walks. There are some fine ones on rights of way – for instance, up Clougha Fell from Quernmore; above Tarnbrook Wyre; up Dunsop Fell from Slaidburn or Dunsop Bridge; up Fairsnape and Wolf Fell from Chipping or Bleasdale. Beacon Fell Country Park is an atmospheric place to wander through, and there are some pleasant walks around the Coronation Arms at Horton. Don't be confused by road signs by the Rivers Ribble and Hodder claiming some of the territory for Yorkshire (as in the past indeed it was).

FORMBY DUNES SD2808
Reached from the NW edge of Formby, a large tract of sweeping sandy dunes which in some areas is being stabilised by pine plantations; broad beaches and good walks through the adjacent pinewoods, made interesting by the chance of seeing and even feeding red squirrels (you can buy nuts here); £2.70 per car. Best in spring and autumn – can be busy in summer; parking in some places may cost £1.50, but keep looking – a number of other spots are free.

GARSTANG SD4945
Quite an attractive small market town, with a good deal of canal activity (and a fine aqueduct crossing the River Wyre). The entertaining waterside Owd Tithebarn (with a canal museum upstairs) is fun for lunch, and the **Discovery Centre** (High St) is a useful introduction to the area's natural history.

GLASSON DOCK SD4456
Once an important port for Lancaster, this still has the occasional coaster berthing, but is mainly a lively summer boating place now, in pleasant countryside. The Victoria on the dock is a popular dining pub, as is the 17th-c Stork up on the A588.

GREAT MITTON SD7139
Great Mitton church Attractive,

with an outstanding range of memorial tombs.

HELMSHORE SD7821
Helmshore Textile Museums 🏛
(Holcombe Rd) Two stone mills with comprehensive collections of textile machinery, much still in working order. Easily one of the best textile museums in the country, but if social history and machinery aren't your things it's unlikely to convert you. Snacks, shop, disabled access; cl am, Sat, and Nov–Mar; (01706) 226459; £3. The Duke of Wellington on the B6232 W of Haslingden is a reliable family dining pub in fine surroundings, with more views further on.

HEYSHAM SD4160
A tremendous contrast with the power station here (no longer open to the public), is the quaint squint-walled little village **church**, partly Saxon, with Norse-carved hogback tombstone inside. The unusual waterside Golden Ball at Heaton with Oxcliffe off the Lancaster road (may be cut off by very high tides) is fun for lunch.

HEYWOOD SD8510
Corgi Heritage Centre (53 York St) Hundreds of die-cast model vehicles from pre-war cars to James Bond's Aston Martin – even a turning Magic Roundabout; of course it's all a huge plug for the company that makes them, but fascinating for collectors. Shop, limited disabled access; cl Tues and Sun, bank hols; (01706) 365812; free. The Egerton Arms off the B6222 Bury road is a good moorland dining pub.

HILBRE SJ1887
The biggest of three tidal islands which you can reach on foot at low tide from West Kirby; Hilbre is a **nature reserve**, once popular with sunbathers, now visited mainly by birds and occasional seals. Make sure you know the tide times – (0151) 648 4371 – as it's easy to be stranded out here.

HOGHTON SD6226
Hoghton Tower (A675) Splendid 16th-c fortified hilltop mansion, with grand state rooms and royal bedchamber, and a collection of dolls and doll's houses. The gardens are lovely (particularly the rose garden) and the surrounding grounds offer wonderful views of the sea, moors,

Lakeland hills and Welsh mountains. Snacks, shop; open Sun and Mon bank hol wknd pms Easter–Aug, plus Mon–Thurs, and Sun pm July–Sept; (01254) 852986; £2 parking and grounds, £3 house. The Royal Oak at Riley Green has decent food.

HOLDEN SD7749

Holden Clough Nursery Old-fashioned nursery with thoroughly up-to-date approach to raising interesting plants in Victorian kitchen garden of Holden Clough Hall; beds of alpines, trough gardens, herbaceous perennials, shrubs and rhododendrons and maybe RHS special events. Shop, disabled access; cl Sun (exc pms Easter and May bank hols), Good Fri, and 25 Dec–1 Jan; (01200) 447615; free. The Copy Nook has good food, and is a useful stop for walkers.

HOYLAKE BEACH SJ2088

These sweeping sands are beautiful, with an unusual partly tidal **nature reserve** at Red Rocks N of the golf links.

HURST GREEN SD6939

Stonyhurst College Magnificent 16th-c manor house, now home to the famous Roman Catholic boarding school. You can see the library, chapel, other historic rooms and the extensive grounds. Snacks, shop, limited disabled access; open pm Aug exc Fri, gardens usually open July–Aug – phone to check; (01254) 826345; £4.50, £1 garden only. The Punch Bowl and Bayley Arms have good food, with fine Ribble Valley walks nearby.

LANCASTER SD4761

Friendly and relaxed despite the grandeur of many of its stone buildings; ambling down the cobbled streets and alleyways (much is pedestrianised), it's hard to believe this was once a major West Indies shipping port. These days the water traffic is more sedate, with punts for hire and canal cruises in summer. Riverside paths are currently being improved, and a new bridge over the Lune should be ready before this book comes out. The Farmhouse Tavern (Scale Hall Farm, A589 Morecambe road) has good food, and other places worth knowing for lunch include the John o' Gaunt (Market St) and canalside White Cross.

Ashton Memorial & Butterfly Park (Williamson Park) A magnificent folly clearly visible from the motorway, set in 54 acres of lovely landscaped parkland; splendid views from the upper galleries. The butterfly house has a good collection of plants and lepidoptera, as well as free-flying birds and various creepy-crawlies. Snacks, shop, disabled access; cl 25–26 Dec, 1 Jan; (01524) 33318; *£3.25.

Judge's Lodging (Church St) 17th-c house with well restored period rooms, plenty of Gillow furniture, and museum of childhood. Shop; open Mon–Sat pm Good Fri–Oct, plus all day wkdys July–Sept, and pm bank hol wknds; (01524) 32808; £2. Other decent collections at the firmly traditional **City Museum** on Market Sq, in a very grand Georgian former town hall (shop, disabled access; cl Sun, 24 Dec–1 Jan; free), and at the **Cottage Museum** opposite the castle, furnished in the style of an early 19th-c artisan's house (open pm Easter–Sept; 75p).

Lancaster Castle Dramatic 12th-c Norman fortress famous for hangings and witch trials, owned by the Queen as Duke of Lancaster. Part of it is still used as a prison, but the cells, tower and 18th-c Gothic Revival Shire Hall can all be visited. Shop; open daily mid-Mar to mid-Dec; (01524) 64998; £4.

Lancaster Maritime Museum (St George's Quay) Up-to-date look at the local maritime trade and fishing industry; the audio-visual show is good fun. Snacks, shop, disabled access; cl am Nov–Easter, 25 Dec and 1 Jan; (01524) 382264; £2 (free to local residents).

Lancaster Priory Dates back to before the Conquest, though the present hilltop building is mainly 14th- and 15th-c; very interesting medieval choir-stalls, needlework and Anglo-Saxon cross fragments. Snacks and shop (open Easter–Oct), some disabled access; cl winter lunchtimes; free. Nearby are the remains of a Roman bath house.

LEIGHTON HALL SD4874

A notably friendly welcome at this neo-Gothic mansion (more restrained inside), still the home of the Gillow family and with early examples of their furniture. The grounds have a collection of birds of prey, nature trails, and beautifully kept gardens. The setting is lovely, with Lakeland hills rising behind. Snacks, shop, disabled access; cl am, all day Sat and Mon (exc bank hols), and all Oct–Apr; (01524) 734474; *£4.50. The nearby New Inn at Yealand Conyers has good food.

LEYLAND SD5422

British Commercial Vehicle Museum (King St) Jazzed up with sound effects, this has over 90 perfectly restored British wagons, buses, trucks, vans, fire engines and even a Popemobile, shining so much you'd think they were new. Snacks, shop, disabled access; open Sun, Tues, Weds and bank hols Apr–Sept, Sun only Oct; (01772) 451011; *£4.

Old Grammar School (Church Rd) The sturdy 16th-c building has changing local history displays; open pm Thurs, all day Tues and Fri, am Sat; (01772) 422041; free.

Worden Park has art displays and craft workshops, walks, gardens, a maze, and miniature golf. Leyland also has a pleasant town trail, and the 15th-c church has some fine stained glass. The friendly little Rose & Crown (A581 S) has decent basic food.

LIVERPOOL SJ3590

The excellent value National Museums and Galleries on Merseyside Eight Pass means you can visit many of the varied family attractions here without straining your pocket: admission to any one of the eight attractions in the scheme (£3, £1.50 concessions) allows unlimited visits for a year to that and the other seven attractions. Many of the fine 19th-c buildings which recall Liverpool's past as one of the world's great ports have been cleaned up in recent years, and the Philharmonic (Hope St), probably the country's grandest late Victorian pub, will have been given the same treatment by the time you read this; nearby the Everyman Bistro has good value food. You can tour the city's trademark Liver Building on wkdys Apr–Sept by arrangement, (0151) 236 2748, though it's best viewed from one of the famous ferries across the Mersey, which leave regularly from Pier Head. The real

commuter ferries operate half-hourly during rush-hours (£1.85 return); the rest of the day the boats are hourly and aimed at visitors, with a commentary (£3.50 return).

Albert Dock Spectacular restoration of previously redundant warehouse buildings by the river, now a lively complex of shops, cafés and exhibitions, with regular entertainers, performers, events, boat trips and of course Fred's weather map. The Baltic Fleet, a majestically restored Victorian dockside pub, is handy for lunch, and the Hope on the Waterfront cybercafé is different for a drink. Some of the listed attractions are housed in the complex – you can easily base a whole day around a visit here.

Beatles Story (Albert Dock) Bouncy tribute to the local boys made good and the sights and sounds of the 60s, inc a reconstruction of the Cavern Club. Shop, disabled access; cl 25–26 Dec; (0151) 709 1963; £6.95. Beatles fans (considering the price you need to have been really devoted) can also go on a 2-hour tour in a Magical Mystery Tourbus around related city sites – it leaves the Beatles Story daily at 12.30 and 3pm; best to book in advance (0151) 709 3285; £10.95, joint ticket with the Beatles Story, £15.

Bluecoat Arts Centre (School Lane) Attractive Queen Anne building housing changing art exhibitions and occasional recitals, plus art, craft and book shops. Meals, snacks, disabled access to ground floor only; gallery cl Mon, centre cl 25–26 Dec, 1 Jan and bank hols; box office (0151) 709 5297; free (exc for events).

Cathedrals Unusually, both Liverpool's cathedrals were built this century, in widely differing styles. Walk along Hope St (the heart of the city's 18th-c area, with many Georgian brick terraces) to the impressive and more obviously modern Metropolitan Roman Catholic cathedral, designed by Frederick Gibberd after a vast earlier scheme by Lutyens ran out of money; blue light from the 16-sided glass tower reflects evocatively on the marble inside. The Anglican cathedral looks much older, but was completed only in 1978. Britain's biggest, it's undeniably powerful, though its soaring proportions and cavernous scale make it impersonal. Both have good concerts.

Conservation Centre (Whitechapel) Intriguing glimpse at the world of museum and gallery conservation; interactive displays and demonstrations explain how various objects are preserved, and exhibits range from a mummified Egyptian crocodile to two Beatles' gold discs; good programme of events. Café, shop, disabled access; cl Sun am, 23–26 Dec, 1 Jan; (0151) 478 4999; £3 Eight Pass – see above (children free).

Croxteth Hall & Country Park (5m NE) Period displays in Edwardian house, and working farm, Victorian walled garden, miniature railway, and country walks in the grounds – a pleasant family trip out. Meals, snacks, shop, some disabled access; house cl Oct–Easter, farm cl 25 Dec–1 Jan, park open all year; (0151) 228 5311; park free, hall, farm and garden £3.75, hall or farm only £1.85, walled garden only £1.10.

Grand National Experience (Aintree Race Course) Takes you behind the scenes of the world's most famous steeplechase. A visitor centre within the County Stand has memorabilia charting the history of the race from its origins in 1839, while in the weighing room you can try on the silks of past winners, test out the scales and experience a steward's enquiry. Perhaps the highlight is the simulator ride – find out what it's like to jump a National fence; guided tours of the racecourse (11am, 2.30pm) include a look around the stables. Meals, snacks, shop, disabled access; cl Mon, mid-Oct to Apr, and all race days; (0151) 522 2921; visitor centre *£3 (with simulator ride and tour *£7).

Liverpool Football Club Museum 🎫 (Anfield Rd) The visitor centre and Anfield tours are a must for the faithful. There are cups, trophies, programmes and other treasured memorabilia as well as films of the club's finest hours. The tour takes in the grounds, dressing room and pitch – you can even sit on the manager's bench. Snacks, shop, disabled access; visitor centre cl 25 Dec, no tours on match days and

booking essential (0151) 260 6677. Shop, some disabled access; £8.50 (visitor centre only £5.50).

Liverpool Museum (William Brown St) You could spend hours at this excellent museum and still not see everything. It currently includes an aquarium, a particularly good planetarium, and a hands-on natural history centre, but will have practically doubled in size by the time it reopens next year, following extensive refurbishment. Snacks, shop, disabled access; best to phone for opening times; (0151) 207 0001; £3 – Eight Pass (see Liverpool), children free. Just along the road you can tour one of the biggest public libraries in Europe; (0151) 233 5858 to book; free.

Merseyside Maritime Museum (Albert Dock) Huge museum spread over six floors, with boats, ships, craft demonstrations and a lively interpretation of what it was like for the millions who travelled from here to the New World. It takes in the Museum of Liverpool Life, vividly re-creating social history from the last century or so, and the Customs and Excise museum, Anything to Declare – a lot more fun than it sounds, with an intriguing look at concealment techniques, and even demonstrations by sniffer dogs. A gallery on transatlantic slavery has divided local historians, who disagree on Liverpool's true role in the slave trade. Meals, snacks, shop, disabled access; cl 23–26 Dec, 1 Jan; (0151) 478 4499; £3 – Eight Pass (see above).

National Wildflower Centre 🎫 Due to open just after we went to press, this £3.4m Millennium Commission project aims to create a conservation centre for endangered British wildflowers in a 35-acre park, formerly the home of the Gladstones. The planting side of things has been masterminded by Landlife, a charity specialising in developing new wildlife habitats on derelict sites. A purpose-built visitor centre will have hands-on activities and exhibitions about conservation; play area. Snacks, shop and plant sales, disabled access; open Weds–Sun plus bank hols Apr–Sept, Weds only Oct–Mar; (0151) 737 1819; £3.

Open Eye Gallery (Wood St) Good changing photography exhibitions; shop, disabled access; cl Sun, Mon and 24 Dec–1 Jan; (0151) 709 9460; free.

Paul McCartney's home (20 Forthlin Rd, Allerton) 1950s terraced council house, the former home of the McCartney family. John, Paul and George met, rehearsed and wrote many of their earliest songs here, inc 'Love Me Do' and 'I Saw Her Standing There'. Open Weds–Sat Apr–Oct, then Sats only till mid-Dec; (0151) 486 4006; access is by minibus only from Speke Hall (see Speke entry on p.355); £5.10 (NT members free).

Robert Cain (Stanhope St) Evening tours of red brick brewery inc buffet and tastings; shop; cl Fri–Sun; (0151) 709 8734; £3.75. The splendidly restored Brewery Tap pub is good.

Sudley House (Mossley Hill Rd) Interestingly unspoilt private Victorian house with good gardens, attractive furniture, and paintings by Turner and Pre-Raphaelites. Wknd snacks, disabled access to ground floor only; cl Sun am, 23–26 Dec, 1 Jan; (0151) 207 0001; £3, Eight Pass (see Liverpool).

Tate Gallery (Albert Dock) Plenty of sculptures, paintings and various special events. All very well presented with especially good use of natural light, though not really for traditionalists. Meals, snacks, shop, disabled access; cl Mon (exc bank hols), Good Fri, 24–26 Dec, 1 Jan; (0151) 709 3223; free, though £3 for special exhibitions.

Walker Art Gallery (William Brown St) One of the finest art collections outside London, with especially notable Italian, Dutch and Pre-Raphaelite works. Meals, snacks, shop, disabled access; cl Sun am, 23–26 Dec, 1 Jan; (0151) 478 4199; £3 Eight Pass (see Liverpool).

Western Approaches 🔳 (Rumford St) Evocatively restored underground command centre for the World War II Battle of the Atlantic; a labyrinth of rooms covering 50,000 sq ft under the city's streets. Snacks, shop; cl Fri, Sun, and Nov–Feb; (0151) 227 2008; *£4.75.

LYDIATE SD3604

Pick your own Popular around here, with lots of places on the flat ground – soft fruit the speciality, late June to

August; **Lydiate Fruit Farm** (Pilling Lane) has a good farm shop in attractive 18th-c former stable buildings. The Scotch Piper (Southport Rd), with a nice garden, claims to be the county's most ancient pub.

LYTHAM ST ANNE'S SD3228

Decorous seaside town that seems a world away from nearby Blackpool. It has a splendidly restored **windmill** by the prom in the centre of breezy Lytham green (shop, limited disabled access; cl 1–2pm, Mon and Fri, and all Sept–Apr exc Easter; donations), and a small **Lifeboat Museum** next door (open Tues, Thurs and wknds, plus Weds pm July–Aug; free). The Taps is a good real ale pub here.

MANCHESTER SJ8398

Manchester's packed with interesting places to visit, and the continuing development of the hugely ambitious city-centre Millennium Quarter now adds to its considerable attraction for visitors. Exciting new developments planned for the future include the grand canalside Imperial War Museum of the North, scheduled to open in 2002. On a fine wknd or summer evening strolling around the very impressive buildings is already a real pleasure; Albert Sq is one of the finest areas, with the great Albert Memorial (predating London's), several key cultural centres, and some lively café-bars. The Town Hall is a massively impressive piece of Victoriana, facing colourful summer gardens; there are guided tours at 2pm on Sat and alternate Weds in summer. The very wide 15th-c **cathedral** with notable choir stalls, lies at the heart of the Millennium Quarter; work is currently under way on a new visitor centre. The small medieval centre around it is now protected by a new park, and nearby the reconstructed 18th-c Sinclairs Oyster Bar (Cathedral Gates) is good value (not just oysters). Just behind is the new pedestrian Exchange Sq, with Europe's biggest Marks & Spencer, a shopping centre in the former Corn Exchange, the Printworks entertainments complex – and a group of tall post-modern stainless steel windmills. Opening later this year across the park from the Corn Exchange, **Urbis** will form the centrepiece of the new quarter, with galleries looking at Manchester's influence on other industrial cities, as well as more new shops and restaurants. Mash & Air (Chorlton St) is currently drawing in the young and fashionable, thanks to its unusual own-brew beers and equally distinctive food. The Castlefield area by the basin where the Bridgewater and Rochdale canals meet is interesting: restored warehouses, viaducts and the like, lots of lively redevelopment inc a tramway and wonderfully light and airy footbridge, also the good Dukes 92 pub (maybe street theatre outside) – and not far off, on the other side of the GMEX exhibition centre, the very smart Bridgewater concert hall (box office (0161) 907 9000). By contrast, the Rochdale canal towpath is a fascinating seamy-side walk. Chinatown here, incidentally, is the second-largest Chinese community in England: lots of authentic restaurants and a Chinese Arts Centre. Young trendies head to Afflecks Palace on Church St for four floors of antique clothing, records, etc, and there's a huge shopping centre with 20-screen cinema at Trafford Park to the N. It's surprisingly quick getting across the city, and the Metrolink trams quickly cover much of Greater Manchester. See also separate entries for Salford and Prestwich.

Chetham's Library (Long Millgate) Nestled among the modern developments of the Millennium Quarter, this is the oldest public library in Britain, founded in 1653. The attractive building itself dates from the 15th c and was originally a college for priests. Many of the original features remain inc fellows' dormitories, and 17th-c reading tables (still used). Heritage grants are funding newer restoration projects. Cl 12.30–1.30pm, wknds, bank hols and 25 Dec–1 Jan; (0161) 8347961; free.

City Art Gallery (Mosley St) Currently undergoing a £25m expansion, this will include cafés, a shop and improved disabled access when it opens in early 2002. It has excellent decorative and applied art collections, and outstanding Pre-Raphaelites.

Gallery of Costume (Platt Hall, Rusholme) The best museum of its kind, a Georgian mansion with comprehensive displays of fashion over the last 400 years. Displays change regularly – though like the styles themselves eventually come back. Shop, disabled access to ground floor only; (0161) 224 5217; free.

Granada Studios Tour (Water St) Having closed for major redevelopment in early 2000, the new-look attraction is supposed to open some time this year, though as we go to press in summer 2000 there is as yet no news about what it will have to offer, or prices (previously, nearly £15) and times. In its previous incarnation, it was largely TV-based with hi-tech add-ons; best to phone for details on (0161) 833 0880.

Heaton Hall (Prestwich) Splendidly decorated 18th-c neo-Classical house in extensive well used public parkland; fine paintings, plasterwork and furniture, unusual circular Pompeiian room, and various recitals and temporary exhibitions. Disabled access; usually cl Mon (exc bank hols, when cl Weds after) and Tues, and Oct–Easter, phone to check; (0161) 773 1231; free. The Victorian Woodthorpe by the main gate has decent food.

John Rylands Library (Deansgate) One of the city's most remarkable buildings, magnificently neo-Gothic, small exhibitions and tours (Weds 12pm, £1); shop, cl Sat pm, all Sun and bank hols, and 24 Dec–1 Jan; (0161) 834 5343; free.

Manchester Jewish Museum (Cheetham Hill Rd, A665 1m N) In a former synagogue, the story of Manchester's Jewish community over the last 200 years, with fascinating recorded recollections of life early last century. Shop, disabled access to ground floor only; cl Fri, Sat and Jewish holidays; (0161) 834 9879; £3.25. The nearby Derby Brewery Arms is a classic Mancunian pub, good value snacks.

Manchester Museum (Oxford Rd) Good Japanese collection, as well as Egyptian relics, and beehive. Shop, limited disabled access; cl Good Fri, 25–26 Dec and 1 Jan; (0161) 275 2634; free.

Manchester United Museum (Old Trafford) Purpose-built football museum, covering the club's history from its foundation in 1878 to the more recent glory days. Hundreds of exhibits (changing almost as frequently as their strip) and tours of the ground (must book in advance, not match days, and limited on the days before). Meals, snacks, shop (not unjustifiably they call it a megastore), disabled access; cl 25 Dec; (0161) 868 8631; £8 tour and museum, £5 museum only.

Museum of Science & Industry in Manchester (Castlefield) One of Britain's most impressive and imaginative museums, built on the site of the oldest passenger railway station in the world. There are hours of things to do, and plenty to touch and fiddle with. The main galleries take a broad and accessible look at power, industry, and transport (going right up to space travel), with highlights inc an exciting simulator in the air and space gallery, a big hands-on interactive science area, and a fascinating exhibition on sanitation. The vast power hall has working engines and railway locomotives, there's a fascinating exhibition on the history of photography, and a comprehensive look at the development of Manchester. The changing exhibitions are particularly good, with one on ancient cultures running until May. Ongoing developments within the museum inc a new interactive gallery to be added later this year. New restaurant, shop, disabled access; cl Dec 24–26; (0161) 832 1830; £6.50 (children are free to the main galleries), exhibitions £2.

Museum of Transport 🖼 (Boyle St, Cheetham) Around 80 vintage local buses and other vehicles, as well as photographs, tickets and memorabilia – even historic bus stops. Snacks, shop, disabled access; usually open Weds, wknds and bank hols, but best to check; (0161) 205 2122; £2.50.

Pankhurst Centre (62 Nelson St, Chorlton on Medlock) Emmeline Pankhurst launched the suffragette movement from this Georgian semi, now with period-furnished parlour and interestingly planted garden. Snacks, shop, disabled access; cl wknds and bank hols; (0161) 273 5673; free.

Pump House People's History Museum (Bridge St) Takes a comprehensive look at the way ordinary folk toiled and struggled to change society. Lots of well put-together displays inc the largest collection of political banners in the world, plus quizzes and games to entertain children; an upstairs gallery hosts changing exhibitions. Meals, snacks, shops, disabled access; cl Good Fri, 24–26 Dec, and 1 Jan; (0161) 839 6061; *£1 (free on Fri).

Royal Northern College of Music (Oxford Rd) Regular concerts, recitals and exhibitions; meals, snacks, shop; box office (0161) 907 5278/9.

Whitworth Art Gallery (Oxford Rd) British watercolours from Sandby to Turner, plus modern paintings and sculpture, and unusual collections of textiles and wallpaper. Meals, snacks, shop, disabled access; cl am Sun, Good Fri, 23 Dec–3 Jan; (0161) 275 7450; free.

MARPLE SJ9688

Peak Forest Canal Reached from Marple, the towpath soon leaves suburbia for green countryside; N is the famous set of Marple locks and aqueduct over the River Etherow. To the S, you can leave the canal at Strines and climb on to Mellor Moor.

MARTIN MERE SD4214

Wildfowl & Wetlands Trust (off A59) Thousands of wild geese, swans, ducks and flamingoes regularly visit the re-created natural open water habitats at this important 376-acre centre. Some birds will feed straight from your hand. Good visitor centre, well organised walks, lively activities for children and adventure playground, and plenty of instructive and entertaining events. Meals, snacks, shop, disabled access; cl 25 Dec; (01704) 895181; £5. The canalside Ship at Lathom is very popular for lunch.

Windmill Animal Farm (Fish Lane, Holmeswood; just N) This friendly 40-acre place has animals and their babies to feed (inc rare breeds), tractor rides, miniature railway, indoor play area and an adventure playground. Snacks, shop, disabled access; cl wkdys mid-Sept–Easter; (01704) 892282; £3.

MORECAMBE SD4264

Five miles of promenade and more of beaches to stroll along at this cheery resort, with pretty sunsets over the bay (beware of colour clashes during their July Punk Festival), and enjoyable guided walks across the sands; (01539) 532165. A lovely seafront statue commemorates the town's funniest son, Eric Morecambe, who so loved the place, he adopted its name. The Dog & Partridge (Bare) has decent fresh food. **Frontierland** Wild West theme park with 30 family rides and attractions (inc circus), and spectacular views across the bay from the top of the bizarre Polo Tower, designed to look like end-to-end tubes of sweets. Meals, snacks, shop, disabled access; usually cl Nov–Easter and some other days outside high season, but best to check; (01524) 410024; free entry to park, rides from 75p.

OFFERTON SD4666
Vast mudflats and sands, home to 200,000 wading birds. Walks over them are easiest from the Cumbrian side, though guided walks are also available from Hest Bank (details from local Tourist Information Centres; the galloping tides and quicksand do make a guide essential).

OSWALDTWISTLE SD7428
Oswaldtwistle Mills (Moscow Mill, Colliers St) Popular shopping village set around a working mill with various craft workshops inc a sweet factory; also garden, wildfowl reserve, textile museum (£1), and summer events. Meals, snacks, disabled access; cl 25 Dec and 1 Jan; (01254) 871025; free.

PADIHAM SD8034
Gawthorpe Hall Early 17th-c manor house with fine panelling and moulded ceilings, minstrel gallery, Jacobean long gallery, and some mid-19th-c alterations made by Sir John Barry. Important collections of costume, embroidery and lace, and paintings from the National Portrait Gallery. Snacks, shop, limited disabled access; house cl am, Mon (exc bank hols), Fri, and Nov–Mar, grounds open all year; (01282) 771004; £3; NT. The hilly cobbled alleys in the town's centre are now a conservation area. The Red Rock (Sabden Rd) has interesting food, with fine views from its garden.

PENDLE HILL SD8240
An excellent network of paths lets you walk round and almost all over it. Although Pendle's witch-persecuting days are happily over, the place still has a haunting elemental appeal. The view that enraptured George Fox, the founder of the Quakers, is as good as ever. The quickest way up is from Barley village.

PORT SUNLIGHT SJ3384
Lady Lever Art Gallery Lord Leverhulme, who had built his Sunlight Soap factory here, donated the village its outstanding gallery. It has interesting Victorian paintings inc Turners and Pre-Raphaelites – many adapted for use in soap ads, to the fury of the artists. Meals, snacks, shop, disabled access; cl Sun am, 23–26 Dec, 1 Jan; (0151) 645 3623; £3 for an Eight Pass ticket, covering seven other galleries in the area (see Liverpool).

Port Sunlight Heritage Centre 🏛
Sets the scene for this most famous of the garden villages built by 19th-c philanthropists, contriving something better than the appalling squalor of northern England's factory towns. Historically important as the precursor of garden cities, garden suburbs and New Towns, it's perfectly preserved, with groups of mock-Tudor cottages, swathes of greenery and parkland: no two groups of houses are alike. Useful village trail leaflets; also period soap packaging (you can buy soap in replica wrappings). Shop, good disabled access; cl Christmas and New Year; (0151) 644 6466; 60p. Nearby Thornton Hough was also built by Lord Leverhulme, as a mock-Tudor estate village – Port Sunlight on a much smaller scale; the Seven Stars there is useful for lunch.

POULTON LE FYLDE SD3439
Quite an attractive pedestrianised market square, with a lovely church (as others in Lancashire, looking a good deal older than in fact it is), and several useful places to eat – the Old Town Hall is particularly good value.

PRESCOT SJ4793
Knowsley Safari Park Five-mile drive through very natural-looking reserves of lions, tigers, rhinos, monkeys and other animals; they have the biggest herd of African elephants in Europe.

New animals this year include giraffes and meerkats, and they've also added a roller-coaster and a pirate ship ride; also pets' corner and miniature railway. Meals, snacks, shop, disabled access; cl wkdys Nov–Feb; (0151) 430 9009; £7 (£5 children). If you have to pass through the town, the **museum** (Church St) has an interesting collection relating to the area's former clock-making industry; cl 1–2, Sun am, Mon (exc bank hols), Tues, Good Fri, 25–26 Dec, 1 Jan; (0151) 430 7787; free. The Clock Face is a pleasant old mansion-house pub here.

PRESTON SD5329

The town has two decent museums: the impressive if rather dour Greek revival **Harris Museum and Art Gallery** on Market Sq (cl Sun and bank hols; free), and the **Museum of Lancashire** on Stanley St (cl Sun and bank hols; £2). There's a good big market (the space is used for car-boot sales instead on Tues and Thurs); Wall Street (Fishergate) has decent food. **Moor Park Observatory** is open most Thurs evenings (exc the second of the month) Sept–Mar (not Dec); (01772) 257181 to check this.

Church of St Mary (Penwortham) 14th-c chancel, and the scant remains of a motte and bailey castle in the churchyard; nearby the Fleece (Liverpool Rd) is useful for lunch.

Ribble Steam Railway (The Docks) Due to open at Easter: around 30 steam, diesel and electric locomotives have been moved from the former Southport Railway Centre, and will either be displayed in a purpose-built museum here or used to pull passengers 1½ miles along the harbourside. Snacks, shop, disabled access; should open most wknds and bank hols (and for special events at other times), but best to check times and prices nearer the time; (0151) 531 9345.

RAMSBOTTOM SD8017

Lovely village with a Saturday market, overlooked by Holcombe Hill and crossed by the River Irwell. Down by the Twine Valley trout lakes, the Fisherman's Retreat has interesting food.

RIBCHESTER SD6535

Attractive little town, many of its buildings incorporating masonry plundered from the former Roman town here: the White Bull pub, with decent food, has a couple of Tuscan pillars for its porch and an excavated Roman bath house behind. The 15th-c **church** stands on the site of the Roman fort, and looks as if it uses much salvaged material from it.

Ribchester Roman Museum 🅰 On the site of a fort occupied between the 1st and 4th c, with lots of coins, pottery and the famous Ribchester helmet. Shop, disabled access; cl 25 Dec; (01254) 878261; £1.50.

Stydd Nursery (Stoneygate Lane) There are excavated Roman granaries behind this nursery specialising in old-fashioned roses and hardy perennials; some disabled access; open pm Tues–Fri, best to check; (01254) 878797; free.

RINGLEY SD7605

Unexpected corner so close to urban areas – village stocks and ancient bridge over the Irwell (and a decent pub).

RIVINGTON RESERVOIRS SD6215

These attractive waters just outside Horwich make good walking territory. Lower Rivington Reservoir has a waterside path along its eastern edge, and a curious mock-up of Liverpool castle built in 1912 as an adornment to the vast and atmospherically decayed gardens of Lever Park, which cover the hillside. A trail guides you around the undergrowth and up to the Pigeon Tower, within a few minutes of Rivington Pike, the summit. The Great House Barn is the place to start, with a good information centre, maps and guides.

RODDLESWORTH VALLEY SD6622

Good woodland walks from the Royal Arms at Tockholes, and maybe on to the ruins of Hollinshead Hall and its restored curative well.

RUFFORD SD4616

Rufford Old Hall 🅰 Lovely timber-framed Tudor house built by the Hesketh family in the 16th c, with an intricate hammer-beam roof in the Great Hall, and impressive collections of 17th-c Lancashire oak furniture, and

16th-c arms, armour and tapestries. Some later rooms too; audio tour. Meals, snacks, shop, limited disabled access (no facilities); cl am, all day Thurs and Fri, and Nov–Mar; (01704) 821254; £3.80, £2 garden only; NT. The Robin Hood just the other side of Mawdesley has good home cooking.

SABDEN SD7737
Attractive village, with a decent antiques centre, on the slopes of Pendle Hill; linked by a scenic drive to another charming Pendle Hill village, Pendleton, where the Swan With Two Necks is a handy stop.

SALFORD SJ8198
Merging almost imperceptibly into Manchester, this owes its distinct place in the popular consciousness mainly to the works of L S Lowry. A giant arts centre dedicated to the artist opened on the quayside last year (see below). The waterside Mark Addy (Stanley St) has a great choice of cheeses and pâtés.
Ordsall Hall Museum (Ordsall Lane) Timbered Tudor manor house with local history and Victorian farmhouse kitchen. Shop, some disabled access; cl 12.30–1.30pm, Sun am, Sat, Good Fri, 25–26 Dec, 1 Jan; (0161) 872 0251; free.
Salford Museum & Art Gallery (Peel Park) The fine showing of L S Lowry paintings formerly housed here has been moved to The Lowry (below), but it's still worth a visit for its nostalgic reconstructed industrial street scene, with some wonderfully over the top period advertisements. Snacks, shop, disabled access; cl 25–26 Dec, 1 Jan, Good Fri; free.
The Lowry (Salford Quays) This £96m waterfront complex includes two theatres, Artworks (a creative interactive gallery), other galleries presenting changing exhibitions, and of course the world's largest collection of works by the eponymous artist, plus a new footbridge and public plaza with bars and restaurants. Meals, snacks, shop, disabled access; cl 25 Dec; box office (0161) 876 2000; centre free, Artworks £3.75.

SAMLESBURY SD6130
Samlesbury Hall 🏚 Well restored half-timbered 14th-c manor house, with good changing exhibitions and craft demonstrations, and sales of antiques. Meals, snacks, disabled access to ground floor only; cl Mon exc bank hols, and mid-Dec–mid-Jan; (01254) 812010; £2.50. The Myerscough Hotel (A59) is good for lunch.

SILVERDALE SD4875
A little-visited peaceful oasis, up beyond the attractive town of Lancaster: hilly countryside well suited both to walkers and to drivers, and a coastline that's particularly interesting to bird-watchers and naturalists. The small town looks out over the tidal sands to the Cumbrian hills, with streets of quiet houses and a church that looks 14th-c but was built barely a century ago. Various crafts are sold at the Georgian buildings of the **Wolf House Gallery** (Gibraltar), which also has an adventure playground and a courtyard garden; snacks, some disabled access (with notice); cl Sun and Mon Apr–Dec, and all wkdys Jan–Mar; (01524) 701405; free. There are good woodland walks behind the town, readers recommend the Waterslack tearooms (past the railway station), and the Silverdale Hotel on Shore Rd is worth knowing.
Leighton Moss Nature Reserve (off Yealand Redmayne Rd) RSPB reserve with several roomy hides looking out on to reedbeds where bitterns, bearded tits and marsh harriers breed; good walks and views. Guided wildlife outings on Thurs evenings in Aug; the visitor centre is currently being refurbished. Meals, snacks, shop, disabled access; cl 25 Dec; (01524) 701601; £4 (RSPB members free). The Moss is also crossed by a (free) public footpath.
Yealand Conyers Friends' Meeting House Unobtrusively charming, in a quiet and pleasant village; the New Inn here is a popular dining pub.

SKIPPOOL SD3540
Lots of yachting activity in an attractive boating area, with a decent small café.

SLAIDBURN SD7152
A perfectly preserved Forest of Bowland village: charming stone cottages, a green with the River Hodder running by, and at the opposite end an early 18th-c schoolhouse and a church with a very 18th-c feel inside. The Hark to Bounty (named after a former squire's dog) is good for lunch

and has comfortable bedrooms. The B6478, and the narrow road N past Stocks Reservoir, have appealing views.

SOUTHPORT SD3217
Smartish Victorian seaside resort, long famed as the most pleasant shopping town in the area, and as the place where the sea doesn't come in. In fact it comes in as often as anywhere else, but doesn't stay quite as long; this could be due to the famously mucky beach – though quite an effort has been made to improve the area around the sea-wall, inc laying new walkways for visitors; for cleaner shores try slightly S at Formby. The promenade is set back quite a way from the sea, and looks over a man-made lake with boats. The Royal Clifton Hotel here is a decent place to eat, and there are plenty of good summer activities inc pleasure flights over the sands; the pier is currently being restored. Lord St is the elegant main shopping street; there's an excellent antiquarian bookshop down the Wayfarers Arcade just off it.
Pleasureland is a typical fairground, its wooden roller-coaster and gut-wrenching Traumatiser ride well regarded by connoisseurs (£13.99 wristband for all rides).
Atkinson Art Gallery (Lord St) Specialises in 19th- and 20th-c watercolours, oil paintings, prints and sculpture. Snacks, shop, disabled access; cl Thurs and Sat pm, all Sun and bank hols; (01704) 533133; free.
British Lawnmower Museum 🖾 (Shakespeare St) Over 200 fully restored and often bizarre machines from the 1830s to the present, inc one of the first racing lawnmowers – the curator used to be a champion. Shop; cl Sun and bank hols; (01704) 535369; *£1.
Churchtown Southport's villagey oldest part, with a number of pretty thatched cottages, and the lakeside **botanic gardens**, which are very attractive as well as being interesting to plantsmen; boats to hire, fernery, pets' corner, and local history MUSEUM (open 11am–3pm Tues-Fri and wknd and bank hol pms; free). Just opposite, **Meols Hall** is worth a look for its paintings, inc works by Ramsey, Reynolds, Romney and Poussin. Disabled access; open pm

mid-Aug to mid-Sept; (01704) 28326; £3. The Hesketh Arms across from the main gate is good for lunch.
Southport Zoo (Princes Park) Has one of the few snow leopards to be bred in captivity in the West, a tropical wader aviary, and a small endangered cat enclosure. Snacks, shop, some disabled access; cl 25 Dec; £3.80.

SPEKE SJ4282
Speke Hall Built around a square courtyard, this is one of the most beautiful and richly timbered black and white houses in the country; the inside is mainly Victorian, though there's a vast Tudor Great Hall. Restored Victorian garden. Hard to believe the centre of Liverpool is just six miles away. Meals, snacks, shop, disabled access; house open pm exc Mon Apr–Oct, plus wknds Nov–mid-Dec, garden open pm exc Mon all year; (0151) 427 7231; £4.20, £1.60 grounds only; NT.

ST HELENS SJ5195
World of Glass (Chalon Way E) Like the National Glass Centre in Sunderland before it, this £14m new attraction hopes to bring some sheen to the world of glass, through a wide range of informative and entertaining displays. The stylish modern building is fronted by a reconstructed traditional conical glasshouse, and includes several themed areas. Children are bound to enjoy the hands-on displays and crazy mirror maze in Glass Magic, while the Glass Revolution show takes a lively look at the importance of glass today. Earth Into Light includes a re-created glassmaker's parlour, and the evolution of glass from ancient times to the present day is studied in Glass Roots. An unexpected highlight is the labyrinth of tunnels to explore beneath a Victorian furnace. Naturally, there are plenty of activities and demonstrations inc glass-blowers in action. Meals, snacks, shop, disabled access; cl 25–26 Dec, 1 Jan; (08707) 444777; £5. The Carr Mill (E Lancs Rd) is a good value family dining pub.

STANAH SD3542
Out on the Wyre estuary, this has a stretch of waterside country with reedbeds, birds and views, attractive despite the chemical works in the

background. On the opposite bank, over the toll bridge past Poulton, the Shard Bridge Inn at Hambleton is nicely placed for lunch.

STOCKPORT SJ8990

Hat Works (Wellington Mill, Wellington Rd S) Fun new look at the town's hat-making heritage, with lots of millinery exhibits from early 19th-c fur hats to fully restored machines. A resident milliner and textile designer are on hand to answer any questions (you can watch them at work, too), and there's quite a lot aimed at children, inc story-telling in a mock-up of a felt tent (recalling the town's trading links with central Asia), and the chance to dress up as a hatter's apprentice. Meals, snacks, shop, disabled access; cl 25–26 Dec; (0161) 355 7770; *£3.95.

Stockport Air Raid Shelters (Chestergate) Displays include a reconstructed canteen, tool stores and first aid post, re-creating a wartime atmosphere in this labyrinth of tunnels designed to protect thousands of people during World War II; guided tours around the more remote tunnels first Weds of month at 7pm (50p extra). Shop, disabled access; cl Sun am, 25–26 Dec and 1 Jan; (0161) 474 1940; £3.25. The Arden Arms (Millgate St) has good value food – and a great collection of working grandfather clocks.

SUNDERLAND POINT SD4255

This unique hamlet is cut off by the tide twice a day; the local legend of Sambo the slave recalls how he was brought to the point by his master who then went away for such a length of time that Sambo died of a broken heart. He died at Upsteps cottage, and a short path leads to his grave on the other side of the peninsula, which has become a shrine where children leave painted stones to mark his memory. The route passes a cottage which sells a publication about the area. The Globe at Overton is handy for a family lunch.

THORNTON-CLEVELEYS SD3342

Marsh windmill 🖾 (B5412) One of the largest in Europe, this working windmill has tours to the top, demonstrations, a good range of craft shops alongside, and wknd entertainment in summer. Snacks,

shop, disabled access to ground floor; cl 25–26 Dec; (01253) 860765; £1.25.

TURTON BOTTOMS SD7315

Turton Tower 15th-c Renaissance house with Elizabethan buildings and earlier peel tower; mostly a museum inside, but there are a couple of period rooms, and a major collection of carved wood furniture. It was interestingly extended by followers of the Romantic and later Arts and Crafts movements in the 19th c. Victorian woodland gardens. Tearoom, shop; open daily (exc Fri) May–Sept (cl 12–1pm for lunch, and am wknds), pm Sat–Weds in Mar, Apr and Oct, and just pm Sun Nov and Feb; (01204) 852203; £3. The Strawbury Duck just N at Entwistle is prettily placed for lunch.

UPPERMILL SD9905

This whole area of mill settlements in steep valleys cut through the moors is full of interest, and Uppermill itself is one of the most attractive places. Up above the town is a lonely moorland church, with good walks around it and an ancient pub opposite. Fine drives around here include the A635 over Saddleworth Moor, and B6197 Delph–Grains Bar then A672 or A640 over the moors.

Saddleworth Museum & Art Gallery (High St) Based around an old mill, and volunteers occasionally dress up in appropriate garb. Shop, limited disabled access, cl 24–25 Dec and 1 Jan; (01457) 874093; £1.25.

WADDINGTON SD7243

Forest of Bowland village, with a fine **church**, and a lovely drive from Longridge. The Waddington Arms has imaginative fresh food.

WHALLEY SD7336

Whalley Abbey Striking remains of 14th-c Cistercian abbey – the monks' quarters, rather than the church which has virtually disappeared – in grounds of 16th-c manor house used as a religious retreat (they do B&B). Two gatehouses are intact, and there's a visitor centre. Good snacks, shop, disabled access; cl 22 Dec–6 Jan; (01254) 822268; £1.50. The separate 13th-c parish **church** has interesting woodwork and three ancient Celtic-Scandinavian crosses. The Freemasons Arms at Wiswell does good food.

WIGAN SD5908
Haigh Hall Country Park (N of Wigan) 250-acre country park with guided walks, nature trails, beautifully set golf course, craft centre, walled gardens, play area, crazy golf and miniature railway. Occasional tours of house – phone for dates, and a good programme of events. Meals, snacks, shops (one excellent for golfers), some disabled access; cl 25–26 Dec; (01942) 832985; park free, charges for parking and attractions.

Wigan Pier 🖭 (Wallgate) Rather different from when Orwell knew it, this is now a dynamic and entertaining wharfside centre demonstrating local life in the early 1900s, with actors performing in a reconstructed mine, pub, school, music hall, houses and even seaside. An ingenious mix of museum and theatre, it's an enormously enjoyable family day out, and you really do get a tangible impression of what life was really like at the turn of the century. A new exhibition takes a nostalgic look at each decade of the 20th c. Meals, snacks, shop, disabled access; cl Fri (exc Good Fri), and 25–26 Dec; (01942) 323666; £6.95.

WIRRAL SJ2484
Its Merseyside parts aren't on the whole that appealing to visitors, especially on the built-up E side (with the notable exception of Port Sunlight). The NW corner can be rather more attractive, particularly along the edges of the Dee, looking across to the mountains of N Wales. The more interesting bits, inc unusual National Trust heathland, are linked by a 12-mile footpath, best joined at the **Wirral Country Park** at Thurstaston, and running down to the Cheshire parts of the Wirral. The Irby Mill at nearby Irby has decent food.

WRAY SD6067
Charming small backwater with venerable cottages; the welcoming George & Dragon, with an attractive garden, has decent food. From here a spectacular drive over Tatham Fells leads to Slaidburn

WYCOLLER COUNTRY PARK SD9339
Lancashire Brontë country (the ruined hall at Wycoller may have been the base for Ferndean Manor in *Jane Eyre*), with walks along a beck to Clam Bridge, an Iron Age slab, and up to Foster's Leap, a finely placed crag.

Other attractive villages, all with decent pubs and great surrounding scenery, include Goosnargh SD5537, Hurst Green SD6838, Tunstall SD6173 (Brontë church) and Wiswell SD7437. Particularly pretty ones in or on the edges of the Forest of Bowland are Gisburn SD8248, Grindleton SD7545 and Newton SD6950.

Pubs well placed for walks include the Hare & Hounds at Abbey Village SD6422, Pack Horse at Affetside SD7513, Bay Horse at Arkholme SD5872, Black Dog at Belmont SD6716, Dog at Belthorn SD7224, White House on Blackstone Edge SD9716, Owd Betts at Cheesden on Ashworth Moor SD8316, Edisford Bridge on the B6243 W of Clitheroe SD7241, Rams Head nr Denshaw SD9710, Diggle Hotel at Diglea Hamlet above Diggle itself SE0008, Wright Arms at Egerton SD7114, Strawbury Duck by Entwistle Station SD7217, Bulls Head on Grains Bar SD9608, Duke of Wellington on the B6232 W of Haslingden SD7522, Egerton Arms off the narrow Ashworth Rd above Heywood SD8513, Green Man at Inglewhite (nr Beacon Fell) SD5440, New Drop on Longridge Fell SD6439, Romper at Ridge End above Marple SJ9686, Kettledrum at Mereclough SD8632, Highwayman at Nether Burrow SD6275 (pretty stretch of the Lune Valley), Old Rosins at Pickup Bank, Old Hoddlesden SD6922, Roebuck on Roebuck Low SD9606 and Railway at White Coppice SD6118. Up on the moors, many of these are closed during lunchtime Mon–Thurs.

Please let us know what you think of places in the *Guide*. Use the report forms at the back of the book or simply write us a letter.

Where to eat

BISPHAM GREEN SD4813 **Eagle & Child** *Maltkiln Lane (01257) 462297* Striking 3-storey dark brick pub with civilised, mainly open-plan bar, fine old stone fireplaces, oriental rugs and some coir on the flagstones, handsome oak settles, imaginative food, well kept real ales, and friendly service; bowling green and croquet behind; open all day Sun; disabled access. £23|£6

BLACKO SD8542 **Moorcock** *Gisburn Rd (01282) 614186* Isolated old stone inn with wonderful views from big picture windows in the spaciously comfortable lounge bar, tasty generous food (inc some Austrian specialities), efficient friendly service; disabled access. £16|£5.50

BLACKPOOL SD3036 **September Brasserie** *15–17 Queen St (01253) 623282* Not far from the seafront and set above a hairdresser's, this busy little airy restaurant's open-view kitchen does particularly good inventive food from a short menu with ideas from all over the world (inc lovely puddings), and a thoughtful wine list; cl Sun, Mon, 2 wks summer, 2 wks winter. £27|£6.50

CHIPPING SD6241 **Dog & Partridge** *Hesketh Lane (01995) 61201* Spotlessly kept and relaxed dining pub with comfortable main lounge, winter log fire, good choice of enjoyable food (inc fine home-made chips), real ales, and quite a few wines and malt whiskies. £22/3-course lunch £12.50

DOWNHAM SD7844 **Assheton Arms** *(01200) 441227* Charmingly set dining pub in prettily preserved village, with rambling beamed bar, a massive stone fireplace, no smoking area, popular bar food (lots of good fresh fish dishes), well kept real ales, and decent wines; disabled access. £20|£5.95

FENCE SD8337 **Forest** *Cuckstool Lane (01282) 613641* Comfortable pub with heavy panelling, lots of paintings, vases, plates, books and a big open fire, no smoking restaurant, varied inventive food, decent choice of wines, and friendly helpful service; disabled access. £22|£4.65

GOOSNARGH SD5536 **Bushells Arms** *Church Lane (01772) 865235* Friendly modernised pub close to Chingle Hall, with excellent range of imaginative food from a constantly changing menu, and a range of wines; cl Mon; no children; partial disabled access. £15|£6

KIRKHAM SD4232 **Cromwellian** *16 Poulton St (01772) 685680* Tiny evening restaurant in 17th-c house with consistently good interesting food from a fixed-price menu – thoughtful wine list, too; cl Sun, Mon, Easter, 2 wks Oct. £25.80

LIVERPOOL SJ3589 **Becher's Brook** *29a Hope St (0151) 707 0006* Popular Georgian restaurant, close to theatres, with downstairs bar, restaurant decorated with Canadian ethnic art, good interesting modern cooking (pre-theatre suppers also), a carefully chosen wine list, and friendly staff; cl Sat am, Sun, Christmas, New Year, bank hols; children before 6.30pm; disabled access. £35

LONGRIDGE SD6137 **Paul Heathcotes** *104 Higher Rd (01772) 784969* Pretty restaurant with flowers, beams and candlelit tables in little interconnected rooms, exceptional modern British cooking, marvellous puddings, and exemplary service; cl Mon, Tues, cl Sat am. £52 dinner, £23.50 lunch

MANCHESTER SJ8498 **Little Yang Sing** *17 George St (0161) 228 7722* Very busy and popular basement restaurant with super Chinese food inc a children's fixed menu, decent wines, and friendly service; cl 25 Dec; disabled access. £29

MANCHESTER SJ8398 **Mark Addy** *Stanley St (0161) 832 4080* Smart pub in converted boat waiting rooms with a good range of food – though its choice of 50 different cheeses is the main feature; extremely big helpings, doggy-bags provided; bread and cheese|£3.50

MANCHESTER SJ8497 **Mash** *40 Chorlton St (0161) 661 6161/1111* In a converted canalside mill, this bustling place has a microbrewery with three real ales to sample, an informal friendly atmosphere, and 'smart' pizzas from wood-fired ovens, grilled sandwiches, salads and so forth; cl 25–26 Dec; disabled access. £28.50

MANCHESTER SJ8491 **Royal Oak** *729 Wilmslow Rd (0161) 445 3152* Busy pub with exceptional choice of cheeses from around the world – rare to be given less than a pound; bread, cheese or pâté and salad (not wknds); no children.|**£3.50**

MANCHESTER SJ8398 **Simply Heathcotes** *Jackson Row, Deansgate (0161) 835 3536* Stylish modern restaurant with high ceilings, polished wood floors, bright paintings on coloured walls, and contemporary furniture, up-to-the-minute brasserie-style cooking inc very good value set lunches, thoughtful wine list, and efficient service; cl bank hols; disabled access. *£22.50*

MANCHESTER SJ8497 **Yang Sing** *34 Princess St (0161) 236 2200* Exceptionally good Chinese food using the best fresh ingredients (tanks of live fish, too), wonderful dim-sum, some unusual dishes among traditional Cantonese specialities, good value set meals, a bustling atmosphere, and efficient service; must book ahead; cl 25 Dec; disabled access. *£22|£8.20*

MELLOR SJ9888 **Oddfellows Arms** *73 Moor End Rd (0161) 449 7826* Fine old building with low ceilings, open fires and a chatty atmosphere in two flagstoned rooms, no smoking restaurant, and a wide range of interesting food inc lots of different types of fresh fish; cl 4 days over Christmas; children must be well behaved; disabled access. *£21|£6.25*

SAWLEY SD7746 **Spread Eagle** *(01220) 441202* Attractive 16th-c hotel with fine views over the River Ribble and valley from big picture windows, a bustling bar, thoughtful wine list, and particularly good interesting modern food in comfortable dining area; Sun pm, Mon, 3 wks Nov; partial disabled access. *£27*

ST MICHAEL'S ON WYRE SD4641 **Mallards** *Garstang Rd (01995) 679661* Well run and busy little restaurant in former village smithy with reliably good straightforward food, good value wines, and helpful service; cl lunchtimes except Sun, cl 1 wk Jan, July, Oct; disabled access. *£24.50*

THORNTON-CLEVELEYS SD3541 **River House** *Wyre Rd, Skippool Creek (01253) 883497* Delightful restaurant with long-serving owners, very good honest cooking using the freshest local ingredients, a decent wine list, fresh flowers and log fires, and fine views; bdrms; cl Sun, 2 wks Aug; children must be well behaved. *£38*

WHALLEY SD7335 **Toby Jug Tea Shop** *20 King St (01254) 823298* 300-year-old listed building with oak beams, old stone fireplaces, and wooden panelling on the upstairs walls, afternoon tea with cream and scones, cakes and cucumber sandwiches (all home-made), lots of teas and coffees, and light lunches with a fine choice of filled sandwiches and rolls; cl Sun, Mon, Christmas; children over 6.|**£4**

YEALAND CONYERS SD5074 **New Inn** *(01524) 732938* Ivy-covered stone dining pub with log fire in little beamed bar, two communicating cottage dining rooms, novel daily specials, fine salads served with meals, friendly professional service, decent wines, well kept ales, and a sheltered side lawn. *£16.85|£6.50*

Special thanks to Arthur and Margaret Dickinson, Miss J Scholes, Mrs Edna M Jones, Mrs M Sharp, Mr and Mrs J Fawcett, Mr and Mrs J Back

LEICESTERSHIRE AND RUTLAND

Sweeping country views, stately houses and castles, some surprising attractions – and not too many tourists

From spring, Leicester will be home to the National Space Science Centre, likely to be one of the Millennium Commission's more successful projects. Elsewhere, family highlights include scientific fun at Snibston Discovery Park (Coalville), the range of primates at Twycross Zoo, the friendly farm parks at Oadby and Tilton on the Hill, and the excellent motorcycle museum and charming 17th-c hall at Swinford; there's a smaller collection of vintage cars at newcomer Stonehurst Family Farm (Mountsorrel).

Some unusual visits here include the Loughborough bell foundry, Leicester's quirky Abbey Pumping Station, and the restored Moira Furnace (with new woodland walks and an improved children's play area); there are more new walks and landscaped trails down the road at the Heart of National Forest Visitor Centre.

The sweeping countryside particularly suits scenic drives or cycle rides, especially in the east: graceful patches of woodland, plenty of charming stone-built villages to potter through, delightful churches. Many of the less busy roads stride along old coach routes, with broad views. There are quite a few good walks, too – and you get out into unspoilt countryside very quickly from the built-up areas.

Rutland Water has the look of a huge natural lake, pleasant to walk around, with quite a lot of varied things to see and do around it.

Leicester is good for day visits, with lots to see from Hindu temples to Roman remains. It sets a splendid example, with its free museums policy.

Where to stay

EMPINGHAM SK9408 **White Horse** *Main St, Empingham, Oakham, Rutland LE15 8PR (01780) 460221* **£63***, plus special breaks; 13 pretty rms, some in a delightfully converted stable block. Attractive, bustling old inn, handy for Rutland Water; a relaxed and comfortable atmosphere, a big log fire and fresh flowers in open-plan lounge, big helpings of excellent food inc fine breakfasts, coffee and croissants from 8am, and cream teas all year; attractive no smoking restaurant, well kept real ales, and efficient friendly service; cots/high chairs; good disabled access

GLOOSTON SP7394 **Old Barn** *Main St, Glooston, Market Harborough, Leicestershire LE16 7ST (01858) 545215* **£49.50**; 2 rms. Attractively restored 16th-c pub with civilised décor and open fire in beamed main bar, charming little restaurant, super inventive food (some produce from their kitchen garden), good breakfasts, and decent real ales; pleasant walks nearby; cl am winter Mon; well behaved dogs allowed

HAMBLETON SK9107 **Hambleton Hall** *Hambleton, Oakham, Rutland LE15 8TH (01572) 756991* **£195**; 17 quiet, spacious rms, inc a separate new house with 2 bdrms, drawing room, breakfast room and own terrace. In attractive grounds by Rutland Water, this complex around a grandly restored Victorian manor house has fine views, elegant day rooms, antiques, open fires, exceptional flower arrangements, and pleasant helpful staff; no smoking restaurant in separate big modern building (which also houses the swimming pool and friendly bar), enjoyable food, stimulating wine list, and a pampering atmosphere; tennis, golf, and a huge play area; no babies in restaurant (except for breakfast); disabled access ☺

MARKET HARBOROUGH SP7387 **Three Swans** *21 High St, Market Harborough, Leicestershire LE16 7NJ* (01858) 466644 **£88**, plus special breaks; 60 rms. Fine old coaching inn, extended this year, with plush lounge bar, attractive conservatory and glorious courtyard, very friendly helpful staff, and good food; cl 1–3 Jan; disabled access

MEDBOURNE SP7992 **Nevill Arms** *Waterfall Way, Medbourne, Market Harborough, Leicestershire LE16 8EE* (01858) 565288 wkdys **£55**; 8 rms, 6 in separate cottage and barn conversion. Bright and busy old mullion-windowed inn just across footbridge over stream, with excellent food, lots of bar games, friendly prompt service, and an inglenook log fire; cl 25 Dec; disabled access

OAKHAM SK8608 **Whipper-In** *Market Pl, Oakham, Rutland LE15 6DT* (01572) 756971 **£75***, plus special breaks; 24 rms. Attractive and well run 17th-c stone coaching inn with oak-beamed and panelled lounge opening into cosy eating area, log fires, good food in restaurant, and well kept ales; disabled access

PACKINGTON SK3514 **Springs Hydro** *Measham Rd, Packington, Ashby-de-la-Zouch, Leicestershire NE65 1TJ* (01530) 273873 **£170** inc full use of all facilities, plus special breaks; 57 rms. Britain's first purpose-built health hydro with all the amenities, good healthy food, and friendly staff; cl 20–26 Dec; no children; disabled access

ROTHLEY SK5712 **Rothley Court** *Westfield Lane, Rothley, Leicester LE7 7LG* (0116) 237 4141 **£95**; 32 rms (the ones in the main house have more character). Mentioned in the Domesday Book, this carefully run manor house with its beautifully preserved 13th-c chapel has some fine oak panelling, open fires, a comfortable bar, conservatory, and courteous staff; seats out on the terrace and in the garden; disabled access

SAXELBYE SK7020 **Saxelbye Manor House** *Church Lane, Saxelbye, Melton Mowbray, Leicestershire LE14 3PA* (01664) 812269 **£45***; 2 rms. Attractive old house (parts are several hundred years old) with marvellous Victoriana, a long passage leading to a fine Elizabethan oak stairway built in the old stone stairwell, helpful friendly owner, and very good traditional evening meals and breakfasts; cl Dec–Mar

STAPLEFORD SK8118 **Stapleford Park** *Stapleford, Melton Mowbray, Leicestershire LE14 2EF* (01572) 787522 **£235**; 51 lavishly decorated rms, plus cottage. Luxurious country house, extravagantly restored, in lovely large grounds with riding and stabling, tennis, croquet, miniature golf, coarse fishing, and clay-pigeon shooting; lots of mahogany, opulent furnishings, fine oil paintings and an impressive library, delicious restaurant food, enthusiastic American owner, and warmly welcoming staff; health spa and indoor swimming pool; cots/babysitting; dogs welcome; disabled access

STRETTON SK9415 **Ram Jam Inn** *Great North Rd, Stretton, Oakham, Rutland LE15 7QX* (01780) 410776 **£68***; 7 comfortable and well equipped rms. Actually on the A1, this civilised place has a comfortable airily modern lounge bar blending into a newly refurbished restaurant, good interesting food quickly served all day, and useful small wine list; large garden and orchard; cl 25 Dec, 1 Jan

UPPINGHAM SP8699 **Lake Isle** *16 High St East, Uppingham, Oakham, Rutland LE15 9PZ* (01572) 822951 **£74***, plus special breaks; 12 rms with home-made biscuits, sherry and fresh fruit, and two cottage suites. In a charming market town, this 18th-c restaurant-with-rooms has an open fire in the attractive pink-walled lounge, a little bar (once a barber's where the schoolboys had their hair cut), excellent imaginative food in the pine-walled country restaurant (delicious breakfasts, too), a fine carefully chosen wine list, and a small and pretty garden

---

Please let us know what you think of places in the *Guide*. Use the report forms at the back of the book or simply write us a letter.

To see and do

Leicestershire & Rutland Family Attraction of the Year

COALVILLE SK4114 **Snibston Discovery Park** 🔲 (Ashby Rd) Other science centres may have overtaken Snibston in the hi-tech stakes in recent years, but for fun and entertainment value this busy 100-acre site still scores highly, and certainly in Leicestershire it's one of the stand-out places to visit. Based around a former colliery (the first shaft was sunk by George and Robert Stephenson), its exhibitions and displays cover a hugely varied range of topics connected to science and industry. Each section has hands-on or working exhibits; children like the Science Alive gallery best, with plenty of experiments and activities designed to make waves or create electricity – there's even the illusion of cycling with a skeleton. Other highlights for younger visitors include the tornado chamber, where you can manipulate the fog that spins up from a hole in the floor, and the Wild Water gallery, featuring experiments with dams and water wheels. Other sections are based around light, transport, mining, and (more incongruously) fashion. For an extra charge (£1), there's an incredible virtual reality gallery: you find yourselves in the middle of an exploding oil rig and have to make a dash for the helicopter pad. Some displays have a local bias, but effectively bring the subject to a more personal and easily understandable level – like finding out whether your feet are bigger than average, or tugging the pulleys in the engineering gallery. Outside the modern building, the landscaped grounds include a huge play area, nature reserve, sculpture trail, and picnic areas, with extra charges for fishing, and the evocative tours of the mine workings by former pitmen (£1). Very young children may not get as much out of it as slightly older ones, and there's no denying that not all sections have the same instant appeal, but there's enough to keep most age groups busy and intrigued for a good chunk of the day. Meals, snacks, shop, disabled access; cl 25–26 Dec and usually a week in Jan; (01530) 510851; £4.75 (£2.95 children). The family ticket, covering two adults and three children, is very good value at £13.50.

ARNESBY SP6192
Arnesby windmill Handsomely preserved, well worth a look.

ASHBY CANAL SK3707
The towpath has good countryside walking, with green fields and stone-arched bridges, as well as coots, moorhens, herons and maybe even the flash of a kingfisher. The best parts run from the tunnel under Snarestone past Gopsall Park, and then on through Shackerstone and Congerstone to pass Shenton Park on an embankment, before heading into Warwickshire and its junction with the Coventry Canal. It also makes an ideal walking link between Bosworth battlefield and the steam railway to the N.

ASHBY-DE-LA-ZOUCH SK3516
Ashby-de-la-Zouch Castle The Norman core and its 15th-c extension were largely destroyed in the Civil War, but the ruins are impressive, and the adjoining fields were the setting for Sir Walter Scott's *Ivanhoe*. Bring a torch for the underground passage. Snacks, shop, limited disabled access; cl 24–26 Dec, 1 Jan, and Mon and Tues Nov–Mar; (01530) 413343; £2.60; EH. There's a little **museum** (open Easter–Oct) next to the Tourist Information Centre on North St, and the Royal Hotel has a good value carvery.

BELVOIR SK8133
Belvoir Castle Pronounced 'Beaver', this is best from the outside, a glorious fantasy of turrets and battlements, pinnacles and towers, surrounded by terraced gardens peopled with sculptures. Inside, only a couple of rooms are grand enough to impress, and some of the contents are starting to look a little shabby. Meals, snacks, shop, limited disabled access – it's quite a walk up the hill; cl Mon (exc bank hols),

Fri, and Nov–Mar; (01476) 870262; £5.25. The Red House down at Knipton has interesting food. Good drives on fine old coach roads centre on Belvoir: for instance, from Long Benington (Lincs) through Bottesford, Harby and Hose, or via Knipton down through Eastwell and past Grimston all the way to Barrow upon Soar.

BOTTESFORD SK8139
Bottesford church Full of elaborate tombs and monuments; they had to raise the roof to fit them all in.

BREEDON ON THE HILL SK4023
Breedon on the Hill church On an interesting, partly quarried Iron Age hill fort, this has some unique Anglo-Saxon carvings.

BURROUGH ON THE HILL SK7510
Burrough Hill Has an enjoyable path along its escarpment. The summit has splendid views, and an imposing Iron Age hill fort, its high ramparts still largely intact (£1 parking charge). The Stag & Hounds has good value food.

CHARNWOOD FOREST SK4515
Charnwood Forest views The friendly Bulls Head (former B587 Whitwick–Copt Oak), with a big garden and lots of animals, has fine views over surviving remnants of this former hunting park, popular for walks; the Copt Oak pub itself, over on the B591, is also a useful base for walks.

CLIPSHAM SK9716
Yew Tree Avenue (just E, off Castle Bytham Rd) Delightfully quirky avenue of 150 yew trees, clipped in sometimes bizarre shapes to represent animals, characters and events; free. The surrounding woods are full of deer (not to mention bluebells in spring). The reopened Olive Branch has good home cooking.

COALVILLE SK4114
Snibston Discovery Park See *separate family panel on p.362.*

COTTESMORE SK8913
Rutland Railway Museum Nearly 40 industrial steam and diesel locomotives, and 60 other wagons and vehicles used in the ironstone quarries and industry. Occasional steam rides, and quite a nice lineside walk to the old Oakham Canal. Snacks, shop, disabled access; open wknds and bank hols – best to tel

(01572) 813203 for dates of steam days; free (£3 steam days). The Sun is good for lunch.

DESERT SK4704
Tropical Bird Gardens 🏛
(Lindridge Lane) This pleasant five-acre woodland garden has over 50 different species, many in walk-through aviaries; the free-flying macaws are particularly spectacular – they may even perch on your shoulder. Meals, snacks, shop, disabled access; cl mid-Oct to Apr; (01455) 824603; *£4.

DONINGTON LE HEATH SK4212
Donington le Heath Manor House Save for some slight 17th-c refurbishment, this medieval house has remained practically untouched since it was built in the 13th c. The developing 17th-c style gardens include a decorative maze. Meals, snacks, shop; disabled access to tearoom and ground floor only, cl 25 Dec–1 Jan; (01530) 831259; free.

DONINGTON PARK SK4225
Donington Collection 🏛 Largest private collection of single-seat racing cars in the world, with vehicles driven by all the greats, and related memorabilia. The price means you really have to be a racing fan to appreciate it. Meals, snacks, shop, some disabled access; cl 1 wk over Christmas; (01332) 811027; *£7. The Nags Head is a good dining pub.

EXTON SK9110
Barnsdale Gardens (The Avenue) Familiar to viewers of *Gardeners' World*; they were developed on the programme by the late Geoff Hamilton. The interesting plants are grown organically using peat-free compost, and there are plenty of useful ideas and techniques. Coffee shop, nursery, disabled access; gardens cl Nov–Feb (nursery cl 2 wks over Christmas only); (01572) 813200; *£5, ticket required for wknds and bank hols, best to phone. S of here towards the A606 the Barnsdale Lodge Hotel has good food, comfortable bedrooms and a neighbouring antiques centre. In the opposite direction, Exton village is a handsome collection of thatched houses around a tree-studded green, with pleasant walks around; the attractive **church** is beautifully placed

in a park, and the Fox & Hounds has decent home cooking.

Rutland Falconry & Owl Centre Small woodland centre with 30 or so falcons and owls. There are plans to add more enclosures, and they hope to offer snacks in the small shop soon; disabled access; (0378) 152814; £3.

EYEBROOK RESERVOIR SP8595 Rewarding for bird-watchers and fishermen, though as it has no hides or facilities appeals mainly to true enthusiasts.

FOXTON SP6989

Foxton Canal Museum Next to an interesting staircase flight of locks, and based around the extraordinary Victorian steam-powered boat lift built to avoid using the lock and so save water – now being restored, they hope to have it up and running by 2011. Meals, snacks, shop, some disabled access; usually cl Mon and Tues in winter; (0116) 279 2657; site free, museum £2. Bridge 61 at the bottom of the locks has basic food and welcomes children (lots of ducks – take plenty of bread). The locks are a good focus for Grand Union Canal towpath walks. The reservoir over at Saddington is a pretty spot, and the Queens Head there is a good dining pub.

GADDESBY SK6812

Gaddesby church Notable for its elaborate 13th-c workmanship.

HINCKLEY SP4594

Burbage Common & Woods (off A47 just E) Ancient forest with lots of footpaths (some accessible by wheelchair), observation hides, and spectacular ground flora. Visitor centre usually open Sun, pm only Sat, Tues and Thurs Apr–Nov, plus Mon and Fri pms Jun–Aug, but best to check; (01455) 633712; free.

KEGWORTH SK4826

Country drive The Cap & Stocking in Kegworth is an interesting old tavern, at the start of a pleasant drive through the Leakes, Wysall, Widmerpool, Kinoulton, Colston Bassett (just over the Notts border – the Martins Arms is the best lunch stop of all), Granby and Orston.

KIBWORTH HARCOURT SP6894

Kibworth Harcourt windmill The county's only remaining post mill, a fine example from the early 18th c. The Three Horseshoes is good for lunch. The old coach road through Kibworth from Uppingham and on to Kilby, Countesthorpe and Cosby is a fine long-striding drive.

KING'S NORTON SK6800

King's Norton church A graceful Gothic Revival building.

KIRBY MUXLOE SK5204

Kirby Muxloe Castle Peaceful 15th-c ruins, barely used by their original owner before he was executed. Shop, disabled access; open wknd and bank hols pm Apr–Nov; (0116) 238 6886; £1.95. The Royal Oak is useful for lunch.

LEICESTER SK5804

In this busy city's mix of ancient and modern, it's the modern which makes the most immediate impression. But a bit of digging around among the shops, office blocks and traffic schemes does turn up reminders of its long and varied past – most notable among some fine old buildings is the 14th-c Guildhall. In stark contrast, the strikingly modern National Space Science Centre will lend the city some space age glamour when it opens at Abbey Meadows in spring. The city's staunch defence of free entrance to museums etc, while places elsewhere are increasingly demanding a fee, is most attractive. Besides those described individually, good ones include **Newarke Houses** (The Newarke), where there's a quiet period garden, and the **Leicestershire Museum and Art Gallery** (New Walk), which has a collection of German Expressionist art that for this country must be unique, and a discovery room with interactive displays for children; both cl Sun am, plus wkdy ams (exc Sat) in winter, but may be reducing opening hours, so best to check; (0116) 2554100. The **Jain Centre** (Oxford St) has some fantastic examples of traditional Indian architecture (disabled access; open pm wkdys; (0116) 254 3091; donations suggested). The **Hindu temple** on Narborough Rd is reckoned to be one of the finest outside India. Towpath walks along both the Grand Union Canal and the River Soar give a relatively tranquil back view of the city's industrial life.

Abbey Pumping Station
(Corporation Rd) Now a museum of
public health with some bizarre displays
inc the Flush With Pride exhibition,
where you flush imitation faeces down a
see-through loo to follow their
movements through the drains. Shop,
disabled access (not to engine room); cl
wkdy and Sun ams, and 24 Dec–1 Jan;
(0116) 299 5111; free (*£3 when beam
engines in steam).

Belgrave Hall (Church Rd, Leicester's
N edge) A fine example of 18th-c
architecture, furnished with period
pieces; charming gardens. Shop,
disabled access to ground floor and
gardens; cl Sun am, 24–26 Dec, 1 Jan;
(0116) 266 6590; free.

Eco House (Western Park, Hinckley
Rd) This extended 1920s house is a
showcase for environmentally friendly
living, with interactive displays in every
room, and an organic garden. Snacks,
shop, disabled access; cl all Mon and
Tues, Weds–Fri am, and 25 Dec–1 Jan;
(0116) 254 5489; free (donations).

Gas Museum (Aylestone Rd)
Comprehensive study of the industry
and its application, from cookers and
washing machines to hairdryers and
magic lanterns. Disabled access to
ground floor only; open Tues–Thurs
pm (exc 24 Dec–1 Jan); (0116) 250
3190; free.

Gorse Hill City Farm (Anstey Lane)
Friendly little community farm with the
usual animals and activities, plus a new
education room, and developing
organic garden. Meals, snacks, disabled
access; (0116) 253 7582; donations.

Jewry Wall Museum and Site (St
Nicholas Circle) Site of 2nd-c Roman
baths, the courtyard now excavated to
reveal porticoes and shops sheltered by
the remains of a massive stone wall.
Excellent collections of mosaic
pavements and painted wall plaster.
Shop, disabled access with prior
arrangement; cl am (exc Sat), and over
Christmas break – best to check before
visiting; (0116) 2473021; free.

National Space Science Centre
(Exploration Drive, off Corporation
Rd) Opening in the spring, this
thoroughly futuristic place promises a
rewarding day out for families. Four

main galleries lead off from a central
'hub' (with restaurant and play areas),
each looking at different aspects of the
cosmos: Into Space presents the human
face of the space industry – from rocket
scientists to the astronauts themselves,
Our Neighbours studies our solar
system, Planet Earth examines the way
space technology affects everyday life,
and Space Now will give up-to-date
news on the latest developments in
space research, with unique views into
Leicester's very own space research
centre. One lively attraction re-creates
the sensation of blasting off, and
children are bound to enjoy making
their own rocket or presenting a
weather forecast. The centre will also
be home to Britain's newest and most
hi-tech planetarium. Among the extra-
terrestrial and rocket-related exhibits,
the most eye-catching of all will
doubtless be the 30-metre tall Thor
Able rocket (which carried the first
weather satellite into space), housed in
a stunning 41-metre three-storey glass
tower. Meals, snacks, shop, disabled
access. They hadn't confirmed their
opening times and prices as we went to
press, but suggested that adult
admission would be around £7 (£5
children); best to phone, (0116) 253
0811.

LOUGHBOROUGH SK5419
Bell Foundry Museum (Freehold St)
Part of the largest working bell foundry
in the world (bell-casting on Thurs),
with a quite remarkable array of bells in
the tuning room. Shop, disabled access;
cl 12.30–1.30pm, Mon (exc bank hols),
most wknds and winter exc by
arrangement, always best to check;
(01509) 233414; £1.50 (£3.80 for tour
of the works). The Swan in the Rushes
(A6) has good home cooking.

Great Central Railway (Great
Central Rd) Main line steam railway to
Leicester, with a museum and engine
sheds this end. Meals, snacks, shop,
disabled access; no trains wkdys
Oct–May (exc Easter hols) – best to
phone; (01509) 230726; £9.50, museum
only £3.

LYDDINGTON SP8796
Bede House This handsome 15th-c
house was a residence of the Bishops of
Lincoln until the Reformation. Notable

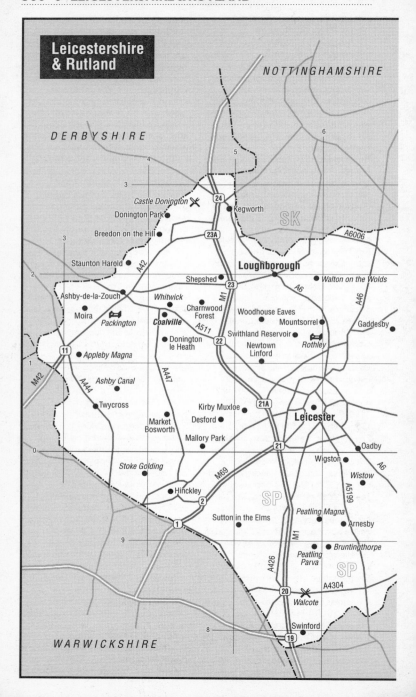

Leicestershire & Rutland

NOTTINGHAMSHIRE

DERBYSHIRE

SK

Castle Donington
Donington Park
Breedon on the Hill
Staunton Harold
Ashby-de-la-Zouch
Moira
Packington
Coalville
Donington le Heath
Appleby Magna
Ashby Canal
Twycross
Market Bosworth
Mallory Park
Stoke Golding
Hinckley
Sutton in the Elms

Kegworth
Shepshed
Loughborough
Whitwick
Charnwood Forest
Woodhouse Eaves
Swithland Reservoir
Newtown Linford
Rothley
Mountsorrel
Gaddesby
Walton on the Wolds

Kirby Muxloe
Desford
Leicester
Oadby
Wigston
Wistow
Peatling Magna
Arnesby
Bruntingthorpe
Peatling Parva
Walcote
Swinford

WARWICKSHIRE

A42, A444, M42, A511, A447, A446, A6, A46, A6006, M1, A426, A5199, M69, A4304

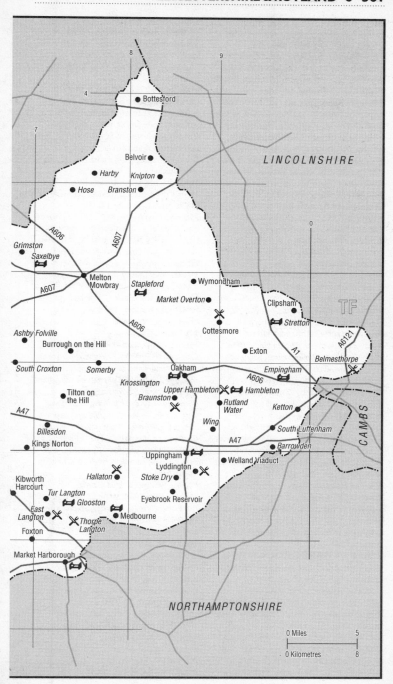

carved ceilings, 15th-c glass, and tranquil garden. Shop, limited disabled access to ground floor only; cl Nov–Mar; (01572) 822438; £2.60. The stone-built village is attractive, and the Old White Hart is good for lunch.

MALLORY PARK SK4500

Mallory Park Circuit 🅱 Motor sport meetings every wknd Mar–Oct, a splendid spectacle if your idea of a day at the races doesn't involve horses – only horsepower. Meals, snacks, shop, disabled access; (01455) 842931; from £8. The Royal Arms at Sutton Cheney is the nearest good eating place.

MARKET BOSWORTH SK3706

Battlefield Steam Railway Line Runs from Shackerstone through Market Bosworth to Shenton by Bosworth Battlefield, a rather nice return trip of just over 9 miles. There's a Victorian tearoom at the Shackerstone end (only open when trains are running), and some displays. Trains usually run wknds and bank hols Mar–Oct, plus Weds July–Aug; (01827) 880754 for timetable; £5 return.

Bosworth Battlefield Visitor Centre Site of the deciding action in the War of the Roses, when Richard III's defeat led to the Tudors' seizing the English throne. The **Bosworth Battlefield Visitor Centre and Country Park** has explanatory films and exhibitions, as well as a detailed trail following the sites of the fighting (now thought to be ever so slightly out). Also an exhibition of armoury from the *Mary Rose*. Meals, snacks, shop, disabled access; cl Nov–Mar; (01455) 290429; £3. The Royal Arms at nearby Sutton Cheney has good food. Market Bosworth village itself is interesting to walk through, and the Black Horse (by the market square alms houses) has good value food.

MARKET HARBOROUGH SP7387 An attractive market town which used to specialise in the production of corsets; bizarre, florid and even agonising examples can be seen in the **town museum** (shop, disabled access with notice; cl Sun am, Good Fri and 24–26 Dec; free). The centre has some fine old Georgian buildings, and above them the gracefully soaring 14th-c spire of the church. The Three Swans Hotel does good lunches.

Little Bowden church (outskirts, nr Sainsbury's) Handsome 12th-c church, set off charmingly by its fine old rectory. The adjacent Cherry Tree has good value food.

MELTON MOWBRAY SK7519 One of the places recently chosen by the English Tourism Council to pilot its 'culinary tourism' scheme, this little town is the home of Stilton cheese and pork pies. Dickinson & Morris (Nottingham St) still make the pies to a traditional recipe. Beside the particularly distinguished church, St Mary's (Burton St), the attractive Anne of Cleves has good value food.

Melton Carnegie Museum (Thorpe End) Celebrates Melton Mowbray's fashionable 19th-c days; shop, disabled access; cl Sun (exc pms in summer), Good Fri and 25–26 Dec; free.

Websters Dairy (Saxelbye) A good place to buy Stilton. In the next village of Grimston, the Black Horse has decent food and a remarkable collection of cricket memorabilia.

MOIRA SK3115

Heart of National Forest Visitor Centre (B5003 W of Ashby) 40 acres of new walks and landscaped trails through traditional broadleaf woodland will be unveiled here at Easter, to coincide with the opening of a new visitor centre with interactive displays about the forest. Meals, snacks, shop, disabled access; (01283) 216633; £2.95 (price may go up when new centre opens). The Rawdon Arms out here is useful for lunch.

Moira Furnace and Craft Workshops Along the same road as the Forest Visitor Centre above, this recently restored 19th-c blast furnace has interactive displays about the operation of the furnace, a few craft workshops, new woodland walks and an improved children's play area. Snacks, shop, disabled access; cl Mon, plus Tues in winter – best to check opening times; (01283) 224667; £3. The towpath beside the canal (the first stretch of the Ashby Canal to be reopened in the county) links the furnace to the attractions listed under Market Bosworth.

MOUNTSORREL SK5715

Stonehurst Family Farm & Motor Museum (Bond Lane) Traditional farm with animals to handle, play barn, trailer rides, nature trail, and a small collection of vintage cars. Meals, snacks, farm shop, disabled access to farmyard and tearoom; cl 25–26 Dec; (01509) 413216; *£3.45.

NEWTOWN LINFORD SK5210
Bradgate Country Park This extensive tract of the former Charnwood Forest hunting park is little changed over the last 750 years. At its heart are the ruins of the 15th-c home of Lady Jane Grey, and a visitor centre tells her sad story. Shop, limited disabled access; visitor centre cl am, Mon, and wkdys Nov–Mar; (0116) 234 1850; parking from £1, visitor centre £1.20. The entrance off the B5328 N of Cropston has better lavatories than the main entrance on the B5327. Fallow deer still roam these heathy slopes among the rock outcrops, and there's general access, plenty of waymarked paths, and lots of opportunities for picnics. Nearby Cropston Reservoir has waterfowl. The Pear Tree in Woodhouse Eaves has good food.

OADBY SK6102
Farmworld (Gartree Rd) Nicely set in charming countryside not far from Leicester, this well organised place has a good range of traditional farm animals and rare breeds. You can feed most of the inhabitants (they sell food, but don't mind your bringing sensible offerings from home), and they usually have some kind of baby or young animals all year round. Milking displays most days, and good play areas for younger children. Snacks, shop, disabled access; cl Christmas–New Year; (0116) 271 0355; £3 (£2.50 children 3–16).

University Botanic Gardens (Stoughton Drive S) Set around student halls of residence, these university gardens are 16 acres filled with a wide variety of plants in different and delightful settings, inc a national hardy fuchsia collection. Some disabled access; cl wknds and bank hols Jan–Mar and Oct–Dec; (0116) 271 7725; free. The Grange Farm (Florence Wragg Way) has imaginative food.

OAKHAM SK8608
Rutland's pint-sized county town is attractive, with a good sense of country bustle about it, and one or two interesting shops; Furleys (High St) has a fine range of very good reproduction furniture. By the church, the 17th-c Wheatsheaf has decent food, and Barnsdale Lodge (just off A606 E) does good lunches. There's a handsome drive through Ashwell, Wymondham and Waltham on the Wolds to Harby.
Oakham Castle The magnificent Norman banqueting hall is all that's left of the building, but earthworks and walls give a good idea of what it must have been like. The hall itself is decorated with a droll collection of extraordinary horseshoes, some grossly opulent, some simply enormously oversized. Shop, disabled access; cl 1–1.30pm, Sun am, court Mons, Good Fri and 25–26 Dec; (01572) 723654; free.
Rutland County Museum (Catmose St) The emphasis is on rural life, though there are some Roman and Saxon finds, and an exhibition on local military regiments. Snacks, shop, disabled access; cl Sun am, Good Fri and 25–26 Dec; (01572) 723654; free.
Rutland Farm Park (Uppingham Rd) This enjoyable farm park is hoping to reopen to the public later this year – phone for details, (01572) 756789.

RUTLAND WATER SK9308
Butterfly & Aquatic Centre 🅰 (off A606 Empingham–Whitwell) Next to the main Rutland Water information centre, there's a butterfly house with a good water feature, and various other insects and reptiles; also a video on the reservoir's construction in the 1970s. Snacks, shop, disabled access; cl Nov–Mar; (01780) 460515; £3.
Rutland Water Europe's biggest man-made lake, oddly shaped, with a number of attractions. On the N side of the lake are nature trails, an unusual drought garden created by the late Geoff Hamilton, places to hire bikes, and hourly **boat trips**; (01572) 787630. The White Horse at Empingham is good for lunch, and other handy dining places are the Finches Arms at Upper Hambleton (the best views over the water), and the Noel Arms at Whitwell. You can fish in various parts of the water, and there's a

fishing centre down at Normanton, as well as a small **museum** in a church modelled on London's St John's, Smith Sq. The refreshingly informal Normanton Park Hotel here has good food.

Rutland Water Egleton Reserve ⌷ This part of the nine-mile reserve is aimed at the more serious bird-watcher, with a comfortable purpose-built observation centre. Varied talks, walks and events; (01572) 770651; usually open every day (exc 25–26 Dec); snacks, shop, excellent disabled access; cl 25 Dec; £3, £2 after 1pm.

Rutland Water Lyndon Reserve ⌷ (off Lyndon–Manton road) This part of the extensive reserve is for the general public, with a useful visitor centre, occasional summer Sun crafts, and varied talks, walks and events. Snacks, shop, disabled access; reserve usually open all year, visitor centre open all wknds, plus Tues–Thurs May–Oct; (01572) 737378; £1.50.

SHEPSHED SK4618
Shepshed windmill Handsomely preserved, well worth a look.

STAUNTON HAROLD SK3720
Ferrers Centre (off B587 N of Ashby) In this pretty village the Ferrers Centre has good craft shops around a striking Georgian courtyard, and special events most summer Suns; snacks, shop, mostly disabled access; cl Mon exc bank hols, 25–26 Dec, and 1 Jan; free. The **church** out here (owned by the NT) was one of the few built during the Commonwealth; open pm only Weds–Sun and bank hols Apr–Sept, plus wknds in Oct; £1 donation suggested.

SUTTON IN THE ELMS SP5093
Falconry Centre (Mill on the Soar, Coventry Rd) Flying demonstrations of owls, hawks, falcons and buzzards; they really try to get the audience involved. On the same site are a fishing lake and thriving family dining pub. Shop, disabled access; cl Mon, and 25–26 Dec; (01455) 285924; *£2.

SWINFORD SP5879
Stanford Hall and Motorcycle Museum 5,000 books line the library of this handsome 17th-c house, an elegant place that still keeps a cosy lived-in atmosphere. Highlights are the painted ceiling in the ballroom, the portraits that accompany the winding grand staircase, and a good costume collection. The excellent motorcycle museum is in the grounds, which also have a lovely 14th-c church with splendid stained glass, walled rose garden, Sun craft centre, and a replica of the first successful flying machine in the country. Snacks, shop, limited disabled access; open pm only wknds, bank hol Mons, and Tues after bank hols Easter–Sept; (01788) 860250; house and grounds £4, grounds only £2.30, motorcycle museum £1 extra. The Cherry Tree at Catthorpe (cl Mon, Tues lunchtime) has good value food.

SWITHLAND RESERVOIR SK5713
Very picturesque reservoir, completely reclaimed by nature, surrounded by woods and trees, with the embankment of the Great Central Railway framing it along one side; you can feed the ducks and swans from the quiet Rothley–Swithland lane which crosses the water. The Griffin has decent food.

TILTON ON THE HILL SK7505
Halstead House Farm ⌷ (Oakham Rd) Farm animals inc some rare breeds, pony (Sun only) and tractor rides, a local history museum with displays of old farming implements, fishing lake, gardens, and a nature trail along a disused railway. Meals, snacks, well stocked farm shop, disabled access; cl Mon (exc bank hols), and Oct–Mar; (0116) 259 7239; £3. The village **church** is notable, and the Rose & Crown is handy for lunch.

TWYCROSS SK3305
Twycross Zoo Park (A444) Specialises in primates, with an enormous range of apes, gibbons, orang-utans, and chimpanzees – every shape, size and species. Plenty of other animals too, inc giraffes, sea-lions, elephants and penguins; the reptile house is 20p extra. Can get crowded on summer afternoons. Meals, snacks, shop, disabled access; cl 25 Dec; (01827) 880250; £6.

UPPINGHAM SP8699
Charming small town with an interesting square (Fri market) and curving 18th/19th-c High St. The Falcon Hotel does nice light lunches and teas.

On most Weds lunchtimes in term-time, musicians from the famous local school (tours Weds and Sat pms mid-Jun–Sept; (01572) 822672; £3.50) give free concerts in the parish church. Handy for Rutland Water.

WELLAND VIADUCT SP9197 (nr Seaton) One of the county's most striking sights: nearly a mile long, swooping across the pastures of the valley, it is the country's longest viaduct.

WIGSTON SP6099

Framework Knitters Museum (Bushloe End) A restored 18th-c knitters' house and workshop, with original hand frames. Open pm only Sun and first Sat of month, plus most bank hols (also by appointment); (0116) 288 3396; £1. The Royal Oak has cheap food.

WOODHOUSE EAVES SK5114

Beacon Hill Country Park This is a good surviving chunk of the former vast Charnwood Forest hunting park. The hill itself (above Woodhouse Eaves) is one of the best viewpoints in the area – an intriguing mix of the industrial and the very rural; it's a popular local beauty-spot, rising almost like a volcano above its lower woodland slopes. From the 245-metre (800-ft) summit, the Jubilee Walk heads N and E through partly wooded country. A trail S makes a small circuit around Broombriggs Farm with boards explaining farming methods by the path (£1 car park charge). The Wheatsheaf is handy for lunch.

WYMONDHAM SK8518

Wymondham windmill One of only four six-sailed mills in the country, with tearoom, craft shops and children's play area. Disabled access; cl Mon exc bank hols, wkdys Nov–Mar, 25 Dec and 1 Jan; free.

Other attractive villages, all with decent pubs, include Appleby Magna SK3109, Ashby Folville SK7011, Barrowden SK9400, Billesdon SK7202, Branston SK8129, Braunston SK8306, Bruntingthorpe SP6089, Cottesmore SK9013, East Langton SP7292, Grimston SK6821, Hallaton SP7896, Harby SK7531, Hose SK7329, Ketton SK9704 (good walks), Knipton SK8231, Knossington SK8008, Market Overton SK8816, Medbourne SP7993 (interesting church too), Peatling Magna SP5992 and Peatling Parva SP5889, Somerby SK7710, South Croxton SK6810, South Luffenham SK9402, Stoke Golding SP3997, Tur Langton SP7194, Walton on the Wolds SK5919, Whitwick SK4316, and Wing SK8902, notable for its small medieval turf maze. Stoke Dry SP8596 and Wistow SP6496 have fine churches.

Pubs useful for walks here include the Pear Tree and Bulls Head in Woodhouse Eaves SK5214; and, all handy for canals, the George & Dragon at Stoke Golding SP3997, Soar Bridge in Barrow upon Soar SK5717, Griffin at Congerstone SK3605, and Navigation at Kilby Bridge SP6097. The Cove Inn spectacularly overlooking the Stoney Cove diving centre nr Stoney Stanton SP4894 is an attractive spot for something to eat.

Where to eat

BELMESTHORPE TF0410 **Blue Bell** *Shepherd`s Walk (01780) 763859* Homely atmosphere in village pub, particularly in the first little beamed cottagey room with its open fire in huge stone inglenook and fresh flowers; as it was originally three cottages, it's on two levels: so you peer down into the bar counter, and a slope winds down round the counter to another area with similar cottagey furniture; well kept real ales, a good choice of wines by the glass, and imaginative bar food. £22.70|**£5.65**

BRAUNSTON SK8306 **Old Plough** *Oakham Rd (01572) 722714* Flower-decked stone inn with heavy beams and a good pubby atmosphere in traditional bar, a stylishly modern no smoking conservatory, seasonally changing and well presented imaginative food, good beers and a well noted wine list; seats out under fruit trees, and boules; disabled access. £20|**£5.95**

CASTLE DONINGTON SK4326 **Nags Head** *Hill Top (01332) 850652*

Civilised low-beamed dining pub with a simple little bar area, an intimate room with three chunky old pine candlelit tables on seagrass and a pretty slate art deco fireplace, and a much bigger, similarly decorated yellow-washed dining area; through an opening to the kitchen you can watch the chefs preparing the beautifully presented imaginative food; very attentive staff and conscientious landlord, well kept ales, 20–30 malt whiskies, and quite a few wines by the glass; handy for Donington Race Track; £23|**£6.95**

COTTESMORE SK9013 **Sun** *25 Main St (01572) 812321* Under new licensees, this 17th-c stone-built thatched village pub has a few tables in the rooms off the bar (best to get there early, or even book), a warm fire in the stone inglenook, sunny yellow walls with some nice sporting prints and other pictures, and stripped pine furnishings; imaginative food, real ales, decent wines, and friendly helpful service; tables and boules in garden. £20.95|**£5.95**

EAST LANGTON SP7292 **Bell** *Main St (01858) 545278* Pretty, creeper-covered inn with a warm inviting atmosphere, a log fire and plain wooden tables in the long stripped stone bar, imaginative food from a seasonally changing menu, OAP wkdy lunches, and a no smoking dining room; own-brewed beers, decent wines, and friendly efficient service; cl 25 Dec; children must be well behaved; partial disabled access. £23|**£6**

HALLATON SP7896 **Bewicke Arms** *1 Eastgate (01858) 555217* Thatched cottage by village green with warm welcome and traditional feel in its two beamed bar rooms, generous helpings of good popular food inc fine puddings, well kept real ales, and friendly service; tearoom and gift shop in the converted stables (disabled access here), and there's a small farm park walk; cl 25 Dec; bdrms; no dogs. £18|**£5.80**

LYDDINGTON SP8796 **Old White Hart** *Main St (01572) 821703* Warm and welcoming 17th-c village inn with just three tables in front of the log fire, heavy bowed beams, and dried flowers in the cosy softly lit bar; an attractive no smoking restaurant with corn dollies and a big oak dresser, and a tiled-floor room with some stripped stone, cushioned wall seats and mate's chairs, and woodburner; very popular imaginative bar food, well kept ales, and picnic-sets and boules in the pretty walled garden; good nearby walks, and handy for the Bede House; no food Sun pm, cl 25 Dec. £25|**£8.95**

THORPE LANGTON SP7492 **Bakers Arms** *Main St (01858) 545201* Extended thatched pub with a warm friendly welcome, simple country furnishings, well presented interesting food (need to book well ahead), helpful service, well kept beer, an extensive wine list, and no smoking snug; cl Mon, wkdy lunchtimes, Sun pm; children over 12. £26.15

UPPER HAMBLETON SK8907 **Finches Arms** *Oakham Rd (01572) 756575* Delightfully placed pub looking over Rutland Water with stylish cane furniture and paintings (for sale) in both the bar and more modern no smoking restaurant, super, imaginative, upmarket food, and real ales; bdrms. £24

WALCOTE SP5683 **Black Horse** *Lutterworth Rd (01455) 552684* Big helpings of authentic Thai food cooked by Thai landlady, unusual drinks, a chatty unpretentious atmosphere, a big open fire, and no smoking restaurant; outside seats for summer; must book; cl am exc Fri; open all day Sun; children in dining area only; disabled access. £17.50 for 5-course meal

Special thanks to Michael and Jenny Back, A E Land, Richard Lewis

LINCOLNSHIRE

Largely undiscovered away from the traditional seaside resorts, with some grand country houses, and a good mix of wildlife attractions; good value

Two features which particularly stand out here are windmills (there are plenty of them, inc the restored five-sailed example at Alford), and stately homes with more than just the family china to look at. Leading the way in this department is Elsham Hall Country & Wildlife Park, the county's Family Attraction of the Year, with its craft demonstrations, adventure playground and eclectic collection of animals. Elsewhere, Doddington Hall hosts regular concerts, children can try on medieval costumes at Tattershall Castle, Isaac Newton's work is displayed in a discovery centre at Woolsthorpe Manor, his former home, and there's a good afternoon's worth of fun to be had at Normanby Hall. Burghley House is well known for its Horse Trials but worth a visit any time of year, and sumptuous Belton is one of the finest Restoration country houses.

Prices here – for places to stay, eating out, and things to do – compare increasingly favourably with those in other areas.

Apart from the lively seaside fairgrounds at Cleethorpes and Ingoldmells, Lincolnshire's other family attractions are mostly wildlife-based, ranging from the enjoyable seal sanctuaries at Mablethorpe and Skegness to the tropical hothouses at Long Sutton's Butterfly & Wildlife Park and at Jungle in Cleethorpes, new to the *Guide* this year.

The Incredibly Fantastic Old Toy Show in Lincoln and the cheerful entertainment museum at Whaplode St Catherine's are fun, the ruined abbey at Thornton Curtis is a little-known romantic gem, and the vintage vehicles at North Hykeham's Road Transport Museum (another newcomer) and the venerable aircraft at Coningsby and East Kirby will charm nostalgia-lovers.

Lincoln is an interesting city with plenty to see and a glorious cathedral; Stamford and Boston too have a good deal of character. N and E of Lincoln, the rolling Wolds countryside makes for enjoyable drives on uncrowded roads, punctuated by attractive villages and charming small towns, and by soaring church spires.

Around The Wash and up the coast towards Wainfleet and Coningsby, the land is very flat, reclaimed from the sea: in springtime the endless bulbfields around Spalding burst into spectacular bloom, and we include an interesting waterside fenland drive S of here. Throughout the county's farmland, huge fields of arable crops can be rather tedious for walkers; speeding past more quickly in a car, bus or train, you're more aware of the shape of the countryside, giving it more appeal, though we have picked out some interesting walks.

In winter, Lincolnshire can be very chilly.

Where to stay

BUSLINGTHORPE TF0985 **East Farm House** *Middle Rasen Rd, Buslingthorpe, Lincoln LN3 5AQ (01673) 842283* **£46***, plus special breaks; 2 rms. 18th-c farmhouse surrounded by family farm, with beams, stripped pine, log fires, relaxed atmosphere, and good breakfasts; tennis and lots of walks; self-catering cottage; cl Christmas

DYKE TF1022 **Wishing Well** *Main St, Dyke, Bourne, Lincolnshire PE10 0AF (01778) 422970* **£49**; 14 rms. The wishing well is at the dining end of the long rambling bar – heavy beams, dark stone, brassware, candlelight and a big fireplace; good popular food, helpful service, friendly atmosphere; gardens and grounds with play area; disabled access

EAST BARKWITH TF1581 **Bodkin Lodge** *Grange Farm, Torrington Lane, East Barkwith, Lincoln, Lincolnshire LN8 5RY (01673) 858249* **£48***; 2 pretty ground floor rms. Run by the same warmly friendly family as the farm, this carefully extended bungalow has a comfortable sitting room with books, fresh flowers, open fire and baby grand piano, good breakfasts in big dining room (evening meals by arrangement), award-winning wildlife farmland trails from the door, and marvellous country views; cl Christmas and New Year; children over 10

EAST BARKWITH TF1581 **Grange** *Torrington Lane, East Barkwith, Lincoln, Lincolnshire LN8 5RY (01673) 858670* **£45**; 2 attractive, airy rms. Welcoming Georgian farmhouse on family-run farm with mature gardens and a grass tennis court; no smoking sitting room with log fire, good Aga-cooked breakfasts, and enjoyable dinner (by arrangement) using fresh local ingredients; farm trail, small lake stocked with trout, and conservation areas; cl Christmas and New Year

HOLBEACH TF3426 **Pipwell Manor** *Washway Rd, Saracens Head, Holbeach, Spalding, Lincolnshire PE12 8AL (01406) 423119* **£44***; 3 rms. Handsome 18th-c farmhouse, welcoming and spotless, with log fire in comfortable sitting room, pretty panelled dining room, afternoon tea with home-made cakes on arrival, good breakfasts with their own eggs and home-made preserves, and a conservatory; free bikes; no smoking and no pets; cl Christmas and New Year

LINCOLN SK9771 **Carline** *1–3 Carline Rd, Lincoln LN1 1HL (01522) 530422* **£42***; 9 well equipped rms. Spotlessly kept and comfortable double-fronted no smoking Edwardian guest house 5 mins from the cathedral, with helpful and cheerful long-serving owners, quiet sitting rooms, and fine breakfasts; cl Christmas and New Year; no baby facilities

LINCOLN SK9871 **D'Isney Place** *Eastgate, Lincoln LN2 4AA (01522) 538881* **£79**, plus special breaks; 17 charming rms. Friendly 18th-c hotel with lovely gardens (one wall of the cathedral close forms its southern boundary), a relaxed and homely atmosphere, good breakfasts using free-range eggs served on bone china in your room (there are no public rooms), and friendly owners; partial disabled access

MARKET DEEPING TF1309 **Caudle House** *High St, Market Deeping, Peterborough, Cambridgeshire PE6 8ED (01778) 347595* **£49.50**; 2 rms. Georgian house with comfortable sitting room, carefully cooked three-course evening meals for residents, a thoughtful wine list, helpful staff, and enjoyable breakfasts (served in the walled garden, weather permitting); cl mid-Nov to Mar

STAMFORD TF0306 **George** *71 St Martins, Stamford, Lincolnshire PE9 2LB (01780) 750700* **£103**, plus special breaks; 47 individually decorated rms. Ancient former coaching inn with a quietly civilised atmosphere, sturdy timbers, broad flagstones, heavy beams and massive stonework, and open log fires; wonderful food in Garden Lounge (tempting help-yourself buffet), restaurant and courtyard (in summer), an excellent range of drinks inc very good value Italian wines, and welcoming staff; well kept walled garden and sunken croquet lawn; disabled access

WINTERINGHAM SE9322 **Winteringham Fields** *1 Silver St, Winteringham, Scunthorpe, Lincolnshire DN15 9ND (01724) 733096* **£90***; 10 pretty, chintzy rms with period furniture (3 off courtyard). Thoughtfully run restaurant-with-rooms in

16th-c manor house with comfortable and very attractive Victorian furnishings, beams and open fires, really excellent inventive food (beautifully presented) in no smoking dining room, fine breakfasts, and courteous friendly service; cl 2 wks Christmas, last wk Mar, first wk Aug

To see and do

Lincolnshire Family Attraction of the Year

ELSHAM TA0311 **Elsham Hall Country & Wildlife Park** 🅳 Good for a leisurely half-day out, this busily undemanding estate has lots going on for families. Leaflets and ads talk about their farmyard animals, but that doesn't really do justice to the range of creatures you'll find here; it's not a massive collection, but as well as the sheep, goats and donkeys you might expect, there are llamas, donkeys, snakes, spiders and all sorts of other things, some of which you can stroke or feed. Taking along some bread or the odd carrot may come in handy. Especially unusual is the carp-feeding jetty, where monster-sized fish will feed straight from your hand; you buy the feed in the shop. They have a talk and demonstration of some of their mini-beasts every day at 1 o'clock, then at 2, weather permitting, they show off some of their birds of prey. Most things are outside, so it's best to visit on a dry day. The family that live here initially opened the park to the public to promote a greater appreciation of the countryside and of arts and crafts, so as well as the attractive grounds (it's very much the kind of place where just wandering around is rewarding) there's a craft centre, with demonstrations by a potter, woodturner and blacksmith, an arboretum, barn theatre, woodland garden, and plenty of space to let off steam. An adventure playground has sections for different age groups, and on bank holidays you might find extra activities such as puppet shows. Special events include lambing days in spring. Meals and snacks (they do a good Sunday lunch), picnic area, shops, garden centre, disabled access; cl Mon and maybe Tues (exc bank and school hols), and all mid-Sept to late Mar; (01652) 688698; £3.95 (£2.50 children over 3).

ABY TF4179
Claythorpe Watermill & Wildfowl Gardens 🅳 Pretty spot around 18th-c water mill (where they've reconstructed an early 1900s bread shop), the grounds full of ornamental wildfowl and poultry, and animals such as wallabies and a miniature pony. Fun to wander through the woods. Meals, snacks, shop, mostly disabled access; cl Nov–Feb; (01507) 450687; *£3.50. The Vine at South Thoresby is a civilised place for lunch.

ALFORD TF4575
Pleasant town with some attractive brick and thatch buildings, and a summer craft market (Fri). The White Horse Hotel and the Half Moon are useful for lunch. W of here, just N of the A16/A1104 junction, the Bluestone Heath hill road past S Ormsby and on to the A157 W of Louth is a splendid scenic drive.
Five-Sailed windmill Tall mid-19th-c restored five-sailed windmill on the road towards Sutton on Sea. Summer teas, shop, disabled access; open every Tues and Sat, plus Sun pm Feb–Oct, Fri Apr–Oct, and daily July–Sept; £2.

ALKBOROUGH SE8821
Overlooks the confluence of the Trent and Humber from a high (for this area) scarp called The Cliff; walks along it on a path leading S to the attractive village of Burton upon Stather.

ASWARBY TF0639
Aswarby church Delightfully set in a well tended park.

BARTON-UPON-HUMBER TA0222
Barton Clay Pits Country Park Informative country park based around former clay pits, with nature reserves, walks, fishing (extensive reed beds), sailing – and good views of the Humber Bridge. Limited disabled access; visitor centre (with in-house sculptor on Sat) open wknds and bank hols Easter–Sept;

(01652) 632034; free.

Baysgarth House Museum (Caistor Rd) This handsome 18th-c house has well displayed local history, especially good on rural crafts. Shop, disabled access to ground floor only; cl Mon (exc bank hols)–Weds, 25–26 Dec, 1 Jan; (01652) 632318; free.

BELTON SK8844

Belton House Splendid Restoration-period mansion with wonderful carvings, ornate plasterwork, and sumptuous furnishings, paintings and ceramics, as well as thousand-acre deer park, orangery and formal Italian garden. Behind-the-scenes tours. Meals, snacks, shop, limited disabled access to house; open Weds–Sun and bank hol Mons Apr–Oct; (01476) 566116; £5.30; NT. The relaxing Brownlow Arms in picturesque Hough-on-the-Hill has good value food.

BOSTON TF3243

Once the country's second-largest seaport, this little town has a number of pretty spots and handsome historic buildings. Most famous is the **Boston Stump**, the graceful tower of the magnificent 14th-c church St Botolph's. Climb to the top for far views over this flat landscape – it's the second-tallest parish church in the country (the tallest is in Louth); the inside is spectacular too. Another prominent feature of the skyline is the waterside **Maud Foster Mill**, the tallest working windmill in the country, and surely one of the most photogenic. The Kings Arms opposite has lovely views of it, and cheap food; Goodbarns Yard (Wormgate) is a popular central pub/restaurant. The surroundings (and the Lincolnshire coast generally) are too flat for driving to be very interesting around here, and side roads which look clear on a map can turn out to be tryingly slow in practice, with muddy agricultural vehicles trundling along slowly; the B1183 and B1192 aren't bad.

Boston Guildhall Museum (South St) In 1607 this was the prison of the Pilgrim Fathers after their unsuccessful attempt to flee to Holland (they did, of course, eventually escape further afield, taking this town's name with them). Displays cover this and the rest of the town's history. Shop, disabled access to ground floor only; cl Sun Oct–Mar, Sun am Apr–Sept, Christmas and New Year; (01205) 365954; £1.25 (free Thurs).

BOURNE WOOD TF0721

(A151 just outside Bourne) Sheltered woodland good for a gentle stroll, esp welcome as so much of the country here is flat, treeless fens. Plenty of bird life, busy at wknds with locals exercising their dogs; parking charge. In the town's market place, there's decent food in the Angel Hotel, opposite an interesting antiques shop.

BRANDY WHARF TF0197

Cider Centre (B1205 SE of Scunthorpe) Pleasingly zany 18th-c riverside cider house with up to 60 different varieties; also orchard and small museum. The enthusiastic owner really knows his stuff. Meals and snacks (not Mon, Tues lunchtime), shop, disabled access; open licensing hours, though cl Mon lunchtimes Nov–Easter and Christmas period; no children under 14; (01652) 678364; free.

BRANT BROUGHTON SK9154

Brant Broughton church spire Elegant and very tall, a landmark for miles around.

BURGH LE MARSH TF4965

Has a notable **church**, and a **windmill** nearby has unusual left-handed sails.

CANDLESBY TF4567

Candlesby Herbs (Cross Keys Cottage) Good range of herb plants and products for sale and on display in the garden; cl Mon; (01754) 890211; free. There's a specialist cactus grower at nearby Candlesby House.

CLEETHORPES TA3108

Big traditional seaside resort with extensive gently shelving tidal sands, and a surprisingly ancient **church** among some attractive older houses in its original core. Some of the seafront buildings are to be restored to their Victorian/Edwardian elegance thanks to a generous English Heritage scheme. The newish road in from the A16 is a big help. Willys (which brews its own beer) is useful for lunch.

Cleethorpes Coast Light Railway (Kings Rd) Gentle trip around local scenery; a new four-arch brick viaduct crosses a canal, and they've recently built a new station. Snacks, shop, disabled coach; cl wkdys Oct–Easter (01472) 604657; *£1.80.

Fuchsia Fantasy (Kings Rd) Hundreds of varieties of fuchsia, and other plants according to season; disabled access; open daily Easter–Sept, best to check other times on (01472) 883075; free.

Humber Estuary Discovery Centre 🖾 (Kings Rd) Unusual spiral-shaped building inspired by seashells, with an interactive journey through time (Cleethorpes lies on the Prime Meridian) looking at local natural and social history; also aquarium and telescopes for bird- and ship-spotting on the Humber estuary. Meals, snacks, shop, disabled access; cl 25–26 Dec, 1 Jan; (01472) 323232; £2.50.

Jungle (Lakeside, Kings Rd) Tropical wildlife from anacondas and iguanas to monkeys and parakeets, with regular handling sessions, plus a children's farm and guinea-pig village; snacks, shop, disabled access; (01472) 291998; £2.50.

Pleasure Island (Kings Road) Family theme park with white knuckle and children's rides, circus, cabaret and various animal shows. Meals, snacks, shop, disabled access; open mid-Apr to mid-Sept, and wknds Sept–Oct; (01472) 211511; £9.

CONINGSBY TF2257

Battle of Britain Visitor Centre 🖾 (A153) Subject to operational commitments you can see the aircraft of the Battle of Britain Memorial Flight – inc the only flying Lancaster in Europe. A visitor centre has exhibitions. Snacks, shop, disabled access; cl wknds, bank hols, and 2 wks at Christmas; (01526) 344041 – check first if you hope to see a particular aircraft; £3.50. The **church** has what's said to be the biggest dial of any clock with just a single hand. Just out of town, the interesting old Leagate Inn is useful for lunch.

CROWLAND TF2410

Crowland church The imposing remains of a once-great abbey, part still used as the parish church – the village also has a three-legged bridge.

DODDINGTON SK9070

Doddington Hall (B1190) Striking lived-in Elizabethan mansion, unchanged externally since it was built, and still with its original walled gardens, gatehouse and family church. The

elegant rooms are mostly Georgian. Regular concerts in the Long Gallery. Teas, shop, disabled access to ground floor and gardens; open pm Weds, Sun and bank hols May–Sept, plus garden also open Sun Feb and Apr; (01522) 694308; £4.30, garden only £2.15. The Stones Arms prettily placed in nearby Skellingthorpe has good value food.

EAST KIRKBY TF3563

Lincolnshire Aviation Heritage Centre 🖾 (A155) Enthusiastic World War II collection on a wartime airfield. The highlight is *Just Jane* the famous Avro Lancaster NX611 lovingly restored by two brothers as a memorial to their brother who died during the Nuremberg Raid in 1944. They hope that one day it will fly again but for the moment are content with taxiing it around the airfield in summer. Snacks, shop, disabled access; cl Sun and 25–26 Dec; (01790) 763207; £4.

ELSHAM TA0311

Elsham Hall Country & Wildlife Park *See separate family panel on p.375.*

EPWORTH SE7803

Old Rectory 🖾 (Rectory St) The childhood home of John and Charles Wesley, built in 1709 by their father. Restored in 1957, with rooms furnished in period style. Snacks, shop; cl Nov–Mar and lunchtimes Mar, Apr, Oct; (01427) 872268; £2.50. They do B&B. Thanks to the Wesley connection, the whole of this pleasant village which is the centre of the Isle of Axholme, with Georgian houses around the market place, has become something of a Methodist centre. The friendly Red Lion has decent food, especially vegetarian.

FOLKINGHAM TF0733

Picturesque village with a fine market place. The Greyhound Inn, crammed with antiques, is good for lunch.

FRAMPTON TF3239

Perhaps the prettiest Fenland village.

FREISTON SHORE TF3942

(off A52 via Freiston) Good paths to the sea wall, with desolate views of myriad birds and even seals on the marshes and banks beyond – don't be tempted out among them, the tides are lethal.

GAINSBOROUGH SK8189

Old Hall 🖾 (Parnell St) Restored medieval manor house with interesting

Great Hall and original kitchen. Good Walkman tour. Snacks, shop, disabled access to ground floor only; cl Sun Nov–Easter and Sun am all year, 25–26 Dec, 1 Jan, Good Fri; (01427) 612669; *£2.50. The Elm Cottage (Church St) has good cheap food, and the lane N along the Trent embankment gives views of the flood plain of this powerful brooding river; the Jenny Wren at Susworth is another good stop. Delicious ice-creams at nearby Blyton Dairy (Old Hall Farm, off A159) include Turkish delight and marshmallow dream.

GEDNEY DROVE END TF4828
Sea walk A good way of seeing The Wash is by following the dyke forming the sea wall; access is from a car park nr Gedney Drove End, from which you can follow the dyke to the mouth of the Nene, with its twin lighthouses either side.

GRANTHAM SK9136
Two rarities The unusually tall spire of the splendid parish church is commemorated in an early 19th-c jingle: 'Grantham, now two rarities are thine, A lofty steeple and a living sign'. The living sign is the hive with living bees – descended from those of that time – still used as an inn sign by the good Beehive pub on Castlegate here.

GREAT STEEPING TF4364
Northcote Heavy Horse Centre Magnificent horses showcased from 11am, with harnessing demonstrations, grooming and wagon rides. Snacks, shop, disabled access; open Sun and Weds Apr–Sept, and daily (exc Sat) July–Aug; (01754) 830286; £4. The Bell at Halton Holegate has good home cooking.

GRIMSBY TA2609
Still important as a fishing port, this is making considerable strides towards attracting visitors. A new road makes access from the A16 much easier. The Abbeygate Centre has reasonably priced antiques shops, also upstairs craft workshops inc lace-making and a café. Alfred Enderby's smoked fish house (Fish Docks Rd) demonstrates traditional methods of smoking salmon, haddock and cod; open 8am–3pm, cl Sun, most Sats and 2 wks at Christmas; (01472) 342984 to check. Cyclists are well catered for by new routes both here and in adjoining Cleethorpes.

National Fishing Heritage Centre (Alexandra Dock) Displays recalling the experiences of a trawlerman of the mid-1950s take you from the back streets of Grimsby, to the fishing grounds of the Arctic Circle and back. Everything in the main centre is under cover, but outside are enjoyable guided tours of a real trawler, the *Ross Tiger*, led by a former trawlerman. Special events and extra activities in the summer, from craft exhibitions to pirate days. Shop, disabled access (not to *Ross Tiger*); cl Fri, 25–26 Dec, 1 Jan; (01472) 323345; £4.95.

Time Trap In the prison cells of the Town Hall the town's social history gets a lively treatment. Interactive games and rather jolly displays cover the building of the docks and the struggle for women's suffrage – and you can see what it's like to be locked in a prison cell; cl Fri–Sun, bank hols; (01472) 324109; free.

GRIMSTHORPE TF0422
Grimsthorpe Castle A patchwork of styles from its medieval tower and Tudor quadrangle to the baroque N front by Vanbrugh; the state rooms and galleries have especially fine furnishings. Outside are formal gardens and parkland with lake (you can take a tour with the ranger in his Land Rover) and red deer tame enough for children to feed. Meals, snacks (inc the bizarre but revelatory courgette cake), shop, some disabled access; open Sun, Thurs and bank hols Easter–Sept, plus Mon–Weds in Aug, house cl am; (01778) 591205; *£6.50 all-in, *£3 park only. The Five Bells at Edenham is a good dining pub (and handy for walkers).

GUNBY TF4666
Gunby Hall (Gunby nr Spilsby; off A158) Interesting neat red brick William III house, with fine oak staircase and clock collection; especially worth visiting for the nine acres of splendid gardens, said to be Tennyson's 'haunt of ancient peace'. Open Weds pm (plus garden only Thurs pm) Apr–Sept; (01909) 486411; £3.60, £2.50 garden only. The Blacksmiths Arms at Skendleby does good value simple lunches.

GUYS HEAD TF4925
Peter Scott Walk A 10-mile walk E from the mouth of the Nene, with its twin lighthouses either side. Scott used to come here to study and paint wildfowl. It leads along the dyke into Norfolk, with access from a car park on the Nene's E bank.

HECKINGTON TF1443
Windmill Set in an understated but pleasant village, this well restored windmill is the only one in Britain with eight sails; shop (selling their flour and locally made bread and ginger cake); open pm Thurs–Sun and bank hols Easter–mid-July, then daily until mid-Sept, and then Sun pm only until Easter; (01529) 461919; £1.50. Nearby the Pearoom is a decent **craft centre**, and the Nags Head is good for lunch. The **church** still has many of its original 14th-c fittings, and is a delight.

HEMSWELL SK9590
Antiques, Craft & Design Centre (signposted off A631) One of the largest craft centres in Britain, with thousands of antiques and bric-a-brac crammed into 270 shops; also a small aircraft museum (wknds only; donations). Good meals and snacks, disabled access; cl 25–26 Dec; (01427) 667066; free.

HORNCASTLE TF2569
Attractive market town popular for antiques, with 30 shops in the Bridge St Antiques Centre. You can still see parts of the town's **Roman wall**. Old Nicks (North St) has a decent carvery, and the Fighting Cocks (West St) is also good value. Some 3 miles N the 'High Street' forking off the A158 is a good drive, following an Iron Age trackway up to Caistor. The A153 to Louth gives some good rolling Wolds views. Another good drive here includes Scrivelsby and its vast deer park, Belchford (Blue Bell useful for lunch), Fulletby (perhaps a stroll on the footpaths here), Somersby (Tennyson's birthplace – his bust is in the church), Old Bolingbroke (castle ruins), Spilsby (good delicatessen in the quiet market place with its statue of Sir John Franklin), and, if you've made good time, Wainfleet and Boston.

INGOLDMELLS TF5666
Fantasy Island (Sea Lane, opposite beach) More elaborate than your average fairground and ideal in any weather – 95% of the rides and other features are inside, with thatched buildings and palm trees nestling under a giant pyramid. Europe's longest roller-coaster opened here a couple of years ago, and other highlights include a volcano theme ride, the IMAX simulator's three roller-coaster-type experiences (the screen is all around you, and your seat slides and shakes), the Balloon Flight, with computer-controlled balloons soaring around the pyramid, a sail-through aquarium, and two water rides – one quite long, the other rather wet. Meals, snacks, shop, disabled access; open July–Oct, wknds only Easter–July; (01754) 872030; free admission to park, 50p a ride.

LINCOLN SK9771
The cathedral and castle, both very striking, share the central hilltop, with enough old buildings around them to keep a sense of unity. There's a lot to appeal up here, and in Steep Hill and Strait St ancient buildings run steeply down to the 15th-c Stonebow Gate at the top of the High St. This lower part of the town is a more normal bustling shopping and working centre, though even here there are a good few interesting old buildings – inc several Saxon churches and the Norman guildhall. The **Greyfriars Exhibition Centre** (Broadgate) is in a lovely 13th-c Franciscan building (open Weds–Sat, cl lunchtime; (01522) 530401; free). The Wig & Mitre and Browns Pie Shop, both on Steep Hill, and Lincolnshire Poacher (Bunkers Hill) are good for lunch, and behind the cathedral and castle the Adam & Eve is a nice old pub. There are some good views from the A607 to Grantham.

Incredibly Fantastic Old Toy Show 🔲 (Westgate) Changing collection of old toys and end-of-pier amusements, close to both the cathedral and castle, so a good treat for unwilling culture buffs. Shop, disabled access; cl Mon (exc bank hol pm), Sun am, wkdys (exc half-term) Oct–Christmas, and all Christmas–Easter; (01522) 520534; *£2.20.

Lincoln Castle 🔲 In beautiful surroundings on a formidable earthwork, this was originally built in

1068 for William the Conqueror, but only two towers and two impressive gateways date from then. One of only four remaining originals of Magna Carta is on display, and there are super views from the ramparts. A 19th-c prison has suitably gruesome exhibits; its chapel is unusually designed so that none of the congregation could see each other. Snacks, shop, limited disabled access; cl 25–26 Dec, 1 Jan; (01522) 511068; *£2.50.

Lincoln Cathedral Many people reckon that this is England's finest. The original building was largely destroyed in an 1185 earthquake, but the magnificent W front survived, and after nearly a century of rebuilding it was complete by 1280. The triple towers rise spectacularly above the nearby rooftops, and are beautifully lit at night. Inside, the carvings and stained glass are stupendous, and the architecture gracefully harmonious. Snacks, shop, disabled access; (01522) 544544; £3.50 suggested donation. The ruins of the once formidable Bishop's Palace are close by.

Museum of Lincolnshire Life and Royal Lincolnshire Regiment Museum 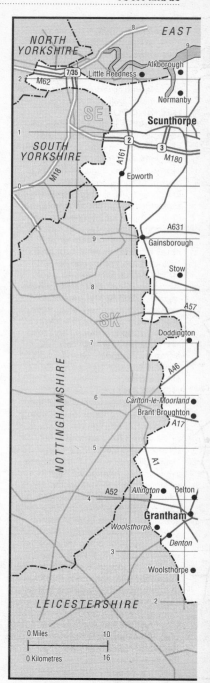 (Burton Rd) County life over the last couple of centuries, well illustrated in big former barracks. Refurbished regimental galleries; snacks, shop, disabled access; cl am Suns Oct–Easter; (01522) 528448; *£2. A lawn in the courtyard makes a good picnic area.

Roman remains These include the high wall along Westgate, and the largely reconstructed Newport Arch N of the cathedral (it had survived intact until a 1964 disagreement with a lorry); the Fossdyke canal between Lincoln and the River Trent is also Roman – you can walk out into the country along it from the city, and the Pyewipe Inn out by the Saxilby road there makes a good destination.

The Lawn In 1820 this was the county's first lunatic asylum; now its landscaped grounds include hands-on history and archaeology, an aquarium and exotic glasshouse, and a restaurant, coffee shop and bar. Shop, disabled access; cl 25–26 Dec, 1 Jan; (01522) 873622; free.

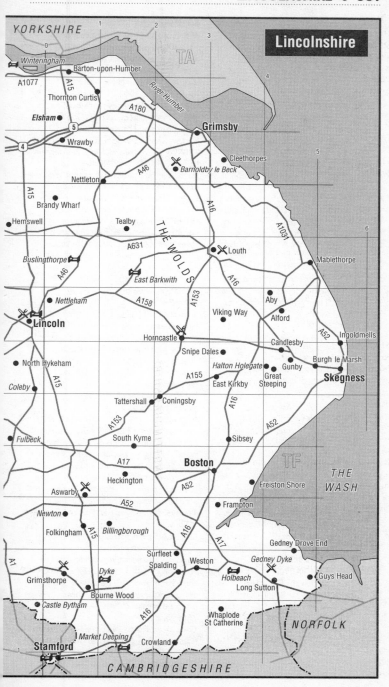

Lincolnshire

YORKSHIRE

Winteringham
Barton-upon-Humber
A1077
A15
Thornton Curtis
A180
River Humber
Elsham
5
Wrawby
4
A46
Nettleton
A15
Brandy Wharf
Hemswell
Tealby
A631
THE WOLDS
Buslingthorpe
A46
East Barkwith
Nettleham
A158
A153
Lincoln
Horncastle
North Hykeham
A15
Coleby
Fulbeck
Tattershall
South Kyme
A153
A17
Heckington
Aswarby
Newton
A52
Folkingham
A15
Billingborough
Grimsthorpe
Dyke
Bourne Wood
Castle Bytham
A16
Market Deeping
Stamford
CAMBRIDGESHIRE

TA

Grimsby
Cleethorpes
Barnoldby le Beck
A16
A1031
Louth
Mablethorpe
A16
Aby
Viking Way
Alford
Candlesby
A52
Ingoldmells
Snipe Dales
Halton Holegate
Gunby
Burgh le Marsh
East Kirkby
Great
Steeping
Skegness
Coningsby
A16
A52
Sibsey
Boston
TF
THE
WASH
A52
Freiston Shore
A16
Frampton
A17
Gedney Drove End
Surfleet
Spalding
Weston
Gedney Dyke
Holbeach
Guys Head
Long Sutton
Whaplode
St Catherine
NORFOLK
Crowland

Usher Gallery 🅰 (Lindum Rd)
Attractive gallery with fine watches, porcelain and miniatures, Tennyson memorabilia, and Peter de Wint watercolours. Snacks, shop, disabled access; cl Good Fri, 25–26 Dec, 1 Jan; (01522) 527980; £2.

LITTLE REEDNESS SE8022
Attractive village with 14th-c **church**, Ouse walks; RSPB **nature reserve** just E at Blacktoft Sands marshes.

LONG SUTTON TF4324
Butterfly & Wildlife Park 🅰 One of Britain's biggest walk-through tropical houses, with hundreds of butterflies flying free. Also creepy-crawly house, reptile land with snakes and crocodiles, wildflower meadows, twice-daily birds of prey displays, good play area and a 9-hole mini-golf course. A well organised place. Meals, snacks, shop, disabled access; cl Nov–Apr; (01406) 363833; *£4.80. The village **church spire** is unusual for the hundreds of tons of lead sheathing it. The 17th-c Olde Ship has good home cooking.

LOUTH TF3186
Hubbard's Hill A walk SW; not in fact a hill, but a river valley – surprisingly deep for the Wolds.
Louth church Elegant 16th-c building with the tallest spire of any parish church in Britain. The tower can be climbed on summer afternoons; hundreds of steps for a fabulous view. The market town is a pleasant stop, with lots of bustle on Weds, and some interesting shops.

MABLETHORPE TF4987
Animal Gardens & Seal Trust (North End) Rescued seals unable to return to the wild find a permanent home here, along with lynx, monkeys, parrots, porcupines, emus, wild cats and many other animals. It's right by the beach. Snacks, shop; cl Nov–Easter; (01507) 473346; £3.50.

NETTLETON TA0900
Potterton & Martin Cottage Nursery (Moortown Rd) This has unusual and interesting plants – mainly alpines and dwarf bulbs and large display gardens; disabled access; cl Christmas–New Year; (01472) 851714; free. Just S towards Normanby le Wold, Caistor Top is the highest point on the Wolds, at 168 metres (550 ft).

NORMANBY SE8816
Normanby Hall Country Park (B1430) Pleasant spot with grazing deer, lots of wildfowl, nature trails, some interesting sculptures, restored Victorian kitchen garden and a farm museum in its 350 busy acres. Period rooms in the Regency mansion. Snacks, shop, disabled access to ground floor only; house and museum open pm Easter–Sept, park open all year; (01724) 720588; £2.90 (North Lincs residents half price). The Sheffield Arms at Burton upon Stather has decent food.

NORTH HYKEHAM SK9368
Road Transport Museum (Whisby Rd, off A46 bypass) Over 45 well restored vintage cars, buses and commercial vehicles; free classic bus rides on special open days – best to phone. Disabled access; open all day Sun and wkdy pms May–Oct, and Sun pm Nov–Apr; (01522) 500566; free (donations welcomed).

SIBSEY TF3551
Trader Mill (A16 N of Boston) The village has a couple of **windmills**, one of them a splendidly restored six-sailed model with fine views from the top. Snacks; open second and fourth Sun of month and 14 May, but may cl for restoration work so best to ring; (01205) 750036; £1.70.

SKEGNESS TF5663
Archetypal 19th-c holiday resort, with the first Butlin's Holiday Camp just up the coast; the beach has clean bathing water. It's a very popular holiday spot so traffic can be very slow in summer. The comfortable old Vine Hotel on the southern edge of the town was here long before the resort, welcoming Tennyson among others; it's pleasant for lunch.
Church Farm Museum 🅰 (Church Rd S) Cluster of restored farmyard buildings and cottage provide good re-creation of daily farm life at the end of the 19th c, also craft demonstrations and special events. Snacks, shop, disabled access; cl Nov–Apr; (01754) 766658; £1.
Gibraltar Point Nature Reserve (Gibraltar Rd) 1,000 acres of sandy and muddy seashore stretching 3m S from Skegness to the mouth of The Wash. The impressive complex of sand dunes

and saltmarsh is good for bird-watching, and home to a wide variety of wildlife; guided walks daily in summer. Shop, disabled access to visitor centre and some hides; reserve open all year, visitor centre cl wkdys Nov–May; (01754) 762677; free (parking £2).

Natureland Seal Sanctuary 🖼 (North Parade) Opposite the beach, this rewarding place is renowned for its seal-rescuing activities. It's fascinating to watch the seals performing tricks – they aren't trained in any way, they just like showing off. Feeding times are announced over the public address system, and other animals include penguins, crocodiles, snakes, insects, and free-flying butterflies May–Sept; also pets' corner and farmyard animals (children can feed them with food from the gift shop). You can see almost everything from covered walkways if it rains. Snacks, shop, disabled access; cl 25–26 Dec, 1 Jan; (01754) 764345; £4.10.

SNIPE DALES TF3368
Country park and nature reserve, managed by the county council, covering 210 acres rich in bird and plant life; the country park is a 90-acre area of pine woods, while the adjacent nature reserve has a trail leading through two valleys and to a viewpoint over the Wolds.

SOUTH KYME TF1650
A fine 14th-c battlemented tower stands alone in a meadow quite nr the road.

SPALDING TF2624
All around this area, the flat fields by the roadside are a mass of colour in spring, first daffodils and then a multicoloured sea of tulips – very Dutch. The riverside Lincolnshire Poacher is useful for lunch.

Ayscoughfee Hall Museum (Church Gate) Spooky-looking medieval manor house, with social history museum, and five acres of gardens and ancient yew hedges. Summer meals and snacks, shop, disabled access to ground floor only; museum cl wknds Nov–Feb, gardens open all year; (01775) 725468; free.

Tropical Forest 🖼 (Rose Cottage Water Garden Centre, Pinchbeck, just N) One of the biggest displays of tropical and subtropical plants in the country. Snacks (summer only and not Mon), shop, water garden centre, disabled access; cl 25 Dec–2 Jan; (01775) 710882; £2.45. The Thatched Ship out here has good value food.

Waterside drive A remarkable fenland drive runs S from Spalding: turn left off B1172 in Little London, keeping alongside the Welland New River. Lagoons and reclaimed land on the right have water birds, with more on the river – maybe even a seal, and on the pastures maybe great percheron horses. At the B1116 a short diversion left takes you to Crowland with a memorable landlocked triangular medieval bridge and what's left of a great abbey. Back towards Deeping the road has more river views, and passes the Exotic Pet Refuge (occasional open days).

STAMFORD TF0307
John Betjeman considered this England's most attractive town. Within the medieval walls are no fewer than 500 listed buildings, inc a good number of attractive medieval **churches** – particularly All Saints in the centre, St George's with excellent 15th-c stained glass, and St Mary's nearby. The George, one of the town's grandest buildings with some parts going back to Saxon times, is excellent for lunch, and there are riverside strolls and quite a few craft and antiques shops.

Burghley House A 20-min walk from Stamford's centre leads to this splendid mansion, built by William Cecil and still the home of his family. The exterior is Tudor at its most solidly showy, but the state rooms inside are largely baroque, with wonderful frescoes by Antonio Verrio – the Heaven Room is astonishing. The peaceful grounds, where the Burghley Horse Trials are held, were landscaped by Capability Brown. Meals, snacks, shop, limited disabled access; cl early Oct–Mar (though gardens may open some dates in Apr for spring flowers display); (01780) 752451; £6.50.

Stamford Museum (Broad St) Local history inc Stamford ware pottery and life-size figures dressed in the clothes of Tom Thumb (only one metre – 3 ft 4 in – tall) and Daniel Lambert, a portly visitor to the town who weighed 218 kg

(50 stone) when he died on a racing outing here. Shop, disabled access to ground floor only; cl Sun pm Oct–Mar, 25–26 Dec, 1 Jan; (01780) 66317; free.

Tolethorpe Hall (off A6121 N) Home to the Stamford Shakespeare company, this has Europe's finest **open-air theatre** in its grounds, with a covered auditorium and a good Shakespeare season of three plays Jun–Aug; box office (01780) 756133; £10–£14.

STOW SK8881

Stow church Notable for its fantastic Saxon arches, with plenty more of interest in this imposing building; the attractive village has a decent pub, the Cross Keys.

SURFLEET TF2528

Leaning spire The tower and spire of Surfleet church lean alarmingly.

TATTERSHALL TF2056

Tattershall Castle 15th-c red brick castle with magnificent 30-metre (100-ft) turreted keep, with fine heraldic chimneypieces and stained glass windows on each of the four storeys; there's a double moat with peacocks and waterfowl, and children can try on medieval costumes. Snacks, shop, some disabled access; cl Jan–Mar, Thurs, Fri April–Oct and Mon–Fri Nov–Dec; (01526) 342543; £3; NT. The 15th-c **church** is also attractive, and just off the A153 towards Sleaford, on the left before you reach Tattershall Bridge, is a preserved steam engine which worked at keeping this area of fens drained for nearly a century. The Abbey Lodge Hotel (B1192 towards Woodhall) has good food.

TEALBY TF1590

The best example of that Lincolnshire speciality – colourful **village cottage gardens**, easily seen from the road. Here, a great variety of neat and charmingly planted gardens front the stone-built cottages, some thatched, on the main street, running down from the 12th-c **church** to a watersplash nr a watermill, and there is more colour in the quaintly named side lanes. The 14th-c Kings Head has good food.

THORNTON CURTIS TA1118

Thornton Abbey (E Halton road) Ruins of 12th-c Augustinian abbey, very atmospheric with its worn spiral stone stairs and dark corridors, well worth a visit. Also small exhibition in magnificent 14th-c gatehouse. Disabled access (not into gatehouse); grounds open daily, gatehouse open only pm third Sun in month, plus pm first Sun too Apr–Sept; (0191) 261 1585; free. EH

VIKING WAY TF3072

Long-distance path helping village-to-village walks, with 'Tennyson country' a popular focus (Tennyson was born at the rectory in Somersby, when his father was rector at Bag Enderby); the Black Horse at Donington on Bain TF2382, Bell at Coleby SK9760 and the Kings Head at Tealby are handy stops.

WESTON TF2924

Baytree Owl Centre (A151) Expanding collection of owls and other birds, with displays in a big arena (11.30am and 1.30pm, Mar–Oct); some birds can be handled. They also have a creepy-crawly house. Good meals and snacks, shop; cl 25 Dec–1 Jan; (01406) 371907; *£1. It's part of a busy little complex, with ducks and rabbits in a landscaped glasshouse, good garden centre, and play area; also donkeys and a mule in a paddock by the car park – regular visitors tell us the latter can't resist carrots.

WHAPLODE ST CATHERINE TF3219

Museum of Entertainment 🏛 (Millgate, off B1165) Unusual and quirky collection tracing the development of entertainment from barrel and church organs to puppets and phonographs, taking in a history of the fairground along the way. Many exhibits are working (there are organ concerts throughout the summer), and the owner clearly loves her subject. Snacks, shop, disabled access; open Sun–Thurs pm Jun–Oct plus Sun pm Easter–Jun; (01406) 540379; £3.

WOOLSTHORPE SK9224

Woolsthorpe Manor 🏛 (nr Colsterworth) Birthplace of Isaac Newton who conducted some of his more important experiments here: geometry workings said to be in his handwriting are scratched into the plasterwork – and of course the garden has a venerable apple tree. An interactive discovery centre exhibits his work; shop, disabled access to ground floor; cl am, Mon, Tues exc bank hols and Nov–Mar (01476) 860338; £3.20; NT. The Rutland Arms by the restored Grantham Canal is a useful family pub.

WRAWBY TA0208

Wrawby Post Mill Working windmill with snacks and a shop; open bank hols and some Suns Apr–Aug – ring Mrs Day to check; (01652) 653699; £1.

Other attractive villages, all with decent pubs, include Allington SK8540 (despite the nearby A1), Barnoldby le

Beck TA2303, Billingborough TF1134, Brant Broughton SK9154, Carlton-le-Moorland SK9058, Castle Bytham SK9819, Coleby SK9760, Denton SK8632, Fulbeck SK9450, Halton Holegate TF4165, Nettleham TF0075, Newton TF0436 and Woolsthorpe SK8435 (the one nr Belvoir). Readers recommend the woods at Stapleford SK8857 for picnics (especially when the rhododendrons are in bloom). Langton by Partney TF3970 has an attractive church.

Where to eat

ASWARBY TF0639 **Tally Ho** *(01529)* 455205 Handsome 17th-c stone inn with beams and open fire in country-style bar, a gently civilised atmosphere, and newspapers to read; good enjoyable food inc fine puddings, well kept real ales, decent house wines, and an attractive pine-panelled restaurant (best to book); bdrms; disabled access. £18|**£7**

BARNOLDBY LE BECK TA2303 **Ship** *Main Rd* (01472) 822308 Carefully run and immaculately kept home to charming Edwardian and Victorian bric-a-brac – stand-up telephones, violins, a horn gramophone, bowler and top hats, old rackets, crops and hockey sticks, stuffed birds and animals, and grandmotherly plants in ornate china bowls; a truly tempting choice of very reasonably priced fresh fish from Grimsby, plus meaty dishes and lovely puddings, too; well kept ales, an extensive wine list with plenty by the glass, tables outside. £21.90|**£6.95**

GEDNEY DYKE TF4126 **Chequers** *Main St* (01406) 362666 Stylishly unassuming but friendly fenland pub with beautifully presented food (super fresh fish and seafood), an open fire, and elegant dining conservatory; well kept beer, decent wines, and helpful service. £25/2-course lunch £10|**£7.95**

GRIMSTHORPE TF0423 **Black Horse** *(01778)* 591247 18th-c coaching inn with log fires, beams, exposed stone and plenty of brass, excellent food with an emphasis on fish and game (all beautifully presented), an intimate candlelit dining room, real ales, an impressive wine list with helpful notes, and friendly staff; pretty bdrms; disabled access. £24|**£4.50**

HORNCASTLE TF2669 **Magpies** *73–75 East St* (01507) 527004 Popular well run restaurant with a relaxed atmosphere and very good French cooking using top-quality fresh local ingredients; cl Mon, Tues, cl am Weds–Sat, pm Sun, 3 wks Aug; disabled access. £26

LINCOLN SK9771 **Browns Pie Shop** *33 Steep Hill* (01522) 527330 Spectacular, really interesting pies (and lots of other food), helpful staff, comfortable seats and pleasant traditional atmosphere; cl 25 Dec and 1 Jan. £20|**£5.50**

LINCOLN SK9771 **Jews House** *15 The Strait* (01522) 524851 Small, intimate and elegantly furnished restaurant in one of the oldest buildings in the city, with very good imaginative food, well schooled friendly service, and upstairs coffee lounge for those who want to smoke after the meal; cl Sun, Mon. £30/3-course lunch £8.50

LINCOLN SK9771 **Wig & Mitre** *30 Steep Hill* (01522) 535190 Ancient, attractive pub with plenty of period features; simpler beamed downstairs bar with exposed stone walls and Gothic furniture on oak floor boards, with sofas in a back area, and a civilised upstairs dining room, light and airy, with views of the castle walls and cathedral; shelves of old books, an open fire, antique prints and more modern caricatures of lawyers and clerics, plenty of newspapers and periodicals; enjoyable (if not cheap) food served all day, starting with full breakfast menu; well kept real ales, an excellent choice of wines, and proper espresso machine. £25|**£6.95**

LOUTH TF3287 **Chuzzlewits** *26 Upgate* Family-run no smoking tearoom with a civilised atmosphere, little glass chandeliers, dining chairs around pretty print glass-covered table-clothed tables, potted palms, and big shop-front windows; wide choice of speciality teas and coffees, home-made cakes, pastries and biscuits, a good range of interesting snacks and light meals, and young waitresses in long black dresses with white frilly aprons and little lacy white caps.|**£4.25**

Special thanks to Michael and Jenny Back, G Poole, Mrs M Sharp, MR and Mrs J Fawcett

We welcome reports from readers

This *Guide* depends on readers' reports. Do help us if you can – in return, we offer a discount on the next edition to people who've helped us with reports for it. Tell us what you think about places already in it, and anything extra you think we should say about them. And send us your ideas for inclusion in the next edition: places to visit, eat at or stay in, attractive drives or walks, maybe even unusual interesting shops you know of. Use the card in the middle, the report forms at the end, or just write – no stamp needed: *The Good Britain Guide*, FREEPOST TN1569, Wadhurst, E Sussex TN5 7BR.

NORFOLK

Rewarding holiday territory, with interesting excursions, historic towns and villages, Broads boating, timeless unspoilt north coast, and a good range of beach resorts

Families are well looked after here, with a welcome diversity of places ranging from the well established zoo at Banham, the attractive Norfolk Wildlife Park, Great Witchingham, and the animal ancestors at Lenwade's Dinosaur Park, to the host of attractions at the ever-expanding Village, Burgh St Margaret, the military collections at Weybourne (regular tank demonstrations), and the gentler charm of a Blakeney seal-spotting boat trip, or a steam train ride at either Sheringham or Wells-next-the-Sea.

Those after an unusual afternoon won't be disappointed either, with the wooded water gardens of the Fairhaven Garden Trust, the ancient sites at Cockley Cley and Grimes Graves, Glandford's delightful Shell Museum, and the combined appeal of flora and steam at the Bressingham Steam Museum & Gardens to choose between.

Castle Acre and Baconsthorpe Castle are both peaceful spots, and tranquil hours can be spent wandering through the rooms and grounds of Blickling Hall, Holkham Hall, Houghton Hall, Felbrigg Hall, and Sandringham, more intimate than other Royal residences.

North Norfolk is charmingly traditional-feeling, with a real sense of place from its Dutch-gabled buildings, flint walls, broad sweeps of sea, saltings and sky, and the odd windmill. A path runs the length of the coast, with often hundreds of sizeable and colourful birds in sight at a time. In summer the twisty coastal A149 is a bumper-to-bumper crawl, but it's a pleasant drive out of season, with a real get-away-from-it-all feel, and inland too, this part then has the same sort of untouristy appeal (though the weather is often kinder on the coast). Hunstanton and Cromer are civilised seaside resorts, and there are many attractive smaller places. Norfolk Buses run coastal tours; (0845) 300 6116. Further down, the coast is dotted with beach resorts, some large and full of life (most obviously, Great Yarmouth), some relaxed and more individual.

Norwich is distinguished yet lively, not overly touristy, with plenty to see inc its bold new library complex and other gems such as the Sainsbury Centre for Visual Arts, the Puppet Theatre, and the Castle Museum, reopening in May after refurbishment.

King's Lynn's rich history is well recounted in several of its museums, and the new Green Quay – an edifying introduction to The Wash – forms the centrepiece of its waterfront regeneration.

Much of the countryside is flat and repetitive – better for cyclists than walkers, with quiet lanes, attractive villages and country churches, and fair views. The best parts – the winding rivers and reed-fringed meres of the Broads – are best seen from a boat, but we've found some good bits for landlubbers.

Prices have increased more here this year than in most places, but there are still plenty of holiday bargains to be found.

Where to stay

BLAKENEY TG0243 **Blakeney Hotel** *Blakeney, Holt, Norfolk NR25 7NE (01263) 740797* **£136**, plus special breaks; 59 very comfortable rms, many with views over the salt marshes and some with own little terrace. Overlooking the harbour with fine views, this friendly hotel has comfortable and appealing public rooms, good food, very pleasant staff, indoor swimming pool, saunas, spa bath, billiard room, and safe garden; very well organised for families, with plenty to do for them nearby; good disabled access ☺

BLICKLING TG1728 **Buckinghamshire Arms** *Blickling, Norwich, Norfolk NR11 6NF (01263) 732133* **£50**, plus special breaks; 3 rms with four-posters, one with own shower. Handsome Jacobean inn in grounds of Blickling Hall, with civilised atmosphere, helpful staff, interesting food in bar and restaurant (best to book), nice breakfasts, well kept ales and good wines

BURNHAM MARKET TF8342 **Hoste Arms** *Market Pl, Burnham Market, King's Lynn, Norfolk PE31 8HD (01328) 738777* **£86**, plus special breaks; 28 comfortable rms. Handsome inn on green of lovely Georgian village, with a smartly civilised atmosphere, attractive bars, some interesting period features, conservatory lounge, stylish food (plus morning coffee and afternoon tea), well kept real ales and good wines, and professional friendly staff; partial disabled access

DOWNHAM MARKET TF6103 **Crown** *Bridge St, Downham Market, Norfolk PE38 9DH (01366) 382322* **£55**, plus special breaks; 9 rms, some cantilevered out over the yard. 17th-c coaching inn with lots of steps, stairs, nooks and crannies, low beams, flagstones and roaring log fire, home to 635 Pathfinder bomber squadron during the war, so appropriate photographs; enjoyable food, restaurant in the former stables, and a welcoming cheerful landlord

GREAT BIRCHAM TF7632 **Kings Head** *Great Bircham, King's Lynn, Norfolk PE31 6RJ (01485) 578265* **£59**; 5 rms. Old-fashioned and rather grand-looking Victorian country inn with an unassuming lounge, a quiet pleasant atmosphere and good log fire; cheerful Italian landlord, generous bar food (quite a few Italian specialities and tempting puddings), a no smoking dining area, decent wines and well kept beers, and a big side lawn with seats and play things; cl 25 Dec

GRIMSTON TF7022 **Congham Hall** *Lynn Rd, Grimston, King's Lynn, Norfolk PE32 1AH (01485) 600250* **£130**, plus special breaks; 14 individually decorated rms. Warmly welcoming and handsome Georgian manor in 30 acres of grounds inc herb, vegetable and flower gardens (herbs for sale and garden open to public), outdoor swimming pool, tennis court, paddock, and orchards – also, walks leaflets; lovely drawing room, a pretty orangery formal restaurant with excellent modern cooking (lighter lunches in bar), and exemplary service; children over 7

KING'S LYNN TF6120 **Tudor Rose** *St Nicholas St, King's Lynn, Norfolk PE30 1LR (01553) 762824* **£60**, plus special breaks; 14 refurbished rms. Attractive half-timbered 15th-c inn with interesting medieval door, a friendly chatty atmosphere, decent food in bar and no smoking raftered restaurant, and good breakfasts; disabled access

MORSTON TG0043 **Morston Hall** *The Street, Morston, Holt, Norfolk NR25 7AA (01263) 741041* **£200*** inc dinner, plus special breaks; 6 comfortable rms with country views. Attractive 17th-c flint-walled house in tidal village, with lovely quiet gardens, two small lounges, one with an old fireplace, and hard-working friendly young owners; particularly fine modern English cooking (they also run cookery demonstrations and hold wine and food events), a thoughtful small wine list, and super breakfasts; croquet; cl 2 wks Jan; dogs welcome away from public rooms

MUNDFORD TL8093 **Crown** *Crown St, Mundford, Thetford, Norfolk IP26 5HQ (01842) 878233* **£55***; 14 good rms. Friendly small village pub, originally a hunting

inn and rebuilt in the 18th c, with an attractive choice of reasonably priced
straightforward food, very welcoming staff, a happy atmosphere, and well kept real
ales; dogs welcome; disabled access

NORWICH TG2208 **Beeches** *4–6 Earlham Rd, Norwich, Norfolk NR2 3DB
(01603) 621167* **£76**, plus special breaks; 36 quiet rms. Three listed Victorian
mansions and an extension only 10-min stroll from city centre but with access to
three acres of English Heritage Victorian gardens; a relaxed, informal atmosphere,
friendly resident owners, enjoyable food in bistro-style restaurant, and good
breakfasts; cl Christmas wk; no children; disabled access

PULHAM MARKET TM1986 **Old Bakery** *Church Walk, Pulham Market, Diss,
Norfolk IP21 4SL (01379) 676492* **£52**; 3 large rms. 16th-c no smoking house with
lots of beams and timbers, an inglenook with a fine log fire in lounge, good
breakfasts, enjoyable evening meal using local produce, and friendly atmosphere; cl
Christmas–New Year; no children

SOUTH LOPHAM TM0381 **Malting Farm** *Blo' Norton Rd, South Lopham, Diss,
Norfolk IP22 2HT (01379) 687201* **£45***, plus special breaks; 3 well furnished rms, 1
with own bthrm. Welcoming no smoking Elizabethan farmhouse on working farm,
with woodburners in inglenooks in both the sitting and dining rooms, big breakfasts
with home-baked bread and preserves around a large table, and a small play area
with toys; the owner's passion is embroidery, patchwork, spinning and quilting and
she holds winter classes; cl Christmas and New Year

SPROWSTON TG2612 **Sprowston Manor** *Wroxham Rd, Norwich, Norfolk NR7
8RP (01603) 410871* **£145**, plus special breaks; 94 individually decorated, spacious
rms. Extended 16th-c manor house in 10 acres of parkland surrounded by
Sprowston Park golf course; comfortable day rooms, fine food in elegant orangery
and attractive restaurant, leisure club with palms and stone balustrades, poolside
bar, and health spa; disabled access

STARSTON TM2386 **Starston Hall** *Hardwick Rd, Starston, Harleston, Norfolk
IP20 9PU (01379) 854252* **£70**, plus special breaks; 3 rms. Of Elizabethan origin and
partly surrounded by the original moat, this attractive house stands in landscaped
gardens on a large estate; carefully restored and with many original features, there
is a spacious and elegant drawing room with beams and an open fire, a candlelit
dining room, enjoyable food using organic produce (available to non-residents
also), and helpful owners; cl Christmas; children over 12; disabled access

STOKE HOLY CROSS TG2302 **Salamanca Farm** *Norwich Rd, Stoke Holy
Cross, Norwich, Norfolk NR14 8QJ (01508) 492322* **£36***; 4 rms. Mainly Victorian
farmhouse (parts are much older) just a short stroll from the River Tas, with guest
lounge, spacious dining room, big garden, and farm shop; no smoking; cl 15 Dec–15
Jan

SWAFFHAM TF8109 **Strattons** *Ash Close, Swaffham, Norfolk PE37 7NH (01760)
723845* **£95***, plus special breaks; 6 interesting, pretty rms. No smoking, Paladian-
style villa with charming warmly friendly owners, and comfortable individually
decorated drawing rooms with family photographs, paintings, lots of china cats (and
several live ones), antiques, patchwork throws, fresh and dried flowers, and open
fires; delicious highly imaginative food using local (and home-grown) organic
produce, a carefully chosen wine list illustrated with Mrs Scott's own watercolours,
and super breakfasts; big cupboard full of toys and games for children; garden with
croquet; cl Christmas; dogs welcome if cat- and child-friendly ☺

THORNHAM TF7343 **Lifeboat** *Ship Lane, Thornham, Hunstanton, Norfolk PE36
6LT (01485) 512236* **£76**, plus special breaks; 14 pretty rms, most with sea view.
Rambling old white-painted stone pub, well placed by coastal flats, with lots of
character in the main bar – open fires, antique oil lamps, low settles and pews
around carved oak tables, big oak beams hung with traps and yokes, and masses of
guns, swords and antique farm tools; several rooms lead off; enjoyable popular food
in bar and elegant restaurant and well kept real ales; sunny conservatory with steps
up to terrace with seats and playground; marvellous surrounding walks; children
welcomed rather than tolerated; partial disabled access

THORPE MARKET TG2434 **Elderton Lodge** *Cromer Rd, Thorpe Market, Norwich NR11 8TZ (01263) 833547* **£100***, plus special breaks; 11 rms. 18th-c shooting lodge for adjacent Gunton Hall, with lots of original features such as old gun cabinets and fine panelling, a relaxing lounge bar with log fire, an airy conservatory where breakfast and lunch are served, and Langtry Restaurant with good food using fresh fish and game; six acres of mature grounds overlooking herds of deer on the thousand acres of Gunton Park; cl 3 wks Jan; children over 10; partial disabled access

TITCHWELL TF7543 **Titchwell Manor Hotel** *Main Rd, Titchwell, King's Lynn, Norfolk PE31 8BB (01485) 210221* **£90***, plus special breaks; 16 light, pretty rms. Comfortable hotel, handy for nearby RSPB reserve, with an open fire, magazines and good naturalists' records of the wildlife, a cheerful bar, attractive no smoking restaurant with French windows on to sheltered neatly kept walled garden, very good food (esp fish), and particularly helpful licensees and staff; lots of walks and footpaths nearby; dogs welcome (bedrooms only); disabled access

WARHAM TF9441 **Three Horseshoes** *The Street, Warham, Wells-next-the-Sea, Norfolk NR23 1NL (01328) 710547* **£56**; 5 rms, one with own bthrm. Basic but cheerful local with marvellously unspoilt traditional atmosphere in its three friendly gaslit rooms, simple furnishings, a log fire, very tasty generous helpings of bar food, decent wines, home-made lemonade, and very well kept real ales; bdrms are in the Old Post Office adjoining the pub, with lots of beams and a residents' lounge dominated by an inglenook fireplace; cl 24–26 Dec; no children

WINTERTON-ON-SEA TG4919 **Fishermans Return** *The Lane, Winterton-on-Sea, Great Yarmouth, Norfolk NR29 4BN (01493) 393305* **£50***; 3 rms, shared bthrm. Traditional 300-year-old pub in quiet village, close to the beach, with warmly welcoming owners, a relaxed lounge bar, open fire, good home-made food inc fresh fish (fine crabs in season), enjoyable breakfasts, and sheltered garden

To see and do

Norfolk Family Attraction of the Year

BANHAM TM0587 **Banham Zoo & Appleyard Craft Court** (B1113) Very much enjoyed by readers, this well established and splendidly organised zoo is beautifully laid out, with over 1,000 animals spread over 35 acres of parkland. There's everything from kangaroos to crocodiles, with particularly good enclosures for their Siberian tigers and ring-tiled lemurs, and an underwater viewing window into Penguin World. It's easy to spend a whole day here: a busy schedule of talks and feeding sessions is spread throughout the day, taking in fur seals, camels, tigers, and, in summer, twice-daily falconry displays. Children can wander among the guinea-pigs, miniature donkeys, goats and sheep in the new Farm Barn, and there's a much better than average adventure play area. Regular visitors tell us new animals are always popping up; unfamiliar faces this year included a striped hyena, and bat-eared and fennec foxes. As we went to press they were about to introduce an unusual red panda – it looks like a cross between a panda, a bear, and a fox. Another recent addition is a shire horse centre. A road train can take you between the enclosures, most of which have particularly helpful explanatory notes. For an extra £1.50, face-painters do a good job of transforming younger visitors into one of the park's residents. Lots of special events throughout the year, inc extra activities around Christmas (though note that last admission in winter is at 3pm). Meals, snacks, shops, disabled access (some of the paths have been resurfaced in recent years); cl 25–26 Dec; (01953) 887771; best to visit outside the summer months, as in peak season admission rises from £6.95 (£4.95 children 3–14) to £7.50 (£5.50 children). It's run by the same people as the Suffolk Wildlife Park at Kessingland (see Suffolk chapter). Across the road are a few shops in converted barns, as well as a working cidery; there's an adjacent campsite.

ACLE TG3910
Acle windmill A fine example.
ATTLEBOROUGH TM0292
Peter Beales Rose Nursery
Specialist in old-fashioned roses that
you won't find for sale elsewhere; you
can wander around the three acres of
gardens; disabled access; cl Sun in Jan,
Christmas and bank hols; (01953)
454707. The 15th-c **church** is
interesting, with an unusual round
tower and a screen decorated with the
arms of the 24 bishoprics in England
when it was built. The White Lodge has
decent food.
AYLSHAM TG1926
Bure Valley Railway 🚂 Steam train
trips along nine miles of narrow-gauge
track between here and Wroxham; you
can combine the journey with a 1½-
hour Broads cruise. The stock isn't very
old, but the people are friendly. Meals,
snacks, shop, disabled access; cl
Jan–Mar and Nov, best to ring for
timetable; (01263) 733858; *£6.90 full
return (£11 inc Broads cruise).
BACONSTHORPE TG1336
Baconsthorpe Castle The
gatehouses, curtain walls and towers
are all that's left of this moated and
semi-fortified 15th-c house, but displays
show what it must have looked like in
its glory. A very pretty peaceful spot,
with swans on the lake adding to its
charm; free. You can find information
booklets at the nearby Post Office.
Light lunches and teas are served in
Margaret's tearooms Mar–Oct.
BANHAM TM0587
**Banham Zoo & Appleyard Craft
Court** See separate family panel on
p.390.
BLAKENEY TG0443
Crabbing is fun from here, and
surprisingly successful. Also a (free)
collection of waterfowl down by the
harbour, long breezy walks, unspoilt
flint cottages, broad sky and sea vistas,
maybe even a seal pup on the beach in
spring. There's a good dyke walk to
Cley-next-the-Sea, with the birds on
the mudflats for company. Blakeney has
a very good tea shop; besides the
Blakeney Hotel, the Manor, White
Horse and Kings Arms are all good. In
summer it gets packed.
Blakeney Point This NT-owned

nature reserve is edged by a good
stretch of the North Norfolk Coast
Path, which gets better as you walk
along it, although the shingle bank needs
patience and is hard on the ankles;
pleasant dunes await at the far end.
Seal boat trips Boats leave from
Morston Quay slightly W on the A149
coast road once or twice a day from
Mar–Oct (times depend on the tide),
and on most winter wknds; when the
tide allows you'll also find trips wending
their way down the creek from the little
harbour at Blakeney itself. Most last
two hours, which takes in an hour or so
exploring the NT-owned bird reserve
at **Blakeney Point**. The highlight
comes just before that, when the boat
goes past the sandbanks at the end of
the point, where dozens of grey and
common seals lie basking happily in the
sun. Several different operators run
boats, with the smaller ones owned by
the Beans our favourites. Booking a few
days in advance is recommended (esp in
summer, when there are crowds of
visitors waiting on the quay), on
(01263) 740038. £5. Local information
centres have full details of operators
and times.
BLICKLING TG1728
Blickling Hall (B1354) Magnificent
house dating mainly from early 17th c,
though the hedges that flank it may be
older. Dramatic carved oak staircase
and splendid paintings (inc a famous
Canaletto), but best of all is the 38-
metre (125-ft) Long Gallery with its
ornate Jacobean plaster ceiling, and the
Chinese bedroom, still lined with 18th-c
hand-painted wallpaper. The gardens
and grounds are lovely, with several
miles of footpaths. Meals, snacks, shop,
plant centre, good disabled access (a lift
in the house); house open Weds–Sun
pm April–Oct, garden also open am,
daily in Aug and winter Sun; (01263)
738030; £6.50, £3.70 garden only; NT.
There's a pleasant walk from the
Buckinghamshire Arms (good for
lunch), and free public access to the
parkland on the W side of the pike-
filled lake with its water birds, with large
tracts of woodland and pasture, as well
as a disused railway line, perhaps even
kingfishers on the River Bure. There are
circular walks within the park.

BRANCASTER TF7944

Scolt Head Miles of dunes, flat coastal saltings, broad tidal beaches: a fine lonely place, largely National Trust and full of birds – Scolt Head island is an important breeding ground, and in good weather a boat takes people across from Brancaster Staithe. Incidentally all along this coast the wading birds, surprisingly approachable, are best seen on a falling tide. The Jolly Sailors is useful for lunch.

BRECKLAND TL9188

East Wretham Heath Nature Reserve (off A1075 NE of Thetford) This shows how the region of poor flat sandy heathland around Thetford looked originally, with scattered shallow meres and scrubby mixed woodland; limited visitor facilities but plenty of wild flowers, nature trails, and hides for watching the birds and deer; free. Elsewhere Breckland is extensively planted now, with pines; there are forest walks, for example from car parks on the A134 NW of Thetford, where you may disturb roe deer. The Crown at Mundford is the best nearby lunch place.

Pingo Trail Starting from Stow Bedon, this is an 8-mile path through the unforested part of the adjacent Breckland grasslands, largely army training ground. It passes through three Sites of Special Scientific Interest (inc Cranberry Rough, an alder swampland), taking you along a disused railway line before joining the Peddars Way at Hockham Heath.

BRESSINGHAM TM0880

Bressingham Steam Museum & Gardens (A1066) The founder, Alan Bloom, has effectively combined his two interests at this rewarding site. The six acres of informal gardens are planted with 5,000 species and cultivars of alpines and perennials in island beds, with lots of the dwarf conifers Bloom has done so much to popularise. Then there's the excellent steam collection, inc 50 road and rail engines, mostly restored to working order, and a charming fairground carousel. Four steam-hauled trains run through the countryside and parts of the garden (all may not be in steam out of high season). A new exhibition is dedicated to that enduring TV favourite, *Dad's Army*. Meals, snacks, shop, disabled access; cl Nov–Easter, phone for train times; (01379) 687382; £6. The Garden House is handy for lunch.

BROADS TG3017

Norfolk's network of linking waterways is not easy to visit on foot or by car; few paths get close enough to the Broads themselves, often tantalisingly out of sight, and once away from the waterside and fenny woodlands you are immediately into the flat, humdrum agricultural landscapes found in much of the rest of the area. There is some scope for strolling along rivers, with pumping-mills, birdlife and the boating scene being the principal features. The best way to see the Broads is undoubtedly by boat. Wroxham with its neighbour Hoveton is a main centre for boat hire, and like the other main centre Horning is probably better thought of as a base for longer spells afloat than short breaks or day trips. If you want a boat for just the day, the quieter reaches of the more northern Broads would probably suit you better – say, from Barton Turf, Hickling, Stalham or Wayford Bridge. Or for a quick taste you can combine a boat trip with the trains on the **Bure Valley railway** at Aylsham.

Berney Arms windmill TG4605 Across the water from Burgh Castle and amazingly remote, this and its nearby pub can be reached not by road but by either boat or train from Great Yarmouth, or as a worthwhile objective for a long walk with a real sense of adventure, across the marshes from Wickhampton or Halvergate, passing other former windpumps. The seven-storey mill dates from the 19th c, when it was used to drain water from the marshes. Cl 1–2pm, maybe Mon and Sat, and all Nov–Mar, best to check; (01493) 700605; £1.60. There's also scope for walking by reedy Breydon Water, the estuarine channel of the River Yare between here and Great Yarmouth.

Boat cruising Broads cruising is generally a week-long affair, but could be worked into a short-stay holiday; the boats nowadays have every mod con and are easy for even a novice to handle, but it's a chilly pastime until summer's well established. Wroxham is the main centre for this, with several boat hire firms. So it's a good place to watch the boating activities from dry land, or to use as the start of a longer cruising holiday. It can be very congested in summer. The Bell has kept more character than many places around.

Day boating The quieter reaches of the more northern Broads are probably more suited to this than the busier parts around Wroxham and Horning. Stalham TG3724, Barton Turf TG3522 and Wayford Bridge TG3424 are possible bases.

Fairhaven Garden Trust TG3713 Charming wooded water gardens set beside the private South Walsham Inner Broad, the waterways linked by little bridges. Rare plants, masses of rhododendrons among the flowers, and a tree – the King Oak – said to be 900 years old. It's an extensive place, running to some 230 acres, inc a big **bird sanctuary** – to visit this part you need permission from the warden. Boat trips every half-hour. Snacks, shop, disabled access – but paths are quite uneven; open daily exc 25 Dec; (01603) 270449; £3. The Ship has good home cooking.

Hickling TG4122 It's normally possible to hire a boat for just the day or maybe an even shorter period here. And walkers have a pleasant path along the N shore.

Horning TG3417 One of the main centres for Broads boat hire, chiefly for longer spells afloat; there are also paddle-boat cruises. So it's a good place to watch the boating activity, perhaps from the Swan or the Ferry, busy Chef & Brewer pubs. There's also some scope for walking along the canalised parts of the River Bure.

Neatishead TG3520 This attractive village, with a decent pub, gives access to the **Barton Broad** nature reserve.

Ranworth Broad TG3514 One of the few broads the cruise boats can't get to. Thanks to a lottery grant, the **conservation centre** here will have new interpretations of local and natural history when it reopens later this year; snacks, shop, disabled access; cl late

Oct–Mar; free. There may be guided tours of the local wildlife on summer Suns; best to book, on (01603) 270479. The village **church** has the best painted rood screen in the county.

River Thurne TG4117 The towpath by the canalised parts gives one of the relatively few opportunities for waterside walks in Broadland.

Strumpshaw Fen TG3306 (off Low Rd, Brundall) Partly drained water meadows and fen between woodland and River Yare, with RSPB hides for watching marsh birds inc harriers and bearded tits, winter geese, and maybe swallowtail butterflies in Jun; (01603) 715191; £2.50 (RSPB members free). The Yare Inn in Brundall is popular for food.

Watching the boats At **Surlingham** TG3006 by the Ferry House pub there's still a rowing-boat ferry. And nearby Coldham Hall is a pub with lovely riverside gardens. **Bramerton** TG2905 gives car access to the waterside; the Woods End pub here is useful. In the pretty village of **Coltishall** TG2719, the Rising Sun pub is on a pretty bend of the River Bure; you can hire bikes from nearby Just Pedalling. At **Stokesby** TG4310, the Ferry House pub is well placed for quite a busy stretch of the River Bure.

Sutton Staithe TG3823 is a lovely quiet waterside spot; the Sutton Staithe Hotel here is useful. **Geldeston** TM3891 is at the navigable head of the River Waveney; down a long track from the road, the Lock, a remote candlelit pub, gives a flavour of how the Broads were 40 years ago – at least out of high season. **Ormesby St Michael** TG4715 gives views from the attractive waterside lawns of the Eels Foot pub.

Dilham TG3325 is one of the few places where by car you can get down to the Norfolk Broads waterside; the Crown pub here is useful.

BURGH CASTLE TG4705 You can still see sections of the massive walls of this coastal Roman fortress, built in the 3rd c to protect the coast from Saxon marauders; free. The Church Farm Inn overlooking the Yare and Waveney has decent food.

BURGH ST MARGARET TG4513 **Village** 🖼 (A1064) Delightful pastiche of a 19th-c village, but an idealised one rather than an authentic set-up along the lines of somewhere like Beamish. Fairground rides (inc traditional Victorian gallopers), candle-making and other crafts, and amusing live shows – the puppet show effectively blends marionettes with people, and a cinema organ accompanies silent comedy films in the 1920s Concert Hall; also narrow-gauge railway, steam-hauled trailer rides, working sawmill, collections of vintage motorbikes and other vehicles, woodland walks, and decent adventure play area, with recently added attractions such as dancing fountains and a junior maze. Meals, snacks, shops, mostly disabled access; cl Nov–wk before Easter; (01493) 369770; *£5.95 (*£2.75 Sat, when less going on: no crafts or live shows).

BURNHAM MARKET TF8342
Handsomely opulent village with a fine green, gatehouse and 13th-c priory remains; the Hoste Arms is a good dining pub.

BURNHAM THORPE TF8541
This hamlet's strong Lord Nelson connections include a pub named after him, with interesting related memorabilia. The lectern in the village church uses wood from HMS *Victory*, and the church has other Nelson mementoes.

CAISTER-ON-SEA TG5012
Caister Castle & Motor Museum
This moated ruin is set back from the town, a little way inland. Falstaff (the original behind Shakespeare's creation) built it on returning from Agincourt; its walls surround a 30-metre (98-ft) tower. The grounds contain a **motor museum** with a good collection of vehicles from 1893 onwards. Snacks, some disabled access; open May–Sept, cl Sat; (01572) 787251; £5.50.

CASTLE ACRE TF8115
A delightful village, with an 18th-c feel along the tree-shaded walk of Stocks Green. The sparse ruins of a great **Norman Castle** are still awe-inspiring. The site is on the Peddars Way, a Roman road following the track of an earlier herding way. West Acre, 2 or 3 miles W, has a few further priory remains, and (like Castle Acre itself) picturesque fords over the River Nar. A

few miles N, some private woodland opens for three wks in late spring for its magnificent azaleas.

Castle Acre Priory Extensive ruins of a Cluniac building by William the Conqueror's son-in-law include the fine arcaded W front of the 11th/12th-c church, and a chapel and 15th-c gatehouse; good Walkman tour, some special events. Well laid out, and very picturesque. Snacks, shop, some disabled access; cl Mon and Tues and 1–2pm in winter, 24–26 Dec; (01760) 755394; £3.20; EH.

CASTLE RISING TF6624
Castle Rising Castle 🏰 Massive earthworks surround this fine Norman keep, a marvellous setting for the summer jousting they occasionally stage here. Shop; cl Mon and Tues Nov–April, 24–26 Dec; (01553) 631330; £3.25. By the church and almshouse in the attractive village the Black Horse is a popular dining pub.

CLEY-NEXT-THE-SEA TG0443
Handy for the bird-sanctuary marshes towards the Blakeney Point sandspit, with excellent hides and plenty of avocets. The pleasant village has an imposing **church**. The neatly restored **windmill** is a more obvious landmark, and has great views from the top (open pm Easter–Oct; (01263) 740209; £1.50), as well as very good accommodation. The George & Dragon and Three Swallows are decent food stops, and there's a long pebbly beach.

COCKLEY CLEY TF8004
Lots of interesting historical things to see around this village (pronounced to rhyme with 'fry'). There's a **museum** in a 17th-c cottage, nature reserve, carriage collection, and 7th-c Saxon church, but most unusual is the **Iceni village**, built as and where it was believed to have existed 2,000 years ago. Snacks, shop, disabled access; open Easter–Oct (01760) 724588; £3.50 covers all attractions. The Twenty Churchwardens is handy for lunch.

CROMER TG2242
Popular seaside resort since Victorian times, with lovely sandy beaches, more sun than the average, bustling markets, golf courses, interesting shops and galleries and lots of entertainments. The pier is one of the last in the country

to present an end-of-pier show – very popular, so worth booking early. The tower of the imposing **church** on Church St – Norfolk's tallest – gives spectacular views of the surrounding countryside. A good local history **museum** next door is spread over five 19th-c fishermen's cottages (shop; cl Mon lunch, Sun am, Good Fri, 23–26 Dec, 1 Jan; £1.80), and on the prom a small **Lifeboat Museum** looks at local lifeboatman Henry Blogg, who over 53 years saved 873 lives (shop, disabled access; cl Oct–Apr; free). Nearby you often find dressed crabs for sale; the crab boats still work from here, and Cromer crabs are the best on England's E coast. The clifftop Dolphin has decent food.

Beacon Hill The only place of any height (a humble 90 metres, 300 ft) on the North Norfolk coast; the Coast Path here detours over the sandy heath and through woodlands.

DENVER SLUICE TF5800
These towering hydraulic sluice gates control water levels in these parts – quite a sight. The riverside Jenyns Arms is a pleasant lunch stop nearby.

DOWNHAM MARKET TF5903
Hermitage Hall (Bridge Farm, A1122 just W) Based around an old chapel used by pilgrims on the way to Walsingham, now with mementoes of local boy Nelson (inc letters, birth certificate and death mask), small collection of cars, Victorian street, and gentle walks down to the Ouse. Snacks, shop, disabled access; open Easter–Christmas, cl Christmas to Easter pm; (01366) 383185; £3.50. In town, the Crown has good value food Thurs–Sun.

EARSHAM TM3188
Otter Trust (off A143) Charitable trust devoted to reintroducing otters to rivers from which they've disappeared; you can see them here in a natural environment. They're obviously cheerful and intelligent, but don't perform on demand and you may have to wait a while to see anything. Snacks, shop, disabled access; open Apr–Oct; (01986) 893470; £5. The Green Dragon in Bungay is a heartening retreat if they don't show.

ERPINGHAM TG2032

Alby Crafts & Gardens Four acres of interesting shrubs, plants and bulbs, with a museum devoted to lace, another concentrating on bottles (over 2,000 of them, mainly from regional brewers) and crafts inc woodturning and stained glass. Very good roses and lilies in July. Meals, snacks, shop, mostly disabled access; cl Mon (exc bank hols), wkdys mid-Dec to mid-Mar (lace museum also cl Sat); (01263) 761226; crafts and lace museum *free, gardens *£2, bottle museum *50p. The Ark, and the Saracens Head out at Wolterton (at the start of a pleasant 2- or 3-hour circular walk), are both very good for lunch.

FAKENHAM TF9429
A pleasant market town; the comfortable Wensum Lodge Hotel has good food (as does the prettily set Sculthorpe Mill off the A148 just W), and the roads N pass through attractive villages.

FELBRIGG TG1939
Felbrigg Hall Magnificent 17th-c house in splendid grounds, inc an orangery with fine collection of camellias, and a colourfully restored walled garden overlooked by a dovecot. The house is decorated with paintings and furnishings from the 18th c, and has a wonderful Gothic library. Meals, snacks, shop, second-hand bookshop; hall and gardens cl Thurs, Fri, and Nov–Mar, hall also cl am; (01263) 837444; £5.70, garden only £2.20; NT. There's public access to the 1,700-acre wooded grounds with their fine mature trees and lake.

FILBY TG4612
Thrigby Hall Wildlife Gardens Popular 18th-c park filled with Asian animals and birds, with tropical and bird houses, tree walk, willow pattern garden, and ornamental wildfowl on the lake. Also a huge jungly swamp hall where crocodiles doze under water. There may be queues on summer wknds. Summer snacks, shop, disabled access; (01493) 369477; *£5.50.

FORNCETT ST MARY TM1694
Industrial Steam Museum Unusual collection of eight giant stationary steam engines rescued from all over the country, inc one that used to open Tower Bridge, and another, the Dover engine, which after 20 years restoration

is finally back to working order. Snacks, shop, disabled access; open May to second wk Nov Mon–Sat, and first Sun of month when the engines are in steam; (01508) 488277; £3.50 (two children free with each adult). The Bird in Hand over at Wreningham is a good value dining pub.

FOXLEY WOOD TG0522
(signed from Foxley village). A big block of ancient woodland, mainly deciduous and grown naturally for many centuries; lovely woodland spring flowers.

GLANDFORD TG0441
Shell Museum 🔳 Curious little museum housing the often very beautiful sea shells and other interesting objects collected by Sir Alfred Jodrell, who lived in nearby Bayfield Hall. Disabled access; cl lunchtimes, cl Sun and Mon (exc bank hols) and Nov–Feb; (01263) 740081; *£1.50. The Kings Head at Letheringsett is quite handy for lunch.

GOODERSTONE TF7602
Attractive village with decent pub, ancient church and nearby watergardens.

GREAT BIRCHAM TF7632
Windmill 🔳 Not far from Houghton Hall, this striking mill is on that Norfolk rarity, a hill – so one of the few places with views. They sell bread baked at the mill's own bakery. Tearooms, shop, some disabled access; open Weds–Sun Easter–Sept; (01485) 578393; £2.50. You can hire bikes. The village is attractive and the Kings Head Hotel (unpretentious despite being a favourite with Sandringham shooting parties) is handy for lunch.

GREAT WITCHINGHAM TG0818
Norfolk Wildlife Park (A1067) 40 acres of attractive parkland filled with a good range of British and European wildlife, with around 500 heron nests up in the trees in spring – a viewing tower brings you eye to eye. The two big play areas will appeal most to slightly older children, with tyres, rope swings and the like. Snacks, shop, disabled access; open Apr–Oct; (01603) 872274; £4. The Old Brewery House in Reepham is the nearest good place for lunch.

GREAT YARMOUTH TG5307
A cross between working town and resort, this still has a busy fishing harbour – used too as a port of call by the Broads cruising boats. There are lots of holiday entertainments, particularly good for families (there's a decent summer fairground too) and some attractions that might well tempt older visitors into the town if they were nearby. The 14th-c **church** of St Nicholas at the top end of the market place has an exceptionally wide nave, and an impressive W front. The smart quay-view Star Hotel has good value bar food.

Amazonia (Sea Front) Indoor tropical paradise with reptiles, insects, butterflies and birds; they have a 4-metre (13-ft) alligator, a python well over 7 metres long (24 ft), and an iguana named Levi. Shop, disabled access; cl 25–26 Dec; (01493) 842202; £3.95.

Elizabethan House Museum (South Quay) This is a patchwork of historical detail – built in 1596, it has a Georgian façade, 16th-c panelled rooms and, among features from later periods, some rooms decorated and furnished in 19th-c style, and a functional Victorian kitchen. Shop; open Sun–Fri Jun–Sept and two wks at Easter; £2. The **Maritime Museum of East Anglia** (Marine Parade) looks at the local fishing industry, with some more incongruous features inc a mummified hand and Indian scalp; open Mon–Fri, Sat and Sun pm Jun–Sept and two wks at Easter; £1. The 13th-c **Tolhouse Museum** (Tolhouse St) used to be the town's gaol and courthouse (you can still see the dungeons). It now has local history, and a brass rubbing centre; times as Maritime Museum above; (01493) 745526 (for all three attractions); £1.

Merrivale Model Village Wellington Pier Gardens) Attractive landscaped gardens with children's rides and remote-controlled cars, and the exceptionally detailed village – featuring a railway, radio-controlled boats and over 200 models. Meals, snacks, shop, disabled access; cl end Oct half-term to Good Fri; (01493) 842097; £3.

Old Merchant's House (Row 117) 17th-c house standing among the narrow lanes or Rows near the waterfront, with some well restored rooms. Shop; cl 1–2pm, and all Nov–Mar; (01493) 857900; £1.85.

Sea Life Centre (Marine Parade) Displays of the kinds of marine life found on the Norfolk coast, as well as underwater tunnels through shark-infested oceans and tropical fish. Meals, snacks, shop, disabled access; cl 25 Dec; (01493) 330631; *£5.75.

GRESSENHALL TF9716

Norfolk Rural Life Museum 🏛 Recently re-displayed, with various exhibits on local life housed in a former workhouse, plus working agricultural reconstructions, rare breeds of farmyard animals in a re-created 1920s farm, and a new adventure play area. Meals, snacks, shop, disabled access; cl Nov–Easter; (01362) 860563; £3.90. The White Horse at Longham has good value food.

GRIMES GRAVES TL8189

Grimes Graves Bring a torch to this Breckland site, as you can climb into one of the 300 pits and vertical shafts which lead down into the galleries – some around 10 metres (33 ft) deep – where the neolithic people mined their flint; the landscape around is pitted by their efforts. No lavatories at the site, but there are some within a mile. Snacks, shop, disabled access; cl 12.30–2pm, all day Mon and Tues Nov–Mar, Christmas; (01842) 810656; £2.

GRIMSTON TF7022

Congham Hall Herb Garden In summer this has around 500 different herbs, in traditional layouts, with many unusual varieties for sale; meals, snacks; open 2–4pm May–Aug (cl Sat); free.

HEACHAM TF6837

Norfolk Lavender (Caley Mill) The largest lavender-growing and distilling operation in the country, along with a national collection of lavender species and cultivars. The guided tour (daily spring bank hol–Sept) really adds interest, and at harvest time they may drive visitors out to the fields. Also rose and herb gardens. Meals and snacks (inc their lavender and lemon scones), shop, disabled access; cl 25–26 Dec, 1 Jan; (01485) 570384; tours (mid-July to mid-Aug) £1.50, £3.95 by minibus. The Gin Trap at Ringstead (with a decent nearby art gallery) and Rose & Crown at

Snettisham both have good food.

HEYDON TG1127 Delightfully unspoilt tucked-away village, with a green that time seems to have passed by, and good food at the unspoilt Earle Arms.

HOLKHAM TF9143

Holkham Hall Splendid Palladian mansion in delightful and very extensive tree-filled grounds with an ornamental lake and 18th-c walled garden. Sumptuously furnished state rooms, with fine paintings by Claude, Rubens, Van Dyck and Gainsborough. An ancestor of the present owner was Thomas Coke, whose revolutionary farming techniques are described in an exhibition in the porter's lodge; there's also a pottery. Snacks, shop, limited disabled access; open pm only Sun–Thurs Whit bank hol–Sept, plus Sun and Mon of Easter and Spring bank hol; (01328) 710227; *£8 for everything, *£5 hall or museum only. Walkers have free access to this coastal estate's driveways; the parkland is a bit sombre, but impressively landscaped with the lake, a temple and obelisk. The Victoria Hotel is handy for lunch. The beach has a bird reserve (and a nudist section). There is a car park quite close to the beach, where pine trees meet the sands; this coastal section of the North Norfolk Coast Path is good for lonely walks – westwards any summer crowds rapidly thin out.

North Norfolk Coast Path From **Overy Staithe** a particularly fine stretch of the path follows a zigzagging dyke – saltmarsh on one side, neat farmland on the other – to the dunes and sandy beach, which never quite looks the same from one day to the next.

HOLME-NEXT-THE-SEA TF6943 From the sandy beach there's a two-mile walk past a rewarding **bird sanctuary** and saltings to Thornham – another good bird-watching place. Another more serious walking possibility is the **Peddars Way** which starts here – an inland link from the Coast Path, running from Holme down through Castle Acre and then in a strikingly straight bee-line right across the county to Knettishall Heath nr Thetford, following ancient-feeling

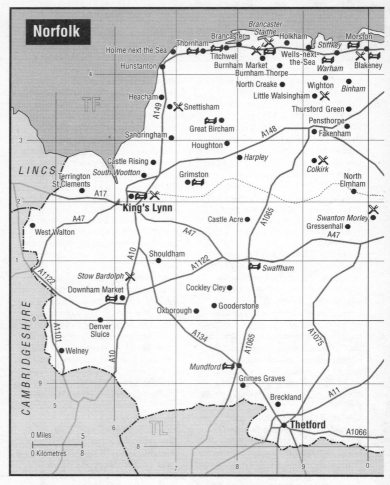

Norfolk

Brancaster Staithe · Holkham · Morston
Brancaster · Stiffkey
Thornham · Wells-next-the-Sea
Holme next the Sea · Titchwell · Warham · Blakeney
Hunstanton · Burnham Market
Burnham Thorpe
North Creake ● · Wighton
Heacham · Little Walsingham ● · Binham
TF · ✗ Snettisham · Thursford Green
Great Bircham · Penthorpe
Sandringham · A148 · Fakenham
Houghton ●
Castle Rising ● · Harpley · Colkirk
LINCS · South Wootton · North Elmham
Terrington St Clements · Grimston
A17 · King's Lynn
West Walton · Castle Acre ● · A1065 · Swanton Morley
A47 · Gressenhall ● · A47
A10 · Shouldham · A47
A1122 · Swaffham
Stow Bardolph · A134
Downham Market · Cockley Cley ● · Gooderstone
Oxborough ●
CAMBRIDGESHIRE · Denver Sluice
A1101 · Welney · A10
A1075
Mundford · A1066
Grimes Graves
Breckland · A11
TL · Thetford · A1066

0 Miles 5
0 Kilometres 8

green ways and quiet lanes. Earnest walkers may find there is a little too much road-walking to sustain interest.
HOLT TG0738
Pleasant little town with some handsome Georgian buildings; Nicholsons in the High St sells anything from clothes to antiques, and has a useful continental-style licensed café; the market-place Feathers has good value food. The terminus of the **North Norfolk Steam Railway** from Sheringham.
HORSEY TG4622
A quiet corner of the coast, below sea level – among the places most at risk of

flooding if the sea defences are breached. There's a good path to the dunes and the sea from the lane past the Nelson Head (good food). On the other side of the main road, **Horsey windpump** is a restored drainage windmill, now in full working order. Teas, small shop; cl Oct–Mar; (01493) 393904; £1.30; NT. This is a good area for a **varied round walk**: a path along quiet reed-fringed Horsey Mere (NT, with wildfowl and otters) and the New Cut to another former drainage windmill – the marshes on the far side of the cut seem alive with birds. Then you can either walk straight back to the

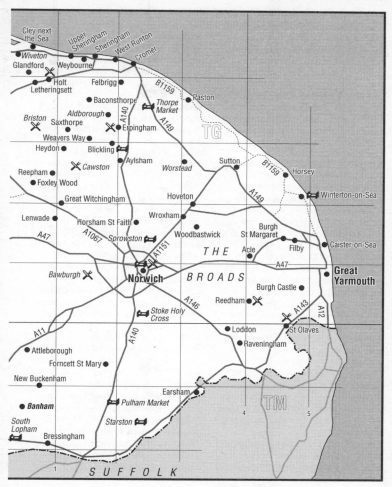

village, or for a total contrast join the beach for sea views nr Horsey Corner.
HORSHAM ST FAITH TG2114
Norwich Aviation Museum 🏛 (Old Norwich Rd) Enthusiastic displays of local aeronautical history, with aircraft (inc Vulcan bomber), engines, and other paraphernalia; on the edge of Norwich Airport, so a good view of the live article too. Snacks, shop; open Tues–Sat, Sun pm and bank hols April–Oct, Weds, Sat and Sun pm Nov–Mar, cl Christmas and New Year; (01603) 893080; £2.50. The thatched Chequers prettily placed at Hainford has good food.

HOUGHTON TF7928
Houghton Hall Built for Robert Walpole and obviously designed to impress, this is a spectacularly grand Palladian mansion set in charming parkland. The state rooms were decorated and furnished by William Kent, and house an important collection of 20,000 model soldiers and other militaria. They occasionally have Shetland ponies and llamas in the stables. Snacks, shop, disabled access; open Thurs, Sun and bank hol pms Easter–Sept; (01485) 528569; £6. Driving along the C road nr North Pole farm you may spot unusual herds of

white deer. The 17th-c Dukes Head at West Rudham has good home cooking.

HOVETON TG3120

Hoveton Hall Gardens Large attractive woodland garden with daffodils and rhododendrons, lakeside walk, kitchen garden and recently redesigned walled old-fashioned herbaceous 'spider garden'. You can stay in a wing of the house. Teas, plant sales; open Weds, Fri, Sat Easter–mid-Sept; (01603) 782798; £3. The Black Horse is useful for lunch.

Wroxham Barns Craft Centre 🔲 (Tunstead Rd) Good for families, with several craft workshops in 18th-c restored farm buildings, as well as a children's farm and traditional fair. Meals, snacks, shop, play area, disabled access; cl 25–26 Dec; (01603) 783762; *£2.25 for farm, otherwise free.

HUNSTANTON TF6740

Clean, fresh and well kept resort with gently shelving tidal sands (summer pony rides), summer boat trips, and pleasant dune walks past the golf course up to the **bird reserve** on Gore Point. On a clear day you can see Boston's Stump across the Wash. The low cliffs around the town are quite colourful, with different rock strata. The Ancient Mariner (part of Le Strange Hotel, Old Hunstanton) is good value, opposite Le Strange Barns (Golf Course road) – an interesting craft gallery, and the Marine Bar (St Edmund's Terrace) has decent food all day.

Oasis Standing out among the typical resort entertainments is this giant leisure park on the prom with tropically heated indoor and outdoor pools and both towering and toddler aquaslides; meals and snacks, disabled access; cl Dec–Jan; (01485) 534227; £3.45.

Sea Life Aquarium (Southern Promenade) An ocean tunnel at this excellent place brings you face to face with deep-water creatures as well as octopuses and toothy conger eels. Snacks, shop, disabled access; cl 25 Dec, Jan; (01485) 533576; £5.50.

KING'S LYNN TF6120

Once England's fourth-largest town, it's quieter now, with pleasant corners, some attractive Georgian brick buildings and a few much older places such as the 17th-c Custom House on the quay by the River Purfleet (now home to the town's Tourist Information Centre), the 15th-c **church** of St Nicholas (Chapel Lane; attractive for festival concerts), the South Gates, Red Mount Chapel and the two medieval guildhalls. The first of these, the 15th-c **St George's Guildhall** (King St), is now the town's theatre, and home of the King's Lynn Festival (open 10am–2pm Mon–Fri, cl bank hols and on concert days so best to ring (01553) 764864); the Tourist Information Centre has details of tours, (01553) 763044. A Tudor warehouse on the South Quay has been converted into a visitor centre for The Wash (see Green Quay below) as part of a £4m project to smarten up the town's waterfront; other plans in the pipeline include improvements to riverside walkways and new facilities for the town's ferry service. On Tues the main market place has some good crafts stalls. The Tudor Rose between there and St Nicholas is good for lunch, and the Globe Hotel on the market place itself is good value.

Green Quay (South Quay) Housed in the Tudor Marriott's Warehouse, this new discovery centre provides a solid introduction to The Wash, with interactive displays explaining how it was formed, and other exhibits inc an aquarium, looking at the wildlife that lives in and around it today. There's a fair bit to interest children inc the chance to make rubbings of animal footprints in the floor, and the Mussel Game, based around the mollusc's daily struggles with local currents. Meals, snacks, shop, disabled access; open daily; (01553) 818500; £3.50.

Lynn Museum (Old Market St) Local history, archaeology and natural history inc skeleton of a Saxon warrior, a surprisingly interesting collection of medieval pilgrim badges, and Victorian fairground gallopers; shop, disabled access, cl Sun, Mon and bank hols; £1.

Tales of the Old Gaol House 🔲 (Saturday Market Pl) Lively journey through the town's rich history; with spirited models, and spooky sights, sounds and smells, this is particularly good for children. Shop, disabled access; cl Weds and Thurs Nov–Easter,

25–26 Dec and 1 Jan; (01553) 774297;
£2.40 (inc audio tour). The tour
includes the 14th-c King John Cup and
other fabulous examples of civic
paraphernalia housed in the Undercroft
of the handsome medieval Trinity
Guildhall.

Town House Museum (Queen St)
Social history told through
reconstructed room settings from the
Middle Ages to the 1950s inc Victorian
kitchen, nursery and town garden.
Shop, limited disabled access; cl Sun exc
pm May–Sept, and bank hols; £1.80.

Trues Yard 🖼 (North St) Restored
old fishermen's cottages giving a good
picture of life here in the last century,
when families of up to 11 were often
squeezed into two little rooms. Snacks,
shop, disabled access; (01553) 770479;
£1.90.

LENWADE TG1017

Dinosaur Park (Weston Park, off
A1067) A splendidly silly treat for small
children, with life-size reconstructions
of dinosaurs hidden in 300 acres of
nicely kept woodland – good for
children to see how big some of these
beasts really were. Themed play areas
(one specially for under-5s) include the
ingenious Climb-a-Saurus, a 23-metre
(75-ft) brontosaurus replica with slides,
ladders, and so on tucked away inside;
also woodland maze, animals to handle
in the new 'secret garden', and other
activities (for a small extra charge) inc a
deer safari and crazy golf. Meals, snacks,
shop, disabled access; open daily mid-
Apr to mid-Sept, plus Fri–Sun and
school hols late Mar–Oct; (01603)
876312; £5.50 (£4.50 children 3–14).

LETHERINGSETT TG0638
The **church** has an unusual round
tower. A restored **watermill** in a
pretty setting still mills flour from local
wheat. Cl Sat pm and all Sun, with
demonstrations wkdy pms
(Tues–Thurs in winter); (01263)
713153; £3 during demonstrations,
otherwise £2. The Kings Head is
pleasant for lunch.

LITTLE WALSINGHAM TF9336
Once as popular a centre of pilgrimage
as Canterbury, thanks to a replica of the
Virgin Mary's home in Nazareth. Things
tailed off when Henry VIII destroyed
the priory and its shrine in 1538, but

picked up again in the 20th c. The Bull
Inn is a good place, with plenty of
pilgrimage customers. The village is also
the terminus of the **Wells &
Walsingham Light Railway** which
runs from Wells-next-the-Sea.

Shirehall Museum 🖼 Emphasis on
the pilgrimage to Walsingham; displays
are in an almost perfect Georgian
courtroom complete with original
fittings. Shop, limited disabled access; cl
Nov–Easter; (01328) 820510; £1 joint
ticket with abbey £3.

Walsingham Abbey Grounds
Plenty of remains of the 12th-c building,
inc the Abbey Gates, Great Arch, part
of the refectory and the Holy Wells.
Pleasant gardens and woodland walks,
with masses of snowdrops in early
spring. Open via the Shirehall Museum
and Tourist Information Centre in
summer, or the estate office in winter
(office hours only), cl wknds Nov–Mar
(exc Feb), and daily from 22 Dec–Jan;
(01328) 820259; £2.50 (joint ticket with
Shirehall Museum £3).

LODDON TM3695

Reads Nursery (Hales Hall, off A146
SE) Specialising for over a century in
unusual conservatory plants, inc a good
range of lemon, orange and other citrus
fruits, also nut trees etc. Disabled
access; cl Mon (exc bank hols) and 24
Dec–5 Jan; (01508) 548395; nursery
free, barn and garden £2. The village is
attractive, and the 17th-c Swan has
home-made food.

NEW BUCKENHAM TM0890
A fine village, largely medieval, with a
decent pub.

NORTH CREAKE TF8539

Creake Abbey All that remains of this
early 13th-c Augustinian priory is the
crossing and east arm, but it's still
worth a passing look, and the village is
charming. Cartwrights at South Creake
has good food.

NORTH ELMHAM TF9821

North Elmham church An attractive
13th-c building, odd in that there's a
step down into it; a little further N are
the interesting ruins of a **Saxon
cathedral**, and there are pleasant
walks. The Kings Head has good food.

NORWICH TG2308
Busy but civilised, the old centre has
quite a concentration of attractive

streets and buildings, with all sorts of surprises in the narrow streets and lanes that still follow its medieval layout. One such surprise is the new sleek horseshoe-shaped, glass-covered building between Bethel St and Theatre St which, come March, will be home to one of Britain's most advanced public libraries (to replace the one destroyed by fire in 1994) with computer links to 30 centres throughout the county, as well as several cafés and new tourist information and heritage centres. Elm St is especially handsome, and there are plenty of antiques shops and so forth. Even the more commercial/industrial centre N of the River Wensum has fine patches (such as Colegate), and the main shopping areas are closed to traffic. Fortunately the visually disappointing university is hidden away out on the W edge, though in term-time its students do bring a good bit of life into the centre. Norwich is the home of Colmans Mustard, and the Mustard Shop (Bridewell Alley) has some varieties you may not have come across before. The ancient Adam & Eve (Bishopgate) is good for lunch, the Gardeners Arms (Timber Hill) is interesting, and other pubs useful for a bite to eat without being overrun by students include the Unthank Arms (Newmarket St) and riverside Ribs of Beef (Wensum St).

Assembly House (Theatre St) Across the road from the new library, this chameleonic building was founded as a hospice in 1248, and has served as priest's college, family home, 18th-c cards house, girls' school and wartime camouflage school. Although the chapel was completely destroyed in 1548, and more recently, a fire ravaged the building in 1995, some of the original buildings remain and the brick-vaulted medieval cellar still lies beneath the restaurant. Meals, snacks, shop, disabled access; cl Sun; (01603) 626402; free.

Boat trips From the River Wensum you can clearly see how some of the city's older buildings were designed for water-borne traffic, rather than road transport.

Bridewell Museum (Bridewell Alley) 14th-c building used as a prison from 1583 to 1828, with exhibits on the town's trade and industries, and reconstructed late 19th-c shops. Usually cl Sun, and Oct–Mar, though best to check; (01603) 493625; £2.

Castle Museum (Castle Meadow) This impressive four-square Norman fortress dominates the city from its hill; it reopens in May following refurbishment. As well as displays of art (with particular emphasis on the Norwich School), silverware (for which the town was famous), ceramics, and natural history, it will include a new lecture theatre, a café in the opened-up rotunda, and an underground passage linking it to a former courtroom in the Shirehall, now a regimental museum; best to phone (01603) 493625, nearer the time.

Dragon Hall 🏛 (King St) Well preserved medieval merchant's hall, with splendid timber-framed roof, intricate carvings, cellars, vaulted undercroft, and some finely painted roundels. Shop, limited disabled access; cl Sun, Sat Nov–Mar, 21 Dec–2 Jan, bank hols; (01603) 663922; *£1.50.

Inspire Hands-on Science Centre 🏛 Popular with readers, in medieval St Michael's church (Coslany St) – hence the witty name. Snacks, shop, disabled access; cl Mon, Christmas wk; *£3.50.

Norwich Cathedral The modern city is firmly shut out by the great medieval gateways of the close. Basically medieval, the church has some fine features from later periods – the flying buttresses for example, and the late 15th-c vaulted roof, spire and west window with Victorian glass. The Norman cloisters are the largest in the country, rebuilt after a serious riot between city and cathedral in 1272, and remarkable for the 400 bosses carved with scenes of medieval life (there are hundreds more in the cathedral itself, though less easy to see). Meals, snacks and shop (not Sun), disabled access; (01603) 764385; suggested donation £3. Free guided tours leave the Welcome Desk at 10.45am and 2.15pm Mon–Sat Jun–Oct, tours at other times by prior arrangement. The extensive precincts make an awe-inspiring impression: medieval alleys and secluded gardens, with all sorts of varied buildings from the cottages of Hooks Walk through the finer houses in the Upper Close to the buildings of Norwich School. The best view of the cathedral is from the river by Pulls Ferry; it's not easy to see from other parts of the town.

Puppet Theatre 🖼 (St James's Church, Whitefriars) Useful diversion for children, ring for performance times. Shop, snacks, disabled access; (01603) 629921; £5, children £3.75, 2 hours' free parking in Anglia Sq car park.

Sainsbury Centre for Visual Arts 🖼 (University of East Anglia, off B1108 W) Striking Norman Foster building with notable 19th- and 20th-c European art and a fascinating range of ethnographic art, inc African tribal sculpture, and Egyptian and Asian antiquities. Meals, snacks, shop, disabled access; cl Mon, 23 Dec–2 Jan; (01603) 593199; £2.

St Peter Hungate Literally dozens of churches, in great variety, are one of the city's joys. Perhaps the finest of all is this one on Princes St, an impressive 15th-c church with grand hammer-beam roof, museum of church art and brass rubbing centre.

OXBOROUGH TF7401

Oxburgh Hall Henry VIII stayed in this pretty moated manor house in 1487, and the room is now decorated with wall hangings worked by Mary Queen of Scots. Unfortunately, most of the house was thoroughly refurbished during Victorian times, but the gatehouse remains as an awe-inspiring example of 15th-c building work, 24 metres (80 ft) high. The garden has a colourfully restored French parterre. Meals, snacks, shop, disabled access to ground floor only; cl Thurs, Fri, and early Nov–Mar, garden also open some wknds Mar, house cl am; (01366) 328258; *£5.40, *£2.70 garden only; NT. The Bedingfeld Arms opposite has decent food.

PASTON TG3135

Paston windmill A fine example.

PENSTHORPE TF9429

Pensthorpe Waterfowl Trust (A1067) This good-sized collection of wild and exotic waterfowl had just been put on the market as we went to press,

but the staff are hopeful that, when a new owner is found, they will continue to run it along similar lines. The visitor centre has displays of wildlife art and photography. Also woodland, meadow, lakeside and riverside nature trails, adventure playground, and very good talks and events. Meals, snacks, shop, disabled access; cl wkdys Jan–Mar, 25 Dec, 1 Jan; (01328) 851465; *£4.80.

RAVENINGHAM TM3996

Raveningham Hall Gardens Interesting collection of rare shrubs, shrub roses, traditional kitchen garden, arboretum, and Victorian conservatory. Teas; open Sun and bank hol Mon pms Apr–July; (01508) 548222; £2.

Raveningham Craft Workshops (Beccles Rd) Victorian farm buildings with furniture-making, piano workshop, antiques and other workshops; teas; free. Loddon's the best nearby place for a meal.

REEDHAM TG4202

Pettitts Animal Adventure Park 🖼 You can still watch the demonstrations of feather craft, though they've become a little swamped by the other attractions here, inc aviaries, gnome village, American-style locomotive ride around the grounds, big adventure playground, miniature horse stud, and crazy golf. New owners take over the park just before this book comes out, but the format is likely to remain the same. Meals, snacks, shop, some disabled access; cl Sat (exc bank hol wknds), and Nov–Easter; (01493) 700094; £6.75. The Railway Tavern (open all day wknds) has good food and brews its own fine beers, and the little car ferry here is fun.

REEPHAM TG0922 Attractive large village or small town with some worthwhile shops and a fine old inn (the Old Brewery House). A cycle route runs past well restored fomer station with cycle hire, tearooms, gift shop and a **nostalgia collection** (cl 25 Dec, 1 Jan).

SANDRINGHAM TF6928

Sandringham House Many people come to this part of the county for its connection with the Royal Family. Sandringham House was bought by Queen Victoria for her son Edward in

1862 and has become famous as the Royal Christmas residence; the 19th-c building is filled with their portraits and those of their European counterparts, and has various gifts presented to the family over the years. Unlike at their other homes, you can see most of the rooms the family use, so there's a much more intimate feel than you'd get at Windsor or Buckingham Palace; expect queues though. The grounds and surrounding country park are lovely, with nature trails, adventure playground, and the parish church of St Mary Magdalene. Lovely rhododendrons in the woods May/Jun. Meals, snacks, shop, disabled access (a train runs between the grounds entrance and the house); open mid-Apr to early Oct, exc during summer Royal visit – best to check for dates; (01553) 772675; £5.50, £4.50 grounds and museum only. In summer pick-your-own lets you sample fruit that might otherwise have graced the Royal table. There's free access to **Sandringham Country Park** with its majestic trees and glades, a notable parkland walking area. The Feathers towards Dersingham is useful for lunch.

SAXTHORPE TG1332
Mannington Gardens The most beautiful feature of these gardens is the summer rose display, but 20 miles of footpaths around the hall and woodland are open all year (£1 parking). Snacks, shop, disabled access; gardens open Weds–Fri Jun–Aug and Sun pm May–Sept; (01263) 874175; £3. Paths lead to the pleasant grounds of Wolterton Park. The Walpole Arms in the pretty nearby village of Itteringham has good food.

SHERINGHAM TG1543
The working fishing harbour has some old buildings around it, though there's a lot of more modern building up behind. The beach is nice, and the Two Lifeboats has good sea views (as well as decent food inc fresh fish).
North Norfolk Railway Full-size steam railway, chugging through over five miles of lovely coastal scenery to Holt. Plenty of railway memorabilia at the Sheringham station, and a collection of steam engines and vintage rolling stock. Meals, snacks, shop, disabled

access; steam trains Apr–Dec and some additional special event wknds; (01263) 822045 for timetable; £6.50 all day ticket.
Sheringham Park Extensive parkland, gloriously landscaped by Humphry Repton (it was his favourite work) with excellent coastal views from its waymarked walks and viewing towers. Also mature trees and fine azaleas and rhododendrons (best late May/June), and good walks to the coast. A restored steam-powered sawmill operates some wknds; Snacks, disabled access; (01263) 823778; free, but parking £2.60; NT.
Upper Sheringham The 14th-c **church** in this quiet flintstone village is very attractive, and the Red Lion is a pleasant stop. Footpaths from here lead to Sheringham Park.

SHOULDHAM TF6709
There are **nature trails** in pleasant woods just N of this attractive unspoilt village, which has a decent pub.

SNETTISHAM TF6833
Park Farm 🖼 Working farm offering good insight into seasonal farming operations – lambing, shearing, and red deer calving. Lots of animals, plus impressive adventure playground, and a craft centre. Meals, snacks, shop, disabled access; cl Mon–Thurs Nov–Jan; (01485) 542425; £3.95 for either farm or 45-min guided ride around deer park, £7 for both. Pretty walks nearby, as well as a nature reserve along the beach. The Rose & Crown is a good dining pub.

ST OLAVE'S TM4599
St Olave's Priory Ruins of 13th-c Augustinian priory; you can still see the fine brick undercroft in the cloister – a remarkable early use of this material; free. The riverside Bell is very old indeed, though much modernised.

SUTTON TG3923
Windmill The most striking mill in Norfolk and the tallest in Britain, nine floors high; shop, limited disabled access; cl Oct–Mar; (01692) 581195; £3.50.

TERRINGTON ST CLEMENT TF5519
African Violet Centre Wide range of plants besides the African violets it's developed so successfully as house

plants. Good tearoom, children's play area; cl 25–26 Dec, 1 Jan; (01553) 828374. The Woolpack at Walpole Cross Keys has decent food.

THETFORD TL8683

Ancient House Museum Early Tudor house with fine oak ceilings, now a local history museum with small period herb garden behind. Shop; cl 12.30–1pm, Sun (exc pm in summer); (01842) 752599; free exc July and Aug, when £1.

Thetford Priory Ruins of 12th-c Cluniac monastery; you can easily make out the full ground plan of the cloisters, and the 14th-c gatehouse still stands; disabled access; free.
Warren Lodge 15th-c flint former hunting lodge, worth a look. The Bell and Thomas Paine are both civilised places for lunch.

THORNHAM TF7243

Walks along the coastline here give marvellous views, and this is good bird-watching terrain, with wading birds, the occasional marsh harrier and maybe even seals. Beware of tides when parking on the seafront, as the lower road can be flooded.

THURSFORD GREEN TF9734

Thursford Collection 🎫 valid till Oct. Bouncy collection of barrel, street and fairground musical organs and a Wurlitzer cinema organ, most demonstrated every day. Also showmen's steam engines, adventure playground, and Venetian Gondola switchback ride. Meals, snacks, shop, disabled access; cl am and Jan–Easter; (01328) 878477; £4.70.

TITCHWELL TF7544

Bird-watching Pleasant coastal village with good RSPB reserve nearby; besides the Manor Hotel, the Three Horseshoes has good value food and bedrooms.

WEAVERS WAY TG1531

This long-distance path can be used as part of a link from the parkland of Blickling Hall to take in walks through and around the **Wolterton Park** and **Mannington Hall** estates, both owned by the Walpoles, who have opened up a network of paths in the area extending NW to **Holt Country Park**. The Saracens Head on the edge of Wolterton Park is a very civilised

dining pub.

WELLS-NEXT-THE-SEA TF9142

Pleasant rather gracious little village-sized town; don't be fooled by the name – the sea is a mile away these days, though there's a particularly good stretch of the North Norfolk Coast Path from here to **Overy Staithe**, where the sandy beach never looks quite the same from one day to the next. The Crown is good for lunch.

Wells & Walsingham Light Railway 🎫 Passing through quietly attractive scenery, this railway is remarkable for being the longest in the world to use a 10¼-inch gauge track, with a steam locomotive built specially for it not long ago. Snacks, shop; cl end Oct–Mar; (01328) 710631 for times; £5.50 return.

WELNEY TL5393

Wildfowl & Wetlands Trust 🎫 (Hundred Foot Bank) Excellent 1,000-acre wild bird reserve, with numerous hides, spacious observatory, and floodlit lagoon. In winter the sights include up to 4,000 migratory Bewick's swans and all sorts of duck; it can be busy then, and you'll need to wrap up well. In spring the emphasis switches to waders and other birds. There's a summer nature trail, and interesting conducted summer walks. Snacks, shop, part disabled access; cl 25 Dec; (01353) 860711; £3.50. In winter some local roads can be flooded, and then you can approach it only from the E.

WEST RUNTON TG2042

Norfolk Shire Horse Centre Extensive collection of draught horses and moorland and mountain ponies. You can hire riding horses by the hour, and there's a children's farm (though some readers feel the aviaries and hutches are a little crowded). Meals, snacks, shop, disabled access; cl Sat (exc bank hol wknds and Aug), and Nov–Easter; (01263) 837339; £4.75. The seaside village itself is attractive, and the Village Inn is useful for lunch.

WEST WALTON TF4713

West Walton church A textbook example of early Gothic architecture; just about all of it dates from the mid-13th c, and there's a cool elegance throughout. The King of Hearts (good for lunch) holds the key.

WEYBOURNE TG1043
Muckleburgh Collection 🏛 (A149)
Around 3,000 military items inc World
War II fighting vehicles on the site of a
former military camp, once the lynch-
pin of defences on this coast. You can
ride in a Gama Goat (a six-wheel
American personnel carrier), and there
are tank demonstrations every Sun,
bank hols and wkdys during summer
school hols. Meals and snacks (in
NAAFI-style café), shop, disabled
access; cl Nov–mid-Feb; (01263)
588210; *£4.50. The Dun Cow
overlooking the Salthouse marshes has
decent food, with a nearby shack selling
very fresh shellfish and samphire.
Salthouse and Kelling back heathy
hinterlands, allowing walkers a mix
between this and the unvaryingly
straight coast.

WIGHTON TF9439
Pleasant village in attractive coastal
area, once home to the sculptor Henry
Moore; the Carpenters Arms is a
decent pub, and the **Old School
House** is a good art gallery. A stop on
the **Wells & Walsingham Light
Railway.**

WINTERTON-ON-SEA TG4919
One of the quieter seaside resorts on
this coast, with a gentle villagey feel, and
a particularly good beach over the
dunes – nice for a wander by the sea;
the 17th-c Fisherman's Return is very
pleasant for lunch.

WOODBASTWICK TG3215
Picturesque thatched estate village,
home to Woodfordes Brewery, one of
Britain's best microbreweries; the Fur
& Feather dining pub is the brewery tap.

WROXHAM TG3017
Barton House Railway (Hartwell
Rd) Miniature railway through a big
riverside garden; open pm third Sun of
month in summer, 40p. Boats leave for
here from Wroxham Bridge.
Other attractive villages here, all
with decent pubs, include Aldborough
TG1834, Binham TF9839, Colkirk
TF9126, Harpley TF7825, Mundford
TL8093, South Wootton TF6422,
Stiffkey (pronounced 'Stewkie')
TF9743, Swanton Morley TG0116,
Wiveton TG0342 and Worstead
TG3025. The Three Horseshoes at
Warham TF9441 is a decent pub in an
attractive coastal area.

Where to eat

BAWBURGH TG1508 **Kings Head** *Harts Lane (01603)* 744977 Bustling old pub
with friendly licensees, four linked rooms with low beams and standing timbers, a
big log fire and a woodburner, imaginative attractively presented food (the weekly
specials are much liked), a no smoking restaurant, and well kept real ales; cl 25 Dec
pm; disabled access. £24.25|**£4.95**
BLAKENEY TG0243 **White Horse** *4 High St (01263)* 740574 Small friendly
hotel nr harbour (if that's not too grand a word), with a good mix of chatty
customers in the attractively decorated long bar, enjoyable food inc local fish, real
ales, up to 11 wines by the glass, a small no smoking area and conservatory
restaurant, and efficient friendly service; bdrms. £18|**£5.95**
BRANCASTER STAITHE TF7944 **Jolly Sailors** *Main Rd (01485)* 210314 On
the edge of thousands of acres of National Trust dunes and salt flats, this stylish old-
fashioned pub has a diary of recent sightings of rare bird species on the bar; a log fire
and good mix of seats in three small rooms, enjoyable often imaginative bar food,
prompt friendly service, well kept real ales, decent wines, and an attractive no
smoking restaurant; nice garden with a terrace, enclosed play area, and tennis
court. £19.20|**£6.95**
BRISTON TG0633 **John H Stracey** *Norwich Rd (01263)* 860891 Neatly kept and
well run country dining pub with a wide choice of well cooked fairly priced bar food,
and popular restaurant with speciality evenings; comfortable seats and log fire, well
kept real ales, and friendly licensees; comfortable bdrms; partial disabled access.
£15.25|**£6.50**
BURNHAM MARKET TF8342 **Fishes** *Market Pl 01328* 738588 Attractive and
homely blue and white decorated restaurant with long-standing owners, friendly

staff, highly enjoyable unpretentious fresh fish and seafood, and good traditional puddings; cl Sun pm, Mon. £23.50/3-course lunch £12.95

CAWSTON TG1422 **Ratcatchers** *Easton Way, Eastgate (01603) 871430* Bustling, warmly welcoming dining pub with a nice mix of wooden tables and chairs in L-shaped beamed bar, an open fire, a quiet and cosy no smoking candlelit dining room and no smoking conservatory, a huge choice of good freshly prepared food inc interesting fresh fish dishes, real ales, and a nice wine list; disabled access. £28|£9

COLKIRK TF9126 **Crown** *Crown Rd (01328) 862172* Unpretentious, friendly village pub with open fires, solid country furniture, a pleasantly informal no smoking dining room, good promptly served food (nice daily specials inc vegetarian choices), well kept real ales, decent wine list, and helpful landlord; own bowling green behind. £17.50|£4.55

ERPINGHAM TG1932 **Ark** *The Street (01263) 761535* Lovely individual food inc home-made bread and home-grown vegetables in simple relaxed cottage; log fire and courteous service; bdrms; cl Sun pm, Mon, winter Tues, part Oct; disabled access. £31/3-course Sun lunch £15.25

ERPINGHAM TG1732 **Saracens Head** *(01263) 768909* Comfortably civilised inn with simple but stylish two-room bar, a nice mix of seats, log fires and fresh flowers, excellent inventive food inc good value 2-course Sun supper and 3-course monthly feasts, very well kept real ales, interesting wines, and a charming old-fashioned gravel stableyard; good bdrms; cl 25 Dec; limited disabled access. £22|£7

HOLT TG0738 **Owl Tea Rooms** *White Lion St (01263) 713232* Georgian building with bakery and tearooms behind, serving home-made bread, scones, quiches and pies served on plates made by the owners; organic local veg, daily specials and vegetarian choices, home-made preserves, and good cream teas; cl Sun, bank hols; disabled access. £12.50|£3.95

KING'S LYNN TF6119 **Rococo** *11 Saturday Market Pl (01553) 771483* Delicious, imaginative modern cooking using fresh local produce in pretty dining room with lots of fresh flowers and paintings; cosy lounge area, a relaxed atmosphere, good informal service, and decent wines; cl Sun, Mon am, 24–31 Dec; disabled access. £36 dinner, £20 lunch

LITTLE WALSINGHAM TF9336 **Old Bakehouse** *33 High St (01328) 820454* In an attractive medieval village, this Georgian-fronted house has high beams in the main restaurant, a smaller dining room with a brick oven dating from 1550, and downstairs bar; sound cooking (evenings only) with plenty of choice, and reasonably priced French wines; bdrms; cl Sun, Mon, Tues, Weds to non-residents, 2 wks Jan, 1 wk Jun, 2 wks Nov; children over 5. £30/3-courses Thurs pm £13.50

NORWICH TG2208 **Adlards** *79 Upper St Giles St (01603) 633522* Warmly friendly and quietly decorated restaurant serving delicious carefully thought-out food from a menu that changes daily, lovely puddings, fine service, and good wine list; cl Sun, Mon am, 1 wk after Christmas; disabled access. £40 dinner, £25 lunch

REEDHAM TG4001 **Ferry** *Ferry Rd (01493) 700429* Perfectly placed pub beside River Yare with plenty of tables to watch boats or swans (good moorings); a secluded back bar with fine log fire, long front bar with big picture windows, no smoking restaurant, and very popular good food; partial disabled access. £15.95|£3.75

SNETTISHAM TF6834 **Rose & Crown** *Old Church Rd (01485) 541382* Pretty white cottage with boldly decorated new no smoking Cellar Bar, cheerfully painted Garden Room, and unchanged back bar; log fires, 5 real ales, 20 wines by the glass, and very good imaginative food; new frozen take-away service, too; lovely walled garden with wooden play fort, guinea-pigs and chipmunks; lovely bdrms; well behaved dogs welcome; disabled access. £27.50|£6.50

ST OLAVE'S TM4599 **Priory Farm** *Beccles Rd (01493) 488432* Good interesting food inc fresh fish and children's menu; right by St Olave's Priory; open all day Jun-Sept (normal hours the rest of the year); disabled access. £15|£6.95

STOW BARDOLPH TF6205 **Hare Arms** *Lynn Rd (01366) 382229* Pretty, creeper-covered pub with old advertising signs, fresh flowers, plenty of tables around its central servery, and a good log fire in welcoming bar; maybe two friendly ginger cats and a sort of tabby; spacious, heated and well planted no smoking conservatory, good, interesting bar food, well kept real ales, a decent range of wines, and quite a few malt whiskies; pretty garden with picnic-sets and wandering peacocks and chickens; cl 25–26 Dec. £30|£8

SWANTON MORLEY TG0217 **Darbys** *Elsing Rd (01362) 637647* Cosy beamed country pub decorated with lots of farm tools and so forth, very well kept real ales, and good, generously served, often interesting bar food (their beef comes from their own farm); log fire, friendly staff, children's room and adventure playground; also bdrms, self-catering, camping, caravan site, horse facilities, country trails; disabled access. £18|£5.50

UPPER SHERINGHAM TG1542 **Red Lion** *The Street (01263) 825408* Relaxing little flint cottage with two quiet small bars, simple furnishings, a big woodburner, newspapers to read, and no smoking snug; good food, well kept real ales and over 30 whiskies. £17.95|**£6.75**

Special thanks to Michael and Jenny Back, Mr and Mrs Walster and J F M West

NORTHAMPTONSHIRE

A bounty of grand houses, and unspoilt countryside dotted with charming gold stone villages; not so much for families

Marketing experts have recently been struggling to find a 'brand name' for this archetypal shire county. Suggestions so far have ranged from 'Diana Country' (the princess is buried at Althorp, her ancestral home), 'Boot Country' (the county's cobbling tradition is well represented at Northampton's Central Museum), and 'Squires and Spires', which, however dire, is perhaps most appropriate because, despite its diminutive stature, Northamptonshire is punctuated by elegant stone spires and has an unrivalled concentration of great houses in grand surroundings.

Of these places, those especially suited for families include richly furnished Boughton House (with its adventure playground), Sulgrave Manor (splendid historically themed events), and the county's Family Attraction of the Year, Holdenby House, replete with lovely gardens, decent falconry centre, and lively bank holiday period re-creations.

Wicksteed Park on the edge of Kettering is a good treat for children, Manor House Museum in the town itself has free children's activities in school holidays, and boat trips are just part of the fun at the Stoke Bruerne Canal Museum.

Oundle's dragonfly centre, Rushton's Triangular Lodge, and Naseby's Civil War model add a touch of the unusual.

The countryside here is very relaxing, with gently appealing partly wooded landscapes, villages built of red or honey-coloured stone, and the fine churches of the Nene Valley.

The county is notable for its lovely stone-built churches, many with elegant spires visible a long way off and a memorable feature of the county's landscape — particularly along the valley of the River Nene. Besides those mentioned above we'd suggest Burton Latimer SP9075, Dodford SP6160 (striking memorials), Earls Barton SP8563 (fine Saxon tower), Easton Maudit SP8858, Great Weldon SP9289, Higham Ferrers SP9669, Kings Sutton SP4936, Lowick SP9780, Middleton Cheney SP4941, Passenham SP7739 (17th-c murals), Raunds SP9972, Rothwell SP8181 and Whiston SP8460. With many of these, the village is well worth seeing, too.

Please let us know what you think of places in the *Guide*. Use the report forms at the back of the book or simply write us a letter.

Where to stay

ASHBY ST LEDGERS SP5768 **Olde Coach House** *Ashby St Ledgers, Rugby, Warwickshire CV23 8UN (01788) 890349* **£65**, plus special breaks; 6 rms. In an attractive thatched stone village, this handsome creeper-covered inn has several comfortable, rambling and atmospheric rooms, a winter log fire, straightforward bar food, well kept beer, and big gardens with children's activity centre; cl 25–26 Dec

BADBY SP5558 **Windmill** *Main St, Badby, Daventry, Northamptonshire NN11 3AN (01327) 702363* **£69**, plus special breaks; 8 rms. Carefully modernised thatched stone inn with beams, flagstones and huge inglenook fireplace in front bar, a cosy comfortable lounge, good generously served bar and restaurant food, and decent wines; fine views of the pretty village from car park

CASTLE ASHBY SP8659 **Falcon** *Castle Ashby, Northampton, Northamptonshire NN7 1LF (01604) 696200* **£95.50**; 16 nicely decorated rms. Smart hotel in attractive preserved village, with stone walls and hops on dark beams in the 16th-c cellar bar, an open fire, and real ales; restaurant overlooking pretty garden, good breakfasts, and welcoming landlord; children over 10 in evening restaurant; disabled access

EAST HADDON SP6668 **Red Lion** *Main St, East Haddon, Northampton NN6 8BU (01604) 770223* **£75**, 5 rms. Rather elegant and substantial golden stone hotel with a smart, well heeled feel in the neat lounge bar, a nice mix of furniture, recessed china cabinets, old prints, and pewter, and small public bar with well kept real ales and decent wines; pretty restaurant, high quality daily-changing food, and enjoyable breakfasts; attractive walled garden; 25–26 Dec

OLD SP7873 **Wold Farm** *Harrington Rd, Old, Northampton, Northamptonshire NN6 9RJ (01604) 781258* **£50**; 5 rms. No smoking 18th-c farmhouse in a quiet village, with spacious interesting rooms, hearty breakfasts in the beamed dining room, attentive welcoming owners, log fire, snooker table, and two pretty gardens

OUNDLE TL0488 **Talbot** *New St, Oundle, Peterborough, Cambridgeshire PE8 4EA (01832) 273621* **£54**, plus special breaks; 39 most attractive big rms. Mary Queen of Scots walked to her execution down a staircase that's now in this carefully refurbished 17th-c hotel; attractive cosy lounges, big log fires, good food in timbered restaurant, and garden

PAULERSPURY SP7245 **Vine House** *100 High St, Paulerspury, Towcester, Northamptonshire NN12 7NA (01327) 811267* **£69***; 6 individually decorated rms. 300-year-old building with carefully preserved original features, a relaxed welcoming atmosphere, cosy bar with open fire, and very good modern English cooking (inc home-made bread and petits fours) in attractive restaurant; pretty cottage garden; cl 1 wk over Christmas

SUDBOROUGH SP9682 **Vane Arms** *Main St, Sudborough, Kettering, Northamptonshire NN14 3BX (01832) 733223* **£45***; 3 rms. Cheerful, relaxed thatched pub on picturesque village street, with comfortable main bar, inglenook fireplaces, friendly helpful staff, no smoking upstairs restaurant, and a marvellous range of real ales; disabled access

We welcome reports from readers

This *Guide* depends on readers' reports. Do help us if you can – in return, we offer a discount on the next edition to people who've helped us with reports for it. Tell us what you think about places already in it, and anything extra you think we should say about them. And send us your ideas for inclusion in the next edition: places to visit, eat at or stay in, attractive drives or walks, maybe even unusual interesting shops you know of. Use the card in the middle, the report forms at the end, or just write – no stamp needed: *The Good Britain Guide*, FREEPOST TN1569, Wadhurst, E Sussex TN5 7BR.

To see and do

Northamptonshire Family Attraction of the Year

HOLDENBY SP6967 **Holdenby House, Gardens & Falconry Centre**
Hardly what you'd call pokey in its present form, this fine-looking house was
originally eight times the size it is now, and the largest house in Elizabethan
England. It was a Royal palace for part of the 17th c, and subsequently a prison,
holding the captured King Charles I at the end of the First Civil War. Along the
King's Walk you can retrace the unhappy monarch's steps around parts of the
garden; his guard was said to find it hard to keep up. Today it's most interesting
to families on Easter, spring and summer bank holiday Suns and Mons, when
there are always special events and extra activities for children. They might re-
create a Victorian Easter – or a 14th-c battle, with the chance to try on armour.
On days like these they'll have free activity packs for younger children, and it's
the only time you'll be able to see inside the house, with its unique collection of
rare and unusual pianos. Though it's not quite so lively on other days (note the
full opening times below), there's still a good deal to see, and more to keep
children amused than at most places in this generally more adult-friendly area.
They've a splendid collection of birds of prey, with regular flying displays of
buzzards, owls and kestrels, plus a working armourer and saddlery. The
gardens are lovely, covering 20 acres, with an Elizabethan garden laid out by
Rosemary Verey that includes only plants that would have been grown in 1580.
Children will probably prefer the reconstructed 17th-c farmstead: as well as
period sights and smells there are rare breeds such as soays (the closest thing
to Stone Age sheep), and white park cattle, wild in Britain in Roman times.
There's also a small play area. The family that live here (the Lowthers) have had
more MPs than any other clan. Teas, shop, limited disabled access; open Sun pm
Apr–Sept, plus bank hols, and daily exc Sat July and Aug (if all you want is the
falconry, that's open daily exc Sat all spring and summer). On event days
admission is £5 (£3 children over 3) if you want to see the house, £4 (£2
children) if you don't; other times it's £3 (£1.75 children) for the gardens and
falconry, or £2 (£1 children) for just the falconry.

ALTHORP SP6864
Althorp (Great Brington) The home of
the Spencer family since 1508,
remodelled several times, especially in
the 17th and 18th c, and now firmly on
the map as the resting place of Diana,
Princess of Wales. You can't see the
grave itself (it's on an islet in the Oval
Lake in a small arboretum just NE of the
house), but you can view the lake, and
the former stable block is now a
museum/memorial filled with her
personal possessions, favourite clothes,
video footage of her life and some of the
thousands of books of condolences
sent to Kensington Palace on her death.
The house itself has a splendid
collection of furnishings and porcelain,
and paintings by Rubens, Van Dyck and
Lely. Snacks, shop, some disabled
access; open pm daily July and Aug but
only by advance booking; (01604)

7702097/592020; *£10. The attractive
church is on the edge of the park; its
graveyard has fine views. On the far side
of the estate there's public access to a
sandy-floored area of wildlife-filled pine
woods and heathland known as
Harlestone Firs, pleasant for walking.
The village itself is charming, and the
Fox & Hounds here has decent food,
and lots of character.
ASHBY ST LEDGERS SP5768
This village is quite a gem: fine manor
house, Lutyens almshouses, and a
remarkable **church** with wall paintings,
pre-Reformation pews and triple-
decker pulpit (few signs of interference
by the Reformers, Cromwell or even
the Victorians). The Olde Coach House
has decent food.
BADBY SP5559
Knightley Way This path takes a
pleasant 12-mile course from the

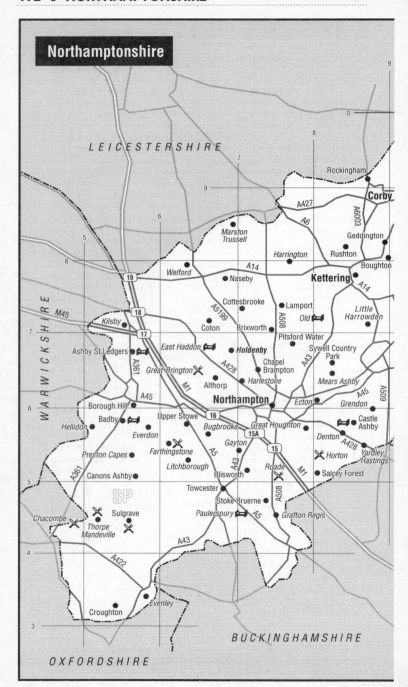

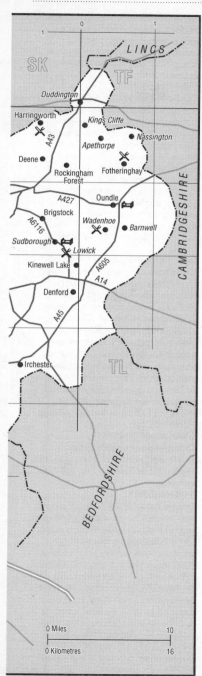

LINCS

SK

TF

Duddington

Harringworth

King's Cliffe

Nassington

Apethorpe

Deene

Rockingham
Forest

Fotheringhay

Oundle

CAMBRIDGESHIRE

Brigstock

Wadenhoe

Barnwell

Sudborough

Lowick

Kinewell Lake

A14

Denford

A45

TL

Irchester

BEDFORDSHIRE

A43

A6116

A427

A605

0 Miles   10

0 Kilometres   16

attractive village of Badby, through an area where gorgeous orange-coloured stone adds to the charm of buildings; it's well waymarked to Greens Norton. The finest part is between Badby Wood and Fawsley Park, where the path drops to landscaped lakes by the hall and estate church. In May the Badby Wood bluebells are lovely.

BLISWORTH SP7253

Grand Union Canal The towpath is popular for country walks, with access among other places from the Royal Oak here, New Inn at Buckby Wharf SP6065, and Navigation Inn at Thrupp Wharf SP7843.

BOROUGH HILL SP5962

This gives the best views in the region, from above the golf course; an Iron Age hill fort shares the top with a formidable array of television and telecommunications masts, but on a clear day the views are tremendous.

BOUGHTON SP8981

Boughton House 🔊 (SE of Geddington) Impressively grand old place often compared to Versailles (some of its treasures were in fact made for there). Richly furnished and decorated, with gorgeous mythical scenes painted on the ceilings, and works by El Greco, Murillo and Caracci lining the walls. Excellent armoury, beautiful parklands, and adventure playground and garden shop. Snacks, shop, disabled access; grounds open pm Sat–Thurs May–Sept, (daily pm Aug), house pm Aug only; (01536) 515731; £6, grounds only £1.50.

BRIGSTOCK SP9485

The **church** has a Saxon tower, and a bell that used to be rung three times a day to help anyone lost in the woods; the Green Dragon is useful for food.

Brigstock Country Park is good for a wander, especially around the wildlife-filled Fermyn Woods on the edge; it can be a little muddy; parking from 50p per hour.

Lyveden New Bield 🔊 Unfinished 'Garden Lodge' started in 1595 but abandoned after the owner Sir Thomas Tresham died. Intriguing and unusual, it was intended to celebrate the Passion of Christ, and is shaped like a Greek cross; the newly restored Elizabethan water gardens and visitor centre are open Weds–Sun and bank hols May–Oct; (01832) 205358; £2; NT. It's a half-mile walk from the car park.

BRIXWORTH SP7471

Brixworth church Particularly fine Anglo-Saxon church, one of England's oldest – mostly 7th-c with much reused Roman material. The George has cheap food.

CANONS ASHBY SP5750

Canons Ashby House (B4525) Exceptional little manor house, more northern-looking than Midlands, beautifully restored with Elizabethan wall paintings and glorious Jacobean plasterwork. The formal gardens have also been carefully restored over the last 20 years, and now closely reflect the layout of the early 18th c. A reasonably sized park has a hilltop 12th–14th-c priory church. Brewhouse café, shop, disabled access; open pm Sat–Weds and bank hols Apr–Oct; (01327) 860044; £4; NT. The Olde House at Home at Moreton Pinkney is handy for lunch.

CASTLE ASHBY SP8659

Castle Ashby House Only the gardens can be visited, but the house is well worth seeing from outside – a splendidly palatial Elizabethan building at the end of a magnificent mile-long avenue planted nearly 300 years ago. The gardens include grand Victorian terraces, sweeping lawns, Italianate gardens with an orangery, and lakeside parkland that may well be the prolific Capability Brown's most enduring achievement. Disabled access; cl 25 Dec; (01604) 696696; £2.50. The **church**, within the park, is very attractive; there's a public path to it. Restored farm buildings nearby house a **Craft Centre and Rural Shopping Yard** (cl Mon). The Falcon in the handsomely preserved estate village has decent food, and the drive through Cogenhoe, Whiston, Grendon and Easton Maudit is pleasant.

CHAPEL BRAMPTON SP7366

Northampton & Lamport Railway (Pitsford Rd) Enthusiastic little railway, with short train rides some wknds and all bank hols mid-Mar to Dec, best to phone (01604) 820327. Snacks, shop, disabled access to train (but not to facilities); £2.80. Its name is a proud

commitment to growth northwards, but for the time being the 14-mile walk and cycle way through pretty countryside by the line is a very pleasant foretaste. The Brampton Halt here has decent food.

COTON SP6771

Coton Manor ⌂ (off A428) Attractive views from charming gardens around 17th-c stone-built manor house (not open); interesting plantings, and water gardens with flamingos, cranes and ornamental waterfowl wandering freely. The wood is lovely at bluebell time. Grooms Cottage in the converted stables is good for a light lunch, and there are interesting plant sales, and disabled access; open pm Weds–Sun and bank hols Easter–Sept; (01604) 740219; *£3.50.

COTTESBROOKE SP7174

Cottesbrooke Hall Very attractive Queen Anne house, reputedly the model for Jane Austen's *Mansfield Park*, with a renowned collection of mainly sporting and equestrian paintings. The lovely garden has formal borders, venerable cedars, a statue walk and extensive wild gardens. Teas, unusual plant sales, disabled access to gardens only; open pm Thurs and bank hols Easter–Sept, plus first Sun of each month, garden also open pm Tues, Weds and Fri Easter–Sept; (01604) 505808; £4, garden only £2.50.

CROUGHTON SP5432

Croughton church Handsome church well worth a visit for its unusual murals, dating from the 14th and 15th centuries.

DEENE SP9592

Deene Park (off A43) Lord Cardigan who led the Charge of the Light Brigade used to live in this beautifully presented partly Tudor house; there's a high-spirited contemporary portrait of him in full attack gallop. Extensive parklands with woodside and lakeside walks, and gardens reflecting continuing interest by the owners over the generations. Cream teas, shop, disabled access to tearooms and garden; open pm Sun Jun–Aug, plus Sun and Mon of bank hol wknds Easter–Aug; (01780) 450223; £5 (gardens only, £3). The Queens Head opposite the church in the pretty village of Bulwick has good value food.

Kirby Hall (W) Splendidly ruined Elizabethan mansion with a bizarre mixture of styles and design; from some angles it still looks intact – even close up. The 17th-c gardens are being restored, and it's a tranquil spot for a picnic. Shop, disabled access; cl wkdys Nov–Mar, 24–26 Dec, 1 Jan; (01536) 203230; £2.50 (inc Walkman tour); EH.

DENFORD SP9976

Denford church Charming in any event (like so many other churches along this river valley); doubly worth a visit for its nature-reserve churchyard by the River Nene, with waterside walks from here. The Cock is an attractive place for lunch.

FOTHERINGHAY TL0793

Lovely village with interesting historical displays in the charming if slightly out-of-proportion 14th-c **church** across a watermeadow from the River Nene. It was part of a small pre-Reformation college and doubles as a memorial to the House of York, with some interesting heraldry. There's only a fragment left of the **castle** where Mary Queen of Scots was imprisoned, beside the castle mound. The Falcon is excellent for lunch.

GEDDINGTON SP8982

The very well preserved elaborate 13th-c cross was erected by Edward I where Queen Eleanor's funeral cortège rested on its way to Westminster. The photogenic packhorse bridge is even older, and there's a 12th-c church.

HARRINGWORTH SP9197

This attractive village is famous for its 82-arch **railway viaduct**. The White Swan has good food.

HOLDENBY SP6967

Holdenby House, Gardens & Falconry Centre See separate family panel on p.411.

IRCHESTER SP9265

Irchester Country Park (Gypsy Lane, Little Irchester) 200 acres of lovely woodland with nature trails, picnic sites, children's play area and even a railway museum; shop, disabled access; cl 25 Dec; (01933) 276866; £1 parking.

KETTERING SP8678

Manor House Museum (Sheep St) This and the adjacent **Alfred East**

Gallery are worth a look if passing; the former has free children's activities in school hols (and a famous mummified cat). Both have shop and disabled access, and are closed Sun and bank hols; free.

Wicksteed Park (off A6, S outskirts) Big amusement park set up in 1921 when they introduced boating on the lake. Some older features still remain (an antique roundabout for example), and more modern attractions include a monorail, roller-coaster and films in the Cine 2000 dome. It's still relatively low-key compared to other leisure parks – thrill rides here are mainly of the dodgems, ferris wheel and pirate ship school – but for many visitors that's precisely the appeal. The grounds are very pleasant for a stroll, with a pitch and putt course, various well laid out gardens, an aviary, paddling pools, and free play areas for younger children. Meals, snacks, shop, disabled access, open daily mid-Apr–early Sept, and wknds in Oct; (01536) 512475; £5 parking charge (less out of season, or after 3pm), then you buy vouchers for the rides, or a wristband with a day's unlimited rides for £11.50.

KINEWELL LAKE SP9979

Well managed local **nature reserve** around former gravel-pit lakes by the River Nene; pleasant walks. The Elizabethan Cock over at Denford has good value food.

LAMPORT SP7574

Lamport Hall (A14) Mainly 17th- and 18th-c house in spacious park, with tranquil gardens containing a remarkable alpine rockery – the home of the first garden gnomes, only one of which now survives. Frequent antique fairs, concerts and other events. Snacks, shop, disabled access to ground floor only; open pm Sun and bank hols Easter–Oct, plus daily guided tours at 3.30pm in Aug (exc Sun); (01604) 686272; £4. The Swan, with great views, has good value food.

NASEBY SP6877

Battle of Naseby Model Model of the crucial Civil War battle set out by the owner of Purlieu Farm, using many hundreds of model soldiers, with a 10-min commentary; open bank hol Sun and Mon pms and by appointment,

(01604) 740241; £2. The nearby Fitzgerald Arms is a good value dining pub. One battle monument (Sibbertoft Rd) marks the position of Cromwell's New Model Army before his devastating counter-attack; there's another on the B4036 towards Clipston (this road from West Haddon and on to Market Harborough in Leics gives a good feel of rural Northants).

NORTHAMPTON SP7560
Daniel Defoe would no longer describe this prosperous shoemaking town as one of the most handsome in the country, but it has a few interesting buildings. There are several fine **churches**, most notably the 12th-c Holy Sepulchre (one of only four remaining round churches in the country), the very grand central All Saints, and the ornate Norman St Peter's in Marefair right by the dual carriageway. The Welsh House (now a china shop) and Hazelrigg House are also very handsome. A social history **museum** in Abington Park is set in the 15th-c home of Shakespeare's granddaughter; cl Sun am, 25–26 Dec; free.

Central Museum (Guildhall Rd) Home to a remarkable collection of boots and shoes, inc an elephant's boot, Margot Fonteyn's ballet shoes, Roman sandals, and Queen Victoria's wedding slippers. Shop, disabled access; cl Sun am, 25–26 Dec; (01604) 238548; free.

OUNDLE TL0488
Charming and elegant stone-built town with a graceful church, several antiques shops and a fine old public school. The ancient Ship does decent food.

Barnwell Country Park (just S) A good spot for a walk, with a variety of birds; the waterside Mill is a pleasant place for lunch.

National Dragonfly Museum (just SE – coming from town take a right at the A605 Oundle roundabout) At pretty Ashton Mill, this unique place has dramatic feeding sessions, several different habitats, and a TV microscope link to the larvae under the water. Fully grown dragonflies put on their best shows on sunny days, though it's a rewarding place in any weather. Teas, craft shop, disabled access; open wknds and bank hols mid-Jun to early Oct;

(01832) 272427; £3. Ashton itself is attractive.

PITSFORD WATER SP7669
Praised for bird-watching, esp in winter when wildfowl flock to the N part of the lake; the S part is popular for fishing. The White Swan at Holcot has decent food.

ROCKINGHAM SP8691
Rockingham Castle 🏰 (A6003) Lovely old house still tucked away behind the curtain wall of the original Norman fortress – obviously quite an effective defence, as the castle was able to resist repeated assaults in the Civil War. The site of the original keep is now a rose garden, but the outline of the two baileys and the drum towers survive, and the later Elizabethan building has a good range of furnishings and art. Meals, snacks, shop, limited disabled access; open pm Sun, Thurs, and bank hols Easter–Sept, as well as Tues in Aug or after bank hols; (01536) 770240; *£4.50, garden only £2.70.

ROCKINGHAM FOREST SP9892
Pleasant back roads through the former Forest of Rockingham give quiet views of a particularly attractive part of the county. This part is good for walks, too, with enough country houses scattered around it to spice interest, and grey-stone cottages are a local feature; on its NW edge the Exeter Arms at Wakerley, a former hunting lodge, gives access to both Wakerley Woods (nice for a picnic) and the Welland Valley.

RUSHTON SP8388
East Carlton Country Park A pleasant spot for strolls, with a few **craft workshops** nr the entrance. **Triangular Lodge** (1m W) Late 16th-c oddity designed by same man as Lyveden New Bield near Brigstock: three walls, three windows and three gables on three sides, and a three-sided chimney, to represent the Holy Trinity. Shop; cl Nov–Mar; (01536) 710761; £1.50; EH. In the attractive village, the Thornhill Arms has decent food.

SALCEY FOREST SP8051
A couple of miles of ancient forest, largely oak, now managed for nature conservation, with well marked trails inc one good for wheelchairs.

STOKE BRUERNE SP7449
Canal Museum Close to a flight of

locks on the Grand Union Canal, with fine old canal buildings (inc a popular pub, the Boat), and lots happening on the water, this is a handsome former corn mill housing a good collection of canal memorabilia, inc a reconstructed traditional narrow-boat cabin complete with immaculately packed-in colourful furniture and crockery. Shop; cl winter Mon, 25–26 Dec; (01604) 862229; £3. Boat trips run from outside the museum to nearby tunnel; (01604) 862107. Good towpath walks from here.

SULGRAVE SP5545
Sulgrave Manor 🏛 (off B4525) The ancestral home of George Washington's family, modest manor with exceptionally good special events when the whole place returns to how it would have been during a particular period. People in period costume go about their daily business, and children can take part in a wide range of activities from wassailing or helping in the kitchen at Christmas, to joining in the harvest during the Apple Day Festival. Still worth a visit on non-event days, with several relics of Washington (he never lived here – it was his great-grandfather who emigrated to America), as well as elegant rooms and well kept gardens. Snacks, shop, disabled access; open wknds (cl 1–2pm) Mar–Dec, and pm wkdys (exc Weds) Apr–Oct, also open ams in Aug and on bank hols, best to check; (01295) 760205; £4 (special events £4.50). Just down the road, the Star is enjoyable for lunch.

SYWELL COUNTRY PARK SP8365
(off A4500) Woodland and lakeside walks, play areas, and a little wildlife display; you can fish on the lake (in fact a reservoir).

TOWCESTER SP6948
This small town (pronounced 'Toaster'), despite some light industry on the edge, has quite a pleasantly villagey feel, and some attractive Georgian and Victorian buildings.

UPPER STOWE SP6456
Old Dairy Farm Centre Sheep, pigs, peacocks, ducks and donkeys, as well as craft workshops, antiques, classic clothes, farm shop and wool collection. Well organised, and decent views – though be prepared for it to be muddy. Restaurant, snacks, shop, disabled access; cl two wks from 25 Dec; (01327) 340525; free, exc special wknds. There are towpath walks on the Grand Union Canal not far off.

Other attractive villages, all with decent pubs, include Apethorpe TL0295, Barnwell TL0484, canalside Bugbrooke SP6757, Denton SP8358, Duddington SK9800, Ecton SP8263, Evenley SP5834, Farthingstone SP6155 (Knightley Way walks), Gayton SP7054, thatched Grafton Regis SP7546, Great Houghton SP7958, Grendon SP8760, Harlestone SP7064, Harrington SP7779, Hellidon SP5158 (pleasant walks nearby), Kilsby SP5671, Litchborough SP6353, Little Harrowden SP8771, Marston Trussell SP6985, Mears Ashby SP8466 (narrow lanes of thatched cottages), Nassington TL0696, Sudborough SP9682, Thorpe Mandeville SP5344, riverside Wadenhoe TL0383, Welford SP6480 and Yardley Hastings SP8656. We'd also recommend rather Cotswoldy King's Cliffe TL0097, and two lovely mellow orange ironstone villages, Preston Capes SP5754 and Everdon SP5957.

Where to eat

CHACOMBE SP4943 **George & Dragon** *I Silver St (01295) 711500* Handy for the M40, this charming village pub has a tidy spacious bar with comfortable seats, beams, flagstones, and logs burning in a massive fireplace, real ales, a wide range of good imaginative food from a changing blackboard (also, afternoon snacks and teas), and friendly and attentive service; bdrms. £20.40|**£7.25**
FARTHINGSTONE SP6155 **Kings Arms** *Main St (01327) 361604* In a pretty village, this handsome 18th-c stone building has homely comfortable sofas and armchairs, a huge log fire in the small bar, lots of decorative plates and pictures, a spacious dining area, a wide choice of good imaginative food, well kept real ales,

decent wines and friendly licensees; nearby walks; cl wkdy lunchtimes; disabled access. £18.50|**£6.75**

FOTHERINGHAY TL0793 **Falcon** *(01832) 226254* Stylish but relaxed old country pub with a good mix of customers, comfortable lounge with fresh flowers and fireplaces at each end, no smoking conservatory and dining room, and little tap bar for locals; excellent food from a varied interesting menu, well kept real ales, and a fine wine list; neat garden; cl Mon but open bank hol lunchtimes; disabled access. £25|**£8.50**

GREAT BRINGTON SP6664 **Fox & Hounds/Althorp Coaching Inn** *Main St (01604) 770651* Golden stone thatched village inn with lots of old beams, big flagstones and bare boards, an attractive mix of country tables and chairs, two fine log fires, and lots of bric-a-brac; a super range of real ales, country wines, an interesting range of enjoyable bar food, and sheltered tables in paved courtyard and side garden. £19.45|**£7.95**

HARRINGWORTH SP9197 **White Swan** *Seaton Rd (01572) 747543* Neatly kept stone-built Tudor pub with generous helpings of enjoyable food, a comfortable lounge/dining area, a quieter dining room, and friendly new licensees; bdrms; cl 25–26 Dec pm; disabled access. £18.50|**£6.50**

HORTON SP8154 **French Partridge** *Newport Pagnell Rd (01604) 870033* Lovely little evening restaurant run by the Partridges for 35 years, with consistently excellent Anglo-French food (marvellous puddings), a relaxed atmosphere, and fine wines; cl Sun, Mon, 2 wks Christmas, 2 wks Easter, 3 wks summer; well behaved children only; disabled access. £35 for 4 courses

LOWICK SP9780 **Snooty Fox** *16 Main St (01832) 733434* Imposing 17th-c inn with a roaring log fire, dark oak beams and neat, attractive dining chairs around well spaced tables in the interesting two-roomed lounge; very good food from a changing blackboard menu, well kept real ales, and plenty of picnic-sets on the grass. £19.35|**£6.95**

ROADE SP7551 **Roadhouse** *16 High St (01604) 863372* Smart and popular restaurant-with-rooms with long-serving owners, comfortable surroundings, courteous service, reliably enjoyable food, and reasonably priced wines; cl pm Sun, Mon and Sat am; disabled access. £30

SULGRAVE SP5545 **Star** *Manor Rd (01295) 760389* Hospitable, small creeper-covered pub with good seasonal food, friendly staff, lots to look at, well kept real ales, and no smoking restaurant; bdrms; cl winter Sun pm, 25 Dec; no children. £17.50

THORPE MANDEVILLE SP5344 **Three Conies** *Banbury Lane (01295) 711025* This friendly stone-built 17th-c dining pub (with a fine wall-mounted sundial) places much emphasis on fresh fish, with more than 15 specials available every day, often with elaborate sauce – other imaginative food, too; real ales, a mix of old and new tables on flagstones, modern art and sculpture on the striking blue walls of the open plan bar, and on red and yellow walls of the dining room, and seats on the spacious back lawn; cl 25 Dec; disabled access. £20|**£5**

WADENHOE TL0183 **Kings Head** *Church St (01832) 720024* In an attractive village of thatched stone houses, this welcoming pub has seats among willows by the River Nene, a bar with woodburner and pale pine furniture, and a little beamed dining room; particularly good imaginative evening and winter lunchtime food (summer lunchtime is limited to soup and sandwiches or ploughman's), well kept real ales, an extensive wine list, pleasant service, and magazines to read; cl Mon am and winter Sun pm; disabled access. £20

Special thanks to Michael and Jenny Back

NORTHUMBRIA

Northumbria – County Durham and Northumberland

A host of opportunities for the tourist; magnificent untouched scenery, Hadrian's Roman legacy, and some excellent new family attractions; very good value.

The continuing new developments within the Tyneside conurbation make it one of the most rewarding places to visit in Britain today. Gateshead's bold new arts complex, the epic Baltic Centre for Contemporary Arts, opens in the autumn, to be followed by the splendid Gateshead Music Centre in 2002. A shimmering new footbridge will provide a handy shortcut to the rash of good free museums and galleries the other side of the Tyne, when it is opened later this year. The Millennium City and Walkergate projects look set to rejuvenate Durham's ancient core over the next few years, too.

Here and elsewhere are plenty of historic highlights, carefully thought through so as to hold genuine appeal for children and adults. Many are outstanding, but if you have time for only two don't miss either the remarkable reconstruction of North of England life a century or two ago, at Beamish, or Hadrian's Wall, striding indomitably across England for nearly 2,000 years – an amazing sight, with Roman forts and engrossing reconstructions and interpretations. Segedunum at Wallsend, Northumbria's Family Attraction of the Year, cleverly blends modern museum technology with ancient excavated remains to give a refreshingly fun and interesting overview of the area's Roman history. Barnard Castle's Bowes Museum has a dazzling display of fine arts, a real treasure-trove in lovely grounds.

A quite eclectic range of enjoyable family attractions have sprung up throughout the county in the last few years. There are the dazzling exhibits of the National Glass Centre, Sunderland, the ever-expanding Historic Quay at Hartlepool, and Newcastle's Life Interactive World, where the mystery of evolution is given surprisingly entertaining treatment.

Other rewarding places for families include the lively Newcastle Discovery (family fun days every Sun), the well organised Preston Hall Museum and Butterfly World in Stockton-on-Tees, and Barnard Castle's Bowes Museum, a treasure trove of fine art, with a room especially given over to children.

New entries to the *Guide* this year include the commendable environmental centre at Bomarsund, the remains of the 14th-c watch-tower at Chathill, and Bowes Railway, joining the profusion of railway centres scattered around George Stephenson's homeland.

People up here are among Britain's friendliest, and prices are low, helped along by welcome saver schemes such as the Power Pass, jointly developed by the Northumbrian Tourist Board and Northern Electric, and available from their electrical shops and Tourist Information Centres throughout the county (£1).

There are great sweeps of largely unspoilt scenery, quiet and uncrowded even in summer – including majestic stretches of coast, with a path along the finest sections. A £10m project aims to restore County Durham's 'black beaches', hoping to reintroduce rare butterflies and flowers and installing contemporary sculpture along a network of cycleways and footpaths. Peaceful lower landscapes are enlivened by streams and woodland, solid stone country buildings, and unhurried small market towns. The area is very good both for walking and for driving, with little traffic (outside the Tyneside/Teesside industrial areas).

May and June are the best months here, with long evenings (stay away from inland waters in later summer, unless you're midge-proof). September can be delightful, but autumn tends to set in quite fiercely in October, and winter is bleak.

Where to stay

ALNMOUTH NU2410 **Marine House Hotel** *1 Marine Rd, Alnmouth, Alnwick, Northumberland NE66 2RW* (01665) 830349 **£94** inc dinner, plus special breaks; 11 rms. 17th-c stone hotel by golf links, with fine sea views; log fire and plenty of books in traditional upstairs residents' lounge, a cosy bar, and enjoyable freshly prepared food in cheerfully decorated no smoking dining room; self-catering also; well behaved dogs welcome; cl Jan; children over 7

CAMBO NZ0584 **Shieldhall** *Wallington, Morpeth, Northumberland NE61 4AQ* (01830) 540387 **£49**; 4 well equipped suites, each with its own entrance. 18th-c stone house and carefully converted farm buildings set around a courtyard, with antiques and other interesting furnishings (Mr Robinson-Gay is a fine cabinet-maker), a library, bar, and cosy lounge with French windows opening on to the neatly kept big garden; enjoyable freshly produced food in candlelit beamed dining room; cl Dec, Jan; children over 10

CHOLLERFORD NY9170 **George** *Chollerford, Hexham, Northumberland NE46 4EW* (01434) 681611 **£120**, plus special breaks; 47 well equipped rms. Quiet hotel with fine gardens sloping down to the river, and the 17th-c bridge over North Tyne visible from the candlelit restaurant; thoughtful attentive service; swimming pool and leisure club; fishing, putting green, and mountain bike hire; limited disabled access

CORNHILL-ON-TWEED NT8842 **Tillmouth Park** *Cornhill-on-Tweed, Northumberland TD12 4UU* (01890) 882255 **£130**, plus special breaks; 14 spacious, pretty rms with period furniture. Solid stone-built country house in 15 acres of parkland, with comfortable relaxing lounges, open fires, a galleried hall, good food in bistro or restaurant, and a carefully chosen wine list; fishing, nearby golf, and shooting; lots to do nearby; dogs welcome; disabled access

CROOKHAM NT9138 **Coach House** *Crookham, Cornhill-on-Tweed, Northumberland TD12 4TD* (01890) 820293 **£72***; 9 individual rms with fresh flowers and nice views, 7 with own bthrm. 17th-c farm buildings around a sunny courtyard, with helpful and friendly long-serving owner, an airy beamed lounge with comfortable sofas and big arched windows, good breakfasts, and enjoyable dinners; lots to do nearby; cl Nov–Easter; good disabled access

DURHAM NZ2742 **Royal County Hotel** *Old Elvet, Durham, Co Durham DH1 3JN* (0191) 386 6821 **£145**, plus special breaks; 151 attractive well equipped rms. Close to the city centre with views of the castle and cathedral, this extended hotel has pleasant furnishings, original Tudor beams, panelling and unusual stained glass ceiling, several restaurants, and lots of leisure facilities; disabled access

GATESHEAD NZ2560 **Eslington Villa** *8 Station Rd, Low Fell, Gateshead, Tyne & Wear NE9 6DR (0191) 487 6017* **£69.50**, plus wknd breaks; 18 rms. Comfortable, extended Edwardian house in quiet residential area with some original features, a lounge with comfortably modern furniture and bay windows overlooking garden, good food in conservatory restaurant, and a friendly atmosphere; cl 25 Dec; disabled access

GREENHEAD NY6667 **Holmhead** *Greenhead, Carlisle, Cumbria CA8 7HY (01697) 747402* **£57**, plus special breaks; 4 cosy rms with showers. Family home, built of Wall stones, once a farmhouse but now a comfortable B&B with moorland, wildlife, Hadrian's Wall and Roman castles all nearby; airy lounge with TV at one end, small bar at the other, games and children's toys, good freshly prepared food using organic farm and local produce eaten family-style around candlelit oak table, and pretty garden with a stream and games (table tennis and snooker in garage); Mrs Staff is a Hadrian's Wall tour guide, and there's a clue trail for children and special learning tour ; cl Christmas and New Year ☺

GRETA BRIDGE NZ0813 **Morritt Arms** *Greta Bridge, Barnard Castle, County Durham DL12 9SE (01833) 627232* **£79.50**, plus special breaks; 23 rms. Smartly old-fashioned coaching inn where Dickens stayed in 1838 to research for *Nicholas Nickleby* – one of the interesting bars has a colourful Dickensian mural; comfortable lounges, fresh flowers, good open fires, and pleasant garden; coarse fishing; pets allowed; play area in garden for children; disabled access

HALTWHISTLE NY7366 **Ald White Craig** *Shield Hill, Haltwhistle, Northumberland NE49 9NW (01434) 320565* **£44**; 3 rms. Homely and neatly kept no smoking 17th-c croft overlooking South Tyne Valley, with prize-winning sheep, rare cattle, dogs, cats and poultry, coal fire and local information in beamed sitting room, good breakfasts around central table in dining room; plenty of walks; self-catering cottages; cl Nov–Mar; no children; disabled access

HAYDON BRIDGE NY8366 **Hadrian Lodge** *Hindshield Moss, Haydon Bridge, Hexham, Northumberland NE47 6NF (01434) 688688* **£45***; 10 comfortable rms. Attractive modern stone-built lodge in 18 acres of pasture close to Hadrian's Wall with residents' summer bar, family tearoom, a self-catering kitchen, small launderette, and two trout lakes with rods for hire; self-catering cottages and bunkrooms; disabled access

HEADLAM NZ1818 **Headlam Hall** *Headlam, Darlington, County Durham DL2 3HA (01325) 730238* **£80**, plus wknd breaks; 36 pretty rms, in the main house and adjacent coach house, plus 2-bedroom cottage in village. Peaceful Jacobean mansion in four acres of carefully kept gardens with little trout lake, tennis court, and croquet lawn; elegant rooms, a fine carved oak fireplace in the main hall, good traditional food in the four individually decorated rooms of the restaurant, and courteous staff; indoor swimming pool, snooker and sauna, and gym; cl 25 Dec; disabled access

HIGH FORCE NY8828 **High Force Hotel** *High Force, Middleton-in-Teesdale, Barnard Castle, County Durham DL12 0XH (01833) 622222* **£50***; 6 rms. Opposite England's highest waterfall (for which it's named), this is a cheerful and friendly place and very popular with walkers; log fires in relaxing bars, good service, decent bar food, a microbrewery, and lots of malt whiskies; no pets

KIRKWHELPINGTON NY9684 **Cornhills** *Kirkwhelpington, Newcastle upon Tyne, Tyne & Wear NE19 2RE (01830) 540232* **£48***; 3 rms. Big no smoking Victorian farmhouse on large stock-rearing farm, with marvellous views towards the coast and Tyne Valley; lots of original features, a comfortable lounge, good breakfasts (local pubs for evening meals), and indoor and outdoor games for children; self-catering also; cl Apr

LONGFRAMLINGTON NU1301 **Embleton Hall** *Longframlington, Morpeth, Northumberland NE65 8DT (01665) 570249* **£85**; 13 comfortable, pretty and individually decorated rms. Charming hotel in lovely grounds surrounded by fine countryside, with a particularly friendly, relaxed atmosphere and courteous staff;

neat little bar, elegant lounge, log fires, excellent value bar meals, and very good food in the attractive dining room; disabled access

LONGHORSLEY NZ1596 **Linden Hall** *Longhorsley, Morpeth, Northumberland NE65 8XF (01670) 516611* **£99**, plus special breaks; 50 individually decorated rms. Georgian hotel in 450 acres of landscaped park with coarse fishing, clay pigeon shooting, mountain biking (bike hire available), 18-hole golf course, pitch and putt, croquet, jogging routes, giant chess, and lots of leisure facilities inc big swimming pool; pubby bar, elegant drawing room, and good food in attractive restaurant; children in main restaurant early evening only; disabled access

NEWCASTLE UPON TYNE NZ2564 **Malmaison** *Quayside, Newcastle upon Tyne, Tyne & Wear NE1 3DX (0191) 245 5000* **£96.50**w; 116 individually decorated and well equipped rms. In a former Co-operative Society warehouse and overlooking the river, this stylish hotel (part of a small chain with other hotels in Edinburgh, Glasgow and Manchester) is boldly decorated throughout with contemporary furniture and artwork, genuinely friendly staff, modern cooking in fashionable brasserie, and decent breakfasts

ROMALDKIRK NY9922 **Rose & Crown** *Romaldkirk, Barnard Castle, County Durham DL12 9EB (01833) 650213* **£86**, plus special breaks; 12 rms – those in the main house have lots of character. Smart and interesting old coaching inn by green of delightful Teesdale village, with Jacobean oak settle, log fire, old black and white photographs, and lots of brass in the beamed traditional bar; a cosy residents' lounge, very good popular food in bar and fine oak-panelled restaurant, and well kept real ales and wines; cl Christmas; disabled access

SEAHOUSES NU2232 **Olde Ship** *Main St, Seahouses, Northumberland NE68 7RD (01665) 720200* **£66**, plus special breaks; 16 rms, inc 4 apartments. Thriving harbourside inn with small rooms full of nautical items and fishing memorabilia, windows looking out towards the Farne Islands, comfortable residents' lounge and sun lounge, popular bar food, five real ales, and good service; ideal for coastal walks; cl Dec–Jan; children over 10; limited disabled access

STANNERSBURN NY7286 **Pheasant** *Stannersburn, Hexham, Northumberland NE48 1DD (01434) 240382* **£64***, plus special breaks; 11 rms. Beautifully located, unpretentious 17th-c stone inn close to Kielder Water and its quiet forests; traditional, comfortable lounge, simple public bar, a happy mix of customers, good food inc excellent fresh vegetables and enjoyable Sun lunch, well kept real ales, a fine choice of malts, good welcoming service, and nice breakfasts; picnic-sets in streamside garden; cl 25–26 and 31 Dec, 1 Jan; disabled access

SWINBURNE NY9374 **Hermitage** *Swinburne, Hexham, Northumbria NE48 4DG (01434) 681248* **£60**; 3 large rms with big baths, overlooking the garden or vegetable patch. Lovely 17th-c country house reached through a grand arch and down a long drive with woodland on either side; graceful rooms with family portraits, prints and antiques, warm and friendly owners, and generous breakfasts; no smoking; several nearby pubs for meals; cl Oct–Feb; children over 10

WOLSINGHAM NZ1037 **Greenwell Farm** *Tow Law, Bishop Auckland, County Durham DL13 4PH (01388) 527248* **£45***, plus special breaks; 6 rms in comfortably converted stone barn. Old farmhouse with fine views, sitting and dining rooms, good food using naturally reared meats and locally grown produce, and spring lambs, calves and chicks, a nature trail, and conservation areas; can bring own horse or mountain bike; self-catering cottage; cl Christmas and New Year; disabled access

---

Please let us know what you think of places in the *Guide*. Use the report forms at the back of the book or simply write us a letter.

To see and do

Northumbria Family Attraction of the Year

WALLSEND NZ3066 **Segedunum** (Buddle St) Opening only a few months before we went to press, this £9 million attraction is an exciting development for the area, unlike any of the other museums you'll find dotted along Hadrian's Wall – perhaps most obviously because it's in the heart of urban, industrial Tyneside, and there's no longer a surviving stretch of the Wall itself (there is a reconstructed section). It's also a lot bigger, and the well put together displays give an excellent idea of everyday life in Segedunum, the fort that once stood here, and an intriguing look at how the site developed over the centuries that followed. For many years Wallsend had rather neglected its heritage as the Wall's (extended) terminus; the remains of the fort lay buried under Victorian housing until the 1970s, after which they were excavated more thoroughly than just about any other site in the Empire: you can see plenty of the finds. The most striking feature of the complex is the spectacular 35-metre (115-ft) viewing tower, which makes it look rather like an airport; this is topped by a virtual reality theatre that overlooks the excavated remains, and while you watch, reconstructs the fort's original buildings on to their original spots. For once we'd recommend not coming on a sunny day: there's a bit of a glare then. Another unique feature is a completely functional reconstructed Roman bathhouse; in the evenings they plan to let pre-booked groups take a dip. Elsewhere are videos, more reconstructions, and plenty of hands-on and touch-screen activities, many at child's height. There are also galleries on mining (there was once a colliery here) and shipbuilding (Swan Hunter are based next door). Children under 6 aren't going to be engaged for long (though they'll have fun sounding the hooter in the shipbuilding section), but older ones can be happily distracted for an hour or two, particularly if they learned about the Romans at school. Snacks, shop, disabled access; cl 25–26 Dec; (0191) 295 5757; *£2.95 (*£1.95 children over 4). A family ticket, for two adults and two children, is £8.50.

ALLENDALE NY8352
The B6305/B6295 is a great scenic drive; lots of walks up there, and the Kings Head in Allendale village is a good stop.
Allenheads Heritage Centre (Allenheads) The history of this former lead-mining village, the highest in England, is told in its heritage centre, blacksmith's shop and engine house; also nature trails. Meals and snacks in the Hemmel café, shop, disabled access; (01434) 685326; £1. The Allenheads Inn is an entertaining stop.
ALNMOUTH NU2410
This pleasant town has attractive beaches, good coastal walks, and a lot for summer visitors; the Saddle has good food.
ALNWICK NU1813
Busy town at the heart of prosperous farming country, with some attractive old streets nr the market square – it

was used in the film *Elizabeth*. The hillside **church** of St Michael and All Angels above the river is a perfect example of a complete Late Gothic building. An impressive number of second-hand books are on sale in the converted Victorian station. The Market Tavern has bargain food.
Alnwick Castle The 'Windsor of the North' dates back to the 11th c, and is the second-largest inhabited castle in the country. Stone soldiers stand guard on the battlements, and inside all is Italian Renaissance grandeur, with a magnificent art collection taking in works by Titian, Van Dyck and Canaletto, and an outstanding Claude. Also a famous collection of Meissen china, Roman remains, refurbished museum with displays on the Duke's own private army and local archaeology, and children's playground. Landscaped grounds by Capability

Brown include a 12-acre walled garden currently being restored to magnificence. Meals, snacks, shop; open 7 Apr–26 Oct; (01665) 511100; £6.25.
Hulne Park Excellent for gentle parkland walks; dogs not allowed. Don't miss the whimsical Brizlee Tower and hermit's cave.

AMBLE NU2604
This attractive small town has a solid old fishing harbour, and modern yacht marina; RSPB **boat trips** around nearby Coquet Island with its colourful eider ducks and puffins, phone (01665) 711975.

AYDON NZ0066
Aydon Castle 13th-c, and remarkably well preserved, in a lovely setting. Snacks, shop, some disabled access; cl Nov–Mar; (01434) 632450; £2; EH.

BAMBURGH NU1835
Bamburgh Castle Stunning huge square Norman castle on a cliff above the sea, its clock serving as timekeeper for the cricket green in the attractive village below. Despite the forbidding exterior, the inside is very much a lived-in stately home, with armour from the Tower of London. Snacks, shop; cl Nov–Mar; (01668) 214515; £4. There's a neo-Gothic shrine to Grace Darling in the yard of the interesting 13th-c **church**. The Lord Crewe Arms is well placed for lunch.
Grace Darling Museum (Radcliffe Rd) Pictures and mementoes of the local heroine, inc the boat in which Grace and her father rescued nine survivors from the wrecked SS *Forfarshire*. Shop, disabled access; cl Sun am and all Nov–Easter; (01668) 214465; free (donations to RNLI).

BARNARD CASTLE NZ0416
Pleasant market town, still coming to life on Weds market day, with several attractive buildings. In the centre, the Old Well, with a terrace over the town walls, has good value food. There's charming gorge scenery nearby, here wooded, romantic and unmistakably lowland in character – making for good walks. The valley path W eventually climbs above the river and follows field routes as it leads towards Cotherstone.
Bowes Museum A beautiful French-style chateau in 20 acres of meticulously kept formal grounds. The 40 rooms are

filled with sumptuous fine arts and an outstanding display of paintings by Canaletto, Goya, El Greco and others; also local history section, and small display of 1950s toys. Relatively few people find their way to this treasure-house, though it's one of the most worthwhile places to visit in the entire country – those readers who have visited, certainly enjoyed it. Meals and snacks (limited in winter), shop, disabled access; cl 25–26 Dec, 1 Jan; (01833) 690606; £3.90.
Castle These dramatically set 12th-c ruins include the original keep and the 14th-c hall. Shop, disabled facilities; cl 1–2pm, Mon and Tues Nov–Mar, 24–26 Dec, and 1 Jan; (01833) 638212; £2.30 (inc audio tour).
Eggleston Abbey Downstream from Barnard Castle, this is reached by a couple of miles of enjoyable riverside walk – or by car. Substantial remains inc gracefully arched windows, and some remnants of the monastic buildings; disabled access; free.
Rokeby Park (just SE) Elegant 18th-c villa in a fine setting, most famous for its *Rokeby Venus* by Velasquez (though the original is now in the National Gallery). The best of the other pictures is probably Pellegrini's *Venus disarming Cupid*. Open May bank hols and the following Tues, then pm only Mon and Tues Jun to first Tues in Sept; (01833) 637334; *£5. The Morritt Arms nearby does good meals. The B6278 to Stanhope and Edmundbyers is a fine drive.

BEADNALL NU2329
On Northumberland's underpopulated coast, this attractive village has boats on the beach, and an interestingly restored waterside limekiln; nearby Benthall is also a pleasant place to visit.

BEAMISH NZ2154
North of England Open-air Museum Perhaps the most rewarding paid attraction in Britain, an amazingly ambitious 300-acre museum exhaustively re-creating life in the North of England in the early 19th and 20th c. No detail is overlooked, and there's something for everyone in the five main sections: a town with streets, shops, houses and businesses, colliery village with mine, chapel, cottages and

school, manor house with formal gardens and orchard, railway station, and home farm with animals and craft demonstrations. A re-created engine shed with a magnificent 1822 locomotive, and a full-scale replica of Stephenson's _Locomotion No. 1_ which carries visitors down a ¼-mile track. Costumed interpreters really bring the place to life. Children can wander round this authentic little world at their leisure, touching everything, and joining in most of the activities, from learning to play hoops and hopscotch to taking part in lessons in the schoolroom (bad handwriting is rewarded by a light rap on the knuckles). A Victorian fairground has rides including a Hall of Mirrors (small extra charge), and working trams and buses join up the different areas. Meals and snacks (inc period pub), good shops, some disabled access; cl Mon and Fri Nov–Mar, and daily from mid-Dec to New Year, best to check; (01207) 231811; £10, or £3 late Oct–Mar when only the town and tramway are open. The Shepherd & Shepherdess not far from the gate is useful for lunch, as is the more individual Beamish Mary (follow sign from A693 to No Place & Cooperative Villas).

BELLINGHAM NY8383
(pronounced 'Bellingjum') A small country town with an attractive 13th-c church, stone-roofed to protect it against arson-minded Border raiders.
Black Middens Bastle House A 16th-c stone-built defensive farmhouse which is 180 metres' walk from the road, is open to the public at all reasonable times; free; EH. There's a pretty walk just N of the town, to the 9-metre (30-ft) cascade of Hareshaw Linn. The Cheviot Hotel does decent food. This is the main town in North Tynedale, one of the least-known and most unspoilt parts of Northumberland, with good scenic drives. Between the Pennines and the Cheviots, it's a peaceful river valley surrounded by wild moorland, with fine scenery and a particularly unrushed atmosphere – very relaxing.

BELSAY NZ1078
Belsay Hall and Gardens 🏛 (A696)
The same family have lived here for nearly 600 years, first in a medieval castle, then a Jacobean manor house and finally a grand mansion designed to look like a Greek classical temple – all can still be seen, but the mansion is strangely eerie, there's no furniture and in some rooms no floors either. The 30 acres of landscaped parkland are very agreeable, with rhododendron garden, formal terraces and woodland walks. Snacks, shop, disabled access; cl 24–26 Dec; (01661) 881636; *£3.80. The Highlander has good food.

BERWICK-UPON-TWEED NT9953
Largely unspoilt, this has some handsome 18th-c buildings and a fine 17th-c church; most people who come here seem to while away at least a bit of time watching the swans on the River Tweed. Alternatively, look out over the sea from the Rob Roy (Spittal Rd), which has good local fish. The town has an extraordinary trio of bridges, and deserves to be approached by walking along the Tweed: there are paths on both banks, starting from the East Ord picnic site by the A1 road bridge. The **town ramparts**, impressively intact, were a masterpiece of 16th-c military planning. Partly grassed over and easy to walk, they give good views. You can hire bikes here (01289) 331476. Berwick has an impressive track record for hospitality: in the early 19th c it boasted a formidable total of 59 pubs and three coaching inns.

Berwick Barracks (The Parade)
Britain's oldest surviving purpose-built barracks, now a local history museum and gallery, with an interesting exhibition on the British soldier, another on early maps, and a contemporary art gallery. Snacks, shop, disabled access; cl Mon and Tues Nov–Mar, 24–26 Dec, 1 Jan; (01289) 304493; £2.60.

Wine & Spirit Museum and Chemist (Palace Green) The mainland base of Lindisfarne mead and country wine makers, with a collection of objects from the wine and spirits industries, working potter, home-made pot-pourri, and Victorian chemist shop. Snacks, shop, disabled access; cl Sun Nov–Easter, and over Christmas; (01289) 305153; free.

BINCHESTER NZ2332
Binchester Roman Fort Quite a lot left of this 1st-c 10-acre fort, inc the best-preserved military baths in the country, with an exceptional hypocaust system. Interesting events include days when you can sample Roman food. Shop, disabled access; open Easter wknd, then May–Sept; (01388) 663089; £1.50. Nearby **Escomb church** is interesting, built in the 7th c from stone from the fort. A 3rd-c fort can be seen a few miles S at Piercebridge (where the riverside George, with its famous grandfather clock which stopped when the old man died, is useful for lunch), and finds from both sites are shown at the Bowes Museum in Barnard Castle.

BISHOP AUCKLAND NZ2130
Auckland Castle 🏛 The main country residence of the Bishops of Durham, a grand series of buildings entered through a splendid Gothic gatehouse in the town's market place. Some rooms are relatively stark, but a highlight is the chapel, splendidly transformed from a 12th-c aisled hall by Bishop John Cosin in the 17th c. The attractive grounds have an unusual 18th-c deercote. Meals, snacks, shop, limited disabled access, with more planned for the first floor later this year; open pm Fri and Sun May–Sept, and daily exc Sat mid-July–Aug; (01388) 601627; *£3.50.

BLANCHLAND NY9650
The archetypal border village, every house looking a stronghold, alone in a great bowl of magnificent scenery; the Lord Crewe Arms here is an interesting hotel, in parts very ancient indeed.

BOMARSUND NZ2784
Earth Balance (signposted off A189 N of Bedlington) Enjoyable place spread over 260 acres, showcasing environmentally friendly living, with organic food and drink made on the premises, a green garden centre, and Re-Dress, where new clothes and textiles are made out of recycled products. A trail takes you around eco-buildings, a willow maze, a nature reserve, and a fishing lake that provides power for the complex. Readers enjoy the Cat & Sawdust pub here, with ales brewed in the site's solar-powered brewery, and there's a good choice of locally made food and crafts in the café and shop. Some disabled access; cl 23 Dec–4 Jan; (01670) 821000; free.

BOULMER NU2613
One of several attractive villages and small towns dotted down Northumberland's scenic and underpopulated coast, this has active fishing boats.

BOWES NY9913
Bowes Castle Within the earthworks of a Roman fort, these remains include the great Norman keep, three storeys high; free. The comfortable Ancient Unicorn, with *Nicholas Nickleby* connections, has decent food.

BURNOPFIELD NZ1857
Gibside Chapel and Grounds Marvellous Palladian mausoleum for the Bowes family in 18th-c landscaped park, with the rather sad ruins of a hall and other estate buildings dotted around. Miles of pleasant walks. Snacks, shop, disabled access; cl Mon (exc bank hols), chapel open by appointment only Nov–Mar; (01207) 542255; £3; NT. The Highlander at White-le-Head has decent food.

BYRNESS NT7702
Chew Green Roman Camps Little-visited spectacular earthworks alone in wild country, well repaying the stiff walk up the Pennine Way through the Redesdale Forest. The Pennines up here contain a great many more unspoilt prehistoric and other archaeological remains – useful goals for walkers in these magnificent hills, often yielding remarkable views. Some areas N of the A68 (which as it approaches the Scottish border is a remarkably dramatic drive) and W of the B6341 may temporarily be put out of bounds by Army training.

CAMBO NZ0283
Wallington House Built in 1688 and altered in the 1740s, with fine plasterwork and porcelain, and works by the pre-Raphaelite circle often found here in the house's 19th-c cultural glory days. Showpiece fuchsias in the conservatory, and over 100 acres of lawns, terraces, lakes and woodland landscaped by Capability Brown. Meals, snacks, shop, plant centre, adventure playground, some disabled access; house cl am, all day Tues, and Nov–Mar,

grounds and garden open all year; (01670) 774283; £5.40, grounds only £3.90; NT. There is free access to the huge surrounding estate, which is laced with footpaths and includes prehistoric sites and more parkland.

CAULDRON SNOUT NY8128

Beyond High Force, the Pennine Way rewards walkers with some truly wild landscape as the Tees rushes along a gorge beneath Cronkley Scar and tumbles down Cauldron Snout, a 60-metre (200-ft) cascade which can be reached from the dam at Cow Green Reservoir (where there is also a nature trail). The pleasant Langdon Beck Inn is a short drive or walk below the dam.

CHATHILL NU1825

Preston Tower Built by the Sheriff of Northumberland as a watch-tower during Border raids of the late 14th c, half of the building was later pulled down to provide stone for surrounding cottages and farm buildings. A scale model shows what it would have looked like originally, and furnishings in the remaining quarters give an idea of what it must have been like to live there in the 15th c; (01665) 589227; *£1.

CHEVIOT HILLS NT9716

Part of the Northumberland National Park, the Cheviots are strikingly empty and solitary, with only the characteristic local breed of hardy sheep for company in most places – an area that suits walkers who really want to get away from other people.

CHILLINGHAM NU0525

Chillingham Castle Striking old castle dating back to the 12th c, full of antiques, tapestries, arms and armour. Formal gardens, woodland walks, lake, and splendid views of the surrounding countryside; occasional concerts and special events. Brave souls can rent one of their haunted apartments (self-catering). Snacks, shop; cl am, Tues (exc July and Aug), and Oct–late Apr (exc Easter wknd); (01668) 215359; £4.50. The Percy Arms at Chatton is good for lunch.

Chillingham Wild White Cattle Park The famous large-horned white cattle have been here for the last 700 years, the only animals of their kind still pure and uncrossed with domestic breeds. As they're potentially

aggressive, tours are led by a warden. Bring binoculars for a closer view. Shop, limited disabled access; cl 12–2 pm, Sun am, all day Tues, and Nov–Mar; (01668) 215250; *£3. Above the park, Ross Castle hill fort has great views.

CHOLLERFORD NY9070

Hexham Herbs (B6318, nr Chesters) Over 800 varieties of herbs beautifully laid out in attractive walled gardens; also old-fashioned roses, many other plants, and woodland walk. Shop, some disabled access, plant sales; telephone for winter opening; (01434) 681483; £1.50.

CLENNEL STREET NT9207

This ancient drove road leading from Coquetdale is a good walking route into the Cheviots – lonely grassy moors (boggy in parts when it's wet), dry stone walls, sheep, dark conifer plantations. You can pick up the route nr Alwinton, and there's a pretty way back, along a track by the River Alwin.

CRASTER NU2519

A pleasant place to visit, with its tidal fishing harbour, good kippering factory, excellent pub, and magnificent clifftop walk to Dunstanburgh Castle.

DARLINGTON NZ2815

Railway Centre & Museum Interesting museum in carefully restored North Rd Station, part of which is still used for train services. Exhibits inc Stephenson's *Locomotion* built in 1825, which pulled the first passenger steam train on a public railway. Steam train rides some summer wknds. Snacks, shop, disabled access; cl 25–26 Dec and all Jan; (01325) 460532; £2.10. An extraordinary £760,000 **brickwork locomotive**, a 40-metre (130-ft) approximation of the pre-war record-breaking *Mallard* complete with clouds of bricky steam, lies beside Morrisons supermarket (Morton Park Way). St Cuthbert's (Church Row) is an interesting Early English **church**. No 22 (Coniscliffe Rd) has decent food and brews its own good beer.

DURHAM NZ2742

The ancient core of the town stands on a crag defended by an almost complete loop of the River Wear, with a rewarding riverside path going from Prebends Bridge up to South St (with some of the best views of the cathedral's magnificent pinnacled towers), recrossing the river by Silver St bridge. The old part of town is largely pedestrianised, with attractive cobbled alleys and narrow medieval lanes, and fine medieval buildings among the Georgian and later ones, particularly around the 12th-c pedestrians-only Elvet Bridge (where the Regatta tea rooms have decent food). There are several medieval churches, and interesting little shops. You can hire rowing boats nr Elvet Bridge, which is also the departure point for launches; (0191) 386 9525. The Millennium City, a new complex at the bottom of Claypath inc a 500-seater theatre, heritage centre and Tourist Information Centre plus a large public square and riverside walks, is due to open in early 2002; work is also under way on redeveloping the adjacent Walkergate area into a new leisure centre. Ghostly guided walks leave from the Tourist Information Centre at 6.30pm on Mons July–Sept (also at 8.30pm July–Aug); £3. The Court (Court Lane) has cheap food all day exc Sun; the best value food is out at the Seven Stars at Shincliffe.

Crook Hall & Gardens 🖼 (Frankland Lane, Sidegate) Medieval manor surrounded by delightful gardens, currently being restored. Snacks; open pm only Easter wknd, May bank hols, Sun May–mid-Sept, and daily (exc Sat) late Jun–early Sept; (0191) 384 8028; *£3.75.

dli Museum & Gallery 🖼 (Aykley Heads) Newly refurbished and with a controversial new name – veteran soldiers understandably took umbrage when politically correct councillors demanded the reference to the Light Infantry was dropped from the title – this now incorporates imaginative displays about Durham's illustrious regiment, as well as unusual temporary art exhibitions. Snacks, shop, disabled access; cl 25 Dec; (0191) 384 2214; *£2.50.

Durham Castle Developed from an early Norman motte and bailey. Still a proud building, with original chapel and 13th-c great hall, it's now used for university accommodation, and you can

stay here. Shop; guided tours Mon, Weds and wknds 2–4 pm in term time, usually every day in hols – best to check first; (0191) 374 3800; £3.

Durham Cathedral Huge, and probably England's finest, a fiercely beautiful and unusually well preserved Norman building, breathtaking and very masculine inside; it was the first in Britain to use pointed arches. St Cuthbert's shrine is here, and they say that the Lady Chapel owes its odd position at the W end to his hatred of women; every time they tried to build it in the right place his spirit apparently caused the foundations to collapse. Try to spot the unique bronze knocker that seems to have a cheery grin. Rare books and manuscripts in the 15th-c monks' dormitory. Meals, snacks, shop, disabled access; monks' dormitory open 10am–3.30pm Mon–Sat, 12.30–3pm Sun May–Sept (80p), Treasury cl Sun am (£2), tower cl Sun, during services and inclement weather (£2); entry to the cathedral is free, but a donation of £3 is suggested. The close behind the cathedral has some handsome old houses.

Finchale Priory (3m NE, minor road off A167) St Godric chose this site in 1110 as a place to meditate, and it's still a pleasant spot for contemplation, beside the graceful ruins of the 13th-c church.

Houghall College Gardens (Shincliffe Rd) The county's main horticultural training centre, with 10 acres of hardy plants, a water garden, woodland garden, alpine rock garden, parterre and arboretum. This area records some of the lowest temperatures in the country so if it grows here, it'll grow anywhere. Snacks, plant sales, disabled access; only cl during special events; (0191) 386 1351; free.

Oriental Museum (Elvet Hill) Reopening just before this book comes out following lottery-funded refurbishment, this will have a new Chinese gallery to add to its already exceptional collections of everything from plates, carvings, and paintings to costumes and mummies; also new activity room. Snacks, shop, improved disabled access; cl wknd ams, and

Christmas–New Year; (0191) 374 7911; £1.50.

St Mary le Bow Church [£] (The Bailey) The heritage centre here has exhibitions on the city's history. Shop, disabled access; cl am (exc July–Aug), wkdys (exc bank hols) in Apr and May, and all Oct–Mar; £1.

University Botanic Garden (Hollingside Lane) Hugely enjoyable 18-acre garden in mature woodland with exotic trees from America and the Himalayas, tropical house, cactus house and visitor centre, and unusual sculpture garden. Snacks, plant sales, disabled access; cl Christmas–New Year; (0191) 374 2671; *£1.25.

University Museum of Archaeology On the river bank below the cathedral's SW corner, a former fulling mill with finds from the city and surrounding area. Shop, some disabled access; cl Tues and Weds Nov–Mar, and 24–25 Dec; (0191) 374 3623; £1. Also along these banks is a sculpture of the Last Supper, carved by Colin Wilbourn from 13 trees that died of Dutch elm disease.

EGGLESTON NY9923

Eggleston Hall Gardens A good example of an updated 19th-c country-house garden, with rare and unusual trees, shrubs, perennials and other plants. Happily the newly planted ruined early 17th-c chapel is now open to the general public, with photographs showing what it used to look like – a most tranquil place. They sell plants, organically grown herbs, and fruit and vegetables from the walled kitchen garden. Snacks, some disabled access; (01833) 650403; *50p, or *£1 for a season ticket (money refunded if you buy a plant). The moorside village is attractive.

EMBLETON NU2521

Dunstanburgh Castle Screeching gulls add to the atmosphere at these huge ruins, standing imposingly on the cliff above the North Sea. Turner painted the scene three times. Snacks, small shop; cl Mon and Tues Nov–Mar, 24–26 Dec, 1 Jan; (01665) 576231; £1.80; EH (NT members also free). The Dunstanburgh Castle Hotel does good meals. The NT owns much of this stretch of coastline, inc the pleasantly

bracing walk to Craster – one of the finest sections of the Northumbrian coast path.

ETAL NT9239

Pretty row of white cottages running down to a ford across the river, with a working forge and good thatched pub.

Etal Castle Good Walkman tours guide you round these evocative 14th-c ruins; also exhibition on Border history. Shop, disabled access to exhibition area; cl Nov–Mar; (01890) 820332; £2.60; EH.

FORD NT9338

Built as an estate-workers' model village, for Ford Castle; very attractive, with one or two craft workshops, a well restored working corn mill (cl Oct–Mar; (01890) 820338; £2.50), and the friendly Heatherslaw Bakery making good use of the resulting corn.

Heatherslaw Light Railway Steam or diesel journeys on narrow-gauge railway to Etal, along pretty valley of the River Till. Snacks, shop, disabled access; cl Nov–Mar, exc some wknds before Christmas, (01890) 820317 for times; £3.70.

Lady Waterford Hall Well worth a look: used till 1957 as the village school, with murals showing the village children and their families as characters from well known Bible stories; cl 12.30–1.30pm, open by appointment only Nov–Mar; £1.50.

GATESHEAD NZ2162

The fortunes of this previously much-maligned town are set to be revived by the exciting regeneration projects currently taking shape on its quayside. The monumental **Baltic Centre for Contemporary Arts** (see below) opens in Sept, and work is now under way on the Norman Foster-designed £60m Gateshead Music Centre, set to open in 2002. A graceful steel and aluminium drawbridge for pedestrians and cyclists will link the site with Newcastle's many attractions come the spring. Meantime, the **Metro Centre** (A1 just W) is a useful rainy-day outing from Newcastle, a vast modern shopping and leisure complex with several different themed undercover areas, all sorts of fairground attractions (better for younger children than teenage thrill seekers), even a Roman

Catholic church. Do remember exactly
where you put your car – there are
12,000 parking spaces. In the town
itself, the **Shipley Art Gallery** (Prince
Consort Rd) is worth a look (cl Sun am;
free), the Keelmans riverside walk (off
South Shore Rd) is quite pleasant, and
you'll find it difficult to miss the Angel of
the North, towering over the A1.

**Baltic Centre for Contemporary
Arts** (Quayside) Housed within the
gargantuan frame of a former flour mill
(Rank Hovis who built it named their
mills after various seas), this major new
contemporary arts centre – the biggest
of its kind outside the capital – is one of
the focal points of Gateshead's quayside
regeneration. A formidable northern
counterpart to the similar industrial
conversion currently wowing London's
art-lovers, it aims to be not so much
another art gallery, but a place for
artists to work in, with exhibition areas
ranging from a virtual art 'cave' to the
cavernous 'high art gallery', naturally lit
from above. It doesn't open until
September, but a quick glance at its
website, www.balticmill.com, gives a
foretaste of the type of work you can
expect to see there, from giant
sculpture to performance art. The
centre will also encompass lecture
theatres, workshops, and a library, plus
a café, bookshop and rooftop
restaurant. Phone (0191) 478 1810 for
details.

HADRIAN'S WALL NY7868
An amazing sight, if you've never seen it
before. It's extraordinary to imagine
those Roman military engineers, so far
from their warm homeland, building
this remarkable construction through
such inhospitable surroundings. Many
of its 73½ miles run along the natural
crag of the great Whin Sill, making it
that much more formidable; the overall
sense of grandeur is a definite part of
the appeal. The stone Wall itself, with
its turret watchtowers, milecastles and
more sporadic forts, defines the N side
of a narrow frontier zone, bounded on
its S side by an equally remarkable ditch
between turf ramparts; a military road
runs between wall and ditch. It was this
whole installation rather than just the
Wall which the Romans used to control
trade and cross-border travel. The

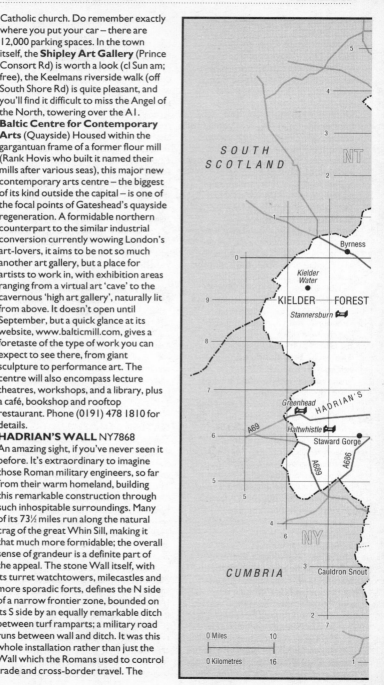

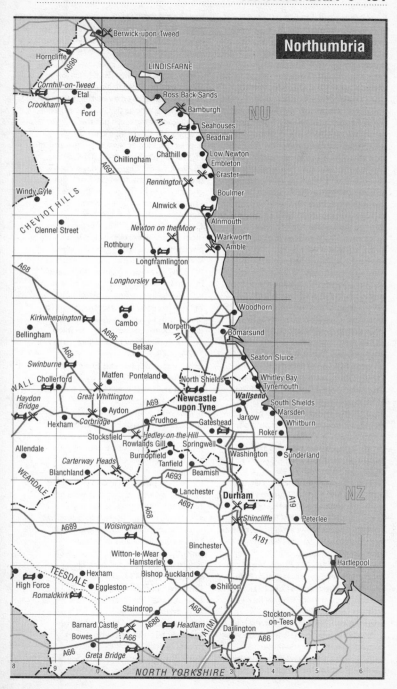

Northumbria

B6318 following the military road is a fine drive, with some of the best views of the Wall. This road also gives walkers easy access to the line of the Wall, with numerous car parks on the way. There's not a lot of point trying to make walks into circuits: all the interest is along the Wall itself, although in places you may prefer to drop down beneath the switchback Whin Sill (the ridge of hard rock on which the Wall stands), which itself can be quite tiring. The views are bleak and exhilarating. Even in fine summer weather the wind can be chilly on the Wall, so go well wrapped up. English Heritage are cutting back on the publicity for some sites – thousands of marauding tourists have caused more damage than centuries of harsh weather and unstable politics ever managed. In summer a tourist bus runs between Hexham and several of the main sites (and even as far as Carlisle), and you can get on or off at any of the stages along the way; check with the information centre on (01434) 605225 for times. The best place to eat nr the main sites is the Milecastle Inn on the B6318 NE of Haltwhistle.

Birdoswald Roman Fort 🏛 NY6166 (Gilsland) Overlooking the Irthing Gorge (and in fact just over the Cumbrian border), this is one of the most impressive sites on Hadrian's Wall, partly because it has so many features in such a small area, and partly for its grand views. Good visitor centre; snacks, shop, some disabled access; visitor centre cl Dec–Feb; (01697) 747602; £2.50.

Carrawbrough Mithraic Temple NY8571 Three 3rd-c altars to Mithras were found here, on the line of the Roman wall nr the fort of Brocolitia. They're now in Newcastle's Museum of Antiquities, but you can see replicas in their original setting.

Cawfield Crags NY7166 One of the best-preserved sections of the Wall.

Chesters Roman Fort NY9170 (B6318, slightly W of Chollerford) The best-preserved example of a Roman cavalry fort in Britain, in an attractive riverside setting. In the bathhouse you can see exactly how the underfloor heating system worked, and a museum has sculptures and inscriptions from

here and other sites. Summer snacks, shop, disabled access; cl 24–26 Dec, 1 Jan; (01434) 681379; £2.80; EH. The Hadrian Hotel at Wall (A6076 S) has good value food.

Corbridge Roman Site NY9864 (slightly NW) Granaries, portico columns and what may be the legionary HQ survive among these 3rd-c remains. The adjacent museum has the magnificent Corbridge Lion. Shop, limited disabled access; cl 1–2pm and all Mon and Tues Nov–Mar; (01434) 632349; £2.80; EH. The village, above the Tyne, is attractive; the Black Bull is good for lunch, and Brocksbushes Farm (2m E) has **pick-your-own** fruit and a farm shop; (01434) 633400.

Cuddys Crag NY7567 Perhaps the most beautiful section of the Wall, very photogenic and giving glorious views.

Greenhead Roman Army Museum NY6767 (Carvoran) Entertaining and informative interpretation of what it was like to be a Roman soldier, with everything you could possibly want to know about his training, pay, and off-duty hobbies. Snacks, shop, disabled access; cl mid-Nov to mid-Feb; (01697) 747485; £3.

Housesteads Roman Fort and Museum NY7969 (B6318) The best-known and most visited section of the Wall (and also one of the best-preserved), pretty much slap bang in the middle. It owes its fine state of preservation partly to the fact that while other stretches were being used as a handy source of free recycled quality masonry, this fort was base camp for a powerful group of Border bandits; woe betide anyone who tried to use their fortifications as material for cowsheds or churches. A museum has altars, inscriptions and models, and there are good walks in either direction. Snacks, shop; cl 24–26 Dec, 1 Jan; (01434) 344363; £2.80; EH.

Once Brewed National Park Centre NY7567 Very useful Northumberland National Park Information Centre, handy for Housesteads and Vindolanda, with exhibitions and audio-visual presentations. Guided walks leave from here (though not every day). Snacks, shop, disabled access; cl wkdys

Nov–mid-Mar; (01434) 344396; free; EH. The walk from here to Housesteads offers some of the best views of the Wall; it's only three miles but is up and down so can take up to two and a half hours.

Vindolanda NY7766 Started well before the Wall itself, this Roman fort and frontier town soon became a base for 500 soldiers. Full-scale reconstructions, lots of well preserved remains and possibly further excavations in progress. The adjacent museum has a fascinating selection of hand-written letters and documents found on the site, inc party invitations, shopping lists and a note that could have been written by many a modern mother: 'I have sent you socks and two pairs of underpants.' Shop, snacks, disabled access to museum but not site; cl mid-Nov to mid-Feb; (01434) 344277; £3.80.

Walltown Crags NY6766 One of the best-preserved sections of the Wall.

HAMSTERLEY NZ1231
Hamsterley Forest 5,000-acre fellside forest with good walks, cycle routes, four-mile forest drive, and visitor centre with local wildlife exhibitions and a new tearoom. Meals, snacks, shop, disabled access; cl Nov–Mar; (01388) 488312; forest drive around £1.50 a car. The Cross Keys at Hamsterley is a useful base.

HARTLEPOOL NZ5132
The developing Historic Quay and Jacksons Landing factory shopping mall (Marina) are enhancing its appeal to tourists. The town itself has some remains of its medieval wall.

Historic Quay At the old docks, this is a vivid open-air re-creation of an 18th-c port, complete with painstakingly reconstructed furnished houses, market, prison, and fully stocked shops. Also a couple of film shows, a dramatic (and noisy) exhibition on fighting ships, and the forthcoming maritime adventure centre, children's playship, and a Virtual Reality Centre giving would-be sailors the chance to try life at sea, without even getting wet. Lots to see, exceptionally well done. Meals, snacks, shop, disabled access; cl 25 Dec, 1 Jan; (01429) 860888; £4.95. The next-door Jacksons Wharf has decent food.

HMS *Trincomalee* (Jackson Dock) This, the oldest British warship afloat, should be completely restored by 2001; cl 25–26 Dec, 1 Jan; (01429) 223193; £3.

Museum of Hartlepool & PSS *Wingfield Castle* 🅰 (The Marina) Excellent local history, with something of a maritime emphasis; the well restored 1934 paddle steamer *Wingfield Castle* is used in part as a café. Meals, snacks, shop, disabled access; cl 25-26 Dec, 1 Jan; (01429) 222255; free.

HEXHAM NY9364
A pleasant market town, not too big, with some attractive stone buildings. The Royal Hotel has good value food.

Border History Museum 🅰 Formerly the country's first purpose-built prison; colourfully charts the chequered contacts between the English and Scots. Shop; open daily Apr–Oct, then Mon, Tues and Sat only Nov, Feb–Mar; (01434) 652351; £2.

Hexham Abbey Founded around 674 by St Wilfrid, once the largest church N of the Alps. The bulk of what is seen today dates from the 12th c, though there are two splendid Saxon survivals – the superbly atmospheric crypt, and the throne of the Bishop (St Wilfrid's Chair or Frith stool). The choir still descend the unique Night Stairs for services. Summer snacks, shop, disabled access; cl Good Fri; free, but donations welcome.

Warden church (just N) Down a lane by the Tyne, this is a fine example of the sturdy northern churches that had to do double duty as holy places and watch-towers to warn of Border raiders.

HIGH FORCE NY8828
High Force waterfall England's most powerful waterfall, this drops into a craggy cauldron at the end of a striking wooded gorge – though you'll have to pay around 50p (on top of parking) for the short path from the B6277 for the best view. From Bowlees Visitor Centre you can make more of a walk of it, first detouring N to Gibson's Cave, a pretty waterfall at the top of a gorge, and then heading S to cross the Tees for an easy two miles upriver, passing Low Force on the way. The nearby High Force Hotel has decent food (and the

highest brewery in England).

HORNCLIFFE NT9450

Chain Bridge Honey Farm Over 1,000 colonies of bees, a good visitor centre, and honey-based products for sale. Limited disabled access with notice; cl am Sun, wknds Nov–Mar, and 2 wks over Christmas; (01289) 386362; free.

JARROW NZ3365

Bede's World The Venerable Bede lived here for most of his 7th/8th-c life, producing the 37 books that encompass much of what is known of life in early Christian England. Along with the other half of the monastery, St Peter's, at nearby Monkwearmouth, the site is still a major Christian shrine. Very little remains of the original monastery, but there's Saxon stained glass in the church, and the chancel incorporates one of the earlier chapels. A museum in adjacent Georgian Jarrow Hall has finely carved Anglo-Saxon stones, more stained glass, and excavated relics. There's an authentically re-created 11-acre period farm, too. Meals, snacks, shop, some disabled access; cl Sun am, all day Mon (exc bank hols), over Christmas and New Year, and Good Fri; (0191) 489 2106; £3.

KIELDER WATER NY6293

This huge reservoir has done a lot to open up a remote part of the Borders; an attractive drive from Bellingham. It's an interesting shape, modelled by the steep folds of the land, and is already beginning to look as if it's always been tucked away in these pine-blanketed hills. You can hire out **rowing boats** for £8 an hour (01434) 250217. Visitor centres can supply fishing permits for the lake. You can rent **log cabins** around the lake by the week; (01502) 500500.

Bakethin Conservation Area Up at the top of Kielder Water, this is particularly rewarding for wildlife.

Kielder Castle Visitor Centre This 18th-c hunting lodge built for the Duke of Northumberland is now a very good Forest Enterprise visitor centre with exhibitions, closed-circuit TV bird-watching and a sculpture trail. Shop, meals and a play area, disabled access; (01434) 250209; cl wkdys Nov–Christmas, then daily till early

Apr; free. Regular guided walks from here into the great surrounding tract of Kielder Forest – miles of pine trees with a good chance of seeing red squirrels, as well as deer. There are also self-guided forest walks (easy to follow) from half a dozen or more points along the road through; and a 12-mile forest drive. The Pheasant at Stannersburn and Blackcock at Falstone have good food.

Kielder cycling The shores of Kielder Water and the surrounding forests have been well developed for cycling – the very friendly Kielder Bikes Company ▣ hire bikes from Kielder Castle (not Fri out of season), and are good for repairs too; (01434) 250392; a good mountain bike costs £10 for three hours.

Leaplish Waterside Park (slightly round to the W) Another good starting point for Kielder Water, with lots to do in summer, inc plenty of walks and cycle trails, mini golf and a swimming pool. Restaurant and bar, shop, disabled access; (01434) 250312; park free, charges for some activities.

Tower Knowe Visitor Centre Down at the foot of Kielder Water, with an exhibition and useful information about the area and its wildlife. Meals, snacks, shop, disabled access; cl Nov–Mar; (01434) 240398; centre free, exhibition £1. **Cruises** start from here too, and call all around the lake (takes about an hour and a half).

LANCHESTER NZ1243

Hall Hill Farm ▣ (B6296 SW) Friendly working farm with lots of animals, nature trails, riverside walk and trailer rides. Snacks, shop; cl Nov–Mar exc Santa wknds in Dec – phone for details; (01388) 730300; £3.20. The Queens Head is good for food.

LINDISFARNE NU1242

Otherwise known as Holy Island, this important centre for Christian pilgrims is linked to the mainland by a causeway which you can drive (or walk) over at low tide. Tide tables are posted at each end, or tel (01289) 330733; it really is worth checking these carefully – the causeway is impassable for two hours before high tide and four hours after. If you want to visit a particular attraction, make sure that the tide and the opening times match on the day you want to go. There are nature-reserve dunes, fishermen's huts made of upturned former boats, old lime-kilns, a small extended village with tourist cafés and pubs (the Ship has good value food), and good views from the close-grazed grassy crags. The three-mile walk around the island's shores is easy but fascinating.

Lindisfarne Castle The rather lonely and austere exterior belies what's within; the 16th-c fortress was restored by Lutyens for the editor of *Country Life* in a suitably monolithic quasi-medieval style. Sumptuous furnishings inc a fine collection of antique oak furniture, and there's a walled garden designed by Gertrude Jekyll to protect against the North Sea winds. Cl am, Fri (exc Good Fri), and Nov–Mar; (01289) 389244; £4; NT. It's a mile's walk fom the car park.

Lindisfarne Priory From here St Aidan and monks from Iona replanted the seeds of Christianity in 7th-c England. These early monks were driven out by Vikings, so it's the extensive remains of a later 12th-c church you can see today; a very peaceful and romantic spot, with graceful red sandstone arches bordered by incongruously neat lawns. Shop, disabled access to visitor centre; cl 24–26 Dec, and 1 Jan; (01289) 389200; £2.80.

St Aidan's Winery Home of Lindisfarne Mead, a fortified wine made from grapes, honey, herbs and water from an artesian well. They make honey too, and the shop has British beers, ciders and cheeses, as well as local pottery and jewellery. Snacks, shop; cl Christmas–New Year, and other times according to tide – best to phone; (01289) 389230; free.

LONGFRAMLINGTON NZ1199
Brinkburn Priory Well preserved 12th-c church (thanks to some Victorian restoration), still with medieval grave slabs, font and double piscina. Occasional services and concerts. Shop, some disabled access; open pm Apr–Oct; (01665) 570628; £1.60; EH. The Granby is useful for lunch.

LOW NEWTON NU2325
A charming seaside village on a fine stretch of little-visited coast, with a **bird reserve** nearby. The Joiners Arms in High Newton is famous for its fish and chips.

MARSDEN NZ3964
Grotto (A183) The Grotto here is unique: a lift (or a hundred or so steps) down to a pub cut into the seaside cliffs.

MATFEN NZ0370
One of the prettiest inland villages in Northumbria, with a riverside village green – and a good pub.

MORPETH NZ2086
The clock tower here is one of only eight non-church bell towers in Britain; it has only one hand, but still rings the curfew every night. The Tap & Spile, open all day, has good value food.

Morpeth Chantry Bagpipe Museum (Bridge St) Harmonious collection of small pipes and bagpipes from around the world. Headphones explain the difference between a rant and a reel. Shop; cl Sun, 25 Dec; (01670) 519466; £1.50. Good **craft centre** next door (cl Sun).

NEWCASTLE UPON TYNE NZ2563
This big industrial conurbation is far from being conventionally pretty, but has a strong vibrant atmosphere, and several excellent free museums. Its best parts are grouped very compactly high above the River Tyne with its three great bridges – particularly what has become almost the city's trademark, the two-decker High Level Bridge for road and rail designed by Robert Stephenson in the 1840s. The **Metro** system makes it quick and straightforward to get around, and to the attractions noted under North and South Shields, Tynemouth and Whitley Bay; a one-day Day Rover ticket (available from stations or the Tourist Information Centre) costs around £3.50 and is good for all Metro trips and stations (and the ferry between North and South Shields). You can still trace some stretches of the medieval **city wall**, especially from St Andrew's Church along the cobbled lane W of Stowell St – Chinese restaurants around here – and past the Heber Tower along Bath Lane. Grey's Monument is now closed to the public – people were throwing pennies and

stones from the top and causing damage below. Fitzgeralds down the street is useful for a bite to eat. Steep alleys and steps lead from the centre down to The Quay, the oldest part of town, with several unexpected and quaintly attractive timber-framed medieval buildings; one of the oldest, the Cooperage, is a decent pub. Downstream, E of the 1920s Tyne Bridge, an area of refurbished 19th-c wharf buildings is enjoyable to walk through, with a traditional market on Sun, and a useful pub for food – the Bonded Warehouse. This whole quayside area is gradually being rejuvenated, with impressive developments taking shape on the other side of the river, too. Another stylish quayside warehouse conversion, the Waterline (by New Law Courts), has good food, as does the Fog on the Tyne overlooking St Peter's Basin marina. Besides the pubs mentioned above, the handsome Crown Posada (The Side, off Dean St) and the Duke of Wellington (High Bridge) are pleasantly civilised.

Bessie Surtees House (Sandhill) Well renovated timbered Jacobean house, with elaborate plaster ceilings and carved panelling. Cl wknds, bank hols and 25 Dec; (0191) 261 1585; free.

Hancock Museum 🏛 (Barras Bridge) Very good natural history museum, with magnificent collections of stuffed birds and mammals, as well as Egyptology displays, fossils and minerals. Lively temporary exhibitions, and plenty for children. Meals, snacks, shop, disabled access; cl Sun am, 25–26 Dec, and 1 Jan; (0191) 222 7418; £2.50–£3.95 (prices vary according to exhibitions).

Laing Art Gallery (New Bridge St) Notable temporary exhibitions, and excellent children's gallery, the activities well designed to encourage young children to think about shapes, texture and patterns. Free guided tours of the main galleries 11.30am Sat. Meals, snacks, shop, disabled access; cl Sun am, Good Fri, 25–26 Dec, and 1 Jan; (0191) 232 7734; free.

Life Interactive World (Times Sq) Housed in a dramatic new building beside the city's main railway station,

this £58m innovative visitor centre explores the origins of life. You'd think anywhere setting out to explain DNA in an accessible way would be on to a loser, but the main exhibition areas put across serious science in a surprisingly entertaining way. A visit starts with the River of Life, a trip back through billions of years of evolution, tracing how mankind has got to where we are today. One highlight is the Mad Motion ride, a simulator ride designed to make you feel you're surfing, roller-blading, and even bungee-jumping, and among numerous other interactive attractions is the chance to score against a virtual goalie. A live show in the Secret of Life explains what we have in common with everything from dinosaurs to daffodils, and a multimedia spectacle (shown in a theatre resembling a giant brain) aims to illustrate the range of emotions and activities going on in our heads. Meals, snacks, shop, disabled access; cl 25 Dec and 1 Jan; (0191) 261 6006; *£6.95 (*£4.50 children).

Museum of Antiquities (The University) Particularly good on Roman remains, with reconstructions of various points along Hadrian's Wall. The displays have been organised in a very user-friendly fashion. Shop, disabled access with notice; cl Sun, Good Fri, 24–26 Dec, 1 Jan; (0191) 222 7846; free.

Newcastle Castle This Norman building gave the city its name; a lot still remains. It's a little spoiled by the main railway line which cuts the gatehouse off from the keep, but as much as of the fortress was rediscovered only during the railway's construction it seems a little churlish to complain. Shop; usually open daily (exc 25 Dec, 1 Jan and Good Fri), but best to check; (0191) 232 7938; £1.50.

Newcastle Cathedral The 14th/15th-c Anglican cathedral is worth a look; a dramatic stone sculpture occupies the Chapel of the Incarnation. Refectory wkdy lunchtimes only, shop (cl Sun), disabled access; cl 12–4pm Sun; free.

Newcastle Discovery (Blandford Sq) Thriving complex with galleries and interactive features on subjects likely to appeal to the whole family – it's the biggest and busiest museum in the area. A highlight is the interactive Science Factory with plenty to push, press and poke: TV effects create the illusion of flying down the Tyne, there's a soft play area for very young children, and lots of mirrors, magnets and microscopes to fiddle with. Other galleries offer a similarly hands-on look at the history of the city (inc the early days of Newcastle United), fashion, shipbuilding, army life, and local inventors. The multimedia gallery which houses the remarkable 30-metre (100-ft) *Turbinia*, once the fastest ship on the seas, had closed for refurbishment as we went to press, but should reopen around the autumn. They run family fun days every Sun, and during the Easter and summer hols. Snacks, shop, disabled access; cl Sun am, Good Fri, 25–26 Dec, 1 Jan; (0191) 232 6789; free.

NORTH SHIELDS NZ3568
Stephenson Railway Museum (Middle Engine Lane) Excellent, with steam train trips along a short section of the North Tyneside Railway, as well as displays on the development of steam and a collection of rolling stock, inc George Stephenson's *Billy*. Centre cl Fri and all Oct–Apr, trains usually in steam Sun and bank hols May–Sept, plus Sat mid-July to Aug – best to check; (0191) 200 7146 for details; site free, £2 steam trips. The Magnesia Bank (Camden St) has good value food.

Wet 'n' Wild (Royal Quays) Children like this well heated indoor water park with exciting flumes and slides (one has a very steep drop). Meals, snacks, disabled access; cl 25 Dec and 1 Jan; (0191) 296 1333; £6.75 wknds and school hols, less at other times.

NORTHUMBERLAND COAST NU2615
This has much to interest walkers along its sandy and rocky shores, but the hinterland is rather dull, so it's better for pottering and for there-and-back walks than for round ones. A coast path covers the finest sections, which we pick out individually on the map.

PETERLEE NZ4338
Castle Eden Dene Nature Reserve The biggest of Durham's wooded coastal ravines, now a picturesque nature reserve with 12 miles of footpaths over 550 acres; free.

PONTELAND NZ1577
Kirkley Hall Gardens (2m NW towards Morpeth) Attractive and thoughtfully maintained, with big collection of herbaceous perennials, Victorian walled garden, pretty sunken garden, woodland garden and unusual trees and shrubs. Plant sales, disabled access; cl Oct–Mar; (01661) 860808; free.

PRUDHOE NZ0963
Prudhoe Castle 12th/14th-c ruined castle on an impressive mound (the name means 'proud hill') overlooking the Tyne, once the stronghold of the powerful Percy family. Remarkable restored gatehouse, and exhibition in nearby 19th-c manor house. Snacks, shop, disabled access; (01661) 833459; cl Oct–Mar; £1.80; EH. The Feathers at Hedley on the Hill does good wknd food.

Stephenson's Birthplace (Wylam) The single room open here is the NT's least visited property; open Thurs, Sat, Sun, Good Fri and bank hol Mon pms Apr–Oct; 80p. The Fox & Hounds (a short walk along the old railway track) and Boathouse have good value food.

ROKER NZ4058
Roker church This interesting church was designed by leading members of the Arts and Crafts movement.

ROSS BACK SANDS NU1339
One of the finest sections of the Northumbrian coast path – splendid windswept solitude, looking out to Holy Island.

ROTHBURY NY9799
Coquetdale Northumberland's most scenic drive is the B6344 following the river past Brinkburn Priory to Rothbury, then W on the B6341 past Hepple, then turning right on the unclassified road past Holystone and Alwinton. Picturesque walks around Holystone (where the Salmon is a useful stop), increasingly desolate up towards Blindburn.

Cragside Opulent Victorian mansion of Lord Armstrong, the armaments king, with spectacular rooms and some of the amazing gadgets he designed. Best of all are the miles of well wooded landscaped grounds, with lakes, glorious rhododendrons, showy formal garden, and a walk illustrating the various elements of the hydro-electric scheme he devised to light the house. Meals, snacks, shop, some disabled access; cl Mon exc bank hols, and Nov–Mar (house cl am, garden, grounds and visitor centre open selected days in winter); (01669) 620333; £6.50, £4 grounds only; NT. The Newcastle Hotel (open all day) has good value food inc (not winter) high teas. Nearby the **Rothbury Terraces** are excellent for gentle parkland walks.

ROWLANDS GILL NZ1456
Derwentcote Steel Furnace (A694 towards Hamsterley, where the Cross Keys does good value food) The earliest and most complete steel-making furnace to have survived, with an exhibition on steel production. Shop, disabled access; open first and third Sun pm of month, Apr–Sept; (01207) 562573; free.

SEAHOUSES NU2232
An unpretentious seaside resort, with amusement arcades and so forth – and a busy fishing harbour, overlooked by a good interesting pub, the Olde Ship. **Farne Islands** From Apr to Sept, weather permitting, **boat trips** from Seahouses let you see the eider ducks, thousands of other seabirds, and grey seals. Breeding season for the birds is usually around May–July, though perhaps a little later for the seals, whose plaintive-voiced pups stay on shore for only a few weeks. Most boats cost £8. Landing on the NT-owned islands is extra (from £3, £4 breeding times). The NT has a shop with information about the islands on Main St, cl winter Mon and Tues; (01665) 721099.

SEATON SLUICE NZ3276
Seaton Delaval ⊞ Vanbrugh's Palladian masterpiece, a splendid design of central porticoed main block and massive outer wings. Not all the interior has survived unscathed, and much of the original park and grounds has been submerged by surrounding developments. Snacks, shop; open pm only May bank hols, then Weds, Sun and bank hol Mon Jun–Sept; (0191) 237 1493; £3. The buildings around the Norman **church** are attractive, and the Waterford Arms nr the low-key

seafront does generous fresh fish.

SHILDON NZ2326
Timothy Hackworth Railway Museum ⊞ (Hackworth Cl, just SE) Restored home of early railway pioneer, with working replica of a steam locomotive in goods yard, and occasional passenger rides along 400 yds of original Stockton & Darlington track bed. Snacks, shop, limited disabled access; cl Mon (exc bank hols), Tues, and Nov–Easter; (01388) 777999; *£2. The nearby Flag & Whistle has good value food.

SOUTH SHIELDS NZ3667
Arbeia Roman Fort (Baring St) Huge variety of remains, as well as re-created scenes of camp life, museum with excellently displayed finds, and plenty for children to enjoy. A barrack block and part of a courtyard house are currently being reconstructed, and should be ready by spring 2002. Snacks, shop, some disabled access; cl Sun exc pm Easter–Sept; (0191) 456 1369; free, £1.50 for Time Quest (splendid hands-on archaeology exhibition). In a great beach-edge spot, the Littlehaven Hotel (River Dr) does good bar meals in its conservatory, and the Marsden Rattler (South Foreshore) is an enjoyable seafront bar complete with two original railway carriages.

Marsden Bay (nr South Shields) The **nature reserve** here gives one of the few reasonable coastal walks in Industrial Tyneside.

South Shields Museum & Art Gallery (Ocean Rd) Good displays, inc some hands-on exhibitions; cl Sun am Easter–Sept, and all Sun Oct–Easter; (0191) 456 8740; free.

SPRINGWELL NZ2858
Bowes Railway On certain days throughout the summer, well restored steam trains tow passengers in brake vans as far as Blackham`s Hill, where you can see two working steam-powered inclines designed by George Stephenson. The railway was developed to carry coal between local mines and on to Jarrow for shipment, and the centre itself houses many of these locomotives and coal wagons, in use up until the last colliery closures in 1974. Snacks and shop when staff available; centre open daily, trains in steam most

bank hol Sun and Mon pms in summer, plus some Sats too, best to phone; (0191) 416 1847; free (£1 on steam days).

STAINDROP NZ1221
Raby Castle Imposing fortress with Saxon origins; vast medieval hall, 14th-c kitchen, and dazzling Victorian octagonal drawing room – restored to its original splendour. From the outside – where there are walled gardens and a deer park – it looks just as a castle ought to. Snacks, shop (selling oven-ready game from the estate), disabled access to grounds only; open bank hol wknd Sat to following Weds, Weds and Sun only May and Sept, and Sun–Fri Jun–Aug, though best to check (castle open pm only); (01833) 660207; £5, £3 park and gardens only. The village is pretty. Up at Butterknowle the Malt Shovel has good value food, evenings and wknd lunchtimes.

STAWARD GORGE NY8063
Part of the Allen Banks estate (NT, with year-round access to the paths along the wooded River Allen – frequented by roe deer – and a ruined peel tower.

STOCKSFIELD NZ0762
Cherryburn (slightly E at Mickley) Well preserved 18th-c farm, the birthplace of artist and naturalist Thomas Bewick, with an exhibition on his life. A nice spot, with farm animals running about the yard, craft demonstrations, and good valley views. Annual special event first May bank hol. Shop, some disabled access; cl am, all day Tues and Weds, and Nov–Mar; (01661) 843276; £3; NT. The Highlander at Ovington has good value food.

STOCKTON-ON-TEES NZ4419
Green Dragon Museum (Theatre Yard) Local history inc a good audio-visual presentation on the birth of the railways here in 1825. Shop, some disabled access (prior notice preferred); cl Sun and bank hols; (01642) 393938; free. There's a railway heritage trail around town. Slightly E along the river, the surprisingly graceful Tees Barrage keeps polluted tidal water from mixing with water from the hills, moors and valleys, which it's hoped will stimulate watersports in the area.

HM Bark *Endeavour* (Castlegate Quay) Full-size replica of Captain Cook's famous vessel with re-created cabins and exhibits from surgeons' knives to telescopes. Shop, disabled access to main exhibition area; cl Oct–Mar; (01642) 676844; £2.50.

Preston Hall Museum (A135 Stockton–Yarm) Very well constructed Victorian high street and other period rooms, plus working craftsmen, aviary, and woodland and riverside walks. Snacks, shop, disabled access to ground floor only; cl Good Fri, 25–26 Dec, 1 Jan; (01642) 781184; £1.10. On the same site **Butterfly World** has a re-created jungle environment with hundreds of exotic butterflies flitting between the trees, rocks and waterfalls. Shop, disabled access; open daily from Feb half-term to Oct half-term; (01642) 791414; £3.30.

SUNDERLAND NZ3959
Monkwearmouth Station Museum (Monkwearmouth Stn) As well as trains, the chance to play in a bus. Cl Sun am; (0191) 567 7075; free.

National Glass Centre (Liberty Way) This dazzling exhibition is a fascinating cross between gallery, museum, and factory visit. Housed in a striking glass structure on a sloping site alongside the River Wear (you can walk along the glass roof, looking down on the exhibitions below), it focuses on how glass is made and used all around the world. You can even have a go at glass-making yourself, with a range of classes and workshops (around £5 extra, must be over 9). The Kaleidoscope Gallery explores the more imaginative ways glass is used, from time-lapse photography to a hall of mirrors. Several exhibits are interactive, with computer displays and activities, and trails and quizzes keep younger children amused. They occasionally have extra activities for children such as painting and story-telling. Meals, snacks, good shop, disabled access; cl 25 Dec, 1 Jan; (0191) 515 5555; £5 (children £2.50).

St Peter's church Sister church of St Paul's at Jarrow, its early years equally well documented by the Venerable Bede. Much of the original Saxon church still remains, inc the west wall and tower. A striking Colin Wilbourn sculpture outside commemorates the church's 7th-c founder Benedict Biscop.

TANFIELD NZ2057

Tanfield Railway (A6076) The world's oldest surviving railway, built in 1725 to carry coal to the Tyne, and set in a picturesque wooded valley. Steam trains still chuff along the route, and you can get off by a wooden gorge spanned by **Causey Arch**, the earliest railway bridge. There's a collection of locomotives, and they often have a blacksmith forging new parts for restoration work. Summer snacks, shop, disabled access; trains usually run every Sun, plus Weds and Thurs in summer hols, and bank hols; (0191) 388 7545 for timetable; fares from £3.50. The friendly Peacock (Tanfield Lea) has decent food.

TEESDALE NY9425

The best of County Durham's scenery; the B6277 below its moors and on to Alston in Cumbria is one of the finest drives in England. Upper Teesdale has much of the best walking in the Durham Pennines, and is famous for its limestone flora, inc rare arctic alpine species and the unique Teesdale violet; Widdybank Fell is a National Nature Reserve. The attractive villages of Middleton-in-Teesdale, Romaldkirk (there's an esp distinguished church here), Eggleston and Cotherstone all have good pubs and inns. A side track with a reward at its end is to the cosy Strathmore Arms in Holwick. There's good fishing on the river or the reservoirs above it, and fine landscapes all the way along.

TYNEMOUTH NZ3769

Castle and Priory Evocative clifftop ruins, high above the Tyne estuary. Little remains of the once-rich 11th-c Benedictine priory beyond its stirring nave and chancel, and the spooky gravestones outside. Even less is left of the 11th/14th-c castle, but it's unusual to find two such ruins next to each other, and it's a great spot for picnics. Shop, disabled access; cl Mon and Tues Nov–Mar, 24–26 Dec, 1 Jan; (0191) 257 1090; £1.80; EH. The Salutation (Front St) is comfortable for lunch.

Sea Life Aquarium 🔾 (Grand Parade, Beaconsfield) The same reliable

mixture as at their other centres, with a spectacular underwater tunnel surrounded by shark-infested water, and a section devoted to unusual tropical creatures. Meals, snacks, shop, disabled access; cl 25 Dec; (0191) 257 6100; £4.50.

WALLSEND NZ3066

Segedunum *See separate family panel on p. 423.*

WARKWORTH NU2305

Hermitage Prettily placed a short way upstream, this 14th-c cell of retreat is cut into the sandstone cliff, with some crude wall carvings and a tiny vaulted chapel; on Weds, Sun and bank hols Apr–Sept a boat can take you, £1.60.

Warkworth Castle The main street of this quietly picturesque small town rises from the riverside Norman church with its finely vaulted chancel to the striking **castle** on its hill above the River Coquet. It's virtually complete, so wandering round the crooked passageways and dark staircases is wonderfully atmospheric. Events here were immortalised in Shakespeare's *Henry IV.* Shop, limited disabled access; cl 1–2pm winter, 24–26 Dec, 1 Jan; (01665) 711423; £2.40; EH. The Hermitage Hotel is good for lunch, there are one or two antiques shops, and this stretch of coast has some lovely beaches.

WASHINGTON NZ3156

Washington Old Hall 🔾 (The Avenue) Well restored stone-built manor dating from the 13th c, for several hundred years the home of George Washington's family, though his ancestors had been established elsewhere (notably Sulgrave Manor in Northants) for quite a while by the time he was born. Re-created Jacobean rooms and garden, and a new exhibition on the hall's spell as a tenement block in the 19th c. Snacks, shop, disabled access to ground floor only; open Sun–Weds Apr–Oct; (0191) 416 6879; £2.80; NT. The unspoilt old village comes as a real surprise when you've penetrated the surrounding New Town. The Washington Arms is good value for lunch, and there's a small **mining museum** down Albany Way (cl 1–1.30pm; free).

Wildfowl and Wetlands Trust 🔾 (District 15, off A1231 E) 100 acres with hides, well laid out walks, adventure play area, and very good visitor centre. Some birds will feed from your hand (you can buy birdseed). Meals, snacks, shop, disabled access; cl 25 Dec; (0191) 416 5454; £4.75.

WEARDALE NY8242
This gave much of Co Durham's wealth, with lead and iron mining along its length and in the moors above. There's little reminder of those days now, but the A689 is a memorable drive. A **riding centre** at Low Cornriggs Farm has lessons, guided rides along scenic former packhorse routes, and farmhouse B&B; (01388) 537600. Along the dale is a string of attractive villages such as Wolsingham (good value food at the Black Bull), as well as pleasant waterside and moorland walks. The Golden Lion at St John's Chapel, open all day in summer, is another useful stop.

North of England Lead Mining Centre Probably the best-preserved lead-mining site in Britain, and unmissable if you're at all interested in industrial history. Equipped with hard hat and lamps, you're led through the mine's dark, chilly passageways to a huge underground waterwheel. Meals, snacks, shop; open daily Apr–Oct, Sun only in Nov; (01388) 537505; £3.40 for surface exhibitions, £5 inc mine trip.

Rookhope This diversion is worthwhile: fine alpine plants nursery, small craft centre, decent pub, more good walks.

Weardale Museum 🖼 (Ireshopeburn) Nr the source of the river, this re-creates life in this high valley's heady lead-mining days, and has an exhibition on John Wesley, who often preached in the adjacent chapel. Shop; cl am, all day Mon and Tues (exc in Aug), and Oct–Apr; (01388) 537417; £1.

WHITBURN NZ4064
Souter Lighthouse 🖼 When built in 1870 this was the most advanced lighthouse of the day, and the first to be powered by electricity; it still has period rooms and equipment. Meals, snacks, shop, disabled access (but not to tower); cl Fri (exc Good Fri), and all Nov–Mar; (0191) 529 3161; £2.80; NT. The Trust also own the Leas, the

spectacular stretch of coastline around here, leading to Marsden Rock with its colony of kittiwakes, cormorants and fulmars. The Jolly Sailor has decent food.

WHITLEY BAY NZ3575
St Mary's Lighthouse Out on St Mary's Island, reached by a causeway at low tide. Good views from the top – for those unable to climb the 137 steps, a camera at the top relays the image to a colour TV at the bottom. Snacks, shop; cl wkdys Nov–Mar (exc school hols), and possibly other times depending on the tide; (0191) 200 8650; £2. When the lighthouse is closed the island is worth a visit for the rock pools alone, and is visited all through the year by a wide range of birds. The Shiremoor House Farm up on Middle Engine Lane, New York (handy too for North Shields and Tynemouth), has some of the best food in this area – good value.

WINDY GYLE NT8515
The high summit by a fine ridge section of the Pennine Way, along the English/Scottish border – the best of the Way's long, lonely plod over the Cheviots' grassy moors. You have to walk some way from the road to reach this main ridge: start from Coquetdale and walk along The Street, an ancient drovers' track. Gradients are mild but the peaty ground can get boggy after rain; not all routes are defined on the ground, but stone boundary walls and forest plantations are useful guides.

WITTON-LE-WEAR NZ1631
Low Barns Nature Reserve 100-acre reserve with nature trails, woodland, grassland, lake and lots of interesting wildlife. Snacks, shop, good disabled access; cl 25–26 Dec, 1 Jan; (01388) 488728; free. The village is attractive, with a tree-lined sloping green; the Victoria is useful for lunch.

WOODHORN NZ2988
Woodhorn church Partly Saxon and Norman, said to be the oldest on this coast; it has a local history museum and craft demonstrations. Shop, disabled access; cl Mon (exc bank hols), Tues, all Nov–Mar; (01670) 817371; free.

Woodhorn Colliery Museum (Queen Elizabeth II Country Park) Former colliery buildings re-creating life in the pit and the communities around it. Also short trips on narrow gauge railway, displays of art by local miners, a new interactive exhibition on the Lindisfarne Gospels, craft workshops, and woodland walks.

Meals, snacks, shop, some disabled access; cl Mon (exc bank hols) and Tues; (01670) 856968; free, though charge for railway.

Where to eat

AMBLE NU2604 **Charlie's Chip Shop** *Albert St (01665) 710206* Popular family-run restaurant serving chips with fish, chicken, and pies, vegetarian options and children's dishes, plus a take-away service; disabled access|**£3.80**

BAMBURGH NU1835 **Copper Kettle Tea Rooms** *21 Front St (01668) 214315* 18th-c cottage nr castle, with beams, panelling, and copper implements; light lunches, home-made scones and cakes, more substantial suppers, a fine range of teas inc many fruit and herb ones, and a good choice of other drinks; no smoking; cl Dec to mid-Feb; limited disabled access. £12|£4

BARNARD CASTLE NZ0516 **Market Place Teashop** *29 Market Pl (01833) 690110* Long-standing tearoom in 17th-c building with flagstones and an open fire, smart uniformed waitresses, home-made cakes, light lunches, a good choice of teas, and a friendly relaxed atmosphere; cl Sun am, all day winter Sun, 24 Dec–6 Jan; disabled access|**£3.30**

BERWICK-UPON-TWEED NT9952 **Foxtons** *26 Hide Hill (01289) 303939* Lively bistro with good, imaginative and varied food that changes daily, decent wine list, and friendly service; cl Sun, bank hols; children over 10. £23|**£5.40**

CARTERWAY HEADS NZ0452 **Manor House Inn** *Kiln Pit Hill (01207) 255268* Popular slate-roofed stone house with fine southerly views over moorland pastures; interesting food from a wide changing menu, a partly no smoking restaurant (with a huge collection of jugs), and a friendly atmosphere; comfortable bdrms, nice breakfasts. £21.20|**£6.95**

CORBRIDGE NY9864 **Valley** *Old Station House, Station Rd (01434) 633434* Extremely friendly Indian restaurant in attractively converted, recently refurbished, sandstone station house with wide choice of very good Indian food and kind service; also, a special train service for parties from Tyneside with uniformed escort and free travel, and your order is phoned ahead to be ready on arrival – good fun; cl lunchtimes, cl Sun, 25 Dec, 1 Jan. £20

CRASTER NU2519 **Craster Restaurant** *(01665) 576230* Upstairs restaurant overlooking the harbour with candles on the tables, exceedingly welcoming staff, and huge helpings of fairly priced really fresh fish from the owners' fish depot – they have their own smoking yard, too; cl Oct–Apr; well behaved younger children lunchtime only, over 12 in evening. £14.85|**£6.60**

DURHAM NZ2643 **Bistro 21** *Aykley Heads House (0191) 384 4354* Former 17th-c farmhouse, now a light and airy Mediterranean-style restaurant, with pine dining chairs on wooden or flagstoned floors, a good choice of very enjoyable interesting modern cooking, a thoughtful wine list, and professional but relaxed service; cl Sun; disabled access. £29|**£9**

GREAT WHITTINGTON NZ0071 **Queens Head** *(01434) 672267* Simple stone inn with two beamed, comfortable and neatly furnished rooms, a wide choice of good interesting food, a no smoking restaurant, log fires, well kept real ales, decent wines, and quite a few malt whiskies; cl Mon exc bank hols; disabled access. £20|**£6.95**

HAYDON BRIDGE NY8364 **General Havelock** *(01434) 684283* Very civilised old stone terraced house with stripped-stone back dining room overlooking the Tyne, good if limited lunchtime food and interesting evening meals, well kept real ales, good wines by the glass, pleasant service, and a friendly local atmosphere; cl Mon, first 2 wks Jan; disabled access. £23.50|**£7**

HEDLEY ON THE HILL NZ0759 **Feathers** *(01661) 843607* Little stone local with three neatly kept traditional bars, woodburners, straightforward furnishings, a charming, relaxed and welcoming atmosphere, imaginative meals, and well kept real ales; cl wkdy lunchtimes exc bank hols; disabled access. £15|**£5.50**

NEWTON-ON-THE-MOOR NU1705 **Cook & Barker Arms** *(01665) 575234* Bustling stone pub with an unfussy, long beamed bar with partly panelled walls, paintings by local artists, a coal fire and coal-effect gas one, and a no smoking area; beautifully prepared imaginative food, changing real ales, decent whiskies and 12 wines by the glass; disabled access. £30|**£6.95**

RENNINGTON NU2119 **Masons Arms** *(01665) 577275* Friendly, well run old coaching inn with good value, quickly served bar food inc nice daily specials, a comfortably modernised beamed lounge bar, friendly helpful staff, real ales, and decent breakfasts; comfortable bdrms; children over 5 in evening. £18|**£5.25**

SHINCLIFFE NZ2940 **Seven Stars** *High St N (0191) 384 8454* Just ten minutes' or so drive from central Durham, this early 18th-c village inn with its pretty window-boxes and creepers has a civilised but largely unspoilt and welcoming atmosphere; the lounge has a coal fire in a handsome Victorian fireplace, copper kettles hanging from the beams, real ales, enjoyable and imaginative bar food from a changing menu (the candlelit dining room is no smoking), and quite a few malt whiskies; parking can be tricky. £23|**£7**

WARENFORD NU1328 **Warenford Lodge** *(01668) 213453* Very individual, old (though rather modern-feeling), dining pub with stripped stonework, a big stone fireplace, comfortable extension with woodburner, really good, attractively presented, imaginative food, and decent wines; children in evening dining room only; cl Mon, Tues, Sun pm in winter, Jan; limited disabled access. £18.30|**£5.20**

Special thanks to Eric Larkham and Norman Fox

We welcome reports from readers

This *Guide* depends on readers' reports. Do help us if you can – in return, we offer a discount on the next edition to people who've helped us with reports for it. Tell us what you think about places already in it, and anything extra you think we should say about them. And send us your ideas for inclusion in the next edition: places to visit, eat at or stay in, attractive drives or walks, maybe even unusual interesting shops you know of. Use the card in the middle, the report forms at the end, or just write – no stamp needed: *The Good Britain Guide*, FREEPOST TN1569, Wadhurst, E Sussex TN5 7BR.

NOTTINGHAMSHIRE

Varied family excursions, some attractive countryside, low prices

Places for families to head for here include the lively Galleries of Justice (putting a fun spin on the 19th-c penal system) and the happy mix of modern science and traditional craftsmanship at Green's Mill and Science Centre, both in Nottingham itself – a lively and interesting city, with a new ice complex to add to its attractions. Elsewhere, the White Post Modern Farm Centre in Farnsfield is particularly good for younger children (as is the fairytale-themed Sundown Adventureland, Rampton), while older brothers and sisters should enjoy the medieval re-creations at Haughton's World of Robin Hood.

For a small county, Nottinghamshire does well for new entries this year, with interesting displays of local history at Mansfield's Museum & Art Gallery and the heritage centre at Eastwood (the latter will also please D H Lawrence fans), and good value vintage train and bus rides at the Nottingham Transport Heritage Centre, Ruddington.

There's a nice mix of unusual attractions too, from the antique clocks at the British Horological Institute, Upton, to the ancient caves at Creswell (occasional story-telling and tours just for children), or the remarkable 1920s time-capsule of Mr Straw's House at Worksop.

The county has some charming and interesting villages, and one or two attractive old towns such as Newark and Southwell. The mansions and families which gave the name of the Dukeries to the countryside in the north are long gone, but broad tracts of landscaped wooded parkland remain, such as Clumber Park, good for letting off steam.

Where to stay

LANGAR SK7234 **Langar Hall** *Church Lane, Langar, Nottingham, Nottinghamshire NG13 9HG (01949) 860559* **£125***, plus special breaks; 10 lovely rms, some in wing and courtyard as well. Fine country house in spacious grounds with beautifully furnished elegant rooms, pillared dining hall with paintings for sale, antiques and fresh flowers, a relaxed informal atmosphere, a lively and friendly owner, and very good food; dogs by arrangement; quite a few facilities for children ☺

NOTTINGHAM SK5640 **H & H Narrowboat Hotels** *7 Bramshill Gardens, London NW5 1JJ (020) 7272 0033* **£255**, per person, full board for 3 nights; 7 oak-panelled cabins. Hotel boat cruises in narrowboats painted in traditional canal colours, with oak and ash panelling, dining lounge, little bar, library and observation saloon, enjoyable food inc breakfast, morning coffee, light lunch, afternoon tea, and 4-course dinner, and helpful informative staff – great fun, plenty of time to explore, themed tours, too; departures from here, among other key canal localities throughout England and Wales; cl Nov to mid-Mar but open Christmas; limited disabled access

SOUTHWELL SK7053 **Old Forge** *Burgage Lane, Southwell, Nottinghamshire NG25 0ER (01636) 812809* **£60***, plus special breaks; 5 rms. 200-year-old former blacksmith's house with welcoming owner, interesting furnishings, super breakfasts in conservatory overlooking the Minster, light supper on request, and pretty terrace; well behaved dogs welcome

SOUTHWELL SK7053 **Saracens Head** *Market Pl, Southwell, Nottinghamshire NG25 0HE (01636) 812701* **£65**; 27 well kept rms. Interesting old hotel (Charles I spent his last free night here) with ancient-feeling beamed main bar, pleasant staff, straightforward bar lunches, and restaurant

To see and do

Nottinghamshire Family Attraction of the Year

FARNSFIELD SK6257 **White Post Modern Farm Centre** (A614, 1m W) This bustling modern working farm really is first-class for families: young children are looked after particularly well, and they have everything from a mouse town to llamas, quails, snakes and fish – with plenty of opportunities to get close to the animals along the way. Especially good fun is their new goat mountain, which lets goats combine two of their favourite activities, climbing and eating. They scramble up a sort of climbing frame as tall as a house, then you can put food in a little box at the bottom, turn a handle for it to go up to the top, then watch them enjoy their meal. There's also a very enjoyable show, where you're talked through a farmer's year – with the help of pigs, rabbits, ducks and rats. Check times for this and other events on the notice board just after the entrance. You can buy food for many of the animals, and younger visitors can generally bottle-feed baby goats, pick up chicks, or fuss the guinea-pigs and rabbits in the farm yard. They're particularly strong on pigs, and you can always watch eggs hatching in their huge incubator. Most displays and animals move indoors if the weather is bad, so it's a good bet all year round (but best to wear suitable shoes if it's likely to be muddy). Play areas are very good – there's an indoor sand pit and plenty of other activities in the field – and as well as things like farm trails and pony rides you'll find more unusual features such as a bat house, aviary, and reptile handling sessions. They sell various insects and reptiles, and have a Reptile Hotel to look after them while you're on holiday. Dogs can't come into the farm, but can be left in attended kennels. Meals, snacks, heated picnic area, good farm shop, disabled access; (01623) 882977; £4.95 (£3.95 children 3–16).

BEACON HILL SK7490
Above the Chesterfield Canal at Gringley on the Hill, this gives magnificent views in all directions; you can make out the towers of Lincoln Cathedral on a clear day.

BLYTH SK6185
An attractive small town, with interesting wall paintings in the **church**; the White Swan by the duck pond is good for lunch.

Hodsock Priory Gardens 🖾 (off B6045 S) Especially lovely at snowdrop time; open 30 days Feb/Mar; (01909) 591204; plant sales; *£3.

CHESTERFIELD CANAL SK7284
This has scope for towpath walks; one quiet stretch is by the Boat at Hayton.

CLUMBER PARK SK6375
One of the great former Dukeries estates, nearly 4,000 acres of farmland,

parks, lake and woodland, with interesting walled garden, and the longest lime avenue in Europe, almost two miles long. The estate is outstanding for its walks, enough for a full-day excursion. You can also hire bikes. Meals, snacks, shop, disabled access; park open all year, cl 25 Dec, 14 July and 18 Aug; (01909) 484977; £3 per car; NT.

COSSALL SK4743
Attractive village in D H Lawrence country: he was once engaged to the girl who lived in Church Cottage.

CRESWELL SK5474
Creswell Crags Visitor Centre
Stone Age man lived in the caves and rock shelters of this limestone gorge right by the Derbyshire border (the village is actually across the border). Even on days when there aren't cave

tours it's an intriguing prehistoric site, with a good visitor centre, reconstructions of Ice Age family life, and other displays and activities. They sometimes have children's stories in one of the caves (booking required), and in the summer there are children's tours. Picnic area, shop, disabled access; cl Nov–Jan exc Sun – best to check for cave tour dates (usually every wknd and daily in summer hols); (01909) 720378; site free, cave tours £2.25. Take a torch. The Greendale Oak at Cuckney has good value food.

CROMWELL SK7961

Vina Cooke Museum of Dolls (Old Rectory) Thousands of toys and objects related to childhood, in an imposing 17th-c rectory. Especially lively on Easter Mon, with morris dancers, crafts and the like. Shop, limited disabled access; cl 12–2pm, all day Fri, 25–26 Dec and 1 Jan; (01636) 821364; *£2.50. The Great Northern at Carlton-on-Trent has decent food.

EASTWOOD SK4647

D H Lawrence Birthplace Museum (8a Victoria St) The writer was born in this typical working-class house in 1885; it's been carefully restored to how he knew it. Shop, limited disabled access; cl 24 Dec–1 Jan; (01773) 763312; £2 (joint ticket with Durban House below, £3.50). Craft workshops next door (usually cl Weds pm and Sun). Another home of Lawrence's, on Garden Rd, is furnished as he described it in *Sons and Lovers*; open by appointment with Ken Roberts on (0151) 653 8710. The chatty Foresters Arms (Newthorpe) is appealing.

Durban House Heritage Centre This decent new centre houses an exhibition on D H Lawrence, with original manuscripts and changing displays such as the copy of *Lady Chatttersley's Lover* used as evidence in the notorious obscenity trial; also changing local history displays, a Tourist Information Centre, and a gift shop selling a complete range of the author's works. Restaurant, disabled access; cl 24 Dec–2 Jan; (01773) 717353; £2 (joint with Birthplace Museum, £3.50).

EDWINSTOWE SK5865

Sherwood Forest Farm Park (Lamb Pens Farm, off A6075) Unusual breeds of traditional farm animals, water buffalo and wallabies, pets' corner, and colourful waterfowl on a sizeable lake. Also an owl garden, adventure playground (with a separate section for the under-5s), and picnic area. They usually have some activities under cover in a barn, but it's very much a place for fine weather. Special events typically include an Easter treasure hunt, and demonstrations of sheep shearing and spinning (best to check exact dates); home-baked teas and snacks, shop, mostly disabled access (can be tricky around the lakes); open daily Easter–Sept, plus wknds till mid-Oct ; (01623) 823558; £4, children £2.50.

Sherwood Forest Visitor Centre With an exhibition on Robin Hood, the visitor centre is a good springboard for the forest itself, only a fraction of what it once was (it used to cover a fifth of the county) but still miles across, though the heathland that Robin himself would have known has largely swallowed up either by farmland or by forestry plantation. Good waymarked paths and footpaths, the most popular being to the Major Oak (a huge tree in the heart of the forest). Meals, snacks, shop, disabled access; park free, car park £1.50 wknds, bank hols and summer hols. **Sherwood Forest Art and Craft Centre** nearby has 17 craft studios housed in a mid-18th-c coach house and stables; cl Mon and Tues Oct–Mar. Near the village church (supposedly where Robin Hood and Maid Marian were married), the Black Swan is handy for something to eat. The best drive is the B6034 N towards Worksop, then the right turn to Carburton and Clumber Park. Sherwood Forest has one of England's three **Center Parcs**, a rewarding place to stay with excellent leisure facilities; (0990) 200300.

ELKESLEY SK6875

Attractive village, with a working potter nr the church. The Robin Hood is useful for lunch.

FARNSFIELD SK6257

White Post Modern Farm Centre *See separate family panel on p.445.*

White Post Wonderland (1m W) Useful enough for families, with free-flying butterflies, a maze, indoor play area, junior roller-coaster and train rides. Meals, snacks, shop, disabled access; cl 24–26 Dec and wkdys in Jan; (01623) 882773; £4. Combs Farm Shop nearby is a good one (cl Sun and Mon).

HAUGHTON SK6872

World of Robin Hood 🏛 With an emphasis on fun that may put off historical purists, this is an enjoyable re-creation of medieval life, placing the Robin Hood stories in their historical context. They've meticulously constructed an entire medieval village complete with costumed guides, but while there are plenty of things to keep children entertained, some of the darker displays may not suit smaller ones; also a small animal farm, and play area. Outside is a deer park and owl sanctuary, with summer activities such as archery. Meals, snacks, shop, some disabled access; cl Nov–Feb; (01623) 860210; *£4.95. The Robin Hood at Elkesley has good value food.

HOLME PIERREPONT SK6339

Holme Pierrepont Hall Early Tudor manor house with interesting early 15th-c timbers, and an elaborate parterre in the formal courtyard garden. Several rooms inc the ball room and billiard room have been recently restored. Teas, shop, disabled access to gardens only; phone for opening; (0115) 933 2371; £3.50, £1.50 garden only. The Round Oak in Radcliffe-on-Trent has decent food.

LAXTON SK7267

Unique for having kept the pattern of its **medieval farming**, with different villagers each owning strips of the three great fields. You can walk the grass paths or sykes which divide groups of these strips, and the Dovecote, a good village pub, has an exhibition in the yard explaining the system. The church has a fine 15th-c screen.

MANSFIELD SK5361

Mansfield Museum & Art Gallery (Leeming St) Very good for local history, with displays of 18th-c porcelain, local watercolours, stuffed birds in the natural history gallery, and a thorough look at Mansfield's industrial heritage; shop, disabled access; cl Sun and bank hols; (01623) 463088; free.

MAPLEBECK SK6961

Delightfully rustic village; the Beehive's a classic country tavern, and nearby Woodborough and Lambley are also worth a look.

NEWARK SK7953

Attractive old market town with some interesting buildings in its side streets, a fine church, and walks by the River Trent, with summer boat trips. The Old Malt Shovel (North Gate) is handy. Useful museums include the **Museum of Social and Folk Life** on Millgate (cl am wknds, bank hols and 25–26 Dec; free), and the local history collection on Appletongate (cl 1–2, Thurs, and Sun exc summer pms; free).

Newark Air Museum 🏛 (Winthorpe, NE) Over 50 assorted aircraft inc rare jet fighters and bombers; half the exhibits are under cover so fine all year round (and the Willow Tree over at Barnby in the Willows is handy for lunch). Snacks, shop, disabled access; cl 24–26 Dec; (01636) 707170; £4.

Newark Castle 🏛 The ruins date from the 11th c, and there's still a fair bit to see; it was destroyed during the Civil War then had periods as a cattle market and a bowling green. The gardens have been relaid as they were in Victorian times. Good explanatory displays at the **Castle Story Exhibition** in the grounds; cl 25–26 Dec, 1 Jan; (01636) 655765; free (£1 for tour of the castle – phone to check times).

NEWSTEAD SK5454

Newstead Abbey (off A60) Splendid former home of Lord Byron, in gorgeously romantic grounds; many of his possessions can still be seen. Rooms are decorated in a variety of styles from medieval through to Victorian, and there are substantial remains of the original abbey. Meals, snacks, shop, limited disabled access; cl am and Oct–Mar (grounds open all year exc last Fri in Nov); (01623) 455900; house and gardens £4, gardens only £2. The Horse & Groom in the attractive nearby village of Linby is a useful stop.

NORTH CLIFTON SK8272

Pureland Meditation Centre & Japanese Garden Peaceful Japanese garden created from 1½ acres of flat field, and more relaxation in the meditation centre (open all year). Snacks, shop, some disabled access (discounted entry); garden cl Mon, and Nov–Mar; (01777) 228567; £3.50.

NOTTINGHAM SK5739

At wknds and summer evenings it quickly loses its big-city character, and is then easy to park in and stroll through, without the rush of traffic that otherwise swarms along its inner ring road. The parts around the parish church (which has some interesting carvings) and the Lace Market are particularly attractive. Besides the museums described below, the **Museum of Costume and Textiles** (43–51 Castle Gate, cl Mon (exc bank hols), Tues, 24 Dec–1 Jan; free) is well worth a look. The town has an amazing number of decent pubs – handy for the thirsty work of serious sightseeing. The new Via Fossa (Canal St) is great fun to look around, and other useful lunch places are Fellows Morton & Clayton (Canal St; brews its own beer), the quaint old Bell (Angel Row), Limelight (attached to the Playhouse) and Lincolnshire Poacher (Mansfield Rd). The city boasts a glistening new leisure attraction in the National Ice Centre, Lower Parliament St (see below).

Attenborough Nature Reserve Unusual reserve with good bird-watching down by Beeston at the extensive partly wooded Attenborough lakes; on the far side a path takes you along the narrow spit of land dividing them from the mighty River Trent. The Manor at Toton is a good nearby dining pub.

Brewhouse Yard Museum (Castle Boulevard) Spread over five 17th-c houses with period rooms and reconstructions, this has very good interactive displays on local life, and several features designed with children in mind (the Feely Boxes are fun). Award-winning historic roses in the cottage garden. Shop, some disabled access; cl winter Fri, 25 Dec, 1 Jan; (0115) 9153600; £1.50 wknds and bank hols, otherwise free.

Castle Museum & Art Gallery On the summit, this dates from the 17th c, but the gateway is from an earlier 13th-c fortress. It now houses an appealing museum, with a history of the site and

the subterranean passageways. Meals, snacks, shop, disabled access; cl 25–26 Dec, 1 Jan and Fri Nov–Mar; (0115) 915 3700; *£2 wknds and bank hols.

Cave tours The rock on which old Nottingham stood is honeycombed with hundreds of galleries, cellars and passageways (one attractive old pub, the Olde Trip to Jerusalem, has a fascinating bar tunnelled right into the rock face). Tours usually leave the castle at 11am, 12.30, 1.30, 2.30 and 3pm Mon–Thurs and Sat, and at 2 and 3pm Fri in summer (less frequently in winter) – in case of occasional rock falls it's always best to call (0115) 915 3700 first. They're quite strenuous; £2.

Caves of Nottingham (Drury Walk) Tour with taped commentary of 750-year-old caverns beneath a busy modern shopping centre, through an underground tannery, Victorian slum, air raid shelters, and pub cellars. Shop; cl 24–26 Dec, 1 Jan and Easter Sun; (0115) 924 1424; £3.25.

Djanogly Art Gallery (University Arts Centre, University Park, SW of centre) Good temporary exhibitions; cl am Sun, am bank hols, 24–26 Dec, 1 Jan; (0115) 951 3189; free.

Galleries of Justice (Shire Hall, High Pavement) The grim realities of a 19th-c trial and prison life are re-enacted with real verve at this growing centre, set around two Victorian courtrooms in use right through to 1986. The award-winning centrepiece – designed very much to entertain children – is called Condemned, and begins with visitors being given a criminal identity number before being sent to trial in the Criminal Court. It's hardly giving the game away to say that the verdict is always guilty – 'Prisoners' are then taken down to the cells, where costumed interpreters posing as prison warders lead them to their fate. Nicked is a similar new police station experience where visitors can help to solve a murder. Meals, snacks, shop, some disabled access; cl Mon (exc bank hols) and 24–26 Dec, 1 Jan; (0115) 952 0555; Condemned £6.95.

Green's Mill and Science Centre (Windmill Lane, Sneinton) Good for families: the restored tower mill still produces flour, and you can try grinding

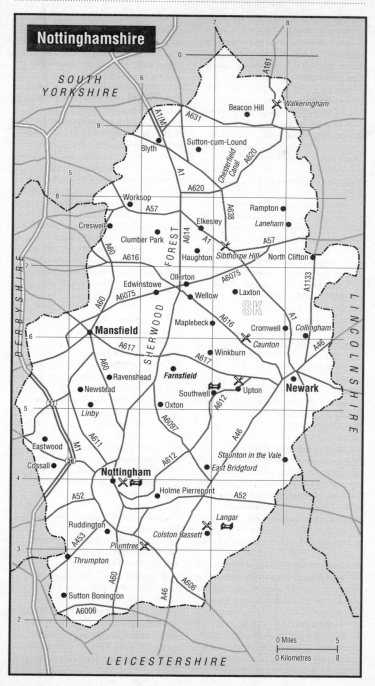

Nottinghamshire

SOUTH YORKSHIRE

DERBYSHIRE

LINCOLNSHIRE

LEICESTERSHIRE

Beacon Hill
Walkeringham
A161
A631
Sutton-cum-Lound
Blyth
A1(M)
Chesterfield Canal
A620
A1
A620
Worksop
A57
A638
Rampton
Laneham
A57
Creswell
Elkesley
A614
A1
Clumber Park
FOREST
Haughton
Sibthorpe Hill
North Clifton
A60
A616
Ollerton
A6075
A1133
Edwinstowe
A60
A6075
Wellow
Laxton
SK
Mansfield
SHERWOOD
Maplebeck
A616
Cromwell
Collingham
A617
Caunton
A46
A60
Winkburn
A617
Ravenshead
Farnsfield
Newstead
Southwell
Upton
Newark
27
Linby
A612
Oxton
A6097
A46
M1
A611
Eastwood
Staunton in the Vale
Cossall
26
A612
East Bridgford
Nottingham
Holme Pierrepont
A52
A52
Ruddington
Langar
A453
Plumtree
Colston Bassett
Thrumpton
A60
A46
A606
Sutton Bonington
A6006

0 Miles 5
0 Kilometres 8

corn on part of an old millstone. Among the exhibits at the hands-on Science Centre next door is a weather satellite receiver showing pictures live from space. Snacks, shop, disabled access; cl Mon (exc bank hols), Tues, and Christmas – best to tel (0115) 915 6878 to check if the mill is working; free.

Lace Centre 🖼 (Castle Rd) This pretty 15th-c house has lace hanging from almost every beam, much of it for sale. Lace-making demonstrations pm summer Thurs. Some disabled access; cl 25–26 Dec and 1 Jan; (0115) 941 3539; free.

Museum of Nottingham Lace 🖼 (High Pavement) Across the road from its former premises in Lace Hall, this tells the story of the city's lace industry, with demonstrations and interesting displays touching on social conditions; their visitor centre arranges self-guided audio tours of the lace market. Shop, limited disabled access; best to check for Christmas opening times; (0115) 989 7365; £2.95.

National Ice Centre Britain's newest ice attraction covering the full range of related sports from ice-hockey (the Nottingham Panthers have regular fixtures here) to speed skating; also regular concerts, and a good programme of courses in the school hols. Snacks when events are on, shop, disabled access; centre open daily, but best to phone for skating times; (0115) 853 3000; skating from £2.80 (£1 extra skate hire).

Tales of Robin Hood 🖼 (Maid Marian Way) Cars carry you through the sights, sounds and smells of a re-created medieval Sherwood Forest, and a film looks at the truth behind the stories. Pretty much for insistent children only – otherwise you might be better going out to Haughton. Meals, snacks, shop, disabled access; cl 25–26 Dec; (0115) 948 3284; £4.95.

Wollaton Hall (Wollaton Park, 3m W) Splendidly ornate Tudor house with the city's natural history collection. The 500-acre grounds are a delight. Shop, some disabled access; cl Fri in winter and 25 Dec; (0115) 915 3900; free wkdys, £1.50 wknds and bank hols, small car parking charge. The adjacent **Industrial Museum** (Courtyard Buildings) looks once again at lace-

making, along with other local industries (usually cl Nov–Mar; phone for steam days (0115) 915 3910; £1.50 wknds, also free wkdys). The Yard Gallery has changing art and natural history exhibitions.

OLLERTON SK6567

Ollerton Mill 🖼 (Market Pl) The only working watermill in the county, still producing flour as it did in the early 18th c, in a pleasant setting on the edge of Sherwood Forest. Award-winning teashop (teashop often open when mill isn't), shop; mill working pm Sun and bank hols Apr–Sept; (01623) 822469; *£1.50. The White Hart opposite the church in the pretty market place has good value food.

Rufford Country Park (off A614 S) Pleasant lakeside spot on edge of Sherwood Forest, with the ruins of a 12th-c abbey, craft centre and family activities most summer weekends; cl 25–26 Dec (£1.50 car park charge).

OXTON SK6251

Attractive village; the lane up hill N below the power lines leads to an Iron Age hill fort.

RAMPTON SK7978

Sundown Adventureland (Treswell Rd; N of A57) Popular with readers, this cheerful little leisure park is best for children between around 4 and 8. It's full of decent life-size representations and tableaux of stories and fairy-tales, from the Wild West to the Three Little Pigs. There are gentle rides, as well as a few animals, and several themed play areas, one under cover (height restrictions apply in here). Good Christmas displays, when every child gets a present from Santa (not everything else is working then). Snacks (mostly fast food), shop, some disabled access; cl 25–26 Dec, wkdys Jan–beginning Feb; (01777) 248274; £4.75 everyone over 2.

RAVENSHEAD SK5654

Longdale Craft Centre 🖼 (Longdale Lane) Very good craft centre, partly set out as a Victorian village street, with rows of period workshops and a small museum. Decent restaurant, snacks, shop, disabled access; (01623) 794858; cl 25–26 Dec; £2. The Little John (B6020) has decent food.

Papplewick Pumping Station ⊞
(Longdale Lane) A working Victorian
waterworks with two beam engines; best
to ring for steam days, though open for
static displays pm most Suns Easter–Oct;
(0115) 963 2938; £1.50 (£3 steam days).
The Burnstump in the Country Park is a
good value family dining pub.

RUDDINGTON SK5732

Framework Knitters Museum ⊞
(Chapel St) Housed in restored 19th-c
workshops, cottages and frameshop,
this museum explores the industry for
which Nottinghamshire was once
famous. Besides reconstructed
cottages you can see the machinery
working, inc the bizarre circular sock-
knitting machines. Snacks, shop; cl end
Dec–Easter, Mon and Tues, and am Sun;
(0115) 984 6914; *£1.50.

**Nottingham Transport Heritage
Centre** (Loughborough Rd) Steam
trains leave every hour from here
between 11.30am and 4.30pm on Suns
and bank hol Mons Apr to mid-Oct; the
track runs as far as Gotham Moor, and
the six-mile round trip lasts 45 mins.
They also run hourly vintage bus rides
(12.30–4.30pm). Meals, snacks, shop,
mostly disabled access; (0115) 940 5705;
£4.50 (inc both train and bus rides).

Village Museum (Church St)
Reconstructed Edwardian shops;
usually open pm Weds, Thurs and bank
hols Apr–Aug, and Weds–Thurs in Sept
– best to phone; (0115) 914 6645; £1.

SOUTHWELL SK7053

Southwell Minster Magnificent 12th-c
church, a fine sight from miles around
(especially at night when it's floodlit),
and glorious to walk through. Fine leaf
carvings and lovely choir screen; it's
worth catching one of the regular
concerts. There's a smart visitor
centre. This attractive old town, small
and quiet, is the home of the bramley
apple, developed by Henry
Merryweather in the 19th c. One of the
original trees still prospers at his
descendant's garden centre on Halam
Rd, where there's a small exhibition on
the subject. The Bramley Apple next
door is good for lunch.

SUTTON BONINGTON SK5025
Pleasant village to saunter through.

SUTTON-CUM-LOUND SK6985
Wetlands Waterfowl Reserve ⊞
(off Loundlow Rd) Lagoons full of birds
from ducks and swans to flamingos, and
many more wild birds inc parrots and
emus in the surrounding countryside.
Also owls, foxes, llamas, wallabies,
prairie dogs and children's farm. Meals,
snacks, shop, disabled access; cl 25 Dec;
(01777) 818099; *£2. The canalside
Boat at Hayton has decent food.

UPTON SK7254

British Horological Institute ⊞
Includes a museum of clocks and
timepieces from marine chronometers
to the first telephone speaking clock.
Some exhibits are over 300 years old,
so don't expect them to keep perfect
time. Snacks, shop, disabled access;
open pm (exc Sat and Mon) Apr–Sept,
and pm Tues–Fri Oct–Mar but best to
check; (01636) 813795; £2.50. The
French Horn has good food.

WELLOW SK6665
An attractive village, unusual for its
permanent maypole – which used to be
the trunk of a Sherwood Forest tree,
but is now metal. It stands on the only
genuine village green in the county, kept
that way since the village was founded in
the 12th c (all the others were just open
spaces used by the villagers and
itinerant traders for buying and selling,
which have been grassed over since all
that stopped). The Olde Red Lion is
good for lunch.

WINKBURN SK7158
Attractive village; unusually, its simple
12th-c village church was formerly a
temple of the Knights Hospitaller.

WORKSOP SK5880
Mr Straw's House (7 Blyth Grove)
One of the NT's most unusual
properties, an ordinary 1920s semi, left
untouched by two brothers who
inherited it when their parents died.
Even the calendar remains unturned. A
fascinating time-capsule, it's open by
prebooked timed ticket only (Tues–Sat
Apr–Oct), but it really is worth taking
the trouble to get one and by limiting
numbers the National Trust ensure that
you can get a really good feeling of what
it was like to live here; (01909) 482380;
£4. The town museum has a display on
the Pilgrim Fathers (cl Sun and pm
Thurs and Sat; free), and the priory
church is worth a look for the elaborate
scrollwork on its 12th-c yew door. The

Newcastle Arms (Carlton Rd) has good value food.

Other attractive villages include Collingham SK8663, East Bridgford SK6943 (the Reindeer has good fresh fish), and, with their more 'Leicestershire-ish' character, Colston Bassett SK7033 (the Haby Lane dairy makes good Stilton), Linby SK5351 and Staunton in the Vale SK8043.

The **River Trent** gives a tremendous sense of power even when it's on its best behaviour, sliding swiftly and massively along; its occasional floods are devastating, and most years it claims lives. Villages giving pleasant access to it include Laneham SK8076 and Thrumpton SK5031.

Decent pubs and inns in good riverside spots include the Hazleford Ferry at Bleasby SK7149, Lazy Otter in Wyke Lane, Farndon SK7651, Bromley Arms at Fiskerton SK7351, Unicorn Hotel at Gunthorpe SK6844 and Ferry at Wilford SK5637.

Where to eat

CAUNTON SK7459 **Caunton Beck** *(01636) 636793* Built in 1820, this roomy and welcoming place was carefully restored using reclaimed oak and Elizabethan timbers, and has an open fire and a wide choice of food ranging from breakfasts to sandwiches to traditional and imaginative modern dishes, served right through the day; friendly staff, a good wine list, and real ales; disabled access. £20.95|**£6.95**

COLSTON BASSETT SK6933 **Martins Arms** *School Lane (01949) 81361* Civilised, rather smart pub with particularly good imaginative food in bar and restaurant (lovely puddings), well kept real ales, a fine choice of malt whiskies, quite a few wines by the glass, an open fire, and smart uniformed staff; no children; disabled access. £29|**£7.95**

NOTTINGHAM SK5639 **Harts Restaurant** *Standard Court, Park Row (0115) 911 0666* Lively, popular brasserie with cheerful modern décor, friendly polite staff, dynamic British cooking with Mediterranean influences (super fish and interesting vegetarian dishes), delicious puddings, and short, thoughtful wine list; theatres nearby; cl 25 Dec; disabled access. £35/2-course lunch £9.90

NOTTINGHAM SK5740 **Lincolnshire Poacher** *161 Mansfield Rd (0115) 941 1584* Cheerful town pub with really tasty, good value, home-made food using fresh local produce (inc lots of vegetarian dishes); interesting real ales, lots of whiskies, a wine of the week, pleasant service, a big wood-floored bar with breweriana, a lively smaller bar, and chatty back snug; popular with young people in the evening. £16|**£4.95**

PLUMTREE SK6132 **Perkins Restaurant and Bar** *Old Railway Station, Station Rd (0115) 937 3695* Delightfully converted old railway station with very popular fresh delicious food (strong French influence), excellent friendly service, and good wines; cl Mon, Sun pm; children must be well behaved. £18.95/2-course lunch £9.75|**£4.50**

SIBTHORPE HILL SK7273 **Mussel & Crab** *Sibthorpe Hill (01777) 870491* Friendly, well run dining pub with spacious lounge bar, a Mediterranean-style restaurant leading off, most enjoyable food with a strong emphasis on fish, a thoughtful wine list (quite a few inc champagne by the glass) with helpful notes, and two outside terraces; good disabled access. £21.95|**£7**

UPTON SK7354 **French Horn** *Main St (01636) 812394* Friendly and bustling dining pub with a neat and comfortable open-plan bar, and a nice relaxed atmosphere; imaginative food inc very good daily specials and lots of puddings (bar food served all day), well kept real ales, several wines by the glass, friendly and efficient service, and a big sloping back paddock. £19|**£7.95**

WALKERINGHAM SK7792 **Three Horse Shoes** *High St (01427) 890959* Warmly welcoming distinctive pub, rather like a French logis, with quite amazing flowers and hanging baskets (using 9,000 plants); a wide choice of often inventive food, and well kept real ales. £17.25|**£6.50**

Special thanks to Mrs J Baker, Rita Cowperthwaite, C Adams

OXFORDSHIRE

Quintessential England, with plenty for the older visitor, from the dreaming spires of Oxford to the antiques shops and markets of charming country towns; richly varied scenery, too

Oxford's rich academic tradition has furnished it with a wealth of striking buildings and fascinating museums, making it the best place here for family days out. The Oxford Story gives a lively (and smelly) account of the city's history, and Curioxity will appeal to children with an interest in science. In summer, an hour or so punting on the river is an ideal way to break up a day spent browsing among the museums, the most rewarding of which are perhaps the Ashmolean (England's oldest) and the exhibit-crammed Pitt Rivers. Another relaxing diversion is the university's botanic garden – the oldest in the world.

Elsewhere, families are best catered for by wildlife attractions, from the good mix of animals and children's activities (they even have their own shop) at the Cotswold Wildlife Park, Burford, to the smaller-scale Wellplace Zoo, Ipsden, and the Waterfowl Sanctuary & Children's Farm at Wigginton Heath, or the enjoyable Victorian re-creations at Cogges Farm Museum, Witney.

Opulent Blenheim Palace (memorable lakeside grounds and good provision for families) by the attractive small town of Woodstock just N of Oxford tops the list of the county's great houses, with other notable buildings at Kingston Bagpuize (charming gardens too), Broughton (interesting furnishings), and Dorchester.

Places with specialist appeal include Benson's Veteran Cycle Museum, the Didcot Railway Centre (impressive collection of locomotives), and the church in Checkendon where part of a unique medieval wall painting has now been uncovered.

Riverside Henley (with its famous summer regatta) and the Cotswold gem of Burford smack of an essential Englishness, and many other villages and small towns are very rewarding, with picturesque stone houses (up in the NW corner many glow with a glorious golden stone), and plenty of antiques and craft shops.

The scenery has considerable variety, from the edge of the Cotswolds in the W and some sweeping downland in the S to the lush fringes of the Chilterns in the E, with some of the finest Thames scenery.

There are very good hotels and places to eat in – at a price.

Where to stay

ASTHALL SP2814 **Maytime** *Asthall, Burford, Oxfordshire OX18 4HW* (01993) 822068 £62.50, plus bargain breaks; 6 quiet rms. Attractive 16th-c Cotswold stone inn with comfortable relaxing dining bar, good food, decent wines, and huge breakfasts; worth an early spring-morning walk through the pretty village, across the fields to Swinbrook and back along the river; disabled access

BAMPTON SP3102 **Morar** *Weald St, Bampton, Oxfordshire OX18 2HL* (01993) *850162* **£46***, plus special breaks; 3 rms. Warmly friendly and neatly kept modern stone house (no smoking) with helpful knowledgeable owners (keen gardeners, barn dancers, and church bell ringers), separate lounge and dining room, lovely English cooking in winter using home-grown produce (home-made bread and preserves, too), pretty flower-filled big garden, and pet sheep, goat and cats; cl 18 Dec–1 Mar; children over 6

BURFORD SP2512 **Burford House** *High St, Burford, Oxfordshire OX18 4QA* (01993) *823151* **£90***, plus winter breaks; 7 cosy, individually decorated rms. Attractive, 14th-c Cotswold partly stone and partly timbered building, with two comfortable lounges (one for residents only), log fires, super breakfasts, and lots of plants in pretty stone courtyard; children over 10

BURFORD SP2412 **Lamb** *Sheep St, Burford, Oxfordshire OX18 4LR* (01993) *823155* **£100**, plus special breaks; 15 rms. Very attractive 500-year-old Cotswold inn with lovely restful atmosphere, spacious beamed, flagstoned and elegantly furnished lounge, civilised public bar, bunches of flowers on good oak and elm tables, three winter log fires, antiques, very good food in airy restaurant, and pretty little walled garden; cl 25–26 Dec

CHARLBURY SP3519 **Bell** *Church St, Charlbury, Chipping Norton, Oxfordshire OX7 3PP* (01608) *810278* **£75**, plus special breaks; 11 comfortable rms. Small, neatly kept, 17th-c hotel with a warm friendly atmosphere, a quiet and civilised flagstoned bar, huge open fire, a short choice of interesting bar lunches and decent restaurant, well kept real ales, and good breakfasts

CHURCH ENSTONE SP3725 **Crown** *Mill Lane, Church Enstone, Chipping Norton, Oxfordshire OX7 4NN* (01608) *677262* **£45**; 3 well appointed rms. Cotswold stone inn in pretty village, with attractive horseshoe bar, conservatory, friendly atmosphere and staff, good food in bar and restaurant, and decent breakfasts; Heritage barn nearby can be viewed by appointment

CLANFIELD SP2802 **Plough** *Bourton Rd, Clanfield, Bampton, Oxfordshire OX18 2RB* (01367) *810222* **£125**, plus special breaks; 12 lovely rms. Rose-clad 16th-c Cotswold stone manor house with armchairs and sofas in relaxed beamed lounge bar, open fire, friendly helpful staff and very good food in elegant restaurant; children over 12

CLIFTON SP4931 **Duke of Cumberlands Head** *Clifton, Banbury, Oxfordshire OX15 0PE* (01869) *338534* **£60**; 6 rms in sympathetic extension. Pretty thatched 17th-c stone inn with a friendly atmosphere, very good food in bar and no smoking back restaurant, enjoyable breakfasts, log fire, well kept beers and wines, and helpful service; tables in garden

CLIFTON HAMPDEN SU5495 **Plough** *Abingdon Rd, Clifton Hampden, Abingdon, Oxfordshire OX14 3EG* (01865) *407811* **£82.50**, plus special breaks; 11 rms with four-posters. Quaint little no smoking village pub close to Thames, run by obliging and idiosyncratic Turkish couple, with marvellously relaxed friendly atmosphere, cosy bar with beams and panelling, two civilised lounge areas, and good fresh food in bar and restaurant; disabled access

CROPREDY SP4646 **Old Manor** *9 Station Rd, Cropredy, Banbury, Oxfordshire OX17 1PS* (01295) *750233* **£54**; 2 rms. In a historic village, this lovely old place has two acres of garden and orchard, a moat with ducks and geese, and Gloucester old spot pigs in the fields bordering the Oxford Canal; guests' sitting room with games and books, breakfast in 15th-c dining room with antiques, clocks and more books, and several dogs and cats; self-catering barn; private motor museum; cl Christmas and New Year; disabled access

DORCHESTER SU5794 **George** *High St, Dorchester-on-Thames, Wallingford, Oxfordshire OX10 7HH* (01865) *340404* **£85**, plus special breaks; 18 distinctive rms. Lovely 500-year-old building with medieval dining room, a comfortably old-fashioned and civilised bar, ancient beams, a big fireplace, good wines, interesting food, and pleasant service; first used as brewhouse for Norman abbey opposite; disabled access

GREAT MILTON SO7874 **Manoir aux Quat' Saisons** *Church St, Great Milton, Oxford OX9 7PD (01844) 278881* **£240***, plus winter breaks; 32 opulent rms. Luxurious Jacobean manor in 27 acres of parkland and lovely gardens with an impeccable kitchen garden; sumptuous lounges with fine furniture, beautiful flowers and open fires, conservatory, exquisitely presented superb food (at a price), and exemplary service; residential cookery courses; disabled access

HENLEY-ON-THAMES SU7482 **Hernes** *Rotherfield Greys, Henley-on-Thames, Oxfordshire RG9 4NT (01491) 573245* **£75**, plus special breaks; 3 rms. In big gardens and grounds surrounded by farmland, this peaceful no smoking family house has a 16th-c heart, comfortable sitting room with panelled ceiling, family portraits, and good breakfasts – dinner by arrangement; cl Christmas and New Year; no children

HENLEY-ON-THAMES SU7682 **Red Lion** *Hart St, Henley-on-Thames, Oxfordshire RG9 2AR (01491) 572161* **£155**, plus special breaks; 26 rms, some with river views. Handsome family-run 16th-c riverside hotel with comfortable public rooms, very good interesting food in elegant Regency-style restaurant, and particularly helpful warmly friendly staff

HORTON-CUM-STUDLEY SP5912 **Studley Priory** *Horton-cum-Studley, Oxford OX33 1AZ (01865) 351203* **£156**, plus special breaks; 18 rms. Once a Benedictine nunnery, this lovely 12th-c Elizabethan manor stands in 13 wooded acres; fine panelling, 16th- and 17th-c stained-glass windows, antiques and open fires in the elegant drawing room and cosy bar, and seasonally changing menus in attractive restaurant; grass tennis court and croquet

KELMSCOT SU2599 **Plough** *Kelmscot, Lechlade, Gloucestershire GL7 3HG (01367) 253543* **£55***, plus special breaks; 8 comfortable rms. Pretty little inn nr Thames with attractively traditional small bar, ancient flagstones, stripped stone walls, and a relaxed chatty atmosphere; a larger cheerfully carpeted back bar, log fires, a wide choice of food, and well kept real ales; boats for hire, and fishing (both nearby), and lots of surrounding walks – on the Oxfordshire cycleway, too; no rooms 24–30 Dec; children over 10

KINGHAM SP2523 **Mill House** *Station Rd, Kingham, Chipping Norton, Oxfordshire OX7 6UH (01608) 658188* **£110**, plus special breaks; 23 good rms with country views. Carefully renovated 17th-c flour mill in seven acres with trout stream; comfortable spacious lounge, open log fire in lounge bar, original features such as two bread ovens, a cosy popular restaurant, and very good interesting food; disabled access

KINGSTON BAGPUIZE SU3997 **Fallowfields** *Southmoor, Kingston Bagpuize, Abingdon, Oxfordshire OX13 5BH (01865) 820416* **£135***; 10 rms. Delightful Gothic-style manor house with elegant, relaxing sitting rooms, open fires, good Aga-cooked food (using home-grown produce) in attractive dining room, courteous helpful service, and two acres of pretty gardens with tennis court; no smoking; lots to see nearby; children over 10

LONG HANBOROUGH SP4214 **Old Farmhouse** *194 Main Rd, Long Hanborough, Witney, Oxfordshire OX8 8JZ (01993) 882097* **£46***; 2 rms, 1 with own bthrm. Welcoming no smoking 17th-c house with lots of charm; stone walls and beams, homely sitting rooms with inglenook fires, a conservatory, good breakfasts with home-made preserves, enjoyable meals using home-grown produce, and a pretty cottagey garden; Oxford only 10-min train ride away, and plenty to do nearby; cl Christmas; children over 12

MINSTER LOVELL SP3211 **Hill Grove Farm** *Crawley Rd, Minster Lovell, Witney, Oxfordshire OX8 5NA (01993) 703120* **£42***; 2 rms. Friendly B&B on family-run 300-acre mixed working farm, with homely lounge and sun room, good breakfasts, and nice views and walks; no smoking; cl Christmas

MOULSFORD SU5983 **Beetle & Wedge** *Ferry Lane, Moulsford, Wallingford, Oxfordshire OX10 9JF (01491) 651381* **£135***, plus special breaks; 10 pretty rms, most with a lovely river view. Civilised riverside hotel where Jerome K Jerome wrote *Three Men in a Boat* and where H G Wells lived for a time (it was the Potwell in *The History of Mr Polly*); informal old beamed Boathouse Bar and lovely conservatory dining room (both with wonderful food – but must book), a carefully chosen wine list, open fires, fresh flowers, a riverside terrace and waterside lawn with moorings, and a warmly welcoming atmosphere; nice walks; disabled access

OXFORD SP5009 **Cotswold House** *363 Banbury Rd, Oxford OX2 7PL (01865) 310558* **£65**; 7 comfortable rms with showers. Beautifully kept modern no smoking Cotswold stone house with particularly helpful owners, residents' lounge, very good breakfasts, pretty flowers throughout, and neat back garden; children over 6

OXFORD SP5106 **Old Bank Hotel** *92–94 High St, Oxford, Oxfordshire OX1 4BJ (01865) 799599* **£155**; 44 distinctive, luxurious rms, with lovely bthrms. Stylish new hotel with a Georgian façade masking a partly Elizabethan building; an impressive collection of 20th-c British art, excellent modern food with an Italian slant in contemporary Quod Bar & Grill with its zinc-topped bar, leather seating, and stone floors, a carefully chosen wine list, courteous helpful staff, and seats out on the terrace, overlooking the garden; cl 24–27 Dec; disabled access

OXFORD SP5107 **Old Parsonage** *1 Banbury Rd, Oxford OX2 6NN (01865) 310210* **£150**; 30 lovely rms. Handsome and civilised 17th-c parsonage, fairly central, with very courteous staff, good breakfasts and excellent light meals in cosy bar/restaurant; small lounge, open fires and fine paintings, and pretty little garden; they provide picnics; cl 24–27 Dec

OXFORD SP5204 **Pine Castle** *290 Iffley Rd, Oxford OX4 4AE (01865) 241497* **£69**, plus wknd breaks; 8 rms. Small family-run Edwardian hotel with comfortable cosy lounge, and good breakfasts in small dining room; cl Christmas and New Year

OXFORD SP5106 **Randolph** *Beaumont St, Oxford OX1 2LN (01865) 247481* **£194**, plus special breaks; 119 rms. Fine neo-Gothic Victorian hotel facing the Ashmolean Museum; elegant comfortable day rooms, a grand foyer, a graceful restaurant with lovely plasterwork ceiling, and cellar wine bar; disabled access

SHILLINGFORD SU5991 **Shillingford Bridge Hotel** *Shillingford Rd, Shillingford, Wallingford, Oxfordshire OX10 8LZ (01865) 858567* **£100**, plus special breaks; 42 rms. Riverside hotel with own river frontage, fishing and moorings, spacious comfortable bars and attractive airy restaurant (all with fine views), squash, outdoor heated swimming pool, and Sat dinner-dance; disabled access

SHIPTON-UNDER-WYCHWOOD SP2717 **Lamb** *Shipton-under-Wychwood, Chipping Norton, Oxfordshire OX7 6DQ (01993) 830465* **£65**; 5 comfortable rms. Ancient Cotswold stone pub with a relaxed and civilised atmosphere, open log fire, highly polished furniture, and newspapers to read in beamed bar, good food in no smoking restaurant, and enjoyable breakfasts

SHIPTON-UNDER-WYCHWOOD SP2717 **Shaven Crown** *High St, Shipton-under-Wychwood, Chipping Norton, Oxfordshire OX7 6BA (01993) 830330* **£85**, plus special breaks; 9 comfortable rms. Densely beamed, ancient stone hospice built around striking medieval courtyard with old-fashioned seats on cobbles, lily pool and roses; impressive medieval hall with a magnificent lofty ceiling, sweeping stairway and old stone walls, log fire in comfortable bar, intimate candlelit restaurant, well chosen wine list, good friendly service, warm relaxed atmosphere, and bowling green; children over 5 in evening dining room; disabled access

SHIPTON-UNDER-WYCHWOOD SP2717 **Shipton Grange House** *High St, Shipton-under-Wychwood, Chipping Norton, Oxfordshire OX7 6DG (01993) 831298* **£65***; 3 rms. Carefully converted no smoking Georgian coach house and stabling, with elegantly furnished sitting rooms, good breakfasts, a friendly welcome, and attractive walled garden; cl Christmas; children over 12

STONOR SU7488 **Stonor Arms** *Stonor, Henley-on-Thames, Oxfordshire RG9 6HE (01491) 638345* **£125***, plus special breaks; 10 individually decorated rms looking over gardens. Carefully restored 18th-c coaching inn, with good imaginative food in conservatory restaurant and Blades Bar; friendly staff; disabled access

UFFINGTON SU3098 **Craven** *Fernham Rd, Uffington, Faringdon, Oxfordshire SN7 7RD (01367) 820449* **£73***, plus special breaks; 5 pretty rms, some with own bthrm. Most attractive 17th-c thatched house with beamed sitting room, log fire in inglenook fireplace, antiques, a friendly relaxed atmosphere, and good food in beamed farmhouse kitchen; lots of nearby walks; disabled access

WOODSTOCK SP4416 **Feathers** *Market St, Woodstock, Oxfordshire OX20 1SX (01993) 812291* **£130**, plus special breaks; 21 individually decorated rms. Lovely old building with a fine relaxing drawing room and study, open fires, first-class friendly staff, a gentle atmosphere, daily-changing imaginative food inc lovely puddings, and a sunny courtyard with attractive tables and chairs

WOODSTOCK SP4416 **Holmwood** *6 High St, Woodstock, Oxfordshire OX20 1TF (01993) 812266* **£80***; 2 pretty rms, both with their own sitting room. Early 18th-c Cotswold stone house with oak beams and antiques, an attractive dining room, and friendly helpful owners; no smoking; cl Jan; children over 12

To see and do

Oxfordshire Family Attraction of the Year

WITNEY SP3609 **Cogges Farm Museum** (Church Lane) A bit different from most farms open to the public, this charming old place gives a useful illustration of rural life in Victorian times. Children enjoy meeting the animals as much as they would at any farm, but adults can get a lot out of it too – particularly those with even the slightest interest in social history. There's something of an instructive bent (it's a favourite on the school-trip circuit), but it isn't too earnest, and the surroundings are pleasant enough to keep most families happy for an unhurried couple of hours. Most popular with children are the demonstrations of cooking in the Victorian kitchen; 'maids' in period costume let you sample old-fashioned cakes and biscuits, and explain how they managed in the days when even the kitchen sink was a far-off luxury. The striking manor house dates back seven centuries in parts; there are taped tours of the upstairs rooms, and an activity room with Victorian toys and games. Younger visitors can usually try on period clothes. Outside are the sorts of animals you'd have found on the farm 100 years ago: shire horses, pigs, cows, chickens and turkeys, with regular feeding displays, and hand-milking in the old dairy. On certain days (usually Tues, Thurs and Sun) they'll demonstrate how Witney blankets were made on their 18th-c hand loom, and they might also have spinning (Tues), lace-making (Weds and Thurs) or butter-making (Sun). The grounds are attractive, with walled gardens, a riverside walk and a peaceful orchard. Some displays seem a little outdated (dummies in corners and roped-off exhibits) but staff are knowledgeable and enthusiastic, and work hard to maintain everyone's enthusiasm. There's a good calendar of seasonal events. Meals, snacks, shop, mostly disabled access; open daily exc Mon from mid-Mar to Oct, plus various days around Christmas; (01993) 772602; £4 (£2 children 3–16). A family ticket is £11.

ABINGDON SU4997

Attractive Thames-side town, until 1974 the county town of Berkshire. Much expanded around its old partly pedestrianised core, which still has a fine old gatehouse, several handsome old buildings and almshouses around the impressive 15th/16th-c **Church of St Helen** (though its steeple is 13th-c), unusually wider than it's long, at the junction of East and West St. The good museum in the 17th-c former county hall (free) has changing exhibitions. Remains of the partly Norman

Benedictine abbey, once the second most powerful in England, have been restored, with part now housing a local theatre. The riverside Old Anchor is prettily placed for lunch, and there's decent food at the Mill House, built into the medieval Town Bridge.

ARDINGTON SU4388

Attractive small village, with a good dining pub, and several craft workshops in the Home Farm buildings.

BANBURY SP4540

The busy shopping town was actually without its famous cross for 250 years, between the Puritans' destroying it in 1602 and the construction of its replacement in 1859. In the church graveyard is the tomb from which Jonathan Swift borrowed the name Gulliver for his traveller. The Tourist Information Centre is to be rehoused in the new canalside shopping complex around Easter, and the decent local history **museum** (cl Sun, and Mon Oct–Mar; free) will have found a new home in restored Tooley's boatyard adjacent, by the end of the year. The Reindeer and the Wine Vaults, both in Parsons St, are useful for lunch. The B4035 towards Sibford Ferris runs through attractive hilly farmland, with good summer **pick-your-own**; the loop N through North Newington, Shutford and Epwell is good too.

BENSON SU6292

Benson Veteran Cycle Museum Private collection of over 500 bicycles from between 1818 and 1930; shop; open am (exc Sun) Easter–early Sept by appointment with Mr Passey, on (01491) 838414; free. Down by the river at the Cruiser station you can hire boats by the day or the hour; (01491) 838304. The footpath beyond the weir bridge leads to Wallingford. The Home Sweet Home at Roke is a charming dining pub.

BIX BOTTOM SU7285

Oxfordshire Way This long-distance path gives one short walk with a palpable sense of peace, from the lane out past Bix Hall to Valley End Farm. **Warburg Reserve** Extensive wildflower-rich rough grassland and ancient beechwood, good for wild orchids and butterflies, besides birds and maybe deer.

BROUGHTON SP4138

Broughton Castle 🏰 (B4035 SW of Banbury) Striking early 14th/16th-c house with proper moat and gatehouse, originally owned by William of Wykeham. Exceptional oak panelling, period furniture, and Civil War relics. Some rooms have bare stone walls under elaborately plastered ceilings, an unusual combination that works rather well. *Shakespeare in Love* was partly filmed here. Snacks, shop, disabled access to ground floor only; open Easter Sun and Mon, then mid-May to

mid-Sept pm Weds, Sun and bank hols, plus Thurs July and Aug; (01295) 262624; £4. There's a decent village **museum**, and the Blinking Owl at North Newington is a comfortable lunch break.

BURFORD SP2512

Lovely little Cotswold town with interesting shops and teashops along its pretty main street. The **church** is particularly intriguing, with a super graveyard, and 17th-c graffiti by some of the 400 Leveller mutineers imprisoned here by Cromwell. The town also has an interesting little **museum** (open pm Apr–Oct; around 50p), and is full of attractive pubs: the best for food and atmosphere is the Lamb, and the Mermaid serves food all day in summer. Burford does get very busy indeed with visitors, and it's worth noting that several smaller and altogether quieter nearby villages are, in their way, as pretty: Taynton, the Barringtons (just over the Gloucs border), Fulbrook, Swinbrook and Asthall. All except the first have the additional attraction of a decent pub. There are attractive walks between these, along the River Windrush for much of the way – the back roads along the Windrush Valley give pleasant drives, too.

Cotswold Wildlife Park 🏰 (Bradwell Grove, A361, 2m S of junction with A40) Well liked by readers and a thoroughly reliable family day out. Hundreds of different creatures from all over the world in spacious re-creations of their natural environment. They have an excellent track record with breeding – rare Asiatic lion cubs are among the latest additions. Various animal encounters and feeding displays, a children's farmyard and good adventure playground as well as, more unusually, animal-themed brass rubbing. A narrow-gauge railway operates Apr–Oct. There are also tropical and reptile houses, aquarium, insect and butterfly house, and a 49-metre (160-ft) walk-through aviary. Meals and snacks (and plenty of space for picnics), shops (one specially for children), disabled access; cl 25 Dec; (01993) 823006; *£6.50 (£4 children 3–16).

BUSCOT SU2496

Buscot Park (A417) What makes this 18th-c house really special is the amazing collection of art and furnishings amassed by its owners; paintings by Reynolds, Gainsborough, Rembrandt, Murillo and several of the Pre-Raphaelites (inc a splendid series by Burne-Jones), with some more recent pictures too. The attractive grounds have formal water gardens and a walled kitchen garden, and maybe pick-your-own in summer. Teas; open Apr–Sept, pm Weds–Fri (plus Mon–Tues garden only) and every second and fourth Sat and Sun in the month; (01367) 240786; £4.40, £3.30 grounds only; NT. The Thames-side Trout (A417 towards Lechlade) is popular for lunch.

CHALGROVE SU6396
Attractive small village, with notable medieval wall paintings in the 11th-c **church** – which owns the village pub.

CHASTLETON SP2429
Chastleton House (off A44 NW of Chipping Norton) This handsome restored Jacobean manor house was little changed by the family who lived in it 1605–1991, really feeling like a well worn-in family house of that period, and not oversmartened despite the lovely plasterwork, beautiful oak and walnut furnishings, embroideries, Jacobite glassware, even the Bible Charles I took to the scaffold. Peaceful Jacobean gardens inc topiary and first standard croquet lawn. Car park up hill from house. Open Apr–Oct pm Weds–Sat; (01608) 674355; £5.10, must have pre-booked timed ticket; NT. There's pleasant walking in the area between this village, Cornwell and (just over the Gloucs border) Adlestrop.

CHECKENDON SU6682
Wall painting (Church of St Peter and St Paul) It wasn't until the church organ was taken away to be repaired last year that this almost perfectly preserved fragment was discovered. Covering 18 sq ft and dating from the 1330s, it depicts a gesturing figure (perhaps that of St Martin) and three knights on horseback, and is thought to belong to a much larger painting destroyed in Victorian times, though experts hope to uncover even more of it now. The Black Horse here is a classic village local. Other churches with fine wall

paintings are those of Shorthampton SP3220, South Leigh SP3908 and South Newington SP4033 (its key is kept by next-door College Farmhouse).

CHINNOR SP7500
Chinnor & Princes Risborough Railway Four-mile train trips up into Buckinghamshire; trains most wknds Apr–Sept, some steam-hauled – (01844) 353535 for timetable and prices (you may need to book for special events).

CHIPPING NORTON SP3127
Chipping Norton Museum of Local History 🖼 Local history in the Co-op Hall of this pleasant old stone-built wool town; shop, cl am, all day Mon exc bank hols, end of Oct–Easter; *£1. The unusually wide market place is being pedestrianised, so traffic may be rather chaotic until its completion; pretty church, some fine 17th-c almshouses, a good few antiques shops, and the Chequers has enjoyable food. The roads to Hook Norton, or B4026/B4022 to Witney, are good Cotswoldy drives.

COLESHILL SU2393
This attractive village is owned by the NT; lots of good walks nearby, and the Radnor Arms has decent food.

COWLEAZE WOOD SU7295
Between Christmas Common and the M40, this has forest art exhibits scattered around as part of a sculpture trail. The Fox & Hounds on Christmas Common is useful for walkers, and now you may see red kites soaring overhead.

CROPREDY SP4646
An attractive village, where you may find sheep grazing the raised churchyard.

CUXHAM SU6695
Pretty thatched houses by the stream which runs along beside the road – and a good village pub.

DEDDINGTON SP4631
Deddington Castle 12th-c fortress remains; there are attractive stone buildings around the village square, inc several antiques shops, and the Deddington Arms and Unicorn (good for lunch).

DIDCOT SU5290
Didcot Railway Centre 🖼 The biggest collection anywhere of Great Western Railway stock, housed under

cover, inc 20 steam locomotives, a diesel railcar and lots of passenger and freight rolling stock. Snacks, shop, disabled access; open wknds all year and wkdys Easter–Sept, best to ring for steam day dates, usually every Sun and Weds in summer hols; (01235) 817200; £4–£7 depending on event. The town itself more or less sprang up around the railway.

DORCHESTER SU5894
Dorchester Abbey Impressive and well preserved abbey, with 12th-c nave and rare lead font. The tower was rebuilt in 1605 and has a 14th-c spiral staircase, as well as a sanctuary with an exceptional Jesse window from the same period, and some mosaic-like 12th-c glass in other windows. The adjacent former guesthouse now houses a little museum. In summer they do very individual ever-so-English teas (Weds–Sun (exc Fri) pm), all home-made and quite addictive. Snacks, shop, disabled access; museum cl Mon, wkdys in Oct and all Nov–Apr; free. The Fleur de Lys opposite does good lunches. The whole Thames-side village is a lovely place to explore, with interesting antiques shops. The River Thames has pleasant walks starting and finishing here; you can cross at Day's Lock, and a short walk brings you to Wittenham Clumps (alternative access from adjacent car park), a pair of hillocks which look across the Chilterns and Berkshire Downs.

EWELME SU6491
One of Oxfordshire's prettiest and most unspoilt villages.

FARMOOR SP4405
Farmoor Reservoir Trout fishing, sailing, bird-watching, and other activities, though you'll need a permit; (01865) 863033 for details and prices.

FILKINS SP2207
Cotswold Woollen Weavers Friendly working woollen mill with demonstrations of traditional production methods in 18th-c buildings. Snacks, well stocked shop, disabled access; (01367) 860491; cl am Sun, 25–31 Dec; free. The Five Alls has good food.

FOREST HILL SP5807
Above Oxford, this gives several pleasant walks from the White Horse pub.

FRILFORD SU4397
Millets Farm Centre Pick-your-own fruit, animals, walks, and an unusually extensive farm shop which takes in a bakery, delicatessen, garden centre, and wine merchant; cl 25 Dec; (01865) 392200.

GREAT COXWELL SU2693
Great Coxwell Barn As noble as a cathedral according to William Morris, a 13th-c stone-built tithe barn 46 by 13 metres (152 ft long, and 44 ft wide), with beautifully crafted timbers supporting the roof; free (donations).

GREAT TEW SP3929
The most charming village in the area (some would say in all England). It's an outstanding series of golden stone 17th- and 18th-c cottages, some thatched and others with stone-slabbed roofs, around an attractive sloping green and among ancient trees, with wooded slopes above. The pub is good.

HENLEY-ON-THAMES SU7781
Pleasant well heeled Thames-side town famed for its summer regatta. You can usually see other rowing races or practices on the river throughout the year, or hire your own boat on (01491) 572035. The informal Anchor (Friday St) and comfortable beamed Old White Horse (Northfield End) are good value pubs nr the river, and the Three Tuns (Market Pl) does food all day.

Greys Court (Rotherfield Greys, 3m W) Attractive gabled Tudor house with interesting ruins of its medieval predecessor; the gardens are even more alluring, with white and rose gardens, ancient wisterias, a kitchen garden, wheelhouse, icehouse and brick maze. Teas, bookstall, some disabled access; open bank hol Mon Apr–Sept, house pm Weds–Fri, garden pm Tues–Sat; (01491) 628529; £4.60, £3.20 gardens only; NT. The village **church** is delightful, and the Maltsters Arms dining pub has lovely country views, and good nearby walks. The B480 to Watlington is a pleasant Chilterns drive.

River and Rowing Museum (Mill Meadows) Housed in a stunning modern building, this has comprehensive displays on the sport inc the Regatta, and the history and life of the river itself. Meals, snacks, shop, disabled access; cl 25–26 Dec, 1 Jan; (01491) 415600; £4.95.

IPSDEN SU6386

Wellplace Zoo Mainly a bird park, but also animals such as lambs, goats, otters, donkeys and monkeys. You can feed several of them, so good for children. Snacks, shop, disabled access; cl wkdys Oct–Easter; (01491) 680473; £2. The King William IV at Hailey is handy for something to eat. Ian Smith can arrange **horse-drawn waggon rides** through these pretty Chilterns fringes; most fine summer days he runs two-horse waggons from Darkwood Farm, Park Corner on a local pub tour; (01491) 641324. Even by car, these are pleasant Chilterns drives – for instance the loop S of Nettlebed through Highmoor Cross, Stoke Row and Nuffield.

KELMSCOT SU2599

Kelmscott Manor The summer home of William Morris until his death in 1896, now with one of the best assemblages of Morris memorabilia, standing out all the more for its domestic setting. Works by other Pre-Raphaelite artists inc splendid paintings by Rossetti, who initially shared the lease. Meals, snacks, shop, disabled access to ground floor only; open Weds (exc 1–2pm) and pm third Sat of month Apr–Sept plus first Sat July–Aug; (01367) 252486; £6. The Plough in the peaceful little Thames-side village is good, and there's a waterside walk of a mile and a half E to the Swan at Radcot Bridge.

KINGSTON BAGPUIZE SU4098

Kingston House (off A415) Charming 17th-c manor house, remodelled in the early 18th c, with lovely panelling, attractive furnishings and friendly unstuffy feel; peaceful garden with mature flowering shrubs, woodland walks, and Georgian gazebo. Shop, disabled access to garden; usually open pm bank hol wknds, and occasional other summer pms – best to ring for exact dates; (01865) 820259; £3.50, £1.50 garden only. The Hinds Head has good value food.

LITTLE ROLLRIGHT SP2931

Rollright Stones Dramatic and mysterious Bronze Age stones, chiefly in a circle about 30 metres (100 ft) across, now thought to date from between 1500 and 2000 BC; legend has it that the stones are a king and his men tricked by a witch into falling under her spell, and petrified. It's supposed to be impossible to count them as you can never tell where you started. The Gate Hangs High nr here is useful for lunch.

LONG HANBOROUGH SP4314

Oxford Bus Museum [img] Around 40 vehicles, from Oxford horse trams to more modern machines up to the 1960s, some roadworthy, others being restored. Disabled access; open Sat, Sun only; (01993) 883617; *£3. The Hand & Shears at Church Hanborough is a very good dining pub.

LONG WITTENHAM SU5493

Pendon Museum of Miniature Landscape and Transport [img] Charming exhibition showing a highly detailed model railway and meticulously researched model 1930s village scenes; you can often see modellers working on the exhibits, and they're always happy to chat. Snacks, shop; open pm wknds and bank hols Jan–Nov, plus Weds pm July–Sept; (01865) 407365; £3. The Machine Man has good fresh food.

MAPLEDURHAM SU6776

Very attractive little community with lovely beechwoods full of birds; the nicest way to reach it is by boat from the Caversham Promenade at Reading (summer only).

Mapledurham House Impressive Elizabethan mansion in pretty Thames-side parkland, with paintings and family portraits, great oak staircases, and moulded Elizabethan ceilings. In the grounds is the last **watermill** on the Thames to use wooden machinery; dating from 1423, it still produces flour, bran and semolina. Also riverside walks and island with picnic area. Teas, shop, disabled access to ground floor only; open pm Sat, Sun and bank hols Easter–Sept; (0118) 972 3350; £6 house and watermill, £4 house only, £3 watermill only. You can stay in a number of lovely cottages on the estate (some thatched).

MILTON SU4892

Milton Manor Elegant 17th-c manor house with splendid Strawberry Hill Gothic library, interesting chapel, walled garden, and unusual collections of teapots and fine china. Open wknd and bank hol Mon pms Easter–Aug; (01235) 862321; £4. The Admiral Benbow has decent food. The cherry orchards around Milton Hill are a fine sight when the white blossom is out in spring, and around July roadside stalls sell plump red-black fresh cherries – the Grove Farm Shop (A4130) is especially friendly.

MINSTER LOVELL SP3211

One of the prettiest and most unspoilt old villages in the area; there's an attractive 15th-c church, village green, and 15th-c bridge over the River Windrush narrow enough for the Welsh drovers to use for counting the sheep in the flocks they brought this way each year. The smart Old Swan does light lunches.

Minster Lovell Hall Imposing and attractively set, this was being used as ramshackle farm buildings until its 'restoration' as neat ruins in the 1930s. Macabre stories about the 15th-c hall usually involve people being shut up in various places and forgotten about until their skeletons are discovered much later. Open every day, free. There's a well restored medieval dovecot nearby.

NORTH LEIGH SP3813

Roman Villa Occupied between the 2nd and 4th c, when it was a very grand place with several dozen rooms, it's now just a few neat but poignant traces, in a very pleasant wooded setting; free. The medieval village church, with a Saxon tower, is lovely inside, and the Woodman is popular for lunch.

NUFFIELD SU6787

Nuffield Place 🖼 The home of Lord and Lady Nuffield 1933–1963, with the original 30s furnishings. Very good gardens with mature trees and shrubs inc rhododendrons, lawns, pond and rockery, as well as Lady Nuffield's own Wolseley and a display of vintage cars. Teas, small shop, limited disabled access; open pm second and fourth Sun each month May–Sept; (01491) 641224; *£3. The Crown pub here has decent food.

NUNEHAM COURTENAY SU5599

Oxford University Arboretum (A4074) Fine conifers and other trees

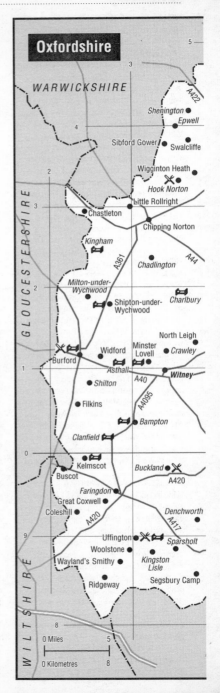

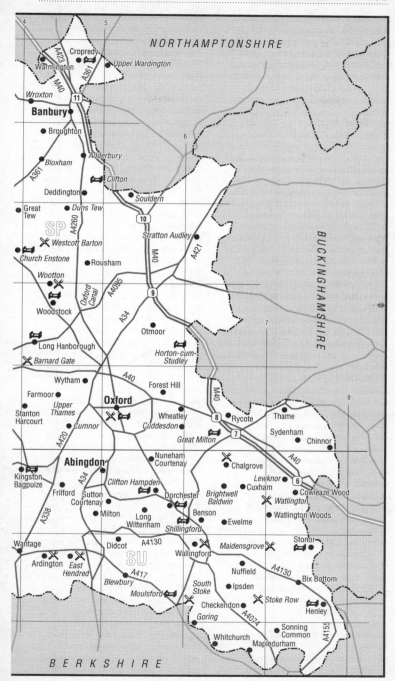

over 55 acres, as well as plants like rhododendrons that won't grow in the soil of Oxford itself. Some disabled access; cl wknds Oct–Apr, and two wks at Christmas; free. About half a mile away, the roses at Notcutts Garden Centre are a blaze of summer colour easily seen from the road; decent meals here.

OTMOOR SP5614

Several square miles of flatland, so poorly drained that in very wet weather its river actually flows backwards, and interesting to walk through (there are several paths). Because serious farming is virtually out of the question, it does have more natural wildlife than most places in the county, and having purchased some of the land from local farmers, the RSPB (backed by local authorities) is working on making it an even more outstanding refuge. The Abingdon Arms at Beckley, with a pretty garden, is one good starting point (and there's a good farm shop there on the B4027 from Stanton St John); the Nut Tree at Murcott does excellent steaks. On one edge, the pick-your-own fruit farm at Elsfield has good views over the wilderness, as well as an unusually wide range of varieties.

OXFORD SP5105

On first impression this can seem quite a frenetic city: the ancient university buildings with their medieval lanes and scholarly corners are surrounded by a bustling largely industrialised town, with a formidable amount of traffic. Some of the major city centre thoroughfares have been pedestrianised in a bid to relieve the nightmarish congestion problems; if you don't come by train or coach, it's certainly a good idea to leave your car at one of the Park and Rides around the ring road. Otherwise, the helpful Tourist Information Centre (Gloucester Green) does a useful car park map, with times and prices. Guided walks around the city (£4.50) usually leave from here at 10.30 and 11am, 1 and 2pm daily (they also operate other themed tours). For first-time visitors, hop-on-and-off **tour buses** from St Aldates, High St, Gloucester Green or Pembroke College take in all the best sites and last

about 1½ hours (£8–£9). Many of the city's oldest or most interesting buildings are grouped around the Bodleian Library, the Sheldonian Theatre and the splendid domed Radcliffe Camera (also a library). This partly cobbled central university area is most attractive, but does sometimes overfill with visitors – students have complained that the noise of tourists puts them off their exams. In the streets and lanes leading off, the honey-coloured stone makes for a harmony that unites different styles and different centuries. There are a few good shops dotted about; Blackwells is the main bookseller, with several branches around the Broad St area (the second-hand section in the main branch is well used by students, and their music shop on Holywell St is rewarding). Near the station, the Oxford Antique Trading Co has 80 dealers under one roof.

Colleges Most allow visitors into at least some of their quads, and do have a wonderful timeless appeal. One of the few they failed to impress was William Cobbett, who wrote in his *Rural Rides* that he 'could not help reflecting on the drones that they contain, and the wasps they send forth'. Newcomers are often surprised to discover that the colleges are all separate bodies with little in common, each firmly maintaining its own dons, rules and traditions; the university itself is little more than an administrative umbrella. Several now charge admission, notably Christ Church, New, Magdalen, Trinity and Brasenose. Access may be more limited in term-time. A few may let you in only with a guide, so a good way of making sure you see a cross-section is to join one of the walking tours that leave the Tourist Information Centre (Old School, Gloucester Green) every day at 10.30 and 11am, 1 and 2pm; £4.50. Afternoon tours are the best, but get there early – places are limited. Guided walks may also leave from the Catte St/High St corner and your guide might turn out to be an enterprising student. Ideally though, it's worth trying to explore at your own pace away from the crowds – again, afternoons are best, with more colleges open then. Besides colleges we pick out individually, more

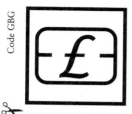

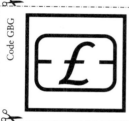

CONDITIONS

1. This discount offer cannot be used in conjunction with any other offer, and is not available as part of a group booking or for more than one child. The voucher is not transferable.
2. Free admission for one child is available only if two adults are paying the full normal tariff.
3. The offer may not be available on bank holidays, or on special event days – in this case our entry for that attraction notes this fact in brackets immediately after the 🎟 sign.
4. A very few attractions are offering some special variation on this offer – their entries spell this out in brackets immediately after the 🎟 sign.
5. This offer expires on 31 December 2001 (or at the close of the attraction's season if that is earlier).

CONDITIONS

1. This discount offer cannot be used in conjunction with any other offer, and is not available as part of a group booking or for more than one child. The voucher is not transferable.
2. Free admission for one child is available only if two adults are paying the full normal tariff.
3. The offer may not be available on bank holidays, or on special event days – in this case our entry for that attraction notes this fact in brackets immediately after the 🎟 sign.
4. A very few attractions are offering some special variation on this offer – their entries spell this out in brackets immediately after the 🎟 sign.
5. This offer expires on 31 December 2001 (or at the close of the attraction's season if that is earlier).

CONDITIONS

1. This discount offer cannot be used in conjunction with any other offer, and is not available as part of a group booking or for more than one child. The voucher is not transferable.
2. Free admission for one child is available only if two adults are paying the full normal tariff.
3. The offer may not be available on bank holidays, or on special event days – in this case our entry for that attraction notes this fact in brackets immediately after the 🎟 sign.
4. A very few attractions are offering some special variation on this offer – their entries spell this out in brackets immediately after the 🎟 sign.
5. This offer expires on 31 December 2001 (or at the close of the attraction's season if that is earlier).

CONDITIONS

1. This discount offer cannot be used in conjunction with any other offer, and is not available as part of a group booking or for more than one child. The voucher is not transferable.
2. Free admission for one child is available only if two adults are paying the full normal tariff.
3. The offer may not be available on bank holidays, or on special event days – in this case our entry for that attraction notes this fact in brackets immediately after the 🎟 sign.
4. A very few attractions are offering some special variation on this offer – their entries spell this out in brackets immediately after the 🎟 sign.
5. This offer expires on 31 December 2001 (or at the close of the attraction's season if that is earlier).

CONDITIONS

1. This discount offer cannot be used in conjunction with any other offer, and is not available as part of a group booking or for more than one child. The voucher is not transferable.
2. Free admission for one child is available only if two adults are paying the full normal tariff.
3. The offer may not be available on bank holidays, or on special event days – in this case our entry for that attraction notes this fact in brackets immediately after the 🎟 sign.
4. A very few attractions are offering some special variation on this offer – their entries spell this out in brackets immediately after the 🎟 sign.
5. This offer expires on 31 December 2001 (or at the close of the attraction's season if that is earlier).

CONDITIONS

1. This discount offer cannot be used in conjunction with any other offer, and is not available as part of a group booking or for more than one child. The voucher is not transferable.
2. Free admission for one child is available only if two adults are paying the full normal tariff.
3. The offer may not be available on bank holidays, or on special event days – in this case our entry for that attraction notes this fact in brackets immediately after the 🎟 sign.
4. A very few attractions are offering some special variation on this offer – their entries spell this out in brackets immediately after the 🎟 sign.
5. This offer expires on 31 December 2001 (or at the close of the attraction's season if that is earlier).

The Good Britain Guide

The Good Britain Guide
FREEPOST TN1569
WADHURST
E. SUSSEX
TN5 7BR

Please use this card to tell us about anything which *you* think should or should not be included in the next edition of *The Good Britain Guide*. Just fill it in and return it to us – no stamp or envelope needed. You can also use the report forms at the end of the book

ALISDAIR AIRD

YOUR NAME AND ADDRESS (BLOCK CAPITALS PLEASE)

☐ *Please tick this box if you would like extra report forms*

REPORT ON *(its name)*

Its address/location

Postcode: Telephone:

What is this? *(hotel, restaurant, garden, village, drive, walk etc)*

Description/why it appeals

REPORT ON *(its name)*

Its address

Postcode: Telephone:

What is this? *(hotel, restaurant, garden, village, drive, walk etc)*

Description/why it appeals

are tucked down some of the town's prettiest streets, such as charming Exeter, Jesus and Lincoln down Turl St, and Corpus Christi and Oriel around Merton Lane and Oriel Sq. This last college has a very attractive and unusual entrance to its dining hall. Trinity on Broad St, though not large, is very grand. Around Radcliffe Sq Brasenose is quaint (and has good views of the surrounding skyline from its quads), and Hertford has its Bridge of Sighs over New College St, in itself worth exploring for some more unusual and less busy views and a good look at the gargoyles on the backs of some of the buildings. Worcester has particularly nice gardens, and many of the other colleges' private Fellows' gardens not usually open to visitors can be seen under the National Gardens Scheme.

Christ Church (St Aldates) The best-known college, a magnificently stately place begun by Cardinal Wolsey in the 16th c, but soon taken over by Henry VIII. The main entrance is through Tom Tower, designed by Christopher Wren and named after its famous bell that rings out 101 times at nine o'clock every night – in less liberal times the hour when students were due back in their rooms. The hall is worth a look, with its remarkable hammerbeam roof, paintings of alumni and benefactors by all the most expensive portrait-painters of the period, and the long tables laid out with silver for meals; there may be teas here some afternoons. The elaborate little cathedral is England's smallest, and doubles as the college chapel. It has some excellent stained glass by Burne-Jones, fantastic pendent vaulting in the choir, and some of the original Norman priory work. Entry into the college may be limited on Suns. A hidden treasure unnoticed by most visitors is the college's Picture Gallery (Canterbury Quad), with an important collection of Old Master paintings and drawings, and various temporary exhibitions. Shop; cl 1–2pm, Sun am, and Christmas and Easter wks, guided tours Thurs at 2.15pm; (01865) 276172; £2.

Keble College (Parks Rd) Brightly Victorian and very red-brick, with perhaps the most famous Pre-Raphaelite painting of all, Holman Hunt's *Light of the World*, in its chapel.

Magdalen College (High St) The most beautiful college, its tower a dramatic sight for visitors entering the city from the S. The quads and cloisters are very pleasant to stroll through, but the chief attraction is the deer park, an unexpected haven in the heart of the bustling city. There's a circular path around this meadow (you can't go in) called Addison's Walk; in spring it's a mass of snowdrops and daffodils, then has hundreds of thousands of fritillaries in later spring, and after that the deer. Over a small bridge is the Fellows' Garden with a small ornamental lake – a very peaceful, sheltered spot.

Merton College (Merton St) The most ancient buildings, with the country's oldest library (tours available).

New College (Holywell St) Impressive chapel, atmospheric wisteria-covered cloisters, and remains of the city wall. Nearby, the tucked-away Turf Tavern is a splendid ancient place.

St Edmund Hall (Queens Lane) The only surviving medieval college, complete with Norman crypt.

University College (High St) Harmonious buildings – and an interesting monument to Shelley despite having thrown him out.

Ashmolean Museum (Beaumont St) The country's first museum, and still one of its finest, opened in 1683 and rehoused in this imposing building from 1845. The well arranged galleries include marvellous European paintings (inc a Titian portrait, bought for a record £2.4m last year), an extensive collection of Pre-Raphaelite pictures, a representative range of work by French Impressionists, and antiquities from ancient Egypt, Greece and Rome. Meals, snacks, shop, disabled access; cl Sun am, all Mon (exc bank hol pms), first wk of Sept (St Giles Fair), Christmas wk, Easter; (01865) 278000; free.

Bate Collection of Musical Instruments (St Aldates) Outstanding constantly developing collection of early keyboards, woodwind, brass, percussion and other instruments. Shop, mostly disabled access; cl am, wknds (exc Sat am during term-time), and a few days at Christmas and Easter; (01865) 276139; free.

Bodleian Library (Broad St) One of the oldest in Europe, its splendidly grand quad dominated by the Tower of the Five Orders. Most of it is closed to the public, but guided tours take in the beautifully vaulted 15th-c Divinity School, which shows some of the library's treasures including the Chancellor's Court, Convocation House and Duke Humfrey's Library, the oldest reading room. (Tours usually leave at 10.30 and 11.30am, 2 and 3pm wkdys, and at 10.30 and 11.30am Sat Mar–Oct; pm only wkdys in winter); (01865) 277224; no under-14s, excellent shop, limited disabled access (notice preferred); cl some bank hols and maybe last wk of Aug; *£3.50. Altogether the library houses over 5,500,000 books, going down six storeys under the centre of the city.

Carfax Tower Right at the traditional centre of Oxford, all that remains of a 14th-c church; good views, and the bells in the tower are interestingly designed. Shop; cl 25 Dec–1 Jan; £1.20.

Castle Mound There isn't much of the Norman castle left save a tower and crypt of the castle church, and an underground well chamber, but the Mound gives quite good views over the city and its surroundings.

Christchurch Meadow An unspoilt expanse of green astonishingly close to the busy city streets. You can gaze across the fields of grazing longhorn cattle to the spires in the distance, or walk under overhanging trees along the banks of the river to the boathouses; college eights row from here all year, in just about any weather.

Covered market (High St) A maze of stalls with something different at every turn; chic boutiques, speciality shops, cafés and old-fashioned butchers and poultry merchants. The Oxford Sandwich Co do excellent take-away sandwiches here, and Ben's Cookies are a favourite with students.

Curioxity (Gloucester Green) The Old Fire Station complex houses a theatre and this interactive science gallery, where visitors can experiment with the exhibits. The staff are helpful, and several sets of parents have told us

it kept their children captivated for a full hour. Meals, snacks, shop; open wknds and daily during school hols; (01865) 794494; £2.10. This area, interestingly rejuvenated with trendy shops, cafés and bustling markets on Weds and Thurs, was once one of the less desirable parts of town. Not far from here among the fashionable shops and boutiques of Little Clarendon St, George & Davies is a good ice-cream parlour.

History of Science Museum (Broad St) Excellent collection of national importance, in one of the city's nicest old buildings (shop, disabled access; probably cl am, Sun, Mon, and a wk at Christmas; (01865) 277280; free). Their extensive refurbishments should be completed by this year.

Iffley Meadows These are conserved for wildlife, and in late spring are a sea of purple snake's-head fritillaries.

Museum of Modern Art (Pembroke St) Modern art museum with the sort of exhibitions and displays not often found in galleries outside London. They open till 9pm on Thurs. Meals, snacks, good bookshop, disabled access; cl Mon, bank hols and 2 wks between exhibitions – worth checking; (01865) 722733; *£2.50.

Museum of Oxford (St Aldates) Interesting little local history museum, with re-created rooms, maps, and period music. Shop; cl Mon, Sun am, Good Fri, 25–26 Dec; (01865) 815559; £2, free for county residents.

Oxford Story (Broad St) One of Europe's longest dark rides, with cars designed as desks taking you through a cheerful and well researched re-creation of university history, complete with sights, sounds and smells. A useful introduction to the city (esp for families), though no substitute for the real thing. Good shop (you can just visit here using the entrance on Ship St), disabled access; cl 25 Dec; (01865) 528822; £5.70. In summer you can get a ticket which also includes entry to Magdalen and New College (£9.70).

Oxford University Museum of Natural History (Parks Rd) Victorian Gothic structure specialising in natural history – outstanding if solidly earnest collection, enlivened by a working beehive in summer; cl am, some days over Easter and Christmas; free.

Pitt Rivers Museum (entrance via University Museum, Parks Rd) Refurbished and fascinating close-packed ethnographic museum off the tourist track. Shrunken heads, totem poles and fertility rites, along with art and ingenuity from all cultures and periods. The million or so exhibits range from Captain Cook's Pacific Islands collection and 18th-c ship models to severed fingertips and an Eskimo coat made from seal intestines. Everything is still displayed in firmly traditional cases or drawers, with neatly handwritten labels, so it has kept something of the Victorian atmosphere that's part of its charm. An exhibition on the art of recycling runs until the autumn. Shop, limited disabled access; cl am, Sun, and a few days over Christmas and Easter; (01865) 270927; free. The adjacent Balfour Building has a gallery of archaeology and a large collection of musical instruments.

Port Meadow This is the best outlying area for Oxford walks, an expanse of waterside common land with grazing horses and flocks of geese, which extends N from Jericho and can be reached on the far side of the Oxford canal via Walton Well Rd, crossing the Thames and turning right along the W bank. Just beyond the far end of Port Meadow is the ruin of 12th-c Godstow Nunnery, where Fair Rosamund the mistress of Henry II is buried; nearby, the riverside medieval Trout pub is touristy but very attractive, and there are often peacocks around here. A second well sited riverside pub, the thatched Perch at Binsey, is another popular walking objective in this direction.

Punting and boat trips Good fun in sunny weather; once you've got the knack it's a very nice way of spending a lazy afternoon. You can hire boats from Magdalen Bridge or Folly Bridge; usually £8–£10 an hour – you'll have to put down a big deposit. Salters run steamer trips from Folly Bridge to Abingdon.

Ruskin walk From the big garden of the Fishes pub at North Hinksey, a footpath towards Oxford partly follows a causeway built originally by John Ruskin to give students experience of healthy outdoor labour.

Sheldonian Theatre (Broad St) A grand classical building, with a lovely painted ceiling. In its time it's been used for parliaments, and nowadays university ceremonies are held here; you may see gowned students heading for these on some wknds, though the theatre is closed to the public then. Nearby, the Kings Arms is a famous university haunt.

St Mary's (High St) Interesting university church with fine views from the tower, and a nice – if busy – café in the crypt; usually cl Sun am; £1.50.

St Michael at the North Gate 🔓 (Cornmarket St) Oxford's oldest building, a Saxon church with displays of silver, clocks and bells; great views from the tower. Shop, disabled access to church; cl Sun am, 25 Dec and Good Fri; £1.50.

University Botanic Garden (High St) Britain's oldest botanic garden, founded in 1621, with 8,000 species of plant from all over the world. It's a lovely place to sit for a while, or wander through on the way to the river. Disabled access; cl Good Fri and 25 Dec; (01865) 286690; £2. They also administer the University Arboretum at Nuneham Courtenay.

University Parks There are countrified walks almost from Oxford's city centre. The parks (primarily playing fields) are the closest place for a good stroll – and in summer you can watch first-class cricket matches for free.

Waterside walks The rivers Thames and Cherwell cut strikingly rural corridors through the city, though walks along the Cherwell may be impeded by closed college gates. They are most likely to be open in mid-afternoon.

OXFORD CANAL SP4816
For towpath walks, there's access from the Jolly Boatman pub at Thrupp SP4816. The towpath is shadowed by the railway, so you can walk by the canal from one village to another, for example from Lower Heyford SP4824 to Nethercott SP4820, and return by train.

RIDGEWAY SU2885
Near the N crest of the downs, the

Ridgeway tracks right across from Wiltshire to Berkshire. This broad grassy trackway was used as a herding highway for some 2,000 years before the Romans came, and after the break-up of the Roman empire came back into use for the same purpose, well into medieval times. It's now part of the long-distance path network, and gives good walking with fine views. The particularly atmospheric short stretch nr Compton Beauchamp takes in the ancient sites of Waylands Smithy, the White Horse and Uffington Castle.

ROUSHAM SP4824

Rousham House Nicely unspoilt 17th-c house embellished by court artists and architects, and remodelled in the 18th c by William Kent to give the external appearance of a Gothic Tudor mansion. It still has Civil War shooting holes in the door. Excellent 18th-c classically landscaped garden with buildings, cascades, statues and vistas in 30 acres of hanging woods above the River Cherwell, and walled flower and vegetable gardens. No children under 15. Some disabled access to grounds; house open pm Weds, Sun and bank hols Apr–Sept, gardens open daily all year; (01869) 347110; *£3 house, *£3 garden. There's a 12th-c church. The Red Lion at Steeple Aston is very good for lunch (no children here, either).

RYCOTE SP6604

Rycote Chapel (off A329) Peaceful little 15th-c private chapel, later visited by both Elizabeth I and Charles I. The wedding scene in the TV production of *Jane Eyre* was filmed here. Shop, disabled access; open pm Fri–Sun and bank hols Apr–Sept; £1.60. The picturesque Kings Head at Great Milton has decent food.

SEGSBURY CAMP SU3883

Extensive Iron Age hill fort, later used by the Romans, with good views; reached by the dead-end lane up past the Sparrow in Letcombe Regis.

SHIPTON-UNDER-WYCHWOOD SP2717

Old houses around a lovely big sloping green, two good inns (one very ancient), and an interesting bookshop.

SIBFORD GOWER SP3537

There are pleasant walks in the countryside around the quiet village of Sibford Gower, where the thatched Wykham Arms is good for lunch.

SONNING COMMON SU7079

Herb Farm 🖼 (Peppard Rd) Extensive range of herb plants and products, with over 200 different species in the display garden. There's an impressive maze (summer only), and agricultural displays in a restored granary. Summer snacks, shop, disabled access; cl 25 Dec–2 Jan; (0118) 972 4220; free, £1.25 for maze. The Greyhound (Gallowstree Common Rd) has good food.

STANTON HARCOURT SP4105

Manor House The medieval Great Kitchen has no chimney – the smoke from ovens and fireplaces collected in the cone of the roof and drifted out through wooden louvres. The gardens too are striking, with neat lawns and topiary, and a wilder wooded area. Teas, shop, disabled access; usually open pm Thurs and Sun fortnightly from mid-Apr–Sept, plus bank hols – best to check first; (01865) 881928; £5, garden only £3. The village is attractive, and the Harcourt Arms nearby does good meals.

STONOR SU7489

Stonor House 🖼 Even older than the stately Tudor façade suggests, with beautiful furnishings, paintings, sculptures and tapestries, and mementoes of Jesuit scholar Edward Campion, one of the many Catholic recusants who found refuge here during the Reformation. There are lovely gardens and a wooded deer park. Snacks, shop; usually open pm Sun and bank hols Apr–Sept, plus pm Weds July–Aug, and pm May and Aug bank hol Sat – best to phone; (01491) 638587; £4.50, chapel and garden only £2.50. The smart Stonor Arms is useful for lunch. The deer park is skirted by an attractive right of way from the village, and you can link this with the famous and unusual Maharajah's Well in the charming village of Stoke Row; or for a longer Chilterns walk you can continue E to Turville in Buckinghamshire.

SUTTON COURTENAY SU5093

An attractive village to stroll through, with things to look out for – like Asquith and Orwell, unlikely bedfellows in their final rest in the graveyard. The

Fish is a good dining pub.

SWALCLIFFE SP3737

Swalcliffe Barn (B4035) Another well preserved tithe barn, with much of its medieval half-cruck timber roof intact. There's a display of agricultural and trade vehicles. Shop, disabled access; open pm Sun and bank hols Easter– end Oct; free. The village is pretty, and the Stags Head has good food.

SYDENHAM SP7301

A charming village, with a lovely church.

THAME SP7006

Well worth a look for its splendid range of unspoilt architecture. The very wide main street has escaped any significant development this century, and has medieval timber-framed buildings next to stately Georgian houses; the 13th-c **church** is attractive. The 15th-c Birdcage Inn used to be the town lock-up; the Rising Sun has decent food – though the best nearby pub for lunch is the Mole & Chicken at Easington out past Long Crendon.

THAMES VALLEY SU7678

Shared with Berks and Bucks, this has a classic, very English sort of beauty, with boating scenes, superb trees and riverside architecture. Riverside walks on the Oxfordshire side are possible only in places, notably between Henley and Sonning – for instance to Shiplake Lock from the Plowden Arms at Shiplake; you can also get down to the Thames from the attractive Perch & Pike at South Stoke SU5983.

UFFINGTON SU3089

Charming village, with decent food at the Fox & Hounds. Opposite here is John Betjeman's former home Garrard Farm, which you can rent in summer, (01328) 851155; as warden of the magnificent 13th-c St Mary's church, he made sure even its oil lamps were preserved.

Tom Brown's School Museum 🏛 (Broad St) Young Mr Brown's schooldays were based on those the author Thomas Hughes passed here; there's an exhibition on his life and work. Shop; open pm wknds Easter–Oct; 60p.

Uffington Castle High above the village, this Iron Age fort covered eight acres but had only one gateway; great views over the vale below. On the hillside a 115-metre (375-ft) **white horse** carved into the chalk is now thought to be around 3,000 years old; it's a striking design, very Celtic. If you stand in the centre of the eye and turn around three times with your eyes closed, any reasonable wish will be granted. This is one good setting-off point for the Ridgeway. The flat-topped little hill below is said to be where George killed the dragon. A bit over a mile E, off the B4507, the turning off up towards the downs opposite the Kingston Lisle road almost immediately passes a cottage on the left which has outside a huge pitted flint rock, locally known as the blowing stone: if you blow in the right hole and in the right way you can produce a splendid deep blast of sound. The pub named after it has good food.

UPPER THAMES SP4001

W of Oxford, the Thames flows through low-lying country, giving the sort of walk you enjoy more for the people you're with than the scenery itself. The Maybush pub on the A415 at Newbridge is a useful focus for pleasant if undramatic riverside strolls through low-lying country, and the Rose Revived here is worth knowing for its big Thames-side lawn. Other pubs handy for quiet Thames walks are the Ferryman off the B4449 S of Stanton Harcourt at Bablock Hythe SP4304, the Talbot on the B4044 nr the Swinford toll bridge SP4409, and the Trout at Tadpole Bridge SP3300 on the unclassified road between Bampton and Buckland.

WALLINGFORD SU6089

Wallingford Museum (High St) Very good sight-and-sound history of the area, complete with reconstructed Victorian street. Shop; cl am (exc Sat), all Mon (exc bank hols), winter Suns, and all Dec–Feb; (01491) 835065; £2. The George nearby has decent food. There are the ruins of a 13th-c castle on a hill, and plenty of places to hire boats or fish around here.

WANTAGE SU3987

Historic town where King Alfred was reputedly born; recently much expanded, though there's an attractive quiet corner by the 13th/15th-c church with its raised graveyard, and in Newbury

St 17th-c almshouses have a courtyard cobbled with bones. The downland roads S into Berks have fine views.

Vale and Downland Museum Centre (Church St) Well displayed local history and geology in a recently restored gallery; the Tourist Information Centre is also situated here. Snacks, shop, limited disabled access; cl Sun am, Good Fri, a few days over Christmas and New Year and some bank hols; £1.50.

Venn Mill 🖼 (A338 N) Still the area's regularly used working corn mill; open 2nd Sun in month Apr–Oct; *£1.

WARMINGTON SP4047

National Herb Centre (Banbury Rd) Wide range of herbs in display gardens set in an attractive valley; also walks, nature trails and a children's activity area. Bistro, herb and plant centre, disabled access; cl 25 Dec–3 Jan; (01295) 690999; free.

WATLINGTON WOODS SU7093 A mass of bluebells in spring, these give great views over Oxfordshire from this steep edge of the Chiltern Hills.

WAYLAND'S SMITHY SU2885 Midway along the Ridgeway between the Uffington White Horse and the B4000 above Ashbury (where the Rose & Crown is ideally placed for walkers), this was even in Saxon times reputed to be the forge of a magic blacksmith, who would invisibly shoe your horse overnight if you left it there with a silver coin – and exact horrid penalties if you tried to slip by without paying. It's an impressive place, alone on the downs, an excavated neolithic burial chamber rather over 5,000 years old, made with massive sarsen stones each weighing several tons; free.

WHEATLEY SP5805 A place of bizarre-shaped buildings: the unusual octagonal windmill is open by appointment (maybe at other times, (01865) 874610; free), while the village lock-up is shaped like a pyramid. Just S at Garsington Jennings Farm Shop has a wide range of produce as well as craft workshops and a working blacksmith's forge. Garsington has decidedly smart open-air operas (and good food at the Three Horseshoes).

WHITCHURCH SU6377 An attractive little village, with nice

walks nearby; the Greyhound does good value food.

Boze Down Vineyard (B471 N) Free tastings pm wknds, and guided tours by appointment, cl Jan–Feb; (0118) 984 4031. Path Hill Farm on Goring Heath nearby has a shop selling organic products.

WIDFORD SP2712

Widford church and lost village (just outside Burford) The church is very simple, but notable for three things – its medieval wall paintings, the remains of a Roman pavement at the west end of the chancel, and its surroundings, a former village that save one solitary house has now virtually disappeared.

WIGGINTON HEATH SP3834

Waterfowl Sanctuary & Children's Farm Set up especially with children in mind, this pleasantly undeveloped place has plenty of baby animals to cuddle, as well as rare breeds, uncommon aviary birds, and 12 well set-out waterfowl ponds, awash with ducks. Wear wellies in wet weather. Snacks, shop, disabled access; cl 25 Dec; (01608) 730252; £3.

WITNEY SP3609 Saxon kings used to hold their meetings, or witans, here – hence the name. It was a prosperous town in the Middle Ages, and is well known for its blankets, made here ever since. Quiet and relaxed, with picturesque stone buildings, market square still with its ancient butter cross and 17th-c clock, and quite a few interesting old buildings such as the 13th-c church and 18th-c blanket hall. Just off Church Green you can see the excavated foundations of a 12th-c palace of the Bishops of Winchester (pm wknds Easter–mid-Sept, free), and the nearby Angel has good value food.

Cogges Farm Museum See separate family panel on p.457.

WOODSTOCK SP4416 Civilised and prosperous small town, with good antiques shops and fine stone buildings. The Feathers Hotel, Bear Hotel and homelier Queens Own (food all day wknds) are all good. The graveyard of nearby Bladon church, where Churchill is buried, has views over Blenheim Park.

Blenheim Palace Undoubtedly one of England's most impressive stately homes: given to the Duke of Marlborough by Queen Anne as a reward for his military achievements, the house itself covers 14 acres, and the grounds stretch for well over 2,000. Churchill was born here, and there's a straightforward exhibition on his life. Highlights within the palace include the sumptuous State Rooms and 56-metre (183-ft) Long Library, along with plenty of opulent furnishings and sculpture; tours leave every 5–10 minutes. The very extensive grounds, landscaped by Capability Brown, are full of interesting paths and tracks; you can picnic. Also butterfly house, miniature railway and play areas with swings, ropes and slides. An extra £1.50 adds a hedge maze, putting green, and model village based on Woodstock and surroundings. You can hire rowing boats (£4 per boat for half an hour) or arrange coarse fishing on the lake (phone first to book). There's enough space to absorb the crowds (Sun is busiest, and Weds is popular with overseas students); the house usually gets quieter after about 3pm. You can avoid having to wait for tickets by arriving early; though most parts are closed till 10.30am, the gates and ticket office open at 9am. Meals and snacks (three different restaurants), several shops and plant centre, some disabled access; house cl Nov to mid-Mar, grounds open all year; (01993) 811325; £9, £6 per car grounds only. There is also a public right of way through the huge estate, with pleasant walks in, for example from the attractive village of Combe.

Oxfordshire County Museum (Fletcher's House) Elegant town house with pleasant gardens and good displays. Snacks, shop, disabled access; cl Sun am, Mon; (01993) 811456; £2.50.

WOOLSTONE SU2987
An attractive village in the Vale of the White Horse; Thomas Hughes reputedly wrote *Tom Brown's Schooldays* in the bar of the White Horse pub here.

WYTHAM SP4708
Charming unspoilt village, all houses owned and preserved by Oxford University; good dining pub.

Other charming small towns and villages, all with decent pubs, include Adderbury SP4635, Bampton SP3103, Blewbury SU5385, Bloxham SP4235 (splendid church spire), Brightwell Baldwin SU6595, Buckland SU3497, Chadlington SP3222, Church Enstone SP3724, Clifton Hampden SU5495, Crawley SP3412, Cuddesdon SP5903, Cumnor SP4603, Denchworth SU3791, Duns Tew SP4528, East Hendred SU4588 (interesting church), Epwell SP3540, Faringdon SU2895, Goring SU6080, Hook Norton SP3533, Kingston Lisle SU3287, Lewknor SU7198, Marsh Baldon SU5699, Milton-under-Wychwood SP2618, Shenington SP3742, Shilton SP2608, Souldern SP5131, Sparsholt SU3487, Stratton Audley SP6026, Upper Wardington SP4945, Wootton SP4320 and Wroxton SP4142.

Where to eat

ARDINGTON SU4388 **Boars Head** *Church Lane (01235) 833254* Civilised and upmarket dining pub with three simply furnished but smart rooms, low beams, bare boards, fresh flowers, and lots of pictures, particularly good wines, well kept real ales, imaginative ambitious food, and no smoking restaurant; good nearby walks; no food Sun pm, cl Mon; disabled access. £25.50|**£8**

BARNARD GATE SP4010 **Boot** *(01865) 881231* Friendly dining pub with an interesting collection of celebrities' boots, a huge log fire, good interesting food, a partly no smoking restaurant, prompt friendly service, decent wines, well kept beers, and big log fire. £23|**£9.95**

BUCKLAND SU3498 **Lamb** *(01367) 870484* Refurbished 18th-c stone dining pub in a tiny village, with a rather sophisticated atmosphere, a civilised little bar with newspapers to read and examples of their own chutneys and jams, popular imaginative food changing seasonally, good value house wines from a strongly French wine list, real ales, and smart helpful service; comfortable bdrms; good walks nearby. £24|**£5.95**

BURFORD SP2512 **Mermaid** *78 High St (01993) 822193* Busy pub with handsome Tudor frontage, an attractive long narrow bar with flagstones, stonework and some panelling, pretty dried flowers, a no smoking dining conservatory, and an upstairs restaurant; a wide choice of interesting food, well kept real ales, and courteous efficient staff; cl 25 Dec; no children in the bars. £30|**£6.95**

CHALGROVE SU6397 **Red Lion** *High St (01865) 890625* Appealing old traditional pub with a smartly contemporary twist to its décor, a log fire and old woodburner, carefully collected prints and period cartoons, and fresh flowers; well kept ales, decent wines, imaginative well presented food, a helpful landlord, and no smoking back dining room; no food Sun pm; cl 25 Dec; disabled access. £20.45|**£5.95**

EAST HENDRED SU4688 **Wheatsheaf** *Chapel Sq (01235) 833229* Attractive black and white timbered 16th-c village pub with a good mix of locals and visitors, high-backed settles, some panelling and an inglenook fireplace, well liked often interesting food, well kept real ales, and decent wines; seats in the colourful garden. £17.50|**£6**

HOOK NORTON SP3533 **Sun** *High St (01608) 737570* In a pretty village and facing the church, this bustling, friendly pub has a flagstoned front bar with a huge log fire and hop-strung beams, a snug carpeted room with comfortable banquettes, and an attractive partly no smoking green-walled restaurant; a wide choice of imaginative popular food (inc a good range of excellent triple-decker sandwiches), real ales, good value wines, and efficient service; bdrms; good disabled facilities. £21|**£7**

MAIDENSGROVE SU6990 **Five Horseshoes** *(01491) 641282* High up in the Chilterns beechwoods, this little 17th-c brick house has fine views from several tables in its extended restaurant, and from the sheltered back garden; rambling bar with log fire and lots of banknotes from around the world, good imaginative food, a decent wine list, well kept real ales, and separate walkers' bar; cl 25 Dec; children in top bar; partial disabled access. £26.95/winter 3-course menu £12.50|**£5.95**

OXFORD SP5106 **Browns** *5–11 Woodstock Road (01865) 511995* Cheerful, bustling brasserie with lots of plants, mirrors, wooden tables and chairs, helpful friendly staff, and a good choice of enjoyable fresh food; half the restaurant is no smoking, and they are kind to children; cl 25–26 Dec; disabled access. £24|**£4.95**

OXFORD SP5106 **Café Moma** *Museum of Modern Art, Pembroke St (01865) 722733* Clean, light and very popular self-service café in the basement, simple modern furnishings, exhibitions on walls, largely vegetarian food from a blackboard, excellent cakes, and efficient friendly service; open till 5pm (till 9pm Thurs only); cl Mon, bank hols; disabled access. £12|**£3.20**

OXFORD SP5107 **Gees** *61a Banbury Rd (01865) 553540* Relaxed, airy atmosphere, fresh herbs and spices to enliven interesting vegetarian pastas, wild mushrooms and so forth as well as good meat and fish dishes, good unusual wines; in genuine old conservatory; cl 25–26 Dec. £25/2-course lunch £9.50

OXFORD SP5007 **Petit Blanc** *71–72 Walton St (01865) 510999* Very popular, stylish and airy two-room brasserie, open all day for breakfast, lunch, afternoon tea and dinner; from the smarter room you can see into the kitchen and watch the preparation of the extremely good Mediterranean food; friendly service and helpful notes against each wine listed; children very welcome; cl 25 Dec; disabled access. £30

SOUTH STOKE SU5983 **Perch & Pike** *The Street (01491) 872415* Just a field away from the Thames, this little brick and flint pub is popular locally; low beams, open fires and comfortable seats in relaxing bar, well kept real ales, a dozen malt whiskies, and enjoyable bar food inc interesting daily specials; pretty window boxes, seats in large flower-bordered lawn, and more on Cotswold stone terrace; they still plan to open bdrms. £20.55|**£7.95**

STOKE ROW SU6884 **Crooked Billet** *Nottwood Lane (01491) 681048* Open-plan beamed dining pub with a relaxed homely atmosphere (rather like a French country restaurant), log fires, a wide choice of good interesting food inc vegetarian menu, decent wines and real ales, and big garden by Chilterns beech woods. £25/2-course lunch £10

UFFINGTON SU3087 **Britchcombe Farm** *(01367) 820667* Working farm in lovely spot below White Horse Hill, afternoon cream teas on Sat, Sun and bank hol Mon with home-made scones, cakes and so forth; very friendly service, log fire in winter, tables outside among the geese and sheep in summer; some fruit and vegetables, home-made mohair knitwear and crafts, caravan for hire, and certified camping/caravan site; disabled access.|**£3**

WALLINGFORD SU6089 **Annie's Tea Rooms** *79 High St (01491) 836308* Prettily decorated and friendly no smoking 17th-c house serving morning coffee, lunches with a home-made daily dish, and afternoon tea inc a fine choice of home-made cakes and quite a few teas; cl Weds, Sun; disabled access|**£3.90**

WATLINGTON SU6894 **Chequers** *Love Lane (01491) 612874* Cheerful, cosy old pub with low beams, candlelight, nice old chairs and antique tables, a conservatory, a wide choice of good popular food, real ales, and a pretty garden; no food Sun pm, 25–26 Dec; no children. £24|**£6**

WESTCOTT BARTON SP4325 **Fox** *Enstone Rd (01869) 340338* Lovely stone-built village pub with enjoyable food under new licensees inc popular pasta dishes, a relaxed little bar with hops on low beams, open fires, high-backed settles and pews on the flagstones, an elegant restaurant, and well kept ales; pleasant garden with wooden play fort. £19|**£5.95**

WOOTTON SP4319 **Kings Head** *Chapel Hill (01993) 811340* Pretty 17th-c Cotswold stone pub with civilised and beamed no smoking lounge, a nice mix of furniture, open log fire, very good imaginative food inc lovely puddings, well kept real ales, and decent wines; children over 12. £30 dinner/£20 lunch|**£8.95**

Special thanks to Keith Arrowsmith, Alan M Dominey, B and K Hypher

---

We welcome reports from readers

This *Guide* depends on readers' reports. Do help us if you can – in return, we offer a discount on the next edition to people who've helped us with reports for it. Tell us what you think about places already in it, and anything extra you think we should say about them. And send us your ideas for inclusion in the next edition: places to visit, eat at or stay in, attractive drives or walks, maybe even unusual interesting shops you know of. Use the card in the middle, the report forms at the end, or just write – no stamp needed: *The Good Britain Guide*, FREEPOST TN1569, Wadhurst, E Sussex TN5 7BR.

SHROPSHIRE

Evocative untouched countryside, some lovely medieval market towns, farmyard fun, and several entertaining family destinations

This being largely rural territory, it is perhaps unsurprising that the majority of family attractions have some connection to farming. Among the pick of the crop are the outstanding Hoo Farm Animal Kingdom at Preston on the Weald (usual animal attractions supplemented by lively activities), Rays Farm Country Matters, Billingsley (atmospheric Christmas events), Acton Scott Historic Working Farm (joint appeal for children and adults), and the excellent developing Park Hall countryside centre at Oswestry, new to the *Guide* this year.

Another newcomer, Mythstories of Shrewsbury (the county's Family Attraction of the Year) tops the eclectic list of other family-friendly places in the county, that takes in the enjoyable Shrewsbury Quest, Cosford's spectacular Royal Air Force Museum, and the excellently preserved and presented industrial heritage at Ironbridge (good value all-in ticket).

Delightful Stokesay Hall is one of the finest medieval manor houses in existence, and other treasures include the architectural whimsy of the Hawkstone Park Follies and the fine interiors of Benthall Hall, Broseley, and newly reopened (and hence new to the *Guide*) Castle Lodge, Ludlow.

Shropshire, particularly in its southern parts, has very attractive unspoilt countryside, with charming places to stay in. Drives and walks pass attractive buildings in stone or black and white timbering, haunting ruins, and a set of uncommonly distinctive hills give sleepy views. The splendid Severn Valley Railway passes through beautiful scenery in the south of the county, as does the Severn Way – a new riverside walk from mid-Wales to Bristol, guides £6.95 from Tourist Inforamtion Centres. In general Shropshire holiday prices are good value.

Where to stay

ALL STRETTON SO4595 **Jinlye** *Castle Hill, All Stretton, Church Stretton, Shropshire SY6 6JP (01694) 723243* **£54**, plus special breaks; 8 spacious comfortable rms with lovely views. Charming 16th-c house in large grounds surrounded by National Trust land; log fires in the comfortable lounges (one has an inglenook fireplace, lots of heavy beams, and a mix of interesting furniture), good home cooking in big no smoking dining room, enjoyable breakfasts, and friendly owners; self-catering also; children over 12; disabled access

BISHOP'S CASTLE SO3288 **Castle Hotel** *Market Sq, Bishop's Castle, Shropshire SY9 5BN (01588) 638403* **£65***; 5 spacious rms with fine views. On the site of the old castle keep, this enjoyable 17th/18th-c hotel has good fires, a relaxed and friendly atmosphere, lovely home-made food, well kept beers, and welcoming owners

CLUN SO2882 **New House Farm** *Clun, Craven Arms, Shropshire SY7 8NJ (01588) 638314* **£50***; 2 rms. Remote 18th-c farmhouse nr the Welsh border with plenty of surrounding hillside walks; homely rooms with copper pans and decorative plates on the walls, packed lunches, good breakfasts, plenty of books, a country garden, and helpful friendly owner; cl end Oct–Easter; children over 5

DIDDLEBURY SO5085 **Delbury Hall** *Diddlebury, Craven Arms, Shropshire SY7 9DH (01584) 841267* **£95**; 4 rms. Beautiful stately Georgian house in 80 acres of landscaped parkland with ornamental duck on the lake, trout fishing, flower-filled gardens, and hard tennis court; large hall with fine oak staircase, spacious drawing room, sitting room and snooker room, enjoyable food using their own vegetables and eggs, a good wine list, and hearty breakfasts; cl Christmas; children by arrangement

GRETTON SO5195 **Court Farm** *Gretton, Cardington, Church Stretton, Shropshire SY6 7HU (01694) 771219* **£50***; 2 rms. Large comfortable no smoking stone-built farmhouse on 330-acre mixed farm, with a warm welcome, a big woodburner in inglenook fireplace, and hearty breakfasts; plenty of places nearby for evening meals; cl Dec–Jan; no children or pets

HANWOOD SJ4409 **White House** *Hanwood, Shrewsbury, Shropshire SY5 8LP (01743) 860414* **£60***, plus special breaks; 6 rms, 3 with own bthrm. Charming 16th-c black and white half-timbered house with two sitting rooms, breakfasts using their own eggs, enjoyable evening meals with some home-grown produce (must pre-book), and two acres of garden; children over 12

HOPESAY SO3883 **Old Rectory** *Hopesay, Craven Arms, Shropshire SY7 8HD (01588) 660245* **£75***; 3 comfortable rms, one with own sitting room. 17th-c rectory with lovely two-acre garden overlooking Hopesay Hill (NT); comfortable drawing room with log fire and baby grand piano, attractive dining room with excellent home cooking, and hearty breakfasts with home-baked bread; no smoking; super walks from the house; cl Christmas and New Year; no children

HOPTON WAFERS SO6376 **Crown** *Hopton Wafers, Kidderminster, Worcestershire DY14 0NB (01299) 270372* **£75**, plus special breaks; 7 rms. Attractive creeper-covered stone inn in pleasant countryside, with interestingly furnished bar, inglenook fireplace, enjoyable food, decent house wines, beers and malt whiskies, friendly efficient service, and streamside garden; children over 12

KNOCKIN SJ3321 **Top Farmhouse** *Knockin, Oswestry, Shropshire SY10 8HN (01691) 682582* **£44**; 3 pretty rms. Most attractive Grade I listed black and white timbered house dating back to the 16th c, with friendly owners, lots of timbers and beams, a log fire in the restful comfortable drawing room, good breakfasts in the large dining room, and an appealing garden; grand piano; children over 10

LONGVILLE SO5393 **Longville Arms** *Longville, Much Wenlock, Shropshire TF13 6DT (01694) 771206* **£46***, plus special breaks; 5 comfortable rms in converted stables with fresh flowers, home-made biscuits, and showers. Warmly friendly inn with two spacious bars, well kept real ales, a wide range of enjoyable food, superb breakfasts, and a neat terraced side garden with play areas for children; partial disabled access

LUDLOW SO5175 **Unicorn** *Corve St, Ludlow, Shropshire SY8 1DU (01584) 873555* **£50**; 5 beamed and timbered rms. Enjoyable 17th-c inn with a warmly atmospheric beamed and partly panelled bar, a huge log fire in big stone fireplace, a good mix of locals and visitors, a candlelit no smoking timbered restaurant, tasty home-made food, real ales, cheerful service, and a pretty little terrace by the modest River Corve

LUDLOW SO5174 **Wheatsheaf** *Lower Broad St, Ludlow, Shropshire SY8 1PQ (01584) 872980* **£45***, plus special breaks; 5 comfortable oak-beamed rms with showers. Attractively furnished small 17th-c pub spectacularly built into medieval town gate; traditional atmosphere, two log fires, lots of hops, timbers, and exposed stone walls, wide range of good food in bar and no smoking restaurant (super steaks), real ales, and friendly owners

MUCH WENLOCK SO6299 **Talbot** *High St, Much Wenlock, Shropshire TF13 6AA (01952) 727077* **£90**, plus special breaks; 6 rms. Dating from 1360 and once part of Wenlock Abbey, this converted 18th-c malthouse is very civilised, with pretty flowers, log fires, prints, pleasant staff, good food in no smoking restaurant and bar, and well kept real ales

NORTON SJ7200 **Hundred House** *Bridgnorth Rd, Norton, Shifnal, Shropshire TF11 9EE (01952) 730353* **£95**, plus special breaks; 10 cottagey rms (some with swing and lavender-scented sheets). Carefully refurbished mainly Georgian inn with quite a sophisticated feel, neatly kept bar with old quarry-tiled floors, beamed ceilings, oak panelling and handsome fireplaces, elaborate evening meals using inn's own herbs, friendly service, good bar food, and excellent breakfast and afternoon tea; delightful garden, no dogs; cl Christmas evening

RHYDYCROESAU SJ2430 **Pen-y-Dyffryn Hall** *Rhydycroesau, Oswestry, Shropshire SY10 7JD (01691) 653700* **£82***, plus special breaks; 10 rms. Handsome Georgian stone-built rectory in five acres with lovely views of the Welsh hills, and trout fishing, hill-walking and riding (shooting can be arranged); log fires in both comfortable lounges, good food using the best local ingredients, and a relaxed friendly atmosphere; well behaved dogs welcome; cl 20 Dec–20 Jan; partial disabled access

SHREWSBURY SJ4917 **Albright Hussey** *Ellesmere Rd, Broad Oak, Shrewsbury, Shropshire SY4 3AF (01939) 290571* **£95**, plus special breaks; 14 lovely rms. Fine moated medieval manor house, partly timber-framed and partly stone-and-brick, in four-acre garden, with particularly good food in timbered and panelled restaurant, and excellent service; children over 3; disabled access

SHREWSBURY SJ4417 **Fitz Manor** *Fitz, Bowmere Heath, Shrewsbury, Shropshire SY4 3AS (01743) 850295* **£50**; 3 rms, shared bthrm. Lovely black and white timbered 15th-c manor house with oak panelling and log fire in comfortable sitting room, a big dining room with antiques, paintings and parquet flooring, good evening meals, big breakfasts, and friendly owners; outdoor heated swimming pool

STREFFORD SO4485 **Strefford Hall Farm** *Strefford, Craven Arms, Shropshire SY7 8DE (01588) 672383* **£46***; 3 rms. No smoking Victorian stone-built farmhouse surrounded by 360 acres of working farm; woodburner in sitting room, good breakfasts (evening meals by arrangement), and lots of walks; cl Christmas and New Year; disabled access

WENLOCK EDGE SO5796 **Wenlock Edge Inn** *Hill Top, Much Wenlock, Shropshire TF13 6DJ (01746) 785678* **£75***, plus special breaks; 3 rms, showers only (served by 58-metre, 190-ft well). Popular and cheerfully welcoming family-run inn by the Ippikins Rock viewpoint, with lots of walks through NT land that runs along the Edge; a chatty and relaxed atmosphere, good fresh home-made bar food inc old-fashioned puddings, fine breakfasts, and wide range of drinks; second Mon evening of month is story-telling night; cl Christmas and New Year; children over 8; disabled access

WESTON SJ5828 **Citadel** *Weston, Shrewsbury, Shropshire SY4 5JY (01630) 685204* **£80**; 3 rms in two turrets. Fine castellated house overlooking Hawkstone Park, with country-house atmosphere, baby grand piano and unusual strapwork ceiling in the elegant sitting room, full-sized table in snooker room, enjoyable food (bring your own wine) in no smoking dining room, and welcoming owners; cl Nov–Mar; no children

WORFIELD SO7595 **Old Vicarage** *Hallon, Worfield, Bridgnorth, Shropshire WV15 5JZ (01746) 716497* **£115**, plus special breaks; 14 pretty rms. Restful and carefully restored Edwardian rectory in two acres; two airy conservatory-style lounges, very good interesting food in no smoking restaurant, a fine wine list, a cosseting atmosphere, and warmly friendly, helpful service; good disabled access

WROCKWARDINE SJ6212 **Church Farm** *Wrockwardine, Telford, Shropshire TF6 5DG (01952) 244917* **£52**; 6 individual well equipped rms, most with own bthrm. Friendly Georgian farmhouse on very ancient site overlooking the attractive garden and church; a relaxed atmosphere, particularly good caring service, beams and log fire in lounge, and good daily changing food in traditionally furnished dining room; cl Christmas; children over 10

To see and do

Shropshire Family Attraction of the Year

SHREWSBURY SJ4812 **Mythstories** (Carnarvon Lane, off Hills Lane) This tucked-away treasure is a real oddity, exploring myths, legends and stories from not just Shropshire but all around the world. The story-telling starts as soon as you go in, with the tale of Tupan, the Amazonian god who inadvertently wreaked havoc on the rain forests as he flew above them on his chariot, but don't expect to find hi-tech versions of the stories, or dramatic reconstructions. The interaction here comes from the imagination, so how much you'll enjoy it depends on how well you like a good yarn. Most of the stories are displayed on the walls, with words and pictures; you can read them for yourself, or push a button to hear a recorded version. You may have some of them memorably recounted in front of you: a storyteller will usually tell you at least one during your visit. There are six galleries in all, taking in everything from Robin Hood's visit to Ludlow (and a claim the legendary law-breaker was a Shropshire lad), through local authors Mary Webb and A E Housman, to a chained library where you can try your hand at untangling the books. Where the stories have a local connection you'll usually find helpful information on how you can visit the sites described. There are a good few hands-on features for children: they can crawl through reeds and find stories connected to the animals said to live in the pretend pond, or draw their tales for possible public viewing on the museum's web site. How long you stay is up to you: you'll need at least an hour to do it justice, but there are so many fantastic stories you'll need a good bit longer to stand any chance of getting through them all. Sofas and books along the way can help stretch a visit. A feast for the mind rather than the eyes, this is a bold idea that deserves encouragement, but it won't appeal to everyone: if your idea of story-telling involves watching a tale unfold on a screen you may be slightly nonplussed. The web site, www.mythstories.com, gives you something of the feel of the place. Teas and cakes, interesting shop; cl Tues, Weds (exc to groups) and all Nov–Mar; (01743) 357140; *£3.25, *£1.75 children 3–16.

ACTON BURNELL SJ5301
Acton Burnell Castle Ruined red sandstone manor house built in the 13th c, but almost abandoned by 1420; disabled access; free. The Plume of Feathers at Harley is fairly handy for lunch.

ACTON SCOTT SO4589
Acton Scott Historic Working Farm (off A49) Vivid introduction to traditional rural life, with plenty of rare breeds, and crops cultivated using old rotation methods; all the work is done by hand or horse power, with period farm machinery. Lots of craft demonstrations, and daily butter-making. Unusually, this is a farm aimed just as much at adults (maybe more) as at children. Meals, snacks, shop, disabled access; cl Mon (exc bank hols), and Nov–Mar; (01694) 781306; £3.95. The handiest place for lunch is the Ragleth in Little Stretton.

ASTLEY ABBOTS SO7096
Astley Abbots Lavender Farm 🖪 (off B4373 N of Bridgnorth) You can pick your own lavender at this friendly farm; also five acres of attractive gardens, and an intriguing look (through an infra-red viewing screen) at bumblebees, busy at work. Tearoom, shop, disabled access; open July–Aug; farm free, gardens £2.50 (inc tea and biscuits). Mrs Hodgson has kindly offered our readers a small discount on lavender purchases.

ATCHAM SJ5409
Attingham Park Splendidly grand late 18th-c house on the site of an old Roman town, with an imposing three-storey colonnaded portico. The extensive picture gallery was designed by Nash, who made imaginative use of early curved cast iron and glass for the

ceiling; attractive mature gardens and deer park outside. Snacks, shop, disabled access by prior arrangement; grounds open daily, house open pm and bank hol Mon Apr–Oct, cl Weds, Thurs; (01743) 708123; house and grounds £4.20, £2 grounds only; NT. The Cholmondeley Riverside towards Cressage has good food.

Home Farm 🖼 Rare breeds and traditional farm machinery; you can watch the milking of the Jersey cows (3.30pm), and play with the pets. Farmhouse teas, shop, limited disabled access; cl am, all day Thurs and Fri (exc school hols), and Oct–Easter; (01743) 709243; £2.75.

BILLINGSLEY SO7183

Rays Farm Country Matters
Traditional farm in pleasant countryside with sheep, horses and cattle and llamas, a good collection of owls and plenty of red and fallow deer – they hope to introduce otters soon. Pleasant woodland walks and indoor and outdoor picnic areas. They have atmospheric activities in the run-up to Christmas. Snacks, shop, disabled access; cl Jan and Feb, exc school hols and some wknds; (01299) 841255; £3.75 (£2.25 children over 2). For longer walks, you can try a section of bridleway starting at the farm, meandering eventually into Wales.

BISHOP'S CASTLE SO3288
Historic little market town with some fine Elizabethan and Georgian buildings, railway and local history museums, good shops, and the curious House on Crutches. It's handy for exploring Offa's Dyke.

Hobbs History of Beer & Brewing
The Three Tuns has a unique Victorian tower brewhouse, still in use – you can usually arrange a tour, (01588) 638797.

BOSCOBEL SJ8308

Boscobel House Interesting old house renowned for sheltering Charles II after the Battle of Worcester, with an unusually well preserved 17th-c garden and cobbled courtyard, and 19th-c décor giving a romanticised view of the King's drama. Good guided tour. Meals, snacks, shop, disabled access to gardens only; usually cl end Dec–Mar and wkdys during Dec; (01902) 850244; £4.30. The **Royal oak** here is said by some to have

been the hiding place of the king, by others to be a descendant, and by still others to be just a fine old tree. The Bell in Tong is good for lunch, and Weston Park at Weston under Lizard (Staffs) is nearby.

White Ladies Priory (just SW) Ruins of Augustinian nunnery destroyed in the Civil War; free.

BRIDGES SO3996
Pleasant quiet village, with a good pub and nearby walks.

BRIDGNORTH SO7193
On the Severn, this old market town is picturesque without being touristy. It's divided into the High Town and Low Town, with steps between the two – though it's easier (and more fun) to take the hair-raising **Cliff Railway**. On the way down you pass some small caves that people lived in till 1856 (they're not open, but labelled). As well as some handsome red brick, High Town has lots of fine timbered buildings, such as the odd town hall built on a sandstone-arched base that straddles the road in the High Street. The **castle** was largely destroyed in the Civil War, but part of the keep remains, left at a scary tilt by the constant bombardment; the grounds are now a park with good views – the best views are from Castle Esplanade. The unusual **church** on nearby East Castle Street was designed by Thomas Telford. The best pubs for food here are the Bear (Northgate) and Punch Bowl (B4364; there is a good carvery and great views).

Costume & Childhood Museum
(Newmarket Building) Lots of old costumes, dolls, and a Victorian nursery. Not open every day (usually cl Tues), but if you find them shut, next-door Beryl's Pantry has a key and can let you in; £1.25.

Daniels Mill (B4555, 1m S) Working cornmill still powered by its big waterwheel; a picturesque old place, run by the same family for 200 years. Snacks, shop; open pm wknds, Weds and bank hols Easter–Sept; (01746) 762753; £2.50.

Severn Valley Railway 🖼 The leading standard-gauge steam railway, with a great collection of locomotives, a splendidly lively atmosphere, and trips through beautiful scenery; for details see entry under Bewdley, in Worcestershire. The Railwayman's Arms in the station is an atmospheric place for a snack.

BROSELEY SJ6701

Benthall Hall (just NW of Broseley) Well liked by readers, an Elizabethan sandstone house with fine oak woodwork and panelling, decorative plasterwork, interesting garden, and 17th-c church (services 3.15pm most Suns). Some disabled access; open pm Weds, Sun and bank hols Apr–Sept; (01952) 882159; £3, £2 garden only; NT. The Foresters Arms is useful for lunch.

Broseley Clay Tobacco Pipe Museum (Duke St) Part of the Ironbridge Gorge Museum (and included in its Passport Ticket); see how they made those long clay pipes that are a trademark of olde-worlde pictures. Shop; cl ams, and early Nov–mid-Apr; £2.65.

BROWN CLEE HILL SO5986 Aptly named, this is Shropshire's highest point at nearly 550 metres (1,800 ft). It has a disappointingly flat top but offers walkers a certain solitary grandeur.

BUILDWAS SJ6404

Buildwas Abbey (B4378) Beautiful remains of 12th-c Cistercian abbey – apart from the roof it's practically all still here. Snacks, shop, reasonable disabled access; cl Oct–Mar; £1.95. It's right next to the gigantic cooling towers of a power station, which this close seem to have a geometrical beauty of their own. The Meadow coming out from Ironbridge has decent food.

BURY DITCHES SO3283 Iron Age ring fort, high on a hill, with superb views of South Shropshire and North Herefordshire.

CAER CARADOC SO4794 (E of Church Stretton) This hill has a pleasingly compact summit, and the pick of the local views. The best start for walks is Hope Bowdler, not far from Shropshire's oldest pub, the Royal Oak at Cardington.

CHIRBURY SO2698 An attractive village, with a famously haunted graveyard.

CLAVERLEY SO7993 An attractive village of black and white

timbered houses. The church has impressive medieval wall paintings.

CLEOBURY MORTIMER SO6775 Civilised small town, most notable perhaps for its church's **crooked spire**, though timbered Tudor buildings among its more elegant Georgian ones are picturesque. A restored **watermill** produces its own stoneground flour. The 16th-c Kings Arms has good value food (and comfortable bedrooms).

CLUN SO3080 Attractive stone-built village on the edge of the **Clun Forest**, a peaceful pastoral area of rolling partly wooded hills. The ruined Norman **castle** gives fine views from the castle mound; free. Down by the River Clun, the 16th-c stone bridge is very picturesque. The Sun and White Horse are useful for lunch.

COSFORD SJ7805 **Royal Air Force Museum** (A41) One of the country's best aviation museums, a spectacular collection of carefully arranged aircraft inc the Victor and Vulcan bombers, Hastings, York and British Airways airliners, and the last airworthy Britannia, as well as lots of missiles and a display of engines. Large modern extension inc art gallery, hands-on exhibits and a display on the history of military photography, due to open this year. Annual airshow in June (phone for date). Snacks, shop, disabled access; cl 24–26 Dec, 1 Jan; (01902) 376200; £5.50. There's a decent farm shop on Holyhead Rd, and the Bell at Tong is a reliable family dining pub.

CRAVEN ARMS SO4282 **Secret Hills Discovery Centre** 📷 (A49 just S) Another of the Millennium Commission's projects, this new grass-roofed structure built into the hillside and set in 25 acres of meadows takes a fresh look at the natural and cultural history of the surrounding countryside. Various galleries house interactive exhibitions on topics as diverse as the geology of landscape, and the art and music it's inspired. A simulated balloon ride over the hills should amuse children, and other attractions include a full-size model of a mammoth skeleton, and craft workshops. Restaurant, shop, good disabled access. As we went to press, they hadn't yet confirmed their opening times, so best to phone to check; (01588) 676000; £4.25 (crafts and meadows free).

ELLESMERE WALKS SJ4035
There are several meres or lakes around here – the Mere by Ellesmere itself, Blake Mere, and Cole Mere, which has a country park around it. This is close enough to the Shropshire Union Canal to include a walk along the towpath, with Colemere village a suitable starting place.

GRINSHILL HILL SJ5223
(between Grinshill and Clive) This gives walkers much wider views than you'd expect from its modest height, and quite an atmospheric summit, where woods open out by sheer quarried rock-faces.

HARMER HILL SJ4921
Pimhill Farm (Lea Hall; A528 S) Organic farm with farm animals, museum of beneficial herbs, farm trail and well priced produce shop. Meals and snacks from their own café; (01939) 290342; free. The Bridgewater Arms is a useful family dining pub.

HAUGHMOND ABBEY SJ5214
Haughmond Abbey (off B5062 E of Shrewsbury) Extensive ruins of Augustinian abbey, inc a fine Norman doorway in the chapter house, some interesting sculpture, and well preserved lodgings and kitchens. Good for picnics. In the grounds are some plants unique to the area. Shop, some disabled access; cl 1–2pm, and Nov–May; (01743) 709661; £1.95; EH.

HAWKSTONE PARK SJ5628
Hawkstone Park Follies Created in the 18th c, this remarkable steeply wooded parkland has been restored after a period of neglect; spectacular views from the monuments dotted around its 100 acres. Highlights include the ruins of a medieval red castle, intricate arches and pathways, and a fantastic underground grotto with tales told by an eerily convincing laser-powered animatron. The full circuit can easily take up to 3 hours and the path isn't always easy going, so sensible shoes are recommended (and you may need a torch for some of the caves and tunnels). The BBC filmed their *Chronicles of Narnia* here. Meals, snacks, shop, limited disabled access; open daily July–Aug, Weds–Sun Easter–Jun and Oct; (01939) 200611; £5. The Caspian Bar of the Hawkstone Park Hotel has good value food.

HODNET SJ6128
Several attractive half-timbered houses here, and some interesting old books in the church.

Hodnet Hall Gardens Sixty acres of lovely landscaped gardens with spacious lawns, lush pools, plants and trees; the astonishingly decorated tearoom is full of big-game trophies. Snacks, shop, disabled access; cl am, Mon, and Oct–Mar; (01630) 685202; £3.25. The Bear Hotel opposite is good for lunch.

IRONBRIDGE SJ6703
This steep town, with intriguing hillside paths and narrow lanes, was the birthplace of the Industrial Revolution: it was Abraham Darby's use here of coke instead of charcoal for smelting which made mass-production of iron possible. Well set among the woods and grassy slopes of the Severn Gorge, it was known as Coalbrookdale until the Darbys built the (recently restored) **iron bridge** across the river that today gives the town its name. As their industry took off they produced the world's first iron rails, boats, trains, and wheels, and for quite some while the valley was the biggest iron-making area in the world. Attractively placed by the riverside, the Meadow, Woodbridge and Olde Robin Hood, and (all handy for Maws craft centre and the Coalport Museum) the Boat and Half Moon at Jackfield and Shakespeare at Coalport are all useful for lunch; there's a pleasant terraced walk between the river and the Golden Ball (Wesley Rd, off Madeley Hill). For a fuller restaurant meal, the Coracle in the square is nice.

Ironbridge Gorge Museum Many of the former industrial sites now make up this outstanding network, one of the most satisfying places to visit in the whole country, scattered over six miles along the gorge. 50-acre **Blists Hill** is the highlight, and the part children like best – a complete reconstructed Victorian village, showing everything from the offices, houses and machinery to the school, pubs, pigsties and swingboats; it's the biggest open-air museum of its kind. Costumed staff add authenticity, and there are extra activities in the school hols. The other main sections include museums devoted to the river, and the iron, china and tile-making industries, with some beautifully restored houses (and wonderful echoes in the brick kilns at Coalport) and a former clay tobacco pipe factory in Broseley. You need only buy tickets for the parts you're interested in (useful leaflets suggest a variety of itineraries, from three hours to a whole day), but a special offer Passport Ticket covering everything is good value – and remains valid indefinitely until you've seen all the bits you want. On bank hols the sites are linked by a bus, otherwise it's best to drive (or walk). Meals, snacks, shops, disabled access; cl 24–25 Dec, 1 Jan and some parts cl Nov–Mar – best to ring first then; (01952) 432166; £10 Passport ticket, or individual tickets to each museum available – Blists Hill is around £7.50.

Maws Craft Centre Across a footbridge from the Coalport tile museum, big centre with 20 workshops selling things as diverse as pottery, puzzles and pictures (cl 25 Dec; free).

Museum of Steel Sculpture 🖻 (Cherry Tree Hill) Dramatic sculptures inspired by the industrial heritage in 10 attractive acres. Cl Mon exc bank hols and all Dec–Feb; £2.

Severn Gorge This has such fascinating and picturesque (though not always exactly pretty) scenery that its industrial monuments cry out for a tour on foot. Steep lanes and paths connect Ironbridge and Coalbrookdale, and an old railway track and a path along the base of Benthall Edge Wood assist walking routes along the gorge. A fine linear walk can be taken from Broseley, descending NW into the gorge via Corbett's Dingle to Coalport. From Coalport, you could even follow the river all the way S to Bridgnorth.

Teddy Bear Museum Next to the Museum of the Gorge, with bears and other furry animals made here by the long-established Merrythought Co; shop, disabled access, cl 25 Dec and 1 Jan; free.

LILLESHALL SJ7314
Lilleshall Abbey Impressive ruins of

12th-c abbey in pleasant setting surrounded by yew trees – it's a nice spot for a picnic, peaceful and undisturbed; open wknds and bank hols; free; EH.

LLANYBLODWEL SJ2422
This attractive village, with a charming ancient riverside pub, has an exuberantly decorated church.

LONG MYND SO4294
The partly heather-covered Long Mynd, England's southernmost grouse moor, has great character, with the much smaller but very striking Caer Caradoc facing it across the valley. For walks, it's best reached from Church Stretton. The bracken-and-bilberry-clad massif has a flat plateau-like top, crossed by the Port Way, an ancient track dating from Neolithic times. Its sides are cut into by a series of narrow, remote-feeling valleys, of which Cardingmill Valley (NT) is best known because of its relative accessibility.

LUDLOW SO5174
Beautiful 12th-c town, its original grid plan still obvious today. The best road in is via Wigmore and Leinthall Starkes – lovely views as you approach. Dotted around are 500 listed buildings, with particularly good examples down Broad Street, a charming mixture of Tudor and Georgian architecture. Book well in advance if you're planning to visit during the Festival in the last wk Jun/first wk July. The most famous building is the lavishly carved and timbered Feathers Hotel on the Bull Ring; some parts inside are almost as striking. The Broadgate, the only one of the town's 13th-c gates to have survived, is interesting. Quite a few antique shops; the Unicorn is the nicest pub for lunch. The town is overlooked by the rather volcanic-looking Titterstone Clee to the NE.

Castle Lodge (Castle Sq) Admired by readers, this atmospheric house tucked up right by the castle walls is reputed to have more wood panelling than any other in England, and was once home to Elizabeth I's Master of Requests. Still inhabited today, it was originally built in the 13th c, rebuilt in 1580, and was finally reopened to the public in 1999. The sparsely decorated rooms with lovely doors and fine ceilings are spread over three floors, and privately funded restoration work continues. The house may be familiar to fans of the recent TV adaptations of *Tom Jones* and *Moll Flanders*. Shop, some disabled access; open daily; (01584) 878098; £2.

Ludlow Castle Dating from around 1086, this splendid fortress has lots of original parts inc the Norman keep, and the chapel with its unusual circular nave. The towers and battlements on their wooded crag over the River Teme have wonderful views, and a properly 'castle-ish' feel. Shakespeare plays are performed here during the Jun/July festival, and there are lots of events throughout the year; shop, cl 25 Dec, and wkdys Jan; (01584) 873355; £3.

Ludlow Museum 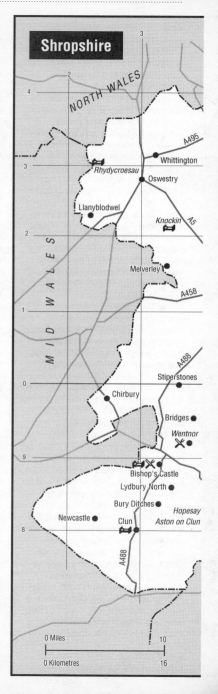 (Castle St) Good local history museum with lots of hands-on activities; cl 1–2pm, all day Sun exc Jun–Aug, and all Nov–Mar; *£1.

Ludlow Parish Church (off King St) Dominating the town almost as much as the castle, with its magnificent pinnacled tower; it's in an attractive tranquil enclave behind the old buttermarket, and has a wonderful sense of timeless peace inside. Magnificently intricate carvings, especially on the ceiling and the choir stalls. In winter it's open 11am–4pm on Sun only, but in summer you can visit all day (exc Sun am); £1 suggested donation.

LYDBURY NORTH SO3485
Walcot Hall Fine Georgian house built for Clive of India; free-standing ballroom, stable yard with matching clock towers, big walled garden, and arboretum with good rhododendrons, azaleas and specimen trees. Mostly disabled access; usually open pm bank hol Mon and the preceding Sun, and by appointment; (020) 7581 2782; £3. You can stay in various wings of the house, and fishing and riding can be arranged.

MARKET DRAYTON SJ6734
The traditional home of gingerbread; the unique local recipe is locked in a bank, but you can still find plenty of toothsome samples in the shops. The Gingerbread Man (Adderley Rd) is a decent family dining pub.

MELVERLEY SJ3316
Craft Centre and Church The stables of the Old Rectory have a craft

Map caption:

Shropshire

NORTH WALES

MID WALES

Rhydycroesau
Whittington
Oswestry
Llanyblodwel
Knockin
Melverley
Stiperstones
Chirbury
Bridges
Wentnor
Bishop's Castle
Lydbury North
Bury Ditches
Newcastle
Clun
Hopesay
Aston on Clun

A495
A5
A458
A488
A488

0 Miles 10
0 Kilometres 16

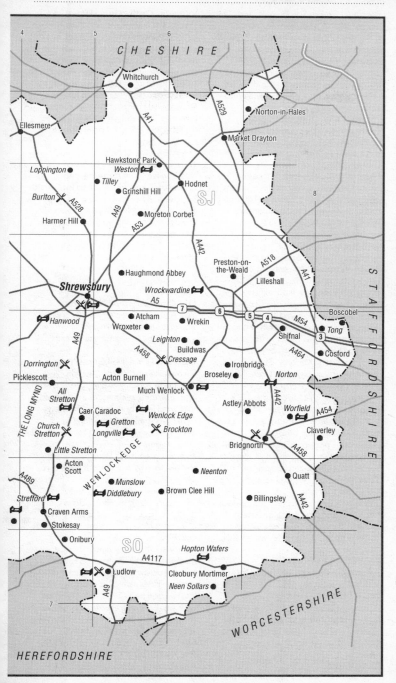

centre (open Fri–Sun Easter–Oct). The beautiful black and white St Peter's Church was rebuilt in 1406 after Owain Glyndwr burned the previous one; it has a fine Jacobean pulpit and chain Bible. The Old Three Pigeons over at Nesscliffe has decent food and all-day coffee, with Kynaston Cave and good cliff walks nearby.

MORETON CORBET SJ5623
Moreton Corbet Castle Destroyed by Parliament in 1644, but you can still see a small 13th-c keep and the substantial ruins of the once-grand Elizabethan house; free. There are some elaborate tombs in the adjacent **church**; the 18th-c Raven at Tilley up towards Wem is a good dining pub.

MUCH WENLOCK SJ6200
Lovely little medieval market town, with lots of timbered and jettied buildings. The Talbot is good for lunch.
Much Wenlock Museum Local history in the Old Market Hall with displays on geology, natural history and local doctor William Penny Brookes, founder of the modern Olympic Games – the town still holds its own version of the games every summer. They plan to revamp their collections over the coming years. Cl 1–2pm , Sun exc Jun–Aug, and all Oct–Mar; free.
Much Wenlock Priory Has its origins in the 7th c, but it's the magnificent remains of the 11th-c building and later additions you can see today. The chapter house has remarkably patterned interlaced arches. Snacks, shop; disabled access; sometimes cl 1–2 pm, and cl Mon and Tues Nov–Mar, 24–26 Dec, 1 Jan; £2.70 (inc audio tour); EH.
Wenlock Edge This very long smooth hill is wooded (and much quarried) along its flanks, but has possibilities for walks. The B4371 along Wenlock Edge has good views.

NEWCASTLE SO2482
An attractive village, with good local walks, and a decent pub.

NORTON-IN-HALES SJ7038
Attractive village with a 13th-c church and a mysterious brading stone on its green. The Hinds Head has good food and attentive service; good nearby walks.

ONIBURY SO4378

Wernlas Collection of Rare Poultry (Green Lane, W of A49) Huge collection of chickens and bantams, along with large fowl, rare breeds of pheasant, unusual European species, plus pigs, donkeys and goats. About 6,000 chicks are hatched each year, so usually some for children to handle or feed. Snacks, shop; cl Mon (exc mid-July–mid-Sept and bank hols), 25 Dec; (01584) 856318; £3. The Hollybush is handy for lunch.

OSWESTRY SJ2929
Cambrian Railway Museum (Oswald Rd) Joint museum with Oswestry Cycle Museum, so lots of old bicycles and a history of cycling (esp good on Dunlop), as well as steam engines and railway memorabilia; one locomotive may be in steam bank hols and last Sun of month. Snacks, shop, some disabled access; cl 25 Dec; (01691) 671749; £1. In the bustling town itself, the Butchers Arms has good value food.

Old Oswestry (just N) Impressive Iron Age hill fort covering 68 acres. The elaborate western defensive entrance and five ramparts remain; free.

Park Hall (Park Hall, Burma Rd) Shropshire's latest countryside attraction, looking at past, present and future farming techniques in restored Victorian farm buildings, with vintage farm machinery inc a working gas engine, and a collection of rare cars and bikes. Animals range from shire horses, and rare breeds of cattle, pigs, sheep and poultry, to more cuddly creatures in the pets' corner; also woodland area with unusual tree carvings and adventure playground, children's driving school (chances to test drive electric vehicles), and a maze cut out of maize (summer only). With milking demonstrations (by hand 12 noon, by machine 1 and 3.30pm), and special events such as horse and tractor-drawn carriage rides as well, it promises at least a good half-day's fun for families with smaller children. Meals, snacks, shop, good disabled access; cl Mon (exc school and bank hols), and all 25 Dec to Feb half-term; (01691) 671123; £3.95.

PICKLESCOTT SO4399
Attractive tucked-away village, with a

delightfully placed ancient pub, and good walking nearby.

PRESTON ON THE WEALD
SJ6814

Hoo Farm Animal Kingdom 🖭 Exceptionally good value traditional working farm, with enough to keep families with very young children happy for a sizeable chunk of the day. All the ingredients you'd expect, from bottle-feeding the lambs and milking demonstrations to a petting corner, egg collecting and nature trails, as well as several more unusual features, such as ostriches, pheasant-rearing, junior quad bikes, an air rifle range and a big walk-in beehive, where a glass window lets you watch the bees at work. Also sheep-racing (summer afternoons at 3pm, not Fri), with a tiny Tote for betting. There's a Christmas tree plantation and a Christmas tree maze, with a story for toddlers to follow as they go round; Father Christmas is here in Dec. Picnic and play areas, and occasional spinning demonstrations. Snacks, shop, disabled access; cl Mon Oct–Nov, and 24 Dec–17 Mar; (01952) 677917; £3.95. The Tayleur Arms over at Longdon upon Tern is a decent family dining pub.

QUATT SO7487

Dudmaston 🖭 (off A442) 17th-c house with the old flower-painting collection of Francis Darby of Coalbrookdale, modern art, and lakeside and woodland walks in the extensive parkland. Snacks, shop, disabled access; open pm Weds–Sun Apr–Sept; (01746) 780866; £3.75 house and garden, £2.75 garden only; NT. There's usually free pedestrian access to the woods all year.
River Severn The Lion at Hampton Loade is a good jumping-off point for riverside walks.

SHIFNAL SJ7407
Much expanded under the influence of nearby Telford, but still with a villagey heart and attractive buildings, inc an interesting church and some worthwhile food pubs such as the Star (Market Pl) and Jaspers (Victoria Rd).

SHREWSBURY SJ4912
The central street layout is still largely medieval, with oddly named streets (Shoplatch, Murivance, Wyle Cop), and plenty of quiet corners up narrow alleys and courtyards among its more modern shops and offices. It's rich in striking architecture, both Tudor timbering and Georgian brick. There's a signposted trail between some of the more interesting buildings. Around The Square numerous buildings reflect the medieval wool fortunes, inc the old market hall; in the adjacent High St, Owens Mansion and Irelands Mansion are fine half-timbered houses worth looking at from outside. Even McDonalds is in a medieval building. The walk up Castle St is worth while, passing the original Grammar School building and the half-timbered Council House Court. Nearby the **church of St Mary** has one of the tallest spires in England. The original town is almost entirely ringed by a loop of the Severn (quiet waterside paths and parks, and you can hire boats along some stretches). Places to mention for food include the Three Fishes (Fish St), Armoury (Victoria Ave), riverside Boat House (New St/Quarry Park), Coach & Horses (Swan Hill/Cross Hill; brews its own beer), cheery Dun Cow Pie Shop (Abbey Foregate), Cromwells (Dogpole) and Shrewsbury (Old Welsh Bridge; food all day).

Mythstories See separate family panel on p.477.

Rowley's House Museum (Barker St) Impressive timber-framed building with social and natural history, and some interesting Roman remains. Shop, disabled access to ground floor only; cl Sun Oct–Easter, all Mons (excl bank hols), and mid-Dec to beginning Jan (01743) 361196; free.

Scenic drive Heading SW from Shrewsbury, the old coach road through Longden and Pulverbatch is an attractive drive – great views the further you go.

Shrewsbury Castle 12th-c, guarding the narrow neck of land between the river's loop. It was refurbished by Thomas Telford in 1790, though still has parts of the earlier building; usually cl Mon and varying times in winter. The **Shropshire Regimental Museum**, set in attractive grounds, has military displays from the American War of Independence to the present day. Shop, some disabled access; cl Mon Apr–Sept,

Sun–Tues Oct–Mar, plus mid-Dec–Jan;
(01743) 358516; £2.

Shrewsbury Quest (Abbey Foregate)
Delightful reconstruction of medieval
monastic life, loosely based around the
Brother Cadfael books by Ellis Peters
(set in medieval Shrewsbury). You can
create your own decorated manuscript
or try your hand at ancient games and
crafts. The carefully researched period
herb garden is a draw in its own right –
quite a few poisonous plants despite the
lovely smell. Meals and snacks (some
inspired by medieval recipes), shop,
disabled access; cl 25–26 Dec, 1 Jan;
(01743) 243324; £4.50. Just opposite,
the impressive 14th-c **abbey** includes a
statue of Edward III, and a memorial to
Wilfrid Owen.

St Julian's Craft Centre (St
Alkmund's Sq) Among other interesting
shops in this part of town is an excellent
craft centre in a 12th-c Julian's church,
with several cheery workshops, a
bustling craft fair every Sat, and a good
restaurant (esp useful for vegetarians).
Some disabled access; cl Sun and bank
hols; (01743) 353516; free. The Old
Post Office nearby (Milk St) does
decent pub lunches.

STIPERSTONES SO3799
The rather eery Stiperstones are
outcrops of harder quartzy rock leaving
strange-shaped boulders, tors and
crests on the skyline – and strange tales
among the people living nearby. The
ridge is crowned by dramatic rocks and
has a splendid view; a short walk from a
nearby car park (you can make an
interesting 8½-mile circuit with a stop
at the More Arms at Shelve), or take
the longish walk up from the former
lead-mining village of Snailbeach.

STOKESAY SO4381
Stokesay Castle (off A49) One of the
finest examples of a medieval manor
house in existence, 13th-c, in a notably
charming setting. The hall with its
cruck-framed roof and early English
windows is just as it was 700 years ago,
and there's a timbered Tudor
gatehouse. Good views from the top of
the tower, and excellent Walkman
tour. Summer snacks, shop; Nov–Mar
cl 1–2pm and all day Mon and Tues, plus
24–26 Dec and 1 Jan; (01588) 672544;
£3.50. The hotel of the same name in

Craven Arms has decent food.

WHITCHURCH SJ5440
Rocking Horse Workshop (Cottage
Farm, B5476 S) Here you can watch the
production and restoration of
traditional rocking horses; cl Sun, 25
Dec; (01948) 666777; free. In town,
there's a lively heritage centre on St
Mary's St (cl Sun; free), and the Horse &
Jockey (Church St) has good value food.

WHITTINGTON SJ3131
(off A5) Handsome remains of 13th-c
Whittington Castle, with good value
food at the Olde Boot alongside.

WREKIN SJ6108
(just W of Telford – and towering
boldly over it) The Wrekin is no
Everest (an easily attained 407 metres,
1,334 ft), but because it's so isolated on
the edge of the Shropshire uplands it
offers walkers a huge panorama,
spanning places over 100 miles apart;
just below, the Huntsman in Little
Wenlock is handy for refreshment.

WROXETER SJ5608
Roman Vineyard Friendly little place
producing several wines; also lavender
farm, rare breeds, and some interesting
glacial stones – not to mention a Roman
wall. Teas, shop (with various lavender-
based products), disabled access;
usually open daily (exc 25 Dec) but
there's not much to see in the winter;
(01743) 761888; free.

Wroxeter Roman City One of the
country's most important Roman sites,
though the majority of the remains are
buried under fields. There's a well
preserved colonnade and municipal
bath, with useful explanatory boards,
and the museum has a good range of
finds from the town (then Britain's
fourth biggest) and the earlier fortress.
Snacks, shop; some disabled access; cl
Mon and Tues Nov–Mar, 24–26 Dec, 1
Jan; (01743) 761330; £3.20; EH. The
Horseshoes at Uckington is a decent
family dining pub.

Other attractive villages, with
decent pubs, include Aston on Clun
SO3982, Leighton SJ6105, Little
Stretton SO4392, Loppington SJ4729,
Munslow SO5287, Neen Sollars
SO6672, Neenton SO6488, Tilley
SJ5027, Tong SJ7907, Wentnor
SO3893 and Worfield SO7696.
Local Tourist Information Centres have

details of **imaginative trails** around the region, centring on the work of Thomas Telford, haunted villages, the novels of Ellis Peters, and sites connected with King Arthur (recent theories suggest the mythical king was a 5th-c warlord ruling from a post-Roman city here – possibly Wroxeter). They also have balloon trip details.

Where to eat

BISHOP'S CASTLE SO3288 **Three Tuns** *Salop St (01588) 638797* Bustling lively atmosphere in simply furnished beamed bar rooms, own-brewed beer from handsome Victorian brewhouse, newspapers to read, a good mix of customers, and tasty home-made bar food. £17.50|**£6.75**

BRIDGNORTH SO7193 **Bear** *24 Northgate (01746) 763250* Attractive cream-painted former coaching inn with two unpretentious bars, some interesting local memorabilia, and a comfortable and friendly bustle; well kept real ales, a good choice of wines by the glass, and enjoyable often interesting bar food; Thursday evening meals are sophisticated and very popular – best to book then; French windows to a small sheltered lawn with picnic-sets; bdrms; disabled access. £19.30|**£6.50**

BROCKTON SO5793 **Feathers** *(01746) 785202* Stylish stone dining pub with charming atmospheric beamed rooms (two are no smoking), a restaurant feel, conservatory, very good interesting food using fresh seasonal produce, efficient, friendly waitress service, and well kept real ales; cl Mon, cl Tues–Fri am. £25

BURLTON SJ4526 **Burlton Inn** *(01939) 270284* Attractively restored pub with three cottagey connecting rooms, fresh flowers, magazines to read, winter open fires, very attractively presented interesting food from a seasonal menu, well kept real ales, and neatly uniformed helpful staff; cl 25 Dec; disabled access. £22|**£6.95**

CHURCH STRETTON SO4593 **Acorn Wholefood** *26 Sandford Ave (01694) 722495* Simple, unpretentious family-run restaurant with friendly service in several no smoking rooms, good filling and daily-changing food (mostly vegetarian), delicious puddings and soups, and cream teas with a choice of 25 teas; cl Tues, Weds (but open Weds during school hols), 2 wks Feb. 2 wks Nov/Dec. £10|**£2.90**

CRESSAGE SJ5605 **Cholmondeley Riverside** *Cound (01952) 510900* Neatly converted 17th-c inn overlooking an exceptionally pretty stretch of the River Severn; church pews, cushioned settles and oak tables in civilised roomy bar, wicker chairs in conservatory with more out on terrace, good imaginative food, well kept beers, a fine choice of wines, and a relaxed friendly atmosphere; coarse fishing; bdrms. £20|**£6.95**

DORRINGTON SJ4702 **Country Friends** *(01743) 718707* Cosy half-timbered no smoking restaurant with consistently enjoyable interesting food inc lovely puddings and British cheeses with home-made bread; super breakfasts; bdrms; cl Sun, Mon, two wks mid-July. £37|**£8.60**

LUDLOW SO5175 **Merchant House** *Lower Corve St (01584) 875438* Two simply furnished rooms in friendly and relaxed Jacobean house with exceptionally good food (wonderful fish and fine game) from set 3-course menu, good value interesting wines, and competent service; cl Sun, Mon, 1 wk Christmas, 1 wk spring; no children. £40

LUDLOW SO5174 **Olive Branch** *2/4 Old St (01584) 874314* Cheery wholefood restaurant in 17th-c former inn with a changing range of tasty lunchtime meals and snacks inc often inventive vegetarian meals, and teas with home-made cakes and scones; cl pm. £16|**£5**

SHREWSBURY SJ4912 **Armoury** *Victoria Quay, Victoria Ave (01743) 340525* Smartly converted warehouse with big arched windows overlooking river, lots of old prints and documents, cabinets with shells and explosives, corks and bottle openers, a good range of well kept real ales, 25 wines by the glass, 70 malt whiskies, and interesting bistro-style food; cl 25 Dec, 1 Jan; no children after 9pm. £22|**£5.95**

SHREWSBURY SJ4912 **Poppy's Restaurant and Tea Rooms** *8 Milk St (01743) 232307* Lovely 17th-c building with really fine timbers in upstairs room, plenty of space for shoppers on ground floor and in courtyard, a little room for smokers, enjoyable lunches with interesting daily-changing salad garnish, and popular morning coffee and afternoon tea; cl Sun; good disabled access. **£12|£4.50**
WENTNOR SO3892 **Crown** *(01588) 650613* 16th-c inn in quiet village with beams, standing timbers, good log fire, collection of china and glass, and mix of tables set for eating in the main area; snug end with comfortable sofas, a good choice of enjoyable food, and a cosy beamed no smoking restaurant; well kept real ales, decent wines, helpful friendly staff, and fine views of the Long Mynd from seats on the neat back lawn; children must be well behaved. **£25|£6**

Special thanks to Mark Holman, Mrs Edna M Jones, Michael and Jenny Back

SOMERSET

Lots for families, with an excellent mix of attractions from first-class city museums to country farms and wildlife centres; also beautiful Bath, charming towns and villages, traditional seaside resorts and some interesting scenery; good value

Bold new developments in Bath and Bristol – the places here with most to offer families – promise to add to their manifold charms. Bristol, the more full-blooded of the two, is packed with interesting places to visit inc the truly modern @Bristol complex (the area's Family Attraction of the Year), the outstanding zoo, and the medley of maritime and industrial heritage in among the docks (enjoyable historic boat trips from here, too). Elegant Bath is easier on the eye, with a profusion of good museums from the fascinating depiction of American life at Claverton to the intriguing miniature sculpture at the Impossible Microworld Museum, new to the *Guide* this year. An exciting new spa development alongside the celebrated ancient baths opens in 2002. Both cities do particularly well for community-based attractions; Create (Bristol) and Envolve (Bath) reflect the growing trend for urban eco-tourism, while the determined campaigning of local people led to the transformation of a wasteland into St Wegburgh's City Farm, half an hour's walk from Bristol's centre. It's a shame Bristol's tourist information service can't match the friendly efficiency of its Bath counterpart.

Other places that serve families well here include a mixture of wildlife attractions such as the new Horse World at Whitchurch (not solely for horse-lovers, with plenty to fill a good chunk of a day), friendly Secret World (a must for badger fans), and Washford's highly enjoyable Tropiquaria (all sorts of exotic animals, and puppet shows as well). The country parks at Keynsham (new play area and lots of animals) and Monksilver are good for letting off steam, Yeovilton is home to one of Britain's more satisfying aviation museums, and the spectacular caves and gorges at Wookey Hole and Cheddar make for unusual days out (with lots to interest children).

Elsewhere there are some fine gardens (the ones at Castle Cary, Cannington College and East Lambrook are particularly memorable), decent local museums at Glastonbury and Taunton, cheerful vineyards and cider mills, steam railways (inc the friendly newcomer at Yenston), the charming miniature city of Wells, and some pleasant walks among the brooding Mendips. On the coast, Minehead is a pleasant traditional resort, and Weston-super-Mare and Clevedon have some appeal.

Over in the W the countryside feels very secluded and self-contained, with each small valley of the Quantocks seeming a private world, and the Blackdown Hills charmingly untouristy, too – classic quiet English countryside with some lovely villages, some with delightfully eccentric names (Exmoor is discussed separately, in the Devon chapter). The Somerset Levels are an interesting contrast – vivid green marshy pastures, rewarding for wildlife and for traditional crafts such as basket-making. Towards the E richer more rolling farmland with small valleys and wooded hillsides offers some gentle country drives.

The countryside is dotted with landmark church towers, pinnacled, turreted and gargoyled. Many churches, particularly in the W, have intriguingly carved 15th- and 16th-c bench ends, also fine oak wagon roofs, brass candelabras and carved screens. In the hillier parts, buildings are generally of stone, varying in colour and character from the Cotswold style of the NE, through the pale limestones of the Mendips and the golden warmth of south Somerset's Ham stone, to the rugged and stolid greys of the hamlets tucked into the green folds of the Quantocks.

Where to stay

BARWICK ST5613 **Little Barwick House** *Barwick, Yeovil, Somerset BA22 9TD* (01935) 423902 **£93**, plus special breaks; 6 rms. Carefully run listed Georgian dower house in 3½ acres of grounds; a lovely relaxed atmosphere, log fire in cosy lounge, excellent food using local produce, a thoughtful wine list, super breakfasts, nice afternoon tea with crumpets, and particularly good service; 2m S of Yeovil; cl Christmas and New Year; dogs by arrangement

BATH ST7464 **Badminton Villa** *10 Upper Oldfield Park, Bath BA2 3JZ* (01225) 426347 **£62***, plus special breaks; 5 rms. Big no smoking Victorian house with marvellous city views, comfortable lounge, good breakfasts, and helpful friendly owners; cl 23 Dec–2 Jan; children over 8

BATH ST7465 **Brocks** *32 Brock St, Bath BA1 2LN* (01225) 338374 **£63***, plus special breaks; 6 rms. Georgian house with fine breakfasts in big dining room, lounge area, helpful staff, and good central position; cl Christmas and New Year

BATH ST7463 **Haydon House** *9 Bloomfield Park, Bath BA2 2BY* (01225) 427351 **£85**, plus special breaks; 5 good rms with sherry and home-made shortbread. Deceptively unassuming-looking Edwardian house with comfortable, elegant and restful rooms, antiques, excellent breakfasts (no evening meals), warmly welcoming owners, and pretty garden; no smoking; children by arrangement

BATH ST7565 **Old Boathouse** *Bath Boating Station, Forester Rd, Bath BA2 6QE* (01225) 466407 **£55**; 4 rms. Edwardian boating station with black and white timbered verandah overlooking river, free launch to Bath centre, punting and rowing boats for hire, sitting room with river views, and separate restaurant; children in cottage only; partial disabled access

BATH ST7464 **Paradise House** *86–88 Holloway, Bath BA2 4PX* (01225) 317723 **£65***, plus special breaks; 11 rms (room 5 has a super view). Classically elegant early 18th-c hotel, lovingly restored, with marvellous views over the city; pretty breakfast room, restful drawing room, log fire, and spacious walled gardens; peaceful, though only 7 mins' walk to centre; cl Christmas

BATH ST7465 **Queensberry** *Russel St, Bath BA1 2QF* (01225) 447928 **£155**, plus special breaks; 29 lovely rms. Three beautifully decorated Georgian town houses in quiet residential street, with comfortable, restful drawing room, open fire, attractive modern restaurant (Olive Tree, see **Where to eat**) and professional service; cl Christmas and New Year

BATH ST7465 **Royal Crescent Hotel** *16 Royal Crescent, Bath BA1 2LS* (01225) 739955 **£230**; 45 luxurious rms. Elegant Georgian hotel in glorious curved terrace, with comfortable antiques-filled drawing rooms, open fires and lovely flowers; imaginative modern cooking in Pimpernel Restaurant and less formal Brasserie Bar, and impeccable service; plunge pool and croquet in quiet garden; they are kind to children; disabled access

BATH ST7565 **Villa Magdala** *Henrietta Rd, Bath BA2 6LX (01225) 466329* **£80***, plus winter breaks; 18 comfortable rms. Overlooking Henrietta Park, this elegant Victorian house is close to the centre and has good breakfasts in attractive dining room, a spacious comfortable lounge, and friendly helpful staff; children over 7

BEERCROCOMBE ST3020 **Frog Street Farm** *Hatch Beauchamp, Taunton, Somerset TA3 6AF (01823) 480430* **£50**, plus special breaks; 3 rms. Peaceful 15th-c listed farmhouse deep in the countryside on a big working farm; beams, fine Jacobean panelling, inglenook fireplaces, a warmly friendly owner, delicious food (much produce from the farm, local game and fish; bring your own wine), and good breakfasts; cl Nov–Mar; children by arrangement

CANNINGTON ST2538 **Blackmore Farm** *Blackmore Lane, Cannington, Bridgwater, Somerset TA5 2NE (01278) 653442* **£42***; 4 rms. Grade I listed manor house dating from 15th c with garderobes, beams and stone archways, good breakfasts around a huge table in the Great Hall, and log fire in comfortable sitting room; no evening meals; good disabled access

HATCH BEAUCHAMP ST3020 **Farthings** *Hatch Beauchamp, Taunton, Somerset TA3 6SG (01823) 480664* **£87**, plus special breaks; 10 rms (inc a cottage suite) with thoughtful extras. Charming little Georgian house in three acres of gardens, with open fires in quiet lounge and convivial bar, and good varied food using fresh local produce; can arrange golf and other activities

HINTON CHARTERHOUSE ST7759 **Homewood Park** *Hinton Charterhouse, Bath BA3 6BB (01225) 723731* **£139**; 19 lovely rms. Charming Victorian hotel on the edge of Hinton Priory and in ten acres of gardens and woodlands; flowers, oil paintings and fine furniture in graceful relaxing day rooms, and an elegant restaurant with very good imaginative food (honey from their own bees – you can help them collect it); tennis, croquet; disabled access

HOLFORD ST1541 **Combe House** *Holford, Bridgwater, Somerset TA5 1RZ (01278) 741382* **£68**, plus special breaks; 16 rms. Warmly friendly former tannery (still has waterwheel) in a pretty spot, with comfortable rooms, log fires, good home-made food, and a relaxed atmosphere; heated indoor swimming pool and tennis court; cl Jan; partial disabled access

HOLFORD ST1541 **Quantock House** *Holford, Bridgwater, Somerset TA5 1RY (01278) 741439* **£42***; 3 rms. Thatched 17th-c house with a large cottagey garden, a big inglenook fireplace in residents' lounge, nice breakfasts, and a friendly welcome; well behaved pets allowed; cl 25 Dec; disabled access

HUNSTRETE ST6461 **Hunstrete House** *Hunstrete, Pensford, Bristol BS39 4NS (01761) 490490* **£170**, plus special breaks; 23 individually decorated rms. Classically handsome, mainly 18th-c country-house hotel on the edge of the Mendips in 92 acres inc lovely walled garden and deer park; comfortable and elegantly furnished day rooms with antiques, paintings, log fires, fresh garden flowers, a tranquil atmosphere, excellent service, and very good food using home-grown produce when possible; croquet lawn, heated swimming pool, all-weather tennis court, and nearby riding; limited disabled access

LANGPORT ST4226 **White House** *Whatley Lane, Langport, Somerset TA10 9QZ (01458) 250892* **£44**; 2 rooms (one with lovely view). Attractive house with marvellous views over the Somerset Levels, and charming owners; drawing room with open fire in hamstone fireplace, fine rugs on the polished wooden floor, and lots of pictures and antiques, snug study with TV, and good full breakfasts with home-made marmalade taken in dining room with French windows leading to conservatory

LOWER VELLOW ST0938 **Curdon Mill** *Lower Vellow, Williton, Somerset TA4 4LS (01984) 56522* **£60**, plus special breaks; 8 smallish but pretty and individually furnished rms. Charming, beautifully furnished, no smoking hotel between the Quantocks and Brendon Hills with 200 acres of working farm to wander over, and a lovely garden; very good evening meals in antiques-filled dining room, substantial breakfasts, and friendly staff (and other guests); the waterwheel and mill shaft have been carefully preserved and still work; outdoor heated swimming pool; civil marriage licence; children over 8

LUXBOROUGH SS9738 **Royal Oak** *Luxborough, Watchet, Somerset TA23 0SH* (01984) 640319 **£65***; 12 simple rms, 11 with own bthrm. Unspoilt and interesting old pub in idyllic spot, with a chatty and friendly beamed bar, log fire, varied real ales, good food in bar and restaurant (plenty of game), and well liked breakfasts; disabled access

MIDDLECOMBE SS9545 **Periton Park** *Middlecombe, Minehead, Somerset TA24 8SW* (01643) 706885 **£99**, plus special breaks; 8 rms (3 no smoking) with views of surrounding countryside. Fine Exmoor-edge Victorian country house with books, log fire, and relaxed atmosphere in comfortable lounge, friendly service, and good food in panelled no smoking dining room; pleasant walks nearby, and they can arrange shooting, fishing or riding at adjacent riding centre; dogs in one rm only; cl Jan; children over 12; disabled access

NORTH PERROTT ST4709 **Manor Arms** *Middle St, North Perrott, Crewkerne, Somerset TA18 7SG* (01460) 72901 **£48***, plus special breaks; 9 rms in restored coach house inc a fine panelled and beamed one. Comfortable and attractive 16th-c inn with friendly helpful licensees, beams, exposed stone, and inglenook fireplace, and good home-made food in small restaurant and bar; garden with play area, and free coarse fishing; free entry to some South Somerset gardens; disabled access

NORTH WOOTTON ST5641 **Riverside Grange** *Tanyard Lane, North Wootton, Wells, Somerset BA4 4AE* (01749) 890761 **£39**; 2 rms. Quietly set converted tannery on river edge and overlooking a cider orchard; charming, welcoming owner and enjoyable breakfasts (places in nearby village for evening meals); no smoking

POLSHAM ST5142 **Southway Farm** *Polsham, Wells, Somerset BA5 1RW* (01749) 673396 **£46***; 3 rms. Friendly Georgian farmhouse on a working farm between Wells and Glastonbury, open fire in comfortable sitting room, attractive dining room, good breakfasts, and pretty garden; cl Nov–Feb

ROADWATER ST0337 **Briar Cottage** *The Old Mineral Line, Roadwater, Watchet, Somerset TA23 0RJ* (01984) 640020 **£40**; 2 rms with fine views. Quietly set cottage, once two railway workers' dwellings, in Exmoor National Park, with a fast-flowing brown trout stream in the grounds, and outdoor heated swimming pool; woodburner in big lounge, small reading lounge, and good breakfast in farmhouse-style kitchen; self-catering also; super walks

ROADWATER ST0337 **Wood Advent Farm** *Roadwater, Watchet, Somerset TA23 0RR* (01984) 640920 **£50**; 4 rms. Relaxed, spacious farmhouse on 340 acres of working farm within Exmoor National Park, great walks; log fire in comfortable lounge, good country cooking using their own produce in attractive dining room with woodburner, grass tennis court, outdoor heated swimming pool, and fishing, clay pigeon and pheasant shooting; children over 10

SOMERTON ST4828 **Lynch Country House** *4 Behind Berry, Somerton, Somerset TA11 7PD* (01458) 272316 **£49**; 5 prettily decorated rms, plus 2 extra in summer cottage. Carefully restored and homely Georgian house, with books in comfortable lounge, and good breakfasts (no evening meals) in airy room overlooking tranquil grounds and lake with black swans and exotic ducks; also self-catering cottages; cl Christmas and New Year

STANTON WICK ST6162 **Carpenters Arms** *Stanton Wick, Pensford, Bristol BS39 4BX* (01761) 490202 **£80**; 12 rms. Warm and attractively furnished tile-roofed inn, converted from a row of miners' cottages; big log fire, woodburner, wide choice of good food inc generous breakfasts, well kept beers, and friendly efficient staff

STOGUMBER ST1037 **Hall Farm** *Station Rd, Stogumber, Taunton, Somerset TA4 3TQ* (01984) 656321 **£37**; 6 rms. Old-fashioned B&B with optional evening meals (bring your own wine) – wonderfully unpretentious, with warmly friendly staff; cl Christmas and New Year; well behaved dogs welcome; disabled access

STOKE ST GREGORY ST3527 **Rose & Crown** *Woodhill, Stoke St Gregory,*

Taunton, Somerset TA3 6EW (01823) 490296 **£50***; 6 rms, some with own bthrm and 2 in annexe. Very friendly 17th-c cottagey inn with a cosy and pleasantly romanticised stable theme, generous helpings of particularly good value food in no smoking dining room, excellent breakfasts, a decent wine list, and efficient service from hard-working family in charge; self-catering nearby; disabled access

STON EASTON ST6254 **Ston Easton Park** *Ston Easton, Bath BA3 4DF (01761) 241631* **£195**; plus special breaks; 21 really lovely rms. Majestic Palladian mansion of Bath stone with beautifully landscaped 18th-c gardens and 26 acres of parkland; elegant day rooms with antiques and flowers, an attractive no smoking restaurant with good food (much grown in the kitchen garden), fine afternoon teas, library and billiard room, and extremely helpful, friendly and unstuffy service; no dogs in rooms (they have kennels), babies and children over 7 welcome by prior arrangement

TAUNTON ST2224 **Castle** *Castle Green, Taunton, Somerset TA1 1NF (01823) 272671* **£150***, plus special breaks; 44 lovely rms. Appealingly modernised partly Norman castle (its W front almost smothered in wisteria), with fine old oak furniture, tapestries and paintings in comfortably elegant lounges, really excellent modern English cooking, good breakfasts, a range of good value wines from a thoughtful list, and efficient friendly service; pretty garden; dogs by arrangement; disabled access

WELLS ST5445 **Infield House** *36 Portway, Wells, Somerset BA5 2BN (01749) 670989* **£49**, plus special breaks; 3 comfortable rms (best view from back one). Carefully restored no smoking Victorian town house with period furnishings and family portraits, elegant lounge (with lots of local guidebooks), good breakfasts in dining room with Adam-style fireplace, evening meals by arrangement, and friendly personal service; cl 1 wk early Dec; children over 12; well behaved pets by arrangement

WOOKEY HOLE ST5347 **Glencot House** *Glencot Lane, Wookey Hole, Wells, Somerset BA5 1BH (01749) 677160* **£86**; 13 rms, many with four-posters or half testers. In 18 acres of gardens and parkland (and with its own cricket pitch), this Jacobean-style Victorian mansion has some fine panelling, carved ceilings, antiques and flowers in the public rooms and hallways, a relaxed friendly atmosphere, and good food in the restaurant; fishing, table tennis, snooker, and small indoor jet stream pool; lots to do nearby; cl first wk Jan; they are kind to children

---

We welcome reports from readers

This *Guide* depends on readers' reports. Do help us if you can – in return, we offer a discount on the next edition to people who've helped us with reports for it. Tell us what you think about places already in it, and anything extra you think we should say about them. And send us your ideas for inclusion in the next edition: places to visit, eat at or stay in, attractive drives or walks, maybe even unusual interesting shops you know of. Use the card in the middle, the report forms at the end, or just write – no stamp needed: *The Good Britain Guide*, FREEPOST TN1569, Wadhurst, E Sussex TN5 7BR.

To see and do

Somerset Family Attraction of the Year

BRISTOL ST6173 **@Bristol** (Harbourside) An astonishing £97 million has been spent on this huge development, and it shows: the displays in the science section are among the most elaborate we've come across. If you want to see everything it's by no means a cheap place to visit, but it easily fills a whole day, and it's hard to imagine many people leave disappointed. Linked by appealingly landscaped squares and avenues, dotted with trees, sculptures, shops and restaurants, there are three main sections: Explore, the very firmly 21st-c science centre, Wildscreen, which looks at life on earth, and a huge IMAX theatre, with a screen four storeys high. All are worth a look, but Explore is the one to head for if you've only limited time: full of interactive and hands-on features, it lets you star in your own TV show, play virtual volleyball, or get an idea of how it feels to be in the eye of a tornado. The latest technology gives a new spin to time-honoured activities like generating electricity or making things fly, and there are some bits you'll never have seen before – the virtual sperm journey for example, or the unique walk-in womb (as they say, 'the only one in the world that takes six people and is wheelchair accessible'). Especially good is the Imaginarium, a next-generation planetarium that looks like a metal sphere and takes you into a 3-D virtual universe; an extra £2 for a 25-min show (though see price info below), this bit is sponsored by a mobile phone company, so there's some focus on the latest in communications. There's an area for under-6s, as well as temporary exhibitions and extra activities such as workshops on how chocolate is made. Meanwhile the Wildscreen area is a well put together walk-through journey around evolution, particularly strong on insects, with lots of videos and multimedia bits. Best of all is the re-created tropical rain forest, with free flying birds and butterflies. Do arrive early if you want to see it all – though the all-inclusive All-Star ticket does allow you to spread it over two days. Meals, snacks, shop, disabled access; cl 25 Dec; (0117) 915 5000; admission to any one of the three attractions is £6.50 (£4.50 children 3–15), with a family ticket (two adults and two children) at £19. For two attractions it's £11 (£8 children), or £32 for a family, and the All-Star ticket, which takes in one single visit to everything (inc Imaginarium) is £15.50 (£11 children) or £50 for families. If all you want is the IMAX, you can save by getting a two-film ticket.

AXBRIDGE ST4354
Pleasant small town with an appealing largely medieval square and narrow winding High St, unusual in this part of the world for its jettied timber-framed buildings. The rambling old Lamb on the corner of the tranquil market square is good for lunch.

BARRINGTON ST3918
Barrington Court 🖻 In the grounds of a splendid 16th-c house, a magnificent series of gardens influenced by Gertrude Jekyll, inc rose garden, and traditional walled kitchen garden, the produce from which is on sale in the shop. The house shows off the reproduction furniture of Stuart Interiors. Meals, snacks, plant centre,

disabled access to garden and ground floor; open Apr–Oct exc Fri; (01460) 241938; £4.20; NT. The village itself is attractive, and the Royal Oak does good lunches.

BATH ST7564
For many this is England's most rewarding old town, though its throngs of summer visitors tend to mask its charms a bit then. Many places enjoyably recall the days of Beau Nash and the building of Bath as a fashionable resort; other draws go back to the Roman Baths, and come right up to date with the city's interesting and unusual shops. If ambitious plans come off, taking the spa waters won't just be something out of Jane Austen: the new

Bath spa complex (see below) should open to the public in 2002. In the meantime our favourite places to visit are the Roman Baths, Museum of Costume at the Assembly Rooms (these attractions offer a good value joint ticket), Pump Room, Building of Bath Museum, Industrial Heritage Centre, No 1 Royal Crescent, and Bath Abbey. The American Museum on the edge of the city at Claverton is very special. Parts not to be missed include the great showpieces of 18th-c town planning, Queen Sq, The Circus and the Royal Crescent; the quieter Abbey Green and cobbled Abbey St and Queen St; and the great Pulteney Bridge (there's a fine view of it from the bridge at the end of North Parade, or the riverside Parade Gardens, where brass bands play in summer). The narrow little lanes between the main streets can be fascinating. In summer lots of informal eating places have tables outside. Good pubs with decent food include the Old Green Tree (Green St) and Richmond Arms (Richmond Pl). Good **street markets** are in Bartlett St (daily), junk to top-drawer antiques, often buzzing with dealers from elsewhere, and Walcot St (Sat am) flea market, good bargains. On the first and third Sat of the month there is a farmers' market with lots of fresh fruit and vegetables adjacent to Green Park Station. The beautifully restored historic **Theatre Royal** presents more pre-West End productions than anywhere else in the country. Don't try to drive around the city: Bath's streets were laid out for travel by sedan chair, not car, and a tortuous one-way system seems designed to deter drivers rather than to make traffic flow more easily. Inadvertently park your car in the wrong place and it may be quickly towed away, despite a lack of proper warnings. Walking around Bath is anyway a delight; there are flat parts, though to make the most of it you have to be prepared to slog up some of the steeper streets. Readers particularly enjoy the somewhat irreverent **Bizarre Bath** walking tours that leave the Huntsman Inn on North Parade Passage at 8pm daily, Apr–Sept (£4.50) – more street theatre than a typical

tour. The rush of a day trip doesn't do justice to the host of things worth seeing; it is best to stay, preferably out of season. On summer days crowds of trippers and school parties tend to spoil the best-known parts, and if you want to visit during Bath's early summer Festival, book accommodation well ahead.

Balloon trips Hot-air balloons give a good view of the city as it's shown in the great architectural drawings. They take off, subject to weather, from the Royal Victoria Park; (01225) 466888; from £125.

Bath Abbey & Abbey Heritage Vaults Particularly renowned for its fan vaulting, the current building is the third great church to be built on this site, begun in 1499. The Elizabethans called it the Lantern of the West because of its profusion of stained glass. Most impressive is the great E window, depicting 56 scenes from the life of Christ. On one side of this is a finely carved memorial to Bartholomew Barnes (1608), and on the other the beautiful medieval carving of the Prior Birde chantry. Restoration work has been returning the interior's gradually blackened Bath stone to its more appealing honey colour. Shop, disabled access; cl Good Fri, 24–26 Dec, 1 Jan, and during private services; £2 suggested donation. A very good exhibition on the abbey's history is in the adjacent carefully restored 18th-c vaults. Disabled access; cl Sun; (01225) 422462; £2. In summer there may be walking tours from the abbey churchyard (usually around 10.30am and 2pm); free.

Bath Postal Museum 🖼 (Broad St) First-class exploration of the development of the postal system since 16th c, inc a full-scale replica Victorian post office; it was from here that the world's first postage stamp was sent in 1840. Snacks, shop, disabled access to ground floor only; cl Sun am; (01225) 460333; £2.90.

Bath Spa Project If all goes well, people will be bathing in the city's ancient natural spa waters in 2002 (a luxury denied since 1978 when the baths were closed down due to doubts over the purity of the source). Just 100 metres from the famous Roman Baths (see below), this stunning Millennium Commission project will comprise one purpose-built and two restored bath houses, with administrative facilities housed in other gentrified buildings. The focal point will be the new Spa complex, designed by the architect of Waterloo's Eurostar terminal and crafted from Bath stone and glass. The building, crowned with a roof-top pool and terrace, is to be styled as a 'centre for well-being', a pleasure-seeker's paradise, replete with whirlpool, steam room, cold plunge, massage rooms, and other restorative perks; also restaurant, gym and visitor centre. When complete, the centre will open daily, and bathing prices will start from around £17; best to phone for details; (01225) 477710.

Beckford's Tower (Lansdown Rd) Italianate tower with fine views from the top, and a little museum commemorating the well travelled collector William Beckford. Shop; open wknds Easter–Oct (01225) 460705.

Boating Cruises leave Pulteney Bridge landing stage at a quarter to and quarter past the hour (not Oct–Easter). Boats and punts can be hired in summer from the Boating Station on the River Avon, Forester Rd, Bathwick: (01225) 466407. The revivified **Kennet & Avon Canal** is one of Bath's pleasures, with quiet towpath walks along to Bathampton (where the George I is popular for lunch); it has quite a few colourful narrowboats in summer. You can cycle right into the centre along the Avon Cycleway, cycle tracks converted from the old Bath and Bristol railway.

Book Museum 🔳 (Manvers St) First and early editions of authors who lived or worked in Bath, especially Jane Austen and Charles Dickens; there's a reconstruction of Dickens's study at Gads Hill on the other side of England. A good chunk of the exhibition is devoted to the history and art of bookbinding, and adjoining this is the shop of **George Bayntun**, who has been binding and selling antiquarian books for over 50 years. Cl 1–2pm, Sat pm, all day Sun and bank hols; (01225) 466000; bookshop customers free, others *£2.

Building of Bath Museum (The Vineyard, Paragon) Fascinating displays on how John Wood and others transformed the town and its architecture, with full-scale reconstructions, original tools, and a fabulous model of the entire city, lighting up when you press the buttons. Shop, disabled access but no facilities – and those who have difficulty walking might notice the floor's slight unevenness; cl Mon (exc bank hols), and Dec–mid-Feb; (01225) 333895; £3.50.

Envolve (Green Park Rd) Visitor centre for the exemplary charity which promotes environmental awareness among the local community. Disabled access; cl Sat pm, all Sun, Mon and bank hols, and over Christmas; (01225) 787910; free.

Georgian Garden (Gravel Walk) Nr Queen Square, another striking reminder of the period, this re-creates the original layout and the kind of plants that would have been used in a small town garden in the 1760s. Given the high ratio of walking-space to plants the emphasis back then was clearly on strolling and chatting rather than horticulture itself. Cl wknds and bank hols, and all Nov–Apr; free.

William Herschel Museum 🔳 (New King St) Interesting Georgian home and workplace of William Herschel, the astronomer (and composer), with period rooms, models of his telescopes, and other scientific equipment. He discovered the planet Uranus from the back garden. Book shop; cl am, and wkdys Nov–Mar; (01225) 311342; *£2.50.

Holburne Museum of Art 🔳 (Gt Pulteney St) Fine old building displaying the decorative and fine-art collection of Sir Thomas William Holburne (1793–1874), inc Old Master paintings, portrait miniatures and Italian bronzes. Meals, snacks, shop, disabled access; cl Sun am, Mon Nov–Easter, and all mid-Dec–mid-Feb; (01225) 466669; £3.50.

Impossible Microworld Museum (Monmouth St) Fascinating museum displaying the ingenious creations of Willard Wigan, who as a dyslexic child discovered his talent for microscopic sculpture by carving a mini-playground for ants. Among the delightful exhibits on show are 'A Herd of Elephants Painted on a Hair', 'A Camel in the Eye of a Needle', and 'Adam & Eve in the Lead of a Pencil'. Last summer the artist became only the fifth person in history to be allowed to display at the Statue of Liberty, where his Lilliputian version of the famous landmark drew huge crowds (not to mention lucrative offers from would-be collectors). Cl 25–27 Dec, 1 Jan; (01225) 333003; £3.95.

Jane Austen Centre 🖾 (Gay St) Jane Austen lived in this street 1801–6, and this enjoyable centre takes a comprehensive look at the much-loved novelist's life, as well as the ways in which the city influenced her writing. Displays include re-creations of a Georgian shop-front and town garden, exhibitions on places mentioned in her novels, and costumes from the BBC's adaptation of *Persuasion*; also news on Austen-related events and walking tours (£3.50 extra). Shop (selling every Austen-related book in print), disabled access; (01225) 443000; £4.

Museum of Bath at Work 🖾 (Julian Rd) Formerly the Industrial Heritage Centre, the highlight here is the engaging **Mr Bowler's Business**, an elaborate re-creation of a factory first established in 1872, providing various services from plumbing and engineering to gas-fitting and bell-hanging. Everything is just as it was then, inc the antique soda fountain that turned out such intriguingly named drinks as Hot Tom and that distant harbinger of today's alcopops, Cherry Ciderette. Snacks, shop, some disabled access by arrangement; cl wkdys Nov–Mar; (01225) 318348; *£3.50.

Museum of Costume & Assembly Rooms (Bennett St) Dazzling – around 200 figures dressed in original costumes from the late 16th c to the present, one of the most impressive displays of fashion and fashion accessories in the world. It's housed in the Assembly Rooms built in 1771 by John Wood the Younger, where the audio-guide has a particularly entertaining commentary – listen out for the bun fight. Summer coffee, shop, disabled access; cl 25–26 Dec, and Assembly Rooms may be cl other dates for functions; (01225) 477785; £4. Along the same street is a small **Museum of East Asian Art**.

No 1 Royal Crescent The most splendid example of the architecture that sprang up in the town's Georgian heyday. In 1768 it was the first house built in Bath's most regal terrace, and now has two floors restored and beautifully furnished in the style of that time. Shop; cl Mon (exc bank hols), and Dec to mid-Feb; (01225) 428126; £4. The Crescent is now closed to traffic at one end, with the hope of reducing damage inflicted by tour buses.

Prior Park Landscape Garden (Ralph Allen Drive, off A3062 S) In a sweeping valley, these striking 18th-c landscaped gardens are being comprehensively restored by the National Trust after a period of neglect. Capability Brown and Alexander Pope helped local entrepreneur Ralph Allen with the original design, and there are plenty of unique ornamental features (inc 18th-c graffiti on the Palladian bridge). Woodland walks offer unusual views over Bath (ring for details of guided walks). Note you can't drive all the way here: there's no car parking on site or nearby. You can walk from town, but the hill is very steep, so best to take the number 2 or 4 bus. Cl am, all day Tues, 25–26 Dec, 1 Jan; (01225) 833977; £4 (£1 off if show bus or train ticket); NT. There's decent food at the Cross Keys over on Midford Rd.

Pump Room This stylish 18th-c mecca for the fashionable was built directly above the Roman temple courtyard; you can catch a glimpse of the baths next door. It now houses a restaurant serving morning coffee, lunches and teas to the gay strains of the Pump Room trio. You can sample the hot spa water, which always comes out at 46°C (116°F).

Roman Baths Founded by AD 75, and undoubtedly one of Britain's most remarkable Roman sites. They were built to service pilgrims visiting a temple to Sulis Minerva, which had been constructed around a sacred hot spring. After this the spring played a dual role – as both a focus for worship, and a reservoir supplying the baths with spa water. The baths were all but forgotten until the 18th c, when workmen chanced upon a bust of Minerva, and it was not until 1878 that most of what you see today was uncovered. The main baths are pretty much intact, though some of the columns are 18th- and 19th-c reconstructions; in August they're open at night and quite beautifully floodlit. A **museum** shows finds made during excavations, inc the bust of Minerva and a remarkable Gorgon's Head pediment (thought by some authorities to depict two a gorgon at all but King Bladud, father of Lear and aeronaut extraordinaire), and a model of the site as it would have appeared in the 4th c. Meals, snacks, shop, some disabled access (though not to baths themselves); cl 25–26 Dec; (01225) 477785; £6.90, inc an audio-guide.

Royal Photographic Society 🖾 (The Octagon, Milsom St) Interactive museum and three galleries with major international exhibitions and useful displays on photographic history, inc the first picture ever taken. Meals, snacks, shop, disabled access (not to restaurant); cl 24–26 Dec and 1 Jan; (01225) 462841; £4 (free to members).

Sally Lunn's Refreshment House & Museum (North Parade Passage) Reputedly the oldest house in Bath, a charming partly timbered medieval structure, still preserving in its cellars the original kitchen of the legendary Sally Lunn, who in the 17th c created her famous brioche bread buns here. Meals and snacks (inc of course the buns, made to a secret recipe), shop; cl 25–26 Dec; (01225) 461634; 30p. They have a sister shop in Windsor.

Victoria Art Gallery (Bridge St) European Old Masters and 18th- to 20th-c British paintings and drawings, as well as decorative arts inc porcelain, glass and watches. Disabled access to ground floor only; cl Sun am, all day Mon, 25–26 Dec and most bank hols; (01225) 477233; free.

BISHOPS LYDEARD ST1729
Attractive village, interesting church with handsome carving.

BITTON SD6769
Avon Valley Railway 🖾 (Bitton Station) Friendly little railway extending lines along the old Midland Railway towards Bath. Snacks, shop, disabled access; open wknds and bank hols, steam trains Sun May–Sept plus bank

hols and Christmas; (0117) 932 7296 for timetable; £3.50.

BRADFORD-ON-TONE ST1722
Sheppy's Cider 🖾 (Three Bridges) The Sheppy family has been making cider here since the early 19th c, and you can follow the entire process over the 370-acre farm. Tastings in the shop, and a small museum. Tearoom (late May–Oct), shop, disabled access to shop and museum; cl Sun (exc 12–2pm Easter–Christmas); (01823) 461233; farm free, museum £1.75. The White Horse has good food.

BREAN DOWN ST2958
Protruding into the Bristol Channel between Weston-super-Mare and acres of holiday camps, this gives the best coastal walk in east Somerset.

BRENDON HILLS SS9738
These give breezy walks with long views; the Royal Oak at Luxborough is a good base.

BRENT KNOLL ST3450
The attractive village has a church with remarkable carved bench-ends; the Red Cow is a popular dining pub. A path leads up to the prominent summit giving the village its name.

BRIDGWATER ST3036
Once you're through the industrial outskirts, some central bits are worth seeing: Castle St is the finest early 18th-c street in the county.

Admiral Blake Museum (Blake St) Now the local history museum, this picturesque house was the birthplace of the Admiral in 1598, and shows his personal possessions (inc his sea chest) and a diorama of his great victory over the Spaniards at Santa Cruz. Shop, disabled access to ground floor only; cl Sun, Mon, Christmas, New Year and bank hols; (01278) 456127; free.

King John's Hunting Lodge (The Square) Actually built around 1500 so having no connection with King John (nor in fact with hunting) – but no less attractive for that. It houses a local history museum. Shop, disabled access to grounds; open pm only Easter–Sept; (01934) 732012; donations; NT.

BRISTOL ST5873
A busy industrial city with the usual big-city problems, this is not the best base for an enjoyable stay, but has all sorts of things to fill a lively day visit. One

excellent initiative here is free entry to five of the city's best museums: City Museum & Art Gallery, Industrial Museum, Georgian House, Red Lodge and Blaise Castle Museum (see separate entries). It's easily reached from Bath or from one of the cosseting nearby country-house hotels we list, and day visits are made easy by good rail connections, and the motorway that plunges right into the city's heart. The city's prosperity still stems from its port, though aerospace now predominates among many other manufacturing interests. There are some striking buildings around the centre, notably the Corn Exchange and the Old Council House on Corn St, and on Broad St the Grand Hotel (1869), the Guild Hall (1843) and the art nouveau façade of the former Edward Everard printing house. The Theatre Royal, opened in 1766, is one of the oldest working theatres in the country. Recent road improvements include the addition of bus lanes, closing off of Queens Square to traffic, and installation of various water features has made the harbourside much more appealing. The best part for leisurely strolls is the elegant suburb of Clifton, with handsome Georgian terraces and its famous suspension bridge. Useful central places for a cheapish lunchtime bite are the Commercial Rooms (Corn St), Cottage (Cumberland Rd), Llandoger Trow (King St) and Le Chateau (Park St). A 250-mile cycle way runs from here to Padstow in Cornwall, keeping off roads as much as possible. **@Bristol** See separate family panel on p.494.

Blaise Castle House Museum (Henbury, 4m NW, off B4047) A spacious and locally popular park with some woodland and refreshments. The late 18th-c house is now a branch of the City Museum, with lots of carefully explained farming equipment, and collections of costume and dolls. The castle itself is a Gothic folly built in 1766 within the now scarcely discernible ramparts of an Iron Age hill fort. Shop, disabled access; museum cl Thurs and Fri, and all Nov–Mar, park open daily; (0117) 950 6789; free. Nearby Blaise Hamlet is a NT-owned estate village

designed by John Nash.

Bristol Cathedral On the other side of the water, this was originally an Augustinian monastery, founded on what's supposedly the spot where St Augustine met the Celtic Christians in the early 7th c. It's a real mix of architectural styles, and perhaps the country's most splendid example of a hall church, where the nave, choir and aisles are all the same height. Highlights include the Chapter House (one of the finest Norman rooms in Britain), and the candlesticks given in thanks by the privateers who rescued Alexander Selkirk (whose adventures inspired Daniel Defoe to write *Robinson Crusoe*). Snacks, shop, some disabled access; (0117) 926 4879; free (donations welcomed).

Bristol Industrial Museum (Princes Wharf) Housed in a converted dockside transit shed, and especially good on transport, with locally built steam locomotives and aircraft (inc a mock-up of Concorde's flight deck), and a good look at the development of the port. Shop, disabled access; open Sat–Weds Apr–Oct, wknds only Nov–Mar; (0117) 925 1470; free. Steam trains run along the docks between here and the SS *Great Britain* every ¼ hour 12–5pm on selected days Mar–Oct; £1.

Bristol Zoo Gardens 🔲 (Clifton Downs; easily reached by buses 8, 9, 508 and 509 from the city centre) One of the most enjoyable zoos in the country, excellent value, lots to see, and plenty of well thought out children's activities. Highlights include the Seal and Penguin Coasts, a transparent underwater walkway that offers an unrivalled view of penguins and seals in their natural environment, Bug World, showing creatures like flat-tailed scorpions and moon jellyfish, and Twilight World, its showcase of wide-awake nocturnal creatures inc a walk-through bat enclosure. Good adventure playground, activity centre with brass-rubbing and face painting, and Zoolympics, a trail around the enclosures that lets children measure their skills and strength against some of the animals. Lots of themed weeks and events. Everything is spread over beautifully laid-out gardens, with spacious lawns and colourful borders. Meals, snacks, shop, good disabled access; cl 25 Dec; (0117) 973 8951; £8.20 (£4.60 children 3–13).

British Empire & Commonwealth Museum Opening just after this book comes out, this enterprising new museum – housed in a former railway station designed by Brunel – aims to tell the story of the Commonwealth from John Cabot's departure for Newfoundland from Bristol in 1497 to the return of Hong Kong to the Chinese mainland 500 years later. Using a variety of mediums (inc an oral history archive with over 700 recorded interviews), Britain's complex overseas history will be looked at in fine detail, from the landing of the Pilgrim Fathers, through the dark days of slavery and transportation, to the rise and fall of the British Empire and the subsequent emergence of the Commonwealth. Exhibits will include historic photographs, rare manuscripts and a collection of costumes from all over the world. Meals, snacks, shop, disabled access; (0117) 925 4980; *£2.

Cabot Tower The attractive park at the end of Great George St is an urban nature reserve, and its tower rewards those willing to climb the hundreds of steps with probably the best views of the city. Snacks, cl 25 Dec; free. Nearby **St George's** has good Fri lunchtime concerts, usually with seats available on the day, but best to check on (0117) 923 0359.

Christmas Steps This famously old-fashioned alley is quaintly lined by steep buildings. At the top is the tiny late 15th-c **Chapel of the Three Kings of Cologne** (the 'three kings' are the three wise men whose shrines are in Cologne Cathedral); the warden of the nearby almshouses can let you in. And at the bottom is the lodge of **St Bartholomew's** – all that remains of the 13th-c hospital and almshouse which once stood on this site. This is a good area for shops selling antiques, stamps and old books.

City Museum & Art Gallery (Queens Rd) Good collections of fine and applied art, archaeology, geology, and history – well worth a look. Meals,

snacks, shop, disabled access; cl 25–26 Dec and 1 Jan; (0117) 922 3571; free. The neo-Gothic Wills Memorial tower next door is a distinctive landmark.

Create Centre (Smeaton Rd, Spike Island) Lively environmental centre with hands-on displays about recycling, some intriguing exhibits inc a column made from 6½ million cans, and an ecohome showcasing methods for greener everyday living. Also changing exhibitions of local art, internet room, and café. Shop, disabled access; cl most wknds, though best to check; (0117) 925 0505; free.

Harveys Wine Cellars 📧 (Denmark St) Unique collection of antique corkscrews, decanters, glasses, bottles, furniture and other items associated with the production and serving of wine, housed in the medieval cellars of this wine company. There's a very good shop, and you may be able to join one of the guided tours with tutored tastings. Restaurant, wine shop; cl Sun and bank hols and occasionally at other times; (0117) 927 5036; £5 (inc a glass of sherry).

Historic Boat Trips (from Princes Wharf) The 1860s steam-tug *Mayflower* gives interesting trips round the dock in the summer – best to check times with the Industrial Museum; (0117) 925 1470; £3. From Apr to Oct the **pleasure steamers** *Waverley* and *Balmoral* run fairly frequent day cruises from here, along the Avon and Severn or to Devon, Wales or Lundy; (0141) 221 8152 for timetable. The *Balmoral* has surprisingly well kept real ale in its bar.

John Wesley's Chapel (Horsefair) Incongruously set in a shopping centre, but much as it was when Wesley preached here (from the famous double-decked pulpit upstairs); the oldest Methodist chapel in the world, built in 1739 and rebuilt in 1748. Guided tours by arrangement. Snacks (not Jan–Easter), shop, disabled access to ground floor only; cl Sun and all bank hols; (0117) 926 4740; free (£2.80 tour).

Lord Mayor's Chapel (Park St) Rare civic church, with glorious 16th-c stained-glass windows, floor tiles and fan-vaulted ceiling; tours by

appointment only; (0117) 929 4350.
Red Lodge (Park St) The house was
altered in the 18th c, but on its first
floor still has the last surviving suite of
16th-c rooms in Bristol, as well as a
wonderful carved stone chimney-piece,
plasterwork ceilings and fine oak
panelling. They occasionally open the
reconstructed Tudor-style garden.
Open Sat–Weds and most bank hols
Apr–Oct; (0117) 921 1360; free. There
are several elegant Georgian streets
round here, notably Great George St,
where the **Georgian House**, built in
1790 for a wealthy sugar merchant, is a
fine illustration of a typical town house
of the day. Three floors are decorated
in period style, inc the below-stairs area
with kitchen, laundry and
housekeeper's room. Times as for Red
Lodge; (0117) 921 1362; free.
SS *Great Britain* On the dockside a
small steam railway on some summer
wknds will whisk you along the old
cargo route to and from this ship,
designed by Brunel as the first iron,
screw-propelled, ocean-going vessel,
and a real departure from what had
gone before. Its continuing restoration
was recently given a boost in the form
of a £7m lottery grant which, among
other things, will go towards re-
creating the sounds and smells of 19th-c
sea travel inside the ship. Snacks, shop;
cl 24–25 Dec; (0117) 926 0680; £6.25.
This includes entry to the **Maritime
Heritage Centre**, with
reconstructions and original machinery
illustrating the city's long history of
ship-building. The nearby diesel-
powered firefloat *Pyronaut* (1934) and
Fairbairn steam-crane (1876) operate
occasional summer wknds.
St Mary Redcliffe (Redcliffe Hill)
Elizabeth I described this as 'the
goodliest, fairest and most famous
parish church in England'. Most of the
current building dates from the late
13th c, inc the wonderful hexagonal
outer porch. Notable features include
the tomb of Admiral Sir William Penn,
the father of the man who founded
Pennsylvania, and the Handel Window,
where eight passages of the *Messiah*
commemorate the great composer's
ties with this church. Wkdy snacks,
disabled access (through South Door).

Maybe free organ recitals Thur
lunchtimes during term-time.
St Wegburgh's City Farm
(Watercress Rd) Another heartening
example of community spirit within the
city, this site might well have remained a
wasteland had local people not
persuaded the council to stump up the
money to develop this working urban
farm. Half an hour's walk from the
centre of Bristol, kept going largely by
volunteers who look after the animals
and tend the various plots inc one for
exotic vegetables; also scented garden
and nature trails designed by students.
Snacks (not Mon or Tues), farm shop,
disabled access; open daily; (0117) 942
8241; free.
University Botanic Gardens (Leigh
Woods) Attractive gardens with
several rock and water features, set
around students' halls of residence. All
the plants are excellently labelled, and
the grounds include BBC *Gardener's
World* microclimate gardens; some
disabled access; cl wknds and bank hols;
(0117) 973 3682; free.
BRISTOL DOCKS ST5872
Being attractively restored, with
distinctive blue and yellow ferries
(Apr–Sept) linking several points. The
old part around King St, between the
waterfront and the Bristol Old Vic, has
quiet cobbled streets of Georgian
buildings, pleasant to wander through,
and elsewhere some of the bigger
warehouses (and even the boats) have
been pressed into service as museums,
café-bars and the like. The Arnolfini, a
big former tea warehouse, is now a
contemporary arts complex with bar,
restaurant, exhibitions, cinema, theatre
and so forth.
BRUTON ST6834
Fascinating little town; worth looking
out for are the Bartons, narrow alleys
leading down from the High St to the
river (which you can cross either by
footbridge or by using stepping stones).
St Mary's church is on the site of a
medieval Augustinian priory and abbey
– the old abbey wall with its buttresses
still stands in Silver St. The church has a
spectacular altar-piece, and in the
chancel is a fine effigy of Sir Maurice
Berkely, a great survivor who was
standard-bearer to Henry VIII, Edward

VI and Elizabeth I. Interesting and individual shops – antiques, books and prints. The Castle Inn is good for lunch, and the delicatessen on High St has a good range of local and French cheeses. The drive up towards Alfred's Tower gives some open views, and below it the Old Red Lion at North Brewham has decent food.

BURNHAM-ON-SEA ST3050
In summer a bustling inexpensive family seaside resort, with wide beaches, sandy dunes, and the usual holiday facilities. Its plain-looking **church** surprises with its collection of Grinling Gibbons carvings from the long-demolished Palace of Whitehall in London.

Animal Farm Country Park 🖼️ (Red Rd, N of Berrow) Good fun for children, with animals and conservation trails, trampolines and play areas. Meals, snacks, shop, disabled access; cl 25–26 Dec (maybe other dates too in winter); (01278) 751628; £3.95. There's a small **nature reserve** in the nearby sand dunes. The Red Cow at Brent Knoll has good food.

BURRINGTON COMBE ST4858
An easy walk by the B3134 (the best drive through the Mendips), this great steeply wooded limestone gorge on the N flank of the Mendips can be combined with walks up on to Black Down for memorable views in all directions, and over the heather and cranberry tops to Dolebury Warren, where the site of an Iron Age hill fort marks a splendid Mendip viewpoint. Other good starting points for Mendips walks include the Crown at Churchill, Swan at Rowberrow and Ring o' Bells at Compton Martin.

BURROW BRIDGE ST3428
Somerset Levels Basket Centre (Lyng Rd) Sells baskets made from local materials cut on the surrounding Levels as well as other crafts. Shop, disabled access; cl Sun and Tues, 25 Dec–1 Jan and maybe over Easter; (01823) 698688; free. The Rose & Crown at East Lyng has good food.

CADBURY CAMP ST4572
This Iron Age hill fort makes a good destination for a walk from the engaging Black Horse in Clapton in Gordano, by a lane past the church, which leads to a footbridge high over the M5. This should not be confused with the more famous Cadbury Castle down towards Yeovil.

CANNINGTON ST2539
Cannington College Heritage Gardens Extensive gardens inc over 10,000 different types of plant, with eight national collections, display and ornamental beds, tropical and sub-tropical glasshouses, and gardens of bees and butterflies. Open pm only Easter Mon–Oct; (01278) 655000; £2. The Malt Shovel at Bradley Green has decent food, and there's a nice drive to Nether Stowey via Combwich and Stogursey.

CASTLE CARY ST6432
Very attractive – basically a medieval market town, now with a useful range of traditional family-run shops and crafts and antiques shops. The 18th-c **Roundhouse** is Britain's smallest prison, and the local museum is worth a look if you've time. The George, a comfortable old thatched coaching inn, has good food.

Castle Cary Vineyard (Honeywick, just E) Produces award-winning wines and welcomes visits; (01963) 351507.

Hadspen Garden 🖼️ (off A371 2m SE) Beautiful five-acre gardens surrounding fine 18th-c house; many old favourite plants, but also lots of exotics. A delightful 17th-c walled garden has all sorts of herbaceous plants and old-fashioned roses, and there's a lily pond and ancient flower meadow. Teas and snacks, nursery, some disabled access; open Thurs–Sun and bank hols Mar–Sept; (01749) 813707; *£3.

CASTLE NEROCHE ST2715
This isolated ruined Norman fortification, with more the aspect now of a hill fort than a castle, is the central feature of well marked woodland walks down towards the Blackdown Hills S of Taunton; fine views at the top.

CHAPEL ALLERTON ST4150
Ashton Windmill The only complete mill left in Somerset, built in the 18th c, with splendid views over the Cheddar Gorge and Somerset Levels. Shop, open pm Sun and bank hols Easter–Sept, plus pm Weds July–Aug (and by appointment in Sept); (01934) 712694; free.

CHARD ST3108
Chard Museum (High St) This local
history museum has good displays on
local industries such as lace-making, and
a bizarre collection of artificial limbs.
Shop, disabled access; cl Sat am, Sun
(exc July and Aug), Nov–early May;
(01460) 65091; £2. There are a couple
of places to hire bikes; the local tourist
board do good cycle routes. **Forde
Abbey**, just over the border in Dorset,
is particularly worth visiting.
Hornsbury Mill 🏚 (just N) 200-year-
old watermill, with landscaped water
garden, trout lake, and play area; you
can stay here. Meals, snacks, shop,
disabled access; cl Jan; (01460) 63317;
*£2. Past here at Combe St Nicholas
the Green Dragon has good value food.

CHEDDAR ST4553
In its older part, this extended village
has a very fine market cross, with some
interesting shops and a tall-towered
14th/15th-c **church**. The Galleries is
quite useful for lunch, and outside are
roadside strawberry stalls and pick-
your-own in summer. Cheddar gets
astonishingly busy in summer, when
every building seems to be either a
tearoom or a shop selling cheese or
cider.
Cheddar Caves and Gorge Two
beautiful caves beneath the gorge; quite
cathedral-like with spectacular
stalagmites and stalactites joining to
form columns. Also an exhibition
devoted to 'Cheddar Man', Britain's
oldest complete skeleton, with a re-
creation of his world of 9,000 years ago.
Good clifftop walks, and plenty of
activities for children, inc the lively
Crystal Quest. Meals, snacks, shop; cl
24–25 Dec; (01934) 742343; £7.50. The
more daring can don hard hats and
boiler suits for what they call
Adventure Caving Expeditions; £10 (no
under-11s).
Cheddar Gorge The area's big
attraction, a magnificent limestone
gorge with picturesque cliffs, formed
when a cavern roof collapsed. Further
up the dramatic B3135 road through
the gorge, it rapidly loses its
commercialised trappings. When you
reach the far end two worthwhile paths
leave the road. At the E end is a quiet
dale with two nature reserves, Black

Rock and Velvet Bottom. On the S side
of the gorge, the West Mendip Way
climbs through woods and gives access
to another path which skirts the top of
the gorge (the views into it are hair-
raising). You can also get up to this
viewpoint via the 274 steps of Jacob's
Ladder from the road at the W
entrance to the gorge, and to make
things easier on the feet, a £2m cable-
car system should open within the next
few years.
Cheddar Gorge Cheese Co Village
(The Cliffs) Shops and traditional crafts
based around a factory that thanks to its
location claims to make the only
genuine Cheddar cheese in the world.
You can watch each stage of the seven-
hour process, and of course taste the
matured product. Also fudge-making,
scrumpy sampling, and less flavoursome
crafts inc lace- and candle-making.
Snacks, shops, disabled access; cl
Nov–late Mar; (01934) 742810; £1.50.

CHEDDON FITZPAINE ST2428
Hestercombe Gardens 🏚 Raised
walks, sunken lawns and a water garden
are all part of the grand design which
Lutyens and Gertrude Jekyll created for
this beautifully restored garden around
what is now Somerset Fire Brigade HQ;
also intriguing landscaped secret
gardens and newly restored Georgian
garden with woodland walks and
classical temples, pleasant even on a
gloomy day. Tearoom, shop (inc plant
sales), limited disabled access; (01823)
413923; £3.60. If you don't want to go
into Taunton, the Bathpool Inn at
Bathpool (A38) is a handy family dining
pub.

CHEW VALLEY LAKES ST5760
The Chew Valley Lake itself and
Blagdon Lake are more popular as
breathing places for people living
nearby than as places for visitors from
afar; both are pleasant large stretches of
water, with managed fishing, and the
B3130 and B3114 have pleasant views.
The New Inn at Blagdon is nicely set for
lunch.

CHEWTON MENDIP ST5952
Chewton Cheese Dairy (Priory
Farm) Another traditional cheese dairy,
one of the few to mature their cheeses
properly, so producing not just the
characteristic rind but also the true

depth of flavour. They start at 7.30am and go on till 3pm, with the best time to watch between 11.30am and 2.30pm. A video shows the stages you may have missed. Meals and snacks, farm shop, disabled access; no cheese-making Thurs or Sun, cl 25–26 Dec; (01761) 241666; free (£2.50 guided tour, 11.30am–1.45pm not Thurs or Sun). The 15th-c **church tower** is perhaps the most magnificent in any village in the area. The Waldegrave Arms has decent food.

CLAVERTON ST7864
American Museum in Britain (Claverton Manor, just SE of the city) Quite a contrast to the rest of Bath's attractions, a fascinating illustration of American history and life, in lovely gracious surroundings. Eighteen rooms are fully furnished and decorated to re-create the style of American homes from the 17th to the 19th c, while the grounds include a replica of part of George Washington's garden at Mount Vernon, and an American arboretum. Collections of folk art and patchwork quilts with sections on Native Americans and Shakers, and good special events. Well liked by readers, it's the only museum in the country completely devoted to our colonial cousins. Snacks, shop, some disabled access; cl am, all day Mon (exc Aug and bank hols), and Nov–Mar; (01225) 460503; *£5.50.

CLEVEDON ST4071
After partly collapsing in 1970, the Victorian **pier** was lovingly restored, and finally reopened in 1998. It is pleasant for a stroll (shop, disabled access; cl Oct–Mar (exc Weds) and there are sailings and fishings from the pier itself; *75p). Above the tollhouse, a gallery sells paintings; shop, disabled access; cl Weds Oct–Mar, and 25 Dec; (01275) 878846. Round the corner in Waterloo House is a **Heritage Centre**; donations. Good views from Church Hill, and in Moor Lane the **Clevedon Craft Centre** has 15 varied workshops and a tearoom; most parts cl Mon. The Little Harp and Moon & Sixpence are seafront family dining pubs with views to Wales.
Clevedon Court (B3130 just E) Most of the original structure of this manor

house, built in 1320, is still intact, though there are interesting additions from other periods inc a charming 18th-c garden. Thackeray wrote part of *Vanity Fair* here. Some disabled access to ground floor; open pm Sun, Weds, Thurs and bank hols Apr–Sept; (01275) 872257; £4; NT.

CLIFTON ST5673
The quiet side of Bristol, with some fine late 18th- and 19th-c terraces, an antiques market (Mall, cl Sun, Mon), a big park right on the spectacular Avon gorge facing the NT woodlands on the crags opposite, and the remarkably modern-looking suspension bridge, based on an 1836 design by Brunel and finished in 1864; a Victorian girl leapt off here after a tiff with her boyfriend, but was saved when her huge skirts acted as a parachute. The Somerset House (Princess Victoria St) is useful for something to eat.

COMBE FLOREY ST1531
Combe Florey church Charming church with attractive carvings; Evelyn Waugh lies buried outside.

COMBE HAY ST7359
This charming steep village has a good pub, and the road to Monkton Combe gives good views.

CRANMORE ST6643
East Somerset Railway Steam trips along what's known as the Strawberry Line, as well as engine shed and workshops, with nine steam locomotives and rolling stock, and art gallery with wildlife paintings by David Shepherd who founded the railway. Meals and snacks (on steam days), shop, disabled access; open daily, though trains don't run every day – best to ring for timetable; (01749) 880417; £5.50, less when no trains running. The Strode Arms in this quiet and pleasant village is very good for lunch.

CREWKERNE ST4409
Thriving town with some decent antiques shops and a number of inexpensive tearooms, restaurants and hotels.

CRICKET ST THOMAS ST3708
Cricket St Thomas Park Within the lovely parkland of a great estate (familiar to fans of *To the Manor Born*), this wildlife centre with a good emphasis on conservation is home to

600 animals, many endangered in the wild. A highlight is a walk through the lemur woods, where you can see the primates swinging happily from the trees above. There's plenty more to amuse children inc a pets' corner and miniature railway. Meals, snacks, shop, cl 25 Dec; (01460) 30111; £4.95 (under-3s free).

CROSCOMBE ST5844

Croscombe is an attractive village, with great 17th-c woodwork in its 15th-c church. The walk from here to Wells gives unforgettable views of the cathedral.

CUCKLINGTON ST7527

Cucklington church 13th-c, with small side chapel dedicated to St Barbara, whose sacred well lies further down in the village.

DOWLISH WAKE ST3712

Perry's Cider Mills They've been making cider here for centuries, and between Oct and Nov you can watch it being produced. The cider mill is in a group of thatched 16th-c buildings around a yard with brightly painted old farm wagons and so forth. Enthusiastically run, with a video on cider-making, liberal tastings and half a dozen different ciders for sale, in old-fashioned earthenware flagons if you want. Shop, disabled access; cl 25–26 Dec, 1 Jan; (01460) 52681; free. The nearby New Inn is very good for lunch.

DUNDRY HILL ST5666

Just S of Bristol's suburbs, this gives walkers views over the city, Chew Magna and Blagdon lakes and the Mendips.

DUNSTER SS9943

Well worth a day of anybody's time, with fine medieval houses along the wide main street below the wooded castle hill, as well as a handsome octagonal former yarn market and market cross, a lovely 15th-c priory **church** with particularly tuneful bells, and a well established **doll museum** in the Memorial Hall (cl Oct–Mar; around 50p). If you plan to visit Exmoor the National Park Information Centre is a useful first stop. The Dunster Castle Hotel has decent food, and there's a wealth of tearooms.

Dunster Castle 🏰 Dramatically set in a 28-acre park rich with exotic flora and even subtropical plants, the castle was largely rebuilt in the 19th-c, but has older features inside such as the 17th-c oak staircase and gallery with its brightly painted wall hangings. Excellent views. Shop in 17th-c stables, disabled access (a buggy avoids the steep climb up the hill); castle cl Thurs, Fri, and all Nov–Mar (gardens open all year); (01643) 821314; £5.50, £3 garden and park only; NT.

Old Dovecote (St George's St) In summer you can go right up this 12th-c dovecote, special for still having its potence or revolving ladder, used for harvesting the plump squabs from the nesting boxes.

Watermill 🏰 Well restored 18th-c mill still grinding and selling flour; teas in a pleasant riverside garden. Cl Fri (exc July–Aug), and all Nov–Easter; (01643) 821759; *£2.10.

EAST COKER ST5412

Charming quiet village; T S Eliot's ashes are buried here, and there's information about his ancestors in the church.

EAST HUNTSPILL ST3345

Secret World 🏰 (New Rd Farm) Very friendly family-run working farm, with an emphasis on wildlife rescue (especially badgers). The best feature is the unique observation badger sett in the Nocturnal House, with glass viewing panels to watch the creatures' life underground. Also farm trail, barn owls, lots of other animals, adventure playground, and special events. Meals, snacks, shop, disabled access; cl Jan; (01278) 783250; £4.95. The Crossways Inn over at West Huntspill is a popular lunch place.

EAST LAMBROOK ST4318

East Lambrook Manor Garden 🏰 Well loved cottage garden around a 15th-c house (not open), started by Walter and Margery Fish in 1937, and described by Mrs Fish in her immensely popular book, *We Made A Garden*. There's a national collection of geraniums here, the original plant nursery area has been restored, and occasional art exhibitions are held in the converted 17th-c malthouse. Snacks, plant sales, shop, some disabled access; cl Sun, best to ring for winter opening times; (01460) 240328; £2.50.

EAST QUANTOXHEAD ST1343
Delightful village with archetypal
duckpond, tiny church with fine oak
carvings, and walks to the coast.

EBBOR GORGE ST5248
If you like Cheddar Gorge but don't like
the souvenir stall, coach parties and all,
then Ebbor Gorge is for you. It's the
same sort of thing, above Wookey
Hole, but altogether quieter and more
unspoilt. It has an attractive nature trail,
and a good walk runs from Wookey
Hole through the Gorge to Pen Hill for
panoramic views. The Hunters Lodge
and New Inn up around Priddy have
sensibly priced food.

FARLEIGH HUNGERFORD
ST8057
Farleigh Hungerford Castle
Extensive ruins of 14th-c castle, with
monuments in the chapel to the
Hungerford family, who once owned
the land from here to Salisbury. Picnics
welcome, shop, limited disabled access;
cl Mon and Tues Nov–Mar, 24–26 Dec
and 1 Jan; (01225) 754026; £2.30 inc
audio tour; EH. The Hungerford Arms
overlooking it has decent food.

GLASTONBURY ST4938
Tales of King Arthur can be found all
over the country, but are especially
prominent here; they like to say that
bones reinterred in the abbey in 1191
were those of Arthur and Guinevere.
The best approach is by the B3151,
showing the town below the famous
Tor. Glastonbury has quite a New Age
feel, probably due to all the legends and
the famous annual rock festival. The
George & Pilgrims, its medieval carved
façade one of the sights of the town, is
quite useful for lunch, and the Who'd A
Thought It has good value food. The
bypass has made the town much more
pleasurable.

Chalice Well (Chilkwell St) Legend
has it that the Holy Grail was hidden
here, now set in a colourful 2½-acre
garden; the spring has apparently
possessed healing powers ever since.
True or not, it's a nice peaceful spot.
Shop, disabled access; (01458) 831154;
*£2.

Glastonbury Abbey These noble
ruins are said to mark the location of
the birth of Christianity in this country.
The story goes that Joseph of

Arimathaea struck his staff into
Wearyall Hill, where it took root.
(Offshoots of the tree, the famous
Glastonbury Thorn, have flourished to
this day and there's a fine specimen in
the abbey.) The remains of the church
date mainly from 1539, though the Lady
Chapel is much older, and massive roof
timbers and richly decorated gable ends
and porches testify to the enormous
wealth of the order who ran it. An
interpretation area has a good range of
stories connected with the site. Snacks
(July–Aug), shop, disabled access; cl 25
Dec; (01458) 832267; £3.

Glastonbury Tribunal (High St)
Glastonbury was formerly an island
rising from a vast inland lake, and you
can almost see this from the top of the
Tor, the highest point of the hills and
ridges among which the little town
nestles, with fantastic views.
Excavations here have revealed a
prehistoric **lake village** covering three
or four acres below it, consisting of
nearly a hundred mounds surrounded
by a wooden palisade. Lots of items and
timbers from the village have been
unusually well preserved thanks to the
waterlogged state of the site, and some
of the finds, providing a fascinating
insight into the life of the settlement,
are displayed in this fine 15th-c
merchant's house. The Tourist
Information Centre is here too, and
there's some notable plasterwork in
the lower back room. Shop, cl 25–26
Dec; (01458) 832954; £2; EH.

Somerset Rural Life Museum
(Chilkwell St) The Abbey Barn and
outbuildings have displays of traditional
regional skills such as cider-making,
peat-cutting and basket-weaving. Also
orchard, rare breeds, and bee garden
with hives. Summer snacks, shop,
mostly disabled access; cl Mon, plus
Suns Nov–Mar, 25–26 Dec and Good
Fri; (01458) 831197; £2.50.

GRABBIST HILL SS9843
Not as famous as Dunkery Hill (and less
frequented even in summer), but
recommended to walkers in search of
rewarding views; it can be climbed from
nearby Dunster.

ILCHESTER ST5222
Charming, with a useful range of well
stocked little shops. Used to be a

Roman town, and one of the houses has a piece of Roman paving. The whole of the green fronting the town hall is said to be the burial ground of Plague victims. The comfortable Ilchester Arms has good food.

ILMINSTER ST3614

Ilminster church Magnificent 15th-c tower, all turrets, pinnacles and gargoyles.

KENNET & AVON CANAL ST6470

Attractively restored, with a good footpath alongside, it runs from Bristol through Hanham (where the Lock & Weir is a charmingly placed pub), Saltford and Bath to the spectacular aqueduct at Avoncliff (and beyond, across Wiltshire and into Berkshire).

KEYNSHAM ST6768

Avon Valley Country Park 🎟 (Pixash Lane) Lots of animals from rare breed pigs to wallabies, deer park, riverside trails (inc plenty of places to fish), an excellent adventure playground, and free boating on the pond. There's also a new soft play area and mini-train rides. Snacks, shop, disabled access; cl Mon (exc summer hols and bank hols), and Nov–Easter; (0117) 986 4929; £3.95. The river-view Lock-Keeper (Keynsham Rd) has decent food.

KINGSBURY EPISCOPI ST4321

Somerset Cider Brandy Co England's first fully licensed cider distillery, with huge copper stills, oak vats and wooden presses, traditional cider orchards to stroll through and tastings of their cider brandy. Shop, limited disabled access; cl Sun, 25–26 Dec; (01460) 240782; free. The village green has an ancient lock-up, and the Wyndham Arms is useful for lunch.

KINGSDON ST5226

Lytes Cary Manor Most of the surviving buildings date from the 16th c, though there are interesting earlier features inc the 14th-c chapel, and the Tudor Great Hall. The attractive garden was designed and stocked by Henry Lyte, a notable Elizabethan horticulturalist, and they are hoping that otters will return to the grounds following improvements to the riverbanks. Plant sales, disabled access to garden only; open Mon, Weds and

Sat pms Apr–Oct (plus Fri pm Jun–Aug); (01985) 843600; £4, £2 garden only; NT. The Kingsdon Inn does good home cooking.

KINGSTON ST MARY ST2229

Pretty village, with attractive church.

LIMINGTON ST5422

Limington church Interesting for its effigies of the Giverney family, dating back to the 1300s.

LONG ASHTON ST5571

Ashton Court Estate 850 acres of woods and grassland with deer enclosures, pitch and putt golf, and views across Clifton and Bristol to the hills beyond. The large manor house (not open) is mostly 19th-c, although some parts date from medieval times. Part of the stables is now a visitor centre (open wknds and some summer wkdys, phone to check; (0117) 963 9174). Café, disabled access; park open all year; free. The Angel has reasonably priced food.

MARTOCK ST4619

The magnificent **church** has a splendid roof; also look out for the old Court House turned into a Grammar School by William Strode in 1661, with the inscription above the door 'Martock neglect not your opportunities' in English, Latin, Hebrew and Greek. The Fleur de Lis in Stoke sub Hamdon is useful for lunch.

Somerset Guild of Craftsmen A big, multi-roomed display of Guild members' work inc jewellery, paintings and furniture. Good coffee shop, disabled access to ground floor only; cl Sun Jan–Mar, 25–26 Dec and 1 Jan; (01935) 825891; free.

MELLS ST7249

Delightful and venerable stone-built village, with marvellous church and graveyard, charming ancient inn, pleasant walks nearby.

MERRIOTT ST4412

Scotts of Merriott Perhaps the last of the big general retail nurseries to raise and grow most of their own trees and shrubs, on 90 acres – a sea of colour when the 500 varieties of roses are in flower in July. Shop; cl 25 Dec, Easter Sun, (01460) 72306; free. In the village **D B Pottery** (Highway Cottage, Church St) make a range of items at good prices using a variety of glazing

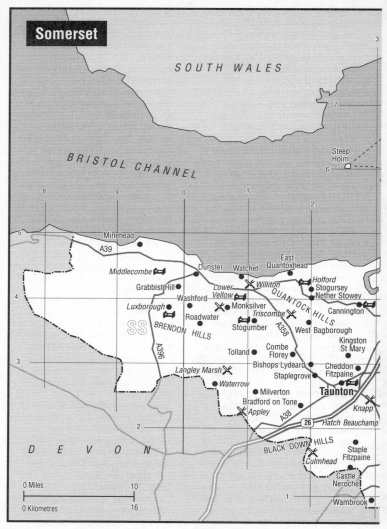

Somerset

SOUTH WALES

BRISTOL CHANNEL

Steep Holm

Minehead
A39
Middlecombe
Dunster
Watchet
East Quantoxhead
Grabbist Hill
Lower Vellow
Williton
Holford
Stogursey
Nether Stowey
Washford
Monksilver
QUANTOCK HILLS
Luxborough
Roadwater
Triscombe
Cannington
SS
BRENDON HILLS
Stogumber
West Bagborough
Kingston St Mary
Tolland
Combe Florey
Bishops Lydeard
Cheddon Fitzpaine
Langley Marsh
Staplegrove
Taunton
Waterrow
Milverton
Bradford on Tone
Knapp
Appley
Hatch Beauchamp
26
A38
DEVON
BLACK DOWN HILLS
Staple Fitzpaine
Culmhead
Castle Neroche
Wambrook

0 Miles 10
0 Kilometres 16

techniques; (01460) 75655; free. The Lord Poulett on the attractive main street of nearby Hinton St George is useful for lunch.

MILVERTON ST1225
The parish church has some fine carving, and there's a little pottery on the charming High St.

MINEHEAD SS9646
There's an easily missed area of sloping streets and thatched cottages around the church, with Church Steps a quaint

steep back lane. Around this original fishing village is a spacious resort, its beach and promenade sheltered by the wooded hills to the NE. It has the usual attractions, a lively harbour, a sizeable holiday camp recently redesigned to be more family-friendly, and a modern shopping area; plans to build England's first new pier for many years were still on hold as we went to press. The Old Ship Aground has good value food and pleasant harbour views. There's an

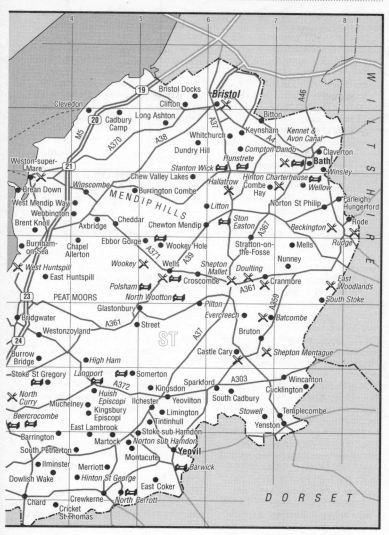

unusual **pottery shop** (cl 12–1.30pm) on Park St, and a little **shoe factory** you can visit on North Rd (cl 1–2pm and wknds exc Sat am). From the harbour you may be able to catch the *Waverley* (paddle steamer) or *Balmoral*, along the Bristol Channel or to Lundy Island. The clifftop Blue Anchor at the end of the B3191 has decent food, great views.

West Somerset Railway Steam trains run from the Minehead terminus along the coast to Watchet and then inland to Bishops Lydeard – a splendid long run stopping at several little stations. Meals, snacks, shop, very good disabled access, with a specially adapted coach; station open daily but no trains Mon (exc bank hols) and Fri in Apr, May and Oct, and none exc Santa specials Nov–Feb, best to ring (01643) 704996 for timetable; £9.40 full return fare.

MONKSILVER ST0737

Combe Sydenham Country Park

(B3188) Over half-way through a 40-year restoration plan, 580 acres of Exmoor-edge woodland, with walks and trails, corn mill, and play areas. They usually do tours of the 16th-c house on summer pms Mon–Thurs. Cl Sat and Nov–Mar; (01643) 702259, £3 car park, charges for some features (house tour £5). The Notley Arms is excellent for lunch.

MONTACUTE ST4917

Montacute House Magnificent 16th-c honeyed stone house in beautiful little village, with a wealth of interesting tapestries, furniture, paintings and ceramics, set in rooms with decorated ceilings, ornate fireplaces and fine panelling. A highlight is the collection of Tudor and Jacobean paintings from the National Portrait Gallery. Impressive formal gardens. Meals, snacks, shop, disabled access to grounds only; cl am, Tues and Nov–Mar; (01935) 823289; £6, £3 garden only; NT. The park is open to walkers. In the village, features worth seeing include the Borough (a quite charming square of two-storey houses), and Abbey Farm and the Monk's House – all that remains of the Norman priory destroyed during the Dissolution. The Phelips Arms is good for lunch.

MUCHELNEY ST4224

Muchelney Abbey The abbey was founded in the 9th c (perhaps earlier), but the well preserved ruins date from the 15th, inc part of the cloister, and the abbot's lodging with its splendidly carved fireplace. Shop, limited disabled access; cl Nov–Mar; (01458) 250664; £1.70. The tiny 14th-c priest's house opposite is worth a quick look; open pm Sun and Mon Apr–Sept; £1.70; NT. The **John Leach Pottery** has a few items on display in the abbey, with the main showroom a couple of minutes' drive S (cl lunchtime, and most Suns).

NETHER STOWEY ST1939

An appealing large village with winding streets, handy for both Exmoor and the Quantocks, with good views over the Levels from the mound of the former Norman castle. The **Quantock Hills Information Centre** in Castle St is a valuable source of information, and the road up wooded Cockercombe gives a lovely sense of the Quantocks' feeling

of peace and timelessness; it's generally the roads on the W side of the hills that give the best views.

Coleridge Cottage (Lime St) The poet moved here in 1796; he lived here with a pig or two, and his friends the Wordsworths resided in considerably more style not far away – the two families were regarded with suspicion by the local population. Open pm Tues–Thurs and Sun, Apr–Sept; (01278) 732662; £2.60; NT. The Ancient Mariner opposite has decent food.

NORTON ST PHILIP ST7756

Norwood Rare Breeds Farm (B3110) Friendly organic farm on high open land with plenty of traditional and rare breeds, nature trails, and good views. You can go right up to the animals, and watch the pigs being fed. Meals, snacks, good farm shop, disabled access; usually cl mid-Sept–Easter; (01373) 834356; £4. The George is a splendid ancient inn building. The B3110 has some steep intricate views.

NUNNEY ST7345

Nunney Castle This 14th-c fort was reduced to ruins in the Civil War, but has one of the deepest moats in the country; it and its feeder stream running through the green of this quaint and quiet village are jostling with ducks. The castle's layout and round towers were supposedly modelled on France's Bastille; free. There's a small covered market place just above the stream, and nearby are 18th-c weavers' cottages. The **church**, as usual in so many Somerset villages, is well worth a look.

PEAT MOORS ST4241

Peat Moors Visitor Centre 🏛 (Shapwick Rd, Westhay) In the heart of the peat-cutting area of the Levels, with an excellent exhibition on the topic, and a reconstructed Iron Age village. Craft demonstrations most summer wknds. Snacks, shop, disabled access; cl Nov–Mar; (01458) 860697; £2.50. The Olde Burtle Inn over past Catcott Burtle has good fresh fish.

QUANTOCK TOPS ST1537

The moorland tops of these hills are quite a different world, where ancient trackways lead past prehistoric cairns and burial mounds; Exmoor, the Bristol Channel, South Wales and the Mendips are in sight. The tiny road crossing the ridge between Nether Stowey and Crowcombe (which has a delightful church) gives walkers easy access to the moor.

QUANTOCK WALKS ST1540

The Quantock Hills have the most for walkers in west Somerset (short of Exmoor). Their secretive quality is illustrated by the dense broad-leafed woodlands on the N side, where shady combes display splendid spring and autumn colours. The village of Holford is a good starting point: the paths begin with helpful signposts, though you may soon get bemused by the complexity of the path junctions. Holford Combe is reasonably easy to find, and a map will get you to the ancient hill fort site capping Dowsborough, from where a moorland track leads gently N to Holford. Another good approach is from Kilve, from where you can take a path to and along the coast, then through East Quantoxhead to the north Quantock slopes for a remarkably varied circuit.

QUANTOCKS – WESTERN SLOPES ST1139

The W slopes of the Quantock Hills, less wooded than the NE side, have some attractive valleys enclosed by plunging slopes, with tracks along the bottom: Bicknoller with its fine **church** (good carvings) is an attractive start for walks, and the Blue Ball at Triscombe is an excellent port of call.

RODE ST8053

Tropical Bird Gardens 🏛 Huge collection of around 200 species of colourful and exotic birds flying through 17 acres of grounds, with ornamental lakes, ponds and masses of trees and shrubs. Also pets' corner and woodland miniature railway (Easter–mid-Sept). Summer meals, snacks, shop (inc sales of clematis, of which they have a notable collection), disabled access; cl 25 Dec; (01373) 830326; £5.70. The Woolpack at Beckington has good food.

SOMERTON ST4928

Built in light grey stone, this market town has a 17th-c market cross and fine old Georgian buildings in the quiet main square, where the Globe has decent food. **St Michael's church** is stupendous, its roof supposedly

created by monks of Muchelney from 7,000 fetter pieces, among which is a beer barrel – apparently a reference to Abbot Bere.

SOUTH CADBURY ST6325

An attractive scatter of golden cottages huddle around the church with its striking gargoyled tower; Waterloo Crescent is a distinctive row of farm workers' cottages built in 1815.

Cadbury Castle Its Arthurian connection is the main draw. The legendary king and his knights are still said to sleep below the turf of this huge hill fort, waking on Christmas Eve to ride down the hill, along what's long been known as King Arthur's Hunting Causeway, and through the village on their pilgrimage to Glastonbury. The castle, covering about 18 acres, is in fact a massive Iron Age camp: many relics have been found there – especially Roman artefacts. It's quite a steep climb, and can be muddy; stout walking shoes recommended. Compton Pauncefoot just E is pretty.

SOUTH PETHERTON ST4317

The **church** has the second-highest octagonal tower in the country.

SPARKFORD ST6127

Haynes Sparkford Motor Museum 🏛 (A359) Huge collection of gleamingly restored vintage and classic cars and motorcycles; you should be able to see some being test-driven outside. Meals, snacks, shop, disabled access; cl 25 Dec, 1 Jan; (01963) 440804; *£4.95. The Sparkford Inn is a nice place for lunch.

STAPLE FITZPAINE ST2618

Pretty village with a fine pub; a quiet drive with good views loops along the S edge of Staple Hill then crosses the B3170 to run over Culmhead (where the Holman Clavel is a good stop), along the Blackdown Hills and past the Wellington Monument.

STAPLEGROVE ST2027

Staplecombe Vineyards 🏛 Friendly little vineyard, with self-guided tours of the fields, then back at the house a cheery couple happy to chat. Shop, disabled access, open pm exc Sun Apr–Oct, or by appointment; (01823) 451217; free. Avoiding Taunton, the Lethbridge Arms at Bishops Lydeard does decent lunches.

STEEP HOLM ST2260
A small island a few miles off shore, its 50 acres a nature reserve teeming with rare plants, wildlife and historic remains. Terrific views from the rugged cliffs. You can get snacks out here, and there's a shop in former Victorian barracks, but it's not really suitable for the disabled. Boat trips to the island run from Knightstone Causeway, Weston, Apr–Oct – Mrs Rendell has dates and times on (01934) 632307; all-day trip £13.

STOGUMBER ST0937
Charming village with cottage gardens, an unblemished main street, and an interesting **church**; the White Horse has good food.
Bee World & Animal Centre (just S of Stogumber Stn) Rather jolly bee farm with observation hives, useful enough exhibition, and plenty of rare breeds and farm animals, some of which children can stroke. Also play area, a crazy golf course, nature trails, and children's pony rides. Staff are helpful and friendly, and you can see trains go past on the West Somerset Railway (combined tickets available). Good meals and snacks, shop, disabled access; cl Nov–Mar; (01984) 656545; £3.50.

STOGURSEY ST2042
Stogursey church Exceptional Norman church with charming carved 15th- and 16th-c pew ends – fascinating figures, faces and grotesques.

STOKE ST GREGORY ST3427
English Hurdle (Curload, towards Athelney) Produces baskets from its own willow plantations, as well as art charcoal. Also working blacksmith and display of willow sculptures. Shop, disabled access; cl Sat pm, Sun, bank hols; (01823) 698418; free. The Rose & Crown at Woodhill on the edge of Stoke St Gregory is popular for lunch.
Willow & Wetlands Visitor Centre (Meare Green Court, towards North Curry) Well liked by some readers, this shows how the area – the most important wetland region in England – developed from marsh and swamp, and looks at its wildlife and industries, especially willow-growing and basket-making (you can tour the resident weaver's workshop – there may be demonstrations, £2). Shop, some

disabled access; cl Sun; (01823) 490249; free.

STOKE SUB HAMDON ST4716
Ham Hill Country Park 140 acres of grassland and woodland, full of wildlife and plants. The hill has provided the stone for many of the villages in the area, producing that distinctive warm honey-coloured look. The elevated area of old stone quarries gives walkers splendid views; you can go E from here on paths past St Michael's Hill, topped by an 18th-c pepperpot tower, to Montacute.
Stoke sub Hamdon Priory The former 14th- and 15th-c priory manor house has long since vanished, but its fine thatched barn and the screens, passage and Great Hall of the chantry can still be seen; free. The village is charming, and the Fleur de Lis is good for lunch. Between here and Montacute is a striking folly, St Michael's Tower; it's one of three, all built by neighbouring friends in the 18th c – whenever one had a flag up it was an invitation for the others to go round for a hearty evening.

STRATTON-ON-THE-FOSSE ST6550
Notable for the spectacular modern (though not modern-looking) Downside Abbey.

STREET ST4836
Shoe Museum Clarks Shoes have been made in Street for quite some while now, and their shoe museum on the High St has examples of footwear from Roman times to the present, along with machinery and advertising material. Shop, disabled access; cl Christmas week; (01458) 842169; free. Behind here **Clarks Village** is an attractively laid out factory shopping centre, with well known names from Jaeger to Black & Decker; some real bargains, plenty of snacks.

TAUNTON ST2224
Busy and prosperous shopping country town with a lively Sat cattle market. It's not of great visual distinction; the best bit is Hammet St, a short street of 18th-c red brick terraces leading to the county's biggest **church**, which has an exceptionally ornate roof, lovely pinnacled tower and lofty Perpendicular chancel. The Tudor House on Fore St is attractive. Just

behind Riverside Pl the **Shakespeare Glassworks** may have demonstrations of glassblowing, and in Bath Pl **Makers** is a decent craft shop selling local hand-made crafts (cl Sun). The Masons Arms in Magdalene St is good for lunch (not Sun).

Somerset County Museum 🎟 Fine museum, housed in part of the former castle (whose 13th-c portcullised gate-tower is absorbed into the County Hotel), with a rare Bronze Age shield. Shop, disabled access to ground floor only; cl Sun, Mon (exc bank hols), Good Fri, 24 Dec–2 Jan; (01823) 320200; £2.50.

Somerset Cricket Museum 🎟 (Priory Bridge Rd) Old building, thought to have been the gatehouse for the priory that once stood adjacent to the cricket ground: bats, balls and blazers, cards, cuttings and caps, and a cricketing reference library too. Some disabled access; open wkdys Apr–Oct, plus wknds when there's a match on; (01823) 275893; £1.

TEMPLECOMBE ST7022
Ancient village with stocks still in place; the name comes from the medieval order of Knights Templar, dedicated to the protection of the Holy Sepulchre and pilgrims to it. The church, supposedly founded by King Alfred's daughter, houses a 13th-c painting of Christ, found by accident in an outhouse 30 years ago; possibly an early copy of the Turin Shroud, which the Knights Templar may have had in their possession for a while.

TINTINHULL ST5020
Tintinhull House Garden Colourful and attractive 1930s formal garden sheltered by walls and hedges, around 17th-c house with Queen Anne façade (not open). Teas, some disabled access; open pm Weds–Sun Apr–Sept; (01935) 822545; £3.80; NT. The nearby Crown & Victoria is good.

TOLLAND ST1131
Gaulden Manor (B3224) The gardens of this nicely tucked-away medieval manor house distinguished for its early plasterwork (open only for parties) are pleasant, with a rose garden and bog garden. Teas, shop, plant sales, disabled access; garden open pm Sun, Thurs and bank hols early Jun–Aug; (01984) 667213; £3.

WAMBROOK ST2908
Attractive village, in quiet countryside suiting both walkers and cyclists; the Cotley Inn here is useful.

WASHFORD ST0440
Cleeve Abbey (signed S) Remarkably well preserved 12th-c Cistercian abbey, the gatehouse, dormitory and refectory all in good condition. Fine timbered roof, detailed wall paintings and traceried windows, and an exhibition on monastic life. Snacks, shop, some disabled access; cl winter lunchtimes, 24–26 Dec, 1 Jan; (01984) 640377; £2.60; EH. The Notley Arms at Monksilver is the closest good place for a meal.

Tropiquaria (A39 – easy to spot by tall radio masts) This enjoyable place is an amazing transformation of a 1930s BBC transmitting station into an indoor jungle with high waterfall, tropical plants, free-flying birds and weird and wonderful animals. You can touch all sorts of creatures: plenty of snakes and lizards, maybe a millipede if you're lucky. There's an aquarium beneath the hall, while out in the landscaped gardens are birds, lemurs, chipmunks, guinea-pigs and wallabies, as well as a couple of good play areas. A delightful puppet theatre (for many, the highlight) below the café, has 20-min marionette and shadow puppet shows (usually hourly in summer, but at other times much less frequent – so worth checking first). Also an intriguing collection of vintage radios and televisions. Meals, snacks, shop, disabled access (not to aquarium); open daily Easter–Oct, then weekends and school hols Nov, Feb and Mar, and a wk after Christmas; (01984) 640688; £4.75. The nearby station on the steam line from Minehead has a little **railway museum** devoted to the old Somerset & Dorset Railway; cl Nov–Feb; (01984) 640869; £1.

WATCHET ST0743
This small working port has fishing boats and coasters using its tidal harbour, and enough industry to keep it from being too touristy – though it's by no means unattractive. The West Somerset Hotel has good cheap food.

WEBBINGTON ST3956
West Mendip Way This long-distance footpath, all the way between

Wells and Weston-super-Mare, crosses the Mendip plateau; there are some stunning views from this section along Crook Peak, Compton Hill and Wavering Down.

WELLS ST5546

With a population of only 9,500 this delightful place wouldn't normally even qualify as a big town, but in fact it's England's smallest city. The **Vicars Close** is said to be one of the oldest complete medieval streets in Europe; the cathedral's Vicars Choral still live here, passing the 15th-c Chain Gate to the cathedral itself. There are a good few other attractive old buildings, many now used as offices and shops (inc several antiques shops), and several grouped around the Market Pl; the City Arms is a pleasant place for lunch, and there's a big cheese shop not far away. The B3139 through Wedmore and side roads off it give a good feel of the dead flatness of the Somerset Levels.

Bishop's Palace Moated and fortified, approached through a 14th-c gatehouse; it's quite dramatic going across the drawbridge. The beautiful series of buildings still has some original 13th-c parts, notably the banqueting hall and undercroft, as well as several state rooms and a long gallery hung with portraits of former bishops. The grounds are the site of the wells that give the town its name, producing on average 150 litres (40 gallons) of water a second. Also lovely gardens, decent arboretum and a rather clever pair of swans, trained to ring a little bell under the gatehouse window when they're hungry (so many people feed them in summer that this isn't terribly often). Snacks, disabled access to ground floor; open Tues–Fri plus bank hols and Sun pm Easter–Oct, daily in Aug; (01749) 678691; £3, maybe more for special exhibitions.

Wells Cathedral Stunning structure right in the centre, its three towers stretching up against the Mendip foothills. The spectacular W front is reckoned by many to be the finest cathedral façade in the country; dating from the 13th c, it carries 293 pieces of medieval sculpture. Unmissable oddities inside include the wonderful scissors-shaped inverted arches, the

north transept's 14th-c clock where horsemen still joust every quarter of an hour, and the fine carvings in the south transept, inc various victims of toothache and four graphic scenes of an old man stealing fruit and getting what for. The embroidered stallbacks in the choir (1937–1948) are a riot of colour, and the library, with documents dating back to the 10th c, is at 51 metres (168 ft) the longest medieval library building in England. Evensong is at 5.15pm wkdys (not Weds), 3pm Sun. Meals, snacks, shop, disabled access; £4 suggested donation.

Wells Museum 🏛 (Cathedral Green) Tudor building with good local history museum inc notable embroidery samplers, and stone figures originally on the W front of the cathedral, but now too fragile to be returned there. Shop, disabled access to ground floor only; cl Tues Nov–Easter; (01749) 673477; *£2.50.

WEST BAGBOROUGH ST1733 Tiny village well placed below the Quantocks, with a traditional working **pottery**, and fresh generous food (and comfortable bedrooms) at the Rising Sun.

WEST MENDIP WAY ST3956 This long-distance footpath, all the way between Wells and Weston-super-Mare, crosses the Mendip plateau, poor windswept sheep pasture on top, pocked with unseen caverns used by potholers, and more visible Bronze Age funeral barrows; there are some stunning views from this section along Crook Peak, Compton Hill and Wavering Down. A path up from Compton Bishop ST3955 gives good access.

WESTON-SUPER-MARE ST3161 Friendly family seaside resort, its Latin epithet added in the 19th c in an attempt to be one up on the fashionable French resorts. The seafront Pavilion (Knightstone Parade) is a rather stylish family dining place, and there are pleasant walks (and a toll road) through the woods around the Iron Age fort above the town. The quietest beaches are to the N, around Sand Bay.

Helicopter Museum 🏛 (B3146, was A370) An unexpected find with over 50 helicopters and autogyros on display.

Usually on the second Sun each month (May–Oct), they have an Open Cockpit Day, when some helicopters are opened up for visitors to inspect, and others even offer flights. Snacks, shop, disabled access; cl Mon, Tues Nov–Mar, and mid-Dec–26 Dec, 1 Jan; (01934) 635227; *£3.50.

Heritage Centre (Wadham St) Displays on local history; snacks, shop, disabled access to ground floor only; cl Sun; (01934) 412144; £1.

Sea Life Centre (Marine Parade) Another in the reliable chain, right by the beach, with walk-through underwater tunnel, and plenty of sharks. Snacks, shop, disabled access; cl 25 Dec (phone for winter opening times); (01934) 641603; *£4.75.

Time Machine (Burlington St) Refurbished local history museum, focusing mainly on Victorian domestic life, with reconstructed shops and lots of seaside displays; it includes adjacent Clara's Cottage, a typical Westonian home of the 1900s with period kitchen, parlour and bedroom. Snacks, shop, disabled access on ground floor only; cl 25–26 Dec, 1 Jan; (01934) 621028; £3.

WESTONZOYLAND ST3534
Steam museum 🖭 Pretty village with a **steam pumping station**; snacks, shop, disabled access; open pm only every Sun, Thurs Jun–Aug; in steam first Sun of month Apr–Oct, plus Sun and Mon bank hol wknds; (01823) 275795; £2.50 (£3 steam days).

WHITCHURCH ST6167
Horse World (Staunton Lane) An absolute must for horse lovers, this new centre has been developed by the Friends of Bristol Horses Society, and has just about everything there is to know about the equine world. The sanctuary is home to over 200 rescued and retired horses, ponies and donkeys, but what makes this place particularly special is the range of other attractions on offer, with easily enough to fill a busy half-day. Housed in pleasantly restored farm buildings, these include an interactive museum examining the origins of the horse and its influence on the human world, a video theatre, a donkey house (where you can pet the docile beasts), and an extensive collection of tack and harnesses. There's a twice-daily Parade of Horses (11.30am and 2.30pm), a nature trail around the paddocks, a horse-themed play area, plenty of space for picnics, and other animals to meet such as goats, lambs, chickens and rabbits. Meals, snacks, shop, disabled access; cl wkdys Jan–Feb; (01275) 540173. Entry to the site is free, but a self-guided tour (taking in all the areas mentioned above) costs *£3.50.

WINCANTON ST7128
Fine Georgian houses and many of the multitude of inns and hotels survive from the coaching era; many still have old coach-entry gates. The **church porch** has a medieval relief of St Eligius. The cheerful Nog (South St) has decent food.

WOOKEY HOLE ST5347
Wookey Hole Caves & Papermill
🖭 Guided tours of half a mile of dramatic subterranean tunnels and caverns, using remote-controlled lighting and special effects to spotlight the geological features and bring to life associated history and myths. Just along the river the papermill demonstrates paper production, and also houses an authentic Edwardian fairground, Magical Mirror Maze and an Old Penny Arcade. A bustling place, all under cover, so ideal when the sun's not shining. Meals and snacks (readers find them a little pricey), shop, disabled access exc to caves; cl 17–25 Dec; (01749) 672243; £7.20. The Burcott Inn nearby is good for lunch.

YENSTON ST7121
Gartell Light Railway The friendly staff who run this 2-ft gauge railway running along the track of the defunct Somerset & Dorset Railway, try hard to ensure passengers enjoy their trip through ¾ mile of attractive Blackmore Vale countryside. The trains leave every 15 mins, and for a small extra charge you can visit the Templecombe Railway Museum with displays on the former local station and various railway memorabilia. Picnic area by small lake, snacks, shop; open bank hol Mons and some Suns May–Oct, plus two Santa wknds in Dec – best to phone; (01963) 370752; £3 (for a day's unlimited travel).

YEOVIL ST5515

Little in the town to interest visitors, but the **Museum of South Somerset** (Hendford) is worth a look if passing, with a good range of local history and reconstructed Roman and Georgian rooms (shop, disabled access; cl Sun and Mon, plus Sats Oct–Mar; free); there's also a dry-ski centre and partly 14th-c church.

YEOVILTON ST5423

Fleet Air Arm Museum 🖼 (Royal Naval Air Station, off A359) Big place concentrating on the story of aviation at sea from 1908, and the history of the Royal Naval Air Service. Lively displays on the WRENS, the Falklands and Gulf Wars, jets and helicopters, as well as nearly 50 historic aircraft, and lots of models, paintings, weapons and photographs, plus a new exhibition on supersonic flight. Viewing galleries look out over the aircraft using this busy base. Also adventure playground, and hi-tech flight simulator. You could easily spend a good few hours here. Meals, snacks, shop, disabled access; cl 24–26 Dec; (01935) 840565; £7. The Kingsdon Inn is the best nearby place for lunch.

Other interesting churches with fine carvings include Bicknoller ST1139, Broomfield ST2231 and Spaxton ST2237.

Particularly attractive villages, all with decent pubs, include Batcombe ST6838, Compton Dando ST6464, Evercreech ST6438, Hinton St George ST4212, Huish Episcopi ST4226, Litton ST5954, Luxborough SS9837, North Perrott ST4709, Norton sub Hamdon ST4615, South Stoke ST7641 (picturesque views from the steep nearby lanes), Waterrow ST0425 and Wellow ST7458. High Ham ST4330, Pilton ST5940, Stowell ST6822 and Winscombe ST4157 are also well worth a visit.

Where to eat

APPLEY ST0621 **Globe** *Appley (01823) 672327* Cheerfully run and unspoilt 15th-c pub with a relaxed chatty atmosphere, generous helpings of good interesting food inc adventurous specials and vegetarian meals, and super puddings; no smoking dining room; cl Mon lunch exc bank hols. £20|**£5.95**

BATCOMBE ST6838 **Three Horseshoes** *(01749) 850359* Honey stone, slate-roofed pub serving very popular food in bustling main room decorated with pretty ivy stencils and artificial ivy, fruit and flower decorations, and a few naive farm animal paintings on the lightly ragged dark pink walls; a woodburner and big open fire, attractive stripped stone dining room, well kept real ales, a good choice of wines, and big well equipped play area in garden. £20|**£8**

BATH ST7265 **Lettonie** *35 Kelston Rd (01225) 446676* Super restaurant-with-rooms in lovely Georgian house in gardens with fine views; spacious reception area, convivial bar, elegant restaurant with paintings by Mr Blunos's Latvian uncle, beautifully presented exceptional food (French with Latvian touches), a relaxed atmosphere, and helpful keen French staff; comfortable, pretty bdrms; cl Sun/Mon, 2 wks Aug, 2 wks after Christmas; disabled access. £57.50 dinner, £34 lunch/2 courses £15

BATH ST7464 **Moody Goose** *7a Kingsmead Sq (01225) 466688* Stylish basement restaurant with large namesake pottery goose, paintings on whitewashed walls, fresh flowers on crisp white tablecloths, deft modern English cooking, and a thoughtful wine list; cl Sun, 2 wks Jan; children over 7. £33/2 courses £12

BATH ST7464 **Old Green Tree** *12 Green St* Genuinely unspoilt pub with a bustling cheerful atmosphere in its three oak-panelled little rooms, a no smoking back bar, several well kept real ales, lots of malt whiskies, a nice little wine list with a dozen by the glass, and enjoyable lunchtime bar food; they do not take bookings; cl 25 Dec, 1 Jan; children over 12|**£5**

BATH ST7465 **Olive Tree** *Russel St (01225) 447928* Light and airy no smoking basement restaurant in the Queensberry Hotel; stylishly simple modern décor, friendly helpful service, super Mediterranean cooking (delicious fish and tempting puddings), and good value wines; cl Sun am, 4 days over Christmas. £40/2 courses £13.50

BATH ST7564 **Rajpoot** *4 Argyle St (01225) 466833* Exceptionally good carefully cooked Indian food in attractively decorated restaurant, particularly good service (you are met at the door by a colourfully uniformed doorman), and used by stars of screen and stage; cl 25–26 Dec; disabled access (by arrangement). £22|**£6.95**

BECKINGTON ST8051 **Woolpack** *Warminster Rd (01373) 831244* This old inn has a spacious, light and modern interior with an attractive no smoking lounge, antique furnishings, a lively flagstoned public bar with a good log fire, cosy candlelit no smoking dining room, imaginative daily specials, and real ales and decent wines; comfortable bdrms. £21|**£7.50**

BRISTOL ST5872 **Harveys Wine Cellars** *12 Denmark St (0117) 927 5034* Attractive restaurant in 13th-c wine cellars with lots of interesting memorabilia (old sherry casks, wine bottles, and old silver and glassware), very good imaginative food, an exceptional cheese board, friendly knowledgeable staff, and a wonderful wine list; guided tours and tastings and wine merchants and wine shop; cl Sun, bank hols, 1 wk Feb, 2 wks Aug; children over 5. £26.50

BRISTOL ST5672 **Neil's** *112 Princess Victoria St, Clifton (0117) 973 3669* Cosy and brightly decorated family-run lunchtime restaurant with friendly owner and a good choice of imaginative French/English food; cl Sun, Mon, 3 wks Christmas. £22

BRISTOL ST5872 **River Station** *The Grove (0117) 914 4434* Converted ex-River Police HQ on waterfront with informal ground-floor bistro, airy first-floor restaurant, modern furnishings, enjoyable popular modern British cooking with Mediterranean slant, and a marvellous choice of wines by the glass; cl 25–31 Dec; disabled access downstairs only. £26.50

CASTLE CARY ST6432 **George** *Market Pl (01963) 350761* Lovely thatched coaching inn with huge black elm mantlebeam said to be over a thousand years old over log fire in beamed front bar, a civilised relaxed atmosphere, no smoking restaurant and inner no smoking bar, well kept ales, decent wines by the glass, enjoyable food, and pleasant staff; bdrms. £20.40|**£7.50**

COMBE HAY ST7359 **Wheatsheaf** *(01225) 833504* Popular country pub in a pretty setting, with pleasantly old-fashioned rooms, a big log fire, shuttered windows, reliably good food (plenty of game and fish), well kept real ales, decent wines, and friendly staff; cl 25–26 Dec; disabled access. £21|**£5.50**

CRANMORE ST6742 **Strode Arms** *(01749) 880450* Neatly kept former farmhouse with charming country furnishings, newspapers to read, log fires in handsome fireplaces, generous helpings of good interesting food in bar and restaurant, well kept real ales, and decent wines; cl winter Sun pm; children in restaurant only; disabled access. £18.50|**£4.75**

CULMHEAD ST2216 **Holman Clavel** *(01823) 421432* Friendly free house high up in the Blackdown Hills, with a relaxed atmosphere, a roaring log fire, ancient skittle alley, simple furnishings, imaginative and enjoyable daily-changing food using organic produce and free range eggs, real ales, and 15 wines by the glass; disabled access. £25|**£4.95**

DOUTLING ST6545 **Waggon & Horses** *Beacon (01749) 880302* 18th-c inn with stone mullioned latticed windows, a rambling bar with interesting pictures for sale, two no smoking rooms, a wide choice of enjoyable robustly flavoured food, decent house wines, cocktails, real ales, and a lovely big walled garden with some remarkable fancy fowl (they sell the eggs), a goat and horses; big raftered gallery for art shows and classical music; children must be well behaved. £19.20|**£6.40**

EAST WOODLANDS ST7944 **Horse & Groom** *(01373) 462802* Small civilised pub on the edge of Longleat estate with a pleasant little bar, comfortable lounge, sizeable no smoking dining conservatory, imaginative food cooked by the new licensees, well kept real ales, good wines by the glass, and seats in attractive garden. £18|**£6.50**

HALLATROW ST6356 **Old Station** *Wells Rd (01761) 452228* Extraordinary pub packed with a formidable collection of bric-a-brac in its dimly lit bars, a handsome beer counter with well kept real ales, a mix of furniture, surprisingly good enjoyable food (given the style of the place), and a no smoking railway carriage

restaurant in a garden with a well equipped play area; bdrms; disabled access.
£19|**£5.60**

KNAPP ST3026 **Rising Sun** *(01823) 490436* Rather smart 15th-c longhouse with
a genteel landlord, a friendly atmosphere, stripped beams and stonework, two
inglenook fireplaces, good food with a strong emphasis on fish, a partly no smoking
restaurant, well kept real ales, farm ciders, a decent wine list, and welcoming staff
(and dogs); bdrms; some disabled access. £24|**£5.50**

LANGLEY MARSH ST0729 **Three Horseshoes** *(01984) 623763*
Unpretentious red sandstone pub with short changing choice of imaginative food
(inc vegetarian dishes and always a game casserole), veg from their own garden, no
chips or fried food, a wide choice of often unusual real ales, farm ciders, no fruit
machines or pool tables, skittle alley, beer garden, and sloping back garden with play
area and farmland views; good nearby walks; cl winter Mon; children must be well
behaved. £15|**£4.95**

MONKSILVER ST0737 **Notley Arms** *(01984) 56217* Immensely well liked,
friendly pub with beamed L-shaped bar, candles and fresh flowers, woodburners,
reasonably priced very good food (they don't take bookings, so must get there
early), well kept beers, and neatly kept cottagey garden running down to a swift
clear stream; pub games, skittle alley, and table tennis; disabled access.
£17.25|**£6.50**

NORTH CURRY ST3125 **Bird in Hand** *Queen Sq (01823) 490248* Friendly
village pub with new licensee, flagstones, original beams and timbers, log fires in
inglenook fireplaces, imaginative food inc plenty of fish, popular Sun roasts, separate
restaurant area with conservatory for more formal dining, well kept real ales, and
summer barbecues. £20.75|**£6**

RUDGE ST8251 **Full Moon** *(01373) 830936* Attractive rustic pub with friendly
licensees, a lot of character in the different rooms, a gently upmarket atmosphere,
small flagstoned dining room (and separate plush restaurant), generous helpings of
imaginative bar food inc a bargain 3-course set lunchtime and early evening meal,
and well kept real ales; comfortable bdrms. £24|**£6**

SHEPTON MALLET ST6144 **Blostins** *29 Waterloo Rd (01749) 343648* Friendly
little candlelit evening bistro with consistently good interesting food inc lovely
puddings, and fairly priced wines; cl Sun, Mon, 1 wk Jan, 1 wk Easter, 2 wks Aug.
£21.50/2 courses £13.95

SHEPTON MONTAGUE ST6731 **Montague Inn** *(01749) 813213* Tastefully
furnished country pub with stripped wooden tables, kitchen chairs and a log fire in
the attractive inglenook fireplace, a slightly upmarket atmosphere, particularly good
food using the best local produce and fish delivered fresh twice a week from
Cornwall, well kept real ales, fine wines, disarmingly swift service, elegant candlelit
dining rooms (one is no smoking), and paintings for sale; pretty back garden and
terrace with nice views; no children. £20.50/£5.95|**£5.95**

TRISCOMBE ST1535 **Blue Ball** *(01984) 618242* Carefully improved little pub,
now thatched, with quite a few original features and new decking at the top of the
woodside terraced garden with peaceful hill views; good food, cheerful landlord, a
marvellous wine list of 400 bottles (they will open any under £20 if you want a glass
only), well kept real ales, a dozen malt whiskies, and farm cider. £25|**£5.75**

WELLS ST5045 **City Arms** *69 High St (01749) 673916* 16th-c pub reached
through a charming cobbled courtyard with white metal seats and tables, Virginia-
creepered walls, and attractive side verandah; cellar-like bar with pillars in arched
doorways, homely sofas and other seats, a really relaxed friendly atmosphere, a fine
open-beamed upstairs restaurant, good interesting food, real ales, and neat,
cheerful staff. £17|**£6**

WEST HUNTSPILL ST3244 **Crossways** *Withy Rd (01278) 783756* Popular
dining pub with a buoyant atmosphere and plenty of space, enjoyable food (esp daily
specials), well kept real ales, and decent wines; comfortable bdrms; cl 25 Dec;
disabled access. £14.50|**£5**

WESTON-SUPER-MARE ST3261 **Reflections** *22 Boulevard (01934) 622454*

Informal family-run restaurant, a good but ordinary café at lunchtimes (exc Sun, when decent set lunch), but transformed Thurs, Fri and Sat evenings with elaborate and well presented high quality meals; cl Sun–Weds pms, 1 Jan for 10 days. £26/2-course Thurs/Fri pm meal £12.95

WILLITON ST0741 **White House** *11 Long St (01984) 632777* Charming shuttered Georgian hotel under the same owners for over 30 years, with antiques and more modern furnishings, paintings and ceramics, very good enjoyable carefully cooked food using the best local produce, and a fine choice of reasonably priced wines; good breakfasts; bdrms; cl Nov–mid-May; partial disabled access. £40

WOOKEY ST5245 **Burcott Inn** *Wookey Rd (01749) 673874* Little roadside pub, close to Wells, neatly kept and friendly with two simply furnished small front bars, an open fire, a roomy attractive back restaurant, nice bar food, well kept real ales, and a sizeable garden; no food Sun or Mon pms; cl 25 Dec, 1 Jan; children must be well behaved; disabled access. £21|**£5.25**

Special thanks to B and K Hypher, Richard Webber, B M Eldridge, R J Cox, Mr and Mrs G Girdin

STAFFORDSHIRE

Britain's best theme park, Potteries porcelain, and some lovely countryside with good walking opportunities

Leaps and bounds ahead of its competition, Alton Towers remains the number one place for families here – increasing its range of attractions every year. Elsewhere, Drayton Manor Park combines white knuckles with wildlife, the prettily set zoo at Winkhill has a new indoor exhibition (not to mention its children's farm or under-5s play room), and Fletchers Garden Centre, Eccleshall, and busy Amerton Farm at Stowe-by-Chartley, have more fun for families than their names might suggest. There's also plenty to interest children and their parents at striking Tamworth Castle, and at those splendid great houses in similarly splendid grounds, Shugborough and Weston Park at Weston under Lizard. Tamworth's Snowdome, new to the *Guide* this year, boasts a full gamut of winter sports from skiing to Sunday morning tobogganing.

The area around Stoke-on-Trent is brimful with museums and show-places reflecting the local pottery industry (the revamped Wedgwood visitor centre is a highlight), and the breweries of Burton upon Trent present beer-making at either end of the scale.

The NE gives beautiful walks and drives in glorious Peak District limestone country (Dove Dale, shared with Derbyshire, is described under that county). In the more industrial S, Cannock Chase has miles of fine landscape, and the canal network allows some unusually attractive walks.

Where to stay

BETLEY SJ7847 **Adderley Green Farm** *Heighley Castle Lane, Betley, Crewe, Cheshire CW3 9BA* (01270) 820203 **£45***; 3 rms. Georgian farmhouse on big dairy farm, with good breakfasts in homely dining room, and large garden; fishing on adjoining farm; cl Christmas and New Year; children over 5

BLACKSHAW MOOR SK0061 **Three Horseshoes** *Buxton Rd, Blackshaw Moor, Leek, Staffordshire ST13 8TW* (01538) 300296 **£65***, plus special breaks; 6 rms. Large, well appointed family-run pub with lots of nooks and crannies, open fire, no smoking area, good atmosphere, generous food served by young friendly staff in bar carvery and separate candlelit restaurant, well kept real ales, and a decent wine list; no accommodation Christmas

CAVERSWALL SJ9542 **Caverswall Castle** *Blyth Bridge Rd, Caverswall, Stoke-on-Trent, Staffordshire ST11 9EA* (01782) 393239 **£75**; 6 oak-panelled rms with four-posters. Castle dating from 1270 with turrets, dungeon, portcullis and moat; lots of atmosphere, fine panelling and paintings, comfortable restful day rooms, grand dining room, and big billiard room; indoor swimming pool and two lakes for fishing; self-catering in restored stone turrets; cl 1 Nov–1 Mar (but self-catering open then); disabled access

CHEADLE SK0044 **Ley Fields Farm** *Leek Rd, Cheadle, Stoke-on-Trent, Staffordshire ST10 2EF* (01538) 752875 **£38**; 3 rms. Listed Georgian farmhouse on working dairy farm in lovely countryside with lots of walks; traditional furnishings in lounge and dining room, good home cooking, and friendly welcome; cl Christmas and New Year

CHEDDLETON SJ9651 **Choir Cottage** *Ostlers Lane, Cheddleton, Leek, Staffordshire ST13 7HS* (01538) 360561 **£55***; 2 pretty rms with four-posters in 17th-c cottage next to owners' home. No smoking cottage with comfortable lounges, attractive dining room with country views, and good breakfasts; cl Christmas; children over 5

ECCLESHALL SJ8329 **George** *Castle St, Eccleshall, Stafford, Staffordshire ST21 6DF* (01785) 850300 **£50**w, plus special breaks; 9 rooms. Friendly 18th-c hotel with open fire in big brick inglenook in cosy, beamed bar, ales from their own microbrewery, and good food in bistro

OAKAMOOR SK0544 **Bank House** *Farley Lane, Oakamoor, Stoke-on-Trent, Staffordshire ST10 3BD* (01538) 702810 **£70**; 3 lovely big rms. Carefully restored no smoking country home in neat gardens on the edge of the Peak National Park and with lovely views; log fire in comfortable drawing room, library, piano in the inner hall, and most enjoyable food (by prior arrangement using home-grown and local produce) – super home-made breads, brioches, pastries and jams and marmalade at marvellous breakfast; friendly dog and cats; lots to do nearby; cl Christmas wk

OAKAMOOR SK0747 **Tenement Farm** *Three Lows, Oakamoor, Stoke-on-Trent, Staffordshire ST10 3BW* (01538) 702333 **£45***; 8 rms with showers. Comfortable no smoking house on traditional beef and sheep farm surrounded by fine countryside, with airy homely lounge, licensed bar, and sunny conservatory; also self-catering cottage; cl Nov–Feb

ROLLESTON ON DOVE SK2327 **Brookhouse Hotel** *Station Rd, Rolleston on Dove, Burton upon Trent, Staffordshire DE13 9AA* (01283) 814188 **£85***, plus wknd breaks; 19 comfortable rms with Victorian brass or four-poster beds. Handsome ivy-covered William & Mary brick building in five acres of lovely gardens with comfortable antiques-filled rooms, and good food in elegant little dining room; children over 12; disabled access

WARSLOW SK0858 **Greyhound** *Warslow, Buxton, Derbyshire SK17 0JN* (01298) 84249 **£35**; 4 clean and comfortable rms with shared bthrms. Warm, welcoming atmosphere in comfortably refurbished slated stone inn handy for Peak district, with generous helpings of home-made food inc hearty breakfasts, live Sat evening entertainment; cl Christmas; children over 12

WETTON SK1055 **Olde Royal Oak** *Wetton, Ashbourne, Staffordshire DE6 2AF* (01335) 310287 **£40**, plus wknd breaks; 4 rms. Shuttered old stone village inn in lovely NT walking country, with a warmly cheerful welcome; an attractive older part leads into a more modern-feeling area, with open fires, country furniture, a sun lounge overlooking a small garden, decent food, and nice breakfasts; children by arrangement

---

Please let us know what you think of places in the *Guide*. Use the report forms at the back of the book or simply write us a letter.

To see and do

Staffordshire Family Attraction of the Year

ALTON SK0743 **Alton Towers** (off B5032) We searched really hard for an alternative to this 200-acre giant as Staffordshire's stand-out family attraction, but, despite the temptation of the Snowdome's Sunday morning tobogganing (see Tamworth entry) if truth be told there's nowhere in the vicinity with such broad appeal. This year they've worked hard to end the queues at the most popular features, fearsome roller-coasters Oblivion and Nemesis. If you book in advance you get to enter the park early, and go on these rides before the main gates have opened (you can save a bit on admission costs too). And at other times you can get a timed ticket, which should mean you won't have to wait longer than 20 minutes. Not sure what you're letting yourself in for? Oblivion is a three-minute horror that climaxes with a 70mph vertical drop, and Nemesis whisks you through unfeasible angles at a greater G-force than that faced by astronauts during a space shuttle launch; both are unsuitable for anyone under 1.4 metres. Other highlights (if you like that sort of thing) are a ride that spins you round three complete loops before leaving you dangling 15 metres (50 ft) above ground (while being attacked by jets of water from handily placed fountains), and the spooky new Hex, a hi-tech haunted house. Though it's these rides that draw the crowds, they've deliberately set out to appeal to whole families rather than just daredevil teenagers: Storybook Land for example has quite a range of gentle rides aimed at children up to around 7 (toddlers love the singing barn), and some live shows now feature Barney, the inexplicably popular purple dinosaur (pre-booked tickets guarantee you front row seats). Dozens of other distractions, from log flumes to lovely extensive gardens that anywhere else would be worth a visit in their own right. There's even a splendidly zany (but thoroughly comfortable) hotel, with a bizarre cross between a galleon and a hot-air balloon in the lobby, and a room which keeps dishing out chocolate; you'll need to book well in advance for themed rooms, such as the Peter Rabbit burrows. Some rides still have a bit of a wait (ten minutes, on average), and you'll need the whole day and some fairly organised planning to get the most out of it. Nor is it cheap, but the presentation and facilities are excellent – if you don't normally like theme parks you may be pleasantly surprised. They usually end the season with a series of spectacular firework displays. Meals, snacks, shops, disabled access (on most rides too); open mid-Mar to early Nov; (01538) 702200; £21 (£17 children 4–13). The family ticket – covering 2 adults and 2 children, or 1 adult and 3 children – can save a bit of money, as will booking in advance, either by phone or online at www.alton-towers.com. They've introduced off-peak tickets that can be up to £5 cheaper than normal; these are available wkdays out of season, so not great for children, but ideal for adults free to flee the office. You can usually buy a good value ticket for a second day's entry from any of the information booths or ticket offices.

ABBOTS BROMLEY SK0824
Quite a lot of attractive buildings, with pleasant countryside around.
ALTON SK0743
Alton Towers See *family panel above.*
BIDDULPH SJ8858
Biddulph Grange Garden (Grange Rd) Notable and really quite charming high Victorian garden, extensively restored; divided by its founder into a number of smaller themed gardens to house specimens from all over the world. Snacks, shop; cl am wkdys, all day Mon (exc bank hols), Tues, and Nov–Mar (exc wknds Nov–mid-Dec); (01782) 517999; £4.30 (£2 Nov/Dec); NT. You can get a joint ticket with Little Moreton Hall, six miles away in Cheshire.
BLYTHE BRIDGE SJ9441

Foxfield Steam Railway Five miles through scenic countryside; a return ticket gives unlimited travel for the whole day (exc during special events). Staff are particularly friendly, and there's a collection of locomotives and rolling stock. Usually open wknds and bank hols Apr–Oct (and occasional days in winter) but best to check; (01782) 396210; £4. The Ship at Teanford has decent food.

BREWOOD SJ8808
Charming small town, with many attractive Georgian and older buildings.

BURTON UPON TRENT SK2523
🔁 The town is dominated by its connections with the brewing industry, and the **Bass Museum** (Horninglow St) explores this topic in some detail – with an emphasis on Bass and the company's shire horses. You can tour the brewery (no under-13s); also indoor and outdoor play areas. Summer special events and occasional lunchtime brass-band concerts. Meals, snacks, shop, disabled access; cl 25–26 Dec, 1 Jan; (01283) 511000; £4.50.

Burton Bridge Brewery A complete contrast to the giant breweries that dominate the town, this shows brewing at the very opposite end of the scale. There's an attached pub; or the Queens Hotel is a comfortable place for lunch, as is the Marquis Suite carvery at the New Talbot Hotel on Anglesey Rd.

River Trent Boat Trips The Boat House at Stapenhill has river and wetland views (boat trips leave on the hour from the ferry bridge from midday onwards in summer). Nearby Rangemore has a good **garden centre**, with farm animals for children.

CALDON CANAL SK0348
The towpath gives many miles of good interesting walks. There's usually something happening at the Froghall Wharf canal terminus (maybe inc barge trips – (01538) 266486), with an interesting walk along the canal to Consallforge (unusual remote pub here). The nearby **nature park** continues this strange lost-valley scenery. There's also good access to this, the most attractive of Staffordshire's canals, from the good Boat pub at Cheddleton, and from Denford nr Leek.

CANNOCK CHASE SK0215
Miles of lovely woodland and rolling heath, threaded with quiet side roads – the breathing space for the more industrial part of Staffordshire. Dotted around the 17,000 acres are Iron Age hill forts, nature trails, streams, pools and springs, and lovely spots for picnics or dramatic views; fallow deer are often seen. There's an information centre at Marquis Drive, and decent campsites. The canalside Moat House at Acton Trussell does decent food.

Castle Ring This large hill fort has fine views over the forests of Cannock Chase to the Trent Valley.

CAULDON SK0749
Notable for its pub, the **Yew Tree**; a very unpretentious place packed with an extraordinary and delightfully higgledy-piggledy collection of remarkable bygones, esp mechanical music.

CHARTLEY SK0228
Chartley Castle (just over 6 miles W of Uttoxeter) A fine old ruin, with good views.

CHEDDLETON SJ9752
Cheddleton Flint Mill (Cheadle Rd) Fully preserved 17th- and 18th-c water mills, with a little museum. Shop, disabled access to ground floor; usually cl Fri, am most wkdys and Nov–Jan; (01782) 502907; free. The Boat does decent lunches, with pleasant canal walks from it.

Churnet Valley Railway 🔁 (Station Rd) Small steam locomotive museum in Victorian station building, complete with signal box and engine sheds. Short steam and diesel runs in attractive surroundings. Snacks, shop; open wknds Easter–mid-Oct, plus Weds in Aug and for various special events (inc in Dec); trains running Sun Apr–Oct, plus Sat July and Aug and Weds Aug; (01538) 360522; £4.50 (less when no trains running).

Old School Craft centre Readers like this well set out craft centre, with its pleasant tearoom.

CHURNET VALLEY SK0545
Very pretty walks from Alton or Oakamoor; the best goes through Hawksmoor and Greendale to pass the broad fishponds in wooded Dimmings Dale and comes back down to the river

past an old smelting mill – and a good café called the Ramblers Retreat. Hawksmoor Wood is itself an attractive nature reserve, and the Talbot in Alton is useful for lunch.

CLIFTON CAMPVILLE SK2510

Clifton Campville church One of those rare country churches that seems practically perfect in every way. The Green Man has good value food.

CODSALL SJ8604

Notable in summer for its profusion of lupins. Moors Farm has a good farm shop and small country restaurant.

CROXDEN ABBEY SK0639

Ruins in quiet surroundings, with some towering arches surviving. The Raddle at Hollington is a good family country pub.

ECCLESHALL SJ8329

Fletchers Garden Centre (Bridge Farm, Stone Rd) Plenty to amuse children, inc adventure playground, animals, falconry displays, crazy golf and (wknds, bank hols and school hols Easter–Oct) a miniature railway, (01785) 851057; £1.40 for crazy golf, 80p return train ticket. The George (Castle St) has good home cooking, and on the other side of town the Star out at Copmere End is prettily set overlooking the lake.

ENVILLE SO8287

Staffordshire Way This way-marked footpath offers scope for walking; the Cat at Enville is a useful place to join it.

FRADLEY JUNCTION SK1513

Trent & Mersey Canal Generally less opportunity for towpath walks than with other Staffordshire canals, but Fradley Junction, with a waterside pub and lots happening on the water, is an attractive place for a stroll.

GREAT HAYWOOD SJ9923

There are interesting **canal walks** from here, and the longest **pack-horse bridge** in the country is nearby.

HANBURY SK1728

The Cock pub at Hanbury is a start for several attractive walks, inc a poignant one to the vast crater left by the 1944 Fauld bomb dump explosion, a tragedy understandably not much publicised at the time.

ILAM SK1350

Attractive estate village, in lovely countryside. Wooded Ilam Park shows

the Manifold Valley at its most sheltered.

INGESTRE SJ9824

Ingestre church Designed by or under Christopher Wren, and reckoned by some to be the finest small 17th-c church outside London.

KINVER SO8582

(the one right over in the W) Interesting village, with some of Britain's only rock houses nearby, still lived in 30 years ago; there are good views from the Iron Age fort on the ridge above.

LEEK SJ9856

Coombe Valley bird reserve This nearby RSPB reserve has a shop, and disabled access; cl 25 Dec (01538) 384017; free. The A53 high moorland road N has good views, and E of here the B5053 gives an excellent impression of the dales country (the Jervis Arms at Onecote is a good family stop).

LICHFIELD SK1109

The attractive centre is largely pedestrianised, with many 18th-c and older buildings among the more modern shops (and antiques shops). The **cathedral**, with its three graceful spires and close with lovely buildings around it, is magnificent inside, and its W front is memorable, esp at dusk or in the dark when shadows seem to bring the profusion of statues to life. Wonderful illuminated gospels in the chapter house. On Sat from May–Sept you can see the remains of a 16th-c gaol behind the Guildhall (Bore St); 40p.

Heritage Exhibition and Treasury (Market Sq) Worth a look, in a sympathetically restored chapel site; cl 25–26 Dec and 1 Jan; £2. You may be able to go up to the viewing platform in the spire, which has splendid views of the surrounding countryside (£1).

Samuel Johnson Birthplace Museum (Breadmarket St) Dr Johnson was born here in 1709; the house is now furnished in period, with many mementoes of him. Shop; cl Sun Nov–Jan; (01543) 264972; £2, free entry on Sat nearest to Dr Johnson's birthday, 16 Sept.

LONGNOR SK0865

This attractive small town, despite its grand church, has a pleasantly villagey feel (and a good craft centre). The interesting Olde Cheshire Cheese has good value food.

LONGSDON SJ9655

Deep Hayes Country Park (Sutherland Rd; village off A53, 2m SW of Leek) Pleasant mixture of two freshwater pools, woods and meadows redeveloped from a former reservoir built in the mid-19th c by the Potteries Waterworks Company. A visitor centre (open wknds, Sun pm only in winter) has details of ranger-led and self-guided walks in and around the park, as well as a shop and disabled facilities – one path is suitable for wheelchairs; (01538) 387655; free (inc parking).

MANIFOLD VALLEY SK1350

This has many good walks, with fewer of the sensational rock features that abound in Dove Dale, but plenty of charm – more or less steep riverside pastures, ancient woodland in the narrower steeper gorges, waterside caves; there's good access to the hills above it, such as Wetton Hill, which have attractive views. The best viewpoint of all, not to be missed, is Thor's Cave, high above the dale. The branch off up Hamps Dale is extremely pretty. There are good pubs nearby at Warslow, Wetton and Hulme End.

MEERBROOK SJ9959

Tittesworth reservoir Large reservoir with visitor centre and restaurant, nature trails and bird hides, adventure playground and a sensory garden for the partially sighted; cl 25 Dec (restaurant and shop cl Mon–Tues Nov–Mar); (01538) 300224; £1 parking.

NEWCASTLE UNDER LYME SJ8349

Heritage Narrow Boats Electric narrow boats to hire by the day; cl Nov–Easter; (01782) 785700; £50–£75 wkdys for up to 12 people (£65–£90 wknds) – very satisfying, gliding along in silence.

ROACHES SJ9963

These form an impressive western barrier at the edge of the Dark Peak; this is perhaps the most exhilarating of several moorland walks from the side roads off the A53 N of Leek. A walk here can be combined with the path through the unspoilt Dane Valley to Danebridge on the Cheshire border;

hidden in the woods above the Dane is Lud's Church – not a church, but a miniature chasm reputed to have been a hiding place for religious dissenters.

RUDYARD LAKE SJ9459

Though man-made it's perhaps one of Staffordshire's prettiest sights (a certain Mr Kipling liked it so much he named his son after it); you can hire a boat, and the muddy marshland provides a haven for wading birds. The meadows and forested slopes above are pleasant for walks and picnics.

RUGELEY SK0418

Quite a few attractive old buildings, inc a beautiful 12th-c **church**.

SHALLOWFORD SJ8729

Izaak Walton Cottage 🏠 (Worston Lane) Smartly rethatched home of the author of *The Compleat Angler*, with displays on the development of angling, period herb garden and picnic orchard. Snacks, shop, limited disabled access; cl ams, Mon–Tues (exc bank hols), and Nov–Mar; (01785) 760278; £2.10. The Worston Mill at Little Bridgeford is attractive for lunch.

SHUGBOROUGH SJ9921

Shugborough Hall & County Museum (A513) Imposing ancestral home of the Earls of Lichfield, begun in the late 17th c and enlarged in the 18th; magnificent state rooms, restored working kitchens, interesting marionette collection, and exhibition of the present Earl's photography. The park has a variety of unusual neo-classical monuments, working rare-breeds farm, and restored corn mill. Meals, snacks, shop, disabled access; open Easter–Sept, plus Sun in Oct; (01889) 881388; entry to estate £2 (payable by NT members), museum and servants' quarters £4 (NT members £3), house £4, farm £4 (NT members £3); NT. An all-in ticket is quite expensive at £8 – better value on one of their special event days, when there are more activities (such as hands-on Victorian cookery displays) for no extra cost. The canalside Wolseley Arms towards Rugeley is a handy food stop.

STAFFORD SJ9223

Greengate St has what's said to be the biggest timber-framed house in the country, built with local oak in 1595; period room settings and an

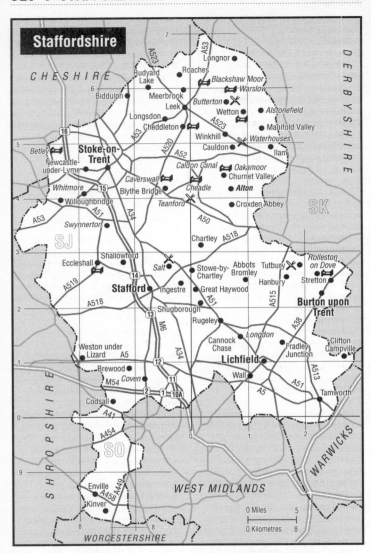

information centre. The Picture House (Bridge St/Lichfield St) has decent food all day.

Shire Hall Gallery (Market Sq) Handsome former county hall complete with courtrooms that were used until 1992; exhibitions of art, craft and photography, and good craft shop. Snacks, disabled access. Cl Sun, Mon during exhibition changes, and bank hols; (01785) 278345; free.

Stafford Castle Visitor Centre (A518 SW) Norman remains, rebuilt in Gothic Revival style in the early 19th c, then allowed to fall into disrepair. Good visitor centre, and a medieval herb garden. Teas Sun only, shop, disabled access to visitor centre; cl Mon (exc spring and summer bank hols), 25 Dec–2 Jan; (01785) 257698; £2.10.

STOKE-ON-TRENT SJ8745

The Potteries The five linked towns

within the Stoke-on-Trent conurbation still produce some of the finest china and pottery in the country. You can tour several of the factories, and most have museums or a visitor centre; a good local bus service connects them all, taking you through a memorable urban landscape, the buildings clinging to small steep hills.

Etruria Industrial Museum (Lower Bedford St, Etruria) This well restored and enjoyable museum sandwiched between two canals and based around the only surviving steam-powered potter's mill in the country (grinding flint right up to 1972) will include a new exhibition hall and tearoom when it reopens at the start of 2001. There is also a working blacksmith on site. Museum open Weds–Sun all year (exc Christmas), engine in steam one wknd each month Apr–Dec, usually the first, but best to check; (01782) 233144; £1.50. The Plough (off A53 opposite Festival site in Etruria) is our current lunch recommendation for the Potteries.

Ford Green Hall 🖼 (Smallthorne) An interesting little 17th-c house with occasional informal performances of period music and other special events. Snacks, shop, limited disabled access, cl am, Fri, Sat and 25 Dec–1 Jan; (01782) 233195; £1.50.

Gladstone Pottery Museum 🖼 (Uttoxeter Rd, Longton) Particularly engrossing, a complete Victorian pottery made much more appealing to families over the last few years, with lively demonstrations and interpretation. It's very much hands-on, and even hands-in – they're quite keen to get your fingers round the clay. It's quite possible to spend up to half a day here. Meals, snacks, shop, mostly disabled access; cl Christmas week; (01782) 319232; £3.95.

Penkhull Despite the development of the Potteries on the slopes below and all around, this hilltop enclave somehow preserves an undisturbed village feel.

Potteries Museum & Art Gallery (Bethesda St, Hanley) The best place to see the full range of ceramics produced locally over the centuries, also reconstructed shops and other local

history – even a Spitfire, produced by local son R J Mitchell. Meals, snacks, shop, disabled access; cl Sun am, 25 Dec–1 Jan; (01782) 232323; free.

Royal Doulton Visitor Centre 🖼 (Nile St, Burslem) Potted history of the famous fine china company, with craft demonstrations, and a well displayed collection of Royal Doulton figures. Factory tours wkdys (exc bank hols) at 10.30am and 2pm (1.30pm Fri), booking recommended; no under-10s. Meals, snacks, good shop, disabled access to visitor centre only; cl Christmas, New Year, but best to check first; (01782) 292434; visitor centre and tour £6.50, visitor centre only £3.

Spode 🖼 (Church St) The birthplace of fine bone china, this is the oldest manufacturing ceramic factory in the Potteries, and still the most atmospheric. A museum has rare and precious pieces, esp in the beautifully laid-out Blue Room, and you can have a go at making a piece yourself. Meals, snacks, factory shop, disabled access; no tours wknds though shop and visitor centre open daily, cl 25–26 Dec, 1 Jan and Easter Sun; tours by appointment, (01782) 744011; £4.75 inc factory tour, or £2.75 just visitor centre and museum.

Wedgwood Visitor Centre (Barlaston) Following a £4.5m renovation, this new-look visitor centre tells the story of that favourite item on wedding lists through a range of interactive and audio-visual displays. A self-guided audio tour leads you round various exhibitions on the history of the pottery, the factory itself, a design room showcasing the famous porcelain, and a demonstration area where you can throw your own pot. Restaurant and bistro, good shop, disabled access; cl over Christmas and New Year; (01782) 204218; £4.95.

STOWE BY CHARTLEY SJ9927 **Amerton Farm** Farm shop, trails, garden centre, craft workshops, pottery, Wildlife Rescue Centre and little steam railway (Sun and bank hols Apr–Oct, diesel summer Sats). Meals and snacks (with ice-cream made on the premises), shop, disabled access; cl 25–26 Dec and 1 Jan; (01889) 270294. This busy place stands out all the more because admission is free (£1.50 for wildlife centre, £1.20 train). The Plough opposite is handy for lunch.

STRETTON SK2624

Claymills Pumping Station Well preserved Victorian pumping station with a period workshop and blacksmith's forge; various summer events when the four 1885 beam engines and five 1937 Lancashire boilers are in steam. Snacks, shop; station open every Sat, plus several wknds mid-May to Oct half-term – best to check; (01283) 509929; donations (£2 on steam days).

TAMWORTH SK2003

A decent town trail links a number of historic buildings; there's also a unique indoor ski slope with real snow (see below). **St Editha's church** has windows by William Morris.

Drayton Manor Family Theme Park (off A4091 S of Tamworth) Popular theme park, with 50 rides and attractions inc a small zoo. Meals, snacks, shop, disabled access; cl Nov–Mar; (01827) 287979; £14. The good Twycross Zoo is a few miles E, just over the Leics border.

Snowdome (River Drive) Try your luck at skiing, snowboarding or even hi-tech tobogganing on real snow at this indoor centre, the first of its kind in Europe. Competent skiers can take to the pistes whenever they wish, but novices will require a lesson first (must book in advance). Various regular events inc lively snowboard sessions accompanied by music and light shows. Bar and restaurant overlooking the slope, mountain sports shop, disabled access (and lessons); cl 25 Dec; (0990) 000011; hourly ski or snowboard sessions start from £16 (inc ski/board hire), family tobogganing Sun and bank hol ams Good Fri–Sept only, £5.50 for 45 mins (£3.50 children).

Tamworth Castle (off Market St) Glorious mixture of architectural styles from the original Norman motte and bailey walls through the Elizabethan timbered hall to the fine Jacobean state apartments. Perhaps more museum than historic home, but plenty to see, with a fair amount to please children, inc high-tech talking heads. Shop, disabled access to ground floor; under

new management so best to phone to check times and prices; (01827) 709626.

TUTBURY SK2129

Pleasant village: the Norman church has a notable W doorway and elaborate carvings; there are two crystal works, craft shops, an attractive ruined castle with good views, and the Olde Dog & Partridge with decent food.

WALL SK0806

Wall Roman Site (Watling St) An important military base from around AD 50; excavations began in the 19th c and revealed one of the most complete Roman bath houses in the country. Good audio-tour, and finds from the area. Snacks, shop; cl 1–2 pm, and all Nov–Mar; (01543) 480768; £2.30. The Black Bull at Shenstone is useful for lunch.

WESTON UNDER LIZARD SJ8010

Weston Park 🖼 (A5) Striking richly decorated 17th-c house, with a fine collection of paintings inc works by Van Dyck, Rubens, Gainsborough and Constable, and Disraeli letters that still somehow catch the imagination. The deer park and grounds, landscaped by Capability Brown, feature a restored 18th-c terrace garden, brightly planted broderie garden, and interesting trees and shrubs; in the last century it took 37 gardeners to look after it all. Also play area, pets' corner, and miniature railway through the woodland. Meals, snacks, shop, some disabled access; usually open pms Easter, then wknds and bank hols mid-Apr to mid-Sept, and daily in summer hols but best to check; (01952) 852100; £5.50, £4 park and gardens only. The Bell at Tong is a reliable food pub; there are several interesting places close by, just over the Shropshire border.

WETTON SK1055

Peak District School of Hang Gliding Adventurous souls can learn to hang glide here; (01335) 310257; 2-day courses start at £119.

WILLOUGHBRIDGE SJ7539

Dorothy Clive Garden (A51) Woodland gardens created by the late Col Harry Clive in memory of his wife; at their best perhaps in spring and early summer, but lovely all year.

Rhododendrons, azaleas, old roses, water garden, rock garden and stunning views of the surrounding countryside. Tearoom with good home-made cakes, disabled access; cl Nov–Mar; (01630) 647237; £3. The Falcon in Woore does good food.

WINKHILL SK0551

Blackbrook Zoological Park 🔲 Unusual species and aviaries, as well as waterfowl, insects and reptiles, under-5s playroom and children's farm – all much enjoyed by readers. Tearooms, shop, disabled access (although paths are steep); cl wkdys Nov–Mar, 25–26 and 31 Dec, 1 Jan; (01538) 308293; £4.95. At pretty Waterhouses nearby you can hire bikes from the Old Station Car Park, (01538) 308609; around £6.50 for three hours. The attractively

set Cross there has decent food – or treat yourself at the Old Beams.

Other attractive villages, with decent pubs, include Alstonefield SK1355, Butterton SK0756, Coven SJ9006, Longdon SK0714, Rolleston on Dove SK2427, Salt SJ9527, Swynnerton SJ8535 and Whitmore SJ8141.

There's good **canal** access from the **decent pubs** at Amington SK2304 (the Gate), Armitage SK0816, Gnosall Heath SJ8220, Norbury Junction SJ7922, Filiance Bridge in Penkridge SJ9214, Shebden SJ7626 (great echoes under the aqueduct) and Wheaton Aston SJ8412.

Moseley Old Hall near Wolverhampton is listed in the Warwickshire chapter.

Where to eat

BUTTERTON SK0756 **Black Lion** *(01538) 304232* Homely 18th-c stone inn with neat rambling rooms, plenty of interesting things to look at, a good log fire, well liked changing food, real ales, wknd evening cocktail bar, games room, seats on terrace, and pleasant views over the Peak National Park; bdrms; cl Mon am; disabled access. £24|£6

SALT SJ9627 **Holly Bush** *(01889) 508234* Thatched house dating in part from 14th c, with pretty hanging baskets and a big back lawn, some ancient beams in several cosy spreading areas, a more modern back extension, coal fires, extremely good popular food (the daily specials are the thing to go for), Sun roasts, well kept ales, and friendly, efficient service; children in eating area until 8.30pm; disabled access. £17.50|£6.50

TEANFORD SK0040 **Ship** *(01538) 722253* Busy little local with generous choice of good home-made food (esp bread and puddings), changing daily specials, good value Sun lunch, and friendly staff; cl Mon am; disabled access. £12.75|£4

TUTBURY SK2129 **Olde Dog & Partridge** *High St (01283) 813030* Popular carvery in half-timbered dining inn with stylish layout, well kept beers, good wines, and friendly helpful service; nice bdrms; brasserie cl Sat am, Sun pm, Mon; disabled access. £18|£5.50

WATERHOUSES SK0850 **Old Beams** *Leek Rd (01538) 308254* Very pretty restaurant-with-rooms, surrounded by flowers and creepers, with oak beams, antique furniture, a cosy friendly atmosphere, excellent carefully cooked food, and good service; bdrms; cl Sat am, Sun pm, Mon, Tues am, all Jan; disabled access. £45/2 courses £16.95

Special thanks to B M Eldridge

SUFFOLK

Nicely unhurried, with sleepy villages, attractive medieval market towns, rewarding country houses, and lonely beaches – ideal for getting away from it all

Easton Farm Park, our Family Attraction of the Year for Suffolk, could be regarded as a neat summation of the county's main appeals, in that it's less developed but better value than many of its peers. Elsewhere, family highlights include the excellent reconstructions at Stowmarket and West Stow Country Park, the unique African animals at Suffolk Wildlife Park in Kessingland (with good provision for children in the school holidays), and the day-filling possibilities at Fritton's Country World. There's a busy mix of birds and other animals at Stonham Aspal (plus various craft workshops to keep adults happy), and those who can't be tempted by the myriad riding opportunities at Wickham Market's Valley Farm Riding & Driving Centre, new to the *Guide* this year, can enjoy their collection of white animals and Camargue horses for free.

Most commendably, several of the splendid country houses here seem to cater as much for children as they do for adults, with lively period re-creations at Kentwell Hall in Long Melford, special events and activities for children at Ickworth House, Horringer, and some fun touches in the gardens of Somerleyton Hall.

Among the county's several gardens, those at Coddenham, Helmingham and Rougham Green deserve special mention.

Places with more specialist appeal include the wonderful collection of music machines at Cotton, Southwold's amber museum (another new entry), and the lovingly restored vehicles at the East Anglia Transport Museum, Lowestoft. In general, prices are quite appealing – both for things to do and for places to stay in.

Southwold, Walberswick, Aldeburgh and Orford are ideal for a seaside stay in understated civilised surroundings. Even in summer you can walk for miles along fairly empty beaches and long stretches of coastal bird country here and elsewhere, for instance near the attractive drowning village of Dunwich, or on the Shotley peninsula: these wide sea and skyscapes are very restorative.

Inland there are delightful villages with colour-washed timbered buildings, glorious churches, attractively restored windmills – and lots of antiques shops. Long Melford, Lavenham, Clare and Cavendish stand out.

Bury St Edmunds has a good range of interesting places to visit (with the unusual Moyses House Museum soon to be refurbished), and anyone interested in racehorses could spend a very enjoyable weekend based at Newmarket.

Constable country, around East Bergholt by the border with Essex, has had more than a comfortable share of summer visitors, but it is very pretty, and people interested in traditional British painting can easily combine visits to Flatford Mill (scene of *The Haywain*), Christchurch Mansion in Ipswich (free) and Gainsborough's House in Sudbury.

Suffolk is excellent for cycling – quiet back roads, lots of villages, gentle gradients, and a very low accident rate; for an especially safe route, try the one at Alton Water – a nice place for a family picnic in summer.

Where to stay

ALDEBURGH TM4656 **White Lion** *Market Cross, Aldeburgh, Suffolk IP15 5BL (01728) 452720* **£97**, plus special breaks; 38 rms, some with sea view. Popular family-run 16th-c seafront hotel with comfortable lounges, two bars, log fires, good food in recently refurbished panelled and beamed restaurant, and cheerful friendly staff; limited disabled access

BEYTON TL9363 **Manorhouse** *The Green, Beyton, Bury St Edmunds, Suffolk IP30 9AF (01359) 270960)* **£46**; 4 pretty rms, 2 in house, 2 in barn conversion. Overlooking the village green, this charming no smoking long-house has lots of beams and panelling in the sitting/dining room, fine china figurines and paintings by the friendly owner's mother, super breakfasts, enjoyable dinners (by arrangement), and large garden; no children, no dogs

BILDESTON TL9949 **Crown** *High St, Bildeston, Ipswich, Suffolk IP7 7EB (01449) 740510* **£55**, plus special breaks; 12 individually furnished rms. Lovely timber-framed Tudor inn with a comfortable well furnished beamed lounge, open fires, good food in popular restaurant, welcoming courteous service, an attractive two-acre informal garden – and resident ghost; self-catering apartment; disabled access

BURSTALL TM0944 **Mulberry Hall** *Burstall, Ipswich, Suffolk IP8 3DP (01473) 652348* **£40***; 3 comfortable rms with showers. Once owned by Cardinal Wolsey, this lovely old farmhouse has a fine garden, an inglenook fireplace in the big beamed sitting room, excellent food (ordered in advance) in pretty little dining room, very good breakfasts with home-baked bread, and helpful friendly owners; tennis and croquet; cl Christmas

BURY ST EDMUNDS TL8564 **Angel** *3 Angel Hill, Bury St Edmunds, Suffolk IP33 1LT (01284) 753926* **£106***, plus special breaks; 66 individually decorated rms. Thriving creeper-clad 15th-c country-town hotel (upgraded throughout this year), with particularly friendly staff, comfortable lounge and relaxed bar, log fires and fresh flowers, and good food in elegant restaurant and downstairs medieval vaulted room (Mr Pickwick enjoyed a roast dinner here); disabled access

CAMPSEA ASHE TM3255 **Old Rectory** *Station Rd, Campsea Ashe, Woodbridge, Suffolk IP13 0PU (01728) 746524* **£60**, plus special breaks; 7 comfortable, pretty rms. Very relaxed and welcoming, no smoking Georgian house by church, with log fire in comfortable and restful drawing room, lovely food from a set menu in summer conservatory or more formal dining rooms with more log fires, a good wine list, and peaceful gardens; dogs allowed (not in dining rooms); cl Christmas, 3 wks Feb/Mar

FRAMLINGHAM TM2863 **Crown** *Market Hill, Framlingham, Woodbridge, Suffolk IP13 9AP (01728) 723521* **£70***, plus special breaks; 12 comfortable rms. Bustling and friendly Tudor coaching inn, with a pleasantly old-fashioned feel, open fire in comfortable lounge, cosy bar with heavy beams and another log fire, enjoyable bar and restaurant meals, friendly helpful staff, and attractive small courtyard

HADLEIGH TM0242 **Edgehall** *2 High St, Hadleigh, Ipswich, Suffolk IP7 5AP (01473) 822458* **£55***, plus special breaks; 9 pretty rms. Friendly family-run Tudor house with Georgian façade, comfortable carefully restored rooms, personal service, traditional English cooking in no smoking dining room, and attractive walled garden with croquet

HARTEST TL8453 **Hatch** *Cross Green, Hartest, Bury St Edmunds, Suffolk IP29 4ED (01284) 830226* **£56**; 2 pretty rms. Charming 15th-c thatched cottage with warmly welcoming owners, a lovely beamed drawing room with antiques, separate dining room for enjoyable breakfasts, log fires, conservatory, seats out on terrace, and peaceful garden; occasional evening meals, and the nearby Crown does good food; no smoking; cl Christmas; children over 9 (though babies welcome); limited disabled access

HIGHAM TM0335 **Old Vicarage** *Higham Rd, Higham, Colchester, Essex CO7 6JY (01206) 337248* **£58**, plus special breaks; 3 rms. Charming Tudor house nr quiet village with very friendly owners, pretty sitting room with fresh flowers, log fire and antiques, enjoyable breakfasts in attractive breakfast room, and grounds and fine gardens with river views, tennis court and heated swimming pool

HINTLESHAM TM0743 **College Farm** *Hintlesham, Ipswich, Suffolk IP8 3NT (01473) 652253* **£42***; 3 spacious rms, 1 with own bthrm and 2 with TV. Late 15th-c no smoking house on 600-acre farm with neat garden, guests' lounge with TV and log fire in inglenook fireplace, hearty Aga-cooked breakfasts in separate dining room, and friendly owners; walks around the farm, and riding and golf nearby; cl mid-Dec to mid-Jan; no pets; children over 12

HINTLESHAM TM0843 **Hintlesham Hall** *Hintlesham, Ipswich, Suffolk IP8 3NS (01473) 652334* **£120**, plus special breaks; 33 lovely rms. Magnificent mansion, mainly Georgian but dating from Elizabethan times, in 175 acres with big walled gardens, 18-hole golf course, outdoor heated swimming pool, croquet, and tennis; restful and comfortable day rooms with books, antiques and open fires, fine modern cooking in several restaurants, a marvellous wine list, and exemplary service; snooker, sauna, steam room gym, and beauty salon; well behaved children over 10 in evening restaurant

LAVENHAM TL9149 **Angel** *Market Pl, Lavenham, Sudbury, Suffolk CO10 9QZ (01787) 247388* **£70***, plus special breaks; 8 comfortable rms. 15th-c inn with original cellar and pargeted ceiling in residents' lounge, several Tudor features such as a rare shuttered shop window front, civilised atmosphere, good food in bar and restaurant (they smoke their own meat and fish), lots of decent wines, several malt whiskies, well kept real ales, thoughtful friendly service, and maybe live classical piano Fri pm; cl 25–26 Dec; disabled access

LAVENHAM TL9149 **Swan** *High St, Lavenham, Sudbury, Suffolk CO10 9QA (01787) 247477* **£138**; 61 smart rms. Handsome and comfortable Elizabethan hotel with lots of cosy seating areas, interesting historic prints and alcoves with beams, timbers, armchairs and settees, good food in lavishly timbered restaurant (actually built only in 1965), afternoon teas, intriguing little bar, and friendly helpful staff; disabled access

LONG MELFORD TL8645 **Bull** *Hall St, Long Melford, Sudbury, Suffolk CO10 9JG (01787) 378494* **£100**, plus special breaks; 25 rms, ancient or comfortably modern. An inn since 1580, this fine black and white hotel was originally a medieval manorial hall, and has handsome and interesting carved woodwork and timbering, and an old weavers' gallery overlooking the courtyard; a large log fire, old-fashioned and antique furnishings, a lovely calm atmosphere, good food, and pleasant friendly service

MILDENHALL TL7174 **Riverside** *17 Mill St, Mildenhall, Bury St Edmunds, Suffolk IP28 7DP (01638) 717274* **£88**, plus special breaks; 30 rms. 18th-c country house by the River Lark with a relaxed restaurant overlooking the lawns, a comfortable bar, welcoming staff, enjoyable food, and real ales; croquet; disabled access

NEEDHAM MARKET TM1053 **Pipps Ford** *Norwich Rd, Needham Market, Ipswich, Suffolk IP6 8LJ (01449) 760208* **£60***, plus winter breaks; 7 pretty rms with antiques and fine old beds, 4 in converted Stables Cottage. Lovely 16th-c farmhouse in quiet garden surrounded by farmland alongside attractive river; log fires in big inglenook fireplaces, good imaginative food using home-baked bread, locally produced meats, honey, eggs, and preserves, and organic local vegetables and herbs, and conservatory with subtropical plants (some meals can be communal); cl 20 Dec–6 Jan; children over 5; disabled access

NEWMARKET TL6463 **White Hart** *High St, Newmarket, Suffolk CB8 8JP*

(01638) 663051 **£55.95**; 19 rms. Comfortable hotel with racing pictures and open fire in spacious lounge, traditional restaurant, reliable bar food, friendly staff, front bar where the trainers meet, and solid back cocktail bar where they take their more important owners

ROUGHAM TL9063 **Ravenwood Hall** *Rougham, Bury St Edmunds, Suffolk IP30 9JA (01359) 270345* **£90**, plus special breaks; 14 comfortable rms with antiques, some rms in mews. Tranquil Tudor country house in seven acres of carefully tended gardens and woodland; log fire in comfortable lounge, cosy bar, good food in timbered restaurant with big inglenook fireplace (home-preserved fruits and vegetables and home-smoked meats and fish), a good wine list, and helpful service; croquet, heated swimming pool and hard tennis court; they are kind to children; disabled access

SOUTHWOLD TM5076 **Crown** *High St, Southwold, Suffolk IP18 6DP (01502) 722275* **£75**; 12 rms. Outstanding old inn with excellent imaginative food in no smoking restaurant and smart but relaxed main bar, inventive breakfasts, lots of interesting properly kept wines by the glass, well kept real ales, and friendly helpful staff; cl first wk Jan

SOUTHWOLD TM5076 **Swan** *Market Pl, Southwold, Suffolk IP18 6EG (01502) 722186* **£100**, plus winter breaks; 43 rms. 17th-c hotel with comfortable and restful drawing room, upstairs reading room, a convivial bar, interesting enjoyable food in elegant no smoking dining room, fine wines, well kept real ales (the hotel backs on to Adnams Brewery), and polite helpful staff; no dogs in main hotel; cl 2 wks Jan for refurbishment; children must be over 5 in evening dining room; limited disabled access

STOKE-BY-NAYLAND TL9836 **Angel** *Polstead St, Stoke-by-Nayland, Colchester, Essex CO6 4SA (01206) 263245* **£65**; 6 comfortable rms. Civilised and elegant dining pub in Stour Valley with Tudor beams in cosy bar, stripped brickwork and timbers, fine furniture, huge log fire and woodburner, decent wines, and particularly good, imaginative and reasonably priced bar food; cl 25–26 Dec; children over 8

WANGFORD TM4679 **Angel** *High St, Wangford, Beccles, Suffolk NR34 8RL (01502) 578636* **£59**; 7 rms. Neatly kept and handsome Georgian-faced 17th-c inn with a light and airy bar, no smoking restaurant, good value dishes of the day and Sun lunch, well kept real ales, decent house wines, pleasant staff, and garden

WESTLETON TM4469 **Crown** *The Street, Westleton, Saxmundham, Suffolk IP17 3AD (01728) 648777 plus freephone (0800) 328 6001* **£89.50**; 19 quiet, comfortable rms. Smart, extended country inn in lovely setting with good nearby walks; comfortable bar, no smoking dining conservatory, newly refurbished restaurant, a wide range of enjoyable food (nice breakfasts, too), log fires, several well kept real ales, decent wines, and a pretty garden with aviary and floodlit terrace; cl Christmas; disabled access

WOODBRIDGE TM2548 **Seckford Hall** *Seckford Hall Rd, Great Bealings, Woodbridge, Suffolk IP13 6NU (01394) 385678* **£130**, plus special breaks; 32 comfortable rms. Handsome Tudor mansion in 34 acres of gardens and parkland with trout-filled lake, putting, and leisure club with indoor heated pool and gym; fine linenfold panelling, huge fireplaces, heavy beams, plush furnishings and antiques in comfortable day rooms, good food (inc lovely teas with home-made cakes), and helpful service; cl 25 Dec; well behaved dogs welcome; disabled access

WORLINGTON TL6973 **Worlington Hall** *Mildenhall Rd, Worlington, Bury St Edmunds, Suffolk IP28 8RX (01638) 712237* **£65**, plus special breaks; 9 comfortable rms with decanter of sherry and fruit. 16th-c former manor house in 5 acres of grounds with a 9-hole pitch and putt course, comfortable panelled lounge bar with log fire, good food in relaxed candlelit bistro, and friendly staff; pets welcome

---

Please let us know what you think of places in the *Guide*. Use the report forms at the back of the book or simply write us a letter.

To see and do

Suffolk Family Attraction of the Year

EASTON TM2758 **Easton Farm Park** 🔲 In 35 acres of attractive countryside, this is a delightful working farm, less developed but better value than many, and with plenty of opportunities for children to get close to the animals. Most can be stroked or fed (special pellets are on sale at the entrance), and younger visitors can go right up to the friendlier ones in the pets paddock. As well as donkeys, poultry, Suffolk horses, pigs and goats, you'll generally come across young animals: baby goats and piglets were delighting summer visitors as we went to press. Unusually, pony rides are included in the price; they usually have them at wknds and school holidays, but it's worth checking in advance the times and whether they'll be running on the day you plan to visit. You can watch milking displays every afternoon in the modern dairy (2–3.30pm); alongside is the lavishly decorated Victorian original, with a striking marble fountain (once the cooling system) as its centrepiece. There's a good play area, as well as token-operated battery-powered tractors – and a full-size one to scramble over. The owners are keen to encourage interest in the environment, so there's an enjoyable Green Trail showing off indigenous bird and plant species. Other activities include a working blacksmith, face-painting, and vintage farm machinery, and farmers' markets are occasionally held here. Dogs are welcome if kept on a lead. Some readers with very small children have found the gravel paths tricky for pushchairs in places. Meals, snacks, picnic areas, shop, disabled access; cl Mon (exc bank hols and in July and Aug), and all Oct to mid-Mar; (01728) 746475; £4.50 (£3 children over 3). The quaint White Horse has decent food, and the Wickham Mkt–Debenham back road through here via Brandeston and Cretingham has some attractive views.

ALDEBURGH TM4656
Fishing village, once an important port, with quaint little streets running down to the shingle beach where the fishermen still haul in and sell their catch, and a much loved boating pond; touristy, but in a quiet way. Benjamin Britten, founder of the town's annual music festival, and his companion the singer Peter Pears are now buried side by side in the churchyard. The Avocet Gallery (High St) has tin toys and automata to play with. The attractively placed Cross Keys and the Mill are both good for lunch. There's an RSPB reserve just N at North Warren, and the Landmark Trust now offer self-catering accommodation (at a price) in the martello tower, the largest and most northerly of the east coast's defences.
Moot Hall Museum 16th-c brick and timber, with outside staircase; scene of the trial in Britten's *Peter Grimes*. It has displays on maritime history and coastal erosion, and finds from the Anglo-Saxon ship burial at Snape. Shop; open

pm wknds Apr–May, Sept–Oct, plus daily pm Jun–Aug (cl 12.30–2.30pm July–Aug); (01728) 452730; 70p.
ALDRINGHAM TM4461
Craft Market Three extensively stocked galleries of local crafts and fine art. Teas, disabled access; cl 12–2 pm Sun (all am winter Suns), 25–28 Dec, 1 Jan; (01728) 830397; free. The Parrot & Punchbowl has good wines and decent food.
ASHBOCKING TM1855
James White Cider Company (Helmingham Rd) Cider and apple-juice making and tasting, with pick-your-own in season. Farm shop, disabled access; call Louise Downie to book a tour wkdys Sept–Mar; (01473) 890202; free. The Moon & Mushroom over at Swilland has good food.
BARDWELL TL9473
Bardwell windmill Carefully restored and now an attractive sight; open for visits most days. The village green, with ancient church opposite the 16th-c pub, is attractive, too.
BAYLHAM TM1152

Baylham House Rare Breeds Farm 🖾 (Mill Lane) Friendly farm park with rare breeds, pets' corner and picnic area; a visitor centre has information about the Roman site on which the farm is situated. Snacks, shop, disabled access; cl Mon (exc bank hols), and Nov–Easter; (01473) 830264; £3, children £1.50. The Sorrel Horse over at Barham has decent food, and walks nearby.

BECCLES TM4290

Beccles and District Museum (Ballygate) Decent local history museum housed in a 17th-c school; shop, disabled access, cl am, Mon (exc bank hols), Nov–Mar.

William Clowes Print Museum (Newgate) Interesting look at the development of printing from 1800 onwards, with wide range of machinery, woodcuts and books. Open 2–4.30pm wkdys Jun–Sept, or by appointment; (01502) 712884; free. Down the same road is a decent local history **museum**; cl am, Mon (exc bank hols), Nov–Mar. The riverside Waveney House Hotel is a comfortable food stop.

BLYTHBURGH TM4575

Blythburgh church Magnificent building in a lovely setting above the marshes; there's a little working pottery nearby, and the White Hart is a good family dining pub.

BRAMFIELD TM4073

Bramfield church Interesting building, with an unusual detached round tower. The Queens Head has good food.

BRANDON TL7884

Brandon Country Park Largely pine woods, and pleasant to stroll around; for a car-borne impression of Thetford Heath, the best road is the B1106.

Brandon Heritage Centre (George St) Brandon used to be the centre of the Stone Age flint industry, so among the local history here is a reconstructed flint-knappers' workshop; also displays on the fur industry and Thetford Forest. Shop, disabled access; open Sat, Sun pm, and bank hols, Apr–Oct, plus Thurs Jun–Aug; (01842) 813707; 50p.

BRUISYARD TM3266

Bruisyard Vineyard 🖾 (signed off B1119 Framlingham road) Picturesque 10-acre vineyard producing decent English wine, with herb garden, water gardens and woodland picnic area. Snacks, shop, some disabled access; cl 25 Dec to mid-Jan; (01728) 638281; free, tours £3.50.

BUNGAY TM3389

Right in the centre of this historic little market town are the ruins of its Norman **castle**, with twin towers and massive flint walls. Bungay straddles the county border, with the Otter Trust at Earsham close by in Norfolk.

BURY ST EDMUNDS TL8464

This busy shopping town has a good deal of character, with quite a few attractive Georgian and earlier houses, and several antiques shops. The **cathedral** gained that status only in 1913; parts are 15th-c, but the hammer-beamed ceiling is 19th-c, and work on restoring the tower still goes on. The nearby Queens Head (Churchgate St) has good food. Another fine old church, **St Mary's** (Crown St), contains the tomb of Mary Tudor. The Linden Tree (Out Northgate St), Masons Arms (Whiting St) and Cupola House (Traverse) do decent food.

Art Gallery (Market Cross) A fine Robert Adam building with changing exhibitions and a decent craft shop. Shop; cl Sun, Mon, and between exhibitions, Christmas; (01284) 762081; £1.

Manor House Museum (Honey Hill) Georgian mansion with a marvellous collection of watches, clocks and other timepieces, as well as period costumes and quite a few hands-on displays. Snacks, shop, disabled access; cl Mon (exc bank hols), Good Fri, 25 Dec–Jan; (01284) 757072; £2.50, free for locals.

Moyses House Museum 🖾 (Cornhill) Unusual 12th-c flint and stone house with good range of Suffolk history, inc gruesome relics of the 'Murder in the Red Barn' – the murderer's account of his trial is bound in his own skin. Displays are firmly traditional, but there's lots to grab the attention. The museum will close for refurbishment (inc a new lift and conference cente) Mar–Sept. Shop, disabled access; cl Sun am, Good Fri, and 25–26 Dec; (01284) 757488; £1.70.

Samson's Tower Museum Little

remains of the former medieval abbey beyond the 12th- and 14th-c gatehouses, but the tranquil gardens are very pleasant, and a **visitor centre** has a history of the site. Shop, disabled access; cl Tues and Thurs Nov–Easter; (01284) 763110; free. Horse-drawn tours of the city leave from the gardens in summer (usually Weds and Sat); £3. An oddity nearby is the pretty little Nutshell (Traverse), probably the country's smallest pub, with long church connections – it closes on Sundays and Holy Days.

Theatre Royal (Westgate St) Britain's third-oldest working theatre, and very handsome – built in 1819 by William Wilkins, the designer of London's National Gallery. It's owned by the NT, and you can look round when productions or rehearsals are not in progress (not Sun or bank hols), or go behind the wings on a guided tour, Sat am; (01284) 769505; free entry (guided tour £3). Walking tours usually leave the Tourist Information Centre at 2.30pm every day (exc Sat) Jun–Sept.

BUTLEY TM3751
Butley Pottery (Butley Barns, Mill Lane) Working pottery, with café, restaurant and disabled access; cl Mon and Tues (exc Jun–Aug), best to phone for winter opening; (01394) 450785; free. The Oyster pub is good for lunch. The B1084 Woodbridge–Orford is a quietly attractive drive, and the even quieter back road S to Capel St Andrew passes the remains of a medieval abbey gatehouse.

CAVENDISH TL8046
A lovely sight, its green framed by colourfully plastered timbered houses, with the tower of the attractive medieval **church** behind. The 16th-c Bull has good value food. The A1092 from Clare goes on to Long Melford with a back road on to Lavenham – four lovely villages. The back roads N of here are also pleasant drives, with plenty of colour-washed old houses.

CHEDBURGH TL8058
Rede Hall Farm Park 🖼 (A143 just E) Working farm based around agricultural life in the 1930–50s, with rare breeds, huge working horses and seasonal activities. Snacks, shop, disabled access; cl Oct–Mar; (01284)

850695; £4. A little further E, the Plough at Rede has good food.

CLARE TL7645
Another of the area's very special timber-and-plaster villages, with a huge and beautiful **church**, the sketchy ruins of a **castle** on an Iron Age earthwork above the River Stour, some remains of a 13th-c Augustinian priory, and little modern intrusion; nature trails around the castle. There's a three-storey antiques warehouse, and the Bell, Clare Hotel and Swan (which does not allow children) have decent food.

Clare Ancient House Museum 🖼 (High St) Local history in an attractive listed 15th-c building. Shop; open pm Thurs–Sun Easter–Sept; *£1.

CODDENHAM TM1252
Shrubland Hall Gardens Stunning Victorian gardens inc formal terrace and a wild woodland garden. There's a magnificent conservatory (not open) and enchanting follies inc a Swiss chalet. Limited disabled access; open pm Sun and bank hol Mon Apr–Sept; (01473) 830221; £2.50.

COTTON TM0667
Mechanical Music Museum 🖼 Large collection of instruments and musical items taking in not just the expected organs, street pianos, polyphons and gramophones, but dolls, fruit bowls and even a musical chair. Their pride and joy is the Wurlitzer theatre pipe organ in the reconstructed cinema. Teas, shop, disabled access; open Sun pm Jun–Sept, plus the first Sun in Oct, a Fair Organ enthusiasts' day; (01449) 613876; *£3. The Trowel & Hammer is good for lunch.

COVEHITHE TM5281
Covehithe church Attractive building; just down the lane this stretch of coast is good for nature walks, especially out of season.

DEBENHAM TM1763
This attractive village has a fine partly Saxon **church**.

Carters Teapot Pottery (Low Rd) Pottery specialising in unusual teapots. Snacks, shop; cl Sun am, 25–26 Dec, and they don't make pots at wknds; (01728) 860475; free.

DENNINGTON TM2866
Dennington church Interesting and attractive church – with excellent

sermons – in pleasant surroundings. The Queens Head next door is good.

DUNWICH TM4770

Once quite a sizeable town, but it's slipping slowly under the sea – most is now submerged. Some say that on quiet nights, when there's a swell running after a storm, they can hear the bells of a submerged church tolling. There are some fragmentary ruins of a friary up on the cliffs. Excellent coastal walks along the cliffs, beaches and heathland of Dunwich Heath, which has a NT tearoom (£1.70 parking charge).

Dunwich Museum (St James St) Small but very interesting, with exhibitions on the village's gradual erosion; shop, disabled access; cl Nov–Feb; free.

EAST BERGHOLT TM0733

Bridge Cottage, Flatford 17th-c cottage nr the mill immortalised by Constable, with a good interpretative centre for his paintings. Teas (highly recommended by readers), shop, disabled access; cl Mon and Tues (exc May–Sept), wkdys Jan–Feb, and Christmas–New Year, limited opening times in winter so best to phone; (01206) 298260; free; NT. Guided walks through areas that inspired his work leave here several times a day May–Sept, but fill up quickly (£1.80). You can hire rowing boats for trips along the River Stour. The mill itself and its famous partner **Willy Lott's Cottage** are both owned by the NT and leased by them to the Field Studies Council. You can see inside only by taking part in their arts courses or popular wildlife watching wknds; (01206) 298283. The **church** with its uncompleted tower has a unique 16th-c timber-framed bell cage, and the Kings Head (with a haywain out in front!) has good value food. From the village the walk along the water-meadows by the Stour is East Anglia's most famous walk – picturesque views immortalised by Constable, and well worth while. This ties in with the more elevated Essex Way to make a very worthwhile circular walk, from Dedham to Lawford church, then via Manningtree Station (extraordinarily good station buffet) to join the Stour itself.

EASTON TM2758

Easton Farm Park *See separate family panel on p.534.*

ELVEDEN TL8080

Center Parcs A relaxing place to stay on the edge of – indeed, virtually part of – Thetford Forest, with excellent leisure facilities; (0870) 520 0300.

EUSTON TL8978

Euston Hall (A1088) Elegant old house built by Charles II's Secretary of State Lord Arlington. The highlight is probably the excellent art collection, with several portraits of the Merry Monarch and his family and court, inc works by Lely and Van Dyck. The grounds were laid out by John Evelyn, William Kent and Capability Brown, so reflect centuries of development, with stately terraced lawns, fine trees, a lake, lovely rose garden and classical temple. Teas in former kitchen, shop, disabled access to grounds and tearoom; open Thurs pm Jun–Sept, 24 Jun, and 2 Sept; (01842) 766366; £3. The Six Bells at Bardwell has decent food.

EYE TM1473

Eye church Beautiful stonework and rood screen.

FELIXSTOWE TM2832

Quite a busy port, with a ferry (passengers, not cars) across to Harwich, and further afield to Zeebrugge. Thanks to its beaches and relatively dry climate it's developed into a popular low-price family resort. Along the coast N, past a Martello Tower, golf course and quiet sand dunes, is the gently attractive and altogether quieter little settlement of Felixstowe Ferry, with another foot-ferry across the estuary of the River Deben, and good local seafood in the waterside Victoria.

Landguard Fort 18th-c, and well worth a look (open Sun and bank hols Easter–Oct; £2); displays on local history in adjacent museum (open pm Weds, Sun and bank hol Mon Easter–Oct; (01394) ; £1).

FLIXTON TM3288

Norfolk & Suffolk Aviation Museum (Homersfield Rd) Aircraft and related items from the Wright Brothers to the present day, with aeroplanes displayed outside and in the Blister Hangar. Snacks, shop, disabled access; cl Fri and Sat Easter–Oct, plus Mon and Thurs Nov–Mar, and all mid-Dec to mid-Jan; (01986) 896644; donations. The Buck nearby has good food (inc a Sun carvery).

FRAMLINGHAM TM2863

The sloping market square is attractive, and the **church** has an excellent hammerbeam roof. The B1116 to Fressingfield is quite a pleasant drive. **Framlingham Castle** (B1116) 12th-c, where Mary I heard that she had become Queen. Unusually the entire curtain wall has survived (you can walk all the way along it), and there are 13 towers, some 17th-c almshouses, and an array of Tudor chimneys. Good views, interesting museum. Snacks, shop, disabled access to ground floor only; cl 24–26 Dec; (01728) 724189; £3.20; EH.

FRITTON TG4700

Country World (Church Lane) Good for families, with woodland walks, children's farm, fishing, heavy horses, miniature railway, birds of prey (displays 12am and 3pm in summer), golf, rowing, boat trips, craft demonstrations and plenty of space for pottering. Snacks, shop, disabled access; open daily Apr–Sept, then wknds and half-term hol in Oct; (01493) 488208; £5.20.

GREAT BRICETT TM0351

Wattisham Airfield Museum (off B1078) Small exhibition related to adjacent airfield which is now one of the largest helicopter bases in Europe. Disabled access; open Sun pm Apr–Oct; (01449) 728933; free.

GREAT LIVERMERE TL8871

There's a charming shortish walk from the church here, past the Ampton Water lake, to Ampton church. A longer path leads through farmland from Great Livermere to Ixworth.

HADLEIGH TM0242

Old market town with some striking buildings (inc the church, famously painted by Gainsborough); there's a nearby woodland RSPB reserve. The Ram has good value food.

HARTEST TL8352

The village green is attractive; at the end, the Crown is pleasant for lunch. **Giffords Hall** 🖾 (Shimpling, just SE) 33 acres with vineyard and winery, wildflower meadows, rare breeds of sheep, pigs and domestic fowl, and a rose garden. It's perhaps best known among gardeners for its sweet peas, and

they have a Rose and Sweet Pea Festival the last wknd in Jun. Meals, snacks, shop, disabled access; cl Nov–Easter; (01284) 830464; £3.25. They do B&B.

HELMINGHAM TM1857

Helmingham Hall Gardens (B1077) Beautiful gardens pretty much as they were in Tudor times. The grand battlemented house they stand around (not open) is ringed by a moat, over which the drawbridge is still raised each night. Extensive deer park with hundreds of red and fallow deer, as well as Highland cattle and Soay sheep, and magnificent old oak trees. Constable painted a number of views of the woodlands. Teas, shop (inc Helmingham produce), disabled access; open Sun pm last wknd in Apr–early Sept (summer Weds pm by appointment); (01473) 890363; £3.75. The welcoming Dobermann at Framsden has good food.

HERRINGFLEET TM4797

Herringfleet windmill Carefully restored, and an attractive sight above the river if you're passing (though it's rarely open for visits).

HOLTON TM4077

Holton windmill Carefully restored, and an attractive sight if you're passing (though it's rarely open for visits).

HORHAM TM2172

St Mary's churchyard The churchyard here has for generations been conserved as natural grassland around its older graves, just scythed for hay in the first week of July; so from spring onwards it's a mass of wild flowers, with plenty of butterflies (and beehives). The Ivy House in the quiet village of Stradbroke does good value lunches.

HORRINGER TL8261

A serenely attractive village with well spaced colour-washed buildings; on some Suns you can find various crafts in the Community Centre.

Ickworth House, Park and Gardens Very untypical stately home, an oval rotunda 30 metres (98 ft) high, with two curved corridors filled with a fascinating art collection inc pictures by Gainsborough, and an exceptional array of Georgian silver. They try hard to make sure children enjoy their visit with quizzes, trails, handling boxes and a free touch tour, introduced primarily for partially sighted visitors. Outside are formal Italianate gardens, and 1,800 acres of attractive parkland with woodland walks and cycle routes. There's a decent-sized play area, special events and activities for children (perhaps a small extra charge for some of these) and themed events in the run-up to Christmas (best to ring for dates). Meals, snacks, shop, plant centre, good disabled access; house open late Mar–Oct, pm daily exc Mon (though open bank hols) and Thurs; garden cl winter wknds; park open all year; (01284) 735270; £5.70 house, park and garden (£2.20 children); £2.50 park and gardens only (70p children); NT.

IPSWICH TM1644

After King John granted it a charter in the 13th c it flourished as a port sending cloth to the continent; the port is still quite busy. Too busy now to consider as a place to stay in, it has quite a few things to look at on briefer visits (traffic schemes make getting in and out by car rather slow). Cardinal Wolsey set up a college here, but all that remains is the 16th-c gatehouse in College St. The Ancient House in the Butter Market (now a kitchenware shop) has some 15th-c carvings, exceptionally neat pargeting (decoratively patterned external plasterwork) and even a priest's hiding hole – ask staff to show you. Dotted about the town are several attractive **medieval churches**, especially the 15th-c St Margaret's (Soane St); St Mary at the Elms (Elm Rd) has the town's oldest cottages behind it. If you're there on a winter's night, five medieval churches are nicely floodlit. In the central pedestrian area the Great White Horse, a former coaching inn, is useful for snacks; the County (opposite County Hall), Old Rep (Tower St) and Greyhound (Henley Rd) have decent food. The area between the town centre and the docks is to be restored as part of English Heritage's 'humble heritage' scheme.

Christchurch Mansion (Soane St) Perhaps the town's highlight; the original 16th-c house was altered in the following century after a fire, but since then it's escaped any further redevelopment. The rooms are furnished in period style, with a Victorian wing inc servants' quarters, and the Suffolk Artists' Gallery has the best collection of works by Constable and Gainsborough outside London. Shop, disabled access to ground floor only; cl Sun am, Mon (exc most bank hols), 24–26 Dec, 1 Jan, Good Fri; (01473) 253246; free. Another gallery next door has frequently changing exhibitions, and the surrounding park has play areas and a bird reserve.

Ipswich Museum (High St) The natural history section has been painstakingly restored to how it was in its Victorian heyday, and includes the first gorillas brought to Europe in the mid-19th c. Other parts have quite an emphasis on Roman Suffolk. Shop, disabled access to ground floor only; cl Sun, Mon, 24–26 Dec, 1 Jan, Good Fri; (01473) 433550; free.

Peter's Ice Cream Factory Tours ⌘ (Grimwade St) A small museum and tours of the factory, and of course a café where you can sample the finished product. Restaurant, shop, disabled access; tours Mon–Fri, 10am, 12, 2pm and 4pm, but best to ring; (01473) 253265; £3.75.

Tolly Cobbold Brewery (Cliff Rd) Striking waterside Victorian brewery, with tours. Some particularly interesting old equipment, inc a Victorian steam engine, and tastings in the Brewery Tap (which functions as a separate pub). Shop; tours Fri and Mon July–Aug 2pm, best to check for other times; (01473) 231723; £3.90 (inc drink).

Transport Museum (Lupin Rd) In an old trolley-bus depot, a developing collection of around 100 ancient commercial vehicles built or used in the area, from fire engines to buses and milk floats. Snacks, shop, disabled access; open Sun and bank hols Apr–end Nov, and pm wkdys during school hols; (01473) 715666; £2.25.

KEDINGTON TL7046

Kedington church One of Suffolk's many attractive churches, this is unusual for its Saxon crucifix.

KERSEY TM0044

A very pretty one-street village, full of timbering and attractive and colourful plasterwork – though one or two

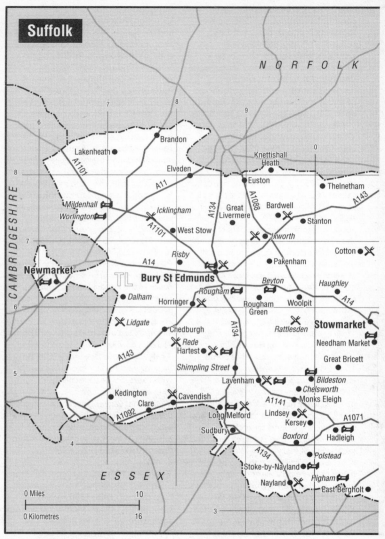

Suffolk

NORFOLK

CAMBRIDGESHIRE

Lakenheath
Brandon
Knettishall Heath
Elveden
Euston
Thelnetham
Mildenhall
Icklingham
Bardwell
Worlington
Great Livermere
Stanton
West Stow
Ixworth
Cotton
Risby
Pakenham
Newmarket
TL
Bury St Edmunds
Beyton
Haughley
Dalham
Rougham
Horringer
Rougham Green
Woolpit
Stowmarket
Lidgate
Chedburgh
Rattlesden
Needham Market
Rede
Hartest
Great Bricett
Shimpling Street
Lavenham
Bildeston
Kedington
Chelsworth
Cavendish
Monks Eleigh
Clare
A1141
Long Melford
Lindsey
Kersey
A1071
Sudbury
Boxford
Hadleigh
Polstead
Stoke-by-Nayland
Nayland
Higham
East Bergholt

ESSEX

0 Miles   10
0 Kilometres   16

buildings look ready for some attention. It runs from the fine 14th-c church down to a ford with ducks, and up the other side; several craft and antiques shops, and the Tudor Bell has decent food.

KESSINGLAND TM5286
Suffolk Wildlife Park (A12) Quite an emphasis on African wildlife at this 100-acre park; some of the animals are the only examples of their type in the

country, inc the wonderfully strange bonteboks (they look like a cross between a horse and a goat with a bit of cow thrown in). Lots for families in summer, with a bouncy castle beside the play areas, animal demonstrations, bird of prey displays (selected days only), crazy golf, and games and activities in summer hols. Feeding times are spread throughout the day. The same people run Banham Zoo in

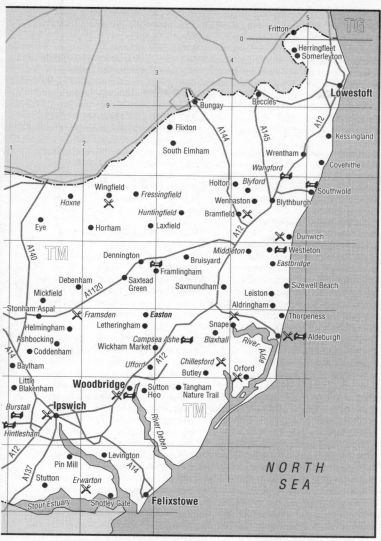

Norfolk. Meals, snacks, shop, disabled access; cl 25–26 Dec; (01502) 740291; £6.95. Kessingland's beach is good, though busy in summer, and it's only three or four miles to Lowestoft.

KNETTISHALL HEATH TL9480
This Country Park has some pleasant strolls – and if you're overflowing with energy (and several days' supplies), you may even be tempted northwards on the Peddars Way, waymarked from

here all the way to Norfolk's N coast.

LAKENHEATH TL7182
Lakenheath church One of Suffolk's elegant and charming churches, though now a bit hidden away among the sprawl edging the nearby huge air base.

LAVENHAM TL9149
One of the finest surviving examples of a small medieval town, this lovely little place has delightfully rickety-looking 14th- and 15th-c timbered buildings

wherever you look; many now house teashops, banks or antiques shops. The old wool hall has been incorporated into the Swan Hotel, itself well worth seeing. Both it (at a price) and the Angel are good for lunch. Self-guided audio tours of the town are available from the pharmacy on the High St (01787) 247284; £3. The A1141 through Monks Eleigh and then the B1115 through Chelsworth to Hitcham is a pretty drive.

Guildhall (Market Pl) Picturesque 16th-c timbered building, at various stages in its career a Town Hall, prison, workhouse and wool store; its beamed interior has interesting local history displays. Disabled access to tearoom (cl Mon) and shop; cl Good Fri, and Dec–Feb; (01787) 247646; £3; NT.

Little Hall (Market Pl) Delightful 15th-c house, attractively repainted, showcasing the Gayer-Anderson collection of books, pictures and antiques, with a pleasant enclosed garden. Open pm Weds, Thurs, Sat, Sun and bank hols Apr–Oct; (01787) 247179; £1.50. There's a good small commercial art gallery nearby.

LAXFIELD TM2972
Laxfield church Well worth a visit, in tucked-away quiet surroundings; nearby is a charmingly preserved very old-fashioned pub, and a small museum (open pm wknds and bank hols mid-May to Sept; free).

LEISTON TM4462
Long Shop Steam Museum 🏭 (Main St) Big industrial museum in preserved buildings of Garrett Engineering Co, with steam engines, steam rollers, traction engines, and memorabilia from the nearby World War II air base. Picnic garden, shop, disabled access; cl Nov–Mar; (01728) 832189; £3. The Engineers Arms opposite has so much memorabilia it seems almost an extension. The sizeable shopping town has the fragmentary remains of a 14th-c abbey off the B1122 just N.

LETHERINGHAM TM2858
Letheringham watermill Pretty, and surrounded by nice gardens, maybe open in summer.

LEVINGTON TM2338
A pleasant spot, with ancient

almshouses, a marina below, and the Ship, a good pub (no children) with estuary views.

LINDSEY TL9744
St James's chapel A charming little thatched flint and stone chapel, built during the 13th c but inc some earlier work too. The White Rose does good food.

LITTLE BLAKENHAM TM1048
Blakenham Woodland Garden Woodland garden richly planted with camellias, rhododendrons, magnolias and the like; lovely in May when the bluebells are out. Lots of rare trees and shrubs. Open pm Sun–Fri Mar–Jun; *£1. The Sorrel Horse over at Barham has decent food (and pleasant walks nearby).

LONG MELFORD TL8645
A very nice old place to stroll around: the fine green and exceptionally long main street (Hall St) are lined with buildings from varied eras, many with lovely timbering, and around 20 of them now antiques shops (not cheap, but interesting). The **church of Holy Trinity** is glorious, with ornate carvings and dozens of spectacular windows; very attractive when floodlit at night. The Bull Hotel, one of the finer old buildings here, does good light lunches, as does the comfortable Black Lion Hotel; the Crown, Hare and George & Dragon are also useful for food.

Kentwell Hall Beautiful Tudor mansion with genuinely friendly lived-in feel, best during their enthusiastic re-creations of Elizabethan and 1940s life (several wknds Apr–Sept), when everything is done as close as possible to the way it would have been done then – even the speech. It's surrounded by a broad moat, and there's a rare breeds farm within the grounds. Snacks, shop, disabled access; house open Sun pm Mar–Oct, 17–20 Apr, and daily mid-July to late Sept; (01787) 310207; most re-creations cost around *£8.20 (*£5.50 children 5–15), though the Great Annual one is *£11.90 (*£8.50 children). On non-event days entry is *£5.70, or *£3.60 garden and farm only.

Melford Hall Turreted Tudor house mostly unchanged externally since Elizabeth I with hundreds of servants and courtiers stayed here in 1578; it also still has the original panelled banqueting hall. Fine collection of Chinese porcelain; the gardens have a Tudor pavilion. Some disabled access; open pm wknds and bank hols Apr–Oct, plus pm bank hols, Weds–Fri May–Sept; (01787) 880286; £4.30; NT.

LOWESTOFT TM5492
Britain's most easterly town, this is the area's main fishing port, so the harbour always has lots to see. It's developed as a resort thanks to its beaches (South Beach has the best bathing water) and proximity to the Broads. Cobbled streets of old buildings survive in the part known as The Scores, and the early medieval **parish church** is imposing and attractive. In the High St the Bayfields Hotel and Volunteer are useful for lunch, as is the seafront Jolly Sailors nr the quaint Pakefield church.

East Anglia Transport Museum 🖼 (Carlton Colville; B1384 SW of Lowestoft) Lots of lovingly restored vehicles around three acres of woodland. The best part is the reconstructed 1930s street scene used as a setting for working trams, trains and trolley-buses. Snacks, shop, some disabled access; open Easter, then Suns May–Sept, plus Weds and Sat pms Jun–Sept, and wkdy pms in summer hols; (01502) 518459; £4. The nearby Crown (A146) does good cheap lunches.

Maritime Museum (Whapload Rd) Housed under the lighthouse on Whapload Rd; cl mid-Oct–Easter; 75p. There's a small **Royal Naval Museum** nearby (cl 12–2pm, Mon pm, Sun am, all day Sat, and mid-Oct to Easter; free).

Mayhem Adventure Play (East Point Pavilion, Royal Plain) Revamped children's play area themed as an underwater world. Meals, snacks, shop, disabled access; cl 25–26 Dec and 1 Jan; adults free, children from £2.95 per hour. It shares the rather grand old pavilion with the tourist information office and good local history displays.

Pleasurewood Hills Theme Park (Corton Rd) Lots of rides and family attractions inc a new spinning roller-coaster; trains and chairlifts speed up travel round the grounds. Meals, snacks, shop, disabled access; open daily mid-May to Aug, and wknds and school

hols Apr–Oct; (01502) 508200; £11.95.

MICKFIELD TM1461
Mickfield Water Garden Centre Two acres of ornamental water gardens and working nursery, with displays of marine and freshwater fish. Wknd teas in summer, garden centre, disabled access; cl Christmas wk; (01449) 711336; free.

MONKS ELEIGH TL9747
Corn Craft (A1141) Traditional corn dollies and their production (demonstrations by appointment). Meals, snacks, big shop, disabled access; cl 25–26 Dec, 1 Jan; (01449) 740456; free. The Swan Hotel is handy.

NAYLAND TL9734
Well rewards a stroll – its fine **church** has an altar painting by Constable; the old White Hart is now a smart restaurant.

NEEDHAM MARKET TM0854
Needham Market church The marvellous hammerbeam roof has been described as 'a whole church seemingly in the air'.

NEWMARKET TL6463
Newmarket has been the centre of horse-racing since 1605, when James I used to slope off here, and in the early morning people driving through are quite likely to have to give way to a string of racehorses. The Tourist Information Centre (occasional exhibitions) is housed in the remains of Charles II's 17th-c palace; cl Sat pm and Sun; (01638) 667200; free. The Rutland Arms (across the road from the Jockey Club) and Bedford Lodge Hotel are useful for lunch.

National Horseracing Museum 🖼 (High St) The stories and scandals of the sport's development through the centuries, with trophies, videos of classic races, a display on the history of betting, and racing relics from saddles to skeletons. You don't have to be interested in racing to get something out of it. Meals, snacks, shop, disabled access; cl Mon (exc bank hols and July–Aug), and Nov–Mar; (01638) 667333; £3.50. They also organise informative tours of the local breeding and racing scene, with a look at horses at work on the gallops, and visits to a training yard, stud and to the handsome Georgian Jockey Club itself; booking essential on (01638) 560622; prices start at around £12.50.

National Stud (A1304 W) Tours of this Mecca of horse breeding by arrangement, (01638) 663464. Snacks, shop, disabled access; guided tours are at 11.15am and 2.30pm wkdys, 11.15am Sat, and 2.30pm Sun, cl Oct–Feb (exc race days); £4. The Kings Head at Dullingham is a good nearby lunch spot.

ORFORD TM4249

Dunwich Underwater Exhibition (Front St) The process of coastal erosion is well illustrated at The Craft Shop; snacks, shop; cl 25–26 Dec; 50p.

Havergate Island Bird-watchers can arrange whole day trips to this marshy RSPB reserve by writing to the warden, Mr Partridge, at 30 Mundays Lane, Orford, Woodbridge IP12 2LX (with SAE); permits usually available every Thurs and alternate wknds Apr–Aug, then in winter just the first Sat of the month; around *£5 inc boat trip from Orford quay.

Orford Castle When Henry II commissioned this castle it was right on the shore, but since then the river has silted so much that it's now slightly inland. It has an amazing 18-sided keep rising to 27 metres (90 ft), supported by three extra towers. Good views from the top (as usual, at the end of a spiral staircase). Shop; cl 1–2pm and Mon–Tues Nov–Mar, 24–26 Dec, 1 Jan; (01394) 450472; £2.60; EH. The **church** has the ruined chancel arches of a Norman predecessor in the graveyard. There's a long lane down to the shore with its quay and old smugglers' inn, the Jolly Sailor. The road through Iken Heath to Snape is a pleasant drive through quiet pinewoods.

Orford Ness After years of belonging to the Ministry of Defence (who barred access to anyone who wasn't in uniform), this magnificently desolate shingle spit just opposite the quay is now owned by the NT and open to the public, though it's more for serious wildlife fans than day trippers. Ferries leave the quay roughly every 15 mins 10am–2pm Thurs–Sat Easter–Oct – you can book if you want; (01394) 450057; £5.40.

PAKENHAM TL9369

Pakenham Water Mill 🖼 (Mill Rd) 18th-c watermill restored to working order by preservation society, pretty mill pond. Snacks, shop, some disabled access; open pm Easter–Sept Weds, wknds and bank hols; or party bookings (01359) 270570; *£2.

Pakenham windmill Carefully restored and now an attractive sight; open for visits on summer Suns.

PIN MILL TM2037

A nice spot below the wooded slopes by the River Orwell, with barges on tidal moorings, and much favoured by artists; the Butt & Oyster here is attractively placed for a bite to eat.

RIVER DEBEN TM3041

Broad winding river close to the coast, best reached from side roads off B1083 S of Shottisham: good walks.

ROUGHAM GREEN TL9261

Netherfield Cottage Herb Garden (Nether St, towards Hessett) Proof that you don't have to have a massive garden to make it very special indeed: hundreds of different herbs, beautifully yet sensibly grouped by how you'd use them, with two small knot gardens and a hedge reshaped to include a window. Best May–Oct, but a peaceful haven at any time. The cheery owner is happy to chat. Cl Nov–Mar; (01359) 270452; free, guided tours by appointment (£5). The Gardeners Arms over at Tostock is an appropriate place for lunch.

SAXMUNDHAM TM3863

This attractive bypassed village has yet another fine **church**. The Poachers Pocket at Carlton just N has decent food, and nearby Yoxford has a couple of good craft workshops.

SAXTEAD GREEN TM2564

Saxtead Green Post Mill (A1120) Traditional Suffolk windmill dating from 1796, meticulously brought back into perfect working order, but it's a steep climb up the staircase; audio tour, shop, cl 1–2pm, Sun, and all Nov–Mar; (01728) 685789; £2.10; EH. Attractive surroundings; the Old Mill House over the green has good home-made food.

SHOTLEY GATE TM2434

At the meeting of the Stour and Orwell estuaries, this is at the hub of a rewarding walk with good views across to Harwich and its shipping. Start inland at Shotley and cross the fields either N to the Orwell or S to the Stour, then follow the waterside. The Bristol Arms has good fresh fish, and up the hill, the colossal mast of HMS *Ganges* (now a police training centre) is a dizzying sight.

SIZEWELL BEACH TL4761
Generally virtually deserted out of season, and pleasurable walking ground despite the rather graceless Sizewell nuclear power plant in the distance. Agate and other semi-precious stones are common among the pebbles, even sometimes amber after stormy E winds, and heathland, an old railway track walk and The Meare (Thorpeness's lake) justify detours inland.

SNAPE MALTINGS TM3957
The converted 19th-c **maltings** are home of the Aldeburgh Music Festival begun by Benjamin Britten, with other concerts throughout the year. The centre is pleasant to wander around, with unusual shops and galleries. The Plough & Sail just outside is good for lunch; up in the village, the Crown (with a bar re-created in *Peter Grimes*) and Golden Key are both good, too.

SOMERLEYTON TM4997
Somerleyton Hall (B1074) Popular with readers, this interesting Jacobean house was rebuilt in the Anglo-Italian style in 1840, and today is still very much lived-in, with period furnishings and paintings. The lovely gardens have a maze and miniature railway and there is occasionally live music in the gardens. Good value snacks, shop, disabled access; open pm only Sun, Thurs and bank hols Easter–Sept, plus Tues and Weds July–Aug; (01502) 730244; £5. The Plough at Blundeston, home of Barkis ('is willing') in *David Copperfield*, is useful for lunch. N of here, with access from the Hall, is wooded **Fritton Lake**, which attracts numerous wildfowl, particularly in the autumn and winter.

SOUTH ELMHAM TM3385
St Peter's Brewery 🏚 Medieval St Peter's Hall has in its outhouses this more modern small brewery, whose excellent bitters, porters and fruit beers (all highly praised by readers) are made with water from their own source. Tours take in the whole brewing process, as well as parts of the

Hall; a visitor centre is planned for later this year. Good meals and snacks, shop, some disabled access; open Fri–Sun, ring for tour times; (01986) 782322; free entry to site, £3.50 tour.

SOUTHWOLD TM5076
Once an important fishing port, now a quite enchanting and civilised little resort with a distinctive lighthouse as its main landmark, an attractive unspoilt green by the sea, and no end of good pubs and inns supplied by the local Adnams brewery (their wholesale wine shop has interesting stock). For food, the Crown is outstanding, and though more straightforward the Kings Head is good, as is the smart Swan Hotel; the Sole Bay and Lord Nelson have the most atmosphere. The Denes is the best beach. Southwold Jack on the tower of the interesting **church** is worth a look: an automaton that rings the bell for services. Across the golf course or along the breezy sea wall you come to the harbour, a tidal inlet, with its cheerful mix of beached fishing boats, multitudes of sailing boats, and tall black fishing shacks; the Harbour Inn here is full of character. There's a rowing-boat ferry over to

Walberswick on the other side of the water – an attractively decorous seaside village, popular with artists ever since Wilson Steer's days there in the 1890s. The Bell here is a striking old inn, and the 15th-c church, parts now destroyed and other bits looking shaky, is attractive. (The drive round by car between Southwold and Walberswick is several miles.)

Amber shop and museum (Market Pl) The longest-standing retailer of amber in Britain, with an impressive collection of related ornaments from 19th-c Chinese scent bottles to fossilised insects. Shop, disabled access; cl over Christmas and New Year; (01502) 723394; free.

Lifeboat Museum (Gun Hill) Always worth a look; open pm daily Jun–Sept; (01502) 722422; free.

River Blyth Broad river winding close to the coast with delightful waterside paths, and marshy and heathy expanses to explore around its mouth.

Southwold Museum (Bartholomew Green) Decent town collections, housed in a 17th-c Dutch gabled cottage; disabled access (but no facilities), open pm Easter–Oct; free.

STANTON TL9671

Wyken Hall Gardens Formal herb, knot and woodland gardens, walled old-fashioned rose garden, copper beech maze, pond, and woodland walk to 7-acre vineyard. A very nice unspoilt estate, just right for exploring. Meals and snacks in medieval barn, unusual country shop, disabled access; open Weds–Fri, Sun and bank hols, and some evenings by appointment Apr–Oct; (01359) 250240; *£2.50. The Six Bells at Bardwell has decent food.

STOKE-BY-NAYLAND TL9836

The lovely 15th-c **church** has a tower familiar from several Constable paintings, and a few handsome Tudor buildings among more ordinary ones; the Angel is excellent for lunch, but get there early.

STONHAM ASPAL TM1459

British Birds of Prey and Conservation Centre 🖼 (Stonham Barns, A1120) Flying displays Apr–Oct, and every species of British owl; also pond-dipping, meerkats, ostriches, goats, rabbits, chickens, deer and guinea-pigs; (01449) 711425; cl 25 Dec; £4.95 (inc nature centre). Around 30 small businesses share the site, inc various craft workshops, bonsai shop, and garden centre.

STOUR ESTUARY WALKS TM1534

Stutton gives access to a fine stretch of the broad Stour estuary just S, with good bird-spotting opportunities.

STOWMARKET TM0458

Museum of East Anglian Life (Iliffe Way) Excellent 70-acre open-air museum. Children look at the reconstructed buildings with a genuine sense of astonishment: did people really live like that? Even the room settings from the 1950s seem prehistoric to fresher eyes. The main buildings (which include a watermill, chapel, smithy and wind pump) are quite spread out, so there's a fair bit of walking involved, inc a nice stroll down by the river. Also a few animals inc Remus the Suffolk punch horse and his friend Blackberry the Shetland pony; adventure playground and occasional basket-

making and wood-turning demonstrations. Snacks, shop, disabled access; cl Nov–Mar – phone for occasional winter opening; (01449) 612229; £4.25. The Magpie (Combs Ford) has decent food.

STUTTON TM1534

Alton Water Reservoir Attractive man-made lake circumscribed by a cycle track which takes in some interesting features on the way inc the Tattingstone Wonder, a folly built for a local squire with pious pretensions who wanted to look across the valley and see a church – the ecclesiastic façade hides a row of almshouses (not open to public); cycle hire is £5.80 for 3 hours; (01473) 328873. Also bird reserve (several hides), a small visitor centre, fishing (first May bank hol to mid-Mar, permits available from visitor centre), and watersports, (01473) 328408. Café (cl Mon), some disabled access (though gravel paths might prove tricky for wheelchairs); reservoir open all year, best to phone for café, cycle hire and visitor centre opening outside school hols; (01473) 328268; one day's parking, £2. In the village itself, the Kings Head has good value food.

SUDBURY TL8741

Gainsborough's House 🖼 (Gainsborough St) The painter was born here in 1727, and the house has an excellent collection of his work; unexpected finds include his efforts at sculpture. Plenty of period furniture and china too, and contemporary arts and crafts. Shop, disabled access to ground floor only; cl Sun am, all day Mon (exc pm bank hols), Christmas–New Year, Good Fri; (01787) 372958; £3. This market town is pleasant, with useful market stalls on Sat; the nearby Waggon & Horses (Acton Sq) has good plain food.

SUTTON HOO TM2849

Sutton Hoo Archaeological Site One of the most famous archaeological sites in the country, where in 1939 the discovery of an Anglo-Saxon ship burial and burial ground of an early 7th-c ruler made historians completely reinterpret the Dark Ages. Most of the finds from here are in the British Museum, but you can see the burial mounds, and an exhibition explains the site's importance. At the moment tours are at 2 and 3pm wknds and bank hols Easter–Oct; *£2 (arrive in good time, there is a 20-min walk from the car park to the site). The NT, who took over the site in 1997, are developing a £3.6 million Lottery-supported visitor and study centre, set to open in 2002. A turn off the B1083 S takes you to the Ramsholt Arms at Ramsholt for lunch among waterside pinewoods, with quiet walks along the Deben estuary.

TANGHAM NATURE TRAIL TM3548

A short walk among the plantations off the B1084 towards Woodbridge specially designed for disabled people; there are also longer walks through the pinewoods here, where red squirrels often show themselves.

THELNETHAM TM0078

Windmill Carefully restored and now an attractive sight; open for visits at least summer Sun pms.

THORPENESS TM4759

At the S end of Sizewell beach, this curious place was built as a holiday village in a deliberately fanciful olde-worlde style, with quite a few attractive mock-Tudor houses (one even masking a water-tower); it has a sizeable artificial but now thoroughly natural-looking picturesque lake, and the **windmill** here was brought over from Aldringham. The Dolphin has good food.

North Warren Miles of RSPB nature reserves stretching along the coast between Thorpeness and Aldeburgh; nature trails, many different birds (esp good for wildfowl in winter), butterflies and dragonflies; free.

WENHASTON TM4275

Wenhaston church Attractive building, with a 15th-c wall painting (in excellent condition) full of lovely devils; it's a nice peaceful village, too.

WEST STOW TL7971

West Stow Country Park Attractive, with 125 acres of heath and woodlands bordered by the River Lark. Over 120 different species of bird have been sighted here, and 25 species of animal; the visitor centre often has art exhibitions. The most interesting feature is the reconstructed **Anglo-Saxon Village**, its buildings erected

using the same methods and tools as in the 5th c. A visitor centre houses original finds from the Anglo-Saxon site. Occasional costumed days, and special events. Meals, snacks, shop, disabled access; cl 25–26 Dec; (01284) 728718; park free, village £4.50. The Red Lion at Icklingham has good food.

WESTLETON TM4369

A pleasant village with an attractive green; the crown has good food.

Minsmere Reserve 🔄 Big RSPB reserve with lots of different species among the heath, woods, marshes and lagoons – good observation hides, and enjoyable walks at any time of year. The heathlands around here are also home to red deer, and are carpeted with spectacular purple heather in summer. Meals, snacks, shop, disabled access; cl Tues, and 25–26 Dec; (01728) 648281; £5 for non-RSPB members. The reserve is skirted by public paths, and one hide is available free for public use, but you need an entry sticker to enter the rest of the reserve. Approach points are Dunwich and Eastbridge. Outside the reserve, much of the flat formerly heathy land nr the coast in this area is now covered with pine plantations: also pleasant for undisturbed walks, with the chance of seeing red deer, and in summer with that lovely fresh foreign pinewood smell.

WICKHAM MARKET TM2956

Valley Farm Riding & Driving Centre (½m W on B1078) Family-run equestrian centre offering a wide range of activities from all-day pony treks to carriage driving, and even stunt riding. They also have a collection of white animals inc sheep, goats, a camel and the only breeding herd of Camargue horses in the country. Snacks, shop, disabled access; cl 25 Dec; (01728) 746916; site free, riding lessons start from £15 for half an hour.

WINGFIELD TM2276

Wingfield College Quite a surprise to find a splendid medieval timber-framed building behind the Georgian façade. One of its 18th-c owners constructed the Palladian exterior to make his home more fashionable, using false ceilings, floors and windows so skilfully that for 200 years the house's earlier parts were forgotten. Striking great hall, and topiary and kitchen gardens. Snacks, shop, disabled access; open pm wknds and bank hols Easter–Sept; (01379) 384888; £3.60. They also organise Wingfield Arts, a varied programme of events in churches, halls and other everyday buildings all over the region; phone for programme. The De La Pole Arms has good food.

WOODBRIDGE TM2749

Quietly attractive and rather dignified market town, with many fine buildings and interesting book and antique shops, and a **church** of great style and interest. The Anchor (Quay St), Kings Head (Market Hill) and Olde Bell & Steelyard (New St) all do decent bar lunches. The B1079 and then B1077 up to Eye is a pleasant drive on an old coach road.

Buttrums Mill £ (Burkitt Rd) Six-storey tower mill, now fully restored, with displays of its history; open pm wknds and bank hols May–Sept; *£1.50.

Tide Mill Restored 18th-c mill on busy quayside, its wheel usually working when tides allow. Shop, disabled access to ground floor only; open daily May–Sept and wknds in Apr and Oct; *£1.50. The Wilford Bridge Hotel nearby at Melton is a good lunch stop – and well placed for river walks.

Woodbridge Museum £ (Market Hill) Looks at the ship burial at nearby Sutton Hoo, as well as the recent Anglo-Saxon finds at Burrow Hill. Shop, disabled access (but no facilities); cl Sun am, all day Mon and Tues (exc bank hols), Weds, and all Nov–Easter;

(01394) 380502; £1 (inc free activity sheets for children).

WOOLPIT TL9762

The **church** here has a hammerbeam roof, and a translation of the village tale that in the 12th c two slightly strange-looking green-skinned children were found by a pit that was suddenly blasted in the earth one night; the boy soon died, but the girl lived, and grew up to marry a local lad and have children. She never said more about her origins than that she'd come from a land far far away. The drive to Buxhall is pretty.

Woolpit & District Museum (The Institute) Small but interesting, with annually changing local history displays (and more on the 12th-c children). Shop, disabled access; open pm wknds and bank hols Easter–Sept; donations.

WRENTHAM TM4982

Wrentham Basketware (London Rd) They make and sell traditional willow baskets and hampers, with up to 320 styles. Cl pm Sun, 25 Dec and occasionally other days; (01502) 675628; free.

Other attractive villages, all with decent pubs, include Bildeston TL9949, Blaxhall TM3657, Blyford TM4277, Boxford TL9640, Chelsworth TL9848, Dalham TL7261, Eastbridge TM4566, Fressingfield TM2677, Haughley TM0262 (its Jacobean manor house in lovely grounds), Hoxne TM1777, Huntingfield TM3374, Ixworth TL9370, Middleton TM4367, Polstead TL9938, Risby TL8066 (with a decent antiques centre), Ufford TM2953 and Shimpling Street TL8752.

Where to eat

ALDEBURGH TM4656 **Regatta** *171–173 High St* (01728) 452011 Bustling seaside restaurant decorated with pennants and seaside murals, and specialising in fresh local seafood – though they also offer interesting meat dishes and fine puddings; a relaxed atmosphere, friendly service, and no smoking area; cl winter Mon, Tues, Weds, Sun pm; disabled access. £20|£5

BARDWELL TL9473 **Six Bells** *The Green* (01359) 250820 Quietly placed 16th-c pub with heavy beams and timbering, attractive decorations, snug dining room and bigger restaurant with conservatory; a wide range of good interesting evening food (light lunches, too), polite service, real ales, good wines, and seats out in front and on back lawn; bdrms; cl Christmas; disabled access. £18|£6

BRAMFIELD TM3974 **Queens Head** *The Street* (01986) 784214 Popular pub with pleasantly relaxed high-raftered lounge bar, a good log fire in impressive fireplace, no smoking side bar, family room, and wide choice of very good interesting food (super puddings); well kept real ales, good wines, and maybe home-made elderflower cordial; cl pms 25 and 26 Dec. £18.60/3-course Sun lunch £12.50|**£5.95**

BURY ST EDMUNDS TL8564 **Maison Bleue** *31 Churchgate St (01284) 760623* Airy French seafood restaurant with big seaside mural, super fish dishes (and some meaty ones too), a thoughtful wine list, and helpful friendly staff; cl Sun, 3 wks Jan; disabled access. £30|**£6.95**

CAVENDISH TL8046 **Bull** *High St (01787) 280245* Cheerful pub hiding an attractive 16th-c beamed interior behind a Victorian frontage; big standing timbers and attractive fireplaces in open-plan rooms, a thriving atmosphere, a big range of enjoyable good food (fresh fish is delivered daily), well kept real ales, and a decent choice of wines by the glass; cl Mon. £20|**£6.95**

CHILLESFORD TM3852 **Froize** *The Street (01394) 450282* Heavy beams and lots of interesting things to look at in big comfortable open-plan dining bar and no smoking restaurant, very generous helpings of excellent food, esp wide choice of particularly good fresh fish, super schoolboy puddings, a fine choice of real ales and good range of wines by the glass; courteous service, hard-working owners, and seats in the garden; bdrms; cl Mon (open bank hol lunches), last wk Feb, first 2 wks Mar, last wk Sept; disabled access. £26|**£8**

COTTON TM0667 **Trowel & Hammer** *Mill Rd (01449) 781234* Big friendly partly thatched and partly tiled white pub with spreading lounge, lots of dark beamery and timber baulks, a big log fire, good interesting food, and a large pretty back garden with swimming pool; cl 25 Dec; no small children in Cotton Club restaurant; disabled access. £18.95|**£6.25**

DUNWICH TM4770 **Flora Tearooms** *Fore St (01728) 648433* Extended former fisherman's hut right on the beach, with great views of the sea and fishing boats, famous for very good fish and chips but also other snacks, teas and home-made cakes; cl 26 Nov–10 Mar; disabled access.|**£5.35**

DUNWICH TM4770 **Ship** *St James's St (01728) 648219* Delightful old pub by the sea with a good bustling atmosphere, friendly helpful staff who cope cheerfully with the crowds, wonderfully fresh fish off the boats on the beach, traditionally furnished bar, conservatory, sunny back terrace, and well kept garden; bdrms; the RSPB reserve at Minsmere is close by; cl 25 Dec pm. £20|**£5.45**

ERWARTON TM2134 **Queens Head** *The Street (01473) 787550* Remote and unspoilt little pub with lovely views, a welcoming unpretentious atmosphere, a cosy coal fire in beamed bar, good well priced bar food inc fresh fish and game in season and decent value Sun lunch, well kept real ales, and friendly service; cl 25 Dec; children in restaurant only; disabled access. £23.95|**£6.50**

FRAMSDEN TM1959 **Dobermann** *The Street (01473) 890461* Charmingly restored thatched pub with twin-facing fireplace separating the friendly spotlessly kept bars, good popular food, and a decent choice of beers and spirits; cl Mon; disabled access; no children. £17.95|**£6.50**

HARTEST TL8352 **Crown** *The Green (01284) 830250* Comfortably modernised and brightly lit pink-washed pub by village green and church (bell ringing practice Thurs pm); lots of space in two no smoking dining areas and large conservatory restaurant, reliably good reasonably priced food inc take-away fish and chips and really good value Mon, Weds and Fri set meals, quick friendly black-tie staff, a chatty local atmosphere, well kept real ales, and a big back lawn and side courtyard; disabled access. £20/3-course Mon pm meal £9.50

HORRINGER TL8261 **Beehive** *The Street (01284) 735260* Particularly well run and pretty ivy-covered pub with extremely helpful service, friendly atmosphere, excellent imaginative food with lots of daily specials and a puddings board, attractively furnished little rambling rooms, woodburner, well kept real ales, and decent wines; no food Sun pm; disabled access. £18.50

ICKLINGHAM TL7872 **Red Lion** *The Street (01638) 717802* Civilised and rather smart thatched pub with a nice mix of wooden chairs, candlelit tables, fresh flowers, fishing rods and various stuffed animals, inglenook fireplace and heavy

beams, very good food, well kept real ales, and country wines; disabled access.
£25|**£7.25**

IPSWICH TM1644 **Mortimers on the Quay** *Wherry Quay (01473) 230225* This
is the place for really fresh daily-changing fish, simply cooked; a thoughtful French
wine list and relaxed atmosphere; cl Sat am, Sun, 23 Dec–5 Jan; disabled access.
£22.50|**£4.50**

IXWORTH TL9370 **Theobalds** *68 High St (01359) 231707* Consistently good
imaginative food (inc vegetarian choice) in 17th-c restaurant with log fires, beams
and standing timbers in cosy rooms, very good wine list, and kind service; cl Sat am,
Sun pm, Mon, 2 wks Aug; children in evening over 8 only. £35|**£9**

LAVENHAM TL9149 **Great House** *Market Place (01787) 247431* Restaurant-
with-rooms in ancient house behind a handsome Georgian façade; bare boards,
antiques, open fires (inc an inglenook in the restaurant itself), very good French
cooking plus lighter lunches and a super French cheeseboard, friendly staff, mainly
French wines, and attractive flower-filled courtyard for outside eating; charming
beamed bdrms; cl Sun pm, Mon, 3 wks Jan. £27.50|**£6.50**

LIDGATE TL7257 **Star** *The Street (01638) 500275* Quaint old place with
interesting small bar, big log fire, handsomely moulded heavy beams and polished
oak and pine tables, chatty Spanish landlady, big helpings of hugely enjoyable food
with Mediterranean hints, good wines and ales, a cosy simple dining room, and
tables in front and in the little rustic back garden; cl Sun pm, 25 Dec, 1 Jan.
£28.50|**£5.50**

LINDSEY TL9744 **White Rose** *(01787) 210664* Civilised thatched and timbered
dining pub with a long beamed main bar, inglenook log fire, country chairs and pine
tables; a second cosy bar opens into a restaurant in former raftered barn, with no
smoking area, attractively presented imaginative bar food from a changing menu,
well kept real ales, good wines, and welcoming service. £20.50|**£6.95**

LONG MELFORD TL8645 **Chimneys** *Hall St (01787) 379806* Lovely beamed
16th-c building with very good carefully prepared interesting food, a thoughtful
wine list, and helpful staff; paintings for sale; cl Sun, bank hols; disabled access.
£37/3-course set meal £18.50

NAYLAND TL9734 **White Hart** *High St (01206) 263382* Smart 15th-c
pub/restaurant with 18th-c coaching frontage, polished tables on wooden floors,
comfortable sofa by log fire, and glass-floored section over wine cellar; good well
presented cooking, a wide choice of wines, real ales, and a relaxed atmosphere;
popular with businessmen and retired folk; cl Mon, Christmas–New Year. £30|**£8**

ORFORD TM4249 **Butley Orford Oysterage** *(01394) 450277* Simple
restaurant with its own oyster beds, fishing boat and smokehouse; very popular
locally and with yachtsmen for its wonderfully fresh fish, decent wines, and brisk
friendly service; disabled access. £25|**£4**

RATTLESDEN TL9758 **Brewers Arms** *Lower Rd (01449) 736377* 16th-c pub
with pleasantly simple beamed lounge and small lively public bar, very welcoming
friendly service, imaginative food, decent wines, well kept ales, and magnificent old
bread oven in main eating area; children must be well behaved; cl Mon; disabled
access. £23.45|**£6**

REDE TL8055 **Plough** *The Green (01284) 789208* Welcoming partly thatched
cottage in lovely spot, with particularly helpful owners, lots of well presented fresh
fish and game in season, imaginative daily specials, good evening restaurant, decent
wine, and lovely sheltered cottagey garden; disabled access. £20.50|**£8**

SNAPE TM3958 **Crown** *Bridge Rd (01728) 688324* Unspoilt smugglers' inn with a
relaxed and warmly friendly atmosphere, old brick floors, beams, big brick
inglenook and nice old furnishings; particularly good interesting well presented
food served by smiling staff, pre- and post-concert suppers, a thoughtful wine list
(12 by the glass inc champagne), well kept real ales, and tables in pretty garden;
bdrms; no children; partial disabled access. £24|**£7.95**

SNAPE TM3957 **Plough & Sail** *The Maltings (01728) 688302* Part of the Snape
Maltings centre with a relaxed and friendly series of attractively furnished rooms,

busy little restaurant, delicious food, well kept real ales, and a fine wine list; cl Sun, Mon pms Christmas–Easter; disabled access. £19|£5

WINGFIELD TM2276 **De La Pole Arms** *Church Rd (01379) 384545* Beautifully restored village inn, tucked away in lovely countryside; deliberately simple yet elegant décor, interesting bric-a-brac, comfortable traditional seating, a pleasantly civilised feel, courteous friendly staff, and very good popular bar food; no smoking restaurant and well kept real ales. £22.25|**£6.95**

WOODBRIDGE TM2748 **Captain's Table** *3 Quay St (01394) 383145* 16th-c cottage with three beamed interlinked rooms, cheerful décor, enjoyable interesting food inc plenty of fresh fish, helpful service, and a thoughtful wine list; cl Sun pm, Mon (open bank hols), 2 wks Jan; disabled access. £20|**£6.50**

Special thanks to Norman Fox, C A Wheelden

SURREY

**Pleasantly traditional family outings, surprisingly peaceful commons
and heaths – perfect for walks; some special gardens**

For fun family days out, the action-packed theme parks at Chessington and
Thorpe Park are always a safe bet, but if it's not white knuckles you're
after then there's a satisfying blend of other attractions elsewhere.
Guildford's lively discovery centre (a newcomer this year) lives up to the
cliché that science can be fun (for children and their parents), while it's not
just adults who enjoy the Rural Life Centre at Tilford (livened up by a
playground and Sunday railway) or the motor-racing memorabilia at the
Brooklands Museum in Weybridge. The county does quite well for family-
friendly wildlife attractions too, from Farnham's bustling Birdworld &
Underwater World to the quieter good value Bocketts Farm Park. Keep a
close eye on the prices we show. A lot of places here have put their prices
up quite sharply this year, but there are still bargains to be had.

In summer especially, there are several opportunities for leisurely
traditional family pursuits: try catching one of the open days at Busbridge
Lakes for a scenic picnic; the scenery around the unique Chatley Heath
Semaphore Tower and Britain's oldest working windmill at Outwood are
other rewarding venues, while a boat trip along the Wey Navigation or a
cycle ride along the Downs Link Path are fun ways of taking in the
countryside.

Leatherhead, Chertsey, Farnham and Godalming are all well served by
decent local history museums, while shoppers might be intrigued by the
unusual ironworks at the Fire & Iron and Forge & Dragon galleries and
inspired by the choice of tempting victuals at stately Loseley Park or the
friendly Hogs Back Brewery at Tongham (over 500 beers).

Unusual outings include the Watts picture gallery at Compton, the
Derby Day Experience (with a wider appeal than you might expect), and
entertaining tours of Denbies Wine Estate or the network of tunnels
hidden under Reigate.

Wonderful gardens here include England's oldest landscape park in
Esher (children's trail and guided walks), the mix of styles at Wisley,
Winkworth Arboretum (glorious autumn colours), the intimate sculpture
garden at Ockley or the unexpected finds at Painshill Landscape Garden.

Despite its commuter-belt image, Surrey is in fact England's most
wooded county, and away from the urban corridors much of the
countryside is beautifully preserved, and quite hilly. The National Trust
owns vast tracts of the finest scenery, and walkers have an excellent
choice, with relatively free access. There are some beautiful villages, too.

Please let us know what you think of places in the *Guide*. Use the report forms
at the back of the book or simply write us a letter.

Where to stay

BAGSHOT SU9062 **Pennyhill Park** *College Ride, Bagshot, Surrey GU19 5ET* (01276) 471774 **£240** inc dinner, plus special breaks; 115 charming spacious rms. Impressive Victorian country house in 120 acres of well kept gardens and parkland; friendly courteous staff, comfortable two-level lounge with panelling and beams, bar with resident pianist, tapestries and fine paintings, and very good imaginative cooking; outdoor swimming pool, tennis, 9-hole golf course, game fishing, and clay pigeon shooting – they can arrange riding too; disabled access

CHERTSEY TQ0467 **Crown** *7 London St, Chertsey, Surrey KT16 8AP* (01932) 564657 **£62**w; 30 comfortable modern rms. Bustling, friendly place with some original features and open fire in large bar, conservatory extension, good food, attractive restaurant, and lovely big garden; disabled access

CHOBHAM SU9760 **Knap Hill Manor** *Carthouse Lane, Woking, Surrey GU21 4XT* (01276) 857962 **£75**; 3 spacious rms with garden views. Really welcoming and relaxing late 18th-c family home with lovely peaceful gardens (tennis and croquet), big comfortable sitting room, delicious breakfasts with home-made preserves, and helpful knowledgeable owners; golf nearby; cl Christmas/Easter; children over 8

EWHURST TQ0840 **High Edser** *Shere Rd, Ewhurst, Cranleigh, Surrey GU6 7PQ* (01483) 278214 **£55***; 3 charming rms, shared bthrm. 16th-c timber-framed farmhouse in lovely countryside, with comfortable residents' lounge, friendly owners, enjoyable food (by arrangement) and open fire in dining room; tennis court in grounds; cl Christmas

FARNHAM SU8145 **Farnham House** *Alton Rd, Farnham, Surrey GU10 5ER* (01252) 716908 **£65**w, plus special breaks; 25 comfortable rms. Attractive Victorian 'gothick' manor house with oak panelling and open fires in comfortable public rooms, split-level restaurant, and tennis court and outdoor heated swimming pool in five-acre gardens

GODSTONE TQ3551 **Godstone Hotel** *87 High St, Godstone, Surrey RH9 8DT* (01833) 742461 **£55***; 8 rms. Well run late 16th-c hotel with open fire in comfortable residents' lounge, good popular food in attractive beamed restaurant, and helpful service from very welcoming owners

HASLEMERE SU9228 **Deerfell** *Blackdown, Haslemere, Surrey GU27 3LA* (01428) 653409 **£44***; 3 comfortable rms. Comfortable no smoking stone coach house with wonderful views and good nearby walks; generous meals in handsome dining room (ordered in advance), open fire in sitting room, pictures, antiques and old rugs, a sun room, good breakfasts, and friendly owners; cl mid-Dec to mid-Jan; children over 6

HASLEMERE SU9232 **Lythe Hill Hotel** *Petworth Rd, Haslemere, Surrey GU27 3BQ* (01428) 651251 **£155.10**, plus special breaks; 41 individually styled rms, a few in the original house. Lovely partly 15th-c building in 20 acres of parkland and bluebell woods (adjoining the NT hillside) with floodlit tennis court, croquet lawn, and jogging track; plush, comfortable and elegant lounges, a relaxed bar, two no smoking restaurants (one with French cooking, the other with traditional English), and good attentive service; disabled access

HOLMBURY ST MARY TQ1144 **Bulmer Farm** *Holmbury St Mary, Dorking, Surrey RH5 6LG* (01306) 730210 **£48***; 8 big comfortable rms, 5 in no smoking barn conversion with own showers. Attractive and welcoming 17th-c farmhouse on 30-acre beef farm in lovely countryside, with oak beams and inglenook fireplace in attractive sitting room, breakfasts with home-made preserves in neatly kept dining room, and large garden; self-catering also; children over 12; disabled access

HORLEY TQ2943 **Langshott Manor** *Langshott, Horley, Surrey RH6 9LN* (01293) 786680 **£165**, plus special breaks; 15 individually furnished rms. Elizabethan house in fine 3-acre garden with roses and lakes; beams, oak panelling, fresh flowers and open fires in elegant rms, and enjoyable traditional cooking in no smoking restaurant; well behaved dogs in their kennels; disabled access

NUTFIELD TQ2950 **Nutfield Priory** *Nutfield, Redhill, Surrey RH1 4EL* (01737) 822066 **£140***, plus special breaks; 60 rms. Impressive Victorian 'gothick' hotel in

40 acres of parkland with lovely elaborate carvings, stained-glass windows, gracious day rooms, a fine panelled library, cloistered restaurant, and even an organ in the galleried grand hall; extensive leisure club with indoor heated swimming pool

To see and do

Surrey Family Attraction of the Year

CHESSINGTON TQ1762 **Chessington World of Adventures** (A243) Considering its size Surrey caters fairly well to families, but this busy theme park (one of two in the area run by the Tussauds Group) is still the best place to head to for unadulterated fun. The big thrill ride is Rameses Revenge, which spins you round 360 degrees at speeds of up to 60mph, while plummeting towards a rock-lined pit where you'll be sprayed by water fountains. Hanging roller-coaster the Vampire is similarly traumatic, and though the more traditional-seeming Rattlesnake looks a little gentler it still packs quite a punch (all have height restrictions). The park is divided into separate areas, the latest of which, Beanoland, is themed around characters from the popular comic: Roger the Dodger's Dodgems is much as you'd expect, but Billy's Whizzer is fun (be prepared to get wet), and there's a well put together stunt show. There's plenty to amuse younger children, from the Dragon River log flume and Action Man Training HQ to the simpler rides around Toytown. They'll also get the most out of the once-famous zoo from which everything else developed; over on the quieter, greener side of the park, it's now rather lost among the other attractions, but there are sea lion and penguin displays at set times throughout the day, and a good insect house. A monorail gives bird's-eye views of the lions, tigers, gorillas and meerkats. It's worth taking advantage of their later opening hours in the summer hols (till 9pm) as the park isn't so busy later in the day; it can be very busy indeed at wknds, and some rides are starting to introduce timed tickets to tackle the queues. The week around Hallowe'en is always fun, with laser light shows, extra entertainment, and the fun of trying everything out in the dark (you need to arrive before 4pm.) Meals and snacks (from McDonalds to a family pub or Mexican diner), shop, some disabled access but best to phone in advance; open late Mar–Oct; (01372) 727227; full-priced entry is rather expensive, at £19.95 (£15.95 children 4–14), though there's a decent saving on the family ticket at £63. But with a bit of planning, you shouldn't have to pay this: booking at least 48 hours in advance either by phone or their website (www.chessington.com) will save £2 on each ticket (and get the family ticket down to £59). Better still, the promotional leaflets you'll find in Tourist Information Centres and the like have included vouchers offering a £4 discount on each admission; for a family of four, that brings the total cost down to £55.80 – still a lot, but if you get here early enough and spend the whole day you won't feel cheated.

ABINGER COMMON TQ1245 Charmingly set village with pretty church, ancient pub and duckpond surrounded by woodland – popular for walks.

ALBURY TQ0547 Attractive village with glimpses of the Victorian mansion Albury Park – or at least its famous chimneys. The Drummond Arms is a civilised place for lunch.

St Peter and St Paul church (Albury Park) This pleasantly set (now redundant) church has some interesting monuments.

BANSTEAD WOOD TQ2657 Popular strolling-ground, surprisingly peaceful despite the proximity of Surrey's northern suburbia and heavily used trunk roads. In Banstead the Mint (Park Rd) is handy for lunch.

BETCHWORTH TQ2149 Attractive village, pleasant for strolls along an annotated trail from a church where *Four Weddings and a Funeral* was filmed, passing a working blacksmith. The Dolphin is a decent pub, and there's a nice drive via Brockham and Newdigate to Rusper in Sussex.

BOX HILL TQ1751
Surrey's most popular viewpoint, with a summit car park and walks on its steep juniper and boxwood slopes: wild orchids and butterflies in early summer, maybe field mushrooms in early autumn; the attractively placed King William IV at Mickleham is excellent for lunch.

CHALDON TQ3155
Attractive church, particularly worth a visit for its unique wall-painting of the *Ladder of Salvation*.

CHARLWOOD TQ2341
Gatwick Zoo & Aviaries ⌨ (Russ Hill) Readers are surprised by the hundreds of mammals and birds here, many in big naturalistic settings – some of which you can walk through, inc the two big tropical houses with plants and butterflies from around the world. Meals, snacks, shop, disabled access; cl 25–26 Dec; (01293) 862312; £5.45. The Greyhound in the attractive village has good value food.

CHERTSEY TQ0467
A good few Georgian buildings in its main streets and pleasant walks by the Thames – for instance from the Boathouse pub (Bridge St).
Chertsey Abbey Medieval remains standing in Abbeyfields Park.
Chertsey Museum (Windsor St) Late Georgian building, displays on the abbey, a good costume collection, a hands-on discovery zone, and a pleasant little garden. Shop, disabled access to ground floor; cl am wkdys, all day Sun, Mon, Easter Sun and Christmas; (01932) 565764; free.
Great Cockcrow Railway ⌨ (Hardwick Lane, Lyne, slightly NW) A notable miniature steam railway, with a unique signalling system. Snacks, shop, disabled access; open Sun pm May–Oct; (01932) 255500; £2. The Golden Grove on St Ann's Hill out towards here is a nice spot for lunch.
Thorpe Park (A320 N) 500-acre leisure park with possibly gentler rides than Chessington and lots for younger children. Rides include the oddly named

roller-coaster X:\No Way Out, hidden in an enormous pyramid (and the park's white-knuckle highlight), a 4-D pirate experience, lively Thunder River and Calgary Stampede, and Loggers Leap (the highest log flume in the country), while at the other end of the adrenaline scale are more sedate play areas, and a man-made beach and pools. Quite a few activities are water-based, and you'll need swimming things for the slides around Wet! Wet! Wet! Across the lake (reached by either a train or waterbus) is a decent-sized traditional working farm with animals and craft centre. Excellent visitor facilities but expect crowds and queues on busy summer days. Meals, snacks, shop, disabled access; cl Nov to mid-Mar; (01932) 562633; £18.50 (£14 children over 1 metre tall and under 14). A good value family ticket is even cheaper if you book in advance.

CHESSINGTON TQ1762
Chessington World of Adventures
See separate family panel on p.554
CHIDDINGFOLD SU9635
Exceptional village in fine surroundings, with one window of its church made up from locally excavated fragments of 13th-c glass made here. The Rams Nest has good value food.
Ramster (A283 S) Splendid Edwardian woodland spring garden. Teas, plant sales, disabled access; open Apr–July; (01428) 654167; *£3.
COBHAM TQ1159
Quite a busy shopping town, with some fine older buildings around the church and in Church St; just SW, Downside Common is a classic cricket green, with cottages scattered around it and an attractive pub – the Cricketers.
Cobham Mill (Mill Rd) Prettily set working watermill, authentically restored by enthusiastic locals. Open pm second Sun of month Apr–Oct; (01932) 867387; free.
Painshill Landscape Garden (A425 slightly W) These beautifully restored 18th-c landscape gardens are a continual surprise, with a Gothic temple, a Chinese bridge, a grotto, a lake with seemingly endless bays and inlets, even a Turkish tent and other follies at every turn. Lots of unusual trees and shrubs. Snacks, shop, limited

disabled access; cl Mon (exc bank hols), also cl Fri Nov–Mar; (01932) 868113; *£4.20. Almost opposite the gates, the Snail brasserie has decent food.

COMPTON SU9547

Watts Picture Gallery (Down Lane) Memorial gallery to Victorian Symbolist painter and sculptor G F Watts (in his time one of the most celebrated artists in the world) with over 250 of his works. In tranquil rural setting. Shop, disabled access to main gallery; cl Thurs, 24–25 Dec and Good Fri, and am Mon, Tues, Fri and Sun; (01483) 810235; free. Just down the road the unique circular Watts Chapel in the village cemetery is covered in Celtic and art nouveau decoration and was designed and built by his wife Mary Watts and villagers. The village church is attractive and the tearoom nearby serves up to 24 different teas.

DEVIL'S PUNCHBOWL SU8936

A spectacular fold of the downs, with nature trails through mixed woodlands, quiet valleys and sandy heaths with scattered ponds. The area is quite developed but the woods and intricacy of the landscape give it a wholesome rurality, and the footpath network is dense. **Gibbet Hill** above the A3 gets a view over most of it.

DORKING TQ1649

Pleasant market town with lots of antiques shops, and a local museum (West St) open Weds, Thurs pm and Sat; 40p; the roads S of the A25 W of here are the county's most pleasant drives, and the steep road up Box Hill N opens a great panorama. The 16th-c Kings Arms in West St has decent food.

Denbies Wine Estate (London Rd) Britain's biggest vineyard, and at 250 acres bigger than most in France. The tour is unique, with road-train rides round the winery, and a 3-D film, where four months of vine growth is condensed into four minutes, and grapes seem to fly out of the screen. You don't have to be a wine buff to enjoy it. Meals and snacks (in unusually designed restaurant), big shop, good disabled access; (01306) 876616; £5 (inc tastings). Fine views and walks nearby.

DOWNS LINK PATH TQ0735

Follows a disused railway track through pleasant countryside – popular for walks and family cycling. The Thurlow Arms at Baynards Station Yard nr Cox Green is handy for access.

DUNSFOLD TQ0036

One of Surrey's most picturesque village greens; the Sun is a pleasant pub.

EAST CLANDON TQ0651

Hatchlands 🆔 (A246) Handsome 18th-c brick house with more floors than are visible from the outside, thanks to an ingenious use of false windows. The grand rooms are especially notable for their ceilings and fireplaces, early examples of the work of Robert Adam. A fine collection of historic keyboard instruments includes a piano once owned by Marie Antoinette. The formal garden was designed by Gertrude Jekyll. Meals, snacks, shop, disabled access (with notice); open Apr–Oct, house and garden pm only Sun, Tues–Thurs and bank hols, plus Fri in Aug, park walks daily from 11am; (01483) 222482; £5, £2 garden and park walk; NT. A visit here is easily combined with Clandon Park at West Clandon (you can get a joint ticket £7.50). The Wishing Well is useful for lunch.

EPSOM TQ2158

Derby Day Experience 🆔 (Queen's Stand) The Derby (first run in 1780) is still the most prestigious race for three-year-olds – and a grand social event. At its home racecourse, this explanation re-creates the excitement, with the help of archive film, interactive displays and various relics and mementoes. Worth a look even if you're not a racegoer – open only one Sun and Tues a month; best to ring (01372) 726311 for dates; £6. The nearby Derby Arms is a reliable food pub. Other famous racecourses in this area include Sandown Park, (01372) 463072; Kempton Park, (01932) 782292; and Lingfield, (01342) 834800; all have good facilities.

Horton Park Children's Farm (B280 W) Plenty of animals to feed and cuddle, tractor rides (a little extra), an adventure playground and indoor play area. Meals, snacks, shop, disabled access; cl 25 Dec; (01372) 743984; £3.65 per child (one accompanying adult free).

ESHER TQ1464
Claremont Landscape Garden (off A307) The oldest surviving landscaped garden in the country, laid out by Vanbrugh and Bridgeman before 1715 and extended and naturalised by William Kent; 49 enchanting acres with lakes, turf amphitheatre, grotto, island, guided walks, children's trail and Braille guide. Meals, snacks, shop, disabled access; cl Mon Nov–Mar and Christmas day; (01372) 467806; £3.20; NT. The Bear (High St) and Prince of Wales (West End Lane) have popular food, and there's a farm shop with **pick-your-own** fruit on Winterdown Rd just N.

FARNHAM SU8346
Handsome town that owed its Georgian heyday to the importance of local corn and hops. Many elegant buildings from this period remain, and there are some even older ones such as the early 17th-c Spinning Wheel. The area around Castle St is especially nice to stroll round, and the Spotted Cow and Fox (both Lower Bourne) are pleasant lunch spots.

Birdworld & Underwater World (Holt Pound, off A325 3m SW – actually just over the Hampshire border) Wide variety of birds from tiny tanagers to ostrich, birds of prey and rare species in 26 acres of garden and parkland. Woodland walks and trails, and adjacent **Underwater World** with tropical and other freshwater and marine fish. Meals, snacks, shop, disabled access; usually cl wkdys Nov and Jan–mid-Feb, phone to check; (01420) 22838; £7.95. The nearby 16th-c Cherry Tree at Rowledge has good food.

Castle 🈸 For 800 years a residence of the Bishops of Winchester. Most of the buildings have been adapted to suit the briefing organisation based here, but the major rooms, inc the great hall, can be seen on a guided tour Weds 2–4pm; snacks, shop; cl Christmas–New Year; (01252) 721194; £1.50.

Castle Keep 🈸 Administered separately; includes the massive foundations and entrance of a Norman tower. Shop; open Apr–Oct; (01252) 713393; £2, inc Walkman tour; EH.

Farnham Museum (West St)

Excellent local history museum; some William Cobbett memorabilia (his picturesque birthplace in Bridge Sq is now a pub named after him), and a pleasant walled garden. Shop, disabled access to ground floor; cl Sun and Mon; free.

Foyer and James Hockey Galleries (Surrey Institute of Art & Design, Falkner Road) Balanced programmes of exhibitions inc art, craft, design and multimedia, housed in two galleries, one a swish modern extension. Shop, disabled access; cl Sun; (01252) 892668; free.

Maltings Gallery (Bridge Sq) Diverse arts and crafts. Snacks, shop, limited disabled access; cl Mon; (01252) 713637; free, although maybe £1 for national exhibitions.

FETCHAM TQ1555
Bocketts Farm Park Working farm in a pretty, historic setting, with traditional and rare breeds, cart rides, falconry, craft demonstrations and their latest attraction – pig racing (wknds and school hols). Meals, snacks, shop, disabled access; cl 25–26 Dec and 1 Jan; (01372) 363764; £3.65.

FOREST GREEN TQ1241
Forge & Dragon Gallery (Ewhurst Road) Picturesque working forge dating from the 16th c, and prettily set by the village green (where the Parrot has good food). A gallery displays the resourceful work of resident ironworker James Davies – usually on hand to discuss any personal requests. Disabled access to parts of forge; cl Sun, and 25 Dec–14 Jan; (01306) 621222; free.

FRENSHAM COMMON SU8540
Popular for walks, with heather and woodland around a lake formed in the 13th c for fish breeding.

GODALMING SU9643
Attractive town with a good few interesting buildings and, because of its narrow streets (part cobbled and pedestrianised), a more old-fashioned feel than most in Surrey. The Inn on the Lake (A3100 S) is good for lunch, and the Star (Church St) has decent snacks.

Busbridge Lakes (Hambledon Rd, off B2130) Very pretty spot with three lakes in fine parkland – exotic waterfowl, peacocks, ornamental

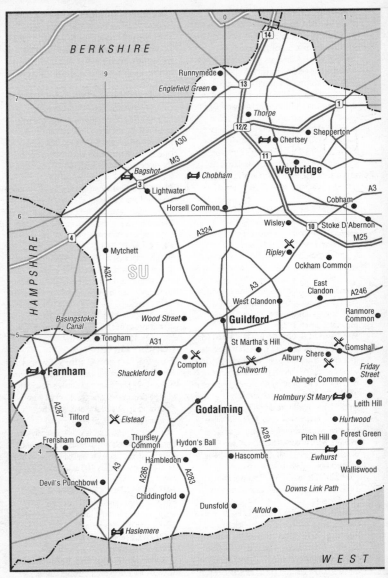

BERKSHIRE

Runnymede
Englefield Green
Thorpe
Chertsey
Shepperton
Weybridge
Bagshot
Chobham
Lightwater
Cobham
Horsell Common
Wisley
Stoke D'Abernon
Mytchett
Ripley
Ockham Common
SU
East Clandon
West Clandon
Ranmore Common
HAMPSHIRE
Basingstoke Canal
Wood Street
Guildford
Tongham
A31
St Martha's Hill
Gomshall
Albury
Shere
Farnham
Compton
Chilworth
Abinger Common
Friday Street
Shackleford
Holmbury St Mary
Leith Hill
Tilford
Elstead
Godalming
Hurtwood
Frensham Common
Thursley Common
Hydon's Ball
Pitch Hill
Forest Green
Hambledon
Hascombe
Ewhurst
Walliswood
Devil's Punchbowl
Chiddingfold
Dunsfold
Alfold
Downs Link Path
Haslemere

WEST

pheasants and many other kinds of bird, as well as follies and grottoes throughout the grounds. Snacks, shop; only open 13–16 Apr, 6–7, 27–28 May, and 26–27 Aug; (01483) 421955; £3.50. **Godalming Museum** (High St) 15th-c house with local history, interactive displays, Gertrude Jekyll gallery and Jekyll-style walled garden. Snacks, shop, some disabled access; cl Mon, Sun and Christmas–New Year; free. The town hall opposite is known affectionately by the locals as the Pepper Pot. **River Wey & Godalming Navigation** This 17th-c canal, passing through some fine scenery, was

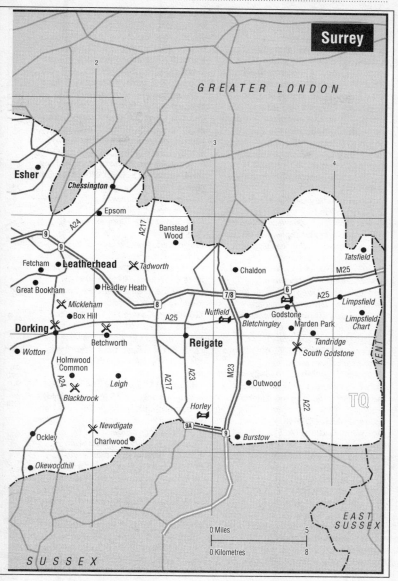

extended here in 1763, to link
Godalming with the Thames. The wharf
has some fine Georgian buildings, and
the locks and towpath have been
restored by the NT – a visitor centre
has exhibitions on Surrey's barge-
building history. A river bus runs to and
from the town centre, and guided

nature walks along the canal take place
throughout the year – best to ring for
dates. Snacks, shop, disabled access;
open Thurs, wknds and bank hols
Apr–Oct; (01483) 561389; £2.50; NT.
You can walk all the way to Weybridge,
some 20 miles, or hire boats from
Farncombe Boat House. Mar–Nov;

(01483) 421306.

GODSTONE TQ3551

Attractive despite its main roads, spread around a broad green with a duck pond, and a pretty group of houses around the imposing **church**, 14th/15th-c with a Norman tower. The Bell is an enjoyable dining pub.

Godstone Farm (Tilburstow Hill) Friendly 40-acre working farm; children are encouraged to touch the animals (and even climb in with some of them). Very good play areas, snacks, shop, disabled access; cl 25 Dec; (01883) 742546; £3.85 per child (accompanied adults free).

Godstone Vineyard (Quarry Rd, just off A22 W of Oxted) Looking up to the downs, this friendly vineyard produces a range of ciders and apple juice on top of its wines; snacks (inc free tastings), shop, disabled access; open all year; (01883) 744590; free. Down the road at Flower Lane (off A22 between Godstone and Oxted), the same people own Flower Farm, with organically grown **pick-your-own** produce; cl Oct–Apr; (01883) 742367.

Pilgrim Harps (Stansted House, Tilburstow Hill Rd S) Make and restore harps of all shapes and sizes; appointment preferred, (01342) 893242. The ancient Fox & Hounds out this way has good food (no children inside).

GOMSHALL TQ0846

Gomshall Gallery (A25) Contemporary arts and crafts for sale; also French wine wholesaler, and house plant sales. Cl Sun and bank hols; (01483) 203795.

GREAT BOOKHAM TQ1352

Polesden Lacey (off A246 S) Attractive Regency house once at the centre of Edwardian high society, now with photographs of some of the notable guests, as well as splendid tapestries, porcelain, Old Masters and other art. The spacious grounds have a walled rose garden and open-air theatre. Meals, snacks, shop, disabled access; house open Weds–Sun and bank hols pm Apr–Oct, grounds open all year; (01372) 458203; £3 house only, £3 grounds only; NT. On the other side of the extended commuter village, the Bookham Commons, with a mixture of thorny scrub (full of birds), small lakes, marshy bits and oak woods, are well wooded and attractive. In Effingham nearby, the Plough and Sir Douglas Haig are both reliable food pubs.

GUILDFORD SU9949

The biggest town in the area, Guildford is older than you might at first think; although many of the buildings are Georgian-fronted, what's behind often dates back much further. The sloping High St has attractive parts as well as its briskly modern shops, with interesting buildings inc the **Abbots Hospital** and the **Grammar School** with its notable chained library; Tunsgate Arch is the start for free guided walks of the city – 2.30pm every Sun, Mon and Weds May–Sept, also 7.30pm Thurs till end Aug.

Guildford Boat House (Millbrook) Old-established boat house where you can hire boats for the Wey Navigation; from £4 an hour; (01483) 504494. Nearby the Jolly Farmer does decent food in a lovely riverside setting.

Guildford Castle 🏰 The hill of the ruined 12th-c castle has fine views of the town, and a garden in the former castle ditch. Shop; open Easter–Sept; (01483) 444702; keep 90p, grounds free.

Guildford Cathedral The cathedral which was begun in 1936 is one of only two entirely 20th-c Anglican cathedrals in the country; it's quite austere, but has a cool elegance inside.

Guildford Discovery Science Centre (Ward St) Primarily for children but enjoyed by adults too, this thoroughly hands-on centre (all the exhibits are designed to be handled) is a lively but thorough introduction to the mysteries of science. The range of activities includes the chance to build your own suspension bridge or send a hot-air balloon to the ceiling, and they have a good programme of events inc science shows and experiments (especially in the school hols). Shop, disabled access with notice; cl Sun am and all Mon; 01483 537080; £2.75 (£2.25 children).

Guildford Museum (Quarry St) Local history from prehistoric man to the Victorians, with a display on Lewis Carroll, who died here in 1898. Shop; cl

Sun and Good Fri; free. Carroll is buried in the cemetery on the Mount, the continuation of the High St.

Guildhall (High St) Mainly Tudor, with one of the few surviving sets of Elizabethan standard measures. Disabled access to ground floor only; cl Sat, Sun; free guided tours at 2 and 3pm Tues and Thurs; (01483) 444035; free.

Loseley Park [££] (off B3000, 3m SW) Most people are familiar with the name from the yoghurts and ice-cream produced here (try the white chocolate and butterscotch). The stately Elizabethan country house was built in 1562, and has fine panelling, ceilings, paintings and tapestries. The gardens include a fountain garden. Meals, snacks, shop, limited disabled access; cl Mon, Tues exc bank hols, house open pm June–Aug, gardens open 11 May–Sept; (01483) 304440; £5 house and gardens, £2.50 gardens only.

HAMBLEDON SU9639
You can climb inside what's said to be a witch's tree in front of the church here; walk round the tree three times and the witch may well appear. Restore your poise in the Merry Harriers.

HASCOMBE SU9940
Lovely village with an interesting **church**; Dirk Bogarde's old local the White Horse is good for lunch (with a great garden), and the B2130 S and then the Dunsfold–Chiddingfold back road is a pleasant drive.

Winkworth Arboretum (B2130 just NW) Nearly 100 acres of lovely hillside woodland, with fine views over the North Downs – esp nice in spring, and with unusual flaring colours in the autumn. Snacks and shop spring–autumn, some disabled access; (01483) 208477; *£3.75; NT.

HEADLEY HEATH TQ2053
Sandy walks and rides through heather, birch woods – and as summer wears on rather too much bracken.

HOLMWOOD COMMON TQ1845
Popular for walks, with undulating oak and birch woods and lots of good paths; the Plough at Blackbrook is good for lunch.

HORSELL COMMON TQ0060
A touch of interest for walkers in the sandpits which inspired and saw the start of H G Wells's *War of the Worlds*; the Bleak House at the Anthonys and Red Lion in Horsell have decent food.

HURT WOOD TQ0943
Large areas of private broadleafed forest around here are open to walkers; relatively unfrequented, so it's a good place to spot birds and wild animals.

HYDON'S BALL SU9739
There's unspoilt walking terrain off the road between Loxhill and Hydestile S of Godalming, with Hydon's Ball a fine viewpoint, though rather hard to find.

LEATHERHEAD TQ1658
Fire and Iron Gallery (Oxshott Rd, A244 N) Unusual exhibitions of ornamental metalwork. Shop; limited disabled access; cl Sun and some bank hols; (01372) 386453; free.

Museum of Local History (Church St) In a pretty timber-framed 17th-c building, and well worth a visit. Shop, disabled access to ground floor; open Sat, Thurs pm and Fri am Apr–Christmas; (01372) 386348; free. The Dukes Head in the pedestrianised High St is pleasant for lunch, and there are riverside walks nearby.

LEITH HILL TQ1343
Perhaps the best stretch of country for walkers in Surrey – which surprises by being England's most wooded county. It has heather, sandy walks, steep pine woods and tremendous views. An 18th-c tower on top of the hill, the highest point in South-East England, is the best viewpoint of all, with an unexpected view of South London – which feels 100 miles away; light snacks, Weds pm and Sat, Sun and bank hols April–Sept, Sat, Sun and bank hols Oct–Mar; £1. Friday Street, which has a fine pub and a lake, is one starting point for switchback routes S through a series of brackeny summits to the tower. Leith Hill can also be approached through attractive farmland from the S, from Ockley or from the Parrot at Forest Green.

LIGHTWATER SU9262
Lightwater Country Park Visitor centre with heathland exhibition and plenty of nature trails. Snacks, shop, disabled access; park open all year, visitor centre open Sun, bank hols and Tues–Fri pm in school hols Apr–Dec; (01276) 479582; free.

MARDEN PARK TQ3653
A peaceful spot for strolls – surprising, as it's so near suburbia and the M25.

MYTCHETT SU8955
Basingstoke Canal 🖼 Now fully rehabilitated; in its Surrey section it does not pass through such fine scenery as the Wey Navigation, but its towpath has been well restored. **Basingstoke Canal Visitor Centre** (Place Rd) has displays on the canal, and good access to its towpath, with boat trips (wknds and bank hols April–Sept, and daily in school hols Easter–Oct). Meals, shop, disabled access; cl Mon (exc bank hols), wknds Oct–Easter; (01252) 370073; information centre and play areas free, exhibition £1.50.

OCKHAM COMMON TQ0858
Chatley Heath Semaphore Tower (Old Lane, off A3 to Effingham) Unique tower rather like a lighthouse, the only surviving member of a chain that once sent messages between the Admiralty in London and Portsmouth; excellent views from the top of the 88 steps. Surrounding it are 700 acres of heath and woodland, with a nature trail and good walks (inc the 20-minute trek from the car park to the tower). Shop; open pm wknds and bank hols Apr–Sept, plus Weds in school hols; (01932) 862762; £2. The extraordinary 'gothick' Hautboy (Ockham Lane) has a good brasserie.

OCKLEY TQ1439
Some attractive old houses along the Roman road here, with the 15th-c Cricketers and the Kings Arms doing good value food; the Scarlett Arms out at Walliswood is a delightful old place.

Hannah Peschar Sculpture Garden 🖼 (Black and White Cottage, Standon Lane) Lush garden filled with contemporary sculpture: the water garden is now more like a tropical rainforest than the cottage garden it started as, and the atmospheric sculptures and ceramics blend perfectly with its unusual design. Some disabled access but no facilities; cl Mon and am Sun, cl winter Sun; (01306) 627269; £7. There's a good big farm shop with **pick-your-own** fruit nearby.

OUTWOOD TQ3245
Spread around an attractive common,

with an antiques shop, and adjacent NT woodlands which are ideal for a picnic. The Bell nr the common and Dog & Duck out towards Coopers Hill are good for lunch.

Outwood Post Mill 🖼 Very well preserved, Britain's oldest working windmill, built in 1665. It's a lovely spot, 120 metres (400 ft) above sea level, with ducks, goats and geese wandering freely in its grounds. In Apr you can walk in the adjacent bluebell woods. Shop, disabled access to ground floor only; open pm Sun and bank hols Easter–Oct; (01342) 843644; £2.

PITCH HILL TQ0842
Though largely wooded, this is good country for walkers, with pleasant views on the relatively open approach from Ewhurst; above the village, the Windmill pub has glorious views from its garden.

RANMORE COMMON TQ1551
Chalk downland with sheep, wild orchids and dense woodlands, within close range of Polesden Lacey. You can walk on the well marked North Downs Way which emerges on to unspoilt downland on Denbies Hillside (car park nearby), a rich site for butterflies; here you look over Dorking and the Weald. The main landmark hereabouts is **St Barnabas church** by Gilbert Scott, the so-called 'Church on the North Downs' of 1859, hinting at the grandeur of his other projects such as the Albert Memorial.

REIGATE TQ2548
Barons Cave tours Below the peaceful castle grounds is a network of old tunnels, notably this splendidly atmospheric passageway with all sorts of myths and stories attached. The tours are enthusiastic and entertaining; open on selected days, best to ring the Wealden Cave and Mine Society on (01737) 823456, for full details and dates; £1–£2. Among the few surviving original buildings in this mainly modern town are one or two timber-framed houses around the High St, where the Market pub (open all day) has decent food.

Windmill church (off A25 W) The 220-year-old former windmill on Reigate Heath was converted into a church in 1882. They still have services at 3pm on the third Sun each month in summer. Disabled access; open all year – if cl, key at golf club clubhouse. There are pleasant walks out here, and the Skimmington Castle is a nice country pub.

RUNNYMEDE TQ0071
A field by a main road; not worth visiting unless you are fascinated by Magna Carta, though up the hill beyond the trees, the nearby memorials to John F Kennedy and the named aircrew who died during World War II are dignified and touching.

SHEPPERTON TQ0766
One of the best places to watch the comings and goings on the **River Thames**, with the **Wey Navigation** joining the river here; the Red Lion (Russell Rd), Warren Lodge Hotel (Church Sq) and handsome Thames Court Hotel (Ferry Lane) all have riverside gardens, and there's a quiet and attractive 18th-c village square with a pleasant church.

SHERE TQ0747
Very picturesque village, with 17th-c timber-framed cottages, a grassy-banked stream with ducks and ford, and lots of interesting corners. In the partly Norman **church** a quatrefoil blocked hole in the chancel wall marks the spot where a 14th-c anchorite had herself walled in, being fed through another hole outside. The Malt House is a decent local history museum, and the ancient White Horse is a good place for lunch. The village is within reach of both the North Downs around Ranmore Common and the greensand hills to the S; the view from the Ewhurst road is particularly memorable.

ST MARTHA'S HILL TQ0348
(E of Guildford) The church on its summit can be reached only on foot, and by starting from the attractive village of Chilworth, where the prettily set pub the Villagers at Blackheath has maps for walkers, you can see the long-abandoned gunpowder mills by the Tilling Bourne.

STOKE D'ABERNON TQ1259
Stoke d'Abernon church Notable for the earliest surviving memorial brass in Britain, dating from the 13th c; set in the floor of the chancel, it's very well preserved.

THURSLEY COMMON SU9040
Mainly pleasant sandy walking country, with heather and quite often unusual birds, also boggy patches with shallow ponds where dragonflies breed.

TILFORD SU8543
Rural Life Centre (Reeds Rd, just W) Carefully displayed private collection of farm implements and machinery, spread over 10 acres of field and woodland, with an arboretum, playground, miniature railway on Suns and 19th-c cricket pavilion. Meals, snacks, shop, disabled access; cl Mon (exc bank hols), Tues, all Oct–Mar; (01252) 795571; £4. The village has a massive oak tree, thought to be 800 years old; the Barley Mow between the river and the goose-cropped cricket green is a pleasant spot for lunch, and it's not far from here to the remains of Waverley Abbey.

TONGHAM SU8848
Hogs Back Brewery 🏛 (Manor Farm, The Street) Tours of friendly little brewery, using traditional methods to produce its nine distinctive ales. The shop has over 500 different English, Belgian and German beers (as well as their own), alongside English wines and farm ciders. Tours 6.30pm Weds Thurs and Fri, 11am and 2.30pm Sat, 2.30pm Sun, other times by arrangement, shop open daily (exc 25 Dec), disabled access; (01252) 783000; tour £5.75 (inc tastings and commemorative glass). Manor Farm also has **pick-your-own** fruit on the same site Jun–Sept.

WALLISWOOD TQ1138
Attractive village, with delightful woodland walk from pub to 13th-c church.

WEST CLANDON TQ0451
Clandon Park 🏛 (A247) Grand 18th-c house with unusual collection of porcelain birds, a Meissen collection, and fine furnishings and paintings. Regular concerts in the grand two-storeyed Marble Hall. Also the Queen's Royal Surrey regimental museum. The gardens have a Maori house brought over from New Zealand in 1892, and a sunken Dutch grotto garden. Meals, snacks, shop, disabled access to ground floor; open Apr–Oct, house from 11.30am Sun, Tues–Thurs and bank hols, gardens every day; (01483)

222482; £5; NT. The smart Onslow Arms is good for lunch, and the 16th-c Bulls Head is popular too.

WEYBRIDGE TQ0862

Brooklands Museum (B374) Exhaustive museum re-creating the racing circuit's 1920s and 30s heyday, with plenty of racing cars, motorbikes and bicycles displayed in the restored clubhouse. Also a restored Wellington bomber and a comprehensive collection of vintage Vickers and Hawker planes. This was the site of the first British Grand Prix (an exhibition telling the history of the race is housed in the converted motoring sheds) and first 100 mph motor ride – just walking round the original banked racetrack is surprisingly enjoyable. Demonstrations and events most wknds. Snacks, shop, good disabled access; cl Mon (exc bank hols), Good Fri, Christmas wk; (01932) 857381; £7. In the town the waterside Old Crown (Thames St) does good value food.

WISLEY TQ0658

Wisley Garden (A3) These 240-acre gardens have come a long way since they were set up in 1904 as experimental gardens for the Royal Horticultural Society; it's a mix of grand landscaped gardens with all sorts of model and trial gardens, even farm, orchard and woodland, alpine meadow. There are exemplary glasshouses. The gardens get very busy (esp at wknds) but are big enough to cope. Meals, snacks, shop (lots of hard-to-get gardening/plant books), garden centre (over 10,000 varieties from wide range of nurseries, but expensive), disabled access; cl Sun (exc to RHS members), 25 Dec; (01483) 224234; £5. The nearby Anchor at Pyrford Lock (turn left down exit road) is well placed for walks along the prettiest section of the **Wey Navigation Canal**, whose towpath gives Surrey's best waterside walks.

Other attractive villages, all with decent pubs, include Alfold TQ0334, Bletchingley TQ3250 (Norman church), Englefield Green SU9970 (handy for Savill Garden in Berkshire), Friday Street TQ1245 (good walks), Holmbury St Mary TQ1144, Hurtwood TQ0845, Leigh TQ2246, Limpsfield TQ4148 (church where Delius is buried), Limpsfield Chart TQ4251 (good walks), Ripley TQ0556, Shackleford SU9345, Thorpe TQ0268 and Wood Street SU9550.

Besides those mentioned, other **churches** worth a look include Burstow TQ3140, Okewoodhill TQ1337, Tandridge TQ3750, Tatsfield TQ4156 and Wotton TQ1247. You'll usually have to get the key from a local keyholder.

Popular starts or finishes for **walks** include the William IV at Little London TQ0646, Sportsman at Mogador TQ2452, Donkey at Charleshill SU8944, Plough high on its hill at Coldharbour TQ1543 and Surrey Oaks at Newgdigate TQ1942.

Besides places already mentioned for the **River Thames**, the Swan in Staines TQ0471 (The Hythe), the Magpie in Sunbury TQ1068 (Thames St), and the Anglers Tavern (off Manor Rd) and Weir (Sunbury Lane) in Walton-on-Thames TQ1066 all have good views and access to the river. The county council has guided walks all year, exploring historical or more usually natural history themes; a typical Sun might have eight or more to choose from. For the current programme ring the Planning Dept, (020) 8541 9463. You can book **balloon trips** on (01252) 844222.

Where to eat

BETCHWORTH TQ2149 **Dolphin** *The Street (01737) 842288* Bustling village local with homely front room, panelled back bar, three open fires, real ales and 18 wines by the glass, very popular good value food, and seats on the front courtyard and on lawn; no children inside. £16|**£6.25**

BLACKBROOK TQ1846 **Plough** *(01306) 886603* Popular pub with award-winning hanging baskets and window-boxes, generous helpings of good imaginative food, very friendly service from smart staff, marvellous choice of wines by the glass, and well kept real ales; pretty cottagey garden with Swiss play house for children – they are not allowed inside; cl 25–26 Dec, 1 Jan; limited disabled access. £18.50|£6.75

CHILWORTH TQ0346 **Villagers** *Blackheath (01483) 893152* Surrounded by quiet woodland and walks, this pub has a pretty terrace and garden, and a path through trees to the cricket green (where Monty addressed thousands of Canadian troups before D-day); rambling beamed main bar, small flagstoned room with big fireplace, decent food, real ales, and pleasant staff; bdrms; disabled access. £18.50|£6

COMPTON SU9547 **Tea Shop** *Down Lane (01483) 811030* Well liked teashop doing morning coffee, light lunches and afternoon tea, home-made cakes, scones and jams, free range eggs, a wide range of drinks inc interesting juices, seltzers, and fruity mineral waters, lots of India, China, herbal, and fruit teas, and different coffees; cl 24 Dec–7 Jan; partial disabled access.|£3.85

DORKING TQ1649 **Partners & Sons Restaurant** *2–4 West St (01306) 882826* Heavily beamed 16th-c building with dining rooms on two floors, very good imaginative modern cooking, and a thoughtful wine list; delicatessen and cookery school, too; cl Sun pm, 25 Dec–11 Jan; disabled access. £29.50

ELSTEAD SU9043 **Woolpack** *Milford Rd (01252) 703106* Cheerfully old-fashioned pub, bustling and friendly, with generous helpings of good interesting bar food inc vegetarian choices and lovely home-made puddings; a fair amount of wool trade memorabilia, open fires, well kept real ales, play area in garden; cl 25 Dec pm–26 Dec; children in family room or dining room only. £20|£5

GOMSHALL TQ0847 **Mulligans** *Station Rd (01483) 202242* Friendly staff in attractively decorated and relaxed fish restaurant with live French café music on Thurs; disabled access. £18

MICKLEHAM TQ1753 **King William IV** *Byttom Hill (01372) 372590* Relaxed and unpretentious pub cut into the hillside with fine views from the snug front bar, a spacious back bar with log fires and fresh flowers, wide range of interesting daily specials inc good vegetarian choice, well kept ales, lovely terraced garden, and nice walks; cl 25 Dec, 1 Jan; children over 12. £19|£7

NEWDIGATE TQ2043 **Surrey Oaks** *Parkgate Rd (01306) 631200* Cheerful little country pub with a small, snug, beamed room in the older part, a woodburner and a coal-effect gas fire, an airy main lounge, games room, very well liked food (esp the daily specials), real ales (small beer festival over Aug bank hol), friendly service, and an elaborate garden with rockery and fountains, a goat, doves, and aviary. £18.45|£5.95

RIPLEY TQ0556 **Michels** *The Clock House (01483) 224777* Charming Georgian house with carefully cooked seasonal food (inc some unusual dishes), a good range of wines, and good service; cl Sat am, Sun pm, Mon; 2 wks Aug. £50/2-course weekday lunch £18

SHERE TQ0747 **Kinghams** *Gomshall Lane (01483) 202168* Beamed 17th-c cottage with a relaxed atmosphere, unpretentious surroundings, cheerful service, good sound cooking from a shortish menu inc daily fish dishes and vegetarian choices, and nice puddings; cl Mon; disabled access. £30|£9.95

SOUTH GODSTONE TQ3549 **Fox & Hounds** *Tilburstow Hill Rd (01342) 893474* Pretty old-fashioned inn in pleasant spot with lots of little nooks and crannies, a cosy low-beamed bar with a good mix of seats and woodburner, popular imaginative food, restaurant with more elaborate dishes, well kept ales, and extensive wine list; cl pms Sun–Tues; children lunchtime only; partial disabled access. £21|£6.75

TADWORTH TQ2356 **Gemini** *28 Station Approach Rd (01737) 812179* Bustling and popular local restaurant with very good modern cooking using influences from all over the world, super puddings, a mainly French wine list, and courteous service; cl Sat am, Sun pm, Mon, 2 wks Christmas; children over 12 (exc Sun lunch when any age welcome); disabled access. £30|£10.50

Special thanks to Ian Downes, Paul Kennedy

SUSSEX

All the ingredients for a rewarding holiday, from the buzz of bohemian Brighton to quieter pleasures – stunning gardens, noble houses, and lovely coastal and downland walks

Sussex is blessed with a welcome diversity of family attractions. The spectacular castles at Bodiam and Herstmonceux offer much more than bricks and mortar alone (though their handsome exteriors merit a visit by themselves), and Newhaven Fort is great fun to explore. Intimate Drusillas zoo (near delightful Alfriston) is ideal for young and old animal lovers (good play areas and holiday events), while Wilderness Wood, Hadlow Down, is good for finding out about forests and their wildlife, and the vintage vehicles and waterfowl (not to mention play areas, craftsmen and miniature steam trains) make a good mix at Bentley Wildfowl & Motor Museum. Other rewarding family destinations include Newhaven's Paradise Park & Planet Earth, Earnley Gardens (quite a busy day out), and the enjoyable Beachy Head Countryside Centre (hands-on exhibitions and decent guided walks).

Unusual outings include a trip on the pretty and well preserved Bluebell steam line (near Sheffield Park), or a brain-teasing bash at the huge maize-maze at Turners Hill; the labyrinthine caves at the atmospheric Smugglers Adventure, Hastings, also keep most ages amused. Amberley and Singleton are home to two bustling open-air museums, both with lots for children.

Sussex has some of the country's finest gardens – Leonardslee at Lower Beeding, Highdown Hill, Nymans at Handcross, Great Dixter at Northiam, Sheffield Park (glorious autumn colours), and the newly restored Borde Hill near Haywards Heath to name but a few. Perhaps the highlight however is Wakehurst Place at Ardingly, with its pioneering new Millennium Seed Bank.

There are handsome houses, too, particularly in West Sussex, with especially impressive furnishings and art collections at Petworth, Goodwood, and Pallant House in Chichester. Charleston Farmhouse at Firle, and Monks House, Rodmell, still have something of the atmosphere brought to them by the Bloomsbury group.

Brighton has elegant Regency architecture, the remarkable Royal Pavilion, good free museums, endless antiques, and also a more raffish and studenty side that gives it a real buzz. By contrast, Eastbourne, sandy Bognor and Worthing are relatively sedate seaside resorts. Rye is an enchanting small town.

The Sussex countryside has very varied yet characteristic scenery: the South Downs with their attractive flint buildings and expansive views, culminating in Beachy Head and its nearby cliffs; the sparsely wooded high sandy heathland of the Ashdown Forest; and the intricate landscapes of the Weald. Much of the coast is developed, but the great sea inlet of

Chichester Harbour has some very attractive places along its shore. Chichester itself has plenty to see in and around it. Various length countryside walks inc trails along the Saxon Shore and a 1066 Country Walk are noted in a free brochure, *Walk South East England*, from most Tourist Information Centres here (and also in Kent and Surrey).

Quite a few of the places we recommend to stay in here are fine buildings in their own right.

Where to stay

ALFRISTON TQ5203 **Star** *High St, Alfriston, Polegate, East Sussex BN26 5TA* (01323) 870495 **£132**, plus special breaks; 37 rms. Fine hotel with fascinating atmospheric front part, built in 15th c as guest-house for pilgrims; lots of medieval carvings, sanctuary post in bar, decent food and drinks, and excellent service; disabled access

AMBERLEY TQ0213 **Amberley Castle** *Church St, Amberley, Arundel, West Sussex BN18 9ND* (01798) 831992 **£170**; 20 very well equipped charming rms. Magnificent 900-year-old castle with suits of armour and weapons in the day rooms – as well as antiques, roaring fires and panelling; friendly service, imaginative food in no smoking 13th-c dining room, and exceptionally pretty gardens; children over 12

ARLINGTON TQ5507 **Bates Green** *Tye Hill Rd, Arlington, Polegate, East Sussex BN26 6SH* (01323) 482039 **£52***, plus winter breaks; 3 rms. Originally an 18th-c gamekeeper's cottage, now a no smoking farmhouse on a 130-acre sheep farm; beams and log fire in oak-panelled sitting room, home-made cake and tea on arrival, and big breakfasts with home-made preserves; sizeable garden (open under the National Gardens Scheme), and a fine wood with lovely May bluebells; cl Christmas; children over 10; no pets

BATTLE TQ7714 **Little Hemingfold Hotel** *189 Hastings Rd, Battle, East Sussex TN33 0TT* (01424) 774338 **£92***, plus special breaks; 12 rms. Partly 17th-c, partly early Victorian farmhouse in 40 acres of woodland, with trout lake, tennis, gardens, and lots of walks (the two Labradors may come with you); comfortable sitting rooms, open fires, restful atmosphere and very good food using home-grown produce at own candlelit table; children can feed farm animals; tennis court; cl 2 Jan–8 Feb; dogs welcome

BATTLE TQ7218 **Netherfield Place** *Netherfield, Battle, East Sussex TN33 9PP* (01424) 774455 **£135***; 13 lovely rms. Handsome Georgian-style hotel in 30 acres of gardens and parkland, with light attractive day rooms, log fire, lovely flowers, a relaxed and friendly atmosphere, and imaginative food using home-grown produce; two hard tennis courts, croquet and putting green; cl 2 weeks Christmas and New Year

BATTLE TQ7414 **Powder Mills** *Powdermill Lane, Battle, East Sussex TN33 0SP* (01424) 775511 **£95**, plus special breaks; 35 rms, some in annexe. Attractive 18th-c creeper-clad manor house in 150 acres of park and woodland with four lakes and outdoor swimming pool, and next to the 1066 Battlefield; country-house atmosphere, log fires and antiques in elegant day rooms, attentive service, and good modern cooking in Orangery restaurant; children over 10 in evening restaurant; well behaved dogs by prior arrangement; disabled access

BOSHAM SU8005 **Kenwood** *Main Rd, Bosham, Chichester, West Sussex PO18 8PH* (01243) 572727 **£52**; 3 large rms. Comfortable and well kept Victorian house with harbour views, plushly furnished lounge, pleasant dining room (with useful fridge and microwave for guests to self cater for light meals), lots of old sporting bats, hockey sticks and tennis racquets, super breakfasts, games room with pool, heated swimming pool, croquet, and free-range poultry; disabled access

BOSHAM SU8004 **Millstream** *Bosham Lane, Bosham, Chichester, West Sussex PO18 8HL* (01243) 573234 **£120***; 33 rms. Warmly friendly small hotel in charming waterside village, with attractive bar and sitting room, open fire and fresh flowers, very good food using fresh local produce, good wine list, streamside garden; disabled access

BRIGHTON TQ3004 **Dove** *18 Regency Sq, Brighton, East Sussex BN1 2FG (01273) 779222* **£69***; 9 rms, 4 with sea view. Lovely, neatly kept bow-windowed Regency house, with warmly welcoming helpful owners, and very good breakfasts in light and airy dining room (enjoyable evening meals by prior arrangement); they are kind to families, with toys and babysitting available ☺

BRIGHTON TQ3004 **Grand** *97–99 Kings Rd, Brighton, East Sussex BN1 2FW (01273) 321188* **£210**, plus special breaks; 200 handsome rms, many with sea view. Famous Victorian hotel with marble columns and floors and fine moulded plasterwork in the luxurious and elegant day rooms; good service, very good food and fine wines, popular afternoon tea in sunny conservatory, a bustling nightclub, and newly refurbished health spa with indoor swimming pool; disabled access ☺

BRIGHTON TQ3004 **Topps** *16–17 Regency Sq, Brighton, East Sussex BN1 2FG (01273) 729334* **£84**; 15 lovely comfortable rms, 11 with gas-effect coal fires and many with sea view. Carefully furnished and well kept Regency town house nr seafront with particularly helpful and genuinely friendly owners, really good breakfasts in attractive basement restaurant, and a library/reception room; disabled access

BURWASH TQ6724 **Ashlands Cottage** *Burwash, Etchingham, East Sussex TN19 7HS (01435) 882207* **£40**; 2 rms, shared bthrm. In a lovely spot nr Batemans, this pretty cottage has marvellous views, a homely sitting room, attractive dining room (no full suppers but pubs nearby), charming owner, and an appealing garden; children over 12

CHICHESTER SU8604 **Bedford Hotel** *36–37 Southgate, Chichester, West Sussex PO19 1DP (01243) 785766* **£88**, plus special breaks; 20 attractive rms, most with own bthrm. Family-run Georgian hotel in centre, with friendly atmosphere, and comfortable no smoking lounge and restaurant opening on to quiet terrace; cl Christmas and New Year

CHICHESTER SU8604 **Suffolk House** *East Row, Chichester, West Sussex PO19 1PD (01243) 778899* **£94***, plus winter breaks; 11 rms, some overlooking garden. Friendly Georgian house in centre with homely comfortable lounge, little bar, traditional cooking in dining room, and small walled garden

CHIDHAM SU7903 **Old Rectory** *Chidham Lane, Chidham, Chichester, West Sussex PO18 8TF (01243) 572088* **£50**; 3 rms. Handsome country house with elegant sitting room, friendly owners, enjoyable breakfasts (good pub nearby for evening meals), and croquet and summer swimming pool in big garden

CLIMPING TQ0000 **Bailiffscourt** *Climping St, Climping, Littlehampton, East Sussex BN17 5RW (01903) 723511* **£150**, plus special breaks; 31 rms, many with four-poster beds and winter log fires, and with super views. Mock 13th-c manor built only 60 years ago but with tremendous character – fine old iron-studded doors, huge fireplaces, heavy beams and so forth – in 30 acres of coastal pastures and walled gardens: elegant furnishings, enjoyable modern English and French food, fine wines, a relaxed atmosphere, and outdoor swimming pool, tennis and croquet; children over 8

CUCKFIELD TQ3024 **Ockenden Manor** *Ockenden Lane, Cuckfield, Haywards Heath, West Sussex RH17 5LD (01444) 416111* **£130**, plus special breaks; 22 pretty rms. Dating from 1520, this carefully extended manor house has antiques, fresh flowers and an open fire in the comfortable sitting room, good modern cooking in fine panelled restaurant, cosy bar, and lovely views of the South Downs from the neatly kept garden (in nine acres of grounds)

EAST GRINSTEAD TQ3634 **Gravetye Manor** *Vowels Lane, East Grinstead, West Sussex RH19 4LJ (01342) 810567* **£242**; 18 lovely rms. Elizabethan manor house in magnificent grounds and gardens – 400 years old this year, and also the 42nd year the Herbert family have been in charge; antiques, fine paintings, and lovely flower arrangements in spacious panelled public rooms, an excellent restaurant using home-grown produce (inc spring water and free-range eggs) and their own home-smoked fish and meats, an exceptional wine list, exemplary service, and a relaxed, almost old-fashioned atmosphere; children over 7 (but babies welcome)

EAST HOATHLY TQ5116 **Old Whyly** *Halland Rd, East Hoathly, Lewes, East Sussex BN8 6EL* (01825) 840216 **£90**; 3 rms. Handsome and historic 17th-c manor house in lovely garden with tennis court and swimming pool and very close to Glyndebourne (hampers can be provided), fine antiques and paintings, and delicious food; plenty of walks nearby

EASTBOURNE TV6198 **Grand** *King Edward's Parade, Eastbourne, East Sussex BN21 4EQ* **£152**, plus special breaks; 152 rms, many with sea views. Gracious and very well run Victorian hotel, with spacious, comfortable lounges, lots of fine original features, lovely flower arrangements, imaginative food in elegant restaurants, and courteous helpful service; leisure club and outdoor pool and terraces; disabled access ☺

ETCHINGHAM TQ6828 **King John's Lodge** *Sheepstreet Lane, Etchingham, East Sussex TN19 7AZ* (01580) 819232 **£65***; 4 rms. The 4-acre gardens surrounding this Jacobean house are lovely — wonderful views, romantic and secret gardens, a wild garden with rose walk, white garden, and lily pond — plants and statuary for sale; guests' private sitting room, stone mullioned windows, heavy beams and inglenook fireplaces, breakfasts served in Elizabethan dining room (on terrace in fine weather), and evening meals by arrangement; swimming pool, tennis court and croquet; cl Christmas; children over 7

FAIRLIGHT TQ8611 **Fairlight Cottage** *Warren Rd, Fairlight, Hastings, East Sussex TN35 4AG* (01424) 812545 **£45***, plus winter breaks; 4 rms, one with four-poster. Comfortable and very friendly no smoking house in fine countryside with views over Rye Bay and plenty of rural and clifftop walks; big comfortable lounge (nice views), good breakfasts in elegant dining room, and generous carefully prepared food (by prior arrangement, but not at Christmas); well behaved pets welcome

FITTLEWORTH TQ0118 **Swan** *Lower St, Fittleworth, Pulborough, West Sussex RH20 1EL* (01798) 865429 **£60***; 11 rms. Attractive 15th-c inn with big inglenook log fire in comfortable lounge, friendly service, enjoyable food in beamed restaurant, attractive panelled side room, and sheltered back lawn; good nearby walks; cl Christmas

FRANT TQ5935 **Old Parsonage** *Church Lane, Frant, Tunbridge Wells, Kent TN3 9DX* (01892) 750773 **£76***, plus special breaks; 3 very pretty rms, 2 with four-posters. Just two miles from Tunbridge Wells, this carefully restored imposing former Georgian rectory has antiques, watercolours and plants in elegant sitting rooms, spacious Victorian conservatory, good food in candlelit dining room, and balustraded terrace overlooking quiet three-acre garden; several nearby walks; children over 7

HARTFIELD TQ4837 **Bolebroke Mill** *Perry Hill, Edenbridge Rd, Hartfield, East Sussex TN7 4JP* (01892) 770425 **£62**; 5 rms, some in the mill and some in adjoining Elizabethan miller's barn. A working mill until 1948, this ancient place was mentioned in Domesday Book, and is surrounded by mill streams and woodland; the internal machinery has been kept intact and steep narrow stairs lead to bedrooms that were once big corn bins; both this and the barn have their own sitting room, breakfasts are marvellous, light suppers enjoyable, and the owners very friendly; no smoking; cl mid-Dec–first wk Feb; children over 8

HELLINGLY TQ6014 **Grove Hill House** *Grove Hill, Hellingly, Hailsham, East Sussex BN27 4HG* (01435) 812440 **£40**; 2 spacious, pretty rooms. Lovely heavily beamed 17th-c farmhouse in quiet countryside, with charming friendly owners, a relaxed and restful atmosphere, traditional furnishings inc antiques and family photographs, fresh flowers and open fire, good hearty breakfasts in separate dining room, enjoyable evening meals (by arrangement) using home-grown produce, and attractive flower-filled garden; cl Christmas; children over 5

MAYFIELD TQ5826 **Middle House** *High St, Mayfield, East Sussex TN20 6AB* (01435) 872146 **£65**; 6 spacious rms. Old-world Elizabethan hotel nr church, with lovely panelled restaurant, red leather chesterfields and armchairs by cosy log fire, chatty locals' bar with big open fire (maybe spit roasts), a wide choice of good interesting bar food, an attractive back garden, and pleasant views

PETWORTH SU9719 **Old Railway Station** *Station Rd, Petworth, West Sussex GU28 0JF (01798) 342346* **£82**, plus special breaks; 6 rms, some in Pullman railway cars. Petworth's former railway station, carefully restored, with large lounge and dining area (the former waiting room with original ticket office windows), fine breakfasts, friendly owners, and terrace (once the platform) and garden; children over 10; disabled access

ROGATE SU8022 **Mizzards** *Rogate, Petersfield, Hampshire GU31 5HS (01730) 821656* **£60**; 3 rms. 16th-c house in quiet country setting with a comfortable and elegant sitting room, vaulted dining room, outside swimming pool, landscaped gardens and lake, and fine farmland views; no evening meals (nearby pubs), no smoking; cl Christmas and New Year; children over 9

RUSHLAKE GREEN TQ6218 **Stone House** *Rushlake Green, Heathfield, East Sussex TN21 9QJ (01435) 830553* **£130**; 7 rms, some with four-posters. In a thousand acres of pretty countryside (with plenty of walks and country sports) and surrounded by an 18th-c walled garden, this lovely house was built at the end of the 15th c and extended in Georgian times; there are open log fires, antiques and family heirlooms in the drawing room, a quiet library, an antique full-sized table in the mahogany-panelled billiard room, wonderful food in the panelled dining room, fine breakfasts, and a cosseting atmosphere; cl 24 Dec–1 Jan; children over 9

RYE TQ9019 **Cadborough Farm** *Udimore Rd, Rye, East Sussex TN31 6AA (01797) 225426* **£60**; 3 large rms. Fine country house in 24 acres with views to the sea over Camber Castle – you can walk across the private fields to the town centre; comfortable drawing room, super breakfasts with home-made preserves, freshly baked breads, their own eggs, and fresh seasonal fruits, log fires, and attractive gardens; self-catering in restored stables and converted dairy; no smoking; cl Christmas and New Year; children over 12; dogs welcome by arrangement

RYE TQ9120 **Jeakes House** *Mermaid St, Rye, East Sussex TN31 7ET (01797) 222828* **£67**, plus special breaks; 12 rms overlooking the rooftops of this medieval town or across the marsh to the sea, 10 with own bthrm. Fine 16th-c building, well run and friendly, with good breakfasts, lots of well worn books, comfortable furnishings, linen and lace, a warm fire, and lovely peaceful atmosphere; children over 12

RYE TQ9220 **Little Orchard House** *West St, Rye, East Sussex TN31 7ES (01797) 223831* **£64**; 2 four-poster rms. Beautifully furnished fine old house with antiques and personal prints and paintings, Georgian panelling, big open fireplace in study, good generous breakfasts (the friendly owners will make evening reservations at any of the many nearby restaurants), and an unexpectedly wonderful secluded garden; children over 12

RYE TQ9220 **Old Vicarage** *66 Church Sq, Rye, East Sussex TN31 7HF (01797) 222119* **£68**, plus bargain breaks; 5 pretty rms with newspaper and glass of sherry. Charming quietly placed mainly 18th-c house with helpful friendly owners, comfortable sitting room or small library, log fire in elegant dining room, and marvellous breakfasts with freshly baked breads, free-range eggs, and home-made jams, jellies and ketchups; no smoking; cl Christmas; children over 8

SHIPLEY TQ1523 **Goffsland Farm** *Shipley Rd, Southwater, Horsham, West Sussex RH13 7BQ (01403) 730434* **£42**; 1 family rm with own sitting/dining rm and own access. 17th-c Wealden farmhouse on 260-acre family farm with good breakfasts, afternoon tea and evening meals by arrangement, and a friendly welcome; good walks

SLINFOLD TQ1131 **Random Hall** *Stane St, Slinfold, Horsham, West Sussex RH13 7QX (01403) 790558* **£90**, plus special breaks; 15 comfortable rms. Restored 16th-c farmhouse with lots of beams, flagstones, copper and brass and fine inglenook fireplace in lounge, a friendly relaxed atmosphere, good breakfasts, and enjoyable modern cooking for candlelit restaurant (or on the terrace); cl 27 Dec–10 Jan

STORRINGTON TQ1015 **Little Thakeham** *Merrywood Lane, Storrington, Pulborough, West Sussex RH20 3HE (01903) 744416* **£180**, plus special breaks; 9

individually decorated rms with stylish fabrics and early antiques. Splendid combination of magnificent Lutyens house, delightfully restored Gertrude Jekyll garden, antiques and Arts and Crafts furniture and objets d'art; log fires, traditional English and French food using local produce, good French wines, and outdoor swimming pool, tennis court, croquet; cl Christmas and New Year; children by arrangement

TILLINGTON SU9622 **Horse Guards** *Tillington, Petworth, West Sussex GU28 9AF (01798) 342332* **£73***; 3 spacious clean rms. Neat, friendly and civilised 17th-c pub in lovely village setting with beamed front bar, very good imaginative food (fresh fish delivered five times a week, and excellent puddings), up to a dozen wines by the glass; no children

UCKFIELD TQ4718 **Horsted Place** *Little Horsted, Uckfield, East Sussex TN22 5TS (01825) 750581* **£155**; 20 individually decorated spacious rms. Stately Victorian country house on extensive estate, with antiques, flowers and log fires in luxurious lounges, delicious food and good wine list in no smoking dining room, and croquet, tennis, indoor heated swimming pool; reduced green fees at East Sussex National Golf Club; children over 8 in restaurant; disabled access

WARTLING TQ6509 **Wartling Place** *Wartling, Hailsham, East Sussex BN27 1RY (01323) 832590* **£70**; 3 individually furnished rms, 2 with four-posters. Handsome Georgian house in lovely secluded gardens, with antiques in residents' drawing room, good breakfasts in elegant dining area (they will arrange picnic hampers), fresh flowers, and helpful owners

WISBOROUGH GREEN TQ0625 **Old Wharf** *Wharf Farm, Wisborough Green, Billingshurst, West Sussex RH14 0JG (01403) 784096* **£70**; 3 rms with views over farmland and canal. Carefully restored no smoking canal warehouse with fine old hoist wheel, comfortable sitting room with log fire, breakfasts using free-range eggs from the farm, walled canalside garden, and friendly atmosphere; cl Christmas and New Year; children over 12; no pets

To see and do

Sussex Family Attraction of the Year

ALFRISTON TQ5205 **Drusillas Park** (up towards A27) Still one of the best organised places for children in the entire country, a small zoo keeping only animals that they can provide with everything they'd have in the wild, so no lions, tigers or elephants, but plenty of smaller and arguably more entertaining creatures in thoughtfully designed enclosures. You watch the meerkats through a little dome in the floor of their spacious home, there's a walk-through fruit bat enclosure, and underwater vantage points in Penguin Bay make it look as if the birds are flying above you. Elsewhere is everything from snakes and other creepy-crawlies to a splendid range of monkeys, inc golden lion-headed tamarins, and the somewhat lugubrious-looking saki monkeys. Everything's designed at child height, and, on the way round, a Zoolympics Trail constantly keeps children asking about the animals. There's a farmyard area, and Pet World gives younger visitors a chance to get closer to rabbits, chinchillas and maybe even snakes. The excellent play areas cover over an acre, with plenty of sliding, climbing and swinging, and areas set aside for toddlers. A jolly little railway chuffs its way around the park and through the llama paddock. Some of the extras have a small additional charge: an activity centre open at wknds and in school holidays costs 50p for mask-making and £1.50 for face-painting, and it's an extra £1 to pan for gold (don't expect to get rich – whoever heard of the East Sussex Gold Rush?). Nearly half the park is under cover – inc one of the play areas – and there are some delightful gardens just outside. Good meals and snacks, picnic areas, shops, excellent disabled access; cl 24–26 Dec; (01323) 870234; £7.60 (£6.50 children 3–12).

ALFRISTON TQ5205
In a sheltered spot below the downs, this is one of Britain's most charming villages – at quieter times of year (in high summer the ice-cream eaters, teashops and curio shops somewhat blunt its appeal). Thatched, tiled and timbered houses, and a fine **church** built on a Saxon funeral barrow, by large green just off the single main street. One of the most engaging buildings in the village is the Star Inn, with its Old Bill, a bright red figurehead lion on one corner taken as a trophy from a 17th-c Dutch ship, and some intricate painted 15th-c carvings among its handsome timbering. Besides the Star, the Market Cross is good for lunch.

Clergy House 🏛 (The Tye) 14th-c, the first building to be taken over by the National Trust. Carefully restored, it now tells a story of medieval life and building methods; charming cottage garden. Shop; cl Tues, Fri and all Nov–Mar; (01323) 870001; £2.50; NT.

Drusillas Park *See separate family panel on p.571.*

English Wine Centre (up by A27) Good cross-section of wines made in this country, as well as regional foods and crafts. Snacks (booked groups only), shop, disabled access; cl 23 Dec–2 Jan; (01323) 870164; free, tours (of vineyard and beyond) and tastings from £4.95.

Litlington On the other side of the Cuckmere valley from Alfriston, notable for its **church** down a footpath – so small there can scarcely be room in it for a congregation of more than about 15. The Plough & Harrow here is useful.

AMBERLEY TQ0212
A delightful thatched village; from the churchyard you can peer into the Castle (now a good hotel), and there is public access to the Wild Brooks, a large expanse of watermeadows which form an important habitat for wetland plants and birds; there's also a way up to the downs here. The unspoilt Black Horse has good food, and there are lovely downs views from the Sportsman's conservatory, balcony and garden.

Amberley Museum (by Amberley Stn) A carefully thought-out open-air museum covering 36 acres of former chalk quarry and limeworks, with plenty of traditional crafts and re-created workshops. Lots going on, from pottery and cobbling to a working village telephone exchange. Meals, snacks, shop, disabled access; cl Mon and Tues (exc school or bank hols), and Nov–mid-Mar; (01798) 831370; £6.25. Nearby the riverside Bridge Inn at Houghton Bridge is great in summer; the B2139 is a pleasant drive.

ARDINGLY TQ3431
Wakehurst Place Garden (B2028) The 'Southern Kew', administered by the Royal Botanic Gardens, with a tremendous variety of interesting trees and shrubs inc many tender rarities. Lakes and water gardens, steep Himalayan glade, woodland walks and fine rhododendron species. Plenty to see throughout the year, and all very peaceful. By the time you read this, the new buildings of the Millennium Seed Bank will finally be open, housing one of the largest international conservation projects ever undertaken. The aim of the project is to safeguard over 24,000 plant species from around the world against extinction, and to secure the future of Britain's flowering plants; exhibitions will give more information about the scheme. Meals, snacks, plant and book sales, disabled access; cl 25 Dec, 1 Jan; (01444) 894066; £5 (free to NT members). Wknd guided walks usually start in front of the mansion at 11.30am and 2.30pm (2pm in winter); 0181 332 5585 to check. The Gardeners Arms (children in garden only), Ardingly Inn and Oak all do good lunches. Nearby **Ardingly Reservoir** offers pleasant strolls by its shores, or you can plan a longer walk around the elevated farmland and woodlands surrounding Wakehurst Place and Balcombe.

ARUNDEL TQ0107
Dating from pre-Roman days, this is dominated by the magnificent walls and towers of the castle on a mound high over the River Arun. Attractive buildings, inc antiques shops and so forth, cluster along the sides of the steep main street climbing from the bridge to the castle. The 19th-c Roman Catholic **cathedral** complements the

castle well, giving rather a French feel to the whole small town. The Swan has decent food. There are public paths along the canalised River Arun and into Arundel Park, with its lakes and woodlands beneath the slopes of the downs.

Arundel Castle Seat of the Dukes of Norfolk for over 700 years – a magnificent sight, a great spread of well kept towers and battlements soaring above the village and the trees around it. The keep is the oldest part; the rest dates mainly from the 19th c. Excellent art collection, inc portraits by Van Dyck, Reynolds, Lely and Gainsborough, as well as 16th-c furniture, and personal possessions of Mary Queen of Scots. Meals, snacks, shop; cl am, Sat, Good Fri and all Nov–Mar; (01903) 883136; £7.

Arundel Museum (High St) Local history and heritage; cl Sun am, and all end Oct–Mar; £1.

Wildfowl & Wetlands Trust (Mill Rd) 55 acres of well landscaped pens, lakes, and paddocks, home to over 1,000 ducks, geese and swans from all over the world. Hides overlook the various habitats, and there are children's activities in school hols. Meals, snacks, shop, disabled access; cl 25 Dec; (01903) 883355; £4.75. The lane past the Trust ends at a little cluster of houses by an isolated church and former watermill. On the way to the Trust, the Black Rabbit has a superb location and does food, and in summer there are **boat trips** from it.

ASHDOWN FOREST TQ4832
A major inland attraction for walkers, part forest, part heathland – sandy tracks, clumps of Scots pines, secretive glades and exhilarating views. A recent Lottery grant will help restore more of the heathland, and new speed limits have made traffic calmer. Don't be put off by the OS map: there are far more walking routes than it suggests (there's a useful 1:30,000 scale walkers' map issued by the Ashdown Forest Centre showing all the paths and rides as well as naming the car parks – an extremely useful idea given the forest's lack of other landmarks). The forest still looks just like the E H Sheppard drawings for A A Milne's Winnie the Pooh stories,

which were set here. Five Hundred Acre Wood is the Hundred Acre Wood of Pooh's world, and with a little searching you can find, SE of Hartfield, a reconstructed Poohsticks Bridge made from locally grown green oak and, by the B2026, Gills Lap (the 'enchanted place' at the top of the forest, near Piglet's house), where a memorial to Milne has been placed nr the triangulation point. Handy pubs for forest walks include the Foresters Arms at Fairwarp, Half Moon at Lye Green and Hatch at Colemans Hatch.

ASHINGTON TQ1317
Holly Gate Cactus Garden (Billingshurst Rd) Over 30,000 succulents and cactus plants from both tropical and arid habitats all over the world – a cactus enthusiast's prickly paradise. Ice-creams, cheap plant sales, disabled access; cl 25–26 Dec; (01903) 892930; *£2. The Franklands Arms at Washington is a useful lunch stop.

BARCOMBE MILLS TQ4316
One of Sussex's secrets, with lazy riverside walks (or boat trips) from the tucked-away Anchor pub here.

BATTLE TQ7515
Takes its name from certainly the most celebrated and perhaps the most disorganised skirmish in English history, thrashed out here in 1066. The main street (carrying a fair bit of traffic, so not exactly peaceful) has a lot of attractive old buildings, some now antiques shops and cafés; beyond them the town extends into spreading new estates. The friendly Olde Kings Head has decent food, and the **church** of St Mary has some 13th-c wall paintings.

Almonry (High St/Virgins Lane) Ancient building with town model, teas, and a pretty little garden (cl Sun, 25–26 Dec and 1 Jan; £1).

Battle Abbey The **battlefield** has a mile-long walk around it with a good audio tour explaining what happened. Four years after the bloodshed William built an abbey on the site as penance, the altar reputedly on the very spot where Harold fell. Not much is left of the original building, but later remains include the monks' dormitory and common room, and the great 14th-c gatehouse which looms over the small market square. Snacks, shop, mostly disabled access; cl 24–26 Dec, I Jan; (01424) 773792; £4; EH.

Battle Museum of Local History (High St) Good local history inc diorama of the Battle of Hastings and a reproduction of the Bayeux Tapestry; shop, disabled access (cl Sun am and all Oct–Easter; £I).

Buckleys Yesterday World 🖭 (High St) Carefully reconstructed period shops, railway station and the like; lots of hands-on activities, and nostalgic film show. Meals, snacks, shop; cl 25–26 Dec, I Jan; (01424) 775378; £4.50.

Weald views The B2096 Heathfield road gives views S to Beachy Head from its highest points, nr Netherfield and just before Dallington. Off this road any of the narrow side roads N into the countryside between Burwash and Dallington take you into the most unspoilt part of the steep Wealden woods and pastures.

BEACHY HEAD TV5997 This towering abruptly cliffy end of the downs is a landmark for miles around, and the giant of this stretch of cliffy headlands: an unspoilt spot with terrific views, inc the lighthouse dwarfed far below. It's easily reached from Eastbourne, and the eponymous hotel, open all day, has decent food.

Beachy Head Countryside Centre Surprisingly enjoyable hands-on exhibitions, as well as indoor and outdoor play areas, and a full programme of guided walks (best to book for these) around cliffs, beaches and wildflower meadows. Meals, snacks, shop, disabled access; usually open daily late Mar–Oct, plus wknds Nov–Christmas (may close lunchtime), with walks wknds and school hols – ring for exact dates; (01323) 737273; free, walks around £2.

BEXHILL TQ7407 A low-key seaside town with a pebble beach interrupted by cumbersome groins – an unlikely setting for a gem of Bauhaus architecture, the shoreside De La Warr Pavilion (open daily; free) designed by Mendelsohn and Chermayeff. The Italian-run café opposite is good value.

Bexhill Museum of Costume 🖭 Set in the delightful grounds of the Old

Manor House up towards the tiny 'Old Town', a good look at 18th- to 20th-c fashions, with accessories and other domestic items as well as the clothes. Shop, disabled access; cl Weds, am wknds, and all Nov–Apr; (01424) 210045; *£1.50.

BIGNOR SU9814 **Roman Villa & Museum** One of the largest villas discovered so far, with marvellous mosaics inc the longest in Britain – 25 metres (82 ft) long, and still in its original position. The quaint thatched buildings in which they are housed (erected by the farmer on whose land the site was found in the 1820s), are now listed buildings themselves. Snacks, shop, some disabled access, and largely under cover; cl Mon (exc bank hols and Jun–Sept), and all Nov–Feb; (01798) 869259; £3.50. The White Horse at nearby Sutton has good food (and good value bedrooms).

BIGNOR HILL SU9813 Up here the trees that obscure views for much of the way in this part of the South Downs give way to open ground; Stane St, a Roman road here relegated to a path, takes a strikingly straight course SW over a woodland and pasture landscape.

BIRDHAM SU8401 **Sussex Falconry Centre** (Lockacre Aquatic Nursery, Wophams Lane) Originally set up as a breeding and rescue centre, then opened to the public with birds such as falcons, hawks, eagles and owls flown throughout the day. Shop, disabled access; cl Mon (exc bank hols), and mid-Oct to mid-Mar; (01243) 512472; £3. This area S of Chichester is flat country, full of nurseries and huge glasshouses; the Lamb towards West Wittering is a popular dining pub.

BODIAM TQ7825 **Bodiam Castle** The perfect picture-book castle, a classic example of 14th-c fortification at its peak, with massive walls rising sheer and virtually complete from the romantic moat, and round drum towers steadfastly guarding each corner. Built to withstand attack from the French, it was only ever besieged by other Englishmen, and on both occasions was rather weedily handed over without a fight. The interior was destroyed around the Civil War, and wasn't repaired until Lord Curzon bought it in 1916; he left the castle to the NT in 1925. Plenty of space for picnics. They have several enjoyable special events, inc a fun day with donkey rides and Punch and Judy, a Christmas Cracker hunt, and children's story-telling. It's worth reading the leaflet they give you on arriving at the car park – most people fail to spot that the lavatories are at this end rather than at the castle itself. Meals, snacks, shop, limited disabled access; cl wkdys Nov to mid-Feb, 24–26 Dec; (01580) 830436; £1.50 for parking, then £3.70 for castle; NT. Next to the castle, Knollys is a good tea shop, and the Salehurst Halt at Salehurst just W does good lunches. In summer you can put together a very enjoyable full day out by taking the 45-minute boat trip to the castle through peaceful countryside from Newenden (they don't run in bad weather); (01797) 280363 for times; £6.50 return. This can then link with a **steam train** on the Kent & East Sussex Railway, from the Tenterden terminus over the Kent border; the trains do now run all the way to Bodiam's recently restored station. Up the hill in Ewhurst Green, the White Dog has interesting food, and **Bodiam Bonsai** grow, show and sell these miniature trees.

BOGNOR REGIS SZ9398
An old-fashioned seaside family resort, popular above all for its sandy beaches. The museum on the High St has a wireless display of 40 years of valve radio, and the Alex (London Rd) has good value food.

BOSHAM SU8004
The Saxon **church** here figures in the Bayeux Tapestry, and the village is a lovely cluster of old cottages around it, the green, and a broad, almost landlocked, inlet of Chichester harbour, busy with boating in the summer. Don't be tempted to park on the shore – the incoming tide is well known for its trick of lapping around parked cars. Very pleasant to stroll around, with good antique shops and craft galleries, esp on Bosham Lane. The Anchor Bleu, right by the water, is popular for lunch.

BOXGROVE SU9007

Boxgrove Priory Now the parish church, this 12th-c building is one of the most outstanding Early English churches in the region, with a surprising 16th-c painted ceiling, free-standing chantry chapel, and the atmospheric remains of various monastic buildings outside.

BRAMBER TQ1810
St Mary's House 🏠 Striking medieval house, with fine panelling, pretty garden with topiary, and unusual Elizabethan painted room. Concerts in spring and autumn. Teas, shop; open pm Sun, Thurs and bank hols Easter–Sept; (01903) 816205; £4. The Bramber Castle has decent food. Adjacent Steyning has some attractive timber-framed and Georgian buildings (and a good Tudor pub, the Chequers).

BRIGHTON TQ3104
Despite its many more modern blocks, huge shopping centre and vast modern sports halls, Brighton still has plenty of glistening white Regency buildings dating from its fashionable days in the 18th c, when the idea that sea-bathing was good for you sent London's finest scurrying to the coast. Still a thriving resort, given a buzzy feel by its vigorous young university and its several language schools for foreign students; there's also a booming gay scene. The most lively part is the Lanes – 17th-c fishermen's cottages squeezed together in narrow twisting byways, now crammed with jewellery and antique shops, restaurants and bars; they're mostly closed to traffic. English's here is entertaining for lunch. The North Laine area is slightly more trendy, with good buskers and cool cafés. Throughout, there's no shortage of simple places to eat, inc the Cricketers (Black Lion St), Greys (Southover St, Kemp Town), Mary Pack's Cliftonville (good local fish; Hove Pl), and, if you like sausages, Sussex Yeoman (Guildford Rd).

Barlow Collection (Brighton University, Falmer; off A27 N) Reckoned to be Europe's finest collection of Chinese ceramics. It's usually open 11.30am–2.30pm Tues and Thurs (exc August and over Easter and Christmas); (01273) 606755; free.

Booth Museum of Natural History (Dyke Rd) Superb well presented collection of animal skeletons (inc some dinosaur bones), as well as the Victorian collection of birds the museum was first built to house. Shop, disabled access; cl am Sun, Thurs, 25–26 Dec, 1 Jan and Good Fri; (01273) 292777; free.

Brighton Fishing Museum (Kings Rd) The seafront Arches across from the Old Ship Hotel used to be occupied by local fishermen, and a couple still are, the rest given over to little craftshops and artists. One houses this collection of local boats, nets, models and pictures. Shellfish stall and fish smokery, shop, disabled access; cl 25–26 Dec, and any day Nov–Apr when the weather is poor; (01273) 723064; free.

Brighton marina (E of centre) This modern place is lively in summer, with lots of boutiques, bars, tables out by the water and so forth. A waterfront entertainment centre inc a factory shopping outlet, bars and restaurants and even a celebrity walk of fame, should be ready by 2002. An electric train runs to here along the beach from the pier.

Brighton market On Sun mornings there's a good market by the station approach; you do have to get there well before breakfast for the bargains, as it's become a major source of supply for the countless Brighton antiques dealers. Nr here **St Bartholomew's church** (Anne St) is an odd building, like a huge brick barn. Film buffs will be well satisfied with the Duke of York's cinema at nearby Preston Circus, which shows the kind of movies not always found outside London.

Brighton Museum and Art Gallery (Church St) The 2-year refurbishment of this outstanding museum, housed in the Prince Regent's stables and riding school, should be completed by the autumn. The excellent collections of art nouveau and art deco will be redisplayed, and a new entrance through the Pavilion gardens will provide a convenient link between the museum and the palace. Best to phone for reopening dates nearer the time; (01273) 290900.

British Engineerium (Nevill Rd, Hove) All sorts of road, locomotive and marine steam engines, as well as tools, models, and a restored Victorian water-pumping station. Shop, limited disabled access; cl wk before Christmas, engines in steam first Sun in month and bank hol Sun and Mon; (01273) 559583; £4.

Foredown Tower (Foredown Rd, Portslade) Very well done, with a **camera obscura** (best on bright days) as well as a weather station with satellite images, astronomy displays, and splendid views. They can arrange visits to Portslade Old Manor, a ruined medieval house a short stroll away. Snacks, shop; cl Mon–Weds, and a few wks over Christmas; (01273) 292092; £2.20.

Hove Museum & Art Gallery (New Church Rd) This grand Victorian villa houses a fine collection of British painting; tearoom, disabled access to ground floor only, cl Sun am, all day Mon, and Christmas wk; (01273) 290200; free.

Museum of Penny Slot Machines (250C Kings Rd Arches) Nostalgic collection of over 50 vintage seaside amusements from penny slot-machines to strength-testers and fortune-tellers; shop, disabled access; open wknd and school hol pms Easter–Aug, plus fine weather Sun pm in winter; free (charge for individual games – they change your money into old coins).

Palace Pier Brighton was one of the earliest resorts to have a pier – that rusting original is now being restored; in the meantime this second pier is a more than satisfactory replacement, and looks magnificent at night.

Preston Manor (A23) Entertaining and vivid illustration of life in Edwardian times, with fully furnished period rooms, and pleasant walled gardens. Shop; cl am Sun and Mon, 25–26 Dec, Good Fri; (01273) 292770; £3.20.

Regency town house Hove, the quieter half of the resort, is just W of Brighton proper. On the way you may be able to visit this Regency house in Brunswick Sq – still being restored so you'll need to make an appointment on (01273) 206306; £3; if not, at least pass St Andrew's Church (Waterloo St), designed by Sir Charles Barry – quite dull from the outside, but inside rather elaborate in places.

Royal Pavilion Nash's flamboyant Indianesque confection should be top of anyone's itinerary: the most eccentric of all royal palaces, a riot of chinoiserie inside. Queen Victoria was the last monarch to own it, but was hardly its greatest fan; if the town council hadn't bought it from her she might well have demolished it. She would no doubt not have been amused to see her apartments restored to their full overblown glory. The gardens have also been returned to the original Regency plan. The whole building is beautifully floodlit at night. It's less busy after 3 o'clock – and better still out of season, when you may find more going on. Snacks, shop, disabled access to ground floor only; cl 25–26 Dec; (01273) 290900; £4.90.

Sea Life Centre (Marine Parade) Lively displays of creatures found off the British coast, with seahorses, touch pools and an undersea soft play area. Meals, snacks, shop, disabled access; cl 25 Dec; (01273) 604234; £5.99.

South Downs In this area the downs are open country; arable farming and the presence of pylons rather detract from the pleasure of walking, but the steep N slopes are still impressive, as at Devil's Dyke (with its tremendous view over Brighton, even more startling at night than by day), Wolstonbury Hill and the Jack and Jill windmills nr Clayton.

Sussex Toy and Model Museum (Trafalgar St) This collection of over 10, 000 objects from Victorian dolls to Meccano hopes to reopen just after this book comes out; best to phone for opening times. Shop, disabled access; (01273) 749494; *£3.

West Blatchington windmill ⌨ (Holmes Ave, Hove) With local history displays; shop, disabled access, open pm Sun and bank hols May–Sept; 70p.

BURPHAM TQ0309
Great views from this attractive hill village, with lovely walks from here along the river or through hilly Arundel Park into Arundel.

BURWASH TQ6724
The single main street of this ridge village has many attractively restored tile-hung cottages, inc an antiques centre with a teashop, with lime trees along its brick pavement. The graveyard of the Norman-towered church gives fine views over the Dudwell Valley, and the Bell opposite is useful for lunch. Around here the intricate landscapes of the Sussex Weald show steep slopes and valleys, ancient woods and hedgerows punctuated by great oaks, pretty villages, tile-hung or weatherboarded oast houses and wood-and-tile barns with their long 'cats'-slide' roofs.

Batemans (off A265) Handsome early 17th-c stone-built ironmaster's house, home to Rudyard Kipling from 1902 to 1936. His study is preserved much as it was then, as is the hefty pipework he installed for a pioneer hydro-electric lighting plant. The attractive gardens have a quaint operating watermill, grinding flour every Sat at 2pm. Dog crèche, snacks, shop, disabled access to ground floor only; cl Thurs, Fri (exc Good Fri), and Nov–Mar; (01435) 882302; £5; NT. Good little-used walks up the wholly unspoilt valley from here, where you can look for Kipling landmarks such as Pook's Hill.

CHANCTONBURY RING TQ1312
One of the great South Downs landmarks, a Romano-British temple site within an Iron Age earthwork, now a prominent hilltop clump of trees, a bracing walk, best reached from Steyning or Washington.

CHICHESTER SU8504
Partly pedestrianised and easy to get around, this handsome former Roman city is one of the country's finest examples of Georgian town planning and architecture. Useful central pubs for food are the Coach & Horses (St Pancras) and Dolphin & Anchor (West St).

Centurion Way This short stretch of disused railway track has been converted to an easy route for cyclists (and walkers) W of Chichester to Mid Lavant.

Chichester Cathedral Mostly Norman, and unusual for rising straight out of the town's streets rather than a secluded close. The spire collapsed in the 1860s (the latest in a long line of structural problems), and was rebuilt, but even now the scaffolding always seems to be up. Highlights include the 14th-c choir stalls, John Piper's Aubusson tapestry, and the window by Chagall. Guided tours (not Sun) at 11am and 2.15pm Easter–Oct. Snacks, shop in the medieval bell tower (23 South St – unusual for being separated from the main building), disabled access; £2 suggested donation. The Bishops Palace gardens are very pleasant.

Guildhall Museum (Priory Park) Began life as a medieval Grey Friars church, now houses the city's archaeological collections; shop, disabled access; usually open Sat pm Jun–Sept, (01243) 784683 to check; free. The Park Hotel opposite has decent food.

Mechanical Music & Doll Collection ▣ (Church Rd, Portfield) A multitude of barrel, fair and Dutch street organs, music boxes and phonographs – all restored and ready to play. Shop, disabled access; open Weds pm Jun–Sept; (01243) 785421; £2.50.

Pagham Harbour (off B2145 S) Peaceful nature reserve, largely silted marshy tidal flats, full of wading birds and wildfowl, particularly in spring and autumn; on the way the Blacksmiths Arms at Donnington, packed with bric-a-brac, has a good children's play area.

Pallant House (North Pallant) Interesting Queen Anne town house with Edwardian kitchen and fine furnishings. The gallery has fine Bow porcelain, and an excellent range of carefully chosen 20th-c art – Sutherland, Klee, Léger, Ben Nicholson and the like. Shop; cl Sun am, all day Mon (exc bank hols), 25–26 Dec; (01243) 774557; £4.

St Mary's Hospital (St Martin's Sq) 13th-c almshouse with some unique misericords in its chapel, and a pretty walled garden; disabled access; usually open wkdys (not 12.30–2pm), but best to check first, (01243) 783377; free.

CHICHESTER HARBOUR SU7702 The most attractive views for walkers are from the shoreside path which skirts the quiet unspoilt peninsulas of Thorney Island and Chidham.

Boat trips Peter Adams runs these around Chichester Harbour, full of yachts and dinghies in summer. They

leave from Itchenor and are best at high tide; (01243) 786418; £5. There's also an hourly passenger ferry between here and the landing at the end of the lane S from Bosham (daily Jun–Aug, wknds only Apr, May and Sept).

East Head A NT-owned promontory on the E entrance of Chichester Harbour, a sandy spit with dunes overlooking the marshes and mudflats of the estuary.

CISSBURY RING TQ1308 Another of the great downland landmarks, a huge ramparted Iron Age hill peppered with much earlier flint mines, and good views over to the Isle of Wight (looking surprisingly near). It's quite close to Findon, where the Gun and Village House are both good lunch places. There's a pleasant walk from here to Chanctonbury Ring.

CLIMPING BEACH TQ0000 This allows an attractive few miles' walk; this bit of coast between Middleton-on-Sea and Littlehampton is the only appreciable undeveloped seaside stretch in W Sussex, apart from Chichester Harbour.

COOMBES TQ1908 **Church Farm** ▣ Trailer rides over farmland and through conservation areas – you have to book, but it's great fun, especially in the lambing season. Snacks, shop, disabled access; open daily Mar to mid-Apr, and Tues, Thurs and Sun at 2.30pm in Aug, otherwise open to groups only (it's always worth phoning to see if you can join a group); (01273) 452028; *£3. They also have a coarse fishing lake.

DELL QUAY SU8303 Attractive waterside hamlet with remains of a Roman quay, harbour views (and fresh fish) from Crown & Anchor.

Apuldram Roses (Apuldram Lane S) Over 300 kinds of old-fashioned and new roses in harbourside field and gardens made from former orchards. The field is at its best from Jun–Sept, after which they have a good end-of-season sale. Snacks, plant sales, some disabled access; usually cl 24 Dec–8 Jan; (01243) 785769; free.

DITCHLING TQ3313 **Ditchling Beacon** ▣ Right by the road, with superb views all around, especially out over the villages and towns to the N; a nice walking area of preserved sheep-cropped unimproved downland, with chalk hill blue butterflies in summer. The village below is pleasant, with a decent **museum** (shop, disabled access; cl Mon (exc bank hols) and wkdys Nov–Mar; £2.50) . The B2116 to Offham has views of the South Downs, and off it the Jolly Sportsman at East Chiltington has good food.

EARNLEY SZ8197
Earnley Gardens (Almodington Lane) This five-acre site is quite a busy day out; as well as the long-established 17 themed gardens, exotic birds and free-flying butterflies, they now have a shipwreck display, small animal farm, and a refreshingly informal nostalgia museum, Rejectamenta. This takes in thousands of everyday objects from the last hundred years, collected over a quarter of a century by a former art student who says she just can't stop. Meals, snacks, shop, disabled access; usually open mid-Mar to end of Oct; (01243) 512637; around £5.50 everything, £3.50 just gardens and butterflies or just nostalgia museum, £1.50 crazy golf.

EAST DEAN TV5597
Seven Sisters Sheep Centre (Gilberts Drive) Very enjoyable family-run downland sheep farm with compact visitor centre, and paved paths between pens of many breeds of sheep. Lambing (mid-Mar to early May), demonstrations of shearing (Jun–early Sept), spinning and milking, and plenty of young animals to cuddle or bottle-feed; also tractor rides (50p extra). The farm shop sells sheep cheeses and yoghurts. Snacks, disabled access; cl am wkdys (exc school hols), all mid-Sept to early Mar, and maybe part of May, best to phone; (01323) 423302; £3. The village itself is prettily set around a sloping green, with an attractive pub, the Tiger. A lane past the farm continues to the **Birling Gap**, a cleft in the coastal cliffs famous since smuggling days, with a lighthouse (moved back 55 ft in 1999 to save it from coastal erosion) and coastguard station; and on to Beachy Head. The Birling Gap Hotel is nicely set just above the shore.

EAST GRINSTEAD TQ3835

Standen (off B2110 W) A fine example of the many talents of the 19th-c Arts and Crafts Movement. Designed by Philip Webb (even down to the unusual light fittings), a friend of William Morris, and little changed since, the interior of the house is decorated with several different William Morris wallpapers, and many of the furnishings are of the period. Snacks, shop, limited disabled access; open pm Weds–Sun end Mar–Oct; (01342) 323029; £5.50, £3 garden only; NT.

EASTBOURNE TV6198
The Duke of Devonshire still owns much of this civilised and restrained seaside resort; as he prohibits seaside tat the place has a more dignified and solid feel than many of its livelier rivals – fun seekers should head elsewhere, but it's perfect for gentle seafront strolling, and a promenade links the smart marina with the beach. The **church** in the Old Town is lavish; next to it the Lamb is a nice old pub.

Lifeboat Museum (Grand Parade) Makes up in enthusiasm what it lacks in size; shop, disabled access, cl Jan–Easter; free.

Museum of Shops 🖼 (Cornfield Terr) One of the most comprehensive collections of its type, 20 reconstructed and very well filled shops and rooms, inc an old seafarers' tavern. Shop, disabled access to ground floor only; cl 24–26 Dec; (01323) 737143; *£3.

Redoubt Fortress 🖼 (Royal Parade) Another splendid tower, housing a more interesting than average military museum. Open-air concerts (usually every Fri Jun–Sept) always end in a firework display. Snacks, shop; cl early Nov–Easter; (01323) 410300; £2.15.

Sovereign Park Shingle Nature Reserve Nature trails around an attractive stretch of shingle coastline, best between Easter and Jun, when most plants are in flower; Easter–autumn, a train connects this with the rest of the seafront. Some disabled access; open all year; free. They try to discourage people from walking across the shingle, as it damages the plantlife.

Towner Art Gallery & Museum (High St, Old Town) Handsome building, with good temporary exhibitions; shop, disabled access; cl am, and all day Mon (exc some bank hols), 25–27 Dec, 1 Jan and Good Fri; charges for some exhibitions.

Wish Tower (King Edward's Parade) Another of the 103 Martello Towers built in case of French invasion; there's a fascinating collection of puppets, some centuries old. Shop; usually open wknds Easter–Oct, plus wkdys mid-July–Aug, but best to check; (01323) 411620; £1.80.

ETCHINGHAM TQ7126
Etchingham church Lovely sturdy ancient semi-fortified building in honey-coloured stone – quaintly, the station is built to match.

FERNHURST SU8928
Nicely varied surrounding countryside for walkers; much is densely wooded, but there are some chances to get out on to the open hillsides as on Woolbeding Common and the S tip of Black Down. The pretty Red Lion has good value food.

FIRLE TQ4707
An attractive quiet village, with a decent pub. **Firle Beacon**, a South Downs landmark, is a lovely walk above the village, with good views.

Berwick church 1940s murals by the Bloomsbury Group; the Cricketers Arms here is a useful lunch place.

Charleston Farmhouse (A27 Firle–Selmeston) Delightful 17th/18th-c house which was the home of Duncan Grant and Clive and Vanessa Bell; decorated by them, it and its magical garden still evoke the atmosphere of those Bloomsbury days. Teas Sat, shop; open pm Weds–Sun and bank hols Apr–Oct, no guided tours Sun and bank hols; (01323) 811265; £5.50. Longer tours on Fri (no under-8s that day); £6.50. Nr here at Alciston, the Rose Cottage has very good home cooking.

Firle Place 🖼 (off A27) Beautiful house, essentially Tudor but remodelled in the 18th c, with some real treasures of European and English painting, and wonderful furnishings. Meals, snacks, shop, some disabled access; open pm Weds, Thurs and Sun Easter–Sept, spring and summer bank hols; (01273) 858335; £4. There are longer unguided tours the first Weds in the month, when more rooms are open

(and the price is higher).

Middle Farm Cider Centre (A27 E) Best known for its excellent farm shop, with a huge range of English ciders and perries, farmhouse cheeses, English wines, good sausages, organic meats, and other produce. Also children's farmyard, and always lots going on at apple harvest time; restaurant, disabled access; cl 25–26 Dec; (01323) 811411; site free, £1 for farmyard.

FISHBOURNE SU8304
Roman Palace (Salthill Rd) This magnificent villa with its 100 or so rooms was occupied from the 1st to the 3rd c, and is the largest known residence from the period in Britain. Some archaeologists now think the Romans first landed here (and not in Kent as was originally supposed), having been invited by a hospitable local chieftain for whom they built this palace. You can see 25 mosaic floors (some are quite remarkable, and it's a bigger collection than anywhere else in Britain), and a garden has been laid out according to its 1st-c plan. Most of the palace is buried beneath nearby housing. Snacks, shop, disabled access; cl mid-Dec to mid-Feb; (01243) 785859; £4.50. The comfortable Woolpack has good food.

FLETCHING TQ4223
Attractive village – often Sussex's Best-Kept Village; and it now has a charming waymarked Millennium Walk.

FONTWELL SU9406
Denmans Garden (off A27) Colourful series of vistas over 3½ acres, inc exuberantly oriental-feeling areas with a gravel stream, ornamental grasses, bamboos and flowering cherries, as well as a beautiful richly planted walled garden. Meals, snacks, plant sales, disabled access; cl Nov–Feb; (01243) 542808; £2.90. In the pretty nearby village of Eartham there is a small but charming church; the George there is a good place to eat.

FRANT TQ5935
Despite the main road this is a charming and rather elegant village, with an ancient church and handsome green. The George has decent food.

GATWICK AIRPORT TQ2740
Skyview 🖼 (South Terminal) Visitor gallery, with a multimedia show

demonstrating a typical airport day, a good explanation of cockpit controls and splendid runway views. Cl 25 Dec, shop, disabled access; (01293) 502244; £3.

GLYNDE TQ4509

Glynde Place Elizabethan manor house in beautiful setting, extensively remodelled inside in the 18th c, but outside left pretty much unchanged. Portraits and mementoes give a good grounding in the family history, while outside are pleasantly wild parklands and lawns. Snacks, shop; usually open pm Sun and bank hols in May, then pm Weds, Sun and bank hols Jun–Sept, plus Thurs July–Aug but best to check; (01273) 858224; £4. There's a neat neo-Palladian **church** nearby, and the Trevor Arms has decent food. The Glyndebourne Festival, with its decidedly smart operas and marvellous auditorium designed by Sir Michael Hopkins, takes place May–Aug.

GOODWOOD SU8808

Goodwood House 🏛 Unusual-looking house in beautiful downland countryside, especially renowned for its paintings, inc works by Canaletto and Stubbs. There's quite a riding feel – it was acquired by the first Duke of Richmond in 1697 so that he could ride with the local hunt, and the stables added during 18th-c alterations seem grander even than the house. The drawing room has been recently restored and now contains 18th-c French furniture. Snacks, shop, disabled access; open pm Sun and Mon Apr–Sept, plus Tues–Thurs in Aug; (01243) 755040; £6. The adjacent **racecourse** is the setting for Glorious Goodwood, and as well as around 19 race days a year, has monthly antiques markets; (01243) 755022 for dates.

Sculpture at Goodwood (Hat Hill Copse, towards East Dean) Excellent changing exhibitions of sculpture in 20 acres of beautiful wooded parkland; it's established an excellent reputation in the few years it's been open, so it's a shame the high admission price limits it to people with more than just a passing interest in the subject. Some disabled access; open Thurs–Sat Mar–Oct; (01243) 538449; *£10. This is a good area for a country drive; the Anglesey

Arms at Halnaker has good food.

GRAVETYE TQ3534

Ingwersens (Birch Farm) Very long-established alpine plants nursery; cl 1–1.30pm, wknds Oct–Feb, two wks at Christmas; (01342) 810236. Out this way, the White Hart at Selsfield (B2028) and Red Lion at Turners Hill are useful for lunch.

HADLOW DOWN TQ5424

Wilderness Wood 🏛 (A272) 62 acres of working woodland, good for learning about forests and their wildlife, or for a pleasant stroll. Several picnic areas and play area, occasional demonstrations of heavy horses and other traditional woodland working methods, and a discovery trail for children. Teas and snacks, shop (they make chestnut furniture and other goods), disabled access; (01825) 830509; £1.90. Nearby Buxted has one of the oldest trees in Britain, a yew thought to be nearly 2,500 years old.

HALLAND TQ4815

Bentley Wildfowl & Motor Museum Busy estate centred around Tudor farmhouse converted into Palladian mansion, filled with fine furnishings and paintings, inc watercolours by local artist Phillip Rickman. The motor museum has gleaming veteran, Edwardian, and vintage vehicles, while the lakes and ponds that surround it are home to a countless variety of rare and exotic wildfowl. There are also woodland trails, a good adventure playground, on-site craftsmen and artists, and miniature trains that steam through the grounds (wknds Easter–Oct plus Weds in Aug). Special events (no extra price) run from veteran and vintage car and other transport rallies to woodcraft, fire brigade and birds of prey displays. Meals, snacks, shop, disabled access; open daily mid-Mar–Oct (house cl Mar and am), and all exc house also open wknds in Nov, Feb and early Mar; (01825) 840573; £4.80, less winter. The Forge is useful for lunch.

HANDCROSS TQ2629

Nymans Garden 🏛 (B2114) Some very impressive rare trees here, inc magnificent southern beeches and eucryphias, as well as fine camellias, rhododendrons and magnolias,

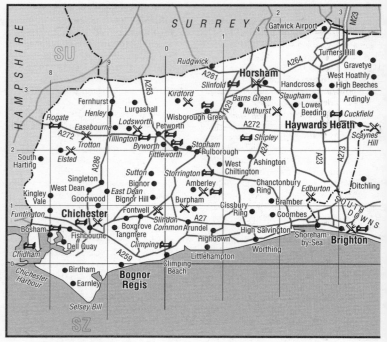

countless other interesting flowering
shrubs, a secluded sunken garden, and
an extensive artfully composed
wilderness. Meals, snacks, plant sales,
shop, disabled access; cl Mon (exc bank
hols), Tues, and wkdys Nov–Feb;
(01444) 400321; £5; NT. The
Wheatsheaf (B2110 W) has decent
food.

HARTFIELD TQ4735
Pleasant village with some attractive
houses. The well stocked shop at Pooh
Corner reflects the fact that
surrounding Ashdown Forest was the
inspiration for A A Milne's tales of
Winnie the Pooh. Perryhill Nursery
(B2026 N) has many unusual plants.

HASTINGS TQ8209
The Old Town up on the cliff at the E
end is very attractive – two medieval
churches, a couple of streets with
raised pavements, lots of medieval
buildings, and relatively unobtrusive
more recent infilling. Down below, the
fishermen still haul their boats up on to
the beach and sell excellent fresh fish by
the unusual tall black wooden net huts.

At each end of the cliffs is an unusual
sloping tracked lift down to sea level
(80p). The First In Last Out in the Old
Town has interesting food and brews its
own beer. The rest of the town is a busy
shopping town, rather run-down in
parts, with 19th-c resort buildings
nearer the seafront, seaside hotels and
B&Bs, a good prom, and shingle beach.
Fairlight Cove A good destination for
walks from Hastings Old Town, by a
path climbing on to the sandstone cliffs
for a rugged couple of miles. The
tumbled appearance of the coast here
bears witness to the occasional cliff-
falls.
Fishermen's Museum (Rock-a-Nore
Rd) Interestingly housed in a former
fishermen's church; shop, disabled
access, cl Good Fri and 25 Dec;
donations.
Hastings Castle Bracingly set above
crumbling cliffs (and the tracked lift),
the evocative Norman ruins are close
to the site of William the Conqueror's
first English motte and bailey castle.
There's a lively audio-visual exhibition

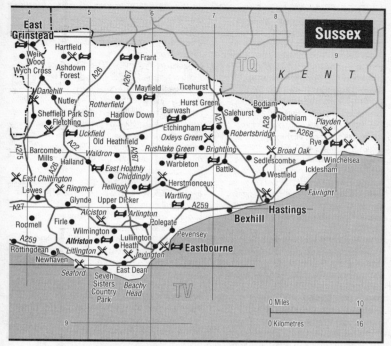

on the Battle of Hastings. Shop, some disabled access; (01424) 422964; £3.

Hastings Museum and Art Gallery (Johns Pl, Bohemia Rd) A little out of the centre, but worth a look for its American Indian displays; children may prefer the dinosaur gallery. Shop, limited disabled access; cl 1–2pm Sat, Sun am, 25–26 Dec and Good Fri, although times may change, so best to check; (01424) 781155; free.

Hastings Tapestry (White Rock Theatre) Ambitious 73-metre (240-ft) tapestry showing great events in British history, created by the Royal School of Needlework; meals, snacks, shop, disabled access; cl over Christmas and all Mar; £2.

Smugglers Adventure (Cobourg Pl) A labyrinth of deep caverns and passages, with models, museum and well done life-size tableaux illustrating life for an 18th-c smuggler. Spooky lighting and sound effects in places. Shop, limited disabled access; cl 25–26 Dec; (01424) 422964; £4.95.

Underwater World (Rock-a-Nore Rd) With walk-through underwater tunnel and a new tropical marine section with coral. Snacks, shop, disabled access; usually cl 24–26 Dec, but best to check first in winter; (01424) 718776; £4.95.

HAYWARDS HEATH TQ3226
Borde Hill Garden (Balcombe Rd, N) Lovely 40-acre gardens with woodland walks through rare maples, oaks, conifers and many other fine trees, as well as a lake, herbaceous borders and magnificent rhododendrons. A Heritage Lottery grant has enabled the restoration of three Victorian greenhouses, and there's a new Mediterranean garden and wildlife pond. You can fish on the lake, and there's an adventure playground. Meals, snacks, plant sales (Blooms of Bressingham), disabled access; cl 25 Dec; (01444) 450326; *£5. The White Harte at Cuckfield does good value simple lunches.

HERSTMONCEUX TQ6410
Herstmonceux Castle ▣ (SE of village) Extensive gardens around

handsome 15th-c brick-built castle, with nature trails, hands-on science centre, and astronomy displays in former buildings of Greenwich Royal Observatory. You can tour the castle itself by arrangement (£2.50). Children's play area; snacks, shop, disabled access; cl Nov–Mar; (01323) 834444; grounds and gardens £3.50, science centre £4.50, all-in ticket £7. The Ash Tree over at Brownbread Street has good old-fashioned home cooking.

Sussex Trug demonstrations (Hailsham Rd) Thomas Smith demonstrates the local art of trug basket-making; disabled access; not wknds (though shop open Sat), bank hols or Christmas–New Year; (01323) 832137.

Windmill Hill From here you can follow paths and tracks for an absorbing walk of about 4 miles past Herstmonceux Castle. And yes, there is a windmill.

HIGH BEECHES TQ2730

High Beeches Gardens (B2110, Handcross) Well worth a visit, 20 acres of landscaped woodland lots of rare plants, water gardens, and wildflower meadows. Snacks, plant sales; open pm daily (exc Weds) Apr–Jun and Sept–Oct, and Sun–Tues July–Aug; (01444) 400589; £4. The Chequers at Slaugham is a good nearby dining pub.

HIGH SALVINGTON TQ1206

High Salvington windmill An 18th-c post mill; open pm first and third Sun Apr–Sept, £1.

HIGHDOWN TQ0903

Highdown Hill (A259) Excellent views from this famous garden, which differs from most of the other great Sussex gardens in that it's on very uncompromising chalk – laid out in and around a chalk pit high on the downs above Angmering; many rarities, inc unusual Chinese plants. Some disabled access; cl wknds Oct–Mar; (01903) 501054; free. There is a nearby Iron Age hill fort, and the Spotted Cow at the foot of the hill does good value food.

HORSHAM TQ1428

Christ's Hospital (just SW) You may be able to join tours of the refreshingly egalitarian public school, where a

remarkable painting by Verrio fills an entire wall of the dining hall. Meals, snacks, shop, disabled access; tours from £3.50 – booking essential; (01403) 211293 for dates.

Horsham Museum (The Causeway) Timber-framed Tudor house with well organised local history, and an extraordinary collection of early bicycles. The small but pretty garden has some unusual wild cyclamen. Shop, some disabled access; cl Sun and bank hols; (01403) 254959; free. The town's much developed, but this quiet corner by the church is particularly attractive. The Black Jug (North St) has good food.

Huxley Experience 🖼 (Brighton Rd) Large collection of birds of prey inc falcons, vultures and even a laughing jackass. Friendly informative staff give flying demonstrations from 2.30pm, and you can handle the creatures at 12 and 2pm. Shop; disabled access; cl Tues and Nov–Apr exc Sun; (01403) 273458; £2.95.

HURST GREEN TQ7327

Merriments Garden (Hawkhurst Rd) Developing four-acre demonstration garden with lots of planting ideas, some unusual plants, and comprehensive nursery inc rare hardy plants. Tearoom, disabled access; garden open Apr–Oct, nursery all year; (01580) 860666; £3.

ICKLESHAM TQ8616
Attractive village despite the main road, with Norman church and country walks.

KINGLEY VALE SU8210
An interesting walk though needing some stamina, whether you approach via the nature trail on the S side or from Stoughton to the N (the Hare & Hounds will fuel you well). This nature reserve is Europe's largest yew forest, a magical place where the trees create some eerie pools of darkness on the S slopes of the downs; above, you can look over Chichester Harbour from a prehistoric burial mound.

LEWES TQ4110
The administrative capital of East Sussex, this is a pleasantly unrushed country town below the quarried white edge of the South Downs. It has some attractive old buildings, mainly Georgian though with a few older

stone-built or timber-framed specimens, particularly along its steep main street and in the little narrow alleys and other streets alongside. This is where you'll see Sussex tile-hanging at its best; there's also quite a lot of 'mathematical tiling' – sham bricks over timbered buildings to make them look more progressive. There are several decent antiques shops, and an attractive complex of **craft shops** in a former candlemaker's factory in Market Lane; café, cl Sun. The Dorset Arms (Malling St) and more bohemian Snowdrop (South St) are useful for lunch. Local brewers Harveys have a brewery tap, the John Harvey (good food in upstairs restaurant), just off Cliffe High St. From Bell Lane on the SW edge you can follow the old Juggs Road track, used by the Brighton fishwives, up past Kingston and the downland nature reserve by Newmarket Hill to the outskirts of Brighton itself. There are more public paths than the OS map suggests; from the town centre you can walk up Chapel Hill, through the golf course and on via an unspoilt dry valley to **Mount Caburn**, rather grandiosely named for its size but capped by an Iron Age fort and with views towards the coast; it's also popular with paragliders.

Anne of Cleves House 🖼 (Southover High St) Henry VIII's wife number four received this fine 16th-c house as part of her divorce settlement. She probably never came here, but its rooms give a good idea of regional life over the following two centuries. Shop; cl Sun am, and all Nov–Feb exc Tues, Thurs and Sat; (01273) 474610; £2.50 (combined ticket with castle £5). Guided tours of the ruined Norman **priory** leave here in summer (usually Tues and Thurs pm), phone David Edy (01273) 486290 for details.

Lewes Castle 🖼 Unusual for being built on not one but two artificial mounds, more recently thought to be part of a prehistoric complex of mounds (Lincoln is the only other such place we know of). The best view of the town is obtained from the roof of the keep, and there's a good archaeological museum. Shop; cl 25–26 Dec and 8 Jan; (01273) 486290; *£4.

Southover Grange Gardens
(Southover Rd) Diarist John Evelyn's handsome boyhood home is now the District Registry Office, but you can visit the attractive gardens; cl 25 Dec, free.

LITTLEHAMPTON TQ0202
Little sign here of its age (it was an important port up to the 1500s), but its long sandy beaches make it a popular simple family resort. Towards the W, beyond the River Arun, there's quite an extensive area of unspoilt dunes between beach and golf course. The 18th-c Arun View right on the river does decent lunches.

Body Shop Tour 🖼 (Watersmead, A259 N) You can book to visit – the 90-min tours are interesting; snacks, shop, disabled access; (08000) 960809. No tours Sun or bank hols; £3.95.

Littlehampton Museum (Church St) Due to open just after we went to press, this refurbished early 19th-c manor house has displays on local history and archaeology; best to call for opening times, prices and facilities; (01903) 738100.

LOWER BEEDING TQ2225
Leonardslee Gardens Enormous Grade I listed garden set in a 240-acre valley with seven beautiful lakes; marvellous rhododendrons, magnolias, oaks and unusual conifers, delightful rock garden, extensive greenhouse and Japanese garden, bonsai exhibition, Victorian motorcar collection and wallaby and deer. The gardens are on the edge of the ancient St Leonard's Forest, and there's a summer wildflower walk. Readers get a great deal of pleasure from coming here. Meals, snacks, plant sales, limited disabled access; cl Nov–Mar; (01403) 891212; May £5 (£6 wknds), other times £4.

LULLINGTON HEATH TQ5401
A rare survival of downland untampered with by modern farming practices, and managed as a National Nature Reserve for its chalkland and heathland flora; a good spot for walks, which can be spun out with a diversion to Wilmington for a view of the enigmatic Long Man.

LURGASHALL SU9327
Attractive small village, with an unusual loggia outside the largely Saxon **church** where parishioners walking in from a

distance could eat their sandwiches. The Noah's Ark here is prettily placed for lunch.

Lurgashall Winery Produces a wide range of traditional country wines, meads and cordials. Tastings, shop, limited disabled access; cl 25–26 Dec, 1 Jan; (01428) 707292; self-guided tours wknds; £1.

MAYFIELD TQ5826
One of Sussex's prettiest villages, with interesting shops, and pleasant hilly terrain around it. A reasonable network of paths includes a short waymarked circular walk.

NEWHAVEN TQ4400
Newhaven Fort (Fort Rd) Built 120 years ago in case of French attack, this is a big place to explore, with underground installations, period reconstructions and tunnels burrowing into the cliffs, super views from its ramparts, and an assault course for children. Snacks, shop; cl wkdys in Mar, and all Nov–Feb; (01273) 517622; £3.95. You can take the ferry to Dieppe in France from here. The harbourside Hope has decent food.

Paradise Park & Planet Earth (Avis Rd) Garden centre with exhibition on the last few million years of evolution, complete with earthquake experience and life-size moving dinosaurs. Also model village with miniaturised Sussex landmarks, and an indoor oriental garden. Meals, snacks, shops, disabled access, cl 25–26 Dec; (01273) 512123; £4.50.

NORTHIAM TQ8225
Great Dixter (turn off A28 at Post Office) Timbered 15th-c house, carefully restored and added to by Lutyens in the early part of this century. He designed the attractive gardens too; originally arranged as a series of distinct areas, they were later stocked more informally with interesting plants by the gardening writer Christopher Lloyd who lives here. Snacks, plant sales, limited disabled access; cl am, all day Mon (exc bank hols) and all Nov–Mar; (01797) 252878; £6, £4.50 gardens only. The Mill (Station Rd) has decent food.

NUTLEY TQ4428
Nutley windmill 17th-c mill saved by enthusiastic locals before such action

became more common; open pm last Sun of month Mar–Sept and second Sat and Sun in May; free. Nearby Camp Hill is one of the best walking areas in the Ashdown Forest.

OLD HEATHFIELD TQ5920
Charming peaceful hamlet – so different from the sprawly small town of Heathfield nearby which sprang up around the now-defunct railway (the town does surprise with an excellent delicatessen specialising in unusual cheeses, a top-class genuinely French patissier, and first-rate farmer/butcher – Pomfrets).

PETWORTH SU9721
Petworth Cottage Museum 🏚 (High St) Interesting reconstruction of an estate worker's cottage; open pm Weds–Sun and bank hols Apr–Oct, *£2.

Petworth House Splendid, its magnificent rooms filled with one of the most impressive art collections in the country, inc Dutch Old Masters and 20 pictures by Turner, a frequent visitor. Other highlights include the 13th-c chapel, grand staircase with frescoes, and the carved room, elegantly decorated by Grinling Gibbons. You can see extra rooms Mon–Weds. Meals, snacks, shop, disabled access; cl am, all day Thurs and Fri, and all Nov–Mar; (01798) 342207; £6; NT. The deer park, with stately trees and prospects still recognisable as those glorified by Turner, is open all year; free. The village is now an antiques honey-pot, with dozens of antiques shops in its narrow streets of attractive old houses – over 100 dealers can now be found here. The Angel Hotel fits in well, and has a good wknd carvery; the Well Diggers (A283 E) has good food too.

PEVENSEY TQ6505
Pevensey Castle Formidable castle based around huge 4th-c Roman fort, with massive bastions and walls of Roman masonry still up to 9 metres (30 ft) high in places. The Norman keep was built by William the Conqueror, and you can see interesting interior details inc fireplaces, dungeons and an oubliette. Shop, some disabled access; cl Mon and Tues Nov–Easter, 24–26 Dec; (01323) 762604; £2.50; EH. The

Castle Cottage restaurant does decent food, inc light summer lunches in the castle garden.

POLEGATE TQ5804

Cuckoo Trail Following the route of a former railway Polegate–Heathfield (with plans for extension beyond), good for traffic-free walking or family cycling; the mileposts, sculpted by local artists, each have a cuckoo hidden in their design.

Filching Manor Motor Museum (Jevington Rd, Wannock) Gleamingly restored vintage cars, shown to great effect in the grounds of a striking manor house. Unique panelling in the minstrel's gallery, acres of woodland and Donald Campbell connections. They also have a go-kart track (open daily; from £10 for 10 mins). Snacks, disabled access; guided tours Sun pm Easter–Oct; (01323) 487838; £5.

PULBOROUGH TQ0518

The town has some attractive buildings down towards the river; the Waters Edge, with lake views, has a good choice of food. There's an RSPB Reserve just S, and the Citrus Centre (off A283 E, just past White Horse pub; cl Mon/Tues) has all sorts of orange, lemon and related trees. The charmingly placed White Hart at Stopham is another nearby place with good food.

Nutbourne Vineyards (Nutbourne Manor) 18-acre vineyard with tours and tastings, visitor centre in a former windmill and a family of llamas; shop; no tours wkdy ams and all mid-Oct–May; (01798) 815196; free.

Parham House Charming Elizabethan house, still a family home, its panelled rooms full of notable portraits, furniture, oriental carpets and rare needlework. The surrounding grounds are really very special – popular with birds, they include a rose garden, a vegetable garden and an apple orchard; there's also a maze designed with children in mind. Lunches in 15th-c kitchen, shop, plant sales; open pm Weds, Thurs, Sun and bank hols Apr–Oct; (01903) 744888; £5.25, £3.25 garden only.

RODMELL TQ4206

Monks House Just a quiet lived-in house, in a pleasant village, but a beautifully kept place of pilgrimage for followers of the Bloomsbury Group, as Leonard and Virginia Woolf lived here from 1919 until Leonard's death in 1969. Open Weds and Sat pm Apr–Oct; (01892) 890651; £2.50; NT. The Juggs at Kingston on the way from Lewes is good for lunch.

ROTTINGDEAN TQ3602

Grange Museum & Kipling Gardens A pretty place, worth a stop. Enthusiastic local volunteers are responsible for preserving both the handsome Georgian grange, now a **museum** (cl Weds, am Sun and 23 Dec–2 Jan), and the pleasant two-acre **Kipling Gardens**, well restored Victorian gardens named after the author who lived here for five years from 1897. Burne-Jones was a resident for a while too, designing the windows made by William Morris for the Early English **church**.

RYE TQ9321

Enchanting, and still relatively unspoilt despite its many charms. Before the wind and sea currents did their work, the little town was virtually surrounded by sea, and as one of the Cinque Ports played an important part in providing men and ships for coastal defence. It's built on a hill crowned by the partly Norman **St Mary's church** (with a notable churchyard, and very early turret-clock, two quarter-jacks by it striking the quarter-hours); up here the largely cobbled streets still follow a 12th/13th-c narrow layout, with most of the houses lining them dating from the 16th c. The town is full of antiques shops, book shops, craft shops and an exceptional kitchenware shop; Rye Art Gallery (107 High St) is a non-profit trust with several floors selling the best of local art and craft. The views are lovely, and steep Mermaid St with its handsome old Mermaid Inn is famously photogenic.

Camber Castle This massive Tudor fort had the sea lapping up to it when it was built, but is now stranded a mile or so inshore by the encroaching shingle (open pm wknds July–Sept; £2). Beyond it the Ship on Winchelsea Beach is a welcoming refuge. On the other side of the river **Camber Sands** is the finest sandy beach in the SE, with plenty of room for walking (though it is massively popular in summer, when roads can be gridlocked; try taking a bike on the train and using the new cycle path from Rye for a less congested journey).

Heritage Centre 💷 (Strand Quay) A useful introduction, with a sound-and-light show based around an intricate town model. Shop, disabled access; cl 24–26 Dec; *£2.

Lamb House (West St) Built in 1723 for former mayor James Lamb, and chiefly devoted to mementoes of the author Henry James, who lived here from 1898 to 1916; after his death E F Benson, who also became mayor, moved here. Open pm Weds and Sat Apr–Oct; (01892) 890651; £2.50; NT.

Rye Castle Museum (just below Church Sq) Lively local history museum now split between two sites: the main gallery is in East St, while other displays are housed in the striking 13th-c Ypres Tower (as in Wipers). Shop, disabled access to East St museum; cl Tues, Weds and wkdys Nov–Mar; (01797) 226728; £2 per site or £3 joint ticket. The Ypres Castle pub just below has good food in a nice setting.

Rye Harbour Because of the build-up of shingle along this coast, it's now a mile or two from the town, though yachts and fishing boats do still come right up the river to the pretty quay. The Inkerman Arms has good fresh fish. Tony Easton will take you **sea fishing** for the day; (01797) 252104; from £25. The expanse of shingle stretching around the river mouth is now preserved as a **nature reserve**, with hides to watch the shore birds.

Treasury of Mechanical Music 💷 (Cinque Ports St) An entertaining collection of music boxes, barrel organs and pianolas, and you can hear them all. Shop, disabled access; cl Tues Nov–Feb; (01797) 223345; £3.

SALEHURST TQ7424
Attractive tucked-away village with 14th-c church and good pub.

SEDLESCOMBE TQ7719
Attractive village, with an unusual organic vineyard.

SELSEY BILL SZ8592
One of the nicest and cleanest **beaches** along the South coast.

SEVEN SISTERS COUNTRY PARK TV5199

(A259, Exceat) Runs down to the sea by the River Cuckmere – protected meadow, saltings, shingle and the flanking chalk headlands; you can hire bikes from the Cuckmere Cycle Co at Granary Barn, (01323) 870310. The chalk cliffs, together with Beachy Head, form the spectacular finale of the South Downs; the South Downs Way long-distance path angles up over them above the flats and the sea at Cuckmere Haven. For an interesting circular walk you can head inland by Friston Forest, West Dean and East Dean. The roomy Golden Galleon at Exceat does good food.

SHEFFIELD PARK TQ4124
Sheffield Park 💷 Wonderful 120-acre garden partly landscaped by Capability Brown, since then imaginatively planted with many varieties of tree unknown to him, especially chosen for their autumn colours. Also marvellous rhododendrons, azaleas and water-lilies on the lakes. Meals, snacks, shop, disabled access; cl Mon (exc bank hols), all wkdys Jan–Feb and 24–31 Dec; (01825) 790231; *£4.50; NT. The Griffin at Fletching nearby is very good for lunch.

SHEFFIELD PARK STATION TQ4023
Bluebell Line (A275) Earliest preserved steam railway in Britain, and one of the best; 9-mile trips through Horsted Keynes to Kingscote (where there are period bus connections to East Grinstead), with splendid stations decked out with period advertisements and wonderful genuine period carriages. The journey passes woodlands that are a mass of bluebells in late spring, usually at their best in mid-May – hence the name of the line. Part of the station is a museum housing the region's largest railway collection, inc some 30 locomotives. The Revd W Awdry based his Fat Controller on the man who organised the railway's restoration in the late 1950s. Pullman dining specials, Santa specials, shop, café, disabled access (with notice); trains wknds all year, daily May–Sept and school hols – (01825) 722370 for timetable; £7.80. The Sloop at Scaynes Hill not far off is good for lunch.

SHOREHAM-BY-SEA TQ2106
Though not one of England's more famous ports, this is quite a busy one, with several attractive old buildings around the harbour. Inland, in Old Shoreham, the early Norman **church** is accompanied by some handsome old houses (among them the good 16th-c Red Lion). Just W is striking **Lancing College Chapel**, begun in 1868, with a soaringly handsome nave, and elaborate stained-glass rose window.

Museum of D-Day Aviation 🖼
(Shoreham Airport) Uniforms, engines, artefacts and a replica Spitfire. Meals, snacks, shop, disabled access; cl wkdys in Mar and Nov, all Dec–Easter; (0374) 971971; *£3. Housed in England's oldest airport, with an appealing 1930s art deco terminal; tours available (£3), good value restaurant with uninterrupted views.

SINGLETON SU8713
Weald & Downland Open Air Museum (A286) Fascinating collection of over 40 historic buildings rescued from all over the SE, dismantled and re-erected here. They're arranged to form an authentic-looking village, with outlying farm and agricultural buildings, a Tudor market hall, blacksmith's forge, tollhouse and Victorian schoolroom. You can buy flour from the medieval farmstead's working watermill, and when it's completed, you'll be able to watch experts restore timber frames in the new futuristic timber-built gridshell building. Well organised children's activities might include brick-laying or basket-making. Snacks, shop, some disabled access, but the site is rather steep; open daily Mar–Oct, then Weds and wknds, plus Christmas wk Nov–Feb; (01243) 811348; £6. The handy Fox & Hounds is a friendly stop.

SOUTH HARTING SU7819
A pretty Downland village, with good value food in the nicely set Ship. The chalk Harting Downs involve no more than a level stroll from the road above the village; the Coach & Horses at nearby Compton is another good base for walks in this area.

Downland drive The roads round here give attractive drives – the B2141 and B2146 S of South Harting, the Walderton–East Mardon back road

between them, and the downs-foot road E through East Harting, Elsted, Treyford and Cocking.

Uppark (B2146 S) Splendid 17th-c house, extensively restored after a disastrous fire in 1989. Incredibly, most of the house's public treasures were rescued, even the wallpaper. The grounds, designed by Humphrey Repton, have a woodland walk and fine views towards The Solent. Meals, snacks, shop, disabled access; open pm Sun–Thurs Apr–Oct; (01730) 825857; £5.50; NT. Entrance is by timed ticket, a few of which can be booked in advance – otherwise get there between 11.30am and 1.30pm. The White Hart has good home cooking.

TANGMERE SU9106
Military Aviation Museum (off A27) Good collection of flying memorabilia based around the former RAF station where H E Bates finished writing *Fair Stood the Wind for France*. Meals, snacks, shop, disabled access; cl Dec–Jan; (01243) 775223; *£3. The nearby Bader Arms has more memorabilia; and there's good food at the Anglesey Arms at Halnaker (with the shell of an 18th-c windmill nearby).

TICEHURST TQ7029
Pashley Manor Gardens (B2099) Eight acres of beautifully restored mainly Victorian formal gardens around handsome house once owned by the Boleyn family. Magnificent old trees, delightfully placed moat and walled garden, views, folly, fine shrubs, roses, herbaceous beds, and clever focal points; very relaxed, charming and peaceful. Tulip festival in Apr, and a summer flower festival in Jun. Snacks, plant sales, limited disabled access; open Tues–Thurs, Sat and bank hols, early Apr–Sept; (01580) 200888; £5. The village is attractive; up a side road at Three Legged Cross, Maynards has good pick-your-own.

TURNERS HILL TQ3335
Amazing Maize Maze 🖼 Huge range of pick-your-own from rhubarb in Apr to beetroot in Oct, as well as a tearoom, good farm shop and of course, the annual crop labyrinth (last year's 3m of castle was reputedly the largest in the world) – don't worry if you get stuck, from a watchtower an

eagle-eyed guide will lead you to the centre via walkie-talkie communication; July to mid-Sept (£4, £3 child). Pick-your-own Apr–Oct, shop open all year; (01342) 718472. The Red Lion has good value food.

UPPER DICKER TQ5509
Michelham Priory Charming 16th-c house based around 13th-c Augustinian priory, with 15th-c gatehouse by the moat (which has plenty of waterfowl). Interesting furniture, tapestries and local ironwork, as well as crafts, working watermill, and rope museum. Meals, snacks, shop, disabled access to ground floor only; open Weds–Sun and bank hols mid-Mar–Oct, daily in Aug; (01323) 844224; £4.70; EH. The Plough is useful for lunch.

WARBLETON TQ6018
Right off the beaten track and as a result very unspoilt – the village has more pre-1750 Sussex barns than anywhere else in the county. The Warbil in Tun is a friendly dining pub.

WEIR WOOD RESERVOIR TQ3935
There's a pleasant waterside walk along its N shore, with paths leading up to Standen House.

WEST CHILTINGTON TQ0918
West Chiltington church Beautiful building in lovely downland countryside – this is windmill country, too.

WEST DEAN SU8612
West Dean Gardens Old roses, 100-yard pergola, wild garden, walled kitchen garden and interesting collection of stately mature conifers in park and arboretum; a splendid downland setting, notably peaceful and relaxed. Meals, snacks, shop, some disabled access, plant sales; cl Nov–Feb; (01243) 818210; £4. The smart White Horse at Chilgrove or Royal Oak a little N of it would be our choice for lunch.

WEST HOATHLY TQ3632
Attractive village tucked quietly away from the road, with tremendous views from the lane down past the ancient Cat dining pub. On a clear day you can see the whole sweep of the South Downs between Chanctonbury Ring and the Long Man of Wilmington.
Priest House Nr the 13th-c church, 15th-c timbered house, now a folk museum with a little cottage garden.

Shop; cl Sun am, and Nov–Feb; (01342) 810479; £2.50. They can arrange guided tours of the village.

WESTFIELD TQ8115
Carr Taylor Vineyard 🅰 One of England's most successful commercial vineyards, producing sparkling wine as well as still (snacks, shop, disabled access; cl Christmas week, and Sun Jan–Feb; (01424) 752501; trails £1.50).

WILMINGTON TQ5403
Long Man of Wilmington Gigantic chalk-cut figure so far impossible to date – guesses hover anywhere between the early 18th c and the Bronze Age. The Giants Rest in the village below has good home cooking.

WINCHELSEA TQ9017
Storms and French raids pretty much put paid to this once-flourishing port's importance; today it's a quiet and pleasant little place, dwarfed by the distances between the three surviving town gates around it. The **Royal Military Canal** runs from here to Hythe in Kent, a never-used Napoleonic defence that was meant as a sort of glorified coastal moat – now a peaceful spot for coarse fishermen. The New Inn is popular for lunch, and the tranquil **church** of St Thomas is elaborately decorated, with some fine old stained glass and medieval tombs. The Fairlight road has clifftop views.

WISBOROUGH GREEN TQ0526
Fishers Farm Park 🅰 (Newpound Lane) Friendly farm, well equipped for families, with animal show and petting areas, good indoor and outdoor play areas, paddling pool and a go-kart track. Meals, snacks, shop, disabled access; cl 25–26 Dec; (01403) 700063; around £7.25, less in winter; also holiday cottages and campsite. The Cricketers Arms on the green has decent food.

WORTHING TQ1402
Restrained but rather charming town, with a pleasant seafront; in the same mould as Brighton but altogether quieter and less gaudy. There's an excellent **herb shop** on Field Row, opposite M&S. The formerly separate village of West Tarring has a 250-year-old fig garden by the 14th-c parish hall, a folklore museum in a row of 15th-c cottages, and a welcoming old pub, the Vine.

Worthing Museum & Art Gallery (Chapel Rd) Extremely rich archaeological collection, and a sculpture garden. Shop, disabled access; cl Sun and some bank hols, best to check; (01903) 239999; free.

WYCH CROSS TQ4235

Ashdown Llama Farm Unusual working llama farm, with big breeding herds of alpacas; sheep and goats too. Snacks, shop, disabled access (but no facilities); cl Mon (exc bank hols), and wkdys Nov–Mar; (01825) 712040; £2.50. The same people run Barnsgate Manor Vineyard a few miles down the road at Herons Ghyll, which has great views from its attractive restaurant.

Other attractive villages, all with civilised pubs doing decent food, include Barns Green TQ1227, Brightling TQ6921 (the pub is at nearby Oxleys Green), Byworth SU9820, Chiddingly TQ5414, Easebourne SU8922, the other East Dean SU9013, Elsted SU8119, Fittleworth TQ0118, Funtington SU7908, Hellingly TQ5812, Henley SU8925, Kirdford TQ0126, Lodsworth SU9223, Robertsbridge TQ7323, Rotherfield TQ5529, Rudgwick TQ0833, Rushlake Green TQ6218, Slaugham TQ2528, Stopham TQ0218, Sutton SU9715, Waldron TQ5419 (ancient church) and West Chiltington TQ0918.

Where to eat

ALCISTON TQ5005 **Rose Cottage** *(01323) 870377* In the same family for over 30 years, this small charming wisteria-covered cottage is full of harness, traps, ironware and bric-a-brac; Jasper is the talking parrot (mornings only); very good promptly served food (esp the simply cooked fresh fish) using organic vegetables and their own eggs, well kept real ales, decent wines and a good range of other drinks like kir and Pimms, a small no smoking evening restaurant, and seats outside; cl 26 Dec; children over 6. £22|**£7.50**

AMBERLEY TQ0211 **Bridge Inn** *(01798) 831619* Nice old white-painted pub by a pretty stretch of the River Arun; a relaxed and friendly bar, attractively furnished two-room dining room, interesting modern portraits and Impressionist-style paintings, generous helpings of good home-made bar food (lots of fresh fish), proper puddings, four Sunday roasts, well kept real ales, friendly helpful service. £19|**£7.25**

BRIGHTON TQ3105 **Black Chapati** *12 Circus Parade (01273) 699011* Particularly good Eastern cooking with Anglo-Indian influences in starkly furnished restaurant with white walls and black tables and chairs, and Breton cider – wine does not always suit the style of food; cl Sun, Mon; disabled access. £29

BRIGHTON TQ3004 **Browns** *3–4 Duke St (01273) 323501* Relaxed and chatty restaurant with an airy spacious feel, bentwood chairs around wooden tables, lots of greenery, ceiling fans, and enjoyable reasonably priced English food with European influences; welcoming for families; disabled access. £19|**£7.50** ☺

BRIGHTON TQ3203 **One Paston Place** *(01273) 606933* Just off the seafront, this airy enjoyable restaurant has a big mural, very good modern British food inc super fish and game dishes, nice puddings, decent house wines, and a friendly atmosphere; cl Sun, Mon, first 2 weeks Jan, first 2 wks Aug; children welcome lunchtimes only. £26.15

BROAD OAK TQ8220 **Rainbow Trout** *Chitcombe Rd (01424) 882436* Pleasant pub with attractive bustling old bar, big restaurant extension, wide range of well cooked food (esp fish) served by friendly waitresses, and well kept real ales; cl 25 Dec, partial disabled access. £17|**£5.25**

BURPHAM TQ0308 **George & Dragon** *(01903) 883131* Smartly comfortable dining pub with splendid views down to Arundel Castle and river; good promptly served food with unusual specials inc good vegetarian dishes, elegant restaurant – worth booking; cl 25 Dec; children over 8. £21|**£6.20**

CHICHESTER SU8606 **Comme Ça** *67 Broyle Rd (01243) 788724* Busy little restaurant close to Festival Theatre with good classic French cooking, popular Sun lunches and children's menu; cl Sun pm, Mon, bank hols; partial disabled access. £24.95|£10.95

CHICHESTER SU8604 **St Martin's Tea Room** *3 St Martin's St (01243) 786715* Handsome brick Georgian-fronted house with pretty garden for summer eating, good lunchtime snacks and meals (mainly vegetarian but with some fish dishes) and afternoon teas using organic produce; cl Sun, bank hols; children must be well behaved; disabled access. £17|£4.50

DANEHILL TQ4128 **Coach & Horses** *(01825) 740369* Cottagey pub in attractive countryside with a really relaxed chatty atmosphere, well kept real ales, a lower part leading to dining area with flowers, candles, woodburner and hops on beams, enjoyable interesting bar food (the specials are well worth checking out), and good wines; big back garden with plenty of seats, with more out in front; £21.45|£6.95

EAST CHILTINGTON TQ3615 **Jolly Sportsman** *Chapel Lane (01273) 890400* Tucked-away Victorian dining pub with stripped wooden floors, chatty little bar, and contemporary light wood furniture and modern landscapes on pale yellow-painted brick walls in the informally civilised restaurant; well kept real ales, a remarkably good wine list, and imaginative cooking from a changing menu; rustic tables and benches under gnarled trees in a pretty cottagey front garden; cl Sun pm, Mon (exc bank hols), 4 days Christmas; disabled access. £29/2-course lunch £10

EASTBOURNE TV6099 **Downland** *37 Lewes Rd (01323) 732689* Pretty candlelit evening restaurant in well run small hotel, with carefully prepared innovative food, good vegetables and lovely puddings, a relaxed atmosphere, and friendly service; bdrms; children over 10. £23

EASTBOURNE TV6199 **Pavilion Tea Rooms** *Royal Parade (01323) 410374* Bustling tearoom by the prom with neatly uniformed friendly staff, attractive bamboo furniture, and morning coffee, enjoyable light lunches, and afternoon teas.|£4.50

EDBURTON TQ2111 **Tottington Manor** *Edburton Rd (01903) 815757* Cosy country house with particularly good food using fresh seasonal produce in bar and restaurant, winter log fire, friendly service and a relaxed atmosphere; bdrms; cl Sat am, Sun pm, first 2 wks Jan; children over 5. £30.50/2-course lunch £12.50

ELSTED SU8320 **Elsted Inn** *Elsted Marsh (01730) 813662* Victorian roadside pub with a warmly friendly welcome, unpretentious bars with open log fires, lots of original wood, candlelit dining room, extremely good interesting cooking using fresh local ingredients (Weds theme night), and very well kept real ales; two dogs, and large garden (with dog-free zone); bdrms; cl 25 Dec pm; partial disabled access. £21.50|£5

ELSTED SU8119 **Three Horseshoes** *(01730) 825746* Cosy Tudor pub in lovely setting with fine views of South Downs from the garden (and good nearby walks); snug rustic rooms with huge log fires, ancient beams and venerable furnishings, very good English country cooking inc lovely puddings, well kept real ales, decent wines by the glass; cl Sun pm Oct–Apr; well behaved children welcome. £25|£7

FLETCHING TQ4223 **Griffin** *(01825) 722890* Civilised old country inn with blazing log fires in quaintly panelled rooms, old photographs and hunting prints, very good innovative food, well kept beers, a good wine list with lots (inc champagne) by the glass, relaxed friendly atmosphere, and lovely garden; bdrms; cl 25 Dec; disabled access. £27.50|£7.50

HARTFIELD TQ4735 **Anchor** *Church St (01892) 770424* Relaxed and friendly pub on the edge of Ashdown Forest, with good bar food, quick service, a chatty heavily beamed bar, dining area, well kept real ales, and popular front verandah; cl 25 Dec pm; disabled access. £15|£5.25

HASTINGS TQ8209 **Harris** *58 High St (01424) 437221* Relaxed, informal and chatty, reasonably priced mainly Spanish food (enjoyable tapas), friendly staff in long white aprons, and decent wine; cl Sun (but open all day Sat). £18.50|£5.50

HASTINGS TQ8009 **Röser's Restaurant** *64 Eversfield Pl (01424) 712218* Extremely rewarding and generous imaginative food using top-quality produce inc home-cured, smoked and pickled ingredients in straightforward-looking little restaurant opposite pier; fine wines, too; cl Sat am, Sun, Mon; disabled access. £23.95 set dinner/ £20.95 set lunch

HERSTMONCEUX TQ6312 **Sundial** *Gardner St (01323) 832217* Pretty and plush 17th-c cottage with excellent carefully cooked food inc lovely vegetables and delicious puddings, a praiseworthy wine list, relaxed atmosphere, formal but warmly friendly service, and terrace and garden for summer eating; cl Sun pm, Mon, 3 wks after Christmas, 3 wks Aug; disabled access. £38.50/2-course lunch £25

HORSHAM TQ1730 **Black Jug** *31 North St (01403) 253526* Most attractively refurbished Edwardian town pub with a relaxed atmosphere, a big airy bar around central servery, lots of old prints and photographs, a plant-filled conservatory, very popular interesting bar food, chilled flavoured vodkas, well kept real ales, decent wines, and small back terrace; no children Sat/Sun pm; cl Sun pm. £21|**£6.95**

JEVINGTON TQ5601 **Hungry Monk** *(01323) 482178* Long-standing popular candlelit evening restaurant (also Sun lunch) with three beamed sitting rooms, bar, little dining room, open fires, a friendly dinner-partyish atmosphere, and good interesting food; cl Mon—Sat am, 24—26 Dec, children over 4. £35

KIRDFORD TQ0126 **Half Moon** *(01403) 820223* Family-run inn with marvellous fresh fish (the family have had Billingsgate links for 130 years) inc some really unusual ones, well kept real ales, local wine and cider, friendly service, simple neat bars, and big garden; cl 25 Dec pm; disabled access. £26|**£6.50**

LITLINGTON TQ5201 **Litlington Tea Gardens** *(01323) 870222* Established 150 years ago, these tearooms still keep their quaint Victorian elegance, with seating on an attractive sheltered lawn under a copper beech or ginkgo, in renovated beach huts with open fronts, or tearoom/restaurant; colourful hanging baskets and flowering tubs, quick efficient service; morning coffee, light lunches, and cream teas; handy for Alfriston; cl end Oct—1 wk before Easter; disabled access.|**£6**

LODSWORTH SU9321 **Halfway Bridge** *Midhurst Rd (01798) 861281* Stylish and civilised but friendly family-run pub with big helpings of inventive home cooking in no smoking restaurant or attractively decorated comfortable bar rooms, log fires, well kept real ales, ciders and wines; cl Sun pm in winter; children welcome over 10. £22|**£5**

NUTHURST TQ1926 **Black Horse** *Nuthurst St (01403) 891272* Warmly welcoming black-beamed pub in lovely walking country with log fire in inglenook fireplace, consistently good promptly served bar food, a no smoking restaurant, very well kept real ales and country wines, friendly service; cl pm 25 Dec. £21|**£6.95**

OXLEYS GREEN TQ7122 **Jack Fullers** *(01424) 838212* Cosy and softly lit dining pub with enjoyable pies and steamed puddings, good side dishes, and some vegetarian choices – all in big helpings; excellent wines (English ones, too), and seats in pretty flower-filled garden with fine views; cl Mon, Tues, 2 wks Feb/Mar, 1 wk Oct; disabled access. £25|**£6.50**

PLAYDEN TQ9122 **Peace & Plenty** *Rye Rd (01797) 280342* Cottagey dining pub with lots of little pictures, china and lamps and a big inglenook with comfortable armchairs on either side in the cosy bar; two intimate dining areas, very well prepared traditional food, well kept ales, and pretty garden; cl 25—26 Dec; disabled access. £18.95|**£5.95**

RINGMER TQ4413 **Cock** *Uckfield Rd (01273) 812040* Civilised heavily beamed country pub with log fire in big inglenook, a fine range of good food, decent wines, two lounges (one no smoking), and seats on the terrace and in the attractive fairy-lit garden; cl 25 Dec, pm 26 Dec. £19.50|**£6.50**

RYE TQ9220 **Flushing Inn** *4 Market St (01797) 223292* Run by the same family for 38 years, this fine old timber-framed inn serves particularly good local fish and seafood (local meat dishes, too) and holds various gastronomic occasions; note the fine 16th-c wall painting; bdrms; cl Mon pm, Tues, first 2wks Jan. £31|**£7**

RYE TQ9321 **Ypres Castle** *(01797) 223248* Popular pub in fine setting nr 13th-c Ypres Tower with unassuming décor, warm friendly atmosphere, enjoyable interesting food inc fresh local fish and seafood, good fresh vegetables, well kept changing ales, good value wine with 20 by the glass, and seats on a sizeable lawn with fine views out over the coastal flats; cl pm 25 Dec. £18|**£6.85**

SCAYNES HILL TQ3825 **Sloop** *Sloop Lane (01444) 831219* Country pub tucked away in a lovely spot with sheltered garden nr Bluebell Line; long saloon bar with pine furniture and comfortable old seats, simple public bar, good bar food, well kept real ales, and decent wines; children must be well behaved; partial disabled access. £20|**£6**

SEAFORD TV4898 **Quincy's** *42 High St (01323) 895490* Enjoyable little cottagey restaurant with homely décor, really friendly service, very good soundly based interesting food (fresh fish from Newhaven and lovely puddings), and a thoughtful wine list; cl Sun pm, Mon, am Tues–Sat, first wk Jan. £30

SLINDON COMMON SU9608 **Spur** *London Rd (01243) 814216* Attractive little 17th-c pub with two big log fires, a good choice of daily changing food, sizeable restaurant, well kept ales, friendly dogs, and pleasant garden; bdrms. £25|**£7.50**

TROTTON SU8322 **Keepers Arms** *(01730) 813724* 18th-c beamed and timbered pub, sofas by big log fire, some unusual pictures and artefacts, interesting medley of old or antique furniture, pretty candelabra, and bowls of fruit and chillis; particularly good interesting food inc yummy puddings, friendly service, relaxed atmosphere, well kept real ales and decent wines; country views from the latticed windows, and tables out on a terrace in front; cl Sun pm, Mon. £18.70|**£5**

Special thanks to Paul Kennedy, Ian Downes

WARWICKSHIRE
(with Birmingham and the West Midlands)

A healthy mix of places to visit including some outstanding museums and art galleries; some enjoyable family days out, too

The range of family attractions here is quite satisfying. As well as the traditional pleasures of friendly farm parks such as those at Middleton, Tanworth-in-Arden, Bodymoor Heath or the Shire Horse Centre & Farm Park at Stratford-upon-Avon, the area offers some unusual and worthwhile excursions in Birmingham's recently expanded Cadbury World or its flagship National Sea Life Centre, the well researched re-creation of a Black Country village at Dudley, and mighty Warwick Castle (lots for children inc lively summer events). Splendid Ragley Hall in Alcester and Coughton Court at Coughton have much to interest all ages, and Charlecote Park is pleasant picnic territory.

Birmingham, a good city for day visits, sets the standard for excellent museums in the region with wonderful collections at the Birmingham Museum and Art Gallery (a must for fans of the Pre-Raphaelite school), the vibrant Ikon Gallery, the Barber Institute of Fine Arts and the fascinating Museum of the Jewellery Quarter (good demonstrations and multiple shopping opportunities), with good botanic gardens, and interesting period houses to boot – refreshingly, many places are free. Elsewhere, the design of the brilliant New Art Gallery in Walsall matches the quality of the artworks within (one interactive gallery is especially designed for children), while Rugby and Leamington Spa (which still has some of the elegance of its spa-resort heyday) both have rewarding new museums.

For more unexpected treats, head for the dazzling displays at the Broadfield House Glass Museum, Kingswinford, or admire the amassed motors at Gaydon and Bickenhill; the gardens at Ryton-on-Dunsmore hold lots of appeal, too.

Warwick has the character and atmosphere to make a short stay enjoyable, and Stratford is the obvious focus for theatre buffs and Shakespeare devotees (there's a money-saving all-in ticket for most Bard-related sites).

Several of Warwickshire's remarkable historic houses hide some lovely secrets within their walls. You'll find splendid sculptures, paintings and fine rococo plasterwork at Farnborough Hall, the art collection at Upton House rivals that of many public art galleries, and Wightwick Manor delights with its idiosyncratic design and furnishings.

The countryside (which edges into the Cotswolds in the S) is quietly attractive, laced with canals and dotted with charming villages and appealing places to stay in.

Where to stay

AVON DASSETT SP4150 **Crandon House** *Avon Dassett, Leamington Spa, Warwickshire CV33 0AA* (01295) 770652 **£40***, plus winter breaks; 5 no smoking rms, 2 in converted dairy. Welcoming farmhouse on small working farm with various livestock, fine views, big garden, comfortable sitting rooms (one with woodburner), and extensive breakfast menu with home-made marmalade and preserves and free-range eggs; cl Christmas; children over 8

BISHOP'S TACHBROOK SP3262 **Mallory Court** *Harbury Lane, Bishop's Tachbrook, Leamington Spa, Warwickshire CV33 9QB* (01926) 330214 **£190**, plus special breaks; 18 wonderfully comfortable and luxurious rms. Fine ancient-looking house — actually built around 1910 — with elegant antiques and flower-filled day rooms, attentive staff, and excellent food using home-grown produce in panelled restaurant; 10 acres of lovely gardens with outdoor swimming pool, tennis, squash, and croquet

BLACKWELL SP2343 **Blackwell Grange** *Blackwell, Shipston-on-Stour, Warwickshire CV36 4PF* (01608) 682357 **£60**; 3 pretty rms. 17th-c Cotswold farmhouse with log fire in comfortable beamed sitting room, large inglenook fireplace in flagstoned dining room, good home cooking using own free-range eggs (evening meal by arrangement; bring your own wine), pretty garden, and nice country views; cl Christmas; children over 12, but parents with younger children stay in annexe; good disabled access

ILMINGTON SP2143 **Howard Arms** *Ilmington, Shipston-on-Stour, Warwickshire CV36 4LT* (01608) 682226 **£65**, plus special breaks; 3 rms. Neatly kept golden stone 17th/18th-c inn opposite village green with pleasant sheltered garden; beamed and flagstoned bar that now incorporates what was the restaurant and is furnished with antiques and country furniture, open fires, friendly service, very good food, and decent wines; children over 5

LEAMINGTON SPA SP3266 **Lansdowne House** *Clarendon St, Leamington Spa, Warwickshire CV32 4PF* (01926) 450505 **£68**, plus special breaks; 14 rms. Enjoyable Regency town house with particularly good service, very attractive public rooms, a tranquil atmosphere, good daily-changing dinners, fine value wine list, and small prize-winning garden; cl 25 and 31 Dec; children over 5; limited disabled access

LITTLE COMPTON SP2630 **Red Lion** *Little Compton, Moreton-in-Marsh, Gloucestershire GL56 0RT* (01608) 674397 **£42**; 3 rms, shared bthrm. Attractive 16th-c stone inn with low beams, log fires, separate dining area, an extensive menu with tasty food, a no smoking area, real ales, large wine list, and seats in the sizeable attractive garden; no dogs; children over 8

LOXLEY SP2755 **Loxley Farm** *Stratford Rd, Loxley, Warwick, Warwickshire CV35 9JN* (01789) 840265 **£60**; 2 suites with their own sitting rooms in attractive barn conversion. Not far from Stratford, this tucked-away, thatched and half-timbered partly 14th-c house has low beams, wonky walls and floors, antiques and dried flowers, open fire, helpful and friendly owners, and good Aga-cooked breakfasts; peaceful garden, and fine old village church; cl Christmas and New Year

SHERBOURNE SP2562 **Old Rectory** *Vicarage Lane, Sherbourne, Warwick, Warwickshire CV35 8AB* (01926) 624562 **£69***, plus special breaks; 14 rms, all with antique brass or brass and iron beds, and some in converted stables. Georgian house not far from Warwick, with cosy sitting room, big log fire, beams, flagstones, honesty bar, large breakfasts and enjoyable evening meals, and pretty walled gardens; no children

STRATFORD-UPON-AVON SP1954 **Carlton** *22 Evesham Pl, Stratford-upon-Avon, Warwickshire CV37 6HT* (01789) 293548 **£44***; 8 homely rms, some with own bthrm. Neatly kept and very welcoming no smoking Victorian house, close to theatre and restaurants, with helpful owners, very good breakfasts in airy dining room, and little garden

STRATFORD-UPON-AVON SP2054 **Melita** *37 Shipston Rd, Stratford-upon-Avon, Warwickshire CV37 7LN* (01789) 292432 **£69***, plus special breaks; 12 well equipped rms. Friendly family-run Victorian hotel with pretty, carefully laid-out garden, comfortable lounge with open fire, extensive breakfasts, and some provision for non-smokers; close to town centre and theatre; cl Christmas; pets by arrangement; partial disabled access

STRATFORD-UPON-AVON SP2055 **Payton** 6 John St, Stratford-upon-Avon, Warwickshire CV37 6UB (01789) 266442 **£56**; 5 charming rms with showers. Quietly set no smoking Georgian house, handy for theatre, with caring owners, very good breakfasts in pretty dining room, and seats in flower-filled courtyard; cl Christmas; children over 12

STRATFORD-UPON-AVON SP2054 **Shakespeare** Chapel St, Stratford-upon-Avon, Warwickshire CV37 6ER (0870) 400 8182 **£168**, plus wknd breaks; 74 comfortable well equipped rms. Smart hotel based on handsome lavishly modernised Tudor merchants' houses, with comfortable bar, good food, quick friendly service, and civilised tea or coffee in peaceful chintzy armchairs by blazing log fires; seats out in back courtyard; 3 mins' walk from theatre; disabled access

STRATFORD-UPON-AVON SP2056 **Welcombe Hotel** Warwick Rd, Stratford-upon-Avon, Warwickshire CV37 0NR (01789) 295252 **£175**, plus special breaks; 64 rms with antiques and luxurious bthrms. Jacobean-style mansion in parkland estate with 18-hole golf course, swimming pool, and two all-weather floodlit tennis courts; deeply comfortable day rooms inc fine panelled lounge, open fires and fresh flowers, elegant restaurant (no children allowed here), and good service; cl first wk Jan; disabled access

SUTTON COLDFIELD SP1394 **New Hall** New Hall Drive, Sutton Coldfield, West Midlands B76 1QX (0121) 378 2442 **£136**w, plus special breaks; 60 lovely rms (the ones in the manor house are the best). England's oldest moated manor house, in 26 beautiful acres, with luxurious day rooms, a graceful panelled restaurant with carefully cooked imaginative food using very fresh (often home-grown) produce, and excellent service; they can hold wedding ceremonies, and have a new leisure club; children over 8; disabled access

WALCOTE SP1258 **Walcote Farm** Walcote, Alcester, Warwickshire B49 6LY (01789) 488264 **£40***; 3 rms with fine views, 1 with a late 16th-c window. Attractive 16th-c farmhouse on working sheep farm with plenty of surrounding walks; a warm welcome from friendly owners, log fires in inglenook fireplaces, beams and flagstones, good breakfasts (several local pubs for evening meals), and pretty garden; no smoking; cl Christmas and New Year

WARWICK SP2864 **Forth House** 44 High St, Warwick, Warwickshire CV34 4AX (01926) 401512 **£65***; 2 appealing and spacious suites – one is almost a garden flat with its own kitchen. Prettily decorated no smoking house with a lovely, surprisingly big garden, and good breakfasts (supper trays by prior arrangement); self-catering flat; disabled access

WILMCOTE SP1658 **Pear Tree Cottage** 7 Church Rd, Wilmcote, Stratford-upon-Avon, Warwickshire CV37 9UX (01789) 205889 **£52**; 7 rms. Charming half-timbered Elizabethan house owned by the same family for three generations, with beams, flagstones, country antiques, a cosy atmosphere, good breakfasts, and sizeable shady garden; self-catering also; cl Christmas–mid-Jan; children over 3

We welcome reports from readers

This Guide depends on readers' reports. Do help us if you can – in return, we offer a discount on the next edition to people who've helped us with reports for it. Tell us what you think about places already in it, and anything extra you think we should say about them. And send us your ideas for inclusion in the next edition: places to visit, eat at or stay in, attractive drives or walks, maybe even unusual interesting shops you know of. Use the card in the middle, the report forms at the end, or just write – no stamp needed: The Good Britain Guide, FREEPOST TN1569, Wadhurst, E Sussex TN5 7BR.

To see and do

Warwickshire Family Attraction of the Year

STRATFORD-UPON-AVON SP1952 **Shire Horse Centre & Farm Park** (just out of town, Clifford Rd – B4632 S) Good fun, and deservedly praised by readers in recent years, this friendly place can easily fill much more of a day than you might expect; it's by no means just for those with an interest in horses. Once used as the battle horses of knights in armour, and later a familiar sight working the fields, the huge shires are far less often seen today – except in centres like this. The noble beasts parade round the ring at 11am and 2pm each day, and there are usually guided tours of the stables, or wagon rides through the fields. Lots of interesting facts about the horses and their glory days, and children can usually have a go at driving one round the yard, walking behind the horse, but steering with the reins (they don't always do this in winter – best to check first then). There are plenty of other animals too, inc rare breeds of cattle, sheep, pigs, goats and poultry, and twice a day (usually 12.15 and 2.15pm) they have Pat-a-Pet sessions when children can handle the rabbits and guinea-pigs; at other times you can feed the ducks and hens. They've made a valiant attempt at re-creating life in a traditional country village, this year adding a short indoor ride through various reconstructed scenes such as a dairy and schoolroom; the models don't move, but the commentary's quite fun, and it's a useful enough introduction to the topic. There's a good play area, with big slides, rope bridges, toy tractors, and an indoor section for younger visitors. Good meals and snacks, shop, disabled access (can be a bit bumpy); cl Thurs and Fri Nov–Feb, and 25 Dec; (01789) 415274; £5.50 (£4.50 children).

ALCESTER SP0755
Ragley Hall (A435) Privately owned family home of the Marquess and Marchioness of Hertford, this perfectly symmetrical Palladian house is set in 400 acres of parkland and formal gardens; excellent baroque plasterwork in Great Hall, fine paintings (inc some modern art) and a mural by Graham Rust; adventure playground, maze and woodland walks in the grounds. Many special events inc good outdoor concerts. Meals, snacks, shop, disabled access; cl Mon–Weds and Good Fri, Oct–Apr; (01789) 762090; £5; grounds also open every day during main school hols; £4. The village itself is attractive, and the Roebuck has good value food; the nearby village of Arrow is interesting to stroll around (despite some development) – as is the pretty stream that divides the two. Fruit farming around here is much rarer than it used to be, but you can still find delicious fresh dessert plums for sale in Sept. The county's best drive (partly in Gloucs) circles Alcester, via Walcote, Aston Cantlow, Wilmcote, Temple Grafton, Wixford, Radford, Inkberrow, Holberrow Green, New End and Kings Coughton.

ARBURY SP3388
Arbury Hall (off B4102 just S of Nuneaton) Splendid-looking mansion, the original Elizabethan house elaborately spruced up in the 19th c to make it one of the best examples of the Gothic Revival style. The writer George Eliot was born on the estate, and her *Mr Gifgil's Love Story* describes some of the rooms – not unreasonably comparing the dining room to a cathedral. Some work by Wren in the stables, and the gardens are a pleasure. Meals, snacks, shop, limited disabled access; open Sun and Mon of bank hol wknds Easter–Sept; (024) 763 82804; £4.50, £2.50 gardens only.

ARMSCOTE SP2444
Picturesque Cotswold stone village, nice pub.

ASHBY CANAL SP3688
Canal towpaths offer some of Warwickshire's nicest walks, and heading off into the Leics countryside from its junction with the Coventry Canal at Marston Junction on the edge of Bedworth this canal has perhaps the

prettiest of them.

ASHORNE SP3057

Nickelodeon (Ashorne Hall, off B4100) Unique collection of mechanically played musical instruments inc self-playing harps, drums and violins, and a vintage theatre, complete with organ rising from the floor (demonstrated Sun at 4.15pm). They show silent comedies and 1950s Pathé newsreels, and have various nostalgic tea concerts and events. There's a miniature railway in the grounds (£2 extra). Meals, snacks, shop, disabled access; open Sun pm Mar–Oct, and maybe other days too – worth checking; (01926) 651444; £7.20. The Cottage has good value food (may cl wkdy lunchtime).

ASTON CANTLOW SP1461
Charming timbered houses and guild-hall, lovely **church** where Shakespeare's parents married, fine old pub.

AUSTREY SK2906
Attractive village with black and white timbered houses and cottages, some thatch.

BADDESLEY CLINTON SP2072
Baddesley Clinton House Romantic 13th-c moated manor house, mostly unchanged since the 17th c. Interesting portraits, priest's holes and garden with chapel and pretty walks. The family history is intriguing. Meals, snacks, shop, some disabled access; house open mid-Feb to mid-Dec Weds–Sun pm (shop and restaurant open till Christmas), grounds open same days mid-Feb to mid-Dec; (01564) 783294; £5 (timed ticket system); NT. The nearby **church** has a lovely E window, and the canalside Navigation at Lapworth and prettily set Cock Horse at Rowington do decent food.

BICKENHILL SP2083
National Motorcycle Museum ⊞ (Coventry Rd) Handy for the NEC, five halls displaying over 650 gleamingly restored motorcycles, all British. Incongruously, they also have the biggest theatre organ in Europe. Meals, snacks, shop, disabled access (not to restaurant); cl 24–26 Dec; (01675) 443311; £4.50. The White Lion at Hampton in Arden has good value food.

BIRMINGHAM SP0786

The city has masses of things to see and do. It has a long heritage despite its mainly modern centre, and a rich and varied industrial history taking in everything from guns to chocolate buttons. Reputedly there are more canals here than in Venice, and redevelopment of old canal buildings has brought a lively new focus to the Gas St/Brindley Pl area. Work is now under way on a grand plan to give the city something of a true heart instead of the vast road systems which characterise its centre, and this may eventually give it enough appeal to encourage a stay. Meanwhile, its strength is as a place for enjoyable day trips, particularly at wknds. Due to open around Sept, **Millennium Point** will house an up-to-the-minute interactive discovery centre inc an area especially developed for younger children, as well as providing a new site for a university engineering and computer technology campus. The city has had a dearth of decent pubs, but now has enough to keep visitors happy, especially around the canal area: Flapper & Firkin (Cambrian Wharf), James Brindley (Gas St Basin) and Malt House (Brindley Pl), with the Fiddle & Bone (Sheepcote St) and Tap & Spile (Brindley Wharf) the current favourites.

Aston Hall (Aston, 2m NE of centre) Strikingly grand Jacobean mansion with panelled long gallery, balustraded staircase and magnificent plaster friezes and ceilings. Snacks, shop, disabled access to ground floor; cl am, and all Nov–Easter; (0121) 327 0062; free (and more satisfying than a good many houses you'd have to pay for).

Barber Institute of Fine Arts (Birmingham University, E gate) Excellent collection of paintings and sculptures, well housed in a very attractive gallery and just the right size to be enjoyable without being overwhelming. Quite a lot of Impressionist works as well as European masters. Shop, disabled access; cl Sun am, 24–26 and 31 Dec, 1–2 Jan, Good Fri; (0121) 472 0962; free. The university (marked out by its huge clock tower) is on the outer fringes of Edgbaston, a couple of miles S of the city centre. This area developed as a smart residential part of town, where industry and commerce gave way to parks and greenery, much of which still remains.

Birmingham Museum and Art Gallery (Chamberlain Sq) Perhaps the best collection of Pre-Raphaelite paintings anywhere, plenty still looking as brilliantly, almost shockingly, fresh and detailed as when they were first painted. Other notable paintings too, and lots of coins and archaeology – one of the first two dozen museums to make the Heritage Secretary's shortlist of excellence and national importance. Meals, snacks, shop, disabled access; cl one week at Christmas and Sun am; (0121) 303 2834; free. Local boy Burne-Jones, a leading light in the Pre-Raphaelite movement, was responsible for four stunning windows in **St Philip's church** on Colmore Row nearby, since 1905 the city's cathedral. The Old Contemptibles (Edmund St) is a useful nearby Edwardian pub, quite striking in its own right.

Birmingham Nature Centre (Pershore Rd) British and European animals in indoor and outdoor enclosures designed to resemble natural habitats. Meals and snacks, shop, disabled access; cl wkdys Nov–Mar; (0121) 472 7775; £1.50.

Birmingham Railway Museum 🄬 (Warwick Rd, Tyseley; A41 3m SE) Working railway museum with fully equipped workshop, steam locomotives, and several historic carriages and wagons. Trains run along a short track, but you can ride on them only in summer, usually first Sun of the month. Meals and snacks, shop, limited disabled access; open Sat, Sun and bank hol Mon; (0121) 707 4696; £2.50.

Blakesley Hall (Yardley, 2m E of centre) This timber-framed 16th-c merchant's house, furnished according to an inventory of 1684, is due to reopen after refurbishment around Sept. Shop, disabled access to ground floor and garden; cl am, and Nov–Mar; (0121) 783 2193; free.

Botanical Gardens 🄬 (Westbourne Rd, Edgbaston) Outstanding: 15 acres featuring a tropical house (with lily pool, bananas and cocoa), palm house,

orangery, a national collection of bonsai, cactus house. The gardens themselves are filled with rhododendrons and azaleas and a goodly collection of trees. Bands play on summer Sun and bank hol pms. Meals, snacks, shop, disabled access; cl 25 Dec; (0121) 454 1860; £4.30, £4.60 summer Suns and bank hols.

Cadbury World (Bournville) Hugely enjoyable place attached to the Cadbury factory, covering everything from how chocolate is made and marketed inc production area, with demonstrators hand-making and decorating chocolates, to the packaging plant where standard bars are wrapped. The latest development here, £2m Cadbury Land, provides a whole new attraction in itself: entered through an old-fashioned style sweetshop, a purpose-built auditorium fitted with interactive buttons lets visitors guide themselves through a candy-covered adventure. Other recent additions include the environmentally minded secret Yowie Kingdom, and Liquid Chocolate, which challenges you to eat freshly made chocolate without licking your lips. Elsewhere is an alternative children's view of chocolate-making offered by Mr Cadbury's Parrot at the Fantasy Factory, as well as Cadabra, a jolly ride through an imaginative chocolate-themed world, a chocolate version of *Coronation St*, and of course, plenty of samples. Book in advance to be sure of getting in; on popular days tickets can be sold out well in advance. Restaurant and picnic areas, good shop (some bargains and unusual varieties), mostly disabled access; open daily Mar–Oct, and usually wknds and at least a couple of other days Nov–Feb, so best to phone but be prepared for a long wait; (0121) 451 4180; £8.

Ikon Gallery (Oozells Sq) Vibrant modern art in stunningly converted school building. Meals, snacks, shop, disabled access; cl Mon and during installation of exhibitions; free.

Museum of the Jewellery Quarter (Vyse St) Birmingham is still Britain's biggest producer of gold jewellery, if not as important to the jewellery trade as it used to be. This excellent centre is built around the perfectly preserved workshops of the Smith & Pepper company, still much as they were at the start of the century. There's a good overview of the industry, as well as tours of the factory and demonstrations of jewellery-making techniques. Snacks, shop, disabled access; cl Sun; (0121) 554 3598; £2.50. Around 100 jewellery shops nearby, so useful for browsing or repairs. The Rosevilla has decent food.

National Sea Life Centre (Waters Edge, Brindley Pl) Very much the flagship of the excellent Sea Life Centre chain that we recommend in quite a few resorts around the country. The hi-tech displays are both fun and instructive, with around 3,000 native British marine and freshwater creatures shown off in careful re-creations of their natural habitats, also themed soft play area and a reconstructed *Titanic* wreck. The highlight is a walk-through tube designed to give the impression of walking along the sea bed, with sharks, rays and other creatures swimming above, alongside and beneath you. Norman Foster designed the building. Meals, snacks, shop, disabled access; cl 25 Dec; (0121) 633 4700; £8. The Figure of Eight (Broad St) is handy for all-day food.

Sarehole Mill (Hall Green, 3m SE of centre) Working 18th-c water mill, with displays explaining the milling process and the new displays on Victorian farming; Tolkien often came here as a child. Limited disabled access; cl am, and Nov–Mar; (0121) 777 6612; free. Other local sites that influenced Tolkien are listed on a leaflet available at Tourist Information Centres.

Selly Manor Museum (Maple Rd, A441 4m S) When the Cadbury family moved their factory out of the city centre in 1879, part of their plans for this new garden suburb involved uprooting timber-framed manor houses from elsewhere and re-erecting them here; two survive as this museum, with herb garden, crafts and various exhibitions. Shop, disabled access to ground floor only; open Tues–Fri, plus bank hols and wknds Apr–Sept pms, best to phone for winter opening; (0121) 472 0199; £2.

Soho House Elegant former home of Matthew Boulton, famous for his development of the steam engine with James Watt, and possibly the first centrally heated house in England since Roman times. Furnished in 18th-c style with Boulton-related displays. Snacks, shop, disabled access; cl Sun am, and all day Mon (exc bank hols); (0121) 554 9122; *£2.50.

BODYMOOR HEATH SP2096
Broomey Croft Children's Farm
Set within Kingsbury Water Park, this friendly working farm has been developed especially with children in mind. There are lots of animals to feed (specially prepared food bags are available for a small charge) inc sheep, pigs, rabbits and goats, and depending on what time of year it is, plenty of activities to watch and join in with, from bottle-feeding the lambs to shoeing horses; also play and picnic areas. Tearoom, shop, disabled access; open daily Easter–Sept, plus Feb and Oct half-terms, wknds only Oct–Mar; (01827) 873844; £2.80 (£2 children). The canalside Dog & Doublet has decent food.

CASTLE BROMWICH SP1489
Castle Bromwich Hall Gardens 🖼
(Chester Rd) Restored 18th-c formal gardens, with authentic collection of period plants, inc historic vegetables and herbs, plus a holly maze. Snacks, plant sales, disabled access; cl am, Mon and Fri, and Nov–Mar, plus wkdys in Apr and Oct; (0121) 749 4100; £3.

CHARLECOTE SP2656
Charlecote Park 250 acres of parkland, full of deer (Shakespeare is said to have poached here), along with the descendants of reputedly the country's first flock of Jacob sheep. Well furnished Great Hall and Victorian kitchen, and an impressive Tudor gatehouse. Three new rooms and a new garden designed by Sir Edmund Fairfax Lucy are now open. Playground, meals, snacks, shop, disabled access; open Fri–Tues Apr–Oct (cl Good Fri); (01789) 470277; £5.40; NT. By the park is a charming little 19th-c estate village of timbered cottages, and a show Victorian church. The Boars Head in pretty Hampton Lucy has decent food.

CLIFFORD CHAMBERS SP1952
Pretty black and white timbered houses

and cottages, and a Tudor former rectory which has some claim to being the true birthplace of Shakespeare.

COUGHTON SP0860

Coughton Court (A435) Several priest's holes are hidden in this mainly Elizabethan house, renowned for its imposing gatehouse and beautiful courtyard; the Throckmortons have lived here since 1409. Notable furniture and porcelain, and an exhibition on the Gunpowder Plot, with a lake, two churches, pleasant walks, formal gardens and play area in the grounds. Meals, snacks, shop, plant sales, limited disabled access; open wknds mid-Mar to end Mar, Weds–Sun Apr–Sept and Tues in Aug and bank hol Mon–Tues, cl Good Fri and Sat nearest 23 June; (01789) 400777; £6.95, £5.10 grounds only; NT. The nearby Moat House, Green Dragon on the fine old green at Sambourne and interesting Old Washford Mill at Studley are all good for lunch.

COVENTRY SP3379

Like Birmingham, more a place to dip into than to fix on as your base for a short holiday. Its most interesting street is Spon St, with one or two ancient buildings that started their lives here and others that have been rescued from elsewhere and rebuilt here (the picturesque Old Windmill does cheap basic lunches). One of the town's most famous inhabitants was Lady Godiva, commemorated best by the Coventry Clock – where she pops out in the pink every hour. The Royal Court Hotel, Greyhound out at Sutton Stop (Aldermans Green/Hawkesbury) and Prince William Henry and William IV (both Foleshill Rd – authentic Indian) are popular for lunch.

Coventry Cathedral (Priory Row) Bombed during the war, the old cathedral ruins have been carefully preserved, and parts of it such as the 14th-c tower remain intact. These have been joined by the new cathedral designed by Sir Basil Spence. It is, perhaps quite rightly, in no way an orthodox church building, but is worth a look for unusual modern art (inc windows by John Piper, tapestry by Graham Sutherland, even holograms); the visitor centre (cl Sun) has more, as

well as a full history of its development. Meals, snacks, shop, disabled access; cl 4 days in July and Nov for degree ceremonies; £2 suggested donation, £2 for visitor centre.

Herbert Art Gallery and Museum (Jordan Well) Lively interactive history of the city. Meals, snacks, shop, disabled access; cl Sun am, and Christmas wk; (024) 7683 2381; free. Browns café-bar nearby serves good food all day.

Lunt Roman Fort (Coventry Rd) Fun reconstruction of 1st-c Roman fort, interesting to see such a site in all its glory. Good interpretative displays. Shop, picnic area, some disabled access; open wknds and bank hols Easter–Oct, plus daily May half-term and late July–mid-Sept exc Weds; (024) 7683 2381; £1.80.

Midland Air Museum (Coventry Airport) Displays of civil and military aircraft spanning more than 70 years. Snacks, shop, disabled access; cl 25–26 Dec; (024) 76301033; £3.75.

Museum of British Road Transport (St Agnes Lane) Huge collection of British road transport displayed in the birthplace of the British motor industry, which developed here as an offshoot of sewing-machine production: cars, commercial vehicles, bicycles, and die-cast models; also the Blitz Experience and fastest car on earth show. Snacks, shop, disabled access; cl Christmas wk; (024) 76832425; free.

St Mary's Guildhall (Bayley Lane) Very well preserved medieval building, with its minstrel's gallery still, and some Flemish tapestries; it's usually open Easter–Sept (exc Fri and Sat), provided there aren't any civic functions, but best to check; (01203) 832381.

Toy Museum (Much Park St) Toys from 1740 to 1990, housed in a 14th-c monastery gatehouse. Shop; cl am, and 25 Dec; (01203) 76227560; £1.50.

DUDLEY SO9591

Black Country Living Museum (Tipton Rd, 1m N of town centre) Good value well thought out open-air museum (with much under cover) giving a good feel of how things used to be in the Black Country, the heavily industrialised and proudly individual areas in the W part of the Birmingham conurbation. It's an authentically reconstructed turn-of-the-century village, complete with cottages, chapel, chemist, baker, pub, and trips along a canal (summer only) or even down a mine, as well as black and white comedies from Laurel and Hardy or Harold Lloyd in the old cinema, school lessons in the school hall, and an old-fashioned working fairground just outside the village (Mar–Nov; extra charges for some rides). Staff in period costumes illustrate traditional crafts and test-drive old vehicles, and there are plenty of extra activities for children during school holidays. Meals and snacks (and space for picnics), shop, mostly disabled access (it may be worth calling first); open daily exc Mon and Tues Nov–Feb, and several days over Christmas; (0121) 557 9643; £7.95

Dudley Museum and Art Gallery (St James's Rd) Some fine paintings, well displayed geology, and appealing temporary exhibitions. Shop, disabled access but no facilities; cl Sun and bank hol Mon, Christmas and New Year; (01384) 815575; free.

Dudley Zoo 🖼 (The Broadway) Based around an impressive **ruined castle**, so the animals enjoy rather special views. Meals, snacks, shop, disabled access; cl 25 Dec; (01384) 215300; £6.75.

Tunnel boat trips The Dudley Canal Trust do boat trips along part of a unique network of canal tunnels and limestone mines. Trips Mar–Nov, and some days in Dec – best to ring for times; (01384) 236275; £2.90.

EARLSWOOD SP1074

Manor Farm Craft Workshops (Wood Lane) Furniture restoration, stained glass, print-making, needlework, vintage car hire, alternative healing centre. Snacks, shop with home-made ice-cream, disabled access; cl Mon, Christmas wk; (01564) 702729; free. The canalside Bluebell and the Red Lion (past the lakes) are useful dining pubs.

EXHALL SP1055

Pretty black and white timbering, and some pleasant gently hilly walks nearby; very quiet, as no through road.

FARNBOROUGH SP4349

Farnborough Hall Palladian villa filled with splendid sculptures, paintings and fine rococo plasterwork; the staircase, hall and two main rooms are on show. The 18th-c landscaped gardens have a couple of ornamental temples, and views from the terrace walk – less impressive than they were thanks to the arrival of the M40. Disabled access to ground floor only; open Weds pm and Sat Apr–Sept, terrace also open pm Thurs and Fri; (01295) 690002; £3, £1 50 terrace walk only; NT. The Butchers Arms nearby is useful.

GAYDON SP3354

Heritage Motor Centre (Banbury Rd) Busy centre with the world's biggest collection of historic British cars – 300 in all, starting with an 1895 Wolseley. Also hundreds of drawings, photographs, trophies and models, hi-tech displays and video shows, and a nature reserve. The design of the building is incredible, esp inside. Meals, snacks, shop, disabled access; cl 24–26 Dec; (01926) 641188; £6. The Malt Shovel is handy for lunch.

HARTSHILL HAYES SP3194

Country park with mixed woodland, opening out at the top for broad views towards the Peak District. The Coventry Canal below allows more extended rambles.

HENLEY-IN-ARDEN SP1565

More small town than village, but a pretty conservation area, with good churches. The Blue Bell and White Swan, both handsome, have decent food.

HONILEY SP2472

The village has virtually gone now, and there are only vestiges of the big house, but you can still sense the vanished settlement around the surviving 18th-c church.

HONINGTON SP2642

Attractive village, its church prettily set on the edge of the lawn of charming late 17th-c Honington Hall (open Weds pm Jun–Aug); (01608) 661434.

ILMINGTON SP2143

Quietly attractive village with peaceful path to partly Norman church, lovely inside; pleasant walks on hills above; Howard Arms good for lunch.

KENILWORTH SP2772

Kenilworth Castle Dramatic castle transformed by John of Gaunt into a

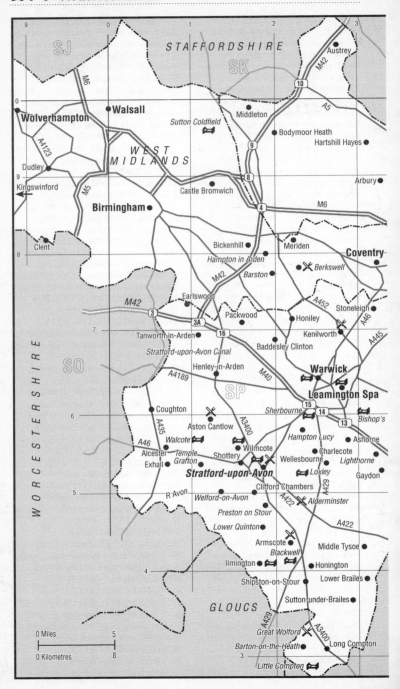

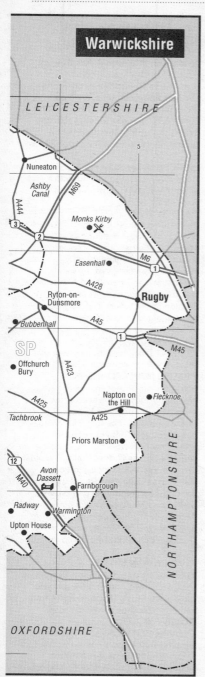

Warwickshire

LEICESTERSHIRE

Nuneaton

Ashby
Canal

A444

Monks Kirby

Easenhall ●

M6

A428

Ryton-on-
Dunsmore

Rugby

● Bubbenhall

A45

M45

SP

● Offchurch
Bury

A23

A425

Napton on ● Flecknoe
the Hill

Tachbrook   A425

Priors Marston ●

NORTHAMPTONSHIRE

Avon
Dassett

● Farnborough

● Radway

Warmington

Upton House

OXFORDSHIRE

spectacular fortress, now one of the
finest castle ruins in the country, with a
still impressive keep and several other
buildings within the sandstone walls.
Also restored Tudor garden, various
re-enactments, open-air plays and
operas, and children's activities most
summer hol wknds. Shop, disabled
access (but no facilities); cl 24–25 Dec,
1 Jan; (01926) 852078; £3.50; EH. The
town itself has a Norman church and
some pleasant strolls, especially around
the castle area. The Clarendon House
(High St) has enjoyable food.

KINGSWINFORD SO8888
Broadfield House Glass Museum
(Barnett Lane) Excellent collection of
glass from nearby Stourbridge,
displayed to dazzling effect. Clever use
of lighting shows off the exhibits quite
spectacularly, and even the audio-visual
shows create a sense of excitement.
One of the area's least expected
treasures. Teas, shop, disabled access
to ground floor; cl ams, Mon (exc bank
hols), 24–28 Dec, 1 Jan; (01384)
812745; free.

LEAMINGTON SPA SP2864
Elegant spa resort popularised by the
rich who came to take the waters in the
18th and 19th c. Still many fine Regency
buildings, though today the town is
better seen as a civilised shopping
centre, and perhaps as a base for sallies
into the surrounding countryside – or
into Warwick, across the River Avon.
The Carpenters Arms (Chandos St) and
Hogshead (Warwick St) are decent
pubs.

Art Gallery & Museum (Royal Pump
Rooms, The Parade) Recently restored
Regency bath house originally built in
1814 but later extended and
remodelled to suit changing fashions.
It's now home to the town's decent
museum and art gallery, as well as its
library and Tourist Information Centre.
Meals, snacks, shop, good disabled
access; cl Thurs am (plus Tues am until
Apr), all Mon, and over Christmas;
(01926) 742700; free. Beautifully laid-
out **Jephson Gardens** opposite are
being redeveloped and are well worth a
look, with wild ducks on the lake.

LONG COMPTON SP2932
This pleasant Cotswoldy village of
thatched stone houses has some

antiques shops; the Red Lion has good food.

LOWER BRAILES SP3139
Attractive Cotswold-edge village with lovely slender-spired church, pretty stone houses, good views, nice old inn.

MERIDEN SP2482
A cross on the green marks what the village feels is the centre of England – one of the streams rising in the village pond ends up in the Severn and the other over in the Humber. The Bulls Head does good value food.

MIDDLE TYSOE SP3344
Charming village – with a very traditional cottage bakery.

Interesting walk The walk S from Upper Tysoe over Windmill Hill (which does have a windmill) takes you to the church on the edge of Compton Wynyates park, giving views of the attractive Tudor manor – a refreshing bit of brick building, in this Cotswold-edge stone country.

MIDDLETON SP1797
Ash End House Farm (off A4091)
Friendly farm set up specifically for children; animals from shire horses to baby chicks and fluffy ducklings, as well as rare breeds of goats, pigs and sheep. A pony ride is included in the price, and there's plenty under cover for wet days. Snacks, shop, disabled access; cl 25–28 Dec, 1 Jan; (0121) 329 3240; £3.60 children (adults half price).

Middleton Hall (A4091) Varied architecture in the house, also nature reserve, walled gardens, orchards and woodland, and a new play area. There's a good craft centre in the stables. Snacks, shop, some disabled access; house open Sun and bank hol pms Apr–Oct; £2; craft centre open Weds–Sun all year; free (01827) 283095; The Green Man is a decent family dining pub.

NAPTON ON THE HILL SP4661
Attractive village on a rounded hill above a curve in the Oxford Canal – perhaps the prettiest canal in this part of the world, with pleasant towpath walks. Great views of seven counties from the hill.

Church Leyes Farm 🎦 Friendly 40-acre family-run organic farm with animals, walks and wildflower conservation headlands by the hedges.

Disabled access with prior notice; cl Sat, and Jewish holy days; (01926) 812143; *£1.

NUNEATON SP3691
Nuneaton Museum & Art Gallery (Coton Rd) Nicely set in colourful Riversley Park, with display on George Eliot; meals, snacks, shop, disabled access; cl Sun am, all day Mon (exc bank hols), and Christmas; (024) 76350720; free. Good craft centre nearby. The central Felix Holt has decent food all day.

OFFCHURCH BURY SP3565
Attractive riverside parkland, with a pleasant walk winding through from the Stags Head.

PACKWOOD SP1772
Packwood House 🎦 (off A34)
Friendly old house with origins as a 16th-c farmhouse, carefully restored and not at all commercialised; interesting panelling, furniture and needlework, and in the garden unusual yew trees clipped to represent the Sermon on the Mount. Snacks, shop, some disabled access; open pm Weds–Sun and bank hols Apr–Oct; (01564) 782024; £4.60, garden only £2.30; NT. The Navigation by the canal at Lapworth has good value food.

PRIORS MARSTON SP4857
Attractive old houses around the village green, and unusual blue brick paths; the ancient Holly Bush is a decent pub. There's a walk up Marston Hill behind, and quite a good network of paths around nearby Priors Hardwick taking you down to the Oxford Canal. The old drovers' Welsh Rd through here via Southam to Cubbington is a pleasant drive; just before Offchurch it crosses the remarkable Fosse Way, a quiet Roman road running dead straight from Brinklow through Stretton-on-Dunsmore and Princethorpe down to Halford.

RIVER AVON SP0950
There is a pleasant riverside walk from the Cottage of Content at Barton; you can buy day fishing tickets from the fruit and vegetable shop across the road.

RUGBY SP5075
Gilberts (St Matthew's St) The game the school invented is commemorated at this shop, that's been making the standard rugby ball since 1842. You can

watch them do it, and there are related displays and collections. Shop, some disabled access; cl Sun and 25–26 Dec and 1 Jan; (01788) 333888; free. The friendly Three Horseshoes Hotel not far off in Sheep St has interesting food.
Rugby Art Gallery & Museum (Little Elborow St) Impressive new centre housed in an attractive modern building, with a fine collection of modern art inc works by L S Lowry and Lucien Freud (you can make an appointment to see paintings not on show) and changing exhibitions, as well as a display of Roman artefacts and a decent look at local social history; the building also houses the town's library. They hope to add a café and a shop soon; disabled access; cl Sun and bank hol ams, and all day Mon; (01788) 533201; free.
Rugby School Founded in 1567, moving to its current site nearly 200 years later. A museum on Little Church St looks at its history and former pupils, such as Rupert Brooke and Lewis Carroll. Shop, disabled access; cl lunchtimes, Sun am and two wks at Christmas; (01788) 556274; £1.50. Guided tours of the school buildings leave here at 2.30pm most days but ring to check; £4.
RYTON-ON-DUNSMORE SP3874
Ryton Gardens (Wolston road, off A45) Home of the Henry Doubleday Research Association, the organic gardening and farming organisation, landscaped with thousands of organically grown plants and trees; herb garden, rose garden, garden for the blind, and shrub borders among the displays, as well as some free-range farm animals, a cooks' garden where all of the plants are edible, and the Paradise Garden which is dedicated to the late Geoff Hamilton. Very good meals and snacks in organic restaurant, shop, disabled access; cl Christmas wk; (024) 76303517; £3.
SHIPSTON-ON-STOUR SP2540
Small town with quite a busy shopping centre, but also rewarding to stroll through, with a good church and a good few handsome old stone buildings, antiques shops among them. The Black Horse (Station Rd) has interesting food.
SHOTTERY SP2055

Anne Hathaway's Cottage A substantial thatched Tudor farmhouse, the home of Anne Hathaway until her marriage to William Shakespeare. Displays of domestic life during the period, and colourful cottage garden. Snacks, shop; cl 23–26 Dec; (01789) 292100; £4.20. There's a craft centre next door, and the Bell is handy for something to eat away from the tourists.
STONELEIGH SP3271
Though primarily known as the showground for the Royal Show, with an increasing number of permanent displays, the village itself has an attractive sandstone Norman church, timber-framed houses, and newly restored Stoneleigh Abbey which will be open Sun and Tues–Thurs from Apr; best to check admission prices nearer the time; (01926) 858585.
STRATFORD-UPON-AVON SP2055
Visitors who look at the town just as a town can be disappointed, but if you have a grounding in Shakespeare's plays the interesting buildings seem that bit more interesting – and not so outnumbered by the workaday ones, the overpriced antiques shops and the gift shops. The gardens by the River Avon make a memorable setting for the Memorial Theatre. If you're looking forward to a good production at the theatre that evening, or, better still, able to run through much of the verse in your head, then you'll love Stratford. But if you've always thought Shakespeare overrated, then you'll think the same about Stratford, too. The pub with the most theatrical Shakespeare connections is the Mucky Duck, or more properly White Swan (Southern Way) – traditionally where the RSC actors and actresses drink; the Arden Hotel has the closest bar to the Memorial Theatre, with good snacks. Useful places for lunch include the Brasserie (Henley St), quaint old Garrick (High St), Vintner Wine Bar (Sheep St) and Slug & Lettuce (Guild St/Union St). Tea in the smart Shakespeare Hotel (Chapel St) is relaxing. Ghost tours around Stratford's more chilling historic sites depart from the Country Artist's

Fountain (in front of the Royal Shakespeare Theatre) at 7.30pm Apr–Sept, other times by appointment; (01789) 204106 £4.50.

Butterfly Farm ⊞ (Tramway Walk) Cascading waterfalls and tropical forests, with up to 1,500 exotic butterflies flying free in a jungle habitat, also an incredible collection of spiders and insects. Shop, disabled access; cl 25 Dec; (01789) 299288; *£3.75.

Hall's Croft (Old Town) Lovely gabled Tudor home of Dr John Hall, who married Shakespeare's daughter; good displays on the medicine of the time, Elizabethan and Jacobean furniture, and a walled garden. Teas, shop, disabled access to ground floor; cl 23–26 Dec; (01789) 292107; £3.50.

Harvard House (High St) Late 16th-c home of the mother of the man who founded Harvard University – no direct connection with Shakespeare, but a striking example of houses of his day with possibly the most ornately carved and timbered frontage in the town, and home to the Neish Collection of pewter. Shop; cl mid-Sept–Jun; (01789) 204507; free.

Holy Trinity church (Waterside) 15th-c, where Shakespeare was baptised and buried; cl Sun am and for other services; 70p to enter the chancel where the grave is.

New Place/Nash's House (Chapel St) Shakespeare died here in 1616; the house was destroyed in the 18th c, but the Elizabethan knot garden remains, and the adjacent house, former home of the writer's granddaughter, has a good collection of furniture and local history. Shop, disabled access to ground floor and gardens only; cl 23–26 Dec; (01789) 292325; £3.50.

Ragdoll Shop (Chapel St) Ragdoll make the children's television programmes *Teletubbies*, *Rosie and Jim*, *Brum* and *Tots TV*. The shop has plenty to amuse small children inc play areas, and they can talk to their favourite characters on the phone. Limited space for disabled access; cl Sun am, 25–26 Dec, 1 Jan; free.

Royal Shakespeare Theatre (Waterside) Shakespeare's plays are of course still performed here by the Royal Shakespeare Company. You can book guided tours of the Royal Shakespeare Theatre and their other theatre, the Swan (usually at 1.30, 5.30pm, and after evening performances; best to phone as they quickly get booked up); the gallery with temporary exhibitions is likely to close soon. Meals, snacks, shop, disabled access for plays but not tours; cl am Sun, 24–25 Dec; (01789) 403405; £2 for gallery, theatre tours *£4. The RSC productions themselves are performed in repertory, so if you're in the area for a few days it's quite possible to see several. Advance booking is recommended – (01789) 403403 – though 100 tickets are kept back for each performance and sold on the day from 9.30am; don't leave it much later, they go pretty fast; a 2-hour guided walk around Shakespeare's Stratford leaves the RSC Thurs, Sat and every day during the Easter hol at 10.30am; (01789) 412602; £5

Shakespeare's Birthplace (Henley St) Though there's no guarantee the playwright really was born here, there are interesting period features, and good interpretative displays. Shop, disabled access to ground floor; cl 23–26 Dec; (01789) 204016; £5.50. If you want to see all the Shakespearian houses it makes sense to buy a joint ticket; this costs £12, and covers this, New Place, Hall's Croft, and the Shottery and Wilmcote sites. You can also buy tickets covering just the three in-town sites for £8.50. A tour bus with commentary links the sites but costs another £8.50; (01789) 294466.

Shire Horse Centre & Farm Park *See separate family panel on p.598.*

Teddy Bear Museum ⊞ (Greenhill St) Delightfully displayed, furry friends of all shapes and sizes – mechanical and musical ones, ones that belonged to famous people, and some that are famous themselves. Shop; cl 25–26 Dec; (01789) 293160; *£2.50.

STRATFORD-UPON-AVON CANAL SP1867

This gives some pleasant towpath walks; the Fleur de Lys at Lowsonford is a good start.

SUTTON-UNDER-BRAILES SP3037

Attractive stone-built village, with some

pleasing Cotswold countryside around it – good walks.

TANWORTH-IN-ARDEN SP1270
Umberslade Children's Farm
Friendly family-run farm with animals to stroke and feed, and play areas for letting off steam. Also nature trails and walks, and goat-milking area. Snacks, shop, disabled access; cl Nov and Jan to mid-Feb; (01564) 742251; £3.50.

UPTON HOUSE SP3745
🖼 (A422 nr Ratley) The exceptional art collection is the main draw here, an enormous range of paintings inc works by Bosch, El Greco, Bruegel and Hogarth, and an exhibition of posters commissioned by Shell all sensibly arranged and displayed. Also Brussels tapestries and Sèvres porcelain. The late 17th-c house was remodelled in the early 19th c. The fine garden has terraces, herbaceous borders, a kitchen garden, 1930s bog garden and ornamental pools as well as the national collection of asters. Teas, shop, some disabled access; open pm Sat–Weds Apr–Oct; (01295) 670266; £5.40, garden only £2.70; NT. There's a timed ticket system on bank hols. Ratley itself is a pretty village, with a lovely church and good home cooking in the Rose & Crown; and the Castle on Edge Hill is a very interesting place for lunch, with terrific views.

WALSALL SP0099
Birchills Canal Museum (Top Lock, Old Birchills) Small museum with a replica boat cabin; shop; open Tues, Weds am, Thurs–Sun pm, cl 22–26 Dec and 1 Jan; (01922) 645778; free.
Jerome K Jerome Birthplace Museum 🖼 (Bradford St) Dedicated to the life and work of the author of *Three Men in a Boat*, with a reconstructed 1850s parlour; cl Sun and bank hols and pm Weds, Fri, open 12–2pm Sat; (01922) 653116; free.
New Art Gallery This imaginative £21m building had architecture critics raving when it opened in February 2000, with some immediately hailing it as a modern classic, but the collection of European art inside is equally impressive with paintings by Rembrandt, Goya, Constable, Manet, Degas, Freud and many others. Equally admirable is the effort that has been

made to make the gallery appeal to all ages and tastes. The centre-piece is the Garman Ryan collection – over 300 works donated to the local people by Kathleen Garman, Jacob Epstein's widow, in 1973, and hung in a sort of two-storey house within the building itself (with the aim being to evoke the feeling of looking at somebody's private collection). Elsewhere, there are changing exhibitions of contemporary and historic art, a children's interactive gallery, and a large shop-window giving passers-by a taste of what's in store for them inside the building. Another welcome feature is the gallery's accessibility and provision for admiring the works in comfort: there are benches everywhere, and the art is mounted lower than usual so you don't have to strain; also restaurant, activity and conference rooms, and a rooftop terrace. Meals, snacks, shop, disabled access; cl Mon; (01922) 654400; free.
Walsall Leather Museum 🖼 (Wisenmore) Well restored Victorian leather goods factory with tours of aromatic workshops and leather-making demonstrations (not Sun). Meals, snacks, shop (lots of local leather goods), disabled access; cl 24–26 Dec, 1 Jan and Easter Sun, Mon (exc bank hols), also Sun am; (01922) 721153; free.

WARWICK SP2864
Though many older buildings survived a major fire in 1694, today's centre is dominated by elegant Queen Anne rebuilding. Some of the oldest structures are to be found around Mill St, which is very attractive to stroll along; there are a good few antiques and other interesting shops. The Rose & Crown (Market Pl) is the best pub here; the Saxon Mill (Guy's Cliffe) is a prettily placed waterside family dining pub, and the Warwick Arms Hotel does good value teas.
Doll Museum (Castle St) Half-timbered Elizabethan house with comprehensive collection of antique dolls and toys. A fun video shows the exhibits come to life. Shop, limited disabled access; cl all Nov–Easter exc Sat; (01926) 495546; £1.
Lord Leycester Hospital (High St) Delightfully wonky half-timbered building built in 1383, still used as a

home of rest for retired servicemen. Fine old guildhall, candlelit chapel, gatehouse and courtyard, and garden with Norman arch and a 2,000-year-old urn from the Nile. Snacks (summer only), shop, disabled access to ground floor only; cl Mon, Good Fri, 25 Dec; (01926) 491422; £3.

Mill Garden Delightful series of plantings in a super setting on the river beside the castle – very nice to stroll through, with plenty of old things to look at along the way; as we went to press the property was on the market but it is hoped that the gardens will be open some wknds, best to ring for details; (01926) 492877.

St John's House (St John's) 17th-c house with exhibits from the county museum, a changing collection of costumes, and several room reconstructions, one of which is soon to be converted into an under-5s discovery room. Shop, disabled access to ground floor only; open Tues–Sat, plus Sun and bank hol Mon pms May–Sept, and over Christmas; (01926) 410410; free.

St Mary's church (Old Sq) Splendid medieval church on the town's highest point, with Norman crypt, chapter house and magnificent 15th-c Beauchamp chapel; in summer you can go up the tower which has excellent views – small admission charge.

Warwick Castle (Castle Hill) One of the country's most splendid castles, this is a lively place, with plenty for children to enjoy (especially in summer). Several displays showing the influence of the Tussauds group who own the site, but purists shouldn't be put off by the gloss or waxwork figures; the rooms are excellently preserved, and their fine furnishings and art well worth braving the crowds for. The marvellous grounds were designed by Capability Brown, and as well as the delightful gardens, have pleasant strolls along the banks of the River Avon; the views from the parklands are dramatic. Meals, snacks, shop, disabled access to grounds only; cl 25 Dec; (01926) 406600; £10.95, £9.75 in winter.

Warwickshire County Museum (Market Pl) In the 17th-c Market Hall, with lots of fossils, and a Sheldon

tapestry map of the county. Shop, disabled access to ground floor; cl Sun exc May–Sept, 25–26 Dec; (01926) 410410; free.

WELLESBOURNE SP2653
Wartime Museum Partly housed in the underground HQ of a former RAF base, a collection of aeronautical archaeology, wartime memorabilia and several aircraft. Shop, some disabled access (not underground); open Sun and bank hols (exc 25–26 Dec) only; £1.50. The Kings Head is a decent pub.

Wellesbourne Watermill 🏠 (B4086) Historic watermill still producing flour in secluded rural setting, with striking wooden wheel. Helpful staff, nature trails and traditional crafts. Meals, snacks, shop; open Thurs–Sun Easter–Sept, maybe other times outside summer, best to phone; (01789) 470237; £3.

WILMCOTE SP1658
Mary Arden's House The picturesque home of Shakespeare's mother, with the barns given over to countryside memorabilia. Daily falconry displays, rare breeds. Snacks, shop, disabled access to ground floor only; cl 23–26 Dec; (01789) 293455; £5. The Mary Arden and Masons Arms have decent food.

WOLVERHAMPTON SJ9400
One of the bookmakers' favourites to become the first new city of the 21st c, this is not really a town for visitors, though its **museum** (Lichfield Rd) is a good one. English Heritage is due to restore some of the town's industrial buildings as part of its humble heritage scheme. Wightwick Manor and Moseley Old Hall (see below) right out on the outskirts are splendid.

Moseley Old Hall 🏠 (Featherstone, off A460/A449 4m N) Tudor house famed as a hiding place for Charles II after the Battle of Worcester. The façade has altered since, but the furnishings and atmosphere in its panelled rooms don't seem to have changed much, and there's a 17th-c knot garden. Readers particularly enjoy the guided tours. Teas, shop, limited disabled access; cl am, Mon (exc bank hols), Thurs, Fri and end Dec–Mar; (01902) 782808; £4; NT.

Wightwick Manor (just off A454, 3m

W) Only a century old, but beautifully and unusually designed by followers of William Morris, and a fine testimonial to the enduring qualities of his design principles. Flamboyant tiles, fittings, furnishings and glass, and lots of Pre-Raphaelite art. Also period garden with yew hedges and topiary. Snacks, shop, some disabled access; open pm Thurs, Sat and bank hol wknds Mar–Dec; (01902) 761108; *£5.50, £2.50 garden only.

Other attractive villages, almost all with decent pubs, include Barston SP2078, Barton-on-the-Heath SP2532 (no pub), Berkswell SP2479 (pretty Norman church), Bubbenhall SP3672, Easenhall SP4679, Flecknoe SP5164, Hampton in Arden SP2081, Hampton Lucy SP2557, upmarket Lighthorne SP3355, Lower Quinton SP1847,

Monks Kirby SP4683 (huge church), Preston on Stour SP2049, Radway SP3748 (we've had no pub recommendation here yet), Temple Grafton SP1255 (Shakespeare's 'Hungry Grafton'), Warmington SP4147 and Welford on Avon SP1452.

Canals give some of the county's best walking opportunities. Besides places already mentioned, useful canalside pubs include the Black Boy and Herons Nest at Knowle SP1876, Waterman at Hatton SP2467 (by a flight of locks), Navigation at Lapworth SP1670, Anchor at Leek Wootton SP2868, Two Boats at Long Itchington SP4164 (the flight of Stockton Locks just E usually has plenty going on), Wharf Inn SP4352 (A423 Banbury–Southam), and Bulls Head at Wootton Wawen SP1563.

Where to eat

ALDERMINSTER SP2348 **Bell** *(01789) 450414* Popular and rather civilised dining pub nr Stratford, with excellent imaginative food using fresh local produce (no fried food), several communicating areas with flagstones and wooden floors, fresh flowers, good wines, real ales, obliging service, and no smoking restaurant; disabled access. £22.70|**£6.95**

ARMSCOTE SP2444 **Fox & Goose** *(01608) 682293* Pretty village pub with contemporary décor but quite a pubby feel, bright crushed velvet cushions and coverings on wooden pews and stools, big mirrors on the walls (a warm red colour in the bar, cream in the eating areas), polished floorboards, and lots of stylish black and white pictures of animals; a stuffed fox and goose guard the dining room's woodburner, and there's a log fire in the flagstoned bar; friendly service, imaginative enjoyable food, well kept real ales, good wines, and lots of soft drinks; elegant new deck area outside overlooking a big lawn with tables, benches and fruit trees; bdrms. £22.35|**£8.50**

ASTON CANTLOW SP1461 **Kings Head** *21 Bearley Rd (01789) 488242* Carefully restored and beautifully timbered Tudor pub with a massive inglenook fireplace and flagstones in comfortable village bar, an old-fashioned snug, a gently upmarket atmosphere, good often inventive food in the carpeted main room, cheerful service, well kept ales, and decent wines; disabled access. £23|**£7.95**

BERKSWELL SP2479 **Bear** *Spencers Lane (01676) 533202* Handsomely refurbished 16th-c timbered pub with a relaxed atmosphere, comfortable snug low-beamed areas, nooks and crannies, beams and panelling, bric-a-brac, well kept ales, decent house wines, and a wide choice of food inc interesting daily specials; seats on back lawn; no children. £19|**£7.50**

GREAT WOLFORD SP2434 **Fox & Hounds** *(01608) 674220* Inviting 16th-c inn with a good mix of locals and visitors in the cosy low-beamed old-fashioned bar; candlelit tables, flagstones and a roaring log fire, really enjoyable imaginative daily specials, over 200 malt whiskies, and a little tap room with several changing real ales; cl Sun evening, Mon; disabled access. £20|**£8**

KENILWORTH SP2872 **Time for Tea** *40 Castle Hill (01926) 512765* Charming and very popular tearoom with pine furnishings and a collection of teapots and tea caddies, a conservatory, delicious home-made cakes and scones, a choice of teas, and a cheerful atmosphere; cl Mon and Tues (open Tues during school summer hols); disabled access.|**£2.50**

MONKS KIRBY SP4682 **Bell** *Bell Lane (01788) 832352* Busy pub with warmly chatty Spanish landlord, timbered and flagstoned rambling rooms, cheerful locals, good tapas (Spanish hors d'oeuvres) as well as more usual bar food, an extensive wine list, well kept real ales, and quite a few whiskies; cl Mon am, 26 Dec, 1 Jan; disabled access. £25|**£4.75**

STRATFORD-UPON-AVON SP2055 **Benson's** *4 Bards Walk (01789) 261116* Close to Shakespeare's birthplace, this light and airy tearoom has lots of plants and flowers, neatly dressed staff, papers and magazines to read, a wonderful patisserie, a marvellous choice of teas and coffees (plus Pimms, buck's fizz and kir), and breakfasts, morning coffee, lunches, and afternoon tea; no smoking; cl winter Sun pm; disabled access. £12|**£5**

STRATFORD-UPON-AVON SP2054 **Opposition** *13 Sheep St (01789) 269980* Small bustling restaurant with friendly atmosphere, generous helpings of very good interesting food – handy for theatres and open for after-show meals; cl 25 Dec, evening 26 Dec. £18|**£6.95**

STRATFORD-UPON-AVON SP2055 **Slug & Lettuce** *38 Guild St (01789) 299700* Cheerfully friendly and popular, with good food, helpful staff, well kept real ales, decent wine, attractive bar with open fire and newspapers, and pretty back terrace. £22.50|**£8**

WILTSHIRE

A charmingly sedate corner of England, with some pleasant surprises for families

With its grand country houses, elegant gardens, and attractive old towns, Wiltshire is largely geared towards the grown-up visitor, but that's not to say that children are completely overlooked. Steam, the liveliest of Swindon's railway-related attractions, is perked up by interactive displays and fun activities which children will doubtless enjoy. Longleat has long been the county's most rewarding family outing, while there's plenty to occupy all ages within the fine estates of Bowood at Calne (wonderful gardens and an outstanding adventure playground), Lacock Abbey (interesting museum), and well organised Wilton House (also with a good play area). The Larmer Tree Pleasure Grounds at Tollard Royal offer family entertainment the Victorian way, and there's a full range of outdoor pursuits at the Woodland Heritage Museum, Brokerswood. The farms at Cholderton and Teffont Magna are particularly good for younger ones.

The small city of Salisbury is nice for a short civilised break, with a lovely cathedral precinct and interesting places to visit tucked quite closely around it. On a smaller scale, Castle Combe is exceptionally pretty, and Bradford-on-Avon, Devizes (home to a first-class local history museum), Marlborough and Malmesbury are all attractive small towns with a good deal of character.

Stourhead landscaped garden at Stourton is quite magnificent, and there are other notable examples at Iford Manor near Bradford-on-Avon, Holt, Middle Woodford, and Avebury Manor, new to the *Guide* this year.

For a different day out, there are fascinating stonemasonry demonstrations at the Bedwyn Stone Museum; or you might consider a drive past the regimental badges cut into the chalk escarpment at Fovant, a rummage through the archives of Swindon's National Monuments Record Centre (another newcomer), or a summer weekend trip to see the oldest working beam engines in the world at Crofton.

One of Wiltshire's most distinguishing features is its profusion of prehistoric sites – best appreciated at quiet times of day, out of season. The great stone circle of Stonehenge needs no introduction, and the various ancient landmarks in and around Avebury make for a veritable archaeological theme park.

The most appealing countryside is along the valleys of the southern chalk streams – intimate scenery with stone or flint houses and sparkling rivers. The northern parts have some quietly attractive drives and walks, especially around Marlborough. Running across the county, the restored Kennet & Avon Canal has lots of scope for enjoyable boat trips or relaxing towpath walks. Wiltshire is also dissected by several cycleways; many Tourist Information Centres have routes and maps, and free advice on cycling and walking in the region can be obtained by phoning (01980) 623255.

Where to stay

BRADFORD-ON-AVON ST8261 **Bradford Old Windmill** *4 Masons Lane, Bradford-on-Avon, Wiltshire BA15 1QN (01225) 866842* **£79**; 3 rms, one suite, one with giant waterbed, another with round bed. Interesting and carefully converted windmill with log fire in attractive circular lounge (former grain store), lots of books, a friendly atmosphere; good vegetarian evening meals with dishes from Thailand, Nepal, Mexico and so forth, and fine breakfasts eaten around communal refectory table; pretty cottagey garden; no smoking; cl Jan–Feb; no children

BRADFORD-ON-AVON ST8359 **Widbrook Grange** *Trowbridge Rd, Widbrook, Bradford-on-Avon, Wiltshire BA15 1UH (01225) 864750* **£105**; 19 pretty rms, many in carefully converted courtyard cottages. Handsome stone ex-farmhouse in 11 acres, with comfortable drawing rooms, good food in elegant dining room, a sunny conservatory, and indoor swimming pool and exercise machines; disabled access

BRADFORD-ON-AVON ST8361 **Woolley Grange** *Woolley Green, Bradford-on-Avon, Wiltshire BA15 1TX (01225) 864705* **£105**, plus winter breaks; 23 rms, with fruit and home-made biscuits. Civilised Jacobean manor house with a relaxed informal atmosphere, lovely flowers, log fires and antiques in comfortable and beautifully decorated day rooms, and pretty conservatory; delicious food using local (or home-grown) produce, often organic, inc home-baked breads and muffins and home-made jams and marmalades for breakfast, marvellous staff, and swimming pool, tennis, badminton, and croquet; particularly well organised for families, with nannies and plenty of entertainment; disabled access ☺

CALNE ST9871 **Chilvester Hill House** *Chilvester Hill, Calne, Wiltshire SN11 0LP (01249) 813981* **£80**; 3 charming spacious rms. Big Victorian house with neat gardens and grounds, particularly helpful friendly owners, comfortable sitting rooms with antiques, good breakfasts and honest no-choice dinners around large table in separate dining room (using home-grown produce), and plenty of local sights; children over 12 (babies allowed)

CASTLE COMBE ST8477 **Manor House** *Castle Combe, Chippenham, Wiltshire SN14 7HR (01249) 782206* **£171**, plus special breaks; 45 lovely rms, some in mews cottage. 26 acres of garden and parkland, inc an Italian garden, around 14th-c manor house; gracious day rooms with panelling, antiques, log fires and fresh flowers, a warm friendly atmosphere, and very good innovative food; 18-hole golf course, croquet, boules, and all-weather tennis court; disabled access

CHICKSGROVE ST9730 **Compasses** *Lower Chicksgrove, Tisbury, Salisbury, Wiltshire SP3 6NB (01722) 714318* **£55**; 4 rms with showers. Lovely thatched house in delightful hamlet with old bottles and jugs hanging from the beams, good home-made food, well kept real ales, and peaceful farm courtyard and garden; children must be well behaved

COLERNE ST8272 **Lucknam Park** *Colerne, Chippenham, Wiltshire SN14 8AZ (01225) 742777* **£226**, plus special breaks; 41 luxurious rms. Noble Georgian house reached by a long beech-lined drive through extensive grounds, with elegant carefully furnished day rooms, panelled library, lovely flowers, antiques and paintings, and excellent food and extremely good service in charming restaurant; snooker, hairdresser, leisure spa with indoor swimming pool, gym and beauty salon, and floodlit tennis courts; croquet; an all-weather equestrian centre; children over 12 in evening restaurant; disabled access

CORSHAM ST8770 **Methuen Arms** *2 High St, Corsham, Wiltshire SN13 0HB (01249) 714867* **£55**, plus special breaks; 24 rms. Georgian inn (a former nunnery) with mullioned windows and heavy oak beams in 14th-c part, comfortable seats in neatly kept bar, good food and friendly staff; pretty walled garden and fine skittle alley; disabled access

CROCKERTON ST8642 **Springfield House** *23 Crockerton, Warminster, Wiltshire BA12 8AU (01985) 213696* **£59***, 3 rms with garden views. Charming and friendly 17th-c house on the edge of Longleat Estate, with tennis in the garden, beams, flowers and open fires, dinner by the inglenook fireplace in candlelit dining room, and lots to do nearby; cl Christmas

CRUDWELL ST9592 **Crudwell Court** *Crudwell, Malmesbury, Wiltshire SN16 9EP (01666) 577194* **£88***; 15 big homely rms. 17th-c former rectory in grounds with walled garden, swimming pool and pond; an airy drawing room, relaxed reading room, enjoyable dinner-party style food in panelled restaurant, afternoon tea, and friendly staff

DEVIZES SU0061 **Bear** *Market Pl, Devizes, Wiltshire SN10 1HS (01380) 722444* **£86**, plus special breaks; 24 rms. Very much at the town's heart, this 16th-c inn has an old-fashioned feel, a wide choice of food from snacks to more elaborate meals served in the oak-panelled Lawrence Room, two more formal restaurants, beams and fresh flowers, and prompt service; cl 25–26 Dec

EBBESBOURNE WAKE ST9924 **Horseshoe** *Ebbesbourne Wake, Salisbury, Wiltshire SP5 5JG (01722) 780474* **£50**; 2 rms. Particularly welcoming pub with beautifully kept little bar, open fire, fresh flowers and interesting bric-a-brac on beams, popular home-made food in bar or no smoking restaurant, big breakfasts and nice Sunday lunches, well kept real ales, pretty little garden, play area, and pets' corner in paddock; well behaved children in some rooms; cl 25 Dec

FORD ST8476 **White Hart** *Ford, Chippenham, Wiltshire SN14 8RP (01249) 782213* **£79**; 11 rms. Very well run, popular and attractive ivy-covered inn in lovely spot by trout stream; an old-fashioned atmosphere, heavy black beams, big woodburner in ancient fireplace, particularly good imaginative food, well kept real ales, malt whiskies and fine wines, attentive cheerful service, and secluded small swimming pool

GASTARD ST8867 **Boyds Farm** *Chapel Knapp, Gastard, Corsham, Wiltshire SN13 9PT (01249) 713146* **£44**, plus special breaks; 3 rms. Friendly and handsome 16th-c house on family-run working farm with pedigree Herefords; homely lounge, woodburner, traditional breakfasts; no evening meals (local pubs nearby)

GRITTLETON ST8680 **Church House** *Grittleton, Chippenham, Wiltshire SN14 6AP (01249) 782562* **£59.50***, plus winter breaks; 4 big comfortable rms. Large Georgian rectory on the edge of a lovely village, in 11 acres of gardens and pasture with a heated indoor swimming pool and croquet; relaxed and friendly house party atmosphere, open fire, antiques and paintings in the drawing room, very good imaginative food using organic home-grown vegetables and fruit (advance notice required), and breakfasts with their own eggs; children under 2 and over 12

HEYTESBURY ST9242 **Angel** *High St, Heytesbury, Warminster, Wiltshire BA12 0ED (01985) 840330* **£49**; 3 comfortable rms. Small 16th-c coaching inn with armchairs, sofas, and a good fire in cosy homely lounge, a long beamed bar with woodburner, quite a few prints, and good service from friendly staff; well kept real ales, decent wines, and a wide choice of consistently good food in charming back dining room that opens on to secluded garden

HINDON ST9132 **Lamb** *High St, Hindon, Salisbury, Wiltshire SP3 6DP (01747) 820573* **£65**, plus special breaks; 13 rms. Solidly built, welcoming and civilised old inn (once a smugglers' haunt) with log fires in fine old bar, attractive lounges, imaginative food, friendly helpful service, and no smoking restaurant

LACOCK ST9168 **At the Sign of the Angel** *Church St, Lacock, Chippenham, Wiltshire SN15 2LB (01249) 730230* **£99**, plus special breaks; 10 charming rms. This fine 15th-c house in a lovely NT village is full of character, with heavy oak furniture, beams and big fireplaces, a restful oak-panelled lounge, and good English cooking in two candlelit restaurants; cl 23 Dec–31 Jan; disabled access

MALMESBURY ST9387 **Old Bell** *Abbey Row, Malmesbury, Wiltshire SN16 0BW (01666) 822344* **£95**, plus special breaks; 32 rms. With some claim to being one of England's oldest hotels and standing in the shadow of the Norman abbey, this fine wisteria-clad building has traditionally furnished rooms with Edwardian pictures, an early 13th-c hooded stone fireplace, two good fires and plenty of comfortable sofas, magazines and newspapers; cheerful helpful service, very good food, and attractively old-fashioned garden; particularly well organised for families ☺

MILDENHALL SU2169 **Fisherman's House** *Mildenhall, Marlborough, Wiltshire SN8 2LZ (01672) 515390* **£60***; 4 lovely rms, 2 with own bthrm. Extremely pretty house with lawns running down to the River Kennet, fresh flowers and stylish furniture, friendly owners, and good breakfasts in airy conservatory; cl Christmas; children over 12

NETTLETON ST8378 **Fosse Farmhouse Hotel** *Nettleton, Chippenham, Wiltshire SN14 7NJ (01249) 782286* **£125***, plus special breaks (inc some interesting craft wknds); 3 rms. 18th-c Cotswold stone house extensively restored with decorative French antique furniture and pretty English chintzes; morning coffee, lunch and cream teas served on the lawns or in very attractive dining room; antiques shop with dried flowers and decorative items in former dairy behind the house

PURTON SU0987 **Pear Tree** *Church End, Purton, Swindon, Wiltshire SN5 9ED (01793) 772100* **£100***; 18 very comfortable, pretty rms. Impeccably run former vicarage with elegant comfortable day rooms, fresh flowers, fine conservatory restaurant with good modern English cooking using home-grown herbs, helpful caring staff, and 7½ acres of grounds inc a traditional Victorian garden; cl 26–30 Dec; disabled access

SALISBURY SU1430 **Farthings** *9 Swaynes Cl, Salisbury, Wiltshire SP1 3AE (01722) 330749* **£50***; 4 rms, some with own bthrm. Spotlessly kept no smoking house with friendly owners, good breakfasts, and pretty garden; nr cathedral; no children

SALISBURY SU1329 **Old Mill** *Town Path, West Harnham, Salisbury, Wiltshire SP2 8EU (01722) 322364* **£70**, plus special breaks; 11 comfortably converted rms. Based on Wiltshire's first paper mill and warehouse – there's been a mill here since 1135 – with good, honest English cooking in restaurant where the mill race rushes through, terrace out by mill pool, and meadow walks with classic cathedral views; good honest English cooking in evening restaurant and beamed bar

SALISBURY SU1428 **Rose & Crown** *Harnham Rd, Harnham, Salisbury, Wiltshire SP2 8JQ (01722) 399955* **£130***, plus special breaks; 28 rms in the original building or smart, modern extension. It's almost worth a visit just for the view – well nigh identical to that in the most famous Constable painting of Salisbury Cathedral; elegantly restored inn with friendly beamed and timbered bar, log fire, good bar and restaurant food, and charming Avonside garden; disabled access

SALISBURY SU1431 **Stratford Lodge** *4 Park Lane, Salisbury, Wiltshire SP1 3NP (01722) 325177* **£60**, plus special breaks; 8 rms. Warmly friendly and relaxed Victorian house with antique furnishings, fresh flowers, generous helpings of very good carefully prepared evening food, super breakfasts in conservatory, and quiet garden; cl 23 Dec–1 Jan; children over 5; limited disabled access

SUTTON VENY ST9041 **Old House** *Sutton Veny, Warminster, Wiltshire BA12 7AQ (01985) 840344* **£68**; 3 rms. Carefully modernised 17th-c thatched house in four quiet acres, with winter log fires, nice food using home-grown vegetables, and good breakfasts; cl Christmas and New Year; children by arrangement

TEFFONT EVIAS ST9931 **Howards House** *Teffont Evias, Salisbury, Wiltshire SP3 5RJ (01722) 716392* **£125**, plus special breaks; 9 rms. Very well run, welcoming and comfortable little hotel in two acres of gardens surrounded by quiet countryside; log fire and lots of fresh flowers from the garden in restful sitting room, delicious food (using their own vegetables and herbs), fine breakfasts, well chosen wines, and extremely good service; cl Christmas

UPPER MINETY SU0091 **Flisteridge Cottage** *Flisteridge Rd, Upper Minety, Malmesbury, Wiltshire SN16 9PS (01666) 860343* **£38***; 3 rms, 1 with own bthrm. Warmly welcoming and homely no smoking cottage with pretty garden, woodburner in sitting room, good breakfasts with home-made preserves (evening meals by arrangement), and friendly helpful owners; children over 11; well behaved pets by arrangement

WARMINSTER ST8944 **Bishopstrow House** *Bishopstrow, Warminster, Wiltshire BA12 9HH (01985) 212312* **£195**, plus special breaks; 32 sumptuous rms, some with jacuzzi. Charming ivy-clad Georgian house in 27 acres with heated indoor and outdoor swimming pools, indoor and outdoor tennis courts, fitness centre and beauty treatment rooms, and own fishing on River Wylye; very relaxed friendly atmosphere, log fires, lovely fresh flowers, antiques and fine paintings in boldly decorated day rooms, and really impressive food; disabled access

WARMINSTER ST8745 **Old Bell** *42 Market Pl, Warminster, Wiltshire BA12 9AN (01985) 216611* **£55**, plus special breaks; 20 comfortable rms. Old-world country-town hotel with traditional bar food, bistro and restaurant, good choice of wines, pretty central courtyard, and friendly service; lots to do nearby

WINSLEY ST7960 **Burghope Manor** *Winsley, Bradford-on-Avon, Wiltshire BA15 2LA (01225) 723557* **£85***; 6 rms with newly refurbished bthrms. Lovely 13th-c family home in attractive countryside, with carefully preserved old rooms and an interesting fireplace engraved with Elizabethan writing, antiques in big drawing room, welcoming caring owners, nice breakfasts, and evening meals by arrangement; wknd self-catering in Dower House in grounds; cl Christmas and New Year; children over 10

WOOTTON BASSETT SU0783 **Marsh Farm Hotel** *Wootton Bassett, Swindon, Wiltshire SN4 8ER (01793) 848044* **£70**w; 38 rms. Handsome Victorian farmhouse in landscaped grounds with particularly warm and friendly atmosphere, comfortable lounge, convivial bar, and enjoyable food in relaxed restaurant; disabled access

To see and do

Wiltshire Family Attraction of the Year

SWINDON SU1385 **Steam** (Kemble Drive, next to the well signed Great Western Designer Outlet Centre) Set in the former works of the Great Western Railway, this is a much enlivened version of the old GWR Museum, brought bang up to date thanks to £11 million from the Lottery, the local council, and the outlet centre next door. At the railway's peak 12,000 people worked here to produce everything needed to keep it running; you can see several of the locomotives built here, but there's as much of an emphasis on the people who worked and travelled on the railways as there is on the trains. Good reconstructions bring to life the sights and sounds of the railway age, and you may come across entertaining talks from people who used to work here. There's plenty to keep small and overgrown children amused, from the various touch screen games and hands-on activities to a tracklay out where younger visitors have fun shunting the trucks. Particularly good fun is a simulator that re-creates the experience of riding on a steam train footplate; it shakes about as if you were moving, and filmed images of the countryside go rushing by. Other displays focus on Isambard Kingdom Brunel and the GWR's days as the 'holiday line', and you can watch restoration work on old engines and carriages. There's a good programme of varied events, and extra activities in the school holidays – in summer that may include actors reliving the 1919 Railway Strike, or even Victorian music hall. This has got much wider appeal than many steam-themed collections, and all ages seem to get something out of it. Meals, snacks, shop, disabled access; cl 25–26 Dec; (01793) 466646; *£4.80 (*£3 children). A family ticket, for two adults and two children, is £13. The Old Pattern Shop has decent food, with good provision for children.

ALTON BARNES SU1061
Kennet & Avon Canal Here the canal lies close enough to Pewsey Down nature reserve for an afternoon's walk to incorporate both features; the spine of the downs here is followed by the Wansdyke, an ancient earthwork which runs across the downs for miles from Morgans Hill nr Calne nearly as far as the Savernake Forest.
ANSTY ST9526
Pleasant village, notable for England's

tallest maypole.

AVEBURY SU1070

Alexander Keiller Museum A succinct introduction to the archaeological wonders of the area. Keiller was the marmalade magnate who was responsible for excavating the site in the 1920s and 1930s, in the most unusual way – he bought the entire village, and re-erected the stones, many of which had become buried or dilapidated. Shop, disabled access; cl 24–26 Dec, 1 Jan; (01672) 539250; £2; NT.

Avebury Manor (behind church on High St) Much altered house, formerly a monastery, with the present buildings dating from the early 16th c, with Queen Anne alterations and then Edwardian renovations. The attractive topiary and flower gardens contain medieval walls and some ancient evergreens. Disabled access to most of garden (but not to house); open pm only Tues, Weds, Sun and bank hol Mons Apr–Oct; (01672) 539250; £3.50, gardens only £2.50; NT.

Avebury Stone Circle This spectacular 4,500-year-old henge monument encompasses the pretty village – where Stones does good vegetarian food, and the Red Lion's position within the circle makes it special too. It's the largest stone circle in Europe, the 200 surviving stones enclosed in a massive earthen rampart nearly a mile in circumference. This itself once surrounded two smaller stone circles.

Fyfield Down SU1470 Primeval-feeling and unkempt, scattered with outcrops known as sarsen stones, the raw material of Avebury stone circle and of part of Stonehenge.

Silbury Hill SU1068 This towering prehistoric mound, purpose unknown, is the largest man-made mound in Europe – it would have taken a thousand men about ten years to build. In May 2000, a hole 12 metres (40 ft) deep and nearly 2 metres (6 ft) wide suddenly appeared at the top; it may be part of a shaft dug in 1776 by treasure-hunters. There's a parking and viewing area, or you can walk the short distance from Avebury car park; there's no access to the summit of the hill.

West Kennett Avenue Leading away from the circle is this 1½-mile avenue of stones, virtually destroyed by ploughing and mostly replaced by modern concrete posts. It leads to the site of the Sanctuary, a stone circle (on the site of an earlier wooden temple) that was similarly razed and marked out in the 20th c with posts.

West Kennett Long Barrow The prehistoric remains of a 5,000-year-old chambered tomb and barrow, where several dozen people were buried – take a torch if you want to venture in behind the massive entrance stone: the chamber with two side chapels runs some 9 metres (30 ft) or more into the barrow. The Waggon & Horses at Beckhampton (of *Pickwick Papers* fame) is quite handy.

Windmill Hill Reached by footpath NW, this, the earliest monument in the area, is a Neolithic enclosure dating back some 5,000 years. There's not a great deal to see apart from mild lumps, but the site is quite evocative.

BARBURY CASTLE SU1476 One of Wiltshire's 4,500 recorded ancient sites. Many are scarcely a lump in the ground, but this Iron Age camp at the northernmost point of the Marlborough Downs, splendidly remote and atmospheric, still has formidable ramparts. There is a car park nearby, but you can also walk up to it from Ogbourne St George along Smeathe's Ridge, a preserved stretch of downland (gorse and all). The Castle is on the long-distance Ridgeway Path.

BISHOPS CANNINGS SU0364 Attractive village, with an outstanding **church**. The Crown has good value food.

BOX ST8268 An attractive up-and-down village, its interesting parts hidden down the steep valley below the A4, with cottages and houses using the same stone that's been quarried nearby since Roman times. There's a story that on 9 Apr, Brunel's birthday, the rising sun shines right through the great railway tunnel he quarried through the hill above here (you can see the restored grand entrance from the A4).

Hazelbury Manor 🏛 (off B3109 just E) Richly varied landscaped gardens, with a medieval archery alley, stone and yew circles, fountain, waterfall, pond, large rockery, formal areas and laburnum walk, all laid out as a sort of giant maze. Open by appointment, (01225) 812952; £2.80. In Chapel Plaister on the way, look out for the 15th-c chapel for Glastonbury pilgrims on the little hilltop green. The Quarrymans Arms tucked away on Box Hill is good for lunch.

BRADFORD-ON-AVON ST8260
Attractive hillside town given a distinguished air by the same sort of golden stone as was used in Bath; it's very steep, and has some handsome buildings reflecting its past wealth as a wool town – and quite a few serious antiques shops. Nr the Norman parish church is a tall narrow late **Saxon church**, unusual for having virtually no later additions. The Dandy Lion (Market St) is good for lunch. A medieval **tithe barn** can be seen at nearby Barton Farm (Pound Lane) down by the river and canal, its massive stone-slab roof supported by an impressive network of great beams and rafters.

Avoncliff A short walk along the canal, this quite steep gorge is shared by canal, river and railway, the canal disdainfully stepping over the river by way of an aqueduct – currently being restored. The Cross Guns has remarkable views over it, and is a good place for lunch.

Iford Manor (just past Westwood) Notable for its stylish Edwardian Italianate riverside terraced garden, with romantic cloisters, colonnade and statues; house not open. Teas wknds and bank hols, May–Aug; open pm Sun and bank hols Apr–Oct, and pm daily (exc Mon and Fri) May–Sept; (01225) 863146; £3.

Westwood Manor (above Avoncliff, just SW) Fully furnished 15th-c stone manor house with its original Gothic and Jacobean windows, fine 17th-c plasterwork, and modern topiary garden. No facilities, open pm only Sun, Tues and Weds Apr–Sept; (01225) 863374; £3.70; NT. The New Inn in Westwood village has decent food, and the **church** has some interesting late medieval stained glass.

BROKERSWOOD ST8352

Woodland Heritage Museum 80 acres of woodland, with lakes, campsites, conservation displays, summer guided walks, adventure playground, and a little railway. Snacks, shop; park open daily; (01373) 823800; £2.50. The Woolpack at Beckington has good food.

BROMHAM ST9464
Sandridge Farm They cure bacon and Wiltshire ham using traditional recipes; also summer nature trail through woodland and pig paddocks (wellies recommended). Shop (good bacon and sausages), disabled access; cl Sun; (01380) 850304; free. The Greyhound in the village has good food, especially fish.

CALNE ST9770
Bowood (off A4) The extensive Capability Brown parkland and colourful pleasure gardens are the glory of Bowood, with their temples, cascades and hermit's cave shielded from the outside world by further miles of partly wooded grounds; in May and Jun a woodland garden is open for rhododendron walks. Much of the main building was demolished in 1955, but there's plenty left, inc the impressive library designed by Robert Adam. Excellent collection of English watercolours, and an outstanding adventure playground. Joseph Priestley discovered oxygen here in 1772. Meals, snacks, shop, garden centre, limited disabled access; cl Nov–Mar; (01249) 812102; £5.90. The Lansdowne Arms at Derry Hill, nr the house, is popular for lunch, and Calne also has a **motor museum**.

CASTLE COMBE ST8477
For many the prettiest village in Britain, this has a classic group of stone-tiled Cotswoldy cottages by the turreted **church** at the bottom of a tree-clad hill running down to a trout stream and its ancient stone bridge. Preservation of the village is taken so seriously that you won't even see television aerials on the houses; several villagers occasionally open their beautifully kept gardens for charity. Best of all during the week out of season; at other times it does get a great many visitors, even though the car park is sited some way up the hill. The charming old Castle Inn has good food.

The village has surroundings that are equally appealing, and attractive paths along deep peaceful valleys.

CASTLE EATON SU1495
Attractive village, by a quiet stretch of the upper Thames, pleasant for strolling.

CHERHILL DOWN SU0469
This large NT area of ancient downland has free access for walkers. A range of man-made features of various periods adorn its slopes, inc a figure of a white horse, an Iron Age hill fort (Oldbury Castle), the mid-19th-c Lansdowne Monument, and an assortment of long barrows, tumuli and ancient field systems; the site is rich in chalkland flora such as orchids, and associated butterfly and bird life.

CHICKSGROVE ST9730
Charming tucked-away hamlet; peaceful walk to Sutton Mandeville church, and back by the Nadder Valley.

CHILMARK ST9732
Attractive village, with a decent partly 13th-c **church**. The Black Dog, with links to early Massachussetts settlers, does interesting food.

CHOLDERTON SU2042
Cholderton Rare Breeds Farm 🖼 (Amesbury Rd, just off the A338) Fun, friendly and well laid out place, good for families with young children. There are plenty of opportunities to get close to the animals inc the youngest of the 60 or so breeds of rabbit they keep. You can also pet pygmy goats and sheep, and other friendly residents include Hannah the shire horse, Coco the donkey, and Ebenezer the goat. A long-standing favourite with visitors is their national Grunt pig-racing (twice a day at wknds and in school hols, usually around 12.30 and 3.30pm); also tractor and trailer rides, pony rides for children, and a couple of play areas, one specifically for under-7s. Nature trails lace through orchards and woodland, and there are recently extended tranquil water gardens in the attractive grounds. Meals, snacks (good cream teas), shop, disabled access; cl Nov–Mar; (01980) 629438; £4.25.

CLEY HILL ST8344
This steep-sided hill just W of Warminster involves a short, puffy stroll to the Iron Age hill fort at its summit, looking across Longleat Park.

CORSHAM ST8770
Corsham Court Fine house and park begun in 1582 but subsequently added to and developed by those busy masters Capability Brown, John Nash, Robert Adam and Humphrey Repton. The paintings are among the best at any stately home in the country, inc works by Caravaggio, Reynolds, Rubens and Van Dyck. In the gardens, the peaceful lake and a Georgian bath house are patrolled by a number of peacocks – if they haven't decided to wander off into the village. Shop, disabled access; cl am, Mon (except bank hols), wkdys Jan–mid-Mar, and all Dec (01249) 701610; £5, £2 garden only. Nearby are some attractive former weavers' cottages; the **church**, on the edge of the park, is largely 12th-c, partly Saxon. The town has a surprising number of antiques shops, some very fine, and the Methuen Arms is good for lunch.

CRANBORNE CHASE ST9319
Some of the finest walking in the S of Wiltshire is to be found here close to the Dorset border, where the county's abundant chalk downland shows at its best. A good example is Ashcombe Bottom N of Tollard Royal, a deep remote valley which plunges into the heart of the Chase.

CRICKLADE SU1093
Small town quietly separated from the busy A419, with some attractive buildings and a glorious tower crowning the fine parish church. At the end of the High St, just N of the Thames, a path on the left off the slip road heading back towards the A419 leads to a broad riverside meadow kept unimproved for decades, and mown only in July after the numerous wild flowers have seeded. The Vale and White Hart have popular food.

CROFTON SU2662
Crofton Beam Engines Still pumping water into the Kennet & Avon Canal, the oldest working beam engines in the world, an 1812 Boulton & Watt, and an 1845 Harveys of Hayle. Snacks, shop; open Easter–Sept, engines usually static, but in steam bank hols and last wknds of Jun, July and Sept; (01672) 870300; static £2, steam wknds £3.50. Nearby Wilton village is picturesque,

with a windmill; the Swan there is good for family lunches, and the Harrow at Little Bedwyn has good food.

DEVIZES SU0061

Lots of grand old buildings in this interesting and friendly town, and a good town trail takes most of them in. The 29 locks of the **Kennet & Avon Canal** coming up Caen Hill from the W form one of the longest flights of locks in the country. The HQ of the Canal Trust on the Wharf has a museum and information centre; (01380) 729489; £1.50. The Bear Hotel, Elm Tree and Castle, all tied to Wadworths the local brewery, are all good for lunch.
Broadleas (Potterne Rd) Rare plants in secluded dell among rhododendrons and other fine flowering shrubs, unusual trees, spring and autumn colour too. Teas Sun, unusual plant sales; open pm Sun, Weds and Thurs, Apr–Oct; (01380) 722035; £3.
Devizes Museum (Long St) First-class local history, particularly good on finds from the area's ancient sites (the Bronze Age gallery is especially interesting); art gallery with John Piper window. Shop, some disabled access; cl Sun, most bank hols, Christmas; (01380) 727369; £3 (free on Mons).

DINTON SU0031

Philipps House and Dinton Park Fine early 19th-c mansion with interesting Portland stone staircase and underfloor heating system. The surrounding parkland offers plenty of scope for a stroll. Some disabled access; house open Sat am and Mon pm Apr–Oct, park open all year; (01985) 843600; house *£3, park free.

EBBLE VALLEY SU0024

The valley of the Ebble chalk-stream winds prettily through a sleepy stream of villages from Odstock to Alvediston – a delightful drive.

FIGSBURY RING SU1833

Iron Age hill fort with good views over Salisbury.

FOVANT SU0128

Regimental Badges Huge chalk carvings on the escarpment (visible from the road), cut by regiments stationed here in World War I – a sight to rival England's various white horses. The Pembroke Arms, with interesting memorabilia of the time, has good value food.

GREAT BEDWYN SU2764

Bedwyn Stone Museum Fascinating little open-air museum demonstrating the ancient art of stonemasonry (the nearby church has fine examples of the finished product). Disabled access but a bit bumpy in places; cl 25 Dec, (01672) 870234; free. The Cross Keys has decent food.

HAYDOWN HILL SU3156

Reached from the E by a walk up from Vernham Dean in Hampshire, this has the ramparts of a hill fort bounded by steep gradients on its S side; the three counties of Berkshire, Hampshire and Wiltshire meet close by at SU350590.

HOLT ST8663

Great Chalfield Manor (N of Holt) Beautiful moated manor house, restored in 1905 and still with its original Great Hall. Open Tues–Thurs pm Apr–Oct, guided tours only, at 12.15, 2.15, 3, 3.45 and 4.30pm; (01225) 782239 to book; *£3.70; NT. Next door is a small parish 13th-c **church**.
The Courts Garden (B3107) Weavers used to come here to settle their disputes; the 15th-c house isn't open, but there are lovely and extensive formal gardens full of yew hedges, pools and borders, with the other half of the grounds given over to wild flowers among interesting trees. Some disabled access; cl am, Sat, and Nov–Mar; (01225) 782340; £3.10; NT. The Toll Gate (Ham Green) now does interesting lunches.

KENNET & AVON CANAL ST8559

This restored canal runs right across the county, and there are pleasant boat trips from several places; Devizes or Wootton Rivers for example, or the notably friendly hire companies at Hilperton and Bradford-on-Avon. In the canal's restoration, a great deal of attention has been paid to the natural environment, so it's attractive for walks alongside; in winter you may even see a kingfisher flashing along it. For a more sedentary view, try the Beehive in Bradford-on-Avon (Trowbridge Rd), Barge Inn at Seend Cleeve ST9361, French Horn at Pewsey Wharf SU1560, Barge at Honeystreet SU1061 or Bridge Inn at Horton SU0563. The Golden

Swan at Wilcot SU1461, Crown at Bishops Cannings SU0363, Somerset Arms at Semington ST3960 and Hop Pole at Limpley Stoke ST7861 are also near it.

LACOCK ST9168

A favourite village of both visitors and film-makers, its grid of quiet and narrow streets a delightful harmony of mellow brickwork, lichened stone and timber-and-plaster. The **church** is 15th-c, and nothing in the village looks more recent than 18th-c. It's remained so remarkably unspoilt because most of its buildings were owned for centuries by the Talbot family, until they left them to the NT in 1944. It gets very busy in summer, but the Trust has preserved it against a surfeit of antiques shops (you'll find all you want in the nearby old market town of Melksham). The village does on the other hand have a splendid collection of pubs – the George is the best.

Lacock Abbey 🔲 Tranquil spread of mellow stone buildings, around a central timber-gabled courtyard, based on the little-altered 13th-c abbey. Tudor additions include a romantic octagonal tower, and there was a successful 18th-c Gothicisation. Surrounded by quiet meadows and trees, this was the setting for Fox Talbot's experiments which in 1835 led to the creation of the world's first photographic negative – a picture of part of the abbey itself. There's an interesting museum devoted to this in a 16th-c barn at the gates, and the gardens are evidence of Fox Talbot's skills in other fields. Limited disabled access; open daily Apr–Oct (plus grounds and museum only in Mar), abbey cl ams and all day Tues; (01249) 730227; £5.80, £3.70 museum, grounds and cloisters only; NT. The photography museum may also open some winter wknds.

LONGLEAT ST8043

(off A362 4m W of Warminster) Easily a full day's activities on this well organised estate, which has been open to the public for over 50 years. Children will probably get most excited about the safari park, which as well as the famous lions includes rhinos, camels, elephants and a rare white tiger.

Among what seem like hundreds of other attractions are displays of parrots, butterflies, and sea lions, a narrow-gauge railway, collection of doll's houses, and exhibitions based around the worlds of Postman Pat and Dr Who. A splendid big play area is themed around a mock castle, and there's a simulator ride and children's pets' corner. Older visitors may prefer the formal gardens laid out by Capability Brown, and of course the handsome 16th-c house itself, much restored inside, but still with impressively grand formal rooms, and the individual murals of the colourful current Marquess of Bath. He has had several mazes and labyrinths built around the grounds; one is still Britain's longest permanent one, another has a slightly saucy shape that can be appreciated only from the Marquis's private roof terrace, and the most bizarre is a bewildering knot of mirrors, with animatronic effects adding to the confusion. Part of the grounds were recently used to film a Bollywood blockbuster. Meals, snacks, shop, disabled access; most attractions, inc safari park, are cl Nov–Apr, but the house is open all year (exc 25 Dec); (01985) 844400; you can get individual tickets to each of the attractions (the house or safari park on their own are £6, and grounds only £2), but it works out much cheaper to buy the all-in Passport ticket for £13 (£11 for children). The Bath Arms at Horningsham at the S entrance to the park, and the White Hart at Corsley on the N side, are good for lunch. One of England's three **Center Parcs** is nearby, a rewarding place to stay with excellent leisure facilities; (0990) 200300.

LUDGERSHALL SU2651

Ludgershall Castle The ruins of a Royal castle and hunting palace, still with some of the original large Norman earthworks, as well as the later flint walling; free. The **church** is also Norman; the Bull & Butcher has reasonably priced food. The nearby area is very pretty and unspoilt, the little villages of the Chutes, Tangley and Vernham Dean straddling the Hampshire border all worth a look (with the pubs over that way worth exploring too).

LYDIARD PARK SU1084 (nr M4 junction 16, or A3102) Painstakingly restored grand Georgian house, with interesting early wallpaper, rare painted glass window, and elegant furnishings much as they would have been when first installed. Extensive lawns, lakes and well wooded parkland, with nature walks and adventure playgrounds. Snacks, shop, disabled access; cl 1–2pm (exc school hols), Sun am, Good Fri, 25–26 Dec; (01793) 770401; car parking £1, house £1.20 – quite a bargain. The adjacent parish **church** has interesting monuments to the St John family, who lived in the house for 500 years.

MALMESBURY ST9387 Yet another charming old town, especially around the green facing its serene Norman **abbey**, from the tower of which a medieval monk called Elmer made one of the earliest semi-successful attempts at flight – he covered a couple of hundred yards, but did break both legs when he crash-landed. The picturesque Old Bell is almost as old as the abbey beside it. The B roads radiating from here are all quite pleasant drives.

MARLBOROUGH SU1868 One of the area's most attractive towns; its very pleasing wide High St has a market each Weds and Sat. Its annual autumn Mop Fair (as in most market towns, formerly for the hiring of servants) has been revived here as a general celebration. Even the more modern additions don't look obtrusively out of place among the harmonious mix of Georgian and Tudor buildings. The Sun (by St Peter's church, where Cardinal Wolsey was inducted as a priest) and Bear are useful for lunch. The Broad Hinton road N gives a good feel of the downs' great open spaces, as does the Manton–Alton Priors road to the SW, passing one of the area's several white horses cut into the chalk, and leading into a pleasant valley drive through Allington and Horton to Devizes. To the E, the quiet road along the Kennet Valley has some attractive views, with good food stops at the Red Lion in Axford and Bell in

Ramsbury, and pleasant walks; there are also walks through the surviving miles of Savernake Forest woodland.

MERE ST8132 Attractive village, dominated by its 30-metre (100-ft) church tower, and with good views from Castle Hill.

White Sheet Hill Easily reached from Mere (via a road bridge over the busy A303) or Stourton, this lofty chalk downland is studded with antiquities – among them a Neolithic causewayed camp and Bronze Age barrows. It's a good site for cowslips, orchids and such butterflies as adonis and chalkhill blues.

MIDDLE WOODFORD SU1236 **Heale Gardens** Eight acres of lovely formal gardens beside the Avon chalk stream, with lots of varied plants; the water garden is especially nice in spring and autumn. Snacks, shop, specialist plant sales with many rare types propagated from the main gardens, shop, disabled access; cl Christmas; (01722) 782504; £3.25. The Wheatsheaf in nearby Lower Woodford is popular for lunch, and this Salisbury road along the Avon's quieter bank is a pretty drive (as is the continuation N of Amesbury, through Fittleworth and East Chisenbury).

NOMANSLAND SU2517 **Forest-edge walks** There are some pleasant walks in countryside that's unusual for Wiltshire, around the Lamb down on the edge of the New Forest at Nomansland.

PEPPERBOX HILL SU2125 (5m SE of Salisbury) Named after the strangely shaped 17th-c tower on its summit. You can't get into the tower, but the site commands fine views over Salisbury itself, and S as far as Southampton. The Hook & Glove at Farley has decent food.

Bentley Wood Beyond East Grimstead N of here, a nature reserve with good walks.

SALISBURY SU1429 A beautiful and gently relaxed city, with a good many fine old buildings, particularly around the lovely cathedral close. The most extensive close in the country, it's always been a distinct area of town, and the gates to it are still locked each night. The buildings cover a variety of architectural styles from the

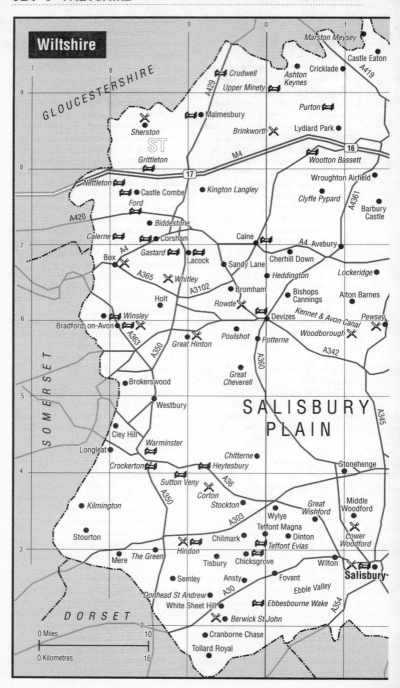

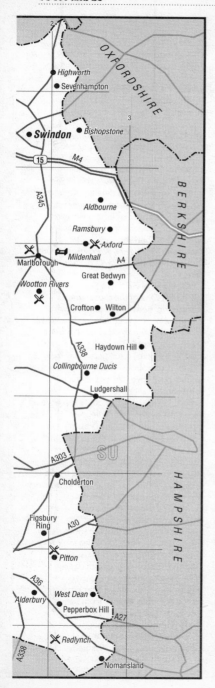

13th c to the present, and while of course its great glory is the elegant cathedral itself, you can't help being struck by how impeccably mown the lawns are. Outside the close, there are some interesting antiques and other shops, and the broad Market Sq still has a traditional market each Tues and Sat; parking in town can be tricky then. The Haunch of Venison (Minster St) is an interesting old town tavern, while the no smoking New Inn (New St) is good for lunch, as is the waterside Old Mill out at West Harnham. Besides places we describe individually below, the close also includes the striking St Anne's Gate, a regimental museum, and the peaceful riverside North Canonry Gardens (occasionally open in summer – check with the cathedral, (01722) 555120).

Medieval Hall (West Walk, The Close) The regular 40-min sound and picture shows in this 13th-c hall provide a colourful introduction to the city and its environs. Snacks, shop, disabled access (but not facilities); performances on the hour from 11am–5pm (doors open 20 mins before each show) Apr–Sept; (01722) 412472; *£1.50.

Mompesson House (The Close) Exquisite Queen Anne building, probably the most interesting in the close, with period furnishings, china and paintings, remarkable collection of 18th-c drinking glasses, and interestingly carved oak staircase. Teas, some disabled access; cl am, all day Thurs and Fri, and Nov–Mar; (01722) 335659; £3.40, 80p gardens only; NT. The NT shop is a couple of minutes' walk away on the High St.

Old Sarum (off A345 2m N) This substantial and easily defended Iron Age hill fort continued as a town right through the Roman occupation and Dark Ages into Norman times. In the early 13th c there was a general move to the much more fertile site of the present city, and the fort gradually fell into decline, becoming a quarry for the new centre; consequently there's not much left, but the views are splendid, and the foundations give interesting clues to ancient architecture and styles. Snacks, shop, limited disabled access; cl 24–26 Dec, 1 Jan;

(01722) 335398; £2; EH.

Salisbury & South Wiltshire Museum (Kings House, The Close) Local history and archaeology in lovely building, with excellent Stonehenge gallery, collections of Wedgwood, costume, lace and embroidery, and some beautiful local watercolours by Turner. One of its more obscure but intriguing exhibits is an aestel, an Anglo-Saxon jewel with links to King Alfred, found by a metal-detector enthusiast in a Wiltshire field. Meals, snacks, shop, disabled access to ground floor; cl Sun exc pm July–Aug, 24–26 Dec; (01722) 332151; £3.

Salisbury Cathedral Begun in 1220 and completed in only 38 years – giving a rare uniformity of style. The magnificent spire (added in 1315 along with the tower) is at 123 metres (404 ft) the tallest in the country, and many would say the finest in the world. Also notable are the 14th-c clock (the oldest working mechanical clock in the world, its mechanism on close view), and the tomb of the first Earl of Salisbury, who gave the church one of only four surviving copies of the Magna Carta; it's still on display in the Chapter House, alongside remarkable early silver. The cloisters stand out too. Snacks, shop, disabled access; cl during services, and on Good Fri; (01722) 555120; £3 suggested donation. The guides are entertaining and knowledgeable. There's a good view of the cathedral from outside the 13th-c Bishop's Palace, though the one immortalised by Constable, and still much as then despite road-scheme threats, is from across the meadows by the River Avon over by West Harnham.

St Thomas's church (off The Close) Built for cathedral workers and in part slightly older than it; has a scary medieval Doom painting.

SALISBURY PLAIN ST9648
Better for driving over than walking – an almost unbroken expanse of rolling high ground, a mixture of pasture and broad unhedged arable fields intersected by tank-training tracks. The A360 gives a good feel of its emptiness. The county council has a leaflet mapping out clearly way-marked walks around the edges of the Army's Imber firing range, totalling some 30 miles for the complete circuit: generally peaceful countryside with large-scale arable farming, but some wide views and maybe the sight of tank and infantry training.

SANDY LANE ST9668
Attractive village; the road from here through Bowden Hill is the prettiest approach to Lacock.

SEMLEY ST8926
Attractive village, with an interesting church; the Benett Arms is good.

SEVENHAMPTON SU2188
Roves Farm The eight-week spring lambing season is the time to come to this friendly sheep farm; pig, sheep and goat racing, trailer rides and shearing in summer. Snacks, shop, disabled access; open Weds–Sun and bank hols Mar–Sept; (01793) 763939; £4. The Saracens Head in Highworth has good value food.

STONEHENGE SU1142
(off A344) One of the most famous prehistoric monuments in the world; everyone knows what it looks like, and how they got the stones here has been pretty much sorted out (the larger ones local, the smaller ones all the way from Wales), but nobody's really sure exactly what Stonehenge (with its careful astronomical alignments) was for. Some experts now reckon it could even have been built by the French. In the interests of conservation, you can't normally go right up to the stones, but you can get pretty close and the fact that people are kept back means that your photos won't be cluttered by the crowds. The best views are very early in the morning from the track from Larkhill, on the other side of the A344, or on a cold clear winter evening looking W past the monument towards the sunset; the ancient stones look very impressive silhouetted against the sky. Even in the crowded light of day the place never quite loses its power to inspire awe, although the car park area would definitely benefit from some investment. The busy main roads nearby detract too, although improvements here are at last in the pipeline. Snacks, shop, disabled access; (01980) 624715; cl 24–26 Dec; *£4 (inc very good Walkman tour); EH. On a

handful of dates through the year you can still wander among the stones by joining one of the coach tours of mysterious sites organised by Astral Travels, (0870) 902 0908; these cost around £50 for a whole day and currently leave only from London, but it's worth it just for the moment when they set you loose at Stonehenge with dowsing rods (the tours take in other local archaeological sites, too). Good walks from here around associated ancient monuments (leaflet available in the car park). There's good pick-your-own fruit late Jun–late July at Rolleston Manor Farm on the B3086 NW.

Woodhenge The scant traces of another prehistoric monument further E which consisted of six rings of timber posts in a ditch; the positions are now marked by concrete posts, and a cairn marks the central spot where the tomb of a little girl ceremonially axed to death was found.

STOURTON ST7835

Stourhead (off B3092) Marvellous 18th-c landscape garden, gradually laid out in Italian style by the banker Henry Hoare II following his return from an Italian tour; a beautifully harmonious landscape of temples, lakes, bridges and splendid trees and other plants. Remarkable views into Somerset from King Alfred's Tower, the tall 18th-c folly at the far end, though there are 221 steps (cl Mon and Fri, and winter). The early Georgian Palladian house has some good Chippendale furniture, and the church in the grounds is in a lovely hillside setting. Meals, snacks, shop, disabled access; garden open all year, house pm daily exc Thurs and Fri, Apr–Oct; (01747) 841152; £8.50 for gardens and house, £4.80 for one or the other (£1.10 less for gardens Nov–Feb) – if you can do only one, make it the gardens; NT. The Red Lion at Kilmington, and Spread Eagle at Stourhead's entrance, are useful for lunch.

SWINDON SU1484

Much older than you might think, this bustling market town and business centre was caught up with a vengeance in the railway age, and in the Railway Village had one of the earliest examples of a planned workers' estate. The Savoy

(Regent Circus) has decent food in an interestingly converted cinema.

National Monuments Record Centre (Great Western Village, off Kemble Drive) The public archive of English Heritage, providing information on the architecture and archaeology of the country. Lots of photographs (inc some from the mid-19th c, and aerial shots of all of England), plus maps, plans and data about historical buildings and ancient sites. A gallery hosts interesting temporary exhibitions; guided tours of the building (the former HQ of the Great Western Railway) leave from here at 2.15pm on one Sat every month – best to check on (01793) 414617, (£2.75). Meals, snacks, shop, disabled access; archive open Tues–Fri and one Sat per month, gallery open Weds–Sun, centre cl Christmas–New Year; (01793) 414600; free.

Railway Village Museum (Faringdon Rd) Restored foreman's house next to the former railway museum, furnished in typical turn-of-the-century working-class style; £1 (free with ticket to Steam). Not far from here, the Gluepot (Emlyn Sq) has decent food.

Steam See separate family panel on p.617.

Swindon & Cricklade Railway (Blunsdon, off B4553 N) One of the only live steam projects in the area, gradually being restored, with occasional trips through the countryside, and small museum. Snacks, shop, disabled access; cl wkdys, 25–26 Dec; (01793) 771615 for train times; around £5.

Swindon Museum & Art Gallery (Bath Rd) Includes works by important 20th-c artists such as Moore and Sutherland. Shop, limited disabled access; cl Sun am, bank hols; (01793) 466556; free.

TEFFONT MAGNA ST9832

Farmer Giles Farmstead Friendly working dairy farm, with 150 cows milked every afternoon; children can feed lambs and other animals, or simply sit and stroke them. Also tractor rides, play areas, old farming equipment, and small vineyard. Meals, snacks, shop, disabled access; cl wkdys Nov–Mar; (01722) 716338; £3.95. The village is very attractive, full of charming stone-built cottages with neatly banked stone-walled gardens; the Black Horse has good food.

TISBURY ST9429

Charming small town, left behind by the main roads so largely unspoilt, with some fine old buildings, riverside church, and just outside to the E an immensely long medieval tithe barn. The lovely old Crown does decent food.

Old Wardour Castle (a couple of miles S) Remains of a substantial 14th-c lakeside castle. Though badly damaged in the Civil War, its walls still stand to their original 18 metres (60 ft), and you can walk almost to the top. It's a lovely peaceful setting, landscaped in the 18th c (and used for Kevin Costner's *Robin Hood* in the 20th). Snacks, shop, disabled access to grounds only; cl 1–2pm and all Mon and Tues Nov–Mar, 24–26 Dec, 1 Jan; (01747) 870487; £2; EH.

TOLLARD ROYAL ST9517

Larmer Tree Pleasure Grounds 🔢 (off A354) Attractive Victorian pleasure gardens in the heart of Cranborne Chase. Laid out by General Pitt Rivers, they were the first privately owned gardens open to the public but then closed for almost a century, opening again a few years back. Pheasants, macaws and peacocks wander about ostentatiously, you can play croquet, and the temples and grottoes are an appealing backdrop to the band concerts they have most Suns; also adventure playground and a small museum. Teas (not Mon or Tues), disabled access; open daily exc Sat and special events Easter–Oct; (01725) 516228; £3.50.

WESTBURY ST8951

To the E you can see the huge Westbury **white horse** cut into the chalk of the downs; late 18th-c, it was an 'improvement' on an altogether older one which may have been Saxon, and which faced in the opposite direction. Above the white horse is an extensive Iron Age hill fort, with good views right down to the Mendips in Somerset.

WHITE SHEET HILL ST9424

The Harepath here is a high track giving sweeping views; you can branch off into a forest plantation. Note that Wiltshire has a second hill with the same name, above Mere.

WILTON SU0931

Wilton House 🔢 One of the most satisfying historic houses we know, well organised and friendly, with lots to see. The original house was damaged by a fire in 1647, and superbly redesigned by John Webb and Inigo Jones, the latter responsible for the magnificent Double Cube room. There's an outstanding art collection inc works by Rubens, Van Dyck and Brueghel, as well as fine furnishings, Tudor kitchen, Victorian laundry, and a display of early photographic equipment. Outside are 21 acres of landscaped parkland, with water and rose gardens, cloister garden, woodland walk, and huge adventure playground. Meals, snacks, shop, disabled access; cl Nov–early Apr; (01722) 746720; £7. The ornately Italianate 19th-c **church** incorporates all sorts of more ancient treasures, esp its magnificent medieval Continental stained glass and 2,000-year-old marble pillars. Wiltons (Market Pl) is good for lunch, the Pembroke Arms has a good Sunday carvery, and the charming Victoria & Albert in nearby Netherhampton is nicely off the tourist track, with a pleasant riverside walk into Salisbury.

Wilton Royal Carpet Factory 🔢 (King St) Surprisingly interesting demonstrations of how they make Wilton weaves and Axminster carpets as well as a museum and carpet making exhibition. Tours four times a day between 11am and 5pm, best to book, on (01772) 742733; disabled access; cl 2pm weeks at Christmas; £4. There's now a shopping village next door.

WILTON SU2861

Wilton windmill (off A338 E of Burbage) Wiltshire's only working windmill, built in 1821 after the construction of the Kennet & Avon Canal had diverted the water previously used to power mills. Now restored, it's beautifully floodlit most evenings. Shop (sells flour milled on site); open pm Sun and bank hols Easter–Sept; (01672) 870427; £2. This little village of Wilton (not to be confused with the larger town nr

Salisbury) is attractive; the Swan has decent food.

WROUGHTON AIRFIELD SU1379

Science Museum A storage facility for London's Science Museum, with national collections of aircraft, rockets, hovercraft, and road transport vehicles. Not really aimed at entertaining the general public, it's usually open around ten times a year at wknds (or by appointment Weds pm and Fri am), with lively special events or air displays; disabled access; (01793) 814466 for 2001 dates; £5.

WYLYE SU0037

Attractive village in delightful valley; one lane is called Teapot St.

Other attractive villages, all with decent pubs, include Aldbourne ST2675, Alderbury SU1827, waterside Ashton Keynes SU0494, Axford SU2370, Berwick St John ST9323 (steep walks nearby), Biddestone ST8773, Bishopstone SU2483, Chitterne ST9843 (good walks), Collingbourne Ducis SU2453, Clyffe Pypard SU0777, Donhead St Andrew ST9124, Great Cheverell ST9754, Great Hinton ST9059, Great Wishford SU0735, Heddington ST9966, Highworth SU2092, Kilmington ST7736, Kington Langley ST9277, Lockeridge SU1467 (good walks), Marston Meysey SU1297, Pewsey SU1560, Pitton SU2131 (wood and downland walks), Potterne ST9938, Poulshot ST9559, Ramsbury ST2771, Sherston ST8585, Stockton ST9738, The Green ST8731 (nr East Knoyle), West Dean SU2527, Winsley ST7961 and Wootton Rivers SU1963.

Where to eat

AXFORD SU2370 **Red Lion** *(01672) 520271* Welcoming brick and flint pub with fine views over valley from sheltered garden or bustling beamed and pine-panelled bar, good popular food in bar and no smoking restaurant (enjoyable daily specials and fresh fish and game), decent wines, and well kept real ales; bdrms and self-catering; disabled access. £25|£5

BERWICK ST JOHN ST9422 **Talbot** *The Cross (01747) 828222* Well run and friendly village pub with simply furnished heavily beamed bar, huge inglenook fireplace and decent fresh food in bar and restaurant; cl Sun pm; children over 7 in evening. £18|£6

BOX ST8369 **Quarrymans Arms** *Box Hill (01225) 743569* Tucked-away unspoilt hillside pub with fine views, two small interesting knocked-together rooms with quarrying memorabilia, a wide choice of good home-cooked food, well kept real ales, and very friendly staff; bdrms. £23.50|£6

BRADFORD-ON-AVON ST8260 **Bridge Tea Rooms** *24a Bridge St (01225) 865537* Old-fashioned no smoking 17th-c tearooms with a large choice of teas, lots of coffees, sandwiches and snacks, lovely home-made cakes and pastries, cream teas; waitresses in mob caps and aprons; cl 25–26 Dec.|£4.95

BRADFORD-ON-AVON ST8261 **Dandy Lion** *35 Market St (01225) 863433* Particularly relaxed and friendly place with an interesting and varied mix of people, big windows on either side of the door with a table and chairs in each, high-backed farmhouse chairs and old-fashioned dining chairs on the stripped wood floor, newspapers to read, nostalgic pop, and a snug little back room; very well liked and reasonably priced food, real ales, good coffee, and candlelit upstairs restaurant; disabled access. £19.95|£4.95

BRINKWORTH SU0184 **Three Crowns** *The Street (01666) 510366* Friendly atmosphere in villagey pub with imaginative food from a changing menu that covers an entire wall, many wines by the glass, well kept real ales, elegant no smoking conservatory, and garden looking out towards church and rolling country; get there early as they don't take bookings and it is very busy; disabled access. £25|£7

CORTON ST9340 **Dove** *(01985) 850109* Charming cottagey country pub with an attractively furnished main bar, huge winter log fire in big central fireplace, a mix of chairs and cushioned wall seats, and dining tables in areas leading off, and no smoking conservatory; good inventive well presented food at sensible prices, real ales, several wines by the glass, attentive friendly staff, and daily papers; tables on the neatly kept back lawn; charming bdrms. £20.45|**£6**

GREAT HINTON ST9059 **Linnet** *(01380) 870354* Attractive old brick pub with pretty summer flowering tubs and window boxes; little right-hand bar with lots of interest on the green walls, comfortable wall banquettes, a biggish rather smart dining room with pink ragged walls, bric-a-brac, plenty of dining chairs and tables, reliably good food inc enjoyable bar snacks and imaginative daily specials and evening choices, real ales, quite a few malts, and nice summer Pimms; cl Mon exc bank hols. £19.50|**£5.95**

HINDON ST9033 **Grosvenor Arms** *High St (01747) 820696* Attractively refurbished 18th-c coaching inn with a good relaxing atmosphere in its traditionally pubby bar, flagstones, a lovely log fire, candlelight, and two very high-backed old settles; another bar on the right, civilised no smoking lounge with country magazines; enjoyable popular food inc imaginative daily specials, neat cheerful staff, well kept ales, good house wines, and daily papers; seats in back courtyard; good bdrms. £22.40|**£7.95**

LOWER WOODFORD SU1235 **Wheatsheaf** *(01722) 782203* Prettily set former farmhouse with the bars in original stables and barn, an indoor goldfish pond (crossed by a miniature footbridge), enjoyable popular food, two no smoking areas, well kept real ales, helpful staff, and a big walled garden; cl 25 Dec; good disabled access. £18.50|**£6.25**

MARLBOROUGH SU1969 **Munchies** *8 The Parade (01672) 512649* Lovely beamed building with marvellous range of really interesting and delicious sandwiches with daily changing home-made fillings using the freshest ingredients; cl Sat–Sun; disabled access|**£2**

MARLBOROUGH SU1869 **Polly Tea Rooms** *26 High St (01672) 512146* In centre of pretty High St, well known for very good cream teas, with home-made bread, scones, jams and cakes; also light lunches and cooked breakfasts; cl evenings, and 25–26 Dec; disabled access; set tea **£4.10**

PEWSEY SU1660 **London House** *Market Pl (01672) 564775* Elegant, popular restaurant with a relaxed bar, open fire in cosy sitting room, particularly good, interesting and well prepared food, a thoughtful wine list, and professional service; cl Sun, Mon am,13–21 Sept; children over 9; disabled access. £32|**£10**

PITTON SU2131 **Silver Plough** *White Hill (01722) 712266* Stylish village inn with lots to look at in comfortable beamed front bar, good bar snacks and more elaborate meals with emphasis on fresh fish and seafood, well kept real ales, country wines, and efficient service; cl pms 25–26 Dec; children in snug and restaurant but must be well behaved. £27.50|**£4.95**

REDLYNCH SU2120 **Langley Wood** *(01794) 390348* Very good innovative food and decent wines in homely and warmly friendly creeper-covered restaurant-with-rooms set in its own grounds; cl Mon, Tues, Sun pms; children must behave (small helpings but no special menu); disabled access. £26|**£8**

ROWDE ST9762 **George & Dragon** *High St (01380) 723053* Interesting old pub with log fire and plenty of dark wood, a simple dining room, exceptional imaginative food (esp delicious fresh fish and lovely puddings), good value set lunches, a relaxed atmosphere, friendly efficient service, and well kept real ales; cl Mon, no food Sun, 25 Dec, 1 Jan. £30|**£6**

SALISBURY SU1429 **New Inn** *New St (01722) 327679* Very attractive pub, no smoking throughout, with ancient heavy beams, timbered walls, inglenook fire, panelled dining room, and unpretentious relaxed atmosphere; good range of well presented home-made food inc nice daily specials and hearty puddings, well kept beer, decent wines, friendly helpful staff, and a pleasant walled garden looking up to the nearby cathedral. £19.20|**£5.95**

SHERSTON ST8586 **Rattlebone** *Church St (01666) 840871* 16th-c pub with low beams, country furnishings, big dried-flower arrangements, and a pleasant relaxed atmosphere in several rambling rooms; wide choice of good interesting food, partly no smoking restaurant, decent wines, well kept real ales, lots of malt whiskies, 20 rums, and pretty little garden; cl 25 Dec am; good disabled access. £21|£5

WHITLEY ST8866 **Pear Tree** *Top Lane (01225) 709131* Attractive honey-coloured stone farmhouse with a civilised, friendly and chatty atmosphere, front bar with cushioned window seats, some stripped shutters, a mix of dining chairs around good solid tables, a variety of country pictures, and a little fireplace on the left, with a lovely old stripped stone one on the right; popular big back restaurant, enticing and delicious food served by first-class staff, well kept real ales, a good wine list with 10 by the glass, and seats on the terrace; boules; bdrms; cl pms 25–26, 31 Dec, and cl 1 Jan. £25|£7

WOODBOROUGH SU1159 **Seven Stars** *Bottlesford (01672) 851325* Civilised pub in seven riverside acres, with attractively moulded panelling in the main bar, a hot coal fire in a range at one end and a big log fire at the other, a pleasant mix of seats and tables, cosy nooks, and retired wine bottles on delft shelves; attractive back dining area, exceptionally good daily changing Anglo/French cooking (inc marvellous vegetables, winter game and summer seafood), exemplary wine list with a dozen by the glass, and very friendly owners; cl Sun pm, Mon (open am bank hols); children must be well behaved. £25|£7.95

WOOTTON RIVERS SU1963 **Royal Oak** *(01672) 810322* Prettily thatched 16th-c pub with a relaxed atmosphere, L-shaped dining lounge with woodburner, comfortably furnished timbered bar, very popular food from a huge menu, well kept beer, decent wines and some interesting whiskies, and friendly service; bdrms with help-yourself breakfasts. £18.50|£7

Special thanks to B and K Hypher

WORCESTERSHIRE

A compact county with some inspiring scenery, old-fashioned black and white timbered villages, and seemingly forgotten corners

Though not perhaps a county with obvious appeal to families, there are nevertheless some highly enjoyable outings to be had among the brooding hills and charming towns and villages here. Avoncroft Museum of Buildings, Bromsgrove, with its salvaged period buildings and other intriguing exhibits, is particularly good value, and is probably best for children during one of its lively re-enactments, as is the lively Commandery in Worcester – a must for the battle-minded. The West Midlands Safari Park at Bewdley is very much a full day out, with rare and exotic animals and lots of fairground rides, and nearer Evesham, the Domestic Fowl Trust at Honeybourne is friendly for children too. Kingsford Country Park in the far N of the county, and the grounds around the Broadway Tower (marvellous views from the top) in the S, are pleasant for picnics, and good places to stretch your legs. There are splendid steam train trips on the Severn Valley Railway – one of Britain's most enjoyable.

Worcester is a busy city, but has interesting finds and good museums (some with activities for children).

The extraordinary ruin and splendid church at Great Witley delight with their architectural whimsy, Hanbury Hall is very handsome, and you can admire unusual artworks as well as the flowers at tranquil Burford House Gardens. Budding horticulturists can pick up good gardening tips at Barnard's Green House, Great Malvern, and Webbs Garden Centre in Wychbold – one of the best in the country – has plenty for children, too.

The Malvern Hills, dominating the view from much of the county, stand as a symbol of Englishness, for many people almost inseparable from thoughts of Elgar's music (Lower Broadheath is the place to start the Elgar trail); they also provide one of Britain's great ridgeway walks. On their flanks the sober town of Great Malvern is attractive, as are Evesham and Cotswolds-edge Broadway.

The orchards make blossom time (usually April through early May) and harvest time (September) attractive: local tourist board trails make it easy to see the best of this, especially in the Vale of Evesham – rich farmland and orchard country, full of farm shops. There's an abundance of fresh local asparagus in May. In winter big log fires and generous central heating are the rule – people here really seem to appreciate their warmth. Prices are generally low, making the area good value for short breaks.

Please let us know what you think of places in the *Guide*. Use the report forms at the back of the book or simply write us a letter.

Where to stay

ABBERLEY SO7367 **Elms** *Stockton Rd, Abberley, Worcestershire WR6 6AT (01299) 896666* £140; 20 comfortable rms. Lovely Queen Anne mansion with fine views from the well kept grounds, elegant restful drawing room with antiques, log fires and flowers, other reception rooms with original ornate plasterwork and finely carved fireplaces, very good food and wines in airy restaurant, and friendly efficient staff; children over 12

BROADWAY SP0937 **Broadway Hotel** *The Green, Broadway, Worcestershire WR12 7AA (01386) 852401* £110, plus special breaks; 20 well kept rms. Lovely 15th-c building, once a monastic guest house, with galleried and timbered lounge, cosy beamed bar, attractively presented food served by attentive staff in airy comfortable restaurant, and seats outside on terrace; dogs by prior arrangement; disabled access

BROADWAY SP0839 **Collin House** *Collin Lane, Broadway, Worcestershire WR12 7PB (01386) 858354* £98, plus special breaks; 6 warm, comfortable and quiet rms. Golden-stone 16th-c Cotswold house in three acres of gardens, orchard, and meadow; restful public rooms, oak beams, log fires, very good English food and carefully chosen wines in candlelit beamed restaurant with mullioned windows, and friendly helpful service; cl 24–28 Dec

BROADWAY SP0937 **Lygon Arms** *High St, Broadway, Worcestershire WR12 7DU (01386) 852255* £176.25, plus special breaks; 65 lovely period rms (some more modern, too). Handsome hotel where Oliver Cromwell and King Charles I once stayed; interesting beamed rooms, oak panelling, antiques, log fires, fine traditional food in the Great Hall with minstrel's gallery and heraldic frieze, excellent service, and charming garden; health spa; children over 8 in evening restaurant; disabled access

CHADDESLEY CORBETT SO8873 **Brockencote Hall** *Brockencote, Chaddesley Corbett, Kidderminster, Worcestershire DY10 4PY (01562) 777876* £135, plus special breaks; 17 individually decorated rms. Grand country-house hotel in 70 acres with half-timbered dovecot and lake; large, airy and attractively furnished rooms, conservatory lounge with garden views, elegant restaurant with enjoyable modern French and English cooking, and very good service; no dogs; disabled access

EVESHAM SP0443 **Evesham Hotel** *Coopers Lane, Off Waterside, Evesham, Worcestershire WR11 6DA (01386) 765566* £102*, plus special breaks; 40 spacious rms. Comfortably modernised and cheerful family-run hotel with a warmly friendly, relaxed and jokey atmosphere, popular restaurant with very good food (esp lunchtime buffet), huge wine and spirits list, and sitting room with games and toys; little indoor swimming pool, and grounds with croquet, swings and putting; particularly well organised for families; cl 25–26 Dec; pets welcome (not in public rooms); partial disabled access ☺

HARVINGTON SP0548 **Mill** *Anchor Lane, Harvington, Evesham, Worcestershire WR11 5NR (01386) 870688* £103, plus special breaks; 21 comfortable rms overlooking grounds. Handsome Georgian hotel in eight acres of parkland with 180 metres (600 ft) of river, mooring for guests' boats, fishing, hard tennis court, and heated outdoor swimming pool; carefully furnished airy lounges with open fires, courteous helpful staff, fine imaginative food using fresh local produce, thoughtful wine list with helpful notes, and good breakfasts; cl Christmas; children over 10

HIMBLETON SO9459 **Phepson Farm** *Phepson, Droitwich, Worcestershire WR9 7JZ (01905) 391205* £45; 6 rms, 2 new ones in renovated farm buildings. Relaxed and friendly 17th-c farmhouse on 170-acre working farm with sheep; comfortable lounge, new guests' lounge, good breakfasts in separate dining room; self-catering apartment; cl Christmas and New Year; pets by arrangement; partial disabled access.

KEMERTON SO9437 **Upper Court** *Kemerton, Tewkesbury, Gloucestershire GL20 7HY (01386) 725351* £105, plus special breaks; 6 rms, plus others in cottages. Lovely Georgian Cotswold manor with Domesday watermill, a lake (lots of wildfowl and free fly-fishing in season), and dovecote in 15 acres of fine gardens, outdoor heated swimming pool, tennis court, croquet, and boating; relaxed atmosphere and many antiques (the owners run an antiques business and there is always something for sale) in elegant rooms, very good food using home-grown produce, and nice breakfasts; cl Christmas; dogs by arrangement; good disabled access

MALVERN SO7647 **Cowleigh Park Farm** *Cowleigh Park, Cradley, Malvern, Worcestershire WR13 5HJ (01684) 566750* **£52***; 3 rms. Carefully restored and furnished black and white timbered 13th-c farmhouse in own grounds, surrounded by lovely countryside, with good breakfasts and light suppers or full evening meals (prior booking); self-catering also; cl Christmas and New Year; children over 7

MALVERN WELLS SO7742 **Cottage in the Wood** *Holywell Rd, Malvern, Worcestershire WR14 4LG (01684) 575859* **£89.50***, plus special breaks; 20 compact but pretty rms, some in separate nearby cottages. Family-run Georgian dower house with quite splendid views across the Severn Valley and marvellous walks from the grounds; antiques, log fires, comfortable seats and magazines in public rooms, and modern English cooking and an extensive wine list in attractive no smoking restaurant

WICKHAMFORD SP0642 **Wickhamford Manor** *Manor Rd, Wickhamford, Evesham, Worcestershire WR11 6SA (01386) 830296* **£65**; 3 rms. Striking timbered manor, first mentioned in the Domesday Book, in 20 acres with 12th-c dovecote and lake, big log fire in beamed drawing room, good breakfasts in the flagstoned kitchen, and a really warm welcome from the friendly owners; tennis and coarse fishing; self-catering cottage; cl Christmas and New Year; children over 11

To see and do

Worcestershire Family Attraction of the Year

BROMSGROVE SO9468 **Avoncroft Museum of Buildings** (2m S at Stoke Prior, by A38 bypass and B4091) Check their events calendar in advance and you can time your visit to this fascinating place to coincide with a battle re-enactment, or a medieval market. These don't go on all the time, but there's usually something happening most wknds, from brick- or hay-making to classic car rallies or miniature train rides. At other times it's quieter, but no less enthralling, and it's surprising how much children enjoy it: several who've visited on school trips quickly return with parents in tow. Around 20 buildings from the last seven centuries have been saved from demolition and rebuilt here: there's a timber-framed merchant's house, a Victorian church and gaol, even a 1946 prefab. A lovely working windmill is particularly popular with children, and, more incongruously, there's a unique collection of telephone kiosks, from Tardis-style police boxes to today's horrid glass ones, with everything in between. This year they added a play area, with the climbing equipment, and there are donkeys, goats and chickens wandering about. Several of the buildings are furnished inside, but it's very much a place to visit on a dry day, when children can make the most of the open space the museum stands on. It's all very low-key and undemanding, but families with an interest in the past can spend a very enjoyable couple of hours strolling around here – without spending much on admission. Meals, snacks, picnic area, shop, disabled access; cl Mon (exc July and Aug), Fri in Nov and Mar, and all Dec–Feb; (01527) 831363; £4.60 (£2.30 children over 5). The family ticket is excellent value at £12.50 for two adults and three children.

ABBERLEY SO7367

Notable for its picturesque, steeply hump-backed packhorse bridge, looking more like a part of Devon or Derbys; ironically, cars have to use a more ancient crossing, the shallow ford beside it. A decent pub nearby is named after John o'Gaunt, the village's former owner.

ABBERLEY HILLS SO7567

(nr Stourport) Little visited by walkers but rewarding for them: partly wooded, with good views and close to the extraordinary ruins of Witley Court.

ABBOTS MORTON SP0255

Charming village, with lovely church and decent pub.

ASHTON UNDER HILL SO9937

Charming black and white timbered houses and a good Norman church; made all the more attractive by the brooding backdrop of Bredon Hill.

BEWDLEY SO7874

Attractive small town, with riverside walks and interesting side streets. The Little Pack Horse (old High St) is full of character.

Bewdley Museum 🎫 (Load St) An 18th-c row of butchers' shops houses this local history museum; shop, disabled access (phone first); cl Nov–Mar; £2.

Severn Valley Railway 🎫 Splendid steam train trips through the Wyre Forest and the Severn Valley between Kidderminster and Bridgnorth in Shropshire, with lots going on – this railway is run with great verve. The station has a fine model railway. Meals, snacks, shop; trains daily May–Sept and most other wknds – (01299) 403816 for timetable; £9.60 for full trip.

West Midlands Safari Park (Spring Grove, just E on A456) Very much a full day out with the main attraction the drive-round animal reserves, home to over 40 species of rare and exotic animals; you can go round as often as you like. Admission covers the entertaining sea lion show, a seal aquarium, reptile house and pets' corner, but you'll have to pay extra for the leisure park, which has around 30 rides from gentle carousels to a roller-coaster and popular log flume. Lots of differently themed shops and places to eat, and the under-cover Dome shows cartoons all day. Meals, snacks, shop, mostly disabled access; open daily end Mar–Oct;

(01299) 402114; the safari park is £5.75 for adults and children over 4; this entitles you to a return visit any time during the rest of the season. At the leisure park, rides are priced individually, or an all-day wristband is £6.75.

BREDON SO9236

Attractive village above River Avon, with magnificent medieval tithe barn and good pub.

Bredon Hill The Vale of Evesham's one notable feature for walkers. It's an outlier of the Cotswolds, distinctively rounded and on cloudy days rather ominous. It's easily reached from Overbury, but the best walk over it is from Bredon's Norton to Elmley Castle.

BRETFORTON SP0944

One of the prettiest black and white thatched villages, with an interesting church and a splendid medieval pub, the Fleece, left to the National Trust after being in the same family for several centuries; a proper pub, it's kept just as it was, with a magnificent collection of Jacobean oak furniture and pewter.

BROADWAY SP0937

Exceptionally harmonious stone-built Cotswold village, with the golden stone and uneven stone-tiled roofs perfectly blending the grand houses and the humbler cottages together, in a long, grass-lined main street. It's decidedly on the coach-tour trail, very busy indeed in summer (though the bypass helps). Fine things for sale in extraordinarily expensive antiques shops, and a very grand old inn, the Lygon Arms, with a useful side wine bar. Our other place-to-stay recommendations do good bar lunches; a good escape from the tourists is the Crown & Trumpet in Church St, an archetypal Cotswold pub, and the Buckland Manor does good teas.

Broadway Tower (off A44 SE) Above the village, this late 18th-c folly has marvellous views that on a clear day – with the help of the telescope – are said to stretch over 12 counties. There are exhibitions on the history of the tower and regular visitor William Morris, while the country park around it has farm animals and nature trails. Meals, snacks, shops, some disabled access; cl wkdys Nov–Mar; (01386) 852390; £3 tower only, £4 tower and park.

Teddy Bear Museum (High St) Decent collection of old bears and toys. Shop; cl 25–26 Dec; (01386) 858323; £1.50.

Vale of Evesham farm shops Good for all manner of local produce inc eggs, jams, pickles and trout as well as fruit and vegetables, but the highlights of the year are asparagus in May and apples and particularly plums in Sept. The A44 W almost always has good pickings.

BROMSGROVE SO9468

Avoncroft Museum of Buildings *See separate family panel on p.634.*

BURFORD SO5968

Burford House Gardens 🖼 (off A456, W of Tenbury Wells) Delightfully set by the River Teme, these tranquil gardens are the home of a national collection of clematis. Lots of other colourful plants too, a new wild flower garden, and the ground floor of the Georgian house is open as a contemporary art gallery. Meals, snacks, plant sales, disabled access; cl 25–26 Dec and 1 Jan; (01584) 810777; £3.50.

CHADDESLEY CORBETT SO8973

Despite the trunk road an attractive village, with a decent pub and a fine partly Norman **church**.

CHILDSWICKHAM SP0738

This streamside village has some delightful timbered stone cottages.

CLENT SO9380

Clent Hills Country Park A fine high hillscape for walkers, open and exhilarating, with waymarked routes. The Holly Bush at Clent is a good lunch break.

CLIFTON UPON TEME SO7161

A pleasant village, with lots of quiet strolls above the orchards.

DROITWICH SO8963

Droitwich Spa Brine Baths (St Andrews Rd) Just the thing after an exhausting morning's sightseeing – you don't drink the water of this famous spa town, but float in it; cl Easter Sun, 25–26 Dec, 1 Jan, the baths open from 11.30 am; (01905) 794894; £6.50 (inc sauna). Interesting buildings include the timbered houses around the High St, and the **Sacred Heart church** (Worcester Rd) with its fine stained-glass mosaics. The Old Cock (Friar St) is good value for lunch.

Heritage Centre (Victoria Sq) Unusual exhibition on radios and broadcasting, and brass rubbing. Shop, disabled access; cl Sun and bank hols; (01905) 774312; free.

ELMLEY CASTLE SO9841

Very old-fashioned village below Bredon Hill, with attractive houses strung out between its lovely church and the millpond, where the Old Mill has good value food.

EVESHAM SP0343

The pedestrianised market square has some fine buildings around it inc a 12th-c abbey gateway; the church's 16th-c bell tower is well preserved, and some altogether more ruined remnants in the town park beyond lead to riverside meadows. The Tourist Information Centre is in another attractive abbey building, the Almonry, a Tudor timbered house with a museum, and nice gardens. The Royal Oak (Vine St) is useful for lunch, and the Green Dragon (Oat St) visibly brews its own ales. In Apr or early May the orchard drive through Harvington, the Lenches, Badgers Hill, Fladbury Cross, Wood Norton and Chadbury is pretty.

FECKENHAM SP0061

Attractive green and some fine Georgian red brick.

FLADBURY SO9946

This appealing village offers walks by the River Avon, a 9th-c Saxon cross, and a handsome Georgian village green. The Chequers is a good dining pub.

GREAT MALVERN SO7745

Elegant hillside spa town with easy access to inspiring hill scenery; the B4232 from Upper Colwall to Wynds Point has some of the best high views, while the B4218 on the E side gives several good views of the hills themselves. A good few craft workshops include musical instrument-makers such as Hibernian Violins (Players Ave); cl wknds. The Foley Arms and Mount Pleasant Hotel have decent food, good views.

Barnard's Green House On the E side of the Malvern Hills, this has an attractive garden with a wide range of gardening ideas around a gracious 17th-c house (not open). The owner is an authority on dried flowers. Teas, plant sales, disabled access; open Thurs (and occasionally Sun) pm Apr–Sept, and other times by appointment; (01684) 574446; *£2. The nearby Bluebell is useful for lunch.

Malvern Hills Forming a splendid backdrop to the Vale of Evesham, these offer good walking. From a distance they look a formidable mountain range, but seem to get milder and more welcoming as you approach. The gentle up-and-down path along their spine makes one of England's great ridge walks, with the Cotswolds and Midland plain on one side and wilder Wales on the other. The Herefordshire Beacon, capped by ramparts of an Iron Age hill fort, is easily reached from the car park on the A449 nr Little Malvern. Great Malvern is well placed for the Worcestershire Beacon, the highest point of the range (425 metres, 1,395 ft), and for long circular walks. The Chase Inn at Upper Colwall and Malvern Hills Hotel by the British Camp car park on Wynds Point are also useful start or finish points.

Malvern Museum ☒ (Abbey Rd) This splendid former gatehouse of a Benedictine monastery houses a museum with displays on local history, Malvern spring water, and Elgar's life. Shop; cl Weds in term-time, all end Oct–Easter; (01684) 567811; £1. The beautifully symmetrical priory just along the road has a notable collection of medieval wall tiles.

Picton Garden (Old Court Nurseries, Walwyn Rd, Colwall) On the W side of the Malvern Hills, this has a nicely laid out cottagey collection of hardy plants and shrubs, best in summer, with a national collection of asters (late summer/autumn) and rock garden. Plant sales, disabled access; cl all day Mon and Tues, and Nov–July; (01684) 540416); £2. The Chase Inn at Upper Colwall is handy for lunch.

GREAT WITLEY SO7765

Witley Court Astonishing ruined shell of Jacobean house transformed into an Italianate palace by the Earl of Dudley, and partly destroyed by fire in 1937. It's an elaborate place, with enormous Perseus fountain, balustraded garden – very atmospheric to wander through, and a new sculpture trail. Overlooking the lake beside it, a

gloriously baroque church is no less dramatic, and one of the county's great finds; it has splendid paintings and stained glass around the largely papier mâché interior. Snacks, shop, some disabled access; cl 24–26 Dec; (01299) 896636; £3.50; EH. The Hundred House is handy for lunch.

HANBURY SO9463

Hanbury Hall 18th-c country house with outstanding painted ceilings and staircase, fine porcelain, and contemporary ice-house and orangery in grounds. The formal gardens are being carefully restored. You can book rooms in the Lodge on the edge of the estate. Snacks, shop, some disabled access; open pm Sun–Weds Apr–Oct; (01527) 821214; £4.60, £2.90 garden only; NT. The church, high on a hill, has superb views over the countryside. The Gate Hangs Well (Woodgate) has a good carvery.

Jinney Ring Craft Centre (B4091 Droitwich Rd) Twelve craft workshops in beautiful timbered barns, from pottery to violin-making; craft gallery and some wknd courses. Meals, snacks, shop, some disabled access; cl Mon exc bank hols; (01527) 821272; free.

HANLEY CASTLE SO8342 Well worth a stop, a rustic little place around a great cedar tree, with an unusually unspoilt pub.

HANLEY SWAN SO8142 An attractive village, with a pleasant traditional pub by the village green and duck pond.

HARTLEBURY SO8371

Hartlebury Castle State Rooms ☒ The official residence of the Bishops of Worcester since 850, now part of the County Museum. You can visit some of the state rooms; snacks, shop, some disabled access; museum cl am Fri and Sun, all day Sat, Good Fri, and all Dec–Jan; (01299) 250416; £2.20 (inc state rooms). The elegant state rooms are usually open Tues–Thurs.

HARVINGTON SP0549 One of the area's oldest villages, brilliantly black and white. The Golden Cross has nice food.

HONEYBOURNE SP1147

Domestic Fowl Trust ☒ (Station Rd) Friendly place with rare breeds of sheep, hens, ducks, geese and turkeys, plus young chicks for children to handle, adventure playground and an indoor play area. You'll need wellies on wet days. Cl 25 Dec, summer snacks, shop, limited disabled access; (01386) 833083; £2.50.

KEMERTON SO9437

Priory 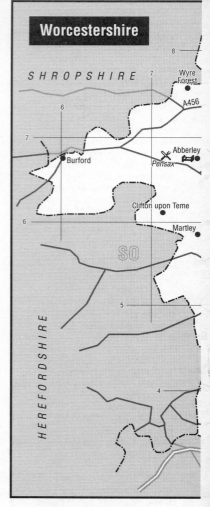 Big garden richly planted with colourful borders; also cool streamside plantings, handsome trees and shrubs and a walled kitchen garden. Plant sales; open Thurs pm May–Oct plus half a dozen Suns (when they do teas); (01386) 725258; £2 (£1.50 in May and June). There are other pretty stone-built houses among the trees of this attractively leafy village, handy for Bredon Hill walks. The Crown is popular for lunch.

KIDDERMINSTER SO8376

Not an alluring place to visit, but a terminus of the excellent Severn Valley steam railway (see Bewdley), with a cheerful replica of Edwardian station refreshment rooms.

Kingsford Country Park (Blakeshall) 200-acre park with pine forests, birch groves and plenty of walks and trails (inc one for the disabled). Very nice unspoilt feel – even the signposts and picnic-sets are made at the saw mill here.

LICKEY HILLS COUNTRY PARK SO9975

A good example of the interesting topography W of Birmingham: high (rising to over 300 metres – 1,000 ft), and densely wooded, a fragment of primeval forest, with the views suddenly opening out over the sprawling city; waymarking makes the maze of paths and tracks less confusing. The Peacock at Forhill has good value food all day.

LOWER BROADHEATH SO8157

Elgar's Birthplace Museum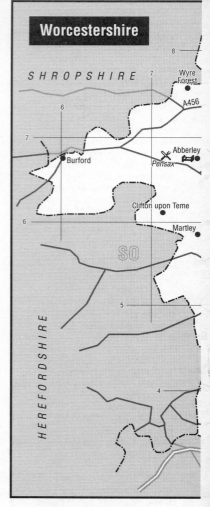
(Crown East Lane) Modest cottage where the composer was born in 1857; now, as he wanted, a museum of his life and work, with displays of photographs and letters, and the desk where he did his writing. A new visitor centre concentrates on his music, with audio-visual displays, manuscripts, musical scores, concert programmes and other memorabilia. Shop, disabled access to centre, gardens, and ground floor of cottage; cl for 4 wks over Christmas, best

to check; (01905) 333224; *£3.50. You can pick up routes and information here about the Elgar Trail around the area. The Bear & Ragged Staff over at Bransford is a very suitable place for lunch.

MARTLEY SO7559

Martley church Notable for its 13th-c wall paintings.

OFFENHAM SP0546

Still has its original gaily striped maypole in its wide black and white main street; a nice village.

OMBERSLEY SO8463

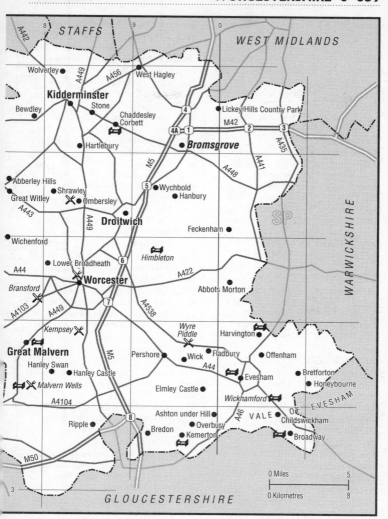

Attractive mix of handsome black and white timbered houses with elegant Georgian brick.

OVERBURY SO9537

Immaculate stone-built estate village, with older buildings and fine church.

PERSHORE SO9445

Very much a working town, the 'capital' of the fruit- and vegetable-growing area around it. It's a pleasant place, largely Georgian, with an impressive abbey, and River Avon walks. The riverside Brandy Cask (Bridge St) has good value

food and brews its own beer. Heading out along the A4104 SW, when you've passed the Oak in Defford keep your eyes skinned for a group of cottages on your right; the last, surrounded by farm animals and without an inn sign, is the Monkey House, a uniquely old-fashioned cider tavern (cl Mon evening, Weds–Thurs lunchtime, all Tues).

RIPPLE SO8737

Appealing village, with finely carved choir seats in its imposing largely 13th-c church.

SHRAWLEY SO7964

Eastgrove Cottage Garden
(Sankyns Green, off A443 E of Great
Witley) Interesting and unusual hardy
and tender perennial plants in a cottage-
garden setting by ancient timbered
house (not open). Good plants for sale,
disabled access; open pm Thurs–Mon
Apr–July, then pm Thurs–Sat Sept–mid-
Oct; (01299) 896389; *£2.

STONE SO8675

Stone House Gardens Unusual
walled garden with colourful plants,
especially climbers and tender
flowering shrubs; interesting plant sales.
Disabled access; open Weds–Sat
Apr–Sept or by appointment; (01562)
69902; £2.50. The Fox at Chaddesley
Corbett has a popular carvery.

WEST HAGLEY SO8979

Falconry Centre 🅴 (Hurrans
Garden Centre, Kidderminster Rd S)
Frequent flying displays of hawks, owls
and other birds of prey; short falconry
courses. Shop, some disabled access;
usually cl 25–26 Dec, 1 Jan and Easter
Sun; (01562) 700014; £2.50. The Holly
Bush (A491 towards Bromsgrove) has
popular fresh food.

WICHENFORD SO7759

Wichenford dovecot Unusually
constructed timber-framed wattle-and-
daub 17th-c dovecot with nearly 600
nesting boxes. Open daily Apr–Oct,
winter by appointment; (01684)
855300; 60p; NT.

WICK SO9645

This riverside village has attractive
houses and a good church.

WOLVERLEY SO8279

Steeply gabled cottages below a brick-
built hilltop church, and the decent
cliffside Lock Inn by the quaint Staffs &
Worcs Canal.

WORCESTER SO8554

Though it's a busy commercial centre,
this has some splendid medieval
buildings dotted about, with lots of half-
timbered houses, particularly around
Friar St, where the Lemon Tree has
good food, and New St. Plenty of shops,
inc some nice specialist ones and cafés
in Hopmarket Yard, a former coaching
inn; the King Charles I (New St) does
good meals. You can tour the
handsome Georgian Guildhall (not
Sun).

Bennetts Farm Park 🅴 (Lower
Wick, SW of city) Working dairy farm
with animals, wknd milking parlour and
vintage machinery museum in pretty
16th-c farm buildings. Walks and fishing
in season. Cl over Christmas, snacks
(inc their own ice-cream), shop;
(01905) 748102; *£3.

City Museum and Art Gallery
(Foregate St) Local and natural history,
with River Severn gallery and children's
activities. Meals, snacks, shop, disabled
access; cl Thurs, Sun, 25–26 Dec, 1 Jan
and Good Fri; (01905) 25371; free.

Commandery (Sidbury) Lively
museum wholly devoted to the English
Civil War, in striking timber-framed
15th-c building. Lots of weaponry,
spectacular audio-visual shows and life-
size talking figures re-creating events
from the war. Unusual special events and
military displays, and brass-rubbing
centre. Meals, snacks, shop; cl Sun am,
25–26 Dec, 1 Jan; (01905) 361821; £3.70.

Greyfriars (Friar St) Beautiful and
carefully restored medieval timber-
framed town house (still lived in), with
delightful walled garden. Open pm
Weds, Thurs and bank hols,
Easter–Oct; (01905) 23571; £2.60; NT.
The nearby Cardinal's Hat is the town's
oldest tavern – lovely panelled back
room.

Museum of Local Life (Friar St) This
15th-c building houses an interesting
museum of local life, with events such as
children's workshops. Shop with
reproduction nostalgiamenta, disabled
access to ground floor only; cl Thurs,
Sun, 25–26 Dec, 1 Jan, Good Fri;
(01905) 722349; free.

Museum of Worcester Porcelain
(Severn St) The country's oldest
continuous producer of porcelain, with
wkdy factory tours (no children under
11), and rare 18th-c porcelain in the
excellent developing museum. Meals,
snacks, shop, disabled access to
museum only; cl 25–26 Dec and Easter
Sun; (01905) 23221; tour £5, museum
£3. The Potters Wheel opposite has
decent food.

Worcester Cathedral Founded on
the site of a Saxon monastery, in a calm
and peaceful setting overlooking the
river. It took from 1084 to 1375 to
build, and has an attractive 14th-c

tower, Norman crypt, and the tombs of Prince Arthur and King John, the latter topped by the oldest Royal effigy in the country. Lots of Victorian stained glass, and some monastic buildings. Guided tours, snacks, shop, some disabled access; £2 suggested donations.
Worcester Woods Countryside Centre (just E off A442) 140 acres of ancient woodland on the edge of the city. Snacks, shop, disabled access; cl 25–26 Dec, 1 Jan; (01905) 766492; free.
WYCHBOLD SO9165
Webbs Garden Centre (A38

towards Bromsgrove) One of the best in the country, attractively laid out, with a massive choice of things to buy, fine amusements for children and good disabled access. The thatched café is exemplary; cl 25–26 Dec; (01527) 860000; free.
WYRE FOREST SO7574
This major broadleaved woodland, on the Shropshire border, has numerous ready-made Forestry Authority trails (leaflets available from the Visitor Centre; the Royal Forester nearby, if open, is useful for lunch).

Where to eat

BRANSFORD SO8052 **Bear & Ragged Staff** *Station Rd (01886) 833399* Stylish dining pub with proper tablecloths, linen napkins, and fresh flowers, very good imaginative food, fine views over rolling country from the relaxed and cheerful interconnecting rooms, open fire, no smoking restaurant, well kept beers, a fine choice of wines, lots of malt whiskies, and willing helpful service. £20.70|£6.50
KEMPSEY SO8548 **Walter de Cantelupe** *34 Main Rd (01905) 820572* Popular roadside pub with friendly relaxed bar, quite a mix of furniture, flowers and candles on tables, a good big fireplace, interesting food, well kept real ales, a good choice of wines by the glass, and hard-working young landlord; bdrms; cl Mon exc bank hols, 1 wk early Mar; children over 3 until 8.15pm; disabled access. £18|£5.50
MALVERN WELLS SO7742 **Croque-en-Bouche** *221 Wells Rd (01684) 565612* Boldly decorated Victorian house with delicious carefully cooked evening food from a shortish menu with marvellous puddings and cheeses, and an exceptional wine list – must book; open Thurs–Sat pm only; cl 1 wk May, 1 wk Sept, Christmas and New Year. £33
OMBERSLEY SO8463 **Kings Arms** *Main Rd (01905) 620142* Big black-beamed and timbered Tudor pub with comfortably informal rambling rooms, various nooks and crannies full of stuffed animals and birds, rustic bric-a-brac and four open fires, excellent varied bar food, well kept real ales, and seats in sheltered courtyard and terrace; cl 25 Dec; children over 8; disabled access. £22
PENSAX SO7468 **Bell** *(01299) 896677* Welcoming and unpretentious mock-Tudor pub with traditional décor, airy no smoking dining room with log fire, enjoyable straightforward food, well kept real ales, and seats in the back garden with fine views over the hills to the Wyre Forest; cl Mon am exc bank hols and summer hols; disabled access. £17.50|£6.50
WORCESTER SO8454 **Browns** *24 Quay St (01905) 26263* Most attractive and spacious warehouse conversion with big windows overlooking river, excellent modern cooking inc fish and vegetarian dishes, and good wines; cl am Sat, pm Sun, Mon, 1 wk Christmas; well behaved children over 8; disabled access. £35 dinner/£19.50 lunch
WORCESTER SO8554 **King Charles House** *29 New St (01905) 22449* Inn from which King Charles made his escape through the back door, closely pursued by Cromwell's forces; enjoyable food, open fires, and a relaxed atmosphere in downstairs restaurant and upstairs bar; cl Sun, bank hols. £30/2 courses £9.95
WYRE PIDDLE SO9647 **Anchor** *Main Rd (01386) 552799* Relaxing 17th-c pub with lovely views over lawn, river and on over the Vale of Evesham; friendly little lounge with log fire, comfortable bar, and good popular food; cl 26 Dec; disabled access. £20|£4.50

Special thanks to Gaynor Hulme

YORKSHIRE

Very friendly, with prices to match – most rewarding for holidays. The city of York itself is excellent for a short break. We have separate sections on the other three main areas, each of which has a great choice of places to visit. With the Dales, first-class walking country, we include Ripon, civilised Harrogate, and their surroundings (virtually all North Yorkshire W of the A19). The Moors and East Yorkshire (North Yorkshire E of the A19 along with the administrative county of East Yorkshire) also include memorable walks and drives, with plenty to keep children amused on the coast. West and South Yorkshire (particularly West Yorkshire) have an outstanding range of unusual visitor attractions, especially for families, often free.

York

A treasure trove of historical interest, with something for all ages

York is full of lovely medieval buildings and twisting alleys, interesting shops and lots of lively cafés, pubs and bars. The magnificent Minster is one of Britain's great sights, the Castle Museum and National Railway Museum (excellent for families) are first-class, and there are plenty of rewarding archaeological attractions from the myriad finds displayed at the Yorkshire Museum (peaceful gardens here, too) to the more children-oriented ARC, and the Jorvik Centre – one of the country's best heritage centres (currently being redeveloped). Just E of the city, busy Murton Park is good for a fair-weather family outing. It is undeniably a tourist city, with summer queues and crowds at the main sites; but most people find that all the other visitors actually seem to add to the atmosphere, rather than detracting from it. York's racecourse is a good one, with monthly meetings; the Ebor Festival in Aug is the biggest event in the northern racing calendar. Within its city walls York is largely pedestrianised – the biggest such area in any similarly sized European city – and very rewarding indeed to walk through. You can do the circuit of the 13th-c city walls and their many towers in a couple of hours or so, mostly on top. One of the best stretches, with good views of the Minster, is between the Monk Bar and Bootham Bar. If you plan on doing the whole circuit it's well worth using one of the Walkman guides rented by the helpful tourist office (Exhibition Sq). If you're travelling to the city by train it's certainly worth exploiting the First Stop York by Train scheme, which offers half-price discounts on many of the major visitor attractions, restaurants, and (from Nov–Mar only) places to stay. The campaign runs Oct–May, and leaflets are available from mainline railway stations or the tourist office mentioned above.

Please let us know what you think of places in the *Guide*. Use the report forms at the back of the book or simply write us a letter.

Where to stay

SHIPTON BY BENINGBROUGH SE5458 **Sidings** *Station Lane, Shipton by Beningbrough, York YO30 1BS (01904)* 470221 **£81**, plus special breaks; 8 rms with showers in two converted coaches. A railway enthusiast's paradise, based on restored former railway carriages with good food served at Pullman-style tables, a decent wine list, railway viewing platform, models, videos, and paintings and artefacts; disabled access

YORK SE5952 **Arnot House** *17 Grosvenor Terrace, York YO30 7AG (01904)* 641966 **£52**, plus winter breaks; 4 rms with four-poster brass beds. Friendly, very well run no smoking Victorian terraced house with lots of original features, antiques and paintings, good breakfasts in neat dining room, and a pleasant relaxed atmosphere; children over 12

YORK SE5849 **Curzon Lodge** *23 Tadcaster Rd, Dringhouses, York YO24 1QG (01904)* 703157 **£70**, plus winter breaks; 10 rms, some in former old coach house and stables. Charming early 17th-c house in marvellous spot just S of city centre overlooking Knavesmire racecourse, with an attractive comfortable drawing room, a sunny farmhouse dining room (enjoyable breakfasts), and parking in grounds; cl Christmas; children over 7

YORK SE6050 **Dairy Guesthouse** *3 Scarcroft Rd, York YO23 1ND (01904)* 639367 **£50***; 5 attractive rms (with thoughtful extras), some with own bthrm. Carefully restored no smoking Victorian house with lots of original features and attention to detail, enjoyable breakfasts with vegetarian choices, warmly hospitable atmosphere, and flower-filled courtyard; cl mid-Dec to end Jan; disabled access

YORK SE6052 **Dean Court** *Duncombe Pl, York YO1 7EF (01904)* 625082 **£125***, plus special breaks; 39 rms. Next to the Minster, this comfortable neatly kept hotel has fresh flowers and plants in airy rooms, very helpful efficient staff, enjoyable food in the elegant restaurant, and tearoom/conservatory serving late breakfasts, light lunches and so forth; good for families with thoughtful extras; children over 6 in evening restaurant ☺

YORK SE5952 **Grange Hotel** *1 Clifton, York YO30 6AA (01904)* 644744 **£125**, plus special breaks; 30 individually decorated rms with antiques and chintz. Close to the Minster, this Regency town house has elegant public rooms, an open fire, newspapers, good breakfasts, excellent restaurant food (there's also a brasserie), and warmly friendly staff; car park; disabled access

YORK SE6052 **Hazelwood** *24–25 Portland St, York YO31 7EH (01904)* 626548 **£63***, plus winter breaks; 14 individually styled rms. Just 4 mins from Minster, this no smoking, neatly kept Victorian house has quite a few original features, a cosy lounge, attractive dining room, helpful owners, and a pretty little garden; off-street parking; children over 8

YORK SE5951 **Holmwood House** *112–114 Holgate Rd, York YO24 4BB (01904)* 626183 **£67**, plus special breaks; 14 pretty rms. Built as two 19th-c houses, this no smoking hotel is 7 mins from the city walls, with open fire in comfortable sitting room, and very good breakfasts; children over 8

YORK SE5947 **Middlethorpe Hall** *Middlethorpe, York YO23 2GB (01904)* 641241 **£184**, plus special breaks; 30 elegant rms, most in the converted stables. Lovely, immaculately restored, William III country house just S of the city, with fine gardens and parkland, antiques, paintings and fresh flowers in comfortable quiet day rooms, and excellent food and service; indoor swimming pool and health and fitness spa; children over 8

YORK SE6052 **Palm Court Hotel** *17 Huntington Rd, York YO31 8RB (01904)* 639387 **£44***; 8 rms. Quiet and spotlessly kept Victorian house 5 mins from Minster, with pleasant sitting room, very good breakfasts, and particularly helpful friendly owners; private car parking; cl Christmas

To see and do

ARC (St Saviourgate) This refreshingly accessible archaeology centre – primarily for children – has recently been redesigned to give visitors an even more hands-on experience than before. With professional archaeologists on hand to give advice, you're encouraged to examine the city's Viking history by yourself, using genuine period relics inc bones, tiles and pottery to piece together a personal impression of Viking-age York. Very much on the school-trips circuit, it's usually open to individuals only in school hols, so best to check out of term-time. It's set in a beautifully restored medieval church, with an interesting old-fashioned garden. Shop, disabled access; cl Sun, and mid-Dec to early Jan; (01904) 643211; £3.60.

Barley Hall 🖼 (Swinegate) The Archaeological Trust that runs the ARC (and the Jorvik Centre) restored this medieval family home, complete with audio tour. Shop, disabled access to ground floor only; cl ams, all Mon and Tues Nov–Feb; (01904) 610275; *£3.50. The nearby Punch Bowl has good value food.

Castle Museum (Tower St) Housed in 18th-c prison buildings on the site of the former castle (part of the outer wall still stands), this is one of the best social history museums in the country, with a huge range of everyday objects from the past four centuries shown in convincingly reconstructed real-life settings, from Edwardian streets to prison cells and more contemporary living rooms. There's even a watermill, by the river outside. They have one of only three Anglo-Saxon helmets in the world, found here in York in the 1980s. Again, best out of term-time. Shop, disabled access ground floor only; cl 25–26 Dec, 1 Jan; (01904) 653611; £5.25.

Churches Besides the Minster, the city has a good few other fine medieval churches, though many are no longer used for services. Most were built during the prosperous 15th and 16th c, and among the finest are Holy Trinity (Goodramgate, which also contains in Our Lady's Row the oldest houses in the city) and St Helen's (St Helen's Sq). All Saints (North St) has some fascinating windows illustrating the last 15 days of the world.

City Art Gallery (Exhibition Sq) Well displayed collections running from Old Masters to the lusciously romantic nudes of William Etty, with some very handsome stoneware pottery. Shop, disabled access; cl 25–26 Dec and 1 Jan; (01904) 551863; £2 (free for York residents).

Clifford's Tower (Tower St) This former castle keep is perhaps York's most interesting building after the Minster. You can walk around the top of the walls, which enclose a garden, and there are good views of the city. It gets its name from Roger Clifford, who was hanged from the tower in chains. There's an unusual Lowry painting of the tower in the City Art Gallery (see entry above). Shop; cl 24–26 Dec, 1 Jan; (01904) 646940; £2. The Tudor Masons Arms is a handy stop.

Fairfax House 🖼 (Castlegate) Magnificently restored mid-18th-c townhouse, probably one of the finest in England, its richly decorated rooms fully furnished in period style. Much of the impressive collection of paintings, pottery, clocks and Georgian furniture was donated by the great-grandson of the confectionery baron Joseph Terry, and there's a re-created mid-18th-c meal. Shop, some disabled access by arrangement (steps at front); cl Fri (exc guided tours, 11am and 2pm), Sun am, and early Jan to late Feb; (01904) 655543; *£4.25.

Guildhall (St Helen's Sq) Exact replica of the original building of 1446, destroyed in a 1940 air raid. The stone walls of the earlier building form the framework of the new one. Disabled access; usually cl wknds Nov–Apr, Sun am in summer, and bank hols; (01904) 613161; free.

Jorvik Viking Centre (below Coppergate Shopping Centre) A £4.8m redevelopment which has spent five years on the drawing board was just about to be implemented here as we went to press. The ambitious scheme will see this excellent heritage centre –

the first place in the country to utilise sights-sounds-and-smells technology – completely re-modelled and expanded to give visitors a wider (and by the sounds of it, more fun) perspective on life in the city of Jorvik. Since it opened in 1984, archaeologists' understanding of the Viking age has increased considerably, and designers are aiming to use this new information to maximise the reality of their re-creations. The new exhibition, depicting a cityscape from later in the Viking age, will give more attention to detail, which means more smells – from the polluted River Foss to the scent of freshly tanned leather, as well as fresh autumnal breezes and the blast from a metalworker's furnace. One important recent historical discovery revealed that by the late 10th c, urban congestion had led the Vikings to build upwards, so new rides will not only take you around the dwellings, but also down sloping river banks, over backyards, and even up through a two-storey house. A new gallery will display ancient objects both as they were found by archaeologists and how they would have appeared in contemporary Jorvik. It takes a lot of courage to change a formula that has proved to be so successful for well over a decade, but we've complete confidence that the new-look centre will provide visitors with an even better-value day out. Jorvik doesn't re-open until Easter, but in the meantime, the adjacent St Mary's church will house a temporary display on the Vikings, featuring a number of sets from the old centre. Best to ring for opening times and prices; (01904) 543400; £5.65.

Merchant Adventurers' Hall (Piccadilly) The largest timber-framed building in the city, and one of the finest in Europe. Built for the powerful Merchant Adventurers' Company in the 1350s and hung with banners of medieval guilds, it has a chapel and undercroft as well as the great hall itself. Cl Suns 7 Oct–23 Mar, plus 23 Dec–2 Jan; (01904) 654818; £2.

Micklegate Bar Museum Another of York's medieval gateways, now housing social history displays. Cl 25–26 Dec, 1 Jan, wkdys Nov–Jan and possibly other times depending on the weather;

(01904) 634436; £1.50.

Murton Park 🄳 (Murton, just E; SE6552) Busy ten-acre park, excellent for children and best known for its **Museum of Farming**, with exhibitions of agricultural equipment, some animals and a Land Army display. Also here, the **Derwent Valley Light Railway** has trips along what was once known as the Blackberry Line, and there's a reconstructed Dark Age settlement and Roman fort (aimed mostly at children). Snacks and picnic area, shop, disabled access; cl over Christmas and New Year, limited facilities Nov–Mar; (01904) 489966; *£3, less in winter.

National Railway Museum (Leeman Rd) You don't have to be a train buff to enjoy this exemplary museum, where they've tried hard to ensure that there's something for the whole family. The great railway age is celebrated with lots of panache, and the background sounds and smells of a steam-era station add to the atmosphere. The centre-piece is the spectacular great hall, in which tracks radiate from a central turntable with a display of two dozen great locomotives from the museum's huge collection, while dotted around are all sorts of carriages and wagons, from the most utilitarian to Queen Victoria's sumptuous royal coach. The surprisingly enjoyable exhibition on the story of the mail is another highlight. Children might get the most out of the Interactive Learning Centre, where plenty of hands-on exhibits and activities vividly explain how trains and railways work, though they're also bound to relish the chance to build their own model train in the excellent new Works wing – home to an array of new exhibits. A miniature railway operates most wknds and school holidays, with steam train rides on certain dates, and there's also an outdoor play area. You can usually get a road train from York Minster to the museum every day in summer, less often in winter (when it may run only at wknds). Meals, snacks (and picnic areas), shop, disabled access; cl 24–26 Dec; (01904) 621261; £6.50, free for children and OAPs. Their all-day car park costs £3.

Richard III Museum (Monk Bar) The most striking and best preserved of

York's four turreted medieval gateways now houses this museum dedicated to the much-maligned monarch (or evil hunchbacked murderer depending on your point of view). Displays are themed as if he were on trial – you put your verdict in the appropriate Guilty or Innocent book on the way out. Shop; cl 25–26 Dec; (01904) 634191; £1.50. The nearby Tap & Spile is a good pub.

Shambles Jettied medieval buildings lean towards each other across these alleys, perked up by witty details such as the red figure of the printer's devil almost opposite the courtyard entry to the Olde Starre (a touristy pub, but genuinely old, with a view of the Minster from seats in its yard). This area has some of the city's most interesting shops, inc good bookshops, all sorts of unusual specialist shops, and, especially in Stonegate, nearer the Minster, and in elegant Micklegate, some serious silver and antiques shops.

St William's College – York Minster Information Centre ⬚ (College St, opposite Minster) 15th-c, with three finely timbered rooms – and a good restaurant. Shop; cl 25–26 Dec, Good Fri, and if they have conferences, so best to phone and check; (01904) 557233; 60p.

Treasurer's House ⬚ (Chapter House St; next to the Minster) There's been a house here since Roman times – this one dates from the 17th c, and the basement has an exhibition on its history. The timbered hall is very fine, as is the period furniture and restored period kitchen. Good meals and snacks; cl Fri, all Nov–Mar; (01904) 624247; £3.50; NT.

York Brewery ⬚ (Toft Green) Tours and tastings (not Sun am, 25–26 Dec or 1 Jan; £4.25 – inc a pint of their beer); (01904) 621162. Just along the road from here the Bar Convent has a museum looking at early Christianity (and decent accommodation); (01904) 643238.

York Dungeon ⬚ (Clifford St) Carefully researched exploration of 2,000 years of superstition, torture and various forms of death, full of grue and gore. There's an extensive Guy Fawkes Experience and Dick Turpin Story, also an exhibition on the Plague. Shop, some disabled access; cl 25 Dec; (01904) 632599; *£6.50.

York Minster A glorious example of Gothic architecture, in soft-coloured York stone, this is Britain's largest medieval building, begun in 1220 and taking a staggering 250 years to build. The richly detailed interior contains more original medieval glass than any other church in England – and indeed is reckoned to house half of all that's known in the country. Look out for the great E window which shows Genesis and Revelations in 27 panels, the splendid five sisters window in the N transept, and the beautiful ceilings of the central tower and chapter house. The choir screen has 15 niches containing statues of the kings of England from William the Conqueror to Henry VI. There's a display on the church's turbulent history in the Foundations Museum and Treasury. Shop, disabled access and facilities (touch and hearing centre, Braille guides, guide dogs welcome); cl Sun am, and occasionally for major services; (01904) 557216; £3 for Museum and Treasury, also small charges for chapter house and crypt. You can climb the tower for good views of the city (£3). Largely traffic-free, the Close outside is fairly quiet, but not enclosed, and without the tranquil serenity of say Exeter, Salisbury or Winchester. Evening ghost trails start from the West End at 7.30pm.

York Model Railway (York BR Station, Tearoom Sq) Painstakingly re-created miniature town and country landscape, running as many as 20 trains at a time; a second much smaller model shows a typical German town at night. Shop, disabled access; cl 25–26 Dec; (01904) 630169; £2.95.

Yorkshire Museum (Museum Gardens) A real treasure-trove, crammed with myriad archaeological finds and riches from Roman, Anglo-Saxon, Viking and medieval times, inc the fabulous medieval Middleham Jewel. All set out very sensibly, with the displays effectively put into context. Shop, disabled access; cl 25–26 Dec, 1 Jan; (01904) 629745; £3.95, less for York residents. Outside are ten acres of botanical gardens by the wall:

peaceful and attractive, around a shapely group of ruins inc the Benedictine St Mary's abbey and the Multangular Tower (medieval, on a Roman base), as well as a working observatory.

Where to eat

YORK SE6051 **Betty's** *6–8 St Helen's Sq (01904) 659142* Famous tearooms opened in 1937 with fine teas and coffees (they import their own), good sandwiches, salads and hot specialities, delicious scones, tea breads and pastries, home-made milk shakes, Alsace wines, and evening pianist; cl 25–26 Dec, 1 Jan|**£6.95**

YORK SE6050 **Meltons** *7 Scarcroft Rd (01904) 634341* Smart little restaurant with paintings for sale, a cheerful mural and collection of cookery books, very good imaginative modern cooking using tip-top ingredients (plenty of vegetarian choice), lovely puddings, fair value wines, and a relaxed friendly atmosphere; cl Sun pm, Mon am, 3 wks Christmas, 1 wk Aug. £26.80|**£5**

YORK SE6052 **St William's College Restaurant** *3 College St (01904) 634830* Lovely 15th-c buildings with enclosed courtyard for outside summer eating next to York Minster, with varied food, and evening jazz and candlelight; cl Good Fri, 25–26 Dec. £20|**£6.95**

YORK SE6052 **Treasurer's House Tearoom** *Minster Yard (01904) 646757* Lovely National Trust property, once home to the medieval treasures of York Minster, with a tearoom in the converted cellars: traditional and herbal teas, good coffee, fruit wines, home-baked cakes and scones, savoury dishes and good puddings, all served by friendly staff; no smoking; cl Fri, cl Nov–end Mar. £25|**£4.50**

The Yorkshire Dales, Harrogate & Ripon

Magnificent countryside with countless walking opportunities; some pleasantly relaxed day trips

Most of the man-made attractions here seem to offer a calm contrast to the dramatic landscape, which includes some of the most invigorating scenery in Britain. The Dales' steep stone-walled pastures, majestic moors, wind-carved limestone crags and rushing streams give drivers and particularly walkers a succession of mouth-watering quickly varying views, and of appealing villages and colourful market towns. Each of the main dales or valleys has its own distinct character (which we describe in the text). The visitor centres at Malham, Aysgarth (scene of a romantic series of waterfalls) and Clapham are all helpful introductions to the area.

For families, the theme park at North Stainley is a reliably fun outing, Kilnsey Park & Trout Farm is good on a sunny day (with a fun-fishing area for children), and the various attractions at stately Beningbrough Hall (good family events in summer) and beautiful Newby Hall can easily fill a decent chunk of the day.

There are well preserved castles at Skipton, Castle Bolton, and Ripley (splendid gardens here, too), and the ruins at Middleham and Richmond make up for in atmosphere what they lack in structure.

The train trip over the Pennines from Settle to Carlisle is memorable on a clear day, and the steam railway that runs between Embsay and tranquil

Bolton Abbey is always pleasurable.

People really enjoy the imaginative tours of the Black Sheep brewery in Masham, and the cheese-making demonstrations at the Wensleydale Creamery in Hawes.

Harrogate is a civilised former spa resort with some of Yorkshire's smartest shops – a comfortable base, in easy reach of both Dales and Moors, with fine gardens at nearby Harlow Carr. Ripon (with one of Britain's largest cathedrals) and Richmond are appealing. Towards the E, Fountains Abbey – the largest monastic ruin in the country – is a most poetic place, with marvellous landscaped gardens opposite.

Where to stay

ALDBOROUGH SE4066 **Ship** *Low Rd, Aldborough, Boroughbridge, York, North Yorkshire YO5 9ER (01423) 322749* **£45**; 5 rms, showers. Friendly and neatly kept 14th-c pub nr ancient church and Roman town, with coal fire in stone inglenook fireplace and old-fashioned seats in heavily beamed bar, ample food, separate restaurant, good breakfasts, well kept real ales, and seats on spacious lawn; no children

ARNCLIFFE SD9371 **Falcon** *Arncliffe, Skipton, North Yorkshire BD23 5QE (01756) 770205* **£62**; 5 rms, some with own bthrm. Delightfully basic Georgian inn with old-fashioned values; functional little rooms and a fire, homely front lounge, airy conservatory, no smoking dining room, and generous plain lunchtime snacks; no B&B Nov–Mar, but self-catering cottage then

BAINBRIDGE SD9390 **Rose & Crown** *Bainbridge, Leyburn, North Yorkshire DL8 3EE (01969) 650225* **£64**, plus special breaks; 12 comfortable rms. 15th-c coaching inn overlooking lovely green, with antique settles and other old furniture in beamed and panelled front bar, open log fires, cosy residents' lounge, big wine list, and home-made traditional food in bar and restaurant; pets welcome by prior arrangement

BOLTON ABBEY SE0753 **Devonshire Arms** *Bolton Abbey, Skipton, North Yorkshire BD23 6AJ (01756) 710441* **£165**, plus special breaks; 41 individually furnished rms with thoughtful extras. Close to the priory itself and in lovely countryside, this civilised former coaching inn owned by the Duke of Devonshire has been carefully furnished with fine antiques and paintings from Chatsworth; log fires, impeccable service, beautifully presented imaginative food in elegant restaurant, super breakfasts; health centre; children over 12 in restaurant; disabled access

BUCKDEN SD9477 **Buck** *Buckden, Skipton, North Yorkshire BD23 5JA (01756) 760228* **£72***, plus special breaks; 14 comfortable rms. Busy pub, popular with walkers and surrounded by moorland views; snug original area and bustling extended open-plan bar, popular food served by smartly uniformed staff in attractive no smoking dining room, decent wines, and well kept real ales; children over 6 in restaurant; disabled access

BURNSALL SE0361 **Red Lion** *Burnsall, Skipton, North Yorkshire BD23 6BU (01756) 720204* **£100***, plus special winter breaks; 11 rms. Pretty, 16th-c, family-run ferryman's inn overlooking the river and village green with its tall maypole; attractively panelled bar with beams and log fires, good food in bar and no smoking restaurant, a decent wine list with 12 by the glass, and big gardens and riverside terrace; 75 yds of private fishing, permits for further seven miles; disabled access

CARPERBY SE0190 **Old Stables** *Carperby, Leyburn, North Yorkshire DL8 4DB (01969) 663590* **£47***, plus special breaks; 3 rms, showers. Carefully converted stables with lots of original features (inc manger in dining room) in unspoilt moorland country with warmly welcoming helpful owners, tastefully furnished rooms, and marvellous breakfasts with home-made preserves; no smoking; cl Nov–Mar; no children or pets

CRAY SD9479 **White Lion** *Cray, Skipton, North Yorkshire BD23 5JB* (01756) 760262 **£50**, plus special breaks; 8 comfortable rms with showers in adjoining barn. Welcoming little pub spectacularly isolated 335 metres (1,100 ft) up with super views, lots of walks, traditional feel with flagstones, beams and log fires, good bar food, and decent wines

DANBY WISKE SE3398 **White Swan** *Danby Wiske, Northallerton, North Yorkshire DL7 0NQ* (01609) 770122 **£36***; 3 comfortable rms, shared bthrm. Cosy little pub in the middle of nowhere, handy for walkers on coast-to-coast footpath, with very friendly licensees, and decent choice of good value food inc free-range eggs from their chickens

FEIZOR SD7967 **Scar Close Farm** *Feizor, Austwick, Lancaster, Lancashire LA2 8DF* (01729) 823496 **£48**, plus special breaks; 4 clean well appointed rms. Friendly converted barn on working farm with big guest lounge, books, magazines and TV, and big breakfasts and homely evening meals – packed lunches, too; lovely quiet countryside; cl 25–26 Dec; disabled access

GRASSINGTON SE0064 **Black Horse** *2 Garrs Lane, Grassington, Skipton, North Yorkshire BD23 5AT* (01756) 752770 **£60**, plus special breaks; 15 rms. On the edge of the cobbled square, this is a bustling place with open fires and beams in comfortable bar, friendly service, and enjoyable food in attractive little restaurant; sheltered terrace

HARROGATE SE2955 **Alexa House** *26 Ripon Rd, Harrogate, North Yorkshire HG1 2JJ* (01423) 501988 **£65***, plus special breaks; 13 rms, some in former stable block. Attractive Georgian house with friendly staff, comfortable lounge, good home cooking in no smoking dining room, and marvellous breakfasts; can use local health club; good disabled access

HARROGATE SE3055 **Balmoral** *16–18 Franklin Mount, Harrogate, North Yorkshire HG1 5EJ* (01423) 508208 **£94**, plus special breaks; 20 lovely rms, many with four-posters. In quiet gardens but nr centre, this popular hotel has restful drawing room (lots of cat decorations), a cosy snug, interesting oriental bar, fine food in elegant restaurant, and helpful friendly staff; you can use the nearby leisure club; cl Christmas–New Year; disabled access

HAWES SD8789 **Cocketts** *Market Pl, Hawes, North Yorkshire DL8 3RD* (01969) 667312 **£59**, plus special breaks; 8 warm rms. Friendly hardworking owners make this a most attractive and enjoyable place to stay with candlelit restaurant, woodburner in small bar, and residents' lounge with books; cl Christmas; children over 10; disabled access

KILNSEY SD9767 **Tennant Arms** *Kilnsey, Skipton, North Yorkshire BD23 5PS* (01756) 752301 **£55**, plus special breaks; 10 rms. In a nice spot nr the River Wharfe, this spacious beamed and flagstoned inn has open fires (one fireplace made from an ornate carved four-poster), friendly service, good value food, and views of spectacular overhanging Kilnsey Crag from restaurant; pets welcome by prior arrangement; cl 25 Dec

KNARESBOROUGH SE3457 **Dower House** *Bond End, Knaresborough, North Yorkshire HG5 9AL* (01423) 863302 **£84**, plus special breaks; 31 clean, comfortable rms. Creeper-clad former dower house with attractively furnished public rooms of some character, good food in Terrace Restaurant, super breakfasts, helpful service, and leisure and health club

LEYBURN SE1190 **Golden Lion** *Market Pl, Leyburn, North Yorkshire DL8 5AS* (01969) 622161 **£64**, plus special breaks; 15 good value rms. Homely inn with comfortable and quietly friendly bay-window two-room bar with light squared panelling, good home-cooked traditional food in bar and evening restaurant, well kept real ales, and helpful service; cl 25–26 Dec; disabled access

LONG PRESTON SD8355 **Maypole** *Main St, Long Preston, Skipton, North Yorkshire BD23 4PH* (01729) 840219 **£46**, plus special breaks; 6 comfortable rms. Neatly kept 17th-c pub with generous helpings of enjoyable traditional food in spacious beamed dining room, open fire in lounge bar, real ales, and helpful service; disabled access

MALHAM SD9062 **Miresfield Farm** *Malham, Skipton, North Yorkshire BD23 4DA (01729) 830414* **£50***, plus winter breaks; 11 rms. Spacious old farmhouse with good freshly prepared food in beamed dining room, pleasant conservatory and two lounges, and lovely garden by stream and village green; disabled access

MARKINGTON SE2764 **Hob Green** *Markington, Harrogate, North Yorkshire HG3 3PJ (01423) 770031* **£105***, plus special breaks; 12 well equipped pretty rms. Lovely gardens and over 800 acres of rolling countryside surround this charming 18th-c stone hotel; comfortable lounge and garden room, log fires, antique furniture, fresh flowers, relaxed atmosphere, good food and friendly service

MIDDLEHAM SE1287 **Greystones** *Market Pl, Middleham, North Yorkshire DL8 4NR (01969) 622016* **£60**, plus special breaks; 5 rms. Friendly family-run Georgian house with log fire, books, magazines and TV in restful lounge, generous helpings of good home-made food using home-baked vegetables and home-made bread, cakes and sweet and savoury biscuits, and enjoyable breakfasts; cl Dec–Feb; disabled access

MIDDLEHAM SE1287 **Millers House** *Middleham, Leyburn, North Yorkshire DL8 4NR (01969) 622630* **£84**, plus special breaks; 7 pretty rms. Neatly furnished Georgian house with fine views, an open fire in pleasant lounge, attractive restaurant with good interesting home-cooked food using vegetables and herbs grown in their garden, lunchtime picnic hampers, and helpful service; cl Jan/Feb; children over 10

NEWTON-LE-WILLOWS SE2189 **Hall** *Newton-le-Willows, Bedale, North Yorkshire DL8 1SW (01677) 450210* **£90**; 3 spacious rms. Handsome Georgian house with quiet gardens and acres of paddocks; lots of fine antiques, paintings and wall hangings, tranquil drawing room with an open fire and French windows into the garden, cosy homely snug with another fire, honesty bar, good breakfasts in light breakfast room (home-made fruitcake, tea and coffee always available), enjoyable food in elegant dining room (by prior arrangement), and a helpful and hospitable owner; children over 13

RAMSGILL SE1171 **Yorke Arms** *Ramsgill, Harrogate, North Yorkshire HG3 5RL (01423) 755243* **£180*** inc dinner, plus special breaks; 13 attractive rms. Enjoyable small former shooting lodge with antique furnishings, log fires, particularly good imaginative cooking in both comfortable dining rooms, fine wines, real ales, courteous service, and lovely surrounding walks; open all day for drinks

RICHMOND NZ1700 **Millgate House** *Millgate, Richmond, North Yorkshire DL10 4JN (01748) 823571* **£50***; 3 rms overlooking the garden. Georgian townhouse with lots of interesting antiques and lovely plants, a peaceful drawing room, warm friendly hosts offering meticulous attention to detail, and good breakfasts in charming dining room which also overlooks the garden; it is this award-winning small garden with views over the River Swale and the Cleveland hills beyond, that is so special, filled with wonderful roses, ferns, clematis and hostas – they have a booklet listing the plants; children over 10

RICHMOND NZ1600 **Old Brewery** *29 The Green, Richmond, North Yorkshire DL10 4RG (01748) 822460* **£44***; 5 rms. In a pretty corner overlooking the village green and castle ruins is this delightful no smoking former inn with Victorian-style renovations and furnishings, a hospitable atmosphere, and nice garden; cl Dec–Jan; no children

RICHMOND NZ1404 **Whashton Springs Farm** *Whashton, Richmond, North Yorkshire DL11 7JS (01748) 822884* **£46**; 8 comfortable rms. Attractive stone-built Georgian farmhouse on 600-acre working mixed farm; log fire in comfortable sitting room, good country breakfasts in attractive dining room (no evening meals) and lovely surrounding countryside; cl Christmas–beginning Feb; children over 5

RIPLEY SE2860 **Boars Head** *Ripley, Harrogate, North Yorkshire HG3 3AY (01423) 771888* **£115***, plus special breaks; 25 charmingly decorated rms. In a delightful estate village, this fine old coaching inn has a relaxed, welcoming atmosphere, with comfortable sofas in attractively decorated lounges, long flagstoned bar, notable wines by the glass, fine food in bar and restful dining room, and unobtrusive service; disabled access

RIPON SE3171 **Ripon Spa** *Park St, Ripon, North Yorkshire HG4 2BU (01765) 602172* **£84***, plus special breaks; 40 individually furnished rms, many overlooking the grounds. Neatly kept friendly and comfortable Edwardian hotel with seven acres of charming gardens, yet only a short walk from the centre; attractive public rooms, and good food in bar and restaurant; disabled access

SEDBUSK SD8790 **Stone House** *Hawes, North Yorkshire DL8 3PT (01969) 667571* **£73**, plus special breaks; 22 rms, 5 with own conservatories. Small, warmly friendly Edwardian hotel in a stunning setting with magnificent views; country-house feel and appropriate furnishings, attractive oak-panelled drawing room, billiard room, log fires, and exemplary service offering good local information; pleasant extended dining room with excellent wholesome food (special needs catered for) inc super breakfasts, and reasonable choice of wines; tennis lawn in the grounds, wonderful walks; P G Wodehouse stayed here as a guest of the original owner who employed a butler called Jeeves – it was on him that Wodehouse based his famous character; cl Jan; dogs welcome; good disabled access

SETTLE SD8163 **Falcon Manor** *Skipton Rd, Settle, North Yorkshire BD24 9BD (01729) 823814* **£90**, plus special breaks; 19 rms. Quietly set imposing Victorian hotel in its own grounds with original features in the spacious public rooms, log fires, fine food and lovely views in elegant restaurant, and obliging service; a well placed touring base; disabled access

STARBOTTON SD9574 **Fox & Hounds** *Starbotton, Skipton, North Yorkshire BD23 5HY (01756) 760269* **£55***; 2 rms with showers. Prettily placed and rather smart little Upper Wharfedale village inn, warmly welcoming, with flagstones, beams and big log fire, imaginative food, and well kept real ales; cl Jan to mid-Feb; no children

STUDLEY ROGER SE2970 **Lawrence House** *Studley Roger, Ripon, North Yorkshire HG4 3AY (01765) 600947* **£90**; 2 spacious, lovely rms. Attractive Georgian house with two acres of garden on the edge of Studley Royal and Fountains Abbey; lovely antiques and fine pictures, log fires, good breakfasts, and delicious evening meals; cl Christmas and New Year; children by arrangement

THORALBY SE0086 **Scarr House** *Thoralby, Leyburn, North Yorkshire DL8 3SU (01969) 663654* **£52**; 3 rms with showers. Relaxed and friendly no smoking 18th-c former farmhouse with lovely views, lots of books, comfortable lounge in converted hayloft with beams, exposed stones and open fire, carefully cooked imaginative food (bring your own wine) at candlelit tables, and nice breakfasts; no children

THORNTON WATLASS SE2385 **Buck** *Thornton Watlass, Ripon, North Yorkshire HG4 4AH (01677) 422461* **£58**, plus fishing and racing breaks; 7 rms, most with own bthrm. Cheerful country pub overlooking cricket green in very attractive village, with interesting beamed rooms, open fire, jazz Sun lunchtime twice a month, good food inc summer barbecues, and lots of nearby walks; cl 24–25 Dec

WATH SE1467 **Sportsmans Arms** *Wath, Harrogate, North Yorkshire HG3 5PP (01423) 711306* **£70**, plus special breaks; 13 rms – most with own bthrm. Friendly, quietly placed 17th-c hotel with lovely views; elegant bar, good range of wines, excellent food (esp fish) in no smoking evening restaurant, super lunchtime bar food, and attentive service; particularly good Sun lunch, and lots of fine cheeses; cl 25 Dec; disabled access

WEST WITTON SE0688 **Wensleydale Heifer** *West Witton, Leyburn, North Yorkshire DL8 4LS (01969) 622322* **£72**, plus special breaks; 14 rms in two adjacent old buildings. Friendly 17th-c coaching inn with comfortable furnishings, log fires and oak beams, and cosy bar; good local game and fresh seafood in bistro or spacious restaurant; well behaved dogs allowed

WIGGLESWORTH SD8056 **Plough** *Wigglesworth, Skipton, North Yorkshire BD23 4RJ (01729) 840243* **£60***, plus special breaks; 12 well equipped rms, some in newer extension. Friendly and well run country inn with popular food in conservatory restaurant and bar; lots of little rooms surrounding bar area – some smart and plush, others spartan yet cosy – friendly service, big breakfasts, packed lunches, and views of the Three Peaks; disabled access

To see and do

AISKEW SE2787
Big Sheep & Little Cow Farm 🔤 Small-scale dairy farm, with friendly sheep and dexter cows (Britain's smallest), pigs and chicks, and a new under-cover animal display – the family in charge love talking to visitors. Snacks, shop selling ewes' milk and ice-cream made here from it, some disabled access; cl Sept–Mar; (01677) 422125; £3.50.

ALDBOROUGH SE4066
Aldborough Roman Town The northernmost civilian Roman town was here, its houses, courts, forum and temple surrounded by a massive 6-metre (9-ft) wall. All that remain are two pavements, the position of the wall and, in the museum, some finds from the site. Shop; open Apr–Oct (cl 1–2pm); (01423) 322768; £1.70, free admission to site only in winter. It's a pleasant village with an impressive church (check out the sundial); the Ship opposite is good for lunch.

ARNCLIFFE SD9371
Charming tucked-away Dales village, well placed for walks. The road up Littondale is pretty, and that to Langcliffe in Ribblesdale runs through dramatic scenery. The Falcon is an archetypal Dales inn.

ASKRIGG SD9491
Delightful collection of elegant stone houses around neat streamside greens, walks to nearby waterfalls, fine 15th-c church, and two decent pubs.

AYSGARTH SE0188
Aysgarth waterfalls The Lower Fall is the most spectacular of this famously romantic series of waterfalls, via a path over the road from the car park. The falls are the National Park's chief visitor honeypot and do get crowded, particularly through Aug (when even parking can be a problem here). They're better in late spring or early autumn, when there tends to be more water in the river and therefore a better show.

In severely cold weather they can be stunning, with wonderful ice sculptures building up. There's generally a small charge to see the Upper Fall (it's on private land), but you can see it almost as well without paying, from the bridge on the road. The main car park (£2 for three hours) has a **National Park Centre**, with displays on the Dales, and useful walks, maps, and guides. Café, shop, disabled facilities; usually cl wkdys and lunchtimes Nov–Mar but best to check for winter opening times; (01969) 663424; free. For more of a walk, you can contrive longer routes along the S bank of the Ure from the delightful village of West Burton.

Yorkshire Carriage Museum (Yore Mill) A collection of Victorian coaches and carriages. Meals, snacks, large charity shop (free entry); cl 25 Dec; (01969) 663399; *£2. The George & Dragon is a good place for lunch.

BAINBRIDGE SD9390
Delightful, its broad sloping green still with the village stocks, and still ringing with the blowing of a buffalo-horn to guide shepherds down through the mists each night at 9pm from the end of Sept till late Feb, as it has done for centuries.

Low Mill 🔤 Restored 18th-c **corn mill** with a collection of fully furnished hand-made dolls' houses, all produced on the premises. Good shop (sells plans to make your own). Open Weds pm July to mid-Sept, maybe bank hols, and by appointment; (01969) 650416; *75p.

BEDALE SE2685
Thorp Perrow Arboretum (off B6268 S) Well laid-out 85-acre landscaped lakeside collection of rare trees and shrubs among some splendid mature specimens that have been growing here for over 400 years. Particularly strong on oaks, ornamental cherries, willows and hazels, and lovely in spring when the bulbs are out; also a new falconry centre. Snacks, shop,

disabled access; (01677) 425323; £7, arboretum only £3.50. In the town the convivial Olde Black Swan does good value lunches.

BENINGBROUGH SE5358
Beningbrough Hall Stately early 18th-c baroque mansion, with a good collection from the National Portrait Gallery, also marvellous staircase with balusters carved in imitation of wrought iron, fine carvings, and a big restored Victorian dairy. Regular events for families, and lovely formal gardens. Meals, snacks, shop, disabled access to ground floor only; cl Thurs, Fri (exc July–Aug), and all Nov–Mar; (01904) 470666; £5, garden only £3.50; NT. The riverside Dawnay Arms at Newton-on-Ouse is useful for lunch.

BISHOPDALE SD9885
One of Wensleydale's tributary dales, broader than the others but still quite dramatic for walkers.

BOLTON ABBEY SE0754
Beautiful spot in lovely rolling wooded parkland on a knoll above the River Wharfe. Most of the priory buildings, dating from the 12th to the 16th c, are in ruins, but the central core of the main church is still used for Sunday services. 19th-c additions such as stained glass (some by Pugin) and murals oddly don't strike a false note. The car park gets rather full in summer (around £3 charge). The Devonshire Arms is very fine for lunch. Attractive walks lead off in most directions: the landscape has a lowland beauty, with the ruined abbey, the turf banks of the Wharfe and the oaks of the Strid Wood, where a leaflet detailing nature trails is available. A steep ascent from Howgill is rewarded by views from Simon's Seat, perched on the edge of moors.

BRIMHAM ROCKS SE2065
(off B6265) Spectacular and extraordinarily weathered gritstone pinnacles, tors and boulders facing the winds at a height of 290 metres (950 ft), conjuring up people, animal heads and other strange figures – a Victorian guidebook declared that they were 'grim and hideous forms defying all description and definition'. Children like them a lot – Henry Moore said that when he was a boy they strongly moulded his imagination. Information

centre, shop and snacks wknds and bank hols Easter–Oct, daily Jun–Sept and school hols – weather permitting, the site is open all year; (01423) 780688; parking £2.30; NT. The Half Moon on the B6265 is handy for food.

CASTLE BOLTON SE0095
Apedale Head This spectacular viewpoint is reached by a 3-mile plod up tracks NW; on fine days it feels like the top of the world, with views encompassing both Wensleydale and Swaledale.

Bolton Castle 🏰 (off A684) A massive 14th-c structure towering over the tiny single-street village built for it. Considering it was partly dismantled in 1645 and has been empty ever since, it's still in fine shape; great views from the 30-metre (100-ft) towers, dungeons and medieval gardens. Meals, snacks, shop; cl 24–25 Dec; (01969) 623981; £4. The Kings Arms at Redmire has good food.

CLAPHAM SD7469
Attractive village that has turned walking and caving into something of an industry. The riverside New Inn is useful for lunch (and a good place for walkers to stay in).

Ingleborough (721 metres – 2,376 ft) Best approached from Clapham, along the Reginald Farrer Trail, past Ingleborough Cave (see below) and Gaping Gill (a vast pot-hole); the panorama extends far across Lancashire and into Cumbria.

Ingleborough Cave One of the most easily visited of the vast network of caverns plunging into the limestone hills around here – and probably the only one that wheelchairs can go all the way through. It's set in the grounds of the outdoors centre at Ingleborough Hall – formerly the family home of the great plantsman Reginald Farrer, who in his short life introduced and eulogised many notable plants from the Himalayas and China. A **nature trail** leads past Farrer's woods and small lake to the cave (40p); unusually, it's a place that looks better in wet weather. Snacks, shop, some disabled access; cl wkdys (unless by appointment) Nov–Feb; (01524) 251242; £4.

National Park Centre Good introductory centre; best to check winter opening, usually wknds only; (01524) 251419; parking around £2 for three hours.

COVERDALE SE0481

Wensleydale's major tributary valley, relatively very quiet; fairly gentle in its lower reaches, climbing high into a wild and untamed-feeling world of lonely sheep farms.

CRAKEHALL SE2490

Crakehall Water Mill 17th-c, on the site of a still earlier one; restored in 1980, it now produces flour again. Even when they're not milling, the wheel should still be turning. Snacks, shop; cl Mon, Tues and end Sept–Easter; (01677) 423240; £1. The Bay Horse in a nice spot on Little Crakehall green has good value food.

CROFT NZ2809

Right on the border with Co Durham is a pleasant **church** where Lewis Carroll's father was parson; there's a plaque in memory of the writer, complete with an enamelled White Rabbit, and an unusual family pew reached by a staircase. If the church is closed, the key is kept at the hotel across the road. Nice river views.

DENTON MOOR SE1450

Above the reservoirs S of Blubberhouses, this offers scope for fairly stretching walks (though nothing to compare with the Dales themselves).

DRUIDS TEMPLE SE1879

Nr the hamlet of Ilton a no-through road leads up to woodlands where you can walk to this scaled-down Stonehenge, built by a landowner in the 1820s as work for local unemployed people.

EMBSAY SE0053

Embsay & Bolton Abbey Steam Railway 🔄 Steam trips along a track prettily set beneath limestone crags, through to Bolton Abbey. There's a cabman's shelter originally at Ilkley, and a collection of old locomotives and carriages. Snacks, two shops (remarkable range of books), disabled access (notice preferred); usually open Sun all year, and other days in summer – best to ring (01756) 795189 for timetable; £5. The well run Elm Tree has good food, and the Wayside Café in nearby Draughton does good scones.

FOUNTAINS ABBEY SE2769

Fountains Abbey & Studley Royal Watergarden (off B6265) The largest

monastic ruin in the country, this romantic place was founded in 1132 by Cistercian monks, in a delightful riverside setting. Said to be haunted by a full choir of ghostly monks, most of the remains are 12th-c, but the proud main tower is 15th-c. Opposite are the lovely landscaped gardens begun by William Aislabie in the 1760s, which include ornamental temples and follies, formal water gardens, lakes aflutter with waterfowl, and 400 acres of deer park. The most beautiful approach is through the extraordinarily ornate Victorian church at the far end (maybe restoration in progress, best to phone for opening), and this 'back-door' entrance is the most tranquil too. A helpful modern visitor centre has been skilfully constructed so that it blends in and doesn't spoil the view. Free guided tours of abbey 11am, 2.30pm, 3.30pm Apr–Oct. Meals, snacks, shop, good disabled access; cl Fri Nov–Jan, and 24–25 Dec; (01765) 608888; *£4.50, deer park – an excellent strolling ground – free; NT. The very civilised Sawley Arms in Sawley just W does good food.

GIGGLESWICK SD7867

Falconry & Conservation Centre 🔄 (top of Crows Nest, off A65 N of Settle) Well organised, with lots of vultures, eagles, hawks, falcons and owls, and regular flying displays (from noon). Meals, snacks, shop, disabled access; cl 25 Dec, maybe other days in winter; (01729) 825164; £4.95.

GLASSHOUSES SE1764

Yorkshire Country Wines (The Mill) Traditional country wines produced in 19th-c flax mill, with free tastings, antiques, and tearoom overlooking the River Nidd; they prefer notice for disabled access. Cl Mon and Tues and wkdys Nov–Easter, winery tours (£2.50) Fri and Sat at 11.45am; (01423) 711947.

GRASSINGTON SE0063

Pleasant small town or large village around a sloping cobbled square, depending a lot on walkers and other visitors, with some attractive shops and a few interesting old buildings; there's a National Park information centre. The

Black Horse has decent food and comfortable bedrooms. The B6160 gives lovely Wharfedale views, and the B6265 to Pateley Bridge also has memorable views (and passes the colourfully lit underground Stump Cross Caverns, well worth a look if you're passing).

GRINTON SE0498
Attractive riverside village with charming church known as the 'cathedral of the Dales', and pleasant walks nearby. The waterside Bridge Inn (open all day) has decent food.

HARROGATE SE3054
This elegant and self-confident inland resort has kept its Victorian spa-town atmosphere despite now filling many of its handsome hotels with up-to-date conferences and so forth. The layout of the town is very gracious, and you couldn't ask for better shops (interesting antiques and some top-notch specialist shops). Almost every available space is filled with colourful plant displays, as if to shake off the gloom of the dark stone buildings. The first thing a visitor notices is the great sweep of The Stray, open parkland which runs right along and through the S side of the centre. The first sulphur well was discovered in the 16th c and named the Tewit Well, after the local word for the lapwings which led a local sporting gent to ride into what was then a smelly bog. It's up on The Stray, grandly encased in what looks like an Italianate mausoleum. The elegant buildings of the compact central area run down from here to the pleasantly laid-out Valley Gardens, very Victorian, their curlicued central tea house run by a friendly Italian family. The relaxed tempo of the place, and the clean bracing climate (it's quite high on the moors), have made it a popular retirement area. Besides the places mentioned in **Where to eat**, the Drum & Monkey (fish restaurant/wine bar, Montpellier Gardens), Hedleys (wine bar, Montpellier Parade) and Regency (off East Parade) are all good for lunch or a snack; the café of the Theatre Royal is also pleasant, as is the Lascelles Arms out in Follifoot.

Harlow Carr Botanical Gardens ⌂ (Crag Lane, off B6162 W) Ornamental and woodland gardens over 68 acres, with streams, pools, rockeries, rhododendrons, spring bulbs and many interesting plants. Also a museum of gardening, model village and scented garden. A place of real peace and fresh moorland air, the finest strolling ground nr Harrogate, and virtually deserted out of season, when the excellent collection of heathers comes into its own. Meals, snacks, plant centre, limited disabled access; (01423) 565418; £4. The adjacent Harrogate Arms has good value food.

Mercer Art Gallery (Swan Rd) An early spa building, with an excellent collection; cl Mon (except bank hols), Sun am, 24–26 Dec and 1 Jan, free.

Royal Pump Room Museum (Royal Parade) The central sulphur wells (there are other outlets all over the town) are housed here, enclosed by glass to contain the reek. You can still order a glass of the water at the original spa counter, now the ticket counter for the museum. The octagonal pump room building contains displays of 19th-c fine china and jewellery, as well as bath chairs and other impedimenta of the golden spa days. Shop, disabled access; cl Sun am, 24–26 Dec and 1 Jan; (01423) 503340; £2.

HAWES SD8789
Busy in summer with hikers and coach-parties, but pretty, and a proper market town, its Tuesday mart full of livestock in late summer. The Crown and White Hart are useful for lunch.

Dales Countryside Museum (Station Yard) Developing centre with interesting displays of local crafts and domestic and industrial life as well as hands-on exhibits, a steam locomotive and displays on transport. Shop, disabled access; open daily Easter–end Oct, phone for winter opening times; (01969) 667450; £3.

Hardraw Force (just N) England's tallest waterfall cascading over a 30-metre (100-ft) lip; it's best after rain (though the paths can be muddy then), and at dry times you may see barely a trickle; small fee at Green Dragon pub. A longer excursion follows the Pennine Way from Hawes and over the River Ure. The valley above the falls is attractive, and this can be a start for the

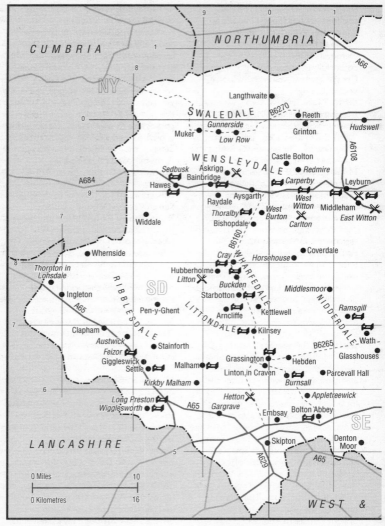

long day's walk to Great Shunner Fell.
Mountain drives The B6255 S to
Ribblehead gives fine mountain views,
and the Buttertubs Pass northwards
through High Shaw over into Swaledale
is a spectacular drive (the Buttertubs
are deep ferny holes nr the summit
where carriers used to cool their
butter in hot weather).
Outhwaites Ropemakers (A684,
Town Foot) They've been making rope
for 200 years – see how it's done. Shop

(not just great hawsers, useful things
too like dog-leads), disabled access; cl
wknds (exc Sats July–Oct, Easter and
spring bank hol), 10 days at Christmas,
and Good Fri; (01969) 667487; free,
self-guided tours £1.70.
Wensleydale Creamery 🏛 (Gayle
Lane) Saved from closure by a timely
management buy-out a few years ago,
this has developed a fascinating
visitor centre, with a well set-out
dairying/cheese museum; you can

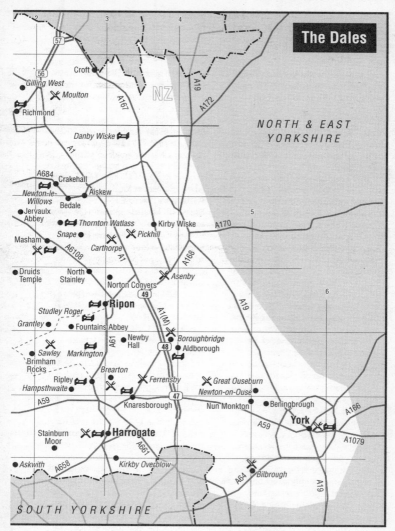

The Dales

NZ

NORTH & EAST YORKSHIRE

SOUTH YORKSHIRE

watch the cheese being made by the traditional method, all by hand. The shop (busy in summer) has samples of their variously flavoured cheeses – our favourite was the one with blueberries. Very good café, disabled facilities; cl 25 Dec; (01969) 667664; *£2.

HEBDEN SE0263

Hebden lead mines There's a rewarding walk up Hebden Beck with its legacy of old lead-mine workings; the route can be extended to take in

Grassington and the path along the River Wharfe.

HUBBERHOLME SD9377

Beautifully placed riverside dales hamlet with a good 13th-c **church**, built on an ancient burial site, with Norman tower, unusual rood loft and pews by Thompson of Kilburn – with their little carved mouse trademark. The charmingly set George, J B Priestley's favourite pub, has good food and bedrooms. A walk not to be missed is up to Scar House and along a level turfy terrace, which commands magnificent views down the dale, to Cray (another good inn there). The walk can be expanded to include Buckden – in fact there are good walks between all the Wharfedale/Littondale places flagged on our map, with good pub food available in each of them.

INGLETON SD7174
White Scar Cave (B6255 towards Hawes) The country's longest cavern and one of the most spectacular, with underground waterfalls and streams, and an Ice Age cavern. Some amazing sights and atmospheric formations, and stunning stalactites and stalagmites that have been here for 100,000 years. Wrap up well – the guided tour takes about 80 mins so gets chilly. Snacks, shop, some disabled access by arrangement; cl 25 Dec (and sometimes after heavy rain); (01524) 241244; £6.25. The Wheatsheaf and Bridge are useful, and the B6255/B6479 is a very scenic long way round to Settle. There is a lovely wooded walk up the River Twiss, over the moor and back down the River Doe, past a series of picturesque waterfalls; not too strenuous, very varied scenery, 2 or 4 hours – the admission fee for this Ingleton Glen is amply justified by the delightful gorge and waterfalls.

JERVAULX ABBEY SE1785
Less imposing than Fountains, Rievaulx and Bolton, but in some ways even more appealing – perhaps because the rough-cropped grass and wild flowers around the shattered walls emphasise the slightly melancholy atmosphere of a place of great worldly wealth and power that's come to nothing. Teas, shop, disabled access; abbey open all year, tearoom cl Nov–Feb; (01677) 460391; £2. The Blue Lion at East Witton nearby has superb food.

KETTLEWELL SD9672
Popular village for walkers, with three decent pubs; there are exhilarating views from the back roads from here up into Coverdale, and to Hawes via Hubberholme.

KILNSEY SD9767
Kilnsey Park & Trout Farm (B6160) Two lakes for fly-fishing, plus a fun-fishing area for children, adventure playground, and good estate shop with fish, oven-ready game and other local produce. There's an aquarium in the visitor centre and a sizeable collection of orchids. You have an even better chance of spotting a red squirrel now (this is a conservation area for these shy creatures), as seven babies were born last year. Good meals and snacks (inc tasty trout from their smokery, and local cheeses), disabled access; cl 25 Dec; (01756) 752150; £2.50 for visitor centre, £3.75 for children's fishery (50p for spectators), and proper fishing from around £15 per half-day. The Tennant Arms has decent food.

KIRBY WISKE SE3684
Sion Hill Hall 🏛 Splendid Georgian mansion, one of the last great country houses to be built, with period furnishings and an enormous collection of antiques, porcelain, paintings and clocks. Snacks, shop (inc antiques), some disabled access; open Weds, Thurs and Sun pm May–Sept, plus a few days in Apr – best to check; (01845) 587206; £4.50.

KNARESBOROUGH SE3557
The little town above the steeply picturesque river gorge, with its spectacular railway viaduct, is pleasant and colourful (esp on Weds market day), with some attractive buildings. The chemist's shop on the square is said to be the oldest in the country; established in 1720, it still has all its original fittings. You can hire **rowing boats** down on the river, and there are pleasant riverside paths and walks: from Abbey Rd for example you should be able to see the intriguing **House in the Rock**, and a 15-min walk down here brings you to St Robert's Cave, the riverside home of a 12th-c hermit. The Mother Shipton and Yorkshire Lass both have good value food.
Knaresborough Castle All that remains are the 14th-c keep (with museum and suitably dank dungeon), gatehouse and some of the curtain wall, but it's easy to imagine what an imposing sight it must have made, glowering over the gorge of the River Nidd – a suitable spot for Thomas à Becket's murderers to hide in. Shop, limited disabled access; cl Oct–Easter; (01423) 503340; £2, also includes

entrance to the 14th-c **Old Court**, now a local history museum.

Mother Shipton's Cave and Well In the 19th c quite a little tourist industry was concocted for the toffs from Harrogate around the alleged 16th-c prophecies of Mother Shipton. The cave she lived in is pleasantly set in 12 acres of riverside parkland, along with this limestone spring, which quickly coats teddy-bears and other unlikely objects in rock so that they can be sold as souvenirs. There are guided tours, and a local history museum (not in winter), but admission to the site is a hefty £4.95 (less in winter). Snacks, shop; (01423) 864600; cl 25 Dec.

LANGTHWAITE NZ0002 Idyllic Dales hamlet, with good circular walks from the nice Red Lion – and the Arkengarthdale road up to the remote but very popular Tan Hill Inn is a very fine drive.

LEYBURN SE1190 Bustling little agricultural town with a proper country atmosphere and lively Friday market: the Sandpiper's the nicest pub, and Tennants is Europe's largest auction room for house clearances and antiques. Off the A684 W are fine drives: up Coverdale to Kettlewell; up Bishopdale on the B6160 and on down past Cray into Wharfedale; up into the Eden Valley's Cumbrian headwaters on the B6269; and the Carperby–Castle Bolton–Reeth road.

Constable Burton Gardens 🖼 (A684 E) A series of fine terraced gardens around a handsome Georgian house (not open); the cyclamen at the end of the short lime avenue flower beautifully in late Aug. Disabled access but no facilities; open late Mar to mid-Oct; (01677) 450428; £2.50. The nearby Wyvill Arms is good.

LINTON IN CRAVEN SD9962 A gem of a Dales village, with lovely stone buildings, set off by lawns running down to a duck-filled stream. The Fountaine is a nice pub.

MALHAM SD9062 This has a good National Parks information centre, and the Listers Arms is a good refuge. A fine if popular walk leads along the beck to Janet's Foss waterfall, and to the romantic severity

of dramatic Gordale Scar, Malhamdale's most memorable natural feature, where a beck makes a spectacular leap from the rocks. The Pennine Way N of Malham waterfall ascends the side of Malham Cove, a great cliff, then crosses a natural rock pavement and heads over a landscape of limestone scars, disappearing streams and green turf to Malham Tarn, a lovely mountain lake skirted on its E side by a nature trail.

Malhamdale One of the smaller dales, its upper stretches cut tortuously and deeply out of the limestone by the River Aire and its steep tributaries, leaving spectacular cliffs, extensive bare upland limestone 'pavements', craggy bowls carved out of the overhanging hillsides, and sparkling waterfalls. This area is understandably a magnet for visitors.

MASHAM SE2280 (pronounced Mazzum) Civilised small market town, with an interesting church, and dignified Georgian houses around its broad market square – which comes to life on Weds and Sat. The Kings Head does decent food.

Black Sheep Brewery (Wellgarth) Set up by a breakaway member of the Theakston family a few years back, its beers since proving very popular. The tours are fun and imaginative: best to book, (01765) 689227 – evening tours are best, with more time to enjoy samples at the end; disabled access; £4.50. Good place for refreshments, too.

Theakston Brewery Centre Next to the big Scottish & Newcastle brewery, this explains the brewing process behind Theakstons beer, inc their Old Peculier. Shop, disabled access; open daily Easter–Oct, and wknds and Weds Nov to mid-Dec; £2.50 (price includes a pint). Enthusiastic tours of the brewery itself are £4; best to book on (01765) 689057; you see more in the mornings; no under-10s.

Uredale Glass (42 Market Pl) Hand-made glassware, with glass-blowing demonstrations (not Sat–Mon); cl Christmas wk, best to phone for opening times in Jan; (01765) 689780; free.

MIDDLEHAM SE1287 Attractive and civilised basically

Georgian stone-built village, still with the style that came from its days as the country's top racehorse-training centre in the 18th and early 19th c. Even now there are times when it seems to have more horses than people: pick up breeding and gallops gossip in the bar of the good Black Swan. This is a good area for self-catering accommodation – and fine walking country.

Middleham Castle This 12th-c structure dwarfs the village. For a time it was the home of young King Richard III. Only the huge keep and some later buildings remain, but there are marvellous views from the top, and an informative exhibition centre. Snacks, shop, disabled access; cl 1–2pm and all Mon and Tues Nov–Mar, 24–26 Dec; (01969) 623899; £2.30; EH.

MUKER SD9197

Attractive Dales hamlet, with very good woollens shop and well liked tearooms. Between here and Keld, the River Swale enters a deeply cut valley and tumbles over waterfalls; there are paths on both sides of the river, or you can take a more upland route over neighbouring Kisdon.

NEWBY HALL SE3568

(off B6265 E of Ripon) In beautiful formal gardens covering 25 acres, this late 17th-c mansion, redesigned inside and out by Robert Adam, has an important collection of classical sculpture and Gobelins tapestries, as well as a good range of Chippendale furniture. In the grounds are a miniature railway, children's adventure garden, paddling pool and woodland discovery walk. Meals, snacks, shop, some disabled access; house cl am, all day Mon (exc bank hols), and Oct–Mar; (01423) 322583; £6.50, £4.70 gardens only.

NIDDERDALE SE1073

This quiet yet beautiful valley has an impressive solitary grandeur. Just outside the National Park, it and the hills above are less liberally laced with footpaths and open-access moorland than the other dales here, and attract far fewer visitors – but there are plenty of relatively unfrequented walks, often on good paved but untarred tracks. The Nidderdale Way allows a fine fairly gentle walk of a couple of hours or so,

up on to the high pastures (see lambs being born in spring) and moorland at Glasshouses and back, with spectacular views almost all the way. It's well signed; start from Dacre Banks and take the lane a couple of hundred yards past the church. The stretch between the attractive small town of Pateley Bridge and the little village of Lofthouse is dominated by the sheltered two-mile waters of Gouthwaite reservoir, serenely set below the hills with some tall trees alongside. From Lofthouse a path runs beside the River Nidd, with picturesque tracks among small woods and ruined farmhouses, to Scar House Reservoir, quite exposed at the valley head (there's also a toll road up to it); high, exposed routes line the N side of the dale up here.

How Stean Gorge To the W of Lofthouse, this is a spectacular ravine pocked with pot-holes and caverns; a footpath snakes between miniature cliffs, with bridges giving views into the gorge; there's also a visitor centre.

NORTH STAINLEY SE2876

Lightwater Valley Theme Park Family fun from the nostalgic pleasure of a steam train to the white-knuckle, green-faced thrills of one of the world's biggest roller-coasters; another roller-coaster is entirely underground. Meals, snacks, shop, disabled access; open wknds and school hols (not Christmas) Easter–Oct, and daily Jun–early Sept; (01765) 635321; £12.50. There's an adjacent factory shopping village, open all year. The Staveley Arms does decent food.

NORTON CONYERS SE3076

(3½ miles N of Ripon) The same family have lived in this late medieval house for over 370 years, and the furniture and pictures reflect the fact that it's still very much a family home. Charlotte Brontë used the building as one of her models for Thornfield Hall. Look out for the hoofprint on the stairs. Attractively planted 18th-c walled garden. Seasonal pick-your-own fruit, shop (with unusual plants and garden fruits), limited disabled access; open pm bank hol Sun and Mon Easter–Aug, then Sun pm from mid-May to mid-Sept, plus pm daily for a wk in July, phone for dates; (01765) 640333; £4. The Freemasons Arms at

Nosterfield is useful for lunch.

NUN MONKTON SE5057

This attractive village is in appearance almost more like France than Yorkshire, with its broad avenue, and the stately meeting of the rivers Nidd and Ouse.

PARCEVALL HALL SE0660

Parcevall Hall Gardens Surrounding an Elizabethan house, 16 acres of woodland gardens charmingly set on a hillside E of the main Wharfedale Valley; superb views from the cliff walk. Tearoom (wknds only), picnic area, plant sales; cl Nov–Easter exc by appointment; (01756) 720311; £3. The Craven Arms at nearby Appletreewick is good for lunch, with lovely views.

PEN-Y-GHENT SD8473

(694 metres – 2,277 ft) Reached from Horton in Ribblesdale; its satisfyingly compact summit is the craggiest feature on the Pennine Way, which near here passes some pot-holes inc Hull Pot.

RAYDALE SD9187

(nr Bainbridge) The most interesting of Wensleydale's subsidiary valleys for walkers. Its lower neck is quite narrow, but it broadens out into quite a broad sheltered bowl of valley, with Semer Water, a sizeable glacial lake which legend has it was conjured up by a wandering beggar to drown a village which had spurned him. It's Yorkshire's third-largest natural lake, and has a path along its half-mile long S side, but to make up circular routes you have to do some road walking. The walled track (a Roman road) just N has wide-ranging views as it descends to Bainbridge.

REETH SE0399

Attractive Dales village with a high, wide, sloping green; the Black Bull and Kings Arms are handy dining pubs. The village is a centre for rambles ranging from pottering along the meadows by the Swale to walks over moors into adjacent Arkengarthdale (where the ascent on to Fremington Edge is memorable).

RIBBLESDALE SD7776

Climbing above Settle into severe and grand mountain scenery, this is craggy and remote: a major magnet for walkers on the Three Peaks Walk, 24 miles taking in the summits of Ingleborough, Pen-y-ghent and Whernside. This is a tough undertaking in its entirety, but each of the peaks on its own is a manageable half-day excursion: choose a clear day – not just for the magnificent views but for your own safety. Below Settle, the valley is less interesting for walkers, and marred by some quarrying.

Upper Ribblesdale This high walking country is riddled with impressive pot-holes, some of them gaping chasms of sensational size that can be admired from the surface, as well as the intricate underground passages that make the area so popular with cavers. Up in the loneliest parts, useful refuges are the cheerful cavers' inn the Old Hill at Chapel le Dale, and the isolated Station Inn at Ribblehead.

RICHMOND NZ1600

A most attractive riverside country town, with steep and pretty streets of old stone buildings, and a splendid broad sloping market square (still cobbled, and perhaps the biggest in the country; market day is Sat). Scollards Hall, built in 1080, is possibly the oldest domestic building in Britain. An attractive riverside walk beneath the towering bulk of its castle heads W through Hudswell Woods, with an extension to Whitcliffe Scar, a cliff above the Swale with an exciting path along its top. The army connection with the town is still strong; nearby Catterick Camp is the biggest in the north. The Black Lion in Finkle St is good value for lunch.

Easby Abbey Extensive remains of a 12th-c Premonstratensian abbey, a pretty riverside walk SE.

Green Howards Museum (Market Sq) In a converted 12th-c church, this includes among duller regimental history the blood-stained pistol holsters of the Grand Old Duke of York. Shop, some disabled access; cl wknds in Feb–Mar and Nov, Sun am mid-May to Oct, and all Dec–Jan; (01748) 822133; £2.

Richmond Castle These austere and intricate ruins dominate the town, and overlook the River Swale from a high rocky outcrop. Shop, some disabled access; cl 1–2pm in winter, 24–26 Dec and 1 Jan; (01748) 822493; £2.60; EH.

Theatre Royal (Victoria Rd) The

country's oldest and most authentic working theatre still in its original form, complete with gallery, boxes and pit. Built in 1788, it doesn't look much from the outside but the immaculately restored interior is really special. Snacks, shop, limited disabled access; guided tours and museum open Mon–Sat Easter–Oct, other times by appointment; (01748) 823021; £1.50.

RIPLEY SE2860

Ripley Castle 🏰 (off A61) Beautifully picturesque castle, in the same family for an amazing 26 generations. Most of the current building dates from the 16th c, inc the tower housing a collection of Royalist armour. For some the main attraction is the splendid gardens, the setting for a national collection of hyacinths and (under glass) a fine tropical plant collection. Also lakeside walk and wildlife trail. Meals, snacks, shop, some disabled access; open Tues, Thurs, Sat and Sun Jan–Mar and Nov–Dec, Thurs–Sun Apr–Jun and Sept–Oct, and daily July–Aug; (01423) 770152; £5, £2.50 gardens only. The attractive village, rebuilt in the 1820s, has a superb delicatessen, and the Boars Head Hotel is a fine old place for lunch.

RIPON SE3171

On Thurs colourful stalls fill the attractive and ancient market square (a few stalls too on Sat); it's largely unspoilt, lined with specialist shops and old inns and hotels. At 9pm each night the Wakeman, a red-coated bugler, blows a buffalo horn here, as one has done for centuries. Going from here down one of the town's engagingly narrow old streets, you're rewarded by a magnificent view of the elegant Early English W front of the cathedral. The Golden Lion just off the market square is useful for a bite to eat. Fountains Abbey is within a walk from here, and Newby Hall and Norton Conyers are also quite close.

Ripon Cathedral Spectacularly floodlit at night, this is one of the largest half-dozen in the country, and has plenty to see, inc very fine carving indeed in both stone and wood, and a 7th-c crypt – the oldest surviving part of any British cathedral building (and probably the oldest surviving crypt outside Italy). Shop, disabled access; £2

suggested donation.

SETTLE SD8163

Market day (Tues) around the Shambles is particularly attractive; look out to the right of here for the Folly, an extraordinary 17th-c town house. Mary Milnthorpe & Daughter is a good antique jewellery and silver shop, and the Golden Lion has good food. Just across the Ribble, Giggleswick is a peaceful contrast to the hectic little town.

Settle–Carlisle Railway A magnificent 70-mile route carved up through Ribblesdale across the wild moors between here and Cumbria, and then dropping down through the lovely Eden Valley; (08457) 484950 for times and fares, £16 for a day return. All year on Sats and some Suns and Weds there's a programme of walks connecting with the moorland stops; they start quite early (8.45am Sat), with dates and times listed on the timetable. Aside from the setting, it's an ordinary Railtrack line: steam trains do run some Sats in summer, but only from cities in the south ((01543) 419472 for routes and times), resulting in the bizarre situation that you can travel by steam if you're coming from Norwich or London, but not if you're in the immediate vicinity. The B6479 is not quite comparable to the train, but a good drive.

SKIPTON SD9851

On Sat the main street has a colourful market (at least some stalls here most other days too, exc Sun, Tues and Thurs). The 14th-c church has a 16th-c rood screen and interesting stained glass. A canal runs through the town, and the Royal Shepherd in an attractive spot has good value quick food.

Skipton Castle 🏰 12th-c, and properly romantic, with sturdy round towers, broad stone steps, and a lovely central flagstoned and cobbled courtyard with a seat around its venerable central yew tree. One of the best-preserved medieval castles in Europe, it really is remarkable how much is left, interior and all – very few other castles have kept their roofs and stayed habitable. The original Norman arched gateway still stands – the word 'Desormais' carved above it is the motto of the family who lived here 1310–1676. Snacks, shop; cl Sun am, 25 Dec; (01756) 792442; £4.20.

STAINBURN MOOR SE2452

The area E of the Dales really has nothing to compare with the Dales themselves for serious walking, but this moorland W of Harrogate has some possibilities for fairly stretching walks, for instance from the car park by the woods along the side road W from Beckwithshaw.

STAINFORTH SD8167

There's a pleasant and gentle Ribblesdale walk from Stainforth Force to Langcliffe.

STARBOTTON SD9574

Tiny but delightful Wharfedale village; a good base for walks, for example along the river to Kettlewell, then back up over the high land; or follow less obvious paths W to Arncliffe in Littondale – which is very similar to the Wharfedale parent valley, though with a flatter damper valley floor.

SWALEDALE SE0098

The northernmost of all the dales, and one of the least visited – giving more chance of getting away from it all at even peak times. Its bold hills, abundant stone barns and extreme tranquillity make it a walkers' favourite. It's grandly austere for the most part, though quite heavily wooded as it drops down towards Richmond. In the steeper parts there are some fine waterfalls. The upper slopes, especially towards the Durham and Cumbrian borders, are wild and empty, except for the huge scattered flocks of hardy clean-limbed Swaledale sheep with their dark faces, grey muzzles, thick fleeces, and curly-horned rams. The meadowland down in the valleys of this dale and its broad tributary Arkengarthdale is largely unimproved, with slow-growing natural grasses and lots of wild flowers. Many of the area's 1,200 traditional stone hay barns which are such a distinctive feature here have been rehabilitated in the last few years, with generous National Parks grant aid. Gunnerside still has around it many of the 'rushes' where lead-miners dammed streams to form torrents that could break up the lead-bearing rock strata below; this whole area was an important lead

centre until Victorian times, and other visible mementoes are ruined mill buildings, tunnel entrances and spoil heaps.

Deep Swaledale Between Muker and Keld the Swale enters a deeply cut valley and tumbles over waterfalls; there are paths on both sides of the river, or you can take a more upland route over neighbouring Kisdon.

WATH SE1467

Attractive Dales hamlet spreading up the valley, with pleasant walks along past the reservoir to Ramsgill – beyond there, there's a splendid moorland drive over to Masham.

WENSLEYDALE SD9889

More expansive in character and not quite as dramatic as Swaledale, but richly picturesque; its unspoilt villages and numerous waterfalls make for pleasurable walking. It used to be one of the richest dales, its broad pastures and countless sheep supporting the wealthy abbeys and castles whose ruins now add so much interest to its scenery. Wensleydale sheep are very distinctive, with long fleecy dreadlock curls. Upper Wensleydale (around and W of Hawes) is steep and wild; E of here the valley starts broadening out, with richer lower pastures, and more regular farmland below Middleham.

WHARFEDALE SE0361

Below Grassington there's an extremely pretty stretch where the valley winds more sinuously past Burnsall, Appletreewick (good riverside car park – around £3) and Bolton Abbey, below hills which though less grand are more varied in shape, with rather sensitively laid-out conifer plantations adding a slightly subalpine feel to some of the views.

Upper Wharfedale With its tributary valley Littondale and its headwaters up in the steep conifer plantations at the top of Langstrothdale, this is one of England's most popular areas for walkers, and very beautiful indeed in parts. The Dales Way follows the River Wharfe for the length of the dale, except between Kettlewell and Grassington. Upper Wharfedale above Grassington has a level floor of sheltered well drained pastures with the river winding through, a few grey stone barns, and steep sides laced with dry-stone walls, gnarled woodland and occasional austere crags, climbing up to high fairly level tops some 365 metres (1,200 ft) above the valley floor. The smaller villages are delightfully private and unspoilt, their grey or whitewashed stonework blending perfectly with the long scars of the limestone terraces above them. Away from the valley floor, stone-walled grassy tracks are the easiest ways of gaining height.

WHERNSIDE SD7381 (736 metres – 2,415 ft) Sometimes criticised by keen walkers as the boring one of the Three Peaks, this is Yorkshire's highest point, and has an exhilarating ridge section; start from the magnificent Ribblehead Viaduct carrying the Settle–Carlisle railway over the head of the dale (the Station Hotel here is a comfortable halt).

WIDDALE SD8287 Widdale is a tributary of Wensleydale, steep-sided and dramatic, with extensive conifer plantations above it.

Other attractive villages include Appletreewick SE0560, Austwick SD7768, Bilbrough SE5346, Boroughbridge SE3967, Brearton SE3261, Buckden SD9477, Burnsall SE0361, Cray SD9379, East Witton SE1586 (ancient houses, long wide green), Gargrave SD9354 (on the Pennine Way), Giggleswick SD8164, Gilling West NZ1804, Grantley SE2369, Gunnerside SD9598, Hampsthwaite SE2659, Hudswell NZ1400, Kirkby Malham SD8961, Kirkby Overblow SE3249, Low Row SD9897 (popular with potholers), Middlesmoor SE0874, Newton-on-Ouse SE5160, Ramsgill SE1271, Redmire SE0591, Snape SE2784, Thornton in Lonsdale SD6873 (Conan Doyle was married in the charming church), Thornton Watlass SE2486, West Burton SE0186 and Wigglesworth SD8157.

Where to eat

ASENBY SE3975 **Crab & Lobster** *Dishforth Rd* (01845) 577286 Old thatched dining pub with a relaxed, informal but civilised atmosphere, interestingly furnished cosy rooms with lots of bric-a-brac, delicious food, and good wines by the glass; opulent bdrms. £30|£9

ASKRIGG SD9491 **Rowan Tree** (01969) 650536 Cosy little candlelit stone barn run by Irish husband and German wife, just a few tables so booking advisable, good imaginative evening meals and reasonably priced wine list; cl Sun, Mon, cl Jan–Feb; children over 12. £27.95 for 5 courses

BILBROUGH SE5346 **Three Hares** *Main St* (01937) 832128 Smart dining pub with welcoming landlord and staff, traditional bar with lots of polished copper and brass, no smoking restaurant, excellent modern cooking using the freshest local produce, interesting wine list, and well kept real ales; children must be well behaved and be gone by 8.30pm; cl Sun pm, Mon; disabled access. £22|£7.95

BOROUGHBRIDGE SE3966 **Black Bull** *6 St James Sq* (01432) 322413 Inn said to date from the 13th c, with big stone fireplace in main bar area (served from an old-fashioned hatch), cosy traditional snug, extended dining room, and well presented food – even the bread, pasta, sorbets and ice-creams are home-made – inc fresh daily fish and lovely puddings; well kept real ales, enjoyable wines with 10 by the glass, afternoon teas (not Sun), friendly attentive service, classical piped music; bdrms; disabled access. £23|£6.50

BREARTON SE3261 **Malt Shovel** (01423) 862929 Popular village pub with friendly, helpful licensees, heavily beamed rooms with open fires and lively hunting prints, good bar food, 5 well kept real ales, and a fine choice of malt whiskies and wines; no food Sun pm, Mon; cl first 2 wks Jan; disabled access. £18.95|£6.25

CARLTON SE0684 **Foresters Arms** (01969) 640272 Friendly, carefully restored inn with log fires, low beams and a nice atmosphere, well kept real ales, a good choice of whiskies, imaginative food in bar and restaurant, and friendly helpful service; good bdrms; no food Sun pm; cl Mon, Tues am, 3 wks Jan; children over 12 in restaurant in evening. £38|£6.95

CARTHORPE SE3083 **Fox & Hounds** *(01845) 567433* Pretty little extended village house with two log fires and some evocative Victorian photographs of Whitby, an attractive high-raftered, no smoking restaurant with lots of farm and smithy tools, enjoyable interesting food (fine daily specials and puddings inc yummy home-made ice-creams), decent wines, and helpful service; cl Mon, first wk Jan; disabled access. £17|**£8.95**

EAST WITTON SE1486 **Blue Lion** *(01969) 624273* Stylish and civilised dining pub with log fire, daily papers, bric-a-brac and rugs on flagstones in the distinctive old rooms, exceptionally good imaginative food, nice breakfasts, decent wines, real ales, and pretty garden; bdrms; disabled access. £19.75|**£6.95**

FERRENSBY SE3660 **General Tarleton** *Boroughbridge Rd (01423) 340284* Bustling 18th-c dining pub with beams and open fires, relaxed atmosphere, delicious food inc super puddings, polite service, and plenty of wines by the glass from a good list; cl 25 Dec; disabled access. £30|**£7**

GREAT OUSEBURN SE4461 **Crown** *Main St (01423) 330430* Cheery and notably friendly village pub (where Ambrose Tiller started his Tiller Girls dancing troupe) with plenty of interest in the warmly welcoming bar, two no smoking eating areas opening off, serving excellent well presented food using home-grown herbs and salad, and well kept real ales; cl Mon–Fri am exc bank hols; disabled access. £18|**£4.95**

HARROGATE SE3055 **Betty's** *1 Parliament St (01423) 502746* Famous cake shop with special blends of teas and coffees, Alsace wines, wonderful light home-cooked meals, traditional afternoon tea, over 75 different delicious cakes and pastries; they also have two tearooms in York, one in Ilkley and one in Northallerton – same details apply to each; cl 25–26 Dec, 1 Jan. £18|**£4.50**

HARROGATE SE2955 **Drum & Monkey** *5 Montpellier Gdns (01423) 502650* Bustling, very popular and long-standing fish restaurant, with downstairs bar (arrive very early for a table) and upstairs dining room (best to book); helpful service, exceptional simply prepared dishes, and very reasonable prices; cl Sun, cl between Christmas and New Year . £15 lunch/£25 dinner|**£7.15**

HARROGATE SE3055 **Tannin Level** *5 Raglan St (01423) 560595* Very good basement wine bar with brick walls and country dining chairs, imaginative food inc lovely puddings, fine wine list, and early evening tapas; cl Sun and bank hols. £25|**£6**

HARROGATE SE2954 **William & Victoria** *6 Cold Bath Rd (01423) 521510* Busy wine bar with upstairs evening restaurant and hearty helpings of decent country cooking; cl Sat am, Sun; first wk Jan; children over 11. £20|**£5.95**

HETTON SD9658 **Angel** *(01756) 730263* Extremely popular dining pub with old-fashioned rambling rooms, consistently excellent imaginative food, very good service from hard-working friendly staff, well kept real ales, and over 300 wines; cl 2 wks Jan; disabled access. £37.50|**£7.75**

LITTON SD9074 **Queens Arms** *(01756) 770208* Welcoming, quietly placed 17th-c inn with good popular food, big collection of cigarette lighters in main bar, another room with more of a family atmosphere, and two coal fires; cl Mon exc bank hols, 3 wks Jan (open 1 Jan); pretty bdrms. £20|**£6.75**

MASHAM SE2280 **Floodlite** *7 Silver St (01765) 689000* Bustling little candlelit restaurant with lots of bric-a-brac, particularly good sound cooking using top local ingredients with emphasis on fish and game, lovely puddings, and a sizeable fairly priced wine list; cl Mon, am Tues–Thurs. £23/2-course lunch £13.50

MIDDLEHAM SE1287 **Waterford House** *Kirkgate (01969) 622090* This most enjoyable restaurant-with-rooms, close to the market square, is filled with all sorts of antiques, has a friendly atmosphere, a superb wine list (they will pour you a glass from any of their 900 bottles), and delicious food using tip-top produce; bdrms (lovely breakfasts); £29.50

MOULTON NZ2303 **Black Bull** *(01325) 377289* Decidedly civilised, well run pub with old-fashioned style and standards of service, memorable bar snacks (excellent smoked salmon), conservatory restaurant or one in the Brighton Belle Pullman dining car, and good wines; cl Sun, 24–27 Dec; children over 7; partial disabled access. £35|£6

PICKHILL SE3483 **Nags Head** *(01845) 567391* Deservedly popular old inn with a nice mix of customers, busy tap room, smarter lounge, no smoking restaurant, particularly good food inc interesting daily specials and lovely puddings, friendly efficient staff, a fine wine list and well kept real ales; bdrms; cl 25 Dec; disabled access. £23|£7.25

SAWLEY SE2467 **Sawley Arms** *(01765) 620642* Rather smart pub with stunning flowering tubs and baskets, several small rooms with log fires and comfortable furniture, daily papers, a no smoking restaurant, good enjoyable bar food (inc interesting soups and fishy starters), and nice house wines; bdrms; cl Sun pm in winter; children over 9. £18|£6.75

North York Moors & East Yorkshire

A real mix of visitor attractions, plus wild open countryside and interesting coastline – great for walking

Families are well catered for here by a refreshingly broad sweep of places to visit. Friendly farm attractions include the buzzing Honey Farm at East Ayton, Staintondale's Shire Horse Farm (good demonstrations and talks), and busy Newham Grange Leisure Farm near Middlesbrough. Developing Nature's World at Acklam presents environmental concerns in a fun and interesting way, there's a satisfying range of traditional distractions at Major Bridge Park (Holme-on-Spalding-Moor) and Sewerby Hall (Bridlington), and the lovely grounds of Sutton Park (Sutton-on-the-Forest) now have the added allure of an adventure playground. The area is spread with haunting ruins, ideal for family picnics, with those at Whitby (fascinating recent archaeological finds), Rievaulx and Byland Abbey worth a special detour. It's easy to see why more people go on the North Yorkshire Moors Railway than any other steam railway in Britain, passing as it does through such wonderful countryside.

The North York Moors National Park is less visited than the Dales, but gives walkers (and drivers) broad and inspiring landscapes; the visitor centre at Danby gives out lots of helpful advice.

North of genteel Scarborough (lots to see and do here, with a good value joint ticket to three of its rewarding museums), the cliffy coast is full of character, with some delightful little fishing villages. The traditional seaside town of Bridlington is also attractive, with a restrained charm, plenty of family amusements, and excellent bird-watching opportunities at Bempton Cliffs and Flamborough Head, just N. Whitby is a working fishing port of real individuality. Hull is bigger, but has lots to interest visitors, with a laudable policy of free entry to all its museums; The Deep, a new waterfront marine centre, is likely to boost tourist numbers to the city when it opens (they hope in the autumn). Inland, Helmsley and Beverley are attractive small towns. The far N of the county makes the most of its Captain Cook connections.

Magnificent Castle Howard tops the list of grand country houses in splendid grounds for its sheer size alone, and the elaborate furnishings at Burton Agnes Hall, Burton Constable Hall, Sproatley, and Sledmere House are most intriguing. Beautifully restored Duncombe Park has marvellous landscaped gardens, and the water-lilies at Burnby Hall are rather special in summer.

More unusual outings include the re-created World War II scenes at Eden Camp just outside Malton, the Skinningrove mining museum, the miniature collections at Nunnington Hall and Robin Hood's Bay (the shoreline here is great for fossil hunting, too), llama trekking in Staintondale, and the extraordinary flowering churchyard at Bolton Percy.

Where to stay

AMPLEFORTH SE5678 **Carr House Farm** *West End, Ampleforth, York, North Yorkshire YO62 4ED* (01347) 868526 **£40**; 3 rms. In peaceful undulating farmland and with an acre of garden, this no smoking 16th-c stone farmhouse has beams and oak panelling, flagstoned dining room with woodburner in inglenook, separate lounge, and good breakfasts using home-made preserves, local bacon, and fresh farm eggs; cl 25 Dec; children over 7; no dogs

BLAKEY RIDGE SE6799 **Lion** *High Blakey, Kirkbymoorside, York, North Yorkshire YO62 7LQ* (01751) 417320 **£59***, plus winter breaks; 10 good rms, most with own bthrm. The fourth-highest inn in England, this has spectacular moorland views, characterful rambling bars, blazing fires, generous helpings of decent food served all day, good breakfasts, candlelit restaurant, quite a few real ales, and genuinely friendly licensees and staff; fine walking country; disabled access

COXWOLD SE5377 **Fauconberg Arms** *Coxwold, York, North Yorkshire YO61 4AD* (01347) 868214 **£55**, plus special breaks; 4 rms. Civilised old stone inn in lovely setting, with a big log fire, some handsome settles and gleaming copper in the two cosy and comfortably furnished rooms of the lounge bar, good food in restaurant and bar, an extensive wine list, afternoon teas (Weds, Sun, bank hols), and decent breakfasts

EGTON BRIDGE NZ8004 **Horse Shoe** *Egton Bridge, Whitby, North Yorkshire YO21 1XE* (01947) 895245 **£50**, plus special breaks; 6 simple rms, most with own bthrm. Beautifully placed inn by River Esk (stepping stones big enough for children to sit on), with lots of friendly wild birds and a pleasant sheltered lawn; open fires, attractive traditionally furnished bars, well cooked food inc excellent breakfasts in cottagey dining room, and decent wines; no accommodation 25 Dec

ESCRICK SE6243 **Church Cottage** *York Rd, Escrick, York, North Yorkshire YO19 6EX* (01904) 728462 **£60**; 7 comfortable, individually furnished rms. Friendly extended house next to church with a spacious no smoking dining room overlooking the landscaped gardens (spit-roast barbecues), a comfortable lounge, and enjoyable breakfasts

FLAMBOROUGH TA2270 **Manor House** *Tower St, Flamborough, Bridlington, East Yorkshire YO15 1PD* (01262) 850943 **£64**; 2 rms, the more expensive room has a 17th-c four-poster. Beautifully restored Georgian house with log fire and books in guest sitting room, lots of antiques (Mrs Berry is an antiques dealer), good breakfasts, and a friendly atmosphere; the old stable block has antiques and intricate local hand-knitted fishermen's sweaters called ganseys for sale; cl Christmas; children over 8

HAROME SE6481 **Pheasant** *Mill St, Harome, Helmsley, North Yorkshire YO62 5JG* (01439) 771241 **£124***inc dinner, plus special breaks; 12 rms. Family-run hotel with a relaxed homely lounge, and traditional bar with beams, inglenook fireplace and flagstones, good very popular food, efficient service, and indoor heated swimming pool; cl Dec–Feb; children over 8; disabled access

HARTOFT END SE7592 **Blacksmiths Arms** *Hartoft, Pickering, North Yorkshire YO18 8EN (01751) 417331* **£63***, plus special breaks; 18 rms. Carefully extended and modernised old inn in lovely surroundings at the foot of Rosedale, friendly traditionally furnished bar, open fires in cosy and comfortable lounges, and enjoyable food in spacious and attractive restaurant; lovely walks all round

HAWNBY SE5690 **Laskill Farm** *Easterside, Helmsley, York, North Yorkshire YO62 5NB (01439) 798268* **£60**; 6 rms, some in beamy converted outside building. Attractive and welcoming creeper-covered stone house on big sheep and cattle farm nr Rievaulx Abbey; open fire and books in comfortable lounge, good food using home-grown produce, and own natural spring water; self-catering also; cl 25 Dec; partial disabled access

HELMSLEY SE6183 **Black Swan** *Market Pl, Helmsley, North Yorkshire YO62 5BJ (01439) 770466* **£130**, plus special breaks; 45 well equipped and comfortable rms. Striking Georgian house and adjoining Tudor rectory with beamed and panelled hotel bar, attractive carved oak settles and Windsor armchairs, cosy and comfortable lounges with lots of character, and a charming sheltered garden

HOVINGHAM SE6675 **Worsley Arms** *High St, Hovingham, York, North Yorkshire YO62 4LA (01653) 628234* **£80**, plus special breaks; 18 individually decorated bedrooms. Stone-built Georgian inn with comfortable and pretty sitting rooms, fresh flowers and open fires, very good modern cooking in elegant restaurant and more informal Cricketers Bistro, and seats out by stream; disabled access

KILBURN SE5179 **Forresters Arms** *Kilburn, York, North Yorkshire YO61 4AH (01347) 868386* **£58***, plus special breaks; 10 clean, bright rms. Friendly old coaching inn opposite the pretty village gardens; sturdy but elegant furnishings made next door at Thompson mouse furniture workshop, a big log fire, and enjoyable food in restaurant and beamed bar; disabled access

LASTINGHAM SE7390 **Lastingham Grange** *High St, Lastingham, York, North Yorkshire YO62 6TH (01751) 417345* **£160**, plus special breaks; 11 rms. Attractive stone-walled country house in 10 acres of neatly kept gardens and fields – with the moors beyond; relaxed homely atmosphere in spacious lounge, open fire, decent food, extremely helpful service, and marvellous walks; good for children with ponies and playground; cl mid-Nov to Mar

MIDDLETON SE7887 **Cottage Leas Country Hotel** *Nova Lane, Middleton, Pickering, North Yorkshire YO18 8PN (01751) 472129* **£79***, plus special breaks; 12 comfortable rms. Delightful, peaceful 18th-c farmhouse with extensive gardens, comfortable informal rooms, beamed ceilings, open log fire in cosy lounge, a well stocked bar, and enjoyable food; pets by prior arrangement; cl 25 Dec pm; partial disabled access

PICKERING SE7984 **White Swan** *Market Pl, Pickering, North Yorkshire YO18 7AA (01751) 472288* **£95**, plus special breaks; 12 comfortable refurbished rms. 16th-c coaching inn with inviting small and quiet, traditional hotel bar, friendly staff and locals, log fires, and antiques in comfortable sitting room; good traditional bar food, an attractive restaurant with fine clarets and daily-changing food using the best local produce, and breakfasts with home-made marmalade; pets welcome

ROSEDALE ABBEY SE7296 **Milburn Arms** *Rosedale Abbey, Pickering, North Yorkshire YO18 8RA (01751) 417312* **£76**, plus special breaks; 11 individual, pretty rms. Friendly 18th-c inn in village surrounded by fine steep moorland; log fire and books in comfortable drawing room, traditionally furnished beamed bar, very good English cooking in attractive restaurant, a decent wine list, excellent breakfasts, and helpful staff; cl 24–26 Dec; pets by prior arrangement

ROSEDALE ABBEY SE7294 **White Horse Farm Hotel** *Rosedale Abbey, Pickering, North Yorkshire YO18 8SE (01751) 417239* **£75**, plus special breaks; 15 rms. Friendly country hotel above the village in 11 acres, with marvellous views, a cosy beamed bar and log fire, comfortable lounge, generously served food, and decent range of wines and malt whiskies; excellent walks; cl 24–25 Dec; dogs by prior arrangement

SCARBOROUGH TA0091 **Wrea Head Hotel** *Scalby, Scarborough, North*

Yorkshire YO13 0PB (01723) 378211 **£120**, plus special breaks; 20 individually decorated rms. Victorian country house in 14 acres of parkland and gardens; friendly staff, minstrels' gallery in oak-panelled hall and lounge, open fires, bow-windowed library, pretty flowers, and good food in airy restaurant; disabled access
WASS *SE5579* **Wombwell Arms** *Wass, York, North Yorkshire YO61 4BE (01347) 868280* **£49**, plus special breaks; 2 individually furnished rms. Attractive, warmly welcoming small inn with a cosy rambling bar, good imaginative food and decent wines in comfortable dining rooms (two are no smoking), and enjoyable breakfasts; cl 2 wks Jan; children over 8
WILLERBY *TA0230* **Willerby Manor** *Well Lane, Willerby, Hull, East Yorkshire HU10 6ER (01482) 652616* **£69**w; 51 individually decorated rms. Family-owned Victorian house in three acres of gardens; airy and attractive conservatory, dining bar and more formal restaurant, good food, helpful service, and health club with swimming pool

To see and do

ACKLAM *NZ4915*
Nature's World 🔳 (Ladgate Lane) Thriving environmental demonstration centre, developing all the time, with organic gardens, nature trails, and a number of re-created natural habitats inc a 400-metre-long model of the River Tees. An innovative new earth-sheltered 'eco-structure' housing displays on the latest in environmental technology (solar and geothermal power and so forth), as well as a futuristic hydroponicum, should be open by the start of 2001. They also hope to build up a seed bank for locally endangered wildflowers. Splendid home-cooked meals and snacks, shop, good disabled access; cl 25 Dec–1 Jan; (01642) 594895; £3.50.
BECK HOLE *NZ8202*
Charming tucked-away village; Birch Hall here is a unique cross between country tavern and village store. The most rewarding way to get here is walking along the historic rail trail along the abandoned line that preceded the current North Yorkshire Moors Railway route, between Grosmont and Goathland.
BEMPTON *TA1973*
Bempton Cliffs The RSPB bird reserve here has the biggest colony of seabirds in the country, with up to a quarter of a million of them nesting in the cliffs. Best views of puffins Jun–July, but plenty of skuas and shearwaters later in summer, with wknd boat trips from Flamborough (North Landing) or Bridlington, though what you'll see

depends on the weather. Snacks, shop, some disabled access; visitor centre cl all Jan, wknds Dec and Feb; (01262) 851179 – book well ahead for the boats; £3 car parking charge. Local fishermen run early summer wknd boats to the cliffs too.
BEVERLEY *TA0339*
Attractive country town, in a way like a small-scale York, with much the same sort of appeal. It's partly pedestrianised, with many fine Georgian buildings, several antiques shops and the like, but unlike York is still very much an honest market town rather than a tourist place. Animals, mainly pigs, are still sold at the Weds market (general market Sat), and the racecourse is central to local life. For meals, the comfortably traditional Beverley Arms and cheap Tiger are good. The B1248 N has rolling Wolds views.
Art Gallery & Museum (Champney Rd) Includes lots of pieces by Fred Elwell the woodcarver, famous for his paintings of the town and its characters; (cl 12.30–1.30pm wknds, all Mon and Tues and bank hols; free).
Beverley Minster Wonderful 13th/14th-c building, considered by some to be one of the most architecturally interesting in Europe, with elegant buttressing and elaborately pinnacled towers. The W front is richly carved yet extraordinarily harmonious. Inside are several delights, inc the intricately carved Percy tomb canopy, the unusual Saxon *fridstol* (one of only two such seats in the country), and the

biggest collection of misericords in Britain. Shop, disabled access; open daily exc 25 Dec, guided tours summer only; £2 suggested donation.

Museum of Army Transport (Flamingate) Huge hangar with all sorts of military vehicles inc planes, tanks and cars, many displayed in realistic settings down to farm-building camouflage for World War II. Children can climb into the jeeps and so on. Some vehicles may be demonstrated on summer Suns. Meals, snacks, shop, disabled access; cl 24–26 Dec; (01482) 860445; £4.50.

St Mary's church (Hengate) The former wealth of the town can be guessed at from the magnificence of another subsidiary church not far from the Minster (and originally intended to be a chapel for that marvellous building); the weather-vane on the SW turret is said to have been the last design by Pugin, who sketched it on the back of an envelope. Opposite is the White Horse, a quaint old gaslit bare-boarded tavern.

BLACKTOFT SE8424

Attractive Humber-side village; its pub the Hope & Anchor, with tables out by the waterside, is great for bird-watchers, right by the RSPB marsh reserve.

BOLTON PERCY SE5341

Behind a medieval gatehouse the 15th-c church has perhaps the most unusual **churchyard** in the country: over 15 years ago local lecturer Roger Brook set about tackling its profusion of weeds, and since then has transformed it into a splendidly colourful garden, with more than a thousand different types of plant creeping around and over the headstones. Rather like a semi-wild cottage garden, it houses part of the National Collection of dicentras and is open all the time. The Crown has generous simple food (not Mon or Tues).

BRIDLINGTON TA1767

Famous for its bracing image in the heyday of the traditional seaside resort, and the way the country rolls down to the long sands of the shore still gives that feeling. The centre is a quay and small harbour, with the usual summer attractions, but the original core of the town is half a mile in from the sea, with

some charming old houses among the more modern ones around the heavily restored **priory church**. A 14th-c gateway (the Baylegate) gives some idea of how imposing the priory must have been before the Dissolution, and houses a local history museum (cl wknds and all mid-Sept to May; £1). Broadacres (A165) has reliable family food inc a carvery. The coast to the S is generally much flatter.

Bondville Model Village 🔲 (Riviera Drive, Sewerby) Readers enjoy this; disabled access; cl Oct–Apr; (01262) 401736; *£2.50. A walk along the low cliff from here towards Flamborough Head soon brings you to a strip of woodland by a stream; if you follow the lane up from here past the car park and along the wood, you come to Iron Age earthworks which cut right across the head – making it a pretty impressive defensive position.

Harbour Museum & Aquarium (Harbour Rd) The best place to find out about the town's seafaring heritage; shop, disabled access; cl Nov–Mar; (01262) 670148; 50p.

John Bull's World of Rock (Carnaby Industrial Estate, off A614 SW) See how they squeeze the words into the candy, and maybe even personalise your own stick of the seaside favourite. Usually cl winter wknds and Christmas, best to check; (01262) 678525; £1 factory and exhibition.

Park Rose Pottery (Carnaby Covert Lane, off A614 SW) Factory visits and a seconds shop, as well as 12 acres of strollable parkland with play areas, owl sanctuary and bee exhibition. Meals, snacks, shop, disabled access; cl 25–26 Dec; (01262) 602823; site entry free, charges for some activities.

Sewerby Hall (NE edge) In spacious parkland right on the coast, with a miniature zoo and aviary (good for children), and a charming garden. The elegant early 18th-c house includes some Amy Johnson memorabilia – the pioneer aviator lived nearby. Snacks, shop, disabled access (but not to the hall); grounds open daily all year, house open Mar–mid-Jan, though only Sat–Tues out of season; (01262) 673769; £3.

BROMPTON SE9582

Wordsworth Gallery (Gallows Hill)
The former home of Mary Hutchinson,
who married William Wordsworth at
Brompton church in 1802. The
medieval barn has an exhibition on the
poet and Samuel Coleridge. Meals,
snacks, shop; cl Mon exc bank hols and
2 wks over Christmas; (01723) 863298;
free. The village is pretty, and the
Cayley Arms does good food.

BUGTHORPE SE7757
Attractive village, especially in spring,
with an interesting **church**.

BURTON AGNES TA1063
Burton Agnes Hall Marvellous richly
decorated Elizabethan house, with
fantastically carved Great Hall, 16th-c
antiques, and some splendid
Impressionist paintings. A fine walled
garden has colourful borders, there's a
pets' corner and topiary bushes. Meals,
snacks, shop, disabled access to ground
floor only; cl Nov–Mar; (01262)
490324; £4.80. The earlier Norman
manor house stands between here and
the church. The attractive **church** at
nearby Kilham has a memorable
Norman door; the 18th-c Bell in
Driffield is pleasant for lunch.

BYLAND ABBEY SE5478
The jagged ruins of this abbey, built for
the Cistercians, date from the 12th and
13th c. Enough detail survives to show
how fine it must have been: look out for
the well preserved floor tiles and
carved stone. Good for picnics. Snacks,
shop, some disabled access; cl 1–2pm,
Nov–Mar; (01347) 868614; £1.70. The
nearby Abbey Inn is most enjoyable for
lunch. The drive past here from Bagby
(SE of Thirsk), Kilburn and Coxwold,
and on via Wass and Ampleforth to
Oswaldkirk is very attractive.

CLEVELAND WAY NZ8215
One of the best ways of encountering
the North York Moors is by this well
marked long-distance path, which takes
a 110-mile horseshoe course from
Helmsley to Filey Brigg around the
moorland escarpments of the
Hambledon and Cleveland hills, before
a coastal finale along the highest cliffs on
the eastern seaboard. Highlights include
Sutton Bank, Roseberry Topping and
the coast around Staithes, Robin
Hood's Bay, Ravenscar and Hayburn
Wake; a particularly fine section can be

reached off the B1257 N of Chop Gate
NZ5703 (where the Buck does good
food). The path westwards on the N
slopes of the moors takes in rock
outcrops. The frequent bus service
between Scarborough and Whitby is
useful for getting you back if you're
walking shorter coastal sections.

COXWOLD SE5377
Neat and very attractive little stone-
built village, very harmonious. The
Fauconberg Arms does good food.
Newburgh Priory (just S) Charming
old house, partly Norman with Tudor
and Georgian additions. One of the
family married Oliver Cromwell's
daughter, who is supposed to have
rescued her father's headless corpse
and had it reburied here; the room with
the tomb is on the tour. Outside is a 40-
acre lakeside and riverside garden with
a fine collection of dogwoods, splendid
formal borders and lots of unusual
plants. Snacks; open pm Weds and Sun
Apr–Jun and Sun and Mon Aug bank hol
wknds; (01347) 868435; £4, £2 grounds
only.
Shandy Hall 🎫 Laurence Sterne's
quaint house has been well restored,
the little study much as it must have
been when he wrote *Tristram Shandy*
here. Outside is a lovely walled garden.
Shop with unusual plant sales; open
Jun–Sept, house pm Weds and Sun,
gardens daily exc Sat; (01347) 868465;
£3.50. Close by is the attractive 15th-c
church of which Sterne was parson – it
still has the box pews it had in his day.

CROPTON SE7588
Cropton Brewery 🎫 The small
family-run brewery has guided tours on
the hour 10am–4pm summer (best to
phone for winter times), and samples of
their robustly flavoured beers, as well
as a children's colouring competition,
and good adjacent pub, the New Inn;
disabled access to ground floor;
(01751) 417330; *£2.95. They sell local
walks leaflets.

DALBY FOREST SE8789
The E part of the National Park has
large forest plantations; this part has
colour-coded trails.

DANBY NZ7108
Moors Centre (Lodge Lane) Helpful
National Park information centre, with
exhibitions, guided walks and events,

and adventure playground; terraced riverside and woodland grounds. Meals, snacks, shop, disabled access to ground floor only; cl wkdys Jan and Feb, 25 Dec, (reduced hours in winter); (01287) 660540; free. This area has decent **horse riding centres**, good for experts and beginners alike; the Moors Centre has the full list, and can also provide numbers for the various cycle hire firms dotted about the region. The Duke of Wellington has good value food.

EAST AYTON SE9985
Honey Farm 🔲 (Betton Farm Centre) Exhaustive exhibition on bees and honey-making, with sales of wax and honey-based products. Also animals, craft shops, farm shop and play area. Meals, snacks, shop, some disabled access; (01723) 864001; £2.95. The Londesborough Arms at Seamer has decent food, and the Forge Valley drive to Hackness runs through ancient woodlands.

EGTON BRIDGE NZ8005
Charming Eskdale village, pleasantly eccentric, twinned with a fictional French one; lovely Esk views, good riverside pub.

ELVINGTON SE6748
Yorkshire Air Museum 🔲 Part of a World War II airfield and base preserved as it was then, with fine aircraft, an old control tower and plenty of other memorabilia inc a Halifax Mk III, engines, models and photographs. Meals, snacks, shop, disabled access; open daily in summer, best to check in winter; (01904) 608595; £4. The St Vincent Arms at Sutton-upon-Derwent is good for lunch.

ESTON NAB NZ5618
Outside the National Park, this gives walkers a massive view over industrial Teesside.

FADMOOR SE6789
Attractive village with good pub, on charming drive from Kirkbymoorside, on over Rudland Slack and past Cockayne to Helmsley.

FANGFOSS SE7653
Rocking Horse Shop Splendid collection of antique rocking horses; you can watch replicas being constructed, and buy either a finished horse or plans for doing it yourself.

Open by appointment (not Sun), (01759) 368737.

FARNDALE SE6697
The largest dale in the National Park, with characteristic North York Moors scenery – lush green fields and red-roofed yellow-stone houses beneath the brooding moorland plateau. It's famous for its miles of wild daffodils in Apr, introduced and naturalised here many centuries ago. They're at their best around Low Mill, and any walk to enjoy them gives the chance of coming back down the ancient green lane of Rudland Rigg, for spectacular views. The friendly Feversham Arms at Church Houses, right next to the daffodil reserve, does very good value food.

FELIXKIRK SE4684
Attractive village, with good drive to Kepwith and Nether Silton; the Carpenters Arms is a good value dining pub.

FILEY TA1180
Much quieter resort than Scarborough, its neighbour up the coast, with the main road dropping down a steep little valley between the church and the old town (and under a footbridge linking the two) to the beach, where fishermen still beach their boats. The rock reef N of the town beyond the sands is interesting; to the S are holiday camps, and the seafront Coble Landing Bar has decent food and great views.
Filey Museum (Queen St) Small and attractively homely summer local museum in former medieval fishermen's cottages; shop, improved disabled access inc good facilities for the blind; cl 12.30–2pm, Sat am, Nov–Easter; £1.25.

FLAMBOROUGH TA2270
A blowy place, high on the headland, with some old houses in the core around the 15th-c **church**; down below past the holiday camp the natural rock harbour is well sheltered, with a lifeboat station, and there are fine views of coast and sea from the point of the headland, by the lighthouse. Flamborough Marine sell a local version of guernseys, weatherproof 'ganseys', hand-knitted in the round. The Seabirds is good for lunch, and the B1259 and B1229 are the most interesting coast

roads. There is some quite exciting walking, particularly around the N side of Flamborough Head, with the cacophony of thousands of kittiwakes sounding within the inlets; puffins can sometimes be seen on rock ledges. A level mile and a half from the lighthouse along clifftops leads to North Landing (café and car park). A longer walk making the Head the midway point starts from the village, skirting fields to join the coast path; to avoid anti-climax, walk the southern cliffs first and keep the real drama for later on. To the N the path follows the coast closely nearly all the way, and hilly country coming right to the coast makes for interest.

FOSTON ON THE WOLDS TA0855

Cruckley Farm 🖼 Friendly working farm, with lots of animals to fuss over – inc some very strange-looking rare breeds. Daily milking displays (usually around 10.45am). Snacks, shop, some disabled access; cl Oct–Apr; (01262) 488337; *£3. The Trout at Wansford has decent food.

GARTON-ON-THE-WOLDS SE9859

Garton-on-the-Wolds church 12th-c, and very High Church inside, with 19th-c mosaics and frescoes.

GOATHLAND NZ8301 In the heart of the moors, this was the picturesque setting for TV's *Heartbeat* (beware coach loads of ardent fans). There are interesting walks from here, inc the short one from opposite the church to **Mallyan Spout**, a waterfall which tumbles into the side of a fine wooded smooth-rocked gorge. The Mallyan Spout Hotel has spacious lounges and does popular food.

GREAT AYTON NZ5610

Captain Cook Schoolroom Museum (High St) Recently revamped museum housed in two rooms of the Postgate School, built in 1704, where James Cook received his early education. Thanks to a Lottery grant, it now features a reconstruction of an early 18th-c school, plus interactive displays about the explorer's early life and later achievements. Open pm Apr–Oct, plus all day July–Aug, other times by appointment only; (01642) 722208; £2.

GUISBOROUGH NZ6116

Gisborough Priory 🖼 12th-c ruined priory, one huge window rising dramatically from the rest of the more or less foundation-level ruins. The gatehouse is fairly well preserved, and it's an atmospheric spot for a picnic. Shop; cl Mon (plus Tues Oct–Mar), 24 Dec–1 Jan; £1. The Fox nearby has decent food, and the market town has attractive corners. Out at Newton (A173) the Kings Head is a popular dining pub by Roseberry Topping viewpoint.

HAWNBY SE5489 Attractive village, on the very scenic Rievaulx Abbey–Osmotherley road; good pub.

HAYBURN WYKE TA0096 From the very well sited hotel here (good value Sun carvery) steep Victorian woodland paths wind down to the cliff-sheltered cove; a clifftop path to the S gives fine views.

HELMSLEY SE6184 Lanes run straight up on to the moors from this attractive small market town (the B1257 is one of the best moorland roads). There's a large cobbled square (busy Fri market), and enough antiques shops and craft shops to please a visitor without seeming too touristy. A lively and bustling place, with a lot of class. A rewarding and very varied drive is past Rievaulx Abbey, Old Byland and Cold Kirby to Sutton Bank, left along the A170 then next right turn to Kilburn, Coxwold, Byland Abbey and back via Ampleforth and Oswaldkirk.

Duncombe Park Beautifully restored early 18th-c house, rebuilt after a fire at the turn of this century. The landscaped gardens, with grand terracing, are magnificent, covering around a tenth of the 300 acres of memorable parkland. Meals, snacks, shop, some disabled access; cl Fri–Sat, and Nov–Mar, best to phone for opening times; (01439) 770213; £6, £4 gardens only. You can wander through the estate (which has nature reserve status) for £2.

Helmsley Castle 🖼 This 12th-c pile, ruined in 1644, stands within enormous earthworks and dominates the town; good for picnics. Shop; cl 1–2 pm, winter Mon and Tues, 24–26 Dec; (01439) 770442; £2.30.

HOLDERNESS TA3029

The area between Wolds, Humber and coast is flat: rich farming country with huge fields and not many buildings, though the fine village churches often with soaring towers or spires reflect the wealth that this fertile land has put into them in the past. The long southern stretch of coast is flat country too, without a great deal of appeal for walkers – except for long lonely off-season walks by the edge of the North Sea.

HOLME-ON-SPALDING-MOOR
SE7838

Major Bridge Park 🖼 (Selby Rd) Private collection of working rural equipment, small rare breeds farm and vintage fairground rides (you can go on these), with nature trails through surrounding countryside. Snacks, shop, disabled access; open Sun May–Sept, daily (exc Sat) in Aug, and some bank hols; (01430) 860992; £2. The Red Lion has good food.

HORNSEA TA2145

Sizeable resort; behind the town, Hornsea Mere, 2m long, is the biggest natural lake in this region, with herons and other birds.

Hornsea Freeport (Rolston Rd) One of the area's most visited attractions, developing leisure centre based around a factory shopping village. Several well known brands and stores (some good bargains), and family features such as butterflies, model village, and indoor and outdoor adventure playgrounds. Meals, snacks, shop, disabled access; usually cl 25–26 Dec but best to check for Christmas opening; (01964) 534222; site free, around £1 (50p children) for family attractions.

Hornsea Museum (Newbegin) Enthusiastic folk museum with re-created period rooms, craft demonstrations and large gardens. Shop, some disabled access (best to phone beforehand); cl Sun am, and all Oct–Easter; (01964) 533443; *£2.

HOVINGHAM SE6675

Attractive village, with good pub and pleasant drive S to Sheriff Hutton and Flaxton.

HOWARDIAN HILLS SE6575

These gentle generously wooded hills have a path along their N flanks, giving intermittent rather patrician views across the plain to the North York Moors.

HOWDEN SE7428

Unpretentiously attractive, with cobbled alleys, a fine market hall, a majestic **minster** with a tall tower, the ruins of a charming medieval chapter house, and a small marshland country park down the lane opposite the minster, with ponds and raised walkways. The White Horse is useful for lunch.

HUGGATE SE8855

Attractive Wolds village, with good pub and easy walks nearby.

HULL TA1028

Kingston-upon-Hull is the full name of this big port, surprisingly pleasant for visitors now that the former docks have been so well tidied up. The landing stage for the former Humber ferry has become an attractive pedestrian enclave with some solid well restored Georgian buildings, and there are Humber views from the waterfront Minerva (which brews its own beer). Nearby, the original dock has become a yacht marina, with quite cheerfully buoyant modern buildings around it. Princes Quay is now a smart shopping centre (with good value food in the Mission, a converted seamen's mission over in Posterngate). The Deep, a £40m waterfront aquarium partly funded by the Millennium Commission, is bound to draw more visitors to Sammy's Point (at the confluence of the rivers Hull and Humber), when it opens (they hope around autumn). Away from the water, some of the most ancient buildings in the narrow streets of the old town have survived, notably on the High St. One of the most delightful old buildings is the Olde Whyte Harte just off Silver St; it was in its heavily panelled upper room that the town's Governor made the fateful decision to lock the town's gate against King Charles in 1642, depriving him of the arsenal that might otherwise have swung the Civil War in his favour. These two enclaves, the old town and former docks, are separated from each other by good main roads through to the modern container and ferry docks; the traffic just sweeps by, leaving them as self-contained islands – very quiet at wknds. Hull's good museums are mostly concentrated in the old town, so it's easy to walk from one to another. A free copy of the city's ale trail (a self-guided tour around the best pubs) is available from the Tourist Information Centre in Paragon St.

Ferens Art Gallery (Queen Victoria Sq) Enterprisingly run general collection, with lots of maritime paintings, Dutch Old Masters and interactive children's gallery. Snacks, shop, disabled access; cl Sun am, 24 Dec–1 Jan, and Good Fri; (01482) 613902; free.

Hands on History (South Church Side) Formerly the Old Grammar School (Hull's oldest secular building, dating from 1583), this is now a rapidly expanding social history collection; shop, disabled access; open all day Sat, Sun pm, and wkdys in school hols; free.

Hull & East Riding Museum (High St) Fine mosaics and a medieval section; cl Sun am, 25 Dec, 1 Jan and Good Fri; (01482) 613902; free.

Hull Maritime Museum (Queen Victoria Sq) This massive yet solidly stylish three-domed Victorian building has good displays on Hull's maritime history. There's a long-established section on whales and whaling, and the huge skeletons on display were mentioned in *Moby Dick*. Shop, disabled access; cl 24–26 Dec, 1 Jan and Good Fri; (01482) 613902; free.

Maister House (High St) Only the staircase and entrance hall are open in this mid-18th-c rebuilding (the rest is still used as offices), but the Palladian staircase is splendid, and the doors ornate and finely carved. Cl wknds and bank hols; 80p; NT.

Spurn Lightship (Princes Dock, Marina) Operating from the 1920s to the 1970s – interesting to go below decks and imagine being confined to this for weeks at a time, not going anywhere, tossed about in storms or blanketed in fog; open daily exc Sun am Apr–Sept; (01482) 613902; free.

Streetlife Museum (High St) Hoping to reopen around May following extensive refurbishment, this substantial collection is devoted mainly to local public transport and bicycles, some weird and wonderful, with a few

interactive displays. Best to phone nearer the time for opening times and prices; (01482) 613902; free.

The Deep (Sammy's Point) Jointly developed by the city's university and council, the European Maritime Institute (to give it its rather grand full title) hopes to open around autumn, and aims to promote awareness about coastal environments through a mixture of interactive displays and live exhibits, looking at sea life from prehistoric times to the present day. Phone (01482) 615789 for more information.

Wilberforce House (High St) William Wilberforce, English philanthropist and anti-slavery campaigner, was born in this 17th-c house, and its Jacobean and Georgian rooms have a good exploration of the horrors of the slave trade and the struggle for its abolition; also a notable collection of dolls. Shop, limited disabled access; cl Sun am, 25 Dec, 1 Jan, Good Fri; (01482) 613921; free. The Olde Black Boy nearby was the site of slave auctions.

HUMBER BRIDGE TA0224

Humber Bridge Country Park At the N end of the longest single-span suspension bridge in the world, nearly a mile between the towers, and a very impressive sweep of engineering (there's a footway across as well as the road). Plenty of woodland and clifftop walks, and an old mill. Meals, snacks, shop, good disabled access; (01482) 640852; free.

HUTTON-LE-HOLE SE7090

🏛 Neat and pretty streamside village at the mouth of Farndale; sheep wander the streets – though they won't be alone in the summer months. Its excellent **Ryedale Folk Museum** is practically a village itself, made up of various old buildings from the area re-erected in the 3-acre grounds, inc an Elizabethan manor house, gipsy caravan, and an Edwardian photographic studio; craft demonstrations most Sat–Weds. Shop, disabled access; cl Nov–Mar; (01751) 417367; £3.25. The Crown here is useful for lunch. There's a pleasant walk (an hour or so) over to Lastingham, and the Blakey Ridge road to Castleton is a great drive with classic moorland views.

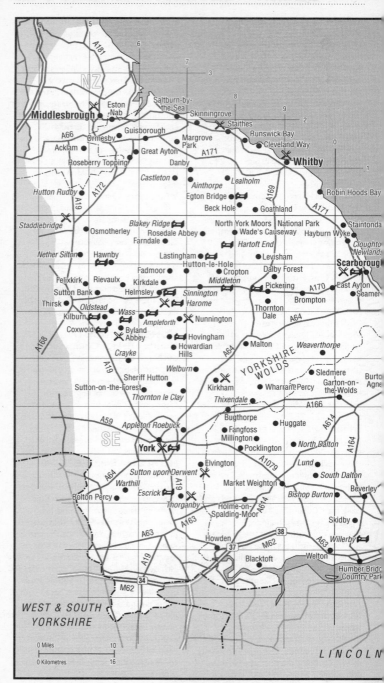

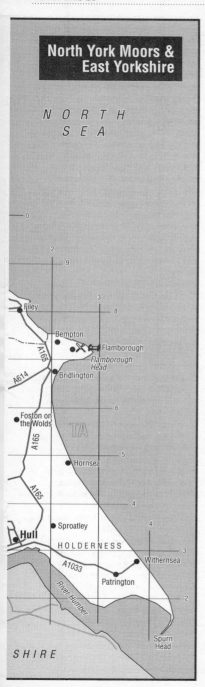

North York Moors & East Yorkshire

NORTH SEA

Filey

Bempton

Flamborough

Flamborough Head

Bridlington

Foston on the Wolds

Hornsea

Hull

Sproatley

HOLDERNESS

Withernsea

Patrington

River Humber

Spurn Head

SHIRE

KILBURN SE5179

Robert Thompson Furniture Workshop The quiet village is almost a place of pilgrimage to this workshop, famous for the unobtrusive little mouse carved as a trademark that you'll see all over North Yorkshire, on church pews and in the better inns and pubs. A visitor centre traces the company history, and you can watch the craftsmen at work. Shop; cl Mon (exc bank hols and Jun–Sept), and Nov–Mar; (01347) 868218; £1.50. They make lovely, simple furniture – though not cheap. The oak they use can be seen all around. Nr the church (with a memorial to Thompson carved by his own craftsmen) the Singing Bird does refreshments, as does the Forresters Arms – full of Thompson work. Up above the village on Roulston Scar is a white horse cut in the turf in 1857 and unique in this part of the country.

Old Mill Furniture (Balk) SE4780 A wide choice of hand-made furniture, with some nice simple designs (one of the craftsmen is an ex-Thompson employee) and competitive prices; cl Sun.

KIRKDALE SE6686

Kirkdale church Saxon, with a unique original sundial, and 7th-c Celtic crosses and carved stones.

KIRKHAM SE7366

Kirkham Priory Remains of Augustinian priory in an attractive quiet spot by the River Derwent; finely sculpted lavatorium, graceful arcaded cloister, and handsome 13th-c gatehouse with some finely carved sculptures and shields. Snacks, shop, disabled access; open Easter–Oct; (01653) 618768; £1.60. The Stone Trough overlooking the ruins is good for lunch, and a pleasant path meanders south by a placid stretch of the River Derwent, to Howsham Bridge and beyond.

LASTINGHAM SE7290

Attractive village, with former **monastery**, once one of the area's most sacred spots of pilgrimage, with an outstanding 11th-c crypt; good pub. The hillside just S gives a classic North Yorks Moors view, and there's a pleasant hour's walk over to Hutton-le-Hole.

LEVISHAM SE8390

A good spot for walkers, with open scenery around it, a track across the blustery moors, and an attractive valley giving separate routes to and from the Hole of Horcum, just below the A169.

MALTON SE7871

Comfortable market town with some interesting side streets, in prosperous farming and racehorse-training country. Sat is a busy market day (the lively livestock mart is on Mon, Tues and Fri). The Royal Oak and Kings Head do good generous food. A scenic road towards York is the old coach road parallel to the A64, from Norton to Buttercrambe and Gate Helmsley.

Castle Howard (off A64 W)

Magnificent 18th-c palace designed by Sir John Vanbrugh, who up to then had no architectural experience whatsoever, but went on to create Blenheim Palace. The striking 90-metre (300-ft) long façade is topped with a marvellous painted and gilded dome, an unforgettable sight beyond the lake as you approach from the N. Splendid apartments, sculpture gallery and long gallery (58 metres (192 ft) long to be exact), magnificent chapel with stained glass by Burne-Jones, and beautiful paintings inc a Holbein portrait of Henry VIII. The grounds are impressive but inviting, inc the domed Temple of the Four Winds by Vanbrugh, a beautiful rose garden and the family mausoleum designed by Hawksmoor. There's a good unobtrusive adventure playground. The palace celebrated its tercentenary in 1999. Meals, snacks, shop, disabled access; cl Nov to mid-Mar; (01653) 648333; £7.50. A grand public road runs through the grounds, from Slingsby on the B1257; the vast estate is also threaded by a few public footpaths which gain glimpses of the great house and the landscaped parts of its grounds.

Eden Camp ⊞ (A64/A169 N)

Elaborately re-created wartime scenes in buildings of former prisoner-of-war camp, very well done with sound, smells and even smoke effects. Covers a wide range of World War II experiences, from the rise of the Nazis to the Blitz and Bomber Command ops room. There's a children's commando assault course, but it's perhaps the wartime generation that will get most out of the place. Meals and snacks in NAAFI, shop, disabled access; cl 2 Dec–early Jan; (01653) 697777; £3.50.

MARGROVE PARK NZ6515

South Cleveland Heritage Centre (Margrove Park) Right on the edge of the moors, with natural history and wildlife exhibitions, and can organise walks and nature trails. Meals, snacks, shop, disabled access; cl Fri, Sat, am Sun, and all Oct–Mar; (01287) 610368; free.

MARKET WEIGHTON SE8741

Neat and pleasant old market town with one or two useful antiques shops. Here the well signposted Wolds Way long-distance path briefly divides in two, allowing walkers a circuit taking in the old railway line, now the Hudson Way, and the villages of Goodmanham and Londesborough with its fine parkland.

MIDDLESBROUGH NZ5116

Captain Cook Birthplace Museum (Stewart Park, Marton, 3m S) The sound of creaking ship's timbers accompanies some of the displays, and the impressive grounds have a conservatory with tropical plants, animals and birds. Meals, snacks, shop, disabled access; cl Mon exc bank hols, 25–26 Dec, 1 Jan; (01642) 311211; £2.40. The nearby Apple Tree has good food.

Dorman Museum (Linthorpe Rd) Currently undergoing refurbishments, this will have extra galleries to house its interesting changing exhibitions, a discovery centre for children, a new café and improved disabled access when it reopens in spring. In summer, they run a programme of activities for children. Best to phone for opening times, (01642) 813781; free.

Newham Grange Leisure Farm ⊞ (Coulby Newham, off A174) Rare breeds and other animals, an agricultural museum with craft displays, reconstructed vet's surgery and saddler's shop, play and picnic areas. Snacks, shop, disabled access; cl wkdys Oct–Mar; (01642) 300202; £1.70.

Transporter Bridge (A178) Unique, with the central section serving as a ferry, every 15 mins shuttling cars and pedestrians across the Tees. A new visitor centre uses interactive displays to tell the story of the town's industrial heritage, as well as the history of the bridge itself; centre open pm only Tues–Sun, plus bank hol Mon; 50p. Bridge only cl Sun am, 25–26 Dec, and 1 Jan; crossing 80p cars, 30p pedestrians.

MILLINGTON SE8351

Wolds Way Good base for round walks based on the well signed Wolds Way, with the landscape here rolling most attractively.

NORTH YORK MOORS NATIONAL PARK SE7199

This has fewer visitors than the Dales: rich valley pastures, with red-tiled stone farmhouses, twisting rivers, quiet roads, and few villages. The higher moorland is generally very grand and empty, mile after mile of heather scoured by breath-snatching winds, where the few walkers have for company scatterings of hardy sheep and the occasional harsh cry of a grouse.

Classic views Surrounded by the interlocking moor and valley landscapes, the graveyard of **Gillamoor church** SE6889 will tempt you to work your camera hard. The lane at SE6188 a bit more than a mile N of Carlton, itself N of Helmsley, gives another fine view.

NUNNINGTON SE6779

Nunnington Hall Big 16th/17th-c house nicely set on the banks of the River Rye, with fine panelling and a magnificent staircase. A family home for nearly 400 years, with the intriguing Carlisle Collection of miniature rooms, each of them ⅛ life-size. Snacks, shop, limited disabled access; cl am, all day Mon (exc bank hols) and Tues (exc Jun–Aug), and all Nov–Mar; (01439) 748283; £4, garden only £1.50; NT. In the attractive village the Royal Oak is good for lunch, and the church has a fine effigy of a knight said to have rid the district of a Loathly Worm.

ORMESBY NZ5317

Ormesby Hall Elegant 18th-c house with elaborate plasterwork, Victorian laundry and kitchen, model railway, and pleasant gardens and grounds. Snacks, shop, disabled access to ground floor only; cl am, all day Mon (exc bank hols), Fri, Sat, and Nov–Mar; (01642) 324188; £3.50, garden & railway only £2.20; NT.

OSMOTHERLEY SE4597

Perhaps more small town than village, but quietly attractive; the Golden Lion is a good dining pub, with tables overlooking the green. A lonely stretch of the Cleveland Way well signed long-distance path runs up over the Hambleton Hills from here, with some road access along the way; and the 44-mile Wyke Way path starts here.

Mount Grace Priory (A19 NW) Carthusian monks not only took a vow of silence but rarely emerged from their own individual cells. One of those cells at this ruined 14th-c priory has been fully restored, giving a good illustration of how the monks must have worked and lived. The ruins are better preserved than those of any other Carthusian establishment in England, and in spring an impressive display of daffodils makes it especially attractive. An adjacent 17th-c manor house has an exhibition, and interesting Arts and Crafts connections. Snacks, shop; cl 1–2pm and Mon–Tues Nov–Mar, 24–26 Dec, 1 Jan; (01609) 883494; £2.80; EH.

North York Moors Adventure Centre (Ingleby Cross) Can organise climbing, caving and canoeing, (01609) 882571.

PATRINGTON TA3122

Patrington church Glorious, with lovely carving inside – its graceful spire beckoning you from a long way off.

PICKERING SE7984

Another attractive small town, usually very quiet (busier Mon market day), with vividly restored medieval murals in the splendid tall-spired **church**. The White Swan has good food; the A169 N has sweeping moorland views (up there the Saltergate Inn is a good stop).

Beck Isle Museum 📷 Charmingly set 17th-c riverside house with a wonderful collection of local bygones and period shops. Shop, disabled access; cl Nov–Mar; (01751) 473653; *£2.50.

North Yorkshire Moors Railway (Pickering Station) Steam trips through some lovely countryside and nostalgically restored stations, a distance of 18 miles; the line was originally built by George Stephenson. The Grosmont end has various locomotives and antique carriages, and you can stop off at Goathland. Meals, snacks, shop, disabled access; cl Jan–Apr (exc Nov and Dec wknds); (01751) 472508 for timetable; £9.50 full return journey. The nearby Station Hotel has decent food.

Pickering Castle 🏰 Ruins of 12th-c keep and later curtain walls and towers, with fine views from its imposing castle mound above the town. Snacks, shop, some disabled access; cl 1–2pm, and Mon and Tues Nov–Mar; (01751) 474989; £2.30.

POCKLINGTON SE8048

An open-faced market town below the Wolds, with a good few handsome buildings; the Feathers is popular for lunch (and has decent bedrooms). The B1246 Driffield road runs through some quite picturesque hills.

Burnby Hall (B1247 S) Famous for their water-lilies, with dozens of varieties in two lakes; also a splendid rose garden, and intriguing collection of all sorts of ethnic material and sporting trophies from across the world. Snacks, shop, disabled access; cl Oct–Mar; (01759) 302068; £2.40. From out here it's not far to the Plough at Allerthorpe (good for lunch).

RIEVAULX SE5785

Rievaulx Abbey Superbly atmospheric ruins of magnificent and once highly prosperous abbey, among the wooded hills of Rye Dale (the most dramatic views are gained by walking down the dale from the N). The nave, dating from 1135, is one of the earliest built in England. Also among the spectacular three-tiered remains is a fine 13th-c choir, and there's a visitor centre with hands-on displays about the history of the site. The graceful colonnades, arches and lancet windows are especially evocative if you get there early or late on a wkdy out of season (if they're not shrouded in scaffolding). Snacks, shop, some disabled access; cl 24–26 Dec, 1 Jan; (01439) 798228; £3.40; EH. Besides the many places in Helmsley not far off, the Hare over in Scawton (a pleasant drive) is good for lunch.

Rievaulx Terrace & Temples This half-mile grass-covered 18th-c terrace overlooks the abbey, with dramatic views. Each end is adorned with a classical temple; one small Tuscan rotunda built to while away the hours in peaceful contemplation, the other, an elaborate Ionic creation, for hunting parties. An ideal spot for a picnic, with good frescoes and an exhibition on landscape design. Snacks, shop; cl Nov–Apr; (01439) 798340; £3; NT.

ROBIN HOOD'S BAY NZ9505

Picturesque fishing village, once popular with smugglers and still largely unspoilt (though there are quite a few shops and cafés for visitors now), its cottages clustered steeply above the rocky shore – a rich hunting-ground for fossil hunters at low tide, when a surprising expanse of sand is exposed beyond the fascinating rock pools. You can walk along a fine section of cliffs to Ravenscar, where a geological trail takes in old alum quarries; an abandoned railway provides an easy walkway back. The Laurel and Olde Dolphin are good value. The village car park is up at the top – quite a climb.

Music in Miniature Exhibition 🏠 (Albion Rd church hall) Charming collection of highly detailed models illustrating English musical history; among the 50 or so doll's house-sized scenes are medieval minstrels, Victorian carol singers, and a 1920s palm court orchestra, all imaginatively put together by one dedicated woman. Shop, disabled access; cl Nov–Easter; (01947) 880512; £1.

ROSEBERRY TOPPING NZ5712

A memorable viewpoint on the extreme N edge of the moors, reached by a moorland walk from Gribdale Gate car park E of Great Ayton; a popular circuit goes by way of Airy Home Farm, the childhood home of Captain Cook.

ROSEDALE SE7296

With its lush fields and red-roofed yellow-stone houses sheltering warmly below the gaunt moorland, this now seems to typify the quiet pastoral countryside of the area. But until 60 or 70 years ago it was a busy iron-working site: the old railway track that once served the quarries loops around the moor above, and makes an easily followed stroll. The hillside at the top of the dreadfully steep Rosedale Chimney road heading S over Spaunton Moor gives motorists too a classic view.

RUNSWICK BAY NZ8016
Very pretty harbourless fishing village, good pubs; an attractive stretch of the well signed Cleveland Way long-distance path runs from here to Staithes (or you can begin closer from tiny Port Mulgrave).

SALTBURN-BY-THE-SEA NZ6621
Originally a superior Victorian seaside resort, with traces of those days still in the Italianate valley garden and the water-operated sloping tramway by the pier. The Ship Inn, a good pub right by the boats pulled up on the beach, is probably the most ancient building. The beach is sheltered by the great headland of Warsett Hill to the S, and a grand section of the well signed Cleveland Way long-distance path takes walkers over this and beyond.

Smugglers Heritage Centre 🖼 (Whitby Rd) Vivid interactive exhibition on the town's smuggling heritage, housed in old seaside cottages. Shop; cl Oct–Easter; (01642) 444318; £1.80.

SCARBOROUGH TA0488
All the usual seaside attractions in a place of some style, its two great curves of firm sandy beach separated by the small harbour below a high narrow headland. Between castle and cliff are the remains of a Roman signal station, one of five such structures built in the 4th c to warn of approaching raiders. To the S is the older part of the resort, with antique tracked cliff lifts between prom and the pleasant streets of the upper town; a house associated with Richard III is here (it now looks a little dilapidated), and there's a small craft centre in a former 14th-c inn. English Heritage is currently funding restoration of the town's Regency architecture. The train station has one of the longest benches in the world; 139 metres (456 ft) long, it can seat 228 people. Interesting churches include medieval St Mary's, where Anne Brontë is buried, and 19th-c St Martin's with elaborate work by Burne-Jones, William Morris and other Pre-Raphaelites. One unique and entertainingly quaint tradition is the summer staging of miniaturised sea battles with all sorts of special effects among the ducks on the lake of Peasholm Park in the more seasidey N part of the town; 3pm Mon and Thurs, late May–Aug. Good views of the bay from the top of Oliver's Mount (and harbour views from the Golden Ball on the front); good value food all day in the very grand Lord Rosebery (Westborough).

Cleveland Way S of Scarborough to Filey is an agreeable few hours' walk along the well signed Cleveland Way, though of less scenic significance than the cliffs further N. Oddly, the Way stops just short of Filey, at the headland of Filey Brigg, although there is nothing to prevent you from walking on into town.

Millennium 🖼 (Harbour) Vivid journey across this last millennium, through Vikings, Normans and the Civil War to the town's early days of rail and Victorian sea bathing – very entertainingly done. Shop, limited disabled access; cl winter wkdys, 25 Dec; (01723) 501000; £2.95.

Rotunda Museum (Vernon Rd) Georgian local history museum, with a Bronze Age skeleton, displays on the resort's Victorian heyday and a new Roman exhibition with activities for children. Shop; cl Mon all year, plus Weds–Fri mid-Oct to May; (01723) 374839; £2 joint ticket with Wood End Museum and Art Gallery.

Scarborough Art Gallery (The Crescent) Striking Italianate villa with good temporary exhibitions; cl Mon, 25–26 Dec and 1 Jan; (01723) 374753; £2 joint ticket with Rotunda and Wood End museum.

Scarborough Castle Looking down over the town from the headland, this stands on the site of British and Roman encampments. It was a royal palace of some importance until the reign of James I. Remains include the 13th-c barbican, medieval chapels and house, and the shell of the original 12th-c keep; great coastal views from the walls. Shop, snacks; cl winter Mon and Tues, 24–26 Dec, 1 Jan; (01723) 372451; £2.30.

Terror Tower 🖼 (Martin Marine, Foreshore Rd) A diversion for children on wet days, with ghoulish reconstructions of horror film sets and actors adding to the tension. Shop, cl winter wkdys; (01723) 501016; £1.95.

Wood End Museum (The Crescent) The Sitwells lived here for 60 years from 1870 (Edith was born here), and there are displays of their work and associated memorabilia. Also lots of fossils, and Victorian conservatory with tropical plants – though not the free-flying birds that once mingled with party-goers. Shop; cl Mon, and also Tues, Thurs and Fri Nov–end May (increased opening hours in school hols, phone to check); (01723) 367326; £2 joint ticket with Rotunda and Scarborough Art Gallery.

SHERIFF HUTTON SE6566 Attractive village, with ruined castle and 12th-c church; good pub.

SKIDBY TA0333 **Windmill** This well restored mill is due to reopen in Jan after refurbishments; open wknds and bank hols plus Weds–Fri in summer hols, mill working Sun only; £1.50. There are gentle country walks nearby, and the Half Moon is useful for something to eat.

SKINNINGROVE NZ7119 **Tom Leonard Mining Museum** 🏛 Good mining museum well demonstrating the reality of work underground. You can see how the stone is drilled, charged with explosives and fired. Shop, phone for disabled access; open am Apr–end Oct; (01287) 642877; £3. The village is industrial, with a steel-rolling mill – far from picturesque, but it has strong local colour, with its odd shantytown of pigeon-fanciers' sheds spreading over the cliff. Walkers can join the well signed Cleveland Way southwards to ascend monumental Boulby Cliff, the highest point on the E coast, before re-entering the National Park.

SLEDMERE SE9365 **Sledmere House** 🏛 Grand 18th-c mansion decorated and furnished in the style of the period, with one showpiece room done in Turkish tiling and a library bigger than many public ones. There's an 18th-c walled garden and the extensive park was landscaped by Capability Brown. They usually play their pipe organ pm Weds, Fri and Sun. Meals, snacks, shop, disabled access. Cl

before 11.30am, all day Mon (exc bank hols), Sat, and Oct–Easter; (01377) 236637; £4.50. The Triton nearby is useful for lunch.

SPROATLEY TA1836 **Burton Constable Hall** The wonderful exterior gives away this delightful house's Elizabethan origins, but the inside was extravagantly remodelled in the 18th c. Around 30 beautifully preserved rooms to see, with a sweeping long gallery and some intriguing collections. Capability Brown landscaped the 200 acres here too, and there's a riding centre in the stables. Teas, shop, disabled access to ground floor only; cl am, all day Fri, and Nov–Easter; (01964) 562400; £4. Camping, caravanning and seasonal fishing are available. The Cock & Bell down at Preston does good value lunches.

SPURN HEAD TA4010 This spit which curls like a claw round the mouth of the Humber Estuary has a rough track open to cars almost to its end: a bleak place to some but a paradise for bird-watchers, who often wait here in spring and autumn for glimpses of rare migrant species. Thanks to the vagaries of nature the peninsula is gradually becoming an island, so best to check tide times carefully. The estuary itself is usually grey, solemn and grim.

STAINTONDALE SE9998 **Llama trekking** Bruce Wright organises this, across the moors or along the coast; the llamas hump your bags while you walk beside them. They can do specialist treks with forest rangers or experts on wild flowers or archaeology. All treks include home-made food; (01723) 871234; from £22 for three hours.

Shire Horse Farm (Staintondale) Friendly little farm with good demonstrations and talks; as well as horses there are various rabbits, small animals and poultry, nature trails, and bracing clifftop walks along part of the Cleveland Way. Snacks, shop, limited disabled access; open Sun, Tues, Weds, Fri and bank hol Mon, Jun–mid-Sept; (01723) 870458; £3.50. The Bryherstones Hotel, off the Cloughton road, has good value food.

STAITHES NZ7818

Steep fishing village, unspoilt down by the shore, where little cottages and the storm-battered Cod & Lobster pose fetchingly against the staggering background of a great red sandstone headland, a striking colour picture as the sun comes up.

Captain Cook & Staithes Heritage Centre 🖼 (High St) This converted Methodist chapel in the village where the great explorer worked as a young man, in 1745, now houses a decent heritage centre, with a reconstructed street scene showing village life at the time; lots of Cook-related artefacts inc a collection of Webber's superb engravings from the voyages. Also displays looking at the importance of local industries such as fishing, mining and smuggling. Shop, disabled access to ground floor only; cl 25–26 Dec, and wkdys Jan; (01947) 841454; £2.25.

SUTTON BANK SE5182

This steep escarpment gives an enthralling view, particularly from the very popular section of the Cleveland Way that runs S from the A170 along the level clifftop to the white horse cut into the hill. Immediately N of the A170 you can combine the path along the top of the slope with a venture down the nature trail into Garbutt Wood, a nature reserve abutting Gormire Lake, the only natural lake in the National Park.

SUTTON-ON-THE-FOREST SE5864

Sutton Park The friendly 1730s manor house itself is now open only Weds and Sun, bank hol Mons and Easter Fri and Sat, but the delightful grounds are open pm daily Easter–Sept, with terraced gardens, a Georgian ice house, lily pond, pleasant woodland walks, nature trails and a new adventure playground. Tearoom; (01347) 810249; £4.50, £2 gardens only. The village with its broad street is pretty, and the smart Rose & Crown has good food.

THIRSK SE4281

World of James Herriot (23 Kirkgate) A lively look at the country's favourite vet as well as his profession, set in the Skeldale House of his novels; you can take part in your own TV programme. Shop, disabled access; cl 25

Dec; (01845) 524234; £4.

THORNTON DALE SE8383

Despite the main road, one of the most delightful villages in this part of Yorkshire – with an attractive forest toll road running NW to Langdale End.

WADE'S CAUSEWAY SE8097

Also known as Wheeldale Roman road, this is a mile-long stretch of broad paved Roman road up over the moors, well restored and maintained. It's open to walkers only, but reached easily by the narrow moorland lane S from Egton Bridge (or a longish walk S from Goathland).

WELTON SE9627

Wolds Way Good area for round walks based on the well signed Wolds Way, with fine views over the Humber in places.

WHARRAM PERCY SE8564

The most famous of the medieval abandoned villages of the Wolds, with lots of grassy humps and an evocative ruined church; English Heritage site, free access. From Thixendale (where the Cross Keys has sensibly priced food) a stretch of the well signed Wolds Way gives walkers a view of the village, and takes in a stretch of classic dry valley.

WHITBY NZ8911

Famous as the port at which Count Dracula came ashore; Bram Stoker got the idea for the book in the fishermen's graveyard of the partly Norman church, 199 steps up from the harbour, with lovely woodwork. Not too far from the abbey on Church Rd is a small but interesting workshop where you can watch jet being crafted into jewellery. Away from the bright waterfront the town is steep and quite attractive, with picturesque old buildings (now often rather smart shops) and some quaint cobbled alleys in its original core E of the busy harbour, where excellent fresh fish is sold straight from the catch. Besides excellent fish and chips from the Magpie café, the Duke of York (Church St, at the bottom of the 199 steps) does decent food all day. In the two wks around the summer solstice the sun both rises and sets above the sea.

Captain Cook Memorial Museum 🖼 (Grape Lane) In the house where the great explorer lived as an apprentice in the shipping trade from 1746; rooms are furnished in period style with models, letters and drawings from Cook's later voyages. Shop; cl Oct–Apr, and wkdys in Mar; (01947) 601900; £2.80.

Dracula Experience 🏛 (Marine Parade) Children probably won't be satisfied until they've visited this vividly spooky re-creation of scenes from the classic tale. Shop; cl winter wkdys, and maybe other times, so best to check; (01947) 601923; £1.95.

Whitby Abbey Impressive set of 13th-c ruins dramatically overlooking the harbour from their windswept clifftop setting, recently designated a World Heritage Site. You can see the skeletal remains of the magnificent 3-tiered choir and the N transept, and it's an evocative spot for a picnic (site of a famous scene in *Dracula*). An earlier building had been the site of the Synod of Whitby, where the dating of Easter was thrashed out in 664. A massive programme of restoration of the surroundings has so far uncovered what archaeologists say is a Celtic Christian cemetery, and a 17th-c stone garden created by descendants of the family who bought the abbey after Henry VIII's dissolution of the monasteries; the garden is being restored and will form a feature of the visitor centre being created in the roofless shell of the old house. Snacks; shop; cl 25–26 Dec; (01947) 603568; £1.70; EH.

Whitby Museum (Pannett Park) Delightfully old-fashioned and crowded, with the only surviving part of Captain Cook's original journal, Queen Victoria's nightdress, some spectacular fossils and the hand of a murderer used as a candle-holder by superstitious burglars. Shop, disabled access; cl Sun am, and in winter cl Tues pm and all day Mon, 25 Dec, 1 Jan; (01947) 602908; £2.

WITHERNSEA TA3428

Withernsea Lighthouse Towering above the houses of this little resort, with fantastic views for those keen enough to climb the 144 steps. Teas, shop, disabled access to ground floor only; open pm wknds and bank hols Mar–Oct, daily mid-Jun–mid-Sept; (01964) 614834; *£1.80. The Commercial Hotel has very low-priced food.

YORKSHIRE WOLDS SE8461

Quiet agricultural chalk country dissected by dry valleys, with extensive views over huge corn fields. The bulk of the off-road walking is found on the well signposted 79-mile Wolds Way from Hessle Haven down on the Humber to Filey Brigg on the coast, where it meets the Cleveland Way. Some of the lesser roads are a delight to walk on, with wide verges, good views and virtually no traffic.

Other attractive villages here, all with decent pubs, include Ainthorpe NZ7008, Ampleforth SE5879 (with its famous school and partly wooded moors), Bishop Burton SE9939, Brompton-by-Sawdon SE9582, Castleton NZ6908 high above the Esk Valley, Cloughton Newlands TA0196, Crayke SE5760, Fadmoor SE6789, Great Ayton NZ5611, Hutton Rudby NZ4706, Lealholm NZ7608, Lund SE9748, Nether Silton SE4692, North Dalton SE9352, Oldstead SE5380, Rosedale Abbey SE7395, Seamer TA0284, Sinnington SE7485, South Dalton SE9645, Thixendale SE8461, Thorganby SE6942, Thornton-le-Clay SE6865, Weaverthorpe SE9771 and Welburn SE7268.

Where to eat

BYLAND ABBEY SE5478 **Abbey** *(01347) 868204* Beautifully placed dining pub opposite abbey ruins, interesting series of rambling old rooms, big fireplaces, polished floorboards, and flagstones; good enjoyable food, decent wines and well kept beers, and big garden; cl Sun pm, Mon am (exc bank hols); limited disabled access. £25

FLAMBOROUGH TA2270 **Seabirds** *Tower St (01262) 850242* Friendly old pub full of shipping memorabilia and a few stuffed birds, with enjoyable food (some fresh fish dishes, too), quite a few wines, and cheerful hard-working staff; cl Mon pm in winter; partial disabled access. £17|£3.75

HAROME SE6482 **Star** *High St (01439)* 770397 Pretty, thatched, 14th-c inn with a charming interior, plenty of bric-a-brac and interesting furniture, two big log fires, daily papers and magazines, and a no smoking dining room; excellent inventive food using the best local produce, well kept real ales, freshly squeezed juices, and quite a few wines by the glass from a fairly extensive wine list; seats and tables on a sheltered front terrace with more in the garden behind; cl Mon am. £22.95|£8

KIRKHAM ABBEY SE7366 **Stone Trough** *(01653)* 618713 Quaint beamed inn with small, cosy and interesting bars, log fires, good lunchtime bar food, an old-fashioned, no smoking restaurant with farmhouse atmosphere, seats outside with valley views; £19.70|£6.25

MIDDLESBROUGH NZ4920 **Purple Onion** *72–80 Corporation Rd (01642)* 222250 Bustling Victorian building filled with bric-a-brac, ornate mirrors, and house plants, an informal atmosphere, downstairs cellar bar with live music, particularly good interesting food, friendly staff, and decent wine list; cl Sun; disabled access. £27.50/2 courses £11.95

NUNNINGTON SE6679 **Royal Oak** *Church St (01439)* 788271 Attractive little dining pub nr Nunnington Hall with log fires, beams hung with copper jugs, antique keys and earthenware flagons, carefully chosen furniture, and generous helpings of enjoyable home-made bar food – super daily specials; cl Mon; children over 8. £23|£7.95

SCARBOROUGH TA0488 **Golden Grid Fish Restaurant** *4 Sandside (01723)* 360922 Very long-standing and famous fish restaurant overlooking the harbour serving snacks, lunches (super daily-fresh fish), vegetarian dishes, and afternoon teas; cl 25 Dec; disabled access. £10.50|£4

STADDLEBRIDGE SE4499 **McCoys Bistro** *Cleveland Tontine (01609)* 882671 A rather special place with a friendly bustling atmosphere in ground-floor bistro, some eccentric furnishings, old-fashioned music, particularly good modern food, a thoughtful wine list, a quieter dining room open only Fri/Sat evenings, and good breakfasts; bdrms. £33

STAITHES NZ7818 **Endeavour** *1 High St (01947)* 840825 Popular little quayside restaurant (lunch by prior booking only) at the bottom of a steep hill, with lovely fresh local fish (delicious meat and game, and vegetarian dishes, too), super puddings, decent good value wine list, and friendly service; bdrms; cl Sun, Mon, cl Nov, 25–26 Dec, cl mid-Jan to mid-Mar; well behaved children only. £25

SUTTON-UPON-DERWENT SE7047 **St Vincent Arms** *Main St (01904)* 608349 Relaxed atmosphere in traditional panelled front parlour with open fire, high-backed old settles, good solid home-cooked food in spacious dining room, friendly staff, well kept beers and good choice of wines; big garden. £19|£7

THORGANBY SE6841 **Jefferson Arms** *Main St (01904)* 448316 Handsome old village inn run by two hard-working sisters, spotlessly kept, stylish and spacious main bar, delightful little beamed lounge with sofas and armchairs, open fire and fresh flowers, and narrow conservatory with grape vines and passion flowers; interesting Swiss röstis (grated and fried potatoes) with various toppings and other good food, real ales, and a careful wine list; quiet bdrms; cl Mon, Tues am; children must be well behaved. £28

WHITBY NZ9011 **Duke of York** *124 Church St (01947)* 600324 Bustling, welcoming pub with fine outlook over harbour entrance and western cliff from the comfortable beamed bar (lots of fishing memorabilia), a wide choice of good value fresh local fish as well as other things, well kept real ales, decent wines, and quick, pleasant service; bdrms. £15.25|£5.95

WHITBY NZ8911 **Magpie Café** *14 Pier Rd (01947)* 602058 Overlooks the town and river, with lots of wonderfully evocative sepia photographs of old Whitby, and much liked for its delicious fresh haddock served by cheerful staff; cl mid-Jan to mid-Feb. £19|£6

Please let us know what you think of places in the *Guide*. Use the report forms at the back of the book or simply write us a letter.

West & South Yorkshire

Excellent museums in the thriving cities and beyond – many of them free; lots of other good family attractions, and some exciting new openings

This part of Yorkshire is chock-a-block with interesting places to visit. It has more than its fair share of first-class museums, and new developments make it all the more appealing for short holiday breaks. At Eureka! in Halifax, the Royal Armouries Museum in Leeds, and Bradford's revamped (and admirably free) National Museum of Photography, Film and Television in Bradford alone, it has three of the most enjoyable places for children in the whole of Britain, with the forthcoming Magna likely to be a tourism catalyst for the less-visited town of Rotherham. The springtime opening of the Millennium Galleries in Sheffield signals the finale of the city-centre rejuvenations there, though lively Leeds still has a clear head start over it – full of appeal to visitors, and a great place for a day trip. Other family favourites include magnificent Harewood House (more than enough for an enjoyable outing, from its splendid furnishings to the famous bird gardens), the Middleton Railway, Leeds, with a nature trail and playgrounds adding to the excitement of a trip on the world's oldest railway, and the interesting industrial heritage centres at Elsecar and Golcar. The eventual completion of the ambitious environmental centre at Denaby Main should make this an enjoyable alternative day out, too. Cannon Hall Open Farm, Cawthorne, has good play areas and some unusual animals, and children are encouraged to touch a host of tropical creatures at the friendly hothouse in North Anston.

A striking feature here is the welcome profusion of 'stately museums': fine houses (many of them free, and often set within attractive grounds) filled with equally fine exhibits. Beautiful Bagshaw Museum, Brodsworth Hall (fascinating glimpses into Victorian life), Shibden Hall & Folk Museum (with its reconstructed 19th-c village), the 1853 Gallery at Saltaire (home to one of the country's largest private art collections – the pioneering industrial village itself is well worth a visit), and Cusworth Hall Museum are all especially rewarding.

Mighty Conisbrough Castle holds lively summer events and guided tours, moated Oakwell Hall is perhaps an unlikely setting for a children's discovery centre, and this year sees sumptuous Nostell Priory reopen its doors to the public following restoration work.

Ilkley on the edge of the moors is attractive, and Hebden Bridge is also worth a trip, with the Hardcastle Crags above, ideal for a peaceful picnic. The Yorkshire Sculpture Park nr Wakefield is pleasant for a stroll.

In the W is a real Yorkshire mix of steep stone cottage terraces, remarkable mill buildings and some dramatic moorland coming right up to the towns, with plenty of exhilarating walking.

With the present counties of South and West Yorkshire, we have included the bottom corner of North Yorkshire, below York itself and the A64.

Where to stay

BRADFORD SE1632 **Victoria Hotel** *Bridge St, Bradford, West Yorkshire BD1 1JX* (01274) 728706 **£70**w, plus wknd breaks; 60 well equipped rms with CD and video (they have a library). Carefully renovated Victorian station hotel with many original features and lots of stylish character, bustling bar, popular and informal brasserie serving good modern food, and marvellous breakfasts; disabled access

HALIFAX SE0829 **Holdsworth House** *Holmfield, Halifax, West Yorkshire HX2 9TG (01422) 240024* **£104**, plus wknd breaks; 40 traditional, individually decorated rms. Lovely 17th-c house a few miles outside, with antiques, fresh flowers and open fires in comfortable lounges, friendly helpful staff, very fine oak-panelled dining room with imaginative food and carefully chosen wines, and garden; dogs by prior arrangement; cl first wk after Christmas; disabled access

HAWORTH SE0237 **Old White Lion** *6–10 West Lane, Haworth, Keighley, West Yorkshire BD22 8DU* (01535) 642313 **£64**, plus special breaks; 14 rms, many with lovely views. Friendly, warm and comfortable 300-year-old inn with three bars, cosy restaurant with enjoyable food, and oak-panelled residents' lounge; nr Brontë museum and church, and Keighley & Worth Valley steam railway

LEEDS SE3033 **42 The Calls** *Leeds, West Yorkshire LS2 7EW* (0113) 244 0099 **£150**w, plus special breaks; 41 attractive rms using original features, with lots of extras, CD stereo with disc library, satellite TV and good views. Stylish modern hotel in converted riverside grain mill with genuinely friendly staff, marvellous food in restaurant and next door Brasserie Forty-Four, and fine breakfasts; cl 5 days over Christmas; limited disabled access

LINTON SE3646 **Wood Hall** *Trip Lane, Linton, Wetherby, West Yorkshire LS22 4JA* (01937) 587271 **£108**; 42 spacious well furnished rms. Grand Georgian mansion in over a hundred acres of parkland overlooking the River Wharfe; comfortable reception rooms, log fire, antiques and fresh flowers, and imaginative cooking in the no smoking restaurant; indoor swimming pool and health centre; disabled access

MONK FRYSTON SE5029 **Monk Fryston Hall** *Main St, Monk Fryston, Leeds, West Yorkshire LS25 5DU* (01977) 682369 **£79**, plus wknd breaks; 30 comfortable rms. Grand recently refurbished manor house in attractive grounds with antiques, log fires and fresh flowers in the oak-panelled bar and lounge, friendly staff, and good food in the original dining room; disabled access

OTLEY SE2143 **Chevin Lodge** *Yorkgate, Otley, West Yorkshire LS21 3NU* (01943) 467818 **£110***, plus special breaks; 50 rms. Built of Finnish logs with walks through 50 acres of birchwood, this comfortable hotel has its own leisure club, good restaurant food, and friendly service; tennis and fishing; disabled access

ROYDHOUSE SE2112 **Three Acres** *37–41 Roydhouse, Shelley, Huddersfield, West Yorkshire HD8 8LR* (01484) 602606 **£70***, plus special breaks; 20 pretty rms. In lovely countryside, this extended 18th-c hotel has a welcoming atmosphere in its traditional bars, good wines and well kept real ales, and excellent food in two restaurants (one with occasional pianist), using fresh local produce; cl 25 Dec

SCISSETT SE2408 **Bagden Hall** *Wakefield Rd, Scissett, Huddersfield, West Yorkshire HD8 9LE* (01484) 865330 **£80**; 17 rms. Handsome hotel in 40 acres of parkland with its own 9-hole par 3 golf course, comfortable airy public rooms inc a conservatory bar, well prepared French and English food, and quietly efficient service; limited disabled access

SHEFFIELD SK3485 **Charnwood Hotel** *10 Sharrow Lane, Sheffield, South Yorkshire S11 8AA* (0114) 258 9411 **£65**w, plus special breaks; 22 comfortable well equipped rms. Friendly extended Georgian house with peaceful lounges, conservatory, and very good food in both the Brasserie and elegant little Henfreys restaurant; cl Christmas; disabled access

---

Please let us know what you think of places in the *Guide*. Use the report forms at the back of the book or simply write us a letter.

To see and do

Yorkshire Family Attraction of the Year

BRADFORD SE1632 **National Museum of Photography, Film and Television** (Princes View) Long considered one of the best and most-enjoyed museums in the country, this splendid place is better than ever since its recent multi-million pound expansion. Five galleries take in everything from John Logie Baird to the toys from *Play School* – and it's all free. You'll pay only to see the films in the cinemas, inc their mammoth IMAX screen. Families really can spend hours here, watching examples of the best and worst of British TV, classic adverts, and early news bulletins. Among the three million items kept here are three key 'firsts': the world's first negative, the earliest television footage, and what's generally considered the first example of moving pictures – Louis Le Prince's 1888 film of Leeds Bridge. Wallace and Gromit and Morph explain the secrets of animation, and you can try your hand at operating a camera or reading the news. Other highlights are the intriguing photography gallery, which includes the cameras used to create the Cottingley fairies, perhaps the best known photographic hoax of all time, and a stunning gallery showcasing the latest digital technology, where you can experiment with virtual reality, or see how long your own Tamagotchi-style creation survives in its virtual world. A fun hands-on section lets you experiment with light, and there are various large-scale temporary exhibitions: The Art of Star Wars runs until 29 Apr. The five-storeys-high IMAX screen regularly shows 3D and 2D films, and more conventionally sized cinemas offer films from around the world. It's worth finding out about special events in advance – some may need to be pre-booked. Meals and snacks (and a room to eat packed lunches), excellent shop, disabled access; cl Mon (exc bank hols), 25 Dec, 1 Jan; (01274) 202030; free. The IMAX cinema is £5.80 (£4 children), or £9.50 (£6.60 children) for a double ticket. They've negotiated special rates with the nearby NCP car park on Hall Ings; you'll need to collect a special voucher from the Box Office before you leave.

ANSTON BROOK SK5184
Reached on foot from South Anston, this flows through a wooded valley that interrupts the monotony of the flat farmlands SE of Rotherham. It can be combined with a walk along the towpath of the derelict Chesterfield Canal.

BATLEY SE2325
Bagshaw Museum (Wilton Park) Beautiful Victorian Gothic mansion in pleasant lakeside park, with one of those excellent miscellaneous collections based on the curio-hunting of an individual enthusiast. Shop, some disabled access; cl wknd ams, Good Fri, 24–26 Dec, and 1 Jan; (01924) 472514; free. The Old Hall at Heckmondwike (B6117), once Joseph Priestley's home, is interesting for lunch.
Skopos Motor Museum (Alexandra Mills) It's worth the trek off the beaten path to visit this good and varied collection of cars, in a pleasant airy

building. Vehicles on display range from Edwardian Rolls-Royces to BMW Isetta and the only surviving Bramham. Shop, disabled access; cl Mon, Tues, 25–26 Dec, and 1 Jan; (01924) 444423; *£2.50.
BRADFIELD SK2692
Attractive two-part village, with interesting church and good walks in great scenery.
BRADFORD SE1632
Though horribly knocked-about by heavy-handed civic designers in the 1960s and 1970s, many buildings survive from what was one of Britain's finest Victorian cities. These, in a solidly unifying northern stone, are a staggering monument to the days when its wools, woollens and worsteds ruled the world: gigantic and confidently Renaissance-style woollen and velvet mills, the imposing Wool Exchange, the opulent city-centre cliffs of heavily ornate merchants' warehouses in Little Germany behind the mostly 15th-c

cathedral, and the florid exuberance of the municipal buildings such as the Gothic city hall, the neo-classical St George's concert hall, even the great Undercliffe cemetery with its sumptuous Victorian memorials (and sweeping Pennine views) – it's been called the most spectacular graveyard in Britain. The city's Asian immigrants have brought a vivid and visible dash of cultural diversity, and there's a feeling of underlying vigour and zest which makes it exciting to visit. Useful places for a pub lunch include the Fountain (Heaton Rd), Office (off City St) and Rams Revenge (Kirkgate), but you might prefer one of the multitude of Indian, Pakistani or Bangladeshi restaurants.

Bolling Hall Museum (off Brompton Ave, S) Classic mainly 17th-c Yorkshire manor house, now home to the city's collection of local furniture. Shop; cl Sun am, Mon (exc bank hols) and Tues; (01274) 723057; free.

Cartwright Hall Art Gallery (Lister Park) Dramatic baroque-style building in attractive floral park, housing the *Brown Boy* by Reynolds and a good representative selection of late 19th- and early 20th-c paintings. Snacks, shop, disabled access; cl Sun am, and all day Mon (exc bank hols), and over Christmas; (01274) 751212; free.

Colour Museum (Grattan Rd) Imaginative study of the use and perception of colour, with interactive displays on the effects of light and colour in general, and particularly the story of dyeing and textile printing. Shop, disabled access; cl Sun, Mon, and 25 Dec–1 Jan; (01274) 725138; £1.50.

Industrial Museum (Moorside Rd, Eccleshill) Former spinning mill well illustrating the growth of the worsted textile industry. Horse-drawn trams carry you up and down the Victorian street, which is complete with workers' cottages, mill owner's house and working Victorian stables with shire horses. Meals, snacks, shop, disabled access; cl Sun am, and all day Mon (exc bank hols), 25–26 Dec, Good Fri; (01274) 631756; free.

National Museum of Photography, Film and Television See *separate family panel on p.688.*

BRAMHAM SE4041
Bramham Park 🏛 The garden here is really quite beautiful, very much in the grand style – Versailles comes to Yorkshire. Long prospects of ornamental lakes, cascades, temples, statuary, grand hedges and stately trees and avenues surround a classical Queen Anne house of great distinction, with lovely period furnishings and paintings. Snacks, shop, should have disabled access by 2001; house open by written appointment only (minimum group of 6 people), gardens open daily Feb–Sept exc during horse trials, usually second wk in Jun, but best to check; (01937) 846005; grounds and gardens £2.95. The Red Lion has decent food.

BRODSWORTH SE5007
Brodsworth Hall and Gardens 🏛 Grand house vividly illustrating life in Victorian times; the family that lived here closed off parts of the house as their fortunes waned, inadvertently preserving the contents and décor exactly as they were (right down to the billiard score-book). Richly furnished rooms, lots of marble statues, and busily cluttered servants' wing. The family commissioned some of the largest and fastest yachts of the Victorian era and an exhibition charts the history of these splendid vessels. The marvellous formal gardens and parkland are gradually being restored. Snacks, shop, some disabled access; cl am, Mon (exc bank hols), and all Nov–Mar; (01302) 722598; £5; EH.

CARL WARK SK2581
On the edge of the Peak District, this hill fort is set handsomely in a great bowl fringed by gritstone outcrops, and offers a more interesting walk than most in South Yorkshire.

CAWTHORNE SE2708
Cannon Hall Open Farm Unusual animals such as wallabies and llamas among the residents at this busy working farm; also baby animals throughout the year, with piglets born regularly. Good play areas, and mostly concreted so doesn't get muddy. Meals, snacks, shop, disabled access; cl 25 Dec; (01226) 790427; £2.10. Cannon Hall itself is now a museum and the grounds an attractive country park. The village is pleasant.

CONISBROUGH SK5198

Conisbrough Castle 🏛 Mightily impressive 12th-c castle with uniquely designed 27-metre (90-ft) keep – circular, with six buttresses and a curtain wall with solid round towers. An added roof and floors re-create something of the original feel, and there's a good audio-visual show. Tours by costumed guides and special events in summer. Meals, snacks, craft shop, limited disabled access; cl 24–26 Dec, 1 Jan; (01709) 863329; *£3; EH. Sir Walter Scott set much of *Ivanhoe* here, writing the novel while staying at the Boat at Sprotbrough nearby; then a riverside farm, it's now a popular dining pub.

CUSWORTH SE5403

Cusworth Hall Museum (Cusworth Lane, just W of Doncaster) Excellent museum of South Yorkshire life, in an elegant 18th-c house. Displays on mining, transport, costume and entertainment, and esp popular gallery of toys and childhood. Tearoom, shop, disabled access to ground floor only; cl Sun am, 25–26 Dec and Good Fri; (01302) 782342; free.

DENABY MAIN SK4999

Earth Centre Perhaps the most ambitious of all the country's environmental centres, this Millennium Commission Project has witnessed the redevelopment over the last decade or so of more than 400 acres left derelict by the decline of the coal industry. Overlooked by mighty Conisbrough Castle, the centre aims to promote environmental issues in an enjoyable way through a range of attractions taking in an interactive nature trail (with pond-dipping, eco-friendly games and an area designed to stimulate all your senses along the way), galleries looking at the history and future of the planet's development, and specially themed gardens dotted with often bizarre-looking constructions; also a fun adventure playground inc a 16-metre (52-ft) play tower. Meals, snacks, shop, disabled access; open daily Feb–Oct; (01709) 512000; £3.50.

DONCASTER SE5802

Not really a great deal to attract visitors apart from its race meetings, but there is some fine architecture, especially around the High St and Market Pl, and a good antiques and junk market on Weds.

Doncaster Museum & Art Gallery (Chequer Rd) Recently refurbished with new archaeology displays and a good deal of natural history (shop, good disabled access; cl Sun am; free).

ELSECAR SK3899

Elsecar Heritage Centre 🏛 (Wath Rd) Developing centre in restored industrial workshops. Lots to see inc a hands-on science centre, a history centre where you can dress up and star in a Victorian melodrama, a beam engine and craft workshops. On summer Suns there's a steam train to the Hemingfield Basin. Meals, snacks, shop, disabled access; cl 25 Dec–1 Jan; (01226) 740203; £3.25 science centre, £1 history centre, £2.50 train, or £5.25 for all.

GOLCAR SE0915

Colne Valley Museum 🏛 (Cliffe Ash) Enthusiastic museum spread over three weavers' cottages, with hand-weaving, spinning and clog-making in gas-lit surroundings, and re-created 1850s living room. Snacks, shop, occasional craft festivals, some disabled access; open pm wknds and some bank hols; (01484) 659762; £1.20. The Sands House up on Crosland Moor is a good dining pub. There's a good year-round walk along the Huddersfield Canal's restored towpath between here and Marsden in *Last of the Summer Wine* country. The Tunnel End pub here is useful for food, as are the Carriage House and Olive Branch a little further off.

GOMERSHAL SE2026

Red House Museum (Oxford Rd) Vividly re-creates the 1830s in its nine carefully furnished period rooms. Charlotte Brontë often stayed at the house (which stands out from its stone neighbours for its unusual red brick), and used it as the basis for Briarmains in her novel *Shirley*. The gardens have been restored in 1830s style. Snacks, shop, disabled access; cl am wknds, Good Fri, best to phone for opening times over Christmas; (01274) 335100; free.

GOOSE EYE SE0240

Interesting preserved village; good

drives around here.

HALIFAX SE0925

Another town with an impressive show of former textiles wealth, interesting to drive through when it's quiet on a summer evening or a Sunday, and surrounded by a splendid ring of moorland. The centre's been cleaned up and partly pedestrianised, which makes it pleasant to potter through, and there are several first-class attractions, with the town now going through something of an artistic renaissance. The medieval **church** has an extremely grand spire and fine carving: look out for Old Tristram, the life-size painted carving of a beggar which was used to collect alms. The Shears (Paris Gates, Boys Lane) down steep lanes among the mill buildings is a pub that embraces much of Halifax's past and atmosphere; the Sportsman (Lee Lane, Shibden – off A647) has a good value carvery and impressive views.

Bankfield Museum (Ackroyd Park, Boothtown Rd) Collection of textiles, costume and contemporary crafts, as well as a regimental museum and display of toys. Shop, disabled access to ground floor only; cl Sun am, all day Mon, best to check for Christmas opening; (01422) 354823; free.

Dean Clough Enormous carpet mill, faced with demolition when it closed down some years ago, but now well restored and home to a thriving complex of galleries and small businesses; best are the Crossley Gallery and Henry Moore Studio, the latter a great showcase for contemporary sculpture (cl am and all day Mon).

Eureka! (Discovery Rd) Remarkable hands-on museum designed exclusively for children; few places are as likely to spellbind anyone between around 3 and 12. Each of the four main galleries ostensibly explores one subject, but in fact covers a multitude of topics and ideas. Particular highlights are the broad-based Things Gallery, full of bright colours and images, the communications gallery (you can put your picture on a front page, save a yacht in distress, or read the TV news), and Living and Working Together,

where children try their hand at grown-up activities like filling a car with petrol at the garage, working in a shop or bank, or making a meal in the kitchen. Easy to see why in the eight years it's been open Eureka! has won just about every award going, from Most Parent Friendly and Best Customer Care to several for Loo of the Year. Meals, snacks, shop, disabled access; cl 24–26 Dec; (01426) 983191; £5.75, children 3–12 £4.75, under-3s free.

Piece Hall (centre) Magnificent Renaissance-looking galleried and arcaded building put up in 1775 by the merchants of Halifax as a market for their cloth. Now it's filled with specialist shops selling books, antiques and bric-a-brac, as well as an art gallery (cl Mon) and other exhibitions. Meals, snacks, shop, disabled access by prior arrangement; cl 25–26 Dec; (01422) 368725; free. The Italianate courtyard comes to life on Fri and Sat when there are 160 bustling stalls; a good few on Thurs too.

Shibden Hall & Folk Museum 🖾 (Godley Lane, off A58 just E) Excellently refurbished 15th-c house, each room illustrating a different period from its history. In the barn a folk museum has an interesting collection of horse-drawn vehicles, while around it is a reconstructed 19th-c village, with workshops, cottage and even a pub. Boating lake, miniature railway, play area and woodland walks in the 90-acre parkland. For many this is a real Halifax highlight. Snacks, shop, limited disabled access; cl Sun am, and usually 2 wks over Christmas, but best to check; (01422) 352246; £2.

Wainhouse Tower (off A646 just W) This 75-metre (250-ft) folly offers good views if you can manage all those steps; shop; usually open only bank hols and a couple of other dates – best to check with the Tourist Information Centre (01422) 368725; £1.70.

HAREWOOD SE3245

Harewood House & Bird Garden 🖾 (A61) The area's most magnificent stately home, inside and out. The 18th-c exterior is splendidly palatial, and inside there's some glorious restored Robert Adam plasterwork. Fine Chippendale furnishings, exquisite Sèvres and

Chinese porcelain, and paintings by Turner, El Greco, Bellini, Titian, and Gainsborough. Capability Brown designed the thousand-acre grounds, which have very pleasing lakeside and woodland walks, an outstanding collection of rhododendron species, and the famous landscaped bird garden (you could spend half a day in just this part). Charles Berry's Terrace has an excellent gallery with contemporary art and crafts. Try to visit the 15th-c **church**, with a splendid array of tombs, and a curious tunnel under the wall of the churchyard, so that servants could arrive unseen by sensitive souls. There's a first-class adventure playground. Meals, snacks, shop, disabled access; cl Nov to mid-Mar and 9 Jun; (0113) 288 6331; £7.25 everything, £6 bird garden and grounds only. TV's *Emmerdale* is filmed on a purpose-built set on the estate. The Harewood Arms opposite has good food, and just N Wharfedale Grange have **pick-your-own** fruit.

HAWORTH SE0237
A touristy village with plenty of craft shops, antiques shops and tea shoppes catering for all the people drawn here by the Brontës (spelt Brunty before father Patrick went posh). A visit out of season catches it at its best, though at any time the steep cobbled main street has quieter more atmospheric side alleys. Most of the family are buried in the churchyard, except Anne, interred in Scarborough. For the most evocative views and atmosphere go up to the moors above town, very grand and not much different from when the Brontës knew them – despite the Japanese footpath signs. The Fleece and Old White Lion are useful for lunch. The A6033 is an interesting drive to Hebden Bridge, and there's a fine old moors road via Stanbury (with its nice Old Silent pub) over to the Colne Valley in Lancashire.

Brontë walks The Pennine moors around here are a favourite stamping-ground for walkers, with a good walk W through Penistone Hill Country Park to the much-visited **Brontë Waterfalls**, and on through a remote valley to Withins, the original Wuthering Heights. There are plenty of paths, though finding the way across fields frequently entails searching for unprominent stone stiles over the dry-stone walls.

Keighley & Worth Valley Railway Actually begins just N at Keighley (where you can connect with BR trains) but is based here. Run by enthusiastic volunteers, the line was built to serve the valley's mills, and passes through the heart of Brontë country. The prettiest station is Oakworth (familiar to many from the film *The Railway Children*). Snacks, shop, some disabled access; usually open wknds all year, daily Jun–early Sept, and most school hols; (01535) 645214 for timetable; £6 return.

Parsonage Museum The Brontës' former home has some 120,000 visitors a year (it was something of a tourist attraction even while Charlotte still lived here). The house is very carefully preserved, with period furnishings, very good changing exhibitions, and displays of the siblings' books, manuscripts and possessions inc the sisters' writing table. Shop; usually cl mid-Jan–mid-Feb, 24–27 Dec; (01535) 642323; £4.50.

HEATH SE3519
Extraordinarily old-fashioned common with gipsy ponies alongside 18th-c mansions (and contrasting views over Wakefield); the gaslit Kings Arms here is good.

HEBDEN BRIDGE SD9927
Engaging small town deep in a valley below the moors, and stepped very steeply up the hillsides. The Robin Hood (A6033 towards Keighley) has good value food. In summer there are **horse-drawn barge trips** along the canal basin, (01422) 845557. The hold of one barge in the marina has been converted into a **visitor centre** with a traditional boatman's cabin (cl Nov–Easter; free).

Hardcastle Crags A beauty spot above the wooded river valley, ideal for walks or a picnic. The Nutclough House on the way up also has decent food.

Heptonstall An interesting and ancient village, a crippling climb up a fearsomely steep cobbled lane above Hebden Bridge; Sylvia Plath is buried in the churchyard. There's a rewarding scenic path along Heptonstall Crags (the cliffs above the wooded valley of Colden Water). An exhilarating old high road leads out to Widdop and beyond (for fine views and walks), and another runs via Colden and Blackshaw Head.

HOLMFIRTH SE1408
Instantly recognisable as the setting for TV's *Last of the Summer Wine*, with evocative little alleys, several good pubs, and a handsome Georgian **church**.

Compo's World (Huddersfield Rd) An exhibition on *Last of the Summer Wine*, the longest-running comedy series in the world. Meals, snacks, shop; cl 25 Dec; (01484) 681408; £1.50.

HUDDERSFIELD SE1416
There's a great sense of style in many of its buildings, especially around the station and central square, and much of the centre is now closed to traffic. The A640 W is a good moorland drive.

Jubilee Tower (Almondbury) Castle Hill is 275 metres (900 ft) high, overlooking the surrounding moors, even the Pennines and Peak District. This tower, with 165 steps, should reopen this year after restoration, and gives unrivalled views; open pm summer wknds and bank hols; £1.25. There's a decent food pub near its base.

Tolson Memorial Museum (Ravensknowle Park) The myths and legends asssociated with Castle Hill are outlined in this former wool baron's mansion, which also has a look at the textile industry, and a collection of horse-drawn vehicles. Snacks, shop, disabled access; phone for winter opening times; (01484) 223830; free.

ILKLEY SE1147
Owes its Victorian and Edwardian spaciousness and style to the mid-19th-c and later craze for hydropathic 'cures', which produced quite a rash of luxurious hydros using the town's pure moorland spring water. Their forerunner was the simple little bath-house built in the mid-18th c around the ice-cold spring up on the moor just S at White Wells – you can still follow the paths the infirm took by donkey. The group of quaintly shaped rocks known as the Cow & Calf up here also makes a pleasant short walk above the town. The **church** has three lovely

Saxon crosses, and just beside it are traces of a Roman fort. There are a good few prehistoric remains around the town, the best known of which is the Bronze Age **Swastika Stone**, a symbol of eternity carved on a flat rock by a moorland path SE of the town, above wooded Hebers Ghyll; the stone is marked on the Ordnance Survey 1:50,000 map, at SE095469. Hebers Ghyll itself is a picturesque ravine with steep Victorian walkways, and the town with its attractive gardens and interesting shops (you can see chocolate being made at Humphreys) makes a nice stop. Ilkley Moor S of the town has potential for satisfying high-level walks (without your hat).

Manor House Gallery & Museum (Castle Yard) One of the few buildings in town to predate the 19th c, an Elizabethan manor house built on the site of a Roman fort, with local history displays. Shop; cl Sun am, all day Mon (exc bank hols) and Tues, 25 Dec and Good Fri; (01943) 600066; free.

KEIGHLEY SE0542
(pronounced 'Keithly') A busy working town with a pleasant centre. The Grinning Rat nr the 16th-c church is useful for lunch.

Cliffe Castle Museum & Gallery (Spring Gardens Lane) 19th-c mansion with French furniture from the Victoria & Albert Museum, as well as various local ephemera. Though quite close to the centre, it's set in a park well above the main road, with an aviary and greenhouses. Shop, disabled access to ground floor only; cl Sun am, all day Mon (exc bank hols), 25–26 Dec, Good Fri; (01535) 618238; free.

East Riddlesden Hall (Bradford Rd, just NE) Interesting early 17th-c oak-panelled stone manor house with attractive plasterwork, period textiles and furniture, and formal walled garden. There's a medieval monastic fishpond, and huge medieval tithe barn. Snacks, shop, some disabled access; open pm Tues, Weds, Sun and Sat Apr–Oct, plus Mon July–Aug; (01535) 607075; £3.50; NT.

LEEDS SE2934
Leeds is now a really rewarding place to visit, with something for all ages: its Royal Armouries Museum is an

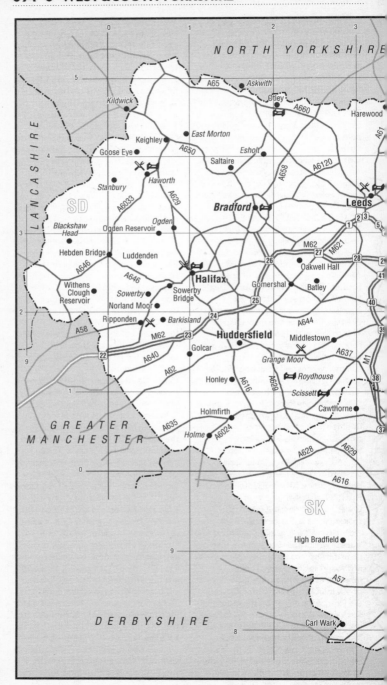

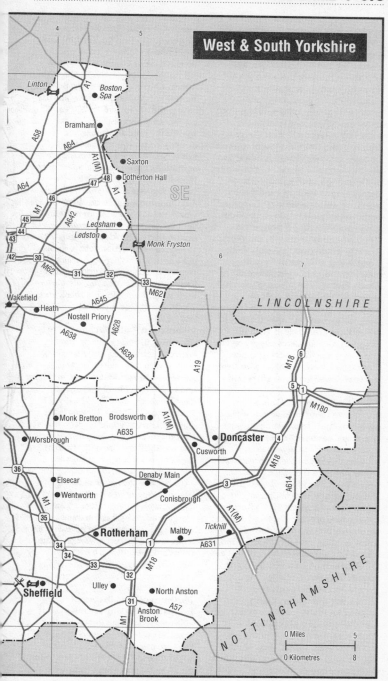

West & South Yorkshire

outstanding family day out, Tropical World is very enjoyable (and free), and there's plenty more to fill a short stay. A great deal of effort has gone into developing a 24-hr café culture here, and behind the hype there really is a surprisingly cosmopolitan city, its compact centre increasingly popular with young people in the evenings (lots of bars and clubs), and ideal for exploring during the day – it's largely free of traffic. There are lots of splendid covered arcades (Victorian, Edwardian and modern), and all sorts of interesting and engaging Victorian architectural details to spot. Shoppers and theatre-goers are well catered for – the former in the exuberantly Venetian/Oriental glass-roofed market, the biggest in Yorkshire, and the latter by the West Yorkshire Playhouse (a useful meeting place with fine city views from its good café/bar) and The Grand (home of Opera North). The imposing town hall is perhaps the high point of Leeds' essentially Victorian centre; and there are good gardens and open spaces. Whitelocks (Turks Head Yard, off Briggate) is a marvellous old city tavern and is very much a Leeds institution. The historic Waterfront area has been well developed for visitors in recent years.

Corn Exchange (Call Lane) This impressive 1860s building is now filled with neat little specialist and designer shops, and has plenty of places for tea, coffee and so forth, as well as an excellent fresh continental bread stall.

Henry Moore Institute (The Headrow) Over a footbridge is this delightful place, with temporary exhibitions of sculpture from Roman times to the present, displayed in quite an unusual building (they don't actually show anything by Henry Moore). Shop, disabled access; cl bank hols; (0113) 234 3158; free. Stays open late on Weds.

Leeds City Art Gallery (The Headrow) Excellent collection of 20th-c British art, as well as English watercolours and sculpture gallery, inc carefully chosen works by Henry Moore (he had his first exhibition here in 1941). Meals, snacks, shop, limited disabled access; cl am Sun and bank hols (stays open late on Weds); (0113) 247

8248; free.

Leeds City Museum Resource Centre (Moorfield Rd, Yeadon) This offers access to the collections of the excellent Leeds City Museum which sadly closed in May 1999. The highlight is Natsef Amun (Keeper of the Bulls), an important Egyptian mummy which has been in the city for almost 200 years, but there are also displays of local wildlife, minerals and fossils, and exhibits from ancient Greece and Rome. Some disabled access (notice preferred); open by appointment only Mon–Fri; (0113) 214 6532; free.

Leeds Industrial Museum (Canal Rd) Once the largest woollen mill in the world, now a huge working museum, its floors given over to a massive display of textile machinery. Also a printing gallery, reconstructions of a turn-of-the-century tailor's shop, clothing factory, and demonstrations of railway locomotives. Snacks, shop, disabled access; cl Sun am, Mon (exc bank hols), 25–26 and 31 Dec, 1 Jan; (0113) 263 7861; £2.

Meanwood Valley Urban Farm 🖾 (Meanwood) Small working organic farm on regenerated waste land N of centre, with rare breeds, organic garden, and environment centre. Meals and snacks (not Mon), shop, good disabled access; (0113) 262 9759; £1.

Middleton Railway Running from Turnstall Rd to Middleton Park, this is the oldest running railway in the world and was the first to be authorised by Parliament. Later it was the first to succeed with steam locomotives, and in 1960 became the first standard-gauge line to be operated by volunteers. With a picnic area, fishing, nature trail and playgrounds as well as the trains, there's plenty for families here. Snacks, shop, disabled access; diesel or steam trains most wknds and bank hols Apr–Christmas, plus some other days in summer; (0113) 271 0320 for timetable; *£2.50.

Museum of the History of Education (Parkinson Court, Leeds University) Small but interesting, inc text and exercise books going back to the 17th c – it's usually best to book with Dr Foster, (0113) 233 4665 (open pm Mon–Fri (exc Tues); free).

Roundhay Park (off A58) 700 acres of rolling parkland, well known for concerts and events. On Princes Avenue here the Canal Gardens are a very pleasant and peaceful corner of the city, with several national flower collections (inc dahlias and violas), lots of roses, and ornamental wildfowl; free. The Roundhay dining pub has very cheap food.

Royal Armouries Museum 🔽 (Clarence Dock, Waterfront) A far cry from the average military museum, this houses the National Museum of Arms and Armour, previously displayed at the Tower of London, but shown off here in a radically different way. It's almost completely interactive, with hi-tech effects and push-button displays, and plenty of costumed demonstrations showing not just how weapons were made and used, but how they affected everyday life; children can try on costumes and helmets, or even test their aim with a crossbow. The building's design is stunning (don't miss the breathtaking Hall of Steel, with 3,000 pieces of gleaming arms and armour on the walls), but the most spectacular feature is outside: the country's only full-size authentically re-created tiltyard, with dramatic exhibitions of jousting, fencing, duelling, and hunting dogs and birds of prey; phone for dates and times. An inside display area often has martial arts displays, and there are demonstrations of traditional skills in the Craft Court. Meals and snacks, shop, good disabled access; cl winter Mons, 24–25 Dec; (0990) 106666; £4.90.

Temple Newsam House 🔽 (5m E, S of A63) That trusty old Capability Brown designed the wonderful 1,200 acres of landscaped parkland and gardens in which this house stands, an extraordinary asset for any city. The house itself dates from Tudor and Jacobean times, and contains the city's very good collections of decorative and fine art, as well as an exceptional assemblage of Chippendale furniture. Rare breeds in the grounds; picnic areas and children's play area. Snacks, shop, disabled access to ground floor only; cl Sun am, all day Mon, and Jan–Feb; (0113) 264 7321; £2 (£1 parking).

Thackray Medical Museum (Beckett St) Dynamic museum at St James's Hospital, well known from the TV series *Jimmy's*. The emphasis is more social history than science, but there are interactive displays on how the body works, and good reconstructions showing the progress of medical care in Britain, inc some deliciously gruesome parts on surgery before the development of anaesthetics. Snacks, shop, disabled access; cl Mon (exc bank and school hols), 24–26, 31 Dec, 1 Jan; (0113) 244 4343; £4.40.

Thwaite Mills Watermill (Stourton, 2m S) This water-powered mill was the focus of a tiny island community perched between the River Aire – which drives the mill wheels – and the Aire & Calder Navigation. The Georgian mill-owner's house has been restored and has displays on the site's history; guided tours of the mill every hour. Snacks, shop, disabled access; cl Sun am, all day Mon (exc bank hols), Christmas, and Jan–Feb; (0113) 249 6453; £2.

Tropical World (Roundhay Park) Huge conservatory with the biggest collection of tropical plants outside Kew, along with all sorts of exotic trees, reptiles, fish, birds, and butterflies, in careful re-creations of their natural settings. Meals, snacks, shop, disabled access; cl 25 Dec; (0113) 266 1850; £1.50.

LOTHERTON HALL SE4436 🔽 (B1217 Garforth–Tadcaster) Edwardian house with displays ranging from oriental art to British fashion, as well as collections of paintings, silver and ceramics and some lovely furnishings. There's a bird garden in the restored grounds. Snacks, shop, some disabled access; cl Mon (exc bank hols), Sun am, and Jan–Feb; (0113) 281 3259; £2 house, grounds free. The Swan at nearby Aberford is popular for lunch.

LUDDENDEN SE0426 Interesting village with Brontë connections; the enormous Oats Royd Mill in the valley is a remarkable sight.

MALTBY SK5489 **Roche Abbey** (off A634 SE) A fine gatehouse to the NW and the still-standing walls of the S and N transepts are all that's left of this 12th-c

Cistercian abbey, but they make an impressive sight. Snacks, shop, some disabled access; cl Nov–Mar; (01709) 812739; £1.60; EH.

MIDDLESTOWN SE2416
National Coal Mining Museum (Caphouse Colliery, New Rd) Exploration of life as a coal miner: no simple reconstruction this – they take you 140 metres (450 ft) underground, down one of Britain's oldest working mine shafts, where models and machinery have been set up to show the methods and working conditions of miners from the 1800s to the present. On the surface (not smart but why should it be?) there are pit ponies, 'paddy train' rides, steam winder, nature trail, and an adventure playground. Dress sensibly if you're going underground. Meals, snacks, shop, disabled access and excellent facilities – helpful to arrange it in advance; cl 24–26 Dec, 1 Jan; (01924) 848806; *£5.75. The Kaye Arms at Grange Moor is a good smart dining pub.

MONK BRETTON SE3706
Monk Bretton Priory The red sandstone remains of an important 12th-c priory, with gatehouse, church and other buildings, as well as some unusually well preserved drains. The ancient Mill of the Black Monks is pleasant at lunchtime (live music for young people most nights).

NORLAND MOOR SE0521
S of Sowerby Bridge, this gives walkers views from the Calderdale Way into adjacent Calderdale, with the Rochdale Canal along its foot.

NORTH ANSTON SK5284
Tropical Butterfly House 🔳 (Woodsetts Rd) Friendly place with insects, reptiles, snakes, birds of prey and farm animals besides the butterflies; they positively encourage you to touch as well as look. Meals (in season and wknds), snacks, shop, disabled access; cl 25–26 Dec and 1 Jan; (01909) 569416; £3.50.

NOSTELL PRIORY SE4017
(off A638) Reopening in Mar following restoration work, this sumptuous Palladian mansion, with an additional wing built by Adam in 1766, has perhaps the best collection of Chippendale furniture anywhere, all designed for this house. Other highlights include the tapestry room, charming saloon, newly opened servants hall and great kitchen, and a remarkably intricate 18th-c dolls' house also said to have been furnished by Chippendale. The most attractive grounds have woodland walks and a lovely rose garden; coarse fishing on the lakes. There's an interesting **medieval church** nr the entrance, and a craft centre in the stables. Snacks, shop, disabled access; house open Weds–Sun pm Apr–Oct, then wknd pms only till early Dec, grounds open same days from 11am; (01924) 863892; house and gardens £4.50, grounds only £2.50; NT. The Spread Eagle has decent food.

OAKWELL HALL SE2127
(signed off A651/A652 S of Birkenshaw) Moated Elizabethan manor house, altered in the 17th c, and still furnished to give something of the atmosphere then; look out for the unusual dog gates at the foot of the staircase. Also period formal gardens, extensive country park with adventure playground, visitor centre and, for children, the Discovery Gallery – a hands-on exploration of the four elements. Snacks, shop, limited disabled access; cl am wknds (Discovery Gallery cl all am), 22–26 Dec and 1 Jan; (01924) 326240; £1.20 house (free Nov–Feb), visitor centre and Discovery Gallery free. The Black Bull opposite the ancient Norman church in nearby Birstall has good value home cooking.

OGDEN RESERVOIR SE0630
N of Halifax, this is well served with paths for walkers (inc a stretch of Roman road).

OTLEY SE2045
Archetypal Yorkshire market town with a most attractive atmosphere (helped by its remarkable number of pubs?).

The Chevin Behind the town, this is not a high hill, but gives walkers a grand view of Wharfedale.

RIPPONDEN SE0318
Rather austerely attractive village, with medieval pack-horse bridge; the B6113 and B6114 above here are interesting moors roads.

ROTHERHAM SK4091
Magna (off Sheffield Rd, Templeborough) Within awesome former steel works, this new centre will put a colourful spin on the story of the steel industry when it opens in Apr. The attraction is made up of four themed 'pavilions' based around the main elements used in steel-making: Earth, housed in the basement, re-creates the drama of working in a quarry, Air is an inflated structure, designed to look like an airship hovering over the main factory floor, Water gives children plenty of excuses to soak their parents, and Fire, set around a giant live flame, uses audio-visual displays to illustrate how man has controlled fire for his benefit, as well as its explosive (and destructive) possibilities. With plenty of emphasis on hands-on activities and interactive experiences, this promises to be fun as well as thoroughly informative. Meals, snacks, shop, disabled access; best to phone for opening times and prices nearer the time; (01709) 720002.

SALTAIRE SE1337
The pioneering industrial village Titus Salt developed in Shipley in the 1850s. Salt's beautifully thought-out classically designed village was so successful that even now it's a favoured place to live. It's well worth looking around, and you might want to try the antique **cable railway**. There's a splendid flight of locks on the Leeds–Liverpool Canal.
1853 Gallery (Victoria Rd) Named from the year when the magnificent mill it's housed in was built, probably one of the largest private collections of contemporary art in the country, inc around 300 works by David Hockney, with some of his intriguing experiments with photography. Huge bookshop, disabled access; (01274) 531163; cl 25–26 Dec; free. Some good smart shops in the building too.
Victorian Reed Organ Museum 🅰 (Victoria Hall, Victoria Rd) Unique, with some eye-opening exhibits, inc one organ no bigger than a family bible. If you're an organ-player you may get the chance to try some of those on display. Shop, limited disabled access (with notice); cl Fri, Sat, and over Christmas; (01274) 585601; *£2.

SAXTON SE4736
Attractive village with decent pub; don't miss the **church**, where Lord Dacre is buried sitting on his war horse – the 1461 Battle of Towton site is just N.

SHEFFIELD SK3281
A vast industrial city (and rather surprisingly, the greenest in England), redeveloped extensively in post-war years. Ongoing initiatives to revitalise the heart of the city can only increase the thriving cultural life of the place, and several places are already rewarding to visit – though needing a street map and quite a bit of journeying. Best to use the comfortably modern tram to get about; it runs out to the giant indoor shopping mall at Meadowhall. By the end of 2001, the Winter Garden temperate plant house should be fully planted, forming an attractive endpiece to the stunning new Millennium Galleries, due to open in spring. Other parts of the scheme, inc new public squares and redesigned gardens, have already opened.
Bishop's House (Meersbrook Park, S Sheffield) Striking 15th- and 16th-c yeoman's house, now a good museum of social history. Limited disabled access; open wknds, otherwise by appointment only; (0114) 278 2600; free.
City Museum and Mappin Art Gallery (Weston Park) Firmly traditional in its approach, but with some interesting collections, inc fine cutlery and a splendid display of antique Sheffield plate. The excellent newly refurbished gallery features works by Renoir, Cézanne, Turner and even Walt Disney. Meals, snacks, shop, disabled access; cl Mon exc bank hol and 25 Dec; (0114) 276 8588; free.
Graves Art Gallery (Surrey St) Well worth a visit, with some fine decorative art; (0114) 2782600; free.
Kelham Island Industrial Museum 🅰 (around Alma St, signed from centre) Lively exploration of Sheffield's industrial development, with all sorts of buildings, workshops and machinery collections (inc formidable working engines), and traditional cutlery craftsmen at work. Snacks, shop, disabled access; cl Fri–Sat; (0114) 272 2106; £3.50. The Fat Cat here has really good cheap food.

Millennium Galleries (Surrey St, opposite Graves Art Gallery) This elegant new £13m complex will form the focal point of Sheffield's central redevelopment when it opens in Apr. As well as providing a new home for the Ruskin collection (previously at Norfolk St), the four climate-controlled galleries will house collections from London's Victoria & Albert Museum (which has been closely involved in the centre's development), displays of metalware showcasing the city's metalworking heritage, and changing exhibitions of art, craft and design work. The Ruskin gallery will lead into a splendid glasshouse, which should be fully completed by the end of the summer. Café, shop, disabled access; best to phone nearer the time for opening times and details; (0114) 278 2600.

National Centre for Popular Music ⊞ It is hoped that the involvement of some big-name pop stars will revive the flagging fortunes of this £15m centre, set in a distinctive building shaped like a pair of drums. Exhibitions look at the development of popular music from classical to hip-hop, with an emphasis on post-1945 sounds. Also a surround-sound auditorium, and you can try your hand at playing an instrument or mixing a record. Meals, snacks, shop, disabled access; (0114) 279 8941; £5.95.

Sheffield Bus Museum ⊞ (Tinsley) Diverse collection of buses with related memorabilia and a big model railway. Shop, snacks, some disabled access; open pm wknds Easter–Christmas for restoration work, with special open days every couple of months when the displays are more lively; (0114) 255 3010; £1.

SOWERBY BRIDGE SE0623 Worth a stop if you're passing; turn down to the canal basin, which always has a lot going on.

ULLEY SK4687 Pleasant walks around a reservoir, also good for fishing and watersports; the Royal Oak is in a lovely setting by the church.

WAKEFIELD SE3221 A number of handsome buildings, inc its **cathedral**, much restored in Victorian times but with some fine 15th-c

masonry and carvings (and a marvellous spire – the tallest in Yorkshire), its rare 14th-c bridge chapel over the River Calder, some Georgian and Regency houses most notably around Wood St and St John's Sq, and its imposing civic buildings.

Wakefield Art Gallery (Wentworth Terrace) Good collection of 20th-c painting and sculpture, internationally famous for its galleries devoted to two famous local sculptors – Barbara Hepworth and Henry Moore. Shop; cl Sun am, all Mon, 25 Dec, 1 Jan; (01924) 305796; free.

Wakefield Museum (Wood St) Recently refurbished to give a much more interactive feel, so that along with the unique collection of preserved animals and exotic birds gathered by local explorer Charles Waterton, and an exhibition of 1940s women's costume, there are plenty of opportunities for hands-on activities. Shop, good disabled access; (01924) 305351; free.

Yorkshire Sculpture Park (Bretton Hall College, West Bretton; A637 SE) Carefully and imaginatively displayed series of major contemporary sculpture set in fine 18th-c landscaped parkland. There are 16 works by Henry Moore in the adjacent country park, often surrounded by grazing sheep. Café, shop, disabled access; cl 24–25 Dec; (01924) 830579; free (though £1.50 car parking charge).

WENTWORTH SK3898 Reckoned by some readers to be the prettiest village they've ever seen.

WITHENS CLOUGH RESERVOIR SD9822 S of Hebden Bridge, this has a path for walkers – and the more energetic can climb up to the prominent monument on Stoodley Pike, for the views.

WORSBROUGH SE3503 **Worsbrough Mill Museum** (A61) Hard to believe this peaceful country park was once a busy industrial area; the only sign of those days is the working corn mill, now a museum but still producing stoneground flour. The 200 acres also include nature trails. Snacks, shop, some disabled access; cl Mon (exc bank hols), Tues, and mid-Dec–early Jan; (01226) 774527; *50p.

Other attractive or attractively placed villages with decent pubs include Askwith SD1648, Barkisland SE0420, Blackshaw Head SD9527, Boston Spa SE4345, East Morton SE1042, Esholt SE1840, High Bradfield SK2692, Holme SE1006, Honley SE1312, canalside Kildwick SE0145, Ledsham SE4529 and nearby Ledston SE4328, Ogden SE0730, Saxton SE4736, Sowerby SE0423, Stanbury SE0037 and Tickhill SK5993 (esp church and semi-ruined castle).

Other useful pubs in fine positions or with good views include Dick Hudsons on the Otley road at High Eldwick above Bingley SE1240, the Castle overlooking the reservoirs nr Bolsterstone SK2796, Brown Cow by open-access woods at Ireland Bridge (B6429) nearer Bingley, Strines nr Strines Reservoir above Bradfield SK2692, Stanhope Arms on Windle Edge Lane nr Winscar Reservoir by Dunford Bridge SE1502, New Inn at Eccup SE2842, Cow & Calf up Skew Hill Lane at Grenoside above Sheffield SK3293, the Malt Shovel at Harden SE0838, Robin Hood at Pecket Well outside Hebden Bridge SD9928, the Cherry Tree on Bank End Lane at High Hoyland SE2710, Fleece at Holme SE1006, Buckstones on the A640 towards Denshaw high above Huddersfield SE1416, Blacksmiths Arms on Heaton Moor Rd at Kirkheaton SE1818, Shepherds Rest and Top Brink on Mankinholes Rd at Lumbutts SD9523 (bracing walks to Stoodley Pike monument), Hinchcliffe Arms at Cragg Vale, Mytholmroyd SE0126 (the B6188 S is a good moors road), Hobbit up Hob Lane, Norland SE0723, Grouse on Harehills Lane, Oldfield, nr Oakworth SE0038, Causeway Foot on the Keighley Rd by Ogden Reservoir SE0631, Waggon & Horses (A6033) and Dog & Gun (off B6141 towards Denholme), both nr Oxenhope SE0335, Pineberry on the A644 Keighley road out of Queensbury SE1030, Brown Cow (A672) dramatically overlooking Scammonden Reservoir SE0215, Clothiers Arms in Station Rd, Stocksmoor, nr Shepley SE1810, White House on the B6107 or Rose & Crown up Cop Hill at Slaithwaite SE0813, Blue Ball nr Soyland SE0120, the Sportsmans Arms at Hawks Stones, Kebcote on Stansfield Moor SD9227, Ring o' Bells on Hill Top Rd at Thornton SE0933, Freemasons Arms on Hopton Hall Lane at Upper Hopton SE1918, Cross Keys overlooking the restored Rochdale Canal at Walsden SD9322, Delvers on Cold Edge Rd and Withens on Warley Moor Rd at Wainstalls SE0428, and Pack Horse at Widdop SD9333.

Where to eat

GRANGE MOOR SE2415 **Kaye Arms** *Wakefield Rd* (01924) 848385 Civilised and popular family-run dining pub with smart dining lounge, particularly good imaginative food, exceptional value house wines from a fine list, lots of malt whiskies, and helpful courteous service; cl Mon, 25–26 Dec; children allowed lunchtime only; disabled access. £23

HALIFAX SE0726 **Design House** (01422) 383242 Stylish modern restaurant in thriving carefully restored carpet mill complex, with enjoyable modern cooking to match; relaxed and friendly atmosphere, good service, and thoughtful wine list; cl Sat am, Sun, Mon pm; disabled access. £23

HAWORTH SE0237 **Weavers** *15 West Lane* (01535) 643822 Charming evening restaurant made up of weavers' cottages, with lots of bric-a-brac, photographs, and spinning mementoes, delicious food, cheerful service, and a good loyal following; bdrms; cl Sun, Mon, 1 wk after Christmas, last wk June. £27.50

LEEDS SE3033 **Brasserie Forty-Four** *42–44 The Calls* (0113) 234 3232 Originally a grain mill (below 42 The Calls, see **Where to stay**), this riverside restaurant is simply furnished with modern designs, and serves enjoyable British and Mediterranean food (very good value early evening set menu), and a good value wine list; cl Sat am, Sun, bank hols; partial disabled access. £28/2-course lunch £9.75

LEEDS SE3033 **Pool Court at 42** *42–44 The Calls* (0113) 244 4242 Cleverly converted quayside grain mill (also incorporating Brasserie Forty-Four and the stylish hotel, 42 The Calls), this is a smart modern restaurant with a calm atmosphere, very accomplished enjoyable food with French leanings (the set meals are good value), lovely puddings, and an interesting wine list; cl Sat am, Sun, 25–26 Dec; no babies and children over 5; disabled access. £47.30/£2 courses £14.50

LEEDS SE2736 **Salvos** *115 Otley Rd, Headingley (0113) 275 5017* Welcoming Italian restaurant run by the same family for over 30 years, with good modern food (popular and interesting daily specials) and cheerful service; cl Sun, 25–26 Dec. £20/2-course special £5

LEEDS SE2933 **Sous le Nez en Ville** *The Basement, Quebec House, Quebec St (0113) 244 0108* Imaginative popular food in fashionable basement restaurant with tiled floors and exposed brick walls, a very good wine list, and efficient service; cl Sun, bank hols (but open Good Fri). £17.50|**£6.95**

RIPPONDEN SE0419 **Old Bridge Inn** *(01422) 822595/823722* Well kept medieval inn by pretty bridge over River Ryburn with interesting rooms, good wines and real ales, and very popular cold buffet wkday lunchtimes (best to book); charming evening restaurant just over the bridge; no bar food Sat, Sun pm; no children; disabled access. £18|**£5.25**

SHEFFIELD SK3187 **Smith's of Sheffield** *34 Sandygate Rd (0114) 266 6096* Very popular restaurant, cheerfully decorated in cream and red with an unusual tented ceiling, relaxed chatty atmosphere, stylish modern cooking using influences from all over the world, and a good wine list; upstairs is perhaps more serious, with an open-plan kitchen and 6 gourmet courses; occasional cookery demonstrations, too; cl Sun pm. £29

Special thanks to Mr and Mrs A Hughes, Mrs S Wrighton, Mrs P Bagnall, S Barber, Norman Fox, Rod Sandford, Mark Holman

LONDON

Rewarding new attractions in the wake of the Millennium rush, some classic institutions getting a 21st-c face-lift, and countless potential for busy days out

With the Millennium madness well behind us, it's interesting to reflect on how the bold new ventures of 2000 lived up to the expectations foisted on them by the press. That the Dome foundered and the new pedestrian bridge wobbled is beyond the realms of debate, but the gallant Tate Modern has slipped effortlessly into its role as a world-class flagship for contemporary art, and perhaps most surprising of all, the London Eye has become an instant tourist icon. Its looming presence has certainly had an influence on the remarkable transformation of County Hall into a hive of activity, with the London Aquarium, new Dali Universe and imaginative Frog Tours all at hand. The gradual establishment of new wildlife habitats is bound to see visitors (feathered and other) flocking to the outstanding new wetland centre in Barnes.

Time will tell how the recently restyled Tate Gallery (they face an uphill battle in trying to persuade us all to think of it as Tate Britain instead) fares against its new sister down river; a free riverbus service ferries you between the two in summer, while Somerset House is becoming a real focus for art lovers, home as it is to the marvellous Courtauld, Gilbert and new Hermitage collections. The restoration of the British Museum's Great Court should have at last been completed by the time this book comes out, and anyone with a serious interest in horticulture won't want to miss the collections at the newly re-housed Lindley Library.

While the South Bank gears itself up for some ambitious redevelopment, Woolwich must be hoping that the new Firepower museum (due to open in May) will attract the same sort of attention that the row of cultural developments has brought to Bankside in recent years.

The great museums of South Kensington all, commendably, offer free admission to children, but with a bit of careful searching, you'll find some rewarding destinations for which a wallet isn't necessary at all, most notably, the delightful Sir John Soane's Museum, the recently improved National Army Museum, the friendly Geffrye Museum, the unusual Museum Of behind the Oxo Tower, Bethnal Green's Museum of Childhood, the lavish Wallace Collection, and a bit further afield at Forest Hill, the Horniman Museum (currently being redeveloped).

As almost everything worth visiting or looking at is concentrated in the relatively small centre, London is quite easy to explore on foot. There is no end of potential walks concentrating on particular interests – architecture, history, royalty or whatever. One of the best overviews of the capital is had by walking along the south bank of the Thames from Lambeth Bridge to Tower Bridge. This walkway gives panoramic views, and is now punctuated by all sorts of points of interest from craft stalls and secondhand bookstalls through occasional free entertainment to interesting refreshment stops. Elsewhere quite a number of people lead guided walks. We have found Original London Walks ((020) 7624 3978) consistently good over the last few years, with a choice of nine or ten a day. Walks last about two hours, usually starting from a tube station; you don't need to book, and the cost is around £5.

Travel Cards are good value cut-price tickets for the day, wknd or longer, valid on buses, tube and rail trains, for as many journeys as you want to make during the day (not the morning rush hour). You can add them to rail fares into London. London's Tube, the underground railway, is a quick and straightforward way of getting around; the Jubilee lines new extension's stations are worth seeing in themselves. Pocket tube and bus route maps are free from ticket offices. In the text, we have grouped things to see and do under the heading of the most convenient tube station, using the ⊖ symbol – or the ⇌ symbol if it's surface rail instead.

Where to stay

22 Jermyn Street Hotel *22 Jermyn St SW1Y 6HP (020) 7734 2353* **£270.88**; 5 rms and 13 suites – spacious with deeply comfortable seats and sofas, flowers, plants, and antiques. Stylish little hotel owned by the same family for over 80 years and much loved by customers; no public rooms but wonderful 24-hr service, helpful notes and suggestions from the friendly owners, in-room light meals, and a warm welcome for children (with their own fact sheet listing shops, restaurants, and sights geared towards them, free video library, old-fashioned and electronic games, and own bathrobes); disabled access ☺

Basil Street Hotel *8 Basil St SW3 1AH (020) 7581 3311* **£251**, plus special breaks; 80 pretty, decent-sized rms. Handy for Harrods and Hyde Park, this very civilised, privately owned Edwardian hotel has a relaxed atmosphere, antiques, fine carpets and paintings in the public rooms, a panelled restaurant with reliably enjoyable food, afternoon teas in lounge, and ladies' club (named after a parrot who had to go when his language became inappropriate); helpful courteous service – many of the staff have been here for years; children free in parents' room

Capital *22–24 Basil St SW3 1AT (020) 7589 5171* **£268**; 48 luxury rms with lovely fabrics, fine paintings, marble bthrms, and tempting extras. Exclusive little hotel nr Harrods with a warm welcome and log fire in reception, intimate panelled bar with good nibbles, a small lounge, exemplary service, and exceptional French-inspired food in chandelier-lit restaurant; disabled access

Chesterfield *35 Charles St W1X 8LX (020) 7491 2622* **£192.25**; 110 well equipped pretty rms. Charming hotel with particularly courteous helpful staff, afternoon tea in panelled library, a relaxed club-style bar with resident pianist, and fine food in attractive restaurant or light and airy Terrace Room

Claridges *Brook St W1A 2JQ (020) 7629 8860* **£397.25**, plus luxury breaks; 197 excellent rms. Grand hotel long used by Royalty and heads of state, with liveried footmen, lift attendants and valets, elegant and comfortable day rooms, and civilised colonnaded foyer where the Hungarian Quartet plays; lovely formal restaurant with mirrored mural and terrace, dinner-dance Fri/Sat pm, and free tennis at Vanderbilt Racquet Club; disabled access

Claverley *13–14 Beaufort Gardens SW3 1PS (020) 7589 8541* **£130**, plus special breaks; 30 individually decorated rms, most with own bthrm. Friendly privately owned Edwardian house with comfortable lounge, panelled reading room, and good breakfasts in cheerful dining room; disabled access

Connaught *Carlos Place W1Y 6AL (020) 7499 7070* **£488.75**; 90 lovely, individually decorated rms inc 24 suites. A very special place with fine old-fashioned dignified values – there's no brochure, no price list; elegant, restful day rooms filled with beautiful flowers and antiques, fine panelling, exemplary service, and outstanding food in the two formal restaurants; disabled access

Conrad *Chelsea Harbour SW10 0XG (020) 7823 3000* **£199**; 160 suites with a light and spacious living room area (many have sofa-beds so two small children could stay with parents at no extra cost). London's first 'suite hotel', tucked away in the quiet modern enclave of the Chelsea Harbour development and overlooking its small marina; enjoyable Mediterranean and Asian-influenced dishes in Aquasia Restaurant and Bar, friendly service, and health club; disabled access

Covent Garden Hotel *10 Monmouth St WC2H 9HB (020) 7806 1000* **£258**; 58 big individual bdrms with smart bthrms. Stylish luxury hotel nr theatres, with wrought-iron staircase from foyer to panelled upstairs drawing room and library, richly coloured interesting furniture, and popular ground-floor brasserie; state-of-the-art screening room for film companies, and for hotel guests' film club; limited disabled access

Durrants *26–32 George St W1H 6BJ (020) 7935 8131* **£159.50**; 92 well equipped rms, with own bthrms; the quietest are at the back. Managed by the same family for over 70 years, this surprisingly quiet central hotel, behind a delightful Georgian façade, has fine paintings and antiques, a clubby bar, and relaxing lounges; cosy panelled restaurant with essentially English cooking, and helpful pleasant staff

Goring *15 Beeston Place SW1W 0JW (020) 7396 9000* **£276.75**, plus special breaks; 74 individually decorated rms, some with balconies overlooking pretty garden. Built in 1910 by the grandfather of the present Mr Goring, this family-run, impeccably kept and very English hotel has a particularly welcoming atmosphere (many staff have been there for years), very good cooking in the elegant restaurant, a super wine list, comfortable lounge for afternoon tea, airy cocktail bar, and staunchly loyal customers; disabled access

Halkin *5 Halkin St SW1X 7DJ (020) 7333 1000* **£344.27**, plus special breaks; 41 stylish well equipped rms, with wonderful marble bthrms. Despite its Georgian exterior, the décor and furnishings here are ultra-modern but enjoyable, and there's a particularly good modern Italian restaurant overlooking the garden; fine breakfasts, and really charming staff; much liked by businessmen, too – lots of facilities for them; new gym; disabled access

Hazlitts *6 Frith St W1V 5TZ (020) 7434 1771* **£205.63**; 23 rms with 18th- or 19th-c beds and free-standing Victorian baths with early brass shower mixer units. Behind a typically Soho façade of listed early Georgian houses, this is a well kept and comfortably laid-out little hotel which could scarcely be handier for the West End; good continental breakfasts served in your bedroom, snacks in the sitting room, lots of restaurants all around; kind, helpful service; disabled access

Knightsbridge Green Hotel *159 Knightsbridge SW1X 7PD (020) 7584 6274* **£161**, plus special breaks; 28 no smoking suites with sitting room. Friendly family-owned hotel, carefully refurbished and neatly kept, with very good in-room breakfasts (no restaurant), bar service, free coffee and tea in lounge, and helpful efficient staff

L'Hotel *28 Basil St SW3 1AS (020) 7589 6286* **£170.38**; 12 well equipped rms. Small family-owned French-style city hotel, nr Harrods, and set above the neatly kept well run Metro wine bar where English and continental breakfasts are served – as well as good modern French café food; friendly staff; disabled access

Leonard *15 Seymour St W1H 5AA (020) 7935 2010* **£270**; 31 rms – mainly luxury suites – with fine paintings, antiques, lovely fabrics, fresh flowers, videos, satellite TV, and hi-fi system; smart 18th-c town house with marvellous staff, light modern meals all day in café bar, and compact exercise room

Meridien Piccadilly *21 Piccadilly W1V 0BH (020) 7734 8000* **£199**w, plus special breaks; 266 luxurious newly refurbished rms. The very best in modern French hotel-keeping, with attractive quiet public rooms, professional and friendly service, popular afternoon tea, marvellous food (one restaurant is the Oak Room of Marco

Pierre White), and free membership of the largest health club in a London hotel; one child under 12 free in parents' room; partial disabled access

One Aldwych 1 Aldwych WC2B 4BZ (020) 7300 1000 **£245**w, plus special breaks; 105 bdrms with daily fresh flowers and fruit, huge beds, TV in bthrms, and lots of extras. Close to theatres and Covent Garden, this fine Edwardian hotel has an impressive foyer with a giant statue of an oarsman in his boat, huge flower arrangements and contemporary paintings throughout, a choice of popular restaurants and bars, and helpful friendly staff; gym, small indoor swimming pool with underwater music, and personal trainers; disabled access

Rubens 39–41 Buckingham Palace Rd SW1W 0PS (020) 7834 6600 **£252.50**, plus special breaks; 173 well equipped rms. Opposite Buckingham Palace and nr Victoria Station, this attractive hotel has comfortable day rooms inc lounge with views of the Royal Mews, restful library, open fire in bar, and attractive split-level restaurant with good food

Swiss House 171 Old Brompton Rd SW5 0AN (020) 7373 2769 **£80**; 15 rms. Festooned with ivy and flower boxes, this is a warmly friendly and good value family-run hotel, relaxed and tidy inside, with very good buffet continental breakfasts – English available, too

Tophams Belgravia 24–32 Ebury St SW1W 0LU (020) 7730 8147 **£140**; 39 cosy rms, 34 with own bthrm. Small, charmingly old-fashioned hotel made up of several town houses with a friendly country-house atmosphere, downstairs bar, attractive lounges, good food in the elegant restaurant, and decent wines; cl Christmas and New Year; disabled access

Windermere Hotel 142/144 Warwick Way, London SW1V 4JE (020) 7834 5163 **£99**∗; 22 individually decorated rms. Small private hotel with a cosy lounge, decent breakfasts, good modern cooking in Pimlico Restaurant, and a friendly informal atmosphere

The West End

This area is world-famous for its shopping and window-shopping, from the daunting bustle of Oxford St, through the bookshops around Charing Cross Rd, the specialist food and cookery shops of Soho, and the elegant stores of Regent St and Piccadilly, to the ultra-smart clothes shops of South Molton St and Bond St. There are great opportunities for window-shopping in the auction houses and fine art galleries. The West End is synonymous with theatre; it's worth knowing that on Leicester Square a half-price ticket booth sells off surplus tickets for that day's performances: open around 12–2 pm for matinee tickets, then from about 2.30pm for evenings – there's usually a queue so it's worth getting there earlier. Highlights here include the National Gallery and Trafalgar Square, Piccadilly with the Royal Academy, the sumptuous Wallace Collection (in a recently remodelled elegant 18th-c house), and Covent Garden (the London Transport Museum here is surprisingly good fun for families). The BBC Experience up by Oxford Circus is great for anyone interested in what goes into TV or radio, not just what comes out. Chinatown is a vivid enclave, Neal St is a focus for vegetarian restaurants and rather alternative shops, and there are staunchly old-fashioned institutions of Englishness and English cooking like Rules or Simpsons – among an extraordinarily eclectic flood of other places to eat.

To see and do

⊖ BOND STREET

Mayfair W of Regent St and N of Piccadilly (and only the shortest of strolls from them; Bond St and Green Park tube stations are handy). This is mostly a quietly discreet area of elegant town houses, smart well established hotels, and richly unobtrusive offices. Despite their famous names, Berkeley Sq and Grosvenor Sq don't have any special appeal for visitors – though you might want to stroll down Brook St to see the neighbouring blue plaques commemorating Handel and Jimi Hendrix living there (Handel House is being restored as a museum). Bond St with its continuation New Bond St is the area's main street for shopping, though unless you want to spend a great deal of money on top-notch designer clothes and shoes, jewellery or oriental rugs this is likely to be confined to the window. Plenty of art and antiques galleries, and a good indoor antique market (124 New Bond St). Asprey's is a remarkable place, famous for its opulent luxury goods and glittering with an awesome tonnage of gems and precious metals. Nearby is a charming life-size sculpture of Churchill chatting to Roosevelt on a bench – you can sit with them. Sotheby's auction rooms are fascinating to wander around. Other small and prestigious art galleries are dotted throughout Mayfair, particularly in nearby Dover St and Cork St; Grays antique market off 58 Davies St has hundreds of indoor stalls. South Audley St has Hobbs of Mayfair, a delicious smart delicatessen, and Goode's, a magnificent glass and china shop. Higgins in Duke St is the Queen's coffee-man. The best Mayfair pub is the Red Lion in Waverton St.

Wallace Collection (Hertford House, Manchester Sq – across Oxford St) Excellent art collection beautifully displayed in an elegant 18th-c house, recently improved and remodelled by the American architect Rick Mather, 100 years after it was first opened as a museum. It's visually very seductive, with probably the best collection of 18th-c French paintings in the world, inc luscious offerings from Watteau, Boucher and Fragonard. Also great Canalettos, fine works by Rembrandt, Rubens and Van Dyck, works by British painters, furniture (mostly 18th-c French), notable assemblage of Sèvres porcelain, and an amazing array of arms and armour, both Oriental and European. It's rarely busy, and in places feels more like a historic home than a museum. There's a new watercolour gallery and public library in the basement, and a café in the glass-covered sculpture garden. Meals, snacks, shop, disabled access with prior warning; cl Sun am, 24–26 Dec, Good Fri, 1 Jan, May Day bank hol; (020) 7935 0687; free.

⊖ ⇌ CHARING CROSS

Trafalgar Square Many people think of this as the heart of central London (distances to and from central London used to be measured from the Cross on the Strand) and there are elaborate plans to pedestrianise part of the square, so as to make it more accessible to visitors (which, if planners get their way, might be under way by the spring). Named for the great naval victory of 1805, it was designed by Nash and completed in 1841; the fountains were added a century later. The centrepiece, **Nelson's Column**, stretches up 56 metres (185 ft), its base guarded by four huge identical lions. Look out for the temporary sculpture of a wizened tree with roots spreading like tentacles over a pile of books. Trafalgar Sq wouldn't be the same without the innumerable pigeons; Nelson has a special coating to protect him from their droppings.

National Gallery This magnificent building right on Trafalgar Sq houses the national collection of Western European painting, with around 2,000 pictures dating from the 13th c to the end of the 19th (some 20th-c works were recently swapped with the Tate, after a decision that 1900 is the date when modern art begins). You'll enjoy it most if you're firm and restrict yourself to just a few of the galleries, rather than trying to see everything. It's hard to pick out highlights (the whole collection is worth studying), but don't miss the Sainsbury Wing, which gives perfect lighting and viewing conditions for its treasure-trove of early Renaissance works. Last summer, David Hockney exhibited a true example of art imitating life, by displaying portraits of attendants currently working at the gallery. It gets very busy, especially on a Sat, or at any time around the Impressionist works. The hi-tech audio tour, with a CD rather than a cassette (so you can skip to whichever bit you want), is well worth the cost, with a commentary on every single picture in the main gallery. Meals, snacks, shop, disabled access; cl 24–26 Dec, 1 Jan, Good Fri; (0171) 747 2885; free, charges for some exhibitions.

National Portrait Gallery (St Martin's Pl, just round the corner) Grandly illustrates British history, with paintings of kings, queens and other notable characters arranged in chronological order from the top floor (medieval) to the present. The new Ondaatje wing, home to the Tudor Gallery – where Shakespeare rubs shoulders with the Rolling Stones – also has a rooftop restaurant (with views across Trafalgar Sq and Whitehall) and a lecture theatre. Meals, snacks, shop (where computer technology allows them to print you a poster of any painting in the gallery), disabled access; cl 24–26 Dec, 1 Jan; (0171) 306 0055; free, charge for some special exhibitions.

St Martin-in-the-Fields This elegant church has frequent lunchtime and evening concerts; (020) 7839 8362 for programme. Unmistakable for its blue clock-dial – the only clock in this part of London that seems always to keep the right time – the church has a busy but very well liked coffee bar in its crypt, with frequent art exhibitions; also brass-rubbing centre, shop (inc all the Academy of St Martin-in-the-Fields CDs), and a good afternoon craft market useful for bargains; all proceeds go towards the running of the church's care centre for the homeless – you're likely to see plenty of bodies huddled in shop doorways in the surrounding streets, a sadly common sight all over London, but especially obvious around

here.

Theatres Theatres abound off Trafalgar Sq, with a group based around this end of Charing Cross Rd, and another up along the Strand. Marked out by the globe on top of the building, the Coliseum (St Martin's Lane) is the home of the English National Opera – you can usually get decently priced seats on the day, from 10am; (020) 7632 8300. Almost next to the Coliseum, the Chandos is a good pub with food all day (upstairs is best), down past the Post Office the underground Tappit Hen is an atmospheric wine bar, and there's no end of smart little coffee shops and cafés near by – Gabys (30 Charing Cross Rd) does perfect hot salt beef sandwiches.

⊖ COVENT GARDEN
Partly pedestrianised, the former vegetable, fruit and flower market with its elegant buildings is now made over to smart cafe-bars, boutiques and stalls, such as those in the covered piazza, selling good but expensive handmade clothes and craft items. There's a bustling cosmopolitan atmosphere and good street entertainers. There's also the Jubilee Market which specialises in different wares on different days. The many bars and restaurants are always lively at night, but again they're not cheap. London's more famous Royal Opera House at Covent Garden has been beautifully restored and extended (at an inordinate cost), and you can look around the refurbished foyer areas and view various exhibitions. A limited number of tickets are available on the day, from here, too; (020) 7304 4000. There are lovely views across Covent Garden from its new Amphitheatre restaurant. One of the delights of this area is its range of unusual or specialist **shops**. In the streets around the Piazza, Knutz (Russell St) has everything for the practical joker, and Penhaligon's (Wellington St) sell lovely old-fashioned toiletries. On the other side of the market, N of the tube station, interesting and unusual shops are set in a labyrinthine network of attractively rejuvenated alleys and streets; you will get lost, but wandering around is great fun, and they all lead back to roughly the same area. Neal St is rewarding for its

small craft and specialist shops, and Neal's Yard is full of healthy living – delightful in summer with its fresh paint and tubs of flowers. Floral St has elegant and expensive clothes and shoe shops (plus the Tintin shop – paradise for the Tintin fan). The Africa Centre on King St may have exhibitions of African art and culture. No shortage of places to eat around here, but useful pubs for lunch or refreshment include the Marquess of Anglesey on Bow St, with a good value upstairs restaurant, and the Lamb & Flag on Rose St, an attractive 300-year-old pub with decent snacks, its back room still much as Dickens described it.

London Transport Museum (The Piazza) On the site of the former Flower Market, this is a surprisingly fun attraction. You can race a tram and a bus, delve into feely boxes, design your own bus and see why a steam train doesn't suit the Underground. The main exhibition is quite traditional, but they don't mind if you climb aboard some of the buses, trams and tube trains, and the touch screens throughout are much more enticing for children than traditional information boards. Costumed actors tell nostalgic transport tales, and there might be story-telling, face-painting or craft workshops in school holidays. Snacks, interesting shop, disabled access; usually cl 24–26 Dec but best to check over Christmas; (020) 7836 8557; £5.50.

St Paul's church The actors' church, full of interesting memorials to performers. Pepys watched the first-ever Punch and Judy show here in 1662. Outside its back gate, facing the covered market, the theatrical tradition continues, with jugglers, clowns, mountebanks and unusual musicians performing on the cobbles.

Theatre Museum (Tavistock St) Exhaustive look at events and personalities on the stage over the last few hundred years. Posters, puppets and props are among the permanent collection, which although astonishingly comprehensive is arranged a little confusingly; it's easy to find yourself going round backwards. The very good temporary displays leave the deepest impression: they sometimes have free stage make-up demonstrations. Shop, disabled access; cl Mon, and bank hols; (020) 7943 4700; £4.50, children free.

Theatre Royal (Drury Lane) The oldest working theatre in the world, first opened in 1663 (Nell Gwynn was one of its earliest performers), but rebuilt several times over the next few centuries. Tours show backstage features inc the intriguing hydraulic lift beneath the stage, still in use. Meals, snacks, shop, disabled access to theatre but not tour; tours 12.30, 2.15 and 4.45pm (exc Weds and Sat when tours are 11am and 1pm); (020) 7240 5357; £7.50.

● LEICESTER SQUARE

All central London's attractions are within easy walking distance of here, with several of the more interesting theatres little more than five mins' stroll. The tube station's various exits are a favourite with Londoners stuck for a place to meet; hordes of them mill around anxiously looking for the friends they finally discover they've been standing next to for half an hour. Around the bustling edges of the pedestrian square, attractively cleaned up in recent years and usually with living statues and other free entertainment, are several huge cinemas, pricy but with excellent sound; you can see films more cheaply at the Prince Charles in Leicester Pl, leading off (where Notre Dame de France has an impressive Jean Cocteau mural). Marked out by its dramatic ornamental gate, **Chinatown** has developed its own character, inviting despite the locals' cool indifference to outsiders; the supermarkets and shops along pedestrianised Gerrard St and in neighbouring streets are fascinating, with their weird and wonderful vegetables, strange squidgy things in little cellophane packets, and odd-smelling dried meats and fish. Plenty of authentic Chinese restaurants, as well as less convincingly adapted telephone boxes. Back by the tube station, this stretch of Charing Cross Rd is justifiably famous for its **bookshops**, specialist and general, new and second-hand. Foyle's is the biggest city bookstore, but trying to find what you want is time-consuming; Waterstones is very friendly and relaxed, with informed staff. The side alleys between here and St Martin's Lane have good second-hand bookshops, several with specialisations such as the occult, antique children's books, or the theatre; Cecil Court is perhaps the best. Two distinctively designed pubs round here are the good value Moon Under Water opposite Blackwells on Charing Cross Rd, and the Salisbury on St Martin's Lane, a splendid Victorian pub, all velvet and cut glass. Not far away on Long Acre is Stanfords, the best map and guidebook shop in Britain, with helpful knowledgeable staff, and books and maps covering all corners of the globe. Leicester Sq is very handy for Soho, described below under Tottenham Court Rd.

◒ MARBLE ARCH

Striking in itself; originally a grand entrance for Buckingham Palace, moved here decades ago, and gleaming after its restoration not so long ago. Over the road **Speakers Corner** on the edge of Hyde Park is where every Sun morning you can still hear impassioned diatribes on all sorts of causes. Traditional debating methods have practically disappeared, and disputes between rival fundamentalist groups have been known to become extremely heated, with the result that extra police armed with hidden cameras now patrol this famous bastion of free speech. Also on Sun you can see what's probably the longest free open-air art exhibition in the world, with the work of 300 artists and craftsmen laid out along the park railings on Bayswater Rd; the Swan opposite gives a pleasant break. The tube station – with so many exits it's a real initiative test finding your way out – is also handy for Oxford St.

Hyde Park Riding Stables (Bathurst Mews) Can organise horse-riding in the park; (020) 7262 3791; £35 an hour (not Mon).

◒ OXFORD CIRCUS

The heart of the city's busiest shopping areas, busy and noisy Oxford St to the left and right, and altogether nicer Regent St to the S. **Oxford St** doesn't have a lot of character, but is full of good stores such as Selfridges, John

Lewis (the self-service restaurant is good for lunch), Marks & Spencer (two major outlets), the two giant music shops HMV and Virgin Megastore, and the usual high street chains. South Molton St and St Christopher's Pl on either side of Oxford St are full of designer clothes shops and smart cafés; St Christopher's Pl also has quite an interesting antiques market. **Regent St** is one of the grandest streets in the whole area, with a splendid curve as it reaches Piccadilly Circus. A harmonious street of considerable character, with the fine shops definitely enhancing its appeal, even if all you want to do is browse. Liberty's is a splendid art nouveau timbered building full of gorgeous soft furnishings and clothes, oriental and leather goods, jewellery and a good gift department. Other high points include Dickins & Jones for designer fashions and accessories; Mappin & Webb for fine china, glass, and jewellery; Hamleys, a marvellous toy shop (not cheap, though); Aquascutum, great for expensive English classic clothes; Waterford/Wedgwood, for lovely china and glass in quite a wide range of prices. The Old Coffee House in Beak St around the corner from here, and Red Lion in Kingly St, are useful for lunch. Carnaby St, tucked away behind, has some rather florid men's shops and good street-fashion houses, but is mainly full of small boutiques with trendy accessories, leather goods and tacky souvenirs; not really worth seeking out.

BBC Experience (Portland Pl) Below the imposing yet rather bullying bulk of Broadcasting House, this excellent visitor centre celebrates the work and programmes of the BBC over the last 75 years, with a mixture of multi-media exhibitions and hands-on displays. You can try your hand at directing · *Eastenders*, or presenting the TV weather or sport, while the radio sections offer an interactive *Desert Island Discs*, and the chance to make a 3-minute play. Plenty for families, but also a great deal to please nostalgic-minded adults, and you'll come out with a much better idea of how programmes are put together. Meals, snacks, big shop, disabled access; cl 25–26 Dec; (0870) 603 0304; £7.50.

⊖ PICCADILLY CIRCUS

Another lively hub of London life, with famous streets radiating off in every direction, each quite different in character; handsome Piccadilly roughly to the W, the theatres of bustling Shaftesbury Avenue to the E, with smarter ones on Haymarket to the S, Regent St coolly curving N towards Oxford Circus – and of course the famous statue of Eros, where all the foreign students sit to be photographed. The streets around here are excellent for shopping. On opposite sides of the traffic islands in Piccadilly Circus are Tower Records, three floors of pop, classical and jazz (open till midnight), and Lillywhites, the long-established sports clothes and equipment store. On Piccadilly, the new Waterstones is the biggest bookshop in Europe, while friendly Hatchards further down is a nicely old-fashioned bookshop where the staff can still sometimes turn vague requests into actual books. Almost next door, Fortnums (Fortnum & Mason) has superior if expensive clothes, as well as the foods for which they're world-famous. Nearby, the Burlington Arcade is an elegant Regency covered arcade of expensive but good shops (excellent cashmere and knife/scissors shops, for instance), with a delightful set of rules, still enforced, that stop people whistling, singing or running in its confines. The Ritz is gorgeously flamboyant inside: well worth the high price of having a frogged and liveried waiter bring you a cup of tea or a perfectly mixed whisky sour. Behind Piccadilly's S side is Jermyn St, where among other splendid but top-of-the-range shops you can buy fine cheeses at Paxton & Whitfield's, briar pipes at Astleys, hand-made shoes at Tricker's, hand-made shirts from Turnbull & Asser, flat hats at Bates, and old-fashioned toiletries at Floris. The Red Lion in Duke of York St just off here is a little gem of a pub, with decent snacks (but very busy on wkdy lunchtimes). A landmark on Haymarket is one of the two branches of Burberrys the mac makers (the other's in Regent St).

Rock Circus (London Pavilion) Exuberant romp through the history of rock and roll, more fun than its stablemate Madame Tussaud's, but still alarmingly high-priced considering its comparative brevity. Wax figures from Elvis to Bono, some interesting archive film, and finale with moving animatronic models. The headsets that provide musical accompaniment are ingeniously designed, though they don't always work properly. Snacks, shop, cl 25 Dec, 1 Jan; (020) 7734 7203; £8.25.

Royal Academy of Arts (Burlington House) Splendid building with excellent changing exhibitions for most of the year, such as the complete series of Botticelli *Divine Comedy* drawings this Mar–Jun, then from early Jun to mid-Aug its famous (often notorious) Summer Exhibition of works by living artists great and small. Meals, snacks, shop, disabled access; cl 25 Dec, Good Fri; (020) 7300 8000; admission charge varies – usually between £6.50 and £10. Work is well under way on the £3m transformation of Burlington courtyard, which should make a great setting for exhibitions of contemporary sculpture, and an attractive public space.

Segaworld Mammoth attraction, and a central redevelopment of the vast preserved Trocadero building, filled with state-of-the-art rides and games. One of the best rides, Aqua Planet, has remarkable 3-D graphics – a multi-tentacled monster seems to leap straight out of the screen. There's also the IMAX Drop, a terrifying free-fall ride, and myriad other flashing and bleeping attractions. All rides have individual charges, though a £10 token covers 4 rides (£20 covers 10).

⊖ TOTTENHAM COURT ROAD

Soho Often heady mix of the tawdry and the fashionable, its coffee bars and cafés swarming with colourful young people in the evenings. Many of Soho's Georgian terraces are rather run-down, with peepshows and naughty video shops stuffed into basements and ground floors. But there are parts that have had much of their original quiet charm restored, like Soho Sq and Meard St, and it's still good for restaurants, and for shops connected with food or cooking. Old Compton St, central London's gayest street, has a good few interesting shops – Italian delicatessens (I Camisa is the best, with fabulous salamis), the Algerian Coffee Store which also sells lots of fruit teas, and two cheap but good wines and spirits shops. Milroys in Greek St has a wonderful collection of hundreds of different malt whiskies. Berwick St has a daily fruit and vegetable market – the lower half is more expensive but has better produce; at Simply Sausages down here you can watch them making some of their 43 different varieties of sausage, which include vegetarian and seafood flavours. The little Dog & Duck in Frith St and Coach & Horses in Poland St (the *Private Eye* pub) are two of the nicest Soho locals; in Romilly St another Coach & Horses is also on the well known Soho characters circuit, and Kettners, now part of the Pizza Express chain, is a very entertaining old building. The area as a whole forms a sort of square, with the tube stations at Leicester Sq, Piccadilly Circus, Tottenham Court Rd and even Oxford Circus all just as handy.

Westminster

This centre of court and government is a pleasant area to walk around, much of it with only light traffic, and with few shops to add extra people to the wide pavements. Westminster Abbey and Buckingham Palace are divided by St James's Park – a fine walk between the two. A tour of the Houses of Parliament during the summer recess is most rewarding. The newly remodelled Tate Britain and Westminster Cathedral are other highlights here, and anyone with an interest in horticulture should seek out the Lindley Library, rehoused at the RHS HQ in Vincent Sq (scene of lovely flower shows).

To see and do

⊖ GREEN PARK
The park itself is the smallest of the parks in central London. It's not a formal garden but, watered by the Tyburn stream which runs below the park, stays genuinely green even in hot summers when London's other grassy spaces are dry and dusty. It's a short stroll to **Shepherd Market**, a colourful place where Mayfair lets its hair down, no longer a market but busy with cafés, good wine bars and a nice pub (the Grapes), and little lanes to wander down.
Clubland The area around St James's St and Pall Mall seems to have more gentlemen's clubs than anything else, but there is a good number of interesting upmarket **shops** too: hand-made shoes at Lobb's, hats at Lock's, wonderful antiques and antiquities at Spink's, fishing equipment at Hardy's, and fine wines at Berry's, or Berry Bros & Rudd to give it its full name. This last is the only shop in London still to look both inside and out just as it did in the early 19th c (they've only just taken down the full-screen shutters), and they are very helpful even if you want just one humble bottle. Farlow's on Pall Mall have everything you might need for that expedition up the Limpopo or into the Gobi Desert. Christie's auction galleries are on King St (the friendly Red Lion off here in Crown Passage is useful for a snack), and there are some other top-of-the-market antiques and book shops nearby, especially up Duke St.
Spencer House (St James's Pl) Overlooking Green Park, this gleaming gilt-filled town house was built for the first Earl Spencer in the mid-18th c. Its sumptuous rooms, restored to their full glory, were among the first neo-classical interiors in Europe. Disabled access; open for guided tours every Sun

(exc Jan and Aug), best to book on
(020) 7499 8620; £6.

St James's Palace Though
comparatively domestic-looking, this is
exceptionally harmonious and carries a
real feel of Old London. It's not open to
the public (its apartments are used by
members of the Royal Family and their
officials), but does provide another
good spot for the **changing of the
guard**, with guardsmen leaving here at
11.15am to go to the Palace, and
coming back at around 12.10pm.

● PIMLICO

Tate Gallery (Millbank) Designed in
classical style to house the collection of
Sir Henry Tate, it has recently been
rebranded as 'Tate Britain', and houses
the greatest collection of British art in
the world, with works from the Tudors
to the Turner Prize, by way of
Constable, Rossetti and Epstein to
name but a few. As part of a
controversial restyling in 2000, the
galleries are now organised by theme
rather than by date, so that a Stubbs
might hang next to work by Gilbert &
George or near a Henry Moore
sculpture. Other rooms are devoted to
individual artists such as Gainsborough,
Hogarth, Sickert and David Hockney,
and more are given over to the art
collected for the nation by the Tate in
the late 20th c. Decent changing
exhibitions (one on Blake runs until
early Feb), and a good hi-tech audio
guide. Other redevelopment has
involved the creation of a new visitor
entrance, and the gardens have been
redesigned to include sculpture courts.
A free river bus service links the gallery
with its new counterpart a mile down
river (Apr–Sept). Meals, snacks, shop,
disabled access; cl 24–26 Dec; (020)
7887 8000; free (exc for special
exhibitions). Though the Tate Gallery
restaurant is a particularly good one,
you might find the Morpeth Arms
nearby useful, with its views of the
glossy MI6 ziggurat across the river.

● ST JAMES'S PARK

This is the best approach to the Palace
(you can get there more quickly, though
less attractively, from Victoria). The
oldest of London's Royal Parks, it was
drained and converted into a deer park
for Henry VIII, redesigned in the style of

Versailles by order of Charles II (who
often went for walks through it), and
then reworked by Nash for George IV –
this is the park which we see today, its
relaxing lakeside environment
particularly enjoyed by lunch-breaking
office workers (and by hundreds of
more or less exotic waterfowl), with a
brass band in summer. It's beautifully
floodlit at night, and on Sun traffic is
barred from its roads. **The Mall**
Running all the way along the top of the
park, this 1,040-metre (3,412-ft) long
ceremonial route was laid out from
1660 for Charles II, with the Palace at
one end and the magnificent Admiralty
Arch at the other. In between, as well as
various grand buildings and government
departments, are a couple of good
contemporary art galleries, with
various changing exhibitions at the **Mall
Galleries** ((020) 7930 6844 for
exhibition info; around £2.50), and a
wonderfully informal little restaurant
and bar at the **ICA**, which with
exhibitions and cinemas too is an
excellent place to spend an afternoon –
and possibly the evening as well (cl am;
(020) 7930 0493; £1.50 day
membership, £2.50 at the wknd).

Buckingham Palace A marvellous
position, surrounded by Royal Parks
and looking commandingly along the
stately Mall towards Admiralty Arch. At
the grand front palace gates the guards
still keep their unflinchingly solemn
positions: you can watch the **changing
of the guard** every day Apr–Aug
(every other day in winter) at 11.30am;
the ceremony may be late or even
cancelled in exceptionally wet weather.

Buckingham Palace tour Now
firmly established as one of London's
most visited attractions, usually
drawing around 400,000 visitors in the
eight weeks it's open. The main appeal
is that this is where the Queen actually
lives – her official London residence,
and where she meets other heads of
state; the Royal Standard flies above it
when she's home. But beyond that,
while perhaps not the most satisfying of
the Royal Palaces, it does pile a
magnificent series of opulent sights into
your walk through the state rooms.
Highlights include the beautiful Picture
Gallery, 46 metres (150 ft) long and

filled with paintings from the Royal collection, the spectacular Grand Staircase, and the throne room with its predominant impression of gold, red and splendour. This last year the ballroom has been added to the tour. Tours are unguided, and there aren't many clues to help you, so it's definitely worth buying the guide book. Theoretically you see everything at your own pace, but in practice you're likely to be carried along in the stream of other people, and you won't get much of a chance to linger. Tickets are sold from an office opposite the palace by the entrance to Green Park, though you can book in advance, on (020) 7839 2233. Busy shop, disabled access (with notice); open early Aug–Sept; £10.50.
Royal Mews (Buckingham Palace Rd) Contains the State Coaches, private driving carriages and even sleighs of the Royal Family, as well as the immaculately turned out carriage horses. The longest painting in the Royal Collection is here too, a 36-metre (120-ft) canvas depicting William IV's Coronation procession. Shop, disabled access; cl Fri–Sun, and am Oct–July; (020) 7839 1377; £4.30.
⊖≷VICTORIA
Lindley Library (80 Vincent Sq) Coinciding with the bicentenary of John Lindley, the distinguished scientist whose collection formed the nucleus of the original library, this assortment of around 50,000 books will be rehoused in the ground floor of the Royal Horticultural Society from early 2001. Recognised as the finest horticultural library in the world, as well as the books (ranging from an 1514 edition of Pliny the Elder's *Historia Naturalis* to contemporary gardening manuals), it will also provide a home for 21,000 paintings and drawings of plants, 1,500 periodicals, and a computer archive with access to 70,000 works; also drawings and exhibition room, darkroom, and good disabled access. Open wkdys; (020) 7821 3600; free. The RHS hold regular flower shows filled with beautifully arranged displays by specialist nurserymen; (020) 7649 1885 for information.
Westminster Cathedral (just off Victoria St) Built in 1903, the red-brick Roman Catholic building is an astonishing structure, very un-English, with handsome mosaics and marble work in its richly ornamental interior. At night its black ceiling seems almost to disappear in the darkness. Its Byzantine splendour is welcome relief from the glassy governmental cliffs of Victoria St. It offers great views over Central London from its tall tower (lift; £2 donation requested).
⊖WESTMINSTER
Banqueting House 🖼 (Whitehall) The only surviving part of the Palace of Whitehall, designed by Inigo Jones and built in 1619; it was a Royal residence until late that century. Charles I was executed here, and it was also the site of his son's restoration. The severely classical hall is pretty much all there is to see, but an entertaining Walkman tour and good audio-visual exhibition keep up your interest for quite some time. The highlight is the wonderful ceiling painted by Rubens, commissioned by Charles I to glorify the Stuart monarchy. They've put mirrored tables underneath so you can study the detail without straining your neck; don't lean on these though – they're on wheels and liable to speed off like errant supermarket trolleys. Shop; cl Sun, 24 Dec–1 Jan, bank hols, and for some government functions; (020) 7839 7569; £3.80. The partly 13th-c Silver Cross is an interesting old pub, the huge and very ornate Lord Moon of the Mall another useful refuge.
Cabinet War Rooms (King Charles St, just off Whitehall) An intriguing series of 21 rooms built to provide Sir Winston Churchill, the War Cabinet and his Chiefs of Staff with a safe place from which to plan their strategies during World War II. The Cabinet Room, Map Room and Prime Minister's Room were preserved intact from the end of the war, and the other rooms have been authentically restored since. Quite basic, they're very evocative, with sound-effects adding to the atmosphere. A museum dedicated to the life of Britain's wartime leader should open here in around three years' time. Shop, disabled access; cl 24–26 Dec; (020) 7930 6961; £5, children free.
Cenotaph (Whitehall) Designed by

Lutyens, this is a sombre reminder of this century's two World Wars, standing indomitably in the centre of the road. Initially it was planned as a temporary symbol, but public opinion was such that the original wooden structure had to be replaced by the stone version you see today.

Downing St Famous as the residence of the Prime Minister at No 10 and the Chancellor of the Exchequer at No 11 (the current incumbents have swapped to give Mr Blair and family more space). You can't get past the gates, but you can at least have a passing look at its surprisingly modest buildings.

Houses of Parliament Across the road from St Margaret's church, these buildings are now of course the main seat of British government, but until Henry VIII moved to Whitehall Palace in 1529, the site was the main residence of the monarch – when they answer the phone today they still call it the Palace of Westminster. The present 19th-c building was designed by Charles Barry, though the 'gothick' detail which has given so much life to what would otherwise be rather a tiresomely deadpan classical façade is by Pugin. One end of the extraordinary 286-metre (940-ft) structure finishes in a lofty Victorian tower (which flies the Union Jack when Parliament is in session), and the other in the clock tower which contains **Big Ben**, the 3½-ton bell whose sonorous hourly rings are one of the best known sounds in the world. Inside, over two miles of passages link the central hall and two chambers – the Houses of Lords and Commons to the N and S of the building respectively. The Commons sits from 2.30pm Mon–Weds, all day from 11.30am Thurs, and from 9.30am–2pm most Fri; to gain entrance to the Strangers' Galleries, you'll need to queue by St Stephen's Gate (on the left for the Commons, right for the Lords – rather appropriate in a way) – or arrange it first with your MP. A letter from your MP can also give access to what's called the Line of Route, going through both Houses and the Members' Lobby and Divisions Lobby, to Westminster Hall, from 1224 to 1882 the chief law court of the country.

It witnessed such trials as those of Sir Thomas More and Charles I, and organising admission is worth the trouble even just to admire the magnificent hammerbeam roof, the earliest surviving example of its kind; alternatively you can book yourself in for a guided tour during the summer recess, early Aug to mid-Sept, (020) 7344 9966; £3.50. The Westminster Arms in Storeys Gate across the square is a good pub, and you're likely to see politicians in the imposing Albert up Victoria St.

Jewel Tower (Parliament Sq) Across the road from the statue of Oliver Cromwell (whose attitude towards Parliaments when he was Lord Protector was not unlike that of Charles I – they were more trouble than they were worth), this 14th-c building has an exhibition on Parliament's history. It was originally a huge treasure chest for Edward III. Cl 24–26 Dec, 1 Jan; (020) 7222 2219; £1.50; EH.

Mounting the Guard (Whitehall) (Whitehall) A survival of the kind of Royal pageantry this area was once full of can be seen in this daily ceremony at Horse Guards Parade, 11am Mon–Sat and 10am Sun.

St Margaret's church (Parliament Sq) The official church of the House of Commons, worth a look particularly for its exceptional 16th-c Dutch stained glass; Sir Walter Raleigh is buried here.

Westminster Abbey Surely one of the most impressive pieces of architecture to survive from the Middle Ages: Edward the Confessor transformed it into the crowning place of English kings, and his body now lies in the great shrine of the present building, erected in the 13th c on the site of his original. Pretty much every king and queen up to George II is buried here; Henry VII's chapel is particularly impressive, and there are splendid tombs erected by James I for his mother Mary, Queen of Scots, and his predecessor Elizabeth I, under whose orders Mary had been executed. Perhaps it's in revenge for this that Elizabeth was lumped in with her sister Mary I, with whom she never got on. The loosely named Poets' Corner takes in a wide range of cultural figures.

There's a small medieval garden in the charming tranquil cloisters. Snacks, shop, disabled access, cl 25 Dec and Good Fri, and Sun (exc for services); £5. If you like history the **museum** in the Norman undercroft shouldn't be missed – it has effigies of many ancestors of the Royal Family made from their death masks, and often wearing their own clothes; £2.50 (which also includes entry to the Chapter House and Pyx Chamber); £7 inc audio tour and entry to all areas of the abbey.

Knightsbridge, Chelsea & Kensington

The three great South Kensington museums between them have something for everyone (inc free admission for children): the visually spectacular collections of the Victoria & Albert; and the lively Natural History and Science Museums (fun science sleep-overs here), both favourites for children. There's grandeur in Kensington Palace, the less-visited but free Leighton House, and across Hyde Park the excellent Apsley House. From the spring onwards, lavishly restored Wellington Arch will afford new park views, and for the latest in contemporary art, head for an exhibition at the Serpentine Gallery. Harrods seems irresistible to most visitors. Down towards the Thames, the Chelsea Physic Garden and the nearby free (and recently improved) National Army Museum are both rather special. A placid grid of clean-cut, subdued Georgian terraced houses contrasts with the ostentatious bustle of the Kings Rd in the S and the hubbub of the Portobello Rd market in the N.

To see and do

London Family Attraction of the Year

● **SOUTH KENSINGTON Natural History Museum** (Cromwell Rd) Newer, more loudly fêted attractions come and go, but this old faithful remains one of the most genuinely appealing places for children in the capital, constantly updating or adding attractions, and with a wealth of displays that could keep most visitors enthralled for a week, never mind a day. Wonderfully varied, it's not at all stuffy or dull, and, best of all, for children admission is completely free. Picking out highlights isn't easy, but younger visitors still most enjoy the parts you'd expect – in particular the dinosaurs. There's a whole gallery devoted to the fearsome beasts, with lots of touch-screen activities and information, and a grisly tableau featuring robotic versions of the monsters devouring one of their much larger cousins; you'll hear constant evocations of their roars as you explore the rest of the exhibition. More gently evocative are the complete skeletons in the museum's main hall; touch-screens around them distract and delight younger visitors, but otherwise they rest undisturbed as they have for decades, a grand and noble sight below the intricately painted ceilings of the remarkable Romanesque building. The creepy-crawlies are another good bet: the displays here are informative and fun, and you can get a taste on their website (www.nhm.ac.uk), which every few seconds displays fresh images from their ant colony. Children also enjoy the new exhibition Rhythms of Life, which entertainingly looks at how nature is affected by the passing of time, taking in changing seasons, sleep patterns, migration, and the growth of flowers; it runs until May 2001. The Earth Galleries are worth putting near the top of your list, not least for the splendid entrance: you walk along an avenue of dramatic sculptures, then ride an escalator towards a huge metal globe. The earthquake simulator here is always popular, and you can see where real earthquakes have occurred in the last few days. There's also an exquisitely glittering collection of rocks and minerals. Elsewhere is everything from how the earth began to some of the most splendid animals from around the world – the only problem can be finding your way round, which you shouldn't even attempt without picking up one of the maps and guides as you go in. It's a vast place, covering four acres, but don't work out your route too precisely: stumbling across something unexpected is one of the museum's great joys. There are regular guided tours: in spring and summer these may take in one of the lesser-known features, the outdoor garden with pond and waterfall. Meals, snacks, shops (one is dinosaur-themed), disabled access; cl 25–26 Dec; 020 7942 5000; entry free to children, over-60s and concessions, otherwise £7.50 (it's free after 4.30pm on wkdays – 5pm at wknds – but closes just before 6pm so you'll need to know what you're heading for to benefit).

✪ FULHAM BROADWAY
The best tube station for the clutch of good value **antiques shops** towards the bottom end of Fulham Rd. You can quickly cut through to the interesting series of more specialised shops on the New Kings Rd, some of which yield unexpected treasures: lovely old clocks, imposing model ships, garden furniture, and ornaments going back to the 16th c. Two shops specialise expensively but magnificently in mirrors, and there's also Christopher Wray's enormous lighting shop which largely fuelled the vogue in Tiffany-style lamps and has almost any sort of lamp fitting you could possibly want. The tube station is also handy for the unfrequented, rather melancholy tranquillity of the somewhat overgrown **Brompton Cemetery**; and for Chelsea Football Club, with the countrified Fox & Pheasant in Billing St just past it making a pleasant break.
Chelsea Harbour (Lots Rd) This modern development includes a striking modern covered mall (mainly luxurious soft furnishings specialists), with popular Deals Restaurant, the stylish Canteen, the smart but relaxed Matt's café, and an adjacent marina. Children like the glass-sided lifts which swoop up into the big dome, and on Sun pms they often have jazz by the marina.
✪ HIGH ST KENSINGTON
Albert Memorial (Kensington

Gardens) Restored to its former glory, a gleaming golden monument to Queen Victoria's beloved husband: intricate mosaics, classic high Victoriana, marvellously grand.
Holland Park One of London's lesser-known open spaces, a wooded park with peacocks, summer open-air theatre and airy restaurant.
Kensington Gardens Surrounding the Palace, and well worth a wander, though less lush than neighbouring Hyde Park. There's a toy boats lake, playground, a fetching statue of Peter Pan, and a tree trunk carved with all sorts of little painted animals. On a sunny day you could be forgiven for thinking you'd stumbled on a beach club, as the grass is covered with prone bodies soaking up the radiation.
Kensington Palace State Apartments (Kensington Gardens) Once-humble town house remodelled by Sir Christopher Wren and then enlarged by William Kent, the birthplace of Queen Victoria, and principal private Royal residence until the death of George II. Diana Princess of Wales lived here until her death; people still leave flowers at the gates. It's still the home of Princess Margaret and Prince and Princess Michael of Kent. Some of the rooms are quite magnificent, with elaborate furnishings and décor, while others are interesting for their comparatively restrained

understatement; a couple of the older ones could even be described as downright poky. Make sure you look up at the ceilings: some are exquisitely painted, inc an effective trompe-l'oeil dome (a couple of the patterns transfer very nicely to stationery in the gift shop). Also pictures and furniture from the Royal collection, and court dress collection. Snacks, shop, disabled access to ground floor only (notice preferred); usually open daily, though best to check in winter; (020) 7937 9561; £9.70.

Kensington shops This is a good area for shopping, especially if you consider yourself young and fashionable. An unusual haven from the crowds is the **Roof Gardens** above BHS on the High St; these extraordinary gardens are often closed for private functions, so you'll need to check first on (020) 7937 7994; free. Their restaurant (open Thurs and Sat evenings) does very good food. Good food pubs in this area include the Windsor Castle (Campden Hill Rd; excellent courtyard garden) and (a walk up Kensington Church St, which has some interesting antique shops) the Churchill Arms – surprisingly good Thai food.

Leighton House (12 Holland Park Rd) This splendid 19th-c house is a uniquely opulent monument to High Victorian Art, its lavish décor and collections created by Lord Leighton, former President of the Royal Academy. The centre-piece Arab Hall has a fountain and an almost dazzling assemblage of Islamic tiles, and there's a fine collection of paintings by Millais, Burne-Jones, and Leighton himself. Shop; cl Tues and autumn-winter bank hols; (020) 7602 3316; free.

Linley Sambourne House (18 Stafford Terrace) The 19th-c home of the celebrated *Punch* cartoonist, unchanged since – a fascinating example of a Victorian town house, with a fine collection of his work. Shop; open Weds and pm Sun, Mar–Oct; (020) 7937 0663; £3.50

Serpentine Gallery (Kensington Gardens) Often has some of London's most interesting exhibitions, concentrating on younger contemporary artists; (020) 7402 6075 for what's on.

✪ HYDE PARK CORNER

Apsley House The Duke of Wellington's elegant former home, designed by Robert Adam. It soon became known as Number One London, as it was the first house within a toll gate at the top of Knightsbridge. The magnificent building has been painstakingly restored; everything gleams and looks as good as new, and works by Correggio, Rubens and Velasquez, amassed by Wellington as gifts from grateful kings and emperors, are back in their original positions (not always to their best advantage). Sumptuous furnishings, décor and sculpture – inc a statue of Napoleon by Canova that has him looking quite different from the usual image. Shop, limited disabled access (though special audio guides for the partially sighted and visitors with learning difficulties); cl Mon (exc bank hols), 25 Dec, 1 Jan, Good Fri, May Day bank hol, 24–26 Dec; (020) 7499 5676; £4.50 inc audio guide, children free.

Hyde Park These 340 acres used to be a Royal hunting park, and in 1851 were the site of the Great Exhibition. Now very much a city park, complete with cycle lanes, roller-bladers, summer sun-bathing and boating lake: you can hire boats, or even swim in parts. At the Park's bottom corner is the relentless torrent of traffic around Hyde Park Corner; the subway can bring you up near the glittering neo-baroque gates erected in honour of the Queen Mother.

Wellington Arch Last occupied some 30 years ago as a police station, Decimus Burton's magnificent triumphal arch, somewhat stranded in a whirl of traffic at Hyde Park Corner, has been lavishly restored by English Heritage. From spring 2001 you can visit the viewing platform and some rooms, and eventually the third floor will have an exhibition on London's monuments, war memorials and statues cared for by English Heritage. Phone (01793) 414910 for more information.

✪ KNIGHTSBRIDGE

Harrods (Knightsbridge) A wonderful place to browse, and has most things anyone could want – there's even a personal shopper available to help you choose. But it's the food halls that visitors to London really enjoy; they're divided into fruit and vegetables, an interesting delicatessen, grocery, meat, poultry, fish (the display of fresh fish at the end of the room is legendary), bread and cakes, flowers, and wines – and the downstairs pantry is not as expensive as you might think. The Scotch House, almost opposite, is not cheap but does have lovely cashmeres, fine woollens, kilts and so forth.

Sloane St Headed by Harvey Nichols, a long-standing fashion store now split into numerous famous-brand boutiques; its 5th-floor food store is superb, alongside a very good bar/restaurant. The street stretching down from here has had something of a renaissance recently, with international designers jostling to open very expensive new stores. In the handsome terraces beyond Sloane St can be found the charming Grenadier (Wilton Row; no food in the bar, but a snug little restaurant) and the surprisingly countryish Nag's Head (Kinnerton St).

⊖ NOTTING HILL GATE

Portobello Rd Famous for its market – fruit and vegetables during the week, antiques on Sat from 7am; with well over a thousand dealers you can still pick up a bargain. The quality and prices are higher at the Notting Hill end; it's more bric-a-brac as you get towards Ladbroke Grove. Portobello Gold has good unusual food in attractive trendy surroundings.

⊖ SLOANE SQUARE

The heart of Chelsea, with Peter Jones, the mecca of the Sloanes, on the square itself (a sister department store of John Lewis, it's good value for money). Just around the corner, the Antelope in Eaton Terrace is a useful lunch stop. The bottom end of Sloane St has two interesting though expensive shops: Partridges, a fancy food shop, and the General Trading Company, with a fine collection of oddities, besides stylish kitchenware, soft furnishings, antiques, glass and so forth.

Carlyle's House (Cheyne Row) The home of the writer from 1834 till his death, with lots of letters and personal possessions, and an early piano played by Chopin. There's a charming little Victorian walled garden. Open Weds–Sun and bank hols Apr–Oct (exc Good Fri); (020) 7352 7087; £3.50; NT. The nearby Kings Head & Eight Bells, across a green and a busy road from the Thames, is almost villagey at the far end of the green, Old Church St past the elegant Chelsea Old Church takes you quickly to a good food pub, the Front Page.

Chelsea Physic Garden (Royal Hospital Rd) If you're tired of the braying crowds of Chelsea, take refuge here. A real haven of peace, it was started in 1673 to study the plants used in medicine by the Society of Apothecaries. It's still used for botanical and medicinal research (there's a unique garden of medicinal plants), but is also full of lovely and unusual plants which thrive here in Thames-side London's warm microclimate. Snacks, shop, disabled access; open pm Weds and Sun Apr–Oct; (020) 7352 5646; £4.

King's Rd Not what it used to be in the 60s and 70s, but you can still find some really individual clothes and shoe shops, and good antique markets. On your way along, refresh yourself at Henry J Beans (197 King's Rd; a rather stylish American-style bar with good quick snacks), La Bersagliera (a pleasantly clattery matriarchal pizza house just past Beaufort St) or the Sporting Page (Camera Pl/Limerston St). S from here, it's quite a short cut through to the Thames.

National Army Museum (Royal Hospital Rd) Surprisingly little visited but well and honestly presented – the history of the men of the British, Indian and Colonial armies from the Battle of Agincourt to the present day, told with photographs, models, uniforms, prints and other mementoes inc the skeleton of Napoleon's horse and a lamp used by Florence Nightingale. New interactive exhibits test your map reading and rank recognition, and there's an astonishingly detailed 70,000 model of the Battle of Waterloo. Portraits by Gainsborough and Reynolds and the collections of the former Museum of the Women's Royal Army Corps. Snacks, shop, disabled access; cl 24–26 Dec, 1 Jan, Good Fri, May Day; (020)

7730 0717; free.

Pimlico Rd An interesting collection of antiques and other small shops (and Peter's Restaurant, a very good value all-day Italian-run café which has been a taxi-drivers' haunt for over 30 years). The Orange Brewery here is a pub brewing its own beers, with decent food.

Royal Hospital (Royal Hospital Rd) Christopher Wren's most glorious secular building, which still houses some 400 Chelsea Pensioners. Cl 12–2pm, Sun am (though you can go to the full dress service in chapel at 11am on Sun); free. The spacious and calm adjacent riverside Ranelagh Gardens are the site of the Chelsea Flower Show in May.

☻ SOUTH KENSINGTON

Brompton Oratory Roman Catholic, and heavily magnificent – sombre despite the pallor of its marble.

Holy Trinity Brompton London's most fashionable and perhaps most lively church. Its gardens lead you into a very peaceful corner of residential London, with a decent pub in Ennismore Mews (the Ennismore Arms, which does Sun lunches).

Natural History Museum *See separate family panel on p.716.*

Royal Albert Hall (Kensington Gore) The home of the summer Promenade Concerts and many other concerts throughout the year; completed in 1871, this huge oval arena was built in honour of Prince Albert. Below its massive metal and glass dome a terracotta frieze shows the progress of Man in the arts and sciences throughout the ages. Before modern technology (in the form of giant suspended mushrooms) got to grips with its acoustics, the hall used to be famous for its echo – it was said that this was the only hall where you could hear the works of modern composers twice.

Science Museum (Exhibition Rd) Amazing museum, with its splendid new Wellcome Wing devoted entirely to contemporary science, medicine and technology. Four new galleries cover as many floors, and look at subjects such as genetics, the internet and the future role of science; there's also a new IMAX cinema (£5.75 extra). The new area has been designed to hold fast-changing, interactive exhibitions with plenty of hands-on displays, workshops and demonstrations, and a multi-sensory activity area aimed at under-8s (but parents seem to love it too). Elsewhere in the museum, exhibits range from Stephenson's *Rocket* to the Apollo 10 space capsule, and there are newly landscaped gardens outside. They hold various special events such as the all-night camp-ins – which enthral children (£25 inc science shows, treasure hunts, workshops and breakfast – must bring a snack and a sleeping bag). Meals, snacks, shop, disabled access; cl 24–26 Dec; (020) 7938 8080; £6.95 (£12 inc IMAX), children free (adults free after 4.30pm wkdys and 5pm wknds).

Victoria & Albert Museum (Cromwell Rd) Britain's national museum of art and design is one of the finest in the world; it was founded in 1851 by Prince Albert, and houses all manner of decorative arts, from all ages and countries. The galleries run to over seven miles, inc a spectacular glass gallery (with touch-screen computer displays), a dazzling silver gallery, and the world's greatest collection of Constables. In spite of all this, it's come under fire for being too dusty recently, but a new management regime has ambitious plans for extensions and improvements over the next few years. Meals and snacks (they do a good Sunday brunch with jazz), shop, disabled access; cl am Mon, 24–26 Dec; (020) 7938 8500; £5 though free after 4.30pm, and any time for children and the unwaged.

Please let us know what you think of places in the *Guide*. Use the report forms at the back of the book or simply write us a letter.

The City & East End

The City's most typical financial buildings are mainly Victorian and Edwardian, and its landmark churches are mostly elegant classical designs, but the ground-plan follows the narrow twisting streets and alleys of medieval times – though because of the Great Fire of 1666 only a handful of buildings are medieval or Tudor. Around St Paul's and the Tower of London (a winner with children), the layout is more open – and far less affected by the City's human tides: most of the rest of the area is packed with worried financial workers during wkdays, then when they leave goes into a catatonic trance in the evening and at wknds. For every person who actually lives in the City, another 60 or 70 flood in each day to work there, then flood out again at night. Besides the Tower, St Paul's and the host of glorious churches, highlights here include some rewarding free museums inc the Geffrye Museum, the Museum of Childhood, and the Ragged School Museum, new to the *Guide* this year. The exhaustive Museum of London is free to children, 18 Folgate St makes for a most unusual guided tour. Two of the river's most striking monuments, the Tower Bridge and the Thames Flood Barrier, both have enjoyable visitor centres. Originally, particular streets came to be associated with particular crafts and trades, and this is reflected in street names throughout the City – Carter Lane, Hosier Lane, Cloth Fair, Ropemaker St, Milk St, Silk St, Coopers Lane and so forth. The great City Livery Companies representing the various trades have effectively run local government in the City for 800 years or more, and it's only now that the franchise is being widened to allow more modern financial institutions a share in local government here. Many guilds have only a tenuous connection with the original crafts involved in their trades. But in Billingsgate Market, still controlled by the ancient Fishmongers Company, you can still see the fish trade being carried on in much the same way as ever (West India Dock Rd, early morning Tues–Sat). Though the halls of the City Livery Companies may have been rebuilt since they were first established in the Middle Ages, they still house some remarkable treasures. Some are open to visit, but only by prior arrangement: you'll have to book well ahead, through the City of London Information Centre, St Paul's Churchyard, EC4; (020) 7332 1456. The liveliest glimpse of East End life nowadays is to be had on Sunday mornings in Brick Lane market.

To see and do

⚓ **ALDGATE EAST**
Brick Lane market London's biggest and most atmospheric street market, a riot of colour, smells and sound, inc some very entertaining market patter. There are plenty of bargains for early risers (and things to avoid – we've even seen someone specialising in second-hand felt-tip pens). The community is largely Asian, so much of the food and other wares are quite exotic; Sun 5am–2pm. Once the terror-stricken

haunt of Jack the Ripper, Whitechapel, the area around here, is still one of London's poorest areas.

Columbia St market Entirely devoted to garden and house plants, has bargains as it closes around 1pm on Sun.

⊖ BANK

Some of the City's finest buildings are around here, though with most you'll have to content yourself with looking at just the outside. Besides the Bank of England itself, handsome or interesting buildings include the neo-classical Custom House on Lower Thames St, Lloyds of London on Lime St, and the Renaissance-style Royal Exchange on Cornhill, with several proud columns in front.

Bank of England Museum (Bartholomew Lane) This neo-classical fortress does still contain oodles of gold – though you can't see it, let alone get your hands on it. There's a small but interesting **museum**, which even shows how computerised currency speculators work. Disabled access; cl wknds and bank hols; (0171) 601 5545; free.

Leadenhall market (Whittington Ave, off Gracechurch St) Victorian iron and glass covered market, vibrant with Cockney humour yet quite smart, and filled with seafood, game, vegetables and fruit; cl around 4pm and wknds. The Lamb's top-floor dining bar gives good views of the market activity.

⊖ BARBICAN

Could be called the north bank's equivalent to the South Bank Centre – certainly its aesthetic equal. This complex includes theatres, exhibition halls, galleries, and what some would say is the city's most comfortable cinema. There's often free entertainment in the foyers.

Museum of London (London Wall; Barbican tube station) No other city museum in the world is quite as comprehensive as this; anyone with just a passing interest in history will find it compelling. London's development is told through chronological reconstructions and period clothes, music and various remains, from a medieval hen's egg to an early (and quite different) tube map – ever heard of the station called Post Office? The

18th-, 19th- and 20th-c sections have almost too much to take in. Under a seven-year redevelopment programme, excellent new galleries cover Roman London (the building adjoins a stretch of original Roman wall), remarkable research on a 14th-c Black Death cemetery nr the Tower of London, and a newly discovered Tudor rubbish dump. Meals, snacks, shop, disabled access; cl Sun am, 24–26 Dec; (020) 7600 0807; £5 – ticket valid for one year, and it certainly is the sort of place you want to come back to, children free.

⊖ BETHNAL GREEN

Museum of Childhood (Cambridge Heath Rd) This very special little museum houses the V&A's collection of toys, dolls, doll's houses, games, puppets and children's costumes. Excellent programme of events, theatre shows, and children's activities (most wknds and several school hols) – most completely free. Snacks, shop, disabled access; cl Fri, 24–26 Dec, 1 Jan; (020) 8980 2415; free.

DOCKLANDS

Once the heartland of Britain's trade-based Empire, these 8½ square miles over the last decade became the largest redevelopment site in Europe, the old warehouses imaginatively converted into smart apartments and office blocks. 244-metre (800-ft) **Canary Wharf** is the great landmark; most of its floors are filled with offices, but there's now a busy covered shopping mall at ground level. A growing cluster of modern but contrasting buildings around the central tower is carefully set off by beautifully designed small public gardens, and this last year Thames-side walkways here have been enlivened by good new café-bars and restaurants. Most parts of Docklands are reached and seen best by the **Docklands Light Railway**; the best bit is between West India Quay and Island Gardens, where you can get off and walk through the foot tunnel under the Thames to Greenwich. The new Jubilee Line tube extension has brought with it some architecturally spectacular stations, the most eye-catching of which are Canary Wharf (designed by Sir Norman Foster) where you descend by escalator from the eyelid-like glass roof entrance to a vast naturally lit hall, and North Greenwich, with its roof cleverly complementing the adjacent Millennium Dome. The earliest docks to be redeveloped are the most visitor-friendly: St Katharine's Dock (Tower Hill tube station is handy), which has a lively marina, a quite cheerful pastiche of a Victorian pub, and lots going on, and Tobacco Dock, with an American-style factory shopping centre. Further E down the river is the gigantic closeable **Thames Flood Barrier**, built to protect the city from freak tides; a Visitor Centre on Unity Way, Woolwich SE18, has an audio-visual exhibition about the barrier, a working scale model and a children's play area; cl Dec–Jan; (020) 8854 1373; £3.40. You can get boats down here from Westminster Pier (020) 7930 3373, £7.25 return).

⊖FARRINGDON

House of Detention 🔒 (Clerkenwell Cl) Well put together displays on crime and punishment in the underground cells of a former prison. Atmospheric without the sensationalised gore of other similar attractions. Shop, cl 24 Dec–1 Jan; (0171) 253 9494; *£4.

Museum of the Order of St John (St John's Lane) Housed in a 16th-c gatehouse and 12th-c crypt, silver, paintings and furniture belonging to the medieval Order, and new interactive gallery relating to the history and work of its more modern offshoot, the St John Ambulance. Shop, disabled access to ground floor; cl Sun, Christmas, Easter, bank hol wknds; (0171) 253 6644; free, £4 donation requested for guided tours of the gatehouse and priory church on Tues, Fri and Sat at 11am and 2.30pm. The Eagle in Farringdon Rd/Bakers Row has outstanding food, and there's an excellent second-hand bookshop opposite the station.

St Bartholomew the Great church (W Smithfield) Mainly Norman, with a 16th-c gateway into the market precincts.

⊖⇌LIVERPOOL STREET

18 Folgate St Guided tours of a quite remarkable house – but be warned, this is no ordinary guided tour, and one far more suited to adults than children. It doesn't do the place justice to say that it's been furnished and decorated in period style – to all intents and purposes you are back in the 18th c, with candles and firelight flickering away, food and drink laid out on the table, even urine in the chamber-pots. Open 2–5pm first Sun of month; (020) 7247 4013; £7. Elaborate candlelit tours first Mon evening of month, £10. In Liverpool St stn, Hamilton Hall is an extraordinarily grand ex-ballroom pub.

⊖MILE END

Ragged School Museum (Copperfield Rd) This canalside warehouse was one of the many 'ragged' (or free) schools set up by Dr Barnado in Tower Hamlets in the late 19th c. Displays concentrate on the school's history (there's a re-created Victorian classroom), life in the East End in the 1890s, and the work of the great philanthropist himself. A new exhibition takes a detailed look at the area's social history over the last 200 years or so, through the eyes of local people inc a former waiter, and an usherette from the People's Palace theatre. Snacks, shop, disabled access to ground floor exhibition only; open Weds, Thurs, and first Sun of month (cl Christmas and New Year); (020) 8980 6405; free.

⊖MONUMENT

Monument (Monument St) A fluted Doric column designed by Wren and Hooke at an exact height of 202 ft (62 metres) to mark the spot where the Great Fire of London began – in Pudding Lane 202ft from its base. The views of the city from the top are tremendous, though there are 311 spiral steps up. The viewpoint was designed as a cage to prevent people jumping off. Cl some bank hols, and occasional other dates; (0171) 626 2717; £1.50.

⊖OLD STREET

Geffrye Museum (Kingsland Rd; Liverpool St/Old St tube stations) One of London's most friendly and interesting museums, yet least-known; 18th-c almshouses converted to show the changing style of the English domestic interior – a sort of historical Through the Keyhole. Displays go from lovely 17th-c oak panelling and furniture through elegant Georgian reconstructions and Victorian parlours to the latest in interior design inc a contemporary loft-style dwelling, though not all is as it seems – out of sight inside the shell of a vintage radio for example there's actually a distinctly modern CD player. They've given the gardens similar treatment, showing trends in domestic horticulture throughout the ages inc a notable herb garden. Excellent programme of exhibitions, special events, talks and activities. Well worth tracking down. Meals, snacks, shop, disabled access; cl Sun am, all day Mon (exc pm bank hols), 24–26 Dec, 1 Jan, Good Fri; (0171) 739 9893; free.

Wesley's House 🏛 (49 City Rd) The father of Methodism had his house and chapel built here in 1778, and they're still much as they were then, with plenty of his personal possessions. You can see Wesley's tomb in the chapel, and the crypt has a museum on the history of Methodism. Shop, disabled access – limited in house but good in museum; cl bank hols, Thurs 12.45–1.30pm, and limited opening Sun (when services); (020) 7253 2262; *£4.

✦ ST PAUL'S

Guildhall (off Gresham St) 15th-c, where the Court of Common Council, over which the Lord Mayor presides, administers the City of London. The Lord Mayor's Banquet is held in the great hall, hung with the banners and shields of the City's 90-odd livery companies. Underneath is the largest 15th-c crypt in the City, and there's also a clock museum, and library with unrivalled collection of City-related manuscripts and books. Disabled access; cl Sun Oct–Apr, and for civic occasions; guided tours, must book, (020) 733 21460; free.

St Anne & St Agnes church (Gresham St) Particularly worth knowing for the Bach cantatas that grace its Lutheran services (usually second Sun in month); (020) 7606 4986 for programme.

St Mary le Bow church 🏛 (Cheapside) With the famous Bow Bells, and often Thurs lunchtime early-music concerts; (020) 7248 5139.

St Paul's Cathedral Despite the attempts of brasher, taller modern buildings to take over, this masterpiece still asserts itself proudly as the area's real landmark, its unmistakable shape repeatedly looming out above the crowded streets. Its huge dome is a pleasing shape after the stolid self-satisfaction of the Victorian and Edwardian masonry which dominates this area. Originally the cathedral was Gothic in style, with a towering 150-metre (500-ft) spire. It fell into disrepair and Wren was assigned to work on its renovation. He didn't relish the job, and no doubt was delighted when the Great Fire of London swept the old church away, allowing him to construct something entirely new. His mainly classical design is unlike any other cathedral in Britain, and took just 35 years to build. The setting for various State occasions, it's full of interesting monuments – the one to John Donne was the only complete figure to be salvaged from the Great Fire. Look out for the wonderful carving on the exterior – some of which is by Grinling Gibbons, who also did the choir stalls. Other highlights include the dizzying Whispering Gallery, the panoramic views from the top (quite a sweat), and the crypt, full of tombs and memorials to notable figures from British history. Snacks, shop, disabled access; cl Sun, Good Fri, 25 Dec and for occasional services; (020) 7236 4128; £5. The City Pipe by the tube station is an enjoyable wkdy wine bar.

✦ TOWER HILL

Tower Bridge Experience Inside the landmark bridge, with wonderful views from its glass-covered walkways, 43 metres (142 ft) above the Thames; animatronic characters and hi-tech displays present the view at various other dates in the bridge's history, with lively multi-media shows designed to leave you feeling proud to be British. The bridge is unusual not just for its design, but because it's still fully operational, raising the roadway from each side drawbridge-style to allow ships to pass; you can see some of the Victorian machinery that used to power this. Snacks, shop, disabled access; cl 24–25 Dec, 17 Jan; (020) 7403 3761; £6.25.

Tower of London Picturesque classic castle, the most notable building to survive the Great Fire of London. A lot of fun to look at even superficially, it dates back to the late 11th c, though the site had been used as a defensive position by the Romans much earlier. Almost every period of English history has witnessed gruesome goings-on here, with not even the highest or mightiest safe from imprisonment or even execution: Walter Raleigh, Lady Jane Grey and two of Henry VIII's wives spent their last days in the Tower. There's a mass of things to see, inc enough armour and medieval weaponry to glut the most bloodthirsty small boy's appetite, the Crown Jewels, the Beefeaters and the ravens. You can also walk along the elevated battlements.

The Jewel House shows off the Crown Jewels to dazzling effect; on the busiest days those tempted to linger are gently drawn along by moving floorway. Two towers that were part of Edward I's medieval palace are furnished in period style, and peopled with appropriately costumed helpful guides; one room in this part has been left untouched to show what a difficult job the restoration was. A reorganisation of the oldest part, the White Tower, has revealed that the inside of the fortress when built was much less imposing than was suggested by the formidable exterior – they were clearly just trying to intimidate the locals. You need a fair bit of time to see everything properly. Snacks, shop, some disabled access; cl 24–26 Dec, 1 Jan; (0171) 709 0765; £11.

Bloomsbury, Holborn & Regent's Park

The British Museum (with its newly restored Great Court) is the outstanding attraction in Bloomsbury and Holborn, a civilised and genteel if slightly faded area of Georgian squares, gardens and courts between the City and Westminster – legal and academic London. Much less well known, the Sir John Soane's Museum is not to be missed, nor are the excellent art collections at Somerset House. The vast modern British Library at King's Cross has some intriguing exhibits, too, and the London Canal Museum (new to the *Guide* this year) combines nicely with a boat trip up the Regent's Canal to Camden. Bloomsbury merges into a more genteel area to the W, over towards Marylebone (inc Madame Tussaud's), with smart Regent's Park (and the Zoo) on its N border; away from the shopping streets of Marylebone High St and Baker St this is largely residential, and the capital of private medicine and dentistry. Bloomsbury does have a large number of hotels, especially for the more budget-conscious visitor, though many are on the tawdry side. Ones which can be recommended include the Academy (17 Gower St WC1E 6HG (020) 7631 4115), the Morgan (24 Bloomsbury St WC1B 3QJ (020) 7636 3735) – both handy for the British Museum – and the George (60 Cartwright Gardens WC1H 9EL (020) 7387 6789).

Please let us know what you think of places in the *Guide*. Use the report forms at the back of the book or simply write us a letter.

To see and do

☻ BAKER STREET

London Planetarium (Marylebone Rd) A satisfying place, showing off one of the most advanced star projectors in the world. Surround-sound gives their enjoyable presentations an added sense of realism. Make sure you get to each show on time – stragglers barely have a moment to find a seat before the lights are dimmed. Plenty of interactive displays too – you can even see how much you'd weigh on another planet. Meals, snacks, shop, disabled access, cl 25 Dec; (0870) 400 3000; £6.30; joint ticket with Madame Tussaud's available. Opposite, the café of St Marylebone church has good value simple vegetarian meals.

Madame Tussaud's (Marylebone Rd) Almost half of overseas visitors place this famous waxworks museum at the top of their list of things to do in London, which explains why the queues can be so long and slow-moving (and perhaps why German TV presenters and Japanese sumo wrestlers now crop up among more familiar simulacrums). Some of the models are uncannily realistic, others rather less so; several members of the Royal Family spring to mind. They've successfully reworked the famous Chamber of Horrors (it no longer has that rather unpleasant emphasis on real-life crime), and the Spirit of London finale is entertaining – you sit in a black cab and are whisked through a cheery interpretation of the city's history. This part is excellently put together, and in places rather witty, but is over a little quickly – like the waxworks as a whole. As you can be in and out of the museum in little over an hour, you're paying more per minute here than practically anywhere else in Britain. Meals, snacks, shop, disabled access; cl 25 Dec; (0870) 400 3000; £11.50.

Sherlock Holmes Museum (221b Baker St) To many people the world over, Baker St calls to mind only one thing – Conan Doyle's great detective. This famous address has various Holmes paraphernalia, and something of the atmosphere of the books re-created in a replica apartment; also waxwork models of 24 characters from the stories. Shop; cl 25 Dec; (0171) 935 8866; *£6. A giant bronze statue of the super-sleuth now stands outside Baker St station.

GOODGE STREET

☻ Pollock's Toy Museum 🔳 (1 Scala St) Housed in a rather charming setting, a wide range of playthings from all over the world and from all periods, almost as if lots of enthusiastic children had just left them scattered through these little rooms. Mechanical and optical toys, teddy bears, furniture, board games and theatres, and a proper toy shop downstairs. Shop, disabled access to ground floor only; cl Sun and bank hols; (0207) 636 3452; £3.

HOLBORN

Legal London A perfect example of the tranquil architecture of this area, **Lincoln's Inn Fields** is a large open space with trees and lawns surrounded by handsome houses, also tennis courts and summer band concerts; it's a pleasant place to spend a summer afternoon. Nearby, the Gothic **Royal Courts of Justice** are impressive, and you can also stroll through the gardens of **Gray's Inn**, said to have been laid out by Francis Bacon around 1600. This area really is legal London, and you'll usually find a good number of lawyers in the splendid Cittie of York (22 High Holborn), an enormous and very atmospheric basement pub with little private booths down one side. Another fine pub in this area is the classic Lamb in Lamb's Conduit St. Dom Vito's Sandwich Bar on Kingsway has superb sandwiches.

Sir John Soane's Museum (13 Lincoln's Inn Fields) One of London's hidden highlights, built by the architect for his splendid collection of pictures, books and antiquities. It's most eccentric, full of architectural tricks and mirrors, which form a complex natural-lighting system for the antiquities covering most of the walls. There's a lovely picture by Turner and an Egyptian sarcophagus, but the highlights are Hogarth's acid series on *The Rake's Progress* and *The Election*. When you've seen them the guide swings open the hinged 'walls' and further treasures emerge inc choice Piranesi drawings and a scale model of the Bank of England. The house is built around a central courtyard monument to his dog ('Alas, poor Fanny!'); you ring the bell to get in, and sign a visitors' book. The guides are very friendly and helpful, the guidebook well worthwhile. Shop, limited disabled access; cl Sun, Mon, Christmas, and Good Fri, open first Tues evening of every month; (020) 7405 2107; free (donations welcome). The breakfast room of Soane's first house, no 12 next door, can also be visited.

⊕ ⇌ KING'S CROSS

British Library (Euston Rd) This vast modern library has good exhibition space for its national treasures such as the Lindisfarne Gospels and Magna Carta, and changes its displays frequently, as well as mounting special exhibitions; also guided tours, and a good programme of events. The entrance courtyard has a gigantic bronze of a crouching seated Sir Isaac Newton, by Paolozzi after William Blake, and impressive entrance gates. Open daily exc 25–26 Dec, and 1 Jan; (020) 7412 7332; free.

London Canal Museum (12–13 New Wharf Rd) The history of London's canal network is told in this former ice warehouse, with displays about the people who strove to make a meagre livelihood by living and working on them, the horses which pulled their boats, and the cargoes they carried. You can peer down into a huge ice well, where the ice was once stored. Temporary exhibitions; book and gift shop; cl Mon exc bank hols, plus 24–26 Dec; (020) 7713 0836; £2.50. A visit here is nicely combined with a trip on the canal. Jason's in Little Venice run enjoyable trips to Camden; (020) 7286 3428; £5.95 return.

⊕ REGENT'S PARK

(Gt Portland St or Regent's Park tube station) Covering over 400 acres, this is the culmination of a glorious swathe of Regency terraces designed by John Nash, which can be seen almost all around it; the buildings of Park Crescent are among the finest. The park was originally intended to be the setting for a palace for the Prince Regent, after whom it was named: now it contains an open-air theatre where Shakespeare and other plays are performed in the summer, the lovely Queen Mary's Rose Garden, the spectacular Avenue Garden (restored to its 1864 glory), a boating lake, bandstand concerts on summer Suns, and plenty of paths to stroll along.

London Zoo (Regent's Park or Camden Town tube station) Despite the presence of lions, giraffes and elephants, it's with smaller creatures that the zoo currently excels. The Web of Life, a live animal exhibition housed in a glass building with a ventilation system inspired by termites' nests, opened in 1999 – their first development since the Mappin Terraces (a sort of animal playground shared by monkeys and sloth bears). It shows how animals adapt to different environments, and how new species evolve; animals chosen to illustrate this include seahorses, a swarm of locusts, and organisms not normally visible to the naked eye, viewed through a micrarium. Other highlights are the irresistible children's zoo, where you can get right up to the animals, the biggest reptile house of any British zoo, and the spellbinding Moonlight World, where day and night are reversed so that you can watch nocturnal creatures such as vampire bats. The 1930s architecture of the penguin pool remains quite something. Meals, snacks, shop, disabled access; cl 25 Dec; (020) 7722 3333; £9.

Primrose Hill Once part of the same hunting park as Regent's Park, now popular strolling ground for this sober residential area. The modest rounded summit gives eye-opening views of the city.

Regent's Canal The Canal offers an excellent walk from Little Venice to Camden Lock, passing by Regent's Park and Primrose Hill (another good viewpoint); boat cruises also operate along here – one-way tickets available. The London Waterbus Company – one of several companies who now run along the stretch of Regent's Canal between Little Venice and Camden Lock – make a stop for passengers who want to get off at the zoo; (020) 7482 2550 for timetable.

⊖ RUSSELL SQUARE

British Museum (Great Russell St) Monumental 19th-c building housing spectacular collections of priceless man-made objects from all over the world, some of them over 3,000 years old. The range is staggering, in which just a few highlights are the Elgin Marbles, the log-book of Nelson's *Victory*, the wonderful and intriguing Egyptian galleries, the comprehensive galleries of Greek vases, the oriental antiquities, and the Amaravati sculpture. With the books now rehoused at the new British Library, there's room for the fascinating collections of non-Western art and culture that had been moved out to the Museum of Mankind. Don't try to take it in all at once – decide what interests you most and stick to that, or your head will start reeling with the extent of this treasure-house before you've got even a tenth of the way through. Try to arrive early as it can get very busy. When the Foster-designed £97m restoration of the Great Court is completed (they hope by the start of 2001), it will create the largest covered public square in Europe, home to an ethnographic collection, as well as cafés, restaurants and lecture theatres; a new public reference library giving visitors access to exhibits not on display will open in the famous Reading Room. Meals, snacks, shop, disabled access; cl am Sun, 24–26 Dec, 1 Jan, May Day, 2 Apr; (0171) 636 1555; free exc for special exhibitions. Just up Gower St, Dillons is a first-class serious bookshop, and in Museum St the Coffee Gallery is super for a really good light lunch or patisserie.

Dickens' House 🏠 (48 Doughty St) Dickens lived here during his 20s, and during that period wrote the *Pickwick Papers*, *Oliver Twist* and *Nicholas Nickleby*. The drawing room has been reconstructed to appear as it was then, and there are original manuscripts and first editions, pictures and personal possessions. His wife's sister died here in 1837, an event which the writer later used as the model for the death of Little Nell in *The Old Curiosity Shop*. Shop,

some disabled access; cl Sun and occasional public hols; (0171) 405 2127; *£4.

⊖ TEMPLE

Dr Johnson's House (17 Gough Sq) A perfect example of early 18th-c architecture, just as Dr Johnson himself was a perfect example of 18th-c barbed slightly flawed gentility. Between 1749 and 1759 he wrote his great *English Dictionary* here, and a first edition of this is on display, along with various memorabilia from his learned life. Shop; cl Sun and bank hols; (0171) 353 3745; *£4. The passages and walkways around here are a good reminder of how London's streets used to be laid out; the 17th-c Olde Cheshire Cheese nearby is a splendid old tavern.

Middle Temple Hall 🏠 Of all the Inns of Court, this is perhaps the most impressive, and it boasts many famous literary figures among its former members. Most of the buildings date from after the reign of Elizabeth I or the Great Fire, but the name points to an older history: the land was owned by the Knights Templar from about 1160. **Middle Temple Hall** is a fine example of Tudor architecture, with a double hammerbeam roof and beautiful stained glass. There is a table made from timber from Sir Francis Drake's *Golden Hind* – he was a member of the Middle Temple – while a single oak tree from Windsor Forest supplied the wood for the 9-metre (29-ft) long High Table. Cl wknds, bank hols, during Aug, and over some vacations – best to check first, (0171) 427 4800; free. The Temple has an unusual round church.

Somerset House (Strand) Built as government offices in the latter years of the 18th c, and for years the HQ of the Inland Revenue, this grand building designed by Sir William Chambers is gradually being handed back to the public. It now houses three major art collections, spread throughout several buildings surrounding a central paved courtyard with a stunning new series of waterspouts. It's long been the home of the **Courtauld Gallery** (North Wing), an outstanding collection of Impressionist and Post-Impressionist paintings inc works by Monet, Renoir, Degas and Cézanne, also Michelangelo,

Rubens, Goya and other masters. In May 2000, the Queen Mother opened the **Gilbert Collection** (South Building), a spectacular assortment of objets d'art (mostly gold and silver) made for the rich and famous over the past 500 years, from six jewel-encrusted gold snuffboxes owned by Frederick the Great of Prussia (valued at over £1m each) to a massive wine cistern weighing nearly 36kg, and even a pair of silver chamber-pots. Around the time this book comes out, the **Hermitage Rooms** will open on the ground floor of the South Building. These galleries will house rotating exhibitions from the famous Winter Palace in St Petersburg, and furnishings will attempt to re-create something of that museum's Imperial Russian splendour. The series of exhibitions kicks off with the treasures of Catherine the Great (running until Sept). Large visitor numbers are expected, so tickets will mostly be sold in advance for specific half-hour slots (with a limited number for sale at Somerset House each day); (020) 7845 4630; £6. Entry to the other two collections is £4 each (a joint ticket is £7). The River Terrace – open as a public promenade for the first time in 100 years – has an open-air café, new restaurant and shop; all the galleries have full disabled access. Open daily exc Sun am, 24–26 Dec, and 1 Jan; (020) 7845 4600.

St Bride's church (Fleet St) A Wren masterpiece, its splendid steeple the influence for today's traditional three-tiered wedding cake; good Sun choir and frequent short lunchtime recitals ((020) 7427 0133 for programme). There's an interesting **museum** in the partly Roman crypt (cl bank hols; free). Caxton set up his first printing press alongside, and ever since St Bride's has been the parish church for anyone involved in the press. This was useful in the days when adjoining Fleet St was the hub of newspaperland; today it's really just a passage between the law courts and the City – but look out for relics of the newspaper kingdoms such as the black-glass former Daily Express Building. The opulent Old Bank of England is now a magnificent pub.

South of the River

South of the river is today home to some of the capital's most exciting attractions inc the pick of the millennium openings. In 2000, the Tate Modern at Bankside opened to thunderous applause from art boffins and casual visitors alike, with the elegant London Eye proving equally popular (at least six other cities worldwide now want their own). County Hall has undergone a most satisfying transformation from bureaucrat's palace to tourist magnet, housing the London Aquarium and the new Dali Universe under its roof, and providing the starting point for London's most unusual sightseeing tour, courtesy of the London Frog Company. The marvellous Imperial War Museum recently opened its permanent exhibition on the Holocaust, and HMS *Belfast*, Britain at War and the Design Museum are other strong draws here. Children particularly like the expensive London Dungeon (with the new Great Fire of London attraction likely to increase visitor numbers), and some of the gruesome surgical instruments at the Old Operating Theatre can send a shiver down your spine, too. Radical plans to redevelop the South Bank arts centre could see the removal of some of London's least-loved buildings, but developers have to come to an agreement on what to replace them with first. Inside, several of the centre's buildings have pleasant bars and so forth, and usually something going on in their foyers — inc free entertainment. Further down river, the stylishly converted Oxo Tower and its environs buzz with a genuinely cheerful atmosphere, especially on summer wknds. Bankside's rich theatrical heritage has been well exploited over the last few years, with the magnificent reconstruction of Shakespeare's Globe Theatre (excellent summer productions and an enjoyable permanent exhibition), and a lively exhibition on the site of its contemporary, the Rose, just round the corner. A stroll along the Thames walkways gives marvellous views across the river, and once the beleaguered new footbridge is reopened, pedestrians will be treated to another unique perspective of the capital. The best views of the Houses of Parliament are from the quiet riverside walk between Westminster Bridge and the ancient palace of the Archbishop of Canterbury by Lambeth Bridge. Though the South Bank and its attractions are well signposted from Waterloo, if you have time to spare the walk is more pleasant over Blackfriars Bridge, or from Westminster. Near the Old Vic just S of Waterloo, La Barca (Lower Marsh St) is an enjoyably theatrical Italian restaurant, and Livebait (The Cut) is renowned for its fish. The café of the Young Vic (The Cut) does very good value light lunches, but you'll feel centuries old if you're out of your 20s.

To see and do

⊖≋ ELEPHANT & CASTLE

Bermondsey market (Bermondsey St/Long Lane) Get up very early on Fri for the bargains: when the antiques dealers start arriving around 5am, other dealers literally pounce on the choice items while they're being set out, and by 8 or 9am things are more ordinary. It's probably the biggest primary source of antiques and bric-a-brac in London, and can be the most exciting. Take a torch in winter.

⊖ LAMBETH NORTH

Florence Nightingale Museum 🔲 (St Thomas Hospital, Lambeth Palace Rd) On the site of the first School of Nursing, a re-created hospital ward in the Crimea, and various artefacts and possessions of the Lady with the Lamp. Shop, disabled access; cl 24 Dec–2 Jan, Good Fri and Easter Sun; (0171) 620 0374; £4.80.

Imperial War Museum (Lambeth Rd; not too far to walk from Westminster) This top-notch museum uses very up-to-date presentation techniques to give a vibrant and sometimes even nerve-wracking exploration of aspects of all wars

involving Britain and the Commonwealth since 1914. The Blitz Experience vividly re-creates London's darkest days, and a Trench Experience gives World War I the same treatment. Small boys of all ages love it, though the tone isn't all gung-ho: the interesting archive recordings of people's experiences of war can leave a deep impression, as do some of the harrowing paintings by official war artists. A new permanent exhibition on the Holocaust covers much of a new six-storey extension. Using original artefacts (many of them lent from former concentration camps) inc a funeral cart from the Warsaw ghetto, letters written by an eight-year old French Jewish boy before his betrayal and deportation to Auschwitz, and a section of a deportation railcar from Belgium, as well as photographs and the testimony of survivors, it will be the largest and most moving memorial to the victims of the Holocaust in the country; also excellent changing exhibitions. Meals, snacks, shop, disabled access; cl 24–26 Dec; (0171) 416 5000; £5.20, free after 4.30pm. It's housed in the former lunatic asylum known as Bedlam, the name a corruption of Bethlehem: the site was originally a hostel set up in the 13th-c by the bishop of that town. There's a clutch of useful tapas bars and the like up past here, around the junction of Kennington Rd and Kennington Lane, and on Waterloo Rd the Fire Station does good food.

Lambeth Palace (S end of Lambeth Bridge) The official residence of the Archbishop of Canterbury, with a charming late 15th-c red-brick exterior. There may be guided tours of the partly early medieval interior, but as we were going to press, they could not confirm when these would be occurring in 2001, so best to phone; (020) 7898 1200. The adjacent **church of St Mary** has the tombs of several archbishops, and Captain Bligh of the *Bounty* is buried here too. Just by the S gateway is a little **Museum of Garden History** founded as a memorial to the Tradescants, father and son, and royal gardeners to Charles I and Henrietta Maria, with a small area planted with plants grown in their time. Snacks, shop, some disabled access; cl Sat, and early Dec–early Mar; (020) 7401 8865; free.

⊖ ₹ LONDON BRIDGE

Bankside This area is very much on the up, with quite a bit of redevelopment going on in the old buildings, and plenty more to come. Riverside promenades offer good Thames and City views – Wren is said to have watched the building of St Paul's from here, and Pepys certainly did watch London burning down in the Great Fire, from nr the interesting old Anchor tavern. One of the best cross-river views of St Paul's is from the modern Founders Arms pubs. For centuries this was London's entertainment centre, full of theatres, bars and licensed brothels. In Clink St are the medieval remains of the Bishop of Winchester's palace, once said to be the biggest building in Europe but now reduced to a single wall and atmospheric rose window. A full-size replica of Francis Drake's *Golden Hind* is moored nearby (cl 25 Dec, but phone to check as it occasionally closes for functions; (0870) 0118 700; £2.50).

Bramah Tea and Coffee Museum (Maguire St, Butlers Wharf) Almost scholarly but surprisingly interesting, meticulously charting the history of these two favourite commodities, with around 1,000 teapots, and lots of ceramics, silver and prints. Teas (good stuff – they're not fans of the tea bag), snacks, shop, disabled access; cl 25–26 Dec; (0171) 378 0222; £4. Nearby the Anchor Tap (just off Shad Thames) is a handy refreshment stop.

Britain at War 🔳 (Tooley St) A splendidly put together re-creation of Blitz-hit London, from reconstructed streets and air-raid shelters to a BBC radio station and GI club. The special effects are suitably dramatic, with lots of smoke, smells and noise. Also authentic period newsreels and front pages, a fully stocked shop and bombed-out pub, and lots of fascinating little details. Shop, disabled access; cl 24–26 Dec; (020) 7403 3171; £5.95.

Design Museum (Butlers Wharf) Intriguing museum showing how design is used in the mass production of everyday objects, from cars and furniture to graphics and ceramics. One gallery has displays of international contemporary design. Snacks, interesting shop, disabled access; cl 25–26 Dec; (0171) 403 6933; £5.50.

Globe Theatre The most famous of Southwark's 1600s theatres, Shakespeare's Globe, has been reconstructed on its original site, where it was open from 1599 to 1642 (when the Puritans closed it down). The late Sam Wanamaker's ambitious project was derided when first mooted, but the theatre has now enjoyed four very successful seasons. It couldn't be more different from the West End: shaped like an O, the three-tiered open-topped theatre is 30 metres (100 ft) in diameter, seating audiences of 1,500 with a further 500 promenaders. Shakespeare's works are performed almost the way they were in the early 1600s – no spotlights, canned music or elaborate sets. Anyone who tells you the seats are uncomfortable has rather missed the point (and you can hire cushions). There are entertaining tours during the day, and displays on the Globes old and new – a good substitute if you can't make a performance. A new exhibition underneath the building looks at the life and works of Shakespeare (the biggest of its kind in the world). Very good café and restaurant with river views, shop, disabled access; tours all day Mon, and ams only Tues–Sun (till 11.30am Sun); (020) 7902 1500; £7.50. The 17th-c galleried George in Borough High St, back past London Bridge station, gives another idea of how the area's buildings used to look back then; NT.

Hays Galleria (off Tooley St) An old dock attractively converted into a shopping arcade, with several places to eat inc a good river-view pub, and a fascinating whimsical pirate-ship working sculpture by David Kemp.

HMS Belfast (E side of Southwark Bridge) Docked permanently in the pool of London, this is the only surviving example of the big-gun armoured warships built for the Royal Navy in the first half of the 20th c. This floating museum has sound and light displays re-creating life at sea, and there's masses to see among its nine decks, from the ship's gun decks to its sick bay. Meals, snacks, shop, limited disabled access; cl 24–26 Dec; (020) 7940 6400; £5, children free.

London Dungeon 🖾 (Tooley St) A sensationalised look at London's seamy underside, so better for unsqueamish children, with witchcraft, torture, black magic and death (inc a grisly Jack the Ripper section) all presented in ghoulishly life-like waxwork scenes. The new £1m Great Fire of London attraction takes you back to the fury of the world's most famous urban inferno, and the Judgement Day water ride treats you to a trip on an executioner's barge. The whole place is very atmospheric and well laid out, though families may find the scariest thing about it is the rather high price. Snacks, shop, disabled access; cl 25 Dec (open later in the evenings mid-July to early Sept); (0891) 600066; £9.95.

Old Operating Theatre (St Thomas St) The church of St Thomas has a unique reconstructed operating theatre in its roof (originally this space was deemed far enough from the rest of the hospital for patients' screams to be out of earshot), and a museum looking at the history of surgery and herbal medicine, with some particularly gruesome bits of surgical equipment on display. Parts of The Madness of King George were filmed here. Shop; cl mid-Dec to early Jan; (020) 7955 4791; £3.25.

Rose Theatre (Park St) Just around the corner from the Globe, this is the site of Bankside's oldest theatre, the Rose, built by Philip Henslowe in 1587. Its remains were rediscovered in 1989 in the basement of an office block, submerged beneath a protective pool of water. A light and sound show brings the story of the theatre to life (inc insights into London as Marlowe and Shakespeare would have known it), and proceeds support the continued excavation and preservation of the site. Shop, disabled access (but no facilities); cl 25–26 Dec, and 1 Jan; (020) 7593 0026; £3.

Southwark Cathedral Off the busy main road and quite a contrast to the buildings cluttered all around it, this is well worth a passing look, with parts over 600 years older than the present late 19th-c nave; interesting memorials to William Shakespeare (whose brother is buried here) and John Harvard, the founder of the American university. They have regular free recitals at Mon and Tues lunchtime. Major restoration work inc cleaning and floodlighting the structure, the creation of a new exhibition area and refectory, and improved disabled access, should be completed by the start of 2001. Shop; open daily (exc during special services); suggested donation £2.50.

Vinopolis (Bank End, Bankside) Cavernous vaulted arches housing a celebration of all things Bacchic. A self-guided audio tour takes you around displays on the world's wine-growing regions, and afterwards you can sample five wines from a choice of 200 (all of which feature in the exhibition). Restaurant, two shops, disabled access; (0171) 495 4909; £10.

⊖ SOUTHWARK

Tate Modern (Bankside) Standing proudly robust on the bank of the Thames opposite St Paul's Cathedral, this masterfully gentrified former power station is a salient landmark amid the cluster of new and exciting developments in this part of the city. Designed by Sir Charles Gilbert Scott in 1947 (the architect of Liverpool's Anglican Cathedral, Waterloo Bridge, and designer of the red telephone box), it stood derelict for nearly 15 years, until the Tate Gallery acquired it in 1994. Today, its cathedral-like windows give splendid views over central London, and a series of stunning top-lit galleries provide perfect lighting for artworks. The collection covers every modern movement from Pop Art to Surrealism, with works by all the great modern artists inc Dali, Picasso, Matisse, and Duchamps, on permanent show for the first time. An insistence on themed displays does rather jumble things up so that the real gems can seem hidden among lesser stuff, but this is a great place. There are around three major loan exhibitions a year, as well as an education centre, auditorium, café with outdoor terrace and a restaurant with river views. Very good disabled access; (020) 7887 8007; cl 24–26 Dec, 1 Jan; free (exc special exhibitions). The building also forms the south bank anchor point of the new **Millennium Bridge**, an elegant and unusual horizontal suspension footbridge, spanning the Thames in a single arch. Designed to create a convenient short cut from the Tate to St Paul's, it unfortunately fell foul of teething problems only one day after it was officially opened. As we went to press, engineers were working on ways to prevent the swaying motion which was leading pedestrians to feel sea-sick; one idea being touted was the introduction of a £1 toll, to keep numbers down.

⊖ ≷ VAUXHALL

London Balloon (Spring Gardens) The world's largest tethered balloon used to soar 150 metres (500 ft) above here, giving a surprisingly affordable and truly unique view of the capital (quite a bit higher than the better-known London Eye). As we went to press they were facing pressures from the local council to build a new balloon, which they hope will be in flight some time in the new year. Phone (020) 7587 1111

for more information.

⊖ ≷ WATERLOO

BFI London IMAX 🅰 (Charlie Chaplin Walk) Britain's largest 3D projection cinema (with a screen the height of 5 double-decker buses) housed in a stunning glass cylindrical building. Café, disabled access; daytime and evening screenings, phone (020) 7902 1234, for details; £6.75.

Gabriel's Wharf (Upper Ground) One of quite a few projects to have brightened up the south bank in recent years: a relaxed place, with a number of cheery designer and craft workshops, along with cafés, events, and Fri craft market.

Museum Of (The Bargehouse, Oxo Tower Wharf) Series of enjoyable temporary exhibitions, with a view to creating a permanent museum about the River Thames here in the future; subjects so far have included collectors, emotions and the unknown, with continuing events and performances. Disabled access to most of the museum; cl am, Mon and Tues, and maybe other times, so best to phone; (020) 7401 2255; free. **Oxo Tower Wharf** itself offers great views over the city from the top of the lavishly restored art deco tower, with its landmark logo (and there's good food).

South Bank Centre This stretch of the riverside, home to a string of world-class theatres, cinemas and galleries (not for nothing do they boast that it's the biggest arts complex) is to undergo a radical redevelopment over the next few years, which might even see the demolition of the much-criticised buildings of the Purcell Room, and even the Queen Elizabeth Hall. Externally, it's not appealing, but a considerable part of the project – funded in part by the Arts Council and Heritage Lottery Fund – aims to tackle this issue, adding landscaped gardens, an open-air amphitheatre, and a new area for skateboarders (they've improvised their own at the moment), beneath which will be built a new home for the British Film Institute, extended space for the new version of the Museum of the Moving Image, and a gargantuan concert hall. Other parts of the scheme include the renovation of the Royal

Festival Hall (due to be completed by 2003), and the erection of towering office blocks and retail outlets whose revenue is supposed to pay for the overall reconstruction. Argument about the plans means that bulldozers may not arrive before 2005 at the earliest. For the time being, occasional open-air festivals, with stalls of books, clothes and jewellery going down to the river, create a buzzing atmosphere on a sunny day. Inside there are frequent free performances and interesting small exhibitions in the foyers of the various halls. The National Theatre, as well as the excellent productions in its three different-sized auditoria, has interesting artistic exhibitions, guided tours behind the scenes, and good places to eat – often accompanied by live music in the foyer of the Olivier Theatre; (020) 7452 3400 to book a tour (£4.75; they don't do them on Sun). The National Film Theatre has good themed screenings and events as well as a riverside café. The Hayward Gallery specialises in world-class art exhibitions. The Royal Festival Hall has a full programme of music and dance; its People's Palace is a good modern restaurant and bar. It's a short walk from here to the London Eye and other attractions in and around County Hall (a rather longer one to the Imperial War Museum).

● WESTMINSTER

Dali Universe (County Hall) London's newest major art gallery is dedicated entirely to the great Spanish Surrealist, and forms part of the exciting new tourist developments clustered around County Hall. Most of the 500 works on display have never been exhibited in Britain before, and among the exhibits are the 124 drawings which accompanied Dali's autobiography *La Vie Secrète*, the spectacular oil painting created for the set of Hitchcock's 1945 film *Spellbound*, and the infamous *Mae West Lips* sofa. Snacks, shop, disabled access; cl 25 Dec and 1 Jan; (020) 7620 2420; £7. Outside, a series of fantastical Dali sculptures have certainly brought some artistic panache to the riverside walkway.

Frog Tours For a totally alternative tour of the sights of central London, this fun new attraction is hard to beat.

Bright yellow amphibious vehicles (used to support the Allied landings in Normandy in 1944, when they were painted a far more practical khaki), take you for a 90-min round trip, taking in – among other places – Parliament Sq, Whitehall, Trafalgar Sq and Hyde Park Corner, before splashing down into the Thames from a slipway nr Vauxhall Bridge for a 30-min cruise along the river. Tours leave daily from 10am from County Hall, and the vehicles seat up to 30 passengers. To pre-book call (020) 7928 3132, but tickets may also be bought from their kiosk outside the front of County Hall; *£13.

London Aquarium (County Hall, a walk across Westminster Bridge from Westminster tube station) This is one of Europe's biggest collections of underwater life, housed in around two million litres of water. The main Atlantic and Pacific tanks are spectacular in their sheer size, giving great views of the sharks, stingrays and conger eels swimming round the Easter-Island style giant heads. The creatures (and occasional divers – often more entertaining than the fish) have plenty of room to swim about, and if you come at a sensible time you'll get several chances to stare at the sharks close-up. The rest of the displays – arranged in different themed areas representing rivers, coral reefs and rainforests – are a more conventional size, so you may have to wait a couple of minutes to get right up to them (for example on our summer holiday visit no-one left the seahorse tank until one of the shy little beasts had finally appeared). Some areas are fairly imaginative, making good use of sound and light effects, and of course the fish and sea life are quite spectacular, with breath-taking colours and patterns; some species haven't been seen in Britain before. Well sized touch tanks let you stroke a ray or gingerly handle a crab. To avoid the crowds at wknds and school holidays, try to come early or late in the day otherwise you may end up having to queue. Snacks, shop, disabled access; cl 25 Dec; (020) 7967 8000; £8.50, free for wheelchair users. Great views of the Houses of Parliament and river from outside.

London Eye (County Hall) This gigantic steel wheel designed, quite literally, to see in the new millennium, took a while to get off the ground, but since it started turning in February 2000 has proved to be one of the most successful and popular of the country's new attractions. The wheel stands nearly 140 metres (450 ft) above the Thames – the fourth tallest structure in London, three times the size of Tower Bridge. On a clear day from its 32 glass pods, passengers can see up to 25 miles in each direction, although pre-booked tickets (the only way to avoid lengthy queues) mean you cannot guarantee perfect viewing conditions. Each rotation (or flight, as British Airways insist on calling them) takes 30 mins, and tickets must be collected from County Hall 30 mins in advance. There's a coffee shop by the ticket office, and every capsule is fully accessible by wheelchair; cl 25 Dec; (0870) 5000 600; £8.50, children (must be accompanied by adults) £5.

Further Afield

We include here only those places which, despite being away from the centre, appeal so much at least to some people that, for them, even a short stay in London would be incomplete without them. A trip down the Thames from Westminster is a fun way to begin a full day out at Greenwich, now a great destination for families, with wonderful alternative views over the city from the park (ideal for picnics), new children's displays at the *Cutty Sark*, and a good value joint ticket to its star attractions, the National Maritime Museum and the Royal Observatory. Kew is also very appealing with its glorious glasshouses reflecting the earlier grandeur of the Great Conservatory at Syon House, Brentford (new to the *Guide* this year, and a rewarding half-day's excursion). Firepower over in Woolwich promises a lively look at the history of the artillery when it opens in May, and the outstanding new Wetland Centre at Barnes not only provides a haven for thousands of birds, but looks after its human visitors too, with a fun discovery centre and full wheelchair access. Wonderfully regal Hampton Court Palace is a popular outing with its famous gardens worth a visit in themselves, and splendid Kenwood in Hampstead provides an idyllic setting for a summer evening concert. Other parts of London do have many treasures tucked away, and though we don't list them, they are well worth Londoners themselves tracking down: prime among them the Whitechapel Gallery in Whitechapel High St E of the City, and, out in W London, Osterley Park, Chiswick Mall (18th-c Thames-side village), Chiswick Park (the first true example of English naturalistic landscaping, with Chiswick House, an early 18th-c partying pavilion), and Sutton House, an improbable 16th-c survival in the heart of Hackney.

Please let us know what you think of places in the *Guide*. Use the report forms at the back of the book or simply write us a letter.

To see and do

🚆 BARNES

Wetland Centre 4m from the heart of the city, this Wildfowl and Wetlands Trust reserve is an incredible feat of environmental transformation. A hundred acres of reservoir have been broken up and resculpted to create over 30 lakes, linked by 27 bridges. With 30,000 trees, and 200,000 aquatic plants, the centre will gradually provide a haven for a spectrum of wildlife, from herons and teals to newts and kingfishers; birds already spotted breeding here include little ringed plover, great crested grebe and lapwing. There are seven hides, and a three-storey viewing tower, but for those who like bird-spotting in comfort, a glass-walled observatory with views across the reserve relays live pictures via CCTV from the hides. A fun-looking discovery centre has lots of hands-on activities for children, with re-created wetland habitats. A visitor centre has touch-screen displays on the wildlife seen at the reserve, along with a café and shop. It's all been designed to accommodate wheelchair access, and there's even a lift in the observation tower. At peak times, the centre provides a riverbus service from Hammersmith, Barnes, and maybe other stations, to prevent traffic from disturbing the wildlife. Cl Sun (exc for WWT members); (020) 8409 4400; £6.50.

🚆 BRENTFORD

Syon Park The London home of the Duke of Northumberland, this was built on the site of a medieval abbey and remodelled from its Tudor original by Robert Adam – it's widely considered to be one of his finest works. The ceiling by Cipriani and the magnificent Scagliola floor are particular highlights, but a visit here can keep the whole family entertained, with 40 acres of grounds to stroll around (landscaped by Capability Brown), Thames-side watermeadows, a giant indoor adventure playground, and the **London Butterfly House** (£3.30 extra). Snacks, shop, disabled access to café and gardens only; house open Weds, Thurs, Sun and bank hol Mon (and all Easter wknd) mid-Mar to Oct, gardens open daily exc 25–26 Dec; (020) 8560 0881; house and gardens £6, gardens only £3.

⊖ CAMDEN TOWN

A bohemian's idyll, with a very wide variety of unusual shops from radical bookshops to fashion workshops, from comic shops to one of London's best brassware and ironmongery shops. Lots of restaurants and cafés too, and good delis serving the area's Italian and Greek communities; try the Parkway Deli for Italian, and Chris Milia (Pratt St) for Greek. The area's biggest draw is its wknd series of lively **markets**, particularly the interesting craft, handmade fashion and other stalls around the attractively converted former warehouses of Camden Lock. There's also a covered market on Camden High St, the Inverness St market for fruit and vegetables, and the Stables, where the best food stalls are to be found. Go and browse, but be warned that you may never again see such huge crowds – the markets here draw 200,000 people every wknd. **Jewish Museum** (129 Albert St) Excellent look at Jewish life, history and religion, with a particularly fine collection of ceremonial art, portraits and antiques, and various audio-visual displays. Shop, disabled access; cl Fri, Sat, all bank and Jewish hols; (020) 7284 1997; £3. They have another branch on East End Road, Finchley, (020) 8349 1143, which traces the history of Jewish immigration and has a moving exhibition on the Holocaust. The Princess of Wales up towards Primrose Hill (Chalcot Rd/Regent's Park Rd) does good bistro food.

🚆 ELTHAM

Eltham Palace (Court Yard) On the site of an early 14th-c royal palace, this splendid 1930s country house, set in attractive grounds, was built around part of a medieval hall erected for Edward IV. Re-created by English Heritage, the art deco interior reflects the glamour of the age in which it was built. Teas; cl Mon (exc bank hols), Tues, Sat, 24–26 Dec and 1 Jan; (020) 8294 2548; house and grounds £5.90, grounds only £3.50; EH.

⇌ GREENWICH

The sort of place you can come back to time and time again; some of our contributors rate Greenwich more highly than anywhere else in the country. Once a favoured residence of the Royal Family, Greenwich has a long and illustrious maritime heritage, still reflected in the museums, boats and grand old ships you can visit. A wknd market has some excellent antiques, junk and secondhand books, also arts and crafts. College Approach has a good wknd covered craft market. You should be able to get boat trips from the Pier up to Westminster (around £5). The Cutty Sark (Lassell St) and Trafalgar (Park Row) are good river-view dining pubs. Three of the best attractions, the Queen's House, National Maritime Museum and Royal Observatory, can be visited on a joint ticket for £10.50. You'll still pay this even if you can visit only one of them, but you don't have to do them all the same day.

Cutty Sark In dry dock not far from Greenwich Pier, this clipper built in 1869 was the fastest of her time – she once sailed 363 nautical miles in a single day. On board, you can watch a video telling her story; there's an impressive collection of ships' figureheads, and new children's display panels and activities. Shop, limited disabled access; cl 24–26 Dec; (020) 8858 3445; £3.50.

Fan Museum 🖼 (12 Crooms Hill, Greenwich) Unique collection of around 3,000 fans and related items from all over the world. They even do fan-making classes. Shop, disabled access (with notice); cl Sun am, and all day Mon; (020) 8858 7879; £3.50.

Greenwich Park Wonderful views from this carefully landscaped park sloping down towards the river; it's a great place for a picnic. A herd of deer graze in a smallish area of woodland and wild flowers known as the Wilderness, and there's the largest children's playground in any Royal Park (as well as the preserved trunk of a tree in which the young Elizabeth I is said to have played).

National Maritime Museum (Romney Rd) 16 galleries all under a spectacular glass canopy house with displays on topics as diverse as plant life, piracy and, of course, sea power. Hundreds of exhibits range from contemporary art and great masterpieces of naval battles, to hands-on activities, Nelson's bloodstained coat, and even hardy yachtsman Tony Bullimore's survival suit. An exhibition about the race to discover the South Pole runs until Sept. It's all great fun and combines nicely with a visit to the Royal Observatory (a joint ticket is £10.50). Meals, snacks, shop, disabled access; cl 24–26 Dec; (020) 8312 6565; £7.50, children free.

Queen's House (Romney Rd) On the site of the original magnificent Royal palace, this early 17th-c house was the first Palladian-style villa in the country, designed by Inigo Jones for Anne of Denmark. An exhibition on naval portraits starts from Easter, best to phone for admission price and opening times. Shop, disabled access; (020) 8858 4422; there may also be a joint ticket with National Maritime Museum and Royal Observatory, phone to check.

Ranger's House (Chesterfield Walk, Blackheath) This lovely stately home with fine furnishings should reopen in spring 2002 following refurbishment. In the 19th c it was the official residence of the Greenwich Park ranger – and Blackheath opposite is a civilised place, good for a pleasant stroll. Phone for more information; (020) 8853 0035.

Royal Naval College With the Queen's House as its focal point, this glorious group of buildings was designed initially by Webb in the late 17th c, then augmented in succession by Wren, Vanbrugh, Hawksmoor and Ripley. It's a magnificently preserved part of old London. Visitors can see an interesting chapel and a notable painted hall. Meals, snacks, shop; cl Sun am, 25–26 Dec; (020) 8269 4747; £3 (free on Sun). The view from across the river (there's a pedestrian tunnel under the Thames here) looks like an 18th-c print come to life.

Royal Observatory (Greenwich Park) The original home of Greenwich Mean Time – standing as it does on zero meridian longitude. The brass line marking the meridian is still there set in the ground: standing over it with one foot in the western hemisphere and one in the east is almost irresistible. The Wren-built observatory was founded by Charles II in 1675, and now houses a comprehensive collection of historic instruments for time-keeping, navigation and astronomy. Good views from the top. The Time Ball is rather confusing – it can go down and up so fast you barely notice it. Meals, snacks, shop; cl 24–26 Dec and 1 Jan; (020) 8858 4422; £6, children free.

⊖HAMPSTEAD

Prides itself on its villagey atmosphere, and off the main streets its maze of twisting lanes is very picturesque and seductively charming. It's home to artistes of all kinds, and well heeled bohemians in general; in some streets a commemorative blue plaque on the front of the house is almost compulsory. Particularly attractive parts include early Georgian Church Row, and Squires Mount (where the Regency-looking house at the end on the left, in fact built in the 1950s, belonged to Richard Burton and Elizabeth Taylor). The gaslit Holly Bush, prettily tucked away up Holly Mount, is a good pub, as is the Flask in Flask Walk (a long-standing favourite of local actors).

2 Willow Road The first Modern Movement house acquired by the National Trust. Designed and built by the architect Erno Goldfinger, it has a good range of work by the artists and intellectuals who lived around Hampstead in the 1930s – as well as the only working TV on show in any NT property. Guided tours from 12.15pm Thurs–Sat Apr–Oct; (0171) 435 6166; £4.20; NT.

Fenton House (Hampstead Grove) Fine William and Mary merchant's mansion, set in a walled garden, with Oriental, English and European china and an exceptional collection of early keyboard instruments. Their period-music concerts on some summer evenings are well worth catching. Open pm Weds–Sun and bank hols Apr–Oct and maybe other times, phone to check; (020) 435 3471; £4.20; NT.

Hampstead Heath North London's best open space, with lakes, hilly

prospects, and some wonderful views of the city skyline – Parliament Hill has a direction-finder pointing out various landmarks. On one edge the ancient Spaniards Inn, still as popular as when Dickens made it famous in the *Pickwick Papers*, faces an 18th-c toll booth notorious for the way its road-narrowing blocks the traffic here.

Kenwood (Hampstead Lane) Achieved its present splendid proportions in the 18th c at the hands of Robert Adam. As part of an £800,000 redecoration scheme, the rooms have been recently repainted in darker hues to better show off the fine collection of paintings, inc old masters, a Rembrandt self-portrait, and 18th- and 19th-c portraits by Reynolds and Gainsborough. Other improvements have included rich carpets covering bare boards, windows draped with opulent curtains, and the return of verdancy to the formerly faded green room. The grounds are lovely, and in summer there are concerts out here, idyllic when it's fine, with the music drifting across the lake with its Japanese bridge, and sometimes a fireworks finale (virtually impossible to park anywhere near – but a free shuttle bus runs from East Finchley tube station from 5pm then). Meals, snacks, shop, disabled access; cl 24–25 Dec, 1 Jan; (020) 8348 1286; free.

Sigmund Freud's House 🔲 (20 Maresfield Gdns) Extraordinary collection of antiques from various ancient cultures, as well as Freud's library, papers and indeed his desk and couch. Shop, some disabled access; open pm Weds–Sun exc Easter and Christmas bank hols; (020) 7435 2002; *£4. The monumental seated statue of Freud by Oscar Nemon can be seen outside the Tavistock Clinic on nearby Belsize Lane.

⇶HAMPTON COURT

Bushy Park Another Royal Park, formerly reserved for hunting. Wren laid out its famous double chestnut avenue, which runs from Teddington Gate to the great house.

Hampton Court Gardens Worth a visit in their own right, especially since the restoration of William III's Privy Garden, damaged in the Palace's 1986 fire. The last time these gardens looked as they do now was in 1702. The elaborately landscaped grounds also include the famous maze, and the annual flower show here is one of the world's biggest. Open as for the Palace; £2.50 gardens only. The Kings Arms, next to the Lion Gate, is useful for something to eat.

Hampton Court Palace An amazing place, just as a Royal palace should be. Begun by Cardinal Wolsey in the early 16th c, the house's splendour soon so pricked Henry VIII's jealousy that Wolsey felt compelled to present it to his king in an attempt to appease him. Successive monarchs have left their architectural marks: the hammer-beamed hall and kitchens were Henry's addition, the Fountain Court was designed by Wren for William and Mary, and much comes from the work of the Victorians (the chimneys mostly date from then). The rooms have managed to keep their distinctive styles, from the starkly imposing Tudor kitchens (themselves taking up 50 rooms) to the elaborate grandeur of the Georgian chambers. The King's Staircase is wonderfully over the top, and the Picture Gallery has the finest Renaissance works from the Royal collection, inc Bruegel the Elder's fascinating *Massacre of the Innocents*. Look out too for the carvings by Grinling Gibbons and the cartoons by Mantegna in the Lower Orangery. There are several excellent audio guides you can pick up and listen to as you go along, with no extra charge. Tudor Christmas activities 27 Dec–3 Jan. Meals, snacks, shops, disabled access; cl 24–26 Dec; (020) 8781 9500; £10.50.

River Thames There are pleasant Thames-side walks around Hampton Court, and summer cruise boats from here back down to Westminster, (0207) 930 4721; £10.

● HIGHGATE

An easy walk across the Heath from Hampstead, this dates largely from the Victorian period and still keeps a villagey atmosphere, centred as it is around the High St. The village is dominated by Highgate School (which Betjeman attended and where T S Eliot

taught). There are lots of pubs in this area, and some smart little cafés. The Grove, a row of very elegant Victorian houses, has been home to such diverse musicians as Yehudi Menuhin and Sting.

Highgate Cemetery (Swains Lane) The most impressive of a series of landscaped and formal cemeteries started in the early decades of Victoria's reign on the outskirts of the city, very well restored over the last 20 years, and still in use. You'll find it hard to miss the tomb of Karl Marx – a monstrous head, frequently daubed with paint and slogans. It's more difficult to search out the graves of Christina Rossetti and George Eliot in the wonderfully atmospheric tangle of trees, shrubs and crumbling ivy-covered monuments. The E cemetery is open all year (exc 25–26 Dec and during funerals), the W by guided tour only (not wkdys Dec–Feb), entry to both cemeteries by appointment, (020) 8340 1834; E cemetery £2, W cemetery £3.

●≋KEW

Kew Bridge Steam Museum 🔄 (Green Dragon Lane) Over the bridge from the gardens, by the tube station, this is a splendid old pumping station housing five Cornish beam engines – one of which you can walk through while it's working. Also a miniature railway, and surprisingly interesting exhibition on the development of London's water supply: there are peepholes into the sewers. It won't engross unless you've at least some interest in the subject – in which case you'll find the engines prime examples of their type. Wknd snacks, shop, some disabled access; cl 25 Dec, Good Fri; (020) 8568 4757; £4 wknds (when engines in steam), £3 wkdys.

Kew Gardens Started in 1759 by George III's mother as nine acres landscaped by Capability Brown. By 1904, they had grown to cover 300 acres, with the foundations of the present wonderful collection firmly laid. The glasshouses include the magnificent modern Princess of Wales range and the remarkable restored Victorian Palm House, as well as an Evolution House displaying plants from up to 400 million years ago. The gardens nr the entrance are largely formally arranged, and drift into attractively landscaped woodland, glades and tree collections further out. The museum was extensively restored a few years ago, and there's also a gallery, and jazz concerts on some evenings in July. A wonderful place you can come back to time and time again – always discovering something new. Meals, snacks, shop, disabled access; cl 25 Dec, 1 Jan; (020) 8332 5622; £5. The Flower & Firkin at Kew Gardens railway station does decent simple food. In summer you can come to Kew by cruise boat from Westminster – see the numbers we give for Hampton Court and Richmond.

Queen Charlotte's Cottage (Kew Gardens) This rusticated summer-house was built for the Royal Family in the 18th c, its interior designed to look like a tent; it's usually open bank hol wknds Apr–Sept; free with admission to the gardens.

Musical Museum (368 Brentford High St, just W of Kew Bridge) Worth a look if you have the time, with a fascinating collection of continuously playing automatic musical instruments. Shop; open pm wknds Apr–Oct, plus Weds pm July–Aug; (020) 8560 8108; £3.20.

⊖≷ RICHMOND

Agreeable if much extended Thames village, with lots of fine 18th-c houses esp around the Green and up Richmond Hill. There are quite a few good dining pubs, inc the riverside White Cross, and the White Swan (Old Palace Lane), Orange Tree (Kew Rd) and Rose of York (Petersham Rd). The river here is really attractive for strolls, and there are summer cruise boats from here back down to Westminster, stopping at

Kew (more fine riverside walks) on the way; (020) 7930 2062.

Ham House (Petersham) A pleasant two-mile walk W along the river from Richmond to this outstanding Stuart mansion. A ghost guide takes you on a tour of haunted rooms (by appointment only). Meals, snacks, shop, disabled access; open pm Sat–Weds Apr–Oct; (020) 8940 1950; £6, £2 garden only; NT. If you happen to be in Twickenham you can get a ferry across.

Richmond Park The most country-like of all London's parks, with great rolling spaces and wildlife (inc herds of deer), model boats on Adam's Pond, and fishing in the 18-acre Pen Ponds. There's a good formal garden at Pembroke Lodge, and the Isabella Plantation's rhododendrons and azaleas are a must-see in season.

≷ WOOLWICH

Firepower (Royal Arsenal West, Warren Lane) Opening in restored former Ministry of Defence research buildings on 26 May as part of the overall redevelopment of the Royal Arsenal, this new museum brings to life the history of artillery since Roman times: plenty of big guns and military vehicles, alongside a unique collection of uniforms, photographs, books and manuscripts. Lots of effort is being made to make the museum appeal to families, with interactive displays and so forth, but some of the exhibitions will have a more personal side to them, with recorded recollections of former servicemen and women, and a poignant display of medals. Meals, snacks, shop, disabled access; cl 25 Dec; (020) 8855 7755; admission should be around £6.50, but best to check.

We welcome reports from readers

This *Guide* depends on readers' reports. Do help us if you can – in return, we offer a discount on the next edition to people who've helped us with reports for it. Tell us what you think about places already in it, and anything extra you think we should say about them. And send us your ideas for inclusion in the next edition: places to visit, eat at or stay in, attractive drives or walks, maybe even unusual interesting shops you know of. Use the card in the middle, the report forms at the end, or just write – no stamp needed: *The Good Britain Guide*, FREEPOST TN1569, Wadhurst, E Sussex TN5 7BR.

More Specialised Expeditions

To see and do

⊖ANGEL

Camden Passage (Angel tube stn) This and the surrounding streets have a great collection of **antiques shops**, well worth the expedition if that interests you. The nearby Island Queen (Noel Rd) does good food in its bar and upstairs restaurant.

⇌ CHISLEHURST

Chislehurst Caves 📷 (entrance off Caveside Close nr the Olde Stationmaster, B264; nr Chislehurst railway station) Atmospheric 45-min lamplit tours of labyrinthine tunnels and passageways carved out of the rock over 8,000 years. They've been used by flint knappers, druids, and as an air-raid shelter during the war. Longer more adventurous tours on Suns and bank hols at 2.30pm. Snacks (wknds and school hols), shop; cl Mon and Tues (exc school hols); (020) 8467 3264; *£3 (£5 longer tour). The Olde Stationmaster is a good value family food pub.

⊖ COLINDALE

RAF Museum 📷 (Grahame Park Way) The story of flight from early times, with 70 full-size aeroplanes, dramatic simulators (inc one which lets you imagine you're piloting a Red Arrow), films and hands-on exhibits (you can have a go at the controls of a modern jet trainer), lively Battle of Britain Experience, and an interesting examination of the impact of flight on history and politics. There's also an interactive Fun'n'Flight gallery. Excellent for enthusiasts and flying-minded children, and warmly recommended by several of our contributors. Meals, snacks, shop, disabled access; cl 24–26 Dec, 1 Jan; (020) 8205 2266; £7.

⇌ FOREST HILL

Horniman Museum (London Rd) They hope to have completed the redevelopment of this art nouveau building in time for its centenary in November. While they're aiming to stay open through much of the year,

some galleries will obviously be shut to the public as work continues, so best to check what's currently on display before visiting. When it reopens, there will be new, larger galleries showing the eclectic mainly ethnographic collections inc a fine group of mummies and religious artefacts, as well as a new home for the remarkable musical instrument collection (interactive computers allow you to hear what some of the extraordinary instruments sound like). Also lots of stuffed animals, and a very well laid out aquarium/ecosystem. Other improvements will include better disabled access, a new café, and a new entrance to the museum from the delightful gardens (with friendly small farm animals). Children love it, despite the old-fashioned feel; good programme of events. Snacks, some disabled access; cl for up to 8 wks early in 2001, plus every Sun am, and 24–26 Dec; (020) 8699 1872; free.

⊖ HIGHBURY & ISLINGTON

Estorick Collection of Italian Art (Northampton Lodge, 39A Canonbury Sq) This outstanding collection of modern Italian art includes fine futurist works by artists inc Balla and Boccioni, as well as later figurative works by Modigliani and Sironi. Meals, snacks, shop, disabled access; cl Mon, Tues and am Sun; (0171) 704 9522; £3.50.

⇌ KNOCKHOLT

South London walks The south-east fringes of London give way to some surprisingly rural North Downs countryside, still within the London borough of Bromley, around Knockholt, High Elms and Downe; paths are plentiful and well maintained. Only the view over South London from behind Knockholt church shows how close you are to the capital.

⊖ NORTH GREENWICH

Millennium Dome The Dome, in virtually everyone's view, has been a financial disaster, soaking up nearly a billion pounds, which could have been spent much better elsewhere. However, as we made clear before it opened, once so much money had been spent, the people who visited it benefited from taking part in an experience which had been funded by far more than the price of their ticket. Almost everyone we know who has visited the Dome has enjoyed it. So in this sense, and for the large (though of course well below target) numbers of people who have visited it, it has been a qualified success. But at what a price! As we go to press, its future is unclear. It seems to us probable that its future development by commercial interests will ensure that, if and when it reopens in a new guise, it will be very different – and probably well worth a look.

⊖≋PADDINGTON

Alexander Fleming Laboratory Museum (St Mary's Hospital, Praed St) The laboratory in which Alexander Fleming discovered penicillin by chance in 1928 has been reconstructed, and an accompanying display and video tell the story of the bacteriologist and the life-saving antibiotic. Shop; cl pms, all Fri–Sun, bank hols, and Christmas–New Year; (020) 7886 6528; *£2.

⊖SOUTHFIELDS

Wimbledon Lawn Tennis Museum (Church Rd) The only museum of its type in the country, with trophies, pictures and other tennis memorabilia tracing the development of the game through the last century. Also highlights of past Wimbledon Championships, and an interesting display on the changes in tennis fashions. You can see the famous Centre Court outside. Tearoom, shop, disabled access; cl Christmas and every day during the Championship fortnight (unless you've gone to watch the tennis); (020) 8946 6131; £5. If you're in London during the Wimbledon fortnight it's always worth popping along to the club in the early evening around 5.30 or 6 – lots of people leave then and their seats are resold cheaply.

Wimbledon Windmill Museum There's an attractive old core around the common, and a striking **windmill** on Windmill Rd (open pm wknds and bank hols Mar–Oct, or all year by appointment; £1). The common, with its ponds and windmill, is one of the best strolling grounds provided by South London's numerous commons and parks.

⊖ST JOHN'S WOOD

Lord's Tour (St John's Wood Rd) Tours of the famous club and grounds inc the new space-age media centre (if available), the players' dressing room, and the excellent MCC Museum, with an exhaustive collection of cricket memorabilia, inc the Ashes urn and 18th-c paintings of the game. Shop, disabled access to most of the ground; tours daily at 12 and 2pm (and at 10am Apr–Sept) exc during major matches and preparation days; (020) 7432 1033; £6. Down in Aberdeen Pl, Crockers is a remarkably opulent Victorian pub with decent food.

Saatchi Gallery (98 Boundary Rd; nearest tube station Swiss Cottage or St John's Wood) Changing exhibitions of challenging modern art. Shop; open pm only Thurs–Sun; (020) 7328 8299; *£5.

≋TWICKENHAM

Museum of Rugby (Rugby Rd) Combines tours of the 75,000-seat home of rugby union with an excellent museum of related memorabilia under the East Stand; interactive displays and period reconstructions illustrate the game's history, and there's plenty of footage from classic matches. Meals, snacks, shop, disabled access; cl Sun am, all Mon (exc bank hols), 24–26 Dec, Good Fri and a day after match days; four tours a day (only one on Sun), best to book on (020) 8892 8877; £5, £3 for either the museum or tour only.

⊖WALTHAMSTOW CENTRAL

William Morris Gallery (Lloyd Park, Forest Rd) William Morris lived here 1846–1858, and the house has an excellent collection of his work: fabrics, furnishings and wallpaper, much of it still fashionable today. Pre-Raphaelite works upstairs include pictures by Burne-Jones and Rossetti. The attractive grounds are ideal for picnics. Shop, disabled access to ground floor only with prior notice – though this is where the main exhibition is; cl 1–2pm, all day Mon, and Sun (exc first Sun in month), and bank hols; (020) 8527 3782; free.

⊖ WARWICK AVENUE

Puppet Theatre Barge (Little Venice) This wonderful floating puppet theatre is as entertaining for adults as it is for children. It seats 50, and is moored here Nov–May, touring the Thames in the summer. Past productions have ranged from *The Three Little Pigs* to *Macbeth*. Snacks, they can accommodate up to 3 wheelchairs, essential to phone in advance; box office (020) 7249 6876; £6.50.

⇌ WEST DULWICH

Dulwich The village still is villagey, with imposing 18th-c houses, duckpond, good pub (Crown & Greyhound), and an almost rural feel (there's even a toll road). There are good walks, in Dulwich Park (best in rhododendron time), and through Dulwich Wood to adjacent Sydenham Hill Wood – the largest fragment of ancient woodland in inner London, and a most surprising place (just big enough to lose your way in), with woodpeckers among the oak and hornbeam trees. The best of the wood is a nature reserve jealously guarded against developers by the London Wildlife Trust; a trail starts from the Crescent Wood Rd entrance on the Sydenham side.

Dulwich Picture Gallery 🏛 (between College Rd and Gallery Rd) This rather austere brick building, designed by Sir John Soane in 1811, was England's first public gallery when it opened six years later. It's home to an impressive collection of 17th- and 18th-c works by artists inc Rembrandt, Van Dyck and Canaletto. Café, shop, disabled access; cl Mon (exc bank hols) and 25 Dec; (020) 8693 5254; *£4.

Where to eat

Alastair Little *49 Frith St W1* (020) 7734 5183 Unassuming-looking from the outside but with paintings of huge vegetables and fruit on the inside walls, very good Italian-based modern food from a sensibly short menu – plenty of strong flavours – enjoyable puddings, an interesting small wine list, and excellent service; cl Sat am, Sun, bank hols. £40 dinner/£32 lunch

Apprentice *Butlers Wharf Chefs School SE1* (020) 7234 0254 The school is a charitable organisation for hopeful chefs and front-of-house personnel; long, simple restaurant and good value modern meals in an enjoyable atmosphere; wknd courses; cl Sat, Sun, 22 Dec–2 Jan; disabled access. £25|£9

Bank *1 Kingsway WC2* (020) 7234 3344 Very modern restaurant with décor to match (the slanted glass decorations hanging from the ceiling are quite a sight), an open kitchen, and interesting food from a very varied menu (as well as lunch and dinner, they also serve breakfasts, from 7am, pre-theatre meals, and wknd brunches inc a children's menu); cl bank hols; disabled access. £40|£9.50

Bertorelli's *33 Floral St WC2* (020) 7836 3969 Cheerful, simply furnished Italian restaurant and slightly cheaper café, excellent for pre-opera meals (it's opposite the stage entrance to the Royal Opera House), with crisp white-clothed tables, exotic flower arrangements, quite a few mirrors, smiling unflappable service, fairly priced Italian wines, and a long choice of good enjoyable Italian food; cl Sun. £25

Bibendum *Michelin House, 81 Fulham Rd SW3* (020) 7581 5817 Magnificent art deco Michelin building housing a light and spacious restaurant with exceptionally good French-style cooking (more elaborate in the evening), marvellous wine list, and courteous well trained staff; the unpretentious downstairs oyster bar is a fine place for a lighter (and cheaper) meal; cl 24–26 Dec; disabled access. £50

Birdcage *110 Whitfield St W1* (020) 7383 3346 Exotically decorated restaurant with antiques from all over the Far East, 18th-c birdcages from France, and so forth, beautifully prepared and presented food with influences from the Orient, India and Europe, interesting puddings, and an eclectic wine list; cl Sat am, Sun. £26 lunch/£38.50 dinner

Bishop's Finger *9–10 West Smithfield EC1* (020) 7248 2341 Swish little bar-cum-restaurant with fresh flowers on elegant tables set on polished bare boards, comfortably cushioned chairs under a wall lined with prints, distinctive food from an open kitchen, well kept real ales, a wide choice of wines, and friendly service;

upstairs evening bar; cl Sat, Sun, bank hols. £16|£4.95

Blue Elephant *4–6 Fulham Broadway SW6 (020) 7385 6595* Luxurious Thai food among waterfalls and exotic jungle greenery, with produce flown in weekly from Thailand; the set meals are better value; cl Sat am, 24–26 Dec; disabled access. £40|£10

Bluebird Café *350 King's Rd SW3 (020) 7559 1000* Former 1920s garage converted to Gastrodrome with a foodmarket offering all sorts of delicious specialist products (inc ready-made dishes), flower market, wine merchant, kitchenware shop, and private dining club; also huge airy first-floor restaurant with kite-like suspended artwork, dark green limestone floor, stainless steel bar at one end with a shellfish bar the other, open-plan kitchen with big woodburning oven, and good modern British cooking served by friendly staff; pre-theatre meals and wknd brunches; cl 25 Dec; disabled access. £42

Bombay Brasserie *Courtfield Cl SW7 (020) 7370 4040* Grand colonial-style furnishings in big restaurant and conservatory, with very good Indian food using recipes from all over India (lots of vegetarian dishes), and courteous helpful staff; cheaper at lunchtime when there's a buffet; cl 25–27 Dec; children over 10; disabled access. £35/£16.95 buffet lunch

Browns *82–84 St Martin's Lane WC2 (020) 7497 5050* Once the City of Westminster's County Courts, this really spacious bar and restaurant has a good relaxed atmosphere, big mirrors and potted plants, bentwood seats and wooden tables, wall banquettes, panelling, helpful service, and enjoyable good value food; other branches in Bath, Brighton, Cambridge, Edinburgh and Oxford. £25/2 courses £9.95 ☺

Café Fish *36–40 Rupert St W1 (020) 7287 8989* Bustling, well run and very popular fish restaurant, plus a brasserie with light meals; super fresh shellfish and fish, fine French cheeses, good puddings, and a fair wine list. £30|£9

Café in the Crypt *St Martin-in-the-Fields Church WC2 (020) 7930 0089* Popular place under the lovely arches of the church with a relaxed atmosphere, good freshly prepared daily-changing food; shop, free lunchtime concerts, candlelit evening concerts, brass rubbing; cl 25 Dec, Good Fri am. £14

Chez Nico at 90 Park Lane *Grosvenor House Hotel W1 (020) 7409 1290* Comfortable, elegant restaurant serving impeccable food (the set lunch is marvellous value) and fine wines (at a price); cl Sat am, Sun, Christmas and Easter; disabled access. £57/3-course set lunch £40|£10

Christopher's American Grill *18 Wellington St WC2 (020) 7240 4222* Fashionable place in a Victorian building in Covent Garden with high ceilings and rococo décor in first-floor restaurant, ground-floor dining room, and basement Speakeasy Bar; highly enjoyable modern American cooking, cheery speedy service, and lots of American wines; cl Sun pm. £40|£15

Chutney Mary *The Plaza, 535 King's Road SW10 (020) 7351 3113* Very good interesting Anglo-Indian food in light conservatory and two dining rooms, plus a verandah bar, a good choice of drinks, and knowledgeable staff; only set lunch available on Sun; cl pm 25–26 Dec; some disabled access. £37/£12.50 2-course lunch

City Rhodes *The Merchant Centre, 1 New St Sq EC4 (020) 7583 1313* Airy light restaurant serving excellent modern inventive British food, cooked by the well known TV chef and beautifully presented, enjoyable puddings, helpful efficient service, and an interesting if pricey wine list; cl wknds, Christmas, New Year, bank hols; children over 9; disabled access. £70|£10

Clarkes *122–124 Kensington Church St W8 (020) 7221 9225* Consistently excellent British/Mediterranean-style food (no choice at dinner, more informal at lunch) in two quietly decorated rooms, friendly staff, and a good choice of wines; cl am Sat and Sun, 10 days Christmas, 2 wks Aug; disabled access. Set 4-course dinner £44

Cork & Bottle *44–46 Cranbourn St WC2 (020) 7734 7807* Basement wine bar we've liked for over 25 years, nr West End theatres – good food inc interesting salads, cold buffet and unusual hot dishes, excellent wines, and cheerful service; cl 25–26 Dec, 1 Jan. £22.50|£7.50

Eagle *159 Farringdon Rd EC1 (020) 7837 1353* Particularly good Mediterranean-style food in popular stylish pub where open kitchen forms part of the bar, well kept real ales, lots of wine by the glass, properly made cocktails, a lively and chatty atmosphere (lots of young media folk), and simple furnishings; cl Sun pm, bank hols, Easter, 1½ wks Christmas. *£21|£7.50*

Ebury Wine Bar *139 Ebury St SW1 (020) 7730 8206* Said to be London's first wine bar (established 1959) with a loyal following, an excellent list of wines by the glass, and very good modern cooking; they have another bar restaurant called Carriages opposite the Royal Mews in Buckingham Palace Rd, and Joe's Brasserie at 130 Wandsworth Bridge Rd; cl 25–26 Dec, 1 Jan. *£31|£6.50*

Fire Station *150 Waterloo Rd SE1 (020) 7401 3267* Remarkable conversion of a former fire station with two chatty front rooms, plenty of wooden pews, chairs and long tables, some brightly red-painted doors, modern art on the walls, newspapers to read, very good imaginative food, a decent choice of wines, and well kept real ales. *£25/2-course early-bird meals £10.95|£7*

Food For Thought *31 Neal St WC2 (020) 7836 9072* Long-established and consistently good unlicensed vegetarian restaurant with take-away service upstairs and communal eating at long tables downstairs – you can also eat at tables outside; no corkage; cl Sun pm, 24 Dec–1 Jan. *£9.50|£3.90*

Footstool *St John's Church SW1 (020) 7222 2779* Partly no smoking restaurant in the church crypt below the concert hall with plants, pictures and stripped brick, and good food from a monthly-changing menu; lighter lunchtime buffet; cl Sat/Sun am; disabled access. *£22|£6.25*

Fortnum & Mason *181 Piccadilly W1 (020) 7734 8040* Famous store with elegant 4th-floor St James's Restaurant (must book), Fountain Restaurant (ground floor), Patio Restaurant, and Salmon and Champagne bar (mezzanine) doing good breakfasts, morning coffee, lunches, fine afternoon tea and pre-theatre meals; cl Sun, bank hols; disabled access. *£26.20/2-course lunch £16.95*

Gavroche *43 Upper Brook St W1 (020) 7408 0881* This put London on the eating map when it was opened by the Roux brothers 30 years ago; drinks and delicious canapés are served in cosy lounge, and the quietly decorated, club-like restaurant with its pictures and table flowers is in the basement; cooking is exemplary classic French with modern touches (lovely puddings and perfect cheeses, too), service from French staff is attentive and professional, and the wine list is classy but expensive (some wines reach four figures); the set lunch is real value; cl Sat, Sun, 22 Dec. *£110/£43.50 set lunch*

Gay Hussar *2 Greek St W1 (020) 7437 0973* Very long-standing and happily unchanging Hungarian restaurant with bags of atmosphere (downstairs has the most), good generous authentic food, and friendly service; cl Sun, bank hols. *£35|£10*

Gordon Ramsay *68 Royal Hospital Rd SW3 (020) 7352 4441* Ensconced in its smart new premises with highly sophisticated and exciting New French cuisine, all beautifully presented, highly trained French staff, and some very fine French wines (at a price); they now take bookings only up to one month in advance. *£60*

Greenhouse *27a Hays Mews W1 (020) 7499 3331* In a mews hidden away in Mayfair, this upmarket, rather sedate restaurant is loved by long-standing customers, and serves very good value and enjoyable English/Mediterranean food (lovely puddings), and a shortish wine list; cl Sat am, bank hols; disabled access. *£70/2-course lunch £10.50*

Hanover Square Wine Bar *25 Hanover Sq W1 (020) 7408 0935* Under the same enthusiastic ownership as the popular Cork & Bottle in Leicester Sq, this bustling wine bar offers a constantly changing cold buffet plus daily hot dishes and charcoal grills, and a particularly good interesting wine list; cl wknds, bank hols. *£22.50|£7.50*

Kalamares Micro *66 Inverness Mews W2 (020) 7727 5082* (Not to be confused with its larger sister restaurant at No 76). Tiny, close-packed authentically Greek restaurant with very good cheap food and friendly service; unlicensed, take your own wine; cl Sun, am, and bank hols; disabled access. *£18|£6*

Mon Plaisir *19–21 Monmouth St WC2 (020) 7836 7243* Bustling French bistro with super atmosphere, good value well prepared food, decent wines, and friendly staff; cl Sat am, all day Sun, bank hols, Christmas, New Year and Easter; disabled access. £30/popular 2-course pre-theatre meal £11.95

Moro *34–36 Exmouth Market EC1 (020) 7833 8336* Simply decorated restaurant with smart bentwood chairs on bare boards, cream and green walls, side bar with high stools, open-plan kitchen, and thriving atmosphere; interesting modern Spanish cooking with influences from North Africa and the Middle East, nice tapas, a short, thoughtful wine list, and informal but punctilious service; cl Sat am, Sun, 2 wks Christmas; disabled access. £27|£14

Nobu *Metropolitan, 19 Old Park Lane W1 (020) 7447 4747* Chic and very fashionable first-floor restaurant overlooking Hyde Park, with innovative beautifully presented Japanese food touched with South American influences, helpful friendly staff, lots of sakis and good choice of wines; prices can quickly add up; cl bank hols; children over 10. £40/set lunch £23.50

Odéon *65–67 Regent St W1 (020) 7287 1400* Long restaurant reached by a rather fine staircase, with nine big semi-circular windows overlooking Piccadilly Circus, lots of tables and banquettes, a bustling atmosphere, classic French provincial cooking with modern additions, good puddings, light menu in bar, afternoon tea, and a well chosen wine list; pre-theatre meals; cl Sun; disabled access. £36|£15

Odette's *130 Regent's Park Rd NW1 (020) 7586 5486* Smart front dining room with lots of gilded mirrors, airy back conservatory, and slightly cheaper downstairs wine bar with good modern English and more unusual dishes, friendly service, and thoughtful wine list; cl Sun pm, bank hols, 1 wk Christmas. £35/£12.50 3-course set lunch

Oxo Tower Restaurant & Brasserie *Oxo Tower Wharf SE1 (020) 7803 3888* Briskly modern brasserie and restaurant on 8th floor of South Bank redevelopment, light and airy, with busy open kitchen, lots of functional tables and chairs, and promptly served modern English food; what stands out, of course, is the panoramic view over the Thames and City – best in summer from tables on the outside terrace; cl 25–26 Dec; disabled access. Restaurant – £60/3-course lunch £33.75, Brasserie – £40/3-course lunch £20

Poons *27 Lisle St WC2 (020) 7437 4549* Atmospheric unlicensed and unmodernised Chinese restaurant with extremely good value tasty barbecued and wind-dried food; cl Good Fri, 24–26 Dec; late opening Sun till 5.15pm. £15. Other branches (more modern and expensive) at 4 Leicester St WC2 (020) 7437 1528, 50 Woburn Pl, Russell Sq WC1 (020) 7580 1188, and 2 Minster Ct, Mincing Lane EC3 (020) 7626 0126

Quaglino's *16 Bury St SW1 (020) 7930 6767* Fashionable restaurant with big stone staircase to antipasti bar overlooking huge dining room with flamboyantly painted pillars, fine flowers, highly modern attractive furnishings, and buoyant buzzing atmosphere; lovely fresh fish and other modern cooking, good wine list, and efficient service; cl pm 24 Dec, 25 Dec, am 26 and 31 Dec, am 1 Jan; no children in bar in evening; disabled access. £35/£12.50 2 courses

Rain Forest Café *20–24 Shaftesbury Avenue W1 (020) 7434 3111* Exciting big restaurant on three floors with amazing special effects such as mist, wildlife noises, thunder and lightning storms, waterfalls, live tropical parrots and aquariums, animatronic trumpeting elephants, gorillas, fluttering butterflies, life-size splashing crocodile and so forth, and 'jungle-esque'-type food (burgers, pizzas, pasta, sandwiches, salad, and appetizers); cl Christmas. £18.50|£7

Rebato's *169 South Lambeth Rd SW8 (020) 7735 6388* Busy and attractive high-ceilinged bar with friendly barman and waiters, good choice of tapas (plenty of fresh fish), and lots of Spanish wines; also Spanish restaurant; cl Sat am, Sun, bank hols, Christmas. £22.50|£4.50

RSJ *13a Coin St SE1 (020) 7928 4554* Relaxed and friendly restaurant with fine modern British and Mediterranean cooking and exceptional Loire wines in simple surroundings; handy for the South Bank; cl Sat am, Sun. £33/3-course set lunch £16.95

Rules *35 Maiden Lane WC2 (020) 7836 5314* One of London's oldest restaurants, smart and very British, with good English food inc fine seasonal game and oysters; an interesting history; cl 4 days over Christmas; partial disabled access. £45|£16.95

Simpsons in the Strand *100 Strand WC2 (020) 7836 9112* There are two restaurants here: Simply Simpsons upstairs has light pink Adam-style décor, serves contemporary British food, and has a smart casual dress code; downstairs is Grand Divan which is much more formal (jacket and tie), with heavy wooden panelling and ornate plasterwork, a club-like atmosphere, and old-fashioned traditional English cooking inc nursery puddings, and roasts carved as you want them at your table on silver-domed trolleys; cl 25–26 Dec; disabled access in Grand Divan only. £35|£14

Sotheby's Café *34–35 New Bond St W1 (020) 7293 5077* Very small but very classy café with simple high-class food inc lovely puddings and good cheeses, a carefully chosen little wine list, and courteous staff; cl Sat, Sun, 2 wks Aug, Christmas; partial disabled access. £27.50|£9.95

Souk *Litchfield St WC2 (020) 7240 1796* Basement restaurant with Moroccan décor – low vaulted ceilings, drapes, ceramic tiles and mirrors, banquettes with colourful cushions, pouffes, low wooden or brass patterned tables, and dim lighting and candlelight; generous and enjoyable Moroccan food, mint tea, and occasional belly-dancing; cl 25–26 Dec, 1 Jan. £20|£5

Square *6–10 Bruton St W1 (020) 7495 7100* Elegant slightly formal restaurant with bold modern drawings on the walls, well spaced tables on the parquet floor, superb English/French cooking with plenty of strong flavours and beautiful presentation, wonderful puddings, a really fine wine list with quite a few burgundies, and exemplary service; cl Sat and Sun am, 25–26 Dec, 1 Jan; disabled access. £75/2 courses £20

Tante Claire *Wilton Pl, SW1 (020) 7823 2003* Classic French restaurant in a wing of the Berkeley Hotel with fine flower arrangements in elegant dining room, more relaxed at lunchtime when the set menu is very good value – courteous service, and some good value French country wines; jacket and tie required; cl Sat am, Sun, 31 Dec; children over 10; disabled access. £80 dinner/£28 3-course set lunch

Tappit Hen *5 William IV St WC2 (020) 7836 9839* Cosy and atmospheric little wine bar, feeling very old-fashioned, with good snacks and good value wines – more for lunchtimes (when the smoked salmon sandwiches are lovely), though you can book for upstairs in the evening; cl Sat, Sun, bank hols. £20|£8

Turner's *87–89 Walton St SW3 (020) 7584 6711* Most enjoyable, elegantly furnished restaurant owned by (though he does not cook any more) the warmly friendly TV cook Brian Turner; extremely good food based on sound classic French techniques, lovely puddings, and a mainly French wine list; very good value fixed price meals; cl Sun, Christmas, bank hols; no children in evening; disabled access. £35/2-course lunch £15

Wagamama *4 Streatham St WC1 (020) 7580 9365* You will have to queue to get into this trendy, simply furnished Japanese basement restaurant with its long tables and benches for communal eating; very friendly cheerful service, noisy informal atmosphere, good healthy food – raw salads, ramens (huge bowls of noodles with meat, vegetables and Japanese additions), rice dishes, sake, grape and plum wines, beer, and free green tea; exceptionally good value; no smoking; cl 25–26 Dec; several other branches too|£5.80

Zafferano *15 Lowndes St SW1 (020) 7235 5800* Many think this the best Italian restaurant in town – smart but relaxed, with carefully set tables, really first-class food (especially nice – and cheaper – at lunchtime), smart friendly staff, perfect coffees, and a good choice of Italian wines. £21.50 lunch/£35.50 dinner

Special thanks to Paul Kennedy

SCOTLAND

South Scotland includes Edinburgh (a great city for a short break) and Glasgow (lots to see here, too), and many of the most interesting places to visit. It has some charming and very peaceful countryside. A 3-hour drive will get anyone living N of Manchester or York well into South Scotland. Beyond that, you really need a longer stay to make the driving worth while. Rail and air, of course, bring Scotland much closer. The fastest trains do the London–Edinburgh run in around 4 hours.

East Scotland has a marvellous variety of scenery from Highland grandeur to placid lochs and rich valleys, from intimate fishing villages and sandy beaches to rugged cliffs. There's also a great variety of interesting places to visit, and the fastest roads run up this side.

West Scotland is on the whole less populated, with a glorious and intricate series of mountain and coastal landscapes. Its magnificent gardens are at their best in May and June. There are interesting family outings, though not nearly so many as in the South and East. We've defined this area as N of the Clyde and S of the Great Glen, with Loch Lomond marking its E edge.

North Scotland, everything N of the Great Glen, has fewer places to visit (and fewer visitors – part of its charm for many); there is magnificent scenery on the W coast and on Skye, a quieter sandy E coast, and some wild and desolate places in the N.

Outside Edinburgh, Glasgow and areas within easy reach, many places close over winter – and others change to shorter winter opening hours in Sept, rather than Oct (the usual month for a change in England). For the scenery, the best time to visit is May and June, when the days are very long, the weather is generally at least as fine as in high summer, and the roads are not yet clogged by summer crowds.

The Scottish Tourist Board do a card that will save money on autumn flights, trains, accommodation and attractions, as well as getting two-for-one entry to the properties of the National Trust for Scotland (NTS) and Historic Scotland (HS). This second organisation looks after most of the castles and abbeys we list. A good value Explorer ticket admits you free to all their properties, for £12 (3 days), £17 (one wk), or £22 (fortnight); from all HS properties, Tourist Information Centres, or in advance (0131) 668 8800. Accommodation is generally very good value here.

Direct flights connect London and some regional airports with Edinburgh, Glasgow, Inverness and Aberdeen, with some local connections from there.

Please let us know what you think of places in the *Guide*. Use the report forms at the back of the book or simply write us a letter.

South Scotland

Masses to see and do, from the multifarious charms of Edinburgh and Glasgow, to country houses, bustling coastal towns and lovely islands

The great cities of Edinburgh and Glasgow naturally have the most going on here, with the latter's new science centre likely to rival the former's Dynamic Earth for Scotland's most innovative family attraction, when it opens in spring. Edinburgh is a most attractive place – aesthetically and in terms of places to visit (even repeated visits won't exhaust its store of treasures). Here too, you can rediscover the pleasures of walking from place to place. The Festival is in Aug and Sept (when to go if that appeals, a time to avoid otherwise). Glasgow may be more industrialised but is easily Edinburgh's equal when it comes to cultural heritage. Some of the most rewarding museums in Britain are to be found here, while the architectural legacy left by Charles Rennie Mackintosh almost parallels that of Gaudi in Barcelona or Lloyd Wright in Chicago; there are some surprisingly green open spaces, too.

The range of places with real family appeal here is kaleidoscopic, taking in the giant inventors' workshop at Irvine, the jolly puppet shows at Biggar, Galloway Forest Park (numerous possibilities for outdoor pursuits), Largs's lively look at the Vikings, and any of the host of industrial-based museums in the area inc the excellent New Lanark living village, the recently redeveloped Scottish Mining Museum at Newtongrange, the authentic Summerlee Heritage Park at Coatbridge, and the eclectic mix of diversions at the Discover Carmichael Visitor Centre or the open-air museum developed around the preserved Victorian ironworks at Patna, both new to the *Guide* this year. Almond Valley Heritage Centre, Livingston, makes a good value excursion, and there are plenty of chances to handle the exotic animals at the Dalkeith hothouse.

This part of Scotland has an abundance of ancient and evocative castles, romantic ruined abbeys, and some glorious gardens and grand houses. As is often the case, many of the stately homes offer a lot more entertainment (for all ages) than you might expect, such as Bowhill House near Selkirk, Drumlanrig Castle by Thornhill, Culzean Castle (with some of the finest grounds in Britain), and romantic Traquair. The adventure playground at Paxton House was designed by the Territorial Army, and the opulent furnishings at Manderston near Duns have to be seen to be believed. Chatelherault at Ferniegair (another new entry) is a pleasant place to while away a sunny afternoon.

There's a particularly interesting mix of gardens across the region as well, from the splendid specialist examples at Stobo, Port Logan and Edinburgh's Royal Botanic collection to the wheelchair-friendly Greenbank Garden in Glasgow (lots of gardening tips here), or the unique restored Victorian fernery on Bute (also new to the book).

Caerlaverock and North Berwick both have outstanding bird-watching facilities – the latter runs a good value all-in ticket with Scotrail.

The Borders hills are grand and relatively little-visited – peaceful get-away-from-it-all walking. A Freedom of the Fairways tourist board pass covers a round on the finest Borders golf courses. The gentler SW corner is one of Britain's friendliest areas, with relatively few tourists.

Where to stay

AUCHENCAIRN NX8149 **Balcary Bay** *Auchencairn, Castle Douglas, Kirkcudbrightshire DG7 1QZ (01556) 640217* **£108***, plus special breaks; 17 rms with fine views. Once a smugglers' haunt, this charming and much liked hotel has wonderful views over the bay, neat grounds running down to the water, comfortable public rooms (one with log fire), a relaxed friendly atmosphere, good enjoyable food inc super breakfasts, and lots of walks; cl Dec–Feb

BEATTOCK NT0603 **Auchen Castle** *Beattock, Moffat, Dumfriesshire DG10 9SH (01683) 300407* **£80**, plus special breaks; 25 pleasantly decorated rms, some in lodge. Smart but friendly country-house hotel in lovely quiet spot with a trout loch and spectacular hill views, good food, and peaceful comfortable bar

CANONBIE NY3976 **Riverside** *Canonbie, Dumfriesshire DG14 0UX (013873) 71512/71295* **£70**, plus special breaks; 7 chintzy rms, 2 in cottage. Civilised little inn with friendly owners, comfortable communicating bar rooms, open fire, attractive furnishings, good imaginative food with home-made breads and preserves and using top-quality produce, a fine wine list, and marvellous breakfasts; cl 14–28 Feb, 1–14 Nov

CLARENCEFIELD NY0669 **Comlongon Castle** *Clarencefield, Dumfriesshire DG1 4NA (01387) 870283* **£100**; 12 rms. 15th-c castle keep with 18th-c mansion house adjoining – suits of armour and a huge fireplace in oak-panelled great hall, good food in Jacobean dining room, and a relaxing drawing room; dungeons, lofty battlements, archers' quarters and haunted long gallery – candlelit tour before dinner if you like; cl first 2 wks Jan

EDINBURGH NT2573 **Balmoral Hotel** *1 Princes St, Edinburgh EH2 2EQ (0131) 556 2414; (0131) 557 3747* **£217***, plus special breaks; 186 luxurious rms. In city centre and handy for visitor attractions. Splendid Victorian hotel with wonderfully opulent entrance hall, elegant day rooms, lovely flowers, particularly friendly helpful staff, and very good food in several restaurants; excellent leisure facilities; good disabled access

EDINBURGH NT2374 **Channings** *South Learmonth Gdns, Edinburgh EH4 1EZ (0131) 315 2226* **£170**, plus special breaks; 48 individually designed bdrms. Originally five Edwardian town houses and now a stylish hotel on a quiet cobbled street overlooking private gardens; relaxed club-like atmosphere, comfortable lounges with open fires, contemporary wine bar and conservatory, and enjoyable modern Scottish and European food in restful downstairs restaurant

EDINBURGH NT2572 **Elmview** *15 Glengyle Terrace, Edinburgh EH3 9LN (0131) 228 1973* **£80***; 3 large rms. Quietly placed in fine Victorian terrace overlooking a park 15 mins' walk from the castle and centre; elegantly furnished, good breakfast and welcome; no children

EDINBURGH NT2674 **Greenside** *9 Royal Terrace, Edinburgh EH7 5AB (0131) 557 0022* **£80**; 15 individually decorated rms. Family-run hotel in Georgian terrace with friendly atmosphere, big lounge, hearty breakfasts, and quiet terraced garden

EDINBURGH NT2574 **Howard** *34 Great King St, Edinburgh EH3 6QH (0131) 315 2220* **£245***, plus special breaks; 15 luxurious rms. Civilised little 18th-c hotel with comfortable, elegant public rooms, courteous friendly service and good food in fashionable modern basement restaurant; cl 24–28 Dec

EDINBURGH NT2776 **Malmaison** *1 Tower Pl, Leith, Edinburgh EH6 7DB (0131) 555 6868* **£131**, plus special breaks; 60 stylish rms with CD players and satellite TV.

Converted baronial-style seamen's mission in the fashionable docks area of Leith with very good food in the downstairs French brasserie, cheerful café bar, gym, and friendly service; free parking; disabled access

ETTRICK VALLEY NT3018 **Tushielaw** *Ettrick Valley, Selkirk TD7 5HT (01750) 62205* **£48***, plus special breaks; 3 small but well furnished rms. Friendly little inn in lovely spot on Ettrick Water, good imaginative restaurant food, intimate bar, fine views, own loch, and shooting and fishing (as well as bird-watching and walking); cl Mon–Weds Nov–Mar

GATEHOUSE OF FLEET NX6056 **Cally Palace** *Gatehouse of Fleet, Castle Douglas, Kirkcudbrightshire DG7 2DL (01557) 814341* **£148**, plus special breaks; 56 rms. 18th-c country mansion with marble fireplaces and ornate ceilings in the public rooms, relaxed cocktail bar, enjoyable food in elegant dining room (smart dress required), evening pianist and Sat evening dinner dance, helpful friendly staff, 18-hole golf course, croquet and tennis, indoor leisure complex with heated swimming pool, private fishing/boating loch; cl Jan, cl wkdys in Feb; disabled access

GIFFORD NT5367 **Tweeddale Arms** *Gifford, Haddington, East Lothian EH41 4QU (01620) 810240* **£65***, plus special breaks; 16 rms. Civilised old inn in quiet village with comfortable sofas and chairs in tranquil lounge, gracious dining room, wide choice of good daily-changing food, and charming service; disabled access

GLASGOW NS5965 **Babbity Bowster** *16–18 Blackfriars St, Glasgow G1 1PE (0141) 552 5055* **£70**; 6 clean simple rms, showers. Warmly welcoming rather continental place with decent breakfasts (served till late), attractively decorated airy bar, and a cheery first-floor restaurant which hosts a gallery as well as a programme of musical and theatrical events; cl 25 Dec, 1 Jan

GLASGOW NS5865 **Malmaison** *278 West George St, Glasgow G2 4LL (0141) 572 1000* **£105**; 72 smartly quirky very comfortable rms. Stylishly converted Nonconformist church with striking central wrought-iron staircase, a relaxed contemporary atmosphere, friendly young staff, enjoyable French food in attractive brasserie/bar, all-day pizzas and modern Mediterranean food in café-bar, and gym; disabled access

GLASGOW NS5567 **One Devonshire Gardens** *Glasgow G12 0UX (0141) 339 2001* **£199**; 27 huge, opulent rms. Elegant cosseting hotel a little way out from the centre, with luxurious Victorian furnishings, fresh flowers, exemplary staff, and fine modern cooking in the stylish restaurant; disabled access

GULLANE NT4983 **Greywalls** *Duncar Rd, Gullane, East Lothian EH31 2EG (01620) 842144* **£210**, plus special breaks; 23 individually decorated rms. Overlooking Muirfield golf course, this beautiful family-run Lutyens house has antiques, open fires and flowers in its comfortable lounges and panelled library, very good food and fine wines in the restaurant, impeccable service, and lovely garden; cl Nov–Mar; disabled access

INNERLEITHEN NT3336 **Traquair Arms** *Innerleithen, Peeblesshire EH44 6PD (01896) 830229* **£70**, plus special breaks; 10 comfortable rms. Very friendly inn with interesting choice of good food in attractive dining room, cosy lounge bar, friendly service, superb local Traquair ale, and nice breakfasts

LOCKERBIE NY1283 **Dryfesdale Hotel** *Dryfebridge, Lockerbie, Dumfriesshire DG11 2SF (01576) 202427* **£87**, plus wknd breaks; 15 rms, 6 on ground floor. Relaxed and comfortable former manse in five acres, open fire in homely lounge, good food in pleasant restaurant, and lovely surrounding countryside; cl 26 Dec; good disabled access

MAYBOLE NS3103 **Ladyburn** *Kilkerran, Maybole, Ayrshire KA19 7SG (01655) 740585* **£145**, plus special breaks; 5 rms. Quietly set family home in lovely wooded countryside with antiques, books and open fires in comfortable day rooms, and friendly staff; shooting and fishing can be arranged; self-catering flat also; cl 2 wks Nov, 4 wks Jan–Mar; no children

MELROSE NT5433 **Burts** *Market Sq, Melrose, Roxburghshire TD6 9PN (01896) 822285* **£88**, plus special breaks; 20 rms. Welcoming 18th-c family-run hotel in delightfully quiet village, close to abbey ruins; coal fire in bustling bar, residents'

lounge, consistently popular imaginative food, exceptional breakfasts, and a decent wine list; cl 26 Dec

MELROSE NT5434 **Dunfermline House** *Buccleuch St, Melrose, Roxburghshire TD6 9LB (01896) 822148* **£46***, plus special breaks; 5 rms. Neatly kept Victorian terraced house nr abbey ruins, with good breakfasts and friendly owners

MINNIGAFF NX4165 **Creebridge House** *Creebridge, Newton Stewart, Wigtownshire DG8 6NP (01671) 402121* **£98***; 19 rms. Attractive country-house hotel in three acres of gardens with relaxed friendly atmosphere, open fire in comfortable drawing room, cheerful bar, and big choice of delicious food inc fine local fish and seafood; disabled access; cl 24–26 Dec

NENTHORN NT6938 **Whitehill Farm** *Nenthorn, Kelso, Roxburghshire TD5 7RZ (01573) 470203* **£46**; 4 rms, 3 with shared bthrm. Comfortable farmhouse on mixed farm with fine views, big garden, log fire in sitting room, and good home cooking; cl Christmas and New Year

PEEBLES NT2344 **Cringletie House** *Cringletie, Peebles EH45 8PL (01721) 730233* **£180**, plus special breaks; 14 pretty rms. Surrounded by 28 acres of garden and woodland and with fine views, very welcoming quiet turreted baronial mansion, delicious food using home-grown vegetables, extensive Scottish breakfasts, and excellent service

PORTPATRICK NW9954 **Crown** *Portpatrick, Stranraer, Wigtownshire DG9 8SX (01776) 810261* **£72**; 12 attractive rms. Atmospheric harbourside inn with rambling and interestingly furnished old-fashioned bar, airy art deco dining room, good food with an emphasis on local seafood, excellent breakfasts, and carefully chosen wines

PORTPATRICK NX0252 **Knockinaam Lodge** *Portpatrick, Stranraer, Wigtownshire DG9 9AD (01776) 810471* **£160** inc dinner, plus special breaks; 10 individual rms. Lovely very neatly kept little hotel with comfortable pretty rooms, open fires, wonderful food, and friendly caring service; dramatic surroundings, with lots of fine cliff walks; children over 12 in evening restaurant (high tea at 6); disabled access except in dining room

QUOTHQUAN NT0140 **Shieldhill** *Quothquan, Biggar, Lanarkshire ML12 6NA (01899) 220035* **£134**, plus special breaks; 16 pretty rms. Partly 12th-c castle in fine setting with comfortable oak-panelled lounge, open fires, library, particularly good food in no smoking restaurant, and warm friendly service

SWINTON NT8347 **Wheatsheaf** *Main St, Swinton, Duns, Berwickshire TD11 3JJ (01890) 860257* **£76***, plus special breaks; 6 rms with baths or showers. Warmly friendly inn with exceptionally good food, a pleasantly decorated and relaxed main lounge plus small pubby area, separate locals' bar, and no smoking front conservatory; garden play area for children; cl 25 Dec and first wk Jan

TURNBERRY NS2005 **Turnberry Hotel** *Turnberry, Girvan, Ayrshire KA26 9LT (01655) 331000* **£310**, plus winter breaks; 132 stylish and comfortable rms. Grand Edwardian country house in spectacular 360-acre coastal setting with two championship golf courses ranked among the world's best. Elegant reception rooms, quite a choice of places to eat inc very good restaurant using tip-top local produce – and plenty of sporting activities: 12-hole pitch and putt (plus the two 18-hole golf courses), indoor swimming pool, health spa, gym, sauna, solarium, squash, and tennis courts; disabled access; cl two wks at Christmas

UPHALL NT0571 **Houstoun House** *Uphall, Broxburn, West Lothian EH52 6JS (01506) 853831* **£139**, plus wknd breaks; 72 comfortable rms, 26 in new extension. 17th-c house divided into three distinct buildings: fine food in three panelled dining rooms, vaulted bars (one with a fire nearly all year), quiet lounge, lovely grounds, and leisure complex with swimming pool, sauna, gym, tennis courts and bistro; disabled access

To see and do

ALLOWAY NS3318

Burns National Heritage Park 🖼️£
A key stop on the Burns Trail: the poet was born here in 1759. The associated local sites are grouped together under the above name. The introductory visitor centre the **Tam O'Shanter Experience** (Murdochs Lane) is a multi-media show bringing Burns's famous poem vividly to life. Up the road you can explore the tiny rooms of the poet's birthplace, thatched Burns Cottage, and there's an adjacent museum of his life, with a good collection of manuscripts and letters. In the other direction, S of the centre, **Burns Monument** was built in 1823 to a fine design by Thomas Hamilton Jr, and is adorned with characters from Burns's poems sculpted by James Thorn. Meals, snacks, shop, disabled access; cl 25–26 Dec, 1–2 Jan; (01292) 443700; *£4.50 for all three sites

ARRAN NS0037
This island is just under an hour by ferry from Ardrossan, a popular public-transport day trip from Glasgow, with summer ferries from Claonaig on Kintyre too; (01475) 650100 for ferry enquiries. It has a marvellous variety of scenery from subtropical gardens to mountain deer forest – and highly regarded (and beautifully set) golf courses. Brodick the main settlement has several places to hire bikes. The Kingsley on Brodick esplanade has decent home cooking, and the Ormidale Hotel has good value food. On the opposite side of the island nr Machrie are several intriguing Bronze Age stone circles. Arran has a good circular walk up and down Goatfell, prominent for miles around, and you can follow the shore right around the N tip, the Cock of Arran. Up near here the waterside Catacol Hotel has decent food. There's a good walk on the W coast, from Blackwaterfoot to the King's Cave, which supposedly sheltered Robert the Bruce.
Arran Brewery With machinery from Jersey and hops from Hereford, one man (originally from High Wycombe) made it his mission to set up the island's first brewery. The result is this

attractive new building, set in the shadow of Brodick Castle (see below), with rewarding views over Brodick Bay and Goatfell Mountain. A viewing gallery in the visitor centre looks over the microbrewery itself, and you can sample some of the beers you've watched being made. Shop, reasonable disabled access; cl Thurs–Sun pm and all day Mon–Weds Dec–Jan; (01770) 302353; *£3.50.
Brodick Castle and Garden Fine old castle, in lovely surroundings between the sea, hills and majestic mountain of Goatfell. Partly 13th-c, and extended in 1652 and 1844, it's very fierce-looking from the outside, but comfortably grand inside – even a little homely in places. There are almost a hundred antlered heads on the walls of the main staircase. It's surrounded by magnificent formal gardens, with the highlight the woodland garden started in 1923 by the Duchess of Montrose, inc many lovely rare and tender rhododendrons. Meals, snacks, shop, limited disabled access; castle cl Nov–Mar, garden and country park open all year; (01770) 302202; £6; NTS.
BALCARY POINT NX8149
On the W side of sandy Auchencairn Bay, this makes for a good peaceful walk from the pretty village of Auchencairn. The Balcary Bay Hotel has good bar food, and lovely views from its terraces.
BALERNO NT1666
Malleny House Garden (off A70) Charming gardens that are home to a national collection of 19th-c shrub roses (best in late Jun), as well as four clipped old yew trees – the survivors of a dozen planted in 1603. Limited disabled access; (0131) 449 2283; around £2; NTS. The handsome Johnsburn House Hotel does good lunches.
BATHGATE NS9970
Cairnpapple Hill (just E of Torpichen, off B792) One of the most important prehistoric sites in the country, a stone circle and series of successive burial cairns that seems to have been used for around 3,000 years from neolithic times to the 1st c BC, and esp during the second millennium BC. Extraordinary

views from this raw and atmospheric hilltop site, known locally as 'windy ways'.

BEARSDEN NS5472

Roman Bath House (Roman Rd) Probably the best surviving visible Roman building in Scotland, built in the 2nd c for the garrison at Bearsden Fort, part of the Antonine Wall defences; free. The appropriately named 55BC (Drymen Rd) has decent food, as does the Beefeater (Station Rd).

BIGGAR NT0437

Several good museums here

Gasworks 🏛 (Gasworks Rd) This striking old building is now a museum on the coal-gas industry (disabled access, open pm Jun–Sept; £1).

Gladstone Court Museum 🏛 (North Back Rd) Houses an entire reconstructed village street (cl Sun am, and all mid-Oct–Easter; £2).

Greenhills Covenanters House 🏛 (North Back Rd) 17th-c farmhouse originally at Wiston but moved piece by piece and reassembled here; cl am, and all Oct–May; £1.

Moat Park Heritage Centre 🏛 Good local history collections, and the centre piece of the town's several worthwhile museums (shop, disabled access, cl Sun am, and all mid-Oct–Easter; £2).

Puppet Theatre (just off A702) Very jolly; when they're not doing shows they sometimes do backstage tours. Teas, shop, disabled access (phone first – they have to remove some seats in the theatre); cl 25 Dec, 1 Jan, and maybe winter Sun; (01899) 220631 for programme and booking; shows £5.

BLANTYRE NS6958

David Livingstone Centre (Station Rd, off A724) The birthplace of the famous explorer, with a museum on his life and work. An African Pavilion looks at the continent today, with contemporary crafts, and there's an adventure playground in the landscaped grounds. Meals, snacks, shop, some disabled access; cl Sun am, and 2 wks over Christmas and New Year; (01698) 823140; £3. The Cricklewood at Bothwell (B7071) is a good dining pub.

CAERLAVEROCK NY0265

Caerlaverock Castle 13th-c, protected not just by its moat but by

the wild swampy marshes around it, it has an unusual triangular inner courtyard, and elaborate projecting tops for dropping missiles on assailants. Snacks, shop, some disabled access; cl 25–26 Dec, 1–2 Jan; (01387) 770244; £2.80.

Wildfowl & Wetlands Trust The Caerlaverock salt marshes are a reserve with outstanding hide facilities and observation towers. Countless wildfowl flock here, especially barnacle geese; between Oct and Apr there are generally around 13,000 of them, very dramatic when they're all in flight. Snacks, shop, some disabled access; cl 25 Dec; (01387) 770200; £3.50 – discounts if you turn up by bike, foot or public transport. The Nith at Glencaple has good value food.

CARDONESS NX5955

Cardoness Castle (A75) Well preserved 15th-c four-storey tower house, overlooking the Water of Fleet; interesting fireplaces. Shop; cl winter wkdys; (01557) 814427; £2. A mile NE, Gatehouse of Fleet has places to eat.

CARMICHAEL NS9338

Discover Carmichael Visitor Centre (A73 N of Biggar) Among the eclectic attractions here are a collection of waxwork models of Scotland's heroes and heroines, various period re-creations inc a Victorian wash-house, a baby animal farm, free horse and cart rides, and an exhibition on wind energy, all within the attractive grounds of the Carmichael Estate. Also indoor and outdoor adventure play areas, and a deer park walk; meals, snacks, shop, disabled access; cl Jan–Mar; (01899) 308169; £2.95.

CASTLE DOUGLAS NX7462

Threave Castle (off minor road Bridge of Dee–Townhead) The Black Douglas, Archibald the Grim, built this in the 14th c; four storeys high, it stands on an islet in the River Dee and you have to get a ferry across (ring the bell and the custodian will come to get you). Shop; cl Oct–Mar (though possibly open in Oct); (0131) 668 8800; £2 inc ferry; HS.

Threave Garden (1m W off A75) The National Trust for Scotland's horticulture school, with plenty to see throughout the year in its walled garden and glasshouses. If you're there in spring, don't miss the massed display of over 200 varieties of daffodil. Meals, snacks, shop, some disabled access; visitor centre cl Nov–Mar; (01556) 502575; £4.50; NTS. The Royal Hotel has good value food.

CLARENCEFIELD NY0669

Comlongon Castle (B725) 15th-c, unusually well preserved, with interesting original features inc dungeons, kitchen, great hall and even privies. Usually open 9am–3pm, but best to phone before visiting; (01387) 870283; *£3.

COATBRIDGE NS7265

Summerlee Heritage Park (off W Canal St) Ambitious centre looking at the local iron, steel and engineering industries. Lots going on, spread over 25 acres of a former iron works; the din from the working machines creates a real feeling of authenticity. Snacks, shop; cl Nov–Apr; (01236) 431261; free (tram 60p).

Time Capsule (Buchanan St) Fun – swimming pools and leisure centre with a loose historic theme: water chutes whizz you through the origins of man, and a woolly mammoth holds court in the centre of the ice rink; (01236) 449572.

CRAMOND NT1877

Charming preserved former fishing village, the once-humble cottages now snapped up by Edinburgh's professionals.

Lauriston Castle Interesting, with mostly Edwardian décor and antiques; shop, disabled access; cl 1–2pm, Fri, wkdys Nov–Mar, 25–26 Dec, and 1–2 Jan; (0131) 336 2060; £4.50.

River Almond walk W of Edinburgh, from the Cramond Brig Hotel on the A90, you can walk along the wooded valley to Cramond, cross the Almond by ferry, then go along the shore past Dalmeny House, and finish below the Forth Bridge at South Queensferry. There are frequent buses back to the start, and to Edinburgh.

CREETOWN NX4759

Gem Rock Museum 🖼 (Chain Rd) Enormous private collection of gem stones and minerals, some displayed in an atmospheric crystal cave. Also a fossilised dinosaur egg. Snacks, shop,

disabled access; cl wkdys Dec and Feb, 23 Dec–Jan; (01671) 820357; *£2.90.

CULZEAN NS2310

Culzean Castle (pronounced 'Cullane') A day here is one of the most popular outings in the region. The 18th-c mansion is one of great presence and brilliance, and the 563 acres of grounds are among the finest in Britain, lushly planted and richly ornamental, with woods, lake, an abundance of paths, bracing clifftop and shoreline walks, and an 18th-c walled garden. The house was splendidly refashioned by Robert Adam, and has been well restored to show off his work to full effect. Meals, snacks, shop, disabled access; house open Apr–Oct, and possibly some winter wknds, park open all year; (01655) 884455; £8 park and castle, £3.50 park only; NTS. You can stay in rather smart self-contained apartments on the top floor.

DALKEITH NT3167

Edinburgh Butterfly & Insect World 🖼 (Dobbies Nursery, off A720 at Gilmerton junction) Gloriously coloured exotic butterflies, as well as scorpions and tarantulas, bee garden, and rainforest frogs. Handling sessions mean you can get even closer to some of the animals. Meals, snacks, shop, disabled access; cl 25–26 Dec, 1–2 Jan; (0131) 663 4932; £4.25. The Sun (Lothianbridge – A7 S) has good value food.

DIRLETON NT5184

Dirleton Castle (A198) Grandly rebuilt after a siege in 1298, only to be destroyed again in 1650. It has a charming garden planted in the 16th c, with ancient yews and hedges around a bowling green. Cl 25–26 Dec, 1–2 Jan; (01620) 850330; £2.50. The Castle Hotel and Open Arms in this pleasant golfing village are both good for lunch.

DRYBURGH NT5932

Dryburgh Abbey Remarkably complete ruins in a lovely setting among old cedars by the River Tweed – its graceful cloisters are very peaceful. Walter Scott is buried here (and on the B6356 N the signposted Scott's View is idyllic). Shop, some disabled access; cl Sun am in winter, 25–26 Dec, 1–2 Jan; (01835) 822381; £2.50. The Buccleuch Arms at St Boswells is a civilised place for something to eat.

DUMBARTON NS4074

Dumbarton Castle 🏰 (A82, Dumbarton) Perched on a rock 73 metres (240 ft) above the River Clyde, with dramatic views of the surrounding countryside. Most of what can be seen dates from the 18th and 19th c, though there are some earlier remains. Snacks, shop; cl Oct–Apr; (01389) 732167; £2. The Ettrick in the picturesque Clydeside village of Old Kilpatrick has good value food.

DUMFRIES NX9775

Another place with close Burns connections. The Globe Tavern (off High St) has two rooms still very much as they were when this was his regular haunt (Anna Park, a barmaid, bore his child).

Burns House (Burns St) Where he lived for the three years before his death; has original letters and manuscripts along with the chair in which he wrote his last poems and songs. Shop; Sun am (all day in winter), winter lunchtimes and winter Mon, 25–26 Dec, 1–2 Jan; (01387) 255297; free.

Burns Mausoleum (St Michael's churchyard) The tomb of Robert Burns, his on-and-off wife Jean Armour, and their five sons; you can usually make an appointment to visit at the Burns House.

Museum and Camera Obscura 🏰 (Church St) In the tower of an 18th-c windmill, this has a camera obscura and local history. Shop, limited disabled access; cl 1–2pm, all day Sun and Mon Oct–Mar, plus am summer Sun, and all 25–26 Dec, 1–2 Jan; (01387) 253374; museum free, camera obscura £1.50.

Robert Burns Centre (Mill Rd) Exhibition and audio-visual display, as well as an interesting scale model of the town at the time he wrote. Meals, snacks, shop, disabled access; cl 1–2pm winter, Sun am (all day in winter), and winter Mons, 25–26 Dec, 1–2 Jan; (01387) 264808; £1.50 for audio-visual exhibition.

DUNBAR NT6779

The harbour here is pretty, with some picturesquely jagged fragments of the medieval castle in the John Muir Country Park, and good walks nearby,

along the cliffs and by the marshy inlets of Belhaven Bay; the harbourside Starfish has good seafood. Quite a few good clean beaches near here, notably Belhaven, nearby Whitesands Bay, and the one at Thorntonloch a few miles down the coast.

DUNDRENNAN NX7547

Dundrennan Abbey (A711) Ruined Cistercian abbey famous as the place Mary, Queen of Scots is thought to have spent her last night in Scotland. Cl Sun am, winter wkdys; (01557) 500262; £1.80.

DUNS NT8054

Edin's Hall Broch Off the A6112 from Duns, this is one of very few such Iron Age strongholds in the Lowlands.

Manderston 🏰 (2m E, off A6105) Splendidly lavish house built for the plutocrat racecourse owner Sir James Miller; he told the architect to spare no expense, so ended up with the world's only silver staircase. Other gloriously extravagant parts are the painted ceilings, and a ballroom decorated in Miller's racing colours. Also fine formal gardens, and an unusual biscuit-tin museum. Teas, shop, limited disabled access; open pm Thurs and Sun mid-May–Sept, and bank hol Mon pm; (01361) 883450; £6, £3.50 grounds only. The Wheatsheaf at Swinton isn't far, for a very good meal.

EAST FORTUNE NT5578

Museum of Flight (East Fortune Airfield, B1347) Good range of aircraft, with 40 aeroplanes from a Spitfire to a Vulcan bomber, and displays on famous flyers and air traffic control. Café, shop, disabled access; cl 25, 31 Dec, 1 Jan; (01620) 880308; £3.

EAST LINTON NT5875

Hailes Castle (minor road SW) Another brief stopping point for Mary, Queen of Scots, now in ruins, but lovely in spring, with wild flowers along the stream; free.

Preston Mill (B1407) One of the oldest working water-driven oatmeal mills left. It's a pretty spot with geese and ducks, and an old dovecote nearby. Shop, limited disabled access; cl 1–2pm, Sun am, wknd ams in Oct, all Nov–May; (01620) 860426; £2.50; NTS. The atmospheric and genuinely pubby Drovers Inn has good food.

EDINBURGH NT2573

Edinburgh is a city of great visual appeal, with lots of interesting places within a pleasant walk of each other; the Festival is in August, with great music and dance and a fun Fringe (but pretty dire drama these days). This is one of Britain's most rewarding cities for visitors, whether you've been dozens of times before or are popping in for the first time. It's dominated by the ancient silhouettes of Edinburgh Castle on its castle cliff and of the long erratic line of tall, thin Old Town buildings stretched along beside it. Up here narrow streets and alleys with steep steps between them and courtyard closes leading off have a real flavour of the distant past, with a good many interesting ancient buildings (and a lot of the city's antiquarian bookshops and other interesting specialist shops). When the authorities decided to redevelop the city in the 18th c, they did it not by knocking down the medieval buildings, but instead by creating an entirely new part of the city, working from scratch. The resulting New Town is a masterpiece of spacious Georgian town planning, stretching out handsomely below the steep crag of Castle Rock and its medieval skyline. As in most cities, there's a hop-on hop-off tour bus, and the ticket gives discounts to some of the places to visit. Walking tours in the evenings are often led by students, and the literary pub tour is particularly good fun; (0131) 226665; £7. The regular bus services have good value daily and weekly passes, and it is worth getting used to the public transport: the city council plans to introduce a radical road-pricing scheme to ease congestion and cut pollution. Edinburgh does put on its best clothes and best events for its Festival; it's easier to see, and truer to itself, at other times of year. If you do visit the Festival, make sure you've got accommodation sorted out well in advance. Edinburgh's pubs and bars are a special delight, chatty places often of great character. Among the best for atmosphere are the Bow Bar (Victoria St), Bannermans Bar (Cowgate), Bennets Bar (Leven St), Café Royal and Guildford Arms (both W Register St), Cumberland (Cumberland St), Athletic Arms (Angle Park Terrace/Kilmarnock Rd), Kays Bar (Jamaica St W) and Milnes (Rose St); for food too, the Abbotsford, Kenilworth and Milnes (all Rose St), Dome (George St), Starbank (Laverockbank Rd), Golf Tavern (Wrights Houses), Braidwoods (West Port) and both Kings Wark and Ship on the Shore (The Shore, Leith). The corner lobby bar of the Balmoral Hotel is a relaxing spot at the hub of the town. For a fuller meal, the city has a remarkable number of good value bistro-style restaurants (as well as the places we mention in the **Where to eat** section). There are lots of good shops dotted around town, especially on or near **Princes St** – its tall, mainly Georgian buildings lining just the one side, giving an expansive view across the sunken gardens to the castle. Parallel is **George St**, with some superior shops, while Rose St, an alley between the two, has plenty of pubs and cafés. More bars around the **Grassmarket** and **Lawnmarket**, a lively area of the Old Town; Victoria St here has interesting shops, notably that of Ian Mellis, who specialises in Scottish, Irish and English farm cheeses. Valvona & Crolla on Elm Row is a dazzling delicatessen.

Arthur's Seat Out beyond Holyrood in Holyrood Park is this saddle-back mountain, a great volcanic mass giving a wonderful panorama over the city, and a pleasant place for wandering, with a hill fort on top and the largely unspoilt Duddingston village below it (the Sheep Heid here is a good pub).

Blackford Hill Virtually a mountain within the city, gives great views.

Calton Hill Dominating the E end of Princes St, with magnificent views over the city. An unusual sight up here is a romantic Doric colonnade, intended to be a full replica of the Parthenon (until the money ran out).

Clan Tartan Centre (Leith Mills, Bangor Rd) Displays of various clans and their costume, computers that allow you to trace your own Scottish heritage, and a factory shop with good value Pringle knitwear and tweeds. Meals, snacks, shop, disabled access; cl 25 Dec, 1 Jan; (0131) 553 5161; free.

Dynamic Earth (Holyrood Rd) This exemplary exhibition shows the story

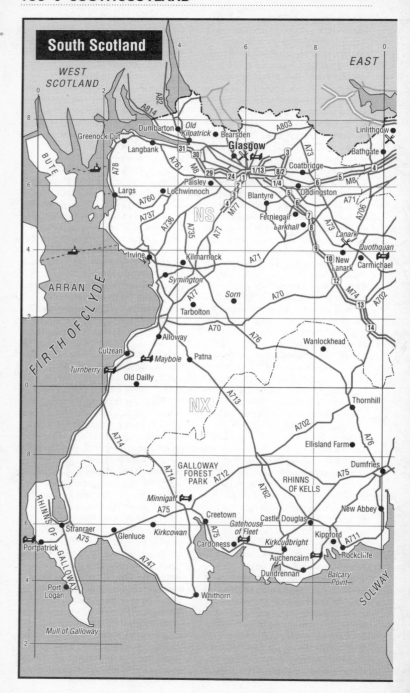

South Scotland

WEST SCOTLAND

EAST

BUTE

ARRAN

FIRTH OF CLYDE

RHINNS OF GALLOWAY

SOLWAY

Greenock Cut
Langbank
Dumbarton
Old Kilpatrick
Bearsden
Linlithgow
Glasgow
Bathgate
A803
A73
Coatbridge
Paisley
Largs
Lochwinnoch
Uddingston
M8
A71
A706
Blantyre
Ferniegair
Larkhall
Lanark
Quothquan
Kilmarnock
New Lanark
Carmichael
Irvine
Symington
Sorn
Tarbolton
A70
A76
Alloway
Wanlockhead
Culzean
Maybole
Patna
Turnberry
Old Dailly
Thornhill
A713
Ellisland Farm
Dumfries
GALLOWAY FOREST PARK
RHINNS OF KELLS
New Abbey
Minnigaff
A75
Creetown
Castle Douglas
Kippford
Stranraer
Glenluce
Kirkcowan
Gatehouse of Fleet
Kirkcudbright
Rockcliffe
Portpatrick
Cardoness
Auchencairn
Dundrennan
Balcary Point
Port Logan
Whithorn
Mull of Galloway

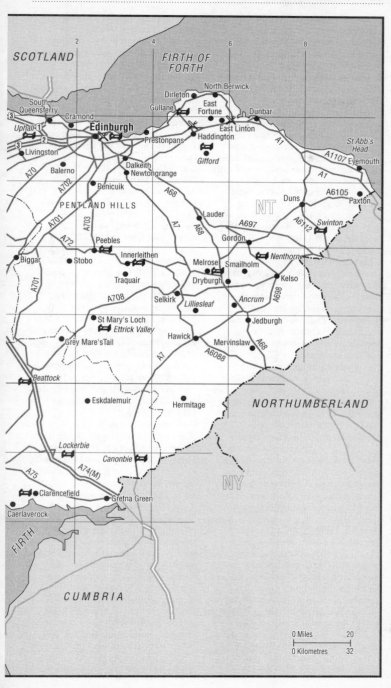

of the planet using hi-tech effects and state-of-the-art displays. It vividly relates the story of evolution using giant screens, dramatic sounds and commentary, and evocative smells, spread over eleven hugely different and often quite spectacular display areas. You can see a volcano erupt, experience an earthquake, watch animals swinging through trees in the rainforest, and take a helicopter flight over the glaciers of Scandinavia. The finale is a colourful film taking in images of storms, hurricanes, and sunsets, with a serious environmental message of course – but hearing it has rarely been so much fun; play area for younger children. Meals, snacks, shop, disabled access; cl Mon and Tues between Nov and Mar, and 25 Dec; (0131) 550 7800; £6.95 (£3.95 children).

Edinburgh Castle Perched on its hill above the city, this is a place of great magnetism; it's been a fortress since at least the 7th c, and excavations show there's been a settlement here for 4,000 years. The oldest building today is the beautiful St Margaret's Chapel, thought to have been built in the 12th c and little changed since. Other highlights include the apartments of Mary, Queen of Scots, Mons Meg (the 15th-c Belgian cannon with which James II cowed the Black Douglases), the Scottish Crown Jewels (centuries older than the English ones), and for romantics the Stone of Destiny or Scottish coronation stone. Glorious views from the battlements, over the Firth of Forth to Fife beyond. You can wander around on your own, but the official guides are a great bonus – they leave from the drawbridge, several times a day. Meals, snacks, shop, mostly disabled access; cl 25–26 Dec and possibly New Year, phone to check; (0131) 225 9846; £7 (inc audio tour). If you're around at lunchtime, look (and listen) for the firing of the One o'Clock Gun from the parapet.

Edinburgh Zoo (Corstorphine Rd; A8 W) Best known for its Penguin Parade every afternoon at 2pm (Apr–Oct) which as we were going to press had been put on hold – by the penguins themselves; some experts believe the birds weren't just sulking but suffering from the lingering effects of avian malaria. There are plenty of other rare and odd-looking animals around the attractive grounds. Children enjoy the yew-hedge maze loosely themed around Darwin's theory of evolution; it has several fountains along the way that periodically shoot out jets of water (summer only). Extra events and activities in summer hols. Meals, snacks, shops (special penguin and polar bear shops in summer), disabled access (though a little hilly); open every day (inc 25 Dec); (0131) 334 9171; £7.

Georgian House (Charlotte Sq) Archetypal period house, part of Robert Adam's magnificent terrace along the N side. The rooms and servants' quarters have been refurbished in the style of 1800. Shop, disabled access to ground floor only; cl Sun am, and Nov–Mar; (0131) 225 2160; £5; NTS. Close by, nr Queen St, beyond a further strip of gardens, is another Georgian area with some interesting shops. Hoggs in the alley behind stately Great King St has a wide choice of malt whiskies at low prices.

Nelson Monument (Calton Hill) Best of all for the views of Edinburgh – if you can face the 31-metre (102-ft) climb to the top. Every day at 1pm (exc Sun) the time ball drops as the gun at the castle goes off. Shop; cl Mon am, and Sun; (0131) 556 2716; £2.

Palace of Holyroodhouse (Canongate) Imposing yet human-scale palace with its origins in the Abbey of Holyrood, founded by David I. Later the court of Mary, Queen of Scots, it was used by Bonnie Prince Charlie during his occupation of Edinburgh, and is still a Royal residence for part of the year. The oldest surviving part is James IV's tower, with Queen Mary's rooms on the second floor, where a plaque on the floor marks where her secretary Rizzio was murdered in front of her. The throne room and state rooms have period furniture, tapestries and paintings from the Royal Collection. Much more inviting than many English palaces, and in the last few years they've really improved visitor facilities. The palace gardens are open Apr–Oct. Directly opposite, construction work continues on the space-age home for the new Scottish Parliament. Shop, limited disabled access by prior arrangement; cl Good Fri, 25–26 Dec, and occasional other dates (if the Queen is in residence for example) – best to check first on (0131) 556 1096; £6.

Royal Botanic Garden (Inverleith Row) Founded as a physic garden in 1670 at Holyrood and then transplanted here (just N of the centre) in the early 19th c. Covering 72 acres, it has various splendid themed areas, with a woodland garden, peat garden, arboretum, Chinese collection and the Glasshouse Experience, inc palm houses, fern house and aquatic house. Guided tours leave from inside the West Gate at 11am and 2pm Apr–Sept. Meals, snacks, shop, disabled access; cl 25 Dec, 1 Jan; (0131) 552 7171; free (tours £2).

Royal Mile Between castle and palace (for most people Edinburgh's two must-sees) is this largely medieval street, around which you'll find all sorts of interesting or historic houses and features, and quaint lanes leading off in all directions. The next ten places (down to Huntly House) are listed in order, as you go down the Mile towards Holyrood. Usefully, it's punctuated with cafés and bars in which to stop and work out your next move, starting with the old-world Ensign Ewart on the left as you leave the castle.

Camera Obscura (Castlehill) Up at the top of the Royal Mile, these 19th-c revolving lenses and mirrors create unique panoramas of the city as soon as the lights go down, with a good commentary; best on a sunny day. Shop; cl 25 Dec; (0131) 226 3709; £4.25.

Scotch Whisky Heritage Centre (Castlehill) Entertainingly illustrates the story of the national drink, starting off with a shortish journey in a barrel-shaped car through well put together sets and tableaux. The full tour is a useful introduction to the distilling process; if you haven't been to a real distillery it's a good substitute, and there's a decent sample and well stocked shop at the end. Meals, snacks, disabled access; cl 25 Dec; (0131) 220 0441; £5.50.

Gladstone's Land (Lawnmarket) Six-storeyed early 17th-c building, still with its arcaded front, and refurnished in period style. The walls and ceilings have remarkable tempera paintings. Shop; cl Sun am, and Nov–Mar; (0131) 226 5856; £3; NTS.

Lady Stair's House (Lady Stair's Close, off Lawnmarket) Named after its 18th-c occupant, this 17th-c building houses the **Writers' Museum**, a collection of manuscripts and objects associated with Robert Burns, Walter Scott and R L Stevenson. Shop; cl Sun exc pm during Festival, 25–26 Dec, 1–2 Jan; (0131) 529 4901; free.

St Giles Cathedral (High St) The Royal Mile widens out briefly around Scotland's High Kirk, the city's most impressive ecclesiastical building, mainly 15th-c, but dating from around 1120. Topped with an ornate crown-like tower, it has monuments to famous Scots from Knox (minister here until his death) to R L Stevenson.

Parliament House (Parliament Sq) Just behind the cathedral, this was the seat of Scottish government until the Union of 1707, and now houses the supreme law courts of Scotland. Don't miss the fine hammerbeam roof in the Hall. Snacks, some disabled access; cl 1–2pm and wknds; (0131) 225 2595; free.

John Knox House (High St) The oldest house on the Royal Mile, where the great reformer is supposed to have died. Now looking every bit of its 500 years, it still has its original timber galleries, oak panelling and splendid painted ceiling. Snacks, shop; cl Sun (exc pms July–Aug), 25–26 Dec; (0131) 556 9579; £2.50.

Museum of Childhood (High St) The first of its type and still one of the best, a charming collection of games, toys and dolls from all over the globe. Shop, some disabled access; cl Sun (exc pm during Festival and July–Aug); (0131) 529 4142; free.

Canongate Tolbooth (Canongate) This elaborate building houses an excellent social history exhibition, the People's Story, with reconstructions built very much around first-hand accounts of Edinburgh life. Shop, disabled access; cl Sun (exc pm during Festival), 25–26 Dec, 1 Jan; (0131) 529

4057; free.

Huntly House (Canongate) 16th-c, housing Edinburgh's main local history museum, with all the exhibits thoughtfully – even artistically – arranged. Shop; cl Sun (exc pm during Festival), cl 25–26 Dec, 1–2 Jan; (0131) 529 4143; free. The Canons Gait nearby is a smart bar.

Royal Museum (Chambers St) A tremendous variety of collections, covering virtually anything you might care to poke around in, now shared between a gloriously light and spacious Victorian building, and its grand new counterpart next door. Children enjoy its intricate working scale models of early engines, but it has something for everyone. Meals, snacks, shop, disabled access; cl Sun am and 25 Dec; (0131) 225 7534; £3 (children free).

Royal Observatory (Blackford Hill) Good range of often lively astronomy displays, inc videos, computer games, and the biggest telescope in Scotland. Glorious views down over the city, and even as far as the Braid Hills. Shop, limited disabled access; cl am Sun, 24 Dec–2 Jan; (0131) 668 8405; £3.50.

Royal Scottish Academy (The Mound) Founded in 1826, in a second neo-classical temple alongside the National Gallery, this will be closed for refurbishment until 2003. Best to phone for information about where the collection is to be rehoused in the meantime; (0131) 225 6671. On either side, like a broad moat for the castle (this was a loch before the New Town was built), are well tended gardens.

Royal Yacht *Britannia* Displays about the yacht and its royal past on an onshore visitor centre, and a chance to explore five decks of the ship in which the Queen and Prince Philip cruised the world. Snacks, shop, disabled access; cl 25 Dec, limited Christmas opening hours; (0131) 555 5566; £7.75.

Scott Memorial (Princes St) After the castle, probably Edinburgh's most memorable building: remarkably ornate, with its handsome if mucky exterior. The historic crypt of St John's episcopal church on Princes St has interesting vegetarian and vegan food.

Scottish National Gallery (The Mound) Fine neo-classical building with particularly good examples of most European schools and periods inc a £20m 1480 Botticelli *Madonna and Child*, barely seen for over a century and acquired thanks to grants from the Heritage Lottery and the National Art Collections funds. Plenty of Scottish paintings too, with many great works by Ramsay, Raeburn, Wilkie and McTaggart. Some art critics have objected to changes in the look of the gallery under its current director, but few would dispute that it's undoubtedly still one of the country's best. Look out for the rather incongruous portrait of one of the donor's dogs – it has to be hung here as a condition of the donation of other pictures. Shop, disabled access; cl 25–26 Dec; (0131) 624 6200; free (exc major exhibitions).

Scottish National Gallery of Modern Art (Belford Rd) Breathtaking collection inc great works by Picasso, Barbara Hepworth and Lichtenstein. Meals, snacks, shop, disabled access; cl Sun am, 25–26 Dec; (0131) 624 6200; free (maybe charges for temporary exhibitions).

Scottish National Portrait Gallery (Queen St) The history of Scotland through a huge and varied collection of portraits in a variety of media. Meals, snacks, shop, disabled access; cl Sun am, 25–26 Dec; (0131) 624 6200; free.

Water of Leith W of the centre and well worth exploring, often very picturesque and ravine-like. By its banks is the quaint little Dean Village, surprisingly close to the heart of the city, yet unaffected by all the New Town building above it. There's a fine series of Georgian crescents around Moray Pl. The river eventually winds down to Leith itself (a once prosperous and separate dockland area now swallowed up by the city, its waterfront reviving again with trendy bars). The Scottish Malt Whisky Society (Giles St), dedicated to cask-strength top-quality malt whiskies, has a downstairs bar/restaurant.

ELLISLAND FARM NX9283 ⊞ (off A76) Robert Burns lived here from 1788 to 1791, trying unsuccessfully to introduce new farming methods. There are displays of material associated with the poet (who wrote *Tam o' Shanter* and *Auld Lang Syne* while living here), and cattle and sheep wander around much as they must have done then. Lovely riverside walk. Shop, some disabled access; cl Sun am, and in winter cl all day Sun and Mon (though if you ring, you may find them open); (01387) 740426; £1.50.

ESKDALEMUIR NY2597
Beautifully set mountain village, famous for its cruel winter weather; it also has an unexpected Tibetan Buddhist temple and monastery.

Borders hill walking The Borders hills have plentiful solitary hill-walking. The Southern Upland Way (which makes a 212-mile coast-to-coast journey over the hills from Portpatrick to Cockburnspath) is a good basis for day walks, though large distances between places often make it hard to find focal points.

EYEMOUTH NT9464
Understated family holiday seaside town around busy but pretty fishing harbour, with a decent beach. The Ship overlooking the harbour has reasonable food.

Eyemouth Museum 🏛 (Market Pl) Good local history museum in former church, with magnificent tapestry commemorating the great fishing disaster of 1881 when 189 fishermen were lost at sea (cl Sun in Oct, all Nov–May; £1.75)

St Abb's A steep and pretty little seaside village nearby, with a sandy beach and old fishing harbour, little used now.

St Abb's Head The best of the E coast scenery for walkers; walk from Eyemouth or St Abb's, with a good path along the cliffs – noisily crowded with breeding seabirds in late spring, with high breezy walks, and a lighthouse. £1 parking, £1 visitor centre (cl Nov–Mar).

FERNIEGAIR NS7453
Chatelherault (Carlisle Rd) Originally built by William Adam as a hunting lodge and summer house for the Dukes of Hamilton; a grand avenue of trees once linked this restored hilltop building with Hamilton Palace (now demolished). The former kennels house a museum with displays on the history of the house, the local area and its wildlife. The Banqueting Hall and Duke's private bedroom can still be seen, and the grounds include restored Georgian gardens, woodland trails, rare white cattle, and a children's adventure playground. Ranger-led walks; meals, snacks, shop, disabled access; cl 25–26 Dec, and 1–3 Jan; (01698) 426213; free.

FIRTH OF FORTH NT4682
Excellent shoreside walks along the sands from Aberlady to North Berwick, with stop-off possibilities at Dirleton and Gullane; a good bus service connects the shoreside villages between North Berwick and Edinburgh, though the hinterland is dull.

GALLOWAY FOREST PARK NX3672
Attractive and easily accessible, taking in around 100 lochs, 300 miles of river, great views, and thousands of hectares of forest, mountain and moorland. Many of the trees are fairly recent replantings, the original woodland having from the 15th c onwards rapidly fallen victim to the demand for timber. Many of the lochs are ringed by waymarked walks and trails, and there are plenty of scenic drives and cycle routes. Visitor centres (Apr–Oct only) at Kirroughtree, Glen Trool and Clatteringshaws all have exhibitions and information to help you make the most of the forests, inc details of where you can camp or fish, and the best places to spot wildlife. Stones mark 14th-c battles between Scotland and England, and the 1680s Killing Time, when Scottish covenanters were hunted down and killed in the government's attempts to impose bishops on the Scottish church.

Loch Trool NX4180 There are particularly attractive trails around the loch, with a good informative summer visitor centre nearby. A memorial stone commemorates a 1307 battle between Robert the Bruce and the armies of Edward I.

Merrick NX4285 The highest point in SW Scotland, a worthwhile but long and strenuous walk up from Glen Trool.

Wood of Cree NX3771 One of the best surviving stretches of ancient forest, with an RSPB reserve among its trees and marshes.

GLASGOW NS5865

There's a real zing and vitality about this proud city, which is making great strides in its efforts to shake off its rather rough image, with the dazzling new Glasgow Science Centre due to provide a shimmering new tourist attraction on the banks of the Clyde come the spring. Besides the excellent art galleries and interesting museums, which the local director of museums has fought hard to keep free, it houses the Royal Scottish Orchestra (with a fine-sounding concert hall), the Scottish Opera and the Scottish Ballet. Though there are many places to see and visit, a snag for visitors is that they are scattered around this sprawling city: the Burrell Collection, one of the most interesting places of all, is out in the suburbs. It's worth investing in a Day Tripper ticket, which allows virtually unlimited train and underground travel, £3.50; this makes it easy to get out to the really attractive parks fringing the city (we list these after the other attractions here, starting with Greenbank Garden). Besides the restaurants and bars mentioned in **Where to eat**, Glasgow is full of places to eat out in, formal and informal; interesting and undaunting pubs and bars include the Auctioneers (St Vincent Pl), Blackfriars (Bell St), Bon Accord (North St), Cask & Still (Hope St) and Horseshoe (Drury St).

Botanic Gardens (730 Great Western Rd) Sloping gently down to the River Kibble, these are famous for their fantastic glasshouses, particularly the half-acre Kibble Palace, with its soaring tree ferns interspersed with Victorian sculpture. Snacks, disabled access; (0141) 334 2422; free.

Burrell Collection (Pollok Country Park, SW Glasgow – see entries for Pollok Country Park and House below) A couple of miles out in the suburbs, but not to be missed – and rarely gets too crowded. Splendidly and imaginatively housed in a modern building created to show its different parts to perfection, the huge collection – far too much to see at one go – includes Egyptian alabaster, Chinese jade, oriental rugs, remarkable tapestries, medieval metalwork and stained glass, even medieval doorways and windows set

into the walls, as well as paintings by Degas, Manet and Rembrandt among others. Good meals and snacks, shop, disabled access; cl 25–26 Dec, 1–2 Jan; (0141) 287 2550; free (parking £1.50).

Pollok Country Park (SW) One of the best of the several parks and gardens you'll find around Glasgow, with waterside and woodland trails, rose garden, Clydesdale horses, and a herd of highland cattle. Shop, snacks, disabled access; (0141) 632 9299; free.

Pollok House (Pollok Country Park) Treasures here include silver, ceramics and porcelain, but it's the paintings that stand out, with a collection of Spanish masters such as Goya and El Greco cannily acquired in the days when they were greatly undervalued. Meals, snacks, shop; cl 25 Dec, 1 Jan; (0141) 616 6410; £4 (free Nov–Mar).

Charles Rennie Mackintosh tours

🖬 Sauchiehall St, a link between the museum/university quarter and the centre, is an ordinary shopping street, but well worth the walk for the ground-breaking designer and architect's most famous building, the Glasgow School of Art (Renfrew St, just off; the tours are highly recommended, (0141) 353 4526), and the decoratively mirrored Willow Tea Room (open till 5pm), furnished to his designs, too; Shop, some disabled access; cl Sun and pm Sat Sept–Jun (limited wknd opening hours in summer); *£5. As well as other places we mention with Mackintosh connections, you can buy works after him at the Glasgow Style Gallery on Gt Western Rd.

Clyde walks A walkway tracks along the Clyde now, its waterfront cleaned up. The veteran pleasure steamer *Waverley* makes some runs from here Jun–Aug – (0141) 221 8152 for times. Some Clydeside pubs well outside Glasgow with decent food and good sea views include the Cardwell at Cardwell Bay in Gourock and the Spinnaker there, and the Lookout down in Troon Marina.

Clydebuilt (Braehead Shopping Centre, off J25a and 26 of M8) The Glaswegian extension of the Scottish Maritime Museum in Irvine tells the story of Glasgow and the Clyde from the tobacco lords of the 18th c, through the city's important status as a global centre for shipbuilding, right up to the present day. Interactive exhibits allow you to steer your own ship, make a fortune as an ocean trader, and for a taste of the real thing can take control of a real steam engine and go aboard the oldest Clyde-built vessel still afloat. Snacks, shop, disabled access; cl 25 Dec and 1 Jan; (0141) 886 1013; £3.50.

Gallery of Modern Art (Queen St) Glasgow's latest big gallery, concentrating on art by living British artists – not just Scottish. Lively café-bar (open some evenings too), shop, good disabled access; cl 25–26 Dec, 1–2 Jan; (0141) 229 1996; free.

Glasgow Art Gallery & Museum (Kelvingrove Park) Huge Victorian building with remarkably rich collection of paintings, esp strong in works by the French Impressionists, Post-Impressionists, and Scottish artists from the 17th c. Also sculpture, silver, porcelain, armour, ethnography and natural history. Meals, snacks, shop, disabled access; cl 25–26 Dec, 1–2 Jan; (0141) 287 2699; free.

Glasgow Cathedral 12th-c, dedicated to St Mungo, the founder of the city. It's very well preserved, though most fittings date from the 19th c; best parts are the crypt, a gracefully vaulted affair built in the mid-13th c, and the Blackadder aisle; summer shop; cl Sun am, 25–26 Dec, 1–2 Jan. The spectacular Necropolis graveyard is closed for restoration, but there's a fine overview from the cathedral. The area around here is the oldest part of Glasgow, though not the most interesting.

Glasgow Science Centre (50 Pacific Quay) This £75m millennium project promises to bring a new wave of innovation to the banks of the Clyde. Opposite the Scottish Exhibition and Conference Centre it received the largest Millennium Commission grant N of the border, and will become Britain's largest science centre when it fully opens in the spring. It will comprise three unique attractions: Scotland's first IMAX cinema (opening around the time this book comes out); a 100-metre (328-ft) tower – the only one in the world with the capability to rotate 360

degrees from the ground up – with a stunning 20-metre (66-ft) panorama of the city from the top, and galleries elsewhere looking at the past and speculating about the future of Glasgow's development; and the sleek Science Mall, where most of the science-related fun will take place. As well as providing a stylish home for 500 or so hands-on exhibits, this last building will house a planetarium, a virtual reality theatre showing activity from within the human body and the earth's crust, displays looking at (among other subjects) space and the planets, digital design and transport, and discovery areas, where visitors will be able to conduct their own experiments; there'll also be a special area for younger children, and a temporary exhibition gallery which will open with a look at science centres around the world. The IMAX cinema and Science Mall will become only the second buildings in Europe (after the Guggenheim in Bilbao) to be clad in shimmering titanium. Listing so many 'firsts', it's easy to lose one's way among the superlatives (always a danger when writing about a new attraction), but given the size, bold design and sheer inventiveness, it should be well worth a visit. Meals, snacks, shop, disabled access; phone (0141) 420 5000 for prices.

House for an Art Lover (Bellahouston Park) Built to 1901 designs by Charles Rennie Mackintosh, with an exhibition on him, and contemporary art exhibitions. Meals, snacks, shop, disabled access; cl every Fri, wknds Oct–Mar (though best to check winter opening times), 24–26 Dec, 1–2 Jan; (0141) 353 4770; £3.50. The Empire Exhibition of 1938 was held on these 171 acres, which now comprise a walled garden, sunken garden and sweeping lawns.

Hunterian Art Gallery (Hillhead St) Dr Hunter bequeathed the core of fine paintings which form the basis of this beautifully hung collection. A grand range of works by Whistler, interesting and well chosen contemporary British art and sculpture, and an amazing re-creation of the home of Charles Rennie Mackintosh (cl 12.30–1.30pm), the designer/architect whose exuberant yet very disciplined and clean-lined art nouveau buildings stand out among the more traditional solidity of much of Glasgow. Shop, disabled access with prior notice; cl Sun; (0141) 330 5431; free.

Hunterian Museum (Hillhead St) Scotland's first public museum, housing the University collections of ethnographic, palaeontological and anthropological material, along with lots of archaeology, and a coin display. Shop, disabled access; cl 12.30–1.30pm, Sun and public hols; (0141) 330 4221; free. The exhibitions were also founded by Dr William Hunter, the 18th-c physician (see above).

Linn Park (Cathcart/Castlemilk) Lots to do – riverside walks, nature trails, golf course, as well as a ruined 14th-c castle, an adventure playground for the disabled (prior arrangement preferred), and an equestrian centre; (0141) 637 3096. Visitor centre open wknd pms only; (0141) 637 1147; free.

McLellan Galleries (Sauchiehall St) Spacious and well lit, these have good changing art exhibitions; snacks, shop, disabled access; cl 25–26 Dec, 1–2 Jan; (0141) 332 7521; free.

Merchant City The area around George Sq and Buchanan St was built on a grid plan in the 19th c, and visually has something in common with New York City – Americans are said to feel at home here. With its proud Victorian buildings cleaned back to their warm sandstone, this smart shopping quarter is the city's most comfortable area to stroll around. Guided walking tours leave the Tourist Information Centre on George Sq daily at 2pm Jun–Sept and there are also evening ghost tours, (0141) 772 0022; £5. The City Chambers here is a spectacular monument to 1880s civic pride, marble everywhere; free tours. The Counting House is a splendid new pub in an opulent converted bank nearby. There are café-bars and bistros off Princes Sq, and antique stalls in Victorian Village (W Regent St). On the SE edge of this area, between Gallowgate and London Rd past the Tolbooth, the Barras (barrows) is an entertaining wknd flea-market. With around 800 stalls it's one of the biggest covered markets in the world, great for bargains or just passing time; try the plump fresh clappie doos (mussels).

Museum of Transport (Kelvin Hall, Bunhouse Rd) Comprehensive collection of vehicles, from trams to ships, very well displayed; the walk-through car showroom is arranged as if some were for sale, with original prices displayed on the windscreens. Snacks, shop, disabled access; cl 25–26 Dec, 1–2 Jan; (0141) 287 2720; free.

Museum quarter NW of the centre, the West End, Kelvingrove and the University quarter have some elegant streets, the main concentration of museums, and the botanic gardens.

People's Palace (Glasgow Green) Very enjoyable refurbished social history museum looking at Glaswegians over the centuries, set in a park just SE of centre; disabled access; cl 25 Dec, 1–2 Jan; (0141) 5540 223; free. The museum's café is in the adjacent Winter Gardens, a massive conservatory with huge tropical plants.

Provan Hall (Auchinlea Park, B806 E) Mansion house virtually unchanged since the 16th c, in a pleasant park with a variety of formal and informal gardens inc a herb garden. Limited disabled access; cl wknds and public hols, 25–26 Dec, 1–2 Jan, best to phone to check; (0141) 771 4399; free; NTS.

Scotland Street School Museum Designed by Mackintosh, this spectacular building originally had a capacity of 1,250 pupils in 21 classrooms, and now houses a lively museum dedicated to education with reconstructed classrooms. It's currently being refurbished, and when it reopens in Jun, it will have more fun re-creations and interesting exhibits. For more information about opening times, phone (0141) 287 0500; free.

St Mungo Museum of Religious Life (Cathedral Precinct, Glasgow) Unique collection of art from all the world's major religions – and some rather obscure ones too. Everything from an Egyptian mummy mask to Dali's *Christ of St John of the Cross*, and in the grounds Britain's only permanent Zen garden. Meals, snacks, shop, disabled access; cl 25–26 Dec,

1–2 Jan; (0141) 553 2557; free.
Tall Ship (Glasgow Harbour, 100
Stobcross Rd) 105-year-old sailing ship,
Glenlee, one of only 5 Clyde-built
sailing ships remaining afloat in the
world; the adjacent pumphouse houses
a gallery, shop and café. Meals, snacks,
shop, disabled access; cl 25 Dec, 1–2
Jan; (0141) 339 0631; £3.50.
Tenement House (145 Buccleuch St)
One-floor late 19th-c flat giving a vivid
impression of life for many Glaswegians
a century ago. The same woman lived
here from 1911 to 1965 and in that time
scarcely changed a thing; its time-
capsule quality was preserved by a
subsequent owner, and then the flat,
still with its original furnishings and
fittings, was left to the National Trust
for Scotland. Open pm Mar–Oct;
(0141) 333 0183; £3.50; NTS.
**University of Glasgow Visitor
Centre** (University Ave) Interactive
displays on the history and life of the
university (founded in 1451), with tours
around some of its grander features,
such as the Lion and Unicorn Staircase,
Bute and Randolph Halls and Memorial
Chapel. Snacks, shop, disabled access; cl
all day winter Sun, plus am summer Sun,
and 2 wks over Christmas and New
Year; (0141) 330 5511; visitor centre
free, tours (11am and 2pm Weds, Fri
and Sat May–Sept, Oct–Apr just 2pm
Weds) £2. You can stay in some of the
university buildings during vacations.
Greenbank Garden (Flenders Rd,
Clarkston, off A726) Aims to
encourage and help owners of small
gardens, so has lots of different shrubs
and flowers to spark ideas. Also garden
and greenhouse designed to meet the
needs of disabled gardeners, with
advice on specially designed tools.
Summer teas, shop, disabled access; cl
25–26 Dec, 1–2 Jan; house open Sun pm
only Apr–Oct; (0141) 639 3281; £3.50;
NTS.
Mugdock Country Park (N
Glasgow) Good strolling ground, with
two castle ruins, a view over Glasgow,
and an attractive loch.
Rouken Glen Park (Thornliebank) A
place of great tranquil beauty, with a
walled garden, gorgeous lawns, and
woodland walks to a waterfall at the
head of the glen.

Victoria Park (Victoria Park Dr
North) Tree-lined park where the fossil
remains in the Fossil Grove, some of
them 230 million years old, were
discovered by workmen digging a path
in the late 19th c.
West Highland Way Level walks can
take in the early stages of the West
Highland Way, which starts at
Milngavie. The determined can press on
along glen routes all the way up to Fort
William – the scenery getting better all
the way.
GLENLUCE NX1858
Glenluce Abbey Ruined Cistercian
abbey founded in the late 12th c, in
beautiful surroundings. Limited disabled
access; cl Sun am, Thurs pm and Fri
Oct–Nov, wkdys and Sun am Dec–Mar;
(01581) 300541; £1.80.
GORDON NT6439
Mellerstain House (just W, off
A6089) William and Robert Adam both
worked on this striking Georgian
house, which has impressive
plasterwork and furnishings, and
paintings by Van Dyck and
Gainsborough. Every great house in
Scotland seems to have something that
belonged to Bonnie Prince Charlie –
this one has his bagpipes. Very pleasant
terraced gardens and parkland, with
fine views towards the distant hills.
Meals, snacks, shop, limited disabled
access; cl am, all day Sat, and Oct–Apr;
(01573) 410225; £4.50. The Gordon
Arms has decent food.
GREENOCK CUT NS2472
Part of an elaborate abandoned water
scheme for Greenock below, this
allows a level walk meandering around a
hillside terrace giving views into the
Highlands.
GRETNA GREEN NY3167
Old Blacksmith's Shop 🏚 It's now
tourists rather than runaway couples
that flock to the Old Blacksmith's Shop
in this little Borders village. More
people come here than to any other
Scottish attraction outside Edinburgh,
despite the fact that there's really very
little to see. An exhibition centre looks
at the once thriving marriage business.
Cl 25–26 Dec, 1 Jan; (01461) 338224;
£2.
GREY MARE'S TAIL NT1814
Spectacular waterfalls, a pretty walk

from the A708 car park NE of Moffat, up a narrow glen. You can continue beyond them along Tail Burn to Loch Skeen.

HADDINGTON NT5173

A pretty market town; the comfortable George and Maitlandfield House hotels, and the correctly named Waterside Inn, all have above-average food.

Lennoxlove 🖾 (B6369 S) The Duchess of Lennox (La Belle Stewart) gave this old house its unusual name in memory of her dead husband. Among reminders of other members of her family are the casket and death mask of Mary, Queen of Scots. In the grounds the Cadzow herd of white park cattle are said to be descended from the sacrificial cattle of the Druids. Meals, snacks, disabled access; cl am, Mon, Tues, Fri, and Nov–Easter; (01620) 823720; £4.

HAWICK NT5014

Drumlanrig's Tower (Towerknowe) Fearsome-looking 16th-c tower with state-of-the-art displays of Borders history, some quite gripping. Shop, disabled access; cl Sun am (all day Sun Nov–Mar); (01450) 377615; £2.

Hawick Museum & Scott Art Gallery 🖾 (Wilton Lodge Park) There's a new Egyptian exhibition at this museum, made considerably more appealing by its setting, a park with riverside walks and gardens. Shop, disabled access to ground floor; cl 12–1pm, am wknds, am wkdys and all day Sat Oct–Mar, 8–9 Jun, 25–26 Dec, 1–2 Jan; (01450) 373457; £1.25*.

HERMITAGE NY4995

Hermitage Castle Almost perfect from the outside, the well restored but very forbidding remains of a 14th-c Borders stronghold reeking of dire deeds. Shop, limited disabled access; cl Fri, and am Thurs Oct–Nov, and all Dec–Easter; (01387) 376222; £1.80.

INNERLEITHEN NT3336

Robert Smail's Printing Works (High St) Fully restored Victorian printer's shop, with water-powered press; you can try your hand at metal typesetting and hand-print your own bookmark. Shop, limited disabled access; cl 1–2pm, Sun am, and all Oct–Apr (exc Sat and pm Sun in Oct); (01896) 830206; £2.50; NTS. The

Traquair Arms is the place to eat.

IRVINE NS2740

Big Idea (Harbour St) In a huge sand-dune-shape building on the tip of the Ardeer Peninsula, this giant inventors' workshop celebrates a century of Nobel Laureates as well as the creations and innovations of the last millennium. A pedestrian drawbridge leads you to a vast array of inventions from life-saving machines to utterly ridiculous contraptions, and hundreds of exhibits with which you can interact thanks to a specially designed electronic key. You're actively encouraged to come up with your own inventions, and best of all, after testing them out, you get to take the end product home. Café, gift shop, disabled access; cl 25 Dec and 1 Jan; (08709)404030; *£7.

Scottish Maritime Museum (Gottries Rd) Down by the harbour, very much a working museum, with lots of restoration work on the good range of historic vessels. Snacks, shop, some disabled access (not to boats); cl Nov–Mar; (01294) 278283; £2.50. The nearby Keys has decent food (all day wknds).

Vennel Gallery Art gallery and museum, and behind, a reconstruction of the Heckling Shop where, as a young man, an unwilling Burns tried to learn the filthy trade of flax dressing. Happily for him, during a New Year's Eve party his aunt knocked over a candle and burnt the building to ashes. Shop, disabled access; cl 1–2pm, all day Sun and Weds; (01294) 275059; free.

ISLE OF BUTE NS0864

This popular Glasgow holiday island is a ½-hour ferry trip from Wemyss Bay/Skelmorlie; it has a mix of fresh air and ebullient summer entertainments. In Rothesay the island's main town the seafront Black Bull has good food. There's lovely open country in the N, its southern tip is rewarding too, and the new West Island Way allows walks with great vistas all along the island's W side – you may see seals on the shore, and there's a bird hide suitable for wheelchairs at Kirk Dam NS0863. There are grand sea views from the Kames Inn, which has food all day.

Bute Museum 🖾 (Stuart St, Rothesay) Decent museum, worth a visit (cl Sun am, and over Christmas and New Year; £1.20). The gents' at the harbour, built in 1899, has ornate wall tiles and fine ceramic mosaic floors.

Monastery of St Blane NS0953 Ruined Norman chapel in a delightful spot, a short way uphill from the road – just sheep and the occasional walker.

Mount Stuart House & Gardens (off A844, just E of Upper Scoulag) In this bracingly bleak landscape, the spectacular Victorian Gothic mansion is quite a shock; the elaborate rooms are splendidly over the top too. The 300 acres of landscaped grounds and woodland include several pretty gardens, as well as a pinetum of mature conifers and a nicely isolated stretch of sandy beach, reached via a lime tree avenue. Snacks, shop, disabled access; cl all day Tues and Thur, and Oct–beginning May; (01700) 503877; £6, garden only £3.50. Scotrail do a special ticket (£15.50) which includes entrance and train, ferry and bus travel from Glasgow Central or Strathclyde stations.

Rothesay Castle 13th-c; shop; cl Sun am, and in winter Thurs pm and all day Fri; £2.

Victorian Fern House and Gardens (Ascog Hall, S of Rothesay) Restored and reopened in 1997, this is the only one of its kind in Scotland. It has been replanted with one of the most impressive collections of ferns to be found outside a botanic garden inc species from South-East Asia, Australasia and South America inc one thought to be over 1,000 years old. Cl Mon, Tues and all mid-Oct to mid-Apr; (01700) 504555; £2.50.

JEDBURGH NT6420

Castle Jail and Museum (Castlegate) Now a local history museum (cl Oct–Easter; £1.25).

Jedburgh Abbey The most complete of ruined 12th-c Borders monasteries founded by David I, and an impressive sight, despite its town setting. Imposing 26-metre (86-ft) tower, splendid W door, and audio-visual show in visitor centre. Snacks, shops, disabled access; cl Sun am Oct–Mar, 25–26 Dec, 1–2 Jan; (01835) 863925; £3. The Pheasant has good food (and makes a point of having good value pheasant in season).

Just off the A68 S of town are the ruins of Ferniehurst Castle.

Mary Queen of Scots House (Queen St) Charming 16th-c fortified dwelling where Mary had to prolong her 1566 stay because of a near-mortal fever (she was later to say she wished she'd died here). There's a good interpretation of her life. Shop; cl Dec–Mar; (01835) 863331; £2.

KELSO NT7035

Floors Castle (1m NW) Magnificent building designed by William Adam in 1721, and much embellished in the next century. It's reputed to be Scotland's biggest inhabited house, with a window for every day of the year. Splendid collection of tapestries and French furniture, and wonderful walled garden (best July–Sept). Good home-made meals and snacks, shop, disabled access; cl Nov–Apr; (01573) 223333; £5.

Kelso Abbey The greatest and wealthiest of the four famous Borders abbeys, though today not much of the building remains. Cobbles (Beaumont St) and the Queen's Head (Bridge St) have good value food.

KILMARNOCK NS4339

Dean Castle (off Glasgow Rd) Very well restored family home, housing a wonderful collection of medieval arms and armour, musical instruments, tapestries, and a display of Burns's manuscripts. It's surrounded by 200 acres of woodland, with nature trails, deer park, riding and other activities. Snacks, shop; open pm daily; (01563) 522702; free. The 18th-c Wheatsheaf in the pretty village of Symington on the other side of town has good original food.

KIPPFORD NX8355

Charming yachting place, usually plenty to watch in summer. The Anchor here is good.

LANGBANK NS3673

Finlaystone 🖾 (A8, 1m W) Some say the garden here is the finest in Scotland – formal and walled, with woodland walks, adventure playgrounds, and picnic areas. The house has connections with Robert Burns and John Knox (unlikely partners), and there's a visitor centre with displays on the Clan Macmillan and Celtic art. Snacks (summer only), shop, disabled access;

gardens open all year; (01475) 540505; £3 house. The modern Langbank Lodge nearby has sensibly priced food (inc afternoon tea and scones) and incredible Clyde views.

LARGS NS2059
The pick of the traditional Clydeside resorts, with boats across the narrow strip of water to the island of Great Cumbrae. The pleasure steamer *Waverley* calls here in summer, and Nardinis (Esplanade) is a vintage tea room – or rather tea palace, with acres of immaculate tables and smartly aproned motherly waitresses.

Vikingar! (Barrfields Centre, Greenock Rd) Lively look at the Vikings in Scotland, from their arrival to their defeat at the Battle of Largs. Very much an 'experience', with lots of interactive displays, and a multi-media show as the centrepiece. There's an adjacent swimming pool. Meals, snacks, shop, disabled access; cl Nov–Feb; (01475) 689777; £3.75.

LAUDER NT5347
Thirlestane Castle ⊞ (off A68 and A697) Charming old castle with restored assemblage of pictures, interesting collection of old toys (some of which children can touch), some outstanding plasterwork in the 17th-c state rooms, woodland walk and picnic areas. Meals, snacks, shop; cl Sat, and Nov–Mar; (01578) 722430; £5.20, £1.50 grounds only. The Eagle and Lauderdale Hotel are useful for lunch.

LINLITHGOW NT0578
House of the Binns (3m E, off A904) The home of the Dalyell family since the 17th c, with some splendid plaster ceilings and a varied collection of furniture and porcelain. Limited disabled access; cl am, all day Fri, and Oct–May; (01506) 834255; £4; NTS.

Linlithgow Palace The birthplace of Mary, Queen of Scots, a magnificently sombre lochside ruin. You can still see the chapel, great hall and a quadrangle with fountain. Shop, limited disabled access, cl 25–26 Dec and 1–2 Jan; (01506) 842896; £2.80. In the town a pleasant old tavern, the Four Marys, is named for her maids-in-waiting Mary Carmichael, Mary Hamilton, Mary Beaton and Mary Seaton, with relevant memorabilia.

LIVINGSTON NT0366
Almond Valley Heritage Centre ⊞ (off A705) Friendly 16-acre museum, with lots to see inc working farm, watermill, and underground shale mine. Also trailer rides (summer wknds and summer hols), adventure playground, and demonstrations of milking and other seasonal activities. Meals, snacks, shop, disabled access; cl 25–26 Dec, 1–2 Jan; (01506) 414957; £2.20.

LOCHWINNOCH NS3558
Nature Centre ⊞ (Largs Rd) RSPB nature reserve with fine views, good woodland and marsh nature trails, and three observation hides. Wknd snacks (wkdys too July and Aug), shop, complete disabled access; cl 25–26 Dec, 1 Jan; (01505) 842663; *£2. The Mossend is a useful dining pub.

MELROSE NT5034
Abbotsford House (B6360 3m W) Set grandly on the River Tweed, this was the home of Walter Scott until his death in 1832. You can still see his mammoth 9,000-volume library, and several of the historical oddities he liked to collect, like Rob Roy's sporran. Snacks, shop, disabled access; cl Sun am (Mar–May and Oct), plus all Nov–mid-Mar; (01896) 752043; £3.80.

Eildon Hills Above the town, these are splendidly compact, giving a very pleasing ridge walk along the top.

Melrose Abbey The ruins are among the finest in the country – best in moonlight, as Scott says (though he admitted he never saw them thus himself). Look out for the wonderful stonework on the 14th-c nave (and the pig playing the bagpipes).
Archaeological investigations now leave little doubt that this was the burial place of Robert the Bruce's heart. Shop; limited disabled access; cl Sun am Oct–Mar, 25–26 Dec, 1–2 Jan; (01896) 822562; £3.

Priorwood Garden (Abbey St) Specialises in flowers suitable for drying, with a herb garden and display orchard illustrating apples through the ages. Shop, disabled access; cl Sun am, and 24 Dec–Feb; (01896) 822493; £2; NTS.

MERVINSLAW NT6713
Jedforest Deer & Farm Park (A68)

Working hill farm with deer as well as other animals inc hawks and several rare breeds. Good for children, and peaceful walks and trails nearby. Snacks, shop, some disabled access; cl mid-Oct–Apr; (01835) 840364; £3.50.

MULL OF GALLOWAY NX1530
Beautifully unspoilt, Scotland's SW toe; good coastal walking.

NEW ABBEY NX9562
Criffel This nearby summit gives walkers an astonishing view of the English Lake District over the Solway Firth.

New Abbey Corn Mill The pretty village has a restored 18th-c corn mill; shop; cl 1–2pm all year, plus Thurs pm, all Fri, and Sun am Oct–Mar; (01387) 850260; £2.50.

Shambellie House of Costume 🖭 (A710) Much extended in recent years, often dazzling displays of costume, thoughtfully arranged in appropriately furnished rooms. Snacks, shop; cl Nov–Mar; (01387) 850375; £2.50.

Sweetheart Abbey (A710) One of the most romantic ruins in the area, with a lofty arched nave open to the sky, and a touching story attached. Shop; cl in winter Sun am, Thurs pm and all day Fri; (01387) 850397, 25–6 Dec, 1–2 Jan; £1.50.

NEW LANARK NS8841
Falls of Clyde The countryside here is spectacular, with a short walk snaking around river cliffs through a verdant gorge to these falls that used to power the mill; a visitor centre here has lots of information on badgers (cl before 11am, and 25–26 Dec). The falls are dramatic when the hydro-electric station up river opens the sluices.

New Lanark (off A73) Founded in 1785 and now the subject of a major conservation programme, this is Scotland's best example of an industrial village, with plenty to keep families amused for a good chunk of the day. Many of the old millworkers' buildings have been interestingly converted to modern accommodation, so it's very much a living village rather than a museum. The village can be busy at wknds; try to visit during the week if you can. Meals, snacks, shop, disabled access; cl before 11am, 25 Dec, 1 Jan; £3.95. In Lanark itself the Crown (Hope

St) has a decent restaurant.

NEWTONGRANGE NT3363
Scottish Mining Museum (Lady Victoria Colliery, A7, Newtongrange) Following a recent £5.2m redevelopment, this new three-storey visitor centre offers an even livelier re-creation of mining days inc a reconstructed coalface, interactive exhibitions and hands-on activities. Meals, home-baked snacks, shop, disabled access; (0131) 663 7519; £4.

NORTH BERWICK NT5585
Scottish Seabird Centre (North Berwick Harbour) Every year over 150,000 seabirds (inc the largest colony of gannets in the world) return to the islands off this town, and this new £3m centre uses remote camera technology to let visitors study the birds in extremely close detail; observation deck, auditorium. Shop, café with wonderful views across the Firth of Forth to Bass Rock, disabled access. Cl 1 day per wk in winter, 25–26 Dec, and maybe New Year, so best to check; (01620) 890202; *£4.50. A good value family ticket covering 2 adults and 2 children costs £12.50, and they also offer a money-saving deal with Scotrail: a return ticket from Edinburgh to North Berwick inc entry to the centre costs £7.90; phone (08457) 484950 for details.

OLD DAILLY NS2401
Bargany Gardens (Old Dailly) Fine ornamental trees, woodland walks winding through springtime glades of snowdrops, bluebells and daffodils, and a lily pond enveloped by azaleas and rhododendrons. Mostly disabled access; cl Oct–Mar; (01465) 871249; £1 donation.

PAISLEY NS4863
Coats Observatory (High St) Displays on astronomy, meteorology and space flight. Shop, cl 1–2pm, and Mon; (0141) 889 2013; free.

Paisley Museum & Art Gallery (High St) Paisley is not just a place but a pattern, so as well as a very wide range of 19th-c art, the appealing museum has a marvellous collection of antique and more modern paisley shawls, along with the looms on which they were made. Shop, some disabled access; cl Sun am and all Mon (exc bank hols), 25–26 Dec,

1–2 Jan; (0141) 889 3151; free. The Anchor (Glasgow Rd) does decent lunches.

PATNA NS4308

Dunaskin Open-air Museum (Dalmellington Rd) Well preserved Victorian ironworks (employing up to 1,400 people in its 19th-c heyday) in attractive rolling countryside, with a period cottage, reconstructed manager's office, industrial machinery, an audio-visual show about Ayrshire life in the 19th and early 20th c, fun play area based around the principles of an iron furnace, and nature trails around the site. Meals, snacks, shop, disabled access; open Apr–Oct (by appointment only Nov–Mar); (01292) 531144; *£4.

PAXTON NT9352

Paxton House (B6461) Built in 1758 by the love-struck Patrick Billie, who hoped to marry a daughter of Frederick the Great; the marriage never took place, but the result was a splendid neo-Palladian mansion, designed and later embellished by the Adam family, and furnished by the Chippendales; 18th-c German/Prussian costume display. Also woodland and riverside walks, huge herd of highland cattle, and adventure playground designed by the Territorial Army. Meals, snacks, shop, disabled access; cl Nov–Apr; (01289) 386291; £5, £2.25 gardens only.

PEEBLES NT2540

Attractive if sedate Borders town, with quite a lot for visitors; the Green Tree (Innerleithen Rd) has reasonably priced food.

Kailzie (B7062, 2 miles SE) Extensive grounds with lovely old trees flanked by azaleas and rhododendrons, formal rose garden, walled garden, and small art gallery. Meals, snacks, shop, disabled access; restaurant and gallery cl Nov–Easter; (01721) 720007; £2.50, (£1 Oct–Apr).

Neidpath Castle (off A72 just W) Spectacularly set, converted from the original 14th-c tower in the late 16th and early 17th c. There's a rock-hewn well, small museum (children like the mummified rat), period kitchen, and a pit prison – not much chance of escape, as some of the walls are 3½ metres (11 ft) thick. Super views from the parapets. Shop; open May bank hol wknds, and

daily July–second wknd in Sept (exc Sun am), phone to check; (01721) 720333; £3.

PENICUIK NT2360

Edinburgh Crystal Visitor Centre (Eastfield) Demonstrations of glass-blowing, cutting and engraving, with an exhibition on the crystal's history. Meals, snacks, shop, disabled access; tours Mon–Fri all year and wknds Apr–Sept (last wknd tour 2.30pm, wkdys 3.30pm), cl 25–26 Dec, 1–2 Jan; (01968) 675128; £3. They run a free minibus service from Waverley Bridge in Edinburgh (on the hour, Apr–Sept only). The Horseshoe out on the Peebles road is a civilised dining pub.

PENTLAND HILLS NT1558

Within easy reach of Edinburgh, genuine uplands with some good high-level walks and attractive reservoirs.

PORT LOGAN NX0942

Logan Botanic Garden (off B7065) A specialist garden of the Royal Botanic Garden of Edinburgh, with a wide range of plants from the warm temperate regions of the southern hemisphere. Snacks, shop, plant sales; cl Nov–Feb; (01776) 860231; £3. The village itself has a natural sea pool where fat fish will eat from your fingers; the Inn does good food. Great sunsets here.

PORTPATRICK NW9954

Attractive harbour town, usually with something going on down by the water, and good food in the waterside inn.

PRESTONPANS NT3874

Industrial Heritage Museum (B1348 Prestongrange Rd) Based around the oldest documented coal mining site in Britain. Reconstructed coalface and colliery workshop, as well as displays on other local industries, from brick and pipe making to brewing and weaving. Lots going on, esp at wknds. Snacks, shop, disabled access; cl late Oct–Mar (but open Christmas week); (0131) 653 2904; free.

RHINNS OF GALLOWAY NX0650

This hammerhead of land in the extreme W of the area is largely empty even in high summer, a very peaceful place, with cliffs (especially on the S point), rocks and small coves.

RHINNS OF KELLS NX7274

This ridge has energetic hill walking

from Forrest Lodge NW of New Galloway.

ROCKCLIFFE NX8453
Attractive yachting village, with a good peaceful walk to Castle Hill Point headland, and beyond by vast stretches of tidal sands.

SELKIRK NT4227
Bowhill House 🖾 (off A708, 3m W)
Outstanding collection of paintings, inc works by Canaletto, Van Dyck, Gainsborough and Claude, as well as impressive furnishings and porcelain, and memorabilia relating to Scott and Queen Victoria. Also restored Victorian kitchen, adventure playground, very active little theatre, and surrounding country park. Snacks, shop, disabled access; grounds cl am, all Fri (exc in July), and all Sept–late Apr; house open daily July only; (01750) 22204; £4.50
Selkirk Glass (off A7 just N)
Demonstrations of paperweight-making; meals, snacks, factory shop, disabled access; usually cl Christmas–New Year; (01750) 20954; free.
Sir Walter Scott's Courtroom
(Market Pl) Low-key exhibition on Sir Walter Scott in the former courtroom where, as sheriff, he dispensed justice to the people of Selkirk; shop, snacks, limited disabled access; cl Sun (exc pm Jun–Aug), ams in Oct, and all Nov–Mar. The decorous town is good for bargain-hunting for the tweeds, woollens and cashmeres which are woven and knitted here; the Queen's Head has freshly cooked food.

SMAILHOLM NT6334
Smailholm Tower (just S, signed off the B6404 NE of St Boswells) Classic 15th-c Borders tower house, very well preserved – all 17metres (57 ft) of it. Display based on Scott's book *Minstrels of the Borders*, and an exhibition of dolls. Shop, limited disabled access; cl Thurs pm, and Fri Oct–Nov, and wkdys Dec–Mar; (01573) 460365; £2.

SOUTH QUEENSFERRY NT1378
Notable for its views of the two great Forth bridges on either side, with piers to potter on; the Hawes Inn, famous from *Kidnapped*, is still going strong.
Dalmeny House (B924, 3m E)
Despite its Tudor Gothic appearance,

this splendidly placed house dates only from the 19th c – there's a superb hammerbeamed roof, as well as fine furnishings, porcelain and portraits. Good walks in the grounds and on the shore. Snacks, disabled access; only open Mon, Tues and pm Sun in July–Aug; (0131) 331 1888; £4.
Hopetoun House (off B904, 2m W)
This huge place is probably Scotland's best example of the work of William and Robert Adam. The magnificent reception rooms have a wonderful art collection with works by Canaletto and Gainsborough, while the superb grounds include a deer park and a flock of rare sheep. You can climb to the rooftop for wonderful views. Meals, snacks, shop, some disabled access; cl Oct–Mar; (0131) 331 2451; £5.30, £2.90 grounds only.

ST MARY'S LOCH NT2320
A pretty spot for walks, tracked by the Southern Upland Way along its E shore; the Tibbie Shiels Inn is a handy stop.

STOBO NT1534
Dawyck Botanic Garden (B712)
Another specialist garden of the Royal Botanic Garden, particularly noted for its arboretum rich in mature conifers (inc a larch believed to have been planted in 1725), with notable Asiatic silver firs and many rarities. Snacks, shop, limited disabled access; cl Oct–Apr (unless by appointment); (01721) 760254; £3.

STRANRAER NX0760
Castle Kennedy Gardens (A75, 4m E) Prettily set between two lochs (with lots of good walks around), these gardens were first laid out in the early 18th c, then after years of neglect were restored and developed in the 19th. They're particularly admired for their walled garden and flowering shrubs. Snacks, shop, limited disabled access; cl Oct–Mar; (01776) 702024; £3.

TARBOLTON NS4327
Bachelor's Club 🖾 (off A77 S of Kilmarnock, and off A76, 7½m NE of Ayr) 17th c thatched house where Burns and his friends formed a debating club in 1780. Shop; open pm daily Easter–Sept, pm wknds only Oct; (01292) 541940; £2.50; NTS.

THORNHILL NX8599
Drumlanrig Castle 🖾 (off A76)

Spectacular and rather unusual pink sandstone castle built in the late 17th c, with a glory of fine panelling and furnishings (mainly Louis XIV), and splendid paintings by Leonardo, Holbein, Rembrandt and Murillo; you can see what's said to be Bonnie Prince Charlie's campaign kettle. Also craft workshops, adventure playground, peacocks wandering over the lawn, working forge, and extensive woodland walks. Meals, snacks, shop, disabled access; cl Sun am, and Sept–Apr; (01848) 330248; £6.

TRAQUAIR NT3336

Traquair House ⌧ (B709) One of the longest-inhabited and most romantic houses in the country; no fewer than 27 English and Scottish kings have stayed here. The Bear Gates have remained closed since 1745 when Bonnie Prince Charlie passed through them for the last time – they won't open again unless the Stewarts regain their place on the throne. An 18th-c brewery still produces tasty beers (£3 for tastings, phone to book), and there's a brewery museum. Traquair is particularly popular with our contributors, and with a maze, art gallery, and antique and craft shops (best on Weds and Thurs) as well as the house and gardens, there's plenty to see. Meals, snacks, shop, some disabled access; cl am (exc Jun–Aug), and all Nov–Easter; (01896) 830323; £5.20, grounds only £2.

UDDINGSTON NS6960

Bothwell Castle Picturesquely set by the river: now ruined, but once the finest stone castle in the country; shop; in winter cl Thurs pm, all day Fri, Sun; £1.50.

Glasgow Zoo (Calderpark) Open-plan zoo, specialising in cats and reptiles (snake-handling every day), with other rare mammals and birds, children's farm, orienteering course, and wknd car boot sales. Falconry and parrot flying displays in winter; Snacks, shop, disabled access; cl 25 Dec; (0141) 771 1185; £4.

WANLOCKHEAD NS8713

Museum of Lead Mining ⌧ (B797) Guided tours of an 18th-c lead mine,

heritage trail and miners' cottages furnished in the styles of 1740 and 1890. You can have a go at panning for gold. Meals, snacks, shop, limited disabled access; cl Nov–Mar; (01659) 74387; £3.95. This remote village is Scotland's highest.

WHITHORN NX4736

Isle of Whithorn Picturesque harbour with boat trips and lots of yachtsmen: the Steam Packet has good local fish.

Whithorn Dig Scotland's first-recorded Christian settlement was established here by St Ninian 1,500 years ago. There have been several churches on the site since, the last of the line the ruined 13th-c priory you can see today. Archaeologists have been hard at work here for some time, and you may be able to watch the dig's progress during the summer. An excellent visitor centre and museum have plenty of the finds, with some fine Celtic crosses. Shop, disabled access; museum and visitor centre cl Nov–Mar (though you can still wander round the priory ruins then); (01988) 500508; £2.70.

Other attractive villages with decent pubs include Ancrum NT6325, Gifford NT5368, Kirkcowan NX3260, Kirkcudbright NX6851 (particularly enjoyable), Lilliesleaf NT5325, Larkhall NS7651, Old Kilpatrick NS4673, Sorn NS5526 and Symington NS3831. Some Clydeside pubs with decent food and good sea views include the Cardwell at Cardwell Bay in Gourock NS2477 and the Spinnaker there, and the Lookout in Troon Marina NS3230. Others with a decent bite to eat and particularly well placed for walkers, drivers or just strollers in these parts include the Murray Arms, Masons Arms and Angel at Gatehouse of Fleet NX5956, Golf Hotel and Old Clubhouse at Gullane NT4882, Breadalbane Hotel at Kildonan NS0231, Swan at Kingholm Quay NX9773, Border at Kirk Yetholm NT8328, Gordon Arms at Mountbenger NT3125 and Buccleuch Arms at St Boswells NT5931.

Where to eat

EAST LINTON NT5977 **Drovers** *5 Bridge St (01620) 860298* Comfortable 18th-c inn with prints and pictures for sale, cosy armchairs, a basket of logs by the woodburner, hops around the bar, very good interesting food (more elaborate in the evening), a good range of real ales, and partly no smoking upstairs restaurant; cl 25 Dec, 1 Jan. £22.50|**£7.25**

EDINBURGH NT2473 **Atrium** *10 Cambridge St (0131) 228 8882* Next to Usher Hall and Traverse Theatre, unusually modern restaurant with wire sculptures, railway sleepers, dim lighting from glass torches, cheerful friendly staff, interesting wine list, and very good imaginative modern Scottish food – lunchtime two-course set menu, too; cl Sun, 10 days Christmas; disabled access. £40|**£12**

EDINBURGH NT2776 **Fishers** *1 Shore (0131) 554 5666* Bustling, lively bistro overlooking the Leith waterfront, with an informal, friendly atmosphere, a dark bar with a few tables and bar counter, and light airy dining room; exceptionally good, imaginative fish dishes, enjoyable straightforwardish puddings, a well chosen, fairly priced wine list, and genuinely helpful, quick, cheerful service. £30

EDINBURGH NT2672 **Kalpna Indian Restaurant** *2–3 St Patrick Sq (0131) 667 9890* Extremely good Indian restaurant with carefully cooked, very fresh and interesting vegetarian food, and polite, efficient service; cl Sun am, 1 Jan; disabled access. £13.50

EDINBURGH NT2776 **Ship on the Shore** *26 The Shore, Leith (0131) 555 0409* Lovely old pub with charming shop model for its hotel sign, a bar with old painted company signs, ship lanterns and nautical equipment, popular food (esp the bargain 3-course lunches), plenty of fish and well liked Sunday breakfasts; no children. £30/3-course lunch £7.95

EDINBURGH NT2676 **Vintners Rooms** *The Vaults, 87 Giles St, Leith (0131) 554 6767* Bustling restaurant – a former fine old sale room, above ancient wine vaults; most enjoyable French provincial cooking plus more modern dishes, super puddings, and a good wine list; you can also choose to eat in the more informal bar; cl Sun, 2 wks from Christmas; partial disabled access. £35/2-course lunch £11.50

GLASGOW NS5667 **Di Maggios** *61 Ruthven Lane (0141) 334 8560* A Glasgow institution with good Italian and other food, and a cheerful atmosphere; cl 25 Dec, 1–2 Jan; disabled access. £18|**£6.25**

GLASGOW NS5965 **Rogano** *11 Exchange Pl (0141) 248 4055* Long-standing restaurant in splendid 1930s ocean liner style with quite an emphasis on fish – vegetarian and meaty dishes, too; Café Rogano (downstairs) is open all day for lighter meals; cl 25 Dec, 1 Jan. £45/3-course set lunch £16.50

GLASGOW NS5667 **Ubiquitous Chip** *12 Ashton Lane (0141) 334 5007* Friendly and informal award-winning restaurant (no chips, hence the name) in Victorian coach house with interesting modern Scottish cooking, outstanding wines, and no smoking areas; disabled access; cl 25 Dec, 1 Jan. Upstairs is similar but cheaper. £40|**£8**

GLASGOW NS5865 **Yes** *22 West Nile St (0141) 221 8044* Stylish bustling restaurant with a relaxed, if fashionable, feel, very good modern cooking taking ideas from all over the world using first-class local produce, courteous service, and a short well chosen wine list; cl Sun. £38.50|**£14.95**

HADDINGTON NT5173 **Waterside** *1–5 Waterside (01620) 825674* A really lovely spot on a sunny day with a fine view across the water, this long two-storey white house has two plush rooms, a woodburner, a more formal stripped-stone conservatory, very good bistro-style food, real ales, and a good range of wines. £25|**£6.95**

LANARK NS8843 **Vigna** *40 Wellgate (01555) 664320* Imaginative Italian menu with good basics, more imaginative dishes, and lots of fresh fish; cl Sun am; disabled access. £26/3-course lunch £10.95

LINLITHGOW NT0378 **Champany Inn** *Champany (01506) 834532* Wonderful Aberdeen Angus beef as well as lovely fresh fish (they also have their own smoke-house), home-made ice-creams, and good wines; cheaper bistro-style meals in their Chop and Ale House next door; main restaurant cl Sat am, Sun (bistro open all week); children over 8 in main restaurant; disabled access. £40.50|£16.75

East Scotland

**Some spectacular sights, from fairytale castles to richly
varied scenery; plenty for families too**

The diversity of family attractions in this part of Scotland really impresses. On the animal front, there's the elaborate aquarium at North Queensferry, the refreshingly wild Highland Wildlife Park at Kincraig, Blair Drummond's rewarding Safari and Leisure Park, and the enjoyable deer centres at Cupar and Glenmore. Dundee's excellent new Sensation science centre should match the Discovery Point for hi-tech thrills, and Satrosphere in Aberdeen will be able to offer even more hands-on high jinks once it has moved into its new premises. There are acres of free fresh air fun at the Aberdeenshire Farming Museum in Mintlaw and the Kinneil Estate at Bo'ness, and other good family days out include Blair Castle at Blair Atholl, Callender House and its surrounding parkland near Falkirk, the Landmark Heritage & Adventure Park in Carrbridge, and Fort George (good special events). The various remains and reconstructions at Archaeolink, Oyne, will appeal to any Indiana Jones wannabes.

The area has so many glorious castles, palaces and great houses that you could devote an entire holiday to seeking them out and still go home disappointed. Those deserving special mention include magnificent Fyvie Castle, Crathes Castle (marvellous interiors), wonderfully grand Haddo House (a busy outing), Leith Hall & Garden (you can stay in its gateway lodge) and friendly Ballindalloch Castle – both newcomers to the *Guide*, Falkland Palace & Garden, and Craigievar Castle, perhaps the most fairytale-romantic of them all.

Garden lovers should head for the celebrated examples at Kildrummy, Kemnay and Muthill.

Elsewhere there's a splendid range of historic smaller towns and villages, and some rewarding museums offer good insights into the history of the region; those in Kingussie and Kirkcaldy immediately spring to mind. More specialised expeditions often turn out to have general appeal: maybe learning about lighthouses at Fraserburgh, or a sheep show at the surprisingly entertaining Scottish Wool Centre in Aberfoyle.

The thriving city of Aberdeen has lots for visitors (many places are free), Dundee has recently added a smart contemporary arts centre to its already considerable appeal (Camperdown Country Park just outside is good for a run around); civilised St Andrews has a quiet charm about it, and students give Stirling some welcome vitality. There's good shopping in Inverness.

The best scenery here is in the N: both Highland, and the valleys – the well known Spey, Dee and Don, and lesser-known places such as the

Angus glens of Glen Clova, Glen Esk and Glen Isla. Further S, the Trossachs are very pretty. The coast has appealing fishing villages in Fife's East Neuk, and a little-known but charming stretch from Nairn to Aberdeen, with good sands, quaint little coves and awesome cliffy crags such as Slains Castle and the nearby Bullers of Buchan.

The relatively few roads through the best parts do tend to get crowded in high summer; to get a feeling of peace, June (when it's still light as midnight approaches) would be much better.

Where to stay

ABERDEEN NJ9305 **Ferryhill House** *169 Bon Accord St, Aberdeen AB11 6UA (01224) 590867* **£79**; 9 rms. Well run small hotel with comfortable communicating spacious bar areas, well over 100 malt whiskies, real ales, friendly staff, a wide choice of food in bar and restaurant and lots of tables on neat well sheltered lawns

ABERFELDY NN8249 **Farleyer House** *Aberfeldy, Perthshire PH15 2JE (01887) 820332* **£180***, plus winter breaks; 19 pretty rms. Charming country house with fine Tay Valley views, log fires, antiques and flowers in library and drawing room, excellent food in airy and elegant restaurant and Scottish bistro; use of nearby leisure club; disabled access

ARDEONAIG NN6634 **Ardeonaig Hotel** *Ardeonaig, Killin, Perthshire FK21 8SY (01567) 820400* **£97**; 12 rms. Extended 17th-c farmhouse on S shore of Loch Tay with log fire in snug and lounge, library with fine views, and tasty, honest food using plenty of fish and game; salmon fishing rights on the loch – as well as fishing for trout and char – a drying and rod room, and boats and outboards; shooting and stalking can be arranged, lots of surrounding walks, and pony trekking; cl Nov–Mar but open for New Year

AUCHTERARDER NN9211 **Gleneagles Hotel** *Auchterarder, Perthshire PH3 1NF (01764) 662231* **£290**, plus special breaks; 219 individually decorated rms. Grand hotel in lovely surroundings with attractive gardens and outstanding leisure facilities: golf courses (inc a championship one designed by Jack Nicklaus), shooting, riding, fishing, health spa, tennis, squash, bowling green, croquet and even falconry, playroom with arts and crafts for children; comfortable, elegant high-ceilinged day rooms, a fine bar, exceptional service, pianists, enjoyable food (inc famous afternoon teas) using local produce (much is home-grown) in four restaurants; disabled access ☺

AVIEMORE NH8810 **Lynwilg House** *Aviemore, Inverness-shire PH22 1PZ (01479) 811685* **£70**; 4 rms, 3 with shower. Attractive, quietly set 1930s-style house in four acres of landscaped gardens with open fire in spacious lounge, lovely breakfasts with their own free-range eggs and home-baked bread, super dinners using home-grown produce, and charming friendly owners; plenty to do nearby; cl Nov–Dec

BALLATER NO3696 **Auld Kirk** *31 Braemar Rd, Ballater, Aberdeenshire AB35 5RQ (013397) 55762* **£52**, plus winter breaks; 6 attractive rms. 19th-c church converted to a hotel in 1990, still with bell tower (the bell is in the main entrance), stained glass and exposed rafters; original pillared pine ceiling in dining room, other public rooms with homely décor, and home cooking; cl Christmas/New Year

BALLATER NO3695 **Balgonie Country House** *Braemar Pl, Ballater, Aberdeenshire AB35 5NQ (01339) 755482* **£120***, plus special breaks. 9 pretty rms. Quietly set and spotless Edwardian house with fine views from four acres of mature gardens, particularly helpful friendly owners, fresh flowers, games and books in lounges, and most enjoyable food using the best local produce in charming dining room; cl Jan–Feb; dogs by arrangement (away from public rooms)

BALQUHIDDER NN4318 **Monachyle Mhor** *Balquhidder, Lochearnhead,*

Perthshire FK19 8PQ (01877) 384622 **£70***; 10 rms with fine views overlooking Voil and Doine lochs. Remote 18th-c farmhouse/hotel six miles W of Balquhidder on 2,000-acre estate with prettily furnished rooms and good food using own game and herbs; private fishing and stalking for guests; no children; partial disabled access

BLAIRGOWRIE NO1244 **Kinloch House** *Blairgowrie, Perthshire PH10 6SG (01250) 884237* **£171***, plus special breaks; 20 individually decorated rms. Creeper-covered 19th-c country house in 25 acres of parkland with highland cattle and fine views; relaxed lounges, comfortable bar, pretty conservatory with lots of plants, and fine choice of carefully prepared food in an elegant dining room; popular sportsmen's room with own entrance, drying facilities, gun cupboard, freezer, game larder and so forth, and new fitness suite; cl 17–30 Dec; no children under 7 in dining room; disabled access

BRIDGE OF CALLY NO1551 **Bridge of Cally Hotel** *Bridge of Cally, Blairgowrie, Perthshire PH10 7JJ (01250) 886231* **£57**, plus winter breaks; 9 rms. In an acre of grounds along the River Ardle, this former drovers' inn is a friendly family-run place with good value home-made food using seasonal game in restaurant and comfortable bar; cl 25–26 Dec; pets welcome

CALLANDER NN6208 **Poppies** *Leny Rd, Callander, Perthshire FK17 8AL (01877) 330329* **£52***; 8 rms. Small private hotel with excellent food in popular and attractive candlelit dining room, convivial bar with RAF theme, comfortable lounge, helpful friendly owners, and seats in the garden; disabled access

CALLANDER NN6307 **Roman Camp Hotel** *Main St, Callander, Perthshire FK17 8BG (01877) 330003* **£110**, plus special winter breaks; 14 individually decorated pretty rms with garden views. Extended over the years since it was built as a hunting lodge in 1625, this pink-painted turreted house has warm open fires and lovely fresh flowers, an elegant drawing room, tranquil library, very good food in candlelit dining room, and 20 acres of grounds; disabled access

CRIANLARICH NN3726 **Allt-Chaorain Country House** *Crianlarich, Perthshire FK20 8RU (01838) 300283* **£60**, plus special breaks; 7 rms. Comfortable small hotel with homely atmosphere, log fire in lounge, honesty bar, sunroom with marvellous views, and good home-cooked food in panelled dining room; lots of fishing, golf and walks nearby; cl 1 Nov–Easter; children over 7; disabled access

DALCROSS NH7451 **Easter Dalziel Farm** *Dalcross, Inverness IV2 7JL (01667) 462213* **£40**; 3 rms with shared bthrm. Early Victorian farmhouse on 210 acres of family-run mixed farm (beef cattle and grain) with friendly helpful owners, log fire in lounge, good Scottish breakfasts in big dining room and – when farm commitments allow – evening meal using own beef, lamb and vegetables; self-catering cottages, too; cl Christmas and New Year

DUNBLANE NN7606 **Cromlix House** *Cromlix, Dunblane, Perthshire FK15 9JT (01786) 822125* **£235***, plus special breaks; 14 rms inc 8 spacious suites. Walking, loch and river fishing or shooting on 3,000 acres around this rather gracious country house; relaxing day rooms with fine antiques and family portraits, an informal atmosphere, very good food using local produce in two dining rooms, and courteous service; cl 2–20 Jan

DUNKELD NN9849 **Kinnaird House** *Kinnaird Estate, Dunkeld, Perthshire PH8 0LB (01796) 482440* **£255***, plus special breaks; 9 spacious individually decorated rms. 18th-c country-house hotel on 9,000-acre estate with very restful civilised atmosphere in deeply comfortable antiques-filled rooms with lovely flowers, family mementoes and pictures, log fires, good creative food in no smoking dining room with early 19th-c frescoes, and a fine wine list; excellent fishing on River Tay and three hill lochs, and shooting; cl Mon–Weds during Jan–Feb; children over 12

EAST HAUGH NN9656 **East Haugh House** *East Haugh, Pitlochry, Tayside PH16 5TE (01796) 473121* **£78***, plus special breaks; 13 rms, 5 in converted bothy, one with open fire. Turreted stone house with lots of character, delightful conservatory bar, house-party atmosphere, helpful cheerful owners, and very good popular food inc local seafood and game in season; excellent shooting, stalking and salmon and trout fishing on surrounding local estates; cl 20–26 Dec; disabled access to one room

ELGIN NJ2163 **Mansion House** *The Haugh, Elgin, Moray IV30 1AW (01343)* 548811 **£120**, plus special breaks; 23 rms. Relaxed and friendly Scottish baronial mansion with prettily furnished public rooms, lovely food inc fine breakfasts, and good wine list; leisure club facilities inc swimming pool; disabled access

FINTRY NS6287 **Culcreuch Castle** *Fintry, Glasgow G63 0LW (01360) 860228* **£80***, plus special breaks; 10 individually decorated rms with lovely views. Scotland's oldest inhabited castle, nearly 700 years old, in beautiful 1,600-acre parkland and surrounding hills and moors, with log fires and antiques in the public rooms, freshly prepared food in candlelit panelled dining room, and a friendly atmosphere, play area; 8 modern Scandinavian holiday lodges, too; disabled access

GLENDEVON NN9705 **Tormaukin** *Glendevon, Dollar, Clackmannanshire FK14 7JY (01259) 781252* **£80**, plus special breaks; 10 refurbished rms, some in converted stable block. Comfortable neatly kept inn in good walking country, with loch and river fishing, lots of golf courses in reach, beamed dining room and softly lit bar, very good food (soup and coffee all day), and fine breakfasts, also recently built self-catering chalet; cl 4 days beginning Jan; disabled access

GLENROTHES NO2802 **Balbirnie House** *Markinch, Glenrothes, Fife KY7 6NE (01592) 610066* **£185***, plus special breaks; 30 rms. Fine Georgian country house in 400-acre park landscaped in Capability Brown style, with fresh flowers, open fires and antiques in gracious public rooms, extremely good inventive food, and a big wine list; disabled access

GRANTOWN-ON-SPEY NJ0227 **Culdearn House** *Woodlands Terrace, Grantown-on-Spey, Moray PH26 3JU (01479) 872106* **£130*** inc dinner, plus special breaks; 9 rms. Carefully run Victorian granite stone house with homely décor inc local watercolours, friendly chatty atmosphere, helpful owners, and enjoyable Scottish food; packed lunches on request; self-catering too; cl Nov–Feb; children over 8; partial disabled access

INVERBOYNDIE NJ6664 **Links Cottage** *Inverboyndie, Banff AB45 2JJ (01261) 812223* **£48**; 3 rms. In an acre of grounds and only a short walk from Banff's marvellous long sandy beach, this neatly refurbished single-storey cottage is comfortable and homely with a friendly atmosphere, hearty breakfasts (places close by for evening meals), and plenty to do nearby; disabled access; cl Nov–Mar

INVERNESS NH6245 **Bunchrew House** *Bunchrew, Inverness IV3 8TA (01463) 234917* **£140**, plus special breaks; 11 individually decorated rms. Friendly 17th-c mansion W of town by Beauly Firth with fine views and landscaped gardens, log fire in the elegant panelled drawing room, and traditional cooking using local produce

KINCLAVEN BY STANLEY NO1437 **Ballathie House** *Stanley, Perth PH1 4QN (01250) 883268* **£160**, plus special breaks; 27 pretty rms, some luxurious. On a vast estate with fine salmon fishing on the River Tay (lodges and facilities for fishermen) and plenty of sporting opportunities, this turreted mansion has a comfortable and relaxed drawing room, separate lounge and bar, good enjoyable modern Scottish cooking, and tennis, croquet, and putting; disabled access

KINGUSSIE NH7500 **Hermitage** *Spey St, Kingussie, Inverness-shire PH21 1HN (01540) 662137* **£42***, plus special breaks; 5 rms. Welcoming house in large garden with fine Cairngorm views, log fires in comfortable lounge, enjoyable home-made set dinners, and hearty Scottish breakfasts; fishing, golf, walking, climbing and bird-watching close by; limited disabled access; cl Christmas

KINNESSWOOD NO1703 **Lomond Country Inn** *Main St, Kinnesswood, Kinross KY13 9HN (01592) 840253* **£64***; 12 comfortable rms, 8 in an extension. Attractive little inn in village centre with views across Loch Leven (nice sunsets), open fires, informal bustling bar, well kept real ales, and good reasonably priced bar and restaurant food using local produce; disabled access

KIRKTON OF GLENISLA NO2160 **Glenisla Hotel** *Glenisla, Blairgowrie, Perthshire PH11 8PH (01575) 582223* **£64**, plus special breaks; 6 rms. Attractively placed peaceful 17th-c coaching inn, prettily restored with natural unpainted wood throughout, happily unmatched furniture, bar with open fire and two real ales, good food, cheerful warm atmosphere; nice garden; dogs welcome; cl 25 Dec

MONYMUSK NJ6715 **Grant Arms** *Monymusk, Inverurie, Aberdeenshire AB51 7HT (01467) 651226* **£65**; 17 rms, most with own bthrm. Smart old inn with dark-panelled lounge bar divided in two by a log fire in the stub wall, simpler public bar, and exclusive right to 15 miles of good trout and salmon fishing on the River Don; ghillie available; disabled access

NAIRN NH8756 **Clifton House** *Viewfield St, Nairn, Moray IV12 4HW (01667) 453119* **£100**, plus special breaks; 12 individually decorated comfortable rms. Lovely, civilised, flower-filled old family hotel (the present owner has lived in this elegant Victorian house all his life and has been running it as a hotel since 1952), individually furnished with antiques, paintings and sculptures; extremely good food using local eggs, fish, meat and game, fine breakfasts with home-made jams, bread, and oatcakes, and an exceptional wine list; during the winter they stage some 20 concerts, plays and recitals; cl mid-Dec to mid-Jan; pets welcome

PEAT INN NO4509 **Peat Inn** *Peat Inn, Cupar, Fife KY15 5LH (01334) 840206* **£145***, plus special breaks; 8 luxurious suites. Famous restaurant with rooms: beams and white plaster walls, log fires and comfortable sofas, friendly service, fine interesting food using the best local produce inc plenty of game and seafood, and an excellent wine list; cl Sun/Mon, 25 Dec, 1 Jan; disabled access

PITLOCHRY NN9162 **Killiecrankie Hotel** *Killiecrankie, Pitlochry, Perthshire PH16 5LG (01796) 473220* **£184*** inc dinner, plus special breaks; 10 spotless rms. Comfortable country hotel in spacious grounds with putting course and croquet lawn, splendid mountain views, mahogany-panelled bar with stuffed animals and fine wildlife paintings, spacious sitting room with books and games, a relaxed atmosphere, very friendly owners, and excellent well presented food in elegant restaurant; cl Jan and Mon–Tues in Dec, Feb–Mar

SCONE NO1526 **Murrayshall House** *Scone, Perth, Perthshire PH2 7PH (01738) 551171* **£120**, plus special breaks; 29 rms, 14 suites, plus lodge which sleeps 6. Handsome mansion in 300-acre park, very popular with golfers (it has its own course); comfortable elegant public rooms, warm friendly staff, relaxed atmosphere, imaginative food, and good wines; dogs welcome; disabled access

SPEAN BRIDGE NN2891 **Letterfinlay Lodge** *Letterfinlay, Spean Bridge, Inverness-shire PH34 4DZ (01397) 712622* **£79**, plus special breaks; 13 rms, most with own bthrm. Secluded and genteel family-run country house with picture window in modern bar overlooking loch; elegantly panelled cocktail bar, popular food, attentive service; grounds run down through rhododendrons to the jetty and Loch Lochy; fishing can be arranged; cl Nov–Mar; disabled access

SPITTAL OF GLENSHEE NO0672 **Dalmunzie House** *Glenshee, Blairgowrie, Perthshire PH10 7QG (01250) 885224* **£84**; 16 rms with own bthrm. Old-fashioned former Victorian shooting lodge, off A93, peacefully set in huge estate among spectacular mountains, plenty of walks within it, and own golf course; family-run atmosphere, enjoyable food using local produce; cl Dec; disabled access

STRATHKINNESS NO4516 **Fossil House & Cottage** *12–14 Main St, Strathkinness, St Andrews, Fife KY16 9RU (01334) 850639* **£46***, plus special breaks; 4 well equipped pretty rms with fresh flowers – particularly good family room. Once a smallholding, the two stone buildings here have a comfortable little guest lounge and sunny conservatory, plenty of books, board games, videos, and lots of ornaments and fighter aircraft pictures, especially helpful, friendly owners, really super breakfasts, and barbecue facilities in the garden; no smoking and no dogs

STRATHYRE NN5617 **Rosebank House** *Strathyre, Callander, Perthshire FK18 8NA (01877) 384208* **£44***, plus special breaks; 4 rms, most with own bthrm. Victorian house with open fires in comfortable lounge and dining rooms, wildlife paintings by the owner, enjoyable evening meals and breakfasts (lovely puddings), and a big quiet garden; plenty to do nearby; cl Christmas

WHITEBRIDGE NH4413 **Knockie Lodge** *Whitebridge, Inverness, Inverness-shire IV2 6UP (01456) 486276* **£125***, plus special breaks; 10 rms. In a wonderfully remote setting by Loch Knockie above Loch Ness, this Georgian hunting lodge has plenty of outside pursuits, a warmly friendly and relaxed house-party atmosphere, lovely flower arrangements, log and peat fires, antiques, and comfortable day rooms, delicious evening meals, and super breakfasts; billiards; cl mid-Oct to mid-Apr; children over 10; dogs by prior arrangement

To see and do

Scotland Family Attraction of the Year

NORTH QUEENSFERRY NT1380 **Deep-Sea World** 🖾 This is probably the UK's most elaborate aquarium, its highlight the spectacular underwater safari. Moving walkways carry you along a transparent viewing tunnel as long as a football pitch, surrounded by all kinds of underwater creatures, and a million gallons of water – the equivalent of two baths a day for the next 60 years. It's divided into different areas to group together the various species: the shallow kelp forests at the start are ideal for small fish and crustaceans, then you'll pass through sandy flats full of turbot and skate, spooky underwater caves with conger eels and small sharks, and some well lit stretches of open sea with everything from deep-sea crabs to the menacing angel shark. You'll generally see a few divers too, hand-feeding the fish or, more surprisingly, taking part in question and answer sessions thanks to waterproof communication systems. You may think they appear a little short: the curve and thickness of the acrylic tunnel makes everything look a third smaller than it really is. You can go round the tunnel as often as you like – it can get busy, but the moving walkways stop delays around the more popular features. Elsewhere are more traditional but no less fascinating displays of marine life – both local and exotic. The sea-horses are popular, and you can stroke some of the creatures kept in the rock-pools (inc a shark). Helpful staff are on hand throughout, and there's a good programme of talks, activities and feeding displays: check the What's On boards as you go in for the schedule. They usually feed the sharks at 12.15pm on Tues, Thurs and Sat, and the piranhas at 11.30am on Sun. The free behind-the-scenes tours give a good insight into the demands of looking after so many creatures, and an introduction to their successful breeding and conservation programmes. Face-painting is included in the admission; the designs are suitably aquatic. They also have a good collection of amphibians, taking in the world's most poisonous frog, and some snakes. Special events include sleepovers for over-8s. Meals, snacks, shop, disabled access; cl 25 Dec; (01383) 411411 (this is the office number – their recorded information line costs 50p a minute); *£6.25 (*£3.95 children over 3). The family tickets offer good savings: £16.95 for two adults and two children, and £18.95 for two adults and three children.

ABERDEEN NJ9305
Scotland's third-largest city, with a large active harbour, well worth pottering around (especially its early morning Fishmarket). The granite centre has wide, orderly streets not unlike Edinburgh's New Town in places, and parks. Markets are regularly held at Castlegate (Union St), and the planetarium on Gallowgate might appeal to star-gazers; (01224) 612323. Leafy Seaton Park is famous for its 14th-c Brig (or bridge) o' Balgownie. The Ferryhill House Hotel (Bon Accord St), Royal Hotel (Bath St) and Athol (King's Gate, W of centre) are useful for lunch, and the Prince of Wales (St Nicholas Lane) is the best proper pub in this part of Scotland.

Aberdeen Art Gallery (Schoolhill) First-class collection of Scottish and English painting since the 16th c, especially strong on contemporary works. Meals, snacks, shop, disabled access; cl Sun am, 25–26, 29 Dec, 1–2 Jan; free.

Aberdeen Maritime Museum (Shiprow) In the town's third-oldest building (very striking), with very good displays on the city's nautical heritage. Snacks, shop, disabled access; cl 25–26 Dec, 1–3 Jan; (01224) 337700; free.

Cruickshank Botanic Garden (St Machar Drive) Eleven acres first planted in the 19th c, and divided into various smaller gardens – rock, water, rose and herbaceous – as well as trees and shrubs and a small terrace garden; disabled access to most areas, cl winter wknds and maybe other times; (01224) 272704; free.

King's College Founded in 1495, and very Oxbridge-like; the chapel is one of the most complete examples of a medieval collegiate church in Britain. A Visitor Centre outlines the history. Snacks (in barrel-vaulted former library), shop, disabled access; cl Sun am, 2 wks at Christmas and occasionally at other times; (01224) 273702; free. It dominates the pedestrianised villagey High St of the Old Town (N of the centre, really too far to walk). Above the River Don, this part seems quite separate, and has other charming old streets, and attractive buildings.

Marischal College (Broad St) The later Protestant rival to King's, though the two were joined to form Aberdeen University in 1860. A splendid neo-Gothic structure, it has a museum with interesting anthropological and archaeological displays; cl Sun am, all day Sat; (01224) 274301; free.

Provost Skene's House 🖼 (Guestrow) Named after its most famous resident, a stately well restored 16th-c house with refurbished period rooms, and remarkable painted ceilings. Snacks; cl am Sun, 25–26 Dec, 1–2 Jan; (01224) 641086; free. The Illicit Still nearby has food all day.

Satrosphere This lively hands-on science and technology centre hopes to have relocated to the Tram Sheds off Constitution St by the time this book is published, where the bigger premises will allow more exhibits and greater space for their fun events. For more information phone (01224) 213232.

St Machar's Cathedral (Old Town) Austere mainly 15th-c church notable for its painted wooden heraldic ceiling. It's the only granite cathedral in the world; shop, disabled access.

ABERFELDY NN8549
This quiet and pleasant small Highland shopping town has a fine 18th-c stone bridge designed by William Adam.

Weem, for a good lunch at the Ailean Chraggan, is close by. There's a well restored **watermill** on Mill St (still mills oatmeal; all parts open to visit, cl mid-Oct to Easter; around £3), and just S of town the delightful verdant 1½-m walk along to the oak-lined Den and Falls of Moness inspired Burns's song *The Birks of Aberfeldy*.

ABERFOYLE NN5200
Lots of woollen shops, and in the heart of Queen Elizabeth Forest Park, so lovely scenery around; you can hire bikes. The Inverard has decent food.

Scottish Wool Centre The story of Scottish wool from sheep to shop, entertainingly told by a live sheep show in the amphitheatre (11am, 12, 2pm, 3pm). They have demonstrations of spinning and weaving. Meals, snacks, good shop, disabled access; cl 25 Dec, 1 Jan; (01877) 382850; *£3.

ALFORD NJ5815
Alford Valley Railway (A944) Narrow-gauge passenger railway with trips in two one-mile sections, and a good static display at the station. Shop, disabled access; trains usually in steam wknds Apr, May, Sept and daily pm Jun–Aug; (019755) 62326; £2.

Grampian Transport Museum 🖼 (A944) Big collection of vintage vehicles, from horse-drawn sledge and carriages to motorcycles, cars and tanks; always plenty going on. Snacks, shop, disabled access; cl Nov–Mar; (01975) 562292; £3.75. There'a dry ski slope on Greystone Rd; (019755) 63024, and the Forbes Arms at Bridge of Alford has decent home cooking.

ALLOA NS8892
Alloa Tower (A907, 6m E of Stirling) This beautifully restored 15th-c tower is all that remains of the ancestral home of the Earls of Mar. Although it was splendidly remodelled by the 6th earl before his exile after the 1715 Jacobite uprising, the tower retains some rare medieval features inc groin vaulting, a complete timber roof, interior well and underground dungeon. Also some attractive furniture and fine paintings inc works by Raeburn and Kneller. Shop, disabled access to ground floor only; open pm only daily Apr–Sept, and wknds only in Oct; (01259) 211701; £2.50; NTS.

ANSTRUTHER NO5603
Pretty East Neuk fishing village;
May–Sept (weather permitting) you can
get boat trips out to the nature reserve
of the **Isle of May**, summer home to
countless puffins and seals; (01333)
310103. The Craws Nest, Dreel and
Smugglers all have good value food.
Scottish Fisheries Museum 🖾 The
many facets of fisher-folk life are
portrayed in this museum, inc the
dangers they face out at sea. There's an
excellent collection of models of old
fishing boats, with 15 full-sized vessels
displayed in a former boatyard and in
the adjacent harbour. Cl winter Sun am,
25–26 Dec, and 1–2 Jan; (01333)
310628; £3.50.

ARBROATH NO6441
Arbroath Abbey Substantial remains
of 12th-c abbey, connected with
Thomas à Becket and Robert the Bruce.
Shop, disabled access to ground floor
only; cl Thurs pm, Sun am and all day Fri
Oct–Mar, 25–26 Dec, 1–2 Jan; (01241)
878756; £2.

AVIEMORE NH8912
Uncompromisingly modern ski-resort
village. There are plenty of places to get
something to eat in this sizeable tourist
development (the Olde Bridge is our
current recommendation).
Cairngorms A ski-lift from Glen More
above the village gives an easy way up to
the summits.
Loch an Eilein A draw for walkers,
nestling beneath the Cairngorms; a
forest track encircles this delightful
little loch, with its castle romantically
placed on an isle – great echoes here.
Strathspey Steam Railway 5m of
great scenery between here and the
Boat of Garten. Snacks, shop, limited
disabled access; usually open daily
Jun–Sept, plus other dates and wknds –
best to ring for timetable; (01479)
810725; £5.40.

BALLATER NO3695
Ballater Station Visitor Centre
(Station Sq) Opening in Apr, this
Victorian railway station has been fully
restored to how it would have been in
the days when Queen Victoria used it
on the way to nearby Balmoral.
Displays will tell the history of its Royal
connections, and lifelike figures will
inhabit the Royal Waiting Room.

Restaurant, shop, disabled access; for
more information about opening times
phone (01224) 288817; free.
Cambus o' May Walks (A93 E)
Extensively quarried until the early
20th c, this pleasantly wooded area is
dissected by several walks inc one
around a small loch (with picnic area),
designed to accommodate wheelchairs.
If you're lucky, you might catch a
glimpse of red deer and capercaillie
among the mix of evergreens.

BALLINDALLOCH NJ1736
Ballindalloch Castle Romantic castle
set in a lovely spot in the heart of the
Speyside distilleries, and still lived in by
the Macpherson-Grants whose
ancestors settled here in mid-16th c.
Furnishings inside are cheerfully light,
and there's a fine collection of 17th-c
Spanish paintings. The Rivers Spey and
Avon run through the grounds which
also include a large rock garden, and the
oldest herd of Aberdeen Angus cattle in
the world. Enjoyable afternoon teas,
well stocked gift shop, disabled access
to tearoom and ground-floor of castle
only; open daily Good Fri–Sept,
otherwise by appointment; (01807)
500206; £5.20.
Glenlivet Distillery The first
Highland malt whisky distillery to be
licensed; (01542) 783220 for opening
times; £2.50.

BALMEDIE COUNTRY PARK
NJ9820
Along a constantly shifting stretch of
coast, this is splendidly bleak-feeling
despite the closeness of Aberdeen.
Visitor centre cl winter wknds, though
best to check; (01358) 742396. The
beaches are clean and safe.

BALMORAL NO2693
Balmoral Castle (off A93) The Royal
Family's Highland residence. Prince
Albert bought the property four years
after he and Queen Victoria had first
rented it in 1848, and had a new castle
built here by 1855. You can't go inside,
but you can explore the wonderful
gardens and woodlands, and there are
various exhibitions in the ballroom.
There are also pony trekking and
pony cart rides. Snacks, meals, shop,
disabled access; open daily 17 Apr–July
(exc Sun Apr and May); (013397)
42334; £4.50.

BANFF NJ6963

Duff House This magnificent example of 18th-c baroque architecture has served as a ducal residence, hotel, sanitarium and prisoner-of-war camp in its time. It now houses a splendid collection of paintings and tapestries from the National Galleries of Scotland, hung in sumptuously furnished rooms inc Chippendale furniture designed by Robert Adam. The extensive grounds laid out alongside the River Deveron are pleasant for strolling in, and include a mausoleum and, rather quaintly, the 19th-c headstones of various dogs. Tearoom with very good home-made food, shop, good disabled access including lifts to gallery, cl Mon–Weds Nov–Mar, 25–26 Dec, and 1–2 Jan; (01261) 818181; £3.50.

BEN VENUE NN4706

Allows some good mountain walks comparable in difficulty to some of the fells of the English Lake District.

BEN VORLICH NN6218

Good walking, for those used to pretty hearty fell walking.

BENNACHIE NJ6623

On the E edge of the Grampians nr Inverurie, this is not that high but gives walkers tremendous views over lowland Grampian; the gently rolling moorland top has several colour-coded Forestry Authority trails (the lower slopes are forested).

BLAIR ATHOLL NN8665

Atholl Country Collection Friendly **folk museum** beside the turn-in for the White Horse, with some unusual exhibits inc the largest known trophy in Britain (awarded for shooting). Open pm Easter wknd then May–mid-Oct, plus wkdy ams July–Sept; £2.

Blair Castle 🏰 (off A9) Nestling among forests and heather-clad hills, this is Scotland's most-visited privately owned house, dating back to the 13th c, though largely renovated in the 18th. You can see about 30 of the rooms, and there's an 18th-c walled garden. A display charts the history of the Atholl Highlanders – the Duke of Atholl's unique private army that turns out here for its annual parade in May. A piper outside every day in summer adds to the atmosphere. Meals, snacks, shop, disabled access to ground floor only; cl Nov–Mar; (01796) 481207; £6, £2 for grounds only. The Atholl Arms has well priced food.

House of Bruar (A9) Country shopping complex with fine specialist foods and clothing; readers like it a lot.

BLAIR DRUMMOND NS7498

Safari and Leisure Park 🏰 (A84) Wild animals in natural surroundings, with plenty of other activities included in the price, from gentle rides for younger children to the exhilarating Flying Fox slide over the lake. You can explore part of the water in pedal-boats, and boat trips circle Chimpanzee Island leaving the chimps to enjoy their natural habitat undisturbed. Feeding times of lions, sea lions, and penguins are posted up nr the entrance. Meals, snacks, shop, disabled access; cl Oct–Apr; (01786) 841456; £8.50 (£4.50 children 3–14) – not bad value if you bring a barbie and make a half-day of it. The Lion & Unicorn at Thornhill does good family lunches.

BO'NESS NS9981

Bo'ness & Kinneil Railway 🏰 Re-creation of the days of steam complete with relocated railway buildings and Scotland's largest collection of locomotives and rolling stock. The 7-mile round trip takes you to the woodlands of the Avon Gorge at Birkhill, for tours of an old clay mine. Meals, snacks, shop, disabled access to railway only; trains usually run wknds Apr–mid-Oct, daily (exc Mon) July and Aug, and for special events in Dec, though you can see the locomotives all year; (01506) 822298; £7.50 mine and train, £4 train only. Discount voucher not valid on special event days.

Kinneil Estate Includes the interesting if not extensive remains of a Roman fortlet, as well as a few later ruins and remains. The converted stables of adjacent Kinneil House have a museum on the site's history, with lots of local pottery. You can still see the workshop where James Watt developed the steam engine, and there are pleasant woodland walks. Shop, limited disabled access; cl am and all day Sun and bank hols; (01506) 778530; free.

BRAEMAR NO1491

One of the most beautifully set

Highland villages; the Fife Arms (very much on the coach routes) is good for lunch. A steep path up Morrone takes the most determined walkers along a route used for a race in Braemar's famous Highland Gathering.

Braemar Castle ☒ (A93 NE) Highly unusual and charming exterior. Snacks, shop; cl Fri (exc July–Aug), and all Nov–Easter; (013397) 41219; £3.

Highland Heritage Centre ☒ (Mar Rd) Good, showing useful film on the area's history and scenery (inc an interesting look at the building of Balmoral Castle), and on the Gathering. Shops, disabled access; cl 21 Dec–1 Jan; (01339) 741944; free.

Linn of Dee NO0689 Not far, giving long glen walks into the Cairngorms along Glen Dee and the Lairig Ghru.

BRODIE CASTLE NH9757 (off A96) Handsome gabled castle with extensive art collection featuring 17th-c paintings of the Dutch school, English watercolours and French Impressionists. Before the National Trust for Scotland took it over in 1980 it had been the seat of the same family since 1160. Outside are woodland walks and wildlife observation hides, and beautiful daffodils in spring. Snacks, shop, limited disabled access; cl Sun am, wkdys in Oct and all Nov–Mar; (01309) 641371; £5; NTS. Their occasional evenings of traditional Scottish music are enjoyed by readers. The nearest really good place for a meal is the Clifton Hotel in Nairn.

BROUGHTY FERRY NO4630 **Broughty Castle Museum** (off A930 4m E of Dundee) 15th-c seaside castle rebuilt in the 19th c to defend the estuary, now a maritime museum. Plenty of harpoons and whaling exhibits – whaling used to be one of Dundee's major industries. Shop; cl Mon from Oct–Mar; (01382) 436916; free. The Fisherman's Tavern and Ship (fantastic view upstairs) are good.

BURNTISLAND NT2385 Once famous for shipbuilding (and shipbreaking), now a popular little resort, with an unusual octagonal **church** where the decision was made to produce the Authorised Version of the Bible in 1601.

CALLANDER NN6207

Quite a busy tourist town, popular in Victorian times thanks to the works of Walter Scott, and still remembered for its appearances in the original *Dr Finlay's Casebook*.

Kilmahog Woollen Mill (just N) Restored flax mill with 250-year-old working wheel, selling tweeds, tartans and other woollen gifts; also maybe whisky tasting. Meals, snacks, shop; cl 25 Dec and 1 Jan; (01877) 330268; free. There is usually a piper outside and Highland dancing some days in summer. The Lade Inn out here has good food.

Rob Roy & Trossachs Visitor Centre (Ancaster Sq) The story of Scotland's most whitewashed rascal (or brave supporter of the downtrodden, depending on your point of view), well told with hi-tech displays. Also information on the beautiful surrounding countryside. Shop, disabled access; cl wkdys Jan–Feb, 25–26 Dec and 1–2 Jan; (01877) 330342; £2.90.

The Trossachs The Highlands in microcosm, beloved by coach tours for their dense conifer forests, steep glens and beautifully framed lochs. Perhaps surprisingly, not brilliant for low-level walks unless you like forests; the route on to Callander Crags from Callander is one of the best. The Byre at Brig o' Turk is a good food stop.

CARRBRIDGE NH9022 **Landmark Heritage & Adventure Park** Good family day out, with films on Highland life (inc one in 3-D), well signposted forest trails (one through the tree-tops), an elaborate adventure playground, water-coaster, and Forestry Heritage Park with fully operational steam-powered sawmill (Apr–Oct). You can sometimes have a go at log-cutting or bark-stripping, and Fred the giant Clydesdale horse may be hauling logs to the mill. Great views from the top of the viewing tower. Meals, snacks, shop, disabled access; cl 25 Dec; (01479) 841614; £6.90. The Dalrachney Lodge Hotel does good lunches.

CASTLE CAMPBELL NS9699 Once known as Castle Gloom, this late 15th-c castle was burned by Cromwell's troops in the 1650s, but still has its courtyard, great hall and barrel roof, as well as splendid views from the tower. Snacks, shop; cl every Sun am, Thurs pm and all day Fri in winter, 25–26 Dec, 1–2 Jan; (01259) 742408; £2.50. The Kings Seat in Dollar has good home-made food.

Dollar Glen An amazing short track takes you up through these spectacular 60 acres of Arthur Rackham-esque woodland – catwalks, rock overhangs, jungle-thick vegetation, and a swirling stream below. Take care, some paths are steep and narrow, and can be dangerous after rain. But this is a gripping approach to Castle Campbell.

CAWDOR NH8449

Cawdor Castle (B9090) Home of the Thanes of Cawdor since the 14th c, this splendid old house is one of the most entertaining as well as interesting places to visit in the whole area. Look out especially for the tree inside a tower and the freshwater well inside the house, as well as the more usual fine tapestries, furnishings and paintings (inc Dali's odd interpretation of the Macbeth tale). The busy grounds have several pretty gardens, craft and wool shops, nature trails, and a little pitch-and-putt course. Meals, snacks, shop, disabled access to ground floor only; open May to mid-Oct; (01667) 404615; £5.60, grounds only £2.90. The nearby Cawdor Tavern is good for lunch.

CLAVA CAIRNS NH7544

A group of circular burial cairns from around 1600 BC surrounded by three concentric rings of great stones, on the banks of the River Nairn.

COLLESSIE NO2712

Fife Animal Park 🅰 (B937) Unique collection of ostriches, emus and rheas – they have birds of all ages (inc maybe newly hatched ones in the incubator house), as well as videos, play area, and animals such as lambs, pigs and wallabies. Meals, snacks, shop, good disabled access, cl Oct–Apr; (01337) 831830; £3.50.

CRAIGELLACHIE NJ2944

Speyside Cooperage Visitor Centre (Dufftown Rd) Working cooperage and visitor centre, with viewing area to watch the craftsmen and a tasting area. Shop (wide range of wood goods), picnic area, disabled access to exhibition only; cl wknds, and

mid-Dec to mid-Jan; (01340) 871108; £2.95. The fine Telford-built bridge here opened in 1814, and carried traffic until 1973. The little Fiddichside Inn (Keith Rd) is a charmingly old-fashioned fishing pub.

CRAIGIEVAR NJ5609

Craigievar Castle (A980) Perhaps the most fairytale-romantic of the area's castles, this picturesque early 17th-c multiple tower dotted with erratically shaped windows soars to a mushrooming of corbels, turrets and crow-stepped gables. Inside, a warren of narrow staircases climbs through a rich series of ornately beamed and plastered rooms. The National Trust for Scotland are worried that too many people come here, so if you do decide to visit (and it is worth while), try to avoid busy times – it's not a place to absorb coach parties comfortably. Castle open pm only Apr–Sept, grounds open all year; (013398) 83635; £6; NTS.

Noah's Ark Country Activity Centre (off A980) You can help to feed and tend to the animals at this friendly place, attractively just S of the castle. Snacks, shop, disabled access; open Apr–Oct (otherwise by appointment only); (01339) 883670; *£3.

CRAIL NO6107

One of the prettiest of the East Neuk fishing villages – the East Neuk being the local name for the E part of the Fife coast.

Secret Bunker (B940 4m W) Beneath an innocuous-looking farmhouse is a network of underground rooms and corridors from where the government would have run Scotland in a nuclear attack (cl Nov–Apr; (01333) 310301; £6.45).

CRATHES NO7596

Crathes Castle (A93) Beautiful 16th-c tower house with wonderful interiors – esp its ceiling paintings, filled with wise old sayings in a mixture of Scots and English. Best of all are the surrounding gardens, inc a four-acre walled garden with a remarkable series of carefully toned colour borders. Meals, snacks, shop, some disabled access; open Apr–Oct; (01330) 844525; £6, £4 garden or castle (£1 car park); NTS.

CRIEFF NN8621

A pleasant airy town, perched on the edge of the Highlands. A modern visitor centre (A822) has two potteries, plant centre and demonstrations of paperweight-making, and there's a Stuart Crystal factory shop on Muthill Rd. The Knock of Crieff, a hill just above, gives walkers a good viewpoint.

CULLODEN NH7445

Culloden Battlefield (B9006) The bleak site of the gruesome massacre in which the 25-year-old Duke of Cumberland destroyed the Highland army of Bonnie Prince Charlie. On the moor a cairn marks this last bloody battle fought on mainland Britain. You can see the Graves of the Clans and the Wells of the Dead, as well as the Old Leanach Cottage around which the battle was fought, now refurbished in period style. Meals, snacks, shop, disabled access; visitor centre cl 24–25 Dec, and first 2 wks in Jan; (01463) 790607; £3.50; NTS. The Snow Goose (E of A9/A96) does good food.

CULROSS NS9885

(off A985) Fascinating small town on the Forth, virtually unchanged since the 16th and 17th c. Until the 1930s this was because no one could afford any improvements, and since then its red pantiled-roofed houses have been carefully restored and preserved by the National Trust for Scotland (they are still lived in). There are the remains of a 13th-c abbey.

Culross Palace The laird's house was the first building the Trust purchased here. It's fully furnished in 17th-c style, and they've re-created a period garden. Guides are good at pointing out those small but fascinating details that make the difference between just another building and a real experience. Snacks, shop; cl am (exc Jun–Aug), wkdys in Oct, and all Nov–Mar; (01383) 880359; £5; NTS. The price includes admission to the Trust's two other main properties here, the Town House (good visitor centre), and the Study, with a Norwegian painted ceiling in the drawing room.

CUPAR NO3313

Scottish Deer Centre 🔲 (Bow of Fife; A91 just W) You can stroke the deer and feed the young fawns at this friendly place, and there are also nature and heritage trails, aerial walkways and observation platforms, and an adventure playground. There's an adjacent holiday shopping courtyard. Snacks, shop, disabled access; cl 25 Dec, 1 Jan; (01337) 810391; £3.95.

DEIL'S CAULDRON NN7624

Beauty spot reached by a signposted circular walk through Glen Lednock from Comrie (the Earthquake House at Comrie records tremors).

DOUNE NN6901

Doune Castle (A84) 14th-c stronghold with two fine restored towers on the banks of the River Teith. Strong associations with Bonnie Prince Charlie and Walter Scott, and the Knights of Ni – the castle was used in the filming of *Monty Python and the Holy Grail*. Shop; in winter cl Thurs pm, Sun am and all Fri; (01786) 841742; £2.50. The village's bridge is said to have been built out of spite by James IV's tailor when the ferryman refused him passage.

DUFFTOWN NJ3240

Glenfiddich Distillery (A491, just N) The only Highland distillery where you can follow the entire whisky production process from barley to bottle – most other distilleries bottle elsewhere. Look out for the friendly distillery cat. Enjoyable tours and generous tastings, shop, disabled access; cl winter wknds, Christmas; (01340) 820373; free. Dufftown has a useful museum.

DULNAIN BRIDGE NH9823

Speyside Heather Centre (Skye of Curr, off A95) Over 300 different types of heather growing in ornamental landscaped garden, along with an exhibition on its various uses, and shop with wide range of heather-based goods. Home-made meals and snacks, garden centre, disabled access; reduced winter opening times, best to phone; (01479) 851359; 75p exhibition.

DUNBLANE NN7801

Cathedral City Museum This small town of ancient origin, its name now tragically familiar all over the world, is of ancient origin, with plenty of old buildings in its narrow streets, esp around the close of its elegant 13th-c cathedral. This incorporates a much older tower, and has a beautiful oval window that you can see only from outside. The museum which explains the interesting background is nearby (cl 1–2pm, all day Sun, and Oct–early May; free). The Stirling Arms has good food.

DUNDEE NO3929

🏛 Beneath the straightforward modern wrappings of this bustling city, you can uncover signs of its distinguished heritage in a number of museums. Recent developments include a fun new science centre and a rewarding contemporary art gallery (see below). You can watch sweets being made at Shaws Factory (Mains Loan; phone for opening times, (01382) 461435; free). The Chequers (South Tay St), Royal Oak (Brook St – Indian), Mercantile (Commercial St) and Number 1 (Constitution Rd) all do good value food.

Camperdown Country Park (off A90) 400 acres of fine parkland with golf course, nature trails, woodland footpaths, and wildlife centre with indigenous animals from wolves and bears to wildcats. Also adventure play area themed around the defeat of the Dutch at the 1797 Battle of Camperdown. Snacks, shop, disabled access; (01382) 432689; free, £2 wildlife centre.

Contemporary Arts Centre (152 Nethergate) £9m centre for contemporary art and film, with two galleries showing changing exhibitions, plus an arts cinema, print studio and activity room for workshops. The trendy Jute Café Bar here has good food; shop, disabled access; centre open daily exc 25–26, 31 Dec and 1–2 Jan, galleries cl Mon; (01382) 432000; free.

Discovery Point (Docks) Excellent lively visitor centre with hi-tech displays on the Royal Research Ship *Discovery*, moored here, which was the first British purpose-built research vessel, commissioned for Scott's first expedition to the Antarctic; displays too on him and others who used the ship. Café, shop, disabled access; cl 25 Dec, 1–2 Jan; (01382) 201245; £5.50.

Frigate *Unicorn* 🏛 (Victoria Dock) This 1824 vessel is the oldest British-built warship still afloat, now with an audio-visual show and a museum of

naval life in her days in commission. Snacks, shop; cl wknds Nov–Mar, 25–26 Dec, 1–2 Jan; (01382) 200900; £3.50.

McManus Museum & Art Galleries (Albert Sq) Important works by 19th-c Scottish and English artists, and a splendid hall with vaulted ceiling and stained glass; cl Sun am, 25–26 Dec, 1–2 Jan; (01382) 434000; free.

Mills Observatory (Balgay Park) Exhibits on space research and astronomy, as well as a small planetarium (by prior arrangement or last Fri in month during winter), and splendid 10-inch refracting telescope. Shop; best to ring for opening times, which vary depending on when the sun sets – in autumn and winter for example they're open 4pm–10pm (cl Mon, limited wknd opening hours); (01382) 435846; free.

Sensation (Greenmarket) This fun new science centre claims to be the only one in Europe devoted entirely to the senses. With more than 60 interactive exhibits, the emphasis is certainly on hands-on fun, with displays ranging from a giant head which children can climb through (they can even slide out of the nose), to various computer-based games inc one based on germination, with individual seeds clammering for your attention – you have to choose what they need to make them grow. Snacks, shop, disabled access; cl 25–26 Dec, and 1 Jan; (01382) 228800; £5 (£3.50 children).

Verdant Works 🏛 (West Hendersons Wynd) Award-winning look at the jute industry, once an important part of the local economy, with films and interactive displays. Snacks, shop, disabled access; cl 25 Dec, 1–2 Jan; (01382) 225282; £5.50.

DUNFERMLINE NT0987

Quite a prosperous light-industry town with a distinguished distant past – it was once Scotland's capital.

Abbot House 🏛 (Maygate) Exhibition on the life of St Margaret of Scotland, a key figure in the town's history; her shrine is outside the abbey nr the East Gate. Meals, snacks, shop; cl 25 Dec, 1 Jan; (01383) 733266; £3. The cave she used to pray in is 84 steps below the Glen Bridge car park (cl

Oct–Easter; free).

Andrew Carnegie Museum
(Moodie St) Focuses on the man who
from humble origins in this house made
a fortune in Pittsburgh steel, then gave
away over $350 million – all the while
claiming he didn't believe in charity. Has
handloom weaving demonstrations the
first Fri of each month, May–Oct. Shop,
disabled access; cl Sun am, and
Nov–Mar; £2.

Dunfermline Abbey The remains of
a Benedictine abbey and later church
buildings are pleasantly set in quiet
precincts away from the busy centre.
The foundations of the original 11th-c
church underlie the more elaborate
Norman nave, and the grave of King
Robert the Bruce is marked by a
modern brass in the choir stalls. The
Palace is the birthplace of Charles I.
Snacks, shop; cl Sun am in Oct, plus
Thurs pm and all Fri Nov–May; (01383)
739026; £2.

Dunfermline Museum (Viewfield
Terrace) Looks at the local
manufacture of damask linen (open pm
wkdys; free).

Pittencrieff House Museum
(Pittencrieff Park) Fine 17th-c mansion
in gently rugged glen, with displays and
paintings (free).

DUNKELD NO0242
Charming small town by the River Tay.
The cathedral has the tomb of the
notorious Wolf of Badenoch,
Alexander Stewart (the illegitimate son
of English king Richard II). There are
pretty preserved cottages (NTS), and
riverside forest walks through National
Trust land around the waterfalls nr the
Hermitage, an 18th-c folly, and so-
called Ossian's Cave; there may be bat
tours and other ranger-led walks in
summer. The Atholl Arms is a useful
stop.

**Beatrix Potter Garden &
Exhibition** A small garden next to the
Birnam Institute re-creates the house
of Mrs Tiggywinkle and Peter Rabbit's
burrow (free); Beatrix Potter spent
holidays here. The institute itself is
currently being refurbished, and when it
reopens in May will have a new building
housing a café, and various exhibitions
inc one on the author herself; (01350)
728970. Birnam is a tiny township, a 15-
min walk from Dunkeld across the
River Tay. Birnam Wood (of *Macbeth*
fame) has a venerable oak, and there's
stirring walking country around.

EDZELL NO5969
Edzell Castle (B966) Some unique
features at this pretty old place – the
walled garden planted here in 1604, and
the charming series of heraldic and
mythical sculptures that decorate the
walls around it; these alternate with
recesses for flowers and nests for birds.
They claim to have captured on camera
the castle's rather active ghost. Shop,
snack, limited disabled access; in winter
cl Thurs pm, all day Fri and Sun am;
(01356) 648631; £2.50. The Ramsay
Arms in Fettercairn has decent food,
and just N there's a lovely drive up Glen
Esk, passing a wayside folk museum.

ELGIN NJ2263
Shopping town of some poise, with
some handsome ancient buildings and
handy for the coast; Thunderton House
has decent food.

Elgin Cathedral Founded in 1224,
and known as the Lantern of the North
and the Glory of the Kingdom because
of its extraordinary beauty and fine-
traceried windows. There's still quite a
lot to see of the ruins: the 15th-c nave
has some ancient Celtic cross slabs with
Pictish symbols, and you can go inside
the spires. A viewing platform in one of
the towers gives unrestricted views.
Shop, some disabled access; cl winter
Thurs pm and all Fri, Sun am, 25–26
Dec, 1–2 Jan; (01343) 547171; £2.50.

Elgin Museum 🔢 (High St) Recently
refurbished thanks to a Lottery grant,
with a world-famous fossil collection
and changing exhibitions (cl Sun am, all
Nov–Apr; £2).

Moray Motor Museum 🔢 (Bridge
St) Decent little place, in a converted
mill (shop, disabled access, cl Oct–Mar;
£2.50).

Pluscarden Abbey (nr Barnhill, 5m
SW) Fascinating; built in the 13th c, it
gradually fell to ruin, but was rebuilt this
century by monks from Prinknash
Abbey down in Gloucestershire – they
now sing a rediscovered chant which
may well have been sung by St Columba
himself; (01343) 890257; free.

Spynie Palace (A941 2m N) Former
residence of the bishops of Moray, the

biggest tower house in Scotland, with good views over Spynie Loch. Shop, disabled access; cl winter Thurs pm, Fri and am Sun; (01343) 546358; £1.80.

ELIE NT4999

Attractive fishing village set around a broad bay – the beach is notably clean and safe (and has a good pub, the Ship, virtually on it).

FALKIRK NS8979

Callender House 🏛 (A803 just E) This huge park, with woodland walks and lots of summer activities, includes Callender House, a striking old house used briefly as HQ by Oliver Cromwell. Remodelled in the 19th c to look like a French château, it's now a museum, with costumed guides interpreting its history. Part of the Antonine Wall, the Roman Empire's farthest frontier, runs through the grounds. Meals, snacks, shop, disabled access; house cl Sun Oct–Mar; (01324) 503770; house £3, park free.

Millennium Link This will bring nearly 70 miles of canal from Glasgow to Edinburgh back to life, rebuilding a link that was severed over 60 years ago when a flight of 19th-c locks was closed. The project (partly funded by Lottery money) has so far seen the removal of obstacles inc filled-in stretches and low bridges, and the refurbishment of locks, and will come to fruition in 2002 with the opening of the spectacular Falkirk Wheel (Lime Rd, Tamfour Hill): a rotating boat lift as high as a nine-storey block of flats which will winch vessels up a 24-metre (80-ft) rise. It has been designed by the same team of architects responsible for the new Scottish Parliament building, who consider it to be a form of contemporary sculpture; a visitor centre will have information about the canal's restoration and the construction of the wheel; phone (0345) 952000 for details. It is hoped that the canal restoration will stimulate economic regeneration.

Rough Castle (6m W) One of the best-preserved sections of the Antonine Wall; not too much is left of the Roman fort that once stood here, but you can still see the ramparts and ditches; free.

FALKLAND NO2507

Falkland Palace & Garden Lovely Renaissance palace of the Stuart kings and queens, set below the Lomond Hills on the main street. Not all is as old as it looks, but it doesn't really matter – accurate restoration work has created a comfortably cosy and genuinely lived-in feel. Pleasant gardens and grounds, with the 1539 tennis courts said to be the oldest in the country. Shop; cl Sun am, and Nov–Mar; (01337) 857397; £5, £2.40 garden only; NTS. Parts of the village are delightful and were Scotland's first conservation area – the Hunters Lodge, opposite the palace, has decent food.

FETTERCAIRN NO6573

The square has a magnificent archway erected to commemorate a visit by Queen Victoria, and the Ramsay Arms has decent food. The drive along the twisting and climbing B974 to Banchory is good, with spectacular views from **Cairn o' Mount** at the top – and when the water's high enough salmon jumping nr the Dee bridge as you enter Banchory.

Fasque 🏛 (just N) Prime Minister William Gladstone lived here 1830–1851, and it still belongs to his family. The main rooms look as if they've scarcely been changed (let alone modernised) since he moved to Wales, and it's quite cluttered with homely odds and ends. Three years ago a parcel of shooting targets turned up behind a chair posted from London in the 1920s and covered with Urgent stickers – but not yet even opened. There's a touching gallery of servants' portraits and lots of Gladstone memorabilia. Shop, limited disabled access; open May–Sept; (01561) 340569; £4.

Fettercairn Distillery (Distillery Rd) One of Scotland's oldest licensed distilleries, with tours, tastings, and good audio-visual show. Shop, disabled access to visitor centre only; cl Sun, and Oct–Apr; (01561) 340205; free.

FINDLATER CASTLE NJ5467

This windswept cliff-edge ruin makes a good destination for a walk; walkers can enjoy other stretches of this coast around Banff, with the bus service along the main road a useful method of return. The Cullen Bay Hotel has good value food.

FOCHABERS NJ3359
Baxters Visitor Centre (A96 just W)
Explores how the grocery shop set up
by George and Margaret Baxter grew
into a company whose food is now sold
all over the world. Landscaped gardens
and woodland walk; meals, snacks, good
shops, some disabled access; cl 24
Dec–7 Jan; (01343) 820393; free,
charges for tastings and
demonstrations.

Folk Museum (High St) Very good;
open Apr–Sept, free. The Gordon
Arms is a reliable food stop in this
pleasant small town.

FORRES NJ0356
Dallas Dhu Distillery (2m S)
Perfectly preserved Victorian distillery,
which you can wander around on your
own. Animatronic models explain
what's happening. Shop (nearly 200
different types of whisky), disabled
access; cl winter Thurs pm, Fri, Sun am;
(01309) 676548; £3.

Falconer Museum (Tolbooth St)
Good fossil collection; cl Sun all year
plus winter Fri and Sat, best to check;
(01309) 673701; free.

Sueno's Stone (E end of town)
Mysterious 9th- or 10th-c stone that
may have been erected to
commemorate a forgotten battle. It's 6
metres (20 ft) high, carved with a cross
on one side and groups of warriors on
the other. In summer you can usually
climb the Nelson Tower in Grant Park
for good views of the Moray Firth; free.

FORT GEORGE NH7656
One of the finest examples of an 18th-c
artillery building, one of three
fortresses built after 1745, when the
Hanoverians were taking no risks in
keeping this area firmly under their
thumb. Very big, with quite a bit to see
and special events all year. Snacks, shop,
disabled access; cl Sun am, 25–26 Dec
and maybe 1–2 Jan; (01667) 462777; £4.
Just off from the fort in the Moray Firth
you may be lucky enough to see one of
the very few inshore schools of
dolphins around the British coast.

FORVIE NK0029
Forvie National Nature Reserve
The fifth-largest sand dune system in
Britain – and the one least disturbed by
people, so lots of wildlife inc Britain's
biggest colony of eider ducks. You have
to stick to the footpaths so as not to
disturb the birds and other wildlife.
Disabled access; visitor centre cl winter
wknds; (01358) 751330; free.

FRASERBURGH NJ9967
Museum of Scottish Lighthouses
(Quarry Rd) Based around a lighthouse
working up to 1991; guided tours take
you to the top and demonstrate how
everything works. Snacks, shop, limited
disabled access; cl 25–26 Dec and 1–2
Jan; (01346) 511022; £3.25.

GLAMIS NO3847
Glamis Castle (A94) The family home
of the Earls of Strathmore, and the
childhood home of the Queen Mother;
a splendid creation, utterly suitable as
the setting for Shakespeare's murder of
Duncan in *Macbeth*. Notable features
include the chapel with its painted
panels and ceiling, and of course there
are those stories about what's locked
away in one of the towers. Meals,
snacks, shop, limited disabled access; cl
early Nov–Mar; (01307) 840393; £6.
The Strathmore Arms is good for lunch.

GLEN ROY NN3088
The glen and its curious Parallel Roads
(not actually roads but the tubmarks of
a former glacier) can be seen from an
easily walked track along its bottom, a
spectacular 4-mile route from Brae Roy
Lodge (return the same way).

GLENMORE NH9809
Cairngorm Reindeer Centre 🔲
(A951) Mingle with free-ranging
reindeer in a pretty stretch of the
Cairngorms; you can feed and stroke
them. Guided walks leave the visitor
centre every day, weather permitting,
at 11am (plus 2.30pm May–Sept). Shop,
disabled access to visitor centre only
(though usually reindeer down here
too); cl 25 Dec, 1 Jan; (01479) 861228;
£5.

HUNTLY NJ5240
Huntly Castle The original medieval
castle here was destroyed and rebuilt
several times, once by Mary, Queen of
Scots. Reconstructed for the last time
in 1602, the ruins are worth a look for
their ornate heraldic decorations. Shop,
disabled access; in winter cl Thurs pm
and Fri; (01466) 793191; *£2.50. In the
square is a little local history museum,
and a ski centre can teach you how to
cross-country ski through the local

forest. On the outskirts of the town not far from the Somerfield supermarket, Deans Shortbread has a good factory shop.

North East Falconry Centre 🖼 (Cairnie, off A96 N) Four flying displays a day in a richly meadowed glade, as well as herd of red deer. Snacks, shop, disabled access; cl Nov–Feb; (01466) 760328; £3.75.

INNERPEFFRAY NN9018
Innerpeffray Library 🖼 Founded in 1680 by the 3rd Lord Madderty, this is Scotland's oldest free lending library; many rare and interesting books inc a particularly fine collection of Bibles. Cl 12.45–2pm, all day Thurs (by appointment only Dec–Jan), but always best to check; (01764) 652 819; *£2.50.

INVERNESS NH6645
The biggest town up here, and the main shopping town for the whole of the N of Scotland. It has an attractive riverside setting and is a handy centre without being at all touristy. James Thins is a good book shop, Nicky Tams (Ness Bank Rd) has decent food, and the Blackfriars (Academy St) is good for local colour. From here the train across to Kyle of Lochalsh gives good Highland views – 2½ hours, the last minutes of which are much the best. There are good walks by a flight of locks on the Caledonian Canal from the Clachnaharry Inn just NW.

Inverness Aquadome (Bught Park) Lively swimming centre with wave machine, log flumes and a health suite inc sauna, steam room and a spa pool; cl 25–26 Dec, and 1–2 Jan.

KEMNAY NJ7212
Castle Fraser (off A944) Once one of the grandest castles of Mar, the z-shaped building incorporates the remains of an earlier one, and there are excellent formal gardens. Snacks, shop; cl wkdys in Oct, and all Nov–Apr (exc Easter), grounds open all year; (01330) 833463; £5, grounds only £2; NTS.

KENMORE NN7644
Scottish Crannog Centre
Interesting reconstruction of a prehistoric loch dwelling. Snacks, shop, disabled access; usually cl Nov–Mar but this year they are hoping to extend their winter opening times, phone to check; (01887) 830583; £3.50. The

attractive estate village is pleasant for a stroll, with a poem pencilled by Burns himself on wall in the welcoming Kemore Hotel.

KENNETHMONT NJ5430
Leith Hall & Garden In over 280 acres of interesting grounds, this mansion was home to the Leith family for over 300 years, and the elegantly furnished rooms reflect their life-style and tastes; an exhibition examines their long tradition of military service. The gardens are breathtakingly beautiful in Jun, and dotted elsewhere around the estate are ponds, nature trails, a bird hide, unusual semi-circular stables, and an ice-house. Staff are very friendly; snacks; house cl am, wkdys in Oct, and all Nov–Mar, grounds open daily; (01464) 831216; £6. Readers tell us that a stay in the gateway lodge here is very enjoyable.

KILDRUMMY NJ4516
Kildrummy Castle Now in ruins, though still with its original 13th-c round towers, hall and chapel, as well as some later remains. Cl Sun am, plus Thurs pm and all day Fri Oct–Nov and all Dec–Mar; (01975) 571331; £2.
Kildrummy Gardens (A97) Very beautiful indeed and of some botanical interest. There's an alpine garden in an old quarry, a water garden, walks in the woods, a video showing the changes through the seasons, and a small museum. Shop, snacks, disabled access; cl Nov–Mar; (01975) 571203; £2. The ruins provide a spectacular backdrop.

KINCRAIG NH8305
Highland Wildlife Park (B9152) Owned by the same charity as Edinburgh Zoo, this 260-acre wildlife park somehow manages to seem a bit wilder than most animal attractions; perhaps it's because they specialise in species once native to the area, so you really get a feeling that the animals could have wandered out of the surrounding woods and mountains. You drive safari-style around enclosures of reindeer, bears, wildcats and enormous bison. The most exciting feature is the wolf territory, where a walkway takes you to a safe vantage point right in the heart of the enclosure. Plenty of rare breeds, inc the wild przewalksi's horses, one of the world's rarest mammals, and you may

see red squirrels feeding in the forest; daily talks and wknd summer face-painting. Snacks and shop in visitor centre (cl winter), disabled access; cl Nov–Mar in bad weather; (01540) 651270; £6.50.

KINGUSSIE NH7500

Highland Folk Museum (Duke St) The first folk museum in Britain, originally opened on Iona in the 1930s. Still a good range of exhibits, inc craft demonstrations and a reconstructed Isle of Lewis black house. Disabled access; cl Sun am, wknds Sept–Oct, best to phone for winter opening times; (01540) 661307; £4 (inc admission to the Highland Folk Park below). The Royal is useful for lunch; the town's pronounced 'Kinoossie'.

Highland Folk Park (A86 E) Demonstrates the life and work of crofters at the turn of the last century; you may be able to help with some of the farming activities. Also a Museum of Highland Sport, which explains why so many of the area's golfers are left-handed. Usually open wkdys Apr–Oct; (01540) 673551; £4 (inc admission to the folk museum above).

KINNOULL HILL NO1423 Just outside Perth, this offers walkers forest tracks and paths, and two folly 'castles' above the River Tay.

KINROSS NO1202

Kinross House Gardens Rather fine and formal, with yew hedges, topiary, roses and herbaceous borders. Disabled access; cl Oct–Apr; (01577) 863680; £2. The Muirs has good value food, as does the Lomond Hotel at Kinnesswood with its quiet views over Loch Leven.

Loch Leven Castle Reached by ferry, the islet fortress where Mary, Queen of Scots was imprisoned for a while; she was rowed to freedom by a page boy, but only after she had been persuaded to abdicate in favour of her infant son. Shop; limited disabled access; cl Nov–Mar, though best to check winter opening; (0131) 668 8800; £3 (inc ferry).

Loch Leven RSPB Visitor Centre At the S end of the lake, with good facilities for watching the birds; in the winter the evening flights and sounds of the thousands of ducks and geese are very moving. Snacks, shop, cl 25–26, 31

Dec, 1 Jan; (01577) 862355; £3. The lake itself is serene rather than dramatic.

KIRKCALDY NT3093 This busy resort and shopping town is not too interesting to visitors, but it has a decent museum and art gallery (see below), and there are some charming old wynds and houses in the eastern suburb of Dysart, which has its own picturesque little harbour. Between here and the main town is 15th-c **Ravenscraig Castle**, perhaps most notable for its symmetrical shape. Great views over the Firth of Forth. Snacks, limited disabled access; free.

Kirkcaldy Museum & Art Gallery In the town's attractive War Memorial Gardens, this houses a superb collection of 18th- to 20th-c Scottish paintings inc perhaps the largest gathering of works by William McTaggart and the Scottish colourist S J Peploe outside the National Galleries of Scotland; also a local heritage museum, and changing exhibitions of art and crafts, photography and natural history. Meals, snacks, shop, disabled access; cl Sun am; (01592) 412860; free.

KIRRIEMUIR NO3854

Barrie's Birthplace (Brechin Rd) The birthplace in 1860 of the writer of *Peter Pan* in 1860: the upper floors are furnished in the style of the period, and next door are displays relating to his work, both literary and theatrical. Teas, shop, disabled access; open daily Apr–Sept (exc Sun am), wknds in Oct; (01575) 572646; £2.50; NTS.

LOCH EARN NN5924 With a trunk road alongside, not one of Scotland's quieter lochs – and largely given over to water-skiing and that sort of thing. Lochearnhead offers a round walk from along a nature trail into Glen Ogle and back via the trackbed of an abandoned railway.

LOCH ERICHT NN6284 Very peaceful but does involve foot-slogging to make the most of it. The road from Dalwhinnie on the A9 at the N end runs along the foot of a steep forested slope; the S end of the loch has more varied scenery, but no road once you reach the end of the little road off the B846 at Bridge of Ericht.

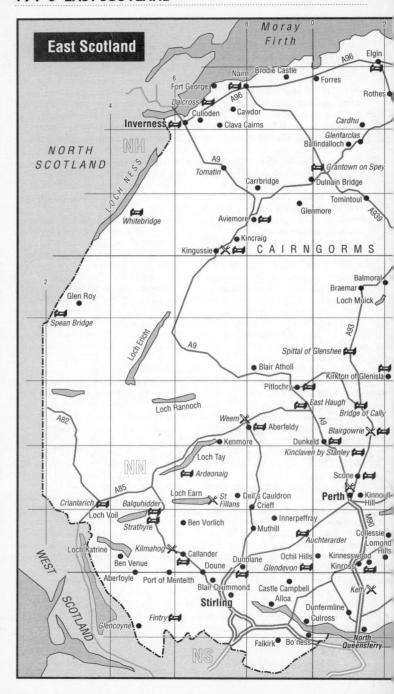

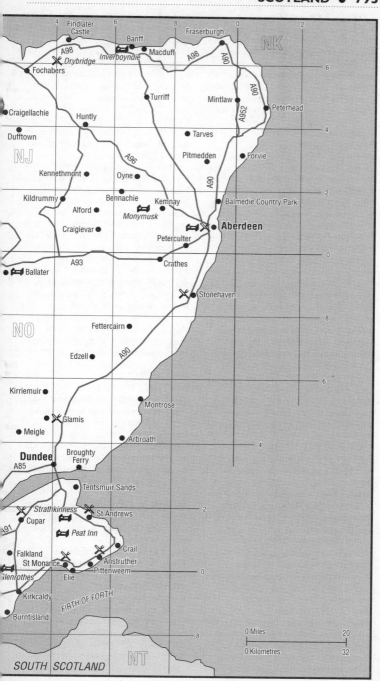

Findlater
Castle
Banff
A98
Inverboyndie
Drybridge
Fochabers
Macduff
A98
Fraserburgh
NK
A90
Craigellachie
Huntly
Turriff
Mintlaw
A90
A952
Peterhead
Dufftown
NJ
Tarves
Kennethmont
A96
Oyne
Pitmedden
A90
Forvie
Kildrummy
Bennachie
Kemnay
Balmedie Country Park
Alford
Monymusk
Craigievar
Peterculter
Aberdeen
A93
Crathes
Ballater
Stonehaven
NO
Fettercairn
Edzell
A90
Kirriemuir
Montrose
Glamis
Meigle
Arbroath
Dundee
Broughty
Ferry
A85
Tentsmuir Sands
Strathkinness
St Andrews
Cupar
Peat Inn
A91
Falkland
Crail
St Monance
Anstruther
Glenrothes
Elie
Pittenweem
Kirkcaldy
FIRTH OF FORTH
Burntisland
NT
SOUTH SCOTLAND

0 Miles 20
0 Kilometres 32

LOCH KATRINE NN4009
A lovely stretch of water that inspired Scott's *Lady of the Lake*, with a Victorian steamer named after the author in summer. The main approach to the E end through the Trossachs does bring a fair bit of summer traffic, but the central part of the loch is served by just a narrow back road, so is fairly peaceful even then.

LOCH MUICK NO2984
Nestling below the summit of Lochnagar, this has paths around its shores, with a car park at the end of the Glen Muick road from Ballater.

LOCH RANNOCH NN6257
Among the quieter and more beautiful lochs, wooded for much of its length. There are peaceful walks from the back road along the S shore.

LOCH TAY NN7745
Remarkably long, with the view seeming to change moment by moment as the clouds flit across the sky. It has a quiet road along its S side. There are easy walks at the E end of the loch, from Kenmore (see above), along the banks of the River Tay, or into the adjacent forest to a viewpoint over the loch.

Ben Lawers This towering bulk, well over 1,200 metres (nearly 4,000 ft), dominates Loch Tay, and is an interesting spot, with alpine wild flowers not found elsewhere in Britain and a quite different feel from other Highland mountains; a steep road leads up the side.

LOCH VOIL NN5220
Served by just a narrow back road, so fairly peaceful even in summer; it's famous for having Rob Roy's grave at Balquhidder. It's worth keeping on the road beyond the far end of the loch; there's some striking scenery around the picnic site at its end.

LOMOND HILLS NO2206
A level walk from the car park by the road above Falkland gives some pleasant rambles – not to be confused with Loch Lomond, this upland gives views over most of SE Scotland.

MACDUFF NJ7064
Marine Aquarium (High Shore) Huge central tank holding nearly half a million litres, open to the sky – a unique design. Emphasis on fish native to the Moray Firth, with touch pools and audio-visual

presentation. Snacks, shop, disabled access, cl 25–26 Dec, 1–2 Jan; (01261) 833369; £3.75.

MEIGLE NO2844
Meigle Museum Outstanding collection of Pictish sculptured stones, all found in or around the churchyard. Shop, disabled access; cl 12.30–1.30pm, and all Dec–Mar; (01828) 640612; £1.80.

MINTLAW NJ9847
Aberdeenshire Farming Museum In over 200 acres of lovely woodland and farmland, criss-crossed with nature trails and with plenty of wildlife, this illustrates two centuries of farming history, with seasonal open-air demonstrations and tours. Meals, snacks, shop, disabled access; park open all year, museum cl Oct–Apr; (01771) 622906; free.

MONTROSE NO6856
Montrose Basin Wildlife Centre (A934) The enclosed estuary is a rich feeding ground for thousands of native and migrant birds, inc oystercatchers, curlews and eider ducks. This centre has great views, interactive displays and high-powered telescopes. Snacks, shop, disabled access; cl 25–26 Dec, 1 Jan; (01674) 676336; £2.50.

MUTHILL NN8616
Drummond Castle Gardens (A822) Majestic formal gardens originally laid out in 1630 by the 2nd Earl of Perth. Lovely views from the upper terrace, splendid early Victorian parterre, and centre-piece sundial designed and built by the master mason of King Charles I. Open pm May–Oct; (01764) 681257; £3.

NAIRN NH8856
A quiet, relaxed and rather discreet old-fashioned resort, with good clean sheltered beaches.

NORTH QUEENSFERRY NT1380
Deep-Sea World *See separate family panel on p.781.*

OCHIL HILLS NS9099
A range of green mountains which rise without preamble from the lowland plain – a striking textbook example of the Highland Fault. A path from Tillicoultry up Mill Glen takes you to Ben Cleuch, the highest point of the range.

OYNE NJ6725

Archaeolink 🖼 This lively centre is a fun exploration of the past. A remarkable turf-roofed building houses an audio-visual presentation, there's an exhibition on myths and legends, and you can try out ancient crafts such as weaving, grinding and arrow-making. Outside are the remains of an Iron Age hill fort, a reconstructed Iron Age farm, a new Roman marching camp and a sandpit play area, where younger members of the family can dig for the past. Meals, snacks, shop, disabled access, cl Nov–Mar; (01464) 851500; £3.90.

PERTH NO1223

Spaciously laid out along the broad River Tay; with an excellent specialist rhododendron nursery at Glendoick Gardens (A90). There are a couple of decent museums and galleries, and the Greyfriars (South St) is popular for lunch.

Branklyn Garden (Dundee Rd) Only about 2 acres but seems much bigger, thanks to a remarkable planting of interesting rhododendrons, small trees, asiatic primulas, meconopsis, lilies and the like. Shop, disabled access; cl Oct–Mar; (01738) 625535; £2.50; NTS.

Caithness Glass (Inveralmond Industrial Estate, N edge) Displays of paperweight-making, with audio-visual theatre, collectors' museum and factory shop. Meals, snacks, shop, disabled access; cl 25–26 Dec, 1–2 Jan, no glass-making wknds (exc occasionally during July and Aug); (01738) 637373; free.

Huntingtower Castle (just W) The main thing to see is its interesting painted ceiling; in winter cl Thurs pm and Fri, 25–26 Dec, 1–2 Jan; £2. The nearby Huntingtower House Hotel has good value food and a streamside garden.

PETERCULTER NJ7900

Drum Castle (off A93) Still looks out over what's left of the medieval forest granted the family by Robert the Bruce. Mainly a much-altered Jacobean mansion, the house is based around a 13th-c keep, one of the three oldest tower houses in Scotland. There's a historic rose garden. Snacks, shop, limited disabled access; cl am, wkdys in

Oct, and all Nov–Easter, grounds open all year; (01330) 811454; £5; NTS. The Lairhillock Inn at Netherley a few miles S is good for lunch.

PETERHEAD NK1246

One of Europe's busiest fishing ports, with a bustling market and rejuvenated marina. There's a good local history **museum** on St Peter St (cl Weds pm, Sun and bank hols; free) and a **heritage centre** (South Rd) with interactive displays on the fishing industry. Shop, meals, snacks, disabled access; cl Sun am and winter wkdys; £2.50.

Ugie Fish House (Golf Rd) Ancient place selling a good range of wild salmon and trout, caught from the adjacent river in season; cl Sat pm, all day Sun; (01779) 476209.

PITLOCHRY NN9458

An inland resort town for a good long time, beautifully set in fine countryside; a happy sort of place, with a comfortable feel. There's lovely woodland on the banks of man-made Loch Faskally, with walks and nature trails. The Westlands and the Moulin Inn (which brews its own beer) have decent food.

Edradour Distillery (A924 E) Scotland's smallest distillery, founded in 1825 and virtually unchanged since Victorian times. Guided tours, tastings, shop, some disabled access; cl Sun am Mar–Oct, all Sun Nov to mid-Dec, and mid-Dec to Feb (exc shop); (01796) 472095; free.

Killiecrankie Visitor Centre (B8079 NW) Queen Victoria was just one of the people to have found this romantic spot beguiling, but it wasn't always so serene. In 1689 it was the site of a fierce battle when the Highlanders routed the troops of William IV, and a Visitor Centre tells the tale. Snacks, shop, disabled access; cl Nov–Apr; (01796) 473233; £1 for parking; NTS. The Killiecrankie Hotel has good food.

Pitlochry Power Station The visitor centre shows how the hydro-electric scheme works, and you may see salmon leaping up the fish ladder; cl Nov–Mar; £2.

PITMEDDEN NJ8828

Pitmedden Garden (A920) Originally planted in the 17th c and pretty much unchanged since, with sundials, fountains and pavilions in elaborate formal gardens. Snacks, shop, limited disabled access; open May–Sept; (01651) 842352; £3.90; NTS. The Redgarth Hotel over at Oldmeldrum has decent food (and good bedrooms).

PITTENWEEM NO5402
Attractive East Neuk fishing village, with some attractive crow-gabled houses (the gables in steps which seagulls rather than crows sit on here).

Kellie Castle & Gardens (B9171)
Fine example of 16th- and 17th-c domestic architecture, though parts date from the 14th c, with good collections of plasterwork, panelling and furniture. Also four acres of gardens inc a Victorian walled garden. Snacks, shop, disabled access to ground floor and gardens; grounds open all year, house cl am, wkdys in Oct, and all Nov–May (exc Easter); (01333) 720271; £4, garden only £1; NTS.

PORT OF MENTEITH NN5700
Inchmahome Priory Famous as the refuge of the infant Mary, Queen of Scots in 1543, this Augustinian priory was founded in 1238 on an island in the middle of the lake, and in spring and summer you can get a boat across. Robert the Bruce prayed here before the Battle of Bannockburn. Snacks, shop; cl Oct–Mar; (01877) 385294; £3 inc ferry.

ROTHES NJ2749
Glen Grant Distillery (Rothes) Founded in 1840 by the brothers Grant, whose malt whisky was one of the first to be bottled and sold as a single malt. Guided tours, tastings, shop, some disabled access; cl Sun am, all Nov to mid-Mar; (01542) 783318; £2.50.

SCONE NO1126
Scone Palace (off A93) The seat of government in Scotland from Pictish times, though the current building is largely 16th-c behind an 18th-c castellated façade. It was the site of the Stone of Destiny – the famous coronation stone – until it was seized by the English in 1296 (it's now been returned to Scotland, though to Edinburgh Castle). Good displays of porcelain, furniture, clocks and needlework, and the grounds are pleasant. Meals, snacks, shop, some disabled access; cl mid-Oct–Apr;

(01738) 552300; £5.90. Pronounced 'Scoon', by the way.

ST ANDREWS NO5116
This civilised university town doubles as rather a dignified seaside resort, with clean, safe beaches. It's outstanding for golfers, though to play on the hallowed greens of the Old Course, you'll need to ring the St Andrews Links Trust on (01334) 466666 before 2pm the day before you want to go, to enter a daily ballot; after that you'll have to tee up £80. There are a few interesting museums on the city's history, some quite lively, and a number of fine buildings belonging to Scotland's oldest university – esp St Leonard's and St Mary's colleges. South St is worth strolling along: attractive riggs or small courts and alleys off, the ancient West Port gateway at the end, and **Holy Trinity church** where John Knox preached his first sermon in 1547. Ma Bells (pleasant seafront views outside), Ogstons, Westport and (a mile S) Grange are all good eating places.

British Golf Museum (Bruce Embankment) Fascinates anyone keen on the game, with interactive and audio-visual displays going right through its 500-year history. Assorted memorabilia include lots of glamorous golfing gear, and the technology is some of the most up-to-date you'll find in any museum. Shop, disabled access; cl Tues and Weds mid-Oct–Easter, 25 Dec–1 Jan (limited opening hours during winter); (01334) 478880; £3.75.

St Andrews Aquarium 🏛 (The Scores) Recently refurbished, with displays of tropical fish, sea-horses and resident seals. Meals, snacks, shop, limited disabled access; phone for winter opening, cl 25 Dec, 1 Jan; (01334) 74786; £4.50.

St Andrews Botanic Garden 🏛 (just off Canongate) Around 18 pleasantly landscaped acres, with a good range of trees and shrubs, and several glasshouses. Disabled access; (01334) 477178; £2.

St Andrews Castle 13th-c, the scene of Cardinal Beaton's murder during a wave of anti-Catholic feeling in 1546. It was largely demolished in the 17th c, but some substantial ruins remain. Shop, disabled access; cl 25–26 Dec,

1–2 Jan; (01334) 477196; £2.50.

St Andrews Cathedral Impressive twin-towered Norman remains; in its time this was the largest cathedral in Scotland, but angry locals sacked it in the 16th c. Shop, limited disabled access; cl 25–26 Dec, 1–2 Jan; (01334) 472563; £2. A joint ticket with the castle costs £3.75. Beside it the very tall and narrow Romanesque **St Rule's Tower** is part of the older church the cathedral was built to replace (perhaps pre-Conquest), and if you can face over 150 steps gives wonderful views from the top.

ST MONANCE NO5201
One of the most attractive East Neuk fishing villages, with an unusual fisherman's church and a restored 18th-c windmill (the Seafood Restaurant has good seafood and sea views).

STIRLING NS7994
Strategically placed on the Firth of Forth, this is a very unstuffy place, with the university students putting quite a bit of buzz into the atmosphere. Dropping down the steep hill on which the castle stands is an attractive and interesting network of old streets, with a lot of character in their old-to-ancient buildings; Argyll Lodgings is an interesting ruined Renaissance-style mansion, and the **Church of Holy Rude** was where Mary, Queen of Scots and James VI were crowned as babies.

Bannockburn Heritage Centre (A872 S) Plenty of information on Robert the Bruce's finest hour, inc an audio-visual show on the battle itself. Café, shop, disabled access; cl Jan–Feb; (01786) 812664; £2.50.

Old Town Jail (St John St) In season, actor-led tours take you through the preserved cells of this 19th-c jail (there's a self-guided audio tour at other times). A glass-sided lift takes you up to roof-top views over the town. Shop, disabled access; cl 25–26 Dec, 1 Jan; (01786) 450050; £3.30.

Smith Art Gallery & Museum (Dumbarton Rd) Good changing exhibitions; cl Sun am, all day Mon; (01786) 471917; free.

Stirling Castle Provides magnificent views from its lofty hilltop site. It became very popular with the Royal family in the 15th and 16th c, and most

of the buildings date from that period. The finest features are the Chapel Royal built by James VI (and I of England), and the Renaissance palace built by James V. A 10-year restoration project has transformed the Great Hall back to its early 16th-c grandeur; crowning the work is a huge new hammerbeam roof made from 350 oak trees and erected by the same craftsmen who assembled the new roof in St George's Hall, Windsor Castle, after the fire of 1992. Snacks, shop; cl 25–26 Dec, 1–2 Jan; (01786) 450000; *£6, parking £2. There's a good visitor centre in a restored building next door. Whistlebinkies (St Mary's Wynd), formerly part of the ancient castle stables, has decent food.

Wallace Monument (top of Abbey Craig, just NE) Perhaps Stirling's most satisfying attraction, a huge 67-metre (220-ft) Victorian tower with dramatic views from the top of its 246 spiralling steps. Each floor has lively audio-visual displays, one on Sir William Wallace, another examining other Scottish heroes. There is a statue of Wallace as portrayed by Mel Gibson in *Braveheart* in the car park. Snacks, shop; cl Christmas, New Year; (01786) 472140; *£3.30.

STONEHAVEN NO8783
Dunnottar Castle (just S) On a precipitous sea-girt crag stands this the bleak and battered but still extensive and well preserved 14th-c ruin, used for the filming of Mel Gibson's *Hamlet*. It sheltered the Scottish Crown Jewels during the Civil War, but has seen much darker episodes in its time. Shop; cl wknds Nov–Easter, 25–26 Dec, 1 Jan; (01569) 62173; £3.50.

Tolbooth Museum (Old Pier) Good local history museum in ancient tolbooth; usually cl am, all day Tues, and Oct–Jun but best to check; (01779) 477778; free. This old fishing town has more seasidey but discreet Victorian streets in its upper part; the harbourside Marine has good reasonably priced food.

TARVES NJ8634
Haddo House (off B999) Wonderfully grand yet still very much a family home; designed by William Adam, and refurbished in the 1880s in the Adam

Revival style. The chapel has stained glass by Burne-Jones. Its choral society is renowned, holding concerts and operas in the adjacent hall; (01651) 851770 for what's on. Meals, snacks, shop, disabled access; house open Easter, then pm May–Sept and wknds in Oct, gardens open all year; (01651) 851440; £5; NTS. Surrounding the house is a 150-acre country park, with wildlife exhibition and guided walks, and a shop selling produce from the estate, and local salmon, venison, whisky and crafts. There's an interesting medieval tomb in Tarves churchyard.

Tolquhon Castle (off B999 S) Impressive remains of a 15th-c castle (cl wkdys and Sun am in winter £1.80).

Tolquhon Gallery Decidedly unstuffy, with contemporary Scottish art and crafts; cl all day Thurs, and wkdys Jan and Feb; free.

TENTSMUIR SANDS NO5024 Five miles of shore walking from Kinshaldy car park on the Fife coast; you may see common and grey seals on the sandbanks, and there are good clean beaches – shorter routes back through the forest.

TOMINTOUL NJ1618 Charming Highland village in attractive scenery, real whisky country; the welcoming Glenavon Hotel has decent food.

TURRIFF NJ7250 **Fyvie Castle** (off A947) Each of the five towers of this magnificent castle was built in a different century by the family that lived here throughout; the oldest parts date back to the 13th c, and the whole building is one of the most fantastic examples of Scottish baronial architecture. Collections of armour and tapestry, and paintings by Raeburn,

Romney and Gainsborough. Snacks, shop; cl am (exc July–Aug), wkdys in Oct, and Nov–Easter; (01651) 891266; £6; NTS. The Towie Tavern does good food.

WHISKY DISTILLERIES open for tours and tastings include **Cardhu** NJ1943 (B9102 nr Knockando), cl wknds exc July–Sept; £2; **Glencoyne** (A81 nr Killearn) (01360) 550229; **Glenfarclas** NJ2138 (Marypark),cl Sun all year plus Sat Oct–May, and over the Christmas hols; £3.50; and **Tomatin Distillery** NH7929, not wknds exc summer Sats, best to phone (01808) 511444.

Worthwhile inns in good spots for walkers, drivers or just strollers (besides those we've mentioned as places to eat at or stay in) include the lochside Achray at St Fillans NN6924, seaview Creel at Catterline NO8778, Loch Ericht Hotel at Dalwhinnie NN6384, Dores Hotel at Dores by Loch Ness NH5930, Clachan overlooking pretty Drymen's green square NS4788, Anchor at Dunipace NS8083, Old Smiddy in the pleasant village of Errol NO2523, Hungry Monk at Gartocharn NS4286, Clova Hotel in Glen Clova NO3373, Old Mill at Killearn NS5285, Cross Keys at Kippen NS6594 (pretty village), Trossachs Hotel nr Loch Achray NN5106, Corriegour Lodge nr Altrua on Loch Lochy NN2390, Loch Tummel Hotel above Loch Tummel NN8460, Meikleour Inn at Meikleour NO1539 (handy for the 30-metre, 100-ft high beech hedge planted in 1746), Pennan Inn in the pretty seaside *Local Hero* village of Pennan NJ8465, Potarch Hotel at Potarch NO6097, Sheriffmuir Inn on wild Sheriff Muir NN8202 and Tomdoun Hotel at Tomdoun NH1501.

Where to eat

ABERDEEN NJ9305 **Babylon** *9 Alford Pl (01224) 595001* On the second floor of a former religious training college, recently refurbished bustling place with bold modern paintings, simple contemporary furniture on bare boards, a bar in what was the altar, innovative brasserie-style cooking, super puddings, and a decent little wine list; cl lunchtimes and Sun–Mon. £30|**£9.95**

ANSTRUTHER NO5603 **Cellar** *24 East Green (01333) 310378* Off a little courtyard nr the harbour, with beams, stone walls, and peat fires – and wonderful fresh fish, good wines; cl Sun, winter Mon, Tues am. £38

BLAIRGOWRIE NO1845 **Cargill's** *Lower Mill St (01250) 876735* Busy bistro, part of a complex with a crafts gallery and coffee shop, antiques warehouse and upholstery business; good varied food inc nice puddings, and several teas and coffees; bright helpful staff; cl winter Mon–Tues; disabled access. £22|**£7.25**

CUPAR NO3714 **Ostlers Close** *25 Bonnygate* (01334) 655574 Cosy unpretentious much-liked restaurant with lovely food using the best local fresh produce, game and fish, and home-grown herbs, a reasonably priced wine list, and friendly owners; children over 6; cl Sun–Mon, cl Weds–Thurs lunchtime and two wks May; £37 dinner/£26 lunch|**£11.95**

DRYBRIDGE NJ4562 **Old Monastery** (01542) 832660 Lovely views from former monastery – as well as very good fish, game and Abderdeen Angus beef, reasonably priced wines and friendly service, cl Sun, Mon, 2 wks Oct, 3 wks Jan; children over 8 in evening. £35

GLAMIS NO3846 **Strathmore Arms** *1 The Square* (01307) 840248 Simply decorated old inn in picturesque unspoilt village, well presented popular food, roaring log fire in lounge, and good caring service; disabled access. £29|**£9.95**

KELTY NT1393 **Butterchurn** *Cocklaw Mains Farm* (01383) 830169 In the courtyard of a farm, this popular restaurant has fine views over Loch Leven, and serves morning coffee, lunch, afternoon teas, snacks, and traditional high teas using fresh local ingredients; they also sell their own products to take away and have a craft and gift centre, farmyard pets for children, and walks and cycle trails; cl 24–26 Dec, 1–2 Jan; disabled access. £20|**£4.95**

KILMAHOG NN6008 **Lade Inn** (01877) 330152 Well run place in lovely wooded surroundings with beamed and partly panelled main bar, Highland prints, no smoking room opening on to terrace and attractive garden, a wide choice of interesting bar food, decent wine list and real ales; disabled access. £24|**£9.95**

KINGUSSIE NH7501 **Cross** *Tweed Mill Brae, Ardbroilach Rd* (01540) 661166 Converted 19th-c stone tweed mill by stream, now a no smoking restaurant-with-rooms, with a relaxed friendly atmosphere, extremely good eclectic Scottish cooking (evenings only) using the best local produce, excellent wine list, marvellous cheeses, and super breakfasts; bdrms; cl Tues pm, 1 Dec–28 Feb; children over 8; disabled access. £42.45 5 courses

PERTH NO1123 **Let's Eat** *77 Kinnoull St* (01738) 643377 Very popular restaurant in what was the Theatre Royal, relaxed friendly atmosphere, enjoyable modern cooking inc proper old-fashioned puddings, and short selective wine list; cl Sun–Mon, 2 wks Jan, 2 wks July; disabled access. £31.45|**£9.95**

ST ANDREWS NO5016 **Vine Leaf** *131 South St* (01334) 477497 Warmly welcoming and attractively laid out dining room overlooking walled herb garden, super food (inc seafood, game and vegetarian dishes), unobtrusive service and decent wines; evenings only; cl Sun, Mon and Jan; disabled access. £30

ST FILLANS NN6924 **Four Seasons** (01764) 685333 Long white family-run hotel with wonderful Loch Earn views, generous helpings of very good Scottish food inc super fish and game dishes; lunchtime snacks, too; can eat in Tarken Bar, on terrace or in smarter restaurant; comfortable bdrms and chalets; cl Jan–Feb, wkdays Nov–Dec. £29.95 4 courses|**£6.95**

ST MONANCE NO5201 **Seafood Restaurant** *16 West End* (01333) 730327 Immaculate, snug and cosy inside, with seafaring models and mementoes on illuminated shelves, plenty of well polished light wood panelling, plainer locals' bar, very good modern cooking inc excellent seafood in no smoking back restaurant, and good bar food; cl Jan and Sun pm and Mon in low season. £35|**£10**

STONEHAVEN NO8595 **Lairhillock** (01569) 730001 Relaxed and friendly extended 18th-c country pub with wide choice of good, popular and imaginative food, well kept real ales, lots of malt whiskies and wines, nice views from cheerfully atmospheric beamed bar, central fire in spacious lounge, and airy conservatory; cl 25–26 Dec, 1–2 Jan; disabled access. £31|**£7.95**

WEEM NN8449 **Ailean Chraggan** (01887) 820346 Small friendly inn with lovely views, very good food inc plenty of fresh fish and enjoyable puddings – you can eat in the bar or restaurant – and a very good wine list; comfortable bdrms; cl 25–26 Dec, 1–2 Jan. £22.75|**£6.50**

West Scotland

Mainland Scotland's finest scenery; glorious coast; a few highlights for children

Oban has quite a lively buzz, Inveraray is interesting, and Glencoe has some of Scotland's most beautiful and wild scenery; all three have things to keep children entertained – as does Barcaldine in its lively sea life centre.

Otherwise places to visit are mostly low-key, suiting the relaxed pace of life here. Hill House is the northern outpost of the work of Charles Rennie Mackintosh (and a wonderful example at that), and the excellently restored Auchindrain Township Museum exudes a real sense of a past community. The great gardens are the high point for most people, and are at their peak in May and June. That's a glorious time to visit this part, with very long days and lots of wild flowers. In high summer the traffic on the twisting roads in the most scenic parts can make driving painfully slow, and the midges become a menace. In autumn the Highland heather's still gorgeous and the weather can be very kind, but the days are shortening dramatically. In winter most hotels here do stay open, and the coast stays very mild. Roads winding slowly along the intricate coast make driving here a succession of glorious sea-and-mountain views.

Where to stay

ARDUAINE NM7910 **Loch Melfort Hotel** *Arduaine, Oban, Argyll PA34 4XG* (01852) 200233 **£110**, plus special breaks; 27 rms, gorgeous sea views. Comfortable hotel popular in summer with passing yachtsmen (hotel's own moorings), nautical charts and marine glasses in airy modern bar, own lobster pots and nets so emphasis on seafood, pleasant foreshore walks, outstanding springtime woodland gardens; cl early Jan to mid-Feb; disabled access

BALLACHULISH NN0559 **Ballachulish House** *Ballachulish, Argyll PA39 4JX* (01855) 811266 **£100**; 8 rms with views. Remote 18th-c house with a friendly atmosphere, spacious antiques-furnished elegant rooms, log fires, honesty bar, hearty helpings of good food using local fish and beef, and billiard room; children over 10

CRINAN NR7894 **Crinan Hotel** *Crinan, Lochgilphead, Argyll PA31 8SR* (01546) 830261 **£130**, plus special breaks; 22 rms. Rather smart hotel by start of canal to Lochgilphead, marvellous views from stylish formal top-floor restaurant and bedrooms, nautical decorations in lounge bar, lots of local fish and large wine list; disabled access; cl Christmas

DERVAIG NM4749 **Druimard Country House** *Dervaig, Tobermory, Isle of Mull PA75 6QW* (01688) 400345 **£125** inc dinner, plus special breaks; 7 rms. Peaceful Victorian country house with wonderful views across the glen and River Bellart, friendly helpful owners, comfortable lounge and conservatory, lots of pictures, books and magazines, good breakfasts, excellent food using the best local produce; the Mull Little Theatre is in the grounds; dogs welcome; cl Nov–end Mar; disabled access

ELLANBEICH NM7417 **Inshaig Park** *Easdale, Oban, Argyll PA34 4RF* (01852) 300256 **£66**; 6 rms. Solid family-run stone building on Seil island (bridge to mainland), a hotel since Victorian times, with stunning sea views, good food inc fresh local seafood, friendly bar and warm welcome

ERISKA NM9041 **Isle of Eriska Hotel** *Ledaig, Oban, Argyll PA37 1SD* (01631) 720371 **£220**, plus winter breaks; 17 rms. In a wonderful position on small island linked by bridge to mainland, impressive baronial hotel with very relaxed country house atmosphere, log fires and pretty drawing room, excellent food, exemplary service, and comprehensive wine list; leisure complex with indoor swimming pool, sauna, gym and so forth, lovely surrounding walks, and 9-hole golf course, windsurfing or waterskiing, clay pigeon shooting, pony trekking, and golf – and plenty of wildlife inc tame badgers who come nightly to the library door for their bread and milk; cl Jan; children over 5 in evening restaurant (high tea provided); disabled access

FORT WILLIAM NN0973 **Grange** *Grange Rd, Fort William, Inverness-shire PH33 6JF* (01397) 705516 **£76**; 4 rms. Charming Victorian house in quiet landscaped gardens with log fire in comfortable lounge, fine breakfasts in dining room overlooking Loch Linnhe, and helpful hard-working owners; cl Nov–Feb; children over 12

ISLE OF GIGHA NR6551 **Gigha Hotel** *Isle of Gigha PA41 7AA* (01583) 505254 **£84**, plus special breaks; 13 rms, most with own bthrm. Attractive small traditional family-run hotel with lots of charm, bustling bar (popular with yachtsmen and locals), neatly kept comfortable residents' lounge, and local seafood in restaurant; self-catering cottages also

KILBERRY NR7267 **Kilberry Inn** *Kilberry, Tarbert, Argyll PA29 6YD* (01880) 770223 **£71***; 3 ground-floor no smoking rms. Homely and warmly welcoming inn on W coast of Knapdale with fine sea views, old-fashioned character, entertaining owner, and outstanding country cooking – everything home-made, from soups and breads to chutney and marmalade; cl mid-Oct to mid-Mar; well behaved children over 8

KILCHRENAN NN0422 **Taychreggan Hotel** *Kilchrenan, Taynuilt, Argyll PA35 1HQ* (01866) 833211 **£114**, plus special breaks; 19 rms. Civilised and extensively refurbished hotel with fine garden running down to Loch Awe, comfortable airy bar with stuffed birds and fish, attractively served lunchtime bar food, polite efficient staff, good freshly prepared food in no smoking dining room, careful wine list, dozens of malt whiskies, and pretty inner courtyard; no children

KILFINAN NR9279 **Kilfinan Hotel** *Kilfinan, Tighnabruaich, Argyll PA21 2EP* (01700) 821201 **£78**, plus special breaks; 11 rms. Friendly former coaching inn, popular locally, in fine scenery with sporting activities such as shooting, fishing and stalking; very good restaurant food, decent bar food, and log fires; children over 12

KILNINVER NM8727 **Knipoch** *Knipoch, Oban, Argyll PA34 4QT* (01852) 316251 **£138**; 16 rms. Elegant very well kept Georgian hotel in lovely countryside overlooking Loch Feochan; fine family portraits, log fires, fresh flowers and polished furniture in comfortable lounges and bars, carefully chosen wines and malt whiskies, and marvellous food inc their own smoked salmon; cl mid-Dec to mid-Mar

OBAN NM8529 **Dungallan House Hotel** *Gallanach Rd, Oban, Argyll PA34 4PD* (01631) 563799 **£96**, plus special breaks; 13 rms, virtually all with own bthrm. Victorian house in neat grounds with fine views over the bay to Mull and Lismore; marvellous food in elegant no smoking dining room, relaxed lounge bar and reading room, warm coal fires, and helpful friendly owners and staff; cl Nov and Feb; limited disabled access

ONICH NN0461 **Allt-Nan-Ros** *Onich, Fort William, Inverness-shire PH33 6RY* (01855) 821210 **£110**, plus special breaks; 20 rms, many with views over the gardens to the water. Victorian shooting lodge with fine Scottish food, friendly atmosphere, bright airy rooms, and magnificent views across Loch Linnhe and the gardens; cl mid-Nov to 28 Dec; disabled access

PENNYGHAEL NM5725 **Pennyghael Hotel** *Pennyghael, Isle of Mull PA70 6HB* (01681) 704288 **£119** inc dinner; 6 rms. Beautifully placed converted byre by Loch Scridain with comfortable little lounge, generous breakfasts, lovely (if limited in choice) evening food using local fish and venison, and really friendly owners and staff; cl end Oct–Easter

PORT APPIN NM9045 **Airds Hotel** *Port Appin, Appin, Argyll PA38 4DF (01631) 730236* **£198***, plus winter breaks; 12 lovely rms – also, 4 cheaper rooms in Linnhe House 60 yds away. Instantly relaxing 18th-c inn with lovely views of Loch Linnhe and the islands of Lismore, blissfully comfortable day rooms, professional courteous staff, and charming owners; the food is exceptional (as is the wine list) and there are lots of surrounding walks, with more on Lismore (small boat every 2 hrs); cl 17–27 Dec, 6–26 Jan; dogs by arrangement

TARBERT NR8768 **Columba Hotel** *Pier Rd, Tarbert, Argyll PA29 6UF (01880) 820808* **£71.90**, plus special winter breaks; 10 rms. In a peaceful position on Loch Fyne with views of the surrounding hills, this family-run hotel has log fires in the friendly bar and lounge, an informal and relaxed atmosphere, very enjoyable food using fresh local produce, and quite a few malt whiskies; cl 24–26 Dec

TARBERT NR8571 **Stonefield Castle** *Stonefield, Tarbert, Argyll PA29 6YJ (01880) 820836* **£144** inc dinner, plus special breaks; 33 rms. With wonderful views and surrounding wooded grounds, this Scottish Baronial mansion has comfortable public rooms and decent restaurant food; snooker room, sauna and solarium; heated swimming pool open in summer only; disabled access

To see and do

ARDUAINE NM7910
Arduaine Gardens (A816) The seaside gardens here, a very sheltered spot with lovely views of the islets and islands, are almost subtropical, with many rarities beside the rhododendrons, camellias and magnolias which flourish so in this part of the world. Disabled access, open all year; (01852) 200366; £2.50; NTS. The comfortable Loch Melfort Hotel, with great sea views, does good bar lunches.
AUCHINDRAIN NN0102
Auchindrain Township Museum (A83) The only communal tenancy township to have remained on its ancient site much in its original form. All the buildings have been excellently restored and simply furnished in period style, so you get a real feeling of stepping back into the past. Snacks, shop; cl Oct–Mar; (01499) 500235; £3.
BARCALDINE NM9240
Sea Life Centre 💷 (A828, Barcaldine) Lively underwater centre, with hi-tech face-to-fish-face displays of native marine life inc jelly fish, and playful seal puppies. Also nature trails and woodland adventure playground. Meals, snacks, shop, mostly disabled access; cl Nov–Feb (open Christmas, New Year and all wknds); (01631) 720386; £6.50. The Lochnell Arms and Falls of Lora down at Connel are reliable lunch stops.
BEN NEVIS NN1671

Though Britain's highest mountain, this is one of the more easily managed summits, with a long, safe path up: expect big crowds in season. Munro-baggers say it's far from being the best viewpoint mountain, though; a 'munro' is any 3,000-ft peak (914 metres), named for Sir Hugh Munro, who first tabulated them (in 1997 climbers relaxing after a lifetime of gaining them all were shocked by publication of a new list adding several more). The mountain was recently sold privately to a conservation charity for less than its market value.
BENMORE NS1391
Younger Botanic Garden (A815) An outstation of the Royal Botanic Garden in Edinburgh, with attractive woodland and glorious rhododendrons. Some enormously tall and magnificent conifers here, and a good many rarities. Nice views too. Meals, snacks, shop, disabled access; cl Nov–Feb; (01369) 706261; *£3.
CAIRNDOW NN1710
Ardkinglas Woodland Garden (off A83) On a hillside overlooking Loch Fyne, the pinetum here includes the tallest tree in Britain, a grand fir well over 61 metres (200 ft) and still shooting upwards. Also rhododendrons, azaleas and other exotic plants, and daffodils in spring. Open all year; disabled access; *£2. The same people run the Tree Shop (about

2m N at the top of the loch), which specialises in specimen trees, indigenous Highland trees, and shrubs. Also lots of well crafted woodware (inc some lovely toys and puzzles); meals, snacks, shop; (01499) 600263. Next door the Loch Fyne Oyster Bar is renowned for its fresh shellfish, which you can eat in the restaurant or buy in the shop; the Cairndow Hotel with a waterside garden is also good.

COLINTRAIVE NS0374
This attractive village spreads along the shore of the sea loch, with gorgeous views (for example from the well run Colintraive Hotel) across the narrow Kyles of Bute. There's a short ferry crossing to Rhubodach on Bute.

CORPACH NN1177
Caledonian Canal From Corpach there are straightforward towpath walks NE, up a flight of locks known as Neptune's Staircase, with mountain backdrops. There's good access to the locks from the Moorings Hotel (good value basement wine bar) at Banavie.
Treasures of the Earth (Mallaig Rd) Award-winning collection of gemstones, crystals and minerals, imaginatively displayed in carefully lit rock cavities. Shop, disabled access; cl 25–26 Dec, 3–31 Jan; (01397) 772283; *£3.

CRINAN CANAL NR7894
Cut through the 9 miles at the top of the Kintyre peninsula at the end of the 18th c, to save coastal sailors many miles of dangerous waters; the end at Crinan is attractive, usually with one or two yachts or even a rare fishing boat waiting to enter the first lock, and the Crinan Hotel is a comfortable lunch stop. The canal towpath allows gentle strolls.

DUNOON NS1878
Brought in easy reach of Glasgow by frequent ferries from Gourock, this late Victorian resort has pleasant views from its fine long promenade; very busy in Aug.

FORT WILLIAM NN1174
A largely Victorian town, partly pedestrianised, that manages to combine its role as a regional centre with its other life as a holiday base, particularly for solid Ben Nevis which rises above it, and for the Caledonian

Canal which leads on up into the Great Glen and across eventually to the North Sea. The Alexandra and Nevis Bank hotels are useful for food, as is the cheerful Grog & Gruel pub; the Nevisport is the place for walking and climbing chat. In summer you can take the Jacobite Express steam train on the **West Highland Line** from here – it goes right up into the Highlands and the views are quite superb.
Inverlochy Castle (NE edge) Partly 13th-c ruins (usually under scaffolding), site of the 1645 battle between Montrose and the Campbells; free.
West Highland Museum 🏛 (Cameron Sq) Refurbished museum, great on Jacobite relics: a secret portrait of Prince Charlie needs a curved mirror to decode it. Shop, limited disabled access; cl Sun (exc July–Aug pms), 25–26 Dec, 1–2 Jan; (01397) 702169; £2.

GLEN NEVIS NN1468
(nr Fort William) Probably the best-known Highland valley, with splendid gorge scenery for an easy long mile's walk to Steall Falls. The Pap of Glencoe and the succession of peaks in the largely unwooded Mamore Forest (access from the Glen) are interesting viewpoint summits; they don't need rock-climbing expertise, just reasonable fitness and plenty of time.

GLENCOE NN1557
The scenery around here is some of Scotland's most beautiful and wild. It's understandably popular with walkers and climbers, who share it with deer, wildcats and golden eagles. The Clachaig and Kings House do food. A forest walk runs from the hospital by Glencoe village past a lochan (small loch) above Loch Leven.
Altnafeadh Good start for walks from the top of the glen. The West Highland Way takes a zigzag route N up the Devil's Staircase and through the mountains to Kinlochleven; another hill walk from Altnafeadh heads E up Beinn a' Chrulaiste, one of Glencoe's more manageable peaks.
Glen Etive Reached from Glencoe by a squelchy walk along glens (or a long track from the A82 E of Glencoe), with close-ups of mighty peaks for reward.
Glencoe Visitor Centre (A82) Has

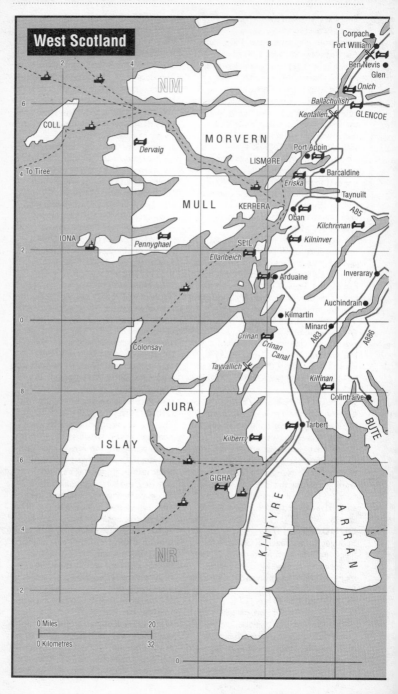

West Scotland

NM

To Tiree

COLL

IONA

Dervaig

MORVERN

LISMORE

MULL

KERRERA

Pennyghael

SEIL

Ellanbeich

Colonsay

Crinan

Crinan Canal

Tayvallich

JURA

ISLAY

Kilberry

GIGHA

NR

Corpach

Fort William

Ben Nevis

Glen

Onich

Ballachulish

Kentallen

GLENCOE

Port Appin

Barcaldine

Eriska

Taynuilt

A85

Oban

Kilchrenan

Kilninver

Inveraray

Arduaine

Auchindrain

Kilmartin

Minard

A83

A886

Kilfinan

Colintraive

BUTE

Tarbert

KINTYRE

ARRAN

0 Miles 20

0 Kilometres 32

the whole story of the massacre of 1692, when billeted troops tried to murder all their MacDonald hosts, as well as useful local information (and fishing permits). Snacks, shop, disabled access; cl Nov–Feb; (01855) 811307; 50p, free parking all day; NTS.

Highland Mysteryworld (Glencoe village) Children enjoy the spooky local myths and legends here. Shop, disabled access; cl Nov–Easter; (01855) 811660; £4.95 (£3.50).

Lost Valley This secret Glencoe pasture-ground was used by the MacDonalds for stolen cattle in times of clan warfare; the walk involves an ascent from the Meeting of the Three Waters.

HELENSBURGH NS2983

Hill House (Upper Colquhoun St) In an area short of many great houses, this is a wonderful example of the work of Charles Rennie Mackintosh; there's an exhibition on his life, and the gardens have been restored to reflect features common to the architect's designs. Snacks, shop; cl am, and all day Nov–Mar; (01436) 673900; £6; NTS – it's one of their busier properties. The dignified resort town, attractively placed on the Clyde, has some good views from its broad streets.

INVERARAY NN0908

Beautifully placed and rather self-consciously elegant, this was built as an estate village in the 18th c, and is now a magnet for visitors. The Loch Fyne Hotel is pleasant for lunch, with stunning views; the George is popular too.

All Saints church The bell tower has the world's second-heaviest ring of ten bells, installed in 1931. Even if there's no-one ringing them you should be able to hear a recording. Shop; cl 1–2pm, all Oct–Apr; (01499) 302259; *£2 for tower, exhibition free.

Argyll Wildlife Park ⊡ (Dalchenna; A83 SW) A collection of local or once-local animals (deer, foxes and wildcats) plus chipmunks, wallabies, racoons and so forth – with some eminently tame wild creatures wandering around. Snacks, shop, disabled access; cl Nov–Apr; (01499) 302264; £4.

Inveraray Castle Built in 1745, and still the home of the Duke and Duchess of Argyll, it has particularly impressive state rooms, and a striking hall. Snacks, shop, ground floor disabled access; cl 1–2pm (exc July and Aug), Sun am, all day Fri (exc July and Aug), and Oct–Mar; (01499) 302203; £4.50. Nearby woodland trails include a view over Loch Fyne from Dun na Cuaiche Tower.

Inveraray Jail [£] (Church Sq) Excellent prison museum, with costumed guides and Katie the Governor's cow really bringing the place to life. You can watch a trial, try your hand at hard labour, and even experience being locked up in one of the sparse little cells. Watch out for the animated surprises. Shop; cl 25 Dec, 1 Jan; (01499) 302381; *£4.90.

ISLE OF GIGHA NR6551 3 miles offshore, linked by frequent ferries from Tayinloan on the A83 down the W coast of Kintyre; the island is a perfect place for really getting away from it all. Apart from the small Gigha Hotel, there are rooms at the Post Office and other places, and you can hire bicycles to explore it properly. Try to see the strange old stones, some of which are supposed to have mysterious powers. Tel (01880) 730253 for ferry times.

Achamore Gardens Created by Sir James Horlick, who bought the island in 1944; a garden of woodlands filled with rhododendrons and azaleas, many plants brought from his home in Berkshire in laundry baskets. Lots of subtropical plants – the climate and soil are perfect for them. Snacks, shop, limited disabled access; £2.

ISLE OF MULL NM5055 For most people this island takes a bit of getting to, but if you are within reach its unspoilt coasts are certainly a dramatic lure. There's a good ferry service from Oban and Lochaline (and in summer from Kilchoan). A couple of castellated mansions, one going back to the 13th c and another, 19th-c **Torosay Castle**, with attractive gardens (tearoom, shop, limited disabled access; open daily Easter–mid-Oct; £4.50), and a small museum in Tobermory, give some rainy-day scope. From May to Sept, the **Mull Experience** runs day trips from Oban to these attractions, inc return

ferry travel and a trip on Mull's unique railway (£17, call (01680) 812421 for details). The interior is less interesting than the coast, with brackeny moors and conifer plantations over much of it, though there is some mountainous hill walking in the S (as usual, not many defined paths).

Iona (off Mull) Lovely, filled with a sense of spirituality as well as its tangible remains of ancient shrines; Scotland's first kings were buried here (as is former Labour leader John Smith).

Isle of Mull Angora Rabbit Farm [£] (Bunessan) Children can cuddle some very fluffy bunnies here, and there is a display system explaining all about the rabbits from the viewpoint of a rabbit. Snacks, shop; cl Sat, and all late Oct–mid-Apr; (01681) 700507; £2.

St Columba Visitor Centre (Fionnphort) Visitor centre dedicated to the saint. The little coastal settlement overlooks Iona, and the boats go from here. The Keel Row has decent food.

KILMARTIN NR8395 **Dunadd Fort** (3m S) This prehistoric hill fort was one of the ancient capitals of Dalriada from which the Celtic kingdom of Scotland was formed. Look out for the carvings nearby of a boar and a footprint, which probably mark the spot where early kings were invested with royal power.

Kilmartin church Plain and Victorian, but it has a stunning 10th-c cross; the graveyard has interesting carved medieval tombstones. The simple Kilmartin Hotel is useful for lunch. A short walk away, tracks link the well signed North, Mid and South Cairns (impressive prehistoric burial mounds – you can climb into the North one via trapdoor and ladder, to see sup-and-ring carvings), and the Templewood stone circles.

Kilmartin House Museum [£] Explains the rich and intriguing archaeology of the area. Meals, snacks, shop, disabled access; open daily 10am–5.30pm, but cl 25–26 Dec, 1 Jan; (01546) 510278; £3.90.

KILMUN NS1781 **Kilmun forest walks** Rare conifers, an arboretum of great beauty, and some striking gum-trees.

LOCH LOMOND NS3884
In spite of being so close to Glasgow and on every coach company's hit list, it does have a serene beauty that seems unspoilt by the visitors. Wee birdies sing and wild flowers spring – and the water is often calm enough to reflect the mountains. The best views are from the narrower N end. Surprisingly, there aren't many paths: the shoreline track, partly metalled, on the quieter E side, comes closest to the water. Cruises round the lake leave from Balloch, as well as from the pretty village of Luss, a good place to hire a boat for pottering about on the water (there's a visitor centre here too). Past the N end of the loch, the Inverarnan Drovers Inn is an entertaining and very idiosyncratic stop.

Balloch Castle Country Park A useful introduction, with a visitor centre, woodland and meadow trails, walled garden, and fine views. Snacks, shop, limited disabled access; cl some lunchtimes, and all Nov–Easter, but best to check winter opening; (01389) 758216; free. The Balloch Hotel has good value bar food all day.

Ben Lomond The southernmost munro (or peak over 3,000 ft, 914 metres), with a good walk up from Rowardennan on the E shore.

Conic Hill Less than half Ben Lomond's height but more accessible, a straightforward but rewarding climb from Balmaha at Loch Lomond's south-east corner.

MINARD NR9799
Crarae Gardens (A83) Lovely gardens noted for their rare ornamental shrubs and rhododendrons, azaleas and conifers, in a beautiful gorge overlooking Loch Fyne. Snacks, shop, and interesting plant sales (all summer only), limited disabled access; visitor centre cl Oct–Easter; (01546) 886614; £3.50

OBAN NM8530
This bustling coastal town is a busy ferry port and a popular place for holidaymakers, with a good cheerful atmosphere; the Oban Inn is fun, and the Lorne has decent food inc fresh local fish. Besides the main ferries, there are boats to Lismore and (just a hop really) Kerrera, for shoreside walks

with the odd ruined fort. A little way S at Cologin, the countrified Barn is useful for lunch, and often has evening folk music.

Dunstaffnage Castle (off A485 4m N) Beautifully set, this was once the prison of Flora MacDonald. It's now in ruins, but you can still see its gatehouse, round towers and massively thick walls. Shop, disabled access to visitor centre only; cl Thurs and Fri Dec–Mar, plus 25–26 Dec, 1–2 Jan; (01631) 562465; £2.

Oban Rare Breeds Farm 🔲 (A816 Oban–Kilmore) A collection of very visitor-friendly animals. Teas, shop, some disabled access; 10am–5.30pm; cl Nov–Mar; (01631) 770608; *£5.

PORT APPIN NM9045
An attractive little settlement, very peaceful, where you can pick wild blueberries by the roadside, catch a boat across to Lismore (shoreside walks), or just sit by the water keeping your eyes open for the seals that are so common around here. This is *Kidnapped* country, with the scene of the Appin Murder not far off, and a monument marking where James of the Glens was wrongly hanged at Ballachulish to the N (the Ballachulish Hotel has decent food and wide views).

RIVER LEVEN NN1861
The glen gives a fine walk through semi-wooded terrain, from Kinlochleven to the dam of the gigantic Blackwater Reservoir – with an awesomely bleak view ahead of empty hills.

SEIL NM7819
This little island is linked to the mainland by a short bridge that people call the Bridge over the Atlantic. There's an attractive walk over to the anchorage on the far side which looks out to Jura.

TARBERT NR8465
Pleasant and quite picturesque small harbourside town; the West Loch Hotel (A83 W) does good local seafood.

TAYNUILT NN0031
Bonawe Iron Furnace (off A85) The most complete remaining charcoal-fired ironworks in Britain, worked until 1876. Iron produced here was used for the cannonballs for Nelson's ships. Shop; cl Dec–Mar with restricted hours

in Oct; (01866) 822432; *£2.50. The lockside Polfearn Hotel does good food.

Inns with decent food, in good places for drivers, walkers or strollers, include the Ardentinny Hotel by Loch Long at Ardentinny NS1887, Village Inn at Arrochar NN2904, Galley of Lorne at Ardfern NM8004, Kilchrenan Inn at Kilchrenan by Loch Awe NN0222, Portsonachan Hotel on the opposite side of that loch NN1227, Whistlefield Hotel by Loch Eck NS1493, Loch Gair Hotel on Loch Gair NR9190 and Oystercatcher at Otter Ferry NR9384.

Where to eat

CAIRNDOW NN1812 **Loch Fyne Oyster Bar** *Clachan Farm* (01499) 600264 Relaxed restaurant in converted farm buildings by Loch Fyne, serving good seafood and smoked fish (they have their own smokehouse); reasonably priced wine list and a warm welcome; cl 25–26 Dec, 1–2 Jan (may close more in Jan for extensions so best to check); disabled access. £24.50|**£8.90**

FORT WILLIAM NN1074 **Alexandra** *The Parade* (01397) 702241 Popular hotel in town square with meals and snacks in the Great Food Stop (open all day) and evening restaurant; disabled access. £18|**£6.25**

KENTALLEN NM9957 **Ardsheal House** (01631) 740227 Particularly good daily-changing evening food in attractive conservatory dining room of fine hotel in 900 acres; very comfortable rooms, antiques, and relaxed atmosphere; lovely bdrms; cl Dec, Jan. £35 4-course dinner

KENTALLEN NN0259 **Holly Tree** (01631) 740292 Super food in carefully converted railway station, cosy public rooms, lovely shoreside setting (best to book in winter); bdrms; cl 28 Nov–Feb; disabled access. £32.50|**£12**

TAYVALLICH NR7487 **Tayvallich Inn** *Kintallen* (01546) 870282 Simply refurbished pub overlooking yacht anchorage with super local seafood (other decent dishes too), dining conservatory (no smoking), and friendly service; cl Mon Nov–Mar; limited disabled access. £25|**£7**

North Scotland

Sensational scenery in the west and on Skye, solitude in the north, empty beaches on the east coast – some surprising gardens

The main draw is the scenery, and the feeling of getting away from it all. The W coast has glorious vistas of sea, mountains and islands. Long empty sandy beaches (and good golf courses) make the E coast suit a quiet summer holiday. The N coast is relatively wild and empty: addictive to some people, harsh and inhospitable to others. Skye is idyllic in good weather. There are a few interesting places to punctuate a visit. Several places have visitor centres, the pick of which are at Armadale Castle on Skye, Auckengill (looks at the region's Viking heritage) and Gairloch, though children will doubtless enjoy the Nessie conspiracy theories at Drumnadrochit the most.

One unexpected pleasure here is the number of interesting gardens, with particular highlights at Strathcarron (excellent water gardens), the bizarre futuristic Hydroponicum at Achiltibuie, and the unmissable Inverewe Gardens at Poolewe.

A dolphin or whale-watching trip from Cromarty can be really special, and the magnificent mountain scenery of Torridon is perhaps the best place to spot local wildlife.

The area is usually at its best between late May and early July, while the days are very long and before the midges have really got into their stride.

Where to stay

ACHILTIBUIE NC0208 **Summer Isles Hotel** *Achiltibuie, Ullapool, Ross-shire IV26 2YQ (01854) 622282* **£98**; 14 comfortable rms. Beautifully placed above the sea towards the end of a very long and lonely road, warm friendly well furnished hotel with delicious set menus using fresh ingredients (in which it's largely self-sufficient), a choice of superb puddings and excellent array of uncommon cheeses; pretty watercolours and flowers; cl Oct–Easter; children over 6

APPLECROSS NG7144 **Applecross Inn** *Shore St, Applecross, Strathcarron, Ross-shire IV54 8LR (01520) 744262* **£60**; 7 rms, some with breathtaking sea views over Sound of Raasay, shared bthrms. Gloriously placed informal inn with tables out by shore, simple comfortable and friendly bar, log or peat fire in lounge, lively landlord, small restaurant with excellent fresh fish and seafood

ARISAIG NM7187 **Arisaig House** *Beasdale, Arisaig, Inverness-shire PH39 4NR (01687) 450622* **£160**, plus special breaks; 12 most attractive recently refurbished no smoking rms with wonderful views. Beautifully furnished extremely comfortable hotel in attractive wooded and terraced grounds nr the shore; elegant drawing room, cosy morning room, lovely flowers, and very good imaginative food using fresh local produce; billiard room, croquet; cl Dec–Feb; children over 10

AULTIVULLIN NC8267 **Catalina** *Aultivullin, Strathy, Thurso, Caithness KW14 7RY (01641) 541279* **£40***, plus special breaks; 1 suite. Extended former croft on wild headland just a short walk from the sea; residents have own wing with private lounge and dining room but owners offer a friendly welcome, good breakfasts, and enjoyable 3-course meals – bring your own wine and they will serve you at whatever time you wish to eat; no children or dogs, no smoking; disabled access

CROMARTY NH7867 **Royal** *Marine Terrace, Cromarty, Ross-shire IV11 8YN (01381) 600217* **£65***; 10 rms. Traditional waterfront hotel with friendly owners and staff, attractive lounges, bars and sun lounge, and Scottish dishes in dining room; gets very busy in summer

DRUMNADROCHIT NH5129 **Benleva Hotel** *Drumnadrochit, Inverness IV63 6UH (01456) 450288* **£70**; 10 rms. Run by particularly helpful and friendly owners, this small family-run hotel is in a fine spot nr Loch Ness with plenty of outside pursuits (the owners will help organise fishing trips); comfortable residents' lounge with open fire, well stocked bar, and homely dining room with a good choice of tasty food using local meat and fish; pets welcome

DRUMNADROCHIT NH4731 **Polmaily House** *Drumnadrochit, Inverness IV63 6XT (01456) 450343* **£128***, plus special breaks; 11 light, pretty rms. Very relaxing and homely hotel in 18 acres, with comfortable drawing room and library, open fires, and excellent food in the no smoking restaurant (wonderful packed lunches too); a happy place for families with well equipped indoor play area with lots of supervised activities, baby sitting and listening, hundreds of children's videos, plenty of ponies and pets, swimming pool, tennis, croquet, fishing, and boating; disabled access; cl Nov–Dec and Feb–Mar ☺

GARVE NH3874 **Inchbae Lodge** *Garve, Ross-shire IV23 2PH (01997) 455269* **£66**, plus special breaks; 15 rms, some in chalet. Former hunting lodge – under new owners – in lovely Highland setting with comfortable homely lounges, winter log fires, small bar (liked by locals), and good fixed-price evening meals using fresh local produce; lots of wildlife, marvellous walks; pets by prior arrangement; cl Christmas; disabled access

GLENELG NG8119 **Glenelg Inn** *Kirkton, Glenelg, Kyle, Ross-shire IV40 8JR (01599) 522273* **£134** inc dinner, plus special breaks; 6 individually decorated and comfortable rms, all with fine views. Overlooking Skye across its own beach, this carefully refurbished homely hotel has a relaxed bar, comfortable sofas and blazing fires, friendly staff and locals, good food using local venison, local hill-bred lamb and lots of wonderfully fresh fish and seafood, and quite a few whiskies; the drive to the inn involves spectacular views from the steep road; open in winter if pre-booked; disabled access

ISLE ORNSAY NG7012 **Eilean Iarmain** *Isle Ornsay, Isle of Skye IV43 8QR (01471) 833332* **£120***, plus winter breaks; 16 individual rms (those in main hotel best), all with fine views. Sparkling white hotel with Gaelic-speaking staff and locals, big cheerfully busy bar, pretty dining room with lovely sea views, and very good food; disabled access

ISLE ORNSAY NG7315 **Kinloch Lodge** *Isle Ornsay, Isle of Skye IV43 8QY (01471) 833214* **£120***, plus winter breaks; 14 rms. Surrounded by rugged mountain scenery at the head of Loch Na Dal, this charming white stone hotel has a relaxed atmosphere in its comfortable and attractive drawing rooms, antiques, portraits, flowers, log fires, and good imaginative food; cookery demonstrations; cl Christmas

LAIDE NG8990 **Old Smiddy** *Laide, Achnasheen, Ross-shire IV22 2NB (01445) 731425* **£64***; 3 pretty rms with thoughtful extras. Really welcoming charming no smoking cottage in lovely spot by loch and mountains, with blazing fire in comfortable homely lounge, and dining room with super breakfasts and delicious evening meals (using local and home-grown produce; bring your own wine); lots of outside pursuits, and pets welcome; cl Nov–Mar; children over 12

LYBSTER ND2436 **Portland Arms** *Lybster, Caithness KW3 6BS (01593) 721721* **£68**; 24 comfortable rms. Staunch old granite hotel with really friendly staff, attractive dining room, generous helpings of good fresh food and fine breakfasts, small cosy panelled lounge bar, and informal locals' bar; shooting/fishing can be arranged; disabled access

MELVICH NC8864 **Melvich Hotel** *Melvich, Thurso, Caithness KW14 7YJ (01641) 531206* **£60**, plus special breaks; 14 rms with showers (also have 4 bthrms). Small traditional hotel in lovely spot with homely furniture and peat fires in the civilised lounge, cosy bar, very relaxing atmosphere, friendly owners and staff, good food (esp local seafood and wild salmon), and fine bay views

PLOCKTON NG8033 **Plockton Hotel** *41 Harbour St, Plockton, Ross-shire IV52 8TN (01599) 544274* **£65***, plus special breaks; 14 rms plus 4 in cottage annexe. Small notably friendly hotel (not to be confused with Plockton Inn around the corner), in a row of elegant houses by a shore lined with palm trees and flowering shrubs, looking over the sheltered anchorage to rugged mountains, with comfortably furnished lively lounge bar, separate public bar, enjoyable food in no smoking restaurant, good breakfasts, a good choice of whiskies, and attentive owners; good disabled access

PORTREE NG4843 **Craiglockhart Guest House** *Beaumont Crescent, Portree, Isle of Skye IV51 9DF (01478) 612233* **£38***; 9 rms, 3 with own bthrm. Small family-run guesthouse overlooking harbour with fine views through picture windows in lounge and dining room, and good breakfasts; cl Dec

PORTREE NG4843 **Rosedale** *Quay Brae, Portree, Isle of Skye IV51 9DB (01478) 613131* **£72**, plus special breaks; 22 rms, many with harbour views. Built from three fishermen's cottages with lots of passages and stairs, this waterfront hotel has two traditional lounges, small first-floor restaurant with freshly cooked popular food, lots of whiskies in the cocktail bar, helpful staff, harbourside garden and marvellous views

RAASAY NG5537 **Isle of Raasay Hotel** *Isle of Raasay, Kyle, Ross-shire IV40 8PB (01478) 660222* **£50***, plus special breaks; 12 rms, plus 6 beds in bunk house. Family-run Victorian hotel with marvellous views over the Sound of Raasay to Skye, popular with walkers and bird-watchers, home-made food with an emphasis on fresh fish; no petrol on the island; disabled access

SCARISTA NG0192 **Scarista House** *Scarista, Harris, Isle of Harris HS3 3HX*

(01859) 550238 **£116**; 5 rms, some in annexe. Marvellously wild countryside and empty beaches surround this isolated small hotel with its antiques-furnished rooms, open fires, warm friendly atmosphere, plenty of books and records (no radio or TV), and good food in candlelit dining room using organic home-grown vegetables and herbs, hand-made cheeses, their own eggs, home-made bread, cakes, biscuits, yoghurt and marmalade, and lots of fish and shellfish; excellent for wildlife, walks and fishing; dogs allowed

SCOURIE NC1641 **Eddrachilles** *Badcall, Scourie, Lairg, Sutherland IV27 4TH* *(01971) 502080* **£87***, plus special breaks; 11 comfortable rms. Well run hotel in its own 320 acres overlooking Badcall Bay, with wonderful island views; popular with nature-lovers – bird sanctuary nearby, seals, fishing and walking; cl 25 Oct–21 Mar; children over 3

SCOURIE NC1544 **Scourie Hotel** *Scourie, Lairg, Sutherland IV27 4SX (01971) 502396* **£80**; 20 rms with views to Scourie Bay. A haven for anglers, with 36 exclusive beats on 25,000-acre estate; snug bar, two comfortable lounges and good food using plenty of local game and fish in smart no smoking dining room; cl mid-Oct to end Mar

SHIEL BRIDGE NG9419 **Kintail Lodge** *Glenshiel, Kyle, Ross-shire IV40 8HL (01599) 511275* **£80**, plus special breaks; 12 good value big rms, most with own bthrm. Pleasantly informal and fairly simple former shooting lodge on Loch Duich, with magnificent views, four acres of walled gardens, residents' lounge bar and comfortable sitting room, good well prepared food inc wild salmon, and fine collection of malt whiskies

SHIELDAIG NG8153 **Tigh an Eilean** *Shieldaig, Strathcarron, Ross-shire IV54 8XN (01520) 755251* **£107.60***; 11 rms. Attractive hotel in outstanding position with lovely view of pine-covered island and sea, private fishing and sea fishing arranged, within easy reach of NTS Torridon Estate and Beinn Eighe nature reserve; pretty, comfortable residents' lounge with well stocked honesty bar, modern dining room with delicious food, warmly friendly owner; cl Nov–Mar

SKEABOST NG4048 **Skeabost House** *Skeabost Bridge, Portree, Isle of Skye IV51 9NR (01470) 532202* **£96**, plus special breaks; 26 rms, 5 in annexe in Garden House. Smart, friendly little hotel with lawn running down to Loch Snizort (good salmon fishing), spacious no smoking lounge (marvellous buffet table), Victorian-style dining conservatory, lovely afternoon tea, log fires, high-ceilinged bar off stately hall, and billiard room; bog-and-water garden, 9-hole golf course; disabled access; cl Dec–Mar exc New Year

STRONTIAN NM7961 **Kilcamb Lodge Hotel** *Strontian, Acharacle, Argyll PH36 4HY (01967) 402257* **£95**, plus special breaks; 11 rms. Warmly friendly little hotel in 30 acres by Loch Sunart, with log fires in two lounges, carefully cooked food using fresh ingredients from organic kitchen garden, fine choice of malt whiskies in small bar, and a relaxed atmosphere, fishing boat, four moorings and jetty; cl Dec–Feb; children over 8 in dining room; disabled access in cottage

TARBERT NB1301 **Leachin House** *Leachin, Harris, Isle of Harris HS3 3AH (01859) 502157* **£90***, plus special breaks; 2 comfortable rms. Meaning 'house among the rocks', this neat and peaceful Victorian stone house on the loch shores (wonderful sunsets) is a haven for nature lovers and walkers – guided trips to look for seals, otters and eagles, fishing, and fine wild flowers in spring and early summer; friendly helpful owners, interesting nautical memorabilia, open fire in the drawing room, and particularly good food using delicious local seafood and lamb, served around a communal table in dining room with original 19th-c hand-painted French wallpaper; cl 18 Dec–18 Jan; children over 10

TORRIDON NG8854 **Loch Torridon Hotel** *Torridon, Achnasheen, Ross-shire IV22 2EY (01445) 791242* **£120***, plus special breaks; 20 comfortable rms. Built in 1887 as a shooting lodge in 58 acres at the foot of Ben Damph by Upper Loch Torridon, this turreted stone house has unusual ornate ceilings and panelling, log fires and innovative cooking; they also run the Ben Damph Lodge nearby; children over 8 in dining room; disabled access

ULLAPOOL NH1192 **Altnaharrie** *Ullapool, Ross-shire IV26 2SS* (01854) 633230 **£330*** inc dinner; 8 rms. Across Loch Broom and reached by a 10-min boat journey, this carefully restored house was originally built for drovers: two lounges with lots of books, an open fire, a mix of Scandinavian and English furnishings, marvellously quiet relaxing atmosphere, room service (they think tea-making facilities in rooms are a sign of neglect), perhaps the best food in Scotland – five set courses with much of the food home-grown or caught locally – and very good wine list; no smoking; cl mid-Nov to Easter; children over 8

ULLAPOOL NH1293 **Ceilidh Place** *12–14 West Argyle St, Ullapool, Ross-shire IV26 2TY* (01854) 612103 **£120***, plus special breaks; 13 rms, most with own bthrm, plus 10 in annexe across the road. White-painted hotel in quiet street with attractive conservatory dining room, stylish café-bar with attractive modern prints and plants, good food served all day, decent wines and cognacs, and a relaxed friendly atmosphere; book shop, live music and theatre

To see and do

ACHILTIBUIE NC0208
Hydroponicum 🖾 Bizarre indoor garden of the future – without any soil. Fascinating guided tours show how plants such as figs, lemons and bananas grow quite happily using the nutrients from the soil, but not the soil itself. Good home-made meals and snacks, shop; disabled access; hourly tours Easter–Sept (cl Oct–Easter); (01854) 622202; £4.

AUCKENGILL ND3664
Northlands Viking Centre 🖾 (Old School) Interesting displays on how the Norsemen came from Scandinavia to Shetland, Orkney and Caithness, with a Viking longship and other relics. Shop, disabled access; cl Oct–May; (01955) 607771; £1.50.

BALMACARA NG8028
(A67) Huge crofting estate surrounding the Kyle of Lochalsh, with challenging walks through breathtaking scenery; you can still see traditional crofting at Drumbuie and Duirnish. The landscape is interspersed with lochs and impressive landmarks like the Five Sisters of Kintail (a fine target for hardened walkers) and Beinn Fhada. **Lochalsh Woodland Garden** 🖾 (A87 3m E of Kyle of Lochalsh) Wonderful woodland gardens, with peaceful walks, collections of rhododendrons, hydrangeas, fuchsias and other plants, and views towards Skye. Open all year; (01599) 566325; *£2; NTS.

BALNAKIEL NC3967
The most NW part of mainland Britain, wild, remote and spectacular, with a little craft village (some bits cl Sun, and limited opening in winter; (01971) 511277; free).

BEINN EIGHE NG9963
One of the easier mountain ascents, with a well marked Mountain Trail making a circular route above Loch Maree.

BETTYHILL NC7062
Strathnaver Museum Good informative memorial to the notorious Highlands Clearances; limited disabled access; cl 1–2pm and all day Sun, and Nov–Mar; (01641) 521418; £1.90. The churchyard has a finely carved 9th-c Celtic stone. The Bettyhill Hotel does decent food. Just S is a wonderful **nature reserve**, and the beach nearby is attractive.

CROMARTY NH7867
Dolphin Ecosse (Bank House) Boat trips out to see the local bottlenose dolphins: they can't guarantee sightings, but nine out of ten of their trips do come across dolphins, and they point out various seabirds and local landmarks along the way. Very friendly and informal, and rated very highly by readers. Whale-watching trips too in Aug and Sept – best to book on (01381) 600323; disabled access. £15. Cromarty itself is a delightfully sleepy place with lots of unspoilt buildings in its well restored core, and a surprisingly good little museum. The friendly Royal Hotel has good value food and lovely views.

DORNIE NG8826
Eilean Donan Castle (off A87)

Connected to the mainland by a causeway, and unforgettably beautiful. First built in 1220, destroyed in 1719, and then restored at the beginning of this century, it's perfectly positioned at the meeting point of Lochs Long, Duich and Alsh. Visitor centre with teas and shop, disabled access; Cl Dec–end Feb; (01599) 555202; £3.75.

DRUMNADROCHIT NH5130
Official Loch Ness Monster Exhibition 🖼 (Drumnadrochit Hotel) Walk-through multi-media experience tracing the legend from its beginnings in Highland folklore to the scientific investigations of recent years using the latest technology, laser animations and special effects. There's a kilt-maker on site. Meals, snacks, shop, disabled access; cl 25 Dec; (01456) 450573; £5.95.
Urquhart Castle (just SE) 14th-c remains, once the biggest castle in Scotland. A piper plays here every day Jun–Sept. Snacks, shop; cl 25–26 Dec, 1–2 Jan; (01456) 450551; £3.80.

DUNCANSBY HEAD ND4073
A grand spot on a fine day, with an absorbing cliff walk S for a good view of the spectacular Stacks of Duncansby, 60 metres (200 ft) offshore rock pinnacles.

DUNNET HEAD ND2074
Mainland Britain's furthest point N, with views to Orkney. Lovely on a clear early summer's day, with spring flowers in the close turf, and puffins pottering around – but wild and unforgiving when the weather changes.

DURNESS NC4067
Attractively placed nr the beautiful sea loch Loch Eriboll, and also has atmospheric boat tours of the Smoo Cave and its underground waterfall; cl Nov–May; (01971) 511259; £2.50.
Cape Wrath In summer you can make an adventurous expedition to this stormy tip of coast, guarded by a lonely lighthouse, by boat across the Kyle of Durness and then along a very long rough track to the lighthouse itself; for details phone Mrs Mackay (01971) 511343.

ELPHIN NC2110
Highland & Rare Breeds Farm 🖼 (A835) Traditional Scottish farm animals close up, on a family-worked croft in attractive setting. They sell fleeces and hand-spun wool. Snacks, shop, some disabled access; cl 20 Sept–20 May; (01854) 666204; *£3.50.

EVANTON NH5864
Clanland & Sealpoint In an attractive restored building on the shores of Cromarty Firth, this lively visitor centre takes a fresh look at the area's local heritage and maritime history. Café, shop, disabled access; cl 25 Dec, 1–2 Jan; (01349) 830000; *£3.50.

FALLS OF GLOMACH NH0125
Tremendous waterfall in a wilderness setting, a fine destination for walkers on Kintail.

FALLS OF MEASACH NH1978
With a mighty drop of 60 metres (200 ft), these are the highlight of the mile-long, sheer-sided Corrieshalloch Gorge, owned by the National Trust for Scotland and equipped with a viewing platform.

FALLS OF SHIN NH5799
(B864 S) There's a good chance of seeing salmon leaping here in June or early July, esp if there's been a dry spell followed by rain so that the river is in spate.

GAIRLOCH NG8076
Gairloch Heritage Museum 🖼 Enthusiastically run, perhaps the best of the several heritage museums in the Highlands, with a new hands-on exhibition. Meals, snacks, shop, disabled access; cl Sun, Nov–Mar exc by arrangement; (01445) 712287; £2.50. The Old Inn here is a useful stop; Gairloch has a beach, and is a good base for hikers.

GLEN AFFRIC NH2124
One of the most majestic inland glens, with a walking route along its floor.

GLENFINNAN NM9080
Jacobite Monument (A830) Built in 1815 to commemorate the Highlanders who fought and died for Bonnie Prince Charlie, in a commanding position at the head of Loch Shiel. A visitor centre has exhibitions on the prince. Good snacks, shop, limited disabled access; visitor centre cl Nov–Mar; (01397) 722250; £1.50; NTS.

GOLSPIE NC8500
Dunrobin Castle (A9) Splendid castle – a gleaming turreted structure with views out to sea and gardens modelled on those at Versailles. The family home

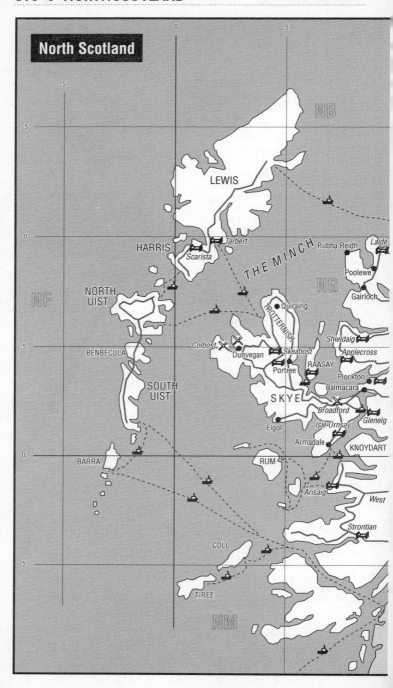

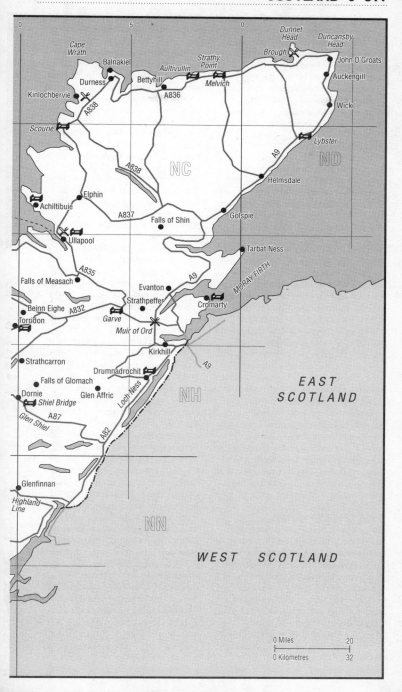

of the Earls and Dukes of Sutherland for longer than anyone can remember, the site was named after Earl Robin in the 13th c; he was responsible for the original square keep. Drastically renovated in the 19th c, it has fine collections of furnishings and art, and a unique collection of Pictish stones; falconry. Snacks, shop; cl Sun am, and mid-Oct–Mar, gardens open all year; (01408) 633177; *£6.

HELMSDALE ND0315

Timespan Visitor Centre (Dunrobin St) Extended centre with reconstructions of scenes in Highland history (with sound effects), art exhibitions and interesting herb garden. Riverside café, shop, disabled access; cl Sun am, Nov–Mar; (01431) 821327; £3.50.

HIGHLAND WALKING NC2617 The Highlands offer ultra-tough mountain walking, but relatively few easier routes on defined paths; shorter circular walks are few and far between. For non-mountaineers the Highlands can be tantalising but problematic: compared to the uplands of England and Wales there are few obvious walking routes (OS maps show hardly any), and the scale of the scenery is often so vast that you need to walk for hours before the views change. The high peaks are mostly for the dedicated (and fit) enthusiast. There is an informal tradition of allowing general access to the mountains, but there are few rights of way, and areas are often closed for at least part of the grouse-shooting season (12 Aug–10 Dec), particularly its first few weeks, or the deer-stalking season (1 July–20 Oct for stags, 21 Oct–15 Feb for hinds).

ISLE OF SKYE NG4829 After Lewis, the biggest of the islands off the Scottish coast, now linked to the mainland by a bridge: islanders who'd campaigned for the bridge didn't expect the high tolls (which were later reduced), and others were initially unnerved by the prospect of easier access bringing floods of visitors and the end of the island's special air of romance – so far neither has happened. The closing of the Kyle of Lochalsh ferry is lamented (though you can still emulate Bonnie Prince Charlie and

Flora MacDonald on one from Mallaig, or the tiny summer one to Kylerhea from past Glenelg). The coasts have plenty of opportunities for gentle pottering, and for finding quiet coves and bays, particularly on the W coast, where for instance Tarskavaig, or the good Stein Inn in the N, are lovely spots to watch the sun go down. The jagged teeth of the Cuillins mountain range to the SE of the centre are unforgettable. Besides places mentioned in **Where to stay** and **Where to eat**, the Misty Isle at Dunvegan, Sligachan Inn at the junction of the A850 and A863 in the middle of the island, the Struan Grill at Struan and the waterside Old Inn at Carbost (handy for the Talisker distillery, which can be visited) all do decent food.

Armadale Castle, Gardens & Museum of the Isles ⌂ NG6404 The castle was built for Lord Macdonald in 1815; it now houses an excellent visitor centre looking at the history of the clan, and the surrounding 40 acres offer beautiful walks among gardens and woodlands. Sleat, this southern peninsula, is known as the Garden of Skye. Very good restaurant, shop, disabled access; cl Nov–Mar (01471) 844305; *£3.90

Dunvegan Castle NG2449 Dramatically set on the sea loch of Dunvegan, this has been the home of the Chief of Macleod for 800 years; no other Scottish castle has been inhabited by the same family for so long. Among its relics is a lock of Bonnie Prince Charlie's hair. Staying here inspired Walter Scott's *Lord of the Isles*. The current clan chief recently hit the headlines when he announced his intention to sell the Black Cuillin mountain range (which his family have owned since Viking times) to raise money to repair the roof and improve public access to the castle. Whatever the outcome, the mountains have been designated a National Scenic Area so the new owners would be able to make very few changes. Good meals and snacks, shops; open daily; cl 25–26 Dec, 1–2 Jan ; (01470) 521206; £5.50, £3.70 gardens only. There are several good self-catering cottages in the attractive grounds, and boat trips go from the jetty to a nearby colony of brown and great grey seals.

Elgol NG5113 A peaceful spot for gorgeous sunset views. There may be summer boat trips to the lonely and dramatic inlet of Loch Coruisk from Elgol. One of the island's lovely shoreside walks runs from Elgol to Loch na Creitheach at the heart of the formidable Cuillins, a mecca for rock-climbers.

Museum of Island Life 🏛 NG2547 (Kilmuir) Worth a look; shop; disabled access; cl Sun, and Nov–Apr; £2.

Portree NG4843 Skye's busiest harbour, attractive and quite picturesque, though in summer it tends to swarm with visitors; the harbourside Pier Hotel is right in the thick of the action, the quieter Cuillins View on the outskirts has good value food in its conservatory.

Quiraing NG4569 A fascinating tumbled rock mass, with a surprisingly manageable path through it.

Raasay (off Skye) Very peaceful island, an ideal place for gentle pottering without lots of competition from other visitors – and for some quite stiff hill walks if that's what you prefer.

Trotternish peninsula (NG5163) Quite extraordinary rock scenery and formations like the Old Man of Storr; the Glenview Hotel at Culnaknock up here has good food, and in season the Flodigarry Hotel serves food all day.

JOHN O' GROATS ND3773 Gets its share of visitors under the mistaken impression that it's the most northerly point on mainland Britain. Increasingly developed for tourists, but still a pleasant spot. The hotel on the harbour looking across to the Orkneys has decent food.

KINLOCHBERVIE NC2156 Friendly village with decent beaches, mountains and scenery around; it's most lively around 6pm on Mon–Thurs (2pm Fri), when the fishing boats return to the pier and auction their catch. There may be boat trips round the harbour.

KIRKHILL NH5543 **Moniack Castle** (A862) Former fortress of the Lovat chiefs, now producing traditional country wines and liqueurs, and interesting meat and game preserves, sauces and coulis, and breakfast preserves. There are tastings and tours, and an amusing video. Shop; cl Sun, 25 Dec; (01463) 831283; *£2.

KNOYDART NG8100 A real Highland wilderness on the W coast, glorious roadless country that's irresistible to hardened walkers – given good weather, full equipment and strong legs. There is a ferry 3 days a week from Mallaig to Inverie, where the Old Forge is very hospitable (and open all day).

LOCH NESS NH5330 Drumnadrochit (see above) is the best place to begin exploring this striking 24-mile loch with the largest volume of fresh water of any lake in the British Isles; up to 215 metres (700 ft) deep in places, so it's not hard to see why stories sprang up of what was hidden in its waters. You can generally take boat trips on the lake, some of them equipped with sonar for monster-spotting.

PLOCKTON NG8033 Idyllic waterside village, with palm trees along the village street; the TV series *Hamish Macbeth* was filmed here. The Plockton Hotel serves generous food.

POOLEWE NG8681 **Inverewe Gardens** (A832) Unmissable beautiful gardens full of rare and subtropical plants, with a magnificent background of mountain scenery. The Atlantic Drift is responsible for the special microclimate which lets these unusual plants flourish even though this is further N than Moscow. Guided walks wkdys at 1.30pm, Apr–Sept. Meals, snacks, shop, limited disabled access; visitor centre, shop and restaurant cl end Oct to 15 Mar; (01445) 781200; £5; NTS.

RUBHA REIGH NG7391 **Rubha Reigh Lighthouse** Remote outpost several miles along a track N of Melvaig; they organise enjoyable walking holidays in the splendidly wild countryside around; tearoom open Sun, Tues and Thurs; cl Jan after New Year; B&B or hostel-style rooms – don't worry about the colour of the water, it's just peaty; (01445) 771263.

STRATHCARRON NG9338 **Attadale Gardens** 🏛 (A890 towards

S) Attractive gardens with excellent water gardens and winding woodland paths, sheltered by the surrounding hills and steep cliffs. Started in the 1890s, they include rhododendrons, azaleas and bamboo. An old sunken garden has been restored along with herb and vegetable gardens, and they are currently developing a nursery garden. Disabled access; cl Sun, and early Nov to early Apr; (01520) 722217; *£2.

STRATHPEFFER NH4858
Originally a fashionable 19th-c spa resort, this has quite a different feel from the rest of the area, with its rather continental appearance of dignified hotels and villas stepped up among its wooded slopes; some call it the Harrogate of the North.

Highland Museum of Childhood ⊞ In restored Victorian railway station, telling the history of childhood in the Highlands among crofters and townsfolk, recorded by oral testimony, displays, photographs and video; fascinating doll and toy collections. Snacks, shop; disabled access; cl Sun am, and Nov–Mar; (01997) 421031; *£1.50.

STRATHY POINT NC8269
(W of Thurso) With a lighthouse at the end of a narrow peninsula, a pleasant stroll along the little road from its car park.

TARBAT NESS NH9487
Jutting from the S side of Dornoch Firth, this is rather isolated, but worth the journey for the walk around the peninsula, from Portmahomack, past the lighthouse, and then along the S coast past a ruined castle to reach Rockfield.

TORRIDON NG9055
Torridon Countryside Centre ⊞ (junction A896 and Diabaig road) Gateway to a huge area of nature reserve in stunning mountain scenery – some say the best in Scotland. It has displays on the scenery and wildlife, as well as a deer park and deer museum. Visitor centre cl Sun am, and all Oct–Apr; £1.50; (01445) 791221; NTS. Nearby at the Mains there are herds of red deer. Torridon is wonderful for challenging walks, and there are a few outstanding easier ones, based for example on Loch Torridon's shores. The Kinlochewe Hotel (A896 E) has

decent food; to reach anywhere N of here by car from the S, incidentally, it's much quicker to go by Inverness than to make your way all the way up the W coast.

ULLAPOOL NH1294
A good centre, with quite a busy harbour, a lot going on for a small place – and good eating (besides the places we've picked out, the fish and chip restaurant is very good, with surprisingly presentable white wines, and the Ferry Boat is useful). You can get a ferry out to the Summer Isles.

WEST HIGHLAND LINE NM9080
A good way of seeing Highlands scenery between Fort William and Mallaig: steam trains in summer, year-round normal trains. The views are terrific.

WICK ND3650
This waterside village has attractive houses and a good church.

Caithness Glass Factory (Wick Airport Industrial Estate) Glass-making demonstrations (not wknds), and factory seconds. Meals, snacks, shop, disabled access; cl Sun Dec–Mar; (01955) 602286; free.

Castle of Old Wick (just S) Ruined four-storey square tower, probably dating from the 12th c.

Wick Heritage Centre In eight buildings by the harbour, this very good centre presents the history of the town; cl Sun, Oct–May; (01955) 605393; £2.

This is a part of the world where inns doing a decent bite to eat are very much at a premium, and a welcome sight indeed after miles of empty road. Besides those listed elsewhere, ones we can recommend for their positions include the Aultbea Inn at Aultbea NG8689, Aultguish Hotel NH3570 on the A835 nr Loch Glascarnoch, Badachro Inn at Badachro NG7773, Royal Hotel at Cromarty NH7867, Northern Sands at Dunnet ND2170, Lock at Fort Augustus NH3709, Cluanie by the loch (walks and maybe eagles) in Glen Shiel NH0711, Garvault Inn extraordinarily isolated on the B871 N of Kinbrace NC8732, Kylesku Hotel at Kylesku NC2234 (the boatman here has taken readers for fascinating 4-hour boat tours), Lewiston Arms at Lewiston

NH5029, Loch Carron Hotel on Loch Carron NG9039, Glenuig Hotel at Lochailort NM7682, Inver Lodge Hotel overlooking Lochinver harbour NC0923, Scrabster Inn at Scrabster ND0970, Ben View at Strontian NM8161, Loch Maree Hotel at Talladale NG8970 and Ben Loyal Hotel at Tongue NC5957. Almost all have bedrooms.

Where to eat

BROADFORD NG6423 **Fig Tree** *(01471) 822616* Enjoyable home-made food inc fresh fish and vegetarian choices in friendly little place; cl Sun, Oct–Feb; disabled access. £22|**£5**

BROUGH ND2273 **Dunnet Head Tearoom** *(01847) 851774* Small traditional unpretentious cottage with good reasonably priced meals and snacks served by warmly friendly owners – fair choice of vegetarian dishes, fresh salmon, local seafood, and local beef; take your own wine; bdrms; open 3–8pm (last orders then), tearoom cl Oct–Easter; children must be well behaved. £12|**£5**

COLBOST NG2050 **Three Chimneys** *(01470) 511258* Simple but stylish no smoking crofter's cottage nr sea with cosy feel in two stone-walled rooms, open fires, friendly owners, thoughtful wine list, and most enjoyable contemporary food with a strong emphasis on fish (though plenty of game and vegetarian choices, too); morning coffee and afternoon teas; good bdrms; cl Sun am, winter am, 3 wks in Jan. £45|**£12.50**

DUNVEGAN NG2351 **Macleod's Table** *The Castle (01470) 521310* Decorated with pine throughout, popular family restaurant with very reasonably priced generous morning coffee, snacks and full meals, and afternoon teas; friendly helpful staff; loch cruises, seal colony, castle gardens and craft shops; cl 1 Nov–19 Mar; disabled access. £20|**£5**

KINLOCHBERVIE NC2256 **Old School House** *Inshegra (01971) 521383* Very good food in old school building with school-related items like photographs, maps, notebooks on tables; home-grown vegetables, local fish and venison, enjoyable puddings, and very good service; bdrms in newish building; disabled access; cl 25 Dec, 1 Jan. £16.25|**£8.25**

MUIR OF ORD NH5251 **Dower House** *(01463) 870090* Very good modern cooking in attractive hotel restaurant, with fine wines, and friendly service; bdrms and lovely gardens; children over 5 in restaurant. £37.50|**£5**

ULLAPOOL NH1195 **Morefield Motel** *North Rd (01854) 612161* Big helpings of exceptionally fresh enterprisingly cooked fish and seafood (owners are ex-fishermen and divers), Aberdeen Angus steaks and roast beef, and vegetarian dishes in smart restaurant of basic hotel, also bar food; restaurant cl 25–26 Dec, 1 Jan; bdrms; disabled access. £20|**£6.25**

Special thanks to Mrs Edna M Jones, David Wallington, Margaret Taylor, Ian M Baillie

We welcome reports from readers

This *Guide* depends on readers' reports. Do help us if you can – in return, we offer a discount on the next edition to people who've helped us with reports for it. Tell us what you think about places already in it, and anything extra you think we should say about them. And send us your ideas for inclusion in the next edition: places to visit, eat at or stay in, attractive drives or walks, maybe even unusual interesting shops you know of. Use the card in the middle, the report forms at the end, or just write – no stamp needed: *The Good Britain Guide*, FREEPOST TN1569, Wadhurst, E Sussex TN5 7BR.

WALES

North Wales (which gets the lion's share of summer visitors) combines glorious unspoilt mountain and valley scenery with plenty of enjoyable and interesting places to visit. West Wales has a beautiful coastline, with lovely walks along it – even in bad weather when upland areas are more or less a write-off, the coast preserves a gloomy magnificence. The new Millennium Coastal Park should revive the appeal of the coastline section around Llanelli, for so long scarred by heavy industry. Mid Wales has fewer tourist attractions: its strength is the grand scenery, which includes the Brecon Beacons National Park, the empty and lonely Cambrian Mountains (wonderful high-level drives here), and the Elan Valley lakes. South Wales has a very good choice of interesting days out, and some pockets of fine scenery.

Besides the medieval castles and spectacular private railways which are almost a Wales trademark, enjoyable days out run from dramatic show caves to grand houses and gardens, from animal parks to Celtic myth-making, from lively historic re-creations to intriguing alternatives for the future. There are some excellent industrial museums – again, full of life.

We have mentioned a few of the Roman and prehistoric sites in which the area abounds. You can get more information from CADW (Welsh Historic Monuments Commission), (029) 2050 0200, which is also responsible for the care of the great majority of the historic castles and other monuments here: if you plan to visit many of their sites, an Explorer Pass (£15 for a week, less for three days – available from most of their sites) is good value as it admits to all.

Wales is relatively cheap for a short break or holiday. And you cut down on transport costs with a seven-day Freedom of Wales train pass (£32, less in winter).

North Wales

Wales's most family-friendly corner, with plenty to visit inc some unusual outings, and some majestic scenery

The landscape varies richly, from Snowdonia's majestic mountain expanses to the intricate and rather intimate landscapes of Clwyd, the luscious Vale of Conwy and the peace of Anglesey. Snowdonia gives plenty of fine walking, both gentle and taxing – somewhere to justify a walking holiday. The much less visited Berwyn Hills further inland also give memorable scenic drives. There are good long beaches and attractive traditional family resorts, yet it's easy to get away from the crowds even in high summer – particularly on the shores of the very Welsh Lleyn Peninsula.

Many of the most rewarding places for families here aren't what you'd call textbook tourist sites – more innovative variations on a traditional theme. Top of the class this year is the enjoyable Llechwedd Slate Caverns, Blaenau Ffestiniog, earning our accolade of Wales Family Attraction of the Year thanks to its exhilarating underground train ride and interesting period village (see Beddgelert's Sygun Copper Mine and the Welsh Slate Museum at Llanberis for other nifty industrial conversions). Elsewhere, the rescued buildings at Holywell are well worth a look, the Greenwood Centre (Y Felinheli) is a delightful celebration of all things arboreal (and good for a rainy day), and Henblas Park at Bodorgan has far more than the average farm park. For a totally different (and relaxing) day out, head for the fairytale holiday village, Portmeirion.

North Wales has some magnificent and remarkably intact castles; the mighty examples at Caernarfon, Conwy and Harlech are especially impressive, and children will perhaps get the most out of Penrhyn near Bangor and Bodelwyddan. This area also lays claim to more than its fair share of picturesque railways, with the Ffestiniog and Snowdon Mountain lines probably the most famous. Erddig offers an unusual glimpse into life in a manor house (both above and below stairs), and the colour schemes inside Rhug chapel, Corwen, are a cheering sight to behold. Glorious Bodnant is one of Britain's greatest gardens, and there are other charming grounds at Bodrhyddan Hall in Rhuddlan, and Plas yn Rhiw.

There is a splendid range of places to stay in, many in superb countryside.

Where to stay

ABERSOCH SH3226 **Porth Tocyn Hotel** *Bwlch Tocyn, Pwllheli, Gwynedd LL53 7BU (01758) 713303* **£88**, plus special breaks; 17 attractive rms, most with sea views. On a headland overlooking Cardigan Bay, a lovely place to stay – with a refreshingly sensible and helpful approach to families (though not solely a family hotel); very friendly hard-working owners and staff, several cosy interconnecting sitting rooms with antiques and fresh flowers, most enjoyable traditional cooking in the restaurant (lots of options such as light lunches, high teas for children as they must be over 7 for dinner in the restaurant, and imaginative Sun lunches), and a happy atmosphere; lots of space in the pretty garden, heated swimming pool in summer, hard tennis court; cl mid-Nov to wk before Easter; disabled access ☺

BEAUMARIS SH6076 **Olde Bulls Head** *Castle St, Beaumaris, Gwynedd LL58 8AP (01248) 810329* **£85**, plus special breaks; 15 rms with antiques and brass bedsteads. Partly 15th-c pub nr castle, with snug alcoves, low beams and open fire in quaint rambling bar, interesting decorations, popular brasserie, very good restaurant food (esp fish), fine wines, and cheery service; entrance to pretty courtyard closed by biggest single-hinged door in Britain; cl 25–26 Dec, 1 Jan; children over 7 in restaurant in evening

BEDDGELERT SH5948 **Sygun Fawr Country House** *Beddgelert, Caernarfon, Gwynedd LL55 4NE (01766) 890258* **£59**, plus special breaks; 9 rms. Marvellous views of Gwynant Valley and Snowdon range from this secluded 17th-c hotel, and lots of surrounding walks; comfortable sitting room, well stocked bar, and home cooking in candlelit traditionally furnished dining room; sauna; cl Jan

BETWS-Y-COED SH7955 **Ty Gwyn** *Betwys-y-Coed, Gwynedd LL24 0SG (01690) 710383* **£56**, plus special breaks; 12 pretty rms, most with own bthrm. Welcoming 17th-c coaching inn with interesting old prints, furniture and bric-a-brac (owners own the antiques shop next door), good food and friendly service; pleasant setting overlooking river and a very good base for the area; children free if sharing parents' room; cl Mon—Weds in Jan; disabled access

BLAENAU FFESTINIOG SH7045 **Queen's Hotel** *I High St, Blaenau Ffestiniog, Gwynedd LL41 3ES (01766) 830055* **£55**, plus special breaks; 12 individually decorated rms. By the famous narrow-gauge railway and surrounded by Snowdonia National Park, this most attractively refurbished Victorian hotel has real ales in convivial lounge bar, good all-day food in bistro (converts to more formal evening restaurant with imaginative dishes), and swift friendly service; lots to do nearby; cl 25 Dec

BRYNSIENCYN SH4866 **Plas Trefarthen** *Brynsiencyn, Llanfairpwllgwyngyll, Gwynedd LL61 6SZ (01248) 430379* **£44**; 9 rms. Happy and comfortable Georgian family house with panoramic views of Caernarfon Castle and Snowdonia, full-size snooker table; Mrs Roberts is a well known soprano soloist for Welsh choirs; self-catering also; cl Christmas

CAERNARFON SH5163 **Seiont Manor** *Llanrug, Caernarfon, Gwynedd LL55 2AQ (01286) 673366* **£140**, plus special breaks; 28 luxurious rms. Fine hotel built from the original farmstead of a Georgian manor house, in 156 acres of mature parkland; open fires and comfortable sofas in lounge, restful atmosphere in library and drawing room, imaginative food in restaurant's four interconnecting areas, leisure suite with swimming pool, gym, sauna and solarium

CAPEL COCH SH4581 **Tre-Ysgawen Hall** *Capel Coch, Llangefni, Gwynedd LL77 7UR (01248) 750750* **£120**, plus special breaks; 19 lavish rms. Handsome Victorian stone mansion with landscaped gardens, plushly comfortable bar, carefully decorated lounge, friendly staff and fine food in conservatory-style restaurant; clay pigeon shooting; cl 24 Dec–2 Jan; disabled access

CAPEL GARMON SH8156 **Tan-y-Foel Country House** *Capel Garmon, Llanrwst, Gwynedd LL26 0RE (01690) 710507* **£120**, plus special breaks; 7 comfortable rms. Charming partly 16th-c no smoking stone hotel N of village, vibrant modern décor in lounge and breakfast room, log fire, warmly friendly relaxing atmosphere, very good robustly flavoured modern food in cosy restaurant using the freshest produce inc local lamb, organic vegetables and home-made bread, interesting wine list; mature gardens and marvellous surrounding countryside; cl Christmas, limited opening Jan; children over 7

CAPEL GARMON SH8155 **White Horse** *Capel Garmon, Llanrwst, Gwynedd LL26 0RW (01690) 710271* **£58***, plus midweek off-season breaks; 6 simple rms (those in newish part are quietest). Comfortable, homely, low-beamed inn with friendly atmosphere, winter log fires, very good home-made food in bar and little no smoking restaurant (some traditional Welsh meals), marvellous breakfasts, magnificent views, delightful surrounding countryside; children over 12

CONWY SH7877 **Castle Hotel** *High St, Conwy, Gwynedd LL32 8DB (01492) 582800* **£80***, plus special breaks; 29 rms. In the heart of the town, early 16th-c inn with fine original oil paintings in public rooms, good food in pretty restaurant, proper pubby bar (popular with locals), friendly helpful staff, decent breakfast, and car parking

GELLILYDAN SH6939 **Tyddyn Du Farm** *Gellilydan, Blaenau Ffestiniog, Gwynedd LL41 4RB (01766) 590281* **£45**; 4 rms with views of hills and mountains, 4 private cottage suites. 400-year-old farmhouse on working farm in heart of Snowdonia, beams and exposed stonework, big inglenook fireplaces in residents' lounge, and wholesome home-made food using own free-range eggs; children can help with the lambs, goats, ducks, sheep and pony; fine walks, inc short one to their own Roman site; partial disabled access

LLANABER SH5919 **Llwyndu Farmhouse** *Llanaber, Barmouth, Gwynedd LL42 1RR (01341) 280144* **£62***, plus special breaks; 7 charming rms, some in a nicely converted 18th-c barn. Most attractive 16th-c farmhouse set just above Cardigan Bay, with a warm welcome from friendly owners, big inglenook fireplaces, oak beams, little mullioned windows, relaxing lounge, enjoyable breakfasts, and good imaginative food in candlelit dining room; cl 25–26 Dec

LLANARMON DC SJ1532 **West Arms** Llanarmon Dyffryn Ceiriog, Llangollen, Clwyd LL20 7LD (01691) 600665 **£79**, plus special mid-week breaks; 15 rms. Charming and civilised old place with heavy beams and timbers, log fires in inglenook fireplaces, lounge bar interestingly furnished with antique settles, sofas in the old-fashioned entrance hall, comfortable locals' bar, good food, and friendly quiet atmosphere; the lawn runs down to the River Ceiriog (fishing for residents); disabled access

LLANDRILLO SJ0337 **Tyddyn Llan** Llandrillo, Corwen, Clwyd LL21 0ST (01490) 440264 **£105**; 10 pretty rms. Restful Georgian house with fresh flowers and antiques in elegantly furnished and comfortable public rooms, charming staff, very good inventive food (using their own herbs) and three acres of lovely gardens; fishing on four miles of River Dee (ghillies available) and fine forest walks (guides available) – can arrange riding and shooting too; dogs by prior arrangement

LLANDUDNO SH7979 **Bodysgallen Hall** Pentywyn Rd, Llandudno, Gwynedd LL30 1RS (01492) 584466 **£182**, plus special breaks; 35 deeply comfortable rms, 19 in hotel, the rest in cottages in grounds. Fine 17th-c house in its own parkland, with mullioned windows, oak panelling, lovely entrance hall and first-floor drawing room, open fires, very good imaginative food in no smoking dining room, and 18th-c walled rose garden and knot garden; tennis, croquet, swimming pool, sauna, gym and beauty salon; children over 8; dogs allowed in cottage suites; disabled access

LLANDUDNO SH7882 **St Tudno** 15 North Parade, Llandudno, Gwynedd LL30 2LP (01492) 874411 **£110**, plus special breaks. Standing opposite the pier, this well run, smart Victorian seaside hotel has genuinely helpful and friendly staff, Victorian-style décor in restful no smoking sitting room, a convivial bar lounge, relaxed coffee lounge for light lunches, and attractive garden-style restaurant with imaginative modern food; good wine list; small indoor pool

LLANDYRNOG SJ1264 **Berllan Bach** Ffordd-las, Llandyrnog, Denbigh, Clwyd LL16 4LR (01824) 790732 **£60**, plus special breaks; 3 rms with French windows on to individual terraces. Carefully converted cottage and barns at the foot of hills in Vale of Clwyd, with woodburner in comfortable sitting room and good food in dining conservatory; marvellous walks, well behaved dogs welcome

LLANERCHYMEDD SH4284 **Llwydiarth Fawr Farm** Llanerchymedd, Gwynedd LL71 8DF (01248) 470321 **£50***, plus special breaks; 3 rms in main house, 2 cottage suites in grounds. Handsome Georgian farmhouse on 850-acre cattle and sheep farm, with a particularly warm homely atmosphere and welcome, comfortable lounge with antiques, log fire, books and lovely views, and very good home-made food using farm and other fresh local produce; terrace, lake for private fishing, nature walks, bird-watching; no smoking; cl Christmas

LLANFAIR DC SJ1355 **Eyarth Station** Llanfair Dyffryn Clwyd, Ruthin, Clwyd LL15 2EE (01824) 703643 **£50***, plus special breaks; 6 pretty rms. Carefully converted old railway station with quiet gardens and wonderful views, a friendly relaxed atmosphere, log fire in airy and comfortable beamed lounge, good breakfasts and enjoyable suppers in dining room (more lovely views), sun terrace and heated swimming pool, and lots of walks; dogs by prior arrangement; disabled access; cl Jan–Feb

LLANFIHANGEL-YNG-NGWYNFA SJ0815 **Cyfie Farm** Llanfihangel, Llanfyllin, Powys SY22 5JE (01691) 648451 **£52**, plus special breaks; 4 rms inc 3 suites with lovely views. Carefully restored 17th-c Welsh stone longhouse on 178 acres of cattle and sheep farm; timbered and beamed rms with fine family furniture, log fire in the residents' lounge, hearty farmhouse cooking in attractive dining conservatory, and relaxed friendly atmosphere

LLANGOLLEN SJ2541 **Bryn Howel** Trevor, Llangollen, Clwyd LL20 7UW (01978) 860331 **£99**, plus special breaks; 36 rms. Extended Victorian mansion with lovely views, comfortable lounges, panelled bar, open fires, and good food using home-grown herbs and fresh local produce in the restaurant; neat grounds, sauna and solarium, and private salmon and trout fishing on River Dee

LLANNEFYDD SH9870 **Hawk & Buckle** Llannefydd, Denbigh, Clwyd LL16 5ED

(01745) 540249 **£55***; 10 modern rms, lovely views. Pleasant 17th-c stone inn, 215 metres (700 ft) up in the hills with remarkable vistas; decent choice of food using fresh local produce, neatly kept beamed and knocked-through lounge bar; a good base for exploring the area – by horse, car or on foot; cl 25–26 Dec; children over 8

LLANSANFFRAID GLAN CONWY SH8075 **Old Rectory** *Llanrwst Rd, Glan Conwy, Colwyn Bay, Clwyd LL28 5LF (01492) 580611* **£139**, plus special breaks; 6 deeply comfortable rms. Georgian house in pleasant gardens with fine views over Conwy estuary, Conwy Castle and Snowdonia; delightful public rooms with flowers, antiques and family photos, delicious food and marvellous wines; good breakfasts, and warmly friendly staff; cl 20 Dec–1 Feb; children under 9 months or over 5

LLANWDDYN SJ0219 **Lake Vyrnwy Hotel** *Llanwddyn, Oswestry, Powys SY10 0LY (01691) 870692* **£110**; 35 rms, the ones overlooking the lake are the nicest – and quietest. Large impressive Tudor-style mansion overlooking lake from hillside in 24,000 acres of forestry, with lots of sporting activities (esp fishing), log fires and sporting prints in the comfortable and elegant public rooms, relaxed atmosphere, clubby bar, and good food using home-made preserves, chutneys, mustards and vinegars and produce from own kitchen garden; nice teas too

NANTGWYNANT SH6555 **Pen-y-Gwryd** *Nantgwynant, Caernarfon, Gwynedd LL55 4NT (01286) 870211* **£54**, plus special breaks; 16 rms. In two acres, this cheery hotel is by the Llanberis Pass in Snowdonia National Park; warm log fire in simply furnished panelled residents' lounge, rugged slate-floored bar that doubles as mountain rescue post; lots of climbing mementoes and equipment, friendly, chatty games room (lots of walkers, climbers and fishermen), hearty, enjoyable food, big breakfasts, and packed lunches; sauna in the trees and outdoor swimming pool, table tennis; cl Nov–New Year and midweek Jan–Feb; disabled access

PENMAENPOOL SH6515 **George III** *Penmaenpool, Dolgellau, Gwynedd LL40 1YD (01341) 422525* **£94**, plus special breaks; 11 low-beamed rms, some in award-winning converted railway station. Cosy 17th-c inn with views over Mawddach estuary, good lunchtime food, imaginative evening restaurant, snug lounge with log fire, beamed and partly panelled bar (real ales), fine nearby walks, and free salmon and trout fishing permits for residents; disabled access

PORTMEIRION SH5837 **Portmeirion Hotel** *Penrhyndeudraeth, Porthmadog, Gwynedd LL48 6ER (01766) 770228* **£155** in village (26 rms), **£145** in hotel (14 rms), plus special breaks. On the edge of an estuary and surrounded by beaches and woods (and traffic-free), this is a remarkable place; the hotel down by the water is quite luxurious – elegant rooms with marble, gilt, and rich colourful fabrics – while behind and in the steeply landscaped grounds above it is a well dispersed very colourful Italianate village, luscious to look at, inc all sorts of characterful cottage bedrooms tucked into the hillside; very romantic when the day visitors have left; lots to do; cl 7 Jan–2 Feb; disabled access. See **To see and do** section ☺

SARON SH4557 **Pengwern** *Saron, Caernarfon, Gwynedd LL54 5UH (01286) 831500* **£44***, plus special breaks; 3 rms. In 130 acres running down to Foryd Bay, this spacious no smoking farmhouse has marvellous views of Snowdonia, and delicious food using home-produced beef and lamb; cl Dec–Jan

TAL-Y-BONT SH7669 **Lodge** *Tal-y-Bont, Conwy, Gwynedd LL32 8YX (01492) 660766* **£70**, plus special breaks; 14 rms. Friendly little modern hotel in over three acres on the edge of Snowdonia, with open fire, books and magazines in comfortable lounge, generous helpings of popular food using lots of home-grown produce in no smoking restaurant, and good service; lots of walks; well behaved pets welcome; good disabled access

TALSARNAU SH6135 **Maes-y-Neuadd** *Talsarnau, Gwynedd LL47 6YA (01766) 780200* **£230** inc 5-course dinner, plus special breaks; 16 luxurious rms. Looking out across Snowdonia, this attractive extended 14th-c mansion is set in eight acres of landscaped hillside; flowers, plants, antiques and open fires, peaceful atmosphere, very good food (herbs and vegetables from their own garden), friendly dogs and cats, and charming staff; children over 8 in evening restaurant; disabled access

TREMEIRCHION SJ0771 **Bach-y-Graig** *Tremeirchion, St Asaph, Clwyd LL17 0UH*

(01745) 730627 **£50***; 3 rms, 2 with brass beds. Wales's first brick-built house with a date-stone of 1567, in 200-acre dairy farm at the foot of the Clwydian Hills; inglenook fireplace in big lounge, home cooking using home-produced beef and lamb and own free-range eggs, and warm welcome; woodland trail, fishing; cl Christmas and New Year

TUDWEILIOG SH2535 **Lion** *Tudweiliog, Pwllheli, Gwynedd LL53 8ND (01758)* *770244* **£44**; 4 basic rms. Extended 300-year-old village pub with good value home-made food in comfortable bar and dining rooms, a welcome for families, play area, lovely views; 10 mins' walk to beach

To see and do

Wales Family Attraction of the Year

BLAENAU FFESTINIOG SH7046 **Llechwedd Slate Caverns** (A470) The same company has been mining and quarrying slate here for over 150 years, and their well organised tours of the huge caverns bring the history of the site vividly to life. There are two underground rides, and it is worth doing both; if you've time for only one, our preference is for the Deep Mine, rather more dramatic, and quite an adventure if you don't mind being underground. You're taken into the depths of the mine in the uniquely designed carriages of Britain's steepest passenger railway: the incline is 1:1.8. The way the 16 floors are named and numbered can be slightly confusing (you board on Floor 2 and alight at Floor A) – all you need to know is that eventually you're 137 metres (450 ft) below the summit of the mountain. Next you'll don your hard hat for a walk through 10 stunning subterranean chambers, each jazzed up for visitors with a sound and light show illustrating the world of a Victorian miner. You'll need to be relatively agile (there are 61 steps going down, and 71 on the way up), and even when it's warm on the surface you'll be glad you brought warm clothing. But the surroundings really are fantastic, the highlight an eerie underground lake, nicely lit to create atmospheric shadows on the water and the steep, craggy walls. The other tour (the Miners Tramway) explains more about the mining process: battery-powered trains take you around the Victorian workings, staying on the level, but passing through splendid man-made caverns, some of which have tableaux or demonstrations of ancient mining skills. You get off at various points along the way, and the guides give useful talks. Back in the brighter world outside you can explore the old buildings of Llechwedd village; the last residents left in the 1970s, but the shops and pub remain open, several stocking Victorian-themed goods which you can buy using period money; most things are priced in old and new currencies, and you can exchange your coins at the former bank, now a museum. Several other exhibitions and displays include some old railway engines and a working smithy, but it's the underground tours that make this worth a detour. You'll need a couple of hours to see everything – longer if you want to potter round the village, or if you have to wait for one of the tours. It's not likely to appeal to very young children. Meals, snacks, shops, some disabled access with prior warning; cl 25–26 Dec, 1 Jan; (01766) 830306; to do both the Deep Mine and Miners Tramway tours costs £10.50 (£7.20 children) – to do just one is £6.95 (£4.80 children). The surface attractions are free.

ABERFFRAW SH3270
Barclodiad y Gawres Some 5,000 years old, this 6-metre (20-ft) underground passage tomb at the top of the cliff is notable for the patterns carved by the entrance and in the side chambers, shown up by a good torch; it's sealed, but you can ask for a key at the Wayside Café in Llanfaelog, about a mile away. Hard to believe now, but Aberffraw was once the Welsh capital. There are some lovely unspoilt coves

and beaches nearby; the beach up the road at Rhosneigr is particularly good (and clean).

BANGOR SH5872

Quiet university town with a pedestrianised High St and a yacht harbour that adds a lively touch in summer; the pier was restored with an EU grant. The Nelson nr the harbour has decent food, as do the Antelope and Union.

Bangor Cathedral Founded 70 years before the one at Canterbury; the present building is restored 13th- to 15th-c, and has an interesting 16th-c carving of Christ bound and seated on a rock, as well as some fine Victorian stained glass; also, unique 14th-c Flemish statues. Disabled access; cl Sat pm, Sun (apart from services), wk after Christmas; free.

Penrhyn Castle (1m E) Splendid 19th-c neo-Norman fantasy built by a slate magnate: the interior is in suitably grand style, with quite remarkable – and often bizarre – panelling, decoration and furnishings. The cathedral-like great hall is heated by the Roman method of hot air under the floor, and one of the beds weighs over a ton – carved from slate. An unexpectedly rich collection of paintings includes works by Rembrandt and Canaletto. In the stableyard is a museum of unique early locomotives, and there's a walled garden and adventure playground. Meals, snacks, shop, disabled access; cl am (exc July and Aug), all day Tues, and Nov–Mar; (01248) 353084; £5, garden only £3.50; NT.

BEAUMARIS SH6076

The most attractive town on Anglesey, with a good deal of character, several old buildings, and a busy waterfront. The 15th-c **church** of St Mary and St Nicholas – easy to spot by its robust square tower – houses the stone coffin of Joan, daughter of King John and wife of the Welsh leader Llewelyn the Great. The Olde Bulls Head and Sailors Return are good for lunch.

Beaumaris Castle 🔳 One of the most impressive and complete of those built by Edward I, despite the struggle over it with Owain Glyndwr in the early 1400s, and the plundering of its lead, timber and stone in later ages.

Beautifully symmetrical, it took from 1295 to 1312 to build (though the money ran out before it could be finished). Shop, good disabled access; cl 24–26 Dec, 1 Jan; (01248) 810361; £2.20.

Beaumaris Gaol Paints a vivid picture of the harshness of the 19th-c prison system, particularly in the dank, poky cells. Shop; open as courthouse, or by appointment, (01248) 810921; £2.75.

Courthouse 🔳 Unique Victorian survival. You can stand in the dock and imagine you're just about to be sentenced. Cl Oct–Mar (exc by advance booking); shop, disabled access; (01248) 811691; court £1.50.

Marine World (Seafront) Displays of the sea life of the Menai Strait. Snacks, shop, disabled access; cl 25 Dec; (01248) 810072; £2.25.

BEDDGELERT SH5948

A quiet village which dreamed up the myth that it was the resting place of Llewelyn's faithful mastiff over a century ago and has been living off it ever since. The Prince Llewelyn does good value food, and there's good Snowdonia walking around the Aberglaslyn Pass (A498 S).

Sygun Copper Mine 🔳 (A498 NE) Interesting tours through often spectacular underground mine workings, with magnificent stalactites and stalagmites and traces of gold and silver in the copper ore veins. You're greeted by a wonderful view of the mountains when you come up at the end. Snacks, shop, some disabled access; cl wkdys Nov–Jan; (01766) 510101; £4.75.

BETWS-Y-COED SH7956

19th-c inland resort village in a beautiful wooded gorge at the head of the Vale of Conwy, on the road to Bangor (and thence Ireland) as well as to Snowdon. Surrounded by picturesque woodland walks, the village has over a century of catering to visitors behind it. One of the best strolls is along the old riverside railway track by the Afon Llugwy W: the raging Swallow Falls and Fairy Glen just W of the village itself are deservedly regarded as two of the area's finest beauty spots. Several interesting bridges nearby, as well as the bizarre Ugly House, which looks like a series of boulders thrown haphazardly together. The Royal Oak Hotel (open all day – afternoon teas, too), Glan Aber Hotel and Ty Gwyn have good food.

BLAENAU FFESTINIOG SH6946
This straggle of village is dwarfed by the vast spoil slopes from the slate mines all around it – once the slate capital of Wales, now with the passing of the industry like a living museum.

Ffestiniog Pumped Storage Power Station ⊞ (Tanygrisiau, off A496 S) Guided tours of the first hydro-electric pumped storage scheme in the country, with dramatic views towards the peaks of Snowdonia. Meals, snacks, shop; cl Sat (exc mid-July–Aug), and end Oct–Easter; some limited disabled access; (01766) 830310; *£2.75. From the information centre there's an attractive (if slightly hairy) drive into the mountains to Stwlan Dam, which also gives super views.

Llechwedd Slate Caverns *See separate family panel on p.827.*

BODELWYDDAN SH9974
Bodelwyddan Castle (off A55) The walled gardens surrounding this showy white limestone castle include a glorious mix of woodland walks, flowering plants, aviary and water features. The house (older than its 19th-c exterior suggests) has been very well restored as a Victorian mansion, with furniture from the Victoria & Albert Museum, and photographs and portraits from the National Portrait Gallery. Plenty for children, inc a woodland adventure playground, and entertaining exhibitions of puzzles, games and optical illusions. Snacks, shop, disabled access; cl Fri (exc July and Aug), and Mon too Nov–Mar; (01745) 584060; £4, grounds only £1.50. The Kinmel Arms at St George has good interesting food.

Bodelwydden Marble Church
19th-c, built entirely of locally quarried stone: an unusual and quite splendid sight.

BODORGAN SH4272
Henblas Park Good range of family activities, from sheep-shearing, falconry and farm animals, through magic shows and juggling workshops, to tractor rides and a neolithic burial chamber. Meals, snacks, shop, disabled access (but no

facilities); open Easter hols, May bank hol wknd, and Sun–Fri late May–Sept; (01407) 840440; £3.75.

BRYNSIENCYN SH4765
Anglesey Sea Zoo (A4080 just S) Excellent collection of local marine life, housed in tanks specially designed to provide as unrestricted and natural an environment as possible. Also walk-through shipwreck, touch pools, adventure playground, and home-made fudge and ice-cream. Meals, snacks, shop, disabled access; cl 18–27 Dec; (01248) 430411; £5.50.

Foel Farm Park Friendly working farm with daily sheep milking, tractor rides, and more home-made ice cream. Snacks, shop, disabled access; cl Nov–Mar; (01248) 430646; £4.25.

Pick-your-own (Gwydryn Hir farm) Pick fruit and vegetables while taking in the view of Snowdonia; open Jun–Oct; (01248) 430344.

Prehistoric burial chamber A couple of miles NW by the back road towards Llangaffo is what looks like a Stone Age hut, but is actually a burial chamber from which the covering earth has been eroded over the millennia.

CAERNARFON SH4763
Surviving lengths of its 13th-c town walls still crowd in its quaintly narrow streets (quaint, that is, unless you're trying to drive through them). The town harbour is busy with yachts in summer, and you can explore a restored steam-powered dredger moored here. The Black Boy and Palace Vaults do decent food.

Air World (Caernarfon Airport, off A499 nr Llandwrog) They encourage you to climb aboard some of the helicopters and aeroplanes here; also a great many model aeroplanes, and pleasure flights. Meals, snacks, shop, disabled access; cl Nov–Feb (exc by appointment); (01286) 830800; £4.

Caernarfon Castle The largest of Edward I's Welsh castles, built after the defeat of Llewelyn the Last, and still quite spectacular. Finished in 1328, it's unusual both for its octagonal towers and for the bands of colour decorating the walls. Edward's son was born here and presented to the people, setting the precedent for future Princes of Wales. The Royal Welch Fusiliers exhibit in the

Queen's Tower and Chamberlain Tower has been recently redeveloped, thanks to help from a big Lottery grant. Shop; cl 24–26 Dec, 1 Jan; (01286) 677617; £4.20. In the square outside, around the statue of former PM David Lloyd George, there's a busy Saturday market.

Segontium Roman Fort & Museum (A4085) Roman fort dating from AD78; excavations have exposed various rebuildings during its three centuries of importance, and a museum shows some of the finds. There's a tradition that Constantine the Great was born here (and the walls of the nearby castle used to be thought to be modelled partly on the walls of Constantinople). Shop; cl am Sun, 24–26 Dec, 1 Jan; (01286) 675625; £1.25.

CAPEL CURIG SH7258
This attractive village is a useful base for enjoyable Snowdonia rambles around the pleasantly landscaped reservoirs N.

CHIRK SJ2938
The quiet little town, important as a staging post on the former road to Ireland, has something of a bypassed-by-time feel now; the Hand and (on the B5070 S) Bridge are quite useful for lunch.

Chirk Castle 🏛 (just W) One of the lucky few of Edward I's castles to survive as an occupied home rather than fall to ruin. The exterior is still much as it was when built 700 years ago, with its high walls and drum towers, though there have been lots of alterations: most of the medieval-looking decorations were by Pugin in the 19th c, the elegant stone staircase dates from the 18th c, and the Long Gallery is 17th-c. The wrought-iron entrance gates are particularly fine, and the formal gardens are magnificent. Meals, snacks, shop, some disabled access; open from 11am; cl Mon, Tues, and Nov–Mar; (01691) 777701; £5; NT. It's right by a well preserved stretch of the earthworks of Offa's Dyke.

COED Y BRENIN SH7226
Forest Park & Visitor Centre (Maesgwn) Excellent introduction to what translates as King's Forest, so called to commemorate the Silver Jubilee of King George V. Some

beautifully varied sights and landscapes, as well as wildlife observation hides, and over 50 miles of walks. Bike hire (it's mainly a mountain bike centre now), snacks, shop, disabled access; cl wkdys Nov–Mar; (01341) 440666; free, 50p short-term parking, £2 all-day parking.

COLWYN BAY SH8480
Though this busy summer seaside resort has all that's wanted for a family beach holiday, it's rather eclipsed by Llandudno just along the coast. The quieter end at Rhos-on-Sea has a puppet theatre; mainly open just school hols; (01492) 548166 for programme. The Rhos Fynach opposite the small harbour at this end, once Capt Morgan's home, does decent food.

Welsh Mountain Zoo (Flagstaff Gardens, Old Highway) Lots of exotic animals in natural-looking habitats, but what really distinguishes this 37-acre zoo from any other is the quite magnificent view over the bay. Also penguin parade and falconry displays. Meals, snacks, shop, mostly disabled access; cl 25 Dec; (01492) 532938; £6.25. In summer a free minibus service usually runs here from the town station. The Mountain View at Mochdre has good value food.

CONWY SH7877
Cheerful old town dominated by its castle, the key part of the town's elaborate defensive system – 21 (originally 22) towers linked by walls some 9 metres (30 ft) high, still the most complete town wall in Wales, with craggy old town gates. You can walk along some parts, looking down over the narrow little streets that still follow their medieval layout. There's a little aquarium by the quay, and you can usually go on summer **boat trips**. The Castle Hotel is a civilised place for lunch.

Aberconwy House 🏛 (Castle St) The only house in the town which survives from the 14th c, once the home of a prosperous merchant. Rooms are furnished in period style, and there's an interesting audio-visual show. Shop; last admission 4.30pm; cl Tues, and late Oct–late Mar; (01492) 592246; £2; NT.

Butterfly Jungle 🏛 (Bodlondeb Park) Tropical butterflies and exotic plants and birds in a re-created jungle environment with rainforest surround-sound; picnic area. Shop, snacks, disabled access; cl Nov–Mar; (01492) 593149; £3.50.

Conwy Castle One of the best-known in Wales, and one of the most important examples of military architecture in the whole of Europe. Built for Edward I in 1283–9, it's very well preserved, still looking exactly as a medieval fortress should – despite the ravages of the Civil War and beyond. There's an exhibition on Edward and the other castles he built, as well as a scale model of the castle and the town in the early 14th c. The top of the turrets offer fine panoramic views; the most dramatic views of the castle itself are from the other side of the estuary. Shop; cl 24–26 Dec, 1 Jan; (01492) 592358; £3.50.

Conwy Mountain Just W of the town, pleasant walking; not a real mountain but with views of Anglesey worthy of mountain status.

Conwy Suspension Bridge 🏛 Built by Telford in 1826, and restored by the National Trust, who have also opened up its toll house, with the rooms furnished as they would have been in the 19th c; disabled access; cl Tues (exc July and Aug) and all Nov–Mar; (01492) 573282; £1. The other, tubular bridge was built by Stephenson in 1848.

Plas Mawr (High St) Elaborate Tudor mansion, carefully restored, its splendid plasterwork, flagstone floors and huge fireplaces all looking as good as new. Small shop; disabled access ground floor only; cl Mon (exc bank hols) and all Nov–Apr; (01492) 580167; £4.

Smallest House Nicely placed on the quayside is Britain's smallest house, barely 2 metres (6 ft) wide and its front wall only 3 metres (10 ft) high. Squeezed into the two rooms (one up, one down) are all the comforts of home, or at least most – there's no lavatory. Shop, limited disabled access; cl Nov–Mar, Good Fri; (01492) 593484; 50p.

Teapot World 🏛 (Castle St) Splendidly silly collection of unusually shaped teapots from the last 300 years – everything from wigwams to cauliflowers. Shop; cl Nov–Mar; (01492) 593429; £1.50.

CORWEN SJ0750
Derwen church (off A494 a few miles N) Interesting medieval building with an elaborately carved rood screen and loft, some old wall paintings, and an excellent Celtic cross in the churchyard.

Llangar church (B4401 S) Built in the 13th c, with remarkable paintings of the seven deadly sins; it's usually visited from Rhug chapel (and covered by the same ticket). The Crown in Corwen has good value food.

Rhug chapel (1m N) 17th-c, not inspiring from the outside, but inside is a riot of colour, almost every available piece of woodwork covered with cheery patterns and paintwork. Cl Mon (exc bank hol wknds), Tues, 24 Sept–1 May; nearby Llangar church (see above) is open 2–3pm; (029) 2050 0200; £2.

CRICCIETH SH4937
Restrained resort with a good sheltered sandy beach. The Prince of Wales is a reliable food pub.

Criccieth Castle 13th-c remains on a rocky, mounded peninsula above the little town, giving superb views over Tremadog Bay. Parts of the inner walls are well preserved, and there's an impressive gatehouse. A cartoon video looks at Gerald of Wales and other Welsh princes. Shop, disabled access; cl Nov–Mar; (01766) 522227; £2.20.

DENBIGH SJ0566
A museum on the High St has interesting finds from nearby Bronze Age sites, and the riverside Brookhouse Mill is popular for lunch, as is the Lion out at Gwytherin (B5384 W).

Denbigh Castle Largely ruined, but still impressive, with a trio of towers and superb archway in the 13th-c gatehouse; the figure on the summit is thought to represent Edward I. Among other remains are what's left of an ambitious church built by the Earl of Leicester, favourite of Elizabeth I. New museum and exhibition in castle and new exhibition in Burgess Gate entrance. Limited disabled access; exhibitions cl Mon exc school and bank hols, cl Oct–Apr; castle open all year; £2; (01745) 813385.

DINAS MAWDDWY SH8513
Meirion Mill Nestling among riverside woods below the mountains on the S

fringes of Snowdonia is this charmingly set woollen mill (you can occasionally see the weaving), in the grounds of the old Mawddwy railway station. Meals, snacks, shop (a huge range of country and outdoor clothing, sheepskin and woollen goods, crafts, and gifts), children's playground, disabled access; cl Jan–Feb; (01650) 531311; free. Nearby is a picturesque pack-horse bridge, and there's a scenic walk to King Arthur's Stone at Camlan; the waterside Dolbrodmaeth has decent food.

DOLWYDDELAN SH7352
Dolwyddelan Castle Picturesquely set on a lightly wooded crag, these old ruins are reputedly the birthplace of Llewelyn the Great. You can still see a restored keep from around 1200 and a 13th-c curtain wall. Summer snacks and shop; cl 24–26 Dec, 1 Jan; (01690) 750366; £2. The village church is attractive, and the Gwydr has cheap food.

FLINT SJ2473
Flint Castle Another fine 13th-c castle, the first built by Edward I to subdue the natives. Parts of the walls and corner towers survive, but the most impressive bit is the great tower or donjon, which is separated by the moat. Overlooking the River Dee, it has a role in Shakespeare's *Richard II*. Cl 24–26 Dec, 1 Jan; free. The Britannia in nearby Halkyn is good for lunch, with fine Dee estuary views from its conservatory.

GRESFORD SJ3454
Gresford church Has some wonderful medieval stained glass, and its bells are often described as one of the Seven Wonders of Wales. A yew tree outside is reputed to be 1,400 years old. The Pant-yr-Ochain has very good food.

HARLECH SH5831
Harlech Castle Splendid-looking structure built in 1283–90 by Edward I, its rugged glory the massive twin-towered gatehouse. It was starved into capitulation by Owain Glyndwr in 1404, and later dogged defence inspired the song 'Men of Harlech'. Before the sea retreated there was a sheer drop into the water on one side, but it now stands above dunes, with wonderful views of

Snowdonia from the battlements. Shop; cl 24–26 Dec, 1 Jan; (01766) 780552; £3. The village around it has all that the crowds of summer visitors to the castle and the good beach could want. The riverside Victoria at Llanbedr does decent food. Some of the most sensationally remote scenery in Wales stretches inland E of Harlech, where a few tortuous roads wind past hill farms towards the splendidly isolated lake of Llyn Cwm Bychan SH6431. From the car park at the end of the road you can walk along a few miles of the Roman Steps (not Roman at all, but an old packhorse route paved with large stone slabs) that heads between some of the most challenging, rock-strewn wilderness in the country; the summits require advanced scrambling skills but the secluded little mountain lake of Llyn Du makes a nicely manageable objective (turn right off the main path at the top of the path).

HOLYHEAD SH2482
Long-established fishing town on little Holy Island, now an unassuming resort with some burial chambers and ancient sites not far away. The Victorian breakwater protecting the harbour is Britain's longest. Across the old Four Mile Bridge at Valley the Bull has good value food.

HOLYHEAD MOUNTAIN SH2183
A dramatic hill giving good walks at the W tip of Holy Island, with an Iron Age fort and Roman watchtower site.

HOLYWELL SJ1977
Greenfield Valley Heritage Centre (A548) Farm museum, and an increasing number of buildings rescued from their original sites and rebuilt here. These include a 17th-c cottage, Victorian farmhouse, and a school, all furnished in period style. Also the remains of a Cistercian abbey and a good few relics of the Industrial Revolution. Snacks, shop, disabled access; cl Nov–Mar; (01352) 714172; £2.25.
St Winefride's Well Source of the holy spring that turned the spot into a centre of pilgrimage – it's supposed to have healing powers. There are pleasant walks from here through the valley to the coast.

LAKE VYRNWY SJ0119
This massive reservoir, created at the

end of the last century, supplies Liverpool with 57 million gallons of water a day. It's an attractive spot, with a visitor centre, waymarked trails, cycle hire, bird hides and a sculpture trail. When the water is low you can see the remains of the original village of Llanwddyn, drowned long ago; shop (wknds only Jan–Mar), limited disabled access. (01691) 870245; free.

LAVAN SANDS SH6473

(nr Aber) Much of the North Wales coast is built on or ribboned by roads, but this is a notable exception: walks by a vast stretch of tidal sands, with flocks of wading birds.

LLANALLGO SH4986

Din Llugwy ancient village Remains of a 4th-c village: a pentagonal stone wall surrounds two circular and seven rectangular buildings; free. The Parciau Arms at Marianglas is the best good place for a meal.

LLANBEDR SH5526

Shell Island (Llanbedr) A causeway leads over the sands to this near-island, appropriately named – after winter storms and high tides it's excellent for beach-combing; there are also wild birds and flowers, and you can fish here. Snacks, shop; (01341) 241453; £4 per car.

LLANBERIS SH5760

Plenty of B&Bs, small hotels, shops and cafés for the summer visitors here for Snowdon, and there are quite a few craft shops dotted along the High St. Sherpa Buses run a good service up the mountain (you can get it from several of the North Wales resorts). Just N of town is a modern working pottery; cl 2 wks at Christmas; (01286) 872529; free.

Dolbadarn Castle (A4086, at the foot of Llanberis Pass) Built in the early 13th c by Llywelyn the Great – it has a fine round keep; free.

Electric Mountain Various changing exhibitions, then a coach whisks you off for a tour of the spectacular Dinorwic pumped storage station (one of Europe's biggest), deep in the mountain. Best to book, (01286) 870636. Snacks, shop, disabled access (with notice); cl Mon–Weds Jan–Easter and 2 wks at Christmas; £5.

Llanberis Lake Railway ⊞ (Padarn Country Park, off A4086) Four-mile trips (they are extending this year) along the shore of Llyn Padarn, using steam locomotives dating from 1889 to 1948. Ideal for those who want the steam-train experience but don't want to spend too long getting it. Snacks, shop, disabled access; cl Sat (exc July–Aug), and all Nov–Mar; (01286) 870549 for timetable; £4.20. The station is set in a super lakeside park with walks through ancient woodland.

Pen-y-Gwryd Hotel (Nantgwynant, A4086/A498 SE) Another good spot for Snowdon walks; also a good place for lunch.

Snowdon Mountain Railway ⊞ (A4086) The best ascent of Snowdon: Britain's only public rack-and-pinion railway, with vintage Swiss steam and modern diesel locomotives. It follows the route of an old pony track, and on a good day takes passengers up over 915 metres (3,000 ft) right to the summit – where in clear weather glorious views might include the Isle of Man and the Wicklow Mountains in Ireland. It's without a doubt one of the most spectacular train journeys in the country. Trains leave when there are more than a couple of dozen people on board – so if there aren't many people about you may have to wait for it to start, and if there are you may have to queue. When trains are running to the summit, you can visit the highest postbox in England and Wales. The mountain summit is crowned by a less-than-elegant café; certainly one of the less successful works of Portmeirion architect Sir Clough Williams-Ellis, it's likely to be replaced in the next few years. It can be chilly, so wrap up well. Meals, snacks, shop, disabled access (with notice); the themed gift shop at Llanberis has been recently refurbished, and there's an adjacent small exhibition area; cl Nov to mid-Mar, and summit section not open till mid/late May because of weather – best to ring first; (01286) 870223; £15.80 return.

Welsh Slate Museum (Padarn Country Park, off A4086) Following Lottery-funded improvements, this intriguing place, stepped steeply into the mountain and once one of the biggest quarries in the country, is now

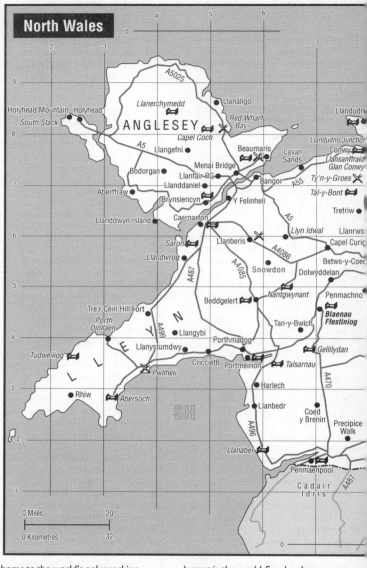

North Wales

Holyhead Mountain · Holyhead
South Stack
Llanerchymedd · Llanallgo
ANGLESEY
Red Wharf Bay
Capel Coch
Llangefni
Beaumaris
Lavan Sands
Bodorgan · Menai Bridge
Llanfair-PG
Llanddaniel
Bangor
Llandudno
Llandudno Junction
Conwy
Llansanffraid Glan Conwy
Ty'n-y-Groes
Aberffraw
Brynsiencyn
Y Felinheli
Tal-y-Bont
Llanddwyn Island
Caernarfon
Trefriw
Saron
Llanberis
Llyn Idwal
Llanrws
Llandwrog
Capel Curig
Snowdon
Betws-y-Coed
Dolwyddelan
Tre'r Ceiri Hill Fort
Beddgelert
Nantgwynant
Penmachno
Porth Dinllaen
Blaenau Ffestiniog
Llangybi
Tan-y-Bwlch
Tudweiliog
Llanystumdwy
Porthmadog
Gellilydan
Criccieth
Portmeirion
Talsarnau
Pwllheli
Harlech
Rhiw
Abersoch
Llanbedr
Coed y Brenin
Precipice Walk
Llanaber
Penmaenpool
Cadair Idris

0 Miles 20
0 Kilometres 32

home to the world's only working incline, carrying wagons up and down a hill, and a row of reconstructed quarrymen's cottages decked out in period furniture from the 1860s, 1900s and 1969. The quarry workshop has been preserved largely in its original state – complete with working craftsmen and machinery. Its water wheel is one of the largest in the world. Snacks, shop, disabled access; cl Sat during Nov–Apr; (01286) 870630; £3.50.

LLANDDANIEL FAB SH5069
Bryn Celli Ddu Restored neolithic passage burial chamber built over a previous stone circle, at the end of a long tunnel, with a carved stone over a burial pit; locked, but key at

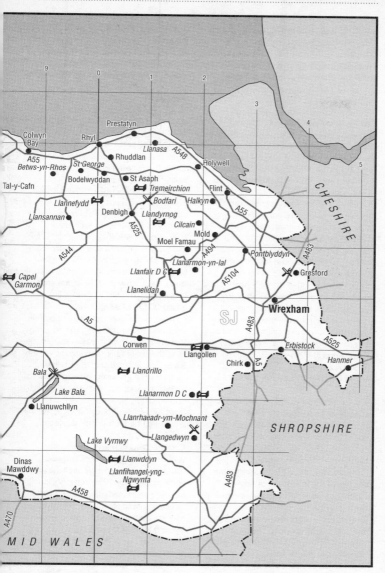

nearby farmhouse; free. Take a torch.

LLANDDWYN ISLAND SH3863

Really a peninsula, making a satisfying walk from Newborough Warren over the lovely beach.

LLANDUDNO SH7882

The main holiday town in the area, and though it does have a long well sheltered curve of good pebbly beach, a prom and a range of resort entertainments, it doesn't feel at all brash. There are charming little shops and boutiques, a well restored pier (from where you can fish), and cable-cars as well as the famously steep quaint tramway up the massive Great Orme headland which protects the main beach – there's a quieter but more exposed beach on the far side. You can walk right up, too; a café on the way has views to justify stopping. At the top there's a 12th-c church, a visitor centre with local geology, and more good walking. On the way down a dry ski slope also has a toboggan run. The Queens Head at Glanwydden, off the Colwyn Bay road, does very good food.

Alice in Wonderland Centre 💷 (Trinity Sq) Jolly exhibition devoted to Alice in Wonderland, with life-size animated tableaux; the real Alice holidayed in Llandudno as a child. Shop, disabled access; cl winter Suns, 25–26 Dec, 1 Jan; (01492) 860082; £2.95.

Conwy Valley Railway Railtrack line from Llandudno to Blaenau Ffestiniog, through magnificent scenery, with several useful stops en route.

Great Orme Mines 💷 4,000-year-old copper mine nr the summit of Great Orme, the biggest such site so far discovered. It's also the only prehistoric metal mine open to the public, with displays of finds, and underground walks through the cavernous workings themselves; weather permitting, you can sometimes see digs in progress. Teas, shop; cl Nov–Jan; (01492) 870447; £4.40.

LLANFAIRPWLLGWYNGYLL SH5372

The record books and tongue-twisting schoolboys add another 39 letters (gocherychwyrndrobwllllantysiliogogo goch) to this village's name, but locals cut it even shorter, to Llanfair PG, or Llanfairpwll. Excellent views of Snowdonia and the Menai Strait from the top of the Marquess of Anglesey's Column, built in 1816 to commemorate the military achievements of Wellington's second-in-command at the Battle of Waterloo. The nearby village of Penmynydd was the ancient home of the Tudor family. The unpretentious, old-fashioned Liverpool Arms at Menai Bridge is the nearest good place for lunch.

Plas Newydd (A4080, 2m S) Fine mountain views from the creeper-covered former home of the Marquess of Anglesey, an elegant 18th-c mansion known best for its mural by Rex Whistler. Other works by the painter as well, along with a collection of relics from Waterloo (the 1st Marquess commanded the cavalry at the Battle of Waterloo), and a good spring garden with rhododendrons (Apr–Jun only) and Australasian arboretum; a woodland gives access to a marine walk on the Menai Strait; boat trips from the jetty (weather permitting). Meals, snacks, shop, disabled access; cl am, Thurs, Fri, all Nov–Mar; (01248) 714795; £4.50; NT.

LLANGEFNI SH4576

Right in the centre of Anglesey, and its 'capital', with a big open-air market every Thurs.

Oriel Ynys Mon 💷 (Rhosmeirch, B5111 N) Excellent gallery with imaginative changing displays on the history of Anglesey, as well as a collection of wildlife paintings by C F Tunnicliffe. You can spend a surprising amount of time here. Meals, snacks, shop, disabled access; cl Mon (exc bank hols), 1 wk between Christmas and New Year; (01248) 724444; £2.25.

LLANGOLLEN SJ2142

Not special in itself despite a good few solid and gracious Georgian and Victorian villas; what makes it attractive is its charming valley setting above the River Dee. It has discreet hotels that cater for the generally older people to whom the area most appeals – though it comes vividly alive during the Eisteddfod. The Abbey Grange, Royal and Wild Pheasant hotels do decent lunches.

Castell Dinas Bran The place for walkers to head for from Llangollen. This hill fort commands views over the vale and is close to the Panorama Walk (actually a surfaced minor road); walks can be linked to the canal towpath below.

Horse-drawn boat trips (Llangollen Wharf) Horse-drawn boat trips along the Vale of Llangollen from here, inc across the Pontcysyllte Aqueduct 38 metres (126 ft) above the River Dee; meals and snacks at the Wharf Centre, shop, prior notice required for disabled access; wknds Mar–Easter, daily Easter–Oct (maybe not Thurs and Fri in Oct), and booked parties only Nov–Dec; (01978) 860702; £3.50. The Sarah Ponsonby close by has decent food.

Llangollen Railway (Abbey Rd) Now

running eight miles, with steam and diesel trains from the pleasantly preserved station to the village of Glyndyfrdwy up the Dee (the Bedwyn Arms in a lovely setting above the river does food). Meals, snacks, shop, special coach for the disabled (you have to book); (01978) 860951 for timetable; around £7.50 full return fare, less for shorter trips.

Lower Dee Exhibition Centre ⌨ (Mill St) Houses a large display of model railways and a collection of memorabilia from the *Dr Who* series, inc many of the monsters bent on exterminating him. Meals, snacks, shop; cl 25–26 Dec, 1 Jan and some Weds in Nov, Jan and Feb; (01978) 860584; £4.75 model railways, £5.75 *Dr Who*. The nearby Corn Mill (Dee Lane) has good food in a striking newly converted windmill.

Motor Museum and Canal Exhibition ⌨ Classic cars and motorcycles and an exhibition on the canal network. Snacks, shop, disabled access; cl Mon, cl Nov–Jan; (01978) 860324; £2. The Sarah Ponsonby nearby has good value food.

Plas Newydd Lady Eleanor Butler and Sarah Ponsonby, the 'Ladies of Llangollen', lived here from 1780 to 1831. The beautiful half-timbered house has stained glass, leather wall coverings and domestic paraphernalia of the period. Pleasant gardens. Shop; cl Nov–Mar; (01978) 861314; £2.50.

Pontcysyllte aqueduct (off A5/A539 E) The longest in Britain, very spectacular to cross – by boat or on foot; the Sun Trevor at Trevor Uchaf above here has good food and more views.

Valle Crucis Abbey (A542 2m N) Substantial remains of the early 13th-c abbey church, and some beautifully carved grave slabs. Shop, limited disabled access; cl 24 Sept–Apr – you can still get into the abbey then, but not into the dormitory or exhibitions; (01978) 860326; £2. The ruins stand at the bottom of the Horseshoe Pass, a nerve-wrackingly steep but extremely scenic mountain drive; the Britannia Inn just above the abbey has exceptional views.

LLANGYBI SH4241
St Cybi's Well Known to the Welsh as Fynnon Gybi, this has been reckoned to have healing properties for over a thousand years. Look out for the corbelled beehive vaulting inside the roofless stone structure, which is ancient Irish in style.

LLANRWST SH7961
Pretty little town with old stone bridge over the Conwy river, said to be the work of Inigo Jones. Gwydir Chapel, added by the influential Wynn family to the parish church in the 17th c, has a stone coffin reputedly that of Llewelyn the Great, as well as a magnificent rood screen from the ruins of Maenan Abbey. The Wynns also constructed the nearby Gwydir Uchaf Chapel, with intriguing ceiling paintings.

LLANUWCHLLYN SH8829
Bala Lake Railway ⌨ Some of the carriages on trains using this delightful 4½-mile route are open to the elements, which seems to make the views of the lake and mountains more vivid. The locomotives were once used to haul slate in the local quarries. Snacks, shop, disabled access (but no facilities); cl Oct–Mar, and certain Mon and Fri early and late in season (open every day July/Aug); (01678) 540666 for timetable; *£7.

LLANYSTUMDWY SH4738
Lloyd George Memorial Museum (A497) Audio-visual displays and memorabilia relating to the life and times of Lloyd George. Between 1861–1880, he lived in nearby Highgate Cottage, with its shoemaking workshop, which has been restored to the way it was then, and has a Victorian garden. Shop, disabled access; cl Nov–just before Easter, cl wknds Apr/May and Oct, cl Sun in June; (01766) 522071; £3. The old-fashioned bar opposite is good value; it's a short stroll from here to where he's buried.

Rabbit Farm (just off A497) Children enjoy this: around 700 rabbits, with other animals and pony rides. Cl Oct–Easter; (01766) 523136; £2.

LLEYN PENINSULA SH3235
Very unspoilt, this peninsula has some good coastal walks around its tip, starting W from Aberdaron, with fine windswept views from Mynydd Mawr (bird reserve nearby), and E of here is the spectacular bay of Hell's Mouth; the

beaches along here have clean bathing water. For a stiffer walk, try Yr Eifl (the Rivals), a 563-metre (1,849-ft) mountain close to the coast.

LLYN IDWAL SH6460
This superbly sited Snowdonia lake beneath Glyder Fach gives pleasant walks along a signed nature trail.

MENAI BRIDGE SH5571
The village takes its name from Thomas Telford's magnificent iron suspension bridge linking Anglesey to the mainland, the first such bridge in the world. The waterside Liverpool Arms has good value fresh food.

Butterfly Palace 🎫 (A5025) Exotic butterflies from all corners of the globe, as well as bird house, insectarium, reptile house, and adventure playground. Meals, snacks, shop, disabled access; 10am–5.30pm (11am–3.30pm Nov–24 Dec); cl 25 Dec–Mar; (01248) 712474; £4.

MOEL FAMMAU SJ1662
The highest point of the Clwydian Range, a bulging massif with clearly marked paths; walk up from the car park on the minor road E of Llanbedr DC through colour-coded forest trails or over open land, for views of much of Snowdonia, the edge of the Peak district and the Wirral.

MOLD SJ2364
A very good theatre, and a richly decorated parish church built to commemorate the victory of Henry Tudor at Bosworth Field in 1485. The Druid in a lovely setting at Llanferres out on the Ruthin road has good food.

PENMACHNO SH8052
Penmachno Woollen Mill Timeless watermill powered by the River Machno, with local weavers explaining and demonstrating the history and craft of the cottage weaving industry. The setting is lovely. Snacks, good shop; cl 25 Dec and maybe winter Sun and Mon; (01690) 710545; free.

Ty Mawr Wybrnant 🎫 (forest road NW) Picturesque, lonely thick-walled medieval cottage, birthplace of Bishop William Morgan who first translated the Bible into Welsh (see St Asaph). Shop, disabled access; cl Mon, Tues, Weds, cl Nov–end Mar; (01690) 760213; £2. NT.

Ty'n-y-Coed Uchaf 🎫 Reached by a pleasant walk along the river from the woollen mill's car park, a fully furnished 19th-c farmhouse, good for showing the traditional way of life in this area. Small shop; cl am, cl Mon, Tues, Weds, Sat, cl Nov–end Mar; (01690) 760229; £2; NT.

PENMAENPOOL SH6717
Its small waterside nature reserve has a very useful nature information centre pointing out promising places throughout this whole area, a good region for walks. One is the walk along the old railway track beside the Mawddach Estuary to Fairbourne, giving magnificent views. The George III is a pleasant place for lunch.

Abergwynant Farm Trekking Centre 🎫 (A493, about a mile SW) Will take beginners out on ponies (experienced riders, too), over scenic routes. Snacks, disabled access; (01341) 422377; from £10 per hour. You can stay at the farm in self-catering cottages and flats; fishing.

PORTHMADOG SH5638
Quite a busy shopping town of low slate-roofed houses, with a spacious harbour and a long causeway road (5p toll) across the estuary. The Ship has decent food, and nearby Black Rock Golden Sands is one of the area's finest beaches.

Ffestiniog Railway 🎫 (Harbour Station) The famous narrow-gauge railway opened in 1836 to carry slate from Blaenau Ffestiniog to Porthmadog by gravity. Closed in 1946, it reopened in 1955 and has gradually been extended to climb the 13¼ miles to Blaenau Ffestiniog; further extensions are planned. Stop off at stations along the way for good walks and views. The railway links with the main line Cambrian Coast Line, hugging the coast from Pwllheli to Machynlleth, with many stops along the way. Meals and snacks (good station bar with seats out on terrace), shop, some disabled access; cl Jan/early Feb and limited winter service, best to phone; (01766) 512340; full return fare £13.80.

Porthmadog Pottery (Snowdon St) See the potters at work or have a go yourself at making a pot, candles, and try out other crafts. Tearoom, big craft shop, two galleries, very good disabled access; cl most wknds, best to check winter opening, cl Christmas hols; (01766) 510910; free.

Welsh Highland Railway (opposite main line station) Overshadowed by its more famous neighbour in size but certainly not in spirit, this enthusiastically restored line runs trains daily in the summer hols and most Suns Apr–Oct. Meals, snacks, shop, disabled access; cl Nov–Easter; (01766) 513402 for timetable; £2.

PORTMEIRION SH6243

Plas Brondanw (Llanfrothen, A4085 N of Penrhyndeudraeth) The ancestral home of Welsh architect Sir Clough Williams-Ellis, and you can visit the architectural garden he designed there – great views; *£1.50.

Portmeirion ⬚ On the steep wooded shores of an inlet from Tremadog Bay, this fairy-tale holiday village designed by Williams-Ellis is set in 175 acres of lush coastal cliff and woodland gardens. Quite charming, it's an Italianate folly – pastel-washed cottages interlaced with grottoes and cobbled squares, a bell tower, castle and lighthouse, and long picturesque flights of steps zigzagging down to the water, which at low tide dries to miles of sand. Enveloping the village are the 60 acres of Gwyllt gardens, with fine displays of rhododendrons, azaleas, hydrangeas and subtropical flora; good wild woodlands, too. You have to pay a toll to enter the village, but once in can see the house where Noel Coward wrote *Blithe Spirit* and the locations for the cult TV series *The Prisoner*; children can play in the playground, on a make-believe schooner apparently moored by the hotel, or, tide permitting, on the beach. A lovely relaxing place, quite unlike anywhere else. Meals, snacks, shops (one specialising in Portmeirion pottery), some disabled access; (01766) 770000; £5. No dogs – though there's a touching dog cemetery in the woods nearby.

PRECIPICE WALK SH7321 Signposted N of Dolgellau, this is an attractive Snowdonia walk.

PRESTATYN SJ0683 Bustling seaside resort standing at one end of the 168-mile route of Offa's Dyke, marked by a stone pillar above

the main beach.

RHIW SH2328

Plas yn Rhiw Charming if unassuming little manor house at tip of Lleyn Peninsula, worth a visit for the gardens and woodland, inc a waterfall, spring snowdrop wood and subtropical specimens. Shop, very limited disabled access; cl Tues, all Oct–Mar; (01758) 780219; £3.20; NT. The setting is lovely, overlooking one of the area's wildest coasts. The beautifully placed Sun over at Llanengan does decent food.

RHUDDLAN SJ0478

Bodrhyddan Hall (A5151 Rhuddlan–Dyserth) Lovely dolls'-house front, and some wonderfully elaborate fireplaces in the drawing room. Also formal French garden, a new woodland garden with four ponds and a Palladian-style summer house, and an interesting well-house built by Inigo Jones. Teas, meals by appointment, shop, disabled access to ground floor only; open pm Tues and Thurs Jun–Sept; (01745) 590414; £4.

Dyserth church Partly 13th-c, with a Jesse window; not far from a plunging 18-metre (60-ft) waterfall.

Rhuddlan Castle Fine old castle, adapted by Edward I from an earlier Norman structure, to guard what was once a busy port (now a sleepy little town). Overlooking the river, it's a pretty spot. Shop, disabled access; cl Oct–Apr; (01745) 590777; £2.

RHYL SJ0081 Rather brash seaside resort; if you're passing with children, the Knights Cavern, a lively interpretation of Welsh history, should amuse them.

Sea Life Aquarium ⬚ (East Parade) One of the very good centres that we've described in several English resorts, with a dramatic Shark Encounter as well as the usual walk-through underwater tunnel. Meals, snacks, shop, disabled access; cl 25 Dec; (01745) 344660; £4.99.

SNOWDON SH6455 This whole area has plenty of fine walking, both gentle and taxing, to fill a walking holiday. Snowdonia's main mountain group soars dramatically, many of its peaks having easily identifiable shapes (when you can see them through the mist). Snowdon itself, the highest mountain in England or Wales, has a number of ways up ranging from the easy path alongside the mountain railway (see Llanberis) to the enthralling Horseshoe Route, which makes its way along knife-edge ridges; the Pyg Track and Watkin Path are among the favourites. For a taste of the mountain without actually going up it, follow the start of the Miners' Track (from the Pen-y-pass car park on the A4086), which really is a track as far as Glaslyn, the last of four lakes passed. The National Trust now owns large areas of the mountain, and is carrying out path improvements alongside careful conservation of the landscape – perhaps with eventual regeneration of some former oak forest.

SOUTH STACK SH2182

Seabird Centre The spectacular cliffs nr the lighthouse are full of seabird breeding colonies, and this 780-acre RSPB reserve has guillemots, razorbills and puffins (esp around May, Jun and July). Lots of colourful wild flowers too, and maybe the odd seal. The newly refurbished visitor centre has closed-circuit TV pictures of nesting birds; guided walks leave here at 2pm Tues and Sat May–Aug. Visitor centre cl Sept–Easter; (01407) 764973; free. Nearby is a large group of the foundations of **hut circles**, probably around 2,000 years old, still with some visible traces of stone sleeping slabs. The RSPB have now opened a second seabird centre at the South Stack lighthouse which also has closed-circuit TV; cl Oct–Easter; (01248) 724444; £2.50.

ST ASAPH SJ0374

St Asaph Cathedral and Museum To match its tiny little city, this is the smallest in Britain, founded in 537. A column in the grounds commemorates its most famous cleric Bishop Morgan (see Penmachno entry) and his work translating the Bible into Welsh. There's a little museum with finds from the site, open by appointment. Shop, disabled access; (01745) 583429; free. The Farmers Arms (The Waen) does proper food.

TAL-Y-CAFN SH7972

Bodnant Garden (off A470) Started in 1875 but improved in 1900, this garden is among Britain's greatest. Part of the 80-acre grounds have a beautiful woodland garden in a sheltered valley, notable for its rhododendrons and azaleas, while below the private house are five terraces in the Italian style, with a canal pool, reconstructed pin mill and an open-air stage on the lowest. Many fine rare plants inc unusual trees and shrubs. Meals, snacks, shop, disabled access (but it is steep in places); cl Nov–mid-Mar; (01492) 650460; £5; NT. The Tal-y-Cafn Hotel is useful for lunch, and the Olde Bull in a delightful setting on the hillside opposite at Llanbedr-y-Cennin does good imaginative food; the Holland Arms at Trofarth is also useful.

TAN-Y-BWLCH SH6945

Plas Tan-y-Bwlch (off A487) The grounds of the Snowdonia National Park's environmental study centre have rewarding strolls through the gardens and extensive woodland; in places the paths cross the Ffestiniog Railway. Woods open all year, gardens summer only; (01766) 590324; £2.50.

TRE'R CEIRI HILL FORT SH3744 Off B4417, just up the hill from Llanaelhaearn, a signed path leads to this evocative place, occupied from the Bronze Age through to the Dark Ages; a massive stone wall, lots of hut foundations, and fine views. At Morfa Nefyn nearby the Bryncynan and (overlooking a lovely sandy bay) Cliff Hotel do good lunches.

TREFRIW SH7863 Used to be a spa, and you can still see the wells on the N outskirts of the village (the water is said to treat rheumatism, indigestion, and homesickness). The village also has a 14th-c church; the Princes Arms has decent food.

Trefriw Woollen Mill (B5106) The same family have run this woollen mill for 135 years; two hydro-electric turbines are driven by the fast-flowing Afon Crafnant, and there's a weaver's garden (best Jun–Sept). Weaving demonstrations and turbine house wkdys all year (even Nov–Easter when the mill itself is closed); hand-spinning demonstrations wkdys from spring bank hol–end Sept. Snacks, shop (selling traditional Welsh bedspreads and tweeds made here); cl Sun exc Easter and May bank hol, and from spring bank hol–end Sept; no weaving over Christmas hols; (01492) 640462; free.

WREXHAM SJ3350

Mostly an industrial town, but its 15th-c church is worth a look, with its magnificent steeple. The A525 to Ruthin is a pleasant drive.

Bersham Industrial Heritage Centre (B5099/B5098 W) Well re-created 18th-c ironworks, with a good overview of other local industries, and occasional demonstrations of various traditional skills. Snacks, shop, limited disabled access; Heritage Centre open all year (exc 25–26 Dec, 1 Jan) but cl 3.30pm in winter; Ironworks cl end Aug–Easter and best to phone for opening hours (01978) 261529; free.

Erddig 🏛 (well signed S) Superb late 17th-c house, especially interesting for the way you can explore the life of those 'upstairs' and 'downstairs' equally as thoroughly; the gallery of servants' portraits is very touching. Enlarged and improved in the early 18th c, the house is filled with splendid original furnishings, inc a magnificent state bed in Chinese silk, and newly reopened butler's pantry with silver collection. Restored outbuildings include a laundry, bakehouse, estate smithy and sawmill, and the surrounding parkland is very pleasant to stroll through. It's one of the most attractive places to visit in all of Wales. Meals, snacks, shop, some disabled access; open 11am–5pm gdns, 12–5pm house (last entry 4pm); cl Thurs, Fri (open Good Fri), cl Nov–end Feb; (01978) 355314; £6, garden and below-stairs £4; NT. The Cross Foxes at Overton Bridge, a few miles S, has good food.

Farm World 🏛 (adjacent to Erddig) Well liked by readers, a 300-acre working dairy farm with all the necessary ingredients. Cl Nov–Feb; (01978) 840697; £3.95.

Y FELINHELI SH5367

Greenwood Centre (off B4366 NE of Caernarfon) An unexpected delight, a lively look at trees and wood from trunks and rainforests to Ethiopian wooden pillows. You can handle most of the exhibits, and there's 17 acres of woodland to explore. Mostly indoors so ideal for rainy days, but worth popping into at any time. Teas, shop, disabled access; open daily in summer, best to ring for winter opening; (01248) 671493; £3.95. The Vaynol Arms at Pentir has good food.

Attractive villages, almost all with decent pubs and in general tending to appeal for their surroundings more than for the beauty of their buildings, include Betws-yn-Rhos SH9174, Cilcain SJ1865, Erbistock SJ3542, Halkyn SJ2172, Hanmer SJ4639, Llanarmon DC SJ1633, Llanarmon-yn-Ial SJ1956, Llanasa SJ1082, Llandwrog SH4456, Llanelidan SJ1150, Llangedwyn SJ1924 in the Tanat Valley, Llanrhaeadr-ym-Mochnant (where *An Englishman Who Went Up A Hill* was filmed) SJ1525, Llansannan SH9466, Pontblyddyn SJ2761, Porth Dinllaen SH2741 (an idyllic seaside spot, but you have to walk to it) and St George SH9576. Other pubs and inns in attractive areas or with notable views include the Porth Tocyn Hotel above the sea at Abersoch SH3226 (excellent clean beach for families here), Castell Cidwm at Betws Garmon SH5458, Sportsmans Arms up on the A543 S of Bylchau SH9863, Bryn Tyrch at Capel Garmon SH8255, Grouse at Carrog SJ1144, T'yn-y-Groes at Ganllwyd SH7224, Eagle & Child in the hilltop village of Gwaenysgor SJ0881, Druid at Llanferres SJ1961 (doing well under new management), Cross Foxes on the Dee at Overton Bridge SJ3643, Ship by acres of sand on the shore of Red Wharf Bay SH5281, Cwellyn Arms at Rhyd-Ddu SH5753 (big playground), White Eagle on Holy Island at Rhoscolyn SH2676 and Caerffynon Hall at Talsarnau SH6236.

Please let us know what you think of places in the *Guide*. Use the report forms at the back of the book or simply write us a letter.

Where to eat

BALA SH9236 **Neuadd-y-Cyfnod** *High St (01678) 521269* Relaxed and informal restaurant in attractive old building (it can trace its history back to 1600), with huge helpings of good value food (morning coffee, lunch, tea and dinner), pleasant service, and attractive furnishings; Welsh lamb a speciality; disabled access; cl beginning Nov–Easter. £15|£5

BEAUMARIS SH6076 **Sailors Return** *Church St (01248) 811314* Bright and cheerful, more or less open-plan pub, with a collection of car-shaped teapots, naval memorabilia and maps and old prints, comfortable furnishings in rich colours, a good mix of customers, well kept real ales, and enjoyable food inc daily specials. £19.75|£6.25

BODFARI SJ0970 **Dinorben Arms** *(01745) 710309* Carefully extended building with warmly welcoming beamed rooms, three open fires, a huge collection of whiskies, well kept real ales and plenty of good wines, popular lunchtime smorgasbord, Fri/Sat carvery, and help-yourself farmhouse buffet Weds/Thurs; disabled access. £12|£4.85

GRESFORD SJ3453 **Pant-yr-Ochain** *Old Wrexham Rd (01978) 853525* Attractively and interestingly decorated spacious pub with country furnishings, open fires, big dining area set out as a library, no smoking room, consistently good interesting food, a decent range of wines, well kept real ales, polite efficient service, and a civilised atmosphere; cl 25–26 Dec; children until 6pm. £22|£6.50

LLANBERIS SH5760 **Y Bistro** *43–45 High St (01286) 871278* Friendly no smoking restaurant with good local produce used in Welsh and English cooking – fine fish and enjoyable puddings; cl Sun, Mon in winter; partial disabled access. £29

LLANDUDNO JUNCTION SH8180 **Queens Head** *Glanwydden (01492) 546570* Busy but comfortable dining pub with a spacious and comfortable modern lounge bar, carefully prepared imaginative food using lots of fine seafood, delicious puddings, real ales, and decent wines; cl 25 Dec; children over 7; disabled access. £25|£6.95

LLANGEDWYN SJ1924 **Green** *(01691) 828234* Very well run ancient place in lovely spot in the Tanat Valley; lots of nooks, alcoves and crannies, a blazing log fire, a good mix of furnishings, pleasant upstairs no smoking restaurant, impressive range of tasty bar food, half-a-dozen real ales, and a good choice of malt whiskies and wines; attractive garden over road with picnic-sets by the river, and fishing permits; disabled access. £18|£5.45

LLANRWST SH7961 **Ty-Hwnt-i'r-Bont** *(01492) 640138* Charming little 500-year-old cottage by bridge, run by Holt family for 26 years, with nice old country furniture under the beams and joists, interesting knick-knacks, light lunches, home-made cakes, shortbread and scones for enjoyable afternoon teas, and quite a choice of teas, coffees and milk shakes; home-made mustards to take away, and old books and bric-a-brac upstairs; cl Mon (exc bank hols), cl Nov–Easter; partial disabled access|£4.80

PWLLHELI SH3535 **Plas Bodegroes** *(01758) 612363* Lovely Georgian manor house in tree-filled grounds with comfortably restful rooms, enjoyable food using superb fresh local produce (esp fish) and very good wine list; bdrms; cl Mon, Dec–Feb. £32/3-course Sun lunch £12.50

RED WHARF BAY SH5281 **Ship Inn** *(01248) 852568* Solidly built old pub looking over miles of cockle-sands, with enterprising bar food, big old-fashioned bars, coal fires, friendly cheerful service, no smoking dining room and cellar room, well kept real ales, quite a few whiskies, and plenty of seats outside. £25|£6.50

TY'N-Y-GROES SH7774 **Groes** *(01492) 650545* Particularly well run family inn with wonderful views from airy no smoking conservatory, rambling low-beamed and thick-walled rooms with welcoming atmosphere and interesting old furnishings, winter log fires, a fine range of good traditional country cooking, well kept real ales, and efficient friendly service; stylish bdrms; children over 10 in restaurant; disabled access (and one specially equipped bdrm). £20.30|£6.50

West Wales

Miles of beautiful unspoilt coastline, some splendid gardens and ruins, and ample opportunities for family fun; ideal for a relaxing break

The big new opening here is the Millennium Coastal Park, the product of a remarkable environmental transformation which should bring more visitors to Llanelli and its outlying areas. While the creation of another open space should be celebrated, this part of Wales already does very well for al fresco activities, from the spectacular 2,000-acre Stackpole Estate, to the wild animals at St Florence, or the numerous attractions at Pembrey Country Park, a great place for families to unwind. Parents looking for a bit of peace and quiet can pack older children off on one of the well supervised adventure days at St David's (a rewarding place, with an excellent aquarium). There are friendly farm animals at Begelly and Gwbert (where you might also catch sight of seals and even dolphins), and a boat trip out to one of the several islands off the coast is always a treat. In Oakwood (Narberth) the region has the only real theme park in Wales (not to mention one of the scariest rides we know), and there's plenty of fun to be had among the dinosaurs at Tenby, which is a good civilised small resort in itself.

The National Botanic Garden of Wales at Llanarthne opened only in May 2000, but already seems to have set a benchmark for 21st-c horticulture; the ancient gardens gradually being redeveloped at Llangathen make a delightfully wistful contrast to its modern extravagances.

The coast is relatively gentle in the S, with level cliffs, sinuous estuaries and some lovely sandy beaches. In the W and N it's much more rugged. The Pembrokeshire Coast Path snaking around the intricate seaboard makes the most of it, as does the new Celtic cycle trail, part of the national Sustrans network.

Where to stay

BROAD HAVEN SM8616 **Druidstone Hotel** *Broad Haven, Haverfordwest, Dyfed SA62 3NE (01437) 781221* **£80**; 9 rms, some with sea view, shared bthrms. Alone on the coast above an effectively private beach with exhilarating cliff walks, this roomy and very informally friendly hotel, with something of a folk-club and Outward Bound feel at times, is extremely winning and relaxing if you take to its unique combination of good wholesome and often memorably inventive food, slightly fend-for-yourself approach amid elderly furniture, and glorious seaside surroundings; self-catering cottages, two with wheelchair access; cl Mon–Fri 5 Nov–12 Dec and 5 Jan–14 Feb; disabled access (see above) ☺
CAREW SN0403 **Old Stable Cottage** *Carew, Tenby, Dyfed SA70 8SL (01646) 651889* **£56**; 3 rms. Originally a stable and carthouse for the castle, this attractive place has an inglenook fireplace and original bread oven, games room, conservatory overlooking the garden, and good Aga-cooked food; children over 3
CRUGYBAR SN6437 **Glanrannell Park** *Crugybar, Llanwrda, Dyfed SA19 8SA (01558) 685230* **£76***, plus special breaks; 8 rms. Surrounded by lawns and overlooking a small private lake in 23 acres of parkland, this very laid-back, peaceful

hotel has two comfortable lounges and a small library, well stocked bar, especially good varied food using fresh local produce where possible, and friendly helpful staff; excellent area for walks and esp bird-watching, also lots of wildlife, pony-trekking, and fishing nearby; cl Nov–Mar

FISHGUARD SM9736 **Gilfach Goch** *Fishguard, Dyfed SA65 9SR (01348) 873871* **£52***, plus special breaks; 6 rms. Traditional carefully modernised 18th-c Welsh stone farmhouse on a 7-acre smallholding with sheep, donkeys, dogs, cats and fowl; lovely views and nr Pembrokeshire coastal path, log fires, homely lounge, good country cooking using many home-produced ingredients, and a safe garden for children; no smoking; self-catering also; cl Oct–Mar; partial disabled access

FISHGUARD SM9537 **Manor House Hotel** *Main St, Fishguard, Dyfed SA65 9HG (01348) 873260* **£48***, plus special breaks; 6 comfortable rms, most with sea views. Georgian house with fine views of harbour from sheltered garden, well planned basement restaurant with interesting home-made food using fresh local produce; cl Christmas

GLYNARTHEN SN3049 **Penbontbren Farm** *Glynarthen, Llandysul, Dyfed SA44 6PE (01239) 810248* **£86**; 10 rms in converted stone outbuildings. Run by a friendly Welsh-speaking family, this Victorian farmhouse is in lovely countryside with nature trails, horse riding, a little farm museum, and nearby beaches; period pine furnishings in bar, lounge and well liked restaurant, good hearty dinners inc some regional dishes, bar lunches, and decent breakfasts; cl 24–28 Dec; disabled access

LLANDELOY SM8527 **Lochmeyler Farm** *Llandeloy, Haverfordwest, Dyfed SA62 6LL (01348) 837724* **£50**, plus special winter breaks; 16 rms. Attractive 16th-c farmhouse on 220-acre working dairy farm; two lounges (one no smoking), log fires, traditional farmhouse cooking in pleasant dining room, mature garden, and Welsh cakes on arrival; can walk around the farm trails; disabled access

NEVERN SN0839 **Trewern Arms** *Nevern, Newport, Dyfed SA42 0NB (01239) 820395* **£50**; 10 rms. Creeper-clad old inn in pleasant riverside hamlet, interestingly decorated slate-floored bar, comfortable lounge bar, decent food, well kept real ales, quiet garden

PENALLY SS1199 **Penally Abbey** *Penally, Tenby, Dyfed SA70 7PY (01834) 843033* **£108**; 12 pretty rms, many with four-posters, and 4 in coach house. 'Gothick'-style country-house hotel in five acres of gardens and woodland with fine views across golf course and Carmarthen Bay; open fire in comfortable lounge, little bar, conservatory, very good food in elegant candlelit restaurant, delicious breakfasts, small indoor swimming pool, snooker and croquet; children over 7 in restaurant; disabled access

RHYDLEWIS SN3447 **Broniwan** *Rhydlewis, Llandysul, Dyfed SA44 5PF (01239) 851261* **£50**; 2 pretty rms. Grey stone house with pine-panelled windows, on small farm surrounded by beech and pine trees, fine views of the Prescelly Hills in the distance, lots of wildlife, and you can help with the calves, hens, and cows; stone barn with games, table tennis and books, woodburner in comfortable sitting room, separate dining room, and good naturally produced food from garden and farm; no smoking; children over 10

SPITTAL SM9822 **Lower Haythog** *Spittal, Haverfordwest, Dyfed SA62 5QL (01437) 731279* **£55***; 6 rms. Centuries-old farmhouse on working dairy farm in 250 acres of unspoilt countryside, with comfortable lounge, log fire, books and games, traditional breakfasts, good cooking in the dining room, and friendly owners; swing and slide in the garden, trout ponds in the woods

ST DAVID'S SM7524 **Warpool Court** *St David's, Haverfordwest, Dyfed SA62 6BN (01437) 720300* **£152***, plus special breaks; 25 rms. Originally built as St David's cathedral school in the 1860s and bordering NT land, this popular hotel has lovely views over St Bride's Bay; Ada Williams's collection of lovely hand-painted tiles can be seen in the public rooms, food in the spacious elegant restaurant is imaginative (good for vegetarians too), and staff are helpful and friendly; quiet gardens, heated summer swimming pool, tennis, exercise room, table tennis, pool and croquet; cl Jan

To see and do

ABERAERON SN4562
The line of colour-washed houses facing the harbour is very pretty; there's a good craft centre here too, and the Harbourmaster and Hive on the Quay are good for food.

AMROTH SN1508
Colby Woodland Garden 🏛 (off A477) Beautiful woodland gardens in sheltered valley – very pleasant and colourful, esp in spring. A walled garden has a 'gothick' gazebo and colourful herbaceous plants. Snacks, gallery, shop; cl Oct–Mar; (01834) 811885; £2.80; NT.

BEGELLY SN1109
Folly Farm (A478) Busy working dairy farm, with the chance to milk a cow – or watch the more modern methods in the milking parlour. Everyone gets a chance to bottle-feed some of the friendly animals. Also indoor traditional fairground, good play areas, a pirate ship, and go-karts. Meals, snacks, shop, disabled access; cl Nov–Feb; (01834) 812731; £3.95. A working pottery is nearby, (01834) 811204.

BURRY PORT SN4100
Pembrey Country Park Good for families to unwind, with 500 acres of woodland, pitch and putt, orienteering, adventure playground, visitor centre, dry ski slope, toboggan run, miniature railway and eight miles of clean sandy beach (no dogs in summer). Meals, snacks, shop, disabled access; park open all year, though most attractions cl winter; (01554) 833913; parking £3 (£5 July–Aug, £1.20 Oct–Mar, charges for some attractions).

CAREW SN0403
Carew Castle & Tidal Mill 🏛
Magnificent Norman castle (the setting for the Great Tournament of 1507), with esp handsome ivy-clad SE tower. The mill is one of just three restored tidal mills in Britain, with records dating back to 1558. Shop; cl Nov–Easter; (01646) 651782; £2.75 both, £1.90 each. By the good Carew Inn nearby is the Carew Cross, an impressive 4-metre (13-ft) Celtic cross dating from the 11th c.

CARMARTHEN SN4120
Busy regional market town, according to legend the birthplace of Merlin, with the remains of a 13th-c castle, and on Priory St an unusual 2nd-c Roman amphitheatre. The Cresselly Arms along the A40 E in the pretty village of Pont-ar-Gothi (pleasant riverside walks) is reliable for lunch.
Carmarthen Museum 🏛 (Abergwili, just E) Good museum in a former palace of the Bishop of St David's, in seven attractive acres. Snacks, shop, disabled access to ground floor only; cl Sun, 25–26 Dec, 1 Jan; (01267) 231691; free.
Gwili Railway 🏛 (Bronwydd, A484 N) Short steam-train trips along a scenic standard-gauge branch line of the old Great Western Railway. Snacks, shop, disabled access; trains daily in Aug, and most Suns and some Weds May–Sept; cl Jan–Mar; (01267) 230666 for timetable; £4.

CARNINGLI COMMON SN0637
(S of Newport) Pleasant walks with some interesting views, on largely unspoilt moorland capped by ancient cairns and other antiquities.

CASTELL HENLLYS SN1138
🏛 (signed off A487 E of Newport) Iron Age hill fort in beautiful countryside overlooking River Gwaun, with interesting reconstruction of three big conical roundhouses. Also a forge, smithy, primitive looms and herb garden. Snacks, shop, some disabled access; cl 1 Nov–31 Mar; (01239) 891319; £2.70.

CASTLE MORRIS SM9032
Llangloffan Farmhouse Cheese (Llangloffan Farm, just N) Delicious traditional farmhouse hard cheeses are hand-made here, and the cheese-making demonstration runs from 10am–12.45pm (not Sun); also friendly animals, a museum-cum-tearoom, children's play area and a picnic spot. The farm shop sells samples of the cheeses, as well as home-made bread and other locally produced foods; cl Sun; (01348) 891241; *£2. The excellent value fish restaurant at Letterston is handy.

CEMAES HEAD SN1249
Gives walkers good views over the mouth of the Teifi estuary and out over the Irish Sea.

CENARTH SN2641
National Coracle Centre 🖼
Unique collection of small hand-made boats from all over the world; they may have demonstrations of how they're made, and there are also various tools used for poaching. A medieval bridge and a pretty waterfall provide the backdrop. Snacks, shop, disabled access; cl Sat, and all Nov–Mar; (01239) 710980; £2.50.
Newcastle Emlyn The attractive main street of this nearby town leads down to an ancient bridge; the Bunch of Grapes and Pelican do decent food.

CILGERRAN SN1943
Cilgerran Castle (off A484) Picturesquely placed on a crag above the River Teifi, this twin-towered Plantagenet fortress has good views from its towers and high walls, though, as usual, you have to go up a spiral staircase. Shop (not Sat), disabled access; (01239) 615007; £2. The ancient Pendre is very good for lunch.
Welsh Wildlife Centre Covering 350 acres, this is one of the richest areas of wetland in the district; the reed bed is the second biggest in Wales. You'll probably see more towards dusk, but even then some bashful creatures might not emerge; a video shows the species you may have missed. Meals, snacks, shop, disabled access; open Easter–Oct half-term; (01239) 621600; *£2.50.

DALE SM8104
Boat trips to Skomer, Skokholm etc Normal base for the National Park boats to the islands of Skomer, Grassholme and Skokholm; sailing times (usually Apr–Oct only) from Dale Sailing Co, (01646) 601636. The Griffin overlooking the anchorage is useful for lunch.
Grassholme The island has 30,000 pairs of gannets: on a clear sunny morning even from the coast you can see it's white with them.
Skokholm This island has Britain's first bird observatory, still tracking migrations.
Dale peninsula At the entrance to the huge natural harbour of Milford Haven, with gentle level-topped terrain giving walkers a bird's-eye view of the shipping activities, reducing the giant oil tankers to a pleasantly toy-like scale.
Skomer 720 acres of spectacular wild scenery with countless birds (inc breeding pairs of short-eared owls) and flowers, as well as seals playing on the shore – maybe common seals briefly in Jun or July, more likely grey seals and their pups in Sept and Oct; it's also remarkable for the easily traced remains of the Iron Age settlement here – there's a well laid out trail.

DINAS HEAD SN0039
The circuit of this nice miniature headland gives about an hour's walk.

DRE-FACH FELINDRE SN3539
Museum of Welsh Woollen Industry (off A484, Dre-fach Felindre) Working museum with textile machinery and tools dating back to the 18th c. Also factory trails, and demonstrations of fabric-making – you may be able to try your hand at spinning. Snacks, shop, disabled access to ground floor; cl Sun during Apr–Sept, cl Sat, Sun during Oct–Mar; (01559) 370929; 50p, children free. There are decent places to eat in Newcastle Emlyn.

FISHGUARD SM9537
The old fishing harbour is surrounded by appropriately small streets of terraced cottages (the Ship here has lots of atmosphere); there's an entirely separate big commercial harbour used by the Irish ferries. In between, the upper town has some attractive old buildings and is pleasant to saunter through. The Royal Oak (scene of the surrender of the last army to invade mainland Britain) is useful here.
Strumble Head You can drive or walk up on to the high headland which protects the harbour; its cliffs are quite grand, particularly where the seas boil through the narrow neck cutting off the rock on which Strumble Head lighthouse stands (there's a car park nearby). Down on the rocks there you quite often see seals even in the spring, though they're more common in late summer. The scenery typifies the rocky, big-dipper coastline of N Pembrokeshire.

GWAUN VALLEY SN0034
Pretty walks along the lushly wooded river either upstream or downstream of Pontfaen.

GWBERT SN1648

Cardigan Island Coastal Farm Park Most notable for its fine clifftop setting overlooking Cardigan Island; there are a good few friendly animals for children, as well as plenty of wild flowers, and a coastal walk to caves where seals breed (best Mar–Nov). You may even see dolphins leaping. Open all year; (01239) 612196; £2.

KIDWELLY SN4007

Kidwelly Castle Remarkably well preserved, this fine castle was built as an earth-and-timber stronghold in 1106, and rebuilt in stone in 1270. Four massive towers, the tremendous gatehouse and much of the impressive outer walls still remain, with steps up to the battlements and turrets. From the walls, the narrow medieval street layout of Kidwelly itself is very obvious. Shop, some disabled access; cl 24–26 Dec, 1 Jan; (01554) 890104; *£2.20 (inc audio tour).

Kidwelly Industrial Museum (Mynyddygarreg, NE; clearly signposted from A484 Kidwelly by-pass) Looks at two great Welsh industries, coal and tin plate. The original tinplate working buildings are still here, and there's an exhibition of coal-mining with pithead gear and a winding engine. Snacks, shop, disabled access; cl Sept–May (open only wkdays and pm wknds Jun, July, Aug, and bank hols); (01554) 891078; free. The riverside Gwenllian Court Hotel out this way has decent food.

LAMPHEY SN0101

Lamphey Palace 🏛 (A4139) Ruined 13th-c palace once belonging to the Bishops of St David's. Shop; cl 25 Dec; (01646) 672224; £2, £1.50 student, child, pensioner.

LAUGHARNE SN3011

The setting on the Taf estuary makes this a rewarding spot for wandering – past Laugharne Castle, Dylan Thomas's Boat House and along the cliff walk (known as Dylan's Walk); in the other direction there's a pleasant walk via Roche Castle. Thomas and his wife are buried in the village churchyard, their grave marked by a simple white cross. Browns Hotel (King St) seems not much changed since Thomas drank there; splendid second-hand bookshop opposite.

Dylan Thomas's Boat House 🏛 (Dylan's Walk) Wales's best-known recent poet lived here while he was writing *Under Milk Wood*, and there are still some of his family photographs and furniture. The writing shed he used for so many poems is nearby. Snacks, shop; open 10am–5pm (3pm in winter); cl 25 Dec; (01994) 427420; £2.75.

Laugharne Castle The ruin Dylan Thomas described as 'brown as owls' is a massive battlemented compilation of styles from 12th- to 16th-c; it has Victorian and Georgian gardens and good views over the estuary. Cl Oct–Apr; (01994) 427906; £2.

LITTLE HAVEN SM8512

Attractive village, with boats pulled up on to the sand, and a good base for seaside walks on the Pembrokeshire Coast Path. There are some attractive sandy-floored rock coves to explore at low tide around here and the Druidstone Hotel to the N, with a good cliff walk N from there to the long sweep of sand and surf at Newgale Sands (food all day from the Duke of Edinburgh).

LLANARTHNE SN5320

National Botanic Garden of Wales The first national botanic garden to be made in Britain for two centuries, this is currently being developed around 18th-c Middleton Hall, in the heart of the attractive Tywi Valley. The centre-piece is the stunning Norman Foster-designed Great Glasshouse – made from 1,000 panes (controlled by computer to vary the climate in different parts) and big enough to cover a football pitch. Plants in here come from as far afield as Southern California, Western Australia and the Canary Islands, and include Britain's rarest tree, the Ley's whitebeam, of which there are only 11 known examples left in the wild. Outside, visitors are treated to a Mediterranean-style landscape with an 18-metre (20-ft) deep ravine, rock terraces, waterfalls and a lake (one of seven on the site). As the gardens gradually establish themselves, other highlights will include a genetic garden and a physic garden displaying herbs and their medicinal uses around the world. The centre will also include a hands-on science centre, and an audio-visual guide around the estate. Meals, snacks, shop, disabled access; cl 25 Dec; (01558) 668768; £6.50.

LLANDEILO SN6222

An attractive sloping town; the Castle Hotel is home to some splendid beers, and past it the Plough at Rhosmaen is a favourite local dining pub.

Dinefwr Park [£] (20 mins' walk from riverside lodge at S edge of Llandeilo; follow Dyfed Wildlife Trust path) Pleasant walks through wooded Capability Brown parkland around isolated, largely 13th-c castle and Newton House. Plenty of deer, but no trace of the medieval town which is known to have stood outside the walls. Meals, snacks, shop, disabled access; cl Nov–Mar; (01558) 823902; £3.

Gelli Aur Country Park (3m W, off B4300) Very relaxing: 60 acres of wooded parkland around a splendid mansion, with an arboretum, nature trails, and specimen trees and shrubs. Meals, snacks, shop, disabled access; cl 25–26 Dec; (01558) 668885; £1.40 parking charge.

LLANELLI SS5099

Millennium Coastal Park One of the most worthwhile millennium projects (the Millennium Commission was impressed enough to provide half of its funding), 14 miles of coastline – once heavily scarred by industry – have been transformed into an attractive new public park over the last five years. Although it doesn't officially open until summer 2001, many of its features are already complete, with attractions along the way from Loughor Bridge to Pembrey (where the Burry Port Harbour is to be restored) inc several new wetland nature reserves, an 18-hole golf course designed by Jack Nicklaus, a National Centre for Angling Excellence, and the restored historic dockyard and new seafront promenade at Llanelli. Lots of public sculpture has been commissioned, gardens and community woodlands have been landscaped, and there are plenty of rewarding new viewpoints over the estuary. The string of sites are linked by a continuous traffic-free cycleway/footpath which will hook up with the **Celtic Trail**, a new 220-mile cycle route that winds its way across

South and West Wales, from the Severn Bridge to the Pembrokeshire Coast National Park.

Parc Howard Art Gallery & Museum In pleasant parkland, the largest collection of the distinctive local pottery in existence, as well as local history, and pictures by local artist J Dickson Innes. Snacks during school hols; shop; cl 1–2pm, and 25–26 Dec, 1Jan; (01554) 772029; free. The Stepney (Park St) is handy for lunch.

Wildfowl & Wetlands Trust (3m E) By Wales's main estuary for wildfowl and waders, with plenty of observation hides and special walkways. Many of the birds will feed from your hand, and at their summer duckery you can hear ducklings calling from inside their eggs. Meals, snacks, shop, disabled access; open 9.30am–5pm (till 4.30pm Oct–Mar); cl 24–25 Dec; (01554) 741087; £5.

LLANGATHEN SN5822

Garden Lost in Time A remarkable survival of a 16th/17th-c garden in the hauntingly attractive grounds of a derelict mansion. Though the garden is very much in its fledgling stage, a walk around the ponds, parapets and arches can be very atmospheric, and as the plants and flowers continue to grow, so too should its appeal to visitors. Snacks, disabled access; cl Nov–Mar; (01558) 668998; £3.95.

LLANGRANOG SN3154

Attractive fishing village with a nice family beach backed by cliffs; there's a pleasant stroll to a headland to the N (otherwise, Cardiganshire lacks a coast path for much of the way). Further N Cwmtydu Cove is pretty – spectacular at sunset.

LLANSTEPHAN SN3410

Llanstephan Castle Sprawling 11th/13th-c ruin, majestically overlooking the Tywi estuary and Carmarthen Bay from an isolated ridge high over the water. Impressive gatehouse with fine vaulted ceiling, and you can still see the slots for drenching intruders with boiling fat or lead; free.

LLANYCEFN SN1024

Penrhos Cottage [£] (off B4313) There can't have been many housing problems around here if local tradition is to be believed; anyone who built a house overnight on common land was entitled to claim it, and this old cottage was such a one, frantically constructed by friends and family. Small shop, disabled access; open by appointment only, (01437) 731328; donations.

MANORBIER SS0697

Manorbier Castle 🖾 Still in the hands of the family who have owned it for over 300 years, this impressive partly 12th-c fortress looking down to the beach has massive medieval outer walls and an early round tower, with a 13th-c chapel (where music is played) and other buildings, and more modern constructions within the walls. Self-catering house. Snacks, shop; cl Oct–Easter; (01834) 871394; *£2. The quiet village is attractive, with a particularly good clean beach, and there's a striking view of the castle from the church. The Castle Inn (open all day in summer) is useful for lunch, and children are made very welcome at the friendly Chives Tea Rooms. Springfields Farm (off A4139) has pick-your-own strawberries and a decent farm shop; (01834) 871746.

MARLOES SM7508

Marloes Deer Park Not actually a deer park, but a wild cliffy headland a couple of miles W, joined to the mainland by quite a narrow isthmus showing steep Iron Age defences; a place to watch birds (choughs breed here) and maybe seals on the offshore rocks. The Lobster Pot is a useful informal family pub, and the beaches are safe for bathing as well as gloriously remote.

Marloes peninsula Gentle terrain above the cliffs, giving views of Skomer Island, and memorable walkers' routes that need only minimal inland walking to complete the circuit.

NARBERTH SN1014

Pleasant little town standing on the imaginary Landsker line separating the 'Little England' of South Pembrokeshire from the more properly Welsh areas to the N. The Angel has good food.

Black Pool Mill 🖾 (Canaston Bridge, 3m W) Striking three-storeyed former corn mill with working machinery, and pleasant walks along the fish-filled river that powered it. Snacks, shop; cl Nov–Mar; (01437) 541233; £2.50.

CC2000 (Canaston Bridge, 3m W)

10–pin bowling, amusements and a reconstruction of TV's *Crystal Maze*; cl 25–26 Dec; (01834) 891622; separate charges for individual attractions.

Cwm Deri Vineyard (Martletwy, off A4075 SW) Self-guided vineyard walk; 350 teddy bears hidden in a shed, and tastings of speciality wines, liqueurs and mead; new winery and shop; picnic area. Maybe cl winter wkdys, and all Jan and Feb (though worth giving them a ring if you're passing); (01834) 891274; free.

Llawhaden Castle 12th-c ruins, surrounded by a deep moat, with the remains of the 13th/14th-c bishop's hall, kitchen and bakehouse; free.

Oakwood (A4075 W) The only real theme park in Wales, and a good one too, especially in the summer hols when they stay open till 10 pm, rounding off every night with a firework display. There's a real mix of things to do, from Europe's biggest wooden roller-coaster to live Mississippi showboat shows. Younger children have their own little roller-coaster (there's another medium-sized one aimed at families), as well as a small farm area, and carousels and the like. The real talking point is the sky-coaster, Vertigo: you're strapped in a harness and winched to a height of up to 43 metres (140 ft), then freefall at 60mph back towards the ground – just before which you'll start swinging like a frantic pendulum. A nightmare cross between bungee-jumping and a parachute drop, this obviously wouldn't suit everyone, so rather than bump up the entry price, there's an extra charge (£30 for up to three people, the maximum number that can go on it at once). This has proved enormously popular, so if you want to try it in peak periods you'll need to get there fairly early to book in. Meals, snacks, shop, disabled access; cl Oct to mid-Dec, then early Jan–Easter; (01834) 891373; £11.50.

NEVERN SN0839

Interesting old riverside village with a medieval bridge over the Nyfer. The church has a tall 10th-c carved Celtic cross and other carved stones, some with Viking patterns, in the graveyard, where the massive yew trees are reputed to weep tears of blood if the

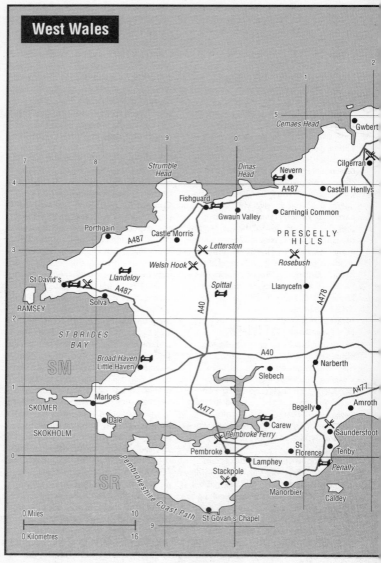

West Wales

Cemaes Head

Gwbert

Cilgerran

Strumble Head

Dinas Head

Nevern

A487

Castell Henllys

Fishguard

Gwaun Valley

Carningli Common

Porthgain

Castle Morris

PRESCELLY HILLS

A487

Letterston

Welsh Hook

Rosebush

St David's

Llandeloy

Spittal

Llanycefn

A487

A40

A478

Solva

RAMSEY

ST BRIDES BAY

A40

SM

Broad Haven
Little Haven

Narberth

Slebech

A477

Marloes

Begelly

Amroth

SKOMER

A477

Dale

Carew

Saundersfoot

SKOKHOLM

Pembroke Ferry

St Florence

Tenby

Pembroke

Lamphey

Penally

SR

Stackpole

Manorbier

Caldey

0 Miles   10

Pembrokeshire Coast Path

0 Kilometres   16

St Govan's Chapel

priest is not Welsh-speaking. The
Trewern Arms is handy for lunch.
Pentre Ifan Burial Chamber (SE
towards Brynberian) One of the most
impressive ancient monuments in
Wales: a striking former long barrow
with the enormous capstone still held
up by three of the four surviving great
upright megaliths. Great views over the

Nyfer Valley.
PEMBROKE SM9801
Museum of the Home 🖾 (Westgate
Hill) Intriguing private collection of all
sorts of everyday objects from the past
300 years, in a pleasant domestic
setting. No under-5s; open Mon–Thurs
May–Sept, 11am–5pm; (01646) 681200;
*£1.20.

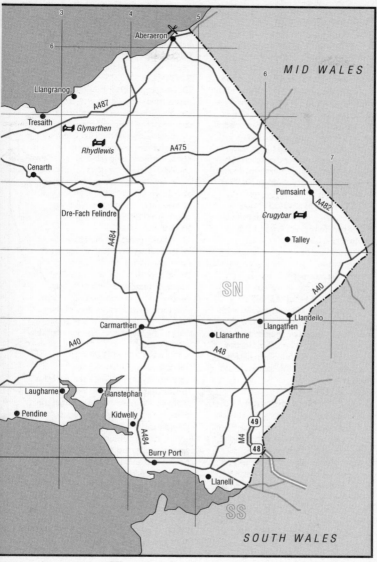

Pembroke Castle 🏛 The birthplace of Henry VII and thus the Tudor dynasty, this impressive 13th-c castle is largely intact, and its endless passages, tunnels and stairways are great fun to explore. The 23-metre (75-ft) tower is one of the finest in Britain. Summer snacks, shop, disabled access; cl 24–26 Dec, 1 Jan; (01646) 684585; *£3 (guided tours by arrangement, Jun–Aug exc Sat, 50p extra). The Pembroke Ferry pub by the water at the foot of the bridge over the estuary does good fresh fish.

PEMBROKESHIRE COAST PATH SR9294
Snaking around the intricate Pembrokeshire seaboard, this makes for notable walks.

PENDINE SN2307
Museum of Speed ⊞ The hard flat
sand on the beaches here made it a
favourite spot for attempting new
speed records; in 1926 J G Parry
Thomas and his 27-litre car Babs set a
short-lived land-speed record of 168
mph, but the careers of both ended the
following year in a grisly accident. The
car spent the next 40 years buried in
the sand but has now been restored,
and in July and Aug (maybe longer)
forms the centre-piece of this small
museum overlooking the beach. Also
local and natural history; shop, disabled
access; cl 1–2pm, Nov–Mar; (01994)
453488; free.

PORTHGAIN SM8132
Quaint small working harbour in tiny
village carefully preserved by the
National Park authorities, former
granite and slate centre – bastions of
former stone works still tower over
water. The Sloop is a good pub, and
there are fine coastal walks.

PRESCELLY HILLS SN0529
(Mynydd Preseli) Pleasant walks with
interesting views, on largely unspoilt
moorland capped by ancient cairns and
other antiquities – for example, the
intriguing Carn Arthur and a hill fort,
both reached from the back road along
the E side.

PUMSAINT SN6640
Dolaucothi Gold Mines (off A482)
2,000 years of gold-mining are the focus
of this unusual mine, in use since Roman
times; tours of both the Roman adits,
Victorian, and 1930s workings,
complete with miners' lamps and
helmets. Visitor centre, woodland
walks, and the chance to have a go at
panning for gold. Stout footwear
recommended. Meals, snacks, shop; site
open Apr–Sept. £2.60. Underground
tours (no under-5s); (01558) 650359.
Estate events – monthly walks and talks
last Fri of every month Apr–Sept;
Roman and archaeology activity days
for families 21–22 July, 4–5 Aug. Fishing,
self-catering, B&B and cycle hire on the
estate (01558) 650707. Get there early
for the underground tours, esp in
summer hols. The nearby Brunant
Arms in fine scenery at Caio has decent
food, and opposite the pub is a Roman
fort and red kite information centre.

SAUNDERSFOOT SN1304
Relaxed extended seaside village, with a
lighthouse on the spit sheltering the
harbour and sandy beach; good fresh
fish at the Royal Oak – which has
heaters for its outside tables.

SLEBECH SN0215
Slebech church (off A40 5m E of
Haverfordwest) Gloriously isolated
ruined 12th-c church, formerly a
temple of the Knights Hospitaller, by
the tidal waters of the East Cleddau.
Though there is a track from the main
road, it's more enjoyable to turn down
the A4075, take the next right turn and
park by the mill, walk over the bridge
and down the track through the woods
above the river. In Haverfordwest,
George's (Market St) has good food.

SOLVA SM8024
One of the prettiest villages on the
coast, with a great deal of character.
From the harbour a good interesting
shortish path runs E to Dinas Fawr, the
opposite headland. This high crag
(enclosed by the ramparts of an Iron
Age fort) gives pretty views of the
attractive little fishing village and the
coast. The Cambrian Arms is a reliable
dining pub.

ST DAVID'S SM7525
The cathedral here has had a
community in residence around it for
longer than any other in Britain, but
thanks to the relative isolation of the
place it's stayed undeveloped, so that St
David's today is little more than a village
– with lots of colourful flowers in
spring. It's a good area for coastal walks,
perhaps to ancient sites such as the
neolithic burial chambers up by St
David's Head to the S or over towards
Solva, to St Non's Chapel, or W to St
Justinian (another chapel here, looking
over Ramsey Island). The Old Cross
Hotel nr the cathedral is a civilised place
for lunch, and the Farmers Arms is
cheap and cheerful. The beach at
Whitesands Bay is good. In summer
(and sometimes in winter depending on
the weather) there are boat trips from
the lifeboat station to rocky Ramsey
Island, where seabirds nest in great
numbers.
Adventure Days Organise well
supervised abseiling, canoeing, rock-
climbing and other activities – ideal for

off-loading active children for the day (over-8s only); (01437) 721611.

Bishop's Palace Impressive ruins, clearly once very grand: plenty of quadrangles, stairways and splendid arcaded walls, with all sorts of intricate and often entertaining details (like the carvings below the arcaded parapets). Atmospheric and tranquil, particularly out of season when you may have it largely to yourself. Shop, limited disabled access; cl am winter Suns, 24–26 Dec, 1 Jan; (01437) 720517; £2.

Oceanarium (New St) Excellent insight into sea and shore life; highlights include the shark tank and rock pool. Talks and demonstrations for children during school hols. Snacks, shop, limited disabled access; cl 25–26 Dec; (01437) 720453; £3.

St David's Cathedral The Norman church had largely collapsed by the 15th c and elaborate repairs had to be made; the resulting roof is an impressive lace-like oak affair, and oak features in most of the rest of the church too. There's a fine collection of Celtic sculptured crosses. Shop, disabled access; cl Sun am; donations.

St David's Farm Park (NE edge, off A487) Commercial farm with rare breed animals as well, and a network of grassy paths giving a view into most fields; playgrounds and picnic areas. Cl Nov–Mar; (01437) 721601; £2.50

St Non's Chapel (about ½ mile N) Reputed birthplace of St Non, the mother of St David; there are lovely sea views from the very scant ruins of the simple coastal chapel here, signed down a track from the useful St Non's Hotel, with a holy well nearby. The walk from St David's is pleasant.

ST FLORENCE SN0802

Manor House Wildlife Park ⌂ (B4318) Around 35 acres of wooded grounds and gardens with exotic birds, reptiles and fish, a pets' corner, playground, model railway and falconry displays (2pm); also natural history museum. Meals, snacks, shop, disabled access; cl Oct–Easter; (01646) 651201; £4.25. The Old Parsonage Farm does quick family food.

ST GOVAN'S CHAPEL SR9692 (past Bosherston, towards St Govan's Head) A simple reroofed 14th-c ruin,

dramatically set halfway down the sea cliffs, and reached via rough rock steps; the former holy well just below has now dried up.

STACKPOLE SR9694

Bosherston lily ponds These ancient elongated lily ponds are a fine sight when in bloom in summer, and well worth a walk; (there are several car parks).

Stackpole Estate (B4319) This spectacular 2,000-acre estate is a real delight to wander through, with lakes, woodlands, cliffs, dunes and beaches offering a range of landscapes to suit every taste and mood. Barafundle Bay is a lovely relatively undiscovered beach. Footpaths lead past a quarry and assorted wildlife over the lake to Bosherston lily ponds. Snacks (at Stackpole Quay); (01646) 661359; car park open Easter–Sept, £1.80 (free to NT members); NT. The Armstrong Arms does good food, and the St Govan's pub is useful too. Further W are the Elegug Stacks, a pair of great rock pinnacles that harbour vast populations of guillemots, herring gulls and kittiwakes.

TALLEY SN6332

Talley Abbey (off B4302) Ruins of once-magnificent 12th-c abbey, still very fine, esp the two pointed archways.

TENBY SN1300

Pleasantly restrained family seaside resort, with sheltered beaches and rock coves. It's a walled town, the splendidly preserved 13th-c wall still with many of its towers left, as well as a magnificent 14th-c arched barbican gateway; a moat used to run the whole length of what is now a tree-lined street. The medieval Plantagenet House, and Coach & Horses and Lamb are all pleasant lunch places.

Caldey Island boat trips Reached by summer boat trips from Tenby harbour (wkdys, plus most Sats May–Sept, weather permitting, £7), still a monastic island, where the Cistercian monks have good cream and honey for sale, as well as more durable crafts and old-fashioned perfume. Besides the modern abbey, there's a 13th-c church with a simple cobbled floor, still in use, on one side of the small cloister of the original priory; these ancient priory buildings (which you can see from outside but not enter) give a better sense of the past than almost anywhere else in West Wales. Sailing times from the Tourist Information Centre, (01834) 842404.

Dinosaur Park (Great Wedlock Farm, Gumfreston – B4318 W) Family fun in a rural setting. Over 20 life-size dinosaurs in glades and swamps along a woodland trail; outdoor and indoor adventure playgrounds, an organised daily activity programme, pets, rides, and computer games; restaurant, indoor and outdoor snack kiosks, and picnic facilities, shop, disabled access; open daily Easter–Sept, and Oct half-term; (01834) 845272; £3.85.

Hoyle's Mouth Cave (off A4139 just SW, Trefloyne Lane towards St Florence; short path through wood on left after 500 yds) Running more than 30 metres (100 ft) back into the hillside, this spooky place has yielded Ice Age mammoth bones, as well as human tools dating back over 10,000 years. Take a torch, but don't go in winter – you'd disturb the hibernating bats.

St Mary's church Interesting 13th-c building with a huge steeple and a plaque commemorating a local invention that many of us use every day – the equals sign.

Tenby Museum and Art Gallery 🖼

There are some remains of the 13th-c castle on the headland above the yachting harbour. Within the castle site is a local history and geology museum, with prehistoric finds and two newly refurbished art galleries with Augustus and Gwen John collections (though not permanently on display). Shop; cl winter wknds and Christmas wk; (01834) 842809; *£2.

Tudor Merchant's House (Quay Hill) Fine example of gabled 15th-c architecture, with a good Flemish chimney and the remains of frescoes on three walls; small herb garden. Shop; cl every Weds, Sun am, all day Sat in Oct, and all Nov–Mar; (01834) 842279; £1.80; NT.

TRESAITH SN2751
Attractive coastal village down steep roads, with a decent pub (and a waterfall to its beach).

Pubs and inns doing food that are noteworthy for their fine positions include the Black Lion at Abergorlech SN5833 (lots of good walks nearby), Forest Arms at Brechfa SN5230, Cresselly Arms by the water at Cresswell Quay SN0406, Stanley Arms on the Cleddau estuary opposite Picton Castle at Landshipping SN0111 and Cennen Arms at Trapp SN6518. The Teifi Netpool at St Dogmaels SN1645 is handy for a walk along to Poppitt Sands.

Where to eat

ABERAERON SN4562 **Hive on the Quay** *Cadwgan Pl (01545) 570445* Cheerful harbourside place on the wharf, based around family honey business (their home-made honey ice-cream is delicious), with lunchtime buffet and popular café – they only open in evenings during Aug and July Seafood Festival – relying heavily on organic produce, and with quite an emphasis on fish from their own boat; also bee exhibition and shop; cl mid-Sept to Spring bank hol. £24.50|**£7.95**

CILGERRAN SN1942 **Pendre** *High St (01239) 614223* Ancient pub with massive stripped 14th-c medieval walls above a panelled dado in the original bar area, some beautifully polished slate flooring, and a comfortable lounge bar and restaurant area; astonishingly cheap and really good interesting food, well kept real ales, prompt welcoming service, and a small terrace with sturdy tables, with more in an enclosed play area; good local wildlife park nearby, and a good area for fishing.|**£3.50**

LETTERSTON SM9429 **Something Cooking** *Haverfordwest Rd (01348) 840621* Enthusiastically run and very friendly fish restaurant with truly outstanding fresh fish, served by neat uniformed waitresses – very reasonable prices too; cl winter Sun, 2 wks Christmas; disabled access. £13.80|**£4.50**

PEMBROKE FERRY SM9704 **Ferry Inn** *(01646) 682947* Former sailors' haunt by the water below Cleddau Bridge (not by the new ferry), with an extensive range of very fresh fish dishes – non-fishy things too – nautical décor, good views, a relaxed pubby atmosphere, well kept real ales, decent malt whiskies, and efficient service; restaurant cl 25–26 Dec. £16|**£4.95**

ROSEBUSH SN0729 **Old Post Office** *(01437) 532205* Quaint bistro with lots of local photos, farming tools and teapots on the ceiling, good value lunches, well prepared traditional cooking in the candlelit dining room, and coffee and afternoon tea; bdrms; some disabled access. £17|**£5.25**

SAUNDERSFOOT SN1304 **Royal Oak** *Wogan Terrace (01834) 812546* In a good spot in the village centre above the harbour, this very well run pub has friendly attentive staff, a buoyant atmosphere in the dining area and carpeted no smoking lounge bar, and enjoyable food inc eight or so fresh fish dishes (increasing to well over a dozen in summer), well kept real ales, 25 malts, an interesting choice of wines with a dozen by the glass, and seats outside, with overhead heaters for cold days. £20.70|**£7.95**

ST DAVID'S SM7525 **Morgan's Brasserie** *20 Nun St (01437) 720508* Smart little brasserie specialising in good fresh fish from a shortish menu, supplemented by daily specials and using good fresh local produce; friendly service, and good value wines; cl Sun (best to phone in winter before visiting), cl Jan, Feb. £30

STACKPOLE SR9896 **Armstrong Arms** *Jason's Corner (01646) 672324* Charming rather Swiss-looking dining pub with neat oak furnishings and glossy beams in four rambling areas, good interesting food (inc fresh local fish), well kept real ales, cheerful uniformed waitresses, and seats in the flower-filled garden; must book Sat pm, Sun am; disabled access. £15|**£4.95**

WELSH HOOK SM9326 **Stone Hall** *(01348) 840212* 14th-c house with imaginative French food and fine wines in beamed and panelled restaurant (evenings only), characterful bar, and lovely grounds; bdrms. £25

Mid Wales

Real seclusion; great untouched landscapes, dramatic natural features, and exhilarating walks; some spectacular steam trips too

Sparsely populated, with far more sheep than people, the lonely heart of Wales is one of Britain's best areas for really getting away from it all. The scenery is spectacular. Though it doesn't quite match the very best of Snowdonia or the West Wales coast, you're not sharing it with as many other visitors. It has very good walking, and little-used former drovers' roads give glorious scenic drives, threading through the huge tracts of forest and moorland around the Llyn Briane reservoir, the Cambrian Mountains and the reservoirs above the Elan Valley. Other kinder ranges of hills tempt out more people, most notably the western Black Mountain, the Brecon Beacons (with some mighty waterfalls in their southern reaches) and the eastern Black Mountains. The area's river valleys are among the finest in Wales: the friendly Usk, the rather more imposing Upper Wye, and above Aberystwyth, the beautiful Vale of Rheidol.

For an area little touched by tourism, there are some pleasantly idiosyncratic places to visit inc the lively Celtica in Machynlleth (also home to the thriving Museum of Modern Art, Wales, a new entry this year), the nearby Centre for Alternative Technology (an innovative transformation of an old slate quarry), and over on the coast, the Borth Animalarium, home to some endangered animals, and another newcomer to the *Guide*.

There's plenty of scope for underground fun as well, from the fascinating series of caves at Craig-y-Nos to the Arthurian legends in the caves of Corris (best for children), or the underground tour at the Llywernog Silver Lead Mine, Ponterwyd. Overground, several steam railways pass through some particularly picturesque countryside. The friendly towns include a string of dignified slightly old-fashioned inland spa towns, with excellently restored historic buildings in Brecon and Presteigne.

There are some very comfortable places to stay in, with glorious countryside more or less on their doorsteps.

Where to stay

ABERDOVEY SN6196 **Penhelig Arms** *Terrace Rd, Aberdovey, Gwynedd LL35 0LT* (01654) 767215 **£69**, plus special breaks; 10 comfortable rms. Carefully refurbished building in fine spot overlooking sea, with cosy bar, open fires, very good food with emphasis on daily-delivered fresh local fish in no smoking restaurant, extensive wine list with 14 by the glass (champagne, too), splendid breakfasts, and friendly service; lovely views of Dovey Estuary; cl 25–26 Dec

ABERDOVEY SN6196 **Preswylfa** *Aberdovey, Gwynedd LL35 0LE* (01654) 767239 **£50***; 3 super rms with lovely views. Friendly and relaxed Edwardian house in pretty, mature garden, courteous genuinely helpful owners, period drawing room with grand piano (all welcome to play), enjoyable evening meals (by arrangement) using home-grown produce in dining room with fine views, and footpath leading to village and beach (4 mins); children over 8

ABERHAFESP SO0595 **Dyffryn** *Bwlch-y-ffridd, Newtown, Powys SY16 3JD* (01686) 688817 **£54***; 2 rms. Carefully restored half-timbered barn on 100-acre sheep and beef cattle farm, with a residents' lounge overlooking the stream, traditional cooking in the dining room, and friendly owners; no smoking; children over 10

CARNO SN9696 **Aleppo Merchant** *Carno, Caersws, Powys SY17 5LL* (01686) 420210 **£45***; 6 rms, most with shower. Warm and friendly 17th-c inn in rural setting, with comfortably modernised beamed lounge bar, public bar and restaurant, fair choice of well liked food, helpful service, and well kept real ales; children over 12

CHURCH STOKE SO2689 **Drewin Farm** *Church Stoke, Montgomery, Powys SY15 6TW* (01588) 620325 **£40**; 2 rms. Attractive 17th-c farmhouse with panoramic views, warm welcome, comfortable beamed lounge, traditional cooking in dining room, and games room with snooker table in converted granary; Offa's Dyke footpath runs through the mixed farm of sheep, cattle and crops; cl Nov, Jan–Feb

CRICKHOWELL SO2118 **Bear** *High St, Crickhowell, Powys NP8 1BW* (01873) 810408 **£61**; 35 rms, the back ones are the best, and some have jacuzzis. Particularly friendly coaching inn with calmly civilised atmosphere, excellent food using local produce and home-grown herbs (some Welsh specialities), fine wines and ports, well kept real ales, and prompt attentive service; lots of antiques, deeply comfortable seats, and a roaring log fire in the heavily beamed lounge, and a partly no smoking family room; children over 5 in restaurant; dogs welcome; disabled access

CRICKHOWELL SO1719 **Gliffaes Hotel** *Gliffaes Rd, Crickhowell, Powys NP8 1RH* (01874) 730371 **£63.50**, plus special breaks; 22 rms, several refurbished this year. Run by the same family since 1948, this imposing house is set in 33 acres of wonderfully peaceful grounds with fine rare trees; enjoyably informal and relaxed atmosphere, comfortable big sitting room, elegant drawing room, pleasant conservatory, glorious Usk Valley views from terrace, good cooking, and cheerful staff; fishing, hard tennis court, golf practice net, and a putting and croquet lawn

EGLWYSFACH SN6796 **Ynyshir Hall** *Eglwysfach, Machynlleth, Dyfed SY20 8TA* (01654) 781209 **£120***; 10 individually decorated, no smoking rms. Carefully run Georgian manor house in 14 acres of landscaped gardens adjoining the Ynyshir coastal bird reserve, with particularly good service, antiques, log fires and paintings in the light and airy public rooms, extremely good food using home-grown vegetables, and delicious breakfasts; lots to do nearby; cl 5–23 Jan; children over 9

GLADESTRY SO2355 **Royal Oak** *Gladestry, Kington, Herefordshire HR5 3NR* (01544) 370669 **£40***; 5 well equipped rms. Unpretentious and welcoming inn on Offa's Dyke, with beams and flagstones, a quiet relaxing atmosphere, good home-cooked bar food (inc nice breakfasts), comfortable lounge, separate bar, and picnic-sets in lovely secluded garden behind

GUILSFIELD SJ2110 **Lower Trelydan** *Guilsfield, Welshpool, Powys SY21 9PH* (01938) 553105 **£50***; 3 rms. Charming black and white farmhouse on beef cattle and sheep farm, with lovely heavily beamed ceilings, fine antiques and comfortable seating, a cosy licensed bar, warm and friendly atmosphere, and delicious farmhouse cooking; pretty garden; also self-catering cottages; cl Christmas; disabled access

HAY-ON-WYE SO2342 **Old Black Lion** *26 Lion St, Hay-on-Wye, Hereford, Herefordshire HR3 5AD* (01497) 820841 **£58.90**, plus special breaks; 10 rms, some in modern annexe. Smartly civilised old hotel with low beams and black panelling, convivial bar, wide choice of carefully prepared food in bar and candlelit no smoking cottagey restaurant, and an extensive wine list; close to fishing (private salmon and trout fishing) and riding; children over 5 and must be over 8 in restaurant

KNIGHTON SO3371 **Milebrook House** *Stanage, Knighton, Herefordshire LD7 1LT* (01547) 528632 **£77.50***, plus special breaks; 10 spacious rms, 4 in a newer smart wing. Charming 18th-c house in three acres surrounded by really unspoilt countryside with River Teme trout fishing; log fires, residents' sitting room, bar (where light lunches are served), and good sound cooking using home-grown vegetables; children over 8; disabled access

LLANDEFALLE SO1034 **Trehenry Farm** *Llandefalle, Brecon, Powys LD3 0UN* (01874) 754312 **£42**; 4 rms. 18th-c farmhouse on 200-acre farm with lovely views of Black Mountains and Brecon Beacons; inglenook fireplaces, beams, TV lounge, good food, and large garden; self-catering also; cl Christmas

LLANDEGLEY SO1263 **Ffaldau Country House** *Llandegley, Llandrindod Wells, Powys LD1 5UD* (01597) 851421 **£46***, plus special breaks; 3 rms. Carefully restored heavily beamed 16th-c country house with flower-filled landscaped gardens, log fire in comfortable lounge, residents' bar, upstairs sitting room with games and books, enjoyable dinners in charming dining room, and fine breakfasts; children over 12

LLANEGRYN SH5905 **Cefn Coch Guest House** *Llanegryn, Tywyn, Gwynedd LL36 9SD* (01654) 712193 **£48***; 5 rms. Traditional coaching inn set in an acre of gardens with fine views, and on the edge of Snowdonia National Park; beams, slate floors, stripped pine, and fresh flowers, Laura Ashley décor, pictures and woodburner in lounge, homely atmosphere, friendly owners, and enjoyable food – they also have a little tearoom; worth visiting the local church, famous for its wooden screen; cl Dec–Jan; children over 12

LLANGAMMARCH WELLS SN9447 **Lake** *Llangammarch Wells, Powys LD4 4BS* (01591) 620202 **£130**; 19 charming, pretty rms with fruit and decanter of sherry. Particularly well run, 1860 half-timbered hotel in 50 acres with plenty of wildlife, well stocked trout lake, clay pigeon shoots, and tennis; deeply comfortable tranquil drawing room with antiques, paintings and log fire, wonderful afternoon teas (in summer under the chestnut tree overlooking the river), courteous discreet service, fine wines and very good modern British cooking in elegant candlelit dining room, and liberal breakfasts; children over 6; disabled access

LLANGORSE SO1329 **Trewalter** *Llangorse, Brecon, Powys LD3 0PS* (01874) 658442 **£44***; 3 rms. Only 10 mins from Hay-on-Wye, this charming and friendly Victorian house has panoramic views across to the Brecon Beacons, an open fire and plenty of games and books in comfortable sitting room, candlelit dinners taken around one big table, and good breakfasts; newly landscaped garden; watersports on lake by village; cl Christmas/New Year; children over 4

LLANWRTYD WELLS SN8746 **Carlton House** *Dolycoed Rd, Llanwrtyd Wells, Powys LD5 4RA* (01591) 610248 **£60**; 7 well equipped rms. Warmly friendly owners run this comfortable Edwardian restaurant-with-rooms, and there's a relaxing little sitting room with plants and antiques, an attractive dining room with original panelling and log fire, serving exceptionally good modern British cooking using top-quality local produce (delicious puddings and home-made canapés and petit fours), super breakfasts with home-made bread and marmalade, and a thoughtful wine list; cl 10–28 Dec

LLYSWEN SO1337 **Griffin** *Llyswen, Brecon, Powys LD3 0UR* (01874) 754241 **£70**, plus special breaks; 7 rms. Old-fashioned and warmly welcoming family-run sporting inn, very well run, with imaginative fresh food in no smoking restaurant (brook trout and salmon caught by the family, local game in season), good breakfasts, interesting comfortable bar with huge inglenook, and helpful service; fishing and shooting courses; disabled access; cl 25–26 Dec

LLYSWEN SO1240 **Llangoed Hall** *Llyswen, Brecon, Powys LD3 0YP* (01874) 754525 **£155**, plus special breaks; 23 very pretty rms with luxurious touches. Fine largely Jacobean mansion beautifully converted into a first-class hotel with lovely house-party atmosphere, handsome hall, elegant and spacious public rooms with antiques, wonderful pictures, fresh flowers and views over the grounds, imaginative modern cooking in charming restaurant, and very good Welsh breakfasts; marvellous surrounding countryside; children over 8

MONTGOMERY SO2296 **Dragon** *Market Sq, Montgomery, Powys SY15 6PA* (01686) 668359 **£74**, plus special breaks; 20 rms. Attractive black and white timbered small hotel with a pleasant grey-stone tiled hall, comfortable residents' lounge, beamed bar, restaurant using local produce; indoor swimming pool, sauna, live jazz Weds pm

NEWTOWN SO1292 **Lower Gwestydd** *Aberbechan, Newtown, Powys SY16 3AY* (01686) 626718 **£42***; 2 rms. Traditional 17th-c black and white half-timbered house on 200 acres of mainly sheep and arable farmland in lovely countryside; comfortable lounge and dining room, and good food with their own fruit and veg, chicken and lamb; children over 5; cl Jan–Apr

OLD RADNOR SO2559 **Harp** *Old Radnor, Presteigne, Powys LD8 2RH* (01544) 350655 **£52**, plus special breaks; 5 pretty rms, most with own bthrm. 15th-c inn in superb tranquil hilltop position, with lovely views and good walks nearby; attentive and hospitable new licensees, traditional bars with good log fires, some slate flooring and antique settles, character dining room, good value home cooking inc good breakfasts, well kept ales; seats outside with play area; cl wkdy lunchtimes

PENNAL SN6799 **Gogarth Hall Farm** *Pennal, Machynlleth, Powys SY20 9LB* (01654) 791235 **£48***; 2 rms. 17th-c house on working farm of suckler cows and sheep with marvellous views of Dovey Estuary – guests welcome to walk around the farm; dining room and lounge, enjoyable breakfasts and evening meals, and utility room for children in wet weather; babysitting available; self-catering also

PRESTEIGNE SO3164 **Radnorshire Arms** *High St, Presteigne, Powys LD8 2BE* (01544) 267406 **£84**, plus special breaks; 16 rms. Rambling handsomely timbered 17th-c hotel with old-fashioned charm and an unchanging atmosphere, elegantly moulded beams and fine dark panelling in the lounge bar, latticed windows, enjoyable food (inc morning coffee and afternoon tea), separate no smoking restaurant, well kept real ales, and politely attentive service

RHANDIRMWYN SN7843 **Royal Oak** *Rhandirmwyn, Llandovery, Dyfed SA20 0NY* (01550) 760201 **£56**; 5 rms, most with own bthrm. Homely, friendly family-run pub in the foothills of the Cambrian Mountains with fine views, superb walking and RSPB Dinas Bird Reserve nearby; simple furnishings, log fire, well kept real ale, decent food, and a warm welcome; dogs by prior arrangement

RHAYADER SN9969 **Beili Neuadd** *Rhayader, Powys LD6 5NS* (01597) 810211

£45*; 3 rms with log fires. Charming partly 16th-c stone-built farmhouse in quiet countryside (they have their own trout pools and woodland), with beams, polished oak floorboards, dormitory accommodation for up to 16 in stone barn with own kitchen; pony-trekking and guided walks nearby; cl Christmas; children over 8

To see and do

ABERDOVEY SN6196
Attractive, restrained resort with very pleasant sheltered beaches but none of the crowds or tat they usually bring. Legend has it there's a lost city beneath the sea, inundated by the crashing waves in a great storm 1,500 years ago. Sometimes at night imaginative people can hear the mournful tolling of its bells. Besides the Penhelig Arms Hotel, the Britannia does good food and has great views.

ABERYSTWYTH SN5981
Low-key resort, scarcely changed in 20 years, with long shingle beaches and sedate cliff railway to large camera obscura high above. Quite a scholarly university town, too, with a good museum, and one of the very few of Edward I's castles in this part of Wales. The university has a large agricultural college attached and as well as the usual sheep, you may see llamas in some of the surrounding fields. There's a pleasant walk along the straight stretch of coast to Borth; you can use the train for the other half of a round trip.
National Library of Wales (Penglais Hill) Imposing neo-classical building looking over the town, with exhibitions of fine early Welsh and Celtic manuscripts and more modern art. Meals, snacks, shop, disabled access. Cl Sun, bank hols and first full wk Oct; free.
Vale of Rheidol Railway (Alexander Rd) The town's main attraction for families, with steam trains for several miles along the picturesque twists of the Rheidol Valley to the dramatic beauty-spot gorge of Devil's Bridge. You can use the railway for attractive round-trip walks. Snacks, shop; trains run most days Easter–Oct, (01970) 625819 for timetable; £10.50 full return fare.

BLACK MOUNTAIN SN8123
The westernmost range in the Brecon Beacons National Park – not to be confused with the Black Mountains to the E. Much of the high terrain is a long way from the road, so this part is more the preserve of the committed long-distance walker. The craggy ridge known as Carmarthen Fan protrudes dramatically above the moors and provides the high point of a long but rewarding walk from the N.

BLACK MOUNTAINS SO2632
Making up the E part of the Brecon Beacons National Park, these finger-shaped ridges have steep-sided valleys between. Most of the best views are from the Offa's Dyke Path along the E flanks: the land eastwards slopes abruptly down to low-lying agricultural Herefordshire, and views far into England give you a feeling of true border country. Circular walks here tend to be long and hefty, often with two major ascents to get you up on to the different ridges, but the scenic Gospel Pass road from Hay-on-Wye lets you drive to within reasonable striking distance of Hay Bluff (670 metres, 2,200 ft). Twmpa (690 metres, 2,263 ft) is better known by its intriguing English name of Lord Hereford's Knob; though it's not itself on the Offa's Dyke Path, it is nearby, and you can combine it with Hay Bluff in a longer walk. Llanthony Abbey, with an atmospheric cellar bar, makes a beautiful objective in the valley below, where diligent map-reading is needed for a cross-fields route from Cwmyoy, with extensions on to the Offa's Dyke Path on the ridge to complete a satisfying circuit.

BORTH SN6086
Borth Animalarium Just a short walk from the beach, this friendly place is committed to the conservation of endangered animals. Residents include lemurs, wallabies, and a family of Geoffreys Cats; also aviaries, bat and reptile houses, a collection of exotic insects, and daily talks and demonstrations. Play and picnic areas, snacks, shop, disabled access; open

Apr–Oct; (01970) 871224; £3.

BRECON SO0428

Enjoyable and interesting small town despite too much traffic, with some fine old buildings around its main square and narrow streets, and a bustling livestock market on Tues and Fri. The striking Norman priory was grandly restored in the 19th c and became a cathedral in 1923. Also the rather sad remnants of a castle, and a couple of decent little museums. The refurbished Camden Arms (Walton) is a comfortable food stop. Some of the highest peaks in the area are a short drive away.

Brecknock Museum & Art Gallery (Captains Walk) Has the town's excellently preserved assize court with an interpretative exhibition, as well as plenty of love spoons and some interesting Celtic crosses. Extensive programme of art, craft, and historical exhibitions. Shop, disabled access; cl 1–2pm Sat, Sun in winter, shut at 4pm Sat during Nov–Feb, Good Fri, 25–26 Dec, 1 Jan; (01874) 624121; £1.

Brecon Beacons Mountain Centre (Libanus) Useful National Parks visitor centre (cl 25 Dec; free, car parking charge from £1 for 2 hours); they can advise on local walks, inc how to get to the spectacular waterfalls nr Glyn Neath. From the centre there's free access to the surrounding area known as Illtud Common, with fine views of the Beacons and an Iron Age hill fort to make for; this can also be used as a starting point for walking up to Craig Cerrig-gleisiad a Fan Frynach National Nature Reserve SN9522, home to Arctic/alpine flora and some 80 bird species.

Cantref Trekking & Riding Centre (Upper Cantref, just S) Can organise pony-trekking through this attractive landscape (£9 half, £22 day), and does farmhouse B&B too; ring Mrs Evans on (01874) 665223.

BRECON BEACONS SO0121

A pair of graceful pointed summits connected by a short ridge that seems to be visible from most of South Wales, and that gives a magnificent high-level walk along the crest, which has massive drops on the northern side. Pen y Fan (886 metres, 2,906 ft) is the highest Welsh summit outside Snowdonia, and

the main E–W upland spine effectively stretches about 5 miles. The most popular walk up from Pont ar Daf, from the A470 to the W, is straightforward enough although there has been some serious footpath erosion, but the N approaches are more exciting and surprisingly little walked.

Brecon Beacons National Park

The southern parts of the park, within easy reach of South Wales, have gentle forest walks in large conifer plantations, where waterfalls and a series of attractive reservoirs are the main features. The abrupt transition from the industrial valleys into this empty wildness is startling.

BUILTH WELLS SO0451

Pleasant small spa town, with good walks in attractive scenery.

CADAIR IDRIS SH7112

This great peak in the S of the Snowdonia National Park offers walkers various ways up its friendly slopes. Good spots are the Arthog waterfalls and nearby lakes, on the lower slopes.

CARREG CENNEN SN6619

Carreg Cennen Castle (nr Trapp, SE of Llandeilo) Few castles can boast as excellent a setting as these old ruins, dramatically dominating their limestone crag high above the river, and overlooking the unspoilt countryside towards the Black Mountains. Rebuilt in the 13th c (and again in the 19th – you can easily distinguish the new stonework), the castle has a mysterious passage in the side of the cliff. Readers enjoy coming here and the staff are very friendly. Meals, snacks, shop; cl 25 Dec; (01558) 822291; £2.50. The Cennen Arms nearby has good simple food.

CORRIS SH7408

Attractive and nicely set beneath the towering crags of Cadair Idris, with lakes and pine forests in the surrounding valley. The whole village seems to be made of slate.

Corris Craft Centre (off A487 towards Corris Uchaf) Craft workshops including working potter, toymaker, goldsmith, leatherworker, and candlemaker, with a restaurant, shop, disabled access, picnic and play areas; best to check winter opening; (01654) 761584; free.

King Arthur's Labyrinth (Upper

Corris, off A487 towards Corris Uchaf) Fun for families; a boat trip takes you to the heart of the underground tunnels and caverns, then it's a half-mile walk through passageways punctuated with scenes from the local version of the Arthurian legends. Wrap up well: it can get cold down here. Meals, snacks, shop; cl mid-Nov to end Mar; (01654) 761584; £4.40.

CRAIG Y NOS SN8316

Craig y Nos Country Park Ideal for a picnic or a stroll: 40 acres of woodland, lake and meadow, landscaped and developed in the last century by the opera singer Adelina Patti. Interactive displays in the visitor centre. Shop, limited disabled access; cl 25 Dec; (01639) 730395; park free, though £1 parking.

Dan-yr-Ogof Showcaves 🖼 (A4067 just N) Fascinating series of caves, well lit to emphasise the extraordinary rock formations. The Cathedral Cave is the largest single chamber open to the public in any British showcave, while 3,000 years ago Bone Cave was lived in by humans. There's also a dinosaur park, Iron Age farm, shire horse centre, and artificial ski-slope, so lots to see. Meals, snacks, shops; cl Nov–Apr (open Feb half-term); (01639) 730284; £7. The Tafarn y Garreg just N does decent food.

CRICKHOWELL SO2118

Pleasant village-sized 'town', with an excellent inn in the Bear, and a fine ancient bridge over the Usk (which the good Bridge End Inn overlooks).

DEVIL'S BRIDGE SN7477

Pretty bridges and dramatic waterfall, tucked away in an atmospheric wooded gorge. The oldest bridge gave this beauty spot its name, when it was built by the Devil in order to trap an old woman into giving him her soul; she outwitted him. Wordsworth was inspired to write a sonnet after a visit here. The entertaining Halfway Inn at Pisgah on the A4120 to Aberystwyth is good for lunch.

ELAN VALLEY SN9365

These four lakes W of Rhayader are the best and most famous of the many man-made reservoirs in Wales. Built at the turn of the last century, they have weathered in well now – even the dams

look good, and there are splendid valley and Cambrian Mountain views, especially from high-level trackways. It's a good spot for bird-watching, particularly in summer, and among the many species you may see red kites. The Elan Valley Hotel (B4518) has decent food.

Elan Valley Visitor Centre (Elan village) Good opening to this attractive area, with a new audio-visual show and displays. Meals, snacks, shop, disabled access. Cl 5 Nov–mid-Mar; (01597) 810880; free (£1 car parking charge). Outside is a statue of Shelley, who lived in a house now lost beneath the reservoirs. Walks from here include woodland walks and strolls along the old railway track by the water's edge – very attractive, and now also suitable for wheelchairs, cyclists, and horse-riders.

FAIRBOURNE SH6112

Fairbourne & Barmouth Steam Railway 🖼 (Beach Rd) Running the spectacular 2½ miles to the end of the peninsula and the ferry for Barmouth, this started life in 1890 as a horse-drawn railway used to carry building materials for the seaside resort of Fairbourne. Meals, snacks, shop; cl last wk Sept–Easter, (01341) 250362 for timetable; £4. The Fairbourne Hotel is quite useful for lunch, as is the 15th-c Last Inn on Barmouth Harbour. The attractively set George III along the estuary at Penmaenpool is quite handy too. Fairbourne and Barmouth both have good clean beaches.

HAY-ON-WYE SO2342

This pleasant small town has become a world centre for secondhand and antiquarian books. There is a growing number of print, junk and antiques shops too, as well as a rather jolly puzzle and teddy bear shop on Broad St. Hay Bluff nearby has lovely walks, and it's within easy reach of the Black Mountains, the Golden Valley over the English border, and the attractive unspoilt countryside just over the Gwent border that we've mentioned in the South Wales section. Besides the fine Old Black Lion, the Kilvert Court (01497) 821042 can be recommended both for food and as a place to stay. Black Mountain Activities just up the road (technically in Herefordshire) can arrange all sorts of exertions; (01497) 847897.

LLANBISTER SO0974

Llananno church Remarkable, with an astonishingly elaborate rood screen that wouldn't be out of place in a cathedral. **Llanbister church** Interesting, with a chimney instead of the usual tower, and presumably a warmer congregation.

LLANDRINDOD WELLS SO0661

Civilised inland resort sheltering below the hills, a largely intact gem of the railway age, with imposing buildings on broad avenues and terraces, wrought-iron frills everywhere, elegant flower displays and Victorian parks, antiques shop-fronts and little canopies along the shopping streets. It was clearly a resort for temperance – though there are places to drink, they're tucked discreetly away. The former spa pump room has been re-opened, there are sedate walks around a very old-fashioned boating lake, and a very helpful Tourist Information Centre is housed in the Old Town Hall. The atmospheric old Llanerch has good home cooking, and the Metropole Hotel generally does some food all day.

Cefnllys Castle A good walk from the town to this impressively sited hill fort with a lonely church below, close to Shaky Bridge (no longer shaky); a nature trail here takes you along the banks of the River Ithon.

National Cycle Collection 🏛 (Temple St) Over 200 cycles, reconstructions of Victorian and Edwardian cycle shops, early lamp collections, displays on past racing stars, and artist exhibitions. Meals, snacks, shop, disabled access; (01597) 825531; £2.50.

Radnorshire Museum (Temple St) Charming district museum, well worth a look, with a gallery showing varying exhibits from early Christian carvings to Victorian paintings. Shop, disabled access to downstairs, cl 1–2pm Tues–Fri, Sun am and all day Mon; (01597) 824513; *£1.

LLANFAIR CAEREINION SJ1006

Welshpool & Llanfair Railway 🏛 (A458, Llanfair Caereinion) Colonial and Austrian steam locomotives are among the wide variety of engines that run along this pretty eight-mile line, and the Welshpool end has an award-winning station reconstruction. Snacks, shop, disabled access (with prior notice); cl Oct–Easter exc Dec Santa Specials, (01938) 810441 for timetable; £7.90. The Goat is useful for lunch.

LLANIDLOES SN9584

Attractive small town, with unique Elizabethan timbered market hall.

LLANWRTYD WELLS SN8746

Pleasant small spa town, said to be Britain's smallest town, with good walks in attractive scenery, also mountain bike hire. The good Neuadd Arms is the focus for all sorts of activities inc man v horse v mountain bike marathons, and bog-snorkelling championships.

MACHYNLLETH SH7400

Wide main street with handsome 24-metre (78 ft) 19th-c clock tower and a very relaxed feel. The White Lion, a big country-town bar, does decent lunches, inc vegetarian.

Celtica Very enjoyable look at the history and legends of the Celts, in an 18th-c mansion. There's a traditionalish museum upstairs, but more fun is the lively walk-through exhibition on the ground floor, special effects bringing ancient villages and druids' prophecies vividly to life. Also a good themed indoor play area for under-8s. It's popular with school trips the last couple of weeks of term. Meals, snacks, good shop, disabled access; cl 25 Dec, 1 Jan; (01654) 702702; *£4.95.

Centre for Alternative Technology (A487 3m N) Technologies for the improvement of the environment have been researched and displayed at this enthusiastic place for over 20 years now, with constantly updated demonstrations of wind power, wave power and solar energy – you can even ride a water-powered cliff-railway (one of Britain's steepest; Easter–Oct only) There's a fun exhibition on what it's like to be in a mole hole. The site, an old slate quarry, has fine views over neighbouring Snowdonia National Park, and they look after children well. Wholesome vegetarian restaurant, good bookshop, disabled access; cl 24–26 Dec, 1 Jan, and two wks mid-Jan; (01654) 702400; £6.90 inc cliff railway, £4.90 without.

They do good value family tickets, and you can save 10% off the entry cost if you arrive by bus, or 50% if you come by bike; you can also halve the cost of hiring a bike from Greenstiles in Machynlleth, (01654) 703543.

Museum of Modern Art, Wales (Penrallt St) This lively modern art gallery has grown up alongside the Tabernacle, a former Wesleyan chapel converted into a centre for the performing arts nearly 15 years ago. Throughout the six galleries, various exhibitions include Showcase Wales (works by Wales's finest contemporary artists), a permanent collection of Welsh modern art, and displays of works by individual artists. The museum runs a busy schedule of events inc workshops (for children as well) in July; there are plenty of recitals and performances in the adjacent auditorium. Shop, disabled access; cl Sun, 24–26 Dec, 1 Jan; (01654) 703355; free.

Parliament House Local history museum in 16th-c building, with a particular emphasis on the rebellion of Owain Glyndwr (it's on the spot where he held parliament). Brass rubbing centre, shop, disabled access; cl 12.30–1.30pm, Sun (unless by appointment), and all Oct–Easter; (01654) 702827; free.

MONTGOMERY SO2793
Tiny town, rewarding for a short exploration on foot, with great views from its castle perched above. Montgomeryshire consists of the quintessential sheep-grazed lands of rural Wales – generally not prime walking country, lacking major objectives for walkers, with few major peaks and fair distances between villages.

OFFA'S DYKE PATH SO2455
The major walkers' attraction in this part; on its coast-to-coast route over the Welsh Marches it takes in some very attractive hill-farm country between Hay-on-Wye and Knighton, including Hergest Ridge (in Herefordshire, but easily reached from the Welsh side) and some well preserved stretches of Offa's 9th-c boundary marker between Knighton and Kington. The George & Dragon in Knighton is worth knowing.

OLD RADNOR SO2559
Old Radnor church Handsome screen and roof, Britain's oldest organ-case and font; delightful surroundings, with hilltop views. The Harp up here has good home cooking.

PLYNLIMON SN7687
(just N of Borth) A major scenic highlight of the coast, with watery views across the vast sands of the Dovey estuary, lots of birds, and an important dune system, habitat for orchids. You can walk round the tip of land jutting into the mouth of the Dovey and then along the shore.

PONTERWYD SN7281
Bwlch Nant-yr-Arian Forest Centre (A44 just W) Designated Kite Country Centre with feeding taking place daily all year (3pm summer, 2pm winter); explore the forest on the scenic way-marked walks and enjoy breathtaking valley views. Plans for new mountain bike trail and new all-ability trail. Visitor centre ((01970) 890694) offers snacks, shop, disabled access; picnic areas and children's play area. Free (parking £1).

Llywernog Silver Lead Mine (A434 just W) A lively place, set against a beautiful sweeping mountainside backdrop. Regular displays of silver panning, sound and light tableaux in the caves and tunnels along the expanded underground tour, and working water-wheels; you can try panning for Fool's Gold or dowsing for mineral veins. Wear sensible shoes in wet weather. Snacks, shop, some disabled access; open mid-Mar to Oct (cl Mon exc July–Aug); (01970) 890620; *£4.95.

Mountain drive There's an eye-opening mountain drive from Ponterwyd N past the partly wooded Nant-y-moch reservoir below the slopes of Plynlimon, and on to Tal-y-bont.

PRESTEIGNE SO3164
Attractive former county town of Radnorshire, with some fine timbered houses and a handsome church. The Radnorshire Arms is good value and readers enjoy the Hat Shop restaurant, which has exhibitions by local artists.

Judge's Lodging (Broad St) Good restoration of the judge's living

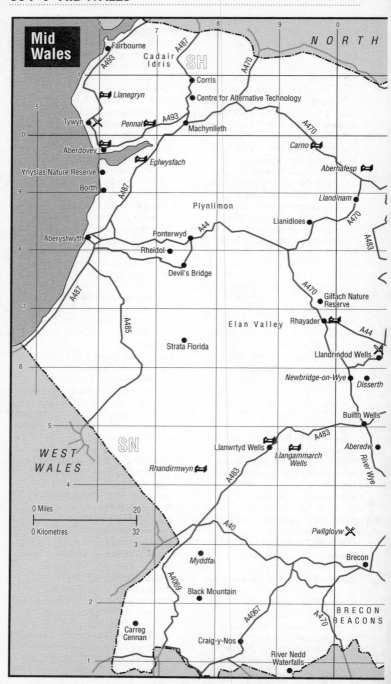

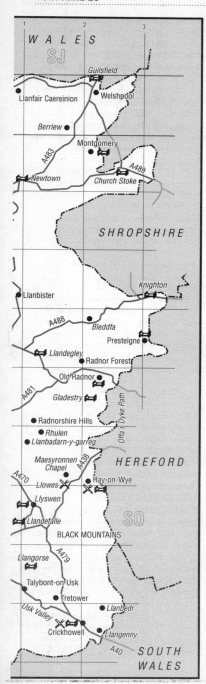

quarters. Unlike in most historic reconstructions you can sit on the chairs and try out the beds for comfort. There's a lively audio tour which leads you to trial in the Victorian court. Shop, disabled access to ground floor only; cl Nov–Feb; (01544) 260650; *£3.75.

RADNOR FOREST SO2160
Open walking country for the most part, with conifers on the northern slopes. Walks include New Radnor to the modest summit of the quaintly named Whimble, and from the A44 between Llanfihangel-nant-Melan (where the Red Lion has decent food) and New Radnor to Water-break-its-neck waterfall (don't miss the path at the top of the fall)

RADNORSHIRE HILLS SO1553
Away from Offa's Dyke, Radnorshire is less well known than it deserves to be, with old drovers' tracks providing some enjoyable escapist walking, and a reasonable network of field paths. There are few major objectives, but this part between Aberedw, Glascwm and Gladestry (where the Royal Oak is on the Offa's Dyke Path) is all very pleasant walking.

RHAYADER SN9867
Gigrin Farm 🏛 (South Rd, just outside) Farm trail with excellent views and red kite feeding station with hides (the birds are fed daily at 2pm); children's play area and picnic site. Also B&B, self-catering and camping. Snacks, shop, disabled access; cl 25 Dec; (01597) 810243; £2.50.

Gilfach Nature Reserve (just N) Includes farmland virtually unchanged in 200 years amid fine craggy mountain backdrops; several well signposted paths inc the Monks' Trod and the nature trail from Gilfach Farm – leading across a defunct railway and close to the otter-populated River Marteg, eventually emerging on the A470 by Pont Marteg, a delightful shady place with a footbridge over the River Wye; Longhouse and visitor's centre, snacks, shop, disabled access; cl Tues–Thurs Apr–June and Sept, and all Oct–Mar; (01597) 870301; £1.50.

Welsh Royal Crystal 🏛 (Brynberth Industrial Estate) Workshop tours; no glassmaking wknds, or some wkdys, best to check first on (01597) 811005.

Snacks, shop, disabled access; cl 25–26
Dec, 1 Jan; £1 workshop tour, £1.50
guided tour. Rhayader is a pleasant little
town, and the Bear, Castle and Cornhill
are useful food stops.

RHEIDOL SN7079
Rheidol Hydro-electric Scheme
(off A44 at Capel Bangor) Guided tours
of power station with unexpected fish
farm. Good nature trails, scenic lakes
and reservoirs, trout fishing. Snacks,
disabled access; cl Nov–Mar; (01970)
880667; free, fishing permits from £6.

RIVER NEDD WATERFALLS
SN9007
A series of mighty waterfalls with few
rivals in Britain grace the deep wooded
gorges of the Nedd, Hepste and Mellte,
just inside the southern Brecon
Beacons park boundary (within easy
reach of South Wales, too). An easy
path leads along the River Nedd from
Pontneddfechan, where the Old White
Horse does generous food.
River Mellte Waterfalls Porth yr
Ogof car park nr Ystradfellte is
convenient for the Mellte. Dire warning
notices ward you off getting too close
to the edge (it is certainly hazardously
slippery), but you can accompany the
river most of the way to its junction
with the Hepste. Here, a path actually
crosses the river by going behind the
curtain of Sgwd yr Eira waterfall – a
rock ledge holds you in safely, but it's an
excitingly damp experience. The Angel
in nearby Ponneddfechan has good
value food.

RIVER WYE SO0847
Pleasant escapist walks around
Aberedw and Boughrood, with a
reasonable network of field paths.

STRATA FLORIDA SN7465
Strata Florida Abbey Little is left of
this once-important centre of learning,
except the ruined church and cloister,
but the surroundings are lovely. 14th-c
poet Dafyd ap Gwilym is thought to be
buried here. Teas, shop, disabled
access; cl Oct–Apr; (01974) 831261;
£2. From Tregaron down the B4343 a
steep road climbs through the pine
forests into the mountains, eventually
reaching the Llyn Brianne reservoir.

TALYBONT-ON-USK SO1122
Attractive village, with friendly boat
hire on the Monmouthshire & Brecon

Canal, opposite the Travellers Rest
(generous food). It's on the Taff Trail
waymarked path.

TRETOWER SO1821
Tretower Court & Castle (off A40)
The medieval manor house dates from
the 14th c, though it has been
developed over the centuries; beside it
is the substantial ruin of an 11th-c
motte and bailey, with massively thick
walls and a three-storey tower. Limited
disabled access; open Mar–late Oct
(longer opening hours in high summer);
(029) 2082 6185; £2.20. The Nantyffin
Cider Mill is a good handy place for
lunch.

TYWYN SH5800
Talyllyn Railway This railway journey
affords glorious views, climbing from
the little seaside resort up the steep
sides of the Fathew Valley and stopping
for passengers to alight and admire
Dolgoch Falls and visit the Nant
Gwernol Forest (there's a waterfall two
mins away from the platform at this
end). The 27-in-gauge railway, the
oldest of this gauge in the world, was
built in 1865 to serve the slate mine at
Abergynolwyn (where the Railway Inn
does decent food in a lovely setting).
Snacks, shop, disabled access with prior
notice; cl 5 Nov–25 Dec, 2 Jan–mid-
Feb; (01654) 710472 for timetable; £9
full return. A museum at the Tywyn
Station shows locomotives, wagons and
signalling equipment whenever the
railway is running.

USK VALLEY SO1519
Walkers can enjoy the lusher swathes,
along the towpath of the 33-mile
Monmouthshire & Brecon canal.

WELSHPOOL SJ2106
Powis Castle (A483, 1m S) Set in
magnificent gardens with splendid 18th-
c terraces, this dramatic-looking castle
was built in the 13th c, but far from
falling into decay like so many others,
has developed into a grand house over
the years. It's been constantly occupied
since its construction, once by the son
of Clive of India – there are displays
about his father's life. Meals, snacks,
shop; cl Mon (exc bank hols), Tues (exc
July and Aug), and Nov–Mar (castle and
museum cl am); (01938) 557018; £7.50,
garden only £5; NT. The Kings Head at
Guilsfield does good home cooking.

Powysland Museum and Canal Centre (Canal Wharf) Respectable local history museum, with canal material too; disabled access; cl 1–2pm, Weds; *£1. The Raven and Royal Oak both have decent food, and the main BR station is rather unusual.

YNYSLAS NATURE RESERVE SN6094
(just N of Borth) A major scenic highlight of the coast, with watery views across the vast sands of the Dovey estuary, lots of birds, and an important dune system, habitat for orchids. You can walk round the tip of land jutting into the mouth of the Dovey and then along the shore.

Attractive villages and small towns in the area, all with decent pubs, include Berriew SJ1801, Llanbedr SO2420, Llandinam SO0388, Llangenny SO2417, Llyswen SO1337, Myddfai SN7730 and Newbridge-on-Wye SO0158. Other pubs doing food that are particularly worth noting for their positions include the Admiral Rodney at Criggion SJ2915, Farmers Arms at Cwmdu SO1823, Dolfor Inn at Dolfor SO1187, White Swan at Llanfrynach SO0725, Coach & Horses above the canal at Llangynidr SO1519 (lovely walks), Stables Hotel at Neuadd Fawr SO2322 (good hill walking) and canalside Royal Oak at Pencelli SO0925.

Some unspoilt and humble rustic **churches** in beautiful settings include Aberedw SO0847, Bleddfa SO2168 (the Hundred House is a good base for walkers), Disserth SO0358, Llanbadarn-y-garreg SO1148, Maesyronnen Chapel SO1740 NW of Hay, and Rhulen SO1349.

Where to eat

CRICKHOWELL SO1920 **Nantyffin Cider Mill** *Talgarth Rd (01873) 801775* Handsome pink-washed dining pub with striking raftered restaurant, a smart, relaxed atmosphere, fresh and dried flowers, a woodburner, comfortable tables and chairs, beautifully presented imaginative food (much organic produce), excellent service, well kept real ales, good wines and charming views; cl Mon, 1 wk Nov, 1 wk Jan; disabled access. £25|**£8.95**

HAY-ON-WYE SO2342 **Kilverts** *Bullring (01497) 821042* Friendly town pub with an informal relaxed atmosphere in the airy high-beamed bar, candles on the good mix of tables, some stripped stone walls and standing timbers, interesting, enjoyable food (esp the daily specials), well kept real ales, local Welsh wines, and efficient easy-going service; bdrms; cl 25 Dec. £18.50|**£4.95**

LLANDRINDOD WELLS SO0561 **Llanerch** *High St (01597) 822086* Welcoming, low-ceilinged 16th-c inn with old-fashioned settles in cheerful, beamed main bar, communicating lounges (one no smoking), popular bar food, well kept real ales, prompt service, peaceful mountain views from the back terrace, and boules and an orchard in the garden; bdrms; cl Christmas. £20|**£5**

LLOWES SO1941 **Radnor Arms** *(01497) 847460* Small, modest and very old place with log fire in the bar, neat little cottagey dining room, enjoyable food (nice puddings), friendly staff, and tables in imaginatively planted garden; cl Sun pm, Mon (exc bank hols), 2 wks Nov, 1 wk June; partial disabled access. £15|**£7.50**

PWLLGLOYW SO0333 **Seland Newydd** *(01874) 690282* Popular with a good mix of people, this former pub has a comfortable lounge, huge fireplace in the bar, and attractive dining room with most enjoyable flavoursome food; a thoughtful little wine list; cl Sun pm, Mon; disabled access. £25|**£7.50**

TYWYN SH5800 **Proper Gander** *High St (01654) 711270* Popular little pink tea shop on two floors with morning coffee, lunches, and good afternoon teas, more elaborate evening restaurant, and good Sun lunch. £20|**£5.50**

Please let us know what you think of places in the Guide. *Use the report forms at the back of the book or simply write us a letter.*

South Wales

Rich in rewarding outings for all ages

Like other places in Britain bereaved by the decline of heavy industry, South Wales has shown particular initiative in exploiting its industrial heritage for tourist purposes. The most obvious examples here are the coal-mining attractions at Trehafod and Blaenavon – two of the most enjoyable days out in all of Wales. Cardiff is gathering appeal for visitors, with several striking new developments, and has plenty for all ages from its Centre for the Visual Arts (home to a fun interactive art gallery) to the excellent Techniquest science centre, and the Museum of Welsh Life just outside (lots of seasonal events). When fully completed, the new development on Cardiff Bay will doubtless draw more visitors to the city. Children and their parents both enjoy Llancaiach Fawr living history museum at Nelson, and other places with universal appeal include busy Margam Park and magnificent Tredegar House.

Swansea has several places of interest (its Maritime & Industrial Museum and Glynn Vivian Art Gallery & Museum both deserve a special mention), and the broad sands of the Gower peninsula are ideal for beach-based entertainment. Monmouth – a small town of real character – is home to a fabulous collection of Nelson memorabilia, and there's an interesting reconstruction of a medieval village at Penarth.

Historic buildings here range from picture-book Caerphilly Castle to the first recorded Norman stone castle at Chepstow, and there's no shortage of atmospheric ruins, from the Roman remains at Caerleon to 14th-c Tintern Abbey – muse to Wordsworth and other like-minded romantics.

Nature-lovers shouldn't miss a trip to see the wildlife at Flat Holm Island, included in the *Guide* for the first time this year.

Even quite close to the built-up and industrialised areas are some unspoilt pockets of attractive scenery.

Where to stay

GILWERN SO2413 **Wenallt Farm** *Twyn-Wenallt, Gilwern, Abergavenny, Gwent NP7 0HP* (01873) 830694 **£48**; 8 rms. Friendly and relaxing 16th-c Welsh longhouse on 50 acres of farmland, with oak beams and inglenook fireplace in big drawing room, a TV room, good food in dining room, and lots to do nearby; dogs welcome

GOVILON SO2513 **Llanwenarth House** *Govilon, Abergavenny, Gwent NP7 9SF* (01873) 830289 **£80***, plus special breaks; 5 spacious, comfortable rms. Fine family-run 16th-c manor house in quiet grounds, with gracious sitting room, log fires, antiques and fresh flowers, fine food using local game and fish and home-produced meat, poultry and garden vegetables in elegant candlelit dining room, and friendly helpful staff; lots to do nearby; croquet; cl late Jan–first wk March exc by prior arrangement; children over 10; partial disabled access

LLANFIHANGEL CRUCORNEY SO2917 **Penyclawdd Court** *Llanfihangel*

Crucorney, Abergavenny, Gwent NP7 7LB (01873) 890719 **£80***; 3 rms with mountain views. Interesting Tudor manor house below Bryn Arw mountain in Brecon Beacons, with an Elizabethan knot garden, herb garden, Norman motte and bailey, and developing yew hedge maze; careful renovation, underfloor heating (to avoid unsightly radiators) and no electricity in dining room (breakfast by candlelight), as well as flagstones, beams and sloping floors, and a friendly relaxed atmosphere; children over 12

MONMOUTH SO5012 **Riverside Hotel** Cinderhill St, Monmouth, Gwent NP25 5EY (01600) 715577 **£68***, plus special breaks; 17 rms. Comfortably refurbished and warmly welcoming bustling hotel overlooking River Monnow and the 13th-c fortified gatehouse, with good value bar meals, extensive restaurant menu, and conservatory; disabled access

MUMBLES SS6087 **Hillcrest House** 1 Higher Lane, Langland, Swansea, West Glamorgan SA3 4NS (01792) 363700 **£65**; 6 individually decorated rms, each themed to represent a different country. Friendly white house with stone terrace two mins from beach yet handy for Swansea; informal welcoming atmosphere, thoughtful individual service, comfortable lounge, imaginative seasonal dishes

OXWICH SS4986 **Oxwich Bay Hotel** Oxwich, Swansea, West Glamorgan SA3 1LS (01792) 390329 **£70***, plus special breaks; 13 rms. Comfortable hotel on edge of beach in a lovely area, with dedicated friendly staff, food served all day, restaurant/lounge bar with panoramic views, summer outdoor dining area, and a welcome for families; cl 24–25 Dec

REYNOLDSTON SS4691 **Fairyhill** Reynoldston, Swansea, West Glamorgan SA3 1BS (01792) 390139 **£140***, plus special breaks; 8 rms. 18th-c hotel in 24 wooded acres with croquet, trout stream and wild duck on lake, log fire in comfortable drawing room, cosy bar, lovely food in attractive dining room, hearty breakfasts, afternoon tea on leafy terrace, and personal friendly service; children over 8

ST BRIDES WENTLOOG ST2982 **West Usk Lighthouse** St Brides Wentloog, Newport, Gwent NP10 8SF (01633) 810126 **£80**; 3 rms. Unusual ex-lighthouse – squat rather than tall – that was on an island in the Bristol channel (the land has since been reclaimed); modern stylish furnishings, lots of framed record sleeves (Mr Sheahan used to work for a record company), informal atmosphere, good big breakfasts, and small dinner-partyish vegan restaurant; flotation tank, aromatherapy and reflexology sessions, lots of walks

TINTERN PARVA SO5200 **Parva Farmhouse Hotel** Tintern, Chepstow, Gwent NP16 6SQ (01291) 689411 **£78**, plus special breaks; 9 comfortable rms. Friendly stone farmhouse rebuilt in 17th c, with leather chesterfields, woodburner and honesty bar in large beamed lounge, books (no TV downstairs), and very good food and wine (inc wine using locally grown grapes) in cosy restaurant; 50 yds from River Wye and lovely surrounding countryside

WHITEBROOK SO5306 **Crown at Whitebrook** Whitebrook, Monmouth, Gwent NP25 4TX (01600) 860254 **£85**, plus special breaks; 11 neat rms. Small modernised hotel with 17th-c heart in beautiful Wye Valley, friendly caring service, relaxed atmosphere, comfortable lounge and bar; small cosy restaurant with fine wines and excellent food combining Welsh ingredients and French style, very good breakfasts; cl 2 wks Jan and 2 wks Aug; children over 12

To see and do

ABERDULAIS SS7799
Aberdulais Falls (A465) Since the 16th c this splendid waterfall has been used to power a range of industries from copper smelting to tinplate. A magnificent water-wheel now generates electricity. Wknd snacks, shop, disabled access (right to the top of the falls thanks to a lift powered by the electricity generated on site); open Apr–Oct, and wknds in Mar; (01639) 636674; £3; NT.
ABERGAVENNY SO2914
There are some attractive ancient

buildings in Nevill St and particularly Market St – where there's a busy Tues and Fri market. The **church** has a remarkable collection of memorials. The Greyhound is a good dining pub, while outside the Lamb & Flag (B4598 SE) is also popular.

Abergavenny Castle ⊞ 12th- and 14th-c remains inc the walls, towers and rebuilt gatehouse; the early 19th-c keep and an adjoining house now contain a local history museum. Shop; cl 1–2pm, all day Sun (exc pm in summer); (01873) 854282; £1.

BARRY ST1166
Lively seaside resort which, along with its jutting-out peninsula Barry Island, grew as a centre for the coal industry. Remains of 13th-c castle, and usual fairground attractions for children. Nearby, the Star in Dinas Powis is good for lunch.

Welsh Hawking Centre ⊞ (Weycock Rd) Cheery centre with over 200 birds of prey. Regular flying demonstrations (12pm, 2.30pm, 4pm), baby birds (May–July), adventure playground, and animals for children to fuss. Snacks, shop, some disabled access; best to phone for winter opening; (01446) 734687; £3.

BARRY DOCK ST2264
Flat Holm The first place to receive a radio message sent across water, this island was once used as a quarantine for sailors, and is now a nature reserve with rare plants, a host of birds inc colourful shelducks and oystercatchers, and thriving populations of lizards and slow-worms; snacks, shop. Boats depart from Barry Island Harbour, Apr–Oct; phone to book (01446) 747661; £9 (inc a guided walk).

BETTWS NEWYDD SO3605
Bettws Newydd church Largely unaltered from the 15th c, with a choir gallery and fine screen. Peaceful village; the Black Bear has enterprising food.

BLAENAVON SO2703
Afon Lwyd Valley Interesting example of post-mining land reclamation between here and Cwmbran New Town, with plantings designed for re-establishment of nature (and for pleasant walking).

Big Pit Mining Museum ⊞ (B4248) Sample the life of a miner by donning a

safety helmet and descending 90 metres (300 ft) in the cage into the Big Pit, which closed as a working coal mine in 1980. Also a reconstructed miner's cottage, and an exhibition in the old pithead baths. Good fun – the guides are former miners so have plenty of anecdotes; you'll need sensible shoes and warm clothing. Children must be over 1 metre tall to go underground. Meals, snacks, shop, disabled access with prior warning; usually cl end Nov–Feb – but worth checking; (01495) 790311; £5.75. The Goose & Cuckoo over the hill at Rhyd-y-Meirch just off the A4042 does good home cooking.

BRIDGEND SS9084
Bryngarw Country Park (just N) Unexpectedly tranquil refuge from the M4, with woodland walks, formal gardens, ornamental lakes and a Japanese garden. Playground, snacks, shop, disabled access; cl 25–26 Dec; (01656) 725155; free (£2 parking school hols and wknds).

Ewenny Priory This riverside ruin is one of the finest fortified religious buildings in Britain.

Newcastle Ruined 12th-c castle with surviving rectangular tower, richly carved Norman gateway and massive curtain walls; collect key from nearby corner shop. The prosperous industrial town below isn't much of a place for visitors, but nearby Merthyr Mawr, with its interesting warren of high sandhills, is attractive, as are Southerndown and Ogmore.

CAERLEON ST3490
Roman Fortress Baths, Amphitheatre & Barracks One of the best examples of an amphitheatre in the country, alongside a similarly well preserved bath house, now under cover. Also the foundations of barrack lines and parts of the ramparts, and the remains of the cookhouse and latrines. Shop, disabled access; cl 24–26 Dec, 1 Jan; (01554) 890104; £2. Caerleon is reckoned in these parts to have been the site of the court of King Arthur. Near the Tourist Information Centre on the High St there's a little art gallery and various craft workshops; the Hanbury Arms has generous food.

Roman Legionary Museum (High St) Gives some idea of the daily life of the garrison; quite a few hands-on activities at wknds and school hols. Shop, disabled access; cl am Sun, 24–26 Dec, 1 Jan; (01633) 423134; £2.20. You can get a joint ticket for the museum and the baths.

CAERPHILLY ST1587

Caerphilly Castle The largest in Wales, with extensive land and water defences. Rising sheer from its broad outer moat, it's a proper picture-book castle, pleasing for this reason to the most casual visitor. It also enthrals serious students of castle architecture with its remarkably complex design of concentric defences. Look out for the incredible leaning tower, which appears ready to topple any second. Shop, disabled access to ground floor; cl 24–26 Dec, 1 Jan; (029) 2088 3143; £2.50. In the oddly strung-out small town, the ancient Courthouse overlooking the castle has a good quick carvery.

CAERWENT ROMAN WALLS ST4790

These massive walls, still some 4½ metres (15 ft) high in places, enclosed the large site of Venta Silurum – over 40 acres, enough for a sizeable town, though none of that's left now; free. The Carpenters Arms up in the attractive village of Shirenewton does good value food.

CALDICOT ST4888

Caldicot Castle (off B4245) The well preserved 12th/14th-c castle was restored as a family home in the 1880s, and lived in until 20 years ago – since when it's been a local museum, surrounded by a country park. Snacks, shop, limited disabled access; cl Sun am, lunchtimes Oct and Mar, and all Nov–Feb; (01291) 424447; £1.50.

CARDIFF ST1876

The civic centre has a range of grand 20th-c white stone civic, governmental or museum buildings around formal Cathays Park. The old city centre is closer to Cardiff Castle, which has Capability Brown's 18th-c landscaped park between it and the river. In the centre, parts are pedestrianised (for example around the fine church of St John the Baptist), and there are many covered shopping arcades, Victorian and modern; multi-ride bus tickets are good value for getting around. After all the furore surrounding the demolition of Cardiff Arms Park, locals have soon taken the magnificent Millennium Stadium to their hearts. The Cottage and Philharmonic (both St Mary's St) and Golden Cross (Custom House St) are quite useful for lunch.

Cardiff Bay Visitor Centre (Bute St) This space-age-style centre explains the ambitious continuing rejuvenation of Cardiff's waterfront and docklands; cl 24–26 Dec; (01222) 463833; free. The area includes Techniquest, a slightly incongruous Norwegian timbered church, and by the end of 2002 it will be home to the Wales Millennium Centre – an arts complex that will house the Welsh National Opera – and the futuristic debating chamber of the Welsh Assembly. The docklands New Sea Lock (Harrowby St) may be Cardiff's most unspoilt pub, the smarter Wharf (Atlantic Wharf) is right on the water's edge. The £197m redevelopment hasn't meant good news for everyone so far: the flooding of one square mile of mudflats to create a purely aesthetic lake completely annihilated the natural habitat of thousands of migrating water birds and wildfowl. Although 1,000 acres of fresh and salt water lagoons have been set aside for birds at nearby Gwent Levels, the RSPB said that the timing of the flooding meant that many had already settled for the winter, and would have thus had difficulty in finding an alternative site.

Cardiff Castle (Castle St) Despite their fairy-tale medieval appearance, the main buildings are largely 19th-c, when the Marquess of Bute employed William Burges to rebuild and restore the place, adding richly romantic wall paintings, stained glass and carvings. Some parts are much older, and in the grounds there's even a piece of a 3-metre (10-ft) thick Roman wall. The Norman keep survives, and there's a 13th-c tower – these two look like proper castle architecture, perched on a little mound. Also two military museums. Snacks, shop; usually cl 25–26 Dec, 1 Jan only, though major development over the next five years may affect opening times – best to phone; (029) 2087 8100; £5 for full guided tour, £2.50 grounds only.

Centre for the Visual Arts (Working St, The Hayes) Wales's largest gallery housed in a listed city-centre building; works by Welsh and international artists, plus regularly changing exhibitions of 20th-c art, and fun interactive art gallery, Fantasmic. Meals, snacks, shop, disabled access; cl Mon (exc bank hols); (029) 2038 8922; £3.50.

Craft in the Bay (Bute St) Demonstrations by potters, jewellers and glass workers, and a large gallery and shop; cl 25–26 Dec, 1 Jan; free.

Llandaff Cathedral (W of centre) Rebuilt several times; it includes some delightful medieval masonry, Pre-Raphaelite works, a marvellous modern timber roof, and a central concrete arch that you may think a mistake. The nearby green has an attractive collection of buildings around it, inc the good Black Lion.

Museum of Welsh Life (St Fagans, A4232 4m W) Excellent 100-acre open-air museum, with a variety of reconstructed buildings illustrating styles and living conditions throughout the ages. Buildings have come from all over Wales, and there are some remarkable exhibits, inc a homely gas-lit Edwardian farmhouse and an entire Celtic village. You can buy things from a period grocery store. Also crafts and lots of seasonal events – there's plenty to fascinate here. Meals and snacks (in 1920s tearoom), shop, limited disabled access; cl 24–26 Dec, 1 Jan; (029) 2057 3500; £5.50, children and OAPs free. The Plymouth Arms is very handy for good value food.

National Museum of Wales (Cathays Park) Lively, with interactive displays and exhibitions on subjects as diverse as ceramics, coins and prehistoric sea monsters. The East Wing has an impressive collection of paintings, with notable French Impressionists, and there's an excellent section on the evolution of the Welsh landscape. Meals, snacks, shop, disabled access; cl Mon exc bank hols, 25 Dec; (029) 2039 7951; £4.50.

Techniquest 🏛 (Stuart St) Fun as well as interest at this high-tech science centre, with around 160 hands-on exhibits and activities, and a planetarium. All exceptionally well done, it's an excellent family excursion. Meals, snacks, shop, very good disabled access; cl 23–26 Dec; (029) 20475475; £5.50.

CHEPSTOW ST5294 A steep but civilised small town, still with its battlemented 13th-c town gate. Stuart Crystal have a workshop opposite the castle, and there's a working pottery on Lower Church St (cl Sun, and sometimes 1–2pm). The civilised Bridge and Castle View are useful for lunch.

Chepstow Castle The first recorded Norman stone castle, proudly standing on an easily defended spot above the Wye, overlooking the harbour. Splendid gatehouse with portcullis grooves and ancient gates, and exhibitions on siege warfare and the English Civil War. Shop, limited disabled access; cl 24–26 Dec, 1 Jan; £3.

Chepstow Museum (Bridge St) Good local history; cl 1–2pm (exc July–Sept), Sun am, and 25 Dec–1 Jan; £1.

CRYNANT SN7904 **Cefn Coed Colliery Museum** (A4109) On the site of former Blaenant Colliery, the story of mining in the Dulais Valley. It still has a steam winding-engine, though the winding gear is now run by electricity. Also a simulated underground mining gallery, boiler house and compressor house. Shop, mostly disabled access; cl Nov–Mar; (01639) 750556; £3.

CWM DARRAN SO1203 (Rhymney Valley, nr Bargoed) Interesting example of post-mining land reclamation, which now provides a wide variety of natural habitats for wildlife and plants, with scenery ranging from the valley floor through forest areas to upland moors giving walkers superb views of the Brecon Beacons.

CWMBRAN ST2795 **Greenmeadow Community Farm** 🏛 (1m W) Founded to protect one of the encroaching new town's last green areas, this friendly farm has a wide range of animals – traditional, rare and cuddly – as well as a deer enclosure, bluebell wood, and craft workshops.

Meals, snacks, shop, disabled access; cl
25–26 Dec; (01633) 862202; £3. Up
towards Pontypool the canalside Open
Hearth (Griffithstown) has good food.
CYNONVILLE SS8194
Afan Forest Park (A4107) 9,000
tranquil acres of forest, with trails for
walking or cycling (you can hire
mountain bikes in summer), picnic and
barbecue areas, and visitor centre; free,
£1 parking charge.
Welsh Miners Museum 🖼 (Afan
Forest Park) Illustrates life as a miner
with coal faces, pit gear and mining
equipment among the displays. Meals,
snacks, shop, disabled access and entry
free; cl 25–26 Dec; (01639) 850564;
£1.20.
EBBW VALE SO1508
Victoria Park (Victoria, A4046 2 m S)
The site of a former Garden Festival,
still full of the lakes, gardens, wetlands
and woodland. Pleasant walks and trails,
woodland craft centre and owl
sanctuary, exhibitions, and some quite
extraordinary sculptures, one made
from 30,000 individually modelled clay
bricks. Also a large factory shopping
centre. Meals, snacks, shop, disabled
access; centre cl 25–26 Dec; (01495)
350010; free (charge for summer land
train).
GOVILON SO2414
Monmouthshire & Brecon Canal A
walk along the Monmouthshire &
Brecon Canal to Llanfoist SO2813 can
tie in with a return along the track of
the former Abergavenny–Merthyr
Tydfil railway line, making a level 4 miles
in all.
GOWER SS4990
This peninsula stretching W of Swansea
has quite a bit of off-putting ribbon
development along the roads entering
it, but it's well worth persevering. Once
beyond the creeping urbanisation W of
Swansea, it encapsulates on a small scale
many different types of Welsh
landscape, with lots of walking
opportunities, and parts of the coast
are lovely (but the N coast is attractive
only at its western end). Busy in
summer (quite a young feel in parts),
even the main places tend to be virtually
empty out of season. The King Arthur
at Reynoldston is the best place here
for food.

Brandy Cove This tiny cove makes an
attractive destination for a walk down
the wooded Bishopston Valley.
Burry Holms Islet with ruined chapel
and Iron Age fort; you can walk out
across the sands at low tide.
Mumbles Pleasantly unspoilt resort
with a gallery collection of traditional
Welsh love spoons (cl Sun), and a
surprisingly active night-life; 14 pubs
line the stretch of Mumbles Rd nr
Mumbles Head, and Swansea students
like to 'go mumbling' between them.
The White Rose does good value food.
Oxwich Bay Dunes and broad sands,
presided over by Oxwich Point on its
W side; good walking. It's also good for
windsurfing – you can hire wet suits
from a windsurfing school at Oxwich
Bay – though the water will never be
more than what might euphemistically
be called invigorating.
Oystermouth Castle 🖼 (Mumbles)
Very complete ruins of the de Breose
family castle, in a small park overlooking
the bay. The gatehouse, chapel and
great hall date from the 13th/14th c. Cl
Oct–Mar; £1.
Port Eynon Point Interesting, with a
huge medieval rock-dove dovecot in
the cliff (birds still use it), and cliff walks
on either side; windsurfing below.
Rhossili Down This rounded
windswept rough-cropped moorland
seems a million miles from Swansea (yet
as the crow flies is only about ten from
the outskirts); it offers Gower walkers
breathtaking coast views. From Rhossili
walks can also take in the long surfers'
sands of the bay. There's an informative
NT visitor centre at Rhossili; cl
Mon–Tues Nov–Jan, and wkdys
Feb–Mar.
Threecliffe Bay From the NT car
park nr Penmaen church a good walk
follows the lane down to this bay, then
heads W along the coast as far as
Nicholaston Farm to end with the mild
ascent of Cefn Bryn, a rounded
moorland hill giving breathtaking views
of both – or all three – Gower coasts.
Weobley Castle (Llanrhidian)
12th/14th-c fortified manor house with
an exhibition on the area's history, and
superb views. Cl 24–26 Dec, 1 Jan;
(01792) 390012; £2. The Welcome to
Town is in a lovely spot above the

estuary, and the long glistening cockle sands – full of interest for walkers.

Whiteford Burrows An extensive nature reserve, with sand dunes, marshy slacks and pine trees – good walks.

Worms Head Nature reserve where you may see seals on the tidal rocks in late summer; walks here can also take in Mewslade Bay, where the south-facing sands are enclosed by limestone cliffs.

LLANTHONY SO2923

Cwmyoy church (Llanthony Valley road) Repeated landslips have left the medieval church twisted, and its tower leans at an angle that makes the Tower of Pisa look positively sober.

Llanthony Priory Graceful ruins of 12th-c priory, the money for its construction put up by Hugh de Lacey when he decided he'd had enough of being a bold bad baron and was thinking of retiring into these lonely hills. It's a very romantic spot, with nothing much but the noise of the sheep to disturb the peace. The remains cover a variety of architectural styles; free. The very ancient crypt bar below the Abbey Hotel, right among the priory buildings, is useful for a snack lunch – a most unusual place. This is a good start or objective for Black Mountains walks.

Partrishow church (nr Llanthony) A remarkable building in the Black Mountains, with a musicians' gallery and a mural of a figure of Death wielding a shovel.

LLANTILIO CROSSENY SO3914

Attractive village with a lovely view of the 13th-c church from the former moat of Hen Cwrt nearby; the Halfway House and Hostry are good for lunch.

White Castle (NW) The remains of the most substantial of the trio of moated castles Hubert de Burgh built to defend the Welsh Marches; £2. The other ruins stand at Skenfrith (the Bell has good value food) and Grosmont, an attractive hillside village with another 13th-c church (the Angel here is also good value).

LLANTRISANT ST0483

The **ancient church** in this attractive hill town has a window by Burne-Jones. Overlooking the Bullring in the centre of the old town, the decent **Model House Craft & Design Centre** has

around ten contemporary craft exhibitions every year; shop; cl Mon (exc bank hols); (01443) 237758; free.

LLANVAPLEY SO3614

Interesting village, with a **church** dating from 860.

MARGAM SS8086

Margam Park (A48) Pretty country park based around splendid 'gothick' mansion, its 850 acres full of natural and historic features and various themed areas, inc a scaled-down nursery-rhyme village for young children. Also a ruined abbey and Iron Age hill fort, marked walks among the parkland and forests, giant maze, deer and cattle, and an adventure playground. Meals, snacks, shop, disabled access; cl winter Mon and Tues; (01639) 871131; £3.85, £1 in winter, when none of the attractions are open (though they have various special events).

MERTHYR MAWR SS8877

Delightful village of thatched cottages, bordered by meadows and woodlands. Nearby Merthyr Mawr Warren is Europe's largest sand dune system, a site of special scientific interest; the ruined 15th-c Candleston castle stands at the edge of the dunes.

MERTHYR TYDFIL SO0511

Brecon Mountain Railway (off A465) The route of this narrow-gauge railway starts at Pant Station, 3 miles N of Merthyr Tydfil, where there's a display of various engines inc vintage locomotives and others from around the world. The journey takes you into the beautiful Brecon Beacons as far as the Taf Fechan reservoir. Snacks, shop, disabled access; cl Nov–Easter exc over Christmas; (01685) 722988 for timetable; £6.20. On a disused railway line, the Dowlais Viaduct is a striking sight, well worth a detour.

Cyfarthfa Castle 🖾 (Cyfarthfa Park) Impressive early 19th-c castellated Gothic mansion, set in beautiful gardens. Now restored to their full Regency glory, the state rooms contain a museum with displays on Egyptology and archaeology. Meals, snacks, shop, disabled access; cl Mon, and am winter wknds, 24–26 Dec, 1 Jan; (01685) 723112; *£1.80.

Garwnant Forest Centre (5m NW, off A470) Looking out over the Llwyn-

On reservoir on the S edge of the National Park, carefully restored old farm buildings with displays on forestry, wildlife and conservation, and information on nature trails and cycle routes (you can hire bikes). Also discovery centre for children. Meals, snacks, shop, disabled access; (01685) 384060; £1 car parking charge.

Joseph Parry's Cottage (Chapel Row, Georgetown) The composer of *Myfanwy* was born here, and the ground floor has been restored and decorated in the style of the 1840s. Shop, limited disabled access; open pm Thurs–Sun Easter–Sept; (01685) 723112; 60p. The Butchers Arms up at Pontsticill has good home cooking.

MONMOUTH SO5113
Attractive market town of considerable character; below the remains of the 12th-c castle where Henry V was born, and the 17th-c Great Castle House (built with enormous blocks of masonry in its precincts), the main Agincourt Sq is surrounded by handsome buildings, inc the imposing central Shire Hall with its arcaded market floor. The town nestles in the crook formed by the River Wye and the River Monnow, with a splendid 13th-c gatehouse bridge over the Monnow. The Punch House is the most enjoyable place here for lunch, and the Gockett (B4293 towards Trelleck) is also useful.

Fairview Rock This lofty crag nr the Biblins suspension bridge makes a good riverside walk from Monmouth, with a level track giving an easy route along the picturesque Lower Wye gorge.

Nelson Museum (Priory St) Tremendous collection relating to Nelson, inc letters, medals and best of all his fighting sword. Nelson has nothing to do with Monmouth, but the collection was originally put together by Lady Llangattock who lived nearby. Shop, some disabled access; cl 1–2pm, am Sun, 24–26 Dec, 1 Jan; (01600) 713519; £1.

NANTGARW ST1285
Nantgarw China Works Museum (Treforest Industrial Estate, off A470) For a brief period early in the 19th c, Nantgarw porcelain was among the finest in the world. They still make pots and clay pipes, and you can watch the craftsmen at work. Snacks, shop; cl Mon, plus winter Tues and Weds, 18 Dec–10 Jan; (01443) 841703; £1.

NASH POINT SS9168
The curious striped cliffs of the Glamorgan coast look over the Bristol Channel to Exmoor. It is worth getting down to shore level to see the cliffs in their full glory.

NEATH SS7597
Borough Museum (Gwyn Hall, Orchard St) Includes finds from a nearby Roman fort. Shop, disabled access; cl Sun, Mon (exc bank hols); (01639) 645726; free.

Gnoll Estate (B4434 NE) Landscaped grounds beautifully restored by the local council. The visitor centre will have you believe they're the finest in Europe, and though this is something of an exaggeration, with some of the features it's not too wide of the mark. Snacks, shop, disabled access; cl over Christmas and New Year; (01639) 635808; free.

Neath Abbey Remains of Cistercian abbey founded in 1130 by Richard de Grainville. Disabled access; free.

NELSON ST1196
Llancaiach Fawr (B4254) Splendidly entertaining and carefully organised living history museum, the Elizabethan manor's Civil War days brought vividly to life by costumed guides who rarely step out of character – they even speak in 17th-c style. Children don't mind visiting a stately home when it's like this – not only are there no ropes or barriers (it's all firmly hands-on), but they can try on historic clothes, handle armour, or even languish in the stocks for a while. Extra activities summer wknds. Meals, snacks, shop; cl Mon Nov–Feb, and Christmas wk; (01443) 412248; £4.50.

NEWPORT ST3187
Museum and Art Gallery (John Frost Sq) Worthwhile collections – inc a mass of teapots; cl Sun and bank hols; free.

Tredegar House (Coedkernew; off A48 SW) Magnificent 17th-c house and gardens set in 90-acre landscaped park on the edge of this industrial town. The Morgans, later Lords Tredegar, lived here for five centuries, and the household's above and below stairs

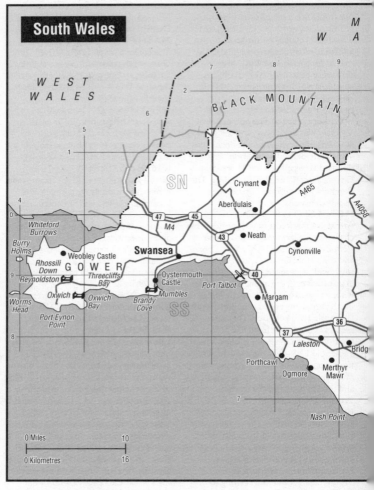

activities are well illustrated in the 30 or so rooms on show. In the grounds are carriage rides, self-guided trails, craft workshops, an Edwardian sunken garden, as well as boating and an adventure playfarm. Meals, snacks, shop, disabled access; cl Mon and Tues (exc Aug), Oct wkdys, and all Nov–Easter; (01633) 815880; £4.75. Past here on the B4239 the Lighthouse Inn at St Brides Wentloog has good food upstairs, and great Severn views.
OGMORE SS8876
Ogmore Castle Three-storeyed 12th-c keep with a preserved hooded

fireplace, a dry moat surrounding the inner ward and a surviving 12-metre (40-ft) W wall. The setting of this ruin is attractive: odd to think that what this impressive fortress was built to defend was the row of stepping stones which still cross the river; free. The Pelican is good for lunch, and the cheery Three Golden Cups along the road at Southerndown gives sea views to Devon on a clear day. Just past it there's a car park by the interestingly preserved remains of the seaside gardens of entirely demolished Dunraven Castle, with walks by the

cliffs over the sands and rock pools, and around to the fragmentary remains of an Iron Age promontory hill fort above the sea.

PENARTH ST1971

An unspoilt seaside resort of some charm, with the usual attractions.

Cosmeston Medieval Village (Lavernock Rd towards Sully) Living museum of medieval life, reconstructed on the site of an actual village which was deserted during the 14th c. Hens and sheep wander between the cottages. Meals, snacks, shop, disabled access; cl 25 Dec; (01222) 708686; £3. It's set in

the Cosmeston Lakes country park, with lakes, woodland and wildlife.

Turner House (Plymouth Rd) Changing exhibits from the National Museum of Wales; disabled access to ground floor; cl all day Mon (exc bank hols), between exhibitions, and occasional lunch times; (029) 2070 8870; £1.25 (free Sun).

PENHOW ST4290

Penhow Castle ⊞ (A48) The oldest lived-in castle in Wales, with tours of the restored rooms taking you from the 12th-c ramparts and Norman bedchamber through the 15th-c Great

Hall with its minstrels' gallery to the Victorian housekeeper's room. There's a choice of several good Walkman tours, one specially for children, and others concentrating on a particular topic, such as the musical or domestic history of the building. You can stay here. Snacks, shop; cl Mon (exc bank hols), Tues, and all Oct–Feb exc Weds and pm occasional Suns; (01633) 400800; £3.60. The Rock & Fountain has good interesting food.

PONTYPOOL SO2801

Valley Inheritance 🏛 (Pontypool Park, off A4042) The story of a typical South Wales valley, well shown in the Georgian stable block of Pontypool Park House. Snacks, shop, disabled access; cl Sun am, 1 wk after Christmas; (01495) 752036; £1.20. The surrounding country park is a microcosm of the Welsh valleys scenery: patches of conifer plantation and rather scrappy moorland rising high above the industrial valleys – not exactly pretty, but its gruff sense of place appeals to some. The Open Hearth just below the canal at Griffithstown is good for lunch.

PORTHCAWL SS8176

Still developing summer resort, with broad sandy beaches, well placed golf club, fairground, fishing from the pier, and what's said to be the largest caravan park in Wales (some say Europe); it's quieter on the W side of the harbour.

RAGLAN SO4108

Raglan Castle Quite magnificent ruins of 15th-c castle, particularly notable for its Yellow Tower of Gwent. Its intricate history is displayed in the closet tower and two rooms of the gatehouse. Shop, some disabled access; cl 24–26 Dec, 1 Jan; (01291) 690228; £2.40. The Clytha Arms (Abergavenny road) has good food.

ST HILARY ST0171

Beaupre Castle (St Hilary) Well preserved ruined Elizabethan courtyard mansion with an extraordinarily elaborate three-storey Italianate porch; free. The Bush is good for lunch, and the village with its thatched houses is pretty.

ST NICHOLAS ST0971

Dyffryn Gardens (off A48) Small themed gardens and seasonal bedding displays help break up the 50 acres of rare plants and shrubs which make up these lovely gardens. Also extensive plant houses, inc a large temperate house and a succulent house, and an arboretum. Summer snacks (open-air theatre then too), shop, limited disabled access; (029) 2059 3328; £3.50, free in winter.

SWANSEA SS6593

Largely post-industrial and commercial, so there are few buildings of any age or great appeal to visitors, but there's a good fresh-food covered market with cockles and laverbread, and long sandy beaches have made it something of a family summer resort. Among some high spots is the 1934 Guildhall, containing the Brangwyn Hall with its 16 huge British Empire murals painted by Sir Frank Brangwyn for the House of Lords – Wales's gain, as they were judged too controversial. There are some castle ruins (you can't go inside, but can see them from outside), inc a striking 14th-c first-floor arcade. The handsome **Dylan Thomas Centre** (Somerset Pl, Marina) is devoted to Welsh literature, with changing exhibitions, restaurant, a good bookshop café (you can peruse the books over your coffee), and disabled access (cl Mon, and some bank hols; (01792) 463980; free, charges for events). From the marina, a cycle and footpath takes you around the bay to Mumbles and Gowerton beyond. The Hanbury in Kingsway is popular for lunch, and the Bankers Draft (Wind St) and Potters Wheel (Kingsway) have good value food all day.

Egypt Centre (University Campus, off Oystermouth Rd) An important collection of Egyptian artifacts. Shop, disabled access; cl Sun and Mon, bank hols and over Christmas; (01792) 295960; free.

Glynn Vivian Art Gallery & Museum (Alexandra Rd) Displays of porcelain from Swansea's all-too-brief but brilliant period of production between 1814 and 1824, and paintings, drawings and sculptures by British, French and, above all, Welsh artists – especially the locally born Ceri Richards. Good changing exhibitions. Shop, disabled access to ground floor; cl

Mon (exc bank hols), 25–26 Dec, 1 Jan;
(01792) 655006; free.

Maritime & Industrial Museum
(Museum Sq, Maritime Quarter) In the
heart of the revitalised docks, with its
collection of historic ships the biggest
and most varied assemblage of floating
maritime exhibits in Wales. Also a
complete working woollen mill. Lots of
thought is put into the displays. Summer
snacks, shop, disabled access; cl Mon
(exc bank hols), 25–26 Dec, 1 Jan;
(01792) 650351; free.

Plantasia (Parc Tawe) Tropical and
desert plants in big futuristic landscaped
glasshouse, also aviary, reptiles and
various creepy-crawlies. Snacks, shop,
disabled access; (01792) 474555; cl
Mon (exc bank hols and July–Aug),
25–26 Dec, 1 Jan; £2.30.

Swansea Museum (Victoria Rd,
Maritime Quarter) The oldest in Wales,
with local history and replicas of the
oldest human bones found in Wales (cl
Mon exc bank hols, and a few days over
Christmas and New Year; free).

TINTERN PARVA SO5300

Tintern Abbey (off A466)
Remarkably well preserved, these 14th-
c ruins were considered an essential
spot for 18th-c artists and poets to visit,
lying as they do in a lovely part of the
steeply wooded Wye Valley.
Wordsworth was just one of many to
find inspiration here. Shop, disabled
access; cl 24–26 Dec, 1 Jan; (01291)
689251; £2.40. The Abbey Mill nearby
has been converted into a little craft
centre, with demonstrations and a
decent coffee shop; cl 25–26 Dec; free.
A visitor centre at Tintern Old Station
can help you make the most of the
surrounding hills and woodland.

TONGWYNLAIS ST1382

Castell Coch (off A470) This
spectacular triangular hillside landmark,
designed in 1875 by William Burges for
the Marquis of Bute, is actually based on
a 13th-c castle in spite of its improbable
appearance, something by Disney out of
Wagner – red sandstone, conical
towers, drawbridge and portcullis.
Though never finished, it's a very
successful pastiche, and inside is just as
impressive: an astonishingly elaborate
mock-medieval idyll of gilt, gorgeous
colours, statues, murals and carvings.

The bedroom of Lady Bute is decorated
on the theme of Sleeping Beauty. Shop,
disabled access to ground floor only; cl
24–26 Dec, 1 Jan; (029) 2081 0101; £2.50.

TREHAFOD ST0290

Rhondda Heritage Park 🅰 (off the
A470) Based around the last colliery
buildings in the area, this well organised
centre uses lively multi-media
exhibitions to re-create the golden days
of the coal-mining industry, evoking
sights, sounds and smells from the life
and work of the miners. The excellent
underground tour showing what it was
like to work a shift is uncannily realistic,
and the twisting simulated trip back to
the surface is a definite highlight. Other
displays look at the wider social
heritage of the valley, with art by locals,
a re-created village street, and from
Easter–Sept, an excellent themed
adventure play area for children. A
good value excursion whatever the
weather. Meals, snacks, shop, good
disabled access (even underground); cl
Mon from Oct–Easter, and 25–26 Dec;
(01443) 682036; £5.60.

USK SO3700

Gwent Rural Life Museum (New
Market St) Interesting collection,
housed in an old barn; cl am wknds and
all Nov–Mar; £2. The little town is
attractive, with the Nags Head
currently the best pub.

WYND CLIFF ST5297
This viewpoint gives walkers an
extensive panorama, a short detour up
steps. Elsewhere, the Wye Valley Walk
between Chepstow and Tintern gives
only occasional views down to the
river, which in this picturesque Lower
Wye gorge makes the boundary
between England and Wales.

Attractive villages or small towns,
all with decent pubs, include Bedwellty
SO1600, Cowbridge SS9974 and
Laleston SS8879. The church and
churchyard of Llancarfan ST0570 are
worth a look.

Pubs or inns elsewhere which are
particularly useful for their attractive
surroundings or views include the Lamb
& Flag out on the Brecon road from
Abergavenny SO2515, Bridgend by the
canal at Gilwern SO2414, Old Glais at
Glais SN7000, Prince of Wales nr the
sand dune nature reserve at Kenfig

SS8383, Old House at Llangynwyd
SS8588, Greyhound at Llantrisant
ST3997, Brynfynnon at Llanwonno
ST0295, Plough & Harrow at Monknash

SS9270, Rowan Tree at Nelson ST1195,
Trekkers at The Narth SO5206 and
Fountain at Trelleck Grange SO4902.

Where to eat

CARDIFF ST1876 **Le Monde** *60–62 St Mary St* (029) 2038 7376 Bustling, cosmopolitan, open-plan wine bar with a big choice of delicious fish and shellfish, super wines, a relaxed atmosphere, and friendly efficient service; cl Sun, 25–26 Dec. £21

LLANDEWI SKIRRID SO3416 **Walnut Tree** *(01873) 852797* Comfortable, stylish dining pub with a marvellously relaxed atmosphere (you can pop in for just a drink or one-course meal), outstanding imaginative and carefully prepared food using tip-top quality produce (wonderful puddings and fine cheeses), an attractive choice of wines (particularly strong on Italian ones), and efficient friendly service; cl Sun, Mon, 1 wk Christmas, 2 wks Feb; disabled access. £33.75|£15

PORT TALBOT SS7489 **Aberavon Beach Hotel** *Princess Margaret Way (01639) 884949* Popular modern hotel opposite a wide sandy beach, with imaginative modern cooking in no smoking restaurant, a thoughtful wine list, helpful staff, and attractive public rooms; all weather leisure centre; comfortable bdrms; good disabled access. £23.50

RAGLAN SO3608 **Clytha Arms** *(01873) 840206* Fine old country inn with a tastefully and solidly comfortable bar, cheerful helpful staff, good carefully prepared food inc delicious puddings and good value Sun lunch in no smoking restaurant, log fires, well kept real ales, and neat garden; bdrms; no food Mon am, 25 Dec. £32|£5.50

TAL-Y-COED SO4115 **Halfway House** *(01600) 780269* Pretty, neat and clean 17th-c cottage with huge wisteria, cosy little no smoking dining room, snug and cosy main bar, lots of Wills cigarette cards, well kept real ales, carefully presented bar food, welcoming service, and a tidy garden; cl ams Mon–Fri; children must be well behaved; disabled access. £18|£5

Special thanks to Mrs Victoria Barrett, Judy Hiam, C J and Sarah Green, Mrs Rosie Lloyd and Ian Downes, E G Parish

We welcome reports from readers

INDEX

This index includes the main places in the **To see and Do** sections.

928 • INDEX

LONDON INDEX

REPORT FORMS

Please report to us: you can use the tear-out card in the middle of the book, the forms on the following pages, or just plain paper – whichever's easiest for you. We need to know what you think of the places mentioned in this edition – especially, whether you think we should add to or change our descriptions of them. We need to know about other places worthy of inclusion. We need to know about ones that should not be included. We try to answer all letters, and readers who send us reports will be offered a discount on the price of the next edition that benefits from their help.

If you are recommending a new entry, the more detail you can put into your description, the better. This will help not just us but also your fellow-readers gauge its appeal. A description of its character and even furnishings is a tremendous boon. Imagine you're writing about it for the *Guide* itself, and put in the sorts of things you'd want to know yourself before deciding whether to choose it.

The atmosphere and character of a holiday hotel or simpler place to stay, or of a restaurant, are very important to us – why it would, or would not, appeal to people who don't know it. But, of course, the quality and type of its food matter a lot, too, so please tell us about that as well. A full address and telephone number is an enormous help.

We'd also very much like you to let us know of places you've enjoyed visiting – anything from a little village to a stately home, from a shop selling unusual things to a factory visit, from an outstanding plant nursery to a hot-air balloon festival, from a hidden-away country church to a cathedral, from a peaceful wood or a nature reserve or a stretch of unspoilt coastal cliff to a theme park or a zoo or a pleasure beach. We're also particularly interested in enjoyable walks and drives. Whatever it is, if you've enjoyed it, please tell us about it.

The card in the middle of the book is a general purpose one for any recommendation. There are also different forms on the following pages: one for endorsement of existing entries; and three forms for more detailed descriptions of places to visit, hotels or restaurants.

When you go to a hotel, restaurant, or anywhere else, don't tell them you're a reporter for *The Good Britain Guide*; we do make clear that all inspections are anonymous, and if you declare yourself as a reporter you risk getting special treatment – for better or for worse! When you write to *The Good Britain Guide* , FREEPOST TN1569, WADHURST, E. Sussex TN5 7BR, you don't need a stamp in the UK. We'll gladly send you more forms (free) if you wish. The information you send us will be stored in our computer files.

Though we try to answer letters, we do have other work to do, besides producing this *Guide*. So please understand if there's a delay. And from June well into autumn, when we are fully extended getting the next edition to the printers, we put all letters and reports aside, not answering them until the rush is over (and after our post-press-day autumn holiday). The end of May is pretty much the cut-off date for reasoned consideration of reports for the next edition – and the earlier the better, if they're suggestions of new entries.

We'll assume we can print your name or initials as a recommender unless you tell us otherwise.

The Good Britain Guide: Endorsement Form

I have been to the following hotels/restaurants/attractions/places in *The Good Britain Guide 2001* in the last few months, found them as described, and confirm that they deserve continued inclusion:

Your own name and address (*block capitals please*)

Please return to:
> *The Good Britain Guide*
> FREEPOST TN1569
> WADHURST
> E. Sussex
> TN5 7BR

The Good Britain Guide: Endorsement Form

I have been to the following hotels/restaurants/attractions/places in *The Good Britain Guide 2001* in the last few months, found them as described, and confirm that they deserve continued inclusion:

Your own name and address (*block capitals please*)

Please return to:
  The Good Britain Guide
  FREEPOST TN1569
  WADHURST
  E. Sussex
  TN5 7BR

The Good Guide to Britain: Report Form

Please use this form to tell us about anything which *you* think should or should not be included in the next edition of *The Good Britain Guide*. Just fill it in and sent it to us – no stamp needed.

ALISDAIR AIRD

☐ *Please tick this box if you would like extra report forms.*

Report on   (*its name*)

Its address:

Postcode: Telephone:

What is this? (e.g. *hotel, restaurant, garden, village, drive, walk*)

Description/why it appeals

Your own name and address (*block capitals please*)

Please return to:
      The Good Britain Guide
      FREEPOST TN1569
      WADHURST
      E. Sussex
      TN5 7BR

The Good Britain Guide: Report Form

Please use this form to tell us about anything which *you* think should or should not be included in the next edition of *The Good Britain Guide*. Just fill it in and sent it to us – no stamp needed.

ALISDAIR AIRD

☐   *Please tick this box if you would like extra report forms.*

Report on   *(its name)*

Its address:

Postcode: Telephone:

What is this? (e.g. *hotel, restaurant, garden, village, drive, walk*)

Description/why it appeals

Your own name and address (*block capitals please*)

Please return to:

The Good Britain Guide
FREEPOST TN1569
WADHURST
E. Sussex
TN5 7BR

The Good Britain Guide: Report Form

Please use this form to tell us about anything which *you* think should or should not be included in the next edition of *The Good Britain Guide*. Just fill it in and sent it to us – no stamp needed.

ALISDAIR AIRD

☐ *Please tick this box if you would like extra report forms.*

Report on *(its name)*

Its address:

Postcode: Telephone:

What is this? (e.g. *hotel, restaurant, garden, village, drive, walk*)

Description/why it appeals

PLEASE GIVE YOUR NAME AND ADDRESS ON THE BACK OF THIS FORM

Your own name and address (*block capitals please*)

Please return to:
  The Good Britain Guide
  FREEPOST TN1569
  WADHURST
  E. Sussex
  TN5 7BR

The Good Britain Guide: **Report Form**

Please use this form to tell us about anything which *you* think should or should not be included in the next edition of *The Good Britain Guide*. Just fill it in and sent it to us – no stamp needed.

ALISDAIR AIRD

☐ *Please tick this box if you would like extra report forms.*

Report on *(its name)*

Its address:

Postcode: Telephone:

What is this? (e.g. *hotel, restaurant, garden, village, drive, walk*)

Description/why it appeals

Your own name and address (*block capitals please*)